Poetry
Criticism

Guide to Gale Literary Criticism Series

For criticism on	Consult these Gale series
Authors now living or who died after December 31, 1959	*CONTEMPORARY LITERARY CRITICISM (CLC)*
Authors who died between 1900 and 1959	*TWENTIETH-CENTURY LITERARY CRITICISM (TCLC)*
Authors who died between 1800 and 1899	*NINETEENTH-CENTURY LITERATURE CRITICISM (NCLC)*
Authors who died between 1400 and 1799	*LITERATURE CRITICISM FROM 1400 TO 1800 (LC)* *SHAKESPEAREAN CRITICISM (SC)*
Authors who died before 1400	*CLASSICAL AND MEDIEVAL LITERATURE CRITICISM (CMLC)*
Authors of books for children and young adults	*CHILDREN'S LITERATURE REVIEW (CLR)*
Dramatists	*DRAMA CRITICISM (DC)*
Poets	*POETRY CRITICISM (PC)*
Short story writers	*SHORT STORY CRITICISM (SSC)*
Black writers of the past two hundred years	*BLACK LITERATURE CRITICISM (BLC)*
Hispanic writers of the late nineteenth and twentieth centuries	*HISPANIC LITERATURE CRITICISM (HLC)*
Native North American writers and orators of the eighteenth, nineteenth, and twentieth centuries	*NATIVE NORTH AMERICAN LITERATURE (NNAL)*
Major authors from the Renaissance to the present	*WORLD LITERATURE CRITICISM, 1500 TO THE PRESENT (WLC)*

ISSN 1052-4851

Poetry Criticism

Excerpts from Criticism of the Works of the Most Significant and Widely Studied Poets of World Literature

VOLUME 26

Laura A. Wisner-Broyles
Editor

GALE GROUP

Detroit
San Francisco
London
Boston
Woodbridge, CT

STAFF

Laura Wisner-Broyles, *Editor*

Lynn Koch, Marie Napierkowski,
Anna Nesbitt, Debra A. Wells, *Assistant Editors*

Maria Franklin, *Permissions Manager*
Kimberly F. Smilay, *Permissions Specialist*
Sandra K. Gore, *Permissions Assistant*

Victoria B. Cariappa, *Research Manager*
Cheryl L. Warnock, *Research Specialist*
Patricia T. Ballard, Wendy Festerling, Tamara C. Knott,
Tracie A. Richardson, Corrine Stocker, *Research Associates*
Timothy Lehnerer, Patricia Love, *Research Assistants*

Mary Beth Trimper, *Production Director*
Dorothy Maki, *Manufacturing Manager*
Cindy Range, *Buyer*

Randy Bassett, *Imaging Database Supervisor*
Robert Duncan, Michael Logusz, *Imaging Specialists*
Gary Leach, *Graphic Artist*
Pamela A. Reed, *Imaging Coordinator*

Library of Congress Catalog Card Number 88-641014
ISBN 0-7876-3074-8
ISSN 1052-4851

Printed in the United States of America

10   9   8   7   6   5   4   3   2   1

Contents

Preface vii

Acknowledgments xi

Preface

A Comprehensive Information Source on World Poetry

Poetry Criticism (PC) provides substantial critical excerpts and biographical information on poets throughout the world who are most frequently studied in high school and undergraduate college courses. Each *PC* entry is supplemented by biographical and bibliographical material to help guide the user to a fuller understanding of the genre and its creators. Although major poets and literary movements are covered in such Gale Literary Criticism Series as *Contemporary Literary Criticism (CLC), Twentieth-Century Literary Criticism (TCLC), Nineteenth-Century Literature Criticism (NCLC), Literature Criticism from 1400 to 1800 (LC),* and *Classical and Medieval Literature Criticism (CMLC), PC* offers more focused attention on poetry than is possible in the broader, survey-oriented entries on writers in these Gale series. Students, teachers, librarians, and researchers will find that the generous excerpts and supplementary material provided by *PC* supply them with the vital information needed to write a term paper on poetic technique, to examine a poet's most prominent themes, or to lead a poetry discussion group.

Coverage

In order to reflect the influence of tradition as well as innovation, poets of various nationalities, eras, and movements are represented in every volume of *PC*. Each author entry presents a historical survey of the critical response to that author's work; the length of an entry reflects the amount of critical attention that the author has received from critics writing in English and from foreign critics in translation. Since many poets have inspired a prodigious amount of critical explication, *PC* is necessarily selective, and the editors have chosen the most significant published criticism to aid readers and students in their research. In order to provide these important critical pieces, the editors will sometimes reprint essays that have appeared in previous volumes of Gale's Literary Criticism Series. Such duplication, however, never exceeds fifteen percent of a *PC* volume.

Organization

Each *PC* author entry consists of the following components:

- **Author Heading:** the name under which the author wrote appears at the beginning of the entry, followed by birth and death dates. If the author wrote consistently under a pseudonym, the pseudonym will be listed in the author heading and his or her legal name given in parentheses in the lines immediately preceding the Introduction. Uncertainty as to birth or death dates is indicated by question marks.

- **Introduction:** a biographical and critical essay introduces readers to the author and the critical discussions surrounding his or her work.

- **Author Portrait:** a photograph or illustration of the author is included when available.

- **Principal Works:** the author's most important works are identified in a list ordered chronologically by first publication dates. The first section comprises poetry collections and book-length poems. The second section gives information on other major works by the author. For foreign authors, original foreign-language publication information is provided, as well as the best and most complete English-language editions of their works.

- **Criticism:** critical excerpts chronologically arranged in each author entry provide perspective on changes in critical evaluation over the years. All individual titles of poems and poetry collections by the author featured in the entry are printed in boldface type to enable a reader to ascertain without difficulty the works under discussion. For purposes of easy identification, the critic's name and the publication date of the essay are given at the beginning of each piece of criticism. Unsigned criticism is preceded by the title of the journal in which it originally appeared. Publication information (such as publisher names and book prices) and parenthetical numerical references (such as footnotes or page and line references to specific editions of a work) have been deleted at the editor's discretion to enable smoother reading of the text.

- **Explanatory Notes:** introductory comments preface each critical excerpt, providing several types of useful information, including: the reputation of a critic, the importance of a work of criticism, and the specific type of criticism (biographical, psychoanalytic, historical, etc.).

- **Author Commentary:** insightful comments from the authors themselves and excerpts from author interviews are included when available.

- **Bibliographical Citations:** information preceding each piece of criticism guides the interested reader to the original essay or book.

- **Further Reading:** bibliographic references accompanied by descriptive notes at the end of each entry suggest additional materials for study of the author. Boxed material following the Further Reading provides references to other biographical and critical series published by Gale.

Other Features

- **Cumulative Author Index:** comprises all authors who have appeared in Gale's Literary Criticism Series, along with cross-references to such Gale biographical series as *Contemporary Authors* and *Dictionary of Literary Biography*. This cumulated index enables the user to locate an author within the various series.

- **Cumulative Nationality Index:** includes all authors featured in *PC,* arranged alphabetically under their respective nationalities.

- **Cumulative Title Index:** lists in alphabetical order all individual poems, book-length poems, and collection titles contained in the *PC* series. Titles of poetry collections and separately published poems are printed in italics, while titles of individual poems are printed in roman type with quotation marks. Each title is followed by the author's name and the volume and page number corresponding to the location of commentary on specific works. English-language translations of original foreign-language titles are cross-referenced to the foreign titles so that all references to discussion of a work are combined in one listing.

Citing *Poetry Criticism*

When writing papers, students who quote directly from any volume in the Literary Criticism Series may use the following general formats to footnote reprinted criticism. The first example pertains to material drawn from periodicals, the second to material reprinted from books:

[1]David Daiches, "W. H. Auden: The Search for a Public," *Poetry* LIV (June 1939), 148-56; excerpted and reprinted in *Poetry Criticism*, Vol. 1, ed. Robyn V. Young (Detroit: Gale Research, 1990), pp. 7-9.

[2]Pamela J. Annas, *A Disturbance in Mirrors: The Poetry of Sylvia Plath* (Greenwood Press, 1988); excerpted and reprinted in *Poetry Criticism*, Vol. 1, ed. Robyn V. Young (Detroit: Gale Research, 1990), pp. 410-14.

Comments Are Welcome

Readers who wish to suggest authors to appear in future volumes, or who have other suggestions, are cordially invited to contact the editors.

Acknowledgments

The editors wish to thank the copyright holders of the excerpted criticism included in this volume and the permissions managers of many book and magazine publishing companies for assisting us in securing reproduction rights. We are also grateful to the staffs of the Detroit Public Library, the Library of Congress, the University of Detroit Mercy Library, Wayne State University Purdy/Kresge Library Complex, and the University of Michigan Libraries for making their resources available to us. Following is a list of the copyright holders who have granted us permission to reproduce material in this volume of **PC**. Every effort has been made to trace copyright, but if omissions have been made, please let us know.

COPYRIGHTED EXCERPTS IN *PC*, VOLUME 26, WERE REPRODUCED FROM THE FOLLOWING PERIODICALS:

American Poetry, v. 3, Fall, 1985. (c) 1985 by Lee Bartlett and Peter White. All rights reserved. Reproduced by permission.—**The American Poetry Review**, v. 5, January, 1976 for an interview with Galway Kinnell by Al Poulin, Jr., and Stan Samuel Rubin; v. X, January-February, 1981 for a review of **As We Know** by Dana Yeaton. Copyright (c) 1981 by World Poetry, Inc. Reproduced by permission of the authors.—**Bulletin of the New York Public Library,** v. 69, November, 1965. (c) 1965 The New York Public Library. Excerpted by permission.—**The Centennial Review**, v. XXX, Winter, 1986 for "Galway Kinnell's Poetry of Transformation" by David Kleinbard. (c) 1986 by The Centennial Review. Reproduced by permission of the publisher and the author—.**Chasqui—Revista de literatura latinoamericana,** v. XXI, November, 1992. Reproduced by permission.—**Christianity and Literature,** v. 37, Summer, 1988. Reproduced by permission.—**The Classical Journal**, v. XXXVI, September, 1992. Reproduced by permission of the publisher.—**Commonweal,** v. 110, March 11, 1983. Copyright (c) 1983 Commonweal Publishing Co., Inc. Reproduced by permission of Commonweal Foundation.—**Contemporary Literature,** v. XXIII, Fall, 1982. (c) 1982 by the Board of Regents of the University of Wisconsin. Reproduced by permission of The University of Wisconsin Press.permission.**The Critical Quarterly,** v. 29, Summer, 1987. Reproduced by permission of Blackwell Publishers—**Essays in Arts and Sciences,** v. X, May, 1981; v. XVIII, May, 1989. Copyright (c) 1981, 1989 by the University of New Haven. Both reproduced by permission.—**Field: Contemporary Poetry and Poetics,** Spring, 1975. Copyright (c) 1975 by Oberlin College. Reproduced by permission—**Index on Censorship,** v. 13, April, 1984. Copyright Writers & Scholars International Ltd. 1984. Reproduced by permission—**Ironwood,** v. 16, Fall, 1980. Copyright (c) 1980 by Ironwood Press. Reproduced by permission.—**Journal of Modern Literature,** v. X, September, 1976. (c) Temple University 1976. Reproduced by permission.—**Language Quarterly**, v. XXIX, Winter-Spring, 1991. Reproduced by permission.—**Letras Femeninas,** v. XIX, Spring-Fall, 1993. Reproduced by permission.—**Modern Language Quarterly,** v. 42, March, 1981. Copyright (c) 1981 by the University of Washington. Reproduced by permission of Duke University Press.—**New Orleans Review** , v.15, Winter, 1988; v. XVII, Summer, 1990. Copyright (c) 1988, 1990 by Loyola University. Both reproduced by permission.—**Nineteenth-Century French Studies,** v. 20, Spring-Summer, 1992. (c) 1992 by **Nineteenth-Century French Studies**. Reproduced by permission.—**Northwest Review,** v. 21, 1983. Copyright (c) 1983 by Northwest Review. Reproduced by permission.—**Philological Quarterly,** v. 74, Summer, 1995 for "Pope, Publishing and Popular Interpretations of the Dunciad Variorum" by Shef Rogers. Copyright (c) 1995 by The University of Iowa. Reproduced by permission of the author.—**PN Review**, v. 16, 1989. Copyright (c) Poetry Nation Review 1989. Rerproduced by permission of Carcanet Press Limited (Manchester)—**Poetry,** v. CXIII, December, 1968 for a review of Body Rags by Michael Benedikt. (c) 1968 by the Modern Poetry Association. Excerpted by permission of the Editor of Poetry and the author.—**Quadrant,** v. XXVII, April, 1983 for "The Repossession of Innocence" by Michael Hulse. Reproduced by permission of the publisher and the author.—**Raritan: A Quarterly Review,** v. XV, Fall, 1995. Copyright (c) 1995 by Raritan: A Quarterly Review. Reproduced by permission.—**Romantic Review,** v. LXVI, 1976. Reproduced by permission.—**Studies in English Literature,** 1500-1900, v. 32, Summer, 1992. c) 1992 Reproduced by permission of The Johns Hopkins University Press.—**Studies in the Literary Imagination**, v. XII, Fall, 1980; v. XIII, Fall, 1980.. Copyright 1980 Department of English, Georgia State University. Both reproduced by permission.—**Symposium,** v. XXIII, Fall-Winter, 1969. Copyright (c) 1969 Helen Dwight Reid Educational Foundation. Reproduced with permission of the Helen Dwight Reid Educational Foundation, published by Heldref Publications, 1319 18th Street, NW, Washington, DC 20036-1802.—**The Denver Quarterly,** v. X, Winter, 1976 for "Reading John Ashbery's Poems" by David Kalstone. Copyright (c) 1976 by the University of

COPYRIGHTED MATERIAL IN *PC,* VOLUME 26, WERE REPRODUCED FROM THE FOLLOWING BOOKS:

Gunn in The 1970s" in **British Poetry Since 1970: A Critical Survey**. Edited by Peter Jones and Michael Schmidt. Persea Books, Inc., 1980. Copyright (c) 1980 Carcanet New Press. All rights reserved. Reproduced by permission.

PHOTOGRAPHS AND ILLUSTRATIONS APPEARING IN *PC,* VOLUME 26, WERE RECEIVED FROM THE FOLLOWING SOURCES:

Conrad Aiken
1889-1973

American poet, novelist, short story writer, essayist, and editor.

INTRODUCTION

A prolific writer of poems as well as fictional and nonfictional prose, Aiken is regarded by some critics as having significantly influenced the development of modern poetry. He was both a contemporary and an associate of such writers as T. S. Eliot and Ezra Pound, but he disliked literary movements and labels. Aiken's work reveals a profound interest in the theories of Sigmund Freud and George Santayana, combining as it does spiritual, philosophical, and psychological elements in its examination of modern existence and the evolution of human consciousness. Much of his poetry draws upon the language and structures of music. Aiken was fascinated with the workings of the conscious and unconscious mind, and with what he termed "that passionate sense of identity which has always been the most preciously guarded possession of the poet." His poetry received nine major literary awards, including a National Book Award, a Bollingen Prize, and a Pulitzer Prize.

Biographical Information

Aiken was the oldest of four children—three boys and a girl—born in Savannah, Georgia, to Anna Potter Aiken and Dr. William Ford Aiken, who were both of Scottish descent. When he was eleven years old Aiken moved to Massachusetts to live with relatives after his father shot his mother and then committed suicide. Profoundly affected by this experience, Aiken later wrote that in discovering his parents' bodies he "found himself possessed of them forever." In 1907, Aiken entered Harvard University, where he studied literature and wrote for the Harvard *Advocate*. T. S. Eliot was one of several well-known classmates at Harvard; Eliot and Aiken developed a lasting personal and professional relationship and critics have debated over which of the two poets influenced the other's work more deeply. After missing classes to complete a translation of a work by nineteenth-century poet Théophile Gautier during his senior year, Aiken was put on probation for absenteeism. His subsequent withdrawal from the university lost him his standing as class poet, and he spent the next year in Europe, visiting Eliot in Paris. He returned to Harvard in the fall of 1911 to complete his degree and afterward pursued a career as a freelance writer. Aiken's early verse, much of which he wrote during the years following his graduation in 1912, has been characterized as reminiscent of the poetry of John Masefield and Edgar Lee Masters while demonstrating Aiken's own initial experiments in adapting musical forms to poetry and his use of common individuals as central characters. In these poems, collected in *Earth Triumphant, and Other Tales in Verse* (1914), *Turns and Movies, and Other Tales in Verse* (1916), *Nocturne of Remembered Spring, and Other Poems* (1917), and the belatedly published *The Clerk's Journal: Being the Diary of a Queer Man* (1971), Aiken used narrative and dramatic verse forms in these collections to examine such themes as disillusionment, guilt, nostalgia, and anxiety. In 1921, Aiken moved his family to England, living at first in London, then later in Rye, Sussex. He continued to write poetry but also worked on prose fiction, and contributed reviews and commentaries on contemporary poetry to London periodicals. In the late 1920s and early 1930s, Aiken experienced a period of deep personal suffering which resulted in divorce from his first wife in 1929, remarriage in 1930, and a suicide attempt in 1932. These years also initiated an extraordinarily productive literary phase during which Aiken produced much of his most enduring and significant work, such as *The Coming Forth by Day of Osiris Jones* (1931) and *Preludes for Memnon; or, Preludes to Attitude* (1931). From 1934 to 1936, Aiken served as London correspondent to the *New Yorker* under the pseudonym of Samuel Jeake, Jr. In 1939, following a divorce from his second wife and his subsequent remarriage, Aiken returned to the United States. His poetry during the next decade reflects his experiences in New England. Collected in the volumes *And in the Human Heart* (1940), *Brownstone Eclogues, and Other Poems* (1942), *The Soldier* (1944), *The Kid* (1947), and *Skylight One: Fifteen Poems* (1949), these works display a variety of stanzaic, rhythmic, and rhyme patterns and focus on Aiken's interest in cultural and ancestral heritage. Aiken's poetry of the 1950s and 1960s is collected in four volumes: *A Letter from Li Po, and Other Poems* (1955), *Sheepfold Hill: Fifteen Poems* (1958), *The Morning Song of Lord Zero: Poems Old and New* (1963), and *Thee: A Poem* (1967). These works emphasize themes relating to language and art while displaying a renewed affirmation of life. Aiken's productive career as a poet spanned nearly sixty years, garnered him numerous awards, and included children's verse and limericks as well as his complex, musically influenced preludes.

Major Works

Between 1915 and 1920, Aiken composed a unified sequence of poems that is regarded as the major work of his early career. These long pieces, which he called "symphonies," strive to achieve the contrapuntal effects of music by juxtaposing patterns of narrative repetition and variation. Aiken traced the origins of his symphonies to a "passing passion for Richard Strauss." However, he abandoned Strauss's smooth, chronological structures in favor of a more modern symphonic tradition consisting of abrupt transitions and elements of cacophony similar to the works of composers Anton Bruckner, Arnold Schoennburg, and Igor Stravinsky. Concerned with themes of personal identity, these poems focus on what has been described as the self-conscious mind's alienation from the outside world and its attempts to reconnect with that world. *The Charnel Rose*, first published in *The Charnel Rose, Senlin: A Biography, and Other Poems* (1918), is Aiken's earliest symphonic composition. Focusing on the theme of nympholepsy, which Aiken defined as a desire for the unattainable, this work features dream-like visions of lamias and death and examines the elusiveness of love. *The Jig of Forslin: A Symphony* (1916) presents the fantasies of an ordinary man haunted by prostitutes, vampires, and demons. Compared by some critics to Berlioz's *Symphonie Fantastique*, with allusions to the hallucinations of characters in the works of Rimbaud, Baudelaire, and Flaubert, this poem portrays the modern world as alienating and hostile. *The House of Dust: A Symphony* (1920), is considered a marked improvement in thematic development and technique over Aiken's previous symphonies. This lengthy and complicated work examines analogies between a city and the human body, centering on the narrator's quest for identity while exploring dimensions of awareness in societies and individuals. In Aiken's *Senlin: A Biography* (published in 1925 and generally considered his most successful symphony) the title character represents an all-encompassing

consciousness that seeks individual form. Even as he assumes the physical appearances of his world in such manifestations as a forest, a desert, a city, and a house, Senlin at the same time exists independently of these appearances. *The Pilgrimage of Festus* (1923) adopts a more concrete image of personality and consciousness in which Festus, searching for truth and knowledge, dreams of encounters with Buddha, Confucius, Jesus Christ, and Mephistopheles. In 1921 Aiken published his narrative poem *Punch: The Immortal Liar, Documents in His History* (1921). It was described by poet Amy Lowell as "one of the most significant books of the poetry renaissance." Based on the figure from the Punch and Judy puppet shows, Aiken's protagonist is presented from several points of view which alternately depict life as mysterious, ironic, and deterministic. Shortly afterward, in *Priapus and the Pool* (1922), Aiken introduced his experiments with serial form, a musical structure based on a series of tones arranged in an arbitrary but fixed pattern in which themes are explored via increment and variation. *Priapus and the Pool* focuses on the many aspects of love as symbolized by the mythical figures Priapus and Narcissus. Aiken turned to a symbolic treatment of death in his collection *John Deth: A Metaphysical Legend, and Other Poems* (1930). This work deals with Freudian ideas of ritual and routine, portrayals of grotesque dream landscapes, and themes of sexuality. In the 1930s Aiken published another major sequence of music-based poems which he called "preludes." First in the cycle is *The Coming Forth by Day of Osiris Jones* (1931), a funerary book of parables, myths, letters, and other documents that borrows from the *Egyptian Book of the Dead* and that serves as a prologue to the two volumes of preludes that follow. *Preludes for Memnon* (1931) furthers Aiken's experiments in serial form begun in *Priapus and the Pool* and addresses the problems encountered in the narrator's search for self-knowledge. Finally, *Time in the Rock: Preludes to Definition (1936)* looks at such themes as the transience of innocence, the nature of love and betrayal, and the attainment of understanding. Highly philosophical and lyrical, these preludes are also concerned with the ability of poetry to extend consciousness and awareness.

Critical Reception

Critical assessment of Conrad Aiken's poetry is, as Louis Untermeyer points out, sharply divided between strong admiration and equally strong dislike. Some commentators complain that Aiken's work is too derivative of Eliot's. Others suggest that his poetry becomes bogged down in its own discussions of poetic technique. Alternatively, several critics have commended Aiken for his attempt to create a new, more accurate poetic language that incorporates music and which is sensitive to the complex workings of the individual mind and the necessary but difficult relationship between the individual mind and the rest of the world.

PRINCIPAL WORKS

Poetry

Earth Triumphant, and Other Tales in Verse 1914
The Jig of Forslin: A Symphony 1916
Turns and Movies, and Other Tales in Verse 1916
Nocturne of Remembered Spring, and Other Poems 1917
The Charnel Rose, Senlin: A Biography, and Other Poems 1918
The House of Dust: A Symphony 1920
Punch: The Immortal Liar, Documents in His History 1921
Priapus and the Pool 1922
The Pilgrimage of Festus 1923
Senlin: A Biography 1925
Priapus and the Pool, and Other Poems 1925
Preludes 1929
Selected Poems 1929
Gehenna 1930
John Deth: A Metaphysical Legend, and Other Poems 1930
Preludes for Memnon; or Preludes to Attitude 1931
The Coming Forth by Day of Osiris Jones 1931
Prelude: A Poem 1932
And in the Hanging Gardens 1933
Landscape West of Eden 1934
Time in the Rock: Preludes to Definition 1936
And in the Human Heart 1940
Brownstone Eclogues, and Other Poems 1942
The Soldier: A Poem 1944
The Kid 1947
The Divine Pilgrim 1949
Skylight One: Fifteen Poems 1949
Collected Poems 1953
A Letter from Li Po, and Other Poems 1955
The Fluteplayer 1956
Sheepfold Hill: Fifteen Poems 1958
Selected Poems [new selection] 1961
The Morning Song of Lord Zero: Poems Old and New 1963
A Seizure of Limericks 1964
Cats and Bats and Things with Wings (children's poetry) 1965
Tom, Sue, and the Clock (children's poetry) 1965
Preludes [contains *Preludes for Memnon* and *Time in the Rock*] 1966
Thee: A Poem 1967
The Clerk's Journal, Being the Diary of a Queer Man: An Undergraduate Poem, Together with a Brief Memoir of Harvard, Dean Briggs, and T. S. Eliot 1971
A Little Who's Zoo of Mild Animals (children's poetry) 1977

Other Major Works

Scepticisms: Notes on Contemporary Poetry (essays and criticism) 1919
Modern American Poets [editor and author of preface] (poetry) 1922
Emily Dickinson, Selected Poems [editor and author of preface] (poetry) 1924
Bring! Bring!, and Other Stories (short stories) 1925
Blue Voyage (novel) 1927
Costumes by Eros (short stories) 1928
American Poetry, 1671-1928: A Comprehensive Anthology [editor and author of preface] (poetry) 1929
Great Circle (novel) 1933
Among the Lost People (short stories and drama) 1934
King Coffin (novel) 1935
A Heart for the Gods of Mexico (novel) 1939
Mr. Arcularis: A Play (drama) 1946
The Short Stories of Conrad Aiken (short stories) 1950
Ushant: An Essay (autobiography) 1952
A Reviewer's ABC: Collected Criticism of Conrad Aiken from 1916 to the Present (essays and criticism) 1958
The Collected Short Stories of Conrad Aiken (short stories) 1960
Selected Letters of Conrad Aiken (letters) 1978

CRITICISM

Calvin S. Brown (essay date 1948)

SOURCE: "The Poetry of Conrad Aiken," in *Music and Literature: A Comparison of the Arts*, The University of Georgia Press, 1948, pp. 195-207.

[*In the following essay, Brown discusses the musical techniques that Aiken used in his early poetry and remarks that unlike many other poets who claim to rely on music, Aiken does so extensively and accurately.*]

Probably no poet has been more concerned with music than Conrad Aiken, or has used it more fruitfully. The interest is visible even in the titles of his poems, where we find nocturnes, tone-poems, variations, dissonants, and symphonies. He describes himself as groping for musical effects from the beginning of his poetic career, and though he has tended to become more metaphysical during the past decade, the influence can still be seen in even such traditional and fixed types as his sonnet sequence, and, to a lesser extent, the *Brownstone Eclogues*. Nevertheless, the principal musical techniques and approaches had been worked out on their most impressive scale before the *Selected Poems* of 1929, and hence we shall concern ourselves primarily with the poems contained in that volume.

Many poets have used titles containing (frequently false) musical implications, and many have been fond of musical references and intricately developed symbols. Aiken's peculiarity does not lie in any one single aspect of the musical influence, but in its extent, richness, and cohesion. The formal arrangement of a good deal of his poetry is based on musical principles rather than on the more widely accepted poetic ones. His symbols are developed and combined in ways analogous to the composer's handling of themes. He has given us, here and there, enough information about the theoretical basis of his work to make it clear that the musical analogies are deliberately and skilfully cultivated. And, finally, this poetry based on music is alive with musical references which reinforce both the implications of its structure and a philosophy in which music is that epitome of the individual and the universe which it was to Schopenhauer.

From the purely formal point of view, Aiken makes extensive and intricate use of the general principles of repetition, variation, and contrast, though he never attempts exact poetic equivalents of the larger musical structures. Frequently, however, we find ABA forms, and these forms often overlap or enclose one another. Thus four of the long poems—*Senlin, The Pilgrimage of Festus, The House of Dust*, and *The Jig of Forslin*—devote an appreciable part of their last sections to repetition, either exact or with slight variation, of material from the first sections. Forslin offers a good example of the complication created by an extension of this principle. The poem as a whole contains the ABA structure just mentioned. But Part IV is also an ABA structure, as is at least one still smaller subdivision, Section iii of Part V. In *Senlin* also we find this type of organization on a smaller scale: the first four sections have the typical musical structure of AABA (a complete form in itself); but the A section is used twice, with new material between the recurrences, at the end of the poem. This habit of returning to the beginning for the end is as common in Aiken's poetry as it is in music,[1] and the source of the device is clearly shown when he has Music, speaking as a character, refer to the

> weak hand that touched, strong hand that held,
>   weak hand
>   that touched;
> eyes that forgetting saw, and saw recalling,
> and saw again forgetting; memory moving
> from wonder to disaster, and to wonder. . . . [2]

Another favorite musical device is parallelism carried to such a point that one passage is clearly a variation on another. Occasionally, as in some of the "Variations," this technique is used for its own sake and thus resembles the musical theme and variations.[3] More frequently, however, as in the larger musical forms, the variation occurs at some distance from the original version as part of a larger pattern. It may take the form of a shift in meter, tense, imagery, tone—almost any kind of change, so long as the original passage is still clearly recognizable. A good example occurs in *Senlin*, where the morning-song[4] contains the quatrain:

> There are houses hanging above the stars
> And stars hung under a sea . . .
> And a sun far off in a shell of silence
> Dapples my walls for me . . .

Eight pages later[5] the passage is varied to

> There are houses hanging above the stars,
> And stars hung under a sea:
> And a wind from the long blue vault of time
> Waves my curtains for me . . .

Variations of this sort are among the most conspicuous structural elements of Aiken's poetry.

Another favorite device, partaking of both repetition and variation, is something of an approximation to the rondo form of music. It consists of two themes which are consistently alternated. In spite of the fact that Aiken speaks of developing such juxtapositions in an attempt to find a poetic equivalent of counterpoint, the device is really parallel to the musical practice of alternation between contrasting themes, strings and woodwinds, loud and soft, etc. One of the most striking examples of this method, a passage alternating between the thoughts of an old man and a young girl living in apartments one above the other, was originally published as a separate poem entitled **"A Counterpoint,"** though it was later incorporated into *The House of Dust*.[6] Another conspicuous example[7] is based on the interplay between the suggestions of the music which a man hears at a concert and the chatter of his companion. Out of numerous other instances of this method we may select the morning-song of *Senlin*[8] as probably the most effective. The two alternating themes are Senlin (his actions and thoughts) and the world outside his window. The first of these, however, is in itself compound and achieves its effect by an alternation between the trivial acts with which the day begins and the sense of the vastness and beauty of the universe which occupies his mind. The first two sections show the interplay of these themes. This alternation is kept up throughout one section of the poem, not with mechanical regularity, for such regularity kills the very effect which the device is designed to produce, but with sufficient consistency and rapidity to give the intended sense of the simultaneity of these diverse elements in Senlin's consciousness.

The border-line between these formal devices of repetition and variation and the development of recurrent symbols is a real one, even though it cannot be exactly located. Up to this point we have dealt with formal elements, but it now becomes necessary to deal with content. In Aiken's longer poems a great deal of attention is given to the development of what, for lack of a better name, we may call symbols or themes. Perhaps the latter is really the better term, since these themes do not symbolize anything in the sense in which Hester Prynne's scarlet letter symbolizes her burden of guilt. Rather, a theme is intended to evoke a state of mind by presenting imagery suggestive of that state. And in this way they are far more like musical themes than like the ordinary subjects of poetry. We may well question whether the primary purpose of a theme in music is to evoke a specific state of mind, but the theme is certainly a thing in itself, both sensuously and intellectually satisfying, and independent of any criteria of objective truth. Its chief function is to be developed so that its own inherent possibilities and its relationships with other themes will be fully exploited. Except that words necessarily have external reference—a fact which Aiken is sometimes inclined to lament—and that there is an external portraying of a state of mind, however indefinable and tenuous, Aiken's themes are essentially like those of the composer.

Their development, then, proceeds along musical lines, with endless modification and combination. A theme already established may be merely suggested in a word or two; a casual phrase may be returned to and expanded until it becomes a full-fledged theme in its own right; two or more themes may be fused to form a single indivisible unit. The anthologists have isolated, for their own purposes, certain sections of Aiken's longer poems in precisely the same way that collections of parlor-music often print merely the statement of a theme from a symphony: the processes are the same, and the nature and extent of the loss are the same.

It is impossible to describe the effect of this technique adequately, but its methods can be shown. Perhaps it will be well to begin with such a short and simple example as **"Evensong."**[9] A girl looked out of her window at twilight, and we are given her train of thoughts and her state of mind, with a background of the sights and sounds which she experienced. "She looked into the west with a young and infinite pity." In the next line the last words are repeated as "a young and wistful pity," and thus one of the recurrent themes of the poem is established. As twilight came on there were slight occasional sounds, such as the murmur of leaves, "and then the hush swept back." As it grew darker, lights were turned on, and the leaves casually mentioned a moment ago are now described in some detail as, wet after rain, they glistened with the street-lights shining up through them. Looking out on this, she felt "a young, and wise, and infinite pity" for the girl without a lover, and went from this feeling into a blending of memories of love with a sense of "tragic peacefulness." She wondered: "Would her lover, then, grow old sooner than she . . . ?" Would he lose interest in the light through the leaves, and the twilight? And her first question came back into her mind. A neighbor sang a child to sleep, and the song was singularly poignant. Because it came up through the leaves of the tree? Or because, as she looked out, she "thought of all the mothers with a young and infinite pity?" The child went to sleep; "the hush swept back." If it were not raining, she thought, there would be a full moon, and the lovers would be in the park—she herself might be going there. Would she grow old and lose interest in love in the park and the latest ways of putting up one's hair? But would her lover grow old sooner than she? And yet, as she watched the city and the wet leaves, once again

> It seemed as if all evenings were the same;
> As if all evenings came,
> Despite her smile at thinking of a kiss,
> With just such tragic peacefulness as this;
> With just such hint of loneliness or pain,
> The perfect quiet that comes after rain.

Short as this poem is, and general as this account of its themes has had to be, something of their development, repetition, variation, and interplay can be seen. The longer poems are infinitely more complex. I have just abandoned an attempt to make a detailed analysis of the themes in *The Jig of Forslin.* The thing cannot be done. One soon reaches the point where, say, the underwater imagery merges with so many other things that it is impossible

to say whether we have one theme or five. Is listening to rain on the roof a reappearance of this theme, or not? And what of the chance (?) occurrence of a word like *eddy* or *flow*? The problem suggests one critic's remark[10] about the omnipresent three-note figure which opens the *Second Symphony* of Brahms: "Presently we see it, even where it is not, as when the sun is in our eyes." Other themes present the same difficulties. Nevertheless, a few examples will illustrate the complexity, if not the subtlety, of the thematic development in *Forslin*.

The first section—slightly less than two pages—introduces five separate themes destined for development in later stages of the work. First comes the motive of twilight, as Forslin sits in his room and his dreams come back to him. But dream and reality merge, and the figure which illustrates the uncertainty in his own mind is the first appearance of the pervasive underwater imagery:

> Now, as one who stands
> In the aquarium's gloom, by ghostly sands,
> Watching the glide of fish beneath pale bubbles,—
> The bubbles quietly streaming
> Cool and white and green . . . poured in silver . . .
> He did not know if this were wake or dreaming;
> But thought to lean, reach out his hands, and swim.

Among other things, he remembered having "stepped in from a blare of sunlight / Over the watery threshold to this gloom"; and this sudden change from light to darkness (or from darkness to light) appears later in various guises. He also remembered music weaving its patterns and opening doors for him—a theme perhaps even more fruitful than the underwater imagery, and frequently combined with it. The idea of music in general is immediately transformed into one of its favorite forms, the music of the café or cabaret. But before this happens the clash of cymbals is compared to "a voice that swore of murder." This hint is taken up a few lines later as Forslin thinks how he sits there in his room: in the world outside, people were dancing and making love, "And the murderers chose their knives." Thus, very unobtrusively, is introduced the theme of the knife-murderer, which is later gradually built up into one of the principal motives. And finally the first section closes with a slightly varied repetition of the lines about the aquarium.

The second section is a single page, but Aiken manages, with the greatest air of casual effortlessness, to introduce into it every one of the five themes stated in the first section, to give a bit more elaboration to some of them (the knife-murderer, for example) and to make the first combination of the two most important ones:

> Deep music now, with lap and flow,
> Green music streaked with gleams and bubbles of
>   light,
> Bears me softly away.

The third section—almost the only piece of "straight" narrative in the poem—goes back to tell who Forslin is and what he is doing there meditating in his room as evening falls. Beyond this point, detailed analysis is impossible. New themes appear, one of them a striking image of a bird falling, seen against the sheer side of a tower. Familiar themes are hinted at, combined, reinterpreted. Familiar phrases are reechoed. The twilight theme is merged with those of music and the aquarium in one passage:[11]

> This is as if, in the going of twilight,
> When skies are pale and stars are cold,
> Dew should rise from the grass in little bubbles,
> And tinkle in music among green leaves.

And near the end of the poem there is a passage of summary in which every phrase evokes associations elaborately built up by earlier treatment of the themes which are here merely mentioned:

> Who am I? Am I he that loved and murdered?
> Who walked in sunlight, heard a music playing?
> Or saw a pigeon tumbling down a wall?
> Someone drowned in the cold floods of my heart.
> Someone fell to a net—I saw him fall.[12]

Though the fact has no bearing on the aesthetic qualities of any single work, it is interesting to note that several of these themes are favorites of Aiken's and occur in a number of his poems of the "symphony" type. So standard do some of them become that in *Time in the Rock*[13] Aiken himself rejects them as so well worn that they are no longer adequate for his purposes:

> But no, the familiar symbol, as that the
> curtain lifts on a current of air, the rain
> drips at the window, the green leaves seen in the
> lamplight are bright against the darkness, these
> will no longer serve your appetite, you must have
> something fresh, something sharp—

But they were good symbols while they lasted, and they achieved remarkable effects in a number of distinguished poems. In the "symphonies" as a group they were employed in much the manner that has already been described for *Forslin*, except that in some later ones (*The House of Dust* and *Senlin*, for example) the transitions between different sections are made smoother and less startling.

What is ultimately the point of all this manipulation of forms and themes? In itself it might seem like a harmless enough kind of solitaire for anyone who happened to find it amusing, but hardly a thing to present to the public as literature. The general answer to these objections is that certain things can be communicated only by devious means, and that these happen to be precisely the things which Aiken wishes to communicate. In an article[14] contributed to *Poetry* in 1919 (ostensibly a review of his own *The Charnel Rose*) he developed at some length the theory on which these works were written, admitting that his views on the subject were not clear at first, since theory has to be developed through practice. He confesses to "some complex which has always given

me a strong bias towards an architectural structure in poetry analogous to that of music," and briefly traces his efforts to achieve this structure until "finally in *Forslin* and *Senlin* it achieved something like a logical outcome."

> What I had from the outset been somewhat doubtfully hankering for was some way of getting contrapuntal effects in poetry—the effects of contrasting and conflicting tones and themes, a kind of underlying simultaneity in dissimilarity. It seemed to me that by using a large medium, dividing it into several main parts, and subdividing these parts into short movements in various veins and forms, this was rendered possible. I do not wish to press the musical analogies too closely. I am aware that the word symphony, as a musical term, has a very definite meaning, and I am aware that it is only with considerable license that I use the term for such poems as *Senlin* and *Forslin*. . . . But the effect obtained is, very roughly, that of the symphony or symphonic poem.

Each section of the poem is colored by what has gone before and, retrospectively, by what is to follow; hence a section repeated will not be exactly the same thing that it was on its first appearance. Furthermore, contrasting tones ("emotion-masses") build up their effects in precisely the same way as contrasting forms. This all leads to an evocative poetry "of which the chief characteristic is its elusiveness, its fleetingness, and its richness in the shimmering overtones of hint and suggestion." In fact, "It is a prestidigitation in which the juggler's bottles or balls are a little too apt, unfortunately, to be altogether invisible."

> It remains, finally, to point out the profound danger of the method I have been outlining: the danger, I mean, that one's use of implication will go too far, and that one will cheat the natural human appetite for something solid and palpable. One cannot, truly, dine—at least every evening—on, as Eliot would remark, "smells of steaks in passage-ways." One must provide for one's symphony a sufficiently powerful and pervasive underlying idea—and, above all, make it sufficiently apparent. Whether the time will come when we shall be satisfied with implication for its own sake, no one, of course, can guess.

This is a well-considered and mild enough statement from the inventor and practitioner of a theory, and objectors will find that Aiken has forestalled them on almost every point. There is, however, one question which it does not raise.

Why did Aiken wish to develop this fleeting and evocative form of poetry? Because he wished to deal, not with the relationships between the individual and other persons or his physical or social environment, but with what goes on in the individual himself. The problem of personal identity, the impossibility of fully communicating anything, the simultaneous complications of thought and feeling—these are the problems which fascinate him. These elusive things can never be stated; but there is a chance that they may be gradually formed in a reader's mind by an indirection comparable to the phenomena themselves. What the metaphysicals set out to do for the consciously thinking mind Aiken wishes to do for the feeling mind, especially in a state of reverie. Once again, his own statement is conclusive. In his novel *Blue Voyage* the rather autobiographical hero Demarest writes a long letter to Cynthia, who has apparently decided to have nothing more to do with him. The letter begins with long accounts of childhood experiences of its author, but is never finished. A second letter,[15] designed to replace this one, tells about the first:

> A long, sentimental reminiscence of my childhood! Yes, I actually believed for a moment that by some such circumferential snare as that I might trap you, bring you within my range, sting, and poison you with the subtle-sweet poison of a shared experience and consciousness. That again is highly characteristic of me. It is precisely the sort of thing I am always trying to do in my writing—to present my unhappy reader with a wide-ranged chaos,—of actions and reactions, thoughts, memories and feelings,—in the vain hope that at the end he will see that the whole thing represents only *one moment, one feeling, one person.* A raging, trumpeting jungle of associations, and then I announce at the end of it, with a gesture of despair, "This is I!"

Or, equally well, this is Forslin, who lived in poverty ten years in order to learn to throw one billiard ball into the air and catch and hold it balanced on another billiard ball; who has performed the feat for the first time in vaudeville and received no applause because it looked too easy; who has decided to kill himself with gas; and who now wanders in his own jungle of associations.

All the verse "symphonies" of Aiken have a similar purpose, and the verse strives to achieve a fluidity by which it can respond to every shift of tone or imagery. The basic form of most of these poems is irregularly rhymed verse employing considerable metrical freedom—an intermediate form which can (and does) pass with ease either to such fixed forms as regularly rhymed quatrains, or to free verse. It is an ideal medium for this purpose. A rigidly followed verse-form cannot give the required fluidity: that is why the attempt at symphonic arrangement in the "fifteen hundred more or less impeccable octosyllabic couplets" of **"Earth Triumphant"** had to be "exceedingly rudimentary," and why **"Disenchantment: a Tone Poem"** could not go much further. On the other hand, imposing form on this type of material is a difficult process at best; hence it is foolish to reject the aid offered by the recurrent patterns of verse. A comparison of the loose prose of Mrs. Bloom's famous sewer of consciousness (or of Demarest's thoughts, influenced by Mrs. Bloom, in *Blue Voyage*) with the verse of ***Forslin***, ***Senlin***, or ***Festus***, leaves no doubt as to the superiority of the latter form.

We can now begin to understand Aiken's artistic preoccupation with musical effects, and our understanding will be aided by a consideration of some of his references to music. Throughout his poetry it is a recurrent theme, not as a superficial ornament, but as an inherent characteristic of his thought. His world is remarkably auditory— so much so that abstractions usually present themselves

in audible form, as in the repeated references to "the horns of glory." Not content with the music of the dance or of the café, he is always hearing strange and solemn music imprisoned in walls and floors, or rising from the depths of earth or sea.

But the music actually heard, even in imagination, forms only a small part of Aiken's musical references. More often, music is a symbolic way of presenting the otherwise inexpressible complications of human thoughts, dreams, even relationships and daily lives. Music and literature are the only arts of movement, and literature can really present only one thing at a time. But music, with its different instruments, its cross-rhythms, its contrapuntal complications, can and does present *simultaneously* a number of different things which are both independent of each other and interrelated. One theory of musical aesthetics is based on the thesis that the laws of musical development are identical with those of human thought.[16] This is certainly Aiken's point of view, and thus we see why, with all his writing about music, he has so very few references to specific composers or works: he does not want the particularity of a specific composition, but rather the generality of the nature of music.

Readers of Aiken's poetry will remember countless passages in which music is symbolically used to represent the complexities of human consciousness, but it may be worth while to select a few of the most striking ones for quotation. In **"Meditation on a June Evening"**[17] the thought of a loved one develops musically in the mind:

> My thoughts turn back to you,
> Like tired music in a tired brain
> Seeking solution in the worn refrain;
> It returns, it returns,
> It climbs and falls, struggles, disintegrates,
> Is querulous, resentful, states, restates;
> But always, like one haunted, comes again
> To that one phrase of pain;
> And that one phrase, you know as well as I,
> Is the remembered pallor of your face;
> And a certain silence, and a certain sky,
> And a certain place.

The main section of Forslin's thoughts is introduced by a statement that

> Things mused upon are, in the mind, like music,
> They flow, they have a rhythm, they close and open,
> And sweetly return upon themselves in rhyme.
> Against the darkness they are woven,
> They are lost for a little, and laugh again,
> They fall or climb.[18]

Not only the individual's secret thoughts, but the relationships between individuals are essentially musical patterns:

> We are like music, each voice of it pursuing
> A golden separate dream, remote, persistent,
> Climbing to fire, receding to hoarse despair.

What do you whisper, brother? What do you tell
    me?
We pass each other, are lost, and do not care.[19]

But beyond this representation of thought and daily life, music opens up other vistas. Aiken frequently comments on the poverty of language and its inability to express the subtleties which he seeks. That is why, in most of his poetry, "we deal in juxtapositions."[20] When words fail, he turns to music; in fact, anything which words cannot adequately express—love and passion, for instance—*is* music.[21] In his later manner, after the period of the "symphonies," Aiken devotes a fine lyric[22] to this difference in the capacities of musical and literary expression:

Music will more nimbly move
than quick wit can order word
words can point or speaking prove
but music heard

How with successions it can take
time in change and change in time
and all reorder, all remake
with no recourse to rhyme!

            . . .

But verse can never say these things;
only in music may be heard
the subtle touching of such strings,
never in word.

Thus the unanswerable problems of the universe can be hinted at only by musical comparisons, for music is in itself a complete and parallel universe. At the conclusion of the speech made by Music in *The Coming Forth by Day of Osiris Jones*[23] we have a clear statement on this point:

O death, in shape of change, in shape of time,
in flash of leaf and murmur, delighting god
whose godhead is a vapour, whose delight
is icicles in summer, and arbutus
under the snowdrift, and the river flowing
westward among the reeds and flying birds
beyond the obelisks and hieroglyphs—
whisper of whence and why, question in darkness
answered in silence, but such silence, angel,
as answers only gods who seek for gods—
rejoice, for we are come to such a world
as no thought sounded.

But this explanation of the ultimate is illusory. When Festus tries to explore human knowledge, "it occurs to him that the possibility of knowledge is itself limited: that knowledge is perhaps so conditioned by the conditions of the knower that it can have little but a relative value."[24] Once again, a musical figure carries the idea. While Festus and the Old Man who represents his *alter ego* are discussing the problems of knowledge they hear a solemn, haunting music which may perhaps be the ultimate expression of the universe.[25] Yet they are forced to realize that

                It is a music

Of mortal origin and fleshly texture.
Who knows if to god's ears it may be only
A scream of pain?

As they draw nearer, they see that it is played by an orchestra of butchers.

    Thus ends our pilgrimage! We come at last,
    Here, in the twilight forests of our minds,
    To this black dream.

Thinking to explore knowledge itself, they have explored only their own mind: whatever man may understand or know about the nature of things is ultimately only his own thought, and the music of the spheres is thus necessarily only the still, sad music of humanity.

Thus we return to music as a symbol of the intricacies of the human consciousness. Frequently in Aiken's poetry there is mention of music muttering behind closed doors, and clearly heard only on those rare occasions when a door is momentarily opened. A long section of *The House of Dust*[26] is devoted to an elaboration and explanation of this symbol. We can quote only a brief part of it here:

        Once, on a sun-bright morning,
    I walked in a certain hallway, trying to find
    A certain door: I found one, tried it, opened,
    And there in a spacious chamber, brightly lighted,
    A hundred men played music, loudly, swiftly,
    While one tall woman sent her voice above them
    In powerful sweetness. . . . Closing the door
    I heard it die behind me, fade to whisper,—
    And walked in a quiet hallway as before.
    Just such a glimpse, as through that opened door,
    Is all we know of those we call our friends. . . .
    We hear a sudden music, see a playing
    Of ordered thoughts—and all again is silence.
    The music, we suppose, (as in ourselves)
    Goes on forever there, behind shut doors,—
    As it continues after our departure,
    So, we divine, it played before we came . . .
    What do you know of me, or I of you? . . .
    Little enough. . . . We set these doors ajar
    Only for chosen movements of the music. . . .

This, then, is the music which haunts Aiken, the music which he so extensively describes and imitates in his verse symphonies. Until fairly recently, the great aim of his poetry was to open those doors, admit us to the room, and let us hear whole concerts of this fleeting, elusive music of the mind. The very nature of the undertaking made complete success impossible, but by means of a musical symbolism and musical techniques Aiken has succeeded farther than anyone else who has made the attempt.

Notes

[1] As other conspicuous examples we may mention "Variations," *Selected Poems* (N. Y., 1929), pp. 66-76, and Time in the Rock (N. Y., 1936), LXV, p. 95.

[2] *The Coming Forth by Day of Osiris Jones* (N. Y., 1931), p. 37.

[3] See *Preludes for Memnon* (N. Y., 1931), Sec. XXXV, for an excellent example.

[4] *Senlin*, II, ii.

[5] *Senlin*, II, x.

[6] First published in *Poetry: A Magazine of Verse*, 1919. Included in *The House of Dust*, IV, iv.

[7] *The Jig of Forslin*, V, iv.

[8] *Senlin*, II, ii.

[9] *Selected Poems*, pp. 3-6.

[10] Goepp, *Great Works of Music*, I, 386.

[11] III, i.

[12] V, v.

[13] *Time in the Rock*, XCII, p. 132.

[14] *Poetry: A Magazine of Verse*, XIV, 152-159.

[15] *Blue Voyage* (N. Y., 1927), pp. 291-292.

[16] See Gehring, *The Basis of Musical Pleasure* (N. Y., 1910).

[17] *Nocturne of Remembered Spring and Other Poems* (Boston, 1917), p. 16.

[18] *The Jig of Forslin*, I, vii.

[19] *The House of Dust*, III, viii.

[20] *The Jig of Forslin*, I, vi.

[21] *Preludes for Memnon*, XVI.

[22] *Time in the Rock*, LXXXIII.

[23] p. 37.

[24] The "Argument" printed as introduction to *The Pilgrimage of Festus* (N. Y., 1923).

[25] *The Pilgrimage of Festus*, V, i.

[26] *The House of Dust*, IV, iii.

Jennifer Aldrich (essay date 1967)

SOURCE: "The Deciphered Heart: Conrad Aiken's Poetry and Prose Fiction," in *The Sewanee Review*, Vol. LXXV, No. 3, July-September, 1967, pp. 485-520.

[*In the following essay, Aldrich examines Aiken's poetry and prose, but speaks of him particularly in terms of a poet who sees and responds to a dual world—the interior, individualized life of the mind, and the exterior, more anonymous world outside.*]

I.

He was standing here—
he that was hurt, he that remembered;
stood here, thought of the thing that hurt him,
the word, the world, the wound—
and I thought with him, remembered with him,
knowing
nothing of his own word or world or wound,
only my own wound that I could share,
my own world that I could give.

O God, is it less than this or more,
that we must give—?

O word is it more than this or less,
that we can say—?

Rashly we give them both,—
the wound, the word; and stand ashamed of shame.

Conrad Aiken's poetry is theoretical, reflective, made of ideas; but his language is concrete, his words drawn from the objects of the actual world. From it he has gathered the things which are meaningful to him, and these make up the world of his writing, with its geography, its botany, its cosmology, and its cast of characters. It is through these "twinned worlds, the inner and outer" that Aiken has laid bare his "visible"—his "deciphered" heart.

Aiken's most successful attempts to set himself truly before the reader occurred after he had written a sizable portion of his poetry, and have usually been within a context of human generality in which the subject is at once highly individual and slightly anonymous. It is in these terms that he discusses poets in general:

They see the world perpetually as both old and new at once: in its complexity they never forget its simplicity; they celebrate its universals, and are therefore dateless; and precisely because they are themselves the most private and individualist of people, by articulating this extreme privacy of awareness they become themselves universals.

Aiken's individual self-awareness has never been in terms of unity; he has sought, rather, to see himself "resolved into his constituent particles: and this with a purpose, that his increased awareness may be put at the service of mankind". His early attempts thus to reveal himself were primarily in terms of the "constituent particles", the things that have an important place in his mind, but he did not at first make clear the distinction, later emphasized, between the actively creative mind and its merely passive function in which it resembles a pool or mirror. An example of this early approach is Aiken's answer to Coleridge's question "What is there in thee Man that can be known?":

> Only this, this process of collection, this mysterious
> process by which the psychic mirror stored away its
> reflections of the ever-changing colors and shapes of
> other psyches, other things. . . . And in the end, one's
> personality was nothing whatever but an anthology of
> these mimicries and adaptations, one was oneself
> simply the compiler. The onomastic.

This is typical of Aiken's shallowest level of self-description or self-definition, the level upon which the self is no more than the memory, the knower. During his life Aiken has extended his belief in the creative ability of the self until he has finally seen it as capable of answering the questions of its existence with its own self-awareness. In the process of deepening his consciousness, however, Aiken has never rejected his earlier levels of self- and world-perception. The statement quoted above is found in the autobiographical essay *Ushant* (1952), and it reiterates an early view which Aiken had retained along with the more mature views which he expresses later in the book. The progress of *Ushant* is simultaneously chronological, following the author's developing awareness from childhood on, and vertical, penetrating the layers of himself to ever deeper strata. The two movements together form a descending spiral which finds, at the deepest level of the self, the earliest memories and associations.

If we take the example of *Ushant*, and, beginning with the simpler, more superficial levels of awareness, descend slowly through Aiken's system of gradually revealed consciousness, we shall begin by exploring the internalized world upon which he has drawn for all his further discoveries; we will then come to the word—the means through which he has come to discover himself and his world; and finally we will uncover the wound, the terror and pity of a human existence, the motive force in his life, and, in existential terms, that part which is the essence of human existence. It is "the wound" which is the deepest level of discovery in *Ushant*; and, in the spiral movement which I have described, this discovery is simultaneous with a return to the earliest objects of perception, the world as apprehended through the senses, now introjected and become the world as himself.

Thus, at the heart of Aiken's work there is a continual flux, but the effort is always the same effort, and it is toward something which is already in existence—which, in fact, has even instigated this effort. It is a teleological motion, with the end always in sight:

> The pages of our lives are blurred palimpsest:
> New lines are wreathed on old lines half-erased,
> And those on older still; and so forever.
> The old shines through the new, and colors it.
> What's new? What's old? All things have double
>   meanings,—
> All things recur.

Three of Aiken's five novels, many of his short stories, and his first long poetic series, **The Divine Pilgrim**, as well as some of the later poems, were all written in the physical form of a journey. The actual vehicles of these journeys seem quite clearly, when looked at together, to be in some way a symbol for consciousness; and the goal is the self. Thus the motif of the "Great Circle" (the title of one of the novels)—for it is the self, also, which set out on the voyage. So, in *Ushant*, Aiken wonders about the "soul's landscape . . . did one ever truly escape, ever—(after a certain point)—change it?"; and he considers whether "an author's writings were often in some degree an anticipation of attitudes yet to be formed, definitions yet to be made, actions yet to be taken". He suggests here that it is through "the word" (by which he means writing; and, by extension, art in general) that the first steps are to be made towards apprehending this landscape of the self. The relationship of the word to the self is not, however, direct. Words tend to be specific; they are better adapted to things than to ideas, to ideas than to feelings—or to feelings than to people. And so,

> Despair, that seeking for the ding-an-sich,
> The feeling itself, the round bright dark emotion,
> The color, the light, the depth, the feathery
>   swiftness
> Of you and the thought of you, I fall and fall
> From precipice word to chasm word, and shatter
> Heart, brain, and spirit on the maddening fact:
> If poetry says it, it must speak with a symbol.
>
> What is a symbol? It is the 'man stoops sharp
> To clutch a paper that blows in the wind';
> It is the 'bed of crocuses bending in the wind,' the
> Light, that 'breaks on the water with waves,' the
> Wings that 'achieve in the gust the unexpected.'
> These, and less than these, and more than these.
> The thought, the ghost of thought, the ghost in a
>   mirror.

The world which is Aiken's has a double meaning because the visible heart of the poet has been deciphered, has been made tangible, physical, for the rest of mankind and for himself. This has not been done easily or quickly, however, but throughout the entire work. It is a summary which must be constantly remade:

> Beloved, there is time,
> between this morning's instant and that wall,
> for such infinitudes of delight and grief,
> such patient addings and subtractions, such
> new sentences, each wider than the last,
> new knowledges, new visions and revisions,
> that we ourselves are like that god; each moment
> is the last wall from which our laughter rings;
> the world summed up; and then a new world
>   found,
> vaster and richer; a new synthesis,
> under the sandgrain, and above the star.

This summary understanding is what he describes elsewhere, in the terms of a Japanese painting of a waterfall, as "pour-in-stillness", in which sense

> there would be no 'progress', . . . of the ordinary sort,
> in a work of art: everything past would be hypothecat-
> ed, everything future would be implied: the move-
> ment of these together would constitute a kind of
> static-dynamic, a stillness of motion round an invis-
> ible center. As action would have preceded any given
> moment in it, so action would follow: but the moment
> itself, *every* moment, was comprehension.

As in the work of art, so in the *opus*, the artist's total work: a student of the total work must approach it through one dimension or the other of the static-dynamic. I have chosen to approach it through the "static" present— through the description of a relatively constant world, or self, toward the discovery of which all of Aiken's motion tends.

Despite the growing existence of a group of people who are very much involved in his work, Aiken has remained "the best known unread poet of the twentieth century", largely, I believe, because so much of his work needs, or at least is improved by, a prior orientation on the read-er's part in Aiken's world. It may or may not be a crit-icism of Aiken that an appreciation of his work requires such a commitment; there certainly have been those who are willing to make it. For these, and for others who have not yet entered Aiken's world, the function which the critic can perform is to help orient the reader in its meanings. The questions which Aiken asks of life are *why* and *how*; but, in order to reach and understand these queries, we must first stand in his place, and we can only do that by asking *what*. That is to say, before it is pos-sible to understand the meaning, to Aiken, of the word, which is his method, or of the wound, which is his meaning, it is necessary to understand his world. In or-der to reach this, I propose to reverse Aiken's process of communication, the effort which he has made to take the readers into his own view, and lend them his ideas by recreating in them his own mood and his own feelings. In the next section of this essay an attempt is made to work backwards through the things that express the mood, to discover the feeling behind each of the things, and so, hopefully, to build up an anthology, an onomasticon, which will reassemble the "treasure-trove" of himself upon which Aiken draws for his writing.

II.

> The landscape
> opens unhesitatingly before us
> hills from rivers roll back
> pathways open to left and right
> our feet are now in the morning brook
> and its clear parable of time
> the tree is under our hands and over our heads
> and as we move to what we do not know
> and can never rightly imagine
> all these become the ambiguous language
> by which we come to pass
> and learn to see

> and mean
> and be.

It must be understood that the meanings behind objects in Aiken's writing certainly have not the rigidity of, for example, the symbolic structure of Yeats's *Mythologies*, or, for that matter, of Jung's theory of the racial uncon-scious and its archetypes—although knowledge of the latter was probably helpful to Aiken in freeing him to accept his own intuitive use of symbols. When he uses the concept, a symbol is, very simply, something which stands for, represents, or evokes something else.

Generally the meanings which Aiken sees behind the words he uses are one commonly understood in our lan-guage: that the short-lived rose should symbolize death in **"The Charnel Rose"**, that Aiken should see the world as a clock, its heartbeats ticking off the seconds until death, that the daisy should seem to be characterized by innocence—none of these ideas is particularly new or surprising to the reader. Other things in his world have achieved the status of symbol because of a more personal meaning which they have for the writer and which becomes evident after the reader has come upon the same idea several times: the bees, for example, which always appear with an atmosphere of warmth and happy comfort; or the bells, which, in *Ushant*, Aiken calls the "bells of time", and which, like a clock striking, seem "as if they were themselves . . . marking out the course of a life". Sometimes he explicitly tells us what he means by an important class of things, as in *Ushant*, when he says:

> in their turn, all the rest of his life, *every*
> house was to become a ship.

Given Aiken's frequent metaphor of himself as a house, houses and ships are both, thus, simultaneously "static" and "dynamic", both the pause of "now" in the move-ment of time.

In the play *Mr. Arcularis* the stars are repeatedly men-tioned in such a way as to make it clear that they rep-resent the infinite which is beyond both life and death. In *The Coming Forth by Day of Osiris Jones* the stars have, as their comment on the universe: "Chaos—hur-ray!—is come again." Polaris, among the rest, has a special significance, as being the "lodestar of our thought" which particularly draws the mind toward thoughts of death. It is with this connection in mind that Aiken warns religious believers:

> O fools that still believe the half-dead prophets,—
> Move south, avoid the North Star, shun the frost.

North is, to him, the direction of death, toward which we are always gravitating, around which we sail continually, whether in boats or in our own houses, until finally we fly straight to it:

> Come dance around the compass
>   pointing north

Before, face downward, frozen,
                        we go forth.

Aiken uses the idea of the great circle in many different ways, or in many different layers of meaning. One of these is the circle from non-being to life, and then to non-being again:

> the flight of bones to the stars, the voyage of dead
>   men,
> those who go forth like dead leaves on the air
> in the long journey, those who are swept
> on the last current, the cold and shoreless ones,
> who do not speak, do not answer, have no names,
> nor are assembled again by any thought, but
>   voyage
> in the wide circle, the great circle. . . .

This Dantesque picture of the souls assembled like dead leaves, ready to be blown away, reminds one also of Genesis: "For dust thou art, and unto dust shalt thou return"; and this, in turn, explains Aiken's almost interchangeable use of *womb* and *tomb*:

>   O pitiful self,
> who of these shapes and shames make all thy
>   meaning
> and draw thy being from disease of chaos
> who of disasters makest thy quick joy
> and now so fearest the womb of night that bore
>   thee. . . .

Another example of this is found in *John Deth: A Metaphysical Legend* where, in part II, Millicent Piggistaile is transformed into a tomb, and Deth into a tree whose dark roots explore her crevices in what is perhaps the most simultaneously erotic and astonishing passage in Aiken's writing. Of trees in general he says in *Ushant*: "Live-oaks, holm-oaks—those were one's first trees, the symbols therefore of all that was tree: . . . in them, one found one's whole notion of greatness and rootedness, of earth-living and earth-dying." This general view, and the specific sexual one mentioned above, are joined in a passage of *Senlin: A Biography* in which the narrator, speaking both for the poet and for humanity, sees himself as a tree such as this one:

> In the hot noon, in an old and savage garden,
> The peach-tree grows. Its ugly cruel roots
> Rend and rifle the silent earth for moisture.
> Above, in the blue, hang warm and golden fruits.
>
>   . . . . .
>
> And these thin leaves, even in windless air,
> Seem to be whispering me a choral music,
> Insubstantial but debonair.
>
> 'Regard,' they seem to say,
> 'Our idiot root, which going its brutal way
> Has cracked your garden wall!
> Ugly, is it not?

A desecration of this place . . .
And yet, without it, could we exist at all?'

The tree, like the person whom it represents, is simultaneously creative and destructive—creative, as it were, in the top half, the more ethereal part of its nature, which gives to the world its leaves and fruits; and destructive in the lower half, which represents man's bestial nature, his ravenous needs for sustenance and gratification. Destructive, also, in that the creative process takes from the world around it the material with which to maintain its creativity.

One of Aiken's more interesting, and least anticipated, symbolisms is that of the leaf. The *leaf*, among other objects and people who make "Remarks on the Person of Mr. Jones" (in *Osiris Jones*), says simply, "You are brief." Here its message is like that of the ephemeral flower. As the product of the tree, however, it has a more distinctive place. In *Time in the Rock* Aiken says, "words words and other words, like leaves, like leaves". The leaves are the human means of self-expression, as they are the output of the tree.

Another somewhat unexpected symbolism in Aiken's Nature is that of the grass-blade. The blade of grass is, to Aiken, a symbol of multiplicity, the one detail among the many:

> The world is intricate, and we are nothing.
> It is the complex world of grass. . . .

The blade of grass is also the symbol of all the human beings who, although small, must not be forgotten: it is the *persona* of the child in man, as the pebble is. It should be kept in mind, however, that while these things have their symbolic meaning, they, like the other symbols which Aiken uses, are also important to him in themselves, in their real, physical existence:

> The idiosyncrasy, the precious idiosyncrasy, of each
> grassblade must be saluted, the individuality of the
> pebble be acknowledged.
>
> The pebble I lift in the palm of my hand
> Laments, 'Lo, you are the one who planned
> This world of horror, this world of grief!
> Of frost and screaming leaf!'

In the second of these quotations there is a confrontation between two personae, the second of which is the creative element in the human character, often seen as father—or as Father. Aiken's own father was to him the original poet, the person with whom he identified himself in order to become a poet—a creator—himself:

> The *persona*, yes, of the father had thus been adopted
> . . . ; and together, too, with this, had proceeded a
> parallel adaptation, the taking over of the father's
> role as a writer.

Aiken's father had killed himself and his wife when his son Conrad was eleven years old, and this sharp and horrifying fact which Conrad had been the first to discover had perhaps served to keep that part of himself which was, like his father, a creator—and which might also, therefore, be a murderer—in some way separate from the rest of himself. The hero of *The Pilgrimage of Festus* sees this creative-destructive element in his character as the god in himself:

> I will not have a god in me!
> I flee in panic, I dart to escape
> This world of horror that flees with me—
> This world that takes its horror of shape
> From my own brain's poor cruelty.
> I flee in terror—: O Festus, find
> Some doorway out of the mind!

Ultimately there is, as in Sartre's play, no exit from the mind, whether the mind itself be seen as a heaven or as a hell. The idea of God in our minds is, itself, a world which we have invented for ourselves, a solution for a problem which no part of Nature except man sees as a problem:

>   —I saw myself and God.
> I saw the ruin in which godhead lives:
> Shapeless and vast: the strewn wreck of the world:
> Sadness unplumbed: misery without bound.
> Wailing I heard, but also I heard joy.
> Wreckage I saw, but also I saw flowers.
> Hatred I saw, but also I saw love . . .
> And thus, I saw myself.
>
>   —And this alone?
>
> —And this alone awaits you, when you dare
> To that sheer verge where horror hangs, and
>   tremble
> Against the falling rock; and, looking down,
> Search the dark kingdom. It is to self you come,—
> And that is God. It is the seed of seeds:
> Seed for disastrous and immortal worlds.
>
> It is the answer that no question asked.

God, then, is simultaneously a symbolic creator of man, invented and projected into symbol by man, and perhaps serving as the archetype for man's own deepest creative resources. Man, as a father, sees the small things about him, among them his children, and loves them; but he is also still the child himself, needing a parent's love. He is the one who, in Freudian terms, has identified with the father, and thus contains the father, with all his creative powers, within himself:

> O god of my imagination, god of my creation,
> whom thus I impersonate, my father, my mother,
> whom I create out of the visible world, as you
>   created me
> out of the invisible, let me be the one
> who loves the seaweed, the starflower, the mussel,
>   the bones of a small fish on
>   the beach
> and I among them like a smooth pebble.

The mind has many other *personae* besides that of the god, the creator: these can be thought of as identifications, some strong, and some, as with a person merely looked upon, very weak. Aiken has said of one of his early poems, **"The House of Dust"**, that it "is really an elaborate progressive analogy between the city, seen as a multicellular living organism, and the multicellular or multineural nature of human consciousness". This similarity is expressed in many different places, of which this line is typical:

> My veins are streets. Millions of men rush
>   through them.

Somewhat similar to the purposes of a city in his writing is the idea which Aiken expresses through rain. Rain, which the Lord "sendeth on the just, and on the unjust", has an all-inclusive quality which makes the poet aware, again, of his participation in humanity:

> Weave, weave, weave, you streaks of rain!
> I am dissolved and woven again.
> Thousands of faces rise and vanish before me.
> Thousands of voices weave in the rain.

Aiken's use of music is similar to this in its function of achieving a transition between the general and the particular. I shall not attempt to discuss Aiken's use of music in the formal structure of his poetry, but simply to describe its symbolic meaning as it appears directly in his writing. Since music has a power, beyond words, of evoking and stimulating emotion, Aiken sometimes uses it to suggest the emotional interaction between two people; at other times he calls on it to intercede between people when words do not seem adequate to the task:

> Let us in joy, let us in love,
> surrender speech to music, tell
> what music so much more can prove
> nor talking say so well. . . .

Particularly in his early poetry, Aiken uses music to suggest a process which it performs for many people, and which it apparently performs very strongly for him: the function of taking the mind out of its immediate surroundings, and allowing it to wander, free of the body, with any strong associations that have been latent:

> You say, before the music starts, while still
> Cacophonies of tuning drawl and mutter,—
> Snarls of horns and cries of violins,—
> That so-and-so has just divorced his wife,
> That Paul is dead, leaving his work unfinished,—
> And what's-her-name was hurried, secretly,
> To an asylum . . . What says the music, then? . . .
>
> Winds pour from the chattering south,
> Warm foam crumbles along lava beaches,
> Parrots are screeching green
> In a sky of smouldering blue.
> Dull broad leaves struggle against the sun.
> And I am there, and you. . . .

Water in general shares the qualities of music and of rain, particularly as it is used in **"Changing Mind"**, where it allows the poet's subconscious and his memories of the important people of his life to flow in free interaction with the world outside of him. When the water is an ocean, it has other properties as well. The hero of *Blue Voyage* is called William Demarest, and he is identified with Andy Cather's psychoanalyst alter-ego, "Bill", in *Great Circle*, and with the central figure, "D.", of *Ushant*. The name *Demarest* can be read as *De mare est*, suggesting that he originates, somehow, in the sea; and if this reading is plausible, it is because the sea has two other meanings: flux and the absolute. Even in the movement of its waves, which heave and swirl without displacing the water itself, the ocean is the archetype for the "static-dynamic . . . stillness of motion around an invisible center". So Aiken, in the process of writing a symbolic poem with the things found by the seaside, says to himself,

> But there is also at your back the sea;
> this too you know; this too you fear; that wide
> unaltering but always altered laughter. . . .

The sea is the positive print of which the rock, or dust, from which we come is the negative; it is not, like God, projected from man's psyche, but rather it is the immutable and absolute state of flux which man can in no way avert or affect; it is the question to which there is no answer. It is, as well, the boundary beyond which no poem can go, the symbol which can be stated only in its physical, never in its abstract, terms:

> . . . your poem becomes the perfect shape it is;
> the sea left out!

> And thus, you know the world.
> Thus, with a phrase, exclude the absolute.

Blue, the color of both sea and sky, represents, like them, the beyond. Because it is a reminder of the unknowable, the unreachable, blue is, for Aiken, "the colour of terror".

Among the rest of the symbols of his world, Aiken includes women:

> . . . the men *were* oneself, the women, no matter how deeply loved, nor with what all-givingness or agony or ecstasy, were not; they paralleled, they accompanied, they counterpointed, but they did not, in the same sense, become intimately the alphabet of one's soul. . . . But all, bless their hearts, a species of constant; a series of constants, each one in turn the x of one's y or the x^1 or x^2 or x^3; or of course even the x^4, unmet, unknown, still locked magically in the imagination.

It is probably at least partly with tongue in cheek that Aiken speaks of man's "inalienable superiority to woman" but it is evident that woman appears to him somewhat strange and distinctly dangerous—as, for example, in the parallel pieces, the short story "Spider, Spider" and poem **"The Wedding"**, in which the woman and the spider symbolize each other, and both represent a sort of greedy lustfulness. Womankind also represents the unconscious:

> . . . woman, that demon of unconsciousness,
> that winged body of delightful chaos,
> that quick embodied treason and deceit. . . .

Sometimes she appears as the repressed *id*:

> 'And on each kite was bound
> A weeping woman, the arms outstretched, the feet
> Nailed at the foot!'

and sometimes the irrepressible *id*:

> And then she smiled, and said—
> 'Ah, it is true! The sensual has its moment.
> The trickster brain—thank God—can be deposed . . .'

Finally, and most generally, woman is the matrix, the womb, the deepest region of creativity—"like the spring earth, she is fruitfulness." Aiken sees woman, not as a being equal with himself, but, like God (which at least puts her in good company), as a symbol of a creative part of himself:

> Thus it comes, thus it comes Ruby,
> woman who art not woman but a wound,
> wound who art not a wound but indeed a word,
> word that art not word but truly a world
> sprung spoken speaking spoiled and spent
> in the brief darkness that the darkness meant.

It would hardly be possible to catalogue all the components of Aiken's world, and all their nuances of meaning. I have been able to discuss only those details which seemed to me most central and most representative, in the hope that the view which I have thereby given of the landscape of Aiken's soul—more, perhaps, through the quotations from his writings than through an explication of them—will serve as enough of an orientation in his world to make it possible to descend to the next level of his "deciphered heart". He himself, as will be seen in the passages quoted from his writing, uses the symbols which have been discussed as important aids in his descent into himself.

III.

> In every part we play, we play ourselves;
> even the secret doubt to which we come
> beneath the changing shapes of self and thing,
> yes, even this, at last, if we should call
> and dare to name it, we would find
> the only voice that answers is our own.
> We are once more defrauded by the mind.

> Defrauded? No. It is the alchemy by which we grow.
> It is the self becoming word, the word
> becoming world. And with each part we play
> we add to cosmic *Sum* and cosmic sum.

Up to now certain assumptions have been made about Conrad Aiken's purpose in writing which should, at this point, be made more explicit. In a statement made near the end of *Ushant* Aiken outlines the theme of his auto-biographical essay:

> How shall the non-knower, who is in process of be-coming the knower, convert himself into a language by which, first, to unravel his own beginnings and outlines against the matrix in which, like a trilo-bite . . . , he found himself embedded, and then, with this basic knowledge, and out of its now co-ordinated constituents, begin a parallel 'arrangement' of the world itself, the world outside and beyond (but with-in oneself too)—the microcosm, with full awareness of the laws and limitations of microcosm . . . receiving into itself the macrocosm, a world within a world—? How indeed!—And nevertheless it was in this really staggering drama that every living human being was involved, to greater or less degree, every day of his life.

This pursuit of consciousness is, in two ways, Aiken's reason for writing: one, that writing was for him a means through which to arrive at the understanding of ever deeper levels of himself; the other, that through his writing he could share his consciousness with others. Thus, a study of "the word" in his writing is a study of his approaches to consciousness and self-conscious-ness.

Aiken has said, "We deal in juxtapositions"; and, in-deed, there is a kind of bifurcation of thought which is typical of him; whenever his consciousness grapples very closely with a single issue, he begins to see that it can be considered in two ways, or as two issues. So there is a "two-voiced theme" which gives Aiken the dual roles of, on the one hand, the "god who knows and mourns himself. . . . Narcissus, and his glass is truth"; and, on the other, of a part of a broader scheme, who can say, "I was a part of nature's plan; / Knew her cold heart, for I was consciousness. . . ." Aiken's consciousness of him-self in the particular adds to the general consciousness of humanity: and through the enriched awareness of humanity, his own consciousness is expanded. There is a back-and-forth motion here, rather like the reiterative relationship with God, as discussed earlier; and, like that relationship, this interaction between the individual poet and the general humanity is ultimately most useful in that it helps to define each in terms of the other. Unlike the idea of God, however, it is presumed that humans do exist "out there", beyond the poet's own consciousness, and for this reason there is more actual giving and taking in the relationship; there is a real conversation as op-posed to one which occurs only on the stage of the poet's mind.

The poet's duty to "give the lowdown on himself, and, through himself, on humanity" sets up the relationship between the individual and the rest of the world which Aiken has explored, in every direction, throughout his writing. In part he sees this as a duty which he has inherited from his family:

This 'thing' of the family's, this accumulated aware-ness, this evolving consciousness, even with its taint of insanity, this it was their duty, and D.'s most of all, as now for the moment their ephemeral spokes-man, to put at the disposal of society—even, if nec-essary, on the chopping-block or the dissecting table.

The self which Aiken thus puts at our disposal is a vac-uum which we are invited to fill: but the vacuum has edges; it has definition. In part this definition has been made in terms of generalities, in order to make it recog-nizable to the largest number possible. There are, to this end, quotes from Shakespeare, Keats, *et al*; and there are statements in which Aiken, taking a somewhat Whit-manesque stance—particularly in the early writings—an-nounces his participation in the generality of humanity. Of **"The Charnel Rose"** he says, "It scarcely needs to be said that the protagonist of the poem is not a specific man, but man in general." And as late as **"The Morning Song of Lord Zero"** we find him saying the same thing, although in more sophisticated terms, and more directly through the personal view as a basis for the general:

> I am your jack-and-jill
> of all trades dubious brother
> panhandler father Cassandra mother
> and yet in the end insidiously
> o indispensably and invidiously
> something more.

When, as he is likely to do in his earlier work, Aiken begins with the general, and does not pointedly place the individual in this shapeless mass, he can be quite dull. When, however, he takes the reader from the generalized idea to a specific self-involvement, and, through that, to the general again, he can, in a very few words, establish a remarkable and exciting sense of perspective, both on the individual and on the generality:

> The eternal mistress lifts her hand,
> To rearrange her hair,
> For the deathless lover who climbs and climbs the
>   stair.
>
> Have we not seen him climb,—or climbed,
>   ourselves,—
> Up the eternal azure of those stairs?
> Ridiculous, to those who stay behind,
> Or chuckle, meditating, from afar:
> The small pathetic back, in silhouette,
> Dwindling against a star.

At times this perspective is gained by concentrating upon the crowd until he suddenly sees himself, and makes the reader see himself, there among the rest. And sometimes he finds the rest of humanity in himself:

> Knock on the door,—and you shall have an answer.
> Open the heavy walls to set me free,
> And blow a horn to call me into the sunlight,—
> And startled, then, what a strange thing you shall
>   see!

Nuns, murderers, and drunkards, saints and sinners,
Lover and dancing girl and sage and clown
Will laugh upon you, and you will find me
   nowhere.
I am a room, a house, a street, a town.

There is here, once again, the shuttling movement, out to the general, and back to the specific—or vice versa; it does not really matter which, for the equation and our participation in it remain the same, no matter which term is given first. As an example of this, Aiken sees in himself both Christ and Judas, in the short story "The Disciple", or in this fragment of **"The Jig of Forslin"**:

   'He writhes his head from side to side.
   O holy Christ I have crucified!—
   I twist there on the cross with you;
   And what you suffer I suffer too.'

The combination of both murderer and murdered in his own creative mind is the theme, also, of the story "Jones and Smith", and of the novel *King Coffin*. The tragedy of the latter is that the central figure, Jasper Ammen, isolated in his refined and individualistic awareness, refuses to recognize concomitant participation (suggested by his punning name, "Am men") in humanity, as symbolized by Jones, whom he wishes to kill. In the end it is himself that he murders. I have suggested before that because of his suicide Aiken's father was to him the symbol of man as both murderer and murdered; and it was through an identification with his father that Aiken probably first achieved the bipolarity in his nature which, in his recognition of it, exploded him, as it were, into all the possibilities of humanity. In realizing that there is no human potential, either for good or for bad, which is not contained within each individual, Aiken took into himself one form of the great circle voyage: by the route of the general, as Mr. Arcularis by the route of the Milky Way (and it is appropriate that both routes should be, in some form, through death), Aiken returns to the specific, to be fully identified with himself. To Senlin's "basic and possibly unanswerable question, *who and what am I*", there is the at least partially satisfactory answer: I am men; and thus, I am a man.

The teleological movement in Aiken's writing, the great spiral into the self, is split in another way; perhaps if we are to stay with a metaphor from geometry, we should see the movement as following the paths of the double helix, the form of the DNA molecule—a not altogether irrelevant comparison. This second bifurcation is in terms of the past as opposed to the present. Aiken's intense interest in psychology justifies the use of Freudian terms here to discuss this split; for what in fact we find reflected here are the concepts of Eros and Thanatos. The first of these is the forward-going stream of self-maintenance and self-improvement; or, in Aiken's terms, of self-creation and self-understanding. This is what Aiken described as "the self-shaping of godhead, or the only thing we knew it by, the mind of man". The reflection of the force of Thanatos is the regressive movement toward death, an attempt to return to one's beginnings:

. . . is it strange that always we should go
Bewildered, in this dance from blood to beauty,—
From beauty back to blood? . . . I am a man:
Sentience wrung from the rock. And in a twinkling
The rock is wrung from sentience.

This is the extreme of the regressive movement. More often Aiken speaks of it in terms of only a partial withdrawal, back to his own childhood:

Hadn't he, ever since, every time he set sail for England, actually been setting sail for that carpeted floor, on which the copy of *Tom Brown's School Days* still lay open at the luminous fragment of verse? Hadn't time stood still, ever since, at that echo of a moment, that phrase of incantation? And hadn't his entire life been simply a *locus* bending itself again and again, after no matter how many interruptions and diversions, as of wars, or storms at sea, to this limit, this perhaps unattainable limit, this imperative and imperishable Ushant?

At other times this reaching for the past extends to Aiken's ancestors, or to the various figures in his cultural past with whom he identified, such as, for example, William Blackstone, the hero of his poem **"The Kid"**. Frequently he finds a satisfying rootedness in his various homes by identifying, not only with the former dwellers there, but with the houses themselves, or the land on which the houses were built. This, in a large measure, explains his attachment to England, the house of his ancestors in poetry, and "the window which looked upon his own racial and cultural past, and thus endowed him with the sense of belonging, of being part of a moving continuum, the evolving series of civilized consciousness".

The mind, reaching into itself both backwards and forwards, completing in both directions the great circle from the womb through life to the tomb—this is what Aiken calls, in *Ushant*, "that unfathomable, and yet to-be-fathomed, pluralism, the plural mind in the plural universe, [which] must forever partly escape the flung net of symbol". He goes on to say:

To bring it all into one solar or lunar and shining parenthesis, one expanding synthesis—the grave of John Keats, the monk in the Borghese Gardens, the thunderous *fiat* on the ceiling of the Sistine, the pitiful dyed flowers of the Piazza di Spagna, or that admirable fresco, on the wall of the lupanarium at Pompeii, which showed the young Roman's penis so emphatically outweighing the heap of gold on the other side of the balance—to bring all this together, well, wasn't that precisely what one was there for? Wasn't one's own *existence* the synthesis, if one used it properly?

Thus, once more, the duality resolves itself in the conscious discovery of self, and we are free to pursue a new theme, a new bifurcation, which appears as soon as consciousness once more bends closely to the study of the self. This is the theme of the relationship of art to life. As with the ambiguous thread of general and particular humanity, so here there is a constant shuttling back and forth between the servant and the served: the life feeds the art—as in the image of the tree sucking life from all around it—and at the same time, when the tree puts forth its leaves and fruit, the art feeds the life. It is "that eternal problem of language, language extending consciousness and then consciousness extending language, in circular or spiral ascent". In this case, the synthesis is found in a new analysis:

> The onomastic making his onomasticon out of words and worlds, adding up the bright syllables and the dark to ever more hermetic meanings and combinations of meaning, even to cancellations, and negations, or contradictions deployed in a fixed counterpoint, or meaning dislimning into meaninglessness; wasn't this precisely the same action as that of love, love finding and making itself in love? They were the two voices of the one flute. . . . And the pursuit of that teasing echo, wherever it might lead, as in the pursuit of love, was the artificer's joy, as if the two pursuits were one and the same.

Were they the same? There is some evidence that Aiken at least half believes so:

> . . . the love was perhaps interchangeably identifiable with one's own consciousness, one's own being and becomingness: it was simply another disguise for the poetic and poietic psyche which is the very center of existence.

It seems probable, in light of the blame laid on the mother in both *Mr. Arcularis* and *Great Circle*, that Aiken felt subconsciously that sex, the illicit half of love, was responsible for the deaths of his parents. It may also be partly for this reason that love from generation to generation, and the identification through which it occurs, is, in the end, more important to Aiken than erotic love. This kind of love particularly has a position very much like that of art in Aiken's mind:

> . . . wasn't there also that obligation, as pointed up by grandfather—both to the ancestors and the descendants—of transmitting the preciously learned inheritance? Weren't the three little D.'s [his children], and his work, in this regard, practically synonymous?

There are, to be sure, occasions when Aiken, in a lyrical mood, takes a more traditional view of the primacy of love and sex over all else:

> In the beginning, nothing; and in the end,
> Nothing; and in between these useless nothings,
> Brightness, music, God, one's self . . . My love,—
> Heart that beats for my heart, breast on which I
>   sleep,—
> Be brightness, music, God, my self, for me.

As this turns out, however, he is only momentarily asking his love to relieve him of the burden of consciousness by which he is committed to discovering brightness, music, God, and all other things, in himself—and himself in all things.

Consciousness necessarily implies consciousness *of*, and it is for this reason, and considering the importance of the idea of consciousness in Aiken's writing, that this paper has had an unusually large emphasis upon content. The forms which Aiken used, vacillating between lyrical and dramatic modes of presentation, between the schools of imagists and realists, were the means, important in themselves, but never the end. When "invited to give his notions of what poetry should be", Aiken turned to the following passage from Santayana's *Three Philosophical Poets*:

> Focus a little experience, give some scope and depth to your feeling, and it grows imaginative; give it more scope and more depth, focus all experience within it, make it a philosopher's vision of the world, and it will grow imaginative in a superlative degree, and be supremely poetical. . . . Poetry, then, is not poetical for being short-winded or incidental, but, on the contrary, for being comprehensive and having range. If too much matters renders it heavy, that is the fault of the poet's weak intellect, not of the outstretched world.

The search for consciousness is a search for meaning which starts with the worlds—he microcosm, and the macrocosm which the microcosm receives into itself—and then seeks to shape the things of it, through words, into a meaning; but the meaning always comes back to the worlds from which it grew. Aiken's most serious concern with language has always revolved around the question of what it can convey, and with what truth. If it is capable of exploring the self, he is still dubious about its ability to go beyond the self or its immediate perceptions:

> are the shoes that await you by the chair
> less true than the dreams from which you wake,
>   the hat
> that hangs in the hall less true than memory
> which remembers it, reaches a hand to it,—
> the door less true than the hand that shuts it?
>
> Move outward, and you only move, poor biped,
> an atom's atom from here to here, never
> from here to there—again your 'self' you meet,
> it is yourself that waits outside the door,
> salutes you on the waking side of dream—

As for the "poetic" function, Aiken sometimes has his doubts about that, also, in light of the curious reciprocal relationship in which he perceives himself with the projection of himself which is God:

> You dream the world? Alas, the world dreamed you.
> And you but give it back, distorted much
> By the poor brain-digestion, which you call
> Intelligence, or vision, or the truth.

In the end, we return once more to the fact that "if poetry says it, it must say it with a symbol." Consciousness, meaning, words, are all grounded in the world, and take their existence from a symbolic extension of the world:

Where will you turn now if not to the rain,
to the curtain in the wind, the leaf tapping the
     window,
these are the wilderness, these are beyond
your pencil with its reflections
your thumbnail with its suggestion of rivers and
     glaciers
now you must go abroad

To the wild night which everywhere awaits you
and the deep darkness full of sounds
to the deep terror in which shines for a moment
a single light, far-off, which is suddenly quenched
this is the meaning for which you seek a phrase
this is your phrase.

In the end, Aiken's first concern is with the thing it-self—the *ding an sich*—and language is above all the medium, employed because he must find expression, and this one is the best he knows. The word is not precious in itself, but important because it is the leaf which grows most naturally on the human tree:

This nature, it appeared, must learn to shape itself in
words; words, and the rhythms of words, were the
medium in which it seemed most likely, or at any rate
most happily and magically, to find the equivalents of
being, the equivalents of the still shadowy self. Here
was the clearest process, and evidence, of growth;
these were the tree's leaves.

At the level of the word we are in a sort of limbo with Aiken; he has used it to pierce through the world, but at this point he comes up against the fact that

who would carve words must carve himself,
first carve himself; and then alas
finds, too late, that Word is only Hand.

If one goes no further than this, he is stranded in a world of word, without meaning.

IV.

O sleeping man, wake, and compose of all
these crystal intricacies of nescience death

of the six words and the six leaves and the
                         six bells
eastward bearing like glass birds the sleeping
                         heart
to the altar of sunrise which the columns
                         uphold
the six crystal columns lucent in sunrise
O sleeping man, wake, it is time to depart,
open your crystal zero, compose your death.

The word is related to the world as a means both of expression and of exploration. The wound is both the reason for searching the world, and, in the end, that thing which the searcher discovers.

To find what Aiken means by "the wound" one first goes back to that terrible shock of his childhood when he discovered both of his parents dead by his father's hand. He early was forced to recognize and to admit, at least implicitly, that "Death is born with us. And I am afraid." The fact of death questions daily the meaning of life; but it is a question asked only by man—or not even neces-sarily by man, if left to follow his instincts, but by the restless intellect of man—by, as Dr. Johnson would have said, "the hunger of the human imagination":

The steeples pointed to the absolute,
Man avoided man, star avoided star,
The rocks were single in hard humbleness;
And thought alone it was that in its weakness
Sought answering thought.

After one has been reading Aiken for a while, one begins to reflect on this question, to wonder when it was, and how, that little Australopithicus—or perhaps it was homo-something-or-other—first posed for himself the questions which we now so naturally find ourselves asking. Aiken points out the fact that many of these problems are self-made. For example, The Tree, in *Three Voices at the Meridian*, says:

                    . . . the devil
by man called conscience or else consciousness
in his unenviable and self-created doom
invented out of time and out of mind
that he might call himself mankind
and who knows why.

The Man's self-justification to The Tree is his own aware-ness; but it is precisely this awareness which is the cause of the problem:

The miracle said 'I' and then was still,
lost in the wing-bright sphere of his own wonder:
as if the river paused to say a river,
or thunder to self said thunder.

As once the voice had spoken, now the mind
uttered itself, and gave itself a name;
and in the instant all was changed, the world
two separate worlds became—

The indivisible unalterably divided;
the rock forever sundered from the eye;
henceforth the lonely self, by self anointed,
hostile to earth and sky.

It is not death itself which puts into question the mean-ing of life, but rather the human consciousness, which, in recognizing the possibility of meaning in life and death, recognizes also the possibility of meaninglessness. "So come we to our mother chaos." This, most deeply, is the wound in human nature. It is the *Angst*, the *nausée* of modern man, which Aiken became aware of at an earlier age than most people, and which he has been struggling with ever since. It is, I believe, his great contribution that, more than any other American writer, he has met this challenge face on and has made a meaning for himself out of the confrontation.

It has been seen that Aiken's role as an individual among the generality of humankind has been both one of giving and one of taking, in giving "the lowdown on himself, and through himself on humanity", and in watching the faces on the street "with an introspective eye". The participation in the generality takes its most concrete shape (although again in the form of a question, at least at first) in the continuity of generations:

> . . . if to wake, to cease to dream, be this,
> to face a self made ready while we slept,
> shaped in the world's shape by the single voice—
> if thus we wake too late and find ourselves
> already weeping, already upon the road
> that climbs past shame and pain to crucifixion—
>
> . . . . .
>
>   ah, can it comfort us,
> us helpless, us thus shaped by a word,
> sleepwalking shadows in the voice-shaped world,
> ah, can it comfort us that we ourselves
> will bear the word with us, we too, we too
> to speak, again, again, again, again,—
> ourselves the voice for those not yet awakened,—
> altering the dreams of those who dream, and
>   shaping,
> while still they sleep, their inescapable pain—?

At best the members of generations gone "will be borne / downstream forever past the later comers", and the thought of each generation flows into the next as a part of "the begin-all-end-all poem, time". Thus Aiken hopes to weld the past and present together in bonds that will at once "exclude the absolute" and make "the nowness of now" supreme. At times. however, the present, seen as an anthology of the past, does not seem to him a broad enough base for the mind's explorations, and he suggests a more courageous use of the powers of consciousness:

> . . . shall we be angelic, close brave wings,
> fall through the fathomless, feel the cold void,
> and sound the darkness of the newly known?—
>
> . . . . .
>
>   ah surely this
> were nobler answer than the glib speech of habit,
> the well-worn words and ready phrase, that build
> comfortable walls against the wilderness?
> Seeing, to know the terror of seeing: being,
> to know the terror of being: knowing, to know
> the dreadfulness of knowledge . . .

Chaos is timelessness, and the little lifetime which, for each human being, contains an infinity of pasts, presents, and futures, is "but lightning on a sea of chaos". This is the "dreadfulness of knowledge". Since chaos cannot be

tamed by seeing or being or knowing one's temporal place in timelessness, Aiken has tried out other medicines for the wound. At times he has turned away from knowledge to feeling, and particularly to love. He has said that "All that we know in love is bitter, / And it is not much." But perhaps it is not what we know in love that matters— "Love is not much: it is a touch: but it is true." Love is, certainly, an important means to an end; it is "the password" to "a world"; but it is not, itself, the end, the world, nor is it the primary means to it. Simply in terms of the frequency with which it is mentioned, the idea of love is preceded by at least two other means to the same end: consciousness and (as a means to consciousness) the word. Before Aiken himself could find any answer in these, however, there was one other possibility with which he had first to dispense. This is the possibility of finding a cure for the wound in religion.

In the later poems, starting with **"Time in the Rock"**, Aiken increasingly addresses the projected *persona* of God as "Lord Zero", or simply "Zero": and finally, as in the quotation which begins this section, this *persona* comes to represent the chaos which it, the imaginative power of man, has the ability to see, and which it has thus, in a sense, invented. Aiken's relationship with God sets the tone for his feelings toward religion in general:

> The thing, of course, was not to retreat, never to
> retreat: never to avoid the full weight of awareness,
> and all that it brought, and above all . . . never to
> seek refuge from it in the comforting placebos of
> religious or mystical myth or dogma.

Thus we come to Aiken's suggested alternative to such a refuge:

> . . . now at last the road was being opened for the
> only religion that was any longer tenable or viable, a
> poetic comprehension of man's position in the uni-
> verse, and of his potentialities as a poietic shaper of
> his own destiny, through self-knowledge and love.

Aiken's greatest hope from self-consciousness is that, through it, he might be able to achieve such understanding as this:

> In the clear shaft of light the man so standing
> alone, but his aloneness known,
> all things accepting, all things gladly heeding,
> the heart beating, the hand bleeding,
> the lost world now again his own
> and marvellous with understanding.

This kind of understanding includes, as an important part of its wisdom, the acceptance of limits which it cannot hope to transcend:

> the drowning one balanced breathless in the wind
> lost in speech
> striving in haste to know the every from the each
> in vain to find

the leaf of leaves the wave of waves
the meaning of meaning

and then came back from the soliloquy of the wind
and listened again to the long soliloquy of the mind;
the spirit humbled, and shaped, and at last resigned,
to the four walls that confined.

The potency of self-knowledge is limited to our own lives; Aiken does not pretend that it can in any way influence chaos itself. The same is true of the word, through which self-knowledge is to be reached:

Shape has no shape, nor will your thinking shape it,
space has no confines, and no borders time;
and yet, to think the abyss is to escape it,
or fix that horror's margin in a rhyme. . . .

The word can still, however, help in self-revelation, and it is through self-revelation that at least the shallowest level of the wound can be healed:

Said he: Thus draw your secret sorrow forth,
Whether it wears a woman's face or not . . .

. . . . .

. . . and bear her forth
Into that landscape that is rightly yours
And dig a grave for her, and thrust her in
All writhing, and so cover her with earth.
Then will the two, as should be, fuse in one.
The landscape, that was dead, will straightway shine
And sing and flower about you, trees will grow
Where desert was, water will flash from dust,
And rocks grow out in leaves. And you, this grief
Torn from your heart and planted in your world,
Will know yourself at peace.

Probably, on this level, the "secret sorrow" represents Aiken's mother whom he had lost even more truly than his father, being without the same opportunity to regain her through identification, and the advice given by him about this subject sounds very like that which might be given by a psychiatrist. It was through poetry that Aiken was able to establish his identification with his father; and it is by writing about his mother's death, incorporating her into the world within his writing, that he hopes also to relieve the pain of her loss. But further than this the word cannot go. With words Aiken again finds himself in the release and the trap of symbols, with their allusive, elusive, illusive qualities; in the end the word, like the memories from the past, cannot go beyond describing the chaos whose outermost fringes, at best, are "fixed in a rhyme":

Here we have sounded, angel!—
O angel soul, O memory of man!—
And felt the nothing that sustains our wings.
And here have seen the catalogue of things—
All in the maelstrom of the limbo caught,
and whirled concentric to the funnel's end,
sans number, and sans meaning, and sans purpose;
save that the lack of purpose bears a name

the lack of meaning has a heart-beat, and
the lack of number wears a cloak of stars.

The world which Aiken creates in words he has already created, in living, by receiving his ancestors unto himself through identification and love; in knowing, by revealing his family unto itself as its "most conscious member"; and in begetting, by passing on those worlds of lives already lived, through himself, to his children. These hopes and memories, times and generations, of the future and of the past, have helped to explain the "begin-all-end-all poem, time", but the need for such an explanation in itself is still a burning wound. And so Aiken suggests that we "let that be our theme . . . —that we must ask a theme."

The self is its own answer even before it is its own question: "It is the answer that no question asked." Inquisitioner and inquisitioned, murderer and murdered, creator and created, the mind is its own most important milieu:

Winter is there, outside, is here in me:
Drapes the planets with snow, deepens the ice on
    the moon,
Darkens the darkness that was already darkness.
The mind, too, has its snows, its slippery paths,
Walls bayonetted with ice, leaves ice-encased.
Here is the in-drawn room, to which you return
When the wind blows from Arcturus. . . .

The mind is a house of many mansions; and it is its own inhabitant. Here it is not only a world touched with winter; it is also the room to which it withdraws from its wintry self when the wind blows on it from the deathly stars. There is all the more urgency for the poet, threatened by the infinite, by chaos, to define and manage his own interior world, shaping the exterior world as he perceives it into a poem:

The world as word
this is the poem which the wise poet writes
in us and through us and around us writes
o and invites
all things created, and all things to come,
each to make tribute and contribution make
to what is never whole
or wholly heard.

If Aiken is making any recommendation, it is that man, driven by the deep wound of his consciousness, turn his consciousness, through the word, and through love, to the now which is his life. "Thirst in the There," he says, "that you may drink the Here." In this sense, Aiken's view is neither optimistic nor pessimistic, for it looks, most importantly, neither backward nor forward; the past is relevant as it is a part of the present, and the future, death, as it influences life. If seen in this way, even death can be an asset to life: of a dying man Aiken says in *Ushant*, ". . . the prospect and immediacy of death had made him a poet." Perhaps the *lacrimae rerum* are most characteristic of "the landscape / With all its nerves and voices", but above all this landscape

         . . . is yours.
Do with it what you will. But never try
To go away from it, for that is death.
Dwell in it, know its houses, and cursed trees,
And call it sorrow. Is this not enough?

Perhaps it is not enough, but it is true; and it is all there is. It is limited in time and space, and Aiken has recognized these limits and made them his. It is, in the physical terms in which it is expressed, a metaphor for the exterior, physical world which is apprehended and made interior through the word and through love. This landscape is, in fact, the poem which the wise poet writes, "the world as word". The existence of this inner world—or word—or wound—created in our consciousness of it, is the pain, the tragedy of human life; but it also *is* this life; and the question which is not asked, but lived, is answered by itself in the living.

Notes

The poetry of Conrad Aiken is copyrighted and is reprinted by permission of the Oxford University Press.

Louis Untermeyer (essay date 1967)

SOURCE: "Conrad Aiken: Our Best Known Unread Poet," in *Saturday Review* (New York), Vol. 50, No. 47, November 25, 1967, pp. 28-9, 76-7.

[*In the following essay, Untermeyer reviews Aiken's prolific career as a poet and observes that his work rarely provokes anything other than strong feelings, whether positive or negative, from its readers.*]

The case of Conrad Aiken is as singular as it is confusing. Practically no criticism of his work has struck anything like a balance. The great quantity of his writing and its stubbornly idiosyncratic quality combine to preclude a tempered estimate. He has been condemned for an all-too-ready rhetoric and he has been exalted for a superb command of the poetic art.

One of the most prolific and definitely the most versatile of poets, Aiken, at the age of seventy-eight, has published twenty-seven volumes of poetry, five novels, five collections of short stories, two books of criticism, three anthologies, two books for children, a play, a quasi-autobiography, and a volume of fifty off-color limericks, to say nothing of works still to appear. He has been called "the best known unread poet of the twentieth century," a man who is famous for having, somehow, missed fame. Not that Aiken has been without honors. He has received all sorts of citations and awards, including the National Book Award, the Shelley Memorial Award, a Pulitzer Prize, a Bollingen Prize, and the coveted Gold Medal from the Institute of Arts and Letters. But, as a full-page "middle" in the London *Times Literary Supplement* put it a dozen years ago, he has received "a recognition too grudging for it to be satisfactory to those who value his writing for its intrinsic worth: for its 'world of symbols shimmering with ambivalences and ambiguities,' and for the fact that it is, unlike much verse of our time, always talk, always the spoken word." The article suggests a specific reason for Aiken's inability to win united acclaim: the poet's penchant for wrapping his themes in "tissue upon tissue of proviso and aspect" on the assumption that "the old unities and simplicities no longer serve."

It is a plausible reason. Readers hot for certainties are bound to be bothered by ambivalences and ambiguities. It has been objected that Aiken is too much the analyst for his own—and the reader's—good; that, prompted by the pronouncements of Freud, he has been unable to resist a central preoccupation: the insistence that men live from dream to dream, from one dubious and always disillusioned ideal to another.

It is, I say, a plausible reason, but it is far from a convincing one. There are too many other factors not closely related. For one thing, there is Aiken's unyielding refusal to try to attract a following. He has made no effort to popularize himself. In an era of publicity-goaded (or self-goading) artists, he has declined to attend fashionable literary gatherings, read his poetry as a performance, deliver lectures, or use the public platform for easy aggrandizement. For another thing, it is hard to "place" Aiken. He has never been in fashion nor part of the poetic mainstream. He will not accommodate himself to any of the convenient categories; he cannot be fitted into academic cubbyholes; he is impossible to handle in perfunctory reviews. Then again, there is the sheer bulk of his work. I know no one—writer or reader—who can keep up with his output. A single volume, his **Collected Poems**, runs to 895 pages, and only a dedicated aficionado can thread his way through the labyrinthine windings of Aiken's internal world.

In common with Yeats's poetry, Aiken's divides itself rather sharply into early and later manners, and those who favor the one rarely like the other. Although students have been taught that it is Yeats's intellectual rather than lyrical poetry which counts, Aiken's readers are not so sure. His position has not yet been, as they say, "finalized."

Essentially a lyrical poet, Aiken began in 1914 with the pseudorealism of **Earth Triumphant**, echoes of the then current vogue for Masefield and W. W. Gibson. This was followed almost immediately by **Turns and Movies**, a grim set of vaudeville vignettes with Masters and Freud lurking in the wings. Every now and then there was an accent that was not borrowed from anyone, and with **The Jig of Forslin**, written in his twenty-sixth year, Aiken discovered his own voice and his own vocabulary. Both are heard in the opening lines:

    In the clear evening, as the lamps were lighted,
    Forslin, sitting alone in his strange world,
    Meditated; yet through his musings heard
    The dying footfalls of the tired day
    Monotonously ebb and ebb away

Into the smouldering west;
And heard the dark world slowly come to rest.
Now, as the real world dwindled and grew dim,
His dreams came back to him. . . .

The tone, to be extended later into symphonic elaborations, is immediately established. It is a tone which is both musical and conversational, a tired but beautiful set of cadences, wavering, blurring, but somehow poignant. It carries the now familiar accents of *Prufrock*, which appeared in England a year after *Forslin* and caused later critics to make invidious comparisons. As an analyst of individual sensibility, Aiken's technique of fusing the mundane with the mysterious was his own, an integral part of his quality—a quality which was captured by Eliot and not, as has been often charged, borrowed from Eliot by Aiken.

Senlin: A Biography is a further advance in the combination of harmonies and dissonances. it purports to be a portrait of an introspective individual—its three sections are entitled "His Dark Origins," "His Futile Preoccupations," and "His Cloudy Destiny"—but the person, as I have written elsewhere, merely acts as the background, the unconscious becomes the hero. Perhaps the most striking and also the most quoted passage is the one beginning:

It is morning, Senlin says, and in the morning
When the light drips through the shutters like the
  dew,
I arise, I face the sunrise,
And do the things my fathers learned to do.

Stars in the purple dusk above the rooftops
Pale in a saffron mist and seem to die,
And I myself on a swiftly tilting planet
Stand before a glass and tie my tie.

Vine leaves tap my window,
Dew-drops sing to the garden stones,
The robin chirps in the chinaberry tree
Repeating three clear tones . . .

There are houses hanging above the stars
And stars hung under a sea.
And a sun far off in a shell of silence
Dapples my walls for me.

The *Pilgrimage of Festus* plays further variations on the suspensions and cadences that characterized the musings of *Forslin* and *Senlin*. Aiken grouped the three, plus two symphonic poems (*The Charnel Rose* and *The House of Dust*), under the heading of *The Divine Pilgrim*. As a student of epistemology who comes to the unhappy conclusion that "knowledge is inconclusive," Festus is blood brother to Forslin and Senlin, all of them searching for the unattainable and all of them trying to explain (if only to themselves) the inexplicable.

A new and sharper note was struck in *Punch: The Immortal Liar*. After the extensions and, in some ways, extenuations of private experiences, after moments of realism drifting into translunar romanticism, the poet speaks with a sudden directness. *Punch* is, first of all, a story or, rather, an alternately light-hearted and scarifying version of a child's myth, a play in which the puppet becomes not the traditional villain but a frustrated visionary, a pathetic dreamer twitched by invisible strings, tortured into making gestures beyond his control. Within the framework of the narrative there are a dozen plangent lyrics, notably those beginning, "Solomon, clown, put by your crown," "Sheba, now let down your hair," "Open a window on the world," "Death, you will wear a chain of gold," and "There is a fountain in a wood."

By the time his *Selected Poems* had won the Pulitzer Prize in 1929, appraisal of Aiken had reached the extremes of derogation and celebration. His succeeding work kept the poles of criticism still further apart. When *And in the Human Heart* appeared, the critics were as divided as ever. Louise Bogan's reaction was negative, and Randall Jarrell's was even more disapproving. Implying that Aiken had little to say, although sometimes saying it beautifully, Jarrell complained that Aiken was "in love with a few dozen words, and their permutations and combinations have assumed for him a weight and urgency that would be quite incomprehensible to his readers if it were not for the fact that most of these are the traditional magic words of English romantic poetry. . . . Any similarity between the poems and reality is purely coincidental." Robert Frost's impatience with what he considered a languid lugubriousness led to a mean pun about "Comrade Aching."

First published in 1952, *Ushant* is a curious combination of autobiography, fiction, a disquisition on the arts—including the art of survival—and a *roman à clef* whose pseudonyms (Rabbi Ben Ezra for Ezra Pound, Tsetse for T. S. Eliot, Hambo for Malcolm Lowry, etc.) were divulged in a later edition. It puzzled some reviewers and pained others. Edward Dahlberg attacked it violently and excused a wanton and scurrilous assault by quoting Samuel Johnson to the effect that to attack a bad book is a benefaction to the commonwealth. More recently, James Dickey dismissed Aiken as "an industrious and unfashionable Historic Personage with space in all the textbooks and anthologies, and very few readers. . . . And yet," Dickey conceded, "through the clouds of poetic vapor, through the long-winded and unworkable analogies, the unprofitable word play, the vagueness of reference, and the on-and-on-and-on of his grave muffled words, a kind of kingdom exists. Perhaps the aim of Aiken's lifelong reverie is to send one into the endlessly ramifying labyrinth of one's memory . . . the vast, ectoplasmic, and often dimly beautiful universe whose only voice he is."

By others, Aiken's gift of eloquence was hailed as evidence that Aiken was not merely a good but a *great* poet. "He has written poetry second to none in our age," said Allen Tate. "He has, through his poetry, and its related arts, exerted a powerful civilizing influence upon the vital current of ideas." Dudley Fitts augmented the commendations by adding, "There are few writers, whether in prose or verse, who can challenge his mastery of language. . . . His writing has the inevitability of the highest art."

The chorus of hosannas reached a climax in an article occupying the first two pages of the April 19, 1963, issue of the London *Times Literary Supplement.* (In general, Aiken has been appreciated more in England than in his own country.) The article was, as usual, unsigned, but it was by the poet Kathleen Raine, who, among other laudations, said that, as a poet, Aiken was not only "supremely American" but that there was also something "Elizabethan, even Shakespearian, in the scope of his humanity; above all, in the recognition of heights no less inescapable than depths." Referring to Aiken's longer compositions, she was "again reminded of Shakespeare's narrative poems, so far have we to go back to find a poet whose thought is lyrical in the parts and in the whole of a work on a major scale."

Kathleen Raine was not the only one to speak of the largeness of Aiken's central concept. Jay Martin, in *Conrad Aiken: A Life of His Art,* and Jennifer Aldrich, in "The Deciphered Heart," a study in the *Sewanee Review,* saw Aiken's works as parts of one gradually accumulating poem, an epic of consciousness. In common with other sympathetic commentators, they agreed that Aiken's preoccupation is a search for recognition, an awareness of the poet as person and of the poet as spokesman for the race, and that this awareness is a painful process expressed by a pervasive sense of hurt—"the word, the world, the wound." Aiken was eleven years old when he was awakened by shots and found that his father had murdered his mother and then killed himself. Such a shock was a trauma from which the grown man could never completely recover and which was bound to color everything he wrote. It is, in consequence, a kind of sadomasochism which drives the hurt ego toward a willed frustration, to seek the very torments it seems to be trying to escape—and make a kind of glory of it.

It has been pointed out that much of Aiken's poetry, several of his short stories, and three of his novels are about voyages, mental as well as physical travels—or travails—or futile escapes—from one confusion to another. In his introduction to *The Collected Novels of Conrad Aiken,* R. P. Blackmur writes that the novels' essential form is the journey, "the finding, declaration, and loss of the self or psyche among the melodramas of love and jealousy, death and immolation, personal power and the frustrated abyss which assault his sensibility. . . . It is the combination of the form with the material that makes the innovation. Let us call the combination the Psychological Picaresque."

Poetry breaks through the prose of the novels, especially *Blue Voyage* and *Great Circle.* It asserts itself above the circuitous plots, the flashing conversations, the interior monologues, the infidelities and ironies. The action continually yields to passages as poetic, personal, and evocative as:

My pride and will were broken before I had come to my seventh year. I was in a state of continual terror. I sneaked in and out of the house, mouselike and secretive, my only purpose to attract as little attention as possible. My favorite story—would you believe it?—was the story of the ugly duckling. This held out a ray of hope for me—I would revenge myself—someday—someday—by turning into a swan. I read this story over and over, memorizing every detail, and as I read it I searched in my soul for signs of the wonder that was to come. How was this to be? What gifts had the good fairies given me, that I might someday astonish and confound my cruel father, my forgetful mother? It could not be strength, for I was weak, and I was constantly ill. It could not be courage, for I hardly ever forgot what it was to be afraid. It could not be beauty, for beauty was not a prerogative of boys. Could it, perhaps, be wisdom?

So much controversy has centered about Aiken's poetry that too little has been said about his prose. His criticism has not had the deserved response from those who have profited by it; yet no one with the exception of Edmund Wilson has shown more sensitivity to the changing patterns of the art of writing. Even less attention has been paid to the influence of his fictions, although more than one novelist has benefited by them. Malcolm Lowry's *Under the Volcano,* to name one indebtedness, has been rapturously rediscovered, but only a precious few have acknowledged Aiken as a begetter of that extraordinary book.

Preludes is another case in point. Originally there were two series: **Preludes for Memnon,** which Aiken first intended to call *Preludes to Attitude,* and **Time in the Rock,** which was to have been called *Preludes to Definition.* When they were combined in a single volume, Aiken furnished a preface in which he explained that the preludes were planned to be "an all-out effort at a probing of the self-in-relation-to-the-world, the formulation of a new *Weltanschauung.* For where was one to go, or what stand upon, now that Freud, on the one hand, and Einstein, on the other, had suddenly turned our neat little religious or philosophic systems into something that looked alarmingly like pure mathematics?"

The **Preludes**—there are ninety-six of them—are a test of Aiken, a severe one for all but the most devoted admirers. There are those who believe them to be his most important work, masterful in style and subtle thought. And there are those who find them difficult and disconsolate, repetitive and prolix. I confess to occupying middle ground. I feel that if the ninety-six were reduced to, say, half, they would be twice as effective, or, as Aiken likes to say, *a*ffective. It is hard to read more than six or seven straight through and enjoy—or even know—what one is reading. Too many of the monologues deal with the use of language and the problem of poetic speech. There is too much of poetry about poetry, of words about words, all of which tends to sound like a not-too-fascinating experiment in tautology. Yet there are many passages and several whole preludes I would not willingly forego. I think particularly of those beginning: "But how it came from earth," "One star fell and another as we walked," "This is not you? These phrases are not you?" "Rimbaud and Verlaine, precious pair of poets," "So death being dead, and love to hatred changes" (with its overtones of Donne), "Misery has no shape" (which recalls Emily Dickinson's "Pain has an element of blank" and reminds one that, long before she became a vogue, Aiken published a revealing selection of her poems), "Winter for a moment takes the mind," and the exquisite mood-picture with its fusion of the beautiful and the banal which opens:

> So, in the evening, to the simple cloister,
> This place of boughs, where sounds of water,
>   softly,
> Lap on the stones. And this is what you are:
> Here, in this dusty room, to which you climb
> By four steep flights of stairs. The door is closed:
> The furies of the city howl behind you:
> The last bell plunges rock-like to the sea:
> The horns of taxis wail in vain. You come
> Once more, at evening, to this simple cloister:
> Hushed by the quiet walls, you stand at peace.

It is obvious that it is the instinctive music rather than the intellect-prodded analysis that wins me. I suspect that sometimes the metaphysical Aiken has misled—or mislaid—Aiken the musician. Years ago I spoke of Aiken's subaqueous melodies and compared them to the music of Debussy, implying that their murmuring rises and dying falls were like echoes heard in a dream. Today it seems that the very wavering sounds are what give the lines their potency. In this regard Aiken is like Poe, who relied on the vaguely suggestive and held that indefiniteness is an integral element of true poetry. Instead of a series of sharp detonations, Aiken luxuriates in kaleidoscopic connotations, an indulgence that becomes a method which (according to an early Aiken note) "takes only the most delicately evocative aspects of sensation, makes of them a keyboard, and plays upon them a music of which the chief characteristic is its elusiveness, its fleetingness, and its richness in the shimmering overtones of hint and suggestion."

Aiken discarded this method in such later works as *The Soldier* and *The Kid*. In these he traced the history of man through the wanderings of the spirit. Aiken accepts war as a brutal but, in the end, beneficial conflict that creates fresh mixtures of people, customs, and cultures: "The history of war is the history of mankind." *The Kid* attempts a panoramic vista, a saga of expanding America with the pioneering William Blackstone of Massachusetts as a symbol of American adventurousness. It is a wholly successful attempt, in some ways Aiken's most consistently solid accomplishment. It achieves a continuity that affords new rewards with each rereading. Blackstone mingles rapt meditations with raw ballads and speaks variously through such real and legendary characters as Thoreau, Audubon, Paul Revere, Ben Franklin, Herman Melville, the Adamses, Whitman, Emily Dickinson, Kit Carson, and Billy the Kid.

These works prove that the passing years have not diminished Aiken's fecundity. On the contrary, since the weighty and enormously inclusive *Collected Poems*, Aiken has published *The Morning Song of Lord Zero*, *A Letter from Li Po*, *Skylight One*, and *Sheepfold Hill*. There has been an increase not only in range but in gusto. His delight in paradox, his skill in wordplay, and his dexterous "vaudeville of the psyche" are apparent not only in *Blues for Rubu Matrix*, which juxtaposes Coney Island's hot dogs with "God's terrific wing," and the shifting levels of *Landscape West of Eden*, but also in the high spirits that prompted the low comedy of *A Seizure of Limericks* and, matching the ingenuity of Milton Glaser's designs, the light humor of his private bestiary in *Cats and Bats and Things with Wings*. At the other extreme, Aiken rises to a mystical love-hate paean (emphasized by Leonard Baskin's remarkable drawings) in the just-published *Thee*. Counterpointing the unhappy reports of man's condition, there is an affirmation not so much of the lives men lead but of life itself, of all that intensifies the sad, still, but triumphant music of humanity. Senlin, Forslin, Festus, Osiris Jones, Demarest, the Preludist, and all the other Aiken simulacra are symbolic figures that are not only viable but ageless.

It is true that Aiken has written too much and too easily. It is also true that he has challenged whatever vogue has been in fashion. When the style demanded a tightly controlled decorum, he spoke up for exuberance; when free verse tended to grow looser and looser, he called for a return to form. He has enriched what might be considered the stock material of poetry with "the renewed inspection of a known thing." He has mounted steadily to the most intense perceptions, if not to Paradise, by the stairway of surprise.

I believe that the future will treat Aiken better than the present. There will be an inevitable winnowing, but the best of his work will stand a long time. I suspect that, of the novels, *Blue Voyage* will be the one most likely to survive, as will several of the short stories, such as the autobiographical "Bring! Bring!," the brilliantly macabre "Mr. Arcularis," and "Silent Snow, Secret Snow," that strange and pathetic story of the little boy quietly vanishing into a muffled white world of madness. Some of the preludes will undoubtedly be anthologized and at least a dozen lyrics will be widely quoted. Besides those I have mentioned, I predict a continuing life for **"Bread and Music"** (which has been reprinted so often that Aiken no longer gives permission for its use), **"Portrait of a Girl," "Annihilation," "At a Concert of Music," "The Quarrel," "And in the Hanging Gardens," "The Road," "The Room,"** and **"The Argument."** Considering how many poets—good poets, too—are known by only a poem or two, who, in the words of another lyricist, could ask for anything more?

Conrad Aiken with Robert Hunter Wilbur (interview date 1968)

SOURCE: "The Art of Poetry IX: Conrad Aiken, An Interview," in *The Paris Review*, Vol. 11, No. 42, Winter-Spring, 1968, pp. 97-124.

[*In the following interview with Conrad Aiken, Wilbur questions the poet regarding his friendships with other writers, such as T. S. Eliot and Malcolm Lowry, discusses with Aiken his poetic theory, and elicits from him his opinion of younger poets.*]

The interview took place in two sessions of about an hour each in September, 1963, at Mr. Aiken's house at Brewster, Massachusetts. The house, called Forty-one Doors, dates largely from the eighteenth century; a typical old Cape Cod farmhouse, the rooms are small but many, opening in all directions off what must originally have been the most important room, the kitchen. The house is far enough from the center of town to be reasonably quiet even at the height of the summer, and it is close enough to the North Cape shore for easy trips to watch the gulls along the edges of relatively unspoiled inlets.

Mr. Aiken dresses typically in a tweed sports coat, a wool or denim shirt, and a heavy wool tie. A fringe of sparse white hair gives him a curiously friarly appearance, belied by his irreverence and love of bawdy puns.

He answered the questions about his own work seriously and carefully, but did not appear to enjoy them; not that he seemed to find them too pressing or impertinent, but rather as if answering them was simply hard work. He enjoyed far more telling anecdotes about himself and his friends and chuckled frequently in recalling these stories.

By the end of each hour Mr. Aiken, who had been seriously ill the previous winter, was visibly tired; but once the tape recorder was stilled and the martinis mixed and poured into silver cups—old sculling or tennis trophies retrieved· from some pawn or antique shop—he quickly revived. He was glad to be interviewed, but more glad still when it was over.

Later, shortly before the interview went to press, a dozen or so follow-up questions were sent to him at the Cape; the answers to these are spliced into the original interview. "You may find you will need to do a bit of dovetailing here and there," he wrote; "the old mens isn't quite, may never be, as sana as before, if indeed it ever was." But there was no real problem; his mind and memory remain clear and precise, despite the physical frailties which age has brought.

[WILBUR]: *In* Ushant *you say that you decided to be a poet when you were very young—about six years old, I think.*

[AIKEN]: Later than that, I think it was around nine.

I was wondering how this resolve to be a poet grew and strengthened?

Well, I think *Ushant* describes it pretty well, with that epigraph from *Tom Brown's School Days*: "I'm the poet of White Horse Vale, Sir, with Liberal notions under my cap." For some reason those lines stuck in my head and I've never forgotten them. This image became something I *had* to be.

While you were at Harvard, were you constantly aware that you were going to be a poet; training yourself in most everything you studied and did?

Yes. I compelled myself all through to write an exercise in verse, in a different form, every day of the year. I turned out my page everyday, of some sort—I mean I didn't give a damn about the meaning, I just wanted to master the form—all the way from free verse, Walt Whitman, to the most elaborate of vilanelles and ballad forms. Very good training. I've always told everybody who has ever come to me that I thought that was the first thing to do. And to study all the vowel effects and all the consonant effects and the variation in vowel sounds. For example, I gave Malcolm Lowry an exercise to do at Cuernavaca, of writing ten lines of blank verse with the caesura changing one step in each line. Going forward, you see, and then reversing on itself.

How did Lowry take to these exercises?

Superbly. I still have a group of them sent to me at his rented house in Cuernavaca, sent to me by hand from the bar with a request for money, and in the form of a letter—and unfortunately not used in his collected letters; very fine, and very funny. As an example of his attention to vowel sounds, one line still haunts me, "Airplane or aeroplane, or just plain plane." Couldn't be better.

What early readings were important to you? I gather that Poe was.

Oh, Poe, yes. I was reading Poe when I was in Savannah, when I was ten, and scaring myself to death. Scaring my brothers and sisters to death, too. So I was already soaked in him, especially the stories.

I see you listed occasionally as a Southern writer. Does this make any sense to you?

Not at all. I'm not in the least Southern; I'm entirely New England. Of course, the Savannah *ambiente* made a profound impression on me. It was a beautiful city and so wholly different from New England that going from South to North every year, as we did in the summers, provided an extraordinary counterpoint of experience, of sensuous adventure. The change was so violent, from Savannah to New Bedford or Savannah to Cambridge, that it was extraordinarily useful. But no, I never was connected with any of the Southern writers.

In what way was the change from Savannah to New England "useful" to you?

Shock treatment, I suppose: the milieu so wholly different, and the social customs, and the mere *transplantation*; as well as having to change one's accent twice a year—all this quite apart from the astonishing change of landscape. From swamps and Spanish moss to New England rocks.

What else at Harvard was important to your development as a poet, besides the daily practice you described?

I'm afraid I wasn't much of a student, but my casual reading was enormous. I did have some admirable courses, especially two years of English 5 with Dean Briggs, who was a great teacher, I think, and that was the best composition course I ever had anywhere.

How did Briggs go about teaching writing?

He simply let us write, more or less, what we wanted to. Then discussion (after his reading aloud of a chosen specimen) and his own marvelous comments: he had genius, and emanated it. Then, at the end of class, we had ten minutes in which to write a short critique of the piece that had been read. This was so helpful to *me* that I took the course for two years.

Was Copeland still teaching then? What did you think of him?

Brilliant reader, not a profound teacher. Vain. At the end of the year he asked me, "Aiken, do you think this course has benefited you?" I was taken aback and replied, "Well, it has made me write often." He replied, "Aiken, you're a very *dry* young man."

Eliot mentioned in an interview with The Paris Review *that while he was reading French poetry at Harvard, you were reading Italian and Spanish poets.*

Yes, I had begun to read Spanish poetry, come to think of it, and Italian, that's true. I'd begun reading Leopardi in 1911, and the French poets I didn't get around to until senior year at Harvard when I discovered Symond's *Symbolist Poets* and swallowed that in one gulp.

None of these foreign readings had anything like the same effect on your work that Eliot's reading of the French symbolists had on his, did they?

I don't think so.

You kept rather to the English Romantic tradition—

Yes, and Whitman had a profound influence on me. That was during my sophomore year when I came down with a bad attack of Whitmanitis. But he did me a lot of good, and I think the influence is discoverable.

What was the good he did? Mainly enabling you to get away from Victorian forms?

General loosening up, yes. He was useful to me in the perfection of form, as a sort of compromise between the strict and the free

Was William James still at Harvard when you were there?

No, he retired the year I got there, or the year before, but was still around and you felt his presence very much. But Santayana was the real excitement for me at Harvard, especially "Three Philosophical Poets," which he was inventing that year as he went along—so we were getting the thing right off the fire.

Santayana's insistence that philosophical content—the "vision" of philosophy—is one of the things that can give the greatest effect to poetry—this, I gather, impressed you quite highly at the time?

Oh, much. Tremendously. It really fixed my view of what poetry should ultimately be.

That it was greatest if it thought most deeply?

That it really had to begin by *understanding*, or trying to understand.

Did you know Eliot quite well at Harvard?

Eliot and I must have met at the end of my freshman year, when I was elected to the *Harvard Advocate*. We saw a great deal of each other, in spite of the fact that we were a year apart, and remained very close.

Was your conversation largely about poetry or did you share other interests and activities?

Of course, at the beginning, on the *Advocate*, we talked chiefly about poetry, or literature in general. But as the friendship, or kinship developed—for in a way I became his younger brother—it widened to take in everything. And we met on very, very many quite frivolous occasions. Sports, comics, everything. We developed a shorthand language of our own which we fell into for the rest of our lives whenever we met, no holds barred—all a matter of past reference, a common language, but basically *affection*, along with humor, and appreciation of each other's minds, and of Krazy Cat. Faced with England, and the New World, and Fraud and all, we always managed to *relax*, and go back to the kidding, and bad punning, and drinking, to the end. It really was marvelous.

Did you see Eliot much after the war brought you back to the States?

Only when he paid his infrequent visits here, when we invariably met to get drunk together. There was a splendid occasion when he and I and our wives dined at "The Greeks'" after he'd received a silver bowl from the Signet Society; he was wearing a cowboy hat, and we all got plastered. We went on to the Red Lion Grill, after many drinks at the Silver Dollar Bar, the two toughest and *queerest* joints in Boston. He couldn't walk, for his ankles were crossed, so Valerie *lifted* him into the taxi.

Did Eliot's early work—such as "Prufrock"—help you in developing your own style?

Oh, "Prufrock" had a tremendous influence on me. You can see it all through the verse symphonies.

The use of the interior monologue in particular?

I don't know whether that came from him. In fact, the whole complex of our relationship is a very subtle thing. I think there was a lot of interchange. For example, I did for English 5 in my extra year at Harvard—the fall of 1911—a poem called **"The Clerk's Journal"** which was about the life of a little stool-sitting clerk in a bank and his mundane affairs, his little love affair, his worry about clothes . . . and telephone wires in the moonlight. This was three years before "Prufrock."

Do you still have this poem?

Yes, I've still got it, with Briggs' comment on the back of it. This was an anticipation. In other words, I was thinking in this direction before "Prufrock," and I have no doubt that Tom saw this poem, **"The Clerk's Journal."** The juices went both ways.

There's a lot of what we now think of as "The Waste Land attitude" in your verse symphonies, isn't there? In **Forslin** *and* **The House of Dust**, *which came well before* The Waste Land?

Yes, there's a lot in *The Waste Land* that owes something, I think, to **The House of Dust** and **Forslin**.

Did you ever see The Waste Land *in manuscript?*

No, I never did. Not as a whole. But I had seen whole sections which prior to *The Waste Land* existed as separate small poems, I believe not then intended for any other purpose, which were later conglomerated into *The Waste Land.*

How did Pound come across "Prufrock"? Did you take it to him or did Eliot do that after he came to England himself?

In 1914 I persuaded Tom to let me take "Prufrock" to England; he wasn't at all sure of it. I tried it everywhere—not even Harold Monro of the famous Poetry Bookshop could see it, thought it crazy; many years later he said it was the Kubla Khan of the Twentieth Century. Then I met Pound, showed it to him, and he was at once bowled over. He sent it to *Poetry.* So, when Tom had to retreat from Germany, when the war started, one of his first moves was to go and see Ezra.

Of course, Tom insisted all his life that I had made him cut a whole page or more out of "Prufrock." I don't remember this, but he claimed it was so—that there was a page or something like that that I thought didn't belong, so he took it out. It may be true, or he may have been confusing it with the major operation that Ezra performed on *The Waste Land.* I'm sorry about it, if so, because there's thirty lines lost!

You knew Maxwell Bodenheim, didn't you? [A new paperback copy of Bodenheim's My Life and Loves in Greenwich Village *was on the coffee table.]*

Oh, very well. He was a great friend of mine. He used to catch me now and then, touring the country. I don't know how he managed it, but periodically he'd show up

in Boston on his way to or from Chicago or New York. He was quite a fascinating creature. He really was a *dedicated* bum and poet.

Did he have an effect on other poets that we've lost sight of?

Yes, I think so. He was a fascinating talker, in spite of the stammer, and he knew everybody. He was a great friend of Bill Williams. You must have heard the story of his broken arm? He called up Williams at Rutherford and said, "I've broken my arm. Can I come and stay with you till it heals?" Bill said, "Certainly." About a month or two went by and Max did nothing about having the cast examined or changed, so finally Bill insisted on looking at it and discovered that there had never been any broken arm.

Did you see a good bit of Pound in the early days?

I saw a lot of him for about six weeks in 1914 in London. I had a letter of introduction to him from Herman Hagedorn, who, it turned out, really didn't know Pound at all. But Pound was extraordinarily kind to me and really took pains to take me around and introduce me to people and to publishers, not always with luck.

Was he any help to you in your own work?

Not a bit. We agreed to disagree about that right off, and I felt right off, too, that he was not for me, that he would become the old man of the sea and be on my shoulders in no time—which is exactly the experience that Williams had with him. I remember Williams describing how when he walked with Pound in London, Pound was always one step ahead. This gradually annoyed Williams to death, so he made a point of being right beside Pound. Very typical that—tells a lot, I think.

How about John Gould Fletcher? You worked with him, were very close to him, in Boston and Cambridge, weren't you?

Yes, just after the war began, about 1915, he came back to Boston and we lived next door to each other for three years. I saw a great deal of him and we swapped notes and what-not; and agreed to disagree about many things because he was more involved in imagism or "Amy"gism than I proposed to be. But I think he had great talent which didn't quite come off somehow.

He's practically unread now.

I know. He wrote me a tragic letter in 1949, I think it was, saying, "You know, Aiken, we are forgotten. We might as well face it." This was only a year or two before he jumped into the lake.

Did Fletcher's organization of material, the sort of thing he was experimenting with in the color symphonies, bear any relation to the work you were doing with music in your verse symphonies?

I don't know. I don't think we influenced each other, but we were interested in the same sort of thing, in a very different way, of course. He was going for this abstract color business and, I think, with more French influence behind him than I had.

When did you first meet Malcolm Lowry?

In 1929. He came to Cambridge to work with me one summer on *Ultramarine*.

How old was he then?

Barely nineteen, I think. He went back to matriculate at Cambridge that autumn.

Later you moved back to England yourself?

Yes, the next year. Then it was that his father turned him over to me *in loco parentis*.

To keep him out of trouble or to teach him poetry?

To take care of him and to work with him. So he spent all his holidays with us in Rye, or went with us if we went abroad. During his years at Cambridge, he was with me constantly.

What was he working on at this time?

He was finishing *Ultramarine*. I've still got about a third of one version of *Ultramarine*. An interesting specimen of his deliberate attempt to absorb me came to light because there was a page recounting the dream of eating the father's skeleton which comes into my own novel, *Great Circle*. He was going to put this in his book and it didn't seem to matter at all that *I'd* had the dream and written it out.

He doesn't put that in the final version?

No. I said, "No, Malcolm, this is carrying it *too* far." *What about* Under the Volcano? *Did you work with him on that also?*

No. The first version was already finished when I arrived in Mexico in 1937. He'd been there two or three years. The extraordinary thing is that it was not published for another ten years, during which time he was constantly revising and rewriting. He changed the end, I think entirely, from the version I saw. But the book was already finished and so was another novel called *In Ballast to the White Sea*, which was lost. I think it was in his shack that burnt down at Dollarton, Vancouver.

That was a remarkable thing too, although very derivative. You could swim from one influence to another as you went from chapter to chapter. Kafka and Dostoevsky and God knows what all. But it was a brilliant thing, had some wonderful stuff in it including, I remember, a description of a drunken steamboat ride up the Manchester Canal from Liverpool to Manchester.

He lived through a lot that he was able to use very effectively.

Oh, he didn't miss a trick. He was a born observer.

Was Lowry a disciplined writer? His life seems to have been so undisciplined.

Yes, when it came to writing, Malcolm was as obsessed with style as any Flaubert, and read enormously to *feed* himself. As I mentioned, he wrote and rewrote *Volcano* for ten years. He once chided me for not taking more pains to "decorate the page."

Do you think writers—fiction writers particularly—should try deliberately to get out and live through the sort of thing he did? Search for experience? I doubt if he did it quite so consciously, but he lived a very active and varied life.

No, I don't think that was the intention, or not wholly the intention in his case. He really had a yen for the sea. And he came by it naturally; I think his mother's father had something to do with the sea. Of course, that's how we met, through his reading *Blue Voyage*. And he always assumed that in some mystic way the fact I had dedicated *Blue Voyage* to C. M. L. was a dedication to him. Those are his initials. Actually these were the initials of my second wife. But he always thought this was the finger pointing.

The very first night he arrived in Hampton Hall, on Plympton Street where I was living, next door to the Crimson Building, he and I and my youngest brother Robert had a sort of impromptu wrestling match. In the course of this I suggested we use the lid of the W.C. tank and each take hold of one end of it and wrestle for possession of this thing. So I got it all right; I got it away from Malcolm but fell right over backward into the fireplace and went out like a light; and when I came to, all I could see was red. I was stripped to the waist and lying in bed by myself. They'd disappeared, of course—we'd been imbibing a little bit—and I galloped down the hall to the elevator not knowing what to do. I thought I'd better get a doctor because blood was pouring down my face. It turned out I had a fracture of the skull, and I was in bed for the next two or three weeks. Malcolm would sometimes remember to bring me a bottle of milk, and sometimes not. And during all this we were working on *Ultramarine*. That was the day's work, always.

To turn to your own work—and the prototypical Paris Review *question: How do you write? You've told me before that you compose on the typewriter.*

Yes, ever since the early twenties. I began by doing book reviews on the typewriter and then went over to short stories on the machine, meanwhile sticking to pencil for poetry.

So your verse symphonies were all written in long hand?

They were all written in little exercise books, with pencil.

When did you start writing poetry on the typewriter?

About the middle of the twenties, I think. It was largely in the intrests of legibility, because my handwriting was extremely small and not very distinct, and the pencil *faded*. And so this was a great advantage and saved me the pains of copying, because in many instances the short stories in *Bring! Bring!* were sent out exactly as written. They were composed straight off my head. I didn't change anything. It's a great labor-saving device—with some risks, because if you lost a copy in the mails it was gone!

You didn't make carbons?

I never used a carbon because that made me self-conscious. I can remember discussing the effect of the typewriter on our work with Tom Eliot, because he was moving to the typewriter about the same time I was. And I remember our agreeing that it made for a slight change of style in the prose—that you tended to use more periodic sentences, a little shorter, and a rather choppier style—and that one must be careful about that. Because, you see, you couldn't look ahead quite far enough, for you were always thinking about putting your fingers on the bloody keys. But that was a passing phase only. We both soon discovered that we were just as free to let the style throw itself into the air as we had been writing manually.

Did writing on the typewriter have any comparable effect on the style of the poetry?

I think it went along with my tendency to compress the poetry, that began about the mid-twenties, '23 or '24, there-abouts. But revision was always done manually. I preferred yellow paper because it's not so responsible-looking and I would just let fly and then put the thing away after it was written and not look at it until the next day. Then go to work on it with a pencil—chop and change and then copy that off again on the yellow paper—and this would go on for days sometimes. There are some instances, especially in later work, when there have been something like twenty versions of a poem.

In the verse symphonies, you did less revising?

Much less. It came out like a ribbon and lay flat on the brush.

Did you often work on two or three poems at once? Particularly when you were doing the shorter poems, like the ones in the two series of **Preludes***?*

No, not so much. I usually stayed with the individual item until it was satisfactory. Although sometimes I would do two or three preludes in a day, first drafts. And then all three would come in for re-tooling, so to speak, the next day or the day after. Those happened very fast, the preludes—especially the *Time in the Rock* ones. They were outpourings as I've only really known during that period. Didn't matter when or where I was. I remember in "Jeake's House" in Rye when carpenters were going through the

kitchen and the dining room all the time, which is where I worked at a long refectory table, and I would just go cheerfully on turning out preludes while hammering and sawing and what-not happened about me.

But most of your other poems have come much more slowly?

Yes, much. Things like *A Letter From Li Po* and "The Crystal" were immensely labored over. Months. Very different procedure entirely. I had the idea but it had to be developed very slowly.

In revising, say, the shorter poems like the **Preludes***, did you usually find it possible to revise so that you were eventually satisfied with the poem, or have you often discarded poems along the way?*

Oh, I've discarded a great many. And occasionally I've discarded and then resurrected. I would find a crumpled yellow ball of paper in the wastebasket, in the morning, and open it to see what the hell I'd been up to; and occasionally it was something that needed only a very slight change to be brought off, which I'd missed the day before.

Do you tend now to look on the two series of **Preludes** *as your major poetry?*

I think those two books are central, along with *Osiris Jones* and *Landscape West of Eden*, but I still don't think the symphonies are to be despised. They've got to be looked at in an entirely different way; and allowances must be made for the diffuseness and the musical structure, which I think I overdid sometimes. Although *Senlin* I think stands up fairly well. And *Festus* too.

You speak of your "verse symphonies." Where did you get the idea of adapting musical structures to poetry?
For one thing, I always hankered to be a composer—I was mad about music, though I never studied seriously, and can't read a note. But I learned to play the piano, and became pretty skillful at improvisation, especially after a drop or two. And from the beginning I'd thought of the two realms as really one: they were saying the same thing, but in two voices. Why not marry them? A young composer named Bainbridge Crist, whom I met in London in 1913, introduced me to the tone-poems of Strauss, and out of this came an early poem, "Disenchantment," now disavowed (though I still like parts of it). And, then, the symphonies. They had the tone of the time, and they married the unlikely couple of Freud and music.

What about your new poem, **Thee***? Is it related to some of this earlier work?*

No, *Thee* is something else again. This is nearer to some of the *Preludes*—not so much aimed at music (pace the title *Preludes)* as at meaning. But this poem, like "Blues for Ruby Matrix," for another example, just came like Topsy. It seized me at lunch, the first section, and I had to leave the table to put it down. Then it finished itself.

In a way I had little to do with it. The theme is much like that of the *Preludes*, but the style very different: I think I'd learned a trick or two from my children's book, *Cats and Bats and Things with Wings*. Short lines, no adjectives, and, for its purpose, very heavy rhyming. None of which was in the least calculated. Who dunnit?

You stress in Ushant *that about the time you were writing* **Landscape West of Eden** *and the* **Preludes** *you were beginning to formulate a view of poetry, or of a poetic comprehension of the world, as the only religion any longer tenable or viable. Should we be seeing this more clearly in the two series of* **Preludes** *than we have, or than most critics have?*

Yes, it was there all right. Actually Houston Peterson in *The Melody of Chaos* got a little close to it although he had only seen the first ten or twelve of *Memnon*. But he, I think, detected the novelty of this approach to the world, or something.

What about your later poems—are **Li Po** *and* **"The Crystal,"** *for example, related to the work you did in the thirties?*

Yes, I think you can see their roots in the *Preludes*. But again, of course, it's a more expanded thing, as the earlier work was more expansive, in a different way. **"The Crystal,"** and the poem about my grandfather, **"Halloween,"** and *Li Po* and **"A Walk in the Garden"**—I think you can see how that whole group grew out of the *Preludes*.

You mention **"Halloween"**—*this has an emphasis on the American past, as does* **The Kid**, *which is quite a bit different from the work you did in England. Is* **The Kid**—

That's sort of *sport* in my career, I would say. And the vaudeville poems are another sort of deliberate divagation. *You mean the ones you were doing very early, in the 1910's?*

Yes. Those were based on observation; I was an addict of vaudeville, and Boston was marvelous for it. You had about three levels of vulgarity or refinement, whichever way you want to put it. The refinement being Keiths at the top, of course, and the bottom being Waldron's Casino, and in between Loews Theatre. And Loews was really the best. It was a wonderful mixture of vulgarity and invention, of high spirits and dirty cracks.

When you started writing fiction—I suppose in the early 20's—what made you turn away from poetry, which you'd been doing up until then? Were you looking for a wider public?

No, it was almost wholly financial. Our income wasn't quite sufficient, and I thought maybe if I could turn out some short stories I could make a little money. But of course that proved to be an illusion, because the sort of stories I wrote could only be sold to things like *The Dial* or *The Criterion*, and I didn't make any more than I would have out of poetry. But then I got involved in it and

found that it was fun, in its different way, and that in fact the short story is a kind of poem, or for *my* purposes it was. And so on it went, parripassu with the poetry.

Some of your stories, like "Mr. Arcularis" and "Silent Snow, Secret Snow," have become classics. Where did you get the ideas for these stories? Dreams? Did reading Freud have anything to do with them?

Of course Freud was in everything I did, from 1912 on. But there was no special influence on these. "Arcularis" did come out of a dream, plus a meeting with a man of that name on a ship. "Silent Snow" was a complete invention; or, let's say, a projection of my own inclination to insanity.

*Then you started working with the longer fiction—*Blue Voyage *and* Great Circle?

Yes, and that was another reason for going into the short stories. Because I actually wrote one chapter of *Blue Voyage* and then stopped dead. I thought no, I really don't know enough about the *structure* of fiction—perhaps I'd better play with the short story for a while, and learn something about this. And also make a little money. So it was after *Bring! Bring!* was finished that I went back to *Blue Voyage*.

Blue Voyage was another matter. I really wanted, sort of in mid-career, to make a statement about the predicament of the would-be artist and just what made him tick and what was wrong with him and why he went fast or slow. Just as *Ushant* was the other end of that statement. "D." of *Ushant* is Demarest of *Blue Voyage*, grown fatter and balder. That was always planned—that I should, as it were, give myself away, to such extent as I could bear it, as to what made the wheels go round. Feeling that this was one of the responsibilities of a writer—that he should take off the mask.

Show just exactly how his own mind and his own experience go into his work—

Yes, and to what extent accidents helped him, and mistakes even, and failures in character, and so forth.

Did you ever meet Freud? Wasn't H. D. trying for a while to get you to go and work with him?

Freud's influence—*and* along with his, that of Rank, Ferenczi, Adler, and (somewhat less) Jung was tremendous. And I wrote one letter to Freud, to which he never replied. I was being groomed by H. D. and Bryher to go to Vienna and take over what H. D. had been doing, i.e., observer: observing: reciprocal analysis. Freud had read *Great Circle*, and I'm told kept a copy on his office table. But I didn't go, though I started to. Misgivings set in, and so did poverty.

You've spoken a couple of times—in Ushant *and more guardedly or more subtly in the poetry—of your faith in consciousness. You speak of the "teleology of conscious-*

ness" at one point. *This sounds almost as if you're looking for a new spiritual attitude toward life, a new religion not based on religious dogma or revelation or a conventional God. Is there anything to this?*

Possibly. I don't know whether I'd put it quite like that. Of course I do believe in this evolution of consciousness as the only thing which we can embark on, or in fact, willy-nilly, *are* embarked on; and along with that will go the spiritual discoveries and, I feel, the inexhaustible wonder that one feels, that opens more and more the more you know. It's simply that this increasing knowledge constantly enlarges your kingdom and the capacity for admiring and loving the universe. So in that sense I think what you say is correct. *Ushant* says this.

One statement that's always impressed me is the preface you recreated for **The House of Dust** *in 1948, in which you wrote that "implicit in this poem was the theory that was to underlie much of the later work—namely, that in the evolution of man's consciousness, ever widening and deepening and subtilizing his awareness, and in his dedication of himself to this supreme task, man possesses all that he could possibly require in the way of a religious credo: when the half-gods go, the gods arrive; he can, if he only will, become divine." Is that too extreme a statement, do you feel now?*

No, I would stand by that. Which is really, in sum, more or less what my Grandfather Potter preached in New Bedford.

When did you first come across your Grandfather Potter's sermons?

I've been carrying the *corpus* of my grandfather—to change the famous saying—with me all my life. I was given very early two volumes of his sermons; and I never go anywhere without them.

What is it in them that's been so important to you?

Well, the complete liberation from dogma; and a determined acceptance of Darwin and all the rest of the scientific fireworks of the nineteenth century.

This was toward the end of the nineteenth century?

Middle of the century. He actually took his parish out of the Unitarian Church. As he put it, "They have defrocked not only me, but my church." For thirty years he and the church, the New Bedford parish, were in the wilderness. Then the Unitarians, about 1890, caught up with him and embraced him. By this time he was president of the Free Religious Association and was lecturing all over the country on the necessity for a religion without dogma.

And this inheritance has been my guiding light: I regard myself simply as a continuance of my grandfather, and primarily, therefore, as a teacher and preacher, and a distributor, in poetic terms, of the *news* of the world, by which I mean new knowledge. This is gone into at some

length in *Ushant*. And elsewhere I have said repeatedly that as poetry is the highest speech of man, it can not only accept and contain, but in the end express best everything in the world, or in himself, that he discovers. It will absorb and transmute, as it always has done, and glorify, all that we can know. This has always been, and always will be, poetry's office.

You once wrote, speaking of the great writers of the American nineteenth century—Whitman, Melville, Hawthorne, James, Poe: "We isolate, we exile our great men, whether by ignoring them or praising them stupidly. And perhaps this isolation we offer them is our greatest gift." It seems to me you didn't receive much attention from the time of your Pulitzer Prize in 1930 until, at best, fairly recently—that you were ignored in the way you speak of for almost thirty years. "This isolation we offer" as "our greatest gift"—would this be true of yourself also?

I think so. I think it's very useful to be insulated from your surrounds, and this gives it to you because it gives you your inviolate privacy, without pressures, so that you can just be yourself. I think that what's happening today, with all the young poets rushing from one college to another, lecturing at the drop of a hat and so on, is not too good; I think it might have a bad effect on a great many of the young poets. They—to quote Mark Twain— "swap juices" a little too much, so that they are in danger of losing their own identity, and don't give themselves time enough in which to work out what's really of importance to them—they're too busy. I think Wordsworth and Coleridge had the right idea too—they deliberately sequestered themselves.

What do you think of the state of poetry today? We sometimes think of the period from 1910 to 1940 or so as being the Golden Era of modern American poetry. Do you think there is anything being done now comparable to the work that was done in those years?

No, I don't think there is. I think we've come to a kind of splinter period in poetry. These tiny little bright fragments of observation—and not produced under sufficient pressure—some of it's very skillful, but I don't think there's anywhere a discernible major poet in the process of emerging; or if he is, I ain't seen him. But I think there's an enormous lot of talent around, and somewhere amongst these I'm sure that something will emerge, given time.

In an interview for The Paris Review *Robert Lowell said: "Poets of my generation and particularly younger ones . . . write a very musical, difficult poem with tremendous skill, perhaps there's never been such skill. Yet the writing seems divorced from culture somehow. It's become too much something specialized that can't handle much experience. It's become a craft, purely a craft, and there must be some breakthrough back into life." He speaks almost as if there's* too *much skill, that it's become something that's holding younger poets back; as if they're concentrating so much on finding the perfect line or the perfect image that they aren't thinking or feeling—*

Well, I don't think that's so, and I think possibly there Lowell is really reflecting one of his own defects, because he *is* a little awkward. What really astonished me in that interview with him is his description of his method of writing verse nowadays—writing out a prose statement first and then trying to translate it to metrics without sacrificing the phrases. Well, this is really the damnedest way of writing a poem that I ever heard of, and I don't think it's any wonder that sometimes his things sound so—so prosaic—if I may go so far.

Poets now seem so wrapped up in the short poem and the perfect small statement; this seems to grow out of the early experiments of Pound and Williams, imagism also. Do you think that these tendencies have taken poets' minds away from larger subjects—from really thinking about what they're going to write about?

I think quite likely. That's a little apropos of what I called the "splinter" stage of poetry. And I think this does go back to the imagists and Pound, T. E. Hulme, and H. D., primarily. And of course that, as a lot of us were quick to see at the time, did impose limitations and very serious ones. That's why I suppose you could say that Williams, for all his power, never really came out with a *final* thing. In fact, I think one of his completest statements is in one of his earliest poems, "The Wanderer," which is much better than *Paterson* because in that he has a real continuing line which goes from one section to another, and it isn't so fragmented.

What about Pound's later works? Do you think that in the Cantos *he's found a way to give a larger organization, make a larger statement, from the earlier techniques?*

No, I don't think so. I think that's a majestic failure. There too it's—he described it himself in one of his own lines: "A broken bundle of mirrors." That's exactly what it is— brilliant fragments here and there, and beautiful—but it doesn't work; there isn't sufficient mind behind it, or organizing theme. He's said this himself—but I take that with a grain of salt.

What do you think about the contemporary poets who talk about "mind-expanding" or "consciousness-expanding"—Ginsberg and his group? Do you think drugs can expand a writer's awareness or perceptions?

I've tried it long ago, with hashish and peyote. Fascinating, yes, but no good, no. This, as we find in alcohol, is an *escape* from awareness, a cheat, a momentary substitution, and in the end a destruction of it. With luck, someone might have a fragmentary Kubla Khan vision. But with no meaning. And with the steady destruction of the observing and remembering mind.

Do you still waver between the view of the artist as simply supplying vicarious experience and your later view that the artist is the leader in the expansion of man's awareness and consciousness?

I think they can function together. I think they do. It's like two parts of the same machine; they go on simultaneously.

When you speak of the artist as the creator and purveyor of new knowledge, doesn't this, to be effective, demand a fairly wide audience?

To be effective?

Yes, socially effective.

No, not necessarily. I mean that can come serially, with time. A small but brilliant advance made today by someone's awareness may for the moment reach a very small audience, but in so far as it's valid and beautiful, it will make its way and become part of the whole world of consciousness. So in that sense it's all working towards this huge audience, and all working towards a better man.

Helen Hagenbuechle (essay date 1980)

SOURCE: "Epistemology and Musical Form in Conrad Aiken's Poetry," in *Studies in the Literary Imagination,* Vol. XIII, No. 2, Fall, 1980, pp. 7-25.

[*In the following essay, Hagenbuechle argues that in Aiken's search for a poetic language and style that would be adequate both to awaken and to articulate human consciousness, he turned to the language of music.*]

Throughout his life Conrad Aiken considered investigation into the human mind as a matter not only of personal concern but also of greatest social consequence, believing "that in the evolution of [his] consciousness . . . man possesses all that he could possibly require in the way of a religious credo."[1] Mankind's ultimate achievement of godhead, by which Aiken means total awareness, cannot be reached without the specific contribution of poetry whose supreme function is to give voice to the unspoken sensibilities of the age. In "Poetry and the Mind of Modern Man," Aiken claims that poetry "must embody the full consciousness of man at that given moment. It cannot afford to lag behind the explorations of knowledge, whether of the inner or outer worlds; these it is its business to absorb and transmute." And the poet concludes that "it has always at last been in poetry that man has given his thought its supreme expression—which is to say that most of all, in this, he succeeds in making real for himself the profound myth of personal existence and experience."[2] An accurate registration of the subtle vibrations of the age, however, is only possible if the poet is both a sharp observer of outward reality and a tireless explorer of the workings of his own mind. Doubtless Aiken wanted to make his readers aware of the special significance he attributed to the Socratic *Gnothi Seauton* when he chose it as an epigraph for *Ushant,* the poetic *summa* of his artistic life. In this autobiography, the poet explains that his epistemological interest is not only the result of a psychological need, but a necessary prerequisite for the use of his medium: for Aiken the problem of consciousness is basically a problem of language.

The distinction between outward reality and the reality of the mind, which experiences the world through language, began to fascinate Aiken when still a boy: "Dogs and horses in one world, indeed! But what about a world of symbols so geometrically and psychologically complex, so shimmering with ambivalences and ambiguities, and algebraic extensions or equivocations, that one's dazzled awareness simply hadn't time to take them in, and was on the run, on the gallop, merely to get a fleeting glimpse of them?" (U, p. 166). Symbolic language is here characterized both in terms of analogies ("algebraic extensions or equivocations") and associations ("ambivalences and ambiguities"). The kaleidoscope that he owned as a child, and which may have started his meditations on the change wrought in objects when reflected in two or more mirrors, later became his central symbol for the complexities of an ever-shifting world[3] reflected in the multiple mirror of the mind: "that unfathomable, or yet to-be-fathomed, pluralism, the plural mind in the plural universe [which] must forever partly escape the flung net of symbol [i. e. language]" (U, p. 167).

Thus Aiken finds himself confronted with two major problems: first, the relationship between the mind and outward reality, and secondly, the nature of the experiencing mind itself. In order to render experience adequately, the poet requires a language capable of expressing consciousness not only in terms of intentionality (Sartre's "consciousness of" or "positional" consciousness) and reflexivity (Sartre's "consciousness of consciousness of" or "non-positional" consciousness), but also as "matrix" or creative principle underlying all mental activities. The experience of the self as an endless series of reflecting mirrors which keep changing both in themselves and in relation to each other, while at the same time the seemingly identical source or form-giving principle keeps producing new perceptions and reflections, is a perplexing problem for the poet. In *Ushant* Aiken describes it in the following words: "if it was the writer's business, or the poet's, to be as conscious as possible, and his primary obligation, then wouldn't this impose upon him the still deeper obligation of being conscious of his *own* workings, the workings of his psyche . . . and along with the work itself, to present, as it were, the *explication*—? . . . He [the protagonist of *Ushant*, called "D"] had discussed, with the farouche John, [John Gould Fletcher], and with the Tsetse [T. S. Eliot], too, the notion, for example, of presenting a poem, or a piece of fiction, complete with the formative matrix, the psychological scaffolding, out of which it was in the act, the very act, of crystallizing" (U, p. 246). In other words, poetic language should not only grasp the content of consciousness (as positional or non-positional "consciousness of"), but should at the same time reveal the very process of becoming conscious.

Conrad Aiken's views of epistemology were strongly influenced by the philosophy of F. H. Bradley, to which T. S. Eliot had introduced him sometime after 1907 while they were still at Harvard. In *Ushant* Aiken speaks about "the

Tsetse's brilliantly analytic and destructive thesis . . . which had contributed much to the 'fixing' of D's implicit intellectual or philosophic position, adding, as it did, the basic 'why' as to the values of knowledge . . ." (U. p. 215). In *Appearance and Reality* (1896) Bradley tries to prove that accurate knowledge of reality is ultimately impossible because cognition breaks that unity of inchoate consciousness and sentience which alone could provide the apprehension of truth. Bradley, like Eliot and Aiken after him, starts with experience and finds that if "we go to experience, what we certainly do *not* find is a subject or an object, or indeed any other thing whatever, standing separate and on its own bottom. What we discover rather is a whole in which distinctions can be made, but in which divisions do not exist. And this is the point on which I insist. . . . when I urge that reality is sentient experience. I mean that to be real is to be indissolubly one thing with sentence . . ."[4] "Reality" is a continuous process of mediation between self and world. But our minds, which Bradley calls "finite centers," can only perceive fractions of this reality, aspects relative to the particular perspective and other conditioning circumstances of the "finite center" at the moment of its contact with reality. In the act of perception, moreover, the mind breaks the original unity of the object with its background, while at the same time polarizing the perceiving mind and the thing perceived. Knowledge and sheer being are therefore incompatible. And yet both appear to be complementary parts of human experience. It is imperative in Aiken's eyes that the poet find ways of expressing this profound paradox characterizing all human awareness.[5]

This problem is the subject of poem XIII from the series *Preludes for Memnon*:

> And how begin, when there is no beginning?
> How end, when there's no ending? How cut off
> One drop of blood from other, break the stream
> Which, with such subtlety, such magnificent power,
> Binds the vast windflower to its throbbing world?
> . . . Shall we be bold, and say, then, 'at this point
> The world begins, the windflower ends?' rip out
> One bleeding atom, pretend it has no kin?
> . . .Or shall we, with the powerful mind, hold off
> The sky from earth, the earth from sky, to see
> Each perish into nothing?
>
> (CP, p. 512)

Aiken here seems to offer two alternative methods to catch the continuum of reality in the net of language. The first one corresponds to what we termed "knowledge," the second one to "immediate being." The "bold" method, which breaks reality into fragments, enables us to understand and control this reality, because the fragments set each other off and define themselves against each other. Yet, the "knowledge" we win in this way cannot be true, because this random division of the whole has been imposed on reality by a mind extraneous to it. The other method proceeds by totalization of one part of reality in that the mind identifies itself with, for example, "the earth" or "the sky." But, no meaning can be won in this way either, because the total absence of comparison makes definition impossible; complete empathy necessarily leads "into nothing."

A passage in *Ushant* further pursues this question. The protagonist dreams about two sages, "the first of whom had discovered the most astounding of all languages, one in which, he said, meaning had been so fragmented into particles and surds [algebraic signs] that it would require a thousand years to assemble enough of them to constitute a single statement; only then to hear the other sage reply that this was nothing, for *he* had discovered a language in which meaning was so concentrated that a single syllable, a single sound, was itself the equivalent of a thousand years" (U, p. 167). The first language tends to be purely referential or denotative, enumerating the objects of this world in their totality; the second is so highly concentrated that it becomes a kind of *Ur*-sound expressing the world not through infinite particularization, but through total implication or connotation. Both languages are artifacts, unable to function in practice. They merely serve as models of two contrary aspects of language, which in actual usage complement each other. This Aiken explains in his essay "Counterpoint and Implication": ". . . it is the aim of every work of art to evoke, or to suggest. . . . Some [artists] think it should be accomplished by methods mainly denotative—or realistic: they argue that the best way to imply is . . . to state. Others believe the method should be mainly connotative: they argue that the best way to state is . . . to imply. Both elements, of course, enter into every work of art, and the only real difference at the bottom is quantitative" (CP, pp. 1025-26). Aiken believes that "the larger the medium in which a poet works, the wider and more frequent will be his ranging of this gamut." He concludes: "It was to make more possible this delicious . . . ranging of the gamut that I evolved the symphonic form . . ." (CP, p. 1026). The two terms, "Counterpoint" and "Implication," denote the two fundamental methods with which poetic language tries to render experience. The language of "counterpoint" attempts to know the world in terms of contrast, opposition. As Melville formulates it in *Moby-Dick* (ch. 11): ". . . there is no quality in this world that is not what it is merely by contrast."

Aiken was hardly alone in his search for a more flexible poetic style. At the end of the nineteenth century and during the first decades of the twentieth, the problem was very much in the air. "Process" was a keyword in much of contemporary philosophy and psychology. Nor is Aiken's "symphonic form" entirely new. Ruskin (following Schopenhauer) remarked that all art tends towards the condition of music. Indeed, artists of the nineteenth century had already tried to reach a kind of absolute art form by combining structural devices belonging to different forms of art. Ideas such as *correspondances, transpositions d' art*, the *Gesamtkunstwerk*, the symphonic poem for orchestra, and program music were then developed by dramatists, poets, musicians and painters alike.[6] At the core of these attempts was the hope to find some form that would have a more direct, more powerful impact on the human soul: the principal purpose of art was to move— in fact, an old Aristotelian demand. Music, and by exten-

sion the musical method of implication, was thought to be the best suited to this effect. Whistler, for example, often painted works in one dominant color and gave them musical titles to indicate that he wanted the spectator to be moved by color and form rather than by the idea or content of the painting: "Symphony in Violet and Blue," "Harmony in Red," "Nocturne in Blue and Green," etc. In poetry, Gautier's "Symphonie en blanc majeur" had far-reaching effects.[7] The poetic genre of the color symphony appealed above all to the imagists. Amy Lowell, Ezra Pound, and especially Aiken's friend John Gould Fletcher tried their hands at it. René Taupin wrote of his symphonies: "Ces poèmes cherchent à être la fusion complète d'une symphonie musicale, d'un tableau et d'une émotion dominante."[8]

The formal ideals of different kinds of art became more and more similar. In his essay on the sculptor Brancusi, Pound wrote that "where Gaudier had developed a sort of form-fugue or form-sonata by a combination of forms, Brancusi has set out to the maddeningly more difficult exploration toward getting all the forms into one form; this is as long as any Buddhist's contemplation of the universe or as any mediaeval saint's contemplation of the divine love,—as long and even as paradoxical as the final remarks in the Divina Commedia."[9] In Conrad Aiken we are dealing with a poet whose untiring search of "absolute poetry" reminds one very strongly of Brancusi. The development begins with his early symphonies and goes on through his experiments with poetry, the short story, and the novel, finding, in my opinion, its apotheosis in his autobiography, *Ushant*. It is in this book that Aiken describes how he gradually became aware of the similarity between his experience of himself as a thinking and feeling continuum and the experience of listening to music. He was convinced "that one should bring music to bear on all his work, the totality of his work."[10] As late as 1967 he confirmed this in an interview with Robert Carlile, remarking: "What I would say is that you should look at all my work, remember that I always have music as a shaping force in the back of my mind, and discover what there is [of music] in the form, the structure of my work."[11] Despite these clear injunctions by the author, neither Carlile nor any other critic I know has yet gone very far beyond a superficial and largely metaphorical understanding of the implication of music in Aiken's poetry.[12] However, Aiken was concerned with applying musical structure to poetic form rather than with the metaphorical use of musical terminology.

Critics rarely understand what is actually at stake in the comparison of music and poetry. This is perhaps less of a surprise if one takes into account the methodological difficulties that any comparison between poetry and music is faced with. One of the best discussions so far can be found in Donald Davie's fascinating book *Articulate Energy*, in which he points to some of the most common errors concerning the term "musical poetry." "When poets say that poetry is or ought to be like music, they often turn out to have only a naive idea of what music is. They take such musical freaks as the imitations of cuckoo-calls, or clocks, or peals of bells, as if they were central to music's nature; and so build up a theory of poetry around the equally freakish poetical device of onomatopoeia. Or else they take music to be 'a cry.'"[13] Poetry is sometimes erroneously thought to be most musical when it tries to rival the harmonies of music by such devices as rhyme, alliteration, assonance, meter, and others. If that were the whole truth, poetry would hardly be worth listening to. Aiken himself laid most stress on the direct presentation of emotion in "musical poetry." Instead of imitating musical sound patterns he attempted to reproduce emotional patterns through the structure of poetic language.

To what extent, we must therefore ask ourselves, is the structure of music embodied in the structure of the human mind or psyche? It is not without interest that the first inspiration to write poetry often consists in a rhythmical or musical motif rather than in a sharply outlined idea or concept. Davie quotes Schiller as saying: "When I sit down to write a poem, what I most frequently see before me is its musical element and not a clear idea of the subject, about which I am often not entirely clear myself."[14] T. S. Eliot testifies to the same experience in "The Music of Poetry": "I know that a poem, or a passage of a poem, may tend to realize itself first as a particular rhythm before it reaches expression in words, and that this rhythm may bring to birth the idea and the image; and I do not believe that this is an experience peculiar to myself."[15] This musical inspiration grows out of the unconscious and can be caught by a faculty that Eliot calls the "auditory imagination." He describes it as "the feeling for syllable and rhythm, penetrating far below the conscious levels of thought and feeling, invigorating every word; sinking to the most primitive and forgotten, returning to the origin and bringing something back, seeking the beginning and the end."[16] Northrop Frye has given the following analysis of the creative act in Eliot: "The poet is concerned not to say anything, but to articulate this rhythm, and in this he resembles the composer; for the poetic structure will first appear in terms of something analogous to 'musical form.' But the articulation itself takes the form of 'clear visual images,' which form the golden mean between 'the extremes of incantation and meaning.'"[17]

It would thus appear that there is some fundamental similarity between musical and poetic inspiration. It may even be argued that all art is first and foremost an expression of rhythm, and that rhythm lies at the basis of inner as well as outer life. It remains, above all, the merit of Susanne Langer to have investigated the correspondence between musical structures and certain dynamic patterns of human experience. In *Philosophy in a New Key* she shows that the fundamental relationships in music are tensions and resolutions and that the patterns generated by these are the patterns exemplified in all art and also in all emotive responses. She comes to the conclusion "that there are certain aspects of the so-called 'inner life'—physical or mental—which have formal properties similar to those of music: patterns of motion and rest, of tension and release, of agreement and disagreement, preparation, fulfilment, excitation, sudden change, etc."[18]

Whenever Aiken speaks of "musical poetry," it is above all this kind of structure and this kind of effect that he has in mind. In the terms "counterpoint" and "implication," the poet has found two complementary concepts on which to focus the highly complex matter of musical poetry. He uses "counterpoint" loosely for all kinds of formal or thematic constructions that have the function of setting each other off by way of contrast. Counterpoint concerns mainly the alternation of structural elements in the horizontal sequence of time. The term "implication," however, which is characterized by elusiveness and "shimmering overtones of hint and suggestions," (CP, p. 1028) seems to refer rather to the vertical, simultaneous combination of elements. By combining counterpoint and implication Aiken hopes to achieve "a kind of underlying simultaneity in dissimilarity" (CP, p. 1027), a poetic effect which he thinks most expressive of the complexity of human experience.

Let us first consider some aspects of Aiken's poetic use of counterpoint. The symphonic form, which favors counterpoint by varying the speed and mood of its "movements" as well as by presenting one subject from several points of view, is the ideal of Aiken's early experimental work of this kind. He invented it with the expressed purpose of effecting all manners of counterpoint: "It seemed to me that by using a large medium, dividing it into several main parts, and subdividing these parts into short movements in various veins and forms, this [the contrapuntal effect] was rendered possible" (CP, p. 1027). **"The Jig of Forslin,"** one of the symphonies, deals with the natural urge to complement the meagreness of ego-confirmation in real life by vicarious wish-fulfillment. The sequence of various types of wish-fulfillment from the cheaply sentimental to the cruelly sadistic affords a great deal of thematic counterpoint. At the same time Aiken tries to invent suitable styles for each episode in order to achieve the desired variety in rhythm and tone: "For my intention has been to employ all methods, attitudes, slants, each in its proper place, as a necessary and vital part of any such study as this. Consequently, it is possible to pick out portions of this poem to exemplify almost any poetic method or tone" (CP, p. 1018).

The poet has chosen an irregular blank verse for the frame of the poem, in which the protagonist is still awake but wishing to fall into a daydream. However, the more he lures his mind into dreaming, the more rhymes occur to express the hypnotic power of the imagination. At the same time, short lines slow the rhythm down to convey a sense of almost dozing off:

> Let us drown, then, if to drown is but to change:
> Drown in the days of those whose days are
>   strange;
> Close our eyes, and drown;
> Wearily, without effort, at our leisure,
> In some strange sea-pool, lit with sun and treasure,
> Sink slowly down
> From the bright waves above our phantom hands
> To vales of twilight sands.
>
>   (CP, p. 56)

The main interest of **"The Jig of Forslin"** lies in the various daydreaming episodes, which are played off against each other. The scene of the juggler, for example, is mostly in blank verse, moving at a moderate speed, with sharp caesuras to mimic the loss of practice and the growing rustiness:

> Practice, practice, practice! That's all it was.
> Three times a year I took the stage again
> To earn the money to keep alive with:
> Used the old tricks, of course, though getting rusty.
>
> > (CP, p. 59)

The highly emotional vampire episode moves more quickly in rhymed tetrameters:

> I heard my heart hiss loud and slow;
> A gust of wind through the curtains came;
> It flapped the upright candle-flame.
> Her famishing eyes began to glow,
> She bared my arm; with a golden pin,
> Leaned, and tenderly pricked the skin.
> And as the small red bubble rose,
> Her eyes grew bright with an evil light,
> She fawned upon me; and my heart froze
> Seeing her teeth so sharp and white.
>
> > (CP, p. 85)

Another type of counterpoint is explored in **"The House of Dust,"** a symphonic poem which moves back and forth between the general and the particular, the external and the internal: ". . . perhaps it would be as well to point out . . . that its theme is essentially contrapuntal: for the entire poem is really an elaborate progressive analogy between the city, seen as a multicellular organism, and the multicellular or multineural nature of human consciousness" (CP, p. 1021). Aiken contrasts the physiological with the psychological, the macrocosmic world of flux as perceived by man with the microcosmic processes going on within the human mind. The perspective alternates between the limited view of an individual persona and the collective consciousness of man in general, between close-up pictures of familiar everyday life and the alienating perspective of a god-like imaginary eye looking at the world from a distant spot in the cosmos.

> I stand by a mirror and comb my hair:
> How small and white my face!—
> The green earth tilts through a sphere of air
> And bathes in a flame of space.
>
> There are houses hanging above the stars
> And stars hung under a sea.
> And a sun far off in a shell of silence
> Dapples my walls for me.
>
> > (CP, p. 206)

In the first two lines the narrator stands in a room facing a wall with a mirror, an everyday human perspective. The next two lines, however, show us the whole planet earth, of which the speaker in his room is himself a small part, tilting through a space in which, we feel, even the earth is only a detail; this we might call the cosmic perspective. In the next stanza the process is reversed. Looking at the earth from outer space, the houses on the lower side seem to be hanging above the stars, just as the stars seem to be hanging under the sea. In the last line we return to the room and look at the wall, but with a difference: the human perspective is now disclosed as an arbitrary fiction, an illusion.

A closer look at the verses quoted above shows that contrasts abound: "stand"—"tilt"; "white"—"green"; "small face"—"earth"; "in the mirror"—"in a flame of space." Then there are also opposite moods: the pale narrator, given to self-reflection, is driven by petty vanity to follow the laws of convention and performs a Prufrock-like action, while the celestial bodies, following great cosmic laws, move in total unawareness and grandiose indifference. The sweep of their pure physical motion is overwhelming in comparison with the shallow narcissism of the narrator, for whom the existence of far-off suns is justified by their dappling his walls for him.

Another kind of counterpoint is created by Aiken through a variation of registers and vocabularies (e.g., poetic versus prosaic style). He blames Alan Seeger for writing poetry "omitting all words which seem to belong to prose" and selecting for his "artificial purpose only the lovely (when taste is at its best) or the merely sensuous or pretty (when taste subsides a little.) One gets, therefore, in reading Seeger's poems a mild and never intense pleasure . . . Nothing disturbs. All is as liquid and persuasive as drifting in a gondola" (Sc, p. 135). Aiken seems to resent the monotony of mood which should be broken occasionally by insertions of realistic or prosaic elements. Almost any poem by Aiken will show that he himself was a master at combining words of different character. The poem **"The Cyclads"** is a case in point; here abstract concepts like "terror of time," "terror of space," "the Absolute," and "Old Repetition" are contrasted with such concrete objects as "dynamos," "endless belt," "corner drugstore," or "cash-tray." Eliot touches on a similar subject in "The Music of Poetry":

> What matters, in short, is the whole poem: and if the whole poem need not be, and often should not be, wholly melodious, it follows that a poem is not made only out of 'beautiful words.' I doubt whether from the point of view of *sound* alone, any word is more or less beautiful than another . . . The music of a word is, so to speak, at a point of intersection: it arises from its relation first to the words immediately preceding and following, and indefinitely to the rest of its context; and from another relation that of its immediate meaning in the context to all the other meanings which it has had in other contexts, to its greater or less wealth of association.[19]

Eliot here confirms Aiken's opinion that the musicality of a poem depends on the poet's effective handling of counterpoint. Moreover he directs our attention to the importance of implication, Aiken's second key-concept, whose ability to evoke a latent meaning derives not only from the immediate context, but also from the larger context of tradition.

Aiken's idea of implication includes the allusive power of words but goes far beyond it. Because the aim of poetry is to move, the poet speaks to convey specific emotions to the reader. These emotions define themselves in relation to each other. Sadness, for example, may be set off by a cheerful mood, which in turn can be followed by fear. Having this type of effect in mind. Aiken writes in "Counterpoint and Implication":

> All this, I must emphasize, is no less a matter of emotional tone than of form; the two things cannot well be separated. For such symphonic effects one employs what one might term emotion-mass with just as deliberate a regard for its position in the total design as one would employ a variation of form. One should regard this or that emotional theme as a musical unit having such-and-such a tone-quality, and use it only when that particular tone-quality is wanted. Here I flatly give myself away as being in reality in quest of a sort of absolute poetry a poetry in which the intention is not so much to arouse an emotion merely, or to persuade of a reality, as to employ such emotion or sense of reality (tangentially struck) with the same cool detachment with which a composer employs notes or chords. Not content to present emotions or things or sensations for their own sakes—as is the case with most poetry—this method takes only the most delicately evocative aspects of them, makes of them a keyboard, and plays upon them a music of which the chief characteristic is its elusiveness, its fleetingness, and its richness in the shimmering overtones of hint and suggestion. Such a poetry, in other words, will not so much present an idea as use its resonance. It is the apotheosis of the poetic method which we have called implication. (CP, p. 1028)

It is clear that Aiken aims at moving the reader in the same way listeners are moved by music. The satisfaction in this type of poetry would ideally come from total empathy of the reader with the essence of the poem—a mental state similar to what Bradley called "immediate being." But the poet has to admit that here, as in the corresponding language of the sage in his dream (the infinitely concentrated single sound), he is chasing an ideal that is hard to realize in practice. The conceptual part of language cannot be totally discarded since it remains the basis of poetic language as well. Eliot approaches the problem more realistically: "My purpose here is to insist that a 'musical poem' is a poem which has a musical pattern of sound and a musical pattern of the secondary meanings of the words which compose it, and that these two patterns are indissoluble and one. And if you object that it is only the pure sound, apart from the sense, to which the adjective 'musical' can be rightly applied, I can only reaffirm my previous assertion that the sound of a poem is as much an abstraction from the poem as is the sense."[20]

Aiken's most radical experiments in the mode of "implication" are his early symphonies. In the preface to **"The Charnel Rose"** he writes:

> 'The Charnel Rose' needs, perhaps, some explanation. Like program music, it is helped by a program: though concrete in its imagery, it avoids sharp statement of ideas; implying the theme, rather than stating it. This theme might be called nympholepsy—nympholepsy in a broad sense as that impulse which sends a man from one dream, or ideal, to another, always disillusioned, always creating for adoration some new and subtler fiction. . . . In the present instance it has been my intention merely to use this idea as a theme upon which one might build wilfully a kind of absolute music. . . . Thus, beginning with the lowest order of love, the merely carnal, the theme leads irregularly, with returns and anticipations as in music, through various phases of romantic or idealistic love . . . finally ending in a mysticism apparently pure. . . . 'The Charnel Rose' is called a symphony, and in some ways the analogy to a musical symphony is close. Symbols recur throughout like themes, sometimes unchanged, sometimes modified, but always referring to a definite idea. The attempt has been made to divest the successive emotions dealt with of all save the most typical or appropriate physical conditions, suggesting physical and temporal environment only so far as the mood naturally predicates it. Emotions, perceptions,—the image-stream in the mind which we call consciousness,—these hold the stage. (CP, pp. 1016-17)

The term "program music" makes it clear that although a poem should express an idea or message, this is to remain as subordinate as the title is to program music. The conceptual part of language should be used mainly as a focal point for the flow of emotions aroused by the sounds, rhythms, and recurring symbols of the poetry.

But although Aiken used the concept of nympholepsy as a unifying idea in **"The Charnel Rose,"** this symphony was not successful. The poet himself was the first to notice that he had overemphasized the element of absolute music: ". . . the variation of tone has not been carried far enough: a little more statement and a little less implication would have been a good thing, for it verges on the invertebrate" (CP, p. 1029). And he concludes his article with a general remark about the danger, "that one's use of implication will go too far, and that one will cheat the natural human appetite for something solid and palpable. One cannot, truly, dine—at least every evening—on, as Eliot would remark, 'smells of steaks in passageways.' One must provide for one's symphony a sufficiently powerful and pervasive underlying idea—and, above all, make it sufficiently apparent. . . . one must compromise . . ." (CP, p. 1029). This compromise leads away from the purely associational towards the more conceptual aspect of language, away from the merely connotative back to the denotative. The remedy lies in "The counterpoint of thought" or "counterpoint of idea."

In his essay, "The Literary Abbozzo: Lola Ridge," Aiken writes: "The provocatively incomplete . . . has its charm, its beautiful suggestiveness; but in proportion as the artist is powerful he will find the *abbozzo*[21] insufficient, he will want to substitute for this charm, this delicate hover, a beauty and strength more palpable. The charm which inheres in the implied rather than the explicit he knows how to retain—he will retain it in the dim counterpart of thought itself" (Sc, p. 87). Aiken seems to suggest that a poem ought not to *present* ideas, but should rather be *expressive of* ideas. Instead of stating the concept itself in the poem, the poet should articulate the music or image or mood or color that this concept dresses in when it appears as poetic inspiration.

The following quotation from *Preludes for Memmon* is an example of "dim counterpoint of thought":

> Or say that in the middle comes a music
> Suddenly out of silence, and delight
> Brings all that chaos to one mood of wonder;
> A seed of fire, fallen in a tinder world;
> And instantly the whirling darkness fills
> With conflagration; upspoutings of delirium;
> Cracklings and seethings; the melting rocks, the bursts
> Of flame smoke-stifled, twisting, smoke-inwreathed;
> Magnificence; the whole dark filled with light;
> And then a silence, as the world falls back
> Consumed, devoured, its giant corolla shrivelled;
> And in the waning light, the pistil glowing,
> Glowing and fading; and on that shrinking stage—
>
> Whisper it, how among the whispering ashes
> Her place bright beauty comes, the moon's dark
>   daughter,
> Lighting those ruins with her radiant madness;
> How swiftly glides, and stoops with what light
>   steps
> Touches the dead face of that desert, comes
> Nearer, bending her face, her divine eyes
> Bright with the brightness of the ineffable;
> Seeking, and finding not; smiling at nothing,
> Blessing the emptiness; her angelic face
> Hopeful at first, then hopeless, and at last
> Weeping; so standing, while her slow tears fall;
> And the long silence begins, the silence that was
> And is and will be; creeps round her; rises coldly;
> And all is still; the world, her hope, and she.
>   (CP, pp. 502-503)

It would be presumptuous to offer a definite interpretation of such a poem. Its imagery and rhythm leave much room for every reader's private associations. All that we can agree on is the outline and structure of the emotional movement conveyed through the poem. Stanza one delineates the emergence of life or order or insight or inspiration out of chaos, its climax and final decline into chaos. The process evolves like the movement of a wave. The second stanza expresses an aftereffect of the first: memory or imagination seeking to restore the epiphany of stanza one, but experiencing only a slight rippling hope before sinking sadly into eternal silence.

Although we cannot precisely define the poem's meaning we feel that it is expressive of something that is only barely conceptual. It is here that Aiken's poetry resembles music most strongly. Lacking the conceptual sense of language, the meaning of music is limited to the revelation of "the rationale of feelings, the rhythm and pattern of their rise and decline and intertwining, to our minds."

"What music can actually reflect is only the morphology of feeling," not any definite emotive or even rational significance. "Articulation is its life, but not assertion; expressiveness, not expression."[22] This well characterizes the prelude quoted above.

Clearly, poetry lacking the "counterpoint of thought" is unsatisfactory, though it may have its own charms. "There are many poets who have the *vox et praeterea nihil* of poetry, and who wisely therefore cultivate that charm; but it is a tragedy when a poet . . . possessing other riches as well, ignores these riches in credulous obeisance to the theory that, since it is the voice, the hover, the overtone, the perfume alone which is important in poetry, therefore poetry is to be sought rather in the gossamer than in the rock. . . . But poetic magic, as George Santayana has said, is chiefly a matter of perspective—it is the revelation of 'sweep in the concise and depth in the clear'—and, as Santayana points out, if this is true we need not be surprised to perceive that the poet will find greatest scope for this faculty in dealing with ideas, particularly with philosophic ideas" (Sc, pp. 236-37). Aiken does not mean to say thereby, that poets be philosophers or logicians. The counterpoint of thought is rather "a matter of perspective," a matter of "vision" (Sc, p. 237). "If the poet's business is vision, he can ill afford to ignore this watchtower [i.e. the 'vision of philosophy']. For if . . . he desires that poetry shall be a king of absolute music . . . a music in which sensations are the notes, emotions the harmonies, and ideas the counterpoint . . . then truly the keyboard of the poet who uses his brain as well as his sensorium will be immensely greater than that, let us say, of the ideal Imagist" (Sc, pp. 237-38).

Although Eliot maintains that poetry and philosophy are profoundly different and that a man could not be both a poet and a philosopher, he basically agrees with Aiken. "The poet who 'thinks' is merely the poet who can express the emotional equivalent of thought. But he is not necessarily interested in the thought itself. . . . I would suggest that none of the plays of Shakespeare has a 'meaning,' although it would be equally false to say that a play of Shakespeare is meaningless. All great poetry gives the illusion of a view of life."[23]

In Aiken's case this saving perspective or vision is his belief, mentioned at the beginning of this essay, that the exploration and evolution of consciousness is the most urgent concern of man. In *Ushant* he describes how this view of the "ever more inclusive consciousness" was first "treated rather as thematic material, something on which to play variations" (U, p. 220), until he realized that his formal interests in musical poetry matched his interests in philosophy. Then, finally, "was the consistent view at last to receive his consistent attention, and to find at last its own expression . . . towards attitude and definition" (U, p. 221). In fact, the symphonies are the structural forerunners of the *Preludes to Attitude* and the *Preludes to Definition*. In his preface to the Oxford edition of the *Preludes* Aiken writes: "It was my hope that in a serial form—separate poems, but constituting a kind of mathematical series—and series does seem to be not only a probability but an inherent necessity in nature—I could approximate some sort of spiral approach to what I thought . . . so desperately needed to be said."[24] When Aiken writes a whole series of poems to approach his vision spirally, he is trying to achieve the same effect of unity in variety which he had earlier sought to achieve by means of counterpoint and implication in the symphonies. The single poems in the series are joined together by the use of leitmotifs and the poet's persistent epistemological interest which serves as "counterpoint of thought." But at the same time these poems are thematically much more independent than are the parts of a symphony. The series, "which seems to be an inherent necessity in nature," on the one hand conforms to the evolutionary process observed in reality, thus intimating a teleogical progress;[25] but on the other hand it is also a most adequate form to describe the multiple and apparently random aspects of things from the points of view of a constantly changing human consciousness. The title *Preludes to Attitude* and *Preludes to Definition* suggest that the reader is not to expect any hard and fast judgments of the world, for in music a prelude is a relatively short independent composition, free in form and resembling an improvisation. At the same time the word "prelude" also implies that the poems ought to be regarded merely as preliminary statements of attitude or definition. The same indeterminacy of meaning, hinted at in the titles, is also expressed in the opening lines of many preludes: "Winter *for a moment* takes the mind"; "*Or say* that in the middle comes a music"; "Ah this is nothing: *All that we said is nothing*" (my italics). Each poem of the series represents one more noncommittal perspective of the problem of consciousness and reality, thus contributing not only to the completion of the series, but also to the cosmic evolution of consciousness.

Ideally, all the fragmentary views presented in the single poems of the series should be seen simultaneously. Aiken describes the supreme art form in *Ushant*: "Everything was to be presented—in this view of the work of art—as on one time-level. As if—for instance—one were to focus, on a given star, an infinite series of telescopes, each of them one light-moment farther off, and, by co-ordinating this infinite series of visions, obtain a simultaneous view of all possible actions and at all possible times. As if the past, the present, and the future, were all presented at once, the single and the multiple, the important and the unimportant, the trivial and the tremendous, the whole of that infinite mechanism, or cosmogony, simultaneously in motion and at rest. . . . In this sense, therefore, there would be no 'progress,' of the ordinary sort, in a work of art: everything past would be hypothecated, everything future would be implied: the movement of these together would constitute a kind of static-dynamic, a stillness of motion round an invisible center" (U, pp. 328-29). Aiken openly admits that his experiments with musical form and his search for serial and spiral patterns to embody the paradoxical stillness in motion are in fact expressions of some profound doubt that the ultimate vision, the intrinsic meaning, might actually remain invisible: the center and goal of evolutionary consciousness is perhaps forever beyond the power of language, even poetic language:

> Despair, that seeking for the ding-an-sich,
> The feeling itself, the round bright dark emotion,
> The color, the light, the depth, the feathery swiftness
> Of you and the thought of you, I fall and fall
> From precipice word to chasm word, and shatter
> Heart, brain, and spirit on the maddening fact:
> If poetry says it, it must speak with a symbol.
>
> (CP, p. 503)

Symbolic language presupposes a basic unity or correspondence between mind and matter and between all the parts and aspects of the world. If this is the case, symbols, metaphors, and similes are meaningful. But in Aiken's world this Emersonian harmony has been lost. It is there only as a hopeless hope. Like Sisyphus, the poet has to go on finding ever new symbolical expressions for the "ding-an-sich," trusting to approach the essence by sheer accumulation of partly true fragments.

> This is not you? these phrases are not you?
> That pomegranate of verses was not you
> The green bright leaf not you, nor the gold fruit
> Burning amongst the leaves, hot fruit of gold
> Nor bird, nor bough, nor bole, nor heaven's blue?
> Alas, dear woman, I have sung in vain.
>
> Let me dishevel then once more the leaves
> Of Cupid's bright thesaurus, and there find
> The word of words, the crimson seed of seeds,
> The aureate sound of sounds; and out of this
> Conceive once more your beauty, and in terms
> Your feminine keen eye will not disdain.
>
> (CP, p. 504)

But all the poetic analogies he collects in stanzas three and four of this prelude are somehow insufficient to describe the nature of the woman. So the poet asks in despair:

> What would you have? Some simple copper coin—
> I love you, you are lovely, I adore you?
> Or, better still, dumb silence and a look?
>
> (CP, p. 504)

We recognize again the two languages of the sages: the "simple copper coin" of factual language being one extreme and "dumb silence" of total implication the other. The poet, however, cannot use either but must find a middle way or else despair:

> No, no, this will not do; I am not one
> For whom these silences are sovereign;
> The pauses in the music are not music,
> Although they make the music what it is.
> Therefore I thumb once more the god's thesaurus,
> For phrase and praise, and find it all for you.
>
> (CP, p. 505)

The solution cannot lie in "chainmaking," i.e., in assembling ever more poetic similes. The poet must step outside of his own perspective and see his very attempt at poetic truth as part of the cosmic "manuscript."

. . . while I turn from these
To the vast pages of that manuscript
On which the stars are stars, the world a world;
And there I find you written down, between
Arcturus and a primrose and the sea.

(CP, p. 505)

Yet even this seemingly ultimate truth is again only the perspective of one particular prelude, which is being superseded by the following poem. For it seems to be, as Aiken had suspected already in the early war years in Boston, "that an author's writings were very often in some degrees an anticipation of attitudes yet to be formed, definitions yet to be made, actions yet to be taken" and "the work of art, of whatever category, [was] therefore, the conscious-unconscious process of arrival at this new point; and, when completed, [it was] itself in a sense the catalyst which would precipitate the new attitude or action" (U, p. 247). Just as no work of art can in itself be final, so the complete *oeuvre* of an artist is only a single thread on the cosmic loom which is weaving the divine texture of the world. The poet's work, in content and form, is designed to express this very insight.

Aiken is not—as many critics suggest—a great philosophical poet just because he is concerned with philosophical and epistemological problems. On the contrary: as a philosopher in the narrower sense he is hardly convincing, and his logic is not always consistent; as a poet he often fails because he tends to speak *about* philosophical ideas instead of using them as "counterpoints of thought." With regard to the weaker part of Aiken's work we cannot but agree with Bollier who, in "Conrad Aiken and T. S. Eliot," comes to the following conclusion: "If Aiken has had difficulty in keeping his 'vision' from becoming argument, one can understand why he has been tempted into talking about this infinitely multiple consciousness rather than rendering it as pure vision, for the very nature of the vision demands that diffuseness, that parallelism and repetition, of presentation which too often amounts to little more than a verbal blur."[26] But I think that Aiken nevertheless deserves the title "philosophical poet," because his preoccupation with musical structure in poetry is at the same time an epistemological concern. His search for a style is also, and above all, a quest for truth.

Notes

[1] Conrad Aiken, *Collected Poems 1916-1970* (New York: Oxford Univ. Press, 1970), p. 1021. This volume will hereafter be cited as CP. Other abbreviated sources in this essay: Conrad Aiken, *Ushant: An Essay* (1952; rpt. Cleveland, Ohio: World Publishing Co., 1962), cited as U; and *Scepticisms: Notes on Contemporary Poetry* (New York: Knopf, 1919), cited as Sc.

[2] Aiken, "Poetry and the Mind of Modern Man," in Howard Nemerov, ed., *Poets on Poetry* (New York: Basic Books, 1966), pp. 6-7.

[3] See *Ushant*, p. 166: "the moving ship on the moving water of a moving world taking its course from a cosmic chronometer of stars which was itself in visible motion. . . ."

[4] F. H. Bradley, *Appearance and Reality*, (1896; 2nd ed., Oxford: Univ. Press, 1930), pp. 128-29. Quoted in E. P. Bollier, "T. S. Eliot and F. H. Bradley: A Question of Influence," *Tulane Studies in English*, 12 (1962), 90.

[5] Again and again Aiken declared that a poet should be free from any kind of intellectually crippling orthodox belief. As an example, let me quote from his essay on Robert Lowell in *Collected Criticism* (London: Oxford Univ. Press, 1968): "between two poets of equal poetic merit, that one will be the greater . . . whose range of reference is wider than any orthodoxy could endow, freer than it would permit; intellectual limitations, there is no gainsaying, are crippling, even if they are only implicit" (p. 363).

[6] cf. Calvin S. Brown, "The Color Symphony Before and After Gautier," *Comparative Literature*, 5:4 (1953), 293.

[7] For the history of the color symphony see Brown's essay.

[8] René Taupin, *L'influence du symbolisme francais sur la poésie américaine* (Paris: H. Champion, 1929), p. 203.

[9] *Literary Essays of Ezra Pound*, ed. T. S. Eliot (London: Faber, 1954), pp. 442-43.

[10] The most thorough attempt to elucidate the function of musical forms and terminology in Aiken's work is found in Robert E. Carlile's doctoral dissertation, "Conrad Aiken's Prose: The Musico-Literary Perspective" (Diss. Univ. of Georgia, 1971). I think, however, that Carlile remains too much on the thematic surface of the problem. A more complete analysis of the syntactical structure or the texture of the imagery or the evolution of plots and subplots would have yielded richer results.

[11] Ibid., p. 146.

[12] Ibid., p. 76. Carlile asks himself to what extent musical analogy can and should be linked to content and/or literary technique when his investigation of Aiken's novels yielded the fact "that music and its terminology in *Great Circle*, not in *Ushant*, is most probably Aiken's way of talking about metaphor." Carlile therefore concludes that "limited analogy is all that is justified."

[13] Donald Davie, *Articulate Energy: An Inquiry into the Syntax of English Poetry* (London: Routledge, 1976), p. 18.

[14] Ibid., p. 31.

[15] *T. S. Eliot: Selected Prose*, ed. John Hayward (London: Faber, 1953), pp. 66-67.

[16] T. S. Eliot, *The Use of Poetry and the Use of Criticism* (London: Faber, 1933), pp. 118-19.

[17] Northrop Frye, *T. S. Eliot* (1963; rpt. London: Oliver and Boyd, 1968), p. 30.

[18] Susanne K. Langer, *Philosophy in a New Key* (Cambridge, Mass.: Harvard Univ. Press, 1942), p. 228.

[19] *Eliot: Selected Prose*, p. 53.

[20] Ibid., p. 60.

[21] The sculptural term "abbozzo" means a sketch or unfinished work.

[22] Langer, p. 238.

[23] *Eliot: Selected Prose*, p. 53.

[24] Aiken, *Preludes* (New York: Oxford Univ. Press, 1966), p. v.

[25] See *Ushant*, pp. 174-75: "Out of this [i.e. the reading of Freud], and the reading at the same time of *The Origin of Species*, and Nietzsche's *Zarathustra* and *Beyond Good and Evil*, was to evolve (since one spoke of evolution, whether of worlds or morals), but so imperceptibly and slowly that he found himself possessed of it before he knew he had been thinking about it, his own later concern with the evolution of consciousness. . . ."

[26] E. P. Bollier, "From Scepticism to Poetry: A Note on Conrad Aiken and T. S. Eliot," *Tulane Studies in English*, 13 (1963), 103.

Harry Marten (essay date 1980)

SOURCE: "The Unconquerable Ancestors: 'Mayflower,' 'The Kid,' 'Hallowe'en'," in *Studies in the Literary Imagination*, Vol. XIII, No. 2, Fall, 1980, pp. 51-62.

[*In the following essay, Marten looks at three of Aiken's poems written in the 1940s after the poet had returned to the U.S. from England and contends that through these poems Aiken succeeded in "rediscovering" and accepting his connections with his homeland and his past.*]

"Do you really feel at home here?"[1] For years Conrad Aiken faced this discomforting question as an American living in Rye, England. But when war in Europe compelled his return to America in 1939, the question, turning suddenly inside-out, became even more disconcerting. Was Aiken at home as an American in America after years abroad? As he tells it, what steered his imagination during this time of dislocation was the heightened sense of ancestry which accompanied his return to New England. "I found," Aiken says simply, "that my ancestral roots claimed me":[2]

> The ancestors, the ancestors, the unconquerable ancestors, whose tongues still spoke so clearly, whose hands still reached so unmistakably . . . Each bud, and then each leaf, each flower, taking up the precious pattern, repeating it; perhaps only with the most infinitesimal variation, the slightest imaginable, and probably accidental, accretion, of one's own. (U, p. 45)

And yet, attention to works written during these years when Aiken found that his "country clock was wound up again" (U, p. 337), suggests that the process of reclamation of, and by, the homeland was a complex one, involving more than one idea of ancestry, and taking the poet down different paths of discovery. **"Mayflower"** (1945), **"The Kid"** (1947), and **"Hallowe'en"** (1949), three central works of the period, mark in particular the intrica-

cies of the process of Aiken's "discovery and acceptance of America" and of "his own ghosts in it" (U, p. 336).[3]

"Mayflower," as the title suggests, is a poem of both departure and arrival. It is Aiken's bridge into the new world, identifying the freshness and immediacy of new experience, and yet affirming, too, a link of old with new as part of perception. Ancestry here seems more a matter of cultural connectedness than a personal feeling of belonging, and yet the discovered ancestral presences, however generalized, offer comfort amidst the confusion of the unfamiliar.

Having arrived on the new world's shore, Aiken discourses with the past, extending the techniques already used in his final novel, *Conversation* (1940), of mingling living voices with quotes and echoes of voices from a long-gone time. "Listen"[4]—Aiken's speaker demands our full attention with his first word in **"Mayflower."** And if we give it, we will hear and learn the ways "the ancient voices hail us from the farther shore" of new world leave-taking, of older times and cultures which are, in fact, continuous with our own. The voices of Aiken's literary godfathers "Will and Ben" (CP, p. 865)—Shake-speare and Jonson—linger on. And in the normal vocabulary men use to record their immediate experiences we recognize the names of things carried from generation to generation.

"Mayflower" flows with sound and speech as the poet experiences "the New England spring" (CP, p. 864). The presence of the past is felt immediately in the imagined "cries and farewells . . . and the praying" of "devout [pilgrim] fathers," and in the vividly onomatopoetic diction which helps to set the scene, marking the clangor of "the hawser falling," the "weeping on the quayside" (CP, p. 864). The assemblage of sounds which establish the vitality of the experience of the past in the present is given more formal, historical resonance as well when Aiken, having cast the moment in the mind's eye, lifts passages into his poem from *Mourt's Relation*, the pilgrim narrative journal he used so pointedly in *Conversation*. The formal language of the record written with an eye toward both posterity and the providential, together with the concrete descriptive images registered by the poet's senses, energize and support one another to inform both poet and reader of the design of permanence-in-change stamped on the face of things.

The controlled excitement of the pilgrims who—

> . . . 'by God's providence,' break of day espied
> land which we deemed to be Cape Cod.'
> 'It caused us to rejoice together and praise God,
> seeing so goodly a land, and wooded to the brink
>   of the sea.'
>
>   (CP, pp. 864-865)

—is indeed very different from nature's intense voices, so alive for the sense aware poet in his New England present. Observing his immediate surroundings, Aiken discovers almost apocalyptic transformations of life: inanimate objects act as if with sentience—"the quick plough breaks dust," while frogs and fish are anthropomorphized and even sunlight seems "altered" by cycles of growth and renewal as "seagulls speak," ale-wives run, the "new snake sleeps in altered light" (p. 865) and the noisy moment surrounds us:

> the pinkwinks shrill, the pinkwinks trill . . .
> *Spring, spring, spring, spring,* they cry,
> water voice and reed voice,
>   . . . *And on his log,*
> the whip-poor-will shrieks and thumps in the bright
>   *May-morning fog.*
>
>   (CP, p. 865)

Yet the poet's receptivity to the vital moment is not, finally, separable from his discovered sense of himself as an inheritor of things seen, ways of seeing and communicating:

> Yes: the ancient voices speak once more. . .
> their spring, still living, now. . . .
> Three hundred years of snow and change,
> the Mermaid voices growing lost and strange; . . .
> Yet not lost wholly:
> in deed, in charter, and in convenant sweetly kept . . .
> and the ballad's melancholy. . . .
> sung at maying, sung at haying,
> shouted at husking to the fiddle's playing, . . .
> And in the names kept too: sorrel and purslane,
> ground-ivy, catnip, elecampane, . . .
> Each child set out and tended his own tree,
> to each his name was given. Thus, they still live,
>   still see:
> Mercy, Deborah, Thankful, Rufus and Amanda
>   Clark,
> trees that praise sunlight, voices that praise the dark.
>   (CP, pp. 865-867)

"All's here" for the poet, "all's kept, for now / spring brings back the selfsame apple bough / that braved the sea three hundred years ago" (CP, p. 869). No longer exiled twice over, but a traveler returned to discover himself a part of an intricate continuum, Aiken has crossed in **"Mayflower"** the threshold of his now not so "alien coast" and sees "in the many-voiced country lane / which parts the fields of poverty grass and clover":

> world without end to love and have it,
> bee-blossom heart to love and live it,
> this holy land, our faith itself, . . .
>
>   (CP, p. 869)

As Aiken tells it in *Ushant*, "the little mayflower poem" provided release "from inhibitory checkings" (U, p. 337). And in freeing the poet from insecurities, from doubts of belonging to the American scene, the poem seems to have provided Aiken with a comfortable starting point for further exploration of the new world experience he was setting out to rediscover in his middle years. Having established for the moment a sense of the basic continuity of new and old which affirms the particularity of each experience, yet suggests, too, the interweaving of past and present in a process of mutual definition, Aiken could

turn to explore more completely the "newness" of the new world experience, concentrating now on his role as inheritor of attitudes that he defined as especially American.

Broadening and depersonalizing the notion of ancestral inheritance in his next important poem, **"The Kid,"** Aiken concentrated on a special ancestral line whose largeness makes clear the poet's intention of offering

> a sort of spiritual history of the U S (old Blackstone, and Anne Bradstreet, and Boone and Crevecoeur and Thoreau and Appleseed and the Quaker martyrs and Kit Carson and Billy the Kid and then Melville and Willard Gibbs and the Adams brothers in starlight (Brooks and Henry) (all ending of course with Emily Dickinson?)?? the "Kid" ideas as the American eponymous hero, whether as pioneer of the inward or outward wilderness. . . . [5]

"The Kid" takes for its subject nothing less than a vision of the American national experience in which newness and uncertainty helped define the shape of groups of people as well as of the individual, nurtured elastic language, produced varieties of geographic directions of exploration and settlement. Americans, as historian Daniel Boorstin has observed,

> were not men moving ever *toward* the west, but men ever moving in the west. The churning, casual, vagrant, circular motion around and around was as characteristic of the American experience as the movement in a single direction.[6]

And Aiken catches the new wanderer perfectly, offering a history of the tantalizing traditional figure of the loner "who sought freedom and privacy in the 'wide open spaces,' or the physical conquest of an untamed continent, and those others, early and late, who were to struggle for it in the darker kingdoms of the soul" (CP, p. 1033). But he provides too, in his ancestral survey, a view of the broader spirit of the American frontier as it was embodied in clusters of transients.

Further, **"The Kid"** dares to suggest what our self-serious literature too often overlooks: that at the foundation of our most solemn American myths humor and high seriousness are joined. As Aiken wrote to his friend John Gould Fletcher, **"The Kid"** is often "*light in tone*, dares a little to be *fun* . . . eschews the portentous, declines to be rigid or pseudo-intellectual or Kierkegaardian or solemn, cuts corners, simplifies, and rollicks its way in carefree ostosyllabic couplets as apparently innocent as a backwoods ballad" (SL, p. 276). In offering his combinations of tone, of high-poetic diction and varieties of slang, vigorous tall tales and gentle or crude songs of the people, Aiken is expressing his concern with an ambiguity which determines much of the transiency, and defined much of the comedy and the heroism of the new world wilderness experience.[7]

The poem, seeking to express the essence of Aiken's "always restless, always moving on" (CP, p. 844) spiritual ancestors, is laced with deliberate ambiguities. Beginning with the prototypically American figure of William Blackstone who found his "untrodden kingdoms in the minde" (CP, p. 851)—and following various mythic-historical incarnations of this wilderness explorer, the "eponymous hero" called the "Kid"—we discover that even seemingly simple definitions of persons and places are impossible. In answer to fairly straightforward questions about the "Kid" in general, for example—

> Who saw the Kid when he rose . . . ?
>
>   (CP, p. 845)
>
> Who heard that lad leap down . . . ?
>
>   (CP, p. 845)
>
> Who bore witness . . . ?
>
>   (CP, p. 847)

—we realize that the "Kid" and the places he passes through can only be understood as mutually defining.

In rendering early impressions of the "Kid" and the land, Aiken gathers a multitude of poetic effects into a small space—crowding together internal rhymes, slant rhymes, assonance, consonance, alliteration, an assemblage of onomatopoetic images. To "witness" seems suddenly an active rather than a passive mode of perception. And as we observe both traveler and natural witnesses, we are drawn, too, to active response by the energy of the language, and in that sense share in the process of definition. While we listen and look, a tongue-twisting catalogue of names, things and places swells into a song of greeting which affects all our senses, enabling us to comprehend and participate in the experience of "moving on." Like a compressed geography or natural history lesson, the list reminds us anew of the existence of what may be familiar, enables us to conjure up the unfamiliar: "And rivers: rivers with their proud hosanna; / Chattahoochee: Tallahassee: Susquehanna / Savannah, high-yaller, and Arkansas, red" (CP, p. 849).

The poem, too, provides a crowded parade of local references and colloquial, informal or semi-formal identifications of things: the "bullbriar patch," "groundhog," "cunning 'possum,'" "hummingbird moth in the scuppernong blossom," "hoarse Monomoy," "Grizzly," "longhorn," "Buffalo spine," "Rattlesnake rattle," "tumbleweed blowing" (CP, pp. 846-847), all hear the "Kid's" approach, know him, admire him. These are, of course, the "Kid's" names for things in the untrodden kingdoms singing back to him in praise. Gaining and giving identity, he is "hailed" and "farewelled" (CP, p. 848) by the noise and activity of nature's constantly changing shape, by the flow of water, and by the "heat-song" (CP, p. 849) and "beast-cry" (CP, p. 850) of wild animals of all kinds and sizes. The "Kid" and his surroundings are perpetually taking form one from the other:

> They caught his hymn as it fell to the sea
> from condor's shadow and sugarpine-tree:
> of might in singleness. . . .
>
>   (CP, p. 848)

> He turned to the land: forgot his name: Hector
> changing and changeless went and came: St. John de
> dedreamed blood-knowledge
>   as he slept in nature: Crececoeur
> sucked blood-knowledge from the blood of the
>   creature . . .
> heartbeat probed in the heartbeat's place. . . .
>
>   (CP, p. 854)

Ambiguities are compounded. Aiken's unbiquitous spiritual ancestor, both a man and more, is at once elusive and substantial. Like an elemental force he rises with the sun and "rid[es] the bridled and fire-bright Beast" (CP, p. 845); seeming to command all space he "span[s] / wide water as only a rainbow can" (CP, p. 846). From the force of his godlike fist comes "the lightening stroke, / the double thunder and a puff of smoke: / the double thunder and the lightening twice" (CP, p. 847). Yet he is a builder and a planter, too, responsive to his world in the limited ways a man can be, shaping it with the tools at his disposal:

> He . . . laid axe to root: John Chapman
> packed his knapsack with the seed of fruit . . .
> framed a corncrib, and plowed up a field,
> planted his corn and brought it to yield: . . .
>
>   (CP, p. 855)

The "Kid" seems both a prime mover—"westward, seaward, he drew the horizon"—and a being whose actions are determined by external circumstances—"following the Sioux who followed the bison" (CP, p. 846). Too, as a man he is capable of a selfless appreciation of the possibilities of the wild—"Lord, lend me wisdom, Lord, let me dream: / spent in thy heart was this sunshine day" (CP, p. 855)—and an arrogant self-serving response to it:

> Said Tidewater Johnny to Bluewater Johnny,
> you got to go west if you want to make money,
> we built up the cities and filled them with people, . . .
> and the cities are pretty, but the forest is best.
>
>   (CP, pp. 855-856)

Even the "Kid's" noble "hymn" of seasons and change often sounds like little more than a folksy squawk, as Aiken juxtaposes majestic visions with such doggerel ballads interpolated into the poem as

> *I'm away, I'm away, I'm away to the west . . .*
> *my pa he can curse, my ma she can cry,*
> *they'll all forgive me in the sweet by-and-by,*
> *I come from heaven and to heaven I'll go,*
> *but what's in between I'm a wantin' to know!*
>
>   (CP, p. 847)

The noble vision seemingly offers no truer glimpse of the "Kid" than the low or comic view does. This is the lesson implicit in realizing, with the help of the poet's ironic subject and image rhyme, that the "Kid" who leaps down "over the night hard hoofbeats pounding" (CP, p. 845) "his hair like fire and his eyes like ice; / and a pinto pony, a wing of flame, / whinnying and gone as quick as it came" (CP, p. 847) is a ghost to bemuse us hovering over the scene when two less than grand "Kids," Catskill Johnny and Swannikin Johnny, enact their own version of things and light out for the territories:

> Said Catskill Johnny to Swannikan Johnny,
> you fetch a horse and I'll find a pony,
> we'll hitch Conestoga to a comet's tail
> and hurry out west on the wilderness trail.
>
> (CP, p. 856)

What the deliberate ambiguities of Aiken's presentations suggest is neither a portrait of men, nor of gods, but rather a paradoxically *unambiguous* representation of a force whose extravagant energies flow through the wide range of the American experience.

The sometimes forced conjoining in "The Kid" of differing dictions, actions, visions, has struck a sour note for a number of Aiken's critics. Perhaps the bristliest, though typical enough, is Frederick J. Hoffman:

> The conception is faulty, the shifts of terms and of the grounds for action, the almost frivolous slightness with which major important ideas are treated, all mark *The Kid* as one of Aiken's conspicuous failures.[8]

And indeed the hoof-pounding rhythms can seem monotonous. Too, the sudden juxtapositions of literary images sufficiently elevated to please the most cultivated connoisseur, with common sing-songs outrageous enough to bring a twinkle to the eye of most popular humorists, can be jarring. Still, we would do well to recall that, as Herman Melville wrote, "There are some enterprises in which a careful disorderliness is the best method."[9] Neither consistently serious nor humorous, Aiken it seems has tried with considerable success to provide something of a bridge between two traditional American literary reactions to the wilderness—ones which, as Aiken rightly sees, are linked by their responsiveness to energies released by the ambiguities of frontier life.

Aiken's singular achievement in "The Kid" is to offer a work which embraces the myths and dreams on which the western movement was based and the harsher, sometimes humorous realities of the frontier experience, without having one cancel the other. Walt Whitman, identified near the end of "The Kid" as one of the hero's late incarnations, once explained the expression of mythic and common experience in a way that we may use to offer our own "hail" and "farewell" to Aiken's substantial accomplishment here. As if summoning the poet-to-be, Walt Whitman wrote in *November Boughs* a year before Aiken's birth:

> Considering Language then as some mighty potentate, into the majestic audience-hall of the monarch ever enters a personage like one of Shakespere's clowns, and takes position there, and plays a part even in the stateliest ceremonies. Such is Slang, or indirection, an attempt of common humanity to escape from bald literalism, and express itself illimitably, which in highest

walks produces poets and poems, and doubtless in pre-historic times gave the start to, and perfected, the whole immense tangle of the old mythologies. For, curious as it may appear, it is strictly the same impulse-source, the same thing.[10]

Aiken himself seems to have understood better than anyone the crux of his problem with "The Kid." Indeed his next major poem, "Hallowe'en," goes a long way toward addressing it. The significant danger of "The Kid's" deliberate ambiguities, of its gathering, without sufficient distinctions, of so many different "Kids" under the general heading of spiritual ancestor, was the loss of centering, explicitly personal, connection with his American inheritance. Although in "Mayflower" Aiken had generally realized his link with America, and he had explored sweepingly in "The Kid" an elemental American vision, he had not yet firmly located himself on the new continent by directly addressing his family roots. In "Hallowe'en," complementing the earlier explorations, the poet completes his discovery of his new found old home by learning to comprehend and accept the presence of his own ghosts in it. For as the poem makes clear in celebrating the days of the dead—All Saints and All Souls Days—

> in forgetting our obligations to the dead
> we have neglected our living and our children's
>   living
> in neglecting our love
> for the dead who would still live within us.
>
> (CP, p. 894)

In contrast to "The Kid," "Hallowe'en" raises ambiguities only to dispel them in the clarity of the poet's dialogue with his grandfather William James Potter. Once more Aiken invites us to observe his new world, and once more we find it at times to be unsettlingly confused. Yet amidst the vagueness, sharply defined presences come forth. In the twilight settings of the poem, when the poet places us somewhere between waking and dreaming, forms and murmuring voices merge, pass into shadow, but reemerge as living images in a ceremony of remembering. With each ritual return, the intensity of ancestral presences and the sense of their world helps to define the poet's own world.

In a kind of enchanted environment where it is difficult to measure the clear outlines of things, where hints of deep mysteries accumulate as words swell in chantlike rhythmic regularity and repetition—

> The moon . . . lights her bonfire
> behind Sheepfold Hill, old corpse-fire
> blazing through oaktrees, the bone-fire
> which, in forests, the priests called *ignis ossium*
>
> (CP, p. 892)

—speaker and reader tense with anticipation of unusual occurrences. The tension is both heightened and relieved by "the homeless" figures that "come to complain and to haunt" (CP, p. 892). For, paradoxically, the apparitions offer the only solidity to be found, compelling our attention to the pains of their displacement.

These figures demand an agony of recognition which, while disconcerting, is less damaging than ignorance. The intensity of their presence clearly invites responses that can begin a process of clarification and change as grandfather and grandson, blending identities, exchange insights:

> In the old time, the old country,
> these two days, these two holy days,
> were devoted to the dead. . . .
> we went in and knelt among bones. And the
>   bones . . .
> joined in complaint and besought us
> for prayers. . . .
>
> In the old time, the old country:
> but now none remembers, . . .
> you come back to abuse and to haunt us,
> you, grandfather . . . and the others:
> to the forgetful house, yourselves not forgetful . . .
> you return once more to remind us. . . .
> it is our ancestors and children who conspire
>   against us
> life unlived and unloved that conspires against us
> our neglected hearts and hearths that conspire
>   against us
>
>   . . . . .
>
> And the spirit, the unappeased houseless spirit,
> whose dwelling should be in ourselves, those who
>   inherit . . .
> homeward once more looks now for prayer and
>   praise
> to be with laurels blest
> and in our breast
> live out his due bequest of nights and days.
>   (CP, pp. 893-895)

Any dwellings we are going to make for ourselves in a new world must have rooms for the still loved presences of our closest ancestors, else, lacking the solid foundation that a sense of personal continuity offers, we will have failed, whatever our efforts, to clear a place in the vast and ambiguous land.

The conclusion of **"Hallowe'en"** brings us from endings full circle to beginnings. Ritual death promotes rebirth, and for Aiken it is a rebirth in memory, a fusion of ritual completion and ritual initiation which, in affirming the interconnectedness of human lives past and present, illuminates for us all the ambiguous places in which we live:

> O you who made magic
> under an oak-tree once in the sunlight
> translating your acorns to green cups and saucers
> for the grandchild mute at the tree's foot,
> and died, alone, on a doorstep at midnight. . . .
> dear scarecrow, dear pumpkin-head!
> who masquerade now as my child, to assure
> the continuing love, the continuing dream,
> and the heart and the hearth and the wholeness—
> it was so, it is so, and the life so lived
> shines this night like the moon. . . .

Rest: be at peace. It suffices to know and to rest.
For the singers, in rest, shall stand as a river
whose source is unending forever.
                         (CP, pp. 896-897)

"Not for nothing," then, as Aiken once wrote, "had been those compulsory war years at the Cape Cod farmhouse, and the prolonged reimmersion in the ancestral scene" (U, p. 297). Secure in Brewster (and later Savannah) at last, and having firmly established in his work both a satisfying general and an intense personal response to American places and people, Aiken would choose, paradoxically, in **"A Letter from Li Po"** and **"The Crystal,"** his major poems of the next decades, to speak from the voice of exile rather than arrival. Aiken once worried in *Ushant* that when

> one felt at home, one would have no more to learn, or would have become so relaxed as to be no longer capable of learning; and one's very purpose for having come there at all, or a very important part of it, would be no longer valid. (U, p. 334)

As if to affirm that being "home" need not mean complacency, that he could still "take on the whole damned world"[11]—even better for planting his creative energy in the rich soil in which he had uncovered ancestral roots— Aiken broadened the range of his final "longer philosophical meditations,"[12] mingling American places with far away locations and his own and ancestral voices with historical and legendary figures. But for now, in **"Mayflower," "The Kid,"** and **"Hallowe'en,"** Aiken had rediscovered his America, "in the delighted acknowledgement of one's debts, one's ties, one's roo one's belongingness" (U, p. 337).

Notes

I am grateful to the American Council of Learned Societies for a fellowship which enabled me to pursue this work.

[1] Conrad Aiken, *Ushant* (1952; rpt. New York: Oxford Univ. Press, 1971), p. 334. Hereafter pages references will be given parenthetically in the text with *Ushant* indicated as U.

[2] Conrad Aiken, "Poetry and the Mind of Modern Man," in *Poets on Poetry*, ed. Howard Nemerov (New York: Basic Books, 1966), p. 2.

[3] Of course these poems were not Aiken's first American theme writings during the period following his return to America in 1939. In part, the subject of American voices and places had long occupied Aiken. These poems, however, are the major works which mark most clearly the process of Aiken's rediscovery of his ability to "enjoy the American scene wholeheartedly again" (U, p. 135). As listed in the Aiken bibliography being prepared by Florence and Fraser Bonnell a version of "Mayflower" first appeared in *The Virginia Quarterly Review*, 21:2 (Spring 1945); "The Kid" appeared in *The Western Review*, 11:3 (Spring 1947); "Hallowe'en" appeared in *The Harvard Alumni Bulletin*, 52:3 (22 October 1949). I am grateful to Mr. and Mrs. Bonnell for allowing me access to their splendid work-in-progress.

[4] Conrad Aiken, *Collected Poems* (New York: Oxford Univ. Press,

1970), p. 864. Hereafter pages references will be given parenthetically in the text, with *Collected Poems* indicated as CP.

[5] Conrad Aiken to Malcolm Lowry, 4 September 1946, in Conrad Aiken, *Selected Letters of Conrad Aiken*, ed. Joseph Killorin (New Haven and London: Yale Univ. Press, 1978), p. 274. Hereafter page references will be given parenthetically in the text, with *Selected Letters* indicated as SL.

[6] *The Americans: The National Experience* (New York: Vintage Books, 1965), p. 95.

[7] Again Boorstin is helpful, summarizing the nature of life in the borderland: "The pervasive ambiguity of American life, the vagueness which laid the continent open to adventure, which made the land a rich storehouse of the unexpected, which kept vocabulary ungoverned and the language fluid—this same vagueness suffused both the comic and the heroic. Both depended on incongruity: the incongruity of the laughable and the incongruity of the admirable" (*The Americans: The National Experience*, p. 332).

[8] *Conrad Aiken* (New York: Twayne, 1962), p. 146.

[9] *Moby-Dick* (Indianapolis, Ind.: The Bobbs-Merrill Co., 1964), p. 465.

[10] *Prose Works 1892, Volume II: Collect and Other Prose*, ed. Floyd Stovall (New York: New York Univ. Press, 1964), p. 573.

[11] Conrad Aiken, "Conversations with Conrad Aiken, the second of two programmes recorded in New York by D. G. Bridson," 1962, p. 1. The typescript of this BBC broadcast which I have used is part of the holdings in Conrad Aiken Collection of the Huntington Library.

[12] Conrad Aiken, "Poetry and the Mind of Modern Man," in *Poets on Poetry*, p. 6.

Steven E. Olson   (essay date 1981)

SOURCE: "The House of Man: Ethical Symbolism in Conrad Aiken's *The Clerk's Journal*," in *Essays in Arts and Sciences*, Vol. X, No. 1, May, 1981, pp. 79-92.

[*In the following essay, Olson refutes the argument that Aiken's early poetry lacks intellectual and ethical depth, and suggests that Aiken uses imagery connected with houses to express his feelings about love and human interconnectedness.*]

The present and ongoing critical estimate of Conrad Aiken continues to be one of modern American letters' most bizarre phenomenons. While a small number of supporters quietly insist that he may justifiably be considered as among the three or four most important poets of the century, his reputation languishes, as it has for decades, amid a detritus of misinformation, faulty generalization, and often well-intentioned but unperceptive commentary. Among the many reasons which can plausibly be brought forward to explain Aiken's obscurity is that following much of the confused response and opprobrium generated by his early verse, he deliberately ceased attempts to "explain" his poetry. Although he published ten volumes of poetry between 1914 and 1925,[1] Aiken's early verse has received essentially no productive reevaluation, as a brief survey of influential critical judgments spanning a period of nearly forty years makes apparent.

Dismissing as nonexistent the ethical content of the poetry contained in Aiken's first nine books, Louis Untermeyer wrote in 1925 that **"The Road"** (in *Priapus and the Pool and Other Poems*, published the same year) constituted "the first poem of Aiken's which expresses compassion for humanity at large and a participation in its struggles."[2] Apparently ignorant of the fact that Aiken's specifically "Freudian" phase ended before 1920, Horace Gregory, in 1942, pigeon-holed Aiken as a decadent:

> The failures and the never-quite-attained successes are as perceptible in his early books as in his latest— the melodious vagueness, the emphasis upon the theme of sexual adventure, reiterated in terms of the slightly soiled, amateur discussions of Freud during the 1920's, the special "artiness" of that same period which never failed to include its heritage of the 1890's from the pages of Henry Harland's *The Yellow Book*.[3]

Despite the fact that Aiken's early poetry bristles with themes and metaphors drawn from an extensive knowledge of natural science and medicine, Frederick Hoffman, twenty years after Gregory, chorused that the first several books contain "*no* intellectual substance."[4] Contrary to such widely held assessments, however, it is emphatically clear that both intellectual principles and ethical beliefs jointly determined the content of Aiken's poetry, from *The Clerk's Journal* (1910-11) through *Thee* (1967). It is with the genesis and moral vision of Aiken's earliest major poem that the present essay shall be concerned.

Conrad Aiken wrote **The Clerk's Journal** during the winter of 1910-11 while a student at Harvard. The poem remained unpublished until 1971, when The Eakins Press brought out a facsimile edition containing an introductory memoir by Aiken. Looking back over a period of some sixty years, the eighty-year-old author called his literally long-lost narrative "unmistakably the work of a very young man."[5] Yet the poem, he went on to suggest, still sounded the note of the "modern." Aiken recalled how he and T. S. Eliot, his friend and classmate, had mutually sought "a new poetic voice, one in which one could think." Forgetting that "The Love Song of J. Alfred Prufrock" had been completed during the summer of 1911, Aiken compared his own poem with his friend's more successful, if not seminal, endeavor:

> Written in 1910, several years before "Prufrock," it is already talking of lunch-counters, plates of beans, the moon among telephone wires, and life being paved with cobblestones. The shift is on.[6]

While for both "the shift" towards modernist aesthetics *was* on, it is essential to keep in mind the very different sensibilities of the two aspiring poets. Aiken, for example, never shared Eliot's anguished spirituality, nor did he seek visionary experiences or wish for prophetic, private knowledge.[7] Aiken's deterministic naturalism precluded, *a priori*, the possibility that one might usefully imagine solutions for despair lying beyond the circumference of the too frequently tawdry quotidian. In his comparison of *The Clerk's Journal* with "Prufrock," Aiken inadvertently obscured the originality and merits of his own poem. By evaluating it "in terms of" Eliot's very different work, he tacitly bolstered the critical position that his early verse failed to achieve a voice of its own. Yet such is not the case: while Aiken participated with Eliot and others in the modernist experiments with language and method, he steadfastly articulated an intellectual and ethical vision uniquely his own. That vision, moreover, owed very little to the contemporary *literary* milieu.

The Clerk's Journal is a two-part verse narrative of close to 450 lines which combines subjective portraiture with reflective analysis. The first part of the poem consists of the clerk's unfolding account of his short-lived romance with a waitress. The second part of the poem consists of the clerk's account of his attempts to diagnose his pain and depression following the break-up of his love affair. Insofar as *The Clerk's Journal* examines the matrix of its own construction, it represents, within the context of Aiken's career, a prototypical "work in progress": we observe the "changing mind" of the clerk as he struggles to create from immediate experience a poetic artifact which can help him to understand his emotions and behavior. He questions and analyzes his fluctuating moods and impulses, which range from an initially laconic cynicism to an intermediately joyful panhumanism to an ultimately resigned scepticism. His feelings are presented and evaluated both as discrete states of mind and as motor reflexes to external events over which he as an individual has little or no control. Taken together, these active and passive dimensions of the protagonist's consciousness allow Aiken to depict the clerk as both catalytic agent and self-scrutinizing specimen.

The Clerk's Journal is valuable today not because it represents an undiscovered "modernist" effort by a major poet, but because it provides insight into the early priorities of Aiken's thought. As early as 1910 it is clear that Aiken believed that the limits of knowledge expand in proportion to man's efforts to seek and disseminate self-knowledge. (The first epigraph in Aiken's autobiography, *Ushant*, published in 1952, is taken from Coleridge's *Self-Knowledge*.) Weighing against man's efforts to increase human intelligence is the retrogressive propensity to imagine that biological limitations can be transcended. Although Aiken did not deliberately attempt to extract an overriding philosophical theme from his psycho-biological interests prior to writing *The Divine Pilgrim* poems between 1915 and 1920, his naturalistic axioms clearly determined the ideational content of the verse written through 1914.

In several respects *The Clerk's Journal* anticipates what Aiken in 1912 described as an interest in making poetry from "the commonplace and sordid."[8] The first of many

pieces set in New York City, his tale in verse arose directly from the previous summer's residence "in a fine, slum boardinghouse near the Twenty-third Street Ferry, by the corner of Death Avenue." There, in 1910, the Harvard junior had tried to "convalesce" from "the Shelley and Keats and Coleridge diseases" picked up from two previous summers spent in the Lake District.[9] By going to New York rather than to England, Aiken sought to repatriate and to urbanize himself by reading such "city" poets as Walt Whitman: "The city, the city . . . the summer in New York was the first real revel in it, the first saturation, and with old Walt, naturally, as guide."[10] Like Whitman, Aiken in *The Clerk's Journal* would seek to celebrate not simply the passions and sufferings of his fictional hero, but also those of the encompassing human community.

Aiken hoped to depict what the Elizabethans understood as "common" behavior: i.e., behavior common to all men regardless of education, wealth, or social position. By using realistic characters and urban slang, he hoped to invigorate his verse and to help get poetry out of the parlor and back into the mainstream of contemporary life. In his initial efforts to "not at all restrict myself to the poetic vocabulary," however, Aiken sometimes attained bathetic heights.[11] The riotously Dreiserian description of a cafe as "a justly far-famed eating-joint," for example, no doubt contributed to his ultimate feeling that *The Clerk's Journal* could be "very funny when it didn't quite mean to be."[12]

Aiken's clerk first appears—as will Forslin, Senlin, and Festus—in an introspective mood, thinking about his immediate situation:

> How these gray days affect the heart!
> My pencil poised in air, I muse
> In melancholy mood, apart
> From life and all its daily news.
>
> (I,1)

Dispirited over the tedium of his drab and unvarying "life of fact," he looks through a "grimy window-pane" at "chimney-pots in wet array." The clerk, like one of Robert Frost's lonely, housebound New Englanders, feels painfully estranged yet at the same time insulated from the world beyond his window. The nature of the world from which he is in temporary retreat is not only drab, but enervatingly and forlornly mechanistic. The clerk views his life as both meaningless and redundant:

> Today, in bed, I wondered why
> Year after year, so patiently,
> I rose at dawn, breakfasted,
> And toiled the day through, wearily,
> And wearily came home, to bed.
> "And what's the use?"—I asked myself;
> Yet every morning, just the same,
> My cheap clock whirs upon its shelf:
> I wake, and rise to daily shame.
>
> (I,1)

Setting yet again an important pattern for subsequent Aiken protagonists, the clerk grapples with the question of his own sanity, so conscious is he of his mind's subjugation to the indifferent, relentless pressure of everyday reality: "Sometimes I think I'll go insane. / This dull life so repeats, so beats / Its tireless echo on my brain" (I,5). The clerk's predicament is one of biological determinism wherein the physiological mechanism of consciousness runs rough-shod over the subsidiary unit of the ego: because he is acutely aware of his inability to control the way his brain *works*, the clerk fears that he likewise cannot actively control the course of his own existence. His *awareness* of his problem persists despite his willed preference to think of other matters. Thus, the problem is compounded: the mind's inability to regulate consciousness becomes an *idee fixe*, a cruelly self-fulfilling prophecy.

Naturalistic determinism persists throughout Aiken's early poetry, though in increasingly complex permutations after 1914. "I have been feeling lately," he wrote to his friend Grayson McCouch in 1913, "that the power of the individual over his destiny has been absurdly exaggerated."[13] Aiken's determinism was seldom synonomous with futility or despair, for he generally accepted it as a phenomenon capable of provoking individual acts of defiance or of conscious courage: the potentially debilitating implications of a mechanistic universe had to be squarely faced and rationally challenged. While neither defiant nor willful (as are other Aiken heroes), the clerk takes sufficient stock of his situation to resolve that he will alter his daily routine. In an effort to combat monotony, he decides to eat lunch at a different cafe:

> —Tush, I am liverish today—
> All's well tomorrow. Think I'll lunch
> At some new place. I've got a "hunch"
> Coffee will drive these blues away.
>
> (I,5)

What was taken to be an insignificant decision changes the clerk's life, for it leads directly to his discovery of the power of love. At the new cafe he orders a second helping of beans to "linger and adore" the waitress-goddess he has stumbled upon:

> She was divine!—And when I left
> She asked, with sweetest irony,
> "All through?"—and smiled. I turned to flee,
> Of every mortal sense bereft.
>
> (I,7)

Eros (possibly flatulently propelled) produces a salubrious state of panic: the clerk's unwholesome lethargy vanishes. Far from transforming the overly introspective clerk into a modern Werther, however, love breaks down the barriers which have helped to keep him locked in selfhood. Love refines and enlarges his vision of life; he begins to think less about himself and more about the mass of suffering humanity around him.

Aiken, like Hawthorne and James, adhered to the moral position that the artist was obligated to combat, rather than perpetuate, the propensities of so-called American "individualism." His ethical and familial heritage, in fact, was remarkably similar to James'. The moral core of James' fiction grew directly out of the Swedenborgian philosophy of Henry James, Sr., who believed that the individual "proprium" (synonomous with egotism and selfhood) must be destroyed before full, productive consciousness was possible, regardless of however horrible a "vastation" it might require. Creative consciousness—the highest human quality—had to supplant the socially engendered, moralistic conscience which, due to its inherently conformist, restrictive tendencies, prevented the individual from becoming fully aware of the reality and integrity of other lives.

Through the influence and writings of his maternal grandfather, William James Potter, Aiken inherited an ethical vision strikingly similar to that which Henry James, Jr., inherited from his father. Potter, a friend of Emerson's, moved from Quakerism to Unitarianism to a rationalistic theology. He renounced both intuitionism and ecclesiasticism in founding the Free Religious Association in New Bedford, Massachusetts. When he moved beyond Unitarianism to "Universal Religion." his congregation moved with him. Potter passed on to his grandson a lively contempt for dogma and myth, as well as a compassionate and progressive moral sensibility.

As the clerk moves outward from his solitary boarding-house room and becomes aware of those around him, he comes to feel a reciprocal bond between himself and his fellow boarders. Much like the relationship between Potter and his devoted congregation,[14] the bond envisioned is one of candor and humility:

> This nondescript gray boarding-house
> Was never much to descant on:
> Dirty, ill-kept, with door-knobs gone.
> Moths' nests, and vestiges of mouse:
> The bedding changed infrequently,
> The table-cloths embossed with egg,—
> All this indeed; yet now I beg
> Its pardon, with humility.
> For there are human beings here,
> Poor beaten things—yet each a gem
> Priceless to me,—because to them
> I have been kind and cavalier.
> Do what I will, my heart will yearn—
> I bless them; and *they* bless, in turn.
>
> (I,12)

Like other writers, Aiken often used houses as cerebral or somatic metaphors (and in fact does so in the second part of *The Clerk's Journal*). *Boardinghouses*, however, were always special to him, and came to occupy an important place in his work. Boardinghouses symbolized for Aiken the essential human condition: in the transitory pilgrimage of his life man in his dependency and weakness must subjugate his willfulness to the common good. Boardinghouses represented the cooperative body politic, the social community; they were seen by Aiken as microcosmic, pluralistic metropolises which flourished in proportion to the degree of selflessness and sensitivity of their residents, who seldom could escape some degree of involvement in the lives of their contiguous neighbors.

The "fine, slum boardinghouse" Aiken lived in during the summer of 1910 also became the setting for a story. In "The Orange Moth" the young hero, Cooke, who is trying to become a writer, savors his temporary residence "in a dirty boarding-house in the great city."[15] At night, freight trains, red-lighted, clank along the Death Avenue tracks. While Cooke fails in his efforts to write passages of incandescent beauty in the vein of De Quincey and Pater, his sensibility expands and he as an individual matures as a result of his spontaneous response to the teeming life around him.

Aiken was born in a Savannah boardinghouse on Whitaker Street, facing Forsyth Park. (The house today is an elegantly restored, single-family residence.) "The first really identifiable 'scene' or action" of his life took place inside the Savannah boardinghouse:

> There were ladies, there were voices downstairs, at the bottom of the echoing stairwell, and they were having tea . . . and into this, down into this, between the dark banisters of the railing, he had released . . . his brother K.'s milk bottle.[16]

In an autobiographical sketch which parallels the *Ushant* account (though it changes the milk bottle from brother's to sister's), Aiken writes: "I was born in a boarding-house, and not a particularly distinguished one. That has always seemed to me an excellent democratic antidote to my family's tradition of being in some way 'well-born.'"[17] Although he was for many years essentially a-political, Aiken's inherited family liberalism rendered him a spiritual democrat, and late in life he actively supported Hubert Humphrey.[18] This aspect of his temperament—so different from Pound's or Eliot's—underlay both Aiken's early appreciation of Whitman and his lifelong fascination with boardinghouses. A similar democratic progressivism and interest in multi-tenanted houses can be found in Hawthorne.

In the matter of boardinghouses we again come upon Aiken's resemblance to Henry James. Both authors as children were deeply influenced by their eccentric, restlessly inquisitive fathers, who dominated the domestic scene. Aiken remembered his father's poems, essays, medical inventions, photographical experiments, and his plans to build a boat in the back-yard. Dr. William Ford Aiken was always "the brilliant enthusiast, the passionate amateur, whose imagination flew in every direction."[19] For his part, the elder Henry James could be equally energetic, equally idiosyncratic: he once spoke of God as "an immense Duck capable only of emitting an eternal quack," and suggested that if human beings were intended to be obedient to the Deity, they would "all have been born webfooted."[20]

Aiken's interest in boardinghouses duplicated essential aspects of the elder James' radical Swedenborgianism. For instance: Swedenborg's description of heaven as a vast, collective, human metropolis caused Henry, Sr., to compare the experience of riding into London on a crowded horse-car to what he imagined heaven must be like.

Writing to a friend, he grotesquely reasoned that a man of normal intelligence could not help but see that this was as close to the New Jerusalem as mortal man could hope to approach:

> I can hardly flatter myself that the frankly chaotic or a-cosmical aspect of our ordinary street-car has altogether escaped your enlightened notice in your visits to the city; and it will perhaps surprise you therefore, to learn that I nevertheless continually witness so much mutual forbearance on the part of its *habitues*; so much spotless acquiescence under the rudest personal jostlings and inconvenience; such a cheerful renunciation of one's strict right; such an amused deference, oftentimes, to one's invasive neighbors; in short, and as a general thing, such a heavenly self-shrinkage in order that "the neighbor" handsome or unhandsome, wholesome or unwholesome, may sit or stand at ease; that I not seldom find myself inwardly exclaiming with the patriarch: *How dreadful is this place! It is none other than the house of God, and the gate of heaven.*[21]

His new awareness of other people enables Aiken's clerk to appreciate how will-lessness, though sometimes destructive of hope, allows his boardinghouse neighbors to practice the "mutual forbearance" which the elder James had discovered amidst the denizens of the crowded horse-car:

> And up and down the stairs I meet
> These poor souls born without a will,
> Resigned long since to life's defeat,
> Whose smiles are sunlight,—for they've lost
> All thought of self, they can be kind;
> They came to Lethe and they crossed,
> Leaving their own souls' dreams behind.
> Life's myriad, nameless souls are they——
> Life's huddled, nebulous multitudes;
> My heart goes out to them and broods;
> How can I make these faces gay?
>
> (I,17)

But while his heart goes out to his fellow boarders, the clerk, anticipating the predicament of Prufrock, cannot discover an appropriate gesture to express his feelings:

> Will a touch of the hand, a word, a glance,
> Work my miracle?—I must try.
> Could I take them all to a play, a dance!
> But alas, no wonder-worker, I.
>
> (I,17)

The clerk's happiness ends abruptly when his adored waitress, without explanation, breaks off their relationship. Cast back into the dull round of his previous existence, he cannot resuscitate his briefly liberating joy and magnanimity. Puzzled and haunted by what he has experienced, the clerk vainly attempts to explain away his pain by positing an innate flaw in the woman he sought to love:

> There was a shrewdness in her eyes—
> A wizened something, old, and wise;
> A dust-speck in the perfect flower,—
> A minute's gray in the golden Hour.
>
> (I,19)

The finest lines in *The Clerk's Journal* emerge in the second part of the poem, where the distraught clerk struggles to comprehend and to diagnose his sorrow. Comparing his heart to a house through which he wanders, he seeks not simply consolation but, more importantly, self-knowledge:

> Your heart's a house . . . sometimes you go
> Into old rooms you scarcely know;
> A mouldy cellar, webbed with grime;
> Or, on a day like this, you climb
> (To flee the hollowness of laughters)
> Among the attic's naked rafters.
> The walls are lathe-and-plaster, bare;
> Old papers, boxes, dust, are there;
> The broken relics of the years
> Too cold and sunless grown for tears . . .
> Turning them with a callous hand
> You muse, and try to understand
> What quality had that or this
> To make you love.
>
> (II,1)

Prior to *The House of Dust*, where it takes on complexly vascular and neurological dimensions, the house image in Aiken's poetry was used primarily as a simple metaphor for the heart, mind, or body. In **"Meditation on a June Evening,"** for example, in a passage which goes on to recall his childhood visits to Duxbury, Aiken writes: "It is as if I visited once more / A house I lived in once, now tenantless."[22] And in **"Improvisations: Lights and Snow,"** he describes his heart as a "forlorn old house" containing locked and secret rooms.[23] While such poets as Poe ("The Haunted Palace") and Eliot ("Gerontion") have also used house imagery in their work, it is the early use of the symbol by Frost which most closely resembles Aiken's.[24]

Frost's "Ghost House," from *A Boy's Will* (1913), strikes the same emotional timbre that one finds in *The Clerk's Journal*, which is the "*un*modern," confessional tone of the personally elegiac:

> I dwell in a lonely house I know
> That vanished many a summer ago,
>   And left no trace but the cellar walls,
>   And a cellar in which the daylight falls
> And the purple-stemmed wild raspberries grow.
>   . . . . .
> I dwell with a strangely aching heart
> In that vanished abode there far apart
>   On that disused and forgotten road
>   That has no dust-bath for the toad.
> Night comes; the black bats tumbled and dart.[25]

Both Aiken and Frost use the image of the house to convey a sense of loss of innocence, and to suggest that what had once been communal has now become lonely, psychologically self-enclosed. In "Ghost House," however, Frost clearly suggests that the surrounding luxuriance of nature will somehow "heal" the speaker, just as it has "healed" an old footpath; the house itself, after all, is being reabsorbed into the landscape.

Aiken's clerk does not suffer passively, but embarks (much like James' Spencer Brydon in "The Jolly Corner") upon an explorational and unpleasant "climb" of deliberate self-confrontation in an effort "to understand" himself. Analytical and bereft of much of the easy sentiment which cloys earlier passages, the second part of *The Clerk's Journal* describes the clerk's determination to dissect and to lay bare the concealed roots of his anguish:

> A week, now—heart and soul I crave
> To yield my dead up, like the grave:
> To utter, word by stillborn word,
> The bitter pain, though no one heard;
> Out of my spirit to exhume
> By wan internal candle-gloom
> Shred after shred the anguish there,
> Fibre by fibre smooth it bare;
> And so, with curious, careful eyes,
> And close-held flame, to scrutinize
> This queer embodiment of pain
> Till it be exorcised or slain.
>
> (II,3)

At the end of the poem the clerk returns to his post at the window to await the coming of spring. Although he partially relapses into the somatic prison of his "pulse's slow reverberant will," his has not been simply (as is Prufrock's) a circular, ineffectual journey. The clerk's progress, if not great, has at least been in the right direction: though returned to himself and condemned to endure the memory of a shattered harmony which reverberates "Like the scattered jargon of a child / Or voices in an ether dream" (II,6), the clerk has taken the tentative but crucial first steps away from ignorance and egotism.

The Clerk's Journal, despite its amateurishness, bears virtually no resemblance to Aiken's juvenilia, as a comparison with his Middlesex *Anvil* poems makes apparent. Nor, for that matter, does it resemble his prior Harvard *Advocate poems*, which are so conventional as to obfuscate—were they not identified as Aiken's—heir authorship altogether. *The Clerk's Journal* is the first of his poems to dramatize and examine behavior modified by love and the loss of love within an essentially naturalistic framework. The poem, like all of Aiken's work, rewards close study. Much greater rewards await the reader who approaches the other early poems—today virtually unknown—without the preformed conviction that they contain neither ideas nor ethical values. To borrow a phrase from *The House of Dust*: Aiken's "errand," even in *Earth Triumphant* (1914), *Turns and Movies* (1916), and *Nocturne of Remembered Spring* (1917), "is not so simple as it seems."[26]

Notes

(I would like to thank the Mabelle McLeod Lewis Memorial Fund for a grant which greatly assisted me in preparing the present article.)

[1]The titles and publication dates of Aiken's early poetry are:

Earth Triumphant and Other Tales in Verse (1914)

Turns and Movies and Other Tales in Verse (1916)

The Jig of Forslin (1916)

Nocturne of Remembered Spring (1917)

The Charnel Rose; Senlin: A Biography, and Other Poems (1918)

The House of Dust (1920)

Punch: The Immortal Liar (1921)

Priapus and the Pool (1922)
The Pilgrimage of Festus (1923)

Priapus and the Pool and Other Poems (1925)

[2] Louis Untermeyer, *Modern American Poetry,* 3rd ed. (New York: Harcourt, Brace and Company, 1925), pp. 488-89.

[3] Horace Gregory and Marya Zaturenska, *History of American Poetry, 1900-1940* (New York: Harcourt, Brace and Company 1942), pp. 217-18.

[4] Frederick J. Hoffman, *Conrad Aiken,* Twayne's United States Authors Series (New Haven: College and University Press, 1962), p. 86.

[5] Conrad Aiken, *The Clerk's Journal* (New York: The Eakins Press, 1971), p. 4.

[6] Ibid.

[7] For a superlatively documented account of Eliot's early spirituality and its place in the poetry, see Lyndall Gordon, *Eliot's Early Years* (New York: Oxford University Press, 1977). Of "Prufrock," Gordon writes: "Despite the poem's mannered surface, Eliot is looking beyond the Jamesian scene and the obligation to cultivate human attachments—towards a characteristic theme of his own, a prophet's obligation to articulate what he alone knows" (p. 47).

[8] *Selected Letters of Conrad Aiken,* ed. Joseph Killorin (New Haven: Yale University Press, 1978), p. 19.

[9] Conrad Aiken, *Ushant* (Cleveland and New York: The World Publishing Company, 1952), p. 71.

[10] Ibid.

[11] *Selected Letters,* p. 19.

[12] *The Clerk's Journal,* p. 4.

[13] *Selected Letters,* p. 21.

[14] An indication of the esteem in which Potter was held by his congregation can be found in Francis Ellingwood Abbot's "Biographical Sketch" in Potter's *Lectures and Sermons:*

> [Potter's life] was such as to command the reverence
> and win the love of an ever increasing circle of those
> whose judgment is the judgment of the universal

conscience. From the beginning to end it was the self-consecration of a pure spirit to universal aims—the devotion of large intellectual powers, great practical wisdom, a strong but never aggressive will, and shy but tender sympathies, to the highest welfare of all. To have lived such a life, in luminous contrast and superiority to the melancholy self-seeking so common among mankind, is to have won the truest and grandest success which can crown any human career.

> Little as he performed the ordinary offices of the conventional 'pastor,' he yet ministered to his people in a way that held them to him with 'hooks of steel,' and rendered him their helper, comforter, and friend. How sweet and gracious and consoling were his sympathies with their sorrows, they knew, if strangers knew not; and the reluctance with which the long pastorate was at last ended tells its own story in these days of swift and frequent change.

See William J. Potter, *Lectures and Sermons* (Boston: George H. Ellis, 1895), pp. vi, lxxv.

[15] Conrad Aiken, *The Collected Short Stories of Conrad Aiken* (Cleveland and New York: The World Publishing Company, 1960), p. 511.

[16] *Ushant,* pp. 35-36.

[17] Conrad Aiken, "Prologue to an Autobiography," *The American Scholar,* 35 (Autumn 1966), 621.

[18] Of his political views Aiken observed:

> It was true that he had once voted for Debs, and that he had twice, too, voted for his great liberal cousin; but he had never found it possible to take more than a casual and superficial interest in practical politics, viewing it, as he did, as inevitably a passing phase, and probably a pretty primitive one, and something, again, that the evolution of consciousness would in its own good season take care of. Revolutions were a waste of time and human material;—you lost a hundred or more years only to find yourself just where you'd begun (*Ushant,* p. 351).

[19] *Ushant,* p. 46.

[20] Quoted without citation of original source by C. Hartley Grattan in *The Three Jameses: A Family of Minds* (New York: New York University Press, 1962), p. 79.

[21] Ibid., pp. 79-80.

[22] Conrad Aiken, *Nocturne of Remembered Spring* (Boston: The Four Seas Company, 1917), p. 21.

[23] Conrad Aiken, *Collected Poems,* 2nd ed. (New York: Oxford University Press, 1970), p. 294.

[24] In terms of temperament, one would be hard-pressed to find two American poets as dissimilar as Aiken and Frost. Where Aiken was

shy, private, and at times recklessly generous in giving away his own ideas and acknowledging his indebtedness to other artists. Frost was self-aggrandizing, public, and almost pathologically protective of his reputation. Yet due to remarkably similar childhood backgrounds, both poets developed into the most masculine, naturalistic, and metaphysically "dark" voices of the American poetry renaissance.

Both writers, though of New England descent, were born elsewhere: Aiken in Savannah, Frost in San Francisco. Both, due to parental deaths, returned, roughly at the same age, to spend their adolescent years in New England. Both had occasion to quit college and both married young and quickly had to support families. Both, for reasons of domestic economy, isolated themselves from the urban centers of poetic activity, and, by doing so, were able to indulge more freely their passionate love of nature (Frost on farms in England and New Hampshire, Aiken on Cape Cod and in Sussex). And, finally, both inherited radicalized versions of nineteenth century transcendentalism: Frost the mystic Swedenborgianism of his mother, Aiken the rational theology of his grandfather Potter. (Eliot, on the other hand, inherited an essentially dogmatic and formalistic Unitarianism.)

[25] Robert Frost, *The Poetry of Robert Frost* (New York: Holt, Rinehart and Winston, 1969), pp. 5, 6.

[26] *Collected Poems*, p. 152.

Helen Hagenbüchle (essay date 1982)

SOURCE: "Antennae of the Race: Conrad Aiken's Poetry and the Evolution of Consciousness," in *The Huntington Library Quarterly*, Vol. 45, No. 3, pp. 215-26.

[*In the following essay, Hagenbüchle asserts that the focus of Aiken's poetry is the relationship between the individual and the world and the difficulty of expressing that relationship.*]

"Surely the basis of *all* poetic activity, its *sine qua non*, its very essence, lies in the individual's ability, and need, to isolate for feeling and contemplation the relation 'I:World.' That, in fact, is the begin-all-end-all business of the poet's life."[1] This sentence contains the gist of Aiken's poetics. The poet sees himself as observer whose object of investigation is the nature and meaning of the human experience. What intrigued Akien throughout his life was the fact that all such investigation implies a threefold difficulty: first, the examination of any object calls for an artificial isolation of that object which necessarily falsifies it; second, both the object under investigation and the recording mind are themselves processes; and third, truth is a matter of total interdependence, in other words, it is a relationship and not a logical true or false value statement. Aiken never lost sight of this preoccupation and constantly reshaped and refined his concept of the relationship "I:World." He did so in his essays, in his short stories, in his novels, and most superbly in his poetry.

Poem XIX of *Preludes for Memnon* is a fine example of Aiken's central concern:

Watch long enough, and you will see the leaf

Fall from the bough. Without a sound it falls:
And soundless meets the grass . . . And so you have
A bare bough, and a dead leaf in dead grass.
Something has come and gone. And that is all.

But what were all the tumults in this action?
What wars of atoms in the twig, what ruins,
Fiery and disastrous, in the leaf?
Timeless the tumult was, but gave no sign.
Only, the leaf fell, and the bough is bare.

This is the world: there is no more than this.
The unseen and disastrous prelude, shaking
The trivial act from the terrific action.
Speak: and the ghosts of change, past and to
      come,
Throng the brief word. The maelstrom has us all.
                                        (CP 520)

By focusing on one isolated object—the leaf—against the background of its seemingly stable surroundings, the poet observes a sudden change. The fall of the leaf is trivial in itself, but a contemplation of the chain of causes bringing about this event leads to the terrifying awareness that whatever change the human mind becomes conscious of is only a minute manifestation of a gigantic invisible commotion, the unceasing microcosmic and macroscosmic "pour of atoms and of stars." The outer world, of which the observer is a small part, is reflected, moreover, in the flux of his own mind: a thought or utterance is always only the "brief word" of a moment, an ephemeral result of the fading insights of the past, anticipating and already initiating the not-yet focused views of the future. The single visible act, like the "brief word," gives us a sense of the passage of time, but is overestimated, like the moment of actual death. In effect everything is caught up in a maelstrom, in which there is neither right nor left nor wrong. Seen in this way, it is impossible to determine if the falling of a leaf, the death of a person, or the destruction of a world is an end, a middle, or a new beginning. The alliteration of "trivial act" and "terrific action" emphasizes the ironic opposition and relativity implied in all existence.

As we have seen, man's awareness of change and time results from the isolation of the observing self from the observed object. Poem LI from *Time in the Rock* demonstrates this dilemma of the mind:

The miracle said 'I' and then was still,
lost in the wing-bright sphere of his own wonder:
as if the river paused to say a river,
or thunder to self said thunder.

As once the voice had spoken, now the mind
uttered itself, and gave itself a name;
and in the instant all was changed, the world
two separate worlds became—

The indivisible unalterably divided;
the rock forever sundered from the eye;
henceforth the lonely self, by self anointed,
hostile to earth and sky.

Alas, good angel, loneliest of heroes!
pity your coward children, who become
afraid of loneliness, and long for rock
as sick men long for home.

(CP 714)

Man only wins his selfhood at the inevitable price of
loneliness, for self-awareness destroys his original union
with nature. In the third stanza Aiken expresses this
concern by two of his favorite symbols, *rock* and *eye*: the
rock stands for undivided existence or sheer being. The
eye, the mind's tool to measure the distance between
itself and the world and to see the world in perspective,
stands for self-awareness; elsewhere Aiken puns on
the homophony of *eye* and *I*. The *good angel* of the last
stanza is the poet-genius. Because of his higher awareness of the human condition, he is even lonelier than
the rest of us. Yet, at the same time, he is beyond the
common fear and terror of daily life as he realizes that it
is precisely due to the alienation of the self that conscious
man has a chance to gain an understanding—however
fragmentary—of himself and of his position in the universe.

Almost all of Aiken's early poetry, including the volumes **Turns and Movies**, **The Divine Pilgrim**, and **John
Deth**, is characterized by an attitude of ironic scepticism:
in a world of flux where the self is not even capable of
knowing its true essence and of distinguishing itself from
the other masked selves that move, like so many vaudeville players, across the stage of life and mind, communication between the different solipsistic selves can only
be illusory. Yet, around 1930, while writing **Preludes for
Memnon**, Aiken begins to turn away from this desperate
view. Change is experienced not only as loss but as the
potential birth of something new. The moment of change
itself may be ephemeral and the word that captures it
brief, yet this is all we have, it is the essential human
experience which reveals the very nature of the relationship "I:World." Therefore, Aiken makes this moment the
focal point of much of his poetry.

Majestic instant,—
Great golden sum of dream whose truth is zero,
Zero of thought whose truth is god, and life,—
Pause in your flight, as if the arrow paused.
Be for our purpose as a rainbow, frozen.

(CP 528)

All language, but above all, the writing of a poem, brings
about a fixation of life's ever-moving kaleidoscope, presenting it—in Aiken's words—"as a rainbow, frozen."
Thus, the artifact seems to give meaning to the instant at
least. But Aiken goes on to ask: "And is this truth? / Or
is the grassblade, by itself, the grass?" The answer is
obviously: no. Only the sum total of all instants and all
things and all thoughts and all poems could be called
"truth." As it is, this poem, as well as all other works of
art, is at best a "prelude," which is only of relative value.
Nevertheless, it is the best we can do to understand our
existence.

It is above all the task of poetry to grasp the critical point
where world becomes language or where the unconscious
turns conscious. For Aiken, the prototype of this process
of transformation is the act of writing. A great part of his
work is therefore poetological, i.e., the process of writing
becomes itself the theme. No wonder Aiken considers
his final versions only as preliminaries. They are structures where "wound" becomes "word" becomes "world,"[2]
or, to put it differently, where immediate individual experience (wound) is translated into linguistic structure (word)
which, in the reader's mind, becomes an independent part
of reality (world) capable of causing new personal experiences. In an essay on Rilke, Aiken writes that "the poem
is simply a part of what is an indivisible *whole* of experience, and itself no more an 'end-product' of anything than
it is the 'beginning' of anything. To Rilke . . . [a]ll things
were to be seen, loved, filtered into the unconscious, there
to be turned magically into names: and then the poetry is
the naming."[3]

The problem of naming is one of the major poetic subjects of Aiken's *oeuvre*. Is there a linguistic equivalent
for experience? Aiken is skeptical.

Despair, that seeking for the ding-an-sich,
The feeling itself, the round bright dark emotion,
The color, the light, the depth, the feathery swiftness
Of you and the thought of you, I fall and fall
From precipice word to chasm word, and shatter
Heart, brain, and spirit on the maddening fact:
If poetry says it, it must speak with a symbol.

(CP503)

"What is a symbol?" The poet asks next, and after enumerating some images which might serve as "objective
correlatives" for some experience, he finally concludes:
"The thought, the ghost of thought, the ghost in a mirror." (CP 503) "The ghost of thought" hints at the loss
of substance inherent in every process of verbalization;
"the ghost in a mirror" refers to the element of reflexivity
characteristic of Aiken's own poetry for, in his poems, he
very often does not transcribe the "process of naming"
itself but instead the process of philosophizing about the
process of naming. This poetological and philosophical
approach to poetry sometimes results in a kind of self-
conscious verse that is more interesting than poetical. T.
S. Eliot, who repeatedly dealt with this problem in his
essays and who, no doubt, discussed these matters with
his friend Conrad Aiken, wrote that, ideally, the poet should
succeed, as Dante did, "in dealing with his philosophy,
not as a theory . . . or as his own comment or reflection,
but in terms of something *perceived*,"[4] that is, in terms of
experience—of poetic truth. This is precisely what Aiken
tries to do in his autobiography *Ushant*, where the experience of thinking about the process of naming translates
itself directly into seemingly endless concatenations of
clauses, subclauses, and interpolations:

How shall the non-knower, who is in process of becoming the knower, convert himself into a language by
which, first, to unravel his own beginnings and outlines
against the matrix in which, like a trilobite . . . he found

himself embedded, and then, with this basic knowl-edge, and out of its now co-ordinated constituents, begin a parallel 'arrangement' of the world itself, the world outside and beyond (but within oneself too)— the microcosm, with full awareness of the laws and limitations of microcosm (but in love with it, just the name, and proud of its prismatic importance) receiving into itself the macrocosm, a world within a world—? How indeed!—And nevertheless, it was in this really staggering drama that every living human being was involved, to greater or less degree, every day of his life." (*Ushant* 324)

In his poems Aiken usually resorts to analogies and met-aphors and frequently uses inner dialogues or exhortative addresses to the soul to express the two-fold process of reflection. In Prelude XXI, for example, Aiken urges the "poor soul" to plunge again and again "from time's colos-sal brink into that chasm," to bring up, with "blood-stained hands," sandgrain after sandgrain, until it finds the "pearl of brightness." The originally biblical pearl symbolizes the poetic vision of beauty and knowledge which dissolves the polarities of inner and outer worlds in a momentary poetic epiphany, a unified vision:

> It is this instant
> When all is well with us: when hell and heaven
> Arch in a chord of glory over madness;
> When Pole Star sings to Sirius; and the wave
> Of ultimate Ether breaks on ultimate Nothing.
> The world's a rose which comes this night to
>   flower:
> This evening is its light. And it is we,
> Who, with our harmonies and discords, woven
> Of myriad things forgotten and remembered,
> Urge the vast twilight to immortal bloom.
>
> (CP 523)

This passage demonstrates Aiken's preference for critical turning points: the breaking wave, the opening up of the rose, the evening, the twilight. We also note the interest-ing detail, that the "immortal bloom" of ultimate truth is made up of "myriad things forgotten" as well as things "remembered," by sandgrains as well as by the pearl. Not only is the consciousness that finds its lasting form in a work of art of importance, but all humanity works together in building up the "Cosmic Sum" of being.

Yet, a haphazard pursuit of single moments of awareness is not Aiken's ultimate goal. By persistently writing about the processes in his mind and then collating what he has written, Aiken tries to create a unified theory of con-sciousness, which he calls his "consistent view." He there-by pursues two aims. He hopes, first, that his method will enable him to understand the difficult phases of his life and the darker levels of his mind and to accept them as meaningful parts of an evolving self; and second, he hopes to be able to put his private experience at the service of society. Every record of an individual consciousness is a step toward the development of man's collective con-sciousness; that these records may outlast their time or be lost and forgotten is, as we have seen in the poem above, of no importance. Partly in a mystical, partly in a genetic

sense, every item of information is forever part of the whole. We are all pilgrims on our way to divine conscious-ness, pioneers in an endless war on the unconscious. This is Aiken's version of two important American *topoi*: as a sort of latter-day Emerson he affirms that "in the evolution of man's consciousness, ever widening and deepening and subtilizing his awareness, and in his dedication of himself to this supreme task, man possesses all that he could possibly require in the way of a religious credo: when the half-gods go, the gods arrive: he can, if he only will, become divine." (CP 1021) As a pioneer of the mind he strives to extend the frontier of consciousness as far into the unknown as possible:

> Live for the frontier of the daily unknown, of terror,
> for the darkness hidden in the striking hand,
> the darkness opening in the thinking mind,
> the darkness under the valve of the beating heart:
> live for the borderland, the daybreak, whence we
>   start
> to live and love, and if we cannot live to forgive:
>
> (CP 870)

The more conscious a human being is, the more forcefully can he fight on the frontier of knowledge. In Aiken's view it is the artist who is equipped with the most sensitive antenna of the mind, as well as with the necessary linguis-tic tools to make the progress of human awareness man-ifest to society. In the essay "Poetry and the Mind of Modern Man," Aiken sums up his philosophy:

> Poetry has always kept easily abreast with the utmost man can do in extending the horizon of his conscious-ness, whether outward or inward. It has always been the most flexible, the most comprehensive, the most farseeing, and hence the most successful, of the modes by which he has accepted the new in experience, realized it, and adjusted himself to it. Whether it is a change in his conception of the heavens, or of the law of gravity, or of morality, or of the nature of con-sciousness, it has always at last been in poetry that man has given his thought its supreme expression— which is to say that most of all, in this, he succeeds in making real for himself the profound myth of per-sonal existence and experience.

> But if poetry is to accomplish this in any age, it must think: it must embody the full consciousness of man at that given moment. It cannot afford to lag behind the explorations of knowledge, whether of the inner or outer worlds: these it is its business to absorb and transmute.[5]

Aiken's need to make "real for himself the profound myth of personal existence and experience" was certainly a powerful motivation for the development of his particu-lar poetic theory. The pervasive image of the "wound" to be turned into "word" is related to that traumatic moment when, as an eleven-year-old boy, Aiken was awakened by revolver shots and discovered that his father had killed his mother and then himself. Even if not all of Aiken's work can be explained as an attempt to reshape that scene so as to come to terms with it, we may safely conclude that this experience has something to do with the characteristic movement of many of his poems. The poet usually begins by describing some personal experience which, however, he does not seem to trust until he has explored its inner causes. Then he moves outward again to generalize his newly won insight by means of an analogy. Aiken's need to discover a meaning in his own life makes him look for recurring patterns; thus, seemingly accidental events take on an aspect of preordained fate and become, in turn, the basis for future meanings. The poet traces the evolution of his personal life back to the lives of his parents and ancestors and sees his poetic vocation as a task inherited from his family. In his autobiography we read:

> This 'thing' of the family's, this accumulated awareness, this evolving consciousness, even with its taint of insanity, this it was their duty, and D.'s [i.e., the narrator's] most of all, as now for the moment their ephemeral spokesman, to put at the disposal of society—even, if necessary, on the chopping-block or the dissecting table. (*Ushant* 305)

But it was his maternal grandfather, the Reverend William Potter, whose sermons Aiken carried with him wherever he went, who had the most marked influence on the shaping of the poet's "consistent view." Aiken admired above all his grandfather's relentless struggle against enslaving dogma and his "determined acceptance of Darwin and all the rest of the scientific fireworks of the nineteenth century."[6] Together with Emerson and Colonel Higginson, the Reverend Potter had founded the Free Religious Association which was intended to unite all the religions of the world. In an interview with Robert Hunter Wilbur, Aiken explained: "this inheritance has been my guiding light: I regard myself simply as a continuance of my grandfather, and primarily, therefore, as a teacher and preacher, and a distributor, in poetic terms, of the *news* of the world, by which I mean new knowledge."[7]

Aiken's most beautiful poetic transformation of his grandfather's views is a passage in **"Hallowe'en,"** a poem, in which the poet addresses his ancestor in a reminiscing inner monologue. After enumerating a number of things that his grandfather might wish to see again, if he could come back among the living, the poet concludes:

> Yet no, not these are your loves, but the timeless
>   and formless,
> the laws and the vision: as you saw on the ship
> how, like an angel, she subdued to her purpose
> the confused power of ocean, the diffused power
>   of wind,
> translating them swiftly to beauty,
> 'so infinite ends, and finite begins, so man
> may make the god finite and viable,
> make conscious god's power in action and being.'
> (CP 896)

Although the metaphor of the ship and its interpretation have been taken literally from his grandfather's diary, it is obvious that Aiken here expresses his own conviction. As we have seen before, *angel*, in Aiken's poetry, sym-

bolizes the poet-genius, the mind in its highest state of consciousness. This lucid mind is likened to a sailboat which, on a windy ocean, transforms the confused power of the unconscious (the ocean) and concentrates the diffused power of the spirit (the wind) into an aesthetic and moral force, able to direct man's life.

But beyond his interest in the history of his personal ancestors, Aiken was also greatly concerned with the roots of American culture and therefore, like Pound and Eliot, emigrated to England, where he continued to live for many years. After his return to New England, however, he admitted: "I preferred the English tradition, and lived there for many years, because that seemed to me what *I* needed. Later, the fortunes of another war sent me back to America, where I found that my ancestral roots claimed me—I should have remained there all the time. / And the truth is that James was wrong, and so were Eliot and myself, and all the others, in thinking that there was an insufficient cultural inheritance in this country: it was there, but neither our teachers nor ourselves were yet aware of it. In Whitman, Melville, Dickinson, Mark Twain, Emerson, Thoreau, Hawthorne, Poe, and James, what more could the ripening consciousness of this country, which in a curious way was both old and young, demand?"[8]

Although Aiken used every conceivable poetic form from sonnet to free verse, much of his poetry is experimental in the sense that he never followed what was fashionable in his time. This fact is often cited as a reason for his lack of popularity. Yet, for all his independence, he was extremely conscious of the poetic tradition: both past and contemporary literature is an integral part of his work. In the form of echoes, quotations, subtexts, images, and thoughts the reader can recognize the subtle presences of Eliot, Pound, Masefield, Whitman, Poe, and Shakespeare. Aiken explicitly commends Eliot for being "inseparably linked with tradition, his genius at war with it, but compelled to speak in its terms," and says, "it is out of such violent conflicts *within the tradition* that new forms, and new works of art, arise."[9] Aiken's notion of the literary tradition may have been slightly more personal than Eliot's, but it is nevertheless similar to it. For both Aiken and Eliot the "articulate formulation of life which human minds make" forms a kind of "ideal order," an order comparable to the one that Eliot advances in "Tradition and the Individual Talent," where he defines "the conception of poetry as a living whole of all the poetry that has ever been written." This concept of literary tradition resembles Aiken's evolving collective consciousness which, like Eliot's "tradition," enables a modern mind to become aware of something vague like "the mind of Europe," a spiritual presence which changes but "which abandons *nothing en route*.[10]

Eliot claimed that at times a poet may have "a feeling of profound kinship, or rather a peculiar intimacy, with another, probably a dead author" and that such an "imperative intimacy arouses for the first time a real, an unshakable confidence" that "we have not borrowed, we have been quickened, and we become bearers of tradition."[11] This, according to Eliot, cannot happen unless the poet "lives in what is not merely the present, but the present moment of the past, unless he is conscious, not of what is dead, but of what is already living."[12] For Aiken, the spirits of his "godfathers, Will and Ben" (i.e., William Shakespeare and Ben Jonson) (CP 869) are not the only ones still pervading his Cape Cod residence; in a poem called **"A Letter from Li Po,"** he also conjures up the spirit of that old Chinese poet:

> Yet to spell down the poem on her page,
> margining her phrases, parsing forth
> the sevenfold prism of meaning, up the scale
> from chicory pink to blue, is to assume
> Li Po himself: as he before assumed
> the poets and the sages who were his.
> Like him, we too have eaten of the word:
> with him are somewhere lost beyond the Gorge:
> and write, in rain, a letter to lost children,
> a letter long as time and brief as love.
>
> (CP 903-904)

Every writer "assumes" his precursors. He is mysteriously connected with the "all-remembering world" carried on the Chinese "Wind Wheel Circle." While composing this poem on Li Po, Aiken was "stirred by the ancient currents" that gave him birth, and felt very much at one with his own ancestors as well as with his spiritual forebears and ultimately with all mankind:

> And they are here, Li Po and all the others,
> our fathers and our mothers: the dead leaf's
>   footstep
> touches the grass: those who were lost at sea
> and those the innocents the too-soon dead:
>   all mankind
> and all it ever knew is here in-gathered,
> held in our hands, and in the wind
> breathed by the pines on Sheepfold Hill.
>
> (CP 915)

The linear time of Aiken's early poetry, symbolized in the falling leaf, has finally been transformed into the spiral time characteristic of his later work. The present moment is no longer conceived merely as transition and loss, but has assumed a quality of *nunc stans*, of mystical continuity. Here we are reminded of Eliot's "Four Quartets," yet, there is a difference in attitude. For Aiken the eternal principle underlying time is not the Christian God; it is rather a consciousness-becoming life-principle, a power which grows ever more manifest to itself in the history of the cosmos and of human consciousness. The individual human being, however, must always experience the moment as transitory: he can at best attain Aiken's confidence that what eludes him is forever preserved in the recollection of the Cosmic Consciousness, where permanence and progress are coeval. By intuiting this Cosmic Consciousness in the act of writing, mind and object, experience and text, become one:

> And all is text, is holy text. Sheepfold Hill
> becomes its name for us, and yet is still
> unnamed, unnamable, a book of trees . . .

> . . . . .
> And in this marriage of text and thing how can we
>   know
> where most the meaning lies? . . .
> . . . . .

>   Which is which?
> The poem? Or the peachtree in the ditch?
> Or is all one? Yes, all is text, the immortal text,
> Sheepfold Hill the poem, the poem Sheepfold Hill,
> and we, Li Po, the man who sings, sings as he
>   climbs,
> transposing rhymes to rocks and rocks to rhymes.

> . . . . .

> Li Yung, the master of the epitaph,
> forgetting about meaning, who himself
> had added 'meaning' to the book of 'things,'
> lies who knows where, himself sans epitaph,
>   his text, too, lost, forever lost . . .
>   And yet, no,
> text lost and poet lost, these only flow
> into that other text that knows no year.
> The peachtree in the poem is still here.
> The song is in the peachtree and the ear.
>
> (CP 910-11)

There can be no doubt that this "other text that knows no year" is—in the last analysis—a secularized and modernized version of the Puritan *topos* of the Book of Life. It is in this "immortal text" that the "trivial acts" of human existence are once more redeemed in the "terrific action" of the ever developing ultratext, Aiken's collective consciousness.

Notes

All excerpts from Aiken's poetry are taken from *Conrad Aiken, Collected Poems 1916-1970* (New York 1970). This volume is cited as CP in the text.

[1] Quoted in John R. Moore, "Conrad Aiken: The Egotistical Sublime," *Sewanee Review* 74 (1966), 699.

[2] Cf. CP 612 and CP 672.

[3] Conrad Aiken, *Collected Criticism* (formerly *A Reviewer's ABC*), (London, 1968), 332.

[4] Quoted in E. P. Bollier, "T. S. Eliot and F. H. Bradley: a Question of Influence," *Tulane Studies in English* 12 (1962), 101.

[5] Conrad Aiken, "Poetry and the Mind of Modern Man," *The Atlantic*, 214 (5), Nov. 1964, 81.

[6] Robert Hunter Wilbur, "Art of Poetry IX: Conrad Aiken, an Interview," *Paris Review*, 11 (1968), 120.

[7] Ibid., 120.

[8] Conrad Aiken, "Poetry and the Mind of Modern Man," 79.

[9] Conrad Aiken, *Collected Criticism*, 386.

[10] T. S. Eliot, "Tradition and Individual Talent," in *The Sacred Wood* (London, 1960), 51.

[11] T. S. Eliot, "Reflections on Contemporary Poetry, IV," *Egoist*, VI (July 1919), 38-40.

[12] T. S. Eliot, "Tradition and the Individual Talent," 59.

Nancy Ciucevich Story (essay date 1989)

SOURCE: "Aiken's *Preludes*: Starting Fresh," in *Essays in Arts and Sciences*, Vol. XVIII, May, 1989, pp. 53-84.

[*In the following essay, Story attempts to provide new insight into the themes, structure, and rhythms of Aiken's* Preludes for Memnon, *arguing that previously, Aiken's poems have been analyzed not in their own right but almost exclusively from the point of view of his parent's violent deaths.*]

A contextualist approach to Conrad Aiken's poetry encounters two obstacles. First is the challenge of identifying his best poems amid the incredible volume of his publications. Second is the distraction of his well known childhood tragedy of parental murder-suicide. With few exceptions,[1] contextualist critics ignore Aiken's work whereas scholars concentrating on the biographical and psychological have produced an abundance of scholarship on the artist and his art. What is called for now is fresh, contextual analysis of Aiken's poetry to complement the wealth of more traditional critiques.

The encyclopedic quality of his writings has led many Aiken scholars to take a panoramic view, sweeping across the vast scope of his poems and novels, pausing here and there to point out how a certain line or paragraph fits into the schema of his life's work. There is a rich tradition of Aiken scholarship that takes the survey approach beginning with Houston Peterson's, *The Melody of Chaos* in 1931, continuing with Jay Martin's *Conrad Aiken: A Life of His Art* in 1962, and finding its most recent expression Ted R. Spivey's 1986 booklength comparison of Aiken and Walker Percy, *The Writer as Shaman*.[2] These volumes, along with a great many other articles and books, form a canon of Aiken scholarship that sheds a great deal of light on the artist and his art. Inherent to the panoramic approach, however, is the broad overview that disallows a sharp focus on the best of his poetry. These kinds of studies place little emphasis on poetic technique and concrete imagery. Nor is there much discussion of experimentation in language, an ironic omission in the criticism of a poet who viewed poetry as experimentation.

The second difficulty with developing a contextual perspective on Aiken's poetry is the dominant tradition of biographical and psychological interpretations in the criticism.[3] These approaches to literature are especially alluring when the life of the artist is marked by parental

suicide, as in the case of Aiken. However, the biographical and psychological critiques fail to account for variations in the quality of his poems and shift attention away from the works of art to the writer's life. Aiken knew better than anyone the lasting psychological effects of his parents' violent deaths. As an artist, he used the events of his life as raw materials for his art. In turn, most of his literary critics have adopted a biographical or psychological explanation of his creativity.

The 100th anniversary of Conrad Aiken's birth in August of 1889 is a choice moment both to reevaluate his art and to redirect the course of Aiken scholarship. What the body of Aiken's literature and the bountiful tradition of Aiken scholarship call out for now is close contextual analysis of his individual works. If Aiken's place among twentieth-century poets is to be defined, the best of his art must be read and judged for its literary merit. Can we dispell the shadow of his parents' suicide, cast out the ghosts of Freudian artistic theory, and examine Aiken's works contextually in the clear light of day?

. . . . .

The ***Preludes for Memnon*** are the first of Aiken's many experiments in writing long poems to succeed in maintaining a consistently high level of artistry. They are among his very best poetry and, along with **"Time in the Rock," "The Coming Forth by Day of Osiris Jones,"** and **"A Letter from Li Po,"** rival the quality of works by Stevens, Williams, and Eliot. The ***Preludes*** incorporate the themes of time, language, and love as vehicles for experimentation with the serial format and the juxtaposition of concrete and abstract imagery alternating with periods of silence. In addition to the suggestion of prophetic song by the reference to Memnon[4] in the title, the word ***Preludes*** describes the poems as a series of beginnings that attempt "to put down, to fix in the eternal form of words, the fragments of consciousness, as many of them as possible, so that the life which the consciousness reflects may be known and judged."[5] The serial form allows the poet to address his feelings and ideas as they come to mind, then dismiss them, and later readdress them, often on a deeper level than before. The movement of the ***Preludes*** is dynamic, allowing for both reflection and prophecy. As Irving Malin has observed, the power and endurance of Aiken's work proceed from its refusal to "stand still," and its continual threat to "get out of focus."[6] For a poet who views existence in terms of process, the series is "not only a probability but an inherent necessity in nature."[7] The serial form is a natural choice for the structure of the ***Preludes*** because it complements the predominant philosophical theme of time.

Time

The flux within linear time is a paradox which is first noticeable in the world outside one's self:

> Watch long enough, and you will see the leaf
> Fall from the bough. Without a sound it falls:
> And soundless meets the grass . . . And so you have

A bare bough, and a dead leaf in dead grass.
Something has come and gone. And that is all.
(Prelude XIX, st. 1, p. 520, *Collected Poems*)

The development of the leaf imagery in this poem relies on the contrast between the vital leaf, attached to the living tree, and the "dead leaf" that withers away when it falls "from the bough": "the fallen leaf, then represents all that can be said about past life, past growth, effort and decay, past love, struggle and pain. It is the inert, trivial vestige of all former vitalities and significances."[8] Soon after the transiency of the world around us becomes apparent, we begin to see the parallel tendency towards change, and ultimately towards death, within ourselves:

The snake and lizard change, yet are the same:
The flowers, many-colored, on the vine,
Open and close their multitude of stars,—
Yet are the same . . . And all these things are you.
(XX, st. 4, pp. 521-22, *CP*)

The correspondence between ourselves and the rest of the natural world as existing in time, then ceasing to exist, is the beginning of our recognition of death. "We move / To doom with all things moving" (XXI, st. 2, p. 522, *CP*). The leaf image in the *Preludes* becomes a symbol of man's transient existence:

Here, we will say, that man is but a leaf,—
Veined like the leaf, and thrilled, and vascular,
And blown as lightly down. He drinks the light,—
Yet in his veins the sap is full of death;
And his own darkness meets him from within.
(XXII, st. 4, p. 524, *CP*)

This transitoriness in man's nature sometimes leads us to see constant change as robbing our lives of all meaning:

They will all perish
The drop of blood, the windflower, and the world;
Sound will be silence; meaning will have no
    meaning.
(XIII, st. 2, p. 512, *CP*)

If everything in existence is subject to change, then all that we perceive as constant—love, value, creativity—are also temporal:

Excellent woman,
Rock over water, field beneath cloud shadow,
Fixed above the changing,
Take comfort if you can in this mad waste.
I am the leaf that dies upon your hand:
Dismiss me with my dying. We are undone
With permanence in impermanence, the flowing
Of shape to shape which means all shapelessness.
Is this my hand in yours? Ah, no such thing.
It is the fog which curtsies to the fog:
The god who finds himself a fraud: the wind
From nowhere blown to nowhere.
(XXIII, st. 4, pp. 526-27, *CP*)

Despite the fact that life is fleeting like that of the leaf (the natural world), we are conscious of our brief actuality in a way that sets us apart from the rest of the natural world. All things are in a continual state of flux, but, to our knowledge, we alone are conscious of the paradox of recurrence, or rebirth, as a form of constancy within this sea of change. This consciousness of the life/death instinct within us cannot alter our ultimate destiny. However, self-consciousness implies the possibility of self-direction, and in the *Preludes*, the creative will is man's most essential characteristic:

And it is we,
Who, with our harmonies and discords, woven
Of myriad things forgotten and remembered,
Urge the vast twilight to immortal bloom.
(XXI, st. 4, pp. 522-23, *CP*)

The use of the word "urge" here proclaims our willful direction of our journey from birth to death, and suggests that we possess some control, albeit temporary, over our destiny. The line, "Urge the vast twilight to immortal bloom" recalls the statue of Memnon in Prelude XLIV, "lifting the sun from the eastern hill, (birth) and then /Handing it to the west—" (death). Like Memnon, we carry within ourselves a sense of the paradoxes embodied in time, the continuum that makes possible and sets the limits to creative action: creation and destruction become confused; the will to live eventuates in the will to die:

Angelic power, divinity, destruction
Perfect in itself—the sword is heartshaped,
The word is bloodshaped, the flower is a coffin,
The world is everlasting—
(XLIV, st. 3, p. 550, *CP*)

Following Socrates' imperative, "know thyself," the *Preludes* assert that man's duty is to "Look with the meanest scrutiny" at himself and all that composes him:

Mistrust it. . . .
This little clock, your slave. You, yourself—
Put up your plumes and crow, you are a clock
Unique, absolved, ridiculous, profound,
The clock that knows, if but it will, its tick
To be a tick, and nothing but a tick.
(LIII, st. 1, pp. 548-49, *CP*)

Ironically, we seem to be the only creatures of time who are aware of our temporality. Yet this self-awareness, that allows for the mortal fear of death we suffer throughout our lives, also makes it possible for us to denounce time to some extent, through memory of the past ("Memory, like a juggler, / Tosses its colored balls into the light, and again / Receives them into darkness," (I, st. 2, p. 499, *CP*), and denial of the future:

What is time, the heart says what is time.
The heart is ticking on the mantelpiece.
The heart says all is past and nothing future.
The heart says heart will never cease.
(XXVIII, p. 533, *CP*)

In this Prelude, the heart is associated with memory, "all is past and nothing future." Like memory, the state of silence in the *Preludes* suggests the ability to withdraw from temporal, chaotic existence into the realm of time-lessness. Reverie usually occurs in silence, and in the state of reverie, our sense of time dissolves into timeless-ness:

> Thus in the evening, in the simple cloister,
> Eternity adds ring to ring, the darker
> Beyond the brighter; and your silence fills
> With such a world of worlds,—so still, so deep,—
> As never voice could speak. . . .
> (XX, st. 5, p. 522, *CP*)

The "simple cloister" here is the retreat into silent reverie that brings about a sense of eternity, incommunicable in words. In Prelude XXIV, silence is directly related to meaning:

> It is a moment between moments, passing
> From one to other; is a syllable,
> Meaningless in itself, which lights a word;
> The pause between two words which makes a
>   meaning;
> The gulf between two stones which makes a world.
> (XXIV, pt. 2, st. 1, p. 528, *CP*)

The emphasis here is on the continuum of experience ("The gulf between two stones"), which we distort by our conception of time as juxtaposed points on a line, dis-tinct from, but adjacent to, one another. The *Preludes* posit that meaning lies within the duration ("moment between moments," "syllable . . . which lights a word," "pause between two words," "gulf between two stones"), and that any interruption of the duration (as occurs when we verbalize our existence) is a distortion of actuality:

> And how begin, when there is no beginning?
> How end, when there's no ending? How cut off
> One drop of blood from other, break the stream
> Which, with such subtlety, such magnificent power,
> Binds the vast windflower to its throbbing world?
> (XIII, st. 1, p. 512, *CP*)

The same meaningful pause, the matrix of existence, oc-curs in musical arrangements also. "The pauses in the music are not music, /Although they make the music what it is" (VI, st. 6, p. 504, *CP*). By virtue of its non-verbal nature, music, like silence and memory, exhibits unspeakable meaning:

> Or say that in the middle comes a music
> Suddenly out of silence, and delight
> Brings all that chaos into one mood of wonder.
> (IV, st. 1, p. 502, *CP*)

Silence also suggests the aura of mystery that clings to life and death:[9]

> Watch long enough, and you will see the leaf
> Fall from the bough. Without a sound it falls:

> And soundless meets the grass.
>
> . . . . .
>
> But what were all the tumults in this action?
>
> . . . . .
>
> Timeless the tumult was, but gave no sound.
> (XIX, st. 1 & 2, p. 520, *CP*)

Silence appears not only as the pauses in daily, chaotic existence, but also as sleep:

> Dream: and between the close-locked lids of dream
> The terrible infinite intrudes its blue:
> Ice: silence: death: the abyss of nothing.
> (III, st. 2, p. 501, *CP*)

Sleep, silence, memory, music, and even death belong to the realm of the "terrible infinite," "the abyss of nothing," because each of these elements of man's experience en-tails the mysterious effect of thwarting, temporarily except for death, the progress of time. Although death, inherent in time, eventually overcomes our will, there have, no doubt, been periods of silence, memory, and reflection in our lives during which we have created momentary re-treats from the transience of time. These respites from the chaos account for the "blue" quality of the "terrible infi-nite" which softens the otherwise sharp, black-and-white contrasts associated with "Ice," "death," and "the abyss."

The images of silence in the poems, reverie, sleep, dreams, pauses, even death, are reinforced structurally by the si-lences between the poems in the series. These quiet paus-es are a reflection of the continuous nature of the process of our experience and, as in Prelude VI, "The pauses in the music are not music, / Although they make the music what it is" (*CP*, st. 6, p. 504); the silences between the poems are essential to the beauty and meaning of the *Preludes*.

Having compared man's ephemeral being to that of the rest of the natural world, and illuminated the differences between self-conscious man and unself-conscious nature, the speaker in the *Preludes* reflects on our sense of in-justice at having to succumb, like unthinking nature, to time's harsh destiny:

> And this, the life-line—means—what does it mean?
> Why, you are brief; you have no meaning; you;
> The clock's tick on the mantel; the heart's heavy
> Dictatorial tick that guides your thought:
> The world beneath the heart that makes you die . . .
> Come, let us hold our hands out to the cloud,
> And ask him if our destinies are just.
> (XL, pt. 2, st. 3, p. 545, *CP*)

The image of man as a clock appears throughout the *Preludes*. Often the clock "on the mantel" (in objective existence) corresponds to our inner-clock: the heart. "The alarm clock ticks, the pulse keeps time with it, / Night and the mind are full of sounds" (L, st. 2, p. 498, *CP*).

Another image of transiency here is the cloud. In the *Preludes*, the cloud generally symbolizes change. In Prelude XL, man's brief actuality, represented by the clock's ticking, seems constant when juxtaposed to the image of the ever-changing cloud. The same is true for Prelude XXIII: "Excellent woman, / Rock over water, field beneath cloud shadow" (CCIII, st. 4, p. 526, *CP*). Conversely, the immensity of the seemingly infinite cosmos often makes individual man seem fragile and finite:

> The clouds flow slowly,
> The idea is slowly changing, like the cloud,
> The mind is changing, like a heaven of clouds,
> The 'I' changes, and with it the 'you.'
>
>   . . . . .
>
> And the cloud, moving, becomes a bird, a dolphin,
> The skeleton of a leaf, a curve, a nothing.
>   (XXIII, st. 2, p. 526, *CP*)

This sense of relativity pervades the *Preludes*, leading, not surprisingly, to a denial of the possibility of absolute truth or falsehood: "Truth is a lie when worshipped as the truth; / The lie a truth when worshipped as a lie" (XL, pt. 2, st. 1, p. 545, *CP*). Since everything in existence is subject to change, the poems suggest we seize the day:

> Let us be reckless of our words and worlds,
> And spend them freely as the tree his leaves;
> And give them where the giving is most blest.
> What should we save them for,—a night of frost . . . ?
> All lost for nothing, and ourselves a ghost.
>   (LVII, st. 4, p. 566, *CP*)

Our distinct nature is one of willful action in the face of a chimerical existence, and we are at our best when we act on our reflections:

> So, let the venom swim toward the heart
> And Romeo hold his breath. Ah here you have
> Poor wretch, poor wretch, the essence of it all:
> Catch here in agony the golden fragment:
> Be conscious, for a fraction of the world:
> Hate, love, desire, suffer with mouth and eye;
> Bruise the poor body that is soon to die;
> And so to bed . . . Alas, and so to bed.
>   (XL, pt. 2, st. 2, p. 545, *CP*)

The emphasis on relishing all of experience is not presented as hedonism in the *Preludes*. In fact, the aim is not mere pleasure, but fulfillment that comes from self-knowledge ("Then say: I was a part of nature's plan; / Knew her cold heart, for I was consciousness;" XLII, st. 4, pp. 547-48, *CP*), acceptance of inevitable change ("The snowflake was my father;" XLII, st. 4, pp. 547-48), and willful action in the face of eventual death ("Come dance around the compass / pointing north / Before, face downward, frozen, / we go forth" (LXII, p. 572, *CP*).

In order to achieve this goal of self-knowledge, and to face all of its deterministic implications, the *Preludes* move

through, and reject as misleading, the dogma of rationality, analytics, and even language itself. The serial structure of the poems is especially appropriate for demonstrating the inconsistency of language because the poems in the series do not merely reiterate and reinforce each other. At times there is a sense of one poem building on another, but just as often there occurs a rephrasing, a modification, or sometimes even a denial of what has come before. The *Preludes* are a series of poems that ultimately reject the supremacy of words as a vehicle for truth.

Language

As experimental poetry, the *Preludes* are not distinct works, but repeated acts of phrasing and rephrasing, affirming and negating, speaking and not speaking. The serial structure, including the periodic silences between the poems, imitates the process of language-making, which in this series is more significant than the meanings of the individual words.

On one level, the *Preludes* are an examination of self and other. Self-consciousness entails objectification, which alienates man from all that he objectifies. His self-awareness is accompanied by the occurrence and development of language that attempts to reunite self and object, but fails in this ultimate task. It is

> the predicament of the consciousness that knows. Consciousness seems always to stop short of its object, and is defined by its limitations. There is a gap, a chasm, all around it, which is the gap between what we know and our knowing.[10]

The *Preludes* reject the belief that language can say anything absolutely meaningful about existence. Thus, they attack religion and rationality as dogmatic. Rather than accept language's false promises in the forms of dogmatic systems of thought, the *Preludes* examine the shortcomings of language, so that what is essentially useful in self-knowledge and communication will become apparent.

The *Preludes* treat consciousness as a continuous endeavor by the human mind to order, through language, the chaotic phenomena of the universe, of which man is an integral part:

> What is the flower? It is not a sigh of color,
> Suspiration of purple, sibilation of saffron,
> Not aureate exhalation from the tomb.
> Yet it is these because you think of these.
>
> What is the frost? It is not the sparkle of death,
> The flash of time's wing, seeds of eternity;
> Yet it is these because you think of these.
> And you, because you think of these, are both
> Frost and flower, the bright ambiguous syllable
> Of which the meaning is both no and yes.
>   (I, st. 4, p. 499, *CP*)

Prelude I sets forth the dialectical movement of consciousness, ordering phenomena (description of "frost and flower"), and likewise being ordered by the phenomena which it perceives ("And you, because you think of these, are both"). Man is "the bright ambiguous syllable / Of which the meaning is both no and yes." This statement describes man as a paradoxical creature who is a participant in what appears to be a dialectical process of existence. We are both "bright" (clear, unclouded, shining) and "ambiguous" (obtuse, cloudy, dull). We are "a syllable, / Meaningless in itself, which lights a word" (XXIV, pt. 2, st. 2, p. 528, *CP*). We are not absolutely meaningful, but relatively so ("the meaning is both no and yes"), and our relative meaning results from the continual combination of self and object. This mixture of self and object manifests itself through language, which the *Preludes* define as a series of symbols that can approximate the relationship of self to object, but can never get at the "thing in itself":

> You dream the world? Alas, the world dreamed you.
> And you but give it back, distorted much
> By the poor brain-digestion, which you call
> Intelligence, or vision, or the truth.
>
> (XII, st. 2, p. 511, *CP*)

In line one of Prelude V, the search for the "thing in itself" is called "Despair," indicating the inability of language to bridge the gap between self and object:

> Despair, that seeking for the ding-an-sich,
> The feeling itself, the round bright dark emotion,
> The color, the light, the depth, the feathery
>   swiftness
> Of you and the thought of you, I fall and fall
> From precipice word to chasm word, and shatter
> Heart, brain, and spirit on the maddening fact:
> If poetry says it, it must speak with a symbol.
>
> (V, st. 1, p. 503, *CP*)

In line two of the above stanza, the "emotion" is described as "bright dark." This image incorporates the same paradox as does the description of man in Prelude I as "bright ambiguous." Lines four, five, and six of the above stanza quite literally describe the failure of language to get at the "thing in itself": "I fall and fall / From precipice word to chasm word, and shatter / Heart, brain, and spirit on the maddening fact." Even poetry, which in the *Preludes* is presented as an attempt to uncover what "is," must resort to symbols. But words are not the only symbols; all of the particulars of experience are symbols of existence:

> The glass breaks, and the liquid is spilled; the string
> Snaps, and the music stops; the moving cloud
> Covers the sun, and the green field is dark.
> These too are symbols: and as far and near
> As those; they leave the silver core uneaten;
> The golden leaf unplucked; the bitter calyx
> Virginal; and the whirling You unknown.
>
> (V, t. 4, p. 503, *CP*)

This stanza stresses the inner-relatedness of all that exists, and the impossibility of one element of existence (man) being able to comprehend the whole, without distorting the whole that it seeks to know.

The presupposition that language can accurately name the "thing in itself" leads to futile search for word-answers to paradoxical questions about life. The *Preludes* remind us that we must look within ourselves in order to know all that can be known about existence, and that our continuous search for transcendent meaning is fruitless and inappropriate:

> What marvels, then, for us, who know already
> All that the waters of the godhead give?
> Let us desist from this forlorn attempt
> To wring strange beauty from a world well known.
>
> (X, st. 4, p. 509, *CP*)

"What marvels" there are, are known to us already; they are the marvels of experience. "All that the waters of the godhead give" are the occurrences within the continuum of time, which are marvelous by virtue of their very existence. Why do we persist in our search for "strange beauty" when we already have the concrete beauty of a "world well known"? The predicament presented here is that of the fool who thirsts although he is surrounded by an abundance of water. To the question, "What is the meaning of all that exists?" The *Preludes* answer, what meaning there is resides in experience itself, which language, as an expression of actuality, helps us to explore. But the exploration is frightening and painful to narcissistic man. We want to see ourselves as surpassing the limits of time, and therefore as eternal:

> And thus Narcissus, cunning with a hand-glass,
> Preening a curl, and smirking, had his say.
> God's pity on us all! he cried (half laughing)
> That we must die. . . .
>
> (XVII, st. 1, p. 518 *CP*)

> Is there a god who knows and mourns himself?
> It is Narcissus and his glass is truth.
>
> (XXVII, st. 5, p. 532, *CP*)

Our regret that we are not eternal is as dangerous to us as it was to Narcissus.

In the legend, Narcissus stares at his own reflection for so long that he transforms into a flower, eternally destined to bend over the stream and admire himself alone. The danger in being afraid to face death is that we cause our own death in life by living on dreams instead of on the actual:

> Deluded sentimentalist, will you stay
> In this one room forever, and hold only
> One withered flower in your withered hand?
> This is the ship that goes to No Man's Land.
>
> (XLVI, st. 5, p. 553, *CP*)

The "withered flower" in the "withered hand" represents our fatally persistent belief in the fairy tale of personal immortality, which prompts us to disregard actuality in favor of delusion. Facing the "abyss" of actuality, although painful and frightening, is a step towards intellectual honesty that the *Preludes* celebrate.[11]

The verge of the "abyss" is symbolized in Prelude XIV (one of the two dialogue poems of the series, the other being Prelude LI) as "The space-defying pine, that on the last / Outjutting rock has cramped its powerful roots." The words "Space-defying" and "powerful roots" indicate that the "abyss" defies conscious categorization. The "frightful language of that place" consists of "The mighty sound / Of pouring elements,—earth, air, and water,— / The cry of eagles, chatter of falling stones" (XIV, st. 2, p. 514, CP). The inarticulate and chaotic sounds of the "abyss" seem "frightful" at first, but the poem soon identifies man's inaccurate verbalizations as attempts to represent the language of this "abyss":

> But these poor words, these squeaks of ours, in
>   which
> We strive to mimic, with strained throats and
>   tongues,
> The spawning and outrageous elements—
> Alas, how paltry are they!
>
>   (XIV, st. 4, p. 515 CP)

Man's language is presented as mimicry in Prelude XI as well:

> And he, this gilding, heard it [Adam's cry], and
>   was moved;
> He mimicked it; he learned its naked vowels;
> He spoke it, sang it, shouted it, although
> Its meaning still escaped him.
>
>   (XI, st. 2, p. 510 CP)

Thus human language is viewed as an unoriginal expression of man's experience. This idea that language is unoriginal defines it as an inexact reflection ("mimicry") of that which lies beneath the surface of consciousness. It has been observed that Aiken "wants only a language for his sensations and his feelings, so that he may better know them."[12] In the *Preludes*, language is viewed as the expression of the meshing of consciousness (sensations) and unconsciousness (feelings). Prelude XI pronounces that "all of nature is shot through with this / Sweet mimicry. This fault, if fault it be, / Is Godlike; as all other things are Godlike." Here is the paradox of language as being "sweet," "Godlike," yet unoriginal which seems contradictory until it becomes apparent that most often in the *Preludes* God is the equivalent of man:

> —I saw myself and God.
> I saw the ruin in which godhead lives:
> Shapeless and vast: the strewn wreck of the world.
>
> And this alone awaits you, when you dare
> To that sheer verge where horror hangs, and
>   tremble
> Against the falling rock; and looking down,
> Search the dark kingdom. It is to self you come,—
> And that is God. It is the seed of seeds:
> Seed for disastrous and immortal worlds.
>
> It is the answer that no question asked.
>
>   (XIV, sts. 6 & 8, p. 515, CP)

The fact that at times in the *Preludes* the word "god" appears without capitalization, and at times capitalized, does not indicate that the capitalized "God" refers to a deity. The capitalization of the word serves the same function as quotation marks serve. In other words, "God" in the *Preludes* sometimes refers to "the whole process of things, be it orderly or chaotic, meaningful or meaningless, and sometimes, perhaps more often, he [Aiken] uses the term to characterize the consciousness that man finds in himself and makes him think the consciousness that man finds in himself and makes him think he is a self."[13] The "dark kingdom" of Prelude XIV calls to mind "the divine dark" of Prelude XXXVIII. Facing the "abyss," and coming to the realization that self equals God, presents man with another paradox: "It is the seed of seeds: / Seed for disastrous and immortal worlds."

Although daring to "that sheer verge" can bring man to the realization that he is God, thus deifying him, it also rules out the existence of a transcendent Deity, which seems "disastrous" to human hopes for individual immortality. The last line of Prelude XIV returns to the idea that our search for transcendent answers to the questions consciousness raises is inappropriate. The "abyss," on the other hand, presents us with the appropriate answer: "It is the answer that no question asked." Here once again, we find that meaning ("the answer") is beyond the grasp of human language and consciousness.

Throughout the *Preludes*, cognition proves inadequate in the quest for meaning: "For what's unguessed / Will have such shape and sweetness as the knowing / Ruins with pour of knowledge" (XIII, st. 4, p. 513, CP). Rationality is criticized for misleading man, carrying him farther and farther away from actuality, whereas "what's unguessed" is "the answer that no question asked," the irrational event of daily experience, which is meaningful by virtue of its existence.

The conscious search for eternal truths is often presented as culminating in death, in the *Preludes*:

> From one bird
> We guess the tree, and hear the song; but if
> Miraculous vision gives us, all at once,
> The universe of birds and boughs, and all
> The trees and birds from which their time has
>   come,—
> The world is lost.
> Love, let us rest in this.
>
>   (XIII, st. 4, pp. 513-14, CP)

The last line of this Prelude contains a play on the word "rest." Once the poem has established that only in "rest" (death) can the limitations of consciousness be overcome, it suggests that the speaker and his love "rest" from seeking eternal truths while conscious, else they find the answer to their search in eternity, through death ("rest"). *The resolution* of life's particularities in an eternal whole *is to rejoice* in the particularities themselves, before they become the eternal generalization, death:

Such that you say, on such and such a day,—
The word you spoke, at such and such an hour,—
Such feeling, or such vision, or such thought—!
                              (XXXII, st. 1, p. 537, *CP*)

The "such" here is the signification of the particular in the form of a word; "It is a sound by tongue and wonder made" (XXXII, st. 2, 1 p. 537, *CP*). Here again language appears as the attempted bridge between self and object. But "such" in this poem is also "less than this" (language), and by being "less than" language, it is more: it is a symbol for the particulars themselves:

It is the flame dropped on a wet leaf;
The blood-drop on the pillow; the breath blown
On the cold windowpane which winter weaves.
. . . . .
It is the history, in item told,
Of ichthyosaurus in a marsh of time;
Of Grimm's law in the forest leaf.
                              (XXXII, sts. 4 & 5, p. 537, *CP*)

All of life's particulars, like meaning in language, will eventually dissolve into the eternal generality:

And yet,
Comes the dark forest, which no heart foretells,
No mind foresees, no will forestalls, and takes
This suchness. . . .
                              (XXXII, st. 6, p. 538, *CP*)

The speaker in the *Preludes* does not forget that all ends in death, and his memory of this makes daily life extremely precious to him. Prelude XXXIII searches memory for a unifying principle of life:

Then I came to the shoreless shore of silence,
. . . . .
Where day was not, not night, nor space, nor time,
Where no bird sang save him of memory.
                              (XXXIII, sts. 1 & 2, p. 538, *CP*)

Memory brings back to the speaker the images of sensational experience in all their brightness, "a sea more bright." He tries to recall one particular of experience that was for him the "most bright," "But still no image came, save that of sea":

No heart or daisy brighter than the rest;
And only sadness at the bright sea lost,
And mournfulness that all had not been praised.
                              (XXXIII, st. 6, p. 539, *CP*)

The search for the "one" in life fails. The outcome of the search is, in fact, that the particulars of life appear as the "bright sea" of sensations, all of which the speaker wishes he had praised while he was conscious.

By finding meaning in all of the paradoxical particulars of sensual existence, and by embracing the "what is" rather than the wished for, the *Preludes* embrace both the beautiful and the ugly, the pure and the filthy, the faithful and

the faithless in life. The *Preludes* denounce the possibility that anything or anyone in life is all beautiful or all honest. Life is described as an indivisible conglomerate of what we term "good" and "bad": "We are the sum of all these accidents— / Compounded all our days of idiot trifles" (XXIX, st. 1, p. 534, *CP*).

There is no good,
No sweet, no noble, no divine, no right,
But it is bred of rich economy
Amongst the hothead factions of the soul.
                              (XXXI, st. 1, p. 536, *CP*)

Again the juxtaposition of seemingly contradictory concepts ("rich economy," "hothead factions of the soul") reveals the impossibility of separating many warring elements in existence. The *Preludes* provide a violent fate for those claiming to be wholly good or noble:

This was the gentlest creature that we knew,
This lamia of men,
. . . . .
God take his bowels out, and break his bones,
And show him in the market as he is:
An angel with peacock's heart, a fraud.
                              (XXXV, st. 1, p. 540, *CP*)

Where is the noble mind that knows no evil,
Gay insubordinations of the worm?
Discords of mishap, rash disharmonies
Sprung from disorders in the spirit's state?
If there is such, we'll have him out in public,
And have his heart out too.
                              (XXXI, st. 1, p. 536, *CP*)

The *Preludes* express a view that insists on the impossibility of the existence of Platonic good. This relativism applies to love as well: "Your Helen of Troy is all that she has seen,— / All filth, all beauty, all honor and deceit" (XXIX, st. 2, p. 535, *CP*). As one critic has observed,

Filth is simply dirt out of place in our domestic order; what is called obscenity or lechery is an incident to fertility in the animal kingdom; the ethical implications are out of place in referring to cockroaches and worms, and so far as we are creatures of nature, they are out of place for us.[14]

The mixture of "honor and deceit," this ultimate relativity, is bound up in the idea of experience as a process, continual change, that denies constancy:

You trust the heart? far better trust the sea.
Or swear with Romeo, by the inconstant moon.
Believe that ripening acorns will not fall.
Turn a dull eye on heaven, a trustful eye,
And think the clouds will keep their rain forever.
                              (XXX, st. 1, p. 535, *CP*)

The word "trust," which generally has favorable connotations, is linked with "dull" in the above Prelude, implying simple-mindedness. Conversely, constant change, rendering everything relative and denying the possibility of objective, permanent values, is posited as necessarily good in the *Preludes*, by virtue of its innately experiential nature:

> . . . . but better blame
> The ignoble blood—or so you'd say—that comes
> From god himself.
>
> . . . . .
>
> It is the sovereign stream, the source of all;
> Bears with it false and true and dead and dying;
>
> . . . . .
>
> Accept this logic, this dark blood of things.
> There is no treason here that is not you.
>   (XXX, sts. 2 & 3, pp. 535-36, *CP*)

Once again, change is seen as "the source of all," and inconstancy as natural to man:

> That stinking wretch whose rot is worse than worst:
> That natural marsh of nature, in which evil
> Is light as hawk to wing.
>
> . . . . .
>
> Why in that heart will come such power as never
> Visits the virtuous, and such sweetness too
> As god reserves for chaos.
>   (XXXI, st. 2, p. 537)

The reference to man as being "natural marsh of nature" is quite apt. There is nothing so "stinking," yet so full of life (therefore virtuous and sweet) as a salt marsh. The "power" that "never visits the virtuous" is an attribute of the brave man who looks chaos in the eye, accepts what he finds there, and lives his life fully in the knowledge that it is, in rational terms, purposeless.

Although the *Preludes* continually stress the importance to man of facing the "abyss," and chastise the one who, out of fear, continues to deceive himself as to the nature of existence (even threatens to "have his heart out"), the fact remains that life is a mixture of all conceivable elements, including fear. Prelude LIV posits fear as natural, although lamentable, in man:

> Go, clap your hands against the sunset, children!
> Invoke dark memory; the witch will tell you
> How god was frightened, when a pebble fell:
> Covered his eyes, because the plum-tree blossomed:
> and weeps for you, his sons, who fear to live.
>   (LIV, st. 8, p. 536, *CP*)

Equating god to man, or to existence, and showing that god is frightened by natural insignificances (the falling pebble and blossoming plum-tree), Aiken points out that fear is as inherent as change in our nature. Prelude LV explores fear in its various forms, and explains that "it is our terrors that delight us, lead / Downward to such Golcondas of soft gold / As warm the thought with thinking." Since fear is native to us, the *Preludes* implore the reader to embrace it:

> Indulge your terror: let him have his claws,
> His goblin snout, his fangs, his huge grimaces
> Which eat the fog, your house, your heart,
>   yourself;
> Entice him; let the cold mist creep upon you;
> Let him lie down beside you in your bed
> And stretch his foul and sweaty reptile body
> Against you, hip and thigh, and close cold hands
> About your throat; feel all his scales and horns;
> And the wet marsh-breath on your cheek.
>   (LV, st. 1, p. 536, *CP*)

This vivid description of fear as a beast with claws and fangs, preying on man as he sleeps, invokes the memory of childhood nightmares, with the dreamer having no control over his destiny. The reference to "marsh-breath" calls up the rich, fertile, yet "stinking" "natural marsh of nature" of Prelude XXXI. It seems that the frightful beast described in Prelude LV is actually "That stinking wretch whose rot is worse than worst" (Prelude XXXI), that is, man himself. Thus, by accepting change and fear of change as innate characteristics of our human nature, we should be able, according to Aiken, to "snap our thumb-bones, then, at frost and rime, / And be, like wise men, ghosts before our time" (LV, st. 3, p. 564, *CP*). "Wise men" is an evocative term in this poem, bringing to mind the "wise men" of the Nativity story while simultaneously denouncing this Biblical echo in defining "wise men" as those who disbelieve dogma and accept relativity.

The *Preludes* present the apparent certainties of rationalism and analytics as dogmatic by reasserting their relativity.

> Come let us take another's words and change the
>   meaning;
> Come let us take another's meaning and change
>   the words,
>   (XXXVII, st. 1, p. 541, *CP*)

In this seemingly cavalier assault on the inexactness and unoriginality of language, the speaker of the *Preludes* challenges the blind acceptance of dogma, established ways of thinking. Undermining the cynical attitude reflected in the poem's message, however, is a sense of child-like playfulness in the tone and structure of the lines, "Come, let us take another's words and change the meaning / Come, let us take another's meaning and change the words." The message of the lines is clear; language is inexact, but what are the implications of the playful repetitive structure and the lack of seriousness in the tone of the lines? Whereas the message that language is not absolute is disturbing, the structure and tone of the lines undercut their seriousness. The result of this tension between content and form is that the tone of the poem as a whole is purposely ambiguous and far from despairing.

Another passage from this poem emphasizes the lack of originality of language, an idea that would seem to negate the significance of words:

With words, but they were not our words, but
others'
Smacked of the kitchen, or of gods, or devils,
Worn and stained by the blood of centuries,

Shall we be slaves to such inheritance?
(XXXVII, st. 1, p. 541, *CP*)

The second line mixes images of the comfort of everyday
life with others from the sublime to the sinister ("smacked
of the kitchen," "gods, or devils"). These references to
the ordinary and the extraordinary are relegated to equal
status by their arbitrary positions in the series. There is
no sense of their being ordered from least to most important, no indication of progress or regression. Are the
kitchen and the devil raised to divine rank by the mention of god, or are god and the devil equated with the
pedestrian status of the kitchen? Even the last two lines
of the passage create an unsettling effect on the reader.
The references to "worn," "stained," "blood," and "slaves"
are followed by the equivocal term, "inheritance." Most
often inheritance has positive connotations as in property, wealth, or social status, but it can also be used in a
sinister way, as to inherit mental illness or the sins of
one's ancestors. Once again, the poem is deliberately
ambiguous in its attitude toward the medium of language.

Nevertheless, the speaker finds peace in the knowledge
that our knowledge is "known," and in the realization
that we "ourselves" are "but as old as stones that sleep
/ In God's midstream of wreckage, worn as smooth"
(XXXVII). The realization that doctrines and dogmas are
merely inherited rationalizations and beliefs of past ages
might lead to the conclusion that any one of these systems of thought is as good, or bad, as any other one. It
has been observed that

> Aiken has realized, better than most psychologists,
> the distortions of presentational immediacy that result
> from our acquired ways of ordering perceptions, of
> dividing the flow of events into arbitrary units, and of
> molding experience to favored formulations.[15]

Once again in the *Preludes*, ultimate relativity undermines the concept of the absolute. "The demon truth,
sharp as a maggot, works / His destined passage through
the Absolute" (XXXVII, st. 3, p. 542, *CP*). However,
seeing relativity as the rule when no ultimate "rule" exists
is paradoxical.

In a systematic philosophy, the contradiction would be
unresolvable. But the *Preludes* are poems of ambiguity,
tension, and paradox. The periodic undermining in one
Prelude of what has been previously set forth in another
is characteristic of the serial form that encourages re-
statement and even contradiction. Thus the series of poems
is organic in that form corresponds to content.

This acceptance of paradox leads to an attack on organized religion as a form of brainwashing. Prelude XXXVIII
presents an interpretation of dogmatic religion as deceit-
ful, and religious leaders as opportunists:

And most of all, oh sly ones, when you sell
So dearly to the poor your grains of wisdom,
Or barter to the ignorant your belief;

Oh think of this belief and think it evil,
Evil for you because you heard it only
From a stone god whose prophecies you mocked;
Evil for them because their hunger buys it;
Evil for both of you, poor pitiful slaves. . . .
(XXXVIII, st. 3, p. 542, *CP*)

It is not the essence of religious feeling that the speaker
finds fault with. This feeling is as much a part of our
nature as are continuous change and the search for the
absolute. Religious dogma is evil because religious leaders preach it as truth and their followers blindly accept
it, without rethinking it, and latch on to religion as a
system of inherited slogans. Therefore, this dogma is not
an immediate expression of religious feeling, but a set of
worn-out rationalizations. It is "evil" because it is mockery; it is also "evil" because the masses accept it out of
their "hunger" for meaning. Prelude XLVII (pp. 553-
554, *CP*) attacks the believers in religious dogma on the
grounds that they are moral cowards:

Oh pitiful servants of a servant's servant,
Eaters of myth, devourers of filth, cowards
Who flee the word's edge as you flee the sword,
Slaves of the clock's heart, serfs of history,
Low minions of the worm—

Through the repetition of "servant," the first line of this
stanza states the complex relationships of priest, god,
and man. The "pitiful servants" are the mass of people
who mechanically attempt to serve God by serving the
church. The church (the priests) is the third "servant" in
the line, the "servant's servant." Thus, the second "servant" is God, who is served by the priests, who in turn
are served by the people. God, in the *Preludes*, is often
the "servant" of man's desire for transcendence. The last
four lines of this passage are a caustic attack on the
"cowards / Who flee the word's edge as you flee the
sword." This line has a Biblical overtone as does much
of the poem. It addresses the "Daughters of Jerusalem"
in the first stanza, in terms of self-righteous suffering.
The repetition of words like "weep" and "blessed," references to the "crucifixion" and the land of "milk and
honey," and "mothers" and "fathers" knowing and begetting us, creates irony in this poem which calls man a
god, and curses "the half-dead prophets." The correspondence of the "word's edge" to the sharp edge of the
sword recalls the image In Prelude XXXVII of the "demon truth, sharp as a maggot."

The rejection of dogma often appears in the *Preludes* as
an act of violence:

When you have done your murder, and the word
Lies bleeding, and the hangman's noose
Coils like a snake and hisses against your neck—
(XLIV, st. 1, p. 550, *CP*)

This rejection of dogma means the giving up of many cherished transcendent ideas which have turned man through centuries of strife:

> Nor will we be in Paradise together,
> Today, tomorrow, or in other years;
> Nor eat of milk and honey, save of that
> Which now we have in seeing what we have.
>
>   (XLVII, t. 3, p. 554, *CP*)

The last two lines of the above passage present our recompense for the death of "the word": intellectual integrity. Prelude XLIV elevates this intellectual honesty to the realm of incommunicable immediacy, through the symbol of an angel's wings:

> Rejoice, gay fool, laugh at the pit's edge, now
> Heaven is come again, you are yourself
> As once you were. . . .
> And you have wings
> Lost from your second day.
>
>   (XLIV, st. 2, p. 550, *CP*)

One may well ask how the vanquishing of dogma can return to us our "wings," and what kind of "wings" we regain. Obviously the "wings" are not an indication of transcendence of the actual, but instead symbolize a heightened experience of incommunicable immediacy. Religious dogma as well as all rational systems of thought attempt to unify the disparate elements of existence, and it is this search for the absolute, where none exists except possibly in death, that the *Preludes* posit as a dangerous deception. The death of "the word" gives rebirth to the "blown wreckage of our flimsy world":

> Yet let us risk
> This tame avoidance of the obvious.
> Inward or outward, let the maze invite
> The poor mind, avid of complexities,
> And wrap it in confusion. It is here,
> When tearing web from web, that we most answer
> The eternal challenge of the absolute.
>
>   (XLVII, st. 3, p. 555, *CP*)

Rationality and analytics, although they have power to tell us useful information about the physical world, are as lame in their ability to get at meaning and value as is religious dogma:

> We have been round the Cape
> With Freud, the sea-gull, Einstein, and the Bear;
> Lived on the sea-moss of the absolute;
> And died in wisdom, and been glad to die.
>
>   (L, st. 2, p. 558, *CP*)

Death is both inevitable and unacceptable to us with or without our rationalizations:

> But let us die as gladly for such reasons
> As have no reason: let us die as fools,
> If so we will; explore the rash heart's folly;
> The marshes of the Congo of the Blood.

Here are such wisdoms—who knows?—as pure wisdom
Knows nothing of. . . .

> Oh humans! Let us venture still, and die,
> Alternately, of madness and of truth.
>
>   (L, st. 4, p. 558, *CP*)

Once again the "rash heart's folly" and the "marshes of the Congo of the Blood," images of man's irrational, conglomerate nature, are praised as being more wise than rational wisdom.

The last two lines of the stanza emphasize man's changing nature and his relative values. Prelude LIX is addressed to "This biped botanist." This poem describes analytical man, who dissects the daffodil, finds that it is composed of parts which he can analyze, but that analysis does not explain the flower's beauty and brightness any more than it explains the tendency towards love and value in man's nature.

Prelude LIX reemphasizes beauty as a function of imagination not rationality by means of the botanist's examinations of the daffodil:

> Pick it dissect and analyze its root:
> It is your heart; then laugh, with fool's delight,
> That heavenly folly made this world so bright.
>
>   (LIX, st. 4, p. 568, *CP*)

This mixture of "folly" and brightness that composes us, and all of experience, is what the *Preludes* would have man celebrate. It is not analytics itself the poems denounce, but the belief that systematized thought in the form of religious, philosophical, or analytical dogma can say anything conclusive about human existence. The *Preludes* question the function of poetry amid this relativity of words. Prelude LII reveals the poetic method in verse form. Much of the poem consists of lists, fragments of memorable occurrences, brought to light through the method of "mental randomness":[16]

> And it was there, at eight o'clock, I saw
> Vivien, and the infinite, together,
> And it was here I signed my name in pencil
> Against the doorpost, and later saw the snow. . . .
>
>   (LII, st. 2, p. 560, *CP*)

At two points in the poem the speaker interrupts his reverie in order to state his method and purpose:

> Put your heart on the table with your hand
> And tell us all those secrets that are known
> In the profound interstices of time.
>
>   (LII, st. 2, p. 560, *CP*)

Lines one and two of this passage describe the method of "mental randomness" as a poetic formula that brings to the surface of consciousness ("table" and "hand"), whatever flows beneath it ("secrets" and "heart"). Line three returns to the image of the interlude ("profound interstices") as being meaningful. This reference to the valuable interlude recalls earlier statements in the **Preludes** where the silent pause is celebrated:

> It is a moment between moments. . . .
>
> . . . . .
>
> The pause, between two words which makes a
> meaning;
>
> (XXIV, pt. 2, p. 528, *CP*)

Once again, the pause is the matrix, the connective, that makes the process possible both within the individual poems and in the series as a whole.

The second time that poetic purpose is mentioned in Prelude LII, the speaker explains the source of poetry and of what it consists:

> Neighbors, I have come
> From a vast everything whose sum is nothing,
> From a complexity whose speech is simple,
> Here are my hands and heart, and I have brought
> Nothing you do not know, and do not fear.
>
> (LII, st. 4, p. 560, *CP*)

Line two of this stanza restates the paradox of multifaceted existence ("vast everything") which cannot be summed up in any one way, unless by death ("whose sum is nothing"). Line three re-emphasizes the inability of "speech," which is "simple," to express the "complexity" which it to some degree reflects. What the speaker has brought to the reader is as much of his rational ("my hands") and irrational ("my heart") self as possible. The depth of the experience that the speaker shares with the reader is revealed in line five of the stanza, "Nothing you do not know, and do not fear." The multifarious experience shared by all human beings includes fear. The **Preludes** attempt to reveal all the shared facets of experience, both those that we generally communicate to one another, and those that we keep hidden, even from ourselves. The aim of Aiken's artistry has been described as "perpetual communication: to see everything—especially whatever the barriers of repression once concealed—to embrace everything and to express everything."[17] Calling once more for intellectual honesty, Prelude LII ends with the following summons:

> Come, we are gods,—let us discourse as gods;
> And weigh the grain of sand with Socrates;
> Before we fall to kissing, and to bed.
>
> (LII, st. 4, p. 561, *CP*)

The last line of this stanza places "Kissing, and to bed" on the same plane as that of weighing "the grain of sand with Socrates." The **Preludes** recognize love as the most effective combatant against the unnerving chaos of everyday life.

Love

Although in these poems, love is as transient as all that exists in time, and although love never completely unifies the creative/destructive tendencies within existence, the **Preludes** derive meaning from love, which is a temporary respite from language's interminable compulsion to come to a consistent understanding of an objectively chaotic universe. One of the most precise definitions of love appears in Prelude XVIII. Here the speaker defines love as a meaningful, unifying force within our short-lived human experience:

> In the beginning, nothing; and in the end,
> Nothing; and in between these useless nothings,
> Brightness, music, God, one's self . . . My love,—
> Heart that beats for my heart, breast on which I
> sleep,
> Be brightness, music, God, myself, for me.
>
> (XVII, st. 1, p. 519 *CP*)

This poem represents existence in terms of linear time, and posits nonexistence at each end of the line in terms of "nothingness" (st. 1), "silence" (st. 2), and "chaos" (st. 3). The speaker in Prelude XVIII implores his love to unite in him all that exists within the interim of experience. The unifying images in the poem that the speaker equates with his love are "Brightness, music, God, one's self" (line 3, st. 1), "the sound of one white flower, opening, closing" (line 3, st. 2), "the vast wonder come between" (line 2, st. 3), "Glory, bewilderment, all sense of brightness" (line 3, st. 3), "star" (line 5, st. 3). The images of "brightness" and "glory" in the **Preludes** are often identified with angels and conscious thought (I, sts. 2 & 5, pp. 498-500, *CP*), both of which are resplendent and nonsubstantive. "Brightness," "glory," and "star," have positive connotations, but "bewilderment" and "vast wonder" reveal a continued awareness of the shortcomings of the cognitive processes in trying to reconcile the apparent dichotomies of existence (order and chaos). Similarly, in Prelude XXXVIII, believers in dogma are pitiable because they "had no heart, when chaos came again, / Who had no love to make the chaos bright" (st. 3, p. 542). Thus love in this poem is able to "make the chaos bright."

Music, as a creative act of the mind ordering chaos, is frequently equated with love in the **Preludes**, as it is in Prelude XVIII ("Brightness, music, God, one's self"). For example, Prelude XXXII incorporates the concepts of "brightness" and of "music" in the image of the lover: "And you, bright flash of time, whose gentle hands / Touch the divine in melody . . ." (XXXII, st. 7, p. 538 *CP*). This description of the lover as "bright flash of time" indicates both the transitoriness of love as well as its meaningfulness. This image embraces the paradox of temporary meaning, and the following line of the poem equates this impermanent divinity with that of music: "Touch the divine in melody." In Prelude IX, stanza two, "Music and love and beauty" are the creative images that offset chaos:

> But there is,—so you tell me,—music, too:
> Music and beauty and the love of love,
> Music and love and beauty and all that.
>
> (IX, st. 2, p. 508, *CP*)

Prelude XVI defines love as music:

> The thing itself—by God, the thing is music,
> For when she touches me, or when she speaks—!
> . . . . .
> Then the brain lights and dizzies . . .
>
> (XVI, st. 4, p. 517, *CP*)

The first line of this passage calls attention to the immediately of music, similar to the immediacy of love. The metaphor of love as music becomes fully established in the description of harmonies and discords:

> It is a sound of many instruments—
> Complex, diverse, an alchemy of voices—
> Brass melting into silver, silver smoothly
> Dissolving into gold; and then the harsh
> And thickening discord: as if chaos yawned.
>
> (XVI, st. 4, p. 517, *CP*)

"God" and "one's self" (the creative individual) are often interchangeable in the *Preludes* (XIV, st. 6, lines 4 & 5, p. 515, *CP*), but in Prelude XVIII, the speaker wishes his love to embody both "God" and himself. "God" in this poem calls up the concept of an omnipotent, omnipresent being. It is the same concept of "God" that appears in Prelude IX, stanza two, in which the speaker calculates the degree of meaning attached to "God" as paltry when compared to that of existence ("this unsubstantial moment"):

> There is a moment, this unsubstantial moment,
> Which has a substance deep as God is deep:
> Deeper, in fact, than thought of God can be.
>
> (IX, st. 2, p. 508, *CP*)

"God" here is the innate desire for whole and permanent truth and meaning. The speaker in Prelude XVIII asks that his love fulfill his desire for truth, by resolving all of the paradoxes of existence. At times in the *Preludes* love is able to defy time, momentarily:

> It [the leaf] was the scene
> Of Tristan, firefly, Isolde, firefly; they glowed
> With timeless rapture upon it, gilded its edges,
> And they and it are gone.
>
> (XXIII, st. 1, p. 526, *CP*)

In this poem, the image of the transitory leaf is offset by the characterization of the lovers as "Tristan" and "Isolde." This characterization aptly communicates love's momentary brightness, as does the image of the glowing fireflies. The last two lines of the passage contain the paradox of the "timeless rapture" of love, that makes life meaningful ("gilded its edges") and then succumbs to time's iron law of change ("And they and it are gone").

In Prelude XVIII, the speaker desires his love to become one with himself. He sees himself as a part of experience and wants to become, through his lover, the whole experience. The "one white flower," in stanza two, is a symbol of the natural world that, in the *Preludes*, does not exclude inanimate objects, but includes all phenomena in existence: "You are what chaos yielded. Be my star" (XVII, st. 3, p. 520, *CP*).

Not only does the speaker in the *Preludes* find love to be a unifying force within chaotic actuality, but sometimes his lover becomes for him the totality of experience. In Prelude VI, the speaker seeks a new language to describe his lover. He chooses symbols for his lover from the natural world, not from romantic ideals:

> while I turn from these [idealistic images]
> To the vast pages of that manuscript
> On which the stars are stars, the world a world;
> And there I find you written down, between
> Arcturus and a primrose and the sea.
>
> (VI, st. 8, p. 505, *CP*)

The definition of love as phenomena places love within the realm of actuality, where it is both real and meaningful. Prelude VII is similar to VI in that the speaker in VII is also preoccupied with finding the proper name, or symbol, although this time the speaker seeks to rename the rain. Whereas in Prelude VI, the speaker defines his love in terms of phenomena, in Prelude VII he defines phenomena in terms of his love:

> In the dark room; and in your heart I find
> One silver raindrop,—on a hawthorne leaf,—
> Orion in a cobweb, and the World.
>
> (VII, t. 3, p. 506, *CP*)

In Prelude XVI the speaker is actually transformed by his lover from an individual into a world: "I become music, chaos, light, and sound; / I am no longer I: I am a World" (XVI, st. 4, p. 1518, *CP*). This respite from an objectively valueless existence with which love presents us is necessarily temporary, and, in some of the *Preludes*, provides only a minimum of transient comfort against ever-threatening death:

> And loose ourselves from terror. . . . Here's my
>   hand,
> The white scar on my thumb, and here's my mouth
> To stop your murmur; speechless let us lie,
> . . . . .
>   And see, beyond this bed,
> That other bed in which we will not move;
> And whether joined or separate, will not love.
>
> (II, st. 2, p. 501, *CP*)

At times in the *Preludes*, the relativity of existence overcomes love's meaningfulness, and the speaker becomes momentarily cynical:

> She will be also the sunrise on the grassblade—
> But pay no heed to that. She will be also
> The infinite tenderness of the morning—
> But pay no heed to that. . . .
>
> (XXIX, st. 2, p. 534, *CP*)

> She will be faithless to you: will have smiles
> Deep from the heart, for other men than you;

Will touch them with the wings of her wide spirit;
Delight and madden them; lead them to darkness.
(XXX, st. 1, p. 535, CP)

But relativity is generally accepted in the **Preludes** as an innate characteristic of all existence, and love is therefore not to be abandoned on that account. Love's nature is as paradoxical as is all of actuality, and should be accepted as such:

> Romeo, Romeo,
> And wherefore art thou Romeo? Not for love,
> Which takes but gives not, gives but takes not,
> lends
> At such a usurer's rate as ruins the heart.
> Generous, yes; magnanimous, sometimes, greedy
> Ah far too often; cautious too.
> (XL, pt. 4, st. 2, p. 544, CP)

Love overcomes the drive to unite self and object more fully than do reflection, music, art, and rationality. Love is not a withdrawing into self, as reflection is, but is a reaching out, a communication (often nonverbal) with another human being. Since love temporarily unites individuals on a one-to-one basis, it is more immediately rewarding than are art and music, which put one in contact with collective humanity. Due to love's nonverbal nature, it celebrates existence and makes it valuable to man in a way that dogma, rationality, and analytics cannot approach:

> Aiken came to believe . . . that consciousness is not self-generative but grows out of the luminous contact with others—in mutual awareness. The self is a product of relations; and . . . it is most fruitfully created in the relation of loving kindness: "caritas."[18]

Above all, the **Preludes** point to love as our most valuable resource and creative capability. Love is the supreme act for mankind because it is the power by which we bridge the chasm between self and other. The counterpart to love is language, especially poetry, the medium, however incomplete, by which we come to know ourselves, our loved ones, and the universe. The **Preludes**, then, embody the wish that we attain the summit of human activity, the goal of knowledge and the gift of love.

The dominant theme of time and the serial structure of the **Preludes** have led more than one critic to view the poems as a study in "the strictest materialism or nihilism" which purports that "whatever is passing in time (ideas, motives, acts) is devoid of reality and meaning simply because it does not persist in time."[19] In the **Preludes**, however, time does not merely limit man's actions, but, more importantly, allows for the possibility of their existence. Time facilitates the two most significant actions man can commit: the search for knowledge and the act of love. Both rely on communication, language, as their vehicle, and the consequence of each is the experience of "meaning" (value and purpose), the fruition of the creative will. The serial structure of the poems as well as the concrete images that seem to shift in meaning and tone from one

poem to the next exemplify Aiken's experimentation in language-making. Moreover, the series of poems taken as a whole includes intermissions of silence that, reinforcing the images of silence occurring throughout the poems, provide a sense of continuity and peace. They reach no final, dark conclusions about man's place in the universe or the function of language and love. Instead, each poem in the series is a chance to begin again, to start fresh.

Both in message and structure, the **Preludes** celebrate potentiality and provide fertile ground for further analysis. The beauty of their imagery, the musical juxtaposition of sound with carefully poised intermittent silences, and the experimental use of the serial method for exploring the dominant themes of time, language, and love are qualities that rank **Preludes for Memnon** among the finest poems of the twentieth century.

Notes

[1] Cleanth Brooks and Robert Penn Warren, Eds., *Understanding Poetry* 4th ed. (New York: Holt, Rinehart, & Winston, 1986), p. 79, include Aiken's "Prelude VII" in their anthology as an example of "precision of observation in poetic effect."

[2] Houston Peterson, *The Melody of Chaos* (New York: Longmans, Green, & Co., 1931); Jay Martin, *Conrad Aiken: A Life of His Art* (Princeton: Princeton Univ. Press, 1962; Ted R. Spivey, *The Writer as Shaman: The Pilgrimages of Conrad Aiken and Walker Percy* (Macon: Mercer Univ. Press, 1986).

[3] Frederick J. Hoffman, *Freudianism and the Literary Mind*, 2nd ed. (Baton Rouge: Louisiana Univ. Press, 1957); and Martin, Conrad Aiken, are two of the finest examples of psychological and biographical criticism on Aiken.

[4] Edith Hamilton, *Mythology* (Mentor Books, 1940; rpt., New York: New American Library of World Literature, 1964), p. 290.

[5] R.P. Blackmur, "The Day Before Daybreak," *Poetry*, 40 (April, 1932), 40.

[6] Irving Malin, "Introduction: Aiken Reflections," *The Southern Quarterly*, 21 (Fall, 1982), 5.

[7] Conrad Aiken, Preface, *Preludes for Memnon and Time in the Rock* (Galaxy Books, New York: Oxford Univ. Press, 1966), p. v.

[8] George Edison, "Thematic Symbols in the Poetry of Aiken and MacLeish," *Univ. of Toronto Quarterly*, 10 (October, 1940), 14.

[9] Edison, 19-20.

[10] Blackmur, 41.

[11] Joseph Warren Beach, *Obsessive Images in the Poetry of the 1930's and 1940's*, ed. William Van O'Connor (Minneapolis: Univ. of Minnesota Press, 1960), p. 62

[12] Blackmur, 43.

[13] Blackmur, 43.

[14] Beach, p. 68.

[15] Henry A. Murray, "Poet of Creative Dissolution," *Wake* 11 (January, 1952), 104.

[16] Murray, 103.

[17] Murray, 103.

[18] Martin, p. 14.

[19] Beach, p. 66.

Robert F. Fleissner (essay date 1992)

SOURCE: "Reverberations of Prufrock's Evening Performance in Aiken's 'Morning Song of Senlin'," in *CLA Journal*, Vol. XXXVI, No. 1, September, 1992, pp. 31-40.

[*In the following essay, Fleissner discusses the similarity of one of Aiken's poems to one of T. S. Eliot's and concludes that Eliot is the more original and profound of the two writers.*]

Because Conrad Aiken was close enough to the youthful Eliot to dub him "Tse-tse," as is well known, conjuring up the possibly fly-like insect image in "Prufrock" (as with "When I am pinned and wriggling on the wall," but compare also "They will say: 'But how his arms and legs are thin!'"), it is worth seeing how he most probably "echoed" the monologue in his well-known **"Morning Song of Senlin"** (also known as **"Morning Song from 'Senlin'"**).[1] To begin, the descriptive phrase ". . . Song of Senlin" may be thought of as a resonance of "Song of . . . Prufrock," whereby the initiatory evening setting takes on a matinal meaning—as if it is meant to represent the very morning after, namely that following the Eliotic night.[2] The dates would clearly fit, for "Prufrock" appeared in England in 1917 in book form; Aiken's poem was in his collection *The Charnel Rose* one year later.[3] Lest these years appear almost too close, it should be remembered that Eliot's monologue was first published in *Poetry*, with Pound's approval and influence, some years before. Indeed, that there is something Prufrockian about **"Senlin"** has not gone unnoticed, though to my knowledge little has been made of it, possibly owing to the connection seeming rather obvious.[4] In this essay, I hereby propose to take up some of the more striking parallels and scrutinize them with special care to see what new illumination they might shed on both poems, particularly on Eliot's.[5]

Because my recent study in book form on the Eliotic monologue made titular mention of a stairway,[6] it is convenient to commence with Senlin's reference to the same effect. Twice he uses the expression "as I descend the stair," thereby harking back to Prufrock's cautious admission "Time to turn back and descend the stair." Does such descent invoke also concomitant ascent, which is to be inferred from my book's title? A query has been duly raised about this (if in public forum, not in any of the reviews to my knowledge), and perhaps it now can be answered, for Aiken *does* admit to ascent as well ("I ascend from darkness"). At one Eliot centenary conference I happened to attend, I was intrigued to hear one of the scheduled speakers suddenly digress from his prepared text to announce that "of course Prufrock ascends the stair" and that "then he descends to meet the Footman." (Because a bound copy of the proofsheets for my book was available on a small display table outside the lecture hall, possibly that accounted for this brief digression, especially because I was seated almost directly under the speaker's nose.) Had I been queried directly how I had the gumption to call my book *Ascending* . . . when only a descent is explicitly forecast in the poem (a point that my Chairperson also gently drew to my attention), my answer would have been manifold: first, my title was ironic, for Prufrock's seeming descent-to-be, in a larger frame of reference, points more to an eventual ascent; hence the poem has been elsewhere likened to Dante's *Commedia*, whereby "Prufrock" represents, in effect, Eliot's *Inferno*, "Ash-Wednesday" a *Purgatorio* (the Florentine having used stair imagery pervasively throughout), and *Four Quartets* the *Paradiso* (with its image of entering a rose-garden). This correlation was definitely on the back of my mind in part, though not mentioned as such in the book, as a reviewer (Dorothy Judd Hall in *Southern Humanities Review*)[7] has been quick to notice. Secondly, common sense would appear to prompt the truism that one cannot descend before one has ascended anyway, thereby providing the inference that the descent-to-be cited in the text admitted of an inherent ascent first. Thirdly, Eliot may have seemingly muddied the waters elsewhere by quoting from Heraclitus and affirming that "the way up and the way down are the same," but his context allowed for appropriate distinctiveness between the two anyhow.[8] Finally, the main titular point I had in mind was that whether or not the speaker himself makes any physical (or for that matter, psychological) ascent, the critical reader is privileged, even obliged, to do it for him, hopefully thereby gaining more understanding of the inner nature of the antihero in the process. For what it is worth, finally, "Portrait of a Lady" does refer explicitly to mounting stairs ("I mount the stairs and turn the handle of the door / And feel as if I had mounted on my hands and knees"), and that poem may well be considered a companion *vers de société* to "Prufrock" (clearly having the same sort of Jamesean mode). In any event, the fact that Aiken's complementary speaker mentions ascent as well as descent should neatly settle the issue of locomotion once and for all.[9]

Because of the link just mentioned with "Portrait," it might be noted that Aiken's passing allusion to "pale rose twilight" relates neatly to a comparable roseate fore-evening in the Eliot monologue—as recently singled out by Cinthia Ozick in her long *New Yorker* article on "T. S. Eliot at 101."[10] Because the general tone of her critique was hardly complimentary, her mentioning that she had once been duly impressed by the roseate turn of phrase in "Portrait" is worth something. Hence the somewhat parallel image in Aiken may be taken as corroborative. We are apt to recall that his poem appeared in a collection of his also titularly citing the rose image.

Prufrock was a man torn between the need for social conformity and his religious conscience—between ethics and morality in one sense—and this split is likewise hinted at in the "Morning Song." For both Eliot's antihero and Aiken's social conformist, the moral issue of accepting conventional religious values appears moot, if not irrelevant, but it is at any rate more *muted* in the Senlin poem (which is somewhat less a dialogue of the mind with itself). For instance, Senlin brings up the phrase "to remember god?"[11] (In the Oscar Williams anthology, the noun is in the lower case, but the Untermeyer collection is more formal and capitalizes it.)[12] The reason for such hesitancy has to do with a kind of neoclassical concern with Deism, with an impersonal "god among the stars" (as Senlin also puts it) rather than with one to whom modernist sophisticates can easily communicate. Thus, Prufrock's decision *not* to make a religious decision is formulated in terms of its questionable relevance apropos of social mores. What would be the sense, he asks, in speaking about returning from the dead if the interlocutor finds the topic embarrassing? Likewise, any other such "overwhelming question" has to be taken *cum grano salis.* Granted, this aspect of the poem has been related to its "insidious" quality (a term helpfully used at the very outset of the monologue itself as if to set the tone), but the effect is more honestly cynical than undermining. For Prufrock never actually denies divinity. He simply would prefer to be on the sidelines, a diffident follower in such matters rather than a leader. In a similar way, Senlin asks his somewhat less-than-overwhelming question: "Should I not pause in the light to remember god?" The question is evidently rhetorical and goes unanswered at first because the posited deity is "immense and lonely as a cloud." Finally, the speaker agrees to dedicate "this moment" to "him alone." And why just such a "moment"? Evidently because he sees himself as having been created in God's image, as being a little "god," as it were, and so sees a reflection of this in the mirror before him. His ritual then consists mainly of combing his hair and tying his tie. This is hardly a very imposing "religious" service, yet it also reflects on J. Alfred's curious question about combing his "hair behind" and wearing a "necktie rich and modest, but asserted by a simple pin." In other words, what counts is primarily appearance, a kind, however, which is seen as an impressionist part of social reality and not at odds with it (as it would be with the critical, often overused, bromide "appearance and reality").[13]

Even as Convention (Nomos) has been traditionally juxtaposed with Nature (Physis), so references to custom or social habitude in "Prufrock" are counterpoised with those to the natural world as most evidently seen in the *evening/ sunrise* imagery patterns, respectively. The notorious metaphysical image at the opening of Eliot's poem, comparing an evening to an etherized patient upon an operating table, one which has been much debated (for example, in terms of relevant source material), is comparable with such a phrase in Aiken as "The stars pale silently. . . ." There the effect is not disconcerting, if only because of its subtlety, yet the meaning is not so far different. After all, what is the fundamental difference between an evening atmosphere about to be dissected and the starry firmament

turning ashen for similar imaginative reasons? One could say that in the first case ennui is suggested, in the second only the diminishing of nighttime and the encroachment of morning—that the first setting is in effect negative, the second basically positive. To some extent, this seems true enough, but if it means that **"Senlin"** is thereby superior *tonally* to "Prufrock," the effect is surely superficial. For even as Eliot's duly hesitant speaker tries to be detached in his boredom, Aiken's subject admits to being likewise "Unconcerned." Of course, such objectifying of emotion need not be taken as solely negative, however much in context it reverts to the French *poètes maudits* like Baudelaire.[14] At best, it points to a healthy enough sense of resignation, a realization that a certain humility is commendable in life, that we are not expected to "win them all."

Much has been made of the temporal element in the Prufrockian monologue (as, for example, revealing the influence of Bergson), and this is mentioned also in Aiken a bit ("My watch is wound"), though only *en passant* and mainly in terms of how it relates to the notion of proper conventionality. Nonetheless, the general time of the day is central to both poems, and much is made of that setting. In certain respects, "Morning Song" might well be seen as an answer to Prufrock's evening lament, even as a solution in kind to his misery. But because Senlin does not get beyond the vague stylistic effects of impressionism, Aiken's portrayal has far less universality and is best known as a period piece.[15]

In keeping with the temporal element is also the musical, another impressionistic aspect but handled more aptly by Eliot. Whereas Prufrock speaks tantalizingly of "music from a farther room" and "the mermaids singing" as background effects, Senlin, in turn, tells only of "Repeating three clear tones," then "two clear tones," and finally about "humming a tune"—somewhat repetitive and clearly unimaginative vocal images.[16] Still, there is something "musical" about the overall structure of **"Senlin."** The arrangement of lines is drawn up in terms of a musical sequence rather than standard form or prosody, albeit this was typical enough of modernism in general.

Lastly, one point of similarity, though seemingly very minor, has its focus of interest: subtle reference to the whiteness of skin. Prufrock's lady with her white arms beneath the lamplight has been metamorphosed into "How . . . white my face!" in Aiken. Does this not suggest something about the stereotyped effects of a primarily white society upon both poets and their speakers? It would appear that way, yet this association has its irony with Eliot because he was also greatly interested in *black* culture, which he made use of in *The Waste Land* and *Sweeney Agonistes*, for example, having studied African athropology at Harvard. See also "The Burnt Dancer" and "little black girl" in "Easter."[17]

In sum, it is natural to associate the poetry of Aiken and Eliot because they both shared the same time period with its aesthetic cultural emphases, they both tried to make their poetry modernist through the use of light conversational modes at first, and they both certainly, in their sophistication, were similarly indebted to Henry James and the traditions of Harvard.[18] They had analogous Southern backgrounds, Aiken having been born in Georgia, Eliot in St. Louis (not only the Gateway to the West but closely tied, particularly by way of the Mississippi and New Orleans, with the South). They both then lived in England, albeit Aiken returned for good to America in 1928. Untermeyer speaks of Aiken's *Nocturne, The Charnel Rose,* and *The House of Dust* as music-like, though the strains are sometimes "tired." He adds: "Even though it is enlivened by injections of T. S. Eliot's conversational idiom, the effect is frequently misty and monotonous."[19] Yet he admits that **"Senlin,"** in particular, is "rich with subtleties of rhythm," the tone being an indulgence in "a delightful whimsicality," surely a special province of Eliot as well. Titles of minor poems of his such as **"Bread and Music"** and **"At a Concert of Music"** tell of Aiken's further musical preoccupations, the latter reminiscent also of the concert in Eliot's "Portrait of a Lady" ("We have been, let us say, to hear the latest Pole / Transmit the Preludes"), and we think in accompaniment of Aiken's own **"Prelude"** and **"Portrait of a Girl."** The influence was also the other way around presumably. Untermeyer reminds us that "[m]ore than any contemporary, except T. S. Eliot (who, I suspect, has learned several tricks in juxtaposition and dissonance from Aiken) he has evolved a subtle subjective poetry which flows as smoothly, as surprisingly as the stream of the subconscious."[20] Perhaps so, but nowadays the term *subconscious* is suspect, for it suggests something somehow inferior to (*sub-*) the conscious, whereas it is part of nature, too. Even as water is so often said to be symbolic of the inner reality (Freud's term *oceanic* reverts to mind), similar watery effects tie "Prufrock" with **"Senlin,"** even as the former's reference to "waves" and "beach" at the end are "echoed" in the latter's "waves" which "Crash on a white sand shore." Yet though Aiken embroiders the seacoast a bit with allusions to bathing, "stars hung under a sea," and "a shell of silence," there is no Prufrockian *tristesse.*[21] We miss the hidden meaning inherent in Eliot's "Love Song" which makes it seem like a Dantean *Inferno* but only the first stage of a *Commedia* which will eventually be sung to Beatrice.[22]

Notes

[1] The former variant title is in Louis Untermeyer, ed., *Modern American Poetry/Modern British Poetry* (New York: Harcourt, 1930), pp. 597-99. The latter is in Oscar Williams, ed., *A Pocket Book of Modern Verse,* rev. ed. (New York: Washington Square, 1930), pp. 358-59. In this paper, my text is that of "Senlin: A Biography," in *Conrad Aiken, Selected Poems* (New York: Oxford UP, 1961), wherein Part II ("His Futile Preoccupations") contains the so-designated "Morning Song," which represents Section 2, commencing "It is morning. Senlin says. . . ." The poem underwent two major revisions, but none seem to have affected the Prufrockian correlations addressed here. From the very outset, the titular notion of futility points back to the wavering Prufrock. References to T. S. Eliot are from the standard text: *T. S. Eliot: The Complete Poems and Plays 1909-1950* (New York: Harcourt, 1952).

[2] Yet, to some extent, the throwback is comparatively to Senlin himself, who begins with an "Evening Song" in I.3. This initiatory section, though hardly so well known or structured, also contains its Prufrockian echolalia, e.g.: (1) Repetitive reference to smoking (I.1); (2) singing "sea-girls" (I.3) as at the end of "Prufrock"; (3) stroll-taking (I.4); (4) the "universe" (Senlin being "conscious of his universe" [I.4], even as Prufrock asks if he should "disturb the universe," which must also be his then); (5) allusions to the "sound of music" (I.6), to the passing of time specifically "like music" (I.7), etc. See notes 3 and 16 infra.

[3] Actually it was a companion poem to that called "The Charnel Rose." Both poems were included in a grouping also called his "Symphonies," thereby accounting, to some extent, for the numerous musical image patterns in "Senlin."

[4] One reason for this is that, ironically, the subject's name means "little old man," as Aiken himself said, which points more to Eliot's "Gerontion" with the same meaning. See Frederick J. Hoffman, *Conrad Aiken* (New York: Twayne, 1962), p. 103. Still, many critics have acknowledged Aiken's key debt in general to "Prufrock," e.g., "Prelude XXVI" in *Time in the Rock* (Helen Hagenbückle, "Metapoetics and the example of *The Prelude,*" in Ted R. Spivey and Arthur Waterman, eds., *Conrad Aiken: A Priest of Consciousness* [New York: AMS Press, 1990], p. 76n); and "Nocturne" (Steven E. Olson, "The Rejection of Nocturne of Remembered Spring," in Spivey and Waterman, p. 44), where "One often cited passage, for example, reads: 'Let us return there, let us return, you and I,— / Through the grey streets of our memories retain / Let us go back again'" (line 11).

[5] A recent critical tendency has been to try to downplay Aiken's debt to Eliot on the grounds that the former was not always derivative, that he has been considered "too imitative of T. S. Eliot" (Olson 37). Nonetheless, Aiken, in a published letter to Houston Paterson, unhesitatingly confessed that "Eliot influenced me a great deal" (Joseph Killorin, ed. *Selected Letters of Conrad Aiken* [New Haven: Yale UP, 1978], p. 145), that he "shamelessly" borrowed from him (ibid.). But if Aiken is not to be accused of plagiarism in this respect, surely Martin Luther King, not himself a "literary" person, should not be. Olson tries to cover for Aiken as follows: "Interestingly enough, however, Aiken says nothing about the enervated tone of Eliot's poems. . . . Aiken might well have found himself embarrassed at aping the worldly lassitude of Eliot's monologuists" (39).

[6] *Ascending the Prufrockian Stair: Studies in a Dissociated Sensibility* (New York: Peter Long, 1988). Although the review in the *CLA Journal* specified 1989 (as did at least one other review), the book actually appeared for the Eliot centenary.

[7] Forthcoming in a fall issue, 1990, at the time of writing.

[8] Comparable are some lines from a draft of *The Waste Land* which have been connected with "Prufrock's pointless swimming": "Like a blind man swimming deep below the surface / Knowing neither up nor down" (see Dominic Manganiello, *T. S. Eliot and Dante* [New York: St. Martin's, 1989], p. 27). Yet the Heraclitean conception scarcely need be thought of as antithetical to Christian tradition, poetically speaking at least, as Hopkins's poem "That Nature Is a Heraclitean Fire and of the Comfort of the Resurrection" makes clear.

[9] The stair imagery is found at great length throughout "Senlin," e.g., "Once more we climb" (II.4), "Up the forbidden stairway" (II.4), "when I climb the stair" (II.8), and "the golden-laddered

stair" (II.8). The notion of ascending stairs for some kind of amorous encounter, presumably with a female, is more explicit in Aiken than in Eliot; this raises the question of whether Eliot did not himself mean to be ambiguous, at least taking into account a spiritual ascent as well.

[10] Ozick, in "A Critic at Large: T. S. Eliot at 101," *The New Yorker*, 20 Nov. 1989, pp. 119-154, mentions "Afternoon gray and smoky, evening yellow and rose" (III.32). Cf. how Aiken "praised Eliot's 'Prufrock' and 'Portrait of a Lady' for their use of free rhyme and 'minimum of sacrifice to form'" (*Collected Criticism* [New York: Oxford UP, 1961], p. 171). He included a generous selection of Eliot's poetry (including "Prufrock") in his *American Poetry 1671-1928*.

[11] On the other hand, "Senlin" deals much with the problem of the subject's identification; he asks if he is a pyramid, house, street, room, door, city, etc. One critic has remarked, "Perhaps god is a giant Senlin?" (Hoffman 106). Prufrock, like Eliot, is too modest to go in for that kind of self-dramatization.

[12] The Oxford ed. also has it in lower case.

[13] A more suitable psycholinguistic dichotomy would be between the "apparent" and the real. Cf. the German *Schein/Sein* dictinction.

[14] "Unlike Eliot, Aiken was not so much influenced by French symbolism" (Hagenbückle 57).

[15] Aiken scholars are self-defensive about this. Apropos of the debt to "Prufrock," Olson observes, "What has not been noted . . . is the extent to which Aiken actually makes the journey into the past that Eliot merely suggests" (44). A nice idea, but does the Prufrockian Eliot already hint at such a journey into the past? The point seems debatable. Hagenbückle writes, "While Eliot describes a young man's world-weary mood in a time of diminished values, Aiken uses similar words to celebrate the age and its infinite options" (76n). "Infinite" in the sense of *not* being so dependent upon merely temporal ties? Yet she cites Aiken's "Beloved, there is time, / between this morning's instant and that wall" as particularly Prufrockian and also very temporal-minded.

[16] Yet we should not forget the singing "sea-girls" also in an earlier portion of "Senlin," which Aiken considered one of his "Symphonies."

[17] Hence the title of my special session for the Modern Language Association Convention (1990): "T. S. Eliot and Ethnicity: The Influence of and on Black Culture."

[18] Cf. an unpublished MS by Aiken, "The Clerk's Journal," which includes an early draft of his "Short Memoir of Harvard, Dean Briggs, T. S. Eliot, in 1911." It reposes in the Huntington Library.

[19] Louis Untermeyer, ed., *Modern American/Modern British Poetry* (New York: Harcourt, 1930), p. 594.

[20] Ibid., p. 595.

[21] Even though Eliot and Aiken conversed regularly with each other (once or twice a week) between 1911 and 1914, and some 65 letters of Eliot to Aiken (1914-1963) are in the Huntington Library (See Sara A. Hodson, "A Letter Long as Time: The Conrad Aiken Collection at the Huntington Library," in Spivey and Waterman, p. 253) and even though Aiken provided the "shrewdest" review of *The Waste Land*, in *The New Republic* (7 Feb. 1923), and spoke highly of his mentor in his *Ushant*, he still lacked the spiritual envolvement which Eliot underwent and so is on record for regretting that the latter "shifted his ground in later years" (Hoffman 21).

[22] After completing this paper I came across Ted R. Spivey's article "Aiken's Eliot: Toward a Revision," *Southern Quarterly*, 17 (1978), 29-41. Spivey compares "Prufrock" and Aiken's "Tetelestai" in terms of castration imagery.

FURTHER READING

Biography

Aiken, Conrad. "Prologue to an Autobiography." *The American Scholar* 35 (Autumn 1966): 621-30.
  Aiken uses poetic language to describe briefly his childhood.

Criticism

Beach, Joseph Warren. "Conrad Aiken and T. S. Eliot: Echoes and Overtones." *PMLA* LXIX, No. 4, Part 1 (September 1954): 753-62.
  Compares Aiken's poetry, beginning with *The Jig of Forslin* (1916) to that of T. S. Eliot of the same era.

Bollier, E. P. "From Scepticism to Poetry: A Note on Conrad Aiken and T. S. Eliot." *Tulane Studies in English* XIII (1963): 95-104.
  Asserts that Aiken's poetry was influenced by and also inferior to the poetry of T. S. Eliot.

DeMott, Benjamin. "Life Carved to a Pointed End." *Saturday Review* LIV, No. 5 (30 January 1971): 23-5.
  Describes the poetry in Aiken's *Collected Poems 1916-1970* as examples of the poet moving toward maturity in his writing.

Denney, Reuel. "Conrad Aiken." In *Six American Poets from Emily Dickinson to the Present: An Introduction*, edited by Allen Tate, pp. 122-58. Minneapolis: University of Minnesota Press, 1969.
  Analyzes the "global" viewpoint of Aiken's poetry.

Dickey, James. "A Gold-mine of Consciousness." *Poetry* XCIV, No. 1 (April 1959): 41-4.
  Assesses Aiken's *Sheepfold Hill,* arguing that it presents Aiken as a "valuable" but not yet "indispensable" poet.

———. "That Language of the Brain." *Poetry* CIII, No. 3 (December): 187-90.
  Asserts that Aiken's *The Morning Song of Lord Zero* (1963) is worth reading even though it is at times "vague" and "long-winded."

Fitts, Dudley. "The Poetry of a Supreme Technician." *The New Republic* 133 (26 December 1955): 19.
Argues that Aiken's *A Letter from Li Po, and Other Poems* (1955) demonstrates "his mastery of language."

Fletcher, John Gould. "The Poetry of Conrad Aiken." *The Dial* 64 (28 March 1918): 291-92.
Contends that Aiken's *Nocturne of Remembered Spring, and Other Poems* (1917) reveals him as "the poet of sexual illusion and disillusion."

———. "Conrad Aiken—Metaphysical Poet." *The Dial* 66 (31 May 1919): 558-59.
Praises the perceptiveness of Aiken's *The Charnel Rose*

Hoffa, William W. "Conrad Aiken: Music and the Poetics of the Preludes." *Four Decades of Poetry 1890-1930* 2, No. 3 (January 1979): 127-44.
Asserts that Aiken's *Preludes* reveal the poet's interest in time, order, and disorder, as well as his desire to be a composer of music.

Hoffman, Frederick J. *Conrad Aiken*. New York: Twayne Publishers, Inc., 1962, 172 p.
Overview of Aiken's work; includes a chronology of his life and a selected bibliography of his works and assessments of his work.

Holmes, John. "A Poet's Voluntary Resumptions." *The Saturday Review* XXXIX, No. 13 (31 March 1956): 18-19.
Suggests that Aiken's *A Letter from Li Po, and Other Poems* (1955) won the Bollingen Award in honor of Aiken's "achievement and purpose" over the years.

Kunitz, Stanley J. "The Poetry of Conrad Aiken." *The Nation* 133 (14 October 1931): 393-94.
Asserts that Aiken's poetry is influenced by the philosopher David Hume

Marten, Harry. *The Art of Knowing: The Poetry and Prose of Conrad Aiken*. Columbia: University of Missouri Press, 1988, 193 p.
Overview of Aiken's works; includes a bibliography of his writings and assessments of his writings.

———. "The Truth in All Its Inconsistencies: Conrad Aiken's 'Senlin: A Biography'." *Essays in Arts and Sciences* XVIII (May 1989): 39-51.

Contends that Aiken's "Senlin" is "a poem that crystallizes its creator's efforts to experiment with ideas of perception and reality."

Mizelle, Vance. "Conrad Aiken's 'Music Strangely Subtle'." *The Georgia Review* 19, No. 1 (Spring 1965): 81-92.
Asserts that in his search for order and harmony, Aiken has given a musical quality to much of his poetry and to his prose work *Ushant*.

Putnam, H. Phelps. "The Pilgrimage of Festus." *The New Republic* 37 (5 December 23): 16, 18.
Reviews Aiken's *Pilgrimage of Festus* and concludes that while clearly expressed, the poem has little to say.

Scott, Evelyn. "A Flight for Angels." *Poetry* XLVI, No. III (June 1935): 162-65.
Reviews Aiken's *Landscape West of Eden*, suggesting that it is a flawed poem by a complex and talented poet.

Spivey, Ted R. "Archetypal Symbols in the Major Poetry of T. S. Eliot and Conrad Aiken." *International Journal of Symbology* 2, No. 3 (November 1971): 16-26.
Describes Eliot and Aiken as two poets who are very different from one another but who share similar patterns of symbols to express themselves in their poetry.

———. "Christ in Savannah: Conrad Aiken's Religious Vision." *Essays in Arts and Sciences* XII, No. 1 (March 1983): 99-112.
Discusses Aiken's grounding in Unitarianism and how his faith and his unhappy past are reflected in his poems.

Theobald, John. "'Where Is It Fled . . . ?'" *Poetry* LXXII, No. IV (July 1948): 224-26.
Reviews Aiken's *The Kid* and sees it as a departure from much of his poetry before it.

Walton, Eda Lou. "The Gentleman of Shalott." *The Nation* 143, No. 17 (24 October 1936): 486, 488.
Negative review of Aiken's *Time in the Rock: Preludes to Definition*.

Willis, Patricia Reynolds. "Unabashed Praise of a Poet." *The Georgia Review* 11, No. 3 (Fall 1967): 373-80.
Favorably compares Aiken the man with his poetry.

Additional coverage of Aiken's life and career is contained in the following sources published by The Gale Group: *Contemporary Literary Criticism*, Vols. 1, 3, 5, 10, 52; *DISCovering Authors: Novelists Module*; *DISCovering Authors: Poets Module*; *Short Story Criticism*, Vol. 9; *Contemporary Authors*, Vols. 5-8R, 45-48; *Contemporary Authors New Revision Series*, Vols. 4, 16; *Concise Dictionary of American Literary Biography, 1929-1941*; *Dictionary of Literary Biography*, Vols. 9, 45, 102; *Major Twentieth-Century Writers*, Vol. 1; and *Something about the Author*, Vols. 2, 30, 73.

Claribel Alegría
1924–

Nicaraguan-born Salvadoran poet, novelist, short fiction writer, biographer, essayist, editor, nonfiction writer, translator, and author of children's books.

INTRODUCTION

Alegría is best known for writings in which she depicts the concerns, histories, and traditions of the peoples of Nicaragua and El Salvador. Mixing geographical, historical, political, and cultural references in her poetry and prose, Alegría attempts to create a literature of social and political awareness from a Latin American perspective.

Biographical Information

Born in Estelí, Nicaragua, in 1924, Alegría lived there until she was nine months old. Due to her father's support of Nicaraguan guerrilla leader Augusto César Sandino, Alegría's family was forced into exile by Anastasio Somoza, a Nicaraguan politician who later became commander-in-chief of the Nicaraguan army and eventually the nation's president. The family settled in Santa Ana, a small town in El Salvador that became the setting for much of Alegría's writing. In 1943 she traveled to the United States to study at George Washington University. While in America, Alegría married Darwin J. Flakoll, who became her frequent collaborator and later translated many of her works into English. Beginning with the 1948 publication of her first volume of poetry, *Anillo de silencio,* Alegría produced diverse works of poetry, fiction, biography, and history, yet her work remained untranslated until 1978, when she was awarded the Casa de las Americas poetry prize for *Sobrevivo.* She returned to Nicaragua for the first time in 1979 after the Sandinista Front for National Liberation overthrew the Somoza government. She continues to comment on Nicaraguan and El Salvadoran politics as well as write collections of poetry and nonfiction work. She has resided in recent years in Nicaragua, El Salvador, and Mallorca, Spain.

Major Works

Alegría's stated aim as a writer is to illuminate the political situation in Central America. War and its consequences are an integral feature of her poetry. In "Estelí," a poem appearing in *Sobrevivo,* Alegría addresses the effects of civil war on El Salvador, focusing on the image of the river that runs through the small town of her birth: "your channel has been filled. / With mud and blood / it has been filled / with empty cartridges / with shirts / pants / and corpses / sticking like algae / to the rocks." Latin American history also pervades her writings. In the bilingual poetry collection *Flores del Volcán / Flowers from the Volcano,* Alegría uses powerful imagery and language to dramatize the imperialistic forces that have exploited Latin America for centuries. A provocative mix of verse and narrative, *Luisa in Realityland* is considered a prime example of magic realism and one of Alegría's best known works. As the document of a young girl's upbringing in a family of "fabulous liars" who are able to convince themselves and others of the validity of their invented stories, *Luisa* juxtaposes personal perspectives and historical events. The work collapses the distinction between inner and outer worlds, emphasizing the importance of spiritual growth in the context of political struggle.

Critical Reception

Throughout her poetry, Alegría emphasizes the value of individual experience, and the memory of that experience, in the face of political turmoil, military campaigns, and civilian massacres. It is this focus on her own experience that makes her poetry at once so intimate and so universal. Critics frequently talk about Alegría "bearing witness" or "offering her testimonial" to events in Central America. Recent critics note her deft treatment of feminist issues such as collectivity and continuity. Because of her interest in political issues, some commentators have asserted that she has neglected aesthetics aspects of her verse. However, recent critics, most notably the commentator Jo Anne Engelbert, reconcile this question by placing Alegría's poems in the European tradition of elegy—poetry that affirms the value of life in the face of death.

PRINCIPAL WORKS

Poetry

Anillo de silencio (poetry) 1948
Suite de amor, Angustia y soledad (poetry) 1951
Vigilias (poetry) 1953
Acuario (poetry) 1955
Huésped de mi tiempo (poetry) 1961
*Vía única (poetry) 1965
†Aprendizaje (poetry) 1970
Pagaré a cobrar y otros poemas (poetry) 1973
Sobrevivo (poetry) 1978
Suma y sigue (poetry) 1981
Flores del volcán / Flowers from the Volcano (poetry) 1982
Y este poema rio (poetry) 1988

Mujer del río / Woman of the River (poetry) 1989
Fugues (poetry) 1993
Variaciones en clave de mi (poetry) 1993
Umbrales = Thresholds: Poems (poetry) 1997

* This volume contains *Auto de fé* and *Communicacíon a larga distancia.*

†This volume incorporates selections from *Anillo de silencio, Vigilias, Acuario, Huésped de mi tiempo,* and *Vía única.*

Other Major Works

Tres cuentos (juvenilia) 1958
New Voices of Hispanic America [editor and translator, with Darwin J. Flakoll] (poetry) 1962
Cenizas de Izalco [with Flakoll] (novel) 1966 [*Ashes of Izalco,* 1989]
Unstill Life: An Introduction to the Poetry of Spanish Poetry of Latin America (anthology) [translator, with Flakoll] 1970
El detén (novel) 1977
Las encrucijada salvadoreña [with Flakoll] (essays) 1980
Cien poemas des Robert Graves (anthology) [editor and translator, with Flakoll] 1981
Nuevas voces de norteamerica (anthology) [editor and translator, with Flakoll] 1981
Nicaragua: La revolución sandinista: Una crónica política, 1855-1979 [with Flakoll] (history) 1982
Poesía viva (anthology) 1983
Despierta, mi bien, despierta (novel) 1986
No me agarran viva: La mujer salvadoreña en lucha [with Flakoll] (biography) 1983 [*They Won't Take Me Alive,* 1987]
Luisa en el país de la realidad (novel) 1987 [*Luisa in Realityland,* 1987]
Albúm familiar (novellas) 1984 [*Family Album: Three Novellas,* 1991]
††*Pueblo de Dios y de Mandinga* (novel) 1991
Somoza: expediente cerrado: la historia de un ajusticiamiento, [with Flakoll] (history) 1993 [Death of Samoza, 1996]
Fuga de Canto Grande [with Flakoll] (history) 1992 [Tunnel to Canto Grande, 1996]

††Contains *El detén, Albúm familiar,* as well as *Pueblo de Dios y de mandinga.*

CRITICISM

Carolyne Wright (essay date 1983)

SOURCE: A review of *Flowers from the Volcano,* in *Northwest Review,* Vol. 21, Nos. 2-3, 1983, pp. 175-83.

[*In the following review, Wright praises Alegría's poetic accomplishments as well as her commitment to political and social justice.*]

With this volume [*Flowers from the Volcano*], Salvadoran poet-in-exile Claribel Alegría is finally able to join the ranks of Ernesto Cardenal, Miguel Angel Asturias, and other politically engaged Central American writers whose work is already available in English translation, and to be added to the still-meagre list of Latin American women poets—among them Gabriela Mistral, Alfonsina Storni, and Rosario Castellanos—who have achieved recognition both in their own countries and on the international level. This bilingual selection, from Alegría's many books in Spanish published in Spain and Latin America, is that of a mature and courageous voice which will expand the North American readers' awareness not only of the repressive and terrifying political realities of the last few decades of Central American history (already given prominence in the media), but also of the ways in which writers committed to social justice and humanitarian values are combatting oppression and institutionalized terrorism in their own countries and abroad.

Alegría herself confronts her nation's bitter history not with the *fusil* (rifle) but with the testimony of her words. Instead of the lyrical decorum and formal grace of an earlier age, *a la* Rubén Darío, we are presented with a stripped and self-effacing language, a *"llanto endurecido"* (hardened weeping) which finds its motive throughout all of revolution-torn Latin America and Spain—from the Spanish Civil War and the murder in Granada of the beloved Federico García Lorca, to the brutal slaying by military police of poet and folklorist Victor Jara in the Estadio Nacional de Chile, to the deaths of Alegría's own countryman, poet Roque Dalton, and the thousands of others in El Salvador and elsewhere. These savage events have already entered the canon of what could, lamentably, be termed the mythos of terrorism in the Spanish-speaking world—events about which a growing number of "people of good will" (as translator Forché has called them) share a common knowledge, as they do about the Nazi Holocaust, the Soviet Gulags, and the Vietnam War. It is tragic that such must be the body of shared knowledge which serves to enhance the accessibility of Latin American poetry *engagé*; and we must also ask ourselves, as we must about the earlier horrors, whether we allow the familiarity of reference to blunt our responses to the reality that the poems represent. As Elie Weisel has said of the literature of the Holocaust, "every word must contain the whole truth," must be charged with a depth and resonance and psychic veracity that mere media coverage cannot begin to approach, so that we do not forget, that we are not condemned to repeat. It is to this task as well that Alegría's poetry has dedicated itself.

Most readers will agree that this poet's style—spare, honed, relentless in its rhythms and incantatory in its litany-like repetition of its "rosary of names" of the dead—is successful in its all-encompassing purpose: to serve as a repository for all that endures in spite of human inhumanity:

> Their persecuted voices are one voice
> dying by torture in prison . . . I am a cemetery,

I have no country
and they are too many to bury.

(from **"We Were Three"**)

It is in memory of this poet in voluntary exile that the dead can "arise" and "rage" and reach beyond their prisons, torture and death toward resurrection in the consciences of all committed people.

Paul Celan, another Holocaust survivor, once said that "a poem can be a message in a bottle, sent out in the (not always greatly) hopeful belief that it may . . . wash up on land." Like Celan's bottle-messages, Alegría's poetry has gone forth into the world with no guarantee that it will be received; although she may not suffer from government-imposed censorship as she would within El Salvador itself, she also cannot reach the very people about whom she is writing. Only by indirection and in translation does her work have a chance to witness on behalf of those who are dead or silenced among her people. In this country, of course, her work will be received, but not necessarily with the same degree of passionate identification that it would be in her own land, her own language. The majority of North American readers will have available to them only the translation, the right-hand side of every page, although there seems to be a heartening increase in the number of those with at least a reading knowledge of the language of this hemisphere's second-largest linguistic group. Moreover, most readers in this country, blessed with relatively safe and sheltered lives, will not be able to empathize with the harshness depicted in poems such as **"Eramos Tres"** (**"We Were Three"**), the final sections of **"Sorrow"** and parts of **"Santa Ana a Oscuras"** (**"Santa Ana in the Dark"**), with the constant awareness of torture and death underlying these poems—poems which are given poignance and an even greater clarity of horror by being overlaid with images of ordinary human interaction and natural beauty:

America is a green, a living stone . . .
It is somber, green, difficult.
The jungle has it by the throat.
The sun seeds its deserts.
Its people are lost
between furrows and rivers.

From the evocative quality of this passage, reminiscent as it is of Neruda's Canto General, Alegría moves to the heart of her concerns, her obsessive awareness:

My America is spilled blood,
the theater of Cain and Abel,
a struggle with no quarter given
against starvation, rage or impotence.

(from **"My Good-byes"**)

In fact, what gives these poems their power is not the violence *per se* of their subject matter, but the uncanny juxtapositions of violence and beauty, of the exquisite and the terrifying, that have always coexisted in the land and the culture. In the title poem, Alegría yearns for the fourteen volcanoes of her "remembered . . . mythical country," but then abruptly reminds us that it is not only "green," but "more red, more gray, more violent" than other countries—not only in its recent political history but on the deepest levels of geography, natural history, and the myths of its pre-Columbian peoples. This land is shaken by volcanic eruptions ("Izalco roars") and haunted by the still-living presences of the sanguinary Mayan gods ("Eternal Chacmol collects blood"), so much so that the present conflicts begin to seem like contemporary enactments of rituals preordained since ancient times:

The priest flees screaming
in the middle of the night
he calls his followers
and they open the *guerrillero's* chest
so as to offer the Chac
his smoking heart.
No one believes in Izalco
that Tlaloc is dead
despite television,
refrigerators,
Toyotas.

(from **"Flowers from the Volcano"**)

The ostensibly innocent and unrelated actions of Mayan *campesino* children, carrying flowers their parents have grown (in the very crater of the volcano once sacred to their ancestors) down to sell to the Salvadoran upper class, become fulfillments to the old prophecies, continuations into modern times of primordial cycles of human sacrifice and tribal renewal—cycles which the currently ascendant civilization wishes to repress and deny, but which are as inexpungible, as invincible now as they were before the pre-Columbian kingdoms fell:

The owners of two-story houses
protected from thieves by walls
peer from their balconies
and they see the red wave descending
and they drown their fears in whiskey.
They are only children in rags
with flowers from the volcano,
with *Jacintos* and *Pascuas* and *Mulatas*
but the wave is swelling,
today's Chacmol still wants blood,
the cycle is closing,
Tlaloc is not dead.

The visionary and ritualistic quality of the title poem is in evidence throughout the collection, especially in the long reminiscence, **"Santa Ana in the Dark,"** and the even longer lament, **"Sorrow."** In the first of these, the poet returns in her imagination to the village of her childhood, and grieves for its slow destruction by the forces of so-called "progress" imposed from outside:

Our house in Santa Ana crumbles
writes my brother.
Little by little we abandon it,

one by one we leave it alone.
The garden once filled with birds is empty.
Poison finished Santa Ana's birds
and the flowers don't grow as before
in the garden of my house.

The extended metaphorical conflict between light and
darkness in this poem, with its repeated Biblical echoes,
underscores the contrast between the idyllic village of
memory and the disintegrated collection of electricity-
deprived dwellings of the present—

Let there be darkness
declared Don Raimundo
the light went out
Santa Ana grew dark . . .
It has been one hundred years
since the death of light
in Santa Ana.

—and transforms what could have been a simple then-
and-now parallelism into a grim recital of the effects of a
destructive power, rendered yet more ominous because
embodied in the figure of the local strongman, Don
Raimundo:

Don Raimundo is accustomed to command.
With the snap of his fingers
all is accomplished . . .
That is why I tell you
Don Raimundo is clever.
God rewards the clever
and punishes those of us who stumble.
Darkness was created
when my father died . . .
Each time a lamp goes out
things grow murkier
and you look without seeing
and say *yes* with your head
no one understands.

Even without direct reference here to death squads, guerrilla warfare, disappearances, and other extreme features
of right-wing terrorism, we feel the grinding oppressive-
ness of daily life under the regime which has put out the
lamps of Santa Ana.

"Sorrow" also involves a mnemonic return, in this instance a pilgrimage to the unmarked grave of Spanish poet
Federico García Lorca, in Granada. The poem resounds
like an echo chamber with the words of other dead poets
and freedom-fighters: Roque Dalton ("*cuando sepas que
he muerto / no pronuncies mi nombre*"), Pablo Neruda
("*puedo escribir los versos más tristes esta noche*"), "Che"
Guevara ("*listos para la muerte / listos para vencer*"),
and García Lorca himself ("*verde que te quiero verde*").
Alegría creates a surrealistic, almost cinematographic series of images, glimpsed as if in fear-dream:

the dark shapes of friends
crying out
that break the fog an instant

a hand with no fingers
strumming a guitar
a single desperate sound
that lifts and escapes
I grope and it supports me
as it recedes.
Is that you, Victor Jara?

After she has evoked with nightmarish compression the
details of the Chilean poet's death by torture, Alegría makes
us privy to her apprehension as she attempts to locate
García Lorca's resting place—and encounters the fear-cen-
sored responses of the people she queries:

I ask at a hotel, in a cafe
the alarmed expressions, the words
and the faces vanish
I do not understand
vague gestures and directions
El crimen fue en Granada . . .
everyone knows that
but no one is capable
of the precise detail

It is still dangerous, forty or more years after the fact, to
pay tribute to the gypsy poet, even to erect a "stone
reading / here lies the poet," but nevertheless the speaker
discovers that some courageous person has "left a tree,
an olive"—the symbol of enduring life in this dry and
stony land—to mark the spot. Still, Granada is not yet free
of its mental and spiritual prison, and those who seek
freedom are as fugitives in their own country:

This mark on our foreheads
betrays us, the obstinate gleam
in our eyes of hunted animals
of vigilance, of calloused tears
we sense one another in the Metro
we seek each other's glance then turn away

The lives of these political exiles, like those of the denizens of police states most North Americans have encountered only in literature—*1984, Farenheit 451, Darkness
at Noon*—are filled with uncertainty, illness, and the constant strain of dissembling in a world in which anyone
may be an informer:

We flee to the museums . . .
and sit for hours pretending to study
a Corot, a Cezanne
if a guard comes near us
we exchange enthusiasms
and stay longer.

No amount of comfort "in the arms of Mother Culture,"
however, will block out the vision of "the slaves . . . trying
to escape the stones that imprison them." Even though
technically free, these exiles are haunted by memories of
their dead or silenced comrades, and by the "stubborn
confused" reports, the "cold, contradictory sentences"
that bring the "implacable news" of the most recent deaths:

the echoes are still coming back
the false accusations
I'll never know who killed you
but you are dead, Roque Dalton,
and they wrap your death in fog.

By the end of the poem, the speaker's identification with her fellow exiles and victims of torture is complete. She moves from the unmarked tomb to the isolation cells of her friends, silenced as they are by pain and terror:

Who raised the bars?
a gray light filters from outside . . .
they have sliced away the sky
I touch my stiff skin
I listen to my own panting
as if from a distance
I need to remain myself
to leave the fog
with a chip of coal I begin to write:
my loneliness, my—
the voices begin coming toward me

In this passage that brings to mind Malamud's *The Fixer* or Jacob Timerman's *Prisoner Without a Name, Cell Without a Number*, the incantatory quality of short, fast-paced lines asserts itself, as the speaker chants her "rosary of names" and accomplishes a near-religious state of union with her dead, to the accompaniment of the howls of those being tortured nearby:

from my solitude I raise my voice
I ask and the answer is clear:
I am Georgina
I am Nelson
I am Raul

From the depths of her "zero hour" the speaker triumphs over horror and isolation to achieve a spiritual and psychic transcendance, both for herself and for those who "will sleep here / on my cot . . . beneath his quota of terror." She knows now that she "is not alone / they are here / the transient guests / only a tissue of time . . . separates us." But even though she is victorious in her assertion of human value in the poem, she still must reiterate the question inescapable in a world as full of inhumanity as this one is: "tell me, in spirit, who / who raised up this prison's bars?"

It is an oft-quoted commonplace that poetry is what gets lost in translation, but in this case, Alegría's straightforward, uncluttered *vers libre*—with its driving syntactical repetitions, catalogues of images, freedom from syllabic or metrical formalities, and minimal dependence on conventional punctuation—transfers quite readily to the target language. These poems tend to be long but short-lined (one to five words), and translator Forché has frequently chosen, therefore, to combine several lines of the original into one in the English version, as in the following, quoted in part above:

Mi América es sangre derramada . . .	My America is spilled blood
una lucha sin tregua quarter	a struggle with no given
con el hambre la rabia, la impotenica.	against starvation, rage or impotence.
Me arranco, me voy.	But I am leaving.
(From **"Mis Adioses"**)	(From **"My Good-byes"**)

Forché has also chosen at times to condense Alegría's more diffuse passages—certainly a translator's prerogative in a largely faithful rendering—to create a tighter poem in the new language. But what I am not certain I understand is the rationale behind the complete elimination of whole lines and phrases, which the bilingual reader can see in the original but which are missing in the English. Usually it is a small detail: in **"Santa Ana in the Dark,"** "*las tormentas con truenos / y relámpagos*" (storms of thunder and lightning) are left out of the list of light-bearing bodies; the faces of maiden aunts in the photo albums that "*se han derrumbado ya*" have not already crumbled in the English; and don Santiago's "*farmacia / bien surtida*" is not said to be *well-stocked*, an important distinction, one would think, in an isolated rural village.

> **What gives these poems their power is not the violence *per se* of their subject matter, but the uncanny juxtapositions of violence and beauty, of the exquisite and the terrifying, that have always coexisted in the land and the culture.**
>
> **—*Carolyne Wright***

Perhaps these details are trivial, or perhaps they and others like them have been inadvertently dropped from the manuscript; but why would Forché choose to eliminate these particular phrases, and not others of equal or arguably lesser importance to the poem's coherence? And why eliminate any of them, since these poems purport to be *translations,* not versions or imitations of the original? If, however, the practice of editing or cutting the original text is germane to Forché's philosophy of translation, why not delete more—even of that which does not make for diffusion in the original—and create consistent versions rather than uneven translations? Since so much of the English does seem to correspond to the tone, vocabulary and intentions of the Spanish, the inconsistencies and deletions that do exist look, to the bilingual reader, like the results of haste or sketchy proofreading. Unfortunately, there are rather numerous typographical errors in the Spanish as well ("*conicienta*" for *cenicienta*; "*oscurridad*" instead of *oscuridad*; "*di*" rather than *de* for the preposition *of*), which could have been avoided with more judicious proofing.

Nevertheless, despite some production problems with this selection of her work, Claribel Alegría's poems will endure as testimonies to the power of memory and dream to confront political horror with courage and constructively-directed indignation. Carolyn Forché, and those whose assistance she acknowledges, are to be commended for introducing Alegría to the English-speaking world. May we all come to know what this poet wishes: "for our America a destiny / that would not fill us with shame."

Claribel Alegría with Carolyn Forché (essay date 1984)

SOURCE: "An Interview with Claribel Alegría," in *Index on Censorship*, Vol. 13, No. 2, April, 1984, pp. 11-13.

[*In the following essay, Alegría discusses her childhood, the pressures of living in exile, and the difficulty of translating poetry.*]

[FORCHÉ]: *Gabriel García Márquez has stated that the most significant period of his life, the richest years, were those of his childhood, before he reached eleven years of age. Is this true for you?*

[ALEGRÍA]: I think García Márquez is correct in that what happens to one in earliest childhood is definitive. I was very much marked by the peasant uprising in El Salvador in 1932. I remember the Guardias Nacionales bringing dozens of prisoners into the fortress across the street from my home with their thumbs tied behind them with bits of cord, shoving them along with rifle butts. I remember the shots at night. I remember the Colonel striking a peasant who had his hands bound behind him, and my father running out of his clinic, his doctor's tunic flapping, to shout: 'Colonel, a real man doesn't hit anyone who can't defend himself.'

I remember the black cloud boiling up behind Santa Ana from the volcano Izalco, which was in continuous eruption during the uprising, the people walking along the street of Santa Ana with handkerchiefs over their noses, volcanic ash dropping from the cloud to powder their hair and coat the streets with a grey film.

I remember a few weeks later a peasant woman from Izalco coming to our door to beg for herself and for her children. She shook her head at my mother's question and replied: 'There is only a handful of us left, señora, only a handful.'

There was the episode of your father and Augusto Cesar Sandino (the leader of the uprising against United States occupation of Nicaragua in the 1930s).

That is another thing that marked me as a child. I remember my father holding my hand in the surf at Acajutla. It was on 22 February 1934. He was telling me, 'They've just murdered Sandino. Tacho Somoza and the gringos betrayed him.' (Anastasio 'Tacho' Somoza was Nicaragua's dictator, put in power by the United States, whose son was overthrown by the 1979 Revolution.)

My father fought earlier with Benjamin Zeledón against the US Marines who were still occupying Nicaragua years later in 1924 when I was born in Estelí. Though I don't remember it directly, I recall my mother telling me how the Marines pointed rifles at her and at me as we passed by their camps on muleback, trying to terrorise her because my father was known to be unfriendly to the gringos. We had to leave for El Salvador when I was only nine months old, though my father helped Sandino's forces until Sandino was assassinated. After that he had a price on his head and could not re-enter Nicaragua for many years.

And your mother?

When I think of my mother, only her good qualities come to the fore. I did not inherit her sweetness, her patient acceptance of whatever happened in life, her regal gentility, her self-effacement, her deep religious faith. Mainly I think I inherited her avid curiosity for places, for people, books, everything.

Could you discuss the development of your work?

My first two books were subjective, lyrical and for the most part, composed of extremely short poems. I see them now as infused with adolescent questioning, with the wonder of a pristine consciousness gazing at the world for the first time.

About half of my third book is made up of sonnets. I felt the need of a formal, pure structure to concentrate what I had to say. In this same book, I published free verse: **'Monólogo de Domingo,'** the poem I now recognise as being the first in which I heard the sound of my own authentic voice, in which I first experimented with a longer narrative style.

In my fourth book, *Acuario,* I deliberately moved away from subjective lyricism and sought for a rather objective, laconic style, occasionally larded with irony, to comment on the world around me rather than on my own feelings and reactions. These poems dealt with domestic themes, city living, the world of human interrelations. They were not political. It was not until *Vía Unica* that I felt the urge to write political poems.

As I think back over my past I can see that, without deliberately intending to do so, I have been elaborating and developing these two strands—subjective lyricism and a more objective, facing-outward type of poetry—and that the two cycles are tending to spiral about their points of origin. I sometimes wonder if they will close on themselves with a definite click—and what I will do if that happens.

How does exile affect your work? In the past four years, there has been a migration of Latin American writers away from their homelands. How do you think this will affect the evolution of Latin American literature?

Let me make it clear that my own exile has been due to force of circumstance, voluntary if you will, rather than induced by political pressures.

Certain things—the odour of jasmine on my terrace or the two paragraph news item in the paper—can revive the memory of my country, or perhaps I should say my countries—but all too frequently I feel that words are growing sterile, that I am reconstructing and extrapolating a memory, an empty evocation of the themes that I prefer to deal with. The sights and sounds and smells, the faces of lost friends, the shorthand expressions by which we immediately understand each other without having to launch into detailed explanations: all of these things, I sometimes fear, are fading, becoming more and more difficult to summon up. I'm on a life raft in a placid sea. I have survived the shipwreck, the slow foundering of half a dozen countries, but I look around at times and ask myself, 'what am I doing here?' Then the guilt surges up.

On the positive side, travel and living in many countries other than one's own is invaluable. Clichés are over-worked truths: travel does broaden one, widen one's horizons. It enables you to take a distance, psychological and emotional as well as geographic, from the problems that form the backdrop of life in your own country and you can become more objective about them rather than being entangled in them.

Certain Latin American stay-at-homes have accused exiled Latin American writers of escapism, but I myself can see no virtue in a defiant, self-satisfied parochialism. Had I remained in El Salvador, I'd have inevitably been caught up in a clique and we'd all have spent our lives taking in each other's laundry in a literary sense. Luckily, I've remained free of that, and living abroad has opened my work to influences, emotions, impressions that I could never have experienced in Santa Ana:

As for the problem of exiled Latin American writers in general, it is not a new phenomenon but it has been much more intense in recent years in the wake of the Pinochet takeover in Chile, Videla's official terrorism in Argentina, and the continuing repression of leftists in Uruguay.

I am not worried about the future of Latin American literature. It is healthy, vital and constantly proliferating. The writers who remain on their home soil to observe the local scene will find publishers even though local censors ban their works, and the writers who have been displaced to other parts of the world and have benefited by a wider frame of reference will each produce his testimony in accordance with his talent and sensitivity. Whatever survives the critical winnowing and the test of time will be known to future generations as Latin American literature.

Your recent works are more rhetorically political. Would you say that this is true? How is the impulse for political poems different?

When I finished writing **Raíces**, I had the strong feeling that I had closed a cycle of subjective, lyrical, somewhat introspective and self-searching poems, and I figuratively dusted off my hands and walked away from that theme which had been a constant in my work.

At the same time I was increasingly horrified by the fratricidal tragedy of Latin America, shocked by the imprisonment, torture, disappearance or assassination of my closest friends. I was obsessed by this spectacle and, I must admit, guilt-stricken that I was sitting here in my Mallorca haven, unable to do anything but scribble verses.

The impulse to write a political poem is a gut reaction of rage, frustration, impotence and, I think, sorrow. They are difficult to write, artistically dangerous because one always runs the risk of becoming no more than a pamphleteer, a propagandist. I rarely plan to write any certain kind of poetry; I write about what most deeply moves me.

In the United States, there has been a growing return to an attentiveness to content. Many people suppose that this is due in part to the influence of Spanish poetry available in translation.

It is true that we Latin Americans have a preference for *content* in contradistinction to word games. We have a lower ratio of ivory tower writers than in other parts of the world. In my own case, the content of what I wish to express is always the motivating force behind each poem, and then I try to express it as truly as I can. Content and manner of expression, or style, always merge and intermingle in any worthwhile work.

How do you think the work of young North Americans differs from that of young South Americans?

I am delighted with the quality and strength of many of the young North American poets I have read. Out of nearly 100 poets whose work I have studied thus far, I consider about 15 to be absolutely first rate, and that is a high percentage. I find many similarities between North and South Americans. The primary difference would be one of socio-political engagement.

North American poets are politically innocuous?

Perhaps politics is absent from North American poetry because, at least to my way of thinking, North American politics is basically so dull. You have two major parties, both of them bourgeois and big-business oriented. In other words, a lighter shade of grey to choose from. In Latin America, politics is always black or white. You are for dictators or against them. You are on the side of the oppressed and dispossessed or you are on the side of the oligarchs, the multi-national corporations, and you defend their and your own interests.

Latin Americans are forced to live in the shadow of an enormously rich, imperial power that has continuously intervened in the internal political affairs of each Latin American nation over the past 150 years, and has been intervening more crudely during the last 25 years to install in power and support oligarchic parties and military dictatorships that will maintain the status quo. (Guatemala, 1954; Cuba, 1961; Santo Domingo, 1965; Chile, 1973 and so on.)

The United States has no such problems. It is the imperialistic status-quo oriented power that creates these problems for us.

You have been translating North American poetry. You have not seen your own poems in translation. Pablo Neruda suggested that when he read his poems in English, he found that their meaning was usually conveyed, but not their atmosphere. Do you find this to be true? What are special problems in working from Spanish to English and vice versa?

Poetry is extremely difficult to translate and some poems are impossible to bring across to another language, but I find it a fascinating challenge and one, furthermore, that has helped me a great deal in mastering and understanding my own language.

I do agree with Neruda that the atmosphere of a poem is frequently left behind in translation, but I think the lack goes deeper than that. I would say that the music and the spirit and special connotations of one language can only rarely survive the sea-change of being cast in another language.

I find that the greatest problem in translating from English to Spanish or vice versa is that English is more succinct than Spanish; what can be said in five words in English takes about eight words to say in Spanish. This, of course, means that the meter of any given poem changes completely. I also think that English has a wider range of synonyms than Spanish, more ways of expressing a precise shade of meaning that we Latins tend to convey with a gesture, a facial expression, some form of body language.

This difference I think is a key to the contrast between the English and the Spanish sensibility. Whereas English is precise, factual, objective, even when employed to tell a children's fairy tale, Spanish seems to me more adequately designed to give free rein to the reader's imagination; by its very looseness and use of generic terms rather than exact ones it forces the reader to open inner doors of fancy and spiritual expansion in order to fill in the details of what the author was trying to express.

But it is difficult for me to be absolutely self-assured and clear-cut about this. You see, from the ages of five to 15 I attended a school where, each day as I entered classes, I encountered a phrase of José Vasconcelos engraved over the portico: 'Por mi raza hablará el espíritu.' (Through my race, the spirit will speak.)

And then, of course, there is the old saying that French is the language of love, English is used for business letters, and Spanish is the language for speaking to God. So I can't be rational about this. I am as atavistic as anyone else.

You have said that you agree with the statement of Shelley—that all poets are writing the same poem.

I believe that human consciousness is evolving, growing ever more complex, understanding more and more about

life, the universe, capable of assimilating and reacting to an ever-increasing flood of data and impressions that assault it from all sides.

As a corollary to this. I feel that each epoch has its own spirit—its own particular set of challenges to overcome, its own kinds of problems to solve.

Just as I believe that the scientist is exploring the frontiers and boundaries (if there are any) of the physical world in an effort to attain a unified field theory or an ultimate set of laws by means of which we can understand how the universe operates, I am convinced that the artist and poet is out on the frontiers of human consciousness in a different direction, searching for clues so tenuous that they slip through the ordinary net of individual consciousness, continually asking why.

It is this deliberate exploration of the frontiers of intuition, inspiration and creativity that qualifies the poet and the artist to serve as precursors, the guides and interpreters of the spirit of the age, and it this kinship of curiosity and adventure, I am sure, that led Shelley to describe the work of individual poets down the ages as 'episodes of that great poem, which all poets, like the cooperating thoughts of one great mind, have built up since the beginning of the world.'

We have all heard it said that poetry and art flourish under repressive regimes or in the face of them. Do you agree with that?

I think this is absolute nonsense, at least under twentieth-century totalitarian regimes. If, in past centuries, poetry and art were produced and somehow flourished under tyrannical regimes, it was simply because the highly efficient, modern machinery of repression had not yet been brought to perfection. I have only to cite the cases of socialist realism in Stalinist Russia, Mao's cultural revolution in China which produced one hundred million copies of the Little Red Book and little else; the ponderous, Wagnerian sterility of German art under Hitler, and, finally, the cultural poverty left by 40 years of Franquismo in Spain.

What is most important to you now, as a poet, as a politica?

I don't feel that I can be compartmentalised, partitioned into different aspects. I am, or try to be, myself, and what I feel is supremely important is human relationships and human warmth.

Why do most of your fellow-writers in Latin America affiliate, at least ideologically, with the left?

I don't see how any person of heightened sensibility who lives under a regime in which a minority with guns, uniforms and off-duty hoodlums carry out officially sponsored reigns of terror against the coerced, intimidated, disorganised majority can possibly favour the Latin American right. All my artist friends feel the same way, and the very few who don't are no longer my friends.

Judith Vollmer (essay date 1990)

SOURCE: "Lines of Pain," in *Women's Review of Books*, Vol. VII, No. 6, March, 1990, pp. 12-13.

[*In the following favorable review of* Women of the River, *Vollmer lauds Alegría's ability to appeal to a wide audience while preserving an "uncanny intimacy" with readers.*]

For years I've looked for the inheritor of the traditions of Neruda and Mistral, for a poet who speaks to both South and North American audiences from her heritage and creates something new—what Alicia Ostriker has called feminist literature's "flying wedge of dissent," a wedge at the forefront of contemporary poetry. I have found that voice in the poems of Claribel Alegría, whose work is now firmly established in the US with the publication of her second book in the Pitt Poetry Series. Carolyn Forché translated Alegría's earlier *Flowers from the Volcano* (1982), and the new book, *Woman of the River*, a collection equally elegant, brutal and mysterious, has been translated by Alegría in collaboration with her husband, Darwin J. Flakoll.

The rich political poems in the collection defy the foreign influences, mostly North American, which continue to damage the Latin American peoples and land. And with dramatic visual, oral and nearly clairvoyant majesty, they praise the known and unknown people, creatures and plush landscapes of Alegría's native Nicaragua and El Salvador. This is a book of tropical fragrances and vegetations, dramatic monologues and stark elegies. The speakers in many of the poems have an oratorical potency whose visual and lyrical roots are in magical realism, and give political concerns a singular resonance, as in **"Documentary"**:

> Trucks and ox-carts
> laden with sacks
> screech down the slopes.
> Besides coffee
> they plant angels
> in my country.
> A chorus of children
> and women
> with the small white coffin
> move politely aside
> as the harvest passes by.
> The riverside women,
> naked to the waist,
> wash clothing.
> The truck drivers
> exchange jocular obscenities
> for insults.
> In Panchimalco,
> waiting for the ox-cart to pass by,
> a peasant
> with hands bound behind him
> by the thumbs
> and his escort of soldiers
> blinks at the airplane:

> a huge bee
> bulging with coffee growers
> and tourists.

Alegría lives in two places—Mallorca and Managua. Many of the poems in this collection, her tenth, express the longings of expatriation, exile and return, and the sharply felt understanding a conscience-stricken, privileged writer feels before the powers who commit atrocities. These are poems of desire for a public forum. **"Though It Only Lasts a Moment," "Farewells," "My Paradise in Mallorca"** and **"Not Yet"** investigate the personal, but while the lover and the speaker's family are in the foreground, Alegría's solos address a huge audience. One woman stands and speaks to her husband, sister, mother at her side, but turns her face to the throngs.

This capacity to speak to so many so plainly and vulnerably recalls Neruda, Akhmatova, Whitman, even Shakespeare. Like each of them, Alegría delivers an expansive rhetorical message, while addressing each of her readers with uncanny intimacy. Neruda holds tiny pieces of agate in his hands and thinks of the forgotten labors of stone carvers. We feel their hands in ours. Whitman loafs on the grass and we feel the brush of his hand against the hair on the back of our necks. Alegría stands beneath a tree; somehow we join her, alert to all of the possibilities of green. Simply put, this is the kind of poetry Denise Levertov described as fully organic—the natural world an extension of the substance of this woman, Claribel Alegría, and she of it.

In **"And I Dreamt I Was a Tree,"** the speaker, a tree-woman, fragrant and heavy with her leaves and shade, decides to free herself "of all that extravagance / of green leaves." In the disrobing, she loses her shields. But while she is shedding her illusions / leaves of beauty, her double consciousness is alerted:

> Again more strongly
> and along with the leaves that scarcely
>   mattered
> fell one I loved:
> a brother
> a friend
> and all my most cherished illusions
> fell to the ground
> and my gods fell
> and my friendly spirits
> shriveled
> and grew wrinkled
> and turned yellow.
> Scarcely any leaves
> were left me:
> four or five at most
> maybe fewer
> and I shook myself again
> more furiously
> and they didn't fall:
> like steel propellers
> they held fast.

Alegría's exquisite melding of body, voice and political alertness is again revealed in **"From the Bridge,"** in which the speaker confronts her girl self—a figure who approaches from the other side of the bridge. The girl makes her approach, ignorant of the killings and betrayals that will befall her in future. The older-self attempts to hold her off, in a riveting soliloquy recalling the brilliant warnings of section IV of Neruda's "Let the Rail Splitter Awake."

"Mater Potens" and **"The Woman of the Sumpul River,"** the poem from which the book's title comes, are two of the finest, most passionate, in the collection. **"Mater"** is a fluid triptych of a daughter who becomes mother to her own mother, then transforms into her pregnant daughter before returning to her self. The title poem works, at first, like **"Documentary,"** with the central speaker leading us inside a volcano to witness the history and atrocity bubbling there. We move concurrently through clouds and trees until we become witnesses to a scene where buzzards hover to hear the story of the woman of the river.

The poem recalls the 1980 massacre in which approximately 600 women, children and elderly people, refugees trying to escape into Honduras, were shot or drowned in the Sumpul River after they were driven from their homes by Salvadoran armed forces. In a rapid juxtaposition of scenes, tenses and perspectives, the poem follows one woman, wounded, her baby son in her arms, into the river. She has lost her three other children and her husband, and she lives to tell her testimony.

> She consoles her baby
> in whispers
> she lulls him with her tears
> she strips leaves from a tree
> and she tells him:
> look at the sun
> through this leaf
> and the baby smiles
> and she covers his face with leaves
> so he won't cry
> so he will see the world
> through the leaves and won't cry
> while the soldiers go past
> mopping up.

Joanne Saltz (essay date 1992)

SOURCE: "The Text as Tortured/Torture in the Text: Claribel Alegría's Luisa in Realityland," in *Chasqui—Revista de literatura latinoamericana*, Vol. XXI, No. 2, November, 1992, pp. 20-6.

[In the following excerpt, Saltz maintains that Luisa in Realityland qualifies as a "poststructural text," connects it to the tradition of insurgent political literature in Latin America, and explores poetic aspects of the work.]

Salvadoran writer Claribel Alegría's **Luisa in Realityland** is a tortured text. It aptly illustrates Angel Rama's obser-vation that while a critical panorama of European literatures evokes a well ordered and cultivated garden, that of Latin American literature calls to mind a confusing jungle in which roads are tortuously carved or often actually incised. Published in 1987, **Luisa in Realityland** presents a problematic which treats that confusion and disjuncture in a passionately critical view of the totalitarian repression and violence in El Salvador, its link to Latin American violence more generally, and to the First World. In presenting such a view, Alegría's work can be situated with those of other Latin American writers such as Gabriel García Márquez, Elena Poniatowska, Antonio Skármeta and Luisa Valenzuela. Like works of Valenzuela, Alegría's text attempts to collapse the physical and psychological marginalization that the politics of repression, violence and torture have imposed upon her homeland and upon her as a writer. In an interview with Carolyn Forché, the North American poet, Alegría explains her motivation for writing political poetry such as **Luisa in Realityland**:

> . . . I was increasingly horrified by the fratricidal tragedy of Latin America, shocked by the imprisonment, torture, disappearance or assassination of my closest friends. I was obsessed by this spectacle and, and I must admit, guilt-stricken I was sitting here in my Mallorca haven, unable to do anything but scribble verses.

> The impulse to write a political poem is a gut reaction of rage, frustration, impotence and, I think, sorrow. They are difficult to write, artistically dangerous because one always runs the risk of becoming no more than a pamphleteer, a propagandist.

In order to explicate the political ramifications in **Luisa in Realityland,** I will also examine Alegría's assault on marginality from several perspectives. This study will first treat the work's formal aspects, which may vary from traditional models of European realism. Such formal innovations are closely linked to the second part of the analysis focusing on narrative perspective, which leads to a discussion of the text's central problematic of political and social protest as it is intertwined with and reciprocally reinforced by the novel's personal (i.e. feminist and autobiographical) elements. Lastly, the [essay] will discuss torture as content, in terms of its historical and textual antecedents and its contemporary manifestations as seen in Alegría's text.

A first and rather obvious observation about **Luisa in Realityland** which marks it as a poststructural text is that its genre is difficult to classify, since its unorthodox form combines narrative and poetry. The text is best described as a collection of poetry incorporating prose poems interspersed with verse and ending with a long poem. Furthermore, the images in the prose sections project a poetic suggestiveness, which might well support the case for categorizing the entire text as poetry. On the other hand, this text might also be classified as a novel on the following grounds. First, it is predominantly narrative, consisting of a series of 71 short fragments which can be viewed as chapters or short stories, and which are connected to the 37 poems in verse form, all of which are given coherence by the theme of the experiences of the main character, Luisa. Second, in terms of content, *Luisa in Realityland* bears a resemblance to the ancient Greek adventure novel of everyday life as discussed by Mikhail Bakhtin, when he notes:

> In this everyday maelstrom of personal life, time is deprived of its unity and wholeness—it is chopped up into separate segments, each encompassing a single episode from everyday life. The separate episodes—this is especially true of the inserted novellas dealing with everyday life—are rounded-off and complete, but at the same time are isolated and self-sufficient. The everyday world is scattered, fragmented, deprived of essential connections. It is not permeated with a single temporal sequence . . .

This quote aptly describes *Luisa in Realityland*, the prose sections of which are complete, but at the same time isolated and disconnected from the everyday world, forming alinear time sequences. Those parts of the text which take the form of poems are interspersed or spliced into the narrative text. Jonathan Culler notes that such a process of insertion may be regarded as grafting,[1] which he characterizes as a model for thinking about the logic of texts, in which graphic or writing operations are combined with processes of insertion and strategies for proliferation. Moreover Culler describes deconstruction in one of its aspects as an attempt to identify grafts in the texts it analyzes, to locate the points of juncture and stress, where one line of argument has been spliced with another. Based on that notion it can be argued that the fragmented form of *Luisa in Realityland,* the short chapters with poetry grafted into the narrative, projects a model of spliced arguments, calling attention to the junctures and stress in a content which displays a discontinuous juxtaposition of images such as love, natural beauty, truth, the quotidian, mythic tradition, religion, lies, illness, poverty, torture, and death. In this sense, the form of the text is tortured, as it is cut, patched, and nonlinear in both chronology and plot.

With its proliferation of themes and approaches the narrative strategy or the poetic voice of *Luisa in Realityland* is likewise a shifting one. While the voice of the verses is obviously in the first person, that of the narrative segments shifts from third person singular to an occasional first person plural, a fact which is not entirely evident upon first examination. The first person singular voice in the poetry sections conveys a feminine view with regard to its content of topos, its psychological elements of emotion, memory, and the surreal, and its social elements which include personal history and myth, political and feminist protest. The writing of some of the narrative segments in the first person plural maintains and generalizes the feminine perspective with which the text concludes, as it sets up the possibility of return to a homeland projected into a future marked by difference from the past.

It is from this female collective position of the narrative portions of *Luisa in Realityland* that various patriarchal myths are conflated and rewritten, while construction of a feminized future is projected. Alegría's family history which has been fictionalized in this work is presented as myth parodied. As Jean Franco notes, all myths are narrated simply, and begin with an emigration and the founding of a city. Related in three chapters entitled "The Nicaraguan Great-Grandfather" Alegria's history can be viewed in contrast to classic myth, which portrays a venerated, valiant hero. Instead the Great-Grandfather is described as a prominent landowner in San Rafael, and one of the most capricious men in the Segovias, whose quarrel with the mayor results in his tearing down his house brick by adobe brick in a fit of pique, and transporting it complete with roof, windowframes, orange and guanabana trees to Concordia on muleback. In his search for a treasure hidden at the bottom of a lake near Concordia, he faces the traditional three obstacles of mythology. The first, which classical myth would regard as supernatural, a winged serpent which is said to guard the prize, is debunked by Great-Grandfather who labels it an Old Wives Tale. The second obstacle is social. In contrast to the classical political struggle, represented by warring armies, Alegría parodies a labor/management struggle, in which reluctant workmen hired to drain the lake find the winged serpent story credible, thus refusing to work. The final obstacle is natural. However, it is not a disaster of mythic proportions, but instead it is personalized and reduced in scale—a persistent headache which hinders Great-Grandfather's clear vision, and which disappears when he discovers the treasure, which is likewise parodied. Unlike the gold of the classics, the treasure is water, the basic element for life and survival, which Great-Grandfather realizes can irrigate the valley if the deep gully leading from the drained lake is dammed.

Just as classical myth is parodied by the myth of the Nicaraguan Great-Grandfather, the latter is also paralleled and contested in the text by a voyage made by Luisa. Unlike the Great-Grandfather, Luisa does not emigrate to found a new society, but playing the part of the prodigal, leaves to study as a young woman, is kept away by political conditions at home, and returns to Central America in middle age. The motif of the voyage in *Luisa in Realityland* closely resembles that of the road in the ancient adventure novel of everyday life, which Bakhtin observes:

> . . . fuses the course of an individual's life (at its major turning points) with his actual spatial course or road—that is, with his wanderings . . . The path itself extends through familiar, native territory, in which there is nothing exotic, alien or strange. . . . setting out the road from one's birthplace, returning home are usually plateaus of age in the life of the individual (he sets out as a youth, returns as a man).

When Luisa and her husband Bud return, it is literally to re-root, as they carry their newborn granddaughter's umbilical cord to be buried in the garden of the house in Nicaragua where Luisa was born. In contrast to the male great-grandfather myth which is notable in that: 1) its purpose is emigratory and public, the founding of a new culture; 2) a male initiates the action; and, 3) females are colonized by the action which includes them but which they never initiate, Luisa's return to her birthplace focuses on the private, rather than the public, in which: 1) there is a return to origin and the natural order, rather than a journey to begin a cultural order; 2) a female, rather than a male, Luisa's daughter, plans the action; and, 3) the journey is undertaken with male accord, since Bud and Luisa travel together. Luisa's return to Central American soil thus differs from the emigration myth of the Great-Grandfather which demonstrates a negation of the volition of the female.

Luisa in Realityland further contests myth in the two chapters entitled "The Myth Making Uncles," in which Luisa names her two uncles' "stories" lies. The first uncle, a philosophy professor, has two favorite stories. First he claims he has met Henri Bergson at the Sorbonne, when he has never been in Europe, and second, he glamorizes his escape from the 1932 Izalco massacre, by claiming to have journeyed alone over the Andes, rather than admit that he had lived in Mexico for two years. The second uncle, a military school trained coffee plantation owner, claims to have been a colonel in World War II, rather than admit that he had never been interested in or involved in battle.

Along with such parodies of classical myths, Alegría also conflates the patriarchal myth which views women as either completely innocent and pure, or entirely corrupt. Malinche, the conqueror Cortez's mistress, is vindicated by madness and by her love for the conqueror.[2] Another myth of women as all good, as pious and sanctified "beatas," or all bad, as prostitutes, collapses when Alegria scrutinizes the social context in which these stereotypical roles appear. Of the two prostitutes depicted, one is a loving mother who grieves for her dead son. The other is the impoverished granddaughter of a president of the republic, who, by convention, would have family status to prevent her political and sexual marginalization. In this example, Alegría emphasizes the violence of poverty, since in the face of being denied other means of economic self-sufficiency, the president's granddaughter turns to prostitution.

Along with contesting these institutionalized portrayals of women in *Luisa in Realityland,* Alegría also inserts bits of folklore in the women's tradition which contest and balance masculine myths and tales. The story teller, Mama Nela, relates the tales of the Siguanaba, a bewitcher of men who leaves them idiots, and of Cipitío, the dwarf who strews flower petals in the path of young girls and recites verses to them from his hiding place.

As a part of Alegría's commitment to human rights, she strongly advocates women's rights on a global scale. In the poem "At the Beach," the narrator explains the practice of foot binding in China as mind-binding to the child, Ximena. Women's roles are projected as participative as well as supportive, when Ximena is admonished not only to carry sand, but to keep opening doors, to always join with others, to act as well as serve.

The poem "First Communion" projects the idea of the avoidance of victimization in the face of male violence, rather than its willful infliction or an improbable utopian family without male members. In the poem, Luisa's special wish at her first communion is to have a baby. Since she knows that she cannot have a child if she is not married, she wishes the hypothetical husband dead immediately after the birth. This desire for the avoidance of victimization by male violence is especially notable in "Aunt Filiberta and her Cretonnes," a story in which Alegría exposes the myth of "they lived happily ever after." Aunt Filiberta, a battered woman with many children, is seen through the eyes of the child, Luisa. Filiberta is portrayed as a woman who leaves her husband time after time for the refuge of Luisa's house, while Luisa's father, who overtly opposes oppression in the male arena public sphere, absents himself, virtually ignoring this problem in the private sphere. The apparently romantic act of Filiberta's husband to retrieve her by hiring musicians to serenade her is exposed as the prelude to a show of force, when he subsequently arrives with truck and pistol. This drama of the private sphere reverberates in the public sphere as the husband's patriarchal rights are supported by political force, depicted in the text by the presence of military Guards who scrutinize the reunion through the barred windows of the fortress across the street. Other witnesses of the reunion are children from the nearby ghetto who surround the truck, their presence acting as an omen to Filiberta and her brood, as it foreshadows their future without the tyrannical father. Under these circumstances, Filiberta is virtually forced to endure the brutal situation. She buys new fabric for curtains and for recovering the furniture, in a ritual which hides the old ugly reality at the same time as it figuratively and temporarily hides her husband's violence on the one hand and projects hope for a better future on the other.

Luisa in Realityland also focuses on the poverty which goes hand in hand with Salvadoran violence and political repression. Furthermore, Alegría links First World wealth with Third World poverty as illustrated in the story "The Versailles Tenement," in which the mirrors in the palace at Versailles proliferate and reverse the image of its opulence, as reflected in the poverty of a Santa Ana tenement also named Versailles. The scene of birds in free flight in the forest surrounding the French palace is transformed in the Santa Ana tenement. The forest becomes a birdcage; the free flying birds become a captive dove. Not only is the bird's freedom restricted, it is condemned to die, a victim of the hungry boy Memo's poverty, since the child has no choice but to eat the dove for dinner in the absence of other food. . . .

Luisa in Realityland concludes with a long poem, "The Cartography of Memory," the theme of which is Luisa's exile from a homeland tortured by the steamrollers, bulldozers and hobnails of foreign boots. In the poem, a child's drawing of heads hanging on a black tree, Malinche's betrayal reiterated at Izalco, and corpse-filled rivers, are superimposed with images of childhood memories, of thick-growing ceiba trees and a proliferation of flowers, with the people waiting for the opportunity for change. The poem and the book end with a vision of a future of return and peace. In regard to form, this poem is divided into seven sections forming a pastiche of the poems "Not

Yet," "Malinche," "The Rivers," "The Ceiba," "Seeds of Liberty," "The Volcanos," and "The Return" which appear earlier in the text. By selecting only certain elements for reiteration of what has already been written, Alegría comments on her own text. Death, torture and absence give way to the desire for return to origin. However, this is no nostalgic return to the past, but rather the projection of a utopian return to a rebellious, feminized future. The idea of return as well as that of the future are both bound up in a nationalism, which Fredric Jameson sees as "both healthy and morbid, since both progress and regress are inscribed in its genetic code from the start." In the vein of progress and regress, I would like to conclude by noting that the tortured elements of the text move in the direction of "progress" as they are rewritten in the final poem, in an attempt for a resolution and unification. On the other hand, the tortured elements call for their own end, the fragments of the text call for an end to fragmentation, and the text, in "regression" points to its own deconstruction.

Notes

[1] Culler comments here on Jacques Derrida's notion of grafting. "One ought to explore systematically not only what appears to be a simple etymological coincidence uniting the graft and the graph (both from the Greek *graphion*: writing instrument, stylus), but also the analogy between the forms of textual grafting and so-called vegetal grafting . . ." (*La Dessemination,* 230/202)

[2] Malinche was the Indian woman whom Cortes used as interpreter and mistress during the conquest of Mexico. See Phillips, Rachel. "Marina/Malinche." *Women in Hispanic Literature: Icons and Fallen Idols.* Beth Miller, ed. Berkeley: University of California Press, 1983: 97-114.

Works Cited

Alegría, Claribel. *Luisa in Realityland.* Willimantic, CT: Curbstone, 1987.

Bakhtin, Mikhail M. *The Dialogic Imagination.* ed. Michael Holmquist. trans. Caryl Emerson & Michael Holmquist. Austin: University of Texas Press, 1981.

Culler, Jonathan. *On Deconstruction: Theory and Criticism after Structuralism.* Ithaca: Cornell UP, 1982.

Forché, Carolyn. "Interview with Claribel Alegría," *Index on Censorship,* April, 1984, Vol. 13, No. 2, p. 11-13.

Foucault, Michel. *Discipline and Punish: The Birth of the Prison.* trans. Alan Sheridan. New York: Vintage, 1979.

Franco, Jean. trans. Carlos Pujol. *Historia de la Literatura hispanoamericana: A partir de la Independencia.* Barcelona: Ariel, 1975.

Jameson, Fredric. *The Political Unconscious.* Ithaca: Cornell UP, 1981.

Phillips, Rachel. "Marina/Malinche." *Women in Hispanic Literature: Icons and Fallen Idols.* Beth Miller, ed. Berkeley: University of California Press, 1983: 97-114.

Rama, Angel. "La generación hispanoamericana del medio siglo: Una generación creadora." *Marcha,* XXVI (1217) 2, (Aug. 7, 1964): 2.

Marcia P. McGowan (essay date 1993)

SOURCE: "Mapping a New Territory: *Luisa in Realityland,*" in *Letras Femeninas,* Vol. XIX, Nos. 1-2, Spring-Fall, 1993, pp. 84-99.

[*In the following essay, McGowan examines the visionary nature of* Luisa in Realityland *and praises Alegría's ability to find new ways of expressing ideas and experiences.*]

Claribel Alegría's ***Luisa in Realityland*** is a truly visionary work; not only does it project the story of one woman's struggle and oppression into a "contagious peace" (***"The Return"***), in which she can, paradoxically, "return / to the future," but it challenges all known genres and refuses to be catalogued or restrained by any one label. Moreover, more than visionary, ***Luisa*** is revisionist, in that it offers new ways of depicting themes, images, realities—literally, a *re-vision.* Adrienne Rich offers a useful frame of reference for ***Luisa in Realityland*** in defining "re-vision" as "the art of looking back, of entering an old text from a new critical direction." Re-vision, Rich says, "is for women more than a chapter in a cultural history: it is an act of survival" (**"When We Dead Awaken"**). As the reader follows Luisa on her Alice-like journey, she sees that traditional literary forms are unable to contain Luisa's quest for survival—that several genres are ransacked along the way, and that the route Alegría chooses for ***Luisa*** maps a new territory, one which not only encompasses the "myths and obsessions of gender" (*Blood, Bread, and Poetry*), but discovers a new "tradition in which political struggle and spiritual continuity are meshed" (*Blood, Bread, and Poetry*).

Reviewers of ***Luisa in Realityland*** have called it a "magical-realist memoir," "an autobiographical odyssey in prose and verse" (Volpendesta); a subtle mosaic of poetry, short stories, prose poems of different textures, densities and colors (Sherman, jacket); and "an autobiographical novel alternately written in verse and anecdotal prose vignettes" (Forché). Its book jacket calls it an "autobiographical prose/ verse novel." Alegría admitted to me in an interview that "though some people call it a novel . . . I don't know what to call it; it is a very special book" (October, 1987). When I told her that I thought of her mixture of prose and poetry an experimental technique that worked remarkably well, she agreed, saying, "I felt that the poetry was needed in order to sort of blend everything that I have there. It was very much needed." To my query about her view of ***Luisa*** as a work in which "political struggle and spiritual continuity are meshed," Alegría replied, yes, but added that it had been "done almost subconsciously."

When she told me the story of Julio Cortázar and his wife Aurora's urging her to record her memories, Alegría said of the experiences of her childhood which she includes in

Luisa, "I didn't think those things had any value whatsoever," but that "it is true that by depicting the things that happened to me . . . my 'magical reality,' because I think that in Latin America, as García Marquez has said very well, all the reality is magic . . . in describing that, I was also describing the political and social situation of my country as . . . a continuity. . . . And you know that I didn't realize this until I finished the book and then I read it, and then I read some reviews . . . but it was something that was there, and it was subconscious" (McGowan interview). This meshing of the personal and political can be found throughout *Luisa,* not only in the prose vignettes, but also in the poems, which Alegría regards as "political poems": "They are love poems," she has said, "love poems to my people" (McGowan interview). It is worth noting that this meshing of the personal with the political, while very much a fact of current Latin American literature, has always been germane to feminist literature as well. Feminist poet and critic Adrienne Rich explains that as early as 1956 she experienced "a rejection of the dominant critical idea that the poem's text should be read as separate from the poet's everyday life in the world. It was a declaration that placed poetry in a historical continuity, not above or outside history" (*Blood*). While this declaration might seem less than startling to the Latin American reader, to whom testimony, as well as fiction and poetry, have become as inseparable from politics as the Gypsy from Luisa, in the academies of North America, old ideas about the apolitical purity of poem as text are still very much ascendant. And it is predominantly feminist and minority literature which insists on the importance of *context* as well as text.

My reading of *Luisa in Realityland* is informed by a North American feminist perspective which honors text but also honors context as paramount to the discovery of cultural traditions. I agree which Carolyn Forché's remark that the accumulation of poems at the end of *Luisa* becomes a ". . . complete utterance of one woman's struggle to preserve her past and redeem her present." It is this redemptive power that raises *Luisa* out of the realm of ordinary autobiographical discourse and gives it the power of testimony, as well as qualities of the novel of woman as artist—a female *Künstlerroman.*

In the past ten years, much important critical work has been done in the genre of autobiography which has broadened traditional definitions to the point where as unorthodox a work as *Luisa* can be encompassed by the term. Although the protagonist is named Luisa, Alegría is clearly drawing on her own experience as a child. So thin is the line between Luisa and Claribel that their husbands share the same name, and they share the same time and history. Although the prose passages are most often cast in the third person, at least one prose vignette (**"Wilf [3]"**) begins in the first person plural: "We never saw Wilf again." By temporarily abdicating the use of third person, Alegría projects into Luisa's experience not only herself, but all of those with whom she interacted at that time in El Salvador. In counterpoint to the third person prose vignettes, she casts her poems predominantly in first person; in the poem **"I Like Stroking Leaves,"** she asserts,

and the earth is my body
and I am the body
of the earth
Claribel.

Claribel, not Luisa. And so, at least temporarily, any arbitrary distinction between fiction and memoir or "fact" is erased by the removal of the Luisa "mask," and the experience is related, as in traditional autobiography, as that of the author. But in a work in which reality is magical, anything can happen. And if Alegría is, after all, to borrow Carolyn Heilbrun's term "writing a woman's life," she is, to some extent, writing it symbolically, with the collective experience of a generation of Central Americans and a generation of women in mind.

In *Writing a Woman's Life*, Carolyn Heilbrun cites feminist critic Nancy Miller in addressing the need for stretching traditional conventions of autobiography to encompass women's lives:

> Unlike the reading of the classics--or of men's lives, or of women's lives as events — the destinies of men—which always include 'the frame of *interpretations* that have been elaborated over generations of critical activity,' reading women's lives needs to be considered in the absence of 'a structure of critical' or biographical commonplaces. . . . It all needs to be invented, or discovered, or resaid.

It is in light of this need that I suggest we examine Luisa, which invents a new form of autobiographical discourse, incorporating elements of fiction, poetry, and testimony and allows the writer a measure of control over her life—control which is rare in women's writing. As Heilbrun has noted, "because many women would prefer (or think they would prefer) a world without evident power or control, women have been deprived of the narratives, or the texts, or the plots, or examples, by which they might assume power over . . . their lives." The text of *Luisa in Realityland*, in its insistence on self-discovery within a personal and political framework, offers its writer control over her life through *re-vision.*

Lest we think that Alegría's version of writing a woman's life is not a radical *revision,* we must remember, as Jill Ker Conway points out, that:

> . . . there is no model for the female who is recounting a political narrative. There are no recognizable career stages in such a life, as there would be for a man. Nor do women have a tone of voice in which to speak with authority . . . the expression of anger has always been a terrible hurdle in women's personal progress. (Qtd in Heilbrun)

Though Conway here seems to be defining "politics" in a career context, its application may be broadened to encompass the shifting of power relationships in a new generation of women in Central America, who, as Alegría has said, "are liberating themselves through the liberation of their country" (McGowan). *Luisa* is a work which is acutely aware of power relationships and different kinds

of oppression, a work which, while often elegiac and testimonial, unashamedly embodies the anger of its author,
as in **"Operation Herod"**:

> For each dead child
> ten guerillas are born
> from each one
> of these mutilated bodies
> the virus of fury sprouts
> it is dust
> it is light
> multiplying itself
> the stifled tears of mothers
> water it
> and the Herods die
> riddled by worms.

This is the prophetic anger of a revolutionary in exile—a
woman who, as yet, cannot return to her country, except
through memory, but can find words to express betrayal,
anger, and revenge. Alegría's ability to transcend her anger is due largely to her ultimate belief, alluded to in
"Personal Creed":

> in the resurrection of the oppressed
> in the Church of the people
> in the power of the people
> forever and ever
> Amen.

In her vision those who have disappeared "will come back
/ to judge their slayers," as she one day will return to her
country, completing her own life cycle, to embrace her
ceiba: "the circle is open / I must still return / to close it."
The circle is, of course, a traditional female symbol of
completion fulfillment. Until the time of return, although
Luisa wants to be "a *chiltolta,* a *clarinero,* a *zenzontle,*"
she is "only a buzzard with stubby wings / who limps
through time / wasting away" (**"Tropical Birdland"**). The
dead, the tortured, weigh heavily upon her: "Don't come
any closer," the poet tells the young Luisa in **"From the
Bridge,"** "there's a stench of carrion / surrounding me."
"From the Bridge" is a poem self-confrontation, in which
the poet in the present confronts past images of herself,
addressing them in the second person:

> you learned the consolations
> of philosophy
> before understanding
> why you had to be consoled.

The poet asks her younger self, images of whom parade
before her, to stop at the point when her arms fill with
children:

> it is easy to distract yourself
> with a mother's role
> and shrink the world
> to a household.
> Stop there
> don't come any closer
> you still wouldn't recognize me

> you still have to undergo
> the deaths of Roque
> or Rodolfo
> all those innumerable deaths
> that assail you
> pursue you
> define you
> in order to dress in these feathers
> (my feathers of mourning)
> to peer out
> through these pitiless
> scrutinizing eyes
> to have my claws
> and this sharp beak.

But as much as she might bemoan the agony of peering
out with her "pitiless / scrutinizing eyes," it is these eyes
which enable her to share with us a vision not only of the
past, but also of a redemptive future.

But before I go on to *Luisa*'s redemptive visions, I should
say a few more words about the formal elements of *Luisa*.
I have mentioned above some autobiographical elements,
and have asserted that *Luisa* is more than the fairly typical experimental venture that Alan West attributes to the
Latin American writer, who, as Borges once stated, "moves
freely beyond European national traditions and, therefore,
combines at will a variety of styles and forms." In an
essay in *Breaking Boundaries: Latina Writing and Critical Readings,* Eleana Ortega and Nancy Saporta Sternbach have referred to a genre "still to be defined and still
emerging, which specifically articulates Latina experience,"
drawing on "the Latina as storyteller," and situating "the
speaking voice in a genre somewhere in between poetry
and fiction, blurring the line between the short story and
the novel, between conversation and literary discourse."
Certainly, Claribel Alegría is a storyteller, but unlike her
Latina sisters in the United States, she is not "blurring the
line between the short story and the novel," but between
fiction and autobiography. If we concede a conversational
quality to her prose, it springs from direct quotation and
dialogue; in her poetry, from apostrophe or direct address.

More useful, it seems to me, in trying to understand the
wonderfully anomalous structure of *Luisa,* is Paul John
Eakin's explanation of the shifting boundaries between
autobiography and fiction in *Fictions in Autobiography:
Studies in the Art of Self-Invention.* Eakin contends that
"autobiographical truth is not a fixed but an evolving
content in an intricate process of self-discovery and self-
creation" and that "the self that is at the center of all
autobiographical narrative is necessarily a fictive structure." The autobiographers he discusses—Jean-Paul Sartre, Mary McCarthy, Henry James, and Maxine Hong Kingston—"freely avow the presence of fiction in their art," and
so, I am sure would Claribel Alegría, for in one of the first
prose vignettes in *Luisa* we are told, "In Luisa's family
there were many fabulous liars, including herself, of course"
(**"The Myth-Making Uncles [1]"**). One of Luisa's uncles,
who has never left Santa Ana, manages to convince himself, the French consul, and many friends not only that he
has studied in Paris, but that he has met Henri Bergson

and traveled with him to the south of France. This is a liar, a "myth-maker," a fictionist extraordinaire. And so is Claribel Alegría, whose magical reality includes ghosts, a deaf-mute woman who can "communicate with everyone in town" and whose cane Luisa and Bud keep in their house in Deyá, and six charming deaf-mute dwarfs who rent the house that once belonged to the deaf-mute woman, which passes, eventually, through Luisa and Bud's intermediary hands.

The text of *Luisa in Realityland,* in its insistence on self-discovery within a personal and political framework, offers its writer control over her life through revision.

—Marcia P. McGowan

Luisa's lies are generally honorable, not only in the tradition of the storyteller, but also in the tradition of her father, who lies to safeguard Farabundo Marti, and in the tradition of the Chilean girl who lies at the bidding of a prisoner who would rather be tortured and killed than have her acknowledge the truth—the she knows him—to the enemy. However, Luisa's lies can be mischievous, as well, as when she denies her own identity in **"Eunice Avilés"** and tells a man who is a painter that she, too, is one, though she regards herself as a failed painter and has abandoned this avocation. Seemingly out of control, she heaps lie upon lie until she sends him to Mikonos with the hope of meeting her there. "Good grief! Why did I do that," she asks herself when he is gone, then consoles herself by thinking, "Maybe something nice will happen to him on the island, and if it hadn't been for my absurd fibs he would never have gone. Besides, who knows? He may find the Gypsy waiting for him when he arrives."

Clearly, Alegría places herself squarely within the tradition of storytellers as "liars." Yet if we concede both a lie and an autobiography to be fictive constructs, we can understand why William Maxwell, whose *So Long, See you Tomorrow* has "equal claims," according to Eakin, "to being a memoir and a novel . . ." can say, "In any case, in talking about the past we lie with every breath we draw" (Qtd Eakin). Eakin says, in alluding to Mary McCarthy's "A Tin Butterfly" in *Memories of a Catholic Girlhood*:

> . . . autobiographical truth is not a fixed but an evolving content, what we call fact and fiction being rather slippery variables in an intricate process of self-discovery. In view of the complex interrelationship between the remembered incident and its expression in art, we must discard any notion of the juxtaposition of story and commentary as representing a simple opposition between fiction and fact, since fiction can have for the author . . . the status of remembered fact.

Adding to this comment Elizabeth Bruss's contention that "there is no intrinsically autobiographical form" (Qtd Eakin), anyone acquainted with the variety of works cus-

tomarily identified as autobiography should recognize that *Luisa* seems to fit rather easily into this genre despite, or perhaps even because of, its many fictions. It is not, however, simply an autobiography, but a peculiarly female autobiography, not only in form, but in many of the issues it confronts.

In examining women's autobiographies through the centuries, Estelle Jelinek notes in *Women's Autobiography: Essays in Criticism* that though men's autobiography is most often chronological, orderly, directional, and possessed of a linear narrative, women's autobiography rejects these characteristics. Jelinek has found that "irregularity rather than orderliness informs the self-portraits of women":

> The narratives of their lives are often not chronological and progressive but disconnected, fragmentary, or organized into self-sustained units rather than connecting chapters. The multidimensionality of women's socially conditioned roles seems to have established a pattern of diffusion and diversity when they write their autobiographies, and so by established critical standards, their life studies are excluded from the genre and cast into the "nonartistic" categories of memoir, reminiscence, and other disjunctive forms.

Although there might at first seem to be no discontinuity in *Luisa in Realityland,* the more discerning reader can perceive interrelationships not only through the numbering of certain prose vignettes, but also through the symbolical connections of each prose vignette with others and with the poetry. Images of blood, trees, birds, claws, violence, mirrors and photographs, circles, masks, monsters, water, the sun, and the rainbow appear throughout *Luisa.* Indeed, it is largely through these symbols that the work moves toward transcendence and redemption. *Luisa in Realityland* is structured symbolically in a manner similar to Virginia Woolf's *To the Lighthouse* and Maxine Hong Kingston's *The Woman Warrior*. In each of these works, it is through images and symbols that the author's identification with place becomes most clear.

The first poem in Luisa, suffused with longing, asks,

> How was my ceiba?
> the one facing the park
> the one to which
> I made a promise?

Alegría senses the map of her homeland in the foliage of the tree which she longs—despite its size—to encircle in an embrace. She must return "to close" the circle, though, as in the Catholic ritual, Stations of the Cross, "the final station / is always the hardest." If the tree signifies home, it is "strange plants" growing defiantly through bulldozed earth to which she attributes the **"Seeds of Liberty"** which must free her country from centuries of oppression. I have already spoken of the author's identification with the earth in **"I Like Stroking Leaves."** In **"Epitaph"** the poet wants no gravestone, but "fresh grass / and a flowering jasmine." By **"Autumn Bonfire"** it becomes clear that she so closely identifies with her tree that she feels able to speak for it, as indeed, she speaks, through transcription, for the Gypsy who appears in her dreams:

> And now everything is covered with smoke
> my roots
> my leaves
> my back
> all burning in the fire
> of this autumn
> dying suddenly
> in another body
> amid a feast of flames
> and murmurs.

The roots of the tree, the author's roots,

> are freedom
> and death
> and labyrinth
> the beginning
> and the end.

Alegría and her roots are inseparable, light and dark, yin and yang. Even as they split apart,

> above the clear abyss
> of a bonfire
> they search
> tangle together
> separate
> explode in sparks
> like an outburst of cries
> and are nucleus
> and memory
> and tomorrow.

Through the vision conveyed by the image of the tree, Alegría achieves simultaneity of past, present, and future. Through the presence of the poems, which, as Suzanne Ruta has so aptly noted, have an incantatory presence, and "like a Greek chorus, deepen the reach of a prose chapter." Alegría achieves not fragmentation, but integration of some of her major themes: time, identity, continuity, exile. In fact, this is a work in which the identification of the author with her land is total, so that not only does she, oracle-like, speak prophetically for the land, but the land, through pathetic fallacy, "speaks," as in **"The Volcanoes,"** to the muchachos. In **"Seeds of Liberty,"** the identification is so complete that:

> The muchachos
> the plants
> climb towards the future
> toward the sun.

It is largely through images like these that the reader is able to feel the hope in this extraordinary work. The balance of such positive images juxtaposed against such horrible images as the bulldozers flattening, ripping, tearing into El Salvador's crust enables the reader to perceive in Alegría not only the agony of exile, but the hope of return. Alegría does not allow the reader to lose sight of the fact that hope can grow from anguish, that a moment can be beautiful and also cause pain. She balances, exquisitely, images of anguish and joy until it seems, as Alan West has noted, that her poems themselves are like trees, "where many things have fallen out of the branches (gods, illusions, friends), and yet a few stubborn leaves remain 'like steel propellers / resisting.'"

Such balance belies the impression that women's autobiography has developed in "discontinuous forms." *Luisa,* which might at first glance seem to be fragmented, is a highly integrated work of art, one which draws upon the public as well as the private nature of women's lives, and takes seriously the possibility that many feminist writers are currently exploring, of "expanding the possibilities of formal autobiography" (Juhasz).

One way in which Alegría expands the possibilities of formal autobiography is through adding some testimonial elements to *Luisa in Realityland. Testimonio,* oddly enough, appears in her poetry as well as in her prose. As John Beverly states in an excellent essay, "The Margin at the Center: On *Testimonio* (Testimonial Narrative)," ". . . *testimonio* is not . . . fiction. We are meant to experience both the speaker and the situations and events recounted, as real. The situation of the narrator in *testimonio* is one that must be representative of a social class or group." I have already described the symbolic and representational quality of *Luisa in Realityland*. What is unusual and innovative is that although the entire work, in the sense of *testimonio,* bears witness to the horrors of living in a particular time and place, the first person narration most often occurs in the poetry, and the *heroine* of the work is the transcriber of the experience. It is the illiterate Gypsy, the easy inhabitant of Luisa's dreamworld, who dictates the poetry for Luisa to transcribe. And the poetry bears witness to the oppression of a people:

> In my country
> some time ago
> the soldiers
> began killing children
> bruising the tender flesh
> of children
> tossing babies
> into the air
> on bayonets.
>
>   (**"Operation Herod"**)

I am well aware that *testimonio* is usually defined as "a novel or novella-length narrative in book or pamphlet . . . form, told in the first person by a narrator who is also the real protagonist or witness of the events he or she recounts, and whose unit of narration is usually a 'life' or a significant life experience" (Beverly). Both the first person poems and third person narrative prose vignettes, however, convey the impression of "bearing witness," for if in the poetry we hear a first person voice often juxtaposed against other voices, in each prose vignette, the third person narrator most often insists that the protagonist speak for him or herself. Listen to the testimonial quality first in a poetic fragment from **"The Rivers"**:

The terrain in my country
is abrupt
the gullies go dry
in the summertime
and are stained with red
in the winter.
The Sumpul is boiling with corpses
a mother said
The Goascaran
the Lempa
are all boiling with the dead.

Then juxtapose a prose fragment addressing Chilean repression from **"The Blue Theater"**:

"There is nothing to be afraid of," [the guard] said, "all you have to do is say yes or no when I ask you a question. Bring him in," he ordered the first man.

"There were only two chairs covered in blue plastic. The guard sat down in one, and I was left standing. A few seconds later, two more guards entered, dragging a young man between them."

Each experience is personalized, yet is indicative of a wider experience in a country that has been so often brutalized by "a heavy boot / with foreign hobnails" (**"Not Yet"**).

I have quoted John Beverly above as saying of *testimonio* that the narrator's situation must be representative of a social class or group. The surrealistic episode of **"The Blue Theatre"** seems all too representative of the brutality of the oppressor toward the oppressed. The voice in the poetic fragment also "speaks for, or in the name of a community or group" (Beverly). Each of these episodes "evokes an absent polyphony of other voices . . . ." (Beverly). Beverly says that testimony is, to use Umberto Eco's slogan, an "'open work' that implies the importance and power of literature as a form of social action . . . ". His essay suggests, as does much of feminist criticism, that there are experiences in the world today that would be betrayed or misrepresented by the forms of literature "as we know them" and that testimony is a response to the inadequacy of conventional literary forms to give representation to social struggle. Testimony, Beverly argues, "is an instance of the New Left and feminist slogan that the personal is the political." And the testimonial elements of *Luisa in Realityland* are one more instance of Alegría's commitment to overcoming oppression of all kinds.

To return in greater detail to the feminist elements in Luisa, Carolyn Heilbrun aptly notes, "the woman who writes herself a life beyond convention . . . has usually recognized in herself a special gift without name or definition. Its most characteristic indication is the dissatisfaction it causes her to feel with appropriate gender assignments." We see Luisa at a very early age beginning to chafe at the constraints of her sex. In **"Taking the Vows"** Luisa and her friend Isabel act as maids of honor for Sor Ana Teresa, who is going to be "married to God": "The mother superior approached the pew where Sor Ana Teresa knelt, removed her bridal veil,

and with a huge pair of shears hacked off her lovely chestnut hair just above the ears." After that Father Agapito announces that she has "died to the world." It becomes clear that Luisa does not see the priests and nuns as God's exemplars in this act of submission to patriarchy:

"Why didn't God show up?" Luisa asked herself.

"If he had, I'll bet he wouldn't have let them cut off all that lovely hair."

When questioned about this story, Alegría replied,

This submission of the nun, this cutting of her hair, this renouncing to the world is very much like it used to be in El Salvador to be a woman. To be a woman, to be born a girl was already a submission. For instance men, always, didn't like to have little girls; they always wanted little boys, because little boys were going to do something . . . But little girls, no . . . To be born a girl was like . . . all of this hair [being cut] and dying to this world. (McGowan)

Alegría is very much aware of the feminist struggle in Europe and North America and has stated that she accepts and admires it, but she emphasizes that the issue of hunger will have to be "solved" in Central America before feminism can advance beyond where it has presently evolved (McGowan).

In **"First Communion"** Luisa participates in another patriarchal religious rite which the women of her household tell her is "the most important day of her life." She decides that her wish upon this occasion is well worth a sacrifice, and after taking the host in her mouth, she prays,

"Dear little Jesus . . . I don't want to be married; I don't like the way men treat women, but I do want to have a baby, Dear Jesus, and Chabe says that only married women can have babies. So that's why I ask you with all my heart to let me get married, and as soon as I have my baby, to let my husband die."

Clearly, Luisa has grown conscious of the treatment to which men often subject women through members of her family like Aunt Filiberta, who arrives at Luisa's house "at least three times a year" in an ox-cart with all her children because of Uncle Alfonso's having beaten her again. Luisa has also refused to believe, in **"I'm a Whore; Are You Satisfied?"** in the collective wisdom of a society which tells her, "Whore was a bad word. Whores were bad women." Instead, after entering into the antiseptically clean and chastely decorated room of a whore who gives Luisa caramels and after recognizing the whore's humanity, Luisa tells her cousin, Carlos, who reiterates society's stereotype, "You're the one who's bad," and runs toward home. It is Luisa's curiosity, her refusal to accept the so-called "wisdom" of her elders in matters of sex and gender, as much as her determination to speak for those who have been silenced, that foreshadows her vocation as a writer.

One poem, in particular, in *Luisa in Realityland*, illustrates Alegría's awareness of the oppressive effects of *machismo* in her society and of male domination of women cross-culturally. In **"At the Beach,"** the adult Luisa is comforting a little girl who has been wounded by her boy cousins. She tells the girl a story of how, in China, women's feet were bound and their nails were let to grow "until they were claws." She explains,

> It's not that they were useless
> it's that their husbands
> their fathers
> their brothers
> wanted them like that
> a luxury object
> or a slave.
> This still happens
> all around the world
> It's not that their feet are bound
> it's their minds, Ximena,
> there are women who accept
> and others who don't.

Then she tells the story of how Rafaela Herrera frightened Lord Nelson into defeat by using firecrackers and flaming sheets. She concludes, unforgettably:

> Your twisted thumb
> is like being a woman
> you have to use it a lot
> and you'll see how well it heals.
> Run along and play now
> don't carry sand for others
> help your cousins
> to build the castle
> put towers on it
> and walls
> and terraces
> and knock it down
> and rebuild it
> and keep on opening doors.
> Don't carry sand
> let them do it
> for a while
> let them bring you
> buckets full of sand.

Certainly, there is a feminist consciousness at work in *Luisa,* a consciousness which acknowledges the damaging effects of male domination, *machismo.* Alegría has said, "*Machismo* is a thing that is very terribly rooted . . . in all Latin America, in Central America. Even women who have important jobs have to wait on men in Cuba, Nicaragua, El Salvador. This is a very hard thing to eradicate . . . and I don't know how many generations it's going to be until men understand . . ." (McGowan). When asked if her travels have revealed to her what is shared cross-culturally among women, she replied, "a sense of oppression," and she sees as a common strength that "we all are struggling to gain the same liberation," as well as a shared interest in peace.

I don't want to belabor Alegría's feminism, but it offers a confirmation of perceptions that she shares cross-culturally with other women, especially with women artists. We have already seen that there is in Alegría what Rich calls "an organic relation between poetry and social transformation" (*Blood*). In *Luisa in Realityland,* the life of the artist, herself, is submerged in a narrative which emphasizes and identifies with the collective lives of her people, the life of her country. Like the autobiographies of Emmeline Parkhurst, Dorothy Day, Emma Goldman, Eleanor Roosevelt, and Golda Meir, Alegría's autobiography fails "directly to emphasize [her] own importance, though writing in a genre which implies self-assertion and self-display" (Spacks). As Linda Huf notes in *A Portrait of the Artist as a Young Woman,* "women have frequently balked at portraying themselves in literature as would-be writers—or as painters, composers, or actresses, who, as self-portraits of their creators, are invariably surrogate authors. Unlike men, women have only rarely written artist-novels; that is, autobiographical novels depicting their struggles to become creative artists—to become, as the Romantics had it, as gods."

In many respects, ***Luisa in Realityland*** is a portrait of the artist as a young woman. Luisa exhibits many characteristics of the artist-heroine. She is "stalwart, spirited" and seemingly "fearless" (Huf). Luisa, like many contemporary artists in the female *Künstlerroman,* "is torn not only between life and art but, more specifically, between her role as a woman, demanding selfless devotion to others, and her aspirations as an artist, requiring exclusive commitment, to her work." She refuses to distract herself "with a mother's role / and shrink the world / to a household." Innumerable deaths "pursue" and "define" her. The Gypsy, who dictates poems to Luisa, disappears for several years and only comes back when Luisa stops having children and takes up painting. The Gypsy functions as more than the traditional muse; Luisa is the transcriber of the Gypsy's poetry.

Linda Huf declares that today's artist-heroine "sees herself as having been reborn—as an artist." Certainly, there are many images of rebirth in *Luisa in Realityland.* Water is a dominant image. In **"The Rivers,"** Alegría says of El Salvador's dead: "the dead sail down / and the sea receives them / and they revive." In her poem **"Rediscovering America,"** she invites her love to "settle / into a world/ that is ours / it's a river / that flows / and is filled with voices." The poet declares,

> This is my world,
> love,
> but different;
> a second birth
> a new world.

And in **"The Cartography of Memory,"** Alegría repeats seven poems that have appeared earlier in *Luisa*—seven, the magic number—the number of the colors in the rainbow: an image of hope and promise. The single candle which illuminates Luisa's view of Wilf and of her small world in the first vignette becomes by the final poetic sequence diffracted, through the prism of art, the prism of the Gypsy and her "iridescent soap bubble," into a spectrum of color capable of bridging the past, present and future. As the last poems, in their repetition, complete the circle that was begun in **"The Ceiba,"** Alegría, through paradox, maps a new territory and offers us her final *re-vision*:

> Once more there'll be peace
> But of a different kind.
> The rainbow glimmers
> tugs at me
> forcefully
> not that inert peace
> of shrouded eyes
> it will be a rebellious
> contagious peace
> a peace that opens furrows
> and aims at the stars.
> The rainbow shatters
> the sky splits open
> rolls up like a scroll
> of shadows
> inviting us to enter
> and be dazzled.
> Come, love, let's return
> to the future.

Works Cited

Alegría, Claribel. *Luisa in Realityland*. Trans. by Darwin J. Flakoll. Willimantic, Ct.: Curbstone Press, 1987.

Beverly, John. "The Margin at the Center: On Testimonio (Testimonial Narrative)." *Modern Fiction Studies* 35, 1 (Spring, 1989): 11-26.

Eakin, Paul John. *Fictions in Autobiography: Studies in the Art of Self-Invention*. Princeton: PUP, 1985.

Forché, Carolyn. "The Ghosts of a Central American Girlhood," *Los Angeles Times*, 15 Nov. 1987: 3-10.

Heilbrun, Carolyn G. *Writing a Woman's Life*. NYC: Norton, 1988.

Horno-Delgado, Asunción, Eliana Ortega, Nina M. Scott, and Nancy Saporta Sternback, eds. *Breaking Boundaries: Latina Writings and Critical Readings*. Amherst: Mass UP, 1989.

Huf, Linda. *A Portrait of the Artist as a Young Woman: The Writer as Heroine in American Literature*. NYC: Ungar, 1985.

Jelinek, Estelle C., ed. *Women's Autobiography: Essays in Criticism*. Bloomington: Indiana UP, 1980.

Juhasz, Suzanne. "Towards a Theory in Form in Feminist Autobiography. Kate Millett's *Flying* and *Sita*; Maxine Hong Kingston's *The Woman Warrior*," in *Woman's Autobiography: Essays in Criticism*. Ed. Estelle C. Jelinek. Bloomington: Indiana UP, 1980.

McGowan, Marcia P. Interview with Claribel Alegría. *ECSU: WECS*, October 1987.

Rich, Adrienne. *Blood, Bread, and Poetry*. NYC: Norton, 1986.

——. "When We Dead Awaken: Writing as Re-vision," *On Lies, Secrets, and Silence*. NYC: Norton, 1979.

Ruta, Suzanne. "Witness to the Persecution." *Village Voice* 2 Feb. 1988: 61.

Spacks, Patricia Meyer, "Selves in Hiding," *Women's Autobiography: Essays in Criticism*. Ed. Estelle C. Jelinek. Bloomington: Indiana UP, 1980.

Volpendesta, David. "Surreal Estate," *In These Times* 16-22 Dec 1987: 24.

West, Alan. "Latin American Writing: Language and Spies, Resistance and Redemption." *AGNI* 28 (Apr 1989): 248-265.

Sandra M. Boschetto-Sandoval (essay date 1994)

SOURCE: "Quasi-Testimonial Voices in Claribel Alegría's *Luisa in Realityland*: A Feminist Reading Lesson," in *Claribel Alegría and Central American Literature: Critical Essays*, edited by Sandra M. Boschetto-Sandoval and Marcia Phillips McGowan, Ohio University Center for International Studies, 1994, pp. 97-110.

[*In the following essay, Boschetto-Sandoval relates* Luisa in Realityland *to women's testimonials and contends that Alegría constructs literary relationships with her readers in order to foster cultural and political change.*]

In a recent analysis of women's testimonials, Lilian Manzor-Coats (1990) writes that the place of *testimonio* in relation to literature is very similar to the place the "disappeared" have within their repressive societies: "at the crossroads between history and fiction, or, better yet, at that limbo site of encounter between untold history and fiction." This site of encounter becomes in women's testimonials a site of resistance, offering the narrator/reader not only an alternative vision to history, but the possibility of her rearticulation in history. The process also foregrounds what Mary Jacobus (1979) describes as feminist metafiction: a "transgression of literary boundaries that exposes those very boundaries for what they are—the product of phallocentric discourse."

Encompassing issues of testimony, memory, boundary fluidity, and feminist reading practice, Elizabeth Meese (1990) points recently to the feminist desire to be inclusive and to reject the "metalogical conflict between theoretical discourses on 'women' and politically committed feminist action in the world." Convinced that criticism is best written and spoken in the dialectic of theory *and* practice, Meese chooses to engage herself with specific texts which present in her words, "reading lessons" concerning the dialectic between critical practice and practical struggle. Meese contends that when readers consider texts by women from other cultures, they not only resist the "geographical imperialism of English studies," they also engage in a subversive praxis, a complicitous negotiation between individual and collective identity. Meese's theoretical framework refigures women's testimonial voice as defining a relationship between the consolidation of identity (individual or personal and collective/feminist) and "the politics of inclusion which threatens the notion of singular identity but appears to be politically necessary for a socially effective and responsible feminism" (Meese 1990).

To read the poeticized testimonial prose/verse novel *Luisa in Realityland* by Claribel Alegría is to expose a feminist reading lesson. Here, indeed, is a text that not only straddles boundaries, but presents a kaleidoscopic approach to the question of relationships among art, politics, language, and identity. Described as a "self-conscious antithesis to the world of 'wonderland'" (Fisher 1989), Alegría's quasi-testimonial novel attempts to invent a linguistic structure that will reach out and accommodate areas of experience (both personal and political) normally inaccessible to language.

Luisa in Realityland, a text which, according to Alegría herself, "doesn't 'fit' comfortably into accepted literary categories" (Agosin 1988), is a novel that alternates some fifty prose vignettes with approximately forty poems, all of differing lengths and formats. Rather than convey a sharp contrast between two overt discourses, one poetic, the other testimonial, Alegría's novel merely elucidates the difficulty of differentiating the personal from the political and ultimately the political from the artistic. The language of the narrator, which constantly shifts between witnessing and self-inventing, is heterogenous, always acknowledging other discourses and establishing a dialogue with other texts. *Luisa in Realityland* exemplifies the hybrid "dialogic" and polyphonic form theorized by Mikhail Bakhtin (Holquist 1981) and, more recently, by Dale Bauer (1988, 13), who describes the dialogical imperative as a "necessary confusion": "'Confused' is the focal term: we are meant to be unsettled by these dialogues . . . just as we are meant to be unsettled by feminist criticism which seeks to shake up the critical communities which do not acknowledge the excluded margins."

Along with the interweaving of poetry, narrative, and document, the polyphonic text of *Luisa* evokes an hallucinatory realm, what Jean Franco (1985) calls the "deterritorialization of feminine space." "Horrible things are happening," recalls Luisa's mother in the novel. Violence and repression have brought about the violation of sacred spaces of refuge for women and children—identified by Franco as home, convent, and brothel. In *Luisa* these former "eulogized spaces" are transformed into sites of resistance: guerilla bunkers to which combatants retreat when necessary. The family home in Santa Ana becomes not only a refuge for victims of violence and massacre (**"Felix"**), but a hiding place, an escape hatch for revolutionaries (**"Farabundo Marti"**). The personal becomes political in the de-eulogized sanctuary of the home where women become signifiers of resistance. "The dead need to be remembered and to be named so they don't fall into limbo," her mother tells Luisa in **"Litanies."** "The increasing number of the dead began to weigh on [Luisa]. . . . The problem was, what could she do to keep the list from becoming endless?" This initial recollection at the beginning of the novel is not merely a foreshadowing of Luisa/Alegría's vocation to speak for those who have been silenced. It also serves to foreground the oppositional

potentialities of the women characters in/outside the novel and the praxis (theory in action of politics) which produces the very text we are reading.

Breaking *with* tradition to signal breaks *in* tradition, the structure of Alegría's text conjoins literary and sociopolitical critique. Through the interplay of narrative and verse, love and death, the reader is invited to (re)imagine, (re)invent, and (re)present a sociohistorical reality. These (re)positionings and (re)inventions also reflect a plurality of resistances. Sandwiched between the mad woman's harangue against social injustice and Roque Dalton's "via crucis," for example, is Alegría's own intrusion of everyday commonplaces, like love, "a torpid gesture," one that enters "through the window / pirouetting on a tightrope."

Along with shaping a (re)visionary revolution in the letter, Alegría's quasi-testimonial novel reflects the shift from a politics of restrictive identity to a potentially productive polyvalence. Luisa embraces a shifting and multiple identity which is in a state of perpetual transition. The images of "dismemberment" in the opening of **"The Ceiba"** reverberate throughout the text. The "sweeping fragments" which "alter [her] rhythm," "that unhinge" the narrator echo in the **"Final Act,"** wherein the little girl is transformed into a lifeless rag doll. While "innumerable deaths" assail, pursue, and eventually *define* the narrator in "well-planned disorder," at the conclusion of the writing she has "freed [herself] at last." In **"The Cartography of Memory,"** memory and imagination have conspired to "write beyond the ending," and to bring a dazzling future into potential view:

> The rainbow shatters
> the sky splits open
> rolls up like a scroll
> of shadows
> inviting *us* to enter
> and be dazzled.
> Come, love, *let's* return
> to the future.
>   (emphasis is mine)

Luisa in Realityland reproduces a strategy common to the majority of women's testimonials, wherein according to Doris Sommer (1988) "self ultimately achieves its identity as an extension of the collective." The slippage between attention to one's own individuality (the autobiographical voice) and a focus on the social constraints of that individuality (the testimonial voice) is a reminder that life "not only continues at the margins of Western discourse, but continues to disturb and to challenge it" (Sommer 1988). The illusion of singularity, "of standing *in* for others as opposed to standing *up* among them," which Doris Sommer (1988) accuses autobiography of nurturing, is dispelled in *Luisa* in various ways. The first-person singular is not the only voice marshaled in *Luisa* to narrate a plural history. The imperializing cult of individuality and even loneliness is replaced with a collective consciousness which extends the collective potential for resistance. What the novel articulates is a quasi-subversion of the autobiographical genre, for here the autobiographer's concern is not the creation of a monolithic self, but rather the construction of the self as a member of multiple oppressed groups, whose political identity can never be divorced from her conditions. *Luisa in Realityland* mirrors, therefore, a testimonial subject construction in which a community of narrators reconstructs the life of a revolutionary subject, in this case Luisa/Alegría. The voice and authority of the narrator, whose "body" cannot be easily located within the text, are replaced in the novel by that of a compiler whose task it is to "agglutinate" diverse sectors of the population, to merge discourse spaces and sites into one collective representativeness.[1] Hence, the revolutionary subject "emerges" ultimately as the collective pueblo. The narrator's **"Personal Creed"** is a dedicatory "standing up among" that collective.

If, as Sommer argues, testimonials are fundamentally about constructing relationships between the self and the reader, in order to invite and precipitate change (revolution), then *Luisa* is a text of complicitous readership. Meese (1990) contends that in women's testimonials "there is always 'more,' some otherness that exceeds the simple projection of identity . . . the simple projection of opposites." In *Luisa in Realityland* the reader must contend with these gaps and slippages between speech and silence as well, between the way in which the symbolic order does or does not (re)present woman, and "the effort of woman to bring herself into representation, to show herself." An example of this "something more" of which Meese speaks is captured in the poem **"Malinche,"** in which Malinche cannot be portrayed as merely perfidious or victimized, but must be depicted as caught in the in between of that symbolic representation.

> The child knows it all
> guesses it
> five hundred years ago
> Malinche
> handed the invader
> her continent
> handed it over out of love
> out of madness.
> He always knew it
> knew it yesterday
> when he watched
> his father's head fall
> while trying
> to tell him something.
> Treacherous Malinche
> the blossoms of her love
> dropped away
> and there remained heads
> dangling like seedpods.
> Fifty years ago
> the bewitched tree
> (the Indian girl repented
> and embraced it weeping)
> again produced
> a harvest of skulls
> Izalco wept
> dry tears
> and the country mourned.
>
>   . . . . .

> The malinche tree is perfidious
> The Indian girl baptized it
> bewitched it.

Alegría represents here an "official/original" language encased in the optics of alien, marginalized discourses, languages against which the speaker speaks. The reading problem of this poem simulates woman's (Luisa's) position in general, always speaking in another language, in another relationship to the language of power. The poem can be read as a "pre-text" reflecting a dialectic of information and counterinformation. **"Malinche"** is in fact a "mixed blood" text, the origin and meaning of which, like the body of Alegría's narrator, remain slippery and unsettling, thus inviting further speculation and questioning. Resistance clearly accompanies all forms of domination. It is not always identifiable, however, because it inheres in the very gaps, fissures, and silences of hegemonic narratives. It is thus that Alegría's "mixed" voice functions as a form of resistance against authority.

The nonhegemonic, negotiating feminism of *Luisa in Realityland* slips equally, then, between speech and silence, the personal and collective identities required of revolutionaries for their very survival. In its multiplicity of gestures, movements, and operations, *Luisa in Realityland* affords the reader an overarching perspective of "feminisms" which permit transgressions and "border crossings," a fluid female boundary wherein identities converge and diverge. In this extension of people, places, things, and time beyond the boundaries, feminism is not segregated from political resistance. Instead it is placed in "metonymic relationship" with it. Sommer (1988) recognizes a fundamental difference between the *metaphor* of autobiography and heroic narrative in general, "which assumes an identity by substituting one (superior) signifier for another (I for we, leader for follower . . .) and *metonymy,* a lateral identification through relationship, which acknowledges the possible differences among 'us' as components of the whole." The singular in *Luisa in Realityland* represents the plural not because it replaces or subsumes the group, but because the speaker is a distinguished part of the whole. In testimonial complicity with such (ex)centric feminisms as those displayed by the prostitute in **"I'm a Whore; Are you Satisfied?",** by Paulina in **"The President's Sheet,"** by Aunt Filiberta and her "flowered cretonnes," by Crazy Pastora in **"The Mad Woman of the Grand Armee,"** and finally by the redhaired, crazy grandmother in **"Granny and the Golden Bridge,"** the narrator challenges us as readers to recognize existing and potential relationships that extend her/our community through the text.

Even if the reader cannot identify with the speaker to imagine taking her place (i.e., in a "politically" resistant manner of speaking), the map of possible identifications through the text of *Luisa* spreads out laterally, enabling the narrator along with her readers to recognize themselves in a metonymic relationship of shared experience and consciousness. Thus, one additional reading lesson of Alegría's narrative is that we cannot identify with a single subject of the narration, but must instead entertain the difficult idea of several simultaneous points of activity, several simultaneous and valid roles.

Feminisms in *Luisa in Realityland* refigure themselves as "strategies," which, as Meese (1990) contends, to remain strategic, must "adopt the clever, chameleonlike hue of the guerrilla fighter—here and then gone again." One such tactic is the narrator's refusal to engage in the consequences of linear narrative—a refusal which stands in defiance of the common expectations of the life stories of women. Prolonged, nondiscursive pauses permeate the text; madness (**"Nightmare in Chinandega"** and **"The Blue Theatre"**), silence, and nonverbal spaces offer a challenge to linearity. The overlapping of prose and verse genres also reflects a discourse imbued with a language of refusal; a negotiated "confusion" between conventional and nonconventional form, between a masculine prosaics and a feminine lyricism.

> **Rather than convey a sharp contrast between two overt discourses, one poetic, the other testimonial, *Luisa in Realityland* merely elucidates the difficulty of differentiating the personal from the political and ultimately the political from the artistic.**
>
> —*Sandra M. Boschetto-Sandoval*

Despite the many silences and the frustrated/frustrating attempts to speak in the gaps, there is no mistaking the oral undertones of the narratives which make up the text, an orality which helps once again to account for the collective nature of *Luisa in Realityland*. The various "mythmaking" aunts, uncles, and grandfathers who populate the text of Alegría's novel reflect not only the rural tradition of storytelling with roots in indigenous survival, but, more significantly, what Manzor-Coats (1990) describes as the "defamiliarization of history into story." Paradoxically, the "reality" effect is not lessened but intensified through this process. Thus, the text of *Luisa* reflects a variety of counterdiscourses, or stories, not so much competing for authority as acknowledging that no one version of history can be ultimately authoritative.

One of the most significant feminist strategies undertaken in Alegría's novel is the simulated and extended conversation between Luisa/Alegría and the so-termed "Gypsy" who, like Luisa, straddles the fiction/reality border in *Luisa in Realityland*. In **"Luisa and the Gypsy,"** we note that Luisa was frightened because the Gypsy is "terribly daring . . . impatient with her fears." The Gypsy encourages Luisa to keep on with her painting, "and started dictating love poems to her. Since she was *illiterate,* she had to dictate them to Luisa who, as soon as she woke, would *write* them down on a special notebook she kept by her bedside." Luisa is left at times unable to understand the Gypsy, this other self who speaks in the gap, who represents the silent exclusion that operates within and at the boundaries of discourse. The narrator notes of the Gypsy that "Despite her love of adventure, her wildness, . . . it is sadness that always leaves

its mark on her face." The extended dialogue between Luisa and the Gypsy refigures the interpellation demanded of *testimonio* between political theorists (intellectuals and professionals of bourgeois or petit bourgeois origin) and political activists (poor, illiterate working-class masses). This connection is not one of subordination or domination, but of interdependence and lateral relationship.[2] The Gypsy's compulsion to speak herself Luisa notes "her Utopian streak and the happiness bubbling up inside her" and her insistence on secrecy, on hiding herself—an apparent contradiction of speaking and not speaking—refigures a double-voiced strategy of political interaction: theory (the speaking of) and praxis (the action of taking Luisa and her opponents by surprise). Spanning a series of contradictory sociocultural locations, **Luisa in Realityland** posits revolutionary literature as in effect involved in and constructed out of a dialectic of oppressor and oppressed, negotiating between the opposing terms of its dichotomies: literature/oral narrative and song, indigenous/elite, action/imagination.

As he or she makes his or her way through *Luisa in Realityland,* the reader is overwhelmed by the sense that the discourse of analysis and struggle is being created in an open-ended and syncretic process of trial, error, and surprise. This freedom from predictability might be termed an exercise in decentering language, sending the apparently stable structures of Western thought into an endless flux in which signifiers are simply destabilized. Like the large canvases that Luisa paints in swatches of different colors with lines of red dots that "began dripping and running just before they went off the canvas," the captioned frames which make up the prose and poetry vignettes of *Luisa in Realityland* convey no signature and no signifier. They are "half-finished." As the narrator explains, for Luisa, "painting was magic . . . because she was certain that in one of the pictures she would discover the secret: suddenly, right there in the center of the painting a door would open to let her into that other reality, which until now she had only conjectured."

The power of unpredictability in the testimonial discourse of *Luisa in Realityland* refigures the power of feminist discourse which depends upon its ability to remain "dislocated, without a home in culture's institutions." The location or "place" of feminist criticism, according to Meese (1990), is the "'some place' of guerrilla fighters, like the *compañeros de la montaña* who steal, hide, attack, and set up camp somewhere else, awaiting the unpredictable moment when they will strike again."[3] The metanarrative poem **"At the Beach"** illustrates Alegría's feminist project of dislocation, contradiction, and unpredictability in perhaps the most concise form. As an exemplary "reading lesson," I include it here almost in its entirety:

> That's nothing to cry over
> come here
> I'll tell you a story if you stop crying
> the story happened in China.
> Do you know where China is?
> She shook her head
> and reluctantly drew near
>
>   . . . . .

A long time ago, I said
as I settled her on my lap,
far away in China
they bound women's feet
their bodies went on growing
only their feet
were imprisoned
beneath the bandages
and the poor women
could hardly walk
they had to let
their fingernails grow
until they were claws
rather than fingernails
and the poor women
could scarcely pick up a cup
to drink their tea.
It's not that they were useless
it's that their husbands
their fathers
their brothers
wanted them like that
a luxury object
or a slave.
This still happens
all around the world
it's not that their feet are bound
it's their minds, Ximena,
there are women who accept
and others who don't.
Let me tell you about
Rafaela Herrera:
with drums
with firecrackers
and flaming sheets
she frightened none other
than Lord Nelson.
Lord Nelson was afraid
he thought the whole town
had risen up
(he came from England to invade
Nicaragua)
and returned home
defeated.
Your twisted thumb
is like being a woman
you have to use it a lot
and you'll see how well it heals.
Run along now and play
don't carry sand for the others
help your cousins
to build the castle
put towers on it
and walls
and terraces
and knock it down
and rebuild it
and keep on opening doors. . . .

The engine of this metanarrative is, of course, the feminine telling, an irresistible dispersion/appropriation of diverse levels of discourse. Suspended between exemplar, apolo-

gy, exploration, and admonition, the story-poem is both an opening onto as well as a turning away from innocence. If innocence is impossible here, it is not because of volition, but because outside forces are invading and shaping the child/mother's (mother/child's) experience. And telling is a form of survival. **"On the Beach"** allegorizes one of the most crucial elements of the relations among writing, memory, consciousness, and political resistance: the creation of a communal (feminist) political consciousness through the practice of storytelling.

"On the Beach" gives a new political dimension to the term and the experience of motherhood; it transcends the private sphere and invades the political one. A new discursive articulation establishes a new speaking subject. The dialogic relationship between mother and daughter, between teacher and pupil, negotiates a network of engagement, which is both theoretical and practical. Lessons from the past must be contextualized; women, like Rafaela Herrera, must be "spoken of" and exemplified. The mother-daughter relationship is necessary in the interest of collectivity and continuity. The breaking of bonds, the freeing of minds and feet remains incomplete, however, without action. "Your twisted thumb is like being a woman," advises the narrator, "you have to use it a lot / and you'll see how well it heals." As the mother admonishes her child to join in the collective effort of rebuilding the castle, Alegría also prescribes a socially responsible feminism, one which "keeps on opening doors."

As we ponder the reading lesson of Rafaela Herrera and her ambiguously polyvalent "flaming sheets," we recall that resistance and women's testimonial discourse are indeed encoded in the practices of remembering, and of writing. It is the loss of one's children or imagining for them a social change and political transformation that motivates the act of writing. The testimonial poem itself, therefore, becomes the symbol for an act of love, and a tribute to the memory of those who have been silenced, and must now be spoken and written. Paradoxically, the "flaming sheets" also evoke the power of language to destroy as it creates: the work of any rewriting. The trick is not to identify the correct discourse and to defend it with dogmatic heroism but to combine, recombine, and continue to adjust the constellation of discourses in ways that will respond to a changeable reality. *Luisa in Realityland* functions precisely in this zone of indeterminacy—between voice and memory, fable and *testimonio*, legend and history, autobiographical memoir and poetic anthology—which constitutes the feminist project. This multigeneric recombination refigures a process of feminization of literature which, as in the closing lines of Alegría's **"Cartography of Memory,"** projects into the future a "rebellious / contagious peace / a peace that opens furrows / and aims at the stars."

Notes

[1] In *Luisa in Realityland*, almost all the anecdotes related in both prose and verse vignettes are quoted, overheard, indirectly authorized second- and third-hand accounts. Thus the narrator serves most obviously as scribe, as recorder, rather than as "author." This technique is not unlike what George Yudice (1985) describes as

taking place in Alegría's *They Won't Take Me Alive* (1983).

[2] As John Beverley and Marc Zimmerman (1990, 176-77) explain, "Testimonio gives voice in literature to a previously voiceless and anonymous collective popular subject, the pueblo, but in such a way that the intellectual or professional, usually of bourgeois or petit bourgeois origin, is interpellated as being part of, and dependent on, this collective subject without at the same time losing his or her identity as an intellectual . . . it suggests as an appropriate ethical and political response the possibility more of solidarity than of charity."

[3] Sommer (1988, 120-21) clarifies that one of the most fascinating features of women's testimonials is their "unpredictable pattern. . . . As working-class or peasant women involved in political, often armed, struggle, the subjects of these narratives move about in a largely unmapped space. Or it is a space on which competing maps are superimposed, where no single code of behavior can be authoritative."

Works Cited

Agosin, Marjorie. 1988. Review of *Luisa in Realityland* by Claribel Alegría. *Christian Science Monitor* (March): 20.

Alegría, Claribel. 1987. *Luisa in Realityland*. Trans. Darwin J. Flakoll. Willimantic, Conn.: Curbstone Press.

Bauer, Dale. 1988. *Feminist Dialogics: A Theory of Failed Community*. Albany, N.Y.: State University of New York.

Beverley, John, and Marc Zimmerman. 1990. *Literature and Politics in the Central American Revolutions*. Austin: University of Texas Press.

Fisher, Carl. 1989. Review of *Luisa in Realityland* by Claribel Alegría, *Small Press Book Review*, (January/February), n.p.

Franco, Jean. 1985. "Killing Priests, Nuns, Women, Children." In *On Signs*, ed. Marshall Blonsky. Baltimore: Johns Hopkins University, 414-20.

Holquist, Michael. 1981. *The Dialogic Imagination: Four Essays by M. M. Bakhtin*. Trans. Caryl Emerson and Michael Holquist. Austin: University of Texas Press.

Jacobus, Mary. 1979. "The Difference of View." In *Women Writing and Writing about Women*, ed. Mary Jacobus. New York: Barnes & Noble.

Manzor-Coats, Lilian. 1990. "The Reconstructed Subject: Women's Testimonials as Voices of Resistance." In *Splintering Darkness: Latin American Women Writers in Search of Themselves*, ed. with Intro. by Lucía Guerra Cunningham. Pittsburgh: Latin American Literary Review Press Series, Explorations, 157-71.

Meese, Elizabeth A. 1990. *(Ex)Tensions: Refiguring Feminist Criticism*. Urbana: University of Illinois Press.

Sommer, Doris. 1988. "Not Just a Personal Story: Women's Testimonios and the Plural Self." In *Life/Lines: Theorizing Women's Autobiography*, ed. Bella Brodzki and Celeste Schenck. Ithaca: Cornell University Press, 107-30.

Yúdice, George. 1985. "Letras de emergencia: Claribel Alegría" *Revista Iberoamericana* 51/132-33: 953-64.

Jo Anne Engelbert (essay date 1994)

SOURCE: "Claribel Alegría and the Elegiac Tradition," in *Claribel Alegría and Central American Literature: Critical Essays*, edited by Sandra M. Boschetto-Sandoval and Marcia Phillips McGowan, Ohio University Center for International Studies, 1994, pp. 183-99.

[*In the following essay, Engelbert asserts that Alegría utilizes the conventions of Hispanic funereal poetry to lament the death and suffering in El Salvador.*]

In his book on Jorge Manrique, Pedro Salinas defines the poet's relation to literary tradition through an extended analogy. Literary tradition, he says, is comparable to "what in natural history is called *habitat,* the zone capable of sustaining life." The poet, he observes, is born to a particular tradition and lives and breathes and creates within its boundaries; the savage acquires the elements of his song by listening to the shaman; the modern poet does do by poring over Horace and Baudelaire. Poetic creation only occurs within the poet's tradition. "Allí es donde crecen las variadas hechuras de la creación poética, complicándose según la tradición se acrece en volumen y densidad. Fuera de esa zona no hay más que el grito inarticulado del cuadrúmano, o el silencio inefable." (That is where the varied creations of poetic art thrive, growing more elaborate as the tradition increases in volume and density. Outside that zone there is nothing but the inarticulate cry of the primate or ineffable silence.) (Salinas 1947)

In a happier time these pronouncements, like those of T. S. Eliot in "Tradition and Individual Talent," had the ring of eternal verities. To reread them now is to realize how deeply the Latin American writer's relation to tradition—always problematic—has been affected by events of the past fifty years. Salinas's untroubled definition of tradition as "natural habitat" and Eliot's conviction that while tradition could not be inherited, it could be "obtained"—albeit at the cost of "great labour"—make us nostalgic for a simpler era.

For Central American writers identified with the forces of change, the question of tradition reached a crisis in the cultural genocide of the period called La Matanza (The Massacre). In 1932 the government of General Hernández Martínez moved against the indigenous peasant population of El Salvador in a campaign of systematic mass killings. Thirty thousand people were killed in a brief period, and the persecution was so horrific that the indigenous population sought to make itself invisible, abandoning forever native dress, customs, and languages. "Indians as a distinct group vanished after 1932: hounded for any feature that might mark them as 'savage,' they had to shed their distinguishing characteristics in order to survive at all. Names, clothes and habits were changed, native languages and traditions suppressed. . . . It became a crime to be a native Salvadoran" (Hopkinson 1987). Intellectuals who identified themselves with the victims eventually found themselves among the host of Latin American *apatrides,* (those without a country) a group so large and so generalized in this hemisphere, Carolyn Forché (1985) observes, as to "move many Latin Americans living abroad to question the validity of the term 'exile' in the modern world."

For many Central American writers, the aftermath of La Matanza precipitated a rupture with respect to the past that compromised their relation to many aspects of Hispanic literary tradition. Mined by successive betrayals of history, the former "habitat" became treacherous terrain. Few elements of the tradition Salinas had defined so serenely remained untainted, and writers of Claribel Alegría's generation did not presume that somewhere there existed a tradition they might simply "obtain" by dint of "great labor."

Ruben Darío was the last great Central American poet who could confidently assume the entire tradition of Western literature. Salinas attributes to him a citizenship that transcends mere latinity. His country was "that of the world's great humanists . . . not *pluripatria,*" a word marred by the idea of number, but *magnipatria,* a space with "no limits but the vision and dreams of mankind" (Salinas 1948). Salinas does not exaggerate. In his elegy to Verlaine, for example, Darío commands sonorities encompassing Greek mythology and the Christian mass, the Spanish baroque and French symbolism; the entire repertoire of Western tradition is his to invoke.

In contrast, an elegist of our times who would memorialize the slain peasantry of El Salvador exists in a no-man's-land, the wild zone described above by Salinas, "where nothing is heard but the inarticulate cry of the primate." Alegría inhabits precisely this precarious zone, and the anguished cry predicted by Salinas can indeed be heard in her poetry: "In her poems," says Forché (1982), "we listen to the stark cry of the human spirit, stripped by necessity of its natural lyricism, deprived of the luxuries of cleverness and virtuosity enjoyed by poets of the north." If Alegría's poetry is stark, if she has stripped and deprived it of ornamentation, it is because she has chosen to forge a poetics on the narrowest possible base, eschewing any traffic in the coin of the culture of domination. The role she has chosen for herself as poet is an extraordinary one: "Soy cementerio apátrida" (I am a cemetery, I have no country), she writes; she is the memorialist of the forgotten, the repository of her rosary of souls. In five decades of Central American poetry deeply preoccupied with the theme of death, Alegría has emerged as a sensitive and original elegist, a role which in all literary traditions has been universally reserved for males. In the process she has helped to forge a New World poetics of solidarity, providing a model for elegizing the nameless and the dispossessed. In order to form a clear idea of the magnitude of her achievement, we need to consider briefly the nature and function of elegiac poetry and its critical relationship to previous tradition.

I should make it clear that I am using the term *elegiac* in the broad sense that includes not only the lament of an individual for the death of a loved one but the expression of grief "originada por un acontecimiento triste para una colectividad entera" (arising from a sad event which affects an entire community collectively) (Camacho Guizado 1969).

The Hispanic Elegiac Tradition

Few genres have a greater claim to a literary tradition or a more clear and functional need for one than the elegiac tradition. There are many reasons why this should be so, chief among them the fact that the writing and recital of elegiac poetry remains a ritualistic act that has an extraliterary dimension for both the individual mourner and the community. Rilke called the elegy "that vibration which charms us and comforts and helps," recognizing the genre's restorative function. By providing a form for language to enact its work of mediation, elegy aims to restore order to life after the chaotic interruption of death. Although it is a reflection on death, elegy is also, inevitably, a reflection on life that leads the mourner and the community of mourners toward catharsis, resolution and reconciliation.

Elegy has the power to mediate, to bridge the devastating dysfunction of separation, to link the survivors to the deceased and to one another and to unite all in a larger design of human continuity. This quasi-sacramental function gives the elegy unique textual authority. It is tempting to speculate that in patriarchal societies the role of elegist may once have been seen as a kind of sacerdotal activity appropriate to males.

In his excellent book *La elegía funeral en la poesía española* (The funereal elegy in Spanish poetry), Camacho Guizado (1969) stresses the social function of elegy:

> The funereal elegy is essentially social in nature in the sense that it reveals a human attitude toward the other. The occasion of the poem is always someone's death, a fact which definitively determines its structure and makes it almost obligatory that the poem reveal the worldview, the beliefs, customs and ideas of an era, the social status of the poet and the deceased and prevailing conceptions of reality, life and death; all of these factors determine the sign that death shall have for this community of survivors.

Obviously, then, a text privileged among all others, figuring not only the shared sorrow of the moment, but prefiguring and mediating the death of the mourners themselves.

In consoling the bereaved the elegy addresses complex emotional needs with a directness infrequent in other genres.

> In every elegy one may discover a consolation; that is, the laments, the imprecations against death constitute a kind of indirect consolation, providing a means of catharsis for pain and grief. The very act of writing a poem on the death of a loved one is a way of objectifying the tragic event, of purging oneself of passion and thus finding consolation. (Camacho Guizado 1969)

Salinas believed that elegiac literature is always, in the last analysis, a protest, a struggle against death, "una lucha con la muerte." Even the elegist whose message is one of serene resignation subverts his or her own message, Salinas (1947) insisted, by the very act of writing:

> Even when poets write of acceptance in the face of death, they belie their own words. The best and noblest form of resignation is silence, and words are spoken here, precisely, in order that something not perish: words themselves—that they may survive that very death whose acceptance is being extolled.

But even the "individual" elegy inevitably has a communal dimension, and, as with any authentic sacrament, the efficacy of the elegy derives in part from a sense of expectancy on the part of all participants, from their common understanding of the meaning of the rite through long experience with its forms, its function, its allusive language and transcendent significance.

Because this is so, the elegy almost as a matter of course self-consciously evokes its own literary tradition, displaying conspicuously the healing sign of continuity. From the melancholy flute songs of ancient Greece to the solemn lyrics of Propertius and Ovid, from the cropped flowers of the pastoral elegy to the lilacs of Whitman or the poppies of Miguel Hernández, the elegies of Western tradition have constantly and deliberately sought to activate the resonance of their forebears.[1]

The Spanish elegiac tradition, one of the richest and most ancient in Western literature, begins with laments, "embedded like diamonds," as Wardropper (1967) puts it, in epic poems. In the *Cantar de Roncesvalles,* Charlemagne, overwhelmed with grief at the death of his brave young nephew Roldán, cries out in pain and incredulity, giving rise to what will become an increasingly significant genre. In unbroken sequence, each age produced elegiac poetry enriching the genre's repertoire of tropes, systems of allusions, and codes. By the Middle Ages, Charlemagne's simple apostrophe had evolved into a genre already having many formal requirements.[2] As the genre continued to develop, the repertoire of stylistic features increased along with a constellation of topics and themes. When Machado asks in a familiar elegy, "¿a dónde fuiste, Darío, la armonía a buscar?" (where did you go, Darío, in search of harmony?), his question has the resonance of centuries. Without tracing the *Ubi sunt?* to its classical origins, but thinking only of the Hispanic tradition, we can find this structure in laments by Juan Ruiz, the Marqués de Santillana, Jorge Manrique, the Romancero, Garcilaso, and Bocángel, as well as in such modern poets as Juan Ramón Jiménez, García Lorca, and Dámaso Alonso.

In the vast tradition of Spanish elegy, strikingly few poems are expressive of collective rather than individual sentiment. Camacho Guizado's comprehensive study devotes scarcely ten pages to this aspect of the genre. Nevertheless, the experience of war—particularly the massive tragedy of the Spanish Civil War—gave rise to a collective sensibility in certain poets. In "Cementerio de Mor-

ette-Gliéres, 1944," for example, José Angel Valente creates an entire stanza from the names of the fallen, and concludes, "all the bodies are / a single burning corpse" (Camacho Guizado 1969). Today, in the opinion of Camacho Guizado (1969), there are few Spanish poets who would not subscribe to the words of Blas Otero: "It is man who interests me, not as an isolated individual, but as a member of a collectivity existing in a particular historical situation."

If Alegría's poetry is stark, if she has stripped and deprived it of ornamentation, it is because she has chosen to forge a poetics on the narrowest possible base, eschewing any traffic in the coin of the culture of domination.

—*Jo Anne Engelbert*

The persistence through time of specific formal elements is a significant aspect of the genre. The fundamental consistency of the elegy across the millennia is quite independent of humanity's changing views of death and the destiny of the deceased: the Western elegy in its expressive possibilities serves Ronsard and Shelley as well as it serves Unamuno and Juan Ramón Jiménez. For the elegy, as Wardropper (1967) points out, does not depend on philosophical or theological tradition but on its own *literary* tradition. Few traditions are more opulent, more varied, or more venerable.

Jorge Boccanera is perhaps the only commentator who has attempted to include the indigenous literatures of Latin American in an account of the elegiac genre. In the introduction to his anthology *El poeta y la muerte* (The poet and death), Boccanera (1981) characterizes this elusive substratum of Central American literature. "For the indigenous peoples of Mesoamerica," he tells us, "death was never a line of demarcation as it is in Christian tradition. In Nahua poetry, for example, life and death are two sides of the same coin; there are no frontiers between one and the other." The elegiac genre was well represented in the poetry of Mesoamerica, as the collections of Angel Garibay, José Alcina Franch, Miguel León Portilla, and others have revealed. This highly conventionalized poetry stresses the transitoriness and illusory quality of life ("We came only to dream. / It is not true, it is not true that we came to live upon the earth; / our hearts will sprout and grow again, / the buds of our hearts will once again unfurl") (Alcina Franch 1957). In the Aztec city-states of the fifteenth century, poets gathered in closely knit societies at court to reflect, to improvise, and to invoke the departed. Many poems of that era express the belief that the communion of the fraternity of poets will persist uninterrupted in the next life, that poets will continue to make verses together "alongside the drums," after death.[3]

Boccanera (1981) calls attention to the Mesoamerican belief in the efficacy of poetry. "The poem," he tells us, "like the

the warm heart of the sacrificial victim, has the power to revive the myths that gave origin to the world." With the Conquest this poetic sensibility, like so many other aspects of indigenous culture, was eclipsed. "America's native sensibility had to go underground," says Boccanera (1981); "Christ and the apostles took the place of Huitzilopochtli and the 400 brothers of the moon." Although it is impossible to demonstrate a continuity of literary tradition, the elements of an underlying indigenous sensibility help to account for certain constants of Central American poetry. The preference of the indigenous tradition for a less individualistic, more collective poetic persona, its distinctive view of life and death, its sublime faith in the efficacy of the word, and its ancient ideal of an eternal community or fraternity of poets are all elements in evidence today in the region's elegiac poetry.

A New Elegiac Sensibility

In the post-Matanza era, elegiac poetry in Central America is eloquent through stark simplicity. The great cathedral organ of Hispanic tradition is sparingly intoned or renounced in favor of an unamplified voice that is at once personal and collective. Death in the Central American isthmus is not *cortés,* as elegized by Manrique; Death as personified by Alegría is the implacable god Tlaloc demanding blood; his victims are the dispossessed, stripped of land, customs, dress, language, and history. The language of elegy must faithfully reflect this; a lament for the children of the Woman of the River Sumpul must of necessity be as pure as water, uncompromised by reliance on the codes of power.

It is not merely the diction of elegy which is problematized by La Matanza, but the very function and nature of this poetry. In the very midst of chaos, who can pretend to comfort, to reconcile? Who perceives an order to be restored or a power capable of restoring it? Classical resignation and spiritual quietude are often replaced in this latitude by exhortation to action. Boccanera (1981) observes, "En pueblos donde la represión y Muerte son ya una costumbre de la barbarie, la poesía pasa de la elegía a la denuncia, de la clandestinidad al exilio, y nada contra la corriente para no perecer ahogada en la sangre del pueblo agredido" (In countries where repression and death have become the praxis of barbarity, poetry moves from elegy to denunciation, from clandestinity to exile, and swims against the current in order not to drown in the blood of the oppressed). In Central America, Alegría and others are creating a new elegiac tradition that does not merely denounce but which essays a new response to the human needs of the bereaved. Its elements are a rigorous sobriety of expression, identification with the oppressed, a poetic persona that is collective rather than individual, and a sensibility that reflects New World beliefs and values. A fundamental departure from received tradition is the emergence of the female elegist.

Some religious communities, as a symbolic gesture, renounce the luxury of instrumental music. "For orthodox Jewry the absence of musical instruments is regarded as a symbol of the absence of the departed glory of the Temple and a reminder of the tragic history of a people scattered over the four quarters of the globe" (Tobin 1961). Similarly, in Alegría's poetry the absence of verbal opulence signifies somber remembrance and complete identification with the subject.

The normal recourses of poetry fail under the weight of this subject matter. Manuel Sorto writes (quoted in Guillén 1985),

> El sangrerío es grande
> demasiado grande
> para medirlo con metáforas.
> Ninguna alucinación se le parece.
>
> (The river of blood is immense
> too great
> to be measured in metaphors.
> No hallucination can equal it.)

The inadequacy of metaphor to the expression of horror is what Neruda alludes to when he writes, "The blood of the children / flowed out into the streets / . . . like the blood of the children" (Forché 1985). No comparison, no simile, no linguistic elaboration can equal the efficacy of the poet's naked, unmediated voice recounting concrete experience. Alegría never speaks about death in the abstract, nor does she speak about "the dead." Rather she speaks, with maternal tenderness, of "mis muertos" (my dead). In her fictional autobiography **Luisa in Realityland**, she recounts the childhood ritual of nightly prayers for her dead and recalls her dread of omitting the name of a single individual whose soul, on her account, might fall into limbo. As she grew older she added name after name to her rosary of souls until the list threatened to become interminable (Alegría 1987). Even now, she tells us (Alegría 1981), her paradise in Mallorca fills with phantoms after dark, the ghosts of all her dead.

As in the indigenous tradition alluded to above in which "death was never a line of demarcation," Alegría blurs and dissolves boundaries. Her dead mingle promiscuously with the living; they come and go at will, appear in the street, vanish in the mist. But it is in life, not in death, that she wishes to remember her host of souls. "Tu muerte me cansa," she tells her father, "Quiero olvidarla ahora / y recordar lo otro" (I am weary of your death, / I want to forget it for a while and remember all the rest). The faces she holds in memory are vibrantly alive; her father's, for example:

> Tu vida y no tu muerte:
> tu rostro aquella tarde
> cuando llegaste humeando de alegría
> y alzándola en vilo
> le anunciaste a mi madre
> que ahora sí,
> que ya es seguro,
> que le salvé la pierna
> a Jorge Eduardo.

(Your life and not your death:
your face that afternoon
when you came in beaming with joy,
held it up for all to admire,
and announced to my mother
that yes, finally, it was certain
that you had saved Jorge Eduardo's leg.)

There are no panegyrics in this poetry. Alegría does not speak *about* the dead; rather, she speaks to them with the naturalness of everyday conversation. "Remember that hot day," she asks her father, "when we stole the only watermelon / and wolfed it down, just the two of us?" She imagines her mother at the age of twelve, face flushed, braids flying, performing a stunt on her roller skates. In the timeless zone of memory she asks her (Alegría 1981),

> ¿Cuándo perdiste
> esa alegría?
> ¿Cuándo te convertiste
> en la muchacha cautelosa
> que colgó los patines?

> (When did you lose that joy?
> When did you become
> that cautious little girl
> who put away her roller skates?)

The dead invoked by Alegría are disconcertingly active; they do not, cannot, rest. They rise and leave the cemeteries to seek justice; they mount guard, harass the living, lie in ambush, ready to accost the passerby. Gesticulating, winking, waving, they pursue the poet, desperate to tell their stories. Their rage is palpable:

> nadie sabe decir
> cómo murieron
> sus voces perseguidas
> se confunden
> murieron en la cárcel
> torturados
> Se levantan mis muertos
> tienen rabia.

> (no one can say
> how they died.
> Their persecuted voices are one voice
> dying by torture in prison
> My dead arise, they rage.)

> (Forché 1982)

They are legion; they form a solid wall that reaches from Aconcagua to Izalco. In desperation the poet struggles to hold them all, to retain them in memory lest they fall into the limbo of oblivion. But they are too many; she cannot contain them all: having described herself as a cemetery apátrida, she says that her dead "no caben," (they do not fit). *Presentes* (present in spirit), like the ghostly guerrilla fighters in poems by Roberto Obregón or Roberto Sosa who rise at night to fight alongside their companions,

these dead in their anger "continue the struggle" (Alegría 1981).

In her book *Poetry in the Wars* Edna Longley observes, "The 'I' of a lyric poem does not egocentrically claim any privilege as structuralists would have it. Strategically individualist, but truly collective, a poem suppresses self in being for and about everyone's humanity" (Longley 1987). The particulars of Alegría's poetic persona—her loneliness, weariness, even the fungus between her toes—are often links to the collective subject (all of the lonely, weary, pauperized expatriates living in Madrid got fungus infections in the public baths where everyone went to "scrub off the stench exile") (Forché 1982). Her poems do not so much suppress self as transform and transcend it; her progressive identification with those who have fallen in the struggle becomes more and more intense with the passage of time. In poem after poem she identifies herself with those who have suffered or died in the struggle. She submerges herself in the collective historical subject and her voice is one with the chorus, the river of voices raised in protest:

> Ya no es una la voz
> es un coro de voces
> soy los otros
> soy yo
> es un río de voces
> que se alza
> que me habla de la cárcel
> del adiós
> del dolor
> del hasta luego
> se confunden las voces
> y los rostros se apagan
> quién le quitó a ese niño
> su alegría?

> (It is no longer a voice
> it is a chorus of voices
> I am the others
> I am myself
> it is a river of voices
> that is rising
> that speaks to me of prison
> of goodbyes
> of suffering
> of so long for a while
> the voices blend together
> the faces dissolve
> who snatched the smile
> from that little boy?)

"Sorrow," the longest and most powerful of Alegría's elegiac poems, actually takes the form of such a chorus or river of voices. Dedicated to Roque Dalton, "Sorrow" is one of the most original and profound elegies in Central American poetry. An entire poetics of solidarity could be extracted from its strategies for voicing a collective lament. The poem is an *arpillera* pieced of fragments, vivid scraps of personal experience commingled with verses by poets and artists who were witnesses to the common struggle.[4]

"Voces que vienen / que van" (Voices that rise and are gone), the poem begins. We recognize them from familiar phrases—"cuando sepas que he muerto / no pronuncies mi nombre," "verde que," "puedo escribir los versos más tristes," "me moriré en París" (when you know that I have died/ do not speak my name) (green, I want you green) (tonight I can write the saddest verses) (I will die in Paris) (Forché 1982). Besides the fraternity of poets—Dalton, Lorca, Neruda, Vallejo, Antonio Machado, and Hernández—others identified with the cause are invoked as well. Victor Jara appears and Violeta Parra, Che Guevara, and Sandino. Their words are stitched together in a graphic representation of solidarity, appliquéed upon the strong fabric of the poem's personal statement. The poem's eight sections are eight stations of the course of mourning. The invocation of the voices is followed by the recollection of a dusty pilgrimage to the grave of Lorca ("no te pusieron lápida / no te hiceron el honor / de arrancar los olivos / combatientes / torcidos") (They didn't give you a grave marker / they did you the honor of tearing up / the twisted, the stubborn olive trees) (Forché 1982). The third section evokes the sense of loss that is the experience of exile. The expatriates floating like wraiths along the cold boulevards of Madrid recognize each other by the mark on their foreheads, the hunted look in their eyes. The next three sections recount the poet's response to the "implacable news" of the death of Roque Dalton. She passes from stunned horror to an elevated experience of identification with all those who have suffered or died for the cause: in the seventh section she prohects herself through prison walls to a narrow cell and lies on a cot listening in the darkness to the screams of the tortured. We recall the ritual of her childhood litanies, now become an exercise in horror: "empiezo a contar nombres / mi rosario de nombres / pienso en el otro / el próximo / que dormirá en mi catre / y escuchará el ruido de los goznes / y cagará aquí mismo en el cano / llevando a cuestas / su cuota de terror" (I begin counting the names / my rosary of names / I think about the other / the next one who will sleep here / on my cot and listen / to the groaning hinges / and shit right here in this open pipe / hunched beneath his quota of terror). The intensity of this emotion is the poem's climax:

> Desde mi soledad
> acompañada
> alzo la voz y pregunto
> y la respuesta es clara.
>
> (from my solitude I raise my voice
> I ask and the answer is clear.)

One by one, voices call out to her in the darkness: "Soy Georgina / soy Nelson / soy Raúl" (I am Georgina / I am Nelson / I am Raúl). The chorus of voices rises, growing more and more powerful, drowning out the voice of the jailer demanding silence. She rends the veil of time that separates her from herself, from the others. Suddenly there are wine and guitars and tobacco, and sorrow has become reunion. She takes a piece of coal and scrawls on the wall, "más solos están ellos / que nosotros" (they are more alone than we are), the only consolation this elegy can offer and the only consolation that it needs.

In this fraternity of suffering the dispossessed have their homeland in each other. Salvadoran guerrillas often repeat, "we have our mountain [i.e., our refuge] in the people." The poets of this era find their mountain, their "habitat," in the consciousness of their counterparts in solidarity, regardless of era or place of birth.

"Sorrow"'s eighth section, an epilogue, parallels traditional elegiac form by referring confidently to the persistence of the poem itself, exactly as Salinas observed ("words are spoken here, precisely, in order that something not perish: words themselves"), with the enormous difference that the poem, in this tradition, is no longer the work of a single individual; this is its precise strength:

> existen los barrotes
> nos rodean
> también existe el catre
> y sus ángulos duros
> y el poema río
> que nos sostiene a todos
> y es tan substantivo
> como el catre
> el poema que todos escribimos
> con lágrimas
> y uñas
> y carbón.
>
> (the bars do exist
> they surround us
> the cot also exists
> with its hard sides
> the river poem
> that sustains us all
> and is as substantial as the cot
> the poem we are all writing
> with tears, with fingernails and coal.)
>
> (Forché 1982)

The poem's final words are not a pious generality but a challenge, an incitement; the function of this poetry is not to reconcile but to engage:

> y surge la pregunta
> el desafío
> *decidme en el alma quién*
> quién levantó los barrotes?
>
> (and the question arises, the challenge
> tell, me, in spirit, who
> who, raised up this prison's bars?)
>
> (Forché 1982)

Using few of the resources of the traditional elegy, Alegría has created a poetry that approximates its weight and scope and resonance. With others of her generation, she has helped define a New World elegiac tradition, individual and collective, unmediated and profound, a poetry "for and about everyone's humanity."

Notes

[1] When Lope writes in his poem "En la muerte de Baltasar Elisio Medinilla" "Y quiere que consagre a tu memoria elegos versos," he uses a term employed by Euripides. The traditions evoked by Spenser in *The Shepeardes Calender* include not only the poetry of Chaucer but that of Theocritus, Virgil, Mantuan, and Petrarch (Sacks 1985, 38). The panegyric in *Llanto por Ignacio Sánchez Mejías* (¿Qué gran torero en la plaza! / ¡Qué amigo de sus amigos! / ¡Qué señor para criados y parientes!) in turn echoes that of the epic (María Rosa de Malkiel demonstrates that Jorge Manrique takes great pains to have us identify his father with the earlier ideal of the "caballero famoso," Fernán González or El Cid).

[2] According to María Rosa Lida, by this time the rhetorical convention "already demanded of the funereal elegy: 'reflections on the topic of death, the formal lament of the survivors and a eulogy for the deceased'" (La convención retórica exigía tres partes al poema fúnebre: "consideraciones sobre la muerte, lamento de los sobrevivientes y alabanzas del difunto") (Camacho Guizado 1969, 16).

[3] "Ha de seguir enlazándose la unión de los amigos, ha de seguir enlazándose la sociedad junto a los atabales" (The union of poet friends shall continue, / the society of poets must persist beside the sacred drums) (Alcina Franch 1957, 87). The poet Nezahualcoyotl memorializes the princes who have left for "the region of mystery" and tells Prince Tezozomoctli, "Has de venir a vernos en la tierra" (You must come to visit us on earth). Centuries later, Nezahualcoyotl was to be memorialized himself in a poem by Darío, "A Roosevelt."

[4] *Arpilleras* are pictures created by the appliqué of scraps of cloth on a burlap ground. This genre of needlework is closely identified with its political use by wives and mothers of the disappeared to convey their anger and grief. The making of Arpilleras is a popular Latin American handicraft.

Works Cited

Alegría, Claribel. 1981. *Suma y sigue* (Add and carry). Prologue by Mario Benedetti. Madrid: Visor.

———. 1987. *Luisa in Realityland*. Willimantic, Conn.: Curbstone Press.

———. 1989. *Woman of the River/ La mujer del río*. Pittsburgh: University of Pittsburgh Press.

Alcina Franch, José, ed. 1957. *Floresta literaria de la América Indígena*. Madrid: Aguilar.

Boccanera, Jorge, ed. 1981. *El poeta y la muerte: Antología de poesías a la muerte*. Mexico: Editores Mexicanos Unidos.

Camacho Guizado, Eduardo. 1969. *La elegía funeral en la poesía española*. Madrid: Editorial Gredos.

Eliot, T. S. 1964. *The Sacred Wood*. First published 1920. London: Methuen & Co.

Forché, Carolyn. 1982. Introduction to *Flowers from the Volcano* by Claribel Alegría. Pittsburgh: University of Pittsburgh Press.

———. 1985. "El Salvador: An Aide Memoire." First published 1981. In *Poetry and Politics: An Anthology of Essays*. New York: Quill.

Guillén, Orlando. 1985. *Hombres como madrugadas*. Barcelona: Anthropos.

Hopkinson, Amanda. 1987. Introduction to *They Won't Take Me Alive* by Claribel Alegría. London: The Women's Press.

Longley, Edna. 1987. *Poetry in the Wars*. Newark, Del.: University of Delaware Press.

Sacks, Peter. 1985. *The English Elegy: Studies in the Genre from Spenser to Yeats*. Baltimore: Johns Hopkins University Press.

Salinas, Pedro. 1947. *Jorge Manrique o Tradición y originalidad*. Buenos Aires: Editorial Sudamericana.

———. 1948. *La poesía de Rubén Darío*. Buenos Aires: Editorial Losada.

Tobin, J. Raymond. 1961. *Music and the Orchestra*. London: Evans Brothers.

Wardropper, Bruce. 1967. *Poesía elegíaca española*. Salamanca: Ediciones Anaya.

FURTHER READING

Criticism

Acevedo, Ramón Luis. "Claribel Alegría." In *Spanish American Authors: The Twentieth Century*, edited by Angel Flores, pp. 19-20. New York: H. W. Wilson Co., 1992.
  Surveys the themes of Alegría's writing, in particular her poetry.

Sternbach, Nancy Saporta. "Claribel Alegría." In *Spanish American Women Writers: An Annotated Bio-Bibliographical Source Book*, edited by Diane E. Marting, pp. 9-19. New York: Greenwood Press, 1990.

John Ashbery
1927-

(Full name John Lawrence Ashbery; also wrote under the pseudonym Jonas Berry) American poet, critic, editor, novelist, dramatist, and translator.

INTRODUCTION

Ashbery is considered one of the most influential contemporary American poets. Much of his verse features long, conversational passages in which he experiments with syntactical structure and perspective, producing poems that seem accessible yet resist interpretation. Although some critics fault Ashbery's works for obscurity and lack of thematic depth, many regard him as an innovator whose works incorporate randomness, invention, and improvisation to explore the complex and elusive relationships between existence, time, and perception.

Biographical Information

Born in Rochester, New York, Ashbery attended Deerfield Academy in Massachusetts. Graduating from Harvard in 1949, he went on to earn a M.A. in English from Columbia University in 1951. He enjoyed early success as a poet when *Some Trees,* his first major publication, was recognized by the Yale Younger Poets series in 1956. After having worked in publishing in New York City for several years, he studied in Paris on a Fulbright scholarship. He remained in Paris for ten years, supporting himself as a poet, translator, and art critic for the *Herald Tribune,* among other publications. He returned to New York in 1966 and was Executive Editor of *Art News* until 1972. In 1974 he began teaching at Brooklyn College where he served as Distinguished Professor of English from 1980-1990. Ashbery has been awarded many of poetry's highest honors, including a NEA grant, a National Book Award, a National Book Critics' Circle Award, a MacArthur Foundation Fellowship, and a Pulitzer Prize. Ashbery currently teaches at Bard College, a post he has held since 1991.

painting by Francesco Parmigianino, an Italian Renaissance artist who painted a portrait of himself at work in his studio reflecting his observations while peering into a convex mirror. Like the painting, the poem offers a distorted and subjective view of reality, leading many critics to assert that this is Ashbery's representation of the human condition. The poet meditates on the painting and his personal life while creating images of himself at work on the poem. The volume established Ashbery as a highly original poet whose works subvert traditional concepts of structure, content, and theme.

Major Works

Ashbery received immediate critical recognition with the publication of his first volume *Some Trees* in 1956; early in his career he was frequently linked by critics to the avant-garde "New York School" of poetry which included such surrealist and abstract impressionist poets as Frank O'Hara and Kenneth Koch. Although many critics rejected the experimental nature of Ashbery's works during the 1960s, his *Self-Portrait in a Convex Mirror,* published in 1975, is widely regarded as a masterpiece in the realm of contemporary poetry. The long title work is based on a

In his 1978 collection *As We Know,* Ashbery explores themes that thread through many of his verses: the instability of personal identity, the passage of time, and the intriguing relationship between art and life. His recent works, including *April Galleons* and his book-length poem *Flow Chart,* have continued to demonstrate his sense of humor and his penchant for bizarre juxtapositions of words and phrases and experimentation with poetic form. These last volumes, as well as his 1994 collection *And the Stars Were Shining,* explore and celebrate Ashbery's experience as a poet.

Critical Reception

Ashbery is considered a prominent and influential figure in the mainstream of American poetry and is among the most highly honored poets of his generation. Critics frequently note the influence of visual art and film in his verse, observing that the poet's experience as an art critic has instilled him with sensitivity to the interrelatedness of visual and verbal artistic mediums. The Abstract Expressionist movement in modern painting, which stresses non-representational methods of picturing reality, is a particularly important presence in his poems, which are often viewed as "verbal canvases." Although some critics have faulted the seemingly rambling and disconnected quality of such works as *The Tennis Court Oath* and *Self-Portrait in a Convex Mirror,* supporters of Ashbery's art assert that his poetry reflects the open-ended and multifarious quality of sensory perception. Although his poetry is occasionally faulted for obscurity, many commentators argue that traditional critical approaches often lead to misinterpretations of Ashbery's works, which are concerned with the process of creating art rather than the final product.

PRINCIPAL WORKS

Poetry

Turandot and Other Poems 1953
Some Trees 1956
The Poems 1960
The Tennis Court Oath 1962
Rivers and Mountains 1966
Selected Poems 1967
Three Madrigals 1968
Sunrise in Suburbia 1968
Fragment 1969
Evening in the Country 1970
The Double Dream of Spring 1970
The New Spirit 1970
Three Poems [With James Brainard] 1972
Self-Portrait in a Convex Mirror 1975
The Vermont Notebook 1975
Houseboat Days 1977
As We Know: Poems 1979
Shadow Train: Fifty Lyrics 1981
A Wave 1984
Selected Poems 1985
April Galleons 1987
Flow Chart 1991
Hotel Lautréamont 1992
And the Stars Were Shining 1994
Can You Hear Me, Bird 1995

Other Major Works

The Heroes (drama) 1952
The Compromise (drama) 1956
The Philosopher (drama) 1964
A Nest of Ninnies [with James Schuyler] (novel) 1969

Penguin Modern Poets [editor] (poetry) 1974
*Three Plays** (drama) 1978
The Best American Poetry, 1988 [editor] (poetry) 1988
Reported Sightings: Art Chronicle, 1957-1987 (criticism) 1989

* Contains *The Heroes, The Compromise* and *The Philosopher.*

CRITICISM

Paul Zweig (review date 1972)

SOURCE: A review of *Three Poems,* in *The New York Times Book Review,* April 9, 1972, pp. 4, 18, 20.

[*In the following essay, Zweig commends Ashbery's use of hermetic language.*]

I read each new book by John Ashbery with the same puzzlement and fascination. Ashbery's finely tuned style never lapses into the commonplace. Every poem creates a mood of density and discretion, which is almost magical. And yet one never knows quite what the poems are about. His fine elaboration of images and arguments forms a concealing net, a sort of camouflage that works not so much by covering over as by fascinating, so that one forgets to pursue one's hunger for logic amid the glories of pure language. Not since Hart Crane has an American poet made difficulty so thoroughly into a means of expression.

Here are the opening lines of **"The Skaters,"** from Ashbery's collection ***Rivers and Mountains***:

> *These decibels*
> *Are a kind of flagellation, an entity of sound*
> *Into which being enters, and is apart.*
> *Their colors on a warm February day*
> *Make for masses of inertia, and hips*
> *Prod out of the violet-seeming into a new kind*
> *Of demand that stumps the absolute because not new*
> *In the sense of the next one in an infinite series*
> *But, as it were, pre-existing or pre-seeming in*
> *Such a way as to contrast funnily with the*
> *   unexpectedness*
> *And somehow push us all into perdition.*

Long before one has made sense of lines like these—I'm still not sure I have—one has consented to them. Ashbery's muted language creates a lyric of analysis and abstraction that is incredibly precise, but impenetrable.

No poet in America resembles Ashbery, although a number of contemporary French poets, such as Michel Deguy, Marcelin Pleynet and Denis Roche, possess a similar gift for lyric abstraction. Ashbery lived for almost 10 years in Paris, and knew these poets well. Yet they are, in fact, more likely to be his disciples than the reverse, since Ashbery's hermetic style began to develop with his first book, and came fully blown almost 10 years ago in *The Tennis Court Oath*.

Difficulties normally are made to be solved; they are subjects for exegesis. But difficulty can also become a way to broaden the energy of language, arresting the emotions, catching the reader in sudden gaps of meaning, the way exotic images do in another sort of poetry. Instead of analyzing the obstacles of language, one can set oneself afloat on them; not fishing for meanings, but launched in a medium of elusive argument. There is a surrealism of ideas, far different from the florid imagery of André Breton, closer perhaps to the strangely argumentative poetry of Tristan Tzara.

This is the mode John Ashbery, alone among American poets, has created for himself. It has permitted him the triumph of poems like **"Civilisation and its Discontents"** (also in *Rivers and Mountains*), with passages like the following:

> There is no longer any use in harping on
> The incredible principle of daylong silence, the dark
>   sunlight
> As only the grass is beginning to know it,
> The wreath of the North Pole,
> Festoons for the late return, the shy pensioners
> Agasp on the lamplit air. What is agreeable
> Is to hold your hand. The gravel
> Underfoot. The time is for coming close. Useless
> Verbs shooting the other words far away.

Perhaps this is what Ashbery has always meant to do with his dense, almost elegiac language: to defend the "daylong silence" by "shooting the other words far away"; to reshape the connected words of everyday speech (what Mallarmé called "the words of the tribe") into a new, wholly suggestive medium.

Ashbery's most recent volume, *Three Poems*, restates his commitment to hermetic language in more extreme terms than ever before. The very modesty of the book's title is a provocation, for these are not poems at all, but meditations couched in a maddeningly elusive prose style. Never, I think, have the simple forms of prose been waylaid so masterfully into statements that defy interpretation. The volume is divided into three sections of varying length, entitled **"The New Spirit," "The System"** and **"The Recital,"** which, we are informed, ought to be read in sequence as a trilogy. The nature of the sequence eludes me, since I can discover little in the way of development or resolution in the over-all movement of the poems. But this, and all my other attempts at explanation, must be taken quite tentatively, since *Three Poems* has a way of keeping its secrets.

The keeping of secrets appears, in fact, to be the subject matter of part one, **"The New Spirit,"** which begins: "I thought that if I could put it all down that would be one way. And next the thought came to me that to leave all out would be another, and truer, way." Ashbery is a master at leaving it all out, but occasionally he sets into his nega-

tive prose a pattern of signs, which are like blazemarks in a wilderness. "Leaving out," we learn, becomes a way to mute the progress of words, concealing their "destinations," (i.e., their meanings) until they have escaped from the needs and aims of ordinary life:

> The shape-filled foreground: what distractions for the imagination, incitements to the copyist, yet nobody has the leisure to examine it closely. But the thinness behind, the vague air: this captivates every spectator. All eyes are riveted to its slowly unfolding expansiveness.

Ashbery's work is located in "the thinness," outside of time and destinations. It becomes an orchestrated paralysis, devoted not to action but to inaction, broad and still like a pool, not swift and flowing like a river. It is the language of what Ashbery calls "the magic world":

> The magic world really does exist. Its dumbness is the proof of this. Indeed any sign of activity on its part would be cause for alarm, since it does not need us, need to signal its clarion certainties into our abashed, timid, half-make-believe commerce of every day.

In **"The New Spirit"** Ashbery proposes a sort of spiritual exercise, "narrowing down" the reader's awareness until he is suspended amid a honeycomb of words. Having entered the timeless pattern of what he calls "weightlessness," having left everything out, we emerge "in the suddenly vast surroundings that open out among [our] features like pools of quicksilver."

Thus, part one of *Three Poems* defines Ashbery's poetic art: by rarifying his language, by converting its movement into stillness (i.e., into hermetic difficulty), the poet invites his reader to follow him away from the connected "map" of statements; he shows the reader how to undo the "chain of breathing," which measures time, and to emerge into a new space, strenuously cold and slow:

> That space was transfigured as though by hundreds and hundreds of tiny points of light like flares seen from a distance, gradually merging into one wall of even radiance like the sum of all their possible positions, plotted by coordinates, yet open to the movements and suggestions of this new life of action without development, a fixed flame.

Part two, **"The System"** pursues this theme from another point of view. Once we have achieved the mystic stillness of "narrowing down," the temporal world returns, and we are carried forward on the current of everyday words, everyday needs. The mystic may rise to purity of vision, but time does not stop for him. Before he can settle into the new space, he is plunged back into the envelope of flesh, carried further and further away from the heights he once scaled. Ashbery is most open and moving in elegiac passages like the following:

> On this Sunday which is also the last day of January let us pause for a moment and take note of where we

are. A new year has just begun and now a new month is coming up, charged with its weight of promise and probable disappointments, standing in the wings like an actor who is conscious of nothing but the anticipated cue, totally absorbed, a pillar of waiting. And now there is no help for it but to be cast adrift in the new month. One is plucked from one month to the next; the year is like a fast-moving Ferris wheel; tomorrow all the riders will be under the sign of February and there is no appeal.

The only resource against time's "self-propagating wind," is memory, which reinvents the past over and over again, until the flow of time curves upon itself like a wheel, circling the central point, which is no longer past or future, but a radiant, remembered present. Memory saves the mystic by filling the "bare room" of his inward life with its "alphabet of clemency," until finally the patterns of memory have been learned so well that they become a second, more spiritual nature:

> You no longer have to remember the principles, they seem to come to you like fragments of a buried language you once knew. You are like the prince in the fairy tale before whom the impenetrable forest opened and then the gates of the castle, without his knowing why.

If these notations seem at all clear, that is only because they misrepresent Ashbery's incredibly complex prose by attempting to analyze it. Indeed, there is far more going on in *Three Poems* that I have yet grasped. The language is everywhere magnificent, although its enthusiasms are curiously chaste. Sexuality, love, the real world appear in the poem like a ballet of abstractions from which the "I" and the "You" are almost absent. The concreteness of objects and images has been vaporized even more thoroughly than in Ashbery's earlier work. The result is a poem that is fascinating, but impossible to evaluate. I fear, ultimately, that *Three Poems* may be a secret too well kept; a marvelous, but maddening grammar of hermetic moments from which the reader, however willing to be seduced, may be excluded.

Fred Moramarco (essay date 1976)

SOURCE: "John Ashbery and Frank O'Hara: The Painterly Poets," in *Journal of Modern Literature,* Vol. X, No. 3, September, 1976, pp. 436-72.

[*In the following excerpt, Moramarco discusses the poetry of John Ashbery and Frank O'Hara in light of the Abstract Expressionist movement in American painting.*]

> "Insight, if it is occasional, functions critically; if it is casual, insight functions creatively."
>
> Frank O'Hara, *Jackson Pollock*

The title poem in John Ashbery's new collection, *Self Portrait in a Convex Mirror*, begins with a precise de-

scription of the remarkable painting by Parmigianino which inspired it. Looking at the poem and painting together,[1] one is struck by Ashbery's unique ability to explore the verbal implications of painterly space, to capture the verbal nuances of Parmigianino's fixed and distorted image. The poem virtually resonates or extends the painting's meaning. It transforms visual impact to verbal precision. I am reminded of an antithetical statement by the Abstract Expressionist painter Adolph Gottlieb, whose haunting canvases juxtaposing luminous spheres and explosive brush strokes have all sorts of suggestive connections with Ashbery's poetry. Gottlieb writes about his own painting:

> I frequently hear the question "What do these images mean?" This is simply the wrong question. Visual images do not have to conform to either verbal thinking or optical facts. A better question would be "Do these images convey any emotional truth?"[2]

It seems to me Ashbery's intention in **"Self Portrait"** is to record verbally the emotional truth contained in Parmigianino's painting. Visual images do not have to conform to verbal *thinking*, as Gottlieb points out, but they can generate a parallel verbal universe, and it is this sort of a universe that Ashbery's poetry has consistently evoked.

More than any other poets since perhaps William Carlos Williams and Gertrude Stein, Ashbery and his close friend Frank O'Hara have demonstrated in their poetry a continuing affinity with developments in contemporary painting. Partially this is a result of their long and close association with one another and of both poets' extensive involvement with contemporary artists. From 1960 through 1965, Ashbery was the art critic for the European edition of the *New York Herald Tribune* and was Paris Correspondent for *Art News* in the mid-60s. During these years, he also wrote for *Art International* and in 1963 became Editor of *Art and Literature,* published in Paris. Later he became Executive Editor of *Art News,* a post he held until 1972. O'Hara worked for the Museum of Modern Art in 1950 and became an editoral associate of *Art News* from 1953 until 1955, when he rejoined the Museum of Modern Art as a special assistant in their International Program. His appointment as Assistant Curator at the Museum represented, as Dore Ashton has noted, "the first authentic evidence of a rapprochement between poets and painters."[3] He worked with the Museum in one capacity or another (organizing exhibitions, editing catalogs, publishing books) until his untimely death on Fire Island in 1966. By that time, he had published two books—*Jackson Pollock* and *Robert Motherwell*—on Abstract Expressionist painters and had written essays on many others.[4] With this mutual background, it is surely not surprising that the work of the two poets reflects an affinity with the painterly esthetic developed by Jackson Pollock, Mark Rothko, Robert Motherwell, Franz Kline, Willem de Kooning, Adolph Gottlieb, and other Abstract Expressionists.

Their work is not an isolated example of this sort of affinity, but it does represent the peak of Abstract Expressionist influence on American poetry. Basically, the revolution in American painting which occurred in New York during the late 1940s and early 50s has been well described by Harold Rosenberg:

> At a certain moment the canvas began to appear to one American painter after another as an arena in which to act—rather than as a space in which to reproduce, redesign, analyze or "express" an object, actual or imagined. What was to go on the canvas was not a picture but an event.[5]

If we change the words "canvas," "painter," and "picture" in this passage to "page," "poet," and "poem," Rosenberg's perceptive statement can describe as well the situation in American poetry at the time. Just as American painters were experiencing the exhilarating freedom of discovering the act of painting as the "event" to be captured and frozen on the canvas, American poets were discovering, in the very act of poetic composition, the subject matter of their poetry. Just as action painters were calling our attention to the basic materials of their art—paint, color, canvas—and seeing the latter as a field of action, poets began calling our attention to the basic materials of theirs—words interacting with one another to fill the white space of a page and create autonomous worlds.

Perhaps the most obvious example of this parallel development is Charles Olson's well-known discussion of "projective verse," in which he describes poetry as a virtual extension of the poet's body and the act of writing poetry as the significant "event" to be recorded in the poem:

> Verse now, 1950, if it is to go ahead, if it is to be of *essential* use, must, I take it, catch up and put into itself certain laws and possibilities of the breath, of the breathing of the man who writes as well as of his listenings.[6]

Olson's essay goes on to discuss the creation of a poem as a transference of energy from the physiology of the poet to the words on the page; he speaks of "field" composition and of the rapid movement of the poet from one perception to the next. The emphasis is upon vitality, action, motion—the creative life force of the poet transformed and captured in a language which conveys the heightened vitality of the creative moment.

Coming back to Rosenberg's description of action painting for a moment—a description which likewise stresses the immediate and physical quality of the creative act—we find him pointing out that

> A painting that is an act is inseparable from the biography of the artist. The painting itself is a "moment" in the adulterated mixture of his life—whether "moment" means the actual minutes taken up with spotting the canvas or the entire duration of a lucid drama conducted in sign language. The act-painting is of the same metaphysical substance as the artist's existence. The new painting has broken down every distinction between art and life.[7]

Rosenberg concludes his essay on action painting, which originally appeared in *Art News* in December 1952, with the statement, "So far, the silence of American literature on the new painting all but amounts to a scandal."

But Olson's essay had appeared in *Poetry New York* in 1950, and the community he led at Black Mountain College since 1948 was long exploring parallel developments between art and literature. Among the many painters who taught or studied at Black Mountain while Olson was there were Josef Albers (the rector of the college), Franz Kline, Willem de Kooning, Robert Motherwell, and Robert Rauschenberg.[8] The *Black Mountain Review,* essentially a literary magazine, nonetheless published reproductions of Kline's work, collages by Jess Collins, and introduced the French Abstract Expressionist René Laubiès to an American audience.

An even more fertile meeting ground for poets and painters than Black Mountain College was New York's Cedar Tavern in Greenwich Village. In "Larry Rivers: A Memoir," Frank O'Hara points out that the social relationships between poets and painters in the early Fifties led to shared esthetic concerns:

> An interesting sidelight to these social activities [that is, writing poems in the Cedar Tavern while listening to painters "argue and gossip"] was that for most of us non-Academic and indeed non-literary poets in the sense of the American scene at that time, the painters were the only generous audience for our poetry, and most of us read first publicly in art galleries or at The Club. The literary establishment cared about as much for our work as the Frick cared for Pollock and de Kooning, not that we cared any more about establishments than they did, all of the disinterested parties being honorable men.[9]

It is in the poetry of New York poets like O'Hara and Ashbery that the painterly esthetic of Abstract Expressionism manifests itself in literary art, though Olson's criticism provides for us its literary rationale.

Ashbery's Introduction to *The Collected Poems of Frank O'Hara* notes that

> O'Hara's concept of the poem as the chronicle of the creative act that produced it was strengthened by his intimate experience of Pollock's, Kline's and de Kooning's great paintings of the late 40s and early 50s and of the imaginative realism of painters like Jane Freilicher and Larry Rivers.[10]

O'Hara's connection with the New York art scene dates from about 1950, when he first worked at the Museum of Modern Art and became acquainted with many of the most innovative painters in the New York area at the time. But I am concerned here less with the biographical relationships between O'Hara, Ashbery, and the New York painters than with the esthetic relationship between their poetry and the canvases of the New York School. The "casual insight" that O'Hara finds at the center of Jackson Pollock's achievement, for example, is a description as well of his own poetic style. Writing about Pollock, O'Hara finds

> the ego totally absorbed in the work. By being "in" the specific painting, as he himself put it, he gave himself over to the cultural necessities which, in turn, freed him from the external encumbrances which surround art as an occasion of extreme cultural concern.[11]

These external encumbrances are precisely what O'Hara liberates himself from in his own poetry. His is not a poetry of extreme cultural concern, but rather is one focused on the momentary and the transient, on the hundreds of minor details which make up all of our days. His poetry is concerned with movies he has seen, friends he has visited, stores he has shopped at, birthdays he has celebrated, meals he has eaten. The "action" of O'Hara's life is in his poetry in the same way that Pollock's creative life is directly captured in his paintings.

So many of O'Hara's poems are playful, "casually insightful" celebrations of the esthetic autonomy of the creative act. The last stanza of "Autobiographia Literaria" (the serious, Coleridge-inspired title, of course, totally at odds with the spirit of the poem) specifically celebrates this esthetic ego involvement:

> And here I am, the
> center of all beauty!
> writing these poems!
> Imagine![12]

The wonder here is a mock-wonder—whimsical rather than Whitmanic—but it is aimed at calling our attention to the "action" of making the poem. Here, as elsewhere in O'Hara's work, the mock-heroic posturing is only superficially satirical. Underlying the casual chronicles of everday events in his work is a deep commitment to the transformative qualities of poetry—its ability to open our eyes, sharpen our perceptions, involve us more totally with the world around us. O'Hara's whimsy is, if I may be permitted an oxymoron, a serious whimsy.

"A Pleasant Thought from Whitehead" provides an excellent illustration of O'Hara's typical stance: his insistence upon incorporating immediate experience into his work, transforming it through the intervention of casually marvelous events. The poem follows the course of its own genesis, from the desk of the poet to the eyes of the reader, a pelican and an editor interceding to provide wonder and delight:

> Here I am at my desk. The
> light is bright enough
> to read by it is a warm
> friendly day I am feeling
> assertive. I slip a few
> poems into the pelican's
> bill and he is off! out
> the window into the blue!
>
> The editor is delighted I
> hear his clamor for more

> but that is nothing. Ah!
> reader! you open the page
> my poems stare at you you
> stare back, do you not? my
> poems speak on the silver
> of your eyes your eyes repeat
> them to your lover's this
> very night. Over your naked
> shoulder the improving stars
> read my poems and flash
> them onward to a friend.
>
> The eyes the poems of the
> world are changed! Pelican!
> you will read them too![13]

The tossed off quality of this poem is deceptive, as it is in most of O'Hara's work. Here he uses language in a particularly painterly way, the look and sound of the words and their placement in relation to other words reflecting the meaning and evoked response. For example, in "my poems stare at you you / stare back, do you not? my," the two "my's" which frame these lines and the three "you's" within them interact with the two "stares" to indeed confront each other. This technique is repeated in the next lines, which themselves deal with repetition: "poems speak on the silver / of your eyes your eyes repeat / them to your lover's. . . ." The repetition of "your eyes" is another painterly touch, and the lack of comma or caesura between them stresses their interaction. . . .

More than any other poets since perhaps William Carlos Williams and Gertrude Stein, Ashbery and his close friend Frank O'Hara have demonstrated in their poetry a continuing affinity with developments in contemporary painting.

—*Fred Moramarco*

The painterly dimension of Ashbery's work is broader than that of O'Hara's and not limited strictly to Abstract Expressionism or Pop-Art, but incorporates a painterly sensibility drawn from various periods of art history. It manifests itself as early as *Some Trees*, in which the well-known poem **"The Instruction Manual"** demonstrates how a verbally imaginative world can evoke an almost tangible physical reality—how words can be used to evoke places, people, events, odors, and colors that seem to materialize before us. The narrator in the poem is bored by his job (having to turn out an instruction manual on the uses of a new metal), and as his mind wanders under the pressure of having to meet the deadline, he begins to daydream about Guadalajara: "City of the rose-colored flowers"[20] he calls it. His vision of Guadalajara fills the remainder of the poem, and we become caught up in the rich, vitalized verbal canvas he has painted for us, transported from the mundane and often tedious realities of our daily lives to this exotic, marvelous world, brimming over with a vitality that is clearly absent in the world of instruction manuals. The point of the poem, I think, is that literature and art can provide these moments of revitalization for us, and although we must always return to the real world, our esthetic encounters impinge upon our sensibilities and leave us altered. At the conclusion of the poem, the narrator stresses the completeness of the imaginative experience, the absolute autonomy of the creative moment:

> How limited, but how complete withal, has been
> our experience of Guadalajara!
> We have seen young love, married love, and the
> love of an aged mother for her son.
> We have heard the music, tasted the drinks, and
> looked at colored houses.
> What more is there to do, except stay? And that
> we cannot do.
> And as a last breeze freshens the top of the
> weathered old tower, I turn my gaze
> Back to the instruction manual which has made me
> dream of Guadalajara.[21]

Also in this collection there is a sestina entitled **"The Painter"** whose end-words—"buildings," "portrait," "prayer," "subject," "brush," and "canvas"—interact with one another to again emphasize the autonomy of art. The painter in the poem is a conduit through whom art passes. Frustrated by his inability to capture nature on his canvas with the materials of his art, he stares at his blank canvas long and long:

> Sitting between the sea and the buildings
> He enjoyed painting the sea's portrait.
> But just as children imagine a prayer
> Is merely silence, he expected his subject
> To rush up the sand, and, seizing a brush,
> Plaster its own portrait on the canvas.[22]

He gives up his notions of representational art and decides to paint an Expressionistic portrait of his wife,

> Making her vast, like ruined buildings,
> As if, forgetting itself, the portrait
> Had expressed itself without a brush.

The painter, encouraged by this new-found freedom, turns back to the sea for his subject, bringing to the task the fruits of his recent experience; trying to capture the sea on canvas this time, he simply "dipped his brush into the sea, murmuring a heartfelt prayer" and dabbed the ocean water directly on to the canvas. This is beyond Abstract Expressionism and almost anticipates the conceptual art of the late 60s, but the point made in the poem is that no one knows what to make of the new art object. Sea water on canvas is an esthetic outrage, and the townspeople and other artists will not put up with it, so the painter gives up painting:

> Finally all indications of a subject
> Began to fade, leaving the canvas
> Perfectly white. He put down the brush,

> At once a howl, that was also a prayer,
> Arose from the overcrowded buildings.

The tercet which concludes the sestina describes what happens to people who confuse art and life, as, of course, the Abstract Expressionists purposely did, for both painter and his painting are drowned in the ultimate spiritual silence of his subject. His painting is not a portrait of the sea, but rather a *self*-portrait, as, I believe Ashbery and the Abstract Expressionists would agree, all major art is:

> They tossed him, the portrait, from the tallest of
> the buildings:
> And the sea devoured the canvas and the brush
> As if his subject had decided to remain a prayer.

But silence is not art, though finding ways to convey the silence may indeed be.

Ashbery's second collection, **The Tennis Court Oath**, is still a book that arouses passions in critics and readers. Shortly after its appearance Norman Friedman railed against its purposeful obscurity,[23] and more recently Harold Bloom has seen it as an anomaly in what he regards as the otherwise steady progression of Ashbery's literary sensibility.[24] For me it becomes approachable, explicable, and even down-right lucid when read with some of the esthetic assumptions of Abstract Expressionism in mind. This is not to say that there is a conscious attempt here to reproduce on the page what Pollock, Rothko, Kline, and others were doing on canvas, but rather, as Ashbery himself put it in a recent interview,

> It's an influence in a loose, general way. I mean, I didn't go and look at a Jackson Pollock painting and decide to try to imitate this in poetry somehow. But it's just the idea of being as close as possible to the original impulse to work, which somehow makes the poem, like the painting, a kind of history of its own coming into being.[25]

The first assumption to keep in mind is the necessity to view each poem in the work as a totally self-contained world, not mimetic in nature, but autonomous and self-expressive like a Pollock canvas. Secondly, the techniques of juxtaposition developed by the Abstract painters, particularly Rothko and Gottlieb, can be related to the verbal juxtaposition we find in **The Tennis Court Oath**, where words clash and interact with one another to invigorate our sense of the creative possibilities of language. Third, it is important to recall the unconscious dimension of Abstract Expressionism—the freedom it allows the artist for self-expression of the deepest sort. With these few presuppositions in mind, the world of **The Tennis Court Oath** yields its potential rather easily to any careful reader.

We open the book to the title poem and find,

> What had you been thinking about
> the face studiously bloodied
> heaven blotted region
> I go on loving you like water but
> there is a terrible breath in the way of all this

You were not elected president, yet won the race
All the way through fog and drizzle
When you read it was sincere the coasts
stammered with unintentional villages the
horse strains fatigued I guess . . . the calls . . .
I worry.[26]

To attempt to read this in any narrative or lyrical sequence is frustrating, because the lines seem to bear no logical relationship to one another, and even within the line the words seem to make little literal or figurative sense. In addition, a poem entitled **"The Tennis Court Oath"** creates certain expectations in the reader. We are prepared to read something about the French Revolution, perhaps some connection between that historical period and our own, yet historical allusions are nowhere to be found in the poem. This is a characteristic technique of Ashbery's, who loves to give poems weighty and portentous titles like **"Civilization and Its Discontents"** and **"Europe"** and then proceed to construct a poem which frustrates the aroused expectations. A painterly analogy here is to the massive color and line canvases of Barnett Newman, where totally formal and abstract patterns are given titles like "Dionysius" and "Achilles." The reader or the viewer is invited to make his or her own connections, to participate in constructing the work's "meaning."

The juxtapositions here are constantly surprising. A face "studiously bloodied" calls our attention to artifice rather than violence. A "heaven blotted region" is like no region we have seen before, unless it is the region depicted in the haunting faces of the Surrealist painter Magritte, in which the features are replaced by clouds and sky. To love someone "like water" seems a particularly trivial love, but on the other hand, it is the very source and sustenance of life itself. A "terrible breath" intervening between the reader and the poem may be the reader's or the writer's own—life huffing and puffing its constant intrusion on the lucid idealities of art. Not being elected president gives the word "race" which concludes that line a political meaning, while the following line—"All the way through fog and drizzle"—forces us to see it in its more literal sense. What we confront here, it seems to me, is constantly shifting verbal perceptions—verbal "events" as a record of their own occurrence. Pollock's drips, Rothko's haunting, color-drenched, luminous, rectangular shapes, and Gottlieb's spheres and explosive strokes are here, in a sense, paralleled by an imagistic scattering and an emotional and intellectual verbal juxtaposition.

The notorious poem, **"Leaving the Atocha Station,"** provides an additional example of Ashbery's method in action. This is a poem about which Harold Bloom has recorded his "outrage and disbelief," as indeed anyone would who approaches it in exclusively literary terms. Bloom's reductionist view of literature has led him to make statements such as

> Poems may be like pictures, or like music, or like what you will, but if they *are* paintings or musical works, they will not be poems. The Ashbery of *The Tennis Court Oath* may have been moved by de Kooning and

Kline, Webern and Cage, but he was not moved to the writing of poems.[27]

Of course *The Tennis Court Oath* poems *are* poems, but they are poems more influenced by paintings than by other poems, and to understand them or respond to them fully requires pursuing that influence, not dismissing it.

In **"Leaving the Atocha Station,"** the title seems more closely related to the poem than is usually the case in this volume. The second line expresses directly what it is we are reading: "And pulling us out of there experiencing it." Since Paul Carroll has assured us that the Atocha station is a small railroad station in Portugal, the subject of this poem seems clearly to be the experience of pulling out of that station.[28] But before we can be sure about what the subject of the poem is, we need to confront the puzzlement of the initial line: "The arctic honey blabbed over the report causing darkness." Carroll has done a careful job of exegesis here, so my comments need only be minimal and restricted to pointing out that the line forces us to consider the reverberations of each word against the next, as the carefully drawn and strategically placed squares in a Hans Hoffman painting intersect one another and force us to see the abstract pattern in the background from a different perspective. "Arctic honey," Ashbery told my class in Contemporary Poetry, "is probably something cold and sweet." "Blue Poles," in the Pollock painting of that name, are probably something dark and mysterious. The darkness caused by the blabbing, the "pulling us out of there experiencing it," all suggest the sound and motion of the immediate experience of leaving a train station.

From this point on, the images the poem conveys are generated by subconscious free association, limited by the confines of the experience being described. It is not too much to say that the poem attempts to capture the totality of that experience by including what is going on (both consciously and subconsciously) in the narrator's mind, what is going on around him in the immediate vicinity of the railroad car (lots of small, fragmented talk, snatches of it entering and receding from the narrator's consciousness), and what is occurring in the larger, external environment (the landscape that is flashing by).

Seen from this perspective, the poem emerges as an experiential canvas recording an individual's perceptions at a selected moment of his life. Phrases such as "The worn stool blazing pigeons from the roof" are a continuum of ordinary perceptions which enter and disappear from the narrator's consciousness but are recorded permanently in the landscape of the poem. They are like Rothko's yellow and oranges: glowing and fixed moments.

Rivers and Mountains (1966), Ashbery's next volume after *The Tennis Court Oath*, seems a much more conventional book of verse, less preoccupied with fragmented syntax, generally less self-conscious about its own techniques. In many ways it seems closer in its esthetic concerns to *Some Trees* than to the more innovative collection, but even here some painterly analogies can be productively drawn.

I spoke with Ashbery about the longest and most accomplished poem in that volume, **"The Skaters,"**[29] in his New York apartment on West 22nd Street. We were discussing the idea of a work of art as a record of its own composition, an idea, as we have seen, drawn from the esthetic of Abstract Expressionist painting. I mentioned a line in **"The Skaters"** which points forward to later developments in Ashbery's poetry. The line—"This leaving out business"— occurs a third of the way through that long poem and anticipates the memorable opening of *Three Poems*, a meditation on the nature of art, which establishes a dialectic for the artist between "leaving out" and "putting in." His response emphasized a particular relationship in his work between poetry and painterly esthetics:

> Also, when you mentioned what I refer to in **"The Skaters"** as "this leaving out business" which seems to be a preoccupation of mine—it's also in *Three Poems* and a lot of other work—I see now that it is really a major theme in my poetry, though I wasn't aware of it as it was emerging. It's probably something that came from painting too. A lot of de Kooning's drawings are partly erased. Larry Rivers used to do drawings in which there are more erasures than there are lines. Rauschenberg once asked de Kooning to give him a drawing so that he could erase it. I got to wondering; suppose he did erase it? Wouldn't there be enough left so that it would be some *thing?* If so, how much? Or if not, how much could be erased and still have the "sense" of the original left? I always tend to think that none of the developments in painting rubbed off on me very much, but then, when it comes down to it, I see that, as in this case, a lot of it did.

"The Skaters" is a poem absorbed by the question of what should go into art. How many of our fleeting moments are worthy of recording, and what about them makes them different from other moments? "Here a scarf flies, there an excited call is heard" is a line which records a visual and aural perception, but why would an artist choose these perceptions (from an almost infinite variety of others) to perpetuate in the work of art?

> The answer is that it is novelty
> That guides these swift blades o'er the ice
> Projects into a finer expression (but at the expense
> Of energy) the profile I cannot remember.
> Colors slip away from and chide us. The human
>   mind
> Cannot retain anything except perhaps the dismal
>   two-note theme
> Of some sodden "dump" or lament.
>
> But the water surface ripples, the whole light
>   changes.

Capturing the fleeting present and charging it with sudden illumination is, after all, the mission of art; it answers the question posed by Ashbery in the next stanza, "But how much survives? How much of any one of us survives?"

The act of skating thus becomes a metaphor for the artist's graceful glide over the flat surface of existence, leaving his or her mark. Ashbery calls our attention to the lines of the poem, an analogy perhaps to the lines the skaters make in the ice, neither "meaningful" in the sense of having further explanations, but each recording its own presence and as well the absence of its creator:

> But calling attention
> Isn't the same thing as explaining, and as I said I
>   am not ready
> To line phrases with the costly stuff of
>   explanation, and shall not,
> Will not do so for the moment. Except to say that
>   the carnivorous
> Way of these lines is to devour their own nature,
>   leaving
> Nothing but a bitter impression of absence, which
>   as we know involves presence, but still.
> Nevertheless these are fundamental absences,
>   struggling to get up and be off themselves.

The theme of art recording both the presence of the artist during the creative moment and his absence in our present experience of it is more fully developed in *Three Poems* but, as Richard Howard has pointed out, "'The Skaters' . . . becomes a meditation on its own being in the world."[30] This self-reflective quality is perhaps the most important continuity Ashbery's work shares with painterly developments.

Earlier in our conversation, Ashbery specified that continuity rather clearly:

> When I came back to New York for two years (1964-65), I first began writing about art and one of the first things I wrote about was a show of Rauschenberg's, and Jasper Johns also had his first exhibition. At that time it seemed as though this was the next logical way in which daring in art could express itself. Somehow the kind of epic grandeur of someone like Pollock already needed to be looked at more closely. I can see now how those junk collages by Rauschenberg influenced me at that point.

Of course, the junk collages' primary influence in Ashbery's poetry seems to be that of presenting otherwise ordinary objects and images in thoroughly extraordinary contexts. Rauschenberg's linking of a one-way street sign, a bent-up license plate, four metal-covered note pads, a starfish, stenciled numbers and paint, and a photograph of the Capitol dome, the materials spilling off the canvas and connected by a rope to a wooden box on the floor marked "open," for example, in a work cryptically titled "Black Market," illustrates this sort of influence. It is a work which seems to tell us, "Robert Rauschenberg was here and made me. You have never seen this particular configuration before and never will again." A poem in *Rivers and Mountains* entitled **"The Ecclesiast"** contains lines which tell us essentially the same thing:

> They are constructing an osier basket
> Just now, and across the sunlight darkness is taking
>   root anew
> In intense activity. You shall never have seen it
>   just this way
> And that is to be your one reward.

The reward of enabling us to see things as we have never seen them before is, of course, the most traditional of esthetic rewards, and it permeates Ashbery's work from *Some Trees* through *Self Portrait in a Convex Mirror*. In *The Double Dream of Spring*, perhaps the most conventional of Ashbery's volumes, we find this esthetic renewal celebrated and underscored. Several of the poems in the volume were originally written in French and translated by Ashbery himself into English "with the idea of avoiding customary word-patterns and association."[31] The freshness of the language is an end in itself for Ashbery, as it should be for almost any poet, but this freshness reveals itself here in painterly terms as well.

"Years of Indiscretion" describes the heightened sensitivity the artist offers for our participation in terms of the "dotted rhythms of colors" in a pointillistic landscape:

> Whatever your eye alights on this morning is yours
> Dotted rhythms of colors as they fade to the color,
> A gray agate, translucent and firm, with nothing
> Beyond its purifying reach. It's all there.
> These are things offered to your participation.[32]

The title of the volume itself is taken from the title of a painting by the Italian Surrealist, Giorgio de Chirico, another artist who seems to have deeply affected Ashbery. "The Double Dream of Spring" is not one of his particularly well-known paintings, but it does demonstrate, as W. S. Di Piero has shown, "the bizarre felicity of art turning back upon itself."[33] In the middle of the canvas is a framed sketch of images drawn from a composite of many of de Chirico's other paintings: a puffing locomotive, the outlines of a statuesque, grandiose figure viewed from the rear, a series of columnar arches characteristic of arcades in many European cities, a coffee cup upon a pedestal, a Parthenon-like building atop a mountain, the edge of a draped, reclining female statue. To the right of the canvas-within-a-canvas is another arcade archway with a typical de Chirico huge mannequin head, featureless, staring out at the viewer. To the left of it is another mannequin figure, viewed from the rear, walking off into the distance. In the background are several shadowy figures, two of which are repeated almost exactly in the sketch. The artist here contains his dream vision of Spring within another dream and presents the single canvas to us as the reality of his art. To complicate matters further, when *Time* magazine reproduced a copy of "The Double Dream of Spring" in its August 23, 1946, issue, it reported that de Chirico had denounced it as a forgery. He later authenticated the canvas and stated he was misquoted by the *Time* reporter.[34] All of this engenders a lot of confusion about what is reality, what is illusion, what is life, what is art. As Di Piero notes,

> Both images are dreams, both are real, both are art. We are not asked to choose between the two visions, but to accept both at once for what they are: realizations of a dream of a realization, the unreality of art derived from an unreal dream of a reality which is not art. De Chirico must have anticipated such double-talk on behalf of his picture and probably would have been delighted by it.[35]

And so, we can be sure, would Ashbery.

In **"The Double Dream of Spring"** Ashbery seems to be alluding to the particulars of the de Chirico painting, but we cannot quite be sure. The poem shares a bit of the painting's imagery (the "churring of locomotives," two figures turning "to examine each other in the dream"), but it evokes also a deep sense of immediately felt experience, an attempt to transform a collage of moments into some cognitive meaning, a lyricism turned narrative:

> Mixed days, the mindless years, perceived
> With half-parted lips
> The way the breath of spring creeps up on you
>   and floors you:
> I had thought of all this years before
> But now it was making no sense. And the song had
>   finished:
> This was the story.[36]

Is the "double dream" of the title Ashbery's dream and de Chirico's? Or is Ashbery creating a world here as complex as de Chirico's in the sense that the real world he describes is a world that we confront as words on a page: "Was it sap / Coursing in the tree / That made the buds stand out, each with a coherency?" These ambiguities leave us at the end of the poem with the only reality we can ever really experience—the reality of one day following another, the sun rising and setting on the perimeters of our experiential world:

> And now amid the churring of locomotives
> Moving on the land the grass lies over passive
> Beetling its "end of the journey" mentality into
>   your forehead
> Like so much blond hair awash
> Sick starlight on the night
> That is readying its defenses again
> As day comes up. . . .

The last three lines here are illustrative of a persistent pattern of imagery in *The Double Dream of Spring* associated with days beginning and ending, a pattern which reflects the paramount philosophical consideration in Ashbery's work, the problem of time passing, of the artist's futile, but nonetheless determined, attempt to seize the moment.

The influence of de Chirico persists in *Three Poems*, a long, meditative prose poem concerned with the traces that the past events of our lives make upon our present, and in turn the traces that each present moment makes upon our future:

> as we begin each in this state of threatened blankness
> which is wiped away so soon, but which leaves certain
> illegible traces, like chalk dust on the blackboard after
> it has been erased. . . .   [37]

The focus here, however, is metaphysics rather than painting, and it is de Chirico's literary work that hovers in the background rather than his paintings. Ashbery has acknowledged the impact that de Chirico's strange and neglected novel *Hebdomeros* has had on him,[38] and it is this source, as well as de Chirico's scattered comments on art, that nourishes *Three Poems*. In some sense, the work seems an orchestration of a few of de Chirico's basic esthetic precepts:

> To become truly immortal a work of art must escape all human limits: logic and common sense will only interfere. But once these barriers are broken, it will enter the regions of childhood vision and dream.

> Everything has two aspects: the current aspect, which we see nearly always and which ordinary men see, and the ghostly and metaphysical aspect which only rare individuals may see in moments of clairvoyance and metaphysical distraction.

> A work of art must narrate something that does not appear within its outline. The objects and figures represented in it must likewise poetically tell you of something that is far away from them and also of what their shapes materially hide from us.[39]

I hear echoes of each of these principles throughout *Three Poems*. From the beginning, the narrator attempts to journey beyond the human experiential moment to the "massed days ahead," a metaphysical realm which is "as impersonal as mountains whose tops are hidden in cloud."[40] There is a constant attempt in the poem to break out of the confines of human subjective experience, to internalize an objective consciousness. Such an attempt is, of course, doomed from the start, because the consciousness is expressed in a language selected by John Ashbery and as such becomes his subjective consciousness. Consequently, *Three Poems* does narrate something that does not appear within the outline—and that something is an idealized, fully contained world, charged with promise and vitality, but paradoxically devoid of individual human subjectivity.

Because *Three Poems* is one of the longest prose poems in English that I know about, it is concerned with many other things as well, but one reads it with the sense of hearing a voice far off, catching snatches of lucidity intermittently, but never quite grasping the whole of a particular sequence. This evasive completeness is purposeful—wholeness, after all, is always beyond our grasp. We perceive the poem through a glass darkly, or, perhaps more appropriately, as a faint, lingering melody,[41] a remembered performance, vaguely recalled, but insubstantial as a waking dream. Its final lines are self-reflective, a comment on the poem's own achievement:

> The performance had ended, the audience streamed out; the applause still echoed in the empty hall. But the idea of the spectacle as something to be acted out and absorbed still hung in the air long after the last spectator had gone home to sleep.[42]

Returning to the collection with which I began this discussion, *Self Portrait in a Convex Mirror*, we find the paint-

erly sensibility evident throughout Ashbery's work linked to the meditative mode that emerged as early as *Rivers and Mountains* but flourished fully in *Three Poems*. The title poem opens with a comment on the distortive quality of art even in its lucidity. In the Parmigianino portrait it describes,

> the right hand
> Bigger than the head, thrust at the viewer
> And swerving easily away, as though to protect
> What it advertises.[43]

What it advertises, of course, is the artist's vision of himself, a vision limited by the confines of the mirror which contains it and misshapen by the contours of that mirror. Ashbery quotes from Vasari concerning the circumstances under which the portrait was made—Parmigianino's determination to copy exactly everything he saw looking into a convex barber's mirror on a similarly shaped piece of wood. The portrait, as we look at it, "Is the reflection once removed," and Ashbery's poem about the portrait removes us yet further from the actual physical reality of Francesco Parmigianino toward a metaphysical reality—a disembodied consciousness evoked by the presence of the portrait. Art captures life, but what is the nature of that life it captures, how much of his life can the artist give to his art and still remain alive? ". . . the soul establishes itself, / But how far can it swim out through the eyes / And still return safely to its nest?"

The soul of the artist was *in* his being as he painted the portrait. In another sense it is *in* the portrait itself; and in still another sense it is *in* our consciousness as we look at the portrait. Or put another way, it is *in* none of the above places, but rather exists apart from time and place in an uncharted region that is ultimately ineffable. The soul—human consciousness—will not stay contained. It is always

> Longing to be free, outside, but it must stay
> Posing in this place. It must move
> As little as possible. *This is what the portrait says.*
> [emphasis mine]

To convert the feelings evoked by, or contained within, the portrait, or within the poet's own self, into poetry means finding words for the ineffable, a paradoxical and doomed endeavor, but one which the poet, as Ashbery views the role, is destined to undertake continually:

> That is the tune but there are no words.
> The words are only speculation
> (From the Latin *speculum*, mirror):
> They seek and cannot find the meaning of the music.

Self-portraiture, then, emerges fully as a major theme in Ashbery's latest book, but it was, as I think we have seen, his theme all along. It is, as Barbara Rose has noted, a "theme with a thousand faces,"[44] including in the broadest sense, the non-mimetic, painterly face of abstract forms, shapes, and colors. It is a theme he shares with Frank O'Hara, who wrote about "what is happening to me, allowing for lies and exaggerations" and with the abstract canvases of William Baziotes, whose paintings tell him what he is "like at the moment." Looking at life through the mirror of words, the work of O'Hara and Ashbery leads us to shatter the esthetic boundaries between painterly and poetic art. They are our painterly poets, and we need to look at a great many paintings to read them well.

Notes

[1] An excellent reproduction of the portrait appears together with the poem in *Art in America,* LXIII (January-February 1975), 74.

[2] *The New Decade* (Whitney Museum of Modern Art, 1955), pp. 35-36.

[3] *The New York School: A Cultural Reckoning* (Viking, 1973), p. 227.

[4] These are collected in *Art Chronicles* (Braziller, 1974).

[5] Harold Rosenberg, *The Tradition of the New,* 2nd ed. (McGraw Hill, 1965), p. 25.

[6] Charles Olson, *Collected Prose* (New Directions, 1966), p. 15. For an additional discussion of the relationship between Abstract Expressionism and Projective Verse, see Michael Davidson, "Languages of Post-Modernism," *Chicago Review,* XXVII (1975), 11-12.

[7] Rosenberg, p. 39.

[8] See Martin Duberman, *Black Mountain: An Exploration in Community* (Dutton, 1972), for a comprehensive account of the painters and poets who studied and taught at Black Mountain College.

[9] *The Collected Poems of Frank O'Hara* (Knopf, 1971), p. 513.

[10] *Collected Poems,* p. ix.

[11] *Jackson Pollock* (George Braziller, Inc., 1959), p. 12.

[12] *Collected Poems,* p. 11.

[13] *Collected Poems,* pp. 23-24.

[19] "Introduction," *Alfred Leslie,* catalogue published by Allan Frumkin Gallery (New York, 1975).

[20] *Some Trees* (Yale University Press, 1956), p. 26.

[21] *Some Trees,* pp. 29-30.

[22] *Some Trees,* p. 65.

[23] "The Wesleyan Poets—III: The Experimental Poets," *Chicago Review,* XIX (1967), 53-56.

[24] "John Ashbery: The Charity of the Hard Moments," *Salmagundi,* No. 22-23 (Spring-Summer 1973), pp. 103-131.

[25] Lewis A. Osti, "The Craft of John Ashbery," *Confrontation,* No. 9 (Fall 1974), p. 89.

[26] *The Tennis Court Oath* (Wesleyan University Press, 1962), p. 11.

[27] *Salmagundi,* p. 107.

[28] *The Poem in Its Skin* (Big Table, 1968), pp. 6-26.

[29] *Rivers and Mountains* (Holt, Rinehart and Winston, 1966), pp. 34-63.

[30] *Alone in America* (Knopf, 1971), p. 36.

[31] *The Double Dream of Spring* (Dutton, 1970), p. 95.

[32] *The Double Dream of Spring,* p. 46.

[33] "John Ashbery, The Romantic as Problem Solver," *American Poetry Review,* I (August-September 1973), p. 39.

[34] James Soby, *Giorgio de Chirico* (Arno, 1966), p. 106.

[35] *American Poetry Review,* p. 39.

[36] *The Double Dream of Spring,* p. 41.

[37] *Three Poems* (Viking, 1972), p. 79.

[38] *Confrontation,* p. 89.

[39] Robert Goldwater and Marco Treves, eds., *Artists on Art* (Pantheon, 1945), pp. 439-440.

[40] *Three Poems,* p. 4.

[41] The influence of music on Ashbery's work is explored in David Shapiro, "Urgent Masks: An Introduction to John Ashbery's Poetry," *Field,* No. 5 (Fall 1971), pp. 32-45.

[42] *Three Poems, p. 118.*

[43] *Self Portrait in a Convex Mirror* (Viking, 1975), p. 68.

[44] *Art in America,* p. 66.

David Kalstone (essay date 1976)

SOURCE: "Reading John Ashbery's Poems," in *The Denver Quarterly,* Vol. X, No. 4, Winter, 1976, pp. 6-34.

[In the following essay, Kalstone traces the thematic and stylistic development of Ashbery's verse.]

In 1972 John Ashbery was invited to read at Shiraz, in Iran, where for several years the Empress had sponsored a festival gathering music, art, and drama remarkable, even notorious, for its modernity: Peter Brook's *Orghast,* Robert Wilson's week-long production *Ka Mountain and*

GUARDenia Terrace, Merce Cunningham's dances, the music of Stockhausen and John Cage. Ashbery and another visitor, David Kermani, reported that "to a country without significant modern traditions, still under the spell of its own great past, where a production of Shaw or Ibsen would count as a novelty, such an effort even might seem quixotic". Taking into consideration Iranian critics who demanded Shakespeare first or Chekhov first, Ashbery's own response was delighted and characteristic: "The important thing is to start from the beginning, that is, the present. Oscar Wilde's 'Take care of the luxuries and the necessities will take care of themselves' might well have been the motto of the festival, and its justification." That oversimplifies his view of tradition and modernism, this poet who has rich and felt connections, for example, to Traherne and Marvell as well as to recent poets like Wallace Stevens and Auden and Marianne Moore. But the present is always Ashbery's point of departure: "Before I read modern poetry, the poetry of the past was of really no help to me."

Familiar notions about a poet's development won't quite apply to Ashbery's work. He doesn't return to objects, figures, and key incidents which, as the career unfolds, gather increasing symbolic resonance. Nor do his poems refer to one another in any obvious way. Ashbery writes autobiography only inasmuch as he writes about the widening sense of what it is like to gain—or try to gain—access to his experience. The present is the poem. "I think that any one of my poems might be considered to be a snapshot of whatever is going on in my mind at the time—first of all the desire to write a poem, after that wondering if I've left the oven on or thinking about where I must be in the next hour." Or, more tellingly, in verse (**"And *Ut Pictura Poesis* Is Her Name"**, a recent poem):

> *The extreme austerity of an almost empty mind*
> *Colliding with the lush, Rousseau-like foliage of its*
>   *desire to communicate*
> *Something between breaths, if only for the sake*
> *Of others and their desire to understand you and*
>   *desert you*
> *For other centers of communication, so that*
>   *understanding*
> *May begin, and in doing so be undone.*

Like Penelope's web, the doing and undoing of Ashbery's poems is often their subject: fresh starts, repeated collisions of plain talk with the tantalizing and frustrating promises of "poetry". The "desire to communicate" erodes, over a pointed line-break, into hasty beleaguered utterance. Nor does an accumulating personal history provide a frame for him with outlines guiding and determining the future: "Seen from inside all is / Abruptness."

> *And the great flower of what we have been twists*
> *On its stem of earth, for not being*
> *What we are to become, fated to live in*
> *Intimidated solitude and isolation.*
>
>   (**"Fragment"**)

In his images of thwarted nature, of discontinuity between present and past, Ashbery has turned his agitation into a

principle of composition. From the start he has looked for sentences, diction, a syntax, which would make these feelings fully and fluidly available. When he used strict verse forms, as he did in much of his first book, *Some Trees*, it was always with a sense of their power to explore rather than certify that he was a poet. There are three sestinas in *Some Trees*, and one, the remarkable **"Faust"**, in his second book *The Tennis Court Oath*.

> These forms such as the sestina were really devices at getting into remoter areas of consciousness. The really bizarre requirements of a sestina I use as a probing tool. . . . I once told somebody that writing a sestina was rather like riding downhill on a bicycle and having the pedals push your feet. I wanted my feet to be pushed into places they wouldn't normally have taken. . . .

Ashbery's rhyming, too, was restless. At the close of **"Some Trees"** his final rhymes create a practically unparaphrasable meaning, the two words inviting overtones they wouldn't have in prose:

> *Placed in a puzzling light, and moving,*
> *Our days put on such reticence*
> *These accents seem their own defense.*

There were other, drastic attempts to get at "remoter areas of consciousness", some of them in *The Tennis Court Oath* close to automatic writing. **"Europe"**, a poem Ashbery now thinks of as a dead end, was "a way of trying to obliterate the poetry that at the time was coming naturally" to him. Exploding any notion of continuity, it consisted of "a lot of splintered fragments . . . collecting them all under a series of numbers". The **"French Poems"** in *The Double Dream of Spring* were first written in French, then translated "with the idea of avoiding customary word-patterns and associations." In *Three Poems*, his fifth book, long prose pieces were a way to overflow the "arbitrary divisions of poetry into lines", another way to an "expanded means of utterance".

What I am getting at is that a great deal of Ashbery's writing is done in an atmosphere of deliberate demolition, and that his work is best served not by thinking about development, but by following his own advice: beginning at the beginning, "that is, the present". *Self-Portrait in a Convex Mirror* (1975) is the present with which I want to begin. The long title poem of that volume is in every sense a major work, a strong and beautiful resolution of besetting and important problems. Ashbery had already broached these problems in *The Double Dream of Spring*, in which he characteristically approached the world as a foreigner, sometimes in the role of explorer, sometimes as a pilgrim, and almost always as someone bewildered by the clutter of a situation which, wryly phrased, "could not be better". The world of that book is often divided, out of bristling necessity, between inside and outside, between *we* and a dimly identified *they*. "They are preparing to begin again: / Problems, new pennant up the flagpole / In a predicated romance." Access to the present was more peremptorily barred than it was to be in *Self-Portrait in a Convex Mirror*.

The Double Dream of Spring had looked at alternatives with grim amusement. In **"Definition of Blue"** the cant words of social engineers, historians, and broadcasters—*capitalism, romanticism, impetuses*—drain away, with their tripping rhythms, into colorless sentences, while the imaginative eye, seeking out materials for escape, finds only that "erosion" has produced:

> *a kind of dust or exaggerated pumice*
> *Which fills space and transforms it, becoming a*
> *medium*
> *In which it is possible to recognize oneself.*

This comic decay of language and the laws of perspective allows us "A portrait, smooth as glass, . . built up out of multiple corrections / And it has no relation to the space or time in which it was lived." The joke is on us, especially the grammatical joke that it is the portrait which lives, fragments of personality out of touch with anything but the mirroring tricks which make it seem to be a likeness. Meanwhile

> *the blue surroundings drift slowly up*
> *and past you*
> *To realize themselves some day, while, you, in this*
> *nether world that could not be better*
> *Waken each morning to the exact value of what you*
> *did and said, which remains.*

The separation of "nether world" from the independent and inaccessible world of plenitude, the blue surroundings which drift past us and "realize themselves", is a source of frustration and mockery.

> *There is no remedy for this "packaging" which has*
> *supplanted the old sensations.*
> *Formerly there would have been architectural screens*
> *at the point where the action became most*
> *difficult. . . .*

Yet Ashbery also takes a rueful "pop" pleasure in the vocabulary of "packaging", allowing it to deflate itself, as in the double take of a "world that could not be better". The feelings here are not totally resolved, nor are they meant to be. Ashbery once said that he was willing for his poems to be "confusing, but not confused".

It seems to me that my poetry sometimes proceeds as though an argument were suddenly derailed and something that started out clearly suddenly becomes opaque. It's a kind of mimesis of how experience comes to me: as one is listening to someone else—a lecturer, for instance—who's making perfect sense but suddenly slides into something that eludes one. What I am probably trying to do is to illustrate opacity and how it can suddenly descend over us, rather than trying to be willfully obscure.

"Definition of Blue" is, on the surface, laconically faithful to expository syntax, the *sinces* and *buts* and *therefores* which lash explanations together. The logical bridges lead into eroded territory, and then unexpectedly back again; the poem moves in and out of focus like a mind bombard-

ed with received ideas. So—"mass practices have sought to submerge the personality / By ignoring it, which has caused it instead to branch out in all directions." Or, with deadpan determination—"there is no point in looking to imaginative new methods / Since all of them are in constant use." Just at the point when imagination seems reduced to novelty, an overloaded switchboard, we learn that this "erosion" with its "kind of dust or exaggerated pumice" provides "a medium / in which it is possible to recognize oneself". A serious challenge peeps through: how far are we responsible for, dependent upon, these denatured senses of identity?

"Each new diversion", Ashbery tells us, "adds its accurate touch to the ensemble." Mischievous saboteur that he is, Ashbery's pun on *diversion* shows how much he enjoys some of the meandering of unfocused public vocabularies and the "accurate touches" they supply (as to a wardrobe?). But, basically, our sense is of someone bristling, boxed in by a maze of idioms, frustrated and diminished by his presence there. Only the mirrored portrait lives "built up out of multiple corrections". Or, to be more exact, in a petrifying shift to a past tense and the passive voice: "it has no relation to the space or time in which it was lived"—a disaffected vision of personality if there ever was one. The world of "packaging" appears to have robbed him of a life, of his access to power and vision.

I have chosen this example, more extreme than some of the others in **The Double Dream of Spring**, because it is so energetically answered and refigured by Ashbery's long poem **"Self-Portrait in a Convex Mirror"**. In that more recent, more encompassing work, the poet takes charge of the emerging self-portrait rather than suffering it as he had in **"Definition of Blue"**. He tests an identity captured by art against the barrages of experience which nourish and beset it. He is sparked by a Renaissance painting, Parmigianino's self-portrait, alongside which he matches what proves to be his own: a mirror of the state of mind in which the poem was written, open to waves of discovery and distraction, and aware of the unframed and unframable nature of experience:

> *Today has no margins, the event arrives*
> *Flush with its edges, is of the same substance*
> *Indistinguishable.*

Parmigianino's work is itself problematic and haunting, done on the segment of a halved wooden ball so as to reproduce as closely as possible the painter's image in a convex mirror exactly the same size. That Renaissance effort, straining to capture a real presence, touches off in Ashbery a whirling series of responses, visions and revisions of what the painting asks of *him*.

. . . . .

"Self-Portrait" begins quietly, not overcommitted to its occasion, postponing full sentences, preferring phrases:

> *As Parmigianino did it, the right hand*
> *Bigger than the head, thrust at the viewer*

And swerving easily away, as though to protect
What it advertises. A few leaded panes, old beams,
Fur, pleated muslin, a coral ring run together
In a movement supporting the face, which swims
Toward and away like the hand
Except that it is in repose. It is what is
Sequestered.

A lot could be said about Ashbery's entrance into poems and his habit of tentative anchorage: "As on a festal day in early spring", **"As One Put Drunk into the Packet Boat"** (title: first line of Marvell's "Tom May's Death"). Such openings are reticent, similes taking on the identity of another occasion, another person—a sideways address to their subject or, in the case of **"Self-Portrait"**, a way of dealing with temptation. The speaker in **"Self-Portrait"** appears to "happen" upon Parmigianino's painting as a solution to a problem pondered before the poem begins. At first glimpse the glass of art and the face in the portrait offer him just the right degree of self-disclosure and self-assertion, the right balance of living spirit and the haunting concentrated maneuvers of art. The judicious give-and-take appeals to him: thrust and swerve; toward and away; protect and advertise. (This is, by the way, one of the best descriptive impressions of a painting I know.) That balanced satisfaction never returns. What at first comforts him, the face "in repose", prompts an unsettling fear: "It is what is / Sequestered." This is the first full sentence of the poem— brief, shocked, and considered, after the glancing descriptive phrases. An earlier draft of the lines was weaker: "protected" rather than "sequestered" and the word placed unemphatically at the end of the line, as if some of the meance to be sensed in the finished portrait hadn't yet surfaced.

From then on the poem becomes, as Ashbery explains it in a crucial pun, "speculation / (from the Latin *speculum*, mirror)", Ashbery's glass rather than Francesco's. All questions of scientific reflection, capturing a real presence, turn instantly into the other kind of reflection: changeable, even fickle thought. The whole poem is a series of revisions prepared for in the opening lines, where in Parmigianino's receding portrait he imagines first that "the soul establishes itself", then that "the soul is a captive". Finally, from the portrait's mixture of "tenderness, amusement and regret":

The secret is too plain. The pity of it smarts,
Makes hot tears spurt: that the soul is not a soul,
Has no secret, is small, and it fits
Its hollow perfectly: its room, our moment of
    attention.

In an earlier draft of the poem it was not quite so clear why such strong feeling emerges:

            that the soul
Has no secret, is small, though it fits
Perfectly the space intended for it: its room, our
    attention.

Rewriting those lines Ashbery allowed more emphatic fears to surface. "The soul is not a soul." Acting on an earlier

hint that Parmigianino's mirror chose to show an image "glazed, embalmed", Ashbery sees it in its hollow (overtones of burial) rather than in the neutral "space intended". "Our moment of attention" draws sparks between the glazed surface of the portrait and the poet's transient interest which awakens it, and places notions like the *soul* irredeemably in the eye of the beholder. When the poet looks at this ghostly double, alive in its mirroring appeal, the emerging fear comes across like Milly Theale's (*The Wings of the Dove*) in front of the Bronzino portrait resembling her, "dead, dead, dead".

Ashbery writes autobiography only inasmuch as he writes about the widening sense of what it is like to gain—or try to gain—access to his experience.

—*David Kalstone*

Throughout **"Self-Portrait in a Convex Mirror"** the poet speaks to the portrait as in easy consultation with a familiar, but with an everchanging sense of whether he is addressing the image, trapped on its wooden globe, or the free painter standing outside his creation, straining to capture a real presence, restraining the power to shatter what may become a prison: "Francesco, your hand is big enough / To wreck the sphere, . . ." An explosion has been building from the start as Ashbery returns over and over, puzzled by that hand which the convex mirror shows "Bigger than the head, thrust at the viewer / And swerving easily away, as though to protect / What it advertises". At first that defensive posture in a work of art attracts him, an icon of mastery. But, a little later, feeling the portrait as "life englobed", he reads the hand differently:

One would like to stick one's hand
Out of the globe, but its dimension,
What carries it, will not allow it.
No doubt it is this, not the reflex
To hide something, which makes the hand loom large
As it retreats slightly.

The hand returns not in self-defense, but

            to fence in and shore up the face
On which the effort of this condition reads
Like a pinpoint of a smile, a spark
Or star one is not sure of having seen
As darkness resumes.

Philosophic questions mount, but always apprehended through gestures, new expressions glimpsed as one stares at the painting—here a glint of self-mockery, as the painter absorbed with prowess finds himself trapped by his medium after all. "But your eyes proclaim / That everything is surface. . . . / There are no recesses in the room, only alcoves." The window admits light, but all sense of change is excluded, even "the weather, which in French is

/ *Le temps,* the word for time". The opening section of **"Self-Portrait"** winds down, the poet bemused but his poetry drained of the emotional concentration which had drawn him to the painting; a glance at the subject's hands sees them as symbolically placed, but inexpressive:

> *The whole is stable within*
> *Instability, a globe like ours, resting*
> *On a pedestal of vacuum, a ping-pong ball*
> *Secure on its jet of water.*
> *And just as there are no words for the surface, that is,*
> *No words to say what it really is, that it is not*
> *Superficial but a visible core, then there is*
> *No way out of the problem of pathos vs. experience.*
> *You will stay on, restive, serene in*
> *Your gesture which is neither embrace nor warning*
> *But which holds something of both in pure*
> *Affirmation that doesn't affirm anything.*

This is not Ashbery's final reading of the portrait's gesturing hand. But it launches a series of struggles with the past, with "art", with the notion of "surface", with the random demands of the present—struggles which are not only at the heart of this poem but a paradigm of Ashbery's work. Parmigianino's portrait has to compete with the furniture of the mind confronting it: the poet's day, memories, surroundings, ambitions, distractions. The solid spherical segment becomes confused, in the Wonderland of the mind, with other rounded images, toys of attention—a ping-pong ball on a jet of water, and then, at the start of the second section, "The balloon pops, the attention / Turns dully away." There is a rhythm to reading this poem, however wandering it may seem. We experience it as a series of contractions and expansions of interest in the painting, depending upon how much the poet is drawn to its powers of foreshortening and concentration, and alternately how cramped he feels breathing its air. The transitions between sections are marked as easy shifts in inner weather, opposed to the weatherless chamber of Parmigianino's portrait:

> *The balloon pops, the attention*
> *Turns dully away.*
>
>   . . . . .
>
> *As I start to forget it*
> *It presents its stereotype again*
>
>   . . . . .
>
> *The shadow of the city injects its own*
> *Urgency:*
>
>   . . . . .
>
> *A breeze like the turning of a page*
> *Brings back your face*

The painting occurs to him at times as a ship: first, a "tiny, self-important ship / On the surface". In mysterious relation to it the enlarged hand in the distorted portrait seems

"Like a dozing whale on the sea bottom". Threatening? Or a sign of throbbing vitality, an invisible part of its world? Later the portrait

> *is an unfamiliar stereotype, the face*
> *Riding at anchor, issued from hazards, soon*
> *To accost others, "rather than man" (Vasari).*

Toward the end of the poem, the ship sails in to confirm some sense of

> *this otherness*
> *That gets included in the most ordinary*
> *Forms of daily activity, changing everything*
> *Slightly and profoundly, and tearing the matter*
> *Of creation, any creation, not just artistic creation*
> *Out of our hands, to install it on some monstrous,*
>   *near*
> *Peak, too close to ignore, too far*
> *For one to intervene? This otherness, this*
> *"Not-being-us" is all there is to look at*
> *In the mirror, though no one can say*
> *How it came to be this way. A ship*
> *Flying unknown colors has entered the harbor.*

Self-important and tiny? Issued from hazards? Flying unknown colors? Through contradictory senses of the ship, Ashbery judges the portrait's relation to risk and adventure, to the mysterious otherness of "arrival" in a completed work of art.

What happens, for example, when we start to imagine the life of cities behind the surface of a work of art, in this case the sack of Rome which was going on where Francesco was at work; Vienna where Ashbery saw the painting in 1959; New York where he is writing his poem? These are ways Ashbery has of summoning up the countless events which nourished the painting and his response to it. That outside life, again imagined in terms of risk, adventure, voyages, can be profoundly disturbing—a life not palpable in a "finished" work

> *a chill, a blight*
> *Moving outward along the capes and peninsulas*
> *Of your nervures and so to the archipelagoes*
> *And to the bathed, aired secrecy of the open sea.*

Such images focus the problem of how much life is lived in and outside a work of art. There is no point in disentangling what is hopelessly intertwined. The images flow toward and counter one another, and the reader accumulates a bewildering sense of what it is to be fulfilled and thwarted by his own grasped moments of vision (all attempts at order, not just artistic creation, Ashbery tries to remind us). Francesco's portrait has the capacity to make us feel at home; we "can live in it as in fact we have done". Or "we linger, receiving / Dreams and inspirations on an unassigned / Frequency". But at another moment the portrait seems like a vacuum drawing upon *our* plenty, "fed by our dreams". If at one point the mind straying from the conical painting is like a balloon bursting, not much later the straying thoughts are imagined as wayward, even sinister progeny of the painting: The balloon has not burst at all. "Actually / The skin of the bubble-chamber's as tough as / Reptile eggs".

Struggling with the past, with art and its completeness, Ashbery is also struggling with the impulses behind his own writing at the very moment of writing.

> you could be fooled for a moment
> Before you realize the reflection
> Isn't yours. You feel then like one of those
> Hoffmann characters who have been deprived
> Of a reflection, except that the whole of me
> Is seen to be supplanted by the strict
> Otherness of the painter in his
> Other room.

The threat is pressed home by a shift from an impersonal "you" to an endangered "me". The finished work of art is like "A cloth over a birdcage", and the poet wary of its invitations:

> Yet the "poetic", straw-colored space
> Of the long corridor that leads back to the painting,
> Its darkening opposite—is this
> Some figment of "art", not to be imagined
> As real, let alone special?

By the closing pages of the poem two irreconcilable views of "living" have proposed themselves. Parmigianino's appears to be a "Life-obstructing task". ("You can't live there.") More than that, the portrait exposes the poet's own efforts in the present:

> Our time gets to be veiled, compromised
> By the portrait's will to endure. It hints at
> Our own, which we were hoping to keep hidden.

When "will to endure" and "life-obstructing" are identified with one another, as they are here in describing our daily fiction-making activities, the psychological contradictions are themselves almost unendurable. Imagining is as alien and miraculous as the ambivalent image he finds for it: "A ship / Flying unknown colors has entered the harbor." Our creations, torn out of our hands, seem installed "on some monstrous, near / Peak, too close to ignore, too far / For one to intervene". Another way of looking at it: "the way of telling" intrudes "as in the game where / A whispered phrase passed around the room / Ends up as something completely different".

An alternative? Though the poem is always pressing us out of the past, it has no unmediated language for the present, which is as hard to locate as other poets' Edens. Where poets describing unknown worlds have always "liken'd spiritual forms to corporal", Ashbery must perform some of the same *likening* to enter the corporal present itself. He knows the present only from before and after, seen as through a terrifying hourglass:

> the sands are hissing
> As they approach the beginning of the big slide

> Into what happened. This past
> Is now here.

Four of these five monosyllables—"This past is now here"—point to the present with all the immediacy of which English is capable, and *past* disarms them all. There is no comfort in the provisional, in being open to the rush of things. In fact, one of the most devastating contemporary critiques of randomness in poetry comes in the final moments of Ashbery's poem. Yet it is a critique from within, in a poem open to the vagaries of mind—and from a writer deeply committed to describing the struggle we have describing our lives. This is his unique and special place among contemporary poets. The blurring of personal pronouns, their often indeterminate reference, the clouding of landscapes and crystal balls, are all ways not only of trying to be true to the mind's confusions but also to its resistance of stiffening formulations.

In the distorting self-portrait of Parmigianino, Ashbery found the perfect mirror and the perfect antagonist—a totem of art and the past caught in the act of trying to escape from itself. Parmigianino's work of art confirms the poet in a vocation which refuses to be rescued by art, except in the moment of creation.

> Hasn't it too its lair
> In the present we are always escaping from
> And falling back into, as the waterwheel of days
> Pursues its uneventful, even serene course?

This is a difficult dialectic to which he submits. Francesco is the indispensable partner in a continuing conversation; yet Ashbery's final reading of the painterly hand in the self-portrait is the boldest stroke of all:

> Therefore I beseech you, withdraw that hand,
> Offer it no longer as shield or greeting,
> The shield of a greeting, Francesco:
> There is room for one bullet in the chamber:
> Our looking through the wrong end
> Of the telescope as you fall back at a speed
> Faster than that of light to flatten ultimately
> Among the features of the room, . . .

The pun on *chamber*—one last gift of the portrait's vocabulary turned against it—the dizzying transformations of rounded room into telescope and gun barrel, are triumphant tributes to all the contradictions of this poem and the hard-won struggle free of them. It would be a shallow reading which sees this poem as a modernist's dismissal of the past. Ashbery translates that *topos* into radical and embracing human terms. The elation we feel comes from the writer's own unwillingness to take permanent shelter in his work. Any work of art—not just those of the distant past—has designs on us, exposes for what it is our "will to endure". Ashbery builds the awareness of death and change into the very form of his work. It is the old subject of Romantic lyric—of Keat's *Ode on a Grecian Urn*—but here without undue veneration for the moments out of time. Ashbery admits into the interstices of his poem a great deal of experience—

confusion, comedy, befuddlement, preoccupation—in which he takes as much joy as in the "cold pockets / Of remembrance, whispers out of time", which he also celebrates. His withdrawal from the privileged moments is never as regretful or as final as Keats's from his "cold pastoral". Nor is it as rueful as Ashbery's own sense of desertion in **"Definition of Blue"** where "you, in this nether world that could not be better / Waken each morning to the exact value of what you did and said, which remains". In that earlier poem Ashbery feels diminished and powerless before a "portrait, smooth as glass, . . built up out of multiple corrections", which "has no relation to the space or time in which it was lived". In the spaciousness of **"Self-Portrait in a Convex Mirror"** Ashbery radiates a new confidence in his ability to accommodate what is in the poet's mind: the concentrated poem and its teeming surroundings. In its achieved generosity and fluidity, in its stops and starts and turns, Ashbery's long poem dispels some of the frustrations of language and form, or assimilates them more closely to the anxieties and frustrations of living.

. . . . .

I said before that **"Self-Portrait in a Convex Mirror"** answers problems posed by Ashbery's poetic past and helps refigure it.

> Every moment is surrounded by a lot of things in life that don't add up to anything that makes much sense and these are part of a situation that I feel I'm trying to deal with when I'm writing.

Ashbery said this to an interviewer in 1972, as if anticipating the free and flexible voice he found for **"Self-Portrait in a Convex Mirror"**. That year he had published the long prose pieces he entitled *Three Poems*, a work which evidently released him into an "expanded sense of utterance":

> . . . the idea of it occurred to me as something new in which the arbitrary divisions of poetry into lines would get abolished. One wouldn't have to have these interfering and scanning the processes of one's thought as one was writing; the poetic form would be dissolved, in solution, and therefore create a much more—I hate to say environmental because it's a bad word—but more of a surrounding thing like the way one's consciousness is surrounded by one's thoughts.

However odd or puzzling that last phrase may be, we can sense the pressure behind its deliberate, almost involuntary awkwardness. In both quotations Ashbery uses the word "surrounded" to suggest the number of seemingly unrelated "thoughts" or "things" at any given moment pressing behind the little that is articulated. This tension is the point of departure for *Three Poems*:

> *I thought that if I could put it all down, that would*
> *be one way. And next the thought came to me that*
> *to leave*
> *all out would be another, and truer, way.*
>
> *clean-washed sea*

The flowers were.

> *These are examples of leaving out. But, forget as we will, something soon comes to stand in their place. Not the truth, perhaps, but—yourself. It is you who made this, therefore you are true.*

We are dealing with rich polarities in Ashbery's work. The impulse to "leave all out" can be felt as early as a poem like **"Illustration"** from his first book. The protagonist of that poem is a nun about to leave behind the irrelevancies of the world by leaping from a skyscraper. As this droll hierophant remarks: "I desire / Monuments. . . . I want to move / Figuratively, as waves caress / The thoughtless shore." The narrator, too, is convinced: "Much that is beautiful must be discarded / So that we may resemble a taller / Impression of ourselves." That was one way of saying it, the way of concision and foreshortening.

But then there is another way to have it, as in **"And Ut Pictura Poesis Is Her Name"**, a more recent poem (1975):

> *You can't say it that way any more.*
> *Bothered about beauty you have to*
> *Come out into the open, into a clearing,*
> *And rest. . . .*
>   *Now*
> *About what to put in your poem-painting:*
> *Flowers are always nice, particularly delphinium.*
> *Names of boys you once knew and their sleds,*
> *Skyrockets are good—do they still exist?*
> *There are a lot of other things of the same quality*
> *As those I've mentioned. Now one must*
> *Find a few important words, and a lot of low-*
>   *keyed,*
> *Dull-sounding ones.*

A difference in approach makes all the difference. **"Illustration"** proposes a "taller / Impression of ourselves", an epigrammatic and visionary avoidance of ordinary "beauty". *"Ut Pictura"* makes space for a flustered, fuller and meandering, version of self. Vision is invited by coming out into a clearing and taking a relaxed view of the surroundings. The poet finds "a few important words" and "a lot of low-keyed, / Dull-sounding ones".

Though these poems come from different periods in Ashbery's career, I don't want to suggest that one voice or approach replaces the other. But with *Three Poems* Ashbery rounded a critical corner. Its *perpetuum mobile* style prepared him, when he returned to verse, for a new fluidity, a way to readmit the self to his poetry. Alive in its present, and determined as any Jack-in-the-Box, that self pops up when any moment of poetic concision threatens to falsify or obliterate it. The discovery comes as a relief, not so much a calculation as a necessity. Leaving things out, "forget as we will, something soon comes to stand in their place. Not the truth, perhaps, but—yourself."

I am talking, then, about complementary gifts or voices in Ashbery's poetry. He has his own deadpan way of putting it: "In the past few years I have been attempting to

keep meaningfulness up to the pace of randomness . . .
but I really think that meaningfulness can't get along
without randomness and that they somehow have to be
brought together." No wonder that the long **"Self-Portrait in a Convex Mirror"** stands as a centerpiece to his
work in the early 1970s; no single short poem could handle such a copious problem. It would be a mistake to see
this merely as an aesthetic question, a poet talking about
poetry, about the relative virtues of condensed vision and
expansive randomness. The emotional coloring that Ashbery gives this conflict, especially in his long poem, suggests psychological dimensions and stresses. Art "leaving things out" involves a sense of melancholy and sacrifice, a restlessness, a threat to vitality.

The Double Dream of Spring is shadowed by such feelings; the short poems of *Self-Portrait in a Convex Mirror* often counter them. Together, these two books five
years apart, with their different moods, give a sense of the
range and playfulness and boldness of Ashbery's emerging work. There are some poems, of course, which might
be in either book. Still, certain characteristic titles belong
to one and not the other: in *Double Dream*, **"Spring
Day"**, **"Summer"**, **"Evening in the Country"**, **"Rural Objects"**, **"Clouds"**; in *Self-Portrait*, **"Worsening Situation"**,
"Absolute Clearance", **"Mixed Feelings"**, **"No Way of
Knowing"**, **"All and Some"**. The latter pick up colloquial
ways of describing the emotional weather of the moment.
Titles from *Double Dream* tend toward the generic and
the pastoral. (Not that any Ashbery title is more than a
clue or point of departure, less a summary and more a key
signature for the poem.)

In *The Double Dream of Spring* Ashbery seems absorbed
in the forms that lie just behind an experience; the day's
events are "Fables that time invents / To explain its passing". Common phrases are challenged; buried meanings
are coaxed out of them so that they surprise us with a life
of their own, or chastize us for a sleepy acceptance of the
"phraseology we become". Ashbery wants to push past
the hardening of life into habit, the way it congeals into
patterned phrase, the metaphysician's equivalent of "You
are what you eat". I don't know whether **"Young Man with
Letter"** is touched off by yet another appearance of a
golden, well-introduced youth into the city which will
absorb him. But the impulse of the poem quickly becomes
something else: to awaken the "fable" sleeping behind a
phrase like "making the rounds".

> Another feeble, wonderful creature is making the
>   rounds again,
> In this phraseology we become, as clouds like
>   leaves
> Fashion the internal structure of a season
> From water into ice. Such an abstract can be
> Dazed waking of the words with no memory of
>   what happened before,
> Waiting for the second click. We know them well
>   enough now,
> Forever, from living into them, tender, frivolous
>   and puzzled
> And we know that with them we will come out right.

The cliché ("making the rounds") is teased alive by the
strange sad comparison with the seasons. Ashbery performs what he then identifies, "dazed waking of the words",
eventually "living into them". Many of the poems in *Double
Dream* perform such discoveries, satisfied with nothing
merely accidental, nothing less refined than "Fables that
time invents / To explain its passing". Still, having gone
beyond gossip in **"Young Man with Letter"**, having absorbed a single bit of tattle into a large melancholy sense
of natural cycles, Ashbery is left with some nagging questions. Once he has sidestepped the "corrosive friends"
and "quiet bickering" in this poem, there is still something
distant and unreal about the "straining and puffing . . .
commas produce":

> Is it not more likely that . . .
>   this ferment
> We take as suddenly our present
> Is our waltzing somewhere else, down toward the view
> But holding off?

The frustration and self-mockery, the sense of being deprived of the present, are inescapably twinned with the discoveries made in such poems. The mood is odd and disqui-
eting; however gratifying the visionary insight, the poet also
seems to feel experience being taken out of his hands. Hence,
the way fresh hopes verge into nightmares in the long suspended sentence at the opening of **"Spring Day"**:

> The immense hope, and forbearance
> Trailing out of night, to sidewalks of the day
> Like air breathed into a paper city, exhaled
> As night returns bringing doubts
>
> That swarm around the sleeper's head
> But are fended off with clubs and knives, so that
>   morning
> Installs again in cold hope
> The air that was yesterday, is what you are

In this supple maze of syntax, things seem over, exhausted, before they begin; "immense hope" turns into "cold
hope" in "the air that was yesterday".

Again, a sense of pleasure in natural cycles is slowly
withdrawn in **"Years of Indiscretion"**.

> Whatever your eye alights on this morning is yours:
> Dotted rhythms of colors as they fade to the color,
> A gray agate, translucent and firm, with nothing
> Beyond its purifying reach. It's all there.
> These are things offered to your participation.
>
> These pebbles in a row are the seasons.
> This is a house in which you may wish to live.
> There are more than any of us to choose from
> But each must live its own time.

The experience offered here, beginning in random pleasures of the eye, seems at first to belong to us, to *our*
wishes and choices. And yet "participation" suggests
limits to our control, and the ambiguous "its" in the last

line shadows independent processes in which we "participate" but do not endure. The grave diction soon removes us into an atmosphere refined and impersonal, our lives roles rather than improvisations. "There ought to be room for more things, for a spreading out, like," Ashbery says of the generalizing screen which stands between us and details of the landscape ("**For John Clare**"). "Alas, we perceive them if at all as those things that were meant to be put aside—costumes of the supporting actors or voice trilling at the end of a narrow enclosed street."

In his images of thwarted nature, of discontinuity between present and past, Ashbery has turned his agitation into a principle of composition. From the start he has looked for sentences, diction, a syntax, which would make these feelings fully and fluidly available.

—David Kalstone

In one of his best short poems, "**Summer**", Ashbery imagines the winter latent in summer branches: "For the time being the shadow is ample / And hardly seen, divided among the twigs of a tree." Winter's poverty emerges later in a full-blown reminiscence of Stevens: "and winter, the twitter / Of cold stars at the pane, that describes with broad gestures / This state of being that is not so big after all". I am struck by the frequency with which Ashbery returns in *Double Dream* to myths of the seasons, as to photographic negatives, for the true contours governing experience—and what's more important, he is looking not for myths of rebirth but for myths of diminution. In "**Fragment**" we learn that

> *Summer was a band of nondescript children*
> *Bordering the picture of winter, which was indistinct*
> *And gray like the sky of a winter afternoon.*

In the poem "**Summer**", "Summer involves going down as a steep flight of steps / To a narrow ledge over the water."

Ashbery takes his title *The Double Dream of Spring* from de Chirico and so puts us on warning that we are stepping through the looking glass into those deep perspectives and receding landscapes of the mind. He leads us, once we are prepared to follow, to yearned-for, difficult states, free of casual distraction.

> *To reduce all this to a small variant,*
> *To step free at last, miniscule on the gigantic*
> * plateau—*
> *This was our ambition: to be small and clear and*
> * free.*

Does the present exist principally "To release the importance / Of what will always remain invisible?" he asks, with some urgency, in "**Fragment**". *The Double Dream of Spring* seems to answer that question in the affirmative. It is Ashbery's most successfully visionary book, however sad its tone. Unlike *Self-Portrait in a Convex Mirror*, which struggles to include and authenticate the present, *Double Dream* finds the most striking images in its glimpses of the fables behind our lives, and it most yearns for the state which is both free and death-like, diminished.

> *The welcoming stuns the heart, iron bells*
> *Crash through the transparent metal of the sky*
> *Each day slowing the method of thought a little*
> *Until oozing sap of touchable mortality, time lost*
> * and won.*

"**Soonest Mended**"—so goes the title of one of the best of these poems, illustrating a point we can scarcely grasp until we supply the first half of a proverb which has been mimetically suppressed: "least said; soonest mended". *Double Dream* calls for tight-lipped irony as well as yearning for visionary release. In "**Soonest Mended**" comic self-awareness and proverbial wisdom are the ways Ashbery finds to deal with the deposits of history and hazard which determine the course of life:

> *They were the players, and we who had struggled*
> * at the game*
> *Were merely spectators, though subject to its*
> * vicissitudes*
> *And moving with it out of the tearful stadium, borne*
> * on shoulders, at last.*

It is entirely in keeping with the tone of this poem that we are left uncertain as to whether we are borne out of the stadium triumphant or dead. Or both. Just as, at the end of "**Soonest Mended**", action is described as

> *　　　　　　this careless*
> *Preparing, sowing the seeds crooked in the furrow,*
> *Making ready to forget, and always coming back*
> *To the mooring of starting out, that day so long ago.*

The brave carelessness here is licensed by some certainty that no matter how many mistakes we make, no matter what happens, we *do* return to the "mooring of starting out". We can also read this as helplessness. The tone is partly elegiac, owning up to the futility of our efforts, with "mooring" sounding as much like death as a new life. The entire poem has this doubleness of feeling. Its long breathy lines shift quickly from one historical hazard to another; it doesn't take long to get from the endangered Angelica of Ariosto and Ingres to Happy Hooligan in his rusted green automobile. Caught up in a whirligig of historical process, the self has no chance to recover balance, and above all, no conceptual means, no language to do so. Still, the energetic lines breathe the *desire* to assert ego and vitality. The poem sees the world as so full of bright particulars that no rules of thumb can keep up with them; and so it is fairly bitter about standard patterns of history and learning, sees them only as shaky hypotheses. "**Soonest Mended**" doesn't yet pretend pleasure in the present, a pleasure Ashbery *does* experience in later poems; and yet the poem doesn't entirely fall back on dreams of another world. Falling back, not with too much conviction, on the proverbial wisdom of the title, Ashbery has found a middle diction: ready to improvise, yielding to but not swamped by randomness.

. . . . .

I have talked about complementary voices and attitudes in Ashbery's work—alternatives between which **"Soonest Mended"** seems poised—the ways of concision and copiousness. Before *Three Poems* Ashbery was strongly attracted to foreshortening, "leaving all out", moving figuratively: discarding things so that we "resemble a taller / Impression of ourselves". It is easy to forget how fierce and compelling that desire was:

> groping shadows of an incomplete
> *Former existence so close it burns like the mouth that*
> *Closes down over all your effort like the moment*
> *Of death, but stays, raging and burning the design of*
> *Its intentions into the house of your brain, until*
> *You wake up alone, the certainty that it*
> *Wasn't a dream your only clue to why the walls*
> *Are turning on you and why the windows no longer*
>   *speak*
> *Of time but are themselves, transparent guardians you*
> *Invented for what there was to hide.*

> > **("Clepsydra")**

Something has happened between that fevered vision and the more relaxed, but still yearning, close of **"Self-Portrait in a Convex Mirror"**: the Parmigianino portrait recedes, virtually assassinated by the poet; it becomes

> *an invitation*
> *Never mailed, the "it was all a dream"*
> *Syndrome, though the "all" tells tersely*
> *Enough how it wasn't. Its existence*
> *Was real, though troubled, and the ache*
> *Of this waking dream can never drown out*
> *The diagram still sketched on the wind,*
> *Chosen, meant for me and materialized*
> *In the disguising radiance of my room.*

Both this passage and the one from **"Clepsydra"** acknowledge a constellation of dreams perhaps more "real" than "real life" ("the certainty that it / Wasn't a dream"). But the version in **"Self-Portrait"** is wistful, rather than driven: Ashbery seems open to the varieties of experience, registers more pleasurably the ache of the veiled and ineluctable dream. He makes his bow to an ironic view of the visionary self ("the 'it was all a dream' / Syndrome") before returning to a hidden truth behind colloquial language ("the 'all' tells tersely / Enough how it wasn't"). The present *disguises* the tempting dream behind Parmigianino's portrait, but disguises it in the "radiance" of the Poet's room. No need to choose between the present and the unseen—and in the pressured light of the passing of time, no *way* to do so.

It is the jumble of everyday pleasures and frustrations that we hear most often in the fluid style of some of the shorter

poems of *Self-Portrait in a Convex Mirror*. Even the longer poem **"Grand Galop"** is almost literally an attempt to keep the poem's accounting powers even with the pace of inner and outer events. Naturally it doesn't succeed. The mind moves in several directions at once, and the poem is partly about the exhaustions and comic waste carried along by the "stream of consciousness":

> *The custard is setting; meanwhile*
> *I not only have my own history to worry about*
> *But am forced to fret over insufficient details related*
>   *to large*
> *Unfinished concepts that can never bring themselves*
>   *to the point*
> *Of being, with or without my help, if any were*
>   *forthcoming.*

At the start of the poem, the mind moves on ahead of some lists of names (weigela, sloppy joe on bun—the end of the line for Whitman's famous catalogues) and then the poem says we must stop and "wait again". "Nothing takes up its fair share of time". Ashbery calls our attention repeatedly, and with frustration rather than exultation, to the fact that the poem's time is not outside time.

"Grand Galop" also laments the generalizing and pattern-making powers which intervene and block our experience of particulars:

> *Too bad, I mean, that getting to know each just for*
>   *a fleeting second*
> *Must be replaced by imperfect knowledge of the*
>   *featureless*
>   *whole,*
> *Like some pocket history of the world, so general*
> *As to constitute a sob or wail unrelated*
> *To any attempt at definition.*

Imperfect and *featureless* fall with deadpan accuracy in lines which expose the hazards of "aping naturalness". Ashbery's **"Man of Words"** finds that

> *All diaries are alike, clear and cold, with*
> *The outlook for continued cold. They are placed*
> *Horizontal, parallel to the earth,*
> *Like the unencumbering dead. Just time to reread this*
> *And the past slips through your fingers, wishing*
>   *you were there.*

Poetry can never be quite quick enough, however grand the "galop", however strong the desire to "communicate something between breaths". This explains some of the qualities of Ashbery's style which trouble readers. What seems strange is not so much *what* he says as the space between his sentences, the quickness of his transitions. "He" will become "you" or "I" without warning as experiences move close and then farther away, photographs and tapes of themselves. Tenses will shift while the poem refers to itself as part of the past. We feel as if something were missing; we become anxious as if a step had been skipped. So does the poet who, in several of the shorter poems, describes himself as a dazed prologue to someone else's play, or longs for a beautiful apocalypse:

> for a moment, I thought
> The great, formal affair was beginning, orchestrated,
> Its colors concentrated in a glance, a ballade
> That takes in the whole world, now, but lightly,
> Still lightly, but with wide authority and tact.

There are moments when Ashbery takes perilous shelter in the world of fable and dream, as in **"Hop o' My Thumb"**, whose speaker, a kind of Bluebeard, imagines possessing his sirens ("The necklace of wishes alive and breathing around your throat") in an atmosphere at once hothouse and **"Lost Horizon"**:

> There are still other made-up countries
> Where we can hide forever,
> Wasted with eternal desire and sadness,
> Sucking the sherbets, crooning the tunes, naming the names.

Yet these worlds, while drawing out some gorgeous imaginings, generate as much restlessness as the confusing world of daytime plenty. We may share the moment in **"Märchenbilder"** when "One of those lovelorn sonatas / For wind instruments was riding past on a solemn white horse". With it goes impatience, the desire to escape, a very rich and suggestive ambivalence. The fairy tales

> are empty as cupboards,
> To spend whole days drenched in them, waiting for the next whisper,
> For the word in the next room. This is how the princes must have behaved,
> Lying down in the frugality of sleep.

The third of the exotic poems in this volume, **"Scheherazade"**, suggests what Ashbery is after in such works. He doesn't retell the story of the Sultan and the ideal storyteller, but he does explore with evident interest and desire the condition of that inventive lady. She is part of a world of dry lands, beneath which are rich hidden springs. "An inexhaustible wardrobe has been placed at the disposal / Of each new occurrence." She loves the "colored verbs and adjectives",

> But most of all she loved the particles
> That transform objects of the same category
> Into particular ones, each distinct
> Within and apart from its own class.
> In all this springing up was no hint
> Of a tide, only a pleasant wavering of the air
> In which all things seemed present, . . .

That love of detail and rich ability to cope with it, an experience of the world without anxiety, without being overwhelmed by plenitude, is rarely felt in *Self-Portrait*, and therefore to be envied in the world of **"Scheherazade"**. Is it available in the randomness of daily life in America? Ashbery has an affectionate eye and an espe-

cially affectionate ear for the comic and recalcitrant details of American life: "sloppy joe on bun" stands not too far from the weigela which "does its dusty thing / In fire-hammered air". In **"Mixed Feelings"** several young girls photographed lounging around a fighter bomber "circa 1942 vintage" summon up a sense of the resistant particulars which tease the imagination. The fading news-shot flirts with the poet's curiosity. He names the girls of that period affectionately—the Ruths and Lindas and Pats and Sheilas. He wants to know their hobbies. "Aw nerts, / One of them might say, this guy's too much for me." Each side has its innings: the girls are imagined as wanting to dump the poet and go off to the garment center for a cup of coffee; the poet, laughing at their "tiny intelligences" for thinking they're in New York, recognizes that their scene is set in California. What's delightful about this poem is the relaxed exchange of imagining mind with imagined objects, a kind of seesaw in which each is given independent play. Though the girls are dismissed, he is fully prepared to encounter them again in some modern airport as "astonishingly young and fresh as when this picture was made".

One of the most engaging things about Ashbery's book is his own susceptibility to American sprawl, while understanding its impossible cost. There is a serious undertone—or is it the main current?—in a poem called **"The One Thing That Can Save America"**.

> The quirky things that happen to me, and I tell you,
> And you instantly know what I mean?
> What remote orchard reached by winding roads
> Hides them? Where are these roots?

Along with a healthy love of quirkiness, Ashbery expresses a bafflement that any individual radiance is ever communicated from one person to another. The "One Thing" that can "Save America" is a very remote and ironic chance that

> limited
> Steps . . . can be taken against danger
> Now and in the future, in cool yards,
> In quiet small houses in the country,
> Our country, in fenced areas, in cool shady streets.

The poem reaches a political point which it would be oversimplifying, but suggestive, to call "populist".

The enemy, over and over again, is *generality*. The generalizing habit, he tells us in **"All and Some"**, draws us together "at the place of a bare pedestal. / Too many armies, too many dreams, and that's / It." I don't mean that *Self-Portrait in a Convex Mirror* gets down to cracker-barrel preaching. There is too much self-mockery for that.

> Do you remember how we used to gather
> The woodruff, the woodruff? But all things
> Cannot be emblazoned, but surely many
> Can, and those few devoted
> By a caprice beyond the majesty

Of time's maw live happy useful lives
Unaware that the universe is a vast incubator.

What I am getting at is that Ashbery's new variety of tone gives him access to many impulses unresolved and frustrated in *The Double Dream of Spring*.

Whitman's invitation for American poets to loaf and invite their souls can't have had many responses more mysterious, peculiar, searching, and beautiful than Ashbery's recent poems. Where he will go from here there is, to use one of his titles, "no way of knowing". What *is* important is that Ashbery, who was on speaking terms with both the formalism of the American 1950s and the unbuttoned verse of the 1960s is now bold and beyond them. His three most recent books have explored apparently contradictory impulses—a melancholy withdrawal, and a bewildered, beguiling openness—which stand in provocative tension with one another. Older readers have tended to find the poems "difficult"; younger readers either do not experience that difficulty or see past it, recognizing gestures and a voice that speak directly to them. Perhaps it is reassuring to them: a voice which is honest about its confusions; a voice which lays claim to ravishing visions but doesn't scorn distraction, is in fact prey to it. Ashbery does what all real poets do, and like all innovators, his accents seem both too close and too far from the everyday, not quite what we imagine *art* to be. He mystifies and demystifies at once.

Grace Schulman (essay date 1977)

SOURCE: "To Create the Self," in *Twentieth Century Literature,* Vol. XXIII, No. 3, October, 1977, pp. 299-313.

[*In the following excerpt, Schulman explores the defining characteristics of Ashbery's visionary poetry.*]

"From this I shall evolve a man,"[1] Wallace Stevens wrote of the mind's efforts to integrate the self by controlling a swarm of external phenomena. And in our time there are poets whose work is built on the awareness of disorder, confusion, and change, and for whom those very conditions generate the discovery of an interior life through powers above the level of reason. That self-discovery is attained by revelation that is not ultimate, as is the mystic's or the saint's; it is, however, genuine, in that the poet has broken through the limitations of conventional vision to see and to proclaim the truth of what has been seen.

The poetry of Arthur Gregor, John Ashbery, and Jean Garrigue is, each in its own way, based on genuine vision and on revelation through clouds of distress and exile. Each has developed a method of meditation through which the soul may strive toward unity of being. Central to the work of each poet is a vision of the integrated self, as well as the unification of all people and the union of people and things. Each poet dramatizes the belief in the power of art to reveal a continuous present and to cut through the limiting divisions of days, hours, and years.

Those notions are related to Plato's idea that the oneness of absolute truth, beauty, and good may be accessible to faculties above the rational. They recall Coleridge's famous concept of the Imagination:

> The poet, described in *ideal* perfection, brings the whole soul of man into activity, with the subordination of its faculties to each other, according to their relative worth and dignity. He diffuses a tone and spirit of unity, that blends, and (as it were) *fuses,* each into each, by that synthetic and magical power to which we have exclusively appropriated the name of imagination. This power, first put in action by the will and understanding . . . reveals itself in the balance or reconciliation of opposite or discordant qualities: of sameness, with difference; of the general, with the concrete; the idea, with the image; the individual, with the representative; the sense of novelty and freshness, with old and familiar objects; a more than usual state of emotion, with more than usual order . . . [2]

Coleridge's statement suggests that the very method of reconciliation is its aesthetic importance. So too, it is not the discovery of truth (which is, actually, the province of the mystic) but the concentration which the act of discovery demands from the poet of genuine vision.

In *The Poetry of Meditation,* Professor Louis L. Martz has discussed the work of seventeenth-century poets in the light of his investigation of Jesuitical methods of meditation. He writes:

> A meditative poem is a work that creates an interior drama of the mind; this dramatic action is usually (though not always) created by some form of self-address, in which the mind grasps firmly a problem or situation deliberately evoked by the memory, brings it forward toward the full light of consciousness, and concludes with a moment of illumination, where the speaker's self has for a time, found an answer to its conflicts.[3]

[Ashbery] has created methods to transform the transcendent experience into art, as well as to reveal the self in its wholeness. . . .

However different their methods, John Ashbery and Arthur Gregor have affinities in creating a poetry of genuine vision and in dramatizing aesthetic revelation. At the center of their work is the belief that art is a medium for knowing a hidden objective reality and revealing its beauty. That principle recalls Marianne Moore's lines: "Above particularities, / These unparticularities praise cannot violate."[8] And like Marianne Moore, who wrote of objects in ways that expressed forces beyond them, both poets use presentative images to capture the intangible nature of things. Observations, rendered with clarity, are transformed in the process of self-discovery, and lead to perceptions of permanence.

John Ashbery's visionary poetry did not begin until later in his career, after he had devised, and discarded, various methods that would enable him to capture and render the invisible world. Since these tendencies illuminate his final achievement, however, they are essential to a study of his great vision.

From the beginning of his career, John Ashbery has been concerned with the fragmentation of modern life, and with the artist's impulse to seize that elusive moment of reality by cutting through the crowded texture of experience. In his first book, *Some Trees* (1956), he juxtaposes images of present life with those of the unseen, combining them as a way of inquiring into the nature of reality. In **"The Instruction Manual,"** the speaker, writing about "the uses of a new metal,"[9] dreams of Guadalajara, a city he "wanted most to see, and most did not see." Escape from the manual affords a glimpse into what is real—and yet this elusive beauty sends him back to the manual and to the ordinary world. Still, the imagined scene lingers, shaping the speaker's experience, its images sharpened by their remoteness from conventional vision:

> How limited, but how complete withal, has been
> our experience of Guadalajara!
> We have seen young love, married love, and the
> love of an aged mother for her son.
> We have heard the music, tasted the drinks, and
> looked at colored houses.
>
> *(Some Trees)*

In that first book, Ashbery's concern with visual perception recalls Whitman's passive observer in *Leaves of Grass,* and is reminiscent also of Emerson's belief, set forth in "The Poet," his essay, that the poet is a seer, standing at the center, courageously accepting the challenge to submit to his vision. Although the image of obtaining knowledge by sight occurs often in the book, it rings insistently in **"Answering a Question in the Mountains"**:

> We see for the first time.
> We shall see for the first time.
> We have seen for the first time.
> The snow creeps by; many light years pass.
>
> *(Some Trees)*

Embodying the young poet's visionary experience is a remarkably original use of set forms. Sestinas, sonnets, canzones, pantoums, eclogues, and other set forms are made new when given natural speech cadences and a unique music; and, in contrast, expanded lines are transformed by the devices of parallelism and internal rhyme. Here Ashbery devises forms that will frame his vision, forms that are traditional and yet sufficiently unbinding to permit the dramatization of moments when an ideal order is perceived at a time of heightened awareness, when one scene is grasped by the integrated sense. The title poem begins:

> These are amazing: each
> Joining a neighbor, as though speech
> Were still a performance.
> Arranging by chance
>
> To meet as far this morning
> From the world as agreeing

> With it, you and I
> Are suddenly what the trees try
>
> To tell us we are:
> That their merely being there
> Means something; that soon
> We may touch, love, explain.
>
> *(Some Trees)*

The Tennis Court Oath (1962), incorporating a radically different approach, veers toward the world of the senses. Ashbery juxtaposes disparate images and presents fragmented scenes to approximate chaotic modern life and human division. He depicts a surface reality that assaults the mind, broken only occasionally by moments of radiant light:

> Nothing can be harmed! Night and day are
> beginning again!
> So put away the book,
> The flowers you were keeping to give someone:
> Only the white, tremendous foam of the street has
> any importance,
> The new white flowers that are beginning to shoot
> up about now.[10]

Ashbery's characteristic means of dramatizing the inward search properly begins with the poems collected in *Rivers and Mountains* (1966). For one thing, he uses the pronoun shift to present the soul splitting apart from the self to achieve a new unity. In **"A Blessing in Disguise,"** he utters:

> And I sing amid despair and isolation
> Of the chance to know you, to sing of me
> Which are you. You see,
> You hold me up to the light . . .
>
>   . . . . .
>
> I prefer "you" in the plural, I want "you,"
> You must come to me, all golden and pale
> Like the dew and the air.
> And then I start getting this feeling of exaltation.[11]

In this and subsequent works, the sudden shift to "you" or "he" has spiritual meaning. Even when, in some instances, "you" refers to a loved one, the pronoun implies a reflection of the eternal being; and when "he" is a human figure, the word also incorporates the renewed spirit.

Another of Ashbery's methods of enacting the interior journey resembles Arthur Gregor's method of creating a familiar scene, moving back into memory and then, in the course of meditation, discovering the relationship between the present view and the unity of seemingly disparate events. So in **"The Skaters"** the speaker, considering present confusion, remembering the past, achieves transcendence: "Here I am then, continuing but ever beginning / My perennial voyage . . ." (*Rivers and Mountains*).

Abandoning this method, Ashbery reached another stage in the development of his visionary poetry. Confounded by surface impressions, he sought to achieve wholeness of self by isolating a fragment of sensory experience. Thus, in **"Fragment,"** placed in *The Double Dream of Spring* (1970), he writes of the urgent present, "A time of spotted lakes and the whippoorwill,"[12] as a key to the invisible, the disguised reality.

Three Poems, consisting of prose poems called **"The New Spirit," "The System,"** and **"The Recital,"** is an account of the revelation enabling him to reattach apparently contradictory things to the whole and to find a unifying order in the fragments of experience. "I thought that if I could put it all down, that would be one way. And next the thought came to me that to leave all out would be another, and truer, way . . ."[13] he begins, describing as well the struggle of his poetry: including all sensory data, leaving them out, putting them in transformed by the poetic act.

Here Ashbery presents the disguises of reality, made of phenomena that baffle the senses:

> Yet so blind are we to the true nature of reality at any given moment that this chaos—bathed, it is true, in the iridescent hues of the rainbow and clothed in an endless confusion of fair and variegated forms which did their best to stifle any burgeoning notions of the formlessness of the whole . . . this chaos began to seem like the normal way of being . . .
>
> *(Three Poems)*

"The New Spirit" evolves from surrendering the self and learning to live in others, seeing all surface reality again but through the eyes of others. Doing so, you find

> you have returned not to the supernatural glow of heaven but to the ordinary daylight you know so well before it passed from your view, and which continues to enrich you as it steeps you and your ageless chattels of mind, imagination, timid first love and quiet acceptance of experience in its revitalizing tide. And the miracle is not that you have returned—you always knew you would—but that things have remained the same.
>
> *(Three Poems)*

Although its style is far from expository, *Three Poems* is a systematic declaration of Ashbery's aesthetic, and it prepares the way for his major work, *Self-Portrait in a Convex Mirror* (1975). The amazing title poem is an enactment of that method of self-revelation in which the artist perceives all surface reality, but through the eyes of another being. Because corporeal truth mirrors the world of the invisible, the artist will see what is permanent by taking in all that is transitory. And he will come to terms with the self precisely by studying another being.

The marvelously outlandish image Ashbery uses for the lens of the other being is a distorted self-portrait painted by the master, Francesco Parmigianino. By studying the artist's likeness in the curved mirror, relinquishing the demands of the finite ego, the speaker envisions a painter who has accepted life's limitations and triumphed over them:

> . . . there is in that gaze a combination
> Of tenderness, amusement and regret so powerful
> In its restraint that one cannot look for long.
> The secret is too plain. The pity of it smarts,
> Makes hot tears spurt: that the soul is not a soul,
> Has no secret, is small, and it fits
> Its hollow perfectly: its room, our moment of
>   attention.[14]

By discovering his kinship with the painter's interior self— for the portrait is, in its very obliquity, of the man's inner world—the speaker sees his own life transformed:

> . . . I see in this only the chaos
> Of your round mirror which organizes everything
> Around the polestar of your eyes which are empty,
> Know nothing, dream but reveal nothing.
> I feel the carousel starting slowly
> And going faster and faster: desk, papers, books,
> Photographs of friends, the window and the trees
> Merging in one neutral band that surrounds
> Me on all sides, everywhere I look.
>   *(Self-Portrait in a Convex Mirror)*

Retreating from the portrait to examine the events of his daily life, the speaker sees all objects in the haze of Francesco's vision, and then alternates between the ideal world of art and the blight, the inertia of modern society ("Can you stand it, / Francesco? Are you strong enough for it?").

Returning to the present, the poet sees with renewed vision. He has sought "a movement / Out of the dream into its codification." And although there are no fundamental changes in the world around him, he sees its fragment made whole by the creative act. That process, we learn, is the immortality of Francesco and the survival of humankind. . . .

Notes

[1] Wallace Stevens, *The Man with the Blue Guitar, Including Ideas of Order* (New York: Knopf, 1952), p. 42.

[2] Samuel Taylor Coleridge, *Biographia Literaria,* ed. J. Shawcross (2 vols., Oxford: Clarendon Press, 1907), II, 12-13.

[3] Louis L. Martz, *The Poetry of Meditation: A Study in English Religious Literature of the Seventeenth Century* (New Haven: Yale Univ. Press, 1954), p. 330.

[8] Marianne Moore, *Complete Poems* (New York: Viking/Macmillan, 1968), p. 142.

[9] John Ashbery, *Some Trees* (New Haven: Yale Univ. Press, 1956), p. 26—hereafter cited in text.

[10] *The Tennis Court Oath: A Book of Poems* (Middletown, Conn.: Wesleyan Univ. Press, 1962). p. 35.

[11] *Rivers and Mountains* (1966; New York: Ecco Press, 1977), p. 26—hereafter cited in text.

[12] *The Double Dream of Spring* (1970; New York: Ecco Press, 1976) p. 87.

[13] *Three Poems* (New York: Viking, 1972), p. 3—hereafter cited in text.

[14] *Self-Portrait in a Convex Mirror* (New York: Viking, 1975), p. 69—hereafter cited in text.

Dana Yeaton (review date 1981)

SOURCE: A review of *As We Know*, in *The American Poetry Review*, Vol. X, No. 1, January-February, 1981, pp. 34-6.

[*In the following positive review, Yeaton praises linguistic aspects of "Litany."*]

Imagine, a sixty-five page poem written in two columns to be read simultaneously. That means you can't read it— alone, anyway. You'll need two readers, male and female for the difference in pitch, but even then, as my friends and I found after taping **"Litany,"** you can't really say you've heard the poem. Concentrating on one of the readers means ignoring the other; listening for the interplay between voices means missing the sense of each. At times they seem to overhear each other, to respond by echoing or by shifting to an aspect of the other's topic. Or one voice stops and the other, filling the silence left, assumes the power of both. Inevitably, they compete for attention, and this is nothing new for followers of Ashbery, though in **"Litany"** he has discovered a form which is perhaps his clearest expression to date of the fact that:

> Sometimes a pleasant, dimpling
> Stream will seem to flow so slowly all of a
> Sudden that one wonders if it was this
> Rather than the other that one was supposed to
>   read.

When the two monologues click, when for example we hear "materialize" and "dematerialize" pronounced at the same time, or "finality" followed by "fatality," or when one voice stops and the other seems to continue the thought, we can only wonder if it was intended or not. Obviously the poems weren't written simultaneously—was it choreography or chance? Of course there are elements of both; what's important is that **"Litany"** keeps us guessing and that the poet has given up, at least in part, his role as controlling presence. With **"Litany,"** Ashbery continues to redefine poetry by changing the status of the poet from one who creates meaning to one who creates the occasion for it.

Of course there's controversy here. Ashbery's "poetry of distraction"—"compositions made of what the day provides"—asks to be read as it is written, that is, by suspending judgment of what the poem is about, what it means and where it's going. "We must learn to read in the dark," he tells us, indicating that the rewards will not go

to the reader who can squeeze coherence out of any text, but to the one who somehow "found the strength / To be carried irresistibly away." Ashbery's poems have been called "fitful," "abstruse," "obsessively autobiographical," and he has been criticized for what is called his "hyper-conscious awareness." (Except for the obsessive bit, he is probably loved for these same characteristics.) But even the critics who have judged his previous work inaccessible or unsociable will agree that in *As We Know* Ashbery has found a way to be simple. Still fitful, still idiosyncratic and likely to "start out with some notion and switch to both," Ashbery has allowed himself startling fits of clarity. We get long discursive passages—on the state of poetry, the need for humanistic criticism, or the need to be taken care of, all written in the baldest prose—that demonstrate Ashbery's enduring commitment to the idea that anything is material for poetry, "as any magic / Is the right thing at the right time." And if this book is to be called obsessively autobiographic, it should be mentioned that the obsession is with writing our biographies as well, because as the title indicates, *As We Know* is about common knowledge—common, but perhaps never before articulated. It's "the same thing we are all seeing, / Our world," he says in **"A Tone Poem,"** but who can say, he asks in **"Litany,"** "Exactly what is taking place all about us?"

> Not critics, certainly, though that is precisely
> What they are supposed to be doing, yet how
> Often have you read any criticism
> Of our society and all the people and things in it
> That really makes sense, to us as human beings?
> I don't mean that a lot that is clever and intelligent
> Doesn't get written, both by critics
> And poets and men-of-letters in general
> But exactly whom are you aware of
> Who can describe the exact feel
> And slant of a field in such a way as to
> Make you wish you were in it, or better yet
> To make you realize that you are in it
> For better or for worse, with no
> Conceivable way of getting out?

Why, John Ashbery of course.

> You knew
> You were coming to the end by the way the other
> Would be beginning again, so that nobody
> Was ever lonesome, and the story never
> Came to its dramatic conclusion, but
> Merely leveled out like linen close up
> In the mirror. So that the roundness
> Was all around to be appreciated, yet somehow flat
> As well, and could never be trusted
> Even though the rushes slanted all one way
> In the autumn wind, and the leaves
> And branches tried to slant with them
> In a poem of harmonious dejection, but it was
> Only picture-making. Under
> The intimate light of the lantern
> One really felt rather than saw
> The thin, terrifying edges between things
> And their terrible cold breath.

And no one longed for the great generalities
These seemed to preclude. Each thought only
Of his private silence, and hungered
For the promised moment of rest.

Picture-making is the trap **"Litany"** wants to avoid by describing, not the mean event, but the feel of "the rushes slanted all one way." The leaves and branches "*tried* to slant with them" because their motion was imagined as effort and that image is now fused with the perception.

Strangely enough, Ashbery's animism has been used as evidence against him. In a review of his last book, ***Houseboat Days***, one critic complained that the poet's "'nature' appeared as a stage version of reality," and called the tendency "narcissistic." (No doubt he'll be interested in Ashbery's argument that landscapes are more human than portraits.) To me, Ashbery's animism is recognition of the fact that "the seeing is taken in with what is seen." **"Tapestry,"** the poem this line appears in, begins by pointing to the difficulty of separating the tapestry from the "room or loom which takes precedence over it"—from our ideas of its origin. His clinical, textbook diction makes it clear that he is not discussing poetic ways of seeing but basic human perception:

> *The eyesight, seen as inner,*
> *Registers over the impact of itself*
> *Receiving phenomena, and in doing so*
> *Draws an outline, or a blueprint,*
> *Of what was just there. . . .*

Ashbery's concern in **"Tapestry"** is not with displaying his own poetic prowess or powers of association but with discussing a shared problem: "We can hear it, even think it, but," he says in **"A Tone Poem,"** try as we might, we "can't get disentangled from our brains." And this is Ashbery's gamble in *As We Know*; he claims to know how and what we think. "You know what I mean," the title seems to say, and the success or failure of the book teeters on his ability to tell us what we know, to say, in his best T. S. Eliot voice, "There comes a time when the moment / Is full of, knows only itself," and have the reader answer, "Yes, come to think of it, there does."

"But this is about people. / Right," Ashbery says in **"Litany,"** reminding himself and us of his promise to speak "to us as human beings." Of course there are only individual testimonies to say that the promise is kept. Even when the outlook is bleak, I find the book consoling because no matter how terrible "the thin, terrifying edges between things" may be, it is soothing to hear them named accurately and compassionately. There is a person on the other end of these poems who is sad, cynical, and a little angry. He is also happy, well-adjusted and has a way of describing our situation that:

> *can end up really reminding us*
> *How big and forceful some of our ideas can be—*
> *Not giants or titans, but strong, firm*
> *Human beings with a good sense of humor*

And a grasp of a certain level of reality that
Is going to be enough—will have to be—

One advantage of "**Litany**'s" format is that it allows for a conversational manner of speaking which might be judged facile, or too much like prose, if each monologue were not complicated by the other. But **"Litany"** doesn't worry about being mundane; in fact, it flaunts it. One monologue begins with "The simple things / Like having toast or / Going to church" and the other ends by asking a simple favor: "I've written several times but / Can't straighten it out—would you / Try?" Here is a long poem which mocks the idea of any invocation and refuses to come to its dramatic conclusion. And shouldn't there be more literary allusions? and what about these wordy, uncondensed sentences that crop up? Here's a poem that doesn't play by the rules.

Maybe it's unfair to read so much revolution into **"Litany"** though. It doesn't protest established notions of poetry as much as it gets along without them.

> *All I want*
> *Is for someone to take care of me,*
> *I have no other thought in mind,*
> *Have never entertained any. . . .*
>
> *But why you*
> *May ask do I want someone to take care of me*
> *So much? This is why:*
> *I can do it better than anyone, and have*
> *All my life, and now I am tired*
> *And a little bored with taking care of myself*
> *And would like to see how somebody else might*
> *Do it, even if that person falls on their face*
> *Trying to, in the attempt.*

Surely this is bad poetry by contemporary standards. It repeats itself. It tells when it should show. Where are the sensual images? Certainly not that person falling on his face; that's the resident cliche, which is followed by a perfect instance of tautology: "Trying to, in the attempt." Surely this is bad poetry and maybe that's what makes it so appealing. Rather than reduce the feeling to a phrase or name or metaphor, Ashbery expands it, luxuriates in it and the common words that express it. Throughout **"Litany"** and the shorter poems which follow, he can be seen mining ordinary language, and not only for the wisdom or humor stored in its sayings, but for the beauty of simple expression:

> *She said this once and turned away*
> *Knowing we wanted to hear it twice. . . .*
>
> *An idea I had and talked about*
> *Became the things I do.*

These lines have what I want to call a totally linguistic appeal. In its context, "She" does not refer to anyone, so that "turned away" does not create a visual image. The image here is in the idea, the shared experience of having heard something we would like to hear again. In the same way, "An idea I had and talked about" is language specific. There are no pretty words referring us to the sensible world, only the familiar, colorless ones which are normally edited in the poetry-making process. We usually demand some roughage in our verse and do without an article there, a preposition here. But rather than shorten the phrase, Ashbery prefers to economize by leaving out the explanation, the controlling context, which would otherwise provide a comfortable transition from one thought to the next. These are the "privileged omissions" which keep us continually off balance, afraid to look anywhere but at our feet. By calling this a poetry of distraction, we miss the sense in which it is a poetry of extreme concentration. In and between the lines it is our "chronic inattention" Ashbery is attacking.

At times the omissions are easily filled. In the first of "**Litany**'s" three sections, one stanza begins, "There was another photograph / In that album," when there's been no mention of photographs or an album. But what more background do we need? The line provides its own; someone was talking about some photos and we've come in in the middle. Yet there's a nagging insufficiency in an explanation like this because it tends to limit possibilities which Ashbery has carefully left open. Having learned to accommodate these, we're still faced with the transitions which occur in a rapid series, intended, apparently, to disorient us. Generally speaking, it's no fun to be lost (**"I Might Have Seen It"** is one exception), and willfully obscure is another name for cheap verse. When Ashbery loses us, however, it's usually with the purpose of finding us again. An elusive and difficult opening to **"Knocking Around"** is followed by the reassurance, "Nothing is very simple." And in **"My Erotic Double,"** just when the poem is leaving its original scene, and us, behind, Ashbery speaks to the confusion and in doing so releases us from it: "We are afloat. . . ." Now enjoy it.

> One destroys so much merely by pausing
> To get one's bearings, and afterwards
> The scent is lost.

The thought is not a new one, to Ashbery or to modern poetry, but in **"Litany"** it takes on special meaning. In the armchair, we can stop and flip back a few pages or sneak a preview, but a public performance will go on without us. Keeping up with **"Litany"** means accepting our uncertainty. Take the scenery in section I: Spain and the Sahara, Greece and the bayou, tumbleweed and tropics, airports, terraces . . . the object is to keep us moving, and this whirlwind tour is only part of the disorientation. There is the chatter of two voices—a kind of sensory overload—and on top of it, the usual difficulties and distractions associated with a public reading.

Book in hand, it's easier to see how **"Litany"** manages to console us in the face of so much confusion. John Holden, writing for *The American Poetry Review* (July/August 1979), has already mentioned Ashbery's predilection for the syntax of a well-reasoned prose paragraph, how Ashbery uses the sound of logic to connect disparate images.

The stanza may begin with a concise topic sentence, as, for instance, "What was green before is homeless." This is supported by the fact that "The mica on the front of the prefecture spells out 'Coastline'. . . ." Nonetheless they "come round to my idea, my hat, as it would be if I were you in dreams and in business only. . . ." Holden's point is that by presenting an argument thoroughly convinced of itself, Ashbery is able to give idiosyncratic associations the credibility of logical extensions. Similarly, by using a word twice for its different functions, he will pivot undetected from one thought to the next. Or, as in **"A Box and Its Contents,"** the phrase "You see" is not repeated but receives a second meaning retroactively:

> You see, only some of the others were crying
> And how your broad smile paints in the wilderness
> A scene of happiness, with balloons and cars.

As abrupt as the transitions in an Ashbery poem may be—as staggering to us cognitively—they are not abrupt to the ear, and this is the triumph of Ashbery's lyricism. In a voice neither manic nor neurotic, he manages to shift from topic to topic, changing postures, overwhelming us with divergent feelings and reactions—signs which in a Berryman or Plath prefigured an early end.

> I was waiting for a taxi.
> It seemed there were fewer
> Of us now, and suddenly a
> Whole lot fewer. I was afraid
> I might be the only one.

A paranoid thought, to be sure, but so wryly expressed we can hardly worry for Ashbery's sanity. "I might be the only one," the left column says in the pause between stanzas on the right. "And I too am concerned that it / Be this way for you," the right begins, "That you / Get something out of it too." Again, simple words expressing a simple desire show a reluctance to "poeticize"—communication so direct, who can doubt its sincerity? It's as though Ashbery cares more for us than for poetry.

Fortunately, he never has to choose; Ashbery has found a means of expression totally adequate to—because inseparable from—its message. Language is not the enemy. The customary struggle with words will not take place, because in fact words *can* express how he feels, what he means, though we may have to change our ideas of expression to see how "It is they who carry news of it / To other places. Therefore / Are they not the event itself?"

"Litany" is not the telling of a story but the story itself, of how someone once sat down and began writing, and certain things occurred to him and were the grammar presiding over what might be said. Easy acceptance of itself makes **"Litany"** a machine—a poetry machine—which produces itself. These would probably be fightin' words if Ashbery did not use the analogy himself:

> But how in
> Heck can I get it operating again? Only

Yesterday it was in perfect working order
And now the thing has broken down again.
Autumn rains rust it. And their motion
Attacks my credulity also, and all seems lost.

It isn't. **"Litany"** goes on for another twenty-five pages
and feels as if it could go for twenty-five more, spontane-
ously generating, an infinitely renewable resource, with
each monologue drawing on the other, just as **"Self-Portrait"** draws on Parmagianino's *Self-Portrait*, and **"Fantasia on 'The Nut Brown Maid'"** draws on its 16th century
pretext, "The Nutbrowne Maide." Ashbery will discuss
his, our, fatigue, but he won't complain about it. In fact
it's a good sign.

Well, this time has been very good
For my working, the work is progressing, and so
I assume it's been good for you too, whose work
Is also doubtless coming along, indeed, I know so
From the sudden aging visible in both of us, tired
And cozy around the eyes, as the work prepares to
take off.

Among the things that **"Litany"** calls itself—"an out-
burst," a "lullaby that is an exclamation," "a blatantly
cacophonous if stirring symphony,"—it is also a writer's
workshop, and this is one of its most pleasant surprises.
For the present, our work is this poem, but throughout it
there are references to our novel, our work outside the
poem.

Therefore
All your story should be phrased so that
Tinkers and journeymen may inspect it
And find it all in place, and pass on
Or suddenly on a night of profound sleep
The thudding of a moth's body will awaken you
And drag you with it vers la flamme,
Kicking and screaming. And then
What might have been written down is seen
To have been said, and heard, and silence
Has flowed around the place again and covered it.

Ashbery acknowledges what most poets prefer to ignore—
that the audience for poetry today is made mostly of poets
and would-be poets. We may not be accustomed to such
direct tips, but we are probably looking for them, and they
are part of what makes *As We Know* such a friendly book.
Kind even.

David Fite (essay date 1981)

SOURCE: "On the Virtues of Modesty: John Ashbery's
Tactics against Transcendence," in *Modern Language
Quarterly*, Vol. XLII, No. 1, March, 1981, pp. 65-84.

[*In the following essay, Fite analyzes the opaque nature
of Ashbery's verse, viewing it as an important aspect in
the development of the poet's "aesthetic strategy."*]

John Ashbery provides our belated time an *ars poetica*
most notable for its determined modesty. Poetry may be
"grace," as our mild-mannered poet comes to assert in his
recent long poem, **"Litany,"** but it is a grace that neither
seeks nor delivers that chimerical Romantic transcendence
which remains the preoccupation of many of our best
poets and critics alike today. Writing cannot *"transcend
life,"* Ashbery tells us in **"Litany,"** precisely because *"it
is both / Too remote and too near."* Writing is at the same
time removed from life, from "what continues," and yet
part of it, part of the ongoingness of things. **"The Wrong
Kind of Insurance"** makes the writer's dilemma explicit:

We too are somehow impossible, formed of so
    many different things,
Too many to make sense to anybody.
We straggle on as quotients, hard-to-combine
Ingredients, and what continues
Does so with our participation and consent.

It is important to note that this is a dilemma that destroys
itself in the very process of formulation: "what continues
/ Does so with our participation and consent." Writing,
any kind of communication, of trying "to make sense,"
indeed any kind of telling-ourselves-tales, is part of that
participation, part of the consent of living; as **"Litany"**
again would have it, *The tales / Live now, and we live
as part of them, / Caring for them and for ourselves, warm
at last."* If mankind is, among other things, a conversation—"We are all talkers / It is true"—then John Ashbery
will serve as rhetor, his work both a commentary on *and*
emblem of what lies "underneath the talk . . . / The moving
and not wanting to be moved, the loose / Meaning, untidy
and simple like a threshing floor."

Thus, in **"Soonest Mended,"** one of Ashbery's finest poems,
is the situation facing the poet defined. The epistemological problems that have plagued our poets for the last two
hundred years—the Cartesian split between mind and world,
the ineluctability of our otherness to each other—are not
so much obliterated by Ashbery as accepted, *consented
to,* as part of the "tales" constitutive of ourselves, our
lives. This is a peculiar modesty, but a modesty nonetheless, for the acknowledgment from the *start* is that "Overall is beyond me"—words that a contemporary poet as
gifted as A. R. Ammons takes years and crisis-poem after
interminable crisis-poem to deliver.[2]

Ashbery's modesty is notably productive. Free not to
have to address himself, with anguished Romantic intensity, to the inaccessibility of ultimate beauty and truth,
Ashbery has given us instead, over the last quarter of a
century, a resonant and capacious poetry that features, in
the words of **"Soonest Mended,"** "a kind of fence-sitting
/ Raised to the level of an esthetic ideal."

Ashbery's work has been met with so much consterna-
tion, misunderstanding, and even anger because an aesthetic strategy based on "fence-sitting" necessarily for-
sakes most of the tactics of Romantic and post-Romantic
poetry in English. Ashbery's work does not feature symbols or Romantic, organic wholeness of form. "I wish to

keep my differences," the poet announces at the beginning of **"Litany,"** and it is a proclamation that could have appeared on the title page of *Some Trees* in 1956. Ashbery has always wished to write a poetry that, to use his own phrasing from a laudatory review of the work of Pierre Reverdy, gives us not "une signification allégorique" or "philosophique," but rather a world of "phénomènes vivants," a world that we seem to see "pour la première fois."[3] "But what I mean is there's no excuse / For always deducing the general from particulars," the poet chides in **"All and Some,"** and this "resistance of stiffening formulations," as David Kalstone has called it,[4] is at the tactical center of Ashbery's work. His poems characteristically take the conventions of two different types of discourse, the argument and the story, and systematically fragment, splinter, distort them. What results in the first instance has been aptly described by Ashbery himself:

> It seems to me that my poetry sometimes proceeds as though an argument were suddenly derailed and something that started out clearly suddenly becomes opaque. It's a kind of mimesis of how experience comes to me: as one is listening to someone else—a lecturer, for instance—who's making perfect sense but suddenly slides into something that eludes one. What I am probably trying to do is to illustrate opacity and how it can suddenly descend over us, rather than trying to be willfully obscure.[5]

The argument is "suddenly derailed"; time and again as we read Ashbery's work, we are confronted with the interesting predicament of not being at all troubled by the logic of the lines—but for the fact that we do not know what the argument itself *is*. Ashbery sees his arguments, as well as his stories, as a kind of "music." "What I like about music," he says, "is its ability of being convincing, of carrying an argument through successfully to the finish, though the terms of this argument remain unknown quantities. What remains is the structure, the architecture of the argument, scene or story. I would like to do this in poetry."[6]

Cultivated "opacity" is the result, then, of Ashbery's distortions of the conventions of both argument and narrative. These distortions are meant to deliver what we might call, appropriating Ashbery's words in praise of Gertrude Stein's *Stanzas in Meditation*, "a general, all-purpose model which each reader can adapt to fit his own set of particulars."[7] Such a "general, all-purpose model" obviously makes great demands on its readers, leaves them bereft of most of the crutches of modern critical convention. Ashbery, elucidating the etiology of one of his ubiquitous "its," tells us in **"Litany"** that *"It emerges as a firm / Enigma, burnished, filled in."* The problem is that it is we, the readers of Ashbery, who have to do most of the filling in, and outside of a few generally not very helpful clues to be found in the French and German Surrealism of early in the century, in the American Abstract Expressionist art of the 1950s, in isolated nooks and crannies of writers as different as Wallace Stevens, W. H. Auden, and Ronald Firbank, we have little to go on.

How should, or rather, how *can* we read Ashbery, then? Perhaps we can trust the teller in the midst of his enigmat-

ic tales. In recent years Ashbery has come to show an increasingly good-humored awareness of the nature of his enterprise as a writer. Here is an observation on stylistics from **"And *Ut Pictura Poesis* Is Her Name"**: "Now one must / Find a few important words, and a lot of low-keyed, / Dull-sounding ones." The reader new to Ashbery's work indeed is likely to be alarmed, or rather, bored, by the frequency of low words creeping along in dull lines therein.

> We talked, and after that went out.
> It was nice. There was lots of time left
> And we could always come back to it, and use it
>   later
> But the flowers dropped in the conservatory
> For this was the last day of the year
> Conclusion of many ups and downs. . . .

Thus, the eloquence of **"Fragment."** We have here a determined ordinariness, indeed a tiredness of language. Everywhere in Ashbery's poetry we have, as commentators have frequently noted, a deliberate refusal of the language of "ecstatic peaks of feeling."[8] Add the number of exclamation marks in "Ode to the West Wind" and "The Aeolian Harp"; the sum cannot be much less than that found in all of Ashbery's works. An exclamation mark in Romantic poetry is often an emblem, to use Pater's words, of "restlessly scheming to apprehend the absolute."[9] There is no such restlessness in Ashbery precisely because there is, by design, no such absolute. Instead, Ashbery gives us the flux of our tales together, a knowing-through-telling that discards, even as a possibility, any peaks of synecdochal Romantic knowing, wherein an ecstatic gnomic naming of the One is sought. Ashbery, in consenting to our tales together, accepts their inevitable mediacy, and thereby removes from his poetry the anguished and intense feelingfulness which is the province of the solitary Romantic quester. "Yet nothing was its essence," he tells us in a cryptic line from **"The Wine"** in *As We Know*, and this is to say that since "essence," or Ammons's "Overall," is describable only in terms of the language of things, it is thus, in effect, abolished as "essence," for we know only what our tales tell us. Ashbery's interest, then, will focus not on chimeras, but on the world of man as a conversation; as a good rhetor, he will be interested in *effects,* in the manners and modes of our tales together.

The tactics engendered by Ashbery's repudiation of strenuous Romantic knowing and feeling feature a constant recourse to the conventions of our tales, the tales of our culture, in an effort, *known to be lost from the start,* exactly to pin down the flux of consciousness. The effort is a losing one because *any* manner of essentialized knowing is recognized now to be chimerical. We see this in Ashbery's characteristically modest and amusing attempt to explain his process of writing in **"Ode to Bill"**:

> What is writing?
> Well, in my case, it's getting down on paper
> Not thoughts, exactly, but ideas, maybe:
> Ideas about thoughts. Thoughts is too grand a
>   word.
> Ideas is better, though not precisely what I mean.

In fact, it is impossible to say of anything "precisely what I mean," for precision of this sort is predicated upon essence, immutability. Ashbery's calculated modesty in forsaking any bold epistemological predication allows him a considerable resourcefulness in his subsequent tactics toward what he calls, in **"French Poems,"** "This banality which in the last analysis is our / Most precious possession." Ordinariness of language is but one weapon in a formidably inclusive arsenal. We need to examine the others.

Ashbery's "all-purpose" models begin with indefiniteness of reference. Crucial to his opacity are his vague pronouns, especially his "it." Ashbery surpasses Stevens in his use of this pronoun, whose very vagueness is an emblem of the poet's epistemological hesitance. Many of Ashbery's poems are, in some way or another, exercises in "it." The title poem of *As We Know*, Ashbery's latest volume, gives us one of the most sustained and resonant of these exercises:

> All that we see is penetrated by it—
> The distant treetops with their steeple (so
> Innocent), the stair, the windows' fixed flashing—
> Pierced full of holes by the evil that is not evil,
> The romance that is not mysterious, the life that is
>   not life,
> A present that is elsewhere.
>
> And further in the small capitulations
> Of the dance, you rub elbows with it,
> Finger it. That day you did it
> Was the day you had to stop, because the doing
> Involved the whole fabric, there was no other way
>   to appear.
> You slid down on your knees
> For those precious jewels of spring water
> Planted on the moss, before they got soaked up
> And you teetered on the edge of this
> Calm street with its sidewalks, its traffic,
>
> As though they are coming to get you.
> But there was no one in the noon glare,
> Only birds like secrets to find out about
> And a home to get to, one of these days.
>
> The light that was shadowed then
> Was seen to be our lives,
> Everything about us that love might wish to
>   examine,
> Then put away for a certain length of time, until
> The whole is to be reviewed, and we turned
> Toward each other, to each other.
> The way we had come was all we could see
> And it crept up on us, embarrassed
> That there is so much to tell now, really now.

"As We Know," like **"The Wine,"** is the story of "it," a story that concludes, as so many of Ashbery's recent tales and arguments do, with a moral observation, with a kind of proverbial wisdom that is all the more convincing—**"As We Know,"** the title reassures us—because we

do not really know quite what it means. The "it" of Ashbery's **"As We Know"** is immanent in the apparently unrelated details of "All that we see"—in the treetops, the stairs, the windows with their "fixed flashing." "It" also penetrates and pierces "full of holes," and "it" can be fingered, rubbed, and done, lending a heavily phallic cast to the "small capitulations / Of the dance." But what *is* "it"? The answer, of course, is that we do not know—and are not meant to know. "It" in **"As We Know,"** like most of Ashbery's "its," exists without a referent and thus stands at the crucial place in his poetry where randomness and meaningfulness meet. The details in which we see "it" manifest are all, in fact, metaphoric machinations for saying what is unsayable—unsayable not because transcendent, but because immanent and ongoing through multifoliate particulars. "It" is an unessentialized naming of the flux, of that "doing" which involves "the whole fabric," and the name must be indefinite, must be itself a turning away from essence, because the implicit recognition is that any attempt to say "it," to give expression to the ongoingness of things, is inadequate. As Ashbery's rigorous sense of limits would have "it," the tale of his poem is just another telling that we live in, a telling, furthermore, that is itself a stiffening formulation that cannot be allowed to be true *as such,* but only partakes of truth in so far as tales are what, after all, we "live in."

It is this sense of limits in Ashbery that gives us not only "it," but also the absences of his poetry, the spacious emptiness of much of his imagery, the indefiniteness of individual being implied by the rest of his vague personal pronouns. Ashbery's entire work is, in fact, "pierced full of holes." His poetry is full of absences, of holes, of empty afternoons and empty horizons, of "interstices, between a vacant stare and the ceiling" where "we live" (**"Saying It to Keep It from Happening"**). In **"The Ice-Cream Wars,"** "the truth becomes a hole, something one has always known, / . . . A randomness, a darkness of one's own." The dreamlike, often haunting, often melancholy tone that we encounter in so many of Ashbery's poems is built upon the fundamental absences of flux realizing itself as truth.

Ashbery's strategy of loss delivers serenity, however, as often as it does melancholy, for of the truth of "it" we may say not only what **"The Ice-Cream Wars"** reductively says, as *I* know (the motto of so many assertive and darkly Romantic geniuses), but also, "as *we* know"—the comforting assurance of the more modest rhetor, Ashbery. This recouping of losses through a turn to "we" is, of course, the key strategic maneuver in Ashbery's poetry. The consequent obliteration of the distinct Romantic "I" has been well expressed by Ashbery himself in a statement that is becoming one of the most famous in modern poetics:

> The personal pronouns in my work very often seem to be like variables in an equation. "You" can be myself or it can be another person, someone whom I'm addressing, and so can "he" and "she" for that matter and "we"; sometimes one has to deduce from the rest of the sentence what is being meant and my point is also that it doesn't really matter very much,

that we are somehow all aspects of a consciousness giving rise to the poem and the fact of addressing someone, myself or someone else, is what's the important thing at that particular moment rather than the particular person involved. I guess I don't have a very strong sense of my own identity and I find it very easy to move from one person in the sense of a pronoun to another and this again helps to produce a kind of polyphony in my poetry which I again feel is a means toward greater naturalism.[10]

"As We Know" displays such an indefiniteness in its personal pronouns—an unspecified "we" dissolves into an unspecified "you," which gets caught up with a "they" with no referent, and so on—because, for Ashbery, "it doesn't really matter very much" to pin a pronoun down to a specified and referential antecedent. Ashbery's position here, which is based on his startlingly diffident assumption that "we are somehow all aspects of a consciousness giving rise to the poem," is manifested in many important ways in his poetry, not only in his "polyphony" of pronouns, but also in his willingness to adopt the posturings, the poses, and the phrases of others.

One of the most important tactics in Ashbery's poetry is the use of clichés and pat phrases, the verbal formulas of our culture. The short poems of *As We Know*, for instance, yield, among many others, expressions such as "tried and true," "put it behind me," "turns tail and disappears."[11] More important for Ashbery than these figures of our conversations, though, are the cultural clichés that have become figures of our collective thought. Ashbery has always had an acute ear for the conventions of stories, films, advertisements, art and literary criticism. We see his talent for mimicry highlighted in the Firbankian posturings of **"Illustration"** in *Some Trees*; in the fractured banality of the tale of **"Idaho,"** in *The Tennis Court Oath*; in the outrageous triteness of the lampooning of that bestselling poetess of the 1920s, Ella Wheeler Wilcox, in **"Variations, Calypso and Fugue"** in *The Double Dream of Spring*. Sometimes a poem will become a veritable frolicking in junk, in recycled phrases, as in **"A Sparkler."**

> But just once come back see it the way
> I now see it
> Sit fooling with your hair
> Looking at me out of the corner of your eye
> I'm so sorry
> For what we haven't done in the time we've
>   known each other.
>
> Then it's back to school
> Again yes the sales are on.

We have everything here from Harlequin Romance to **"Gidget Agonistes"** to **"School Days."** A passage such as this is perhaps best seen as an emblem of Ashbery's fascination for that from which he should, at first glance, recoil. For what is a cliché but a stiffened formulation? Many clichés—"strong as a bull," "stubborn as a mule," "clear as crystal"—are but metaphors rendered dead through overuse. An imagistic comparison is especially apt, so gains wide currency as a formulated simile, and thus loses

its ability to spur a perception of resemblances. Ashbery's work is full of similes and metaphors, many of them banal ("the pebbled shore of truth," "the wood of general indifference" [**"In a Boat"**]), others simply nonsensical. Clichés and empty similes and metaphors are accepted by Ashbery; he consents to them finally because, after all, they contribute to our definition of ourselves.

Of course, Ashbery as a rhetor of the detritus of our culture usually does not choose merely to highlight banality for its own sake. Rather, he uses clichés and verbal formulas to establish a mood, a tonality among the many in the poem as moods flash, dissolve, perhaps reemerge, perhaps become transmogrified, perhaps fade again. Such is the case with **"A Sparkler,"** where the onslaught of clichés early in the poem bespeaks a simple and modest honesty of emotion that does not need eloquence of presentation, that shuns high drama—a simple modesty consolidated in the final observation of the poem:

> What is beheld is whatever lives,
> Is wildly unappetizing and inappropriate,
> And sits, and fits us.

Such is the case, too, with the use of clichés in **"As We Know,"** where the story crystallizes from the vague "day you did it" to the descriptive commonplace, "You slid down on your knees / For those precious jewels of spring water." People in bad novels and bad plays are always sliding to their knees; "precious jewels" is even more banal. And yet the effect here is poignant. We do not really know why the unspecified "you" is desperate, but "you" certainly is. There is that typical Ashbery sense of absence, of loss, here—the price to be paid for his fundamental strategy of loss—and the effect is typically haunting. "You," whoever it is, "had to stop," for "there was no other way to appear," and now "you" is prostrate beside a stream. Next, with an ambiguous "And" (Ashbery's coordinating conjunctions often contain no logical force, either in argument or in narrative), "you" is teetering "on the edge" of a "calm street," confronted by a menace or a specter that could have been taken from any number of bad horror films: "As though they are coming to get you." We do not know if the "And" participates in the subordinate clause or whether it initiates a separate coordinate clause of its own; it probably does not matter. The enticing particulars, with their undertones of anguish, desperation, even fear, are what matter. These particulars—a mossy stream (we assume), a calm street with sidewalks and traffic (how calm, then?)—are, it must be noted, not overly specified. Nor were the "treetops" with "steeple," the "stair," or even the windows with their "fixed flashing," a detail more cryptic than precise.

And thus we encounter another tactic integral to Ashbery's aesthetic: his images are not to be prized for their exactitude or their evocative naturalism. Ashbery, like Pierre Reverdy, may be interested in giving us "un paysage naturel,"[12] but such a natural landscape has little to do with the obsessive rendering of sensory particulars. Ashbery is not competing with the scientists for the honors of a specious exactitude; unlike many other poets of our time, he is not contriving to deliver, in the best modern fashion, all the streaks on a tulip. Such a representational neurosis has, in fact, given us but another set of conventions called realism, to be used by good and bad writers alike. Ashbery, a poet as much among modern painters as his friend Frank O'Hara, gives us particulars that are so enticing precisely because they are so unspecified, so elusive. Even the stock scenes he gives us, the clichés, become, by virtue of their participation in the flux of the tale or argument, tantalizingly unclear, part of the "all-purpose model." This effect, of course, is strongly dependent upon Ashbery's skill in manipulating the precarious ambiguities of his neosurrealist descriptive style. We may be unable finally to articulate in New Critical fashion the stratagems contributing to the mood of an Ashbery scene, but a mood, and not a mere chaos, had better be there. The movement from a mossy stream via an ambiguous conjunction to an urban street may not be explicable in an easy referential manner, but it does need to make sense within the world of the poem.

Needless to say, surrealistic juxtaposition is a technique given to turgidity, to frenzied clottedness of matter. Ashbery has not always successfully skirted the dangers of his method. In particular, his second book, **The Tennis Court Oath**, capitulates almost entirely to the urge to give us a mechanical textbook surrealism, with all the surrealist accouterments: automatic writing, random juxtaposition of fragments, scissors and paste as substitutes for artistic intelligence. Self-indulgence reaches a climax in the long poem **"Europe,"** which Harold Bloom is certainly right to call, along with most of the rest of the volume, a "fearful disaster."[13] As Marjorie Perloff has noted, the disaster develops because Ashbery, at this extreme in his art, has deprived himself of even the possibility of disjunctiveness.[14] **"Europe"** is a huge puzzle of particulars that are not juxtaposed in any real way beyond the virtual accident of their being on the pages of the poem together, and their having been drawn from the same obscure book, *Beryl of the Bi-Planes.*

The fact is that Ashbery's elusive images need to be placed within the more leisurely—that is to say, the more truly inclusive—program of his distorted arguments, his fragmented stories. This is the accomplishment of **"As We Know"**:

> But there was no one in the noon glare,
> Only birds like secrets to find out about
> And a home to get to, one of these days.

No one "coming to get you" apparently, and yet there is no comfort here. Elusive, dissolving particulars give us still another sense of absence, a dreamlike sense of the absence of afternoons. A "glare" is a suffusion, an enveloping emptiness of light. Within it, only "birds like secrets to find out about" await, and the simile lets us know what we might already have assumed: that there may be some unspecified secret behind all of this, behind or perhaps even constitutive of "it." And something else awaits: "a home to get to, one of these days." We did not know there had been a journey; at least, a journey had not been made

explicit until now in the mechanisms of the narrative. We do definitely have a sense of wandering, of exile and awaited return here. The effect of the elusive particulars again is haunting, melancholy—and yet the "home" is there.

Ashbery's poems characteristically take the conventions of two different types of discourse, the argument and the story, and systematically fragment, splinter, distort them.

—David Fite

And thus we move to the moral of the story, and to another important Ashbery tactic. Ever since **The Double Dream of Spring**, Ashbery's poems, arguments and narratives alike, have tended to congeal, often, but not necessarily, at the conclusion, into proverbs, maxims, home-style aphorisms. The Greek rhetoricians called this foregrounded display of sententiousness *gnōmologia,* and it is pertinent to note that the Greek word *gnōmōn* means "one that knows"—here, a knowing that gets expressed through utterance, through our conversations together. Harold Bloom has attempted, with extraordinary resourcefulness, to see this knowing in Ashbery in the same light as he sees all Romantic knowing—as gnomic utterance, a kind of gift from the gods of an obsessive-compulsive Psyche. Perhaps Bloom slights the rhetorical quality of *gnōmologia,* a quality manifest in the conjoining of *gnōmē* as "judgment, maxim" and *logos* as "word, discourse." For the proverbial knowledge that Ashbery gives us in poems like **"As We Know"** and **"Soonest Mended"** is not a knowledge based on the lightning bolt of transcendent Romantic truth suddenly wrested from on high. Rather, the proverbs participate fully in the world of Ashbery's fence-straddling aesthetic, an aesthetic of flux which, we should remember, warns us again and again to resist the stiffening formulations of "always deducing the general from particulars."

This is the warning, and yet we have already seen that Ashbery's work is full of congealed cultural clichés and conventions. Now we see that it is also stuffed with generalized proverbs, maxims. Is the defense simply to announce, in engaging Emersonian fashion, that consistency is the hobgoblin of little minds? Or can we, using that other determined practitioner of inconsistency, Walt Whitman, assert that Ashbery is large, that his work contains multitudes?

Ashbery *is* large, he does contain multitudes, and with a largess a good deal less egotistical than Whitman's. But, in fact, the contradiction is apparent, not real. The clichés and conventions, the precious banality, provide us, we have seen, not easy answers, but rather ourselves in all our difficulty—"the charity" of our "hard moments" (**"Soonest**

Mended"). These stock scenes and phrases in Ashbery's work give the reader something to hold on to, a model of particulars that *are* particulars and yet are so unspecified—because so common—that we are left, not with the referential terms of the story, but with the structure of the story itself, in its complex interplay of tone and feeling. In like manner, the proverbs and aphorisms of Ashbery's poetry provide judgments and knowing—provide, that is, both the hortatory and propositional poles of discourse—but deliver them in a manner that leaves us free from easy generalized answers. Indeed, we are free of easy deductions because, again, although the proverbs make sense to us, we do not really know what they mean, to what they refer. Proverbial wisdom thus becomes a gesture based on the appeal of the epideictic. There is a *sharing* in the gravity of Ashbery's proverbial knowing, a sharing—and a solace—made possible precisely by the lack of a referent for that knowing.

> The light that was shadowed then
> Was seen to be our lives,
> Everything about us that love might wish to
>   examine,
> Then put away for a certain length of time, until
> The whole is to be reviewed, and we turned
> Toward each other, to each other.

This is all perfectly reasonable. The syntax is complicated but coherent: a kernel proposition, followed by a long appositional construction, followed by a conjunctive addition to the original independent clause (quibblers might place the concluding coordinate clause within the preceding subordinate clause, which is itself part of the long apposition). As Jonathan Holden has noted, Ashbery uses syntax in writing as the "equivalent of 'composition' in painting: it has an intrinsic beauty and authority almost wholly independent of any specific context."[15] The authority of the syntax, the grave measured cadence to these solemn thoughts, can almost blind us to the fact that, although we are moved, perhaps comforted, by the lines, we do not know what they are about. The "light" refers to the preceding dreamlike "noon glare," but it is a surrealistic "shadowed" light, and although we accept the equation now established between the light and "our lives," we have no reasons for doing so. Ashbery does not work out a clever and dialectical conceit from the equation. Rather, the syntax tells us to accept it—the syntax, and the cunning use of the passive voice. Perhaps "was shadowed" is itself passive; it is either passive or an odd linking verb with an adjectival subject complement. But the other two uses of passive here are less ambiguous and more important: the light "was seen to be our lives," and the whole "is to be reviewed." Ashbery's battery of tactics within verb phrases is reminiscent of Wallace Stevens's. Both poets eschew active, transitive verbs; both reveal a preference for the copula, for the passive, for qualifiers ("might wish," "as though" in this poem).[16] In Ashbery, these tactics are, again, emblems of his epistemological modesty; nothing is ever certain within the flux. We often do not know for sure who did what to whom and when in Ashbery's poems. The poet is reluctant to make unqualified assertions of precise transitivity. The passive re-

mains especially indeterminate because it is usually accompanied by a deletion of the "by" phrase, a deletion not always justified by our knowledge of the context. The "light" was "seen to be our lives"; we read this and assume "seen by us." But the appositional construction then goes on to make the curious equation: the light that was seen is "Everything about us that love might wish to examine." So perhaps it is "love" that is doing the seeing, but how can "love" see? This is another tactic common in Ashbery, a tactic particularly congruent with his use of the passive. There is a further instance of it later in this same poem: "The way we had come was all we could see / And it crept up on us, embarrassed." Other examples abound in Ashbery's poetry: "Some departure from the norm / Will occur as time grows more open about it," "Time is sorting us all out," "Pursuing time this way, . . . / You find it has doubled back," ". . . the historical past owed it / To itself, our historical present," "What was one day to be / Removed itself as far as possible from scrutiny."[17]

These are all instances, of course, of personification. In his use of this figure Ashbery differs considerably from the Romantics, who employed it with such abandon that one of its permutations came to merit its own name, the "pathetic fallacy." Typically, in its central and most impressive usage, personification would be wed to apostrophe. The Romantic poet would, in addressing a mountain or a bird or the wind, personify the natural object or phenomenon with the hope of investing himself and his work synecdochally in the eternal via what Coleridge called the "translucence" of the image become symbol.[18] Ashbery's personifications, on the other hand, very seldom address natural objects precisely because the natural object does not, for him, furnish a symbolical road to the sublime. Rather, his personifications are a kind of coy shorthand for the flux that we engender in living the tales of our lives. It is no accident that our examples feature the personification of "time." Even when the word itself is not "time," it is a virtual synonym: the "way," the "past," "What was one day to be." We see here that Ashbery does not personify natural objects, but rather the abstract terms that he uses to describe the flux of things—to describe, that is, "it." Perhaps the presupposition behind this tactic is most explicitly stated in **"All Kinds of Caresses"**: "Our gestures have taken us farther into the day / Than tomorrow will understand. / They live us." Our gestures, our tales, constitute us, and so, in a way, live us. But it is our having lived them that enables them to live us. Clichés and conventions are formulated gestures that now live us through having been lived so often; personification and the passive likewise are tactics that tell us we are being lived by what we have ourselves done—and what we have done, however often stiffened into formulation, is flux, is "it."

The proverb progresses: the "whole is to be reviewed," perhaps recalling the "doing" earlier that had to be stopped because it involved "the whole fabric." And then the conclusion:

> . . . and we turned
> Toward each other, to each other.

The way we had come was all we could see
And it crept up on us, embarrassed
That there is so much to tell now, really now.

To turn toward each other is to attempt a balance against the fundamental absences of our being. The obtrusive repetition of the prepositional phrase here, and of the adverb "now" at the end, gives the passage its gravity, its poignancy. The story is over; the moral is drawn. We do not really know what the story was about, but we do know it was about "it," about an unspecified and haunted "you" with "a home to get to, one of these days." Perhaps the last strophe, with its turn "Toward each other," with its conjoining, its "we," is home. Perhaps home is the place where "you" has to go. That this "you" becomes "we" and that the turning toward "each other" is couched within the staid and comforting rhythms of the proverbial are indications of Ashbery's recent serenity, an emblem of his mature acceptance of absence and his concomitant recognition of the enduring possibilities of love.

The motto for *As We Know* might very well be "there is so much to tell now, really now." The predominant serenity of *Houseboat Days*, the willingness to settle for a "ride in common variety" (**"Variations on an Original Theme"**), continues in this most recent volume. The poet, willing to acknowledge, as he does in **"Late Echo,"** that "there really is nothing left to write about," nonetheless sees great value in this exercise in only apparent futility: "Or rather, it is necessary to write about the same old things / In the same way, repeating the same things over and over / For love to continue and be gradually different." The writer thus addresses himself to his art for the sake of ethics, for the sake of continuing, changing love. And he acknowledges, too, that his tactics in this latest volume are not at all different from those he has employed all along. Indeed, one does not read Ashbery with an eye for the development of key images and metaphoric ideas; one does not read Ashbery the way one reads Yeats or Eliot or any other symbolist poets whose works are congenial to the mechanisms of New Critical analysis. It is true that *Three Poems*, with its explicit drive for greater inclusiveness, does seem to mark a turning point in Ashbery's career as a poet. And it is true that **"Self-Portrait in a Convex Mirror,"** so atypical in its tactics, and so solemn a Romantic rumination on the ordering imagination of the artist, seems, with its remarkable concluding supplication for the blurring of life and art, to have prepared Ashbery for the less strained, more serene "common variety" of *Houseboat Days* and *As We Know*. But, in fact, most of Ashbery's typical tactics—everything from similes to clichés to "it," from the use of the passive to the pronoun "polyphony" to the surrealism—have been apparent in his work from the start.

Thus, when we encounter what seems like an aberrant new form in the long, stunning dialogue **"Litany,"** we are justified in seeking hidden precursor principles for such formal tactics in Ashbery's earlier work. They are not hard to find. **"Litany"** gives us, after all, a continuation, an exfoliation, of the dialogue form of **"Fantasia on 'The Nut-Brown Maid,'"** the concluding poem of *Houseboat Days*.

That earlier long poem, with its almost ritualistic and oddly affirmative neurasthenia, presents an unspecified "He" and "She" whose exchanges, one not really distinct from the other, perhaps constitute, in the words of "She," an attempt to "play to our absences and soothe them." "We may as well begin the litany here," "She" says at an early point in **"Fantasia,"** but the principles behind the dialogic form of both **"Fantasia"** and **"Litany"** are in Ashbery's work from the start. For what are Ashbery's dialogues but logical developments of his pronoun "polyphony," culminations of his insistence on a most un-Romantic indeterminacy of identity? "He" and "She" in **"Fantasia"** are *not* specified. One wastes one's time looking for psychological distinctions, character development. Similarly, in **"Litany,"** whose columns are "meant to be read as simultaneous but independent monologues," the two voices sometimes circle, sometimes transfuse, sometimes mimic, sometimes have nothing to do with each other. Neither voice has a distinct character, a distinct identity. Taken together, the voices give us a polyphony, an especially capacious "all-purpose model." But their conjoining does not represent the sum of two different parts, for Ashbery will simply not grant himself the easy generalization of verisimilitude, of stable character according to the conventions of realism.

Similarly, the easy answer of Romantic wholeness of form is not available in **"Litany"**; the poem cannot properly be said to be "about" anything. Certain rough distinctions can be made between the three sections of the poem—the last section, for instance, has the strongest religious cast in its phrasing as the **"Litany"** is realized—but these distinctions probably lack real explanatory power. For the poem is, again, a flux; it lacks *by design* the strategic impulse toward a generalized transcendence that confers upon the great poems of English Romanticism their organic wholeness of synecdochal form. **"Litany"** is, after all, a poem that ends with one column telling us we "need" the "rows of windows overlooking / The deep blue sky behind the factory," and the other busy requesting a rectification of a clerical error made with regard to payments for a tape recording.

This latest long poem by Ashbery represents a culmination of the poet's seriously cultivated modesty, and it displays, in expansive, leisurely fashion, virtually all the tactics toward modesty that we have seen appear throughout most of his work. The triumph in **"Litany"** *is* its leisureliness, the space it allows an Ashbery, unfettered from epistemological despair over the relation between saying and being,[19] to stretch out, to use for poetry, as Kenneth Burke, another genial rhetor, says one should use for criticism, "all that is there to use."[20]

Thus, we get anything and everything in **"Litany"**: posturings and parody, homilies and lectures, absurd rhymes and absurder reasons, and love—always love. It may be love expressed in artifice, in eclogue: "The lovers saunter away. / It is a mild day in May." It may be love expressed in the rhetoric of the greeting card:

Remember me now
Remember me ever

And think of the fun
We had together

A friend.

It may be love discussed in the frank rhetoric of our time: *"We fucked too long, / Though, you see."* More than ever, it is this love—or, rather, the possibility of it—that is at the center of Ashbery's modest and yet so inclusive art:

And I too am concerned that it
Be this way for you. That you
Get something out of it too.

"Litany" is full, as no other Ashbery work is, of images of absence, of loss, of interstices. Sea, sun, sky, the emptiness of time and climates: we return obsessively to these images, to the fundamental absences of being inherent in such spaciousness. But always, too, we have love and a kind of good-humored serenity; always we are told by the poet that "I do care." And furthermore, for all the absence of "joy," of ecstatic peaks of feeling, we are given the telling affirmation that "Happiness has not" finally been "lacking"—for the poet, or, he thinks, for any of us as humans, as *"beings made of / Love and time."* Again, this is modesty—a modest aesthetic, and necessarily, since they are inextricably conjoined, a modest ethic. **"Litany"** is, in this sense, a long voyaging through a flux of epideictic gestures, a voyaging whose ethical center is suggested in **"This Configuration"**:

Or it may be that we are ordinary people
With not unreasonable desires which we can satisfy
From time to time without causing cataclysms
That keep getting louder and more forceful instead
  of dying away.

How many poets since Blake, Coleridge, and Shelley have been able to tell us, as Ashbery does here, that they are, in some way, "ordinary people"—"Brushing the teeth and all that" (**"Soonest Mended."**)—and that there is "happiness" in that modest recognition? Certainly not many lyric poets. For such modesty as Ashbery gives us, and for such a consequent inclusiveness, we have to turn to the world of fiction, to the world of the novel, with its social and encyclopedic thrust. Of course, the novel typically has been bound by the very conventions of realism that Ashbery passes well beyond. But Ashbery's ethics in *As We Know* do remind us, at times, of a figure as remote, and yet as similarly decent, as E. M. Forster. Midway through the second section of **"Litany"** Ashbery says:

Yet the writing that doesn't offend us
(Keats' "grasshopper" sonnet for example)
Soothes and flatters the easier, less excitable
Parts of our brain in such a way as to set up a
Living, vibrant turntable of events,
A few selected ones, that nonetheless have
Their own veracity and their own way of talking
Directly into us without any effort so
That we can ignore what isn't there.

Thus, one of the manifold voices in **"Litany"** gives us as explicit a rendering of Ashbery's *ars poetica*, of his solution to the "problem" of art, as we are likely to get. What is wanted is a "Living, vibrant turntable of events" that solves the dilemma of formulation in art, and its necessary exclusiveness, precisely by being "vibrant" enough in its living opacity, in its rendering of the flux of its own telling, to enable the reader to "ignore" all that inevitably "isn't there." An "all-purpose" model that connects the prose and the subdued passion, but in the connection exalts both—that is what Ashbery gives us in **"Litany."** His long-cultivated tactics against transcendence bear fruit here in a poetry as capacious as any of our time—in a poetry as capacious, in fact, as the fiction to which so many of our best contemporary poets have consigned all too many of their imaginative possibilities. Good art, Ashbery tells us again in **Litany.**

can end up really reminding us
How big and forceful some of our ideas can
* be—*
Not giants or titans, but strong, firm
Human beings with a good sense of humor
And a grasp of a certain level of reality that
Is going to be enough—will have to be,
And so lead us gradually back to words
With names we had forgotten. . . .

These are "words" that have "mattered," as the conclusion of **"Litany"** tells us. For all the difficulty of their determined ordinariness, of their uncertain grasping of the flux of "what continues," these are "words" that are "going to be enough—will have to be" for beings as modest as ourselves. As readers of Ashbery, we need to be attentive to the tactics of their formulation.

Notes

[1] I mention or quote from the following volumes by Ashbery: *As We Know* (New York: Viking Press, 1979); *The Double Dream of Spring* (1970; rpt. New York: Ecco Press, 1976); *Houseboat Days* (New York: Viking Press, 1977); *Self-Portrait in a Convex Mirror* (New York: Viking Press, 1975); *Some Trees* (1956; rpt. New York: Ecco Press, 1978); *The Tennis Court Oath* (Middletown, Conn.: Wesleyan University Press, 1962); and *Three Poems* (New York: Viking Press, 1972). I use the following abbreviations for the first four volumes: *AWK, DDS, HD,* and *SPCM.*

[2] See "Corsons Inlet," in Ammons's *Collected Poems, 1951-1971* (New York: Norton, 1972), p. 148.

[3] "Reverdy en Amérique," *Mercure de France,* 344 (January 1962), 110-11.

[4] "John Ashbery: Self-Portrait in a Convex Mirror," *Five Temperaments* (New York: Oxford University Press, 1977), p. 183.

[5] Louis A. Osti, "The Craft of John Ashbery: An Interview," *Confrontation,* 9 (Fall 1974), 89.

[6] This is from a brief autobiographical statement provided in the "Biographies and Bibliography" section of *A Controversy of Poets:*

An Anthology of Contemporary American Poetry, ed. Paris Leary and Robert Kelly (Garden City, N.Y.: Doubleday, 1965), p. 523.

[7] "The Impossible," *Poetry,* 90, No. 4 (July 1957), 251.

[8] The phrase is from Laurence Lieberman's long essay on Ashbery in *Unassigned Frequencies: American Poetry in Review, 1964-77* (Urbana: University of Illinois Press, 1977), p. 12.

[9] "Coleridge's Writings," *Westminster Review,* n.s., 29 (1866), 108. Harold Bloom provides a typically strenuous perspective on the Paterian view of Coleridge in "Coleridge: The Anxiety of Influence," the opening essay of *Figures of Capable Imagination* (New York: Seabury Press, 1976), pp. 1-17.

[10] Quoted in *The Craft of Poetry: Interviews from "The New York Quarterly,"* ed. William Packard (Garden City, N.Y.: Doubleday, 1974), pp. 123-24.

[11] The first example is from "Sleeping in the Corners of Our Lives," p. 71; the second, "And I'd Love You to Be in It," p. 89; the third, "Figures in a Landscape," p. 75.

[12] "Reverdy en Amérique," p. 111.

[13] "John Ashbery: The Charity of the Hard Moments," *Figures of Capable Imagination,* p. 172.

[14] The perception is advanced in Perloff's "'Mysteries of Construction': The Dream Songs of John Ashbery," which is chapter 7 of her forthcoming book, *The Poetics of Indeterminancy: Rimbaud to Cage* (Princeton University Press).

[15] "Syntax and the Poetry of John Ashbery," *American Poetry Review,* 8, No. 4 (July/August 1979), p. 37.

[16] Perloff is discerning here, as she is on many of the antisymbolist tactics in Ashbery's work.

[17] The first example is from "Saying It to Keep It from Happening" (*HD,* p. 29); the next three examples are from "Fantasia on 'The Nut-Brown Maid'" (*HD,* pp. 73, 81, and 86); the final example is from "Variation on an Original Theme" (*AWK,* p. 107).

[18] Samuel Taylor Coleridge, *The Statesman's Manual* (London, 1816), p. 230.

[19] Holden approaches Ashbery from this angle.

[20] *The Philosophy of Literary Form,* 3rd ed. (Berkeley: University of California Press, 1973), p. 23.

Bonnie Costello (essay date 1982)

SOURCE: "John Ashbery and the Idea of the Reader," in *Contemporary Literature,* Vol. XXIII, No. 4, Fall, 1982, pp. 493-514.

[*In the following essay, Costello explores the relationship between author and reader in Ashbery's verse.*]

"My way is, to conjure you"

—Epilogue, *As You Like It*

It has been fashionable in the last decade to discuss separately the writer's attention to his act of composition and the reader's experience of that composition. But rather little has been said about the writer's idea of the reader, about his dependence on the reader, his sense of the gap between fictive and actual reader, his efforts to overcome or deny that gap. Reading is as much Ashbery's subject as writing is, and it is through his idea of reading that his self-reflexiveness escapes banal solipsism and opens onto larger questions of communication. In *Rivers and Mountains* Ashbery first uses the reader as his model for the experience of otherness and he continues this habit throughout the seventies, increasingly inscribing the reader in the text to the point of a second column in **"Litany."** Such reflections on the reader do not reduce the meaning of the text, but on the contrary give immediacy to its great themes. Here is not the image of experience but experience itself, not the record of a relationship but the establishment of one.

Convexity is Ashbery's paradigm of the psychic and ontological distance between writer and reader, and the circumscribed eternity of the work of art. It marks the artist's yearning and failure to escape the confines of his medium to reach the reader's present. Conversely, it marks the reader's sense of being surrounded but not enclosed in the world of a text, the 180° panorama of art's illusion. By the image of convexity the desire between writer and reader is linked to the larger structure of thought which characterizes Ashbery's work, the paradoxes and patterns of assertion and denial which gesture toward but never yield to the mind of the reader. Convexity in Ashbery is also the spatial equivalent of his concept of temporality, the present no point in a hierarchy but a moment passed through, receding as it arrives like a point along a convex curve. And it is the temporal condition of art, its frustrating pattern of deferral and belatedness, which Ashbery makes his major theme, continuing a meditative tradition from Marvell through Keats to Whitman and Stevens.

Ashbery is of course not merely talking about writing and reading literature, acts which take up a relatively minor part of the average person's life, if a major part of the poet's. The poet's experience of the text becomes his vantage point for considering all experience, and the condition of textuality is for him characteristic of the condition of all consciousness. These themes arise early in his work, but they come into focus for him in the seventies, particularly in the poem **"Self-Portrait in a Convex Mirror"** and the volume named for it, which established him as the major poet of the decade.[1]

An unidentified "you" inhabits the pages of Ashbery's work, especially in the seventies, and critics have speculated variously on the role and nature of this ubiquitous, amorphous "other," suggesting that the "you" serves as a reimagined self, an erotic partner, a syntactic counterword. It serves, of course, all of these functions; its importance lies in its ambiguity. Ashbery's own remarks in a *New York Quarterly* interview are equivocal, but they still help us to understand the function of the second person pronoun in his work:

> my point is also that it doesn't really matter very much, that we are somehow all aspects of a consciousness giving rise to the poem and the fact of addressing someone, myself or someone else, is what's the important thing at that particular moment rather than the particular person involved.[2]

Addressing someone is indeed Ashbery's premise, with all the attendant problems of communication. The actual reader does not, in reading Ashbery, feel that he is overhearing a private confession, as in "To His Coy Mistress"; rather, he becomes that internal audience. He is brought inside the poem, and the rest of the world lies at the periphery of this encounter. Accepting the fruitful ambiguity of the second person pronoun, we find that Ashbery's poetry is not only fictively addressed to another, but actually addressed to us, that at least one very concrete reification of "you" is an actual reader, *hypocrite lecteur, son semblable, son frère.* Indeed, it is difficult, when reading an unspecified second person pronoun, not to take it personally first, however else we might go on to take it, even while we know that Ashbery's sense of us must be an abstract one. We are inscribed as readers everywhere in his pages, not only through imperatives, directives and other forms of direct discourse, but through specific references to the text and to acts of reading.

It is just such a "you" that reaches out to us uncannily from the pages of *Leaves of Grass:* "Who knows but I am enjoying this? / Who knows, for all the distance, but I am as good as looking at you now, for all you cannot see me?"[3] But the self that speaks out of Ashbery's poems has never had the primacy or imperial authority of Whitman (one wonders, for that matter, how much confidence was behind the strong rhetoric of that predecessor). Nor has it the autobiographical grounding of confessional poetry. For Ashbery, identity is a composite reality and the poem a polyphony of writer and reader ("we are somehow all aspects of a consciousness giving rise to the poem"),[4] an equation of which the poem is the function. "I guess I don't have a very strong sense of my own identity and I find it very easy to move from one person in the sense of a pronoun to another and this again helps to produce a kind of polyphony."[5] The polyphony is most often counterpoint, culminating in **"Litany,"** a counterpoint of "I" and "you" which checks equally the dangers of solipsism and of absorption. Some self-splitting is implicit in the act of writing, which predicates a reading, and Ashbery's work of the seventies is drawn increasingly toward the dynamics of this counterpoint.

Harold Bloom is correct, I think, in viewing *The Tennis Court Oath* as a swerve toward a primitive solipsism and disregard of the reader.[6] The poems, while daring in their writerly qualities are finally unreadable in that the reader is excluded from them. They imply a theory of language in which communication is not a primary goal. It is concerned with the "lonesomeness of words." But in the

seventies Ashbery develops a compromise between writerly and readerly qualities, recognizing his need for the reader in order to complete the language-act and thus the objectification of the self, at the same time resisting the closures of the reader's knowledge. Throughout his work of the seventies we find a deep anxiety about the textual captivity of the self, from which the reader can free him so that he is not, as he writes in **"Grand Galop,"** "a first aid kit no one ever uses / Or a word in the dictionary that no one will ever look up." Such images, and there are many, suggest that words are to be used, that their being, and that of their messenger, is suspended in the text until they are used. This anxiety is apparent in Whitman as much as in Ashbery, and is ultimately an anxiety about non-being, an anxiety requiring not writing alone, but the belief in a reader to ward it off. This is, I think, why the dream must be double; why Ashbery casts himself as a beholder, a "reader" of visual art, in **"Self-Portrait in a Convex Mirror"**; why *Three Poems* is concerned with performance and audience; why **"Litany"** inscribes a responsive reading, however unresponsive in tone and content the second column is; why, like Scheherezade, the title of a poem in *Self-Portrait in a Convex Mirror*, Ashbery is so long-winded; and why the dream songs of *The Tennis Court Oath* and *Rivers and Mountains* increasingly give way to public performance in later work, however dreamlike those performances may be. Ashbery knows that an inevitable solipsism infects the process of writing and reading, that the reader will make the writer over in his own image, just as he has himself made the reader in his own image. Nevertheless, in the cross-gesturing something happens, a suture has been made at certain junctions.

Ashbery is certainly beginning to contemplate a "you" in terms of the reader in *Rivers and Mountains*, but his thoughts are colored by a deep ambivalence about his contract with those readers. In **"The Skaters"** he inscribes the reader repeatedly, but in several places he tries to break the contract: "am afraid I'll / Be of no help to you. Good-bye." **"The Recent Past"** concerns the temporality of language, in which meanings dissolve as they arise, but it could almost be autobiographical as well, not only summing up the movement of all of Ashbery's poems, but recapitulating both the tendency in *Some Trees* to double the self, to make "you" a mirror of "me," and the destructive impulse in *The Tennis Court Oath* to erase both parties:

> You were my quintuplets when I decided to
>   leave you
> Opening a picture book the pictures were all of grass
> Slowly the book was on fire, you the reader
> Sitting with specs full of smoke.

"A Blessing in Disguise," which shows the influence of Whitman, once again embraces this affronted you. The terms of the encounter fit precisely the encounter of writer and reader, with its merging and confusing of identities, its simultaneous plural and singular references (readers are one and many):

> And I sing amid despair and isolation
> Of the chance to know you, to sing of me

Which are you. You see,
You hold me up to the light in a way

I should never have expected, or suspected, perhaps
Because you always tell me I am you . . .

I prefer "you" in the plural, I want "you,"
You must come to me, all golden and pale
Like the dew and the air.
And then I start getting this feeling of exaltation.

But this ideal reader, like Shelley's epipsyche, continually evaporates as the writer awakes to the opacity of the page.

The Double Dream of Spring begins a much more readerly phase of Ashbery's poetry, offering a legibility that nevertheless preserves a sense of the world as an illegible text in which everyone's fate is cryptically inscribed. Against the background of this vaster text the writer encounters the reader in "fragments" of communication, exploring the patterns of desire and power implicit in that relationship. The love relation recorded in the sentence fragments and pseudo-narrative of **"Fragment"** is repeatedly enfolded in the immediacy of the text so that it is hard not to identify with the unnamed addressee, not to understand the affair in terms of the bond of art. Writing is indeed for the poet "the only real beginning," "the end of friendship with self alone."

> The stance to you
> Is a fiction, to me a whole. I find
> New options, white feathers, in a word what
> You draw in around you to the protecting bone.
> This page only is the end of nothing
> To the top of that other.

One's reality is always a fiction from the point of view of another and the other is always invented by the imagination that desires it. Such a dynamic is exaggerated in writing, for the writer's audience is necessarily a fiction, his will over it both total and impotent. The reader of a text does not exist without the writer's *fiat,* and yet the reader may be recalcitrant or may remain a fiction never summoned to proof.

> Not forgetting either the chance that you
> Might want to revise this version of what is
> The only real one, it might be that
> No real relation exists between my wish for you
> To return and the movements of your arms and legs.
> But my inability to accept this fact
> Annihilates it. Thus
> My power over you is absolute.
> You exist only in me and on account of me
> And my features reflect this proved compactness.

The slippage in the term "real" here is typical of Ashbery, but it is also characteristic of the double reality of writing and reading, trying to become one reality. The perfect contract would be a countertext offered by the reader in which the points of intersection could be identified: "I

want it all from you / In writing, so as to study your facial expressions / Simultaneously . . . / Your plans run through with many sutured points."

Houseboat Days continues this sense of the poet's ambiguous power and impotence in relation to writing. His will to meaning is caught in temporality, his identity locked in signs, but in the act of writing his idea of a reader saves him from the solipsism and complacency of thought. **"Collective Dawns"** in particular develops this theme:

> The old poems
> In the book have changed value once again. Their
>   black letter
> Fools only themselves into ignoring their stiff,
>   formal qualities. . . .
>
> The time of all forgotten
> Things is at hand.
> Therefore I write you
> This bread and butter letter, you my friend
> Who saved me from the mill pond of chill doubt
> As to my own viability, and from the proud village
> Of bourgeois comfort and despair, the mirrored
>   spectacles of grief.

Such "bread and butter letters" belong to a pattern of mutuality and conflict in Ashbery's story of "you" which is derived from his idea of the reader. The love which occurs, like Donne's, in the portable rooms of the text draws on all the tensions of social and domestic love in the world, the shifting relations of dominance, patterns of dependence, of mutuality and aggression, narcissism and self-effacement, ecstasy and disillusion. Together writer and reader in **"No Way of Knowing"**

>   are trying to spell out
> This very simple word, put one note
> After the other, push back the dead chaos
> Insinuating itself in the background

but this "camaraderie that is the last thing to peel off, / Visible even now on the woven pattern of branches" must also finally be seen as an illusion, a fiction first of the writer's, then the reader's. Ashbery's general cries of desire seem to reach directly to the reader as he vies against the belatedness of reading. "Why can't you spend the night, here in my bed, with my arms wrapped tightly around you." Writing is always in a sense unrequited since no voice responds out of the written page. The artist's desire is to move the beholder in an immediate way ("'Parmigianino wished to impart the sense of novelty and amazement to the spectator'" and for a moment he can seem to succeed, for the beholder will "forget stand-offishness, exact / Bookkeeping of harsh terms but he is always fickle, never keeps his promise of attention." "Pope Clement and his court were 'stupefied' / By it, according to Vasari, and promised a commission / That never materialized."

The fictive reader, unlike the recalcitrant actual reader, is infinitely faithful and submissive. "I want to concentrate on this / Image of you secure and projected how I imagine you / Because you are this way where are you you are in my thoughts." By inscribing the reader in the text ("you reading there so accurately") the writer brings him in close where he can be watched, but at the same time marks him as a fiction, a puppet to be acted on symbolically, with the hopes that this magic will penetrate to the heart of the actual reader. The writer maintains the knowledge that writing and reading require the very solitude and silence they are designed to dispel. Ashbery writes in **"Lithuanian Dance Band"**: "Yet we are alone too and that's sad isn't it / Yet you are meant to be alone at least part of the time / You must be in order to work."

By including a respondent the poet can have his privacy and his validation, although often, as in **"Litany,"** the respondent serves to check the autocracy of the writer and prove the isolation of the reader. But in **"The Tomb of Stuart Merrill"** Ashbery quotes a reader, after the fashion of *Paterson,* as though to prove not only the reality of his reader but his own power over him. Here is a reader who has been perfectly seduced (the erotic model not overlooked) by Ashbery's method of rumoring enlightenment.

> "I have become attracted to your style. You seem to possess within your work an air of total freedom of expression and imagery, somewhat interesting and puzzling. After I read one of your poems, I'm always tempted to read and reread it. It seems that my inexperience holds me back from understanding your meanings.
>
> "I really would like to know what it is you do to 'magnetize' your poetry, where the curious reader, always a bit puzzled, comes back for clearer insight."

This is an image of the infatuated reader and the writer as tease, promising but never following through with the consummation of meaning.

Ashbery is constantly testing his authorial power, underscoring the implicit imperative of all writing (read!). He will provoke the reader with perverse behavior, momentarily suspending the fact that the reader can veto by his indifference.

> Leading liot act to foriage is activity
> Of Chinese philosopher here on Autumn Lake
>   thoughtfully inserted in
> Plovince of Quebec—stop it! I will not.

The reader, "fruit and jewels / Of my arrangement" must follow his bidding. But this self-assurance is repeatedly mocked by images of the reader's forgetfulness, lapses of attention, ultimate silence. The will to be heard carries on after "sleep had stopped definitively the eyes and ears / Of all those who came as audience" and poetry is left "in creases in forgotten letters / Packed away in trunks in the attic." The writer doesn't have the mastery over the reader ("besides, you aren't paying attention any more") or even over his text, except insofar as he has preempted the reader's recalcitrance by including it.

The motive of writing as the desire for a reader can be seen in many of the poems of **Houseboat Days**; indeed in many of the poems in the book writer and reader seem to be the only existences, like a pair on the ark, on the flood of time. **"Friends"** uses as epigraph a note by Nijinsky which characterizes the artist's sense of double identity— creator and audience, echoing each other: "I like to speak in rhymes, / because I am a rhyme myself." The poem begins in the haunted terror of solipsism, but yields to an image of communication, a feeling "like a pearl," a jewel found when the self is pried open by otherness. In the middle Ashbery writes:

> I feel as though I had been carrying the message for
>   years
> On my shoulders like Atlas, never feeling it
> Because of never having known anything else. In
>   another way
> I am involved with the message. I want to put it
>   down
> (In two senses of "put it down") so that you
> May understand the agreeable destiny that awaits us.

In **"Valentine,"** the poem as love not to the reader, the mutuality is described in a process of difficult habitation, first the speaker inhabiting the reader ("the name of the castle is you") until by the end an inversion has taken place, the other's house collapsing until he has inhabited the speaker, who announces "I am the inhabitable one." Both ends of the process are met with ambivalence and difficulty ("like a serpent among roses I coil to and at you") until "[your] base slips out of slight" and the writer establishes him. It is just such a migration that occurs in the process of reading, in which a writer's self dwells in the mind of a reader until that fictive self becomes the reader's reality. And yet "my back is as a door to you." The give and take continues.

The metaphysics of reading is encountered most directly and successfully in **Self-Portrait in a Convex Mirror**. Most of the poems in **Self-Portrait** are concerned in one way or another with the balance of the equation forming writer and reader; they contain frequent direct addresses to the reader and references to the act of reading, as well as related images of story-telling and hearing, message-sending and receiving, performances and audiences.

The volume's title poem is Ashbery's chief meditation on the ontology of art, and on the idea of the beholder. His brilliant choice of Parmigianino's self-portrait permits rich permutations of artist and beholder. Here Ashbery puts himself in the position of the beholder (analogously, the reader) even while he is also creating his own self-portrait in expectation of a beholder. The mirror reminds us that a text, whether we are its writer or its reader, calls for both active and passive responses, that the artist is always both creator and beholder, that he is looking intensely at himself but at the same time at the imagined beholder, who in turn sees intermittently himself and the artist. These multiple identities slide into and out of one another in the course of the poem, as they do in the course of all creative or interpretive activity.

Art is an experience of absorption, but when the image is one of self-absorption, the beholder feels excluded, denied. This problem is raised on several levels in the work. Ashbery shifts in and out of certainty about whether he is invading the privacy of Parmigianino, or whether he as beholder is the true object of the artist's absorption. Similarly we move in and out of certainty as we respond to the "you" in Ashbery's poems, uncertain whether we are addressees or bystanders. The effect is a repeated experience of embarrassment, as when we answer to a call directed to another.

Some of this ambiguity is apparent at the opening of the poem where the poet leads us to expect that he will paint his own self-portrait, after the example of Parmigianino. He lets us discover belatedly, after the true example of the older artist, who "protects what he advertises," that his meditation on the painting is not a prelude to self-portraiture but rather an act of self-portraiture in its own right, as if all beholding (and all reading, by extension) could be understood as self-portraiture, that the self, in fact, can never be drawn directly. Even when the poet's meditation seems to have abandoned the portrait, the painting resurfaces from the palimpsest of reflected selves. Similarly, the primacy of the original portraitist is denied by the succession of beholders who have remade the portrait in their own image. This theme is not only described as Ashbery reflects on the painting, but demonstrated as his own authority over the meditation gives way to a succession of quotations from art critics, part of the "polyphony" of the poem:

> The balloon pops, the attention
> Turns dully away. Clouds
> In the puddle stir up into sawtoothed fragments.
> I think of the friends
> Who came to see me, of what yesterday
> Was like. A peculiar slant
> Of memory that intrudes on the dreaming model
> In the silence of the studio as he considers
> Lifting the pencil to the self-portrait.
> How many people came and stayed a certain time,
> Uttered light or dark speech that became part of you
> Like light behind windblown fog and sand,
> Filtered and influenced by it, until no part
> Remains that is surely you.

The pencil raised to the self-portrait is simultaneously Ashbery's and Parmigianino's here as later, when the textual representation of Ashbery which we as readers behold and the visual representation of the painter, which Ashbery as spectator beholds, merge. "A breeze like the turning of a page / Brings back your face." It is a hall of mirrors in which the original object of reflection cannot be found, in which the necessary priority of artist to beholder is momentarily obscured in a form of *trompe-l'oeil*

> What is novel is the extreme care in rendering
> The velleities of the rounded reflecting surface
> (It is the first mirror portrait),
> So that you could be fooled for a moment

> Before you realize the reflection
> Isn't yours. You feel then like one of those
> Hoffmann characters who have been deprived
> Of a reflection, except that the whole of me
> Is seen to be supplanted by the strict
> Otherness of the painter in his
> Other room. We have surprised him
> At work, but no, he has surprised us
> As he works.

Ashbery does here with his shifting pronouns (you, me, we, he) just what he sees Parmigianino doing. It is an oddly double gesture both supremely realistic and conspicuously an illusion—an illusion, that is, of a reflection—the thing itself already once removed. The image of the mirror is surely, whatever else it is, Ashbery's comment on mimetic art. His self-referential gestures are like the film of Parmigianino's mirror. Like his mannerist predecessor, he offers a superrealism of the moment that itself comments on the fallacy of realism. That thought cannot escape representation ("speculation [from the Latin *speculum,* mirror]") and yet that representation by definition denies the presence of its object, is Ashbery's traditional but revitalized theme in this poem. He introduces it at the outset:

> "he set himself
> With great art to copy all he saw in the glass,"
> Chiefly his reflection, of which the portrait
> Is the reflection once removed.

Is that warped image in the corner of the picture a window or a mirror, Ashbery asks, questioning implicitly the whole meaning of mimetic art. "We see only postures of the dream," representations of a reality enclosed in an inaccessible dimension. For the reader of a self-portrait this reality is the writer/artist whose existence is enclosed within the text like the genie in the bottle crying to be let out, trying to trick the reader into releasing him and his dangerous powers. By breaking the spell of mimesis, by returning Parmigianino (and himself) to the bottle, Ashbery returns us to ourselves, as readers, for better and worse, for absorption in a work of art means not only the illusion of another reality but the consequent forgetting of our own.

The seductions of mimesis are as great for the artist beholding his own work as they are for the reader. The artist at work, lifting the pencil to the canvas, is trying to merge with his work, to deny the need of an audience. To paint or write oneself into a work is to follow it out of time, or through time, but is also to become, like the genie, caught in the text. Ashbery's poems are full of images of figures caught in the mirrors and made-up countries "wasted with eternal desire and sadness, / sucking the sherbets, crooning the tunes, naming the names." This captivity is not only a metaphor for the condition of the soul, but is literally true of the condition of artistic meaning.

> The surface
> Of the mirror being convex, the distance increases
> Significantly; that is, enough to make the point

That the soul is a captive, treated humanely, kept
In suspension, unable to advance much farther
Than your look as it intercepts the picture.

In **"Self-Portrait"** the shape of the mirror is as important and as richly significant as is its capacity to reflect. That the mirror is convex serves to bring to an extreme the problems of writing and reading which concern Ashbery here. Indeed the principle of convexity can be seen throughout the work, not only in various images, but enfolding the themes and structure of the poetry. Convexity offers an image of unfulfilled desire; it captures the pathos of meaning leaning out of but bound by representation. Convexity is the spatial representation of the flow and ebb or arrival and withdrawal that Ashbery sees as the nature of thought and which he imitates in the movement of his verse. Most of all it defines the relationship of writer and reader, those gestures made by the writer toward a listener set physically and psychically apart.

The curve of convexity suggests a completed globe, and thus an autonomous world, "a globe like ours, resting / On a pedestal of vacuum, a ping-pong ball / Secure on its jet of water." It is the same image that inspired Yeats's "Lake Isle of Innisfree." Our impulse toward that world, as beholders, is to enter and walk in it, for while it curves away from us it also seems panoramic, "refusing to surround us, and yet the only thing we see," which is the very nature of fiction, of any absorbing writing. We are absorbed, but inevitably look up to notice our own world at the edges of that fictive one. The writer, in turn, "would like to stick [his] hand out of the globe, but its dimension, what carries it, will not allow it."

But while the curved shape of convexity suggests (without yielding) the perfection of the sphere, it also causes a distortion in what it reflects. This distortion of surface, which in art is the mark of aesthetic intent, promises something "truer" harbored within the sphere of art, a spiritual dimension we do not find on the surface of nature, which we take for granted. The disproportion of hand and face in the portrait suggests different dimensions, the hand, instrument of art, "Like a dozing whale on the sea bottom," "on another scale" from the head, "the tiny, self-important ship on the surface" of consciousness. In terms of writer and reader, the distortion of representational surface is an invitation to communion with the artist's spirit.

Yet Ashbery also knows that these disproportions do not arise from a true transcendence of the barriers of fact, but from convexity, a superillusion, superior to the illusion of natural representation but still a lie. "The eyes proclaim / That everything is surface." As the gesture of the hand looms large, the soul (the head) retreats, a conversity of theme which structurally reinforces the convexity of the mirror. The shape of convexity gives the illusion of depth only by expanding surface. The artist can only tease the beholder with this illusion, he cannot accomplish his wish to transcend surface. Ashbery's lines similarly generate surface as they tantalize the reader with a promise of depth, and analogously, they extend our attention in time

while they tease us out of time. Momentarily this confession that "everything is surface" seems to weigh him down in despair, but he rises again in the revelation that surface "is not superficial but a visible core," "pure affirmation that doesn't affirm anything."

It is, then, by engaging the reader in surface that Ashbery finds his success—not in the transcendence but in the communication of medium. Ashbery's own poetry shows an absorbing love of surface, in spectacle, in casting up images for their own sake, redundant in meaning but infinite in texture.

Reading is as much Ashbery's subject as writing is, and it is through his idea of reading that his self-reflexiveness escapes banal solipsism and opens onto larger questions of communication.

—Bonnie Costello

While Ashbery incorporates his vocational doubt into the statements of the poems, he also makes full use of style to capture and manipulate our attention, to amaze, shock, soothe, outrage, seduce us. In a sense the rhetorical shape of his poems is far more important than their matter, his metaphors more important for their spectacle than for their significance, the prose and verse rhythms more important than logic in drawing us along. He has no divinity but all the skill and equipment of a great magician; he is all surface, and yet he makes us realize that "surface is not superficial."

As "pure affirmation that doesn't affirm anything," as "the shield of a greeting," a gesture toward the reader from the writer's soul but all surface, convexity veers out and in again in the very shape of paradox. The feeling of paradox is ambivalence, and its image, oxymoron. All poetry in a sense has this shape, leaning out toward significances but receding as soon, an image of spirit, thus both disclosing and veiling it. It marks our yearning to be understood or to understand but also our shyness, our fear of possessing or being possessed. The writer's ambiguous gestures both veil and disclose his purpose, a contributing vagueness prolonging the encounter with the reader. The shuttle of assertion and denial is Ashbery's irresistible idiom, occurring in single lines which are swallowed, like little fish, by whole passages which repeat their pattern. Such is the nature of convexity that it never pauses and one gesture is subsumed by another, thought dying on the breeze that brought it to the threshold of thought. Thus the first thrust of convexity suggests that "the soul is a captive" by advancing out of the flat surface, the second that "the soul is not a soul" by receding, and together they form a curve of asserting and denying "Like a wave breaking on a rock, giving up / Its shape in a gesture that expresses that shape."

There are many sources for **"Self-Portrait,"** Eliot's *Four Quartets,* Yeats's "The Lake Isle of Innisfree," Stevens' "To an Old Philosopher in Rome." But the greatest model is Keats's "Ode on a Grecian Urn," in which the poet is also the audience, questioning silent images enclosed in convexity. Ashbery, like Keats, must break the spell of art, reverse the convex lens of the telescope so that the object will recede and return him to life, rather than envelop him in its "frozen gesture," its "cold pastoral." But Ashbery's ending has none of Keats's triumph in life or art, perhaps because in a self-portrait life and art are so closely entwined. Keats has little regard for the maker of the Grecian urn and much for its subjects, but Ashbery cannot avoid Parmigianino because he *is* the subject, and the poem is full of biographical detail. The violence of the closing image of **"Self-Portrait"** has the impact of a personal dread, for to reject the image of an artist is to reject himself, or to recognize that the reader will necessarily reject him in the end. Though here Ashbery himself has been reader, he is also aware that his poem, and thus his liaison with a reader, is concluding.

> There is room for one bullet in the chamber:
> Our looking through the wrong end
> Of the telescope as you fall back at a speed
> Faster than that of light to flatten ultimately
> Among the features of the room, an invitation
> Never mailed . . .
> > The hand holds no chalk
> And each part of the whole falls off
> And cannot know it knew, except
> Here and there, in cold pockets
> Of remembrance, whispers out of time.

As the curve of the convex mirror disappears into the horizon of thought we are left with a correspondingly hollow feeling, returned to our own reality as readers, "concaved into view." It is from the evasion of such suicidal moments, lingering with the reader like Scheherezade, that Ashbery's famous sustained climaxes derive. For in recognizing the temporality of art Ashbery recognizes again his distance from the reader, his isolation in the act of writing, the lonesomeness of words.

Throughout Ashbery's poetry, with increasing frequency after *Rivers and Mountains,* time signatures (hours, days, seasons, tenses) mark out a pattern of waiting and belatedness. Often these signatures are connected with a circuit of communication (messages sent and received) in which objects wait for words to discover them, words for the objects they name, names for readers, readers for words in an endless system of deferred meaning both figured and enacted in the poems. These images may be metaphors for thought, but they particularly register the anxiety a writer might feel in the spatial and temporal distance from his reader. That is, the inherent duality of his activity, the need for a reader, is reinforced by its inherent temporality.

In *The Double Dream of Spring* and later volumes (especially in *Self-Portrait*) we find recurrent images of messages sent and received years later. In **"Sortes Vergilianae,"** for instance,

> It is this blank carcass of whims and
> tentative afterthoughts
> Which is being delivered into your hand like a letter
> some forty-odd years after the day it was posted.
> Strange, isn't it, that the message makes some sense,
> if only a relative one in the larger context of
> message-receiving
> That you will be called to account for just as the
> purpose of it is becoming plain,
> Being one and the same with the day it set out,
> though you cannot imagine this.

Ashbery's own messages, though they appear as "whims" and "after-thoughts," do indeed make sense "in the larger context of message-receiving." We "cannot imagine" it as "being one and the same with the day it set out" because our imaginations as readers necessarily change it. Literature intensifies the truth that there is no present in communication, for the poet is all anticipation toward his reader, the reader all memory toward the poet. All literature exists, then, simultaneously in the past and in the future, but never in the present. The poems in *Self-Portrait* are usually less optimistic in their refrain of loss than were the poems in *The Double Dream of Spring*. In the later volume the messages arrive too late, or not at all, "invitations never mailed" or received after the event they announce has already taken place. In **"The One Thing That Can Save America,"** he writes:

> All the rest is waiting
> For a letter that never arrives,
> Day after day, the exasperation
> Until finally you have ripped it open not knowing
> what it is,
> The two envelope halves lying on a plate.
> The message was wise, and seemingly
> Dictated a long time ago.
> Its truth is timeless, but its time has still
> Not arrived.

Reading exaggerates rather than overcomes the temporality of thought, and rereading is no solution: "Just time to reread this / And the past slips through your fingers, wishing you were there." Stylistically, Ashbery ingeniously enhances the inherent temporality of his medium by undermining the grammatical, syntactic and rhetorical devices which give it stasis. Main clauses are lost in the "forward animation" of the line, subordinate clauses momentarily taking over until yet other clauses replace them. Punctuation, too, is violated, not in any conspicuous way but by allowing the grammatical subject to change in midsentence, giving the effect of a run-on sentence or fragment. Beginnings and endings tend not to match up, and middles evade dénouement, so that when we glance up from our book we are unable to say what we have been reading, even though the words are perfectly clear. Thus, while Ashbery took as his putative object of attention in **"Self-Portrait"** a work of visual art, perhaps because it provided the stationary qualities of a meditative object, his reflections are largely a result of his own medium, language, which has not only the historicity of all works of art, but is also experienced temporally.

Thought, for Ashbery, is caught in temporality, "the idea of what time it is" always arriving "when that time is already past." We have seen that this idea of thought derives from his artistic medium. Indeed, writing and reading become the model of all thought for Ashbery and the drama of writer and reader ultimately enacts the drama of consciousness. When consciousness is conceived as narrative fiction self-consciousness is modeled after the psychic split of a performance and audience or a writer who must imagine a reader. The desire of all consciousness, like the desire of all literature, is to end this duality through absorption. This is a major theme of *Three Poems*: "We know only that our sympathy has deepened, quickened by the onrushing spectacle, to the point where we are like spectators swarming up onto the stage to be absorbed into the play . . .". Theatrical metaphors accrue in *Three Poems* toward an ever postponed climax until the final decayed note of **"Recital"** denies the fusion, and narrative outlives consciousness: "But the idea of the spectacle as something to be acted out and absorbed still hung in the air long after the last spectator had gone home to sleep."

The fear of solipsism returns with the idea of consciousness as narrative. "The film I have been watching all this time may be only a mirror," but outside of the film is an undifferentiated blur. Images of people walking out of theatres into darkness or mist occur everywhere in Ashbery. "This world is not as light as the other one; it is made grey with shadows like cobwebs that deepen as the memory of the film begins to fade." The only alternative is launching on a new narrative path, "plunging into the middle of some other one that you have doubtless seen before." Consciousness can only bring us to the border of narrative, it cannot lead us out of it. It is only at the end of a passage that Ashbery can write, "the allegory is ended, its coils absorbed into the past, and this afternoon is as wide as an ocean" for the ocean has no speech. But what interests Ashbery most is the tension between the allegory and the ocean, between consciousness and dream, between the orders of the text and the grey mist around it. It is only as a play of contrasts that we can experience the present, the unordered force of experience which, by becoming a text, becomes the past. The acts of writing and reading, as metaphors of consciousness, stand ambiguously against the mist, defending us from its dangers but blocking its ecstasies.

That we are bound each to our own script, "It is your chapter, I said" is clear not only in Ashbery's direct statements, but in his use of cliché and his cartoon characters and stock situations. As actual readers of this record of formulaic experience we are placed at several removes from the present of the writer (like the mirror in the mirror of **"Self-Portrait"**), but are also able to recognize the anxieties of our own daily fictions. Our modern narrative is askew; we have the forms of old stories with a scrambled syntax. We approach the world in an allegorical frame

of mind but are left suspended, too many images unexplained in a proscenium range of observation that implies significance but will not yield it. As we read experience we want beginnings, middles, ends, poetic justice everywhere, necessities of character. We find these because we seek them, but they are illegible, jumbled, mocking our pride as interpreters who think we know how information should be received. In **"Soonest Mended,"**

> Happy Hooligan in his rusted green automobile
> Came plowing down the course, just to make sure
>   everything was O.K.
> Only by that time we were in another chapter and
>   confused
> About how to receive this last piece of information.
> Was it information? Weren't we rather acting this out
> For someone else's benefit . . . ?

The readers here have been absorbed by a text, have left their seats in the audience and joined the actors, but the duality remains as they are watched by someone else. They are now "thoughts in a mind / With room enough and to spare for our little problems." This is, in a sense, what happens when Ashbery inscribes the reader in his text, for in such a case we not only witness an author but also ourselves, or an image of ourselves, as readers. Since we as actual readers are reading a story about the fictions of consciousness, our illusion, our comfort in the belief in a fiction, is broken. That is, by making the fictive reader a metaphor for the experience of consciousness, Ashbery withdraws from the actual reader all the securities of fiction. By making us part of a text Ashbery undermines our secure position as beholders, exposes us to the vulnerability of the stage.

Images of experience as textuality arise in nearly every poem of *The Double Dream of Spring*. In this sense **"Sortes Vergilianae"** by its title takes on a special importance in the volume as the metaphor of a text in which all our fates are written, in which the self, the "I" is no authority but an "insatiable researcher of learned trivia, bookworm." To this larger text of consciousness the poem is "just a footnote, though a microcosmic one perhaps, to the greater curve / of elaboration; it asks no place in it, only insertion *hors-texte*."

But the theme of consciousness as narrative reaches its apex in *Self-Portrait*. Even death is absorbed within an idea of narrative closure in **"Forties Flick"**:

> Why must it always end this way?
> A dais with woman reading, with the ruckus of
>   her hair
> And all that is unsaid about her pulling us back to
>   her, with her
> Into the silence that night alone can't explain.
> Silence of the library, of the telephone with its pad,
> But we didn't have to reinvent these either:
> They had gone away into the plot of a story,
> The "art" part—knowing what important details to
>   leave out
> And the way character is developed.

The movie ends with an image of a woman reading, to suggest that we cannot get past this sense of being inside a story, that even our idea of narrative is enclosed within another narrative. On the perimeters of this scene are the metaphors of oblivion, the "dark vine at the edge of the porch," the "shadows of the snake-plant and cacti," parts of a stage setting which rise at the end of the play to significance as symbols for the undoing of that setting. Details in the background, which seem at the beginning of a story mere atmospheric detail, gather significance and become epiphanies by the end of the story.

> Things too real
> To be of much concern, hence artificial, yet now all
>   over the page,
> The indoors with the outside becoming part of you
> As you find you had never left off laughing at death,
> The background, dark vine at the edge of the porch.

Surely this is an image of Ashbery's own reader, of the limits of the intimacy between reader and writer and of the blur each faces outside of their mutual world of the text. Around the act of reading are the objects of another life over which author and reader have no control, a life temporarily blocked out by the act of reading but hemming it in all along. But even this extratextual moment is woven into Gothic convention, absorbed into the decor of the Forties Flick.

Fairytale and fable structures and images, and particularly titles suggesting the teller of these tales, are typical in *Self-Portrait* and extend the theme of consciousness as fiction. **"Scheherezade"** recalls one who was herself, out of self-preservation, the author of an endless string of fables, and shows landscape infinitely converted to language and generated by it: "an inexhaustible wardrobe has been placed at the disposal / Of each new occurrence." "Most of all she loved the particles / That transform objects of the same category / Into particular ones." Through narrative we can make the world seem more copious than it is, can evade our limits. But the delightful sense of the infinite proliferation of experience as story has its panicky side as Ashbery discovers that "all efforts to wriggle free / Involved him further, inexorably, since all / Existed there to be told" and "nothing in the complex story grew outside." Narrative provides the "wardrobe" for all occurrences, but the wardrobe never feels quite natural even while we are absorbed in wearing it.

> I feel as though someone had made me a vest
> Which I was wearing out of doors into the
>   countryside
> Out of loyalty to the person, although
> There is no one to see, except me
> With my inner vision of what I look like.
> The wearing is both a duty and a pleasure
> Because it absorbs me, absorbs me too much.

Narrative compels us to it and entraps us within it. Even those narratives we construct that might survive the moment of telling are, if not belied, still trapped within the temporality of their medium. "Some stories survived the dynasty of the builders / But their echo was itself locked in." We are ourselves trapped in a solipsistic cycle, as both actors and audience of our own movies, but by this process we are nevertheless "restored to good humor as [we issue] / Into the impervious, evening air." As both actors and audience we make the same mistake twice but also redeem our error, objectify our fictions, insure our own readership, our own applause and thus evade doubt. Ashbery gives solipsism its due, especially the mutual solipsism of writing and reading:

> So in some way
> Although the arithmetic is incorrect
> The balance is restored because it
> Balances, knowing it prevails,
> And the man who made the same mistake twice is
>   exonerated.

"Märchenbilder" announces its fictionality, *"Es war einmal,"* but at the same time our resistance. After a series of false starts, we see that only the "frugality of sleep" can prevent the endless getting and spending of consciousness, the cycle of assertion and denial. Since consciousness cannot avoid story we must inevitably surrender to it, but it only takes us astray, removes us from the "rainbow" of illumination. "As we advance, it retreats; we see / We are now far into a cave." Within that cave, though, our complete absorption in story feels like the threshold of illumination. Stories are "empty cupboards" but "beautiful as we people them / With ourselves." Like the genie, the poet makes fools of us by granting our wishes, but "the third wish unspoken" holds out the promise of a humble satisfaction.

The reader's first wish is for the sublimity of truth, his second for beauty—Ashbery shows us the vanity of both wishes by drawing the reader onto the stage of the text. Our third, though, is for something like goodness, not the ideal goodness, sister of truth and beauty, but a sort of second cousin, the simple social virtue of a writer's contact, however qualified, with a reader. Ashbery's line is not destined for the tower of truth, though that is its apparent track, but exists for the pleasure of riding along with the reader, for the sense of communion that can be had on the way to nowhere in particular. What other function is left for the artist who sees all consciousness as trapped in fiction? Mimesis then becomes the production of mere copies, increasing our removes from the truth, as Plato thought. And irony, as Ashbery tells us in **"Self-Portrait,"** is caught in denial.

> Those assholes
> Who would confuse everything with their mirror
>   games
> Which seem to multiply stakes and possibilities, or
> At least confuse issues by means of an investing
> Aura that would corrode the architecture
> Of the whole in a haze of suppressed mockery,
> Are beside the point. They are out of the game,
> Which doesn't exist until they are out of it.

While mimesis and irony are dismissed, "play" is accepted as the natural mode of a "society that exists as a demonstration of itself." Play, unlike mimesis, makes no claim to the abiding truth of its images, only to their ability to satisfy an urge for self-reflection. Unlike irony, it affirms, though it affirms nothing in particular. Wherever the artist and his reader might wish to go, they surrender their will to "necessity" which "circumvents such resolutions / So as to create something new / For itself . . . things / Do get done in this way, but never the things / We set out to accomplish and wanted so desperately / To see come into being." The writer admits this even while he knows the reader will retrospectively "read / The perfectly plausible accomplishment of a purpose" into his "smooth, perhaps even bland (but so / Enigmatic) finish." That reading itself will be something new, an erosion by "necessity" of the author's will, a redefining of the landscape of experience.

Along with this surrender of his art comes a communal spirit which displaces the egotistical sublime. By repeatedly acting out his desires in a formulaic language, Ashbery accomplishes neither vision nor ironic distance. But he does accomplish a sense of community, a shared nostalgia for meaning. The writer's and reader's mutual yearning for each other's presence becomes the absorbing consolation for the failure to transcend the limits of the text. If language fails to name or to command, it still has the power of what anthropologists call "phatic communion," the power to create social bonds through meaningless gestures. The reader must know that the poet has nothing to tell him, but know at the same time that he is communicating with him. Writing becomes a way of perpetuating the writer's contact with other lives, and thus preserving his own. By sharing in a language we recognize as fallen, we redeem it for its social value. This is not the modernist, anti-social redemption which promises to unearth truths by shaking up old ground, whatever the casualties in communication. Rather, it is a ritual danced with the reader upon the old ground, evoking the mystery and complexity of our entrapment.

Notes

[1] *Self-Portrait in a Convex Mirror* (New York: Viking, 1975), title poem pp. 68-83. Subsequent references to this and other books by Ashbery will be made in the text, under the following abbreviations: *ST: Some Trees* (New Haven: Yale Univ. Press, 1956); *TC: The Tennis Court Oath* (Middletown, Conn.: Wesleyan Univ. Press, 1962); *RM: Rivers and Mountains* (New York: Holt Rinehart, 1967); *DDS: The Double Dream of Spring* (New York: Dutton, 1970); *TP: Three Poems* (New York: Viking, 1972); *SP: Self-Portrait in a Convex Mirror; HD: Houseboat Days* (New York: Viking, 1977); *AWK: As We Know* (New York: Viking, 1979).

[2] Janet Bloom and Robert Losada, "Craft Interview with John Ashbery," *New York Quarterly,* 9 (Winter 1972), pp. 224-25.

[3] Walt Whitman, "Crossing Brooklyn Ferry," rpt. in *Complete Poetry and Selected Prose,* ed. James E. Miller (Boston: Houghton Mifflin, 1959), p. 119.

[4] Bloom and Losada, p. 225.

[5] Bloom and Losada, p. 225.

[6] Harold Bloom, "John Ashbery: The Charity of the Hard Moments" in *Figures of Capable Imagination* (New York: Seabury, 1976), p. 171.

Thomas A. Fink (essay date 1984)

SOURCE: "The Comic Thrust of Ashbery's Poetry," in *Twentieth Century Literature,* Vol. XXX, No. 1, Spring, 1984, pp. 1-14.

[*In the following essay, Fink explores the role of humor in Ashbery's verse.*]

Although John Ashbery's poems seldom cause even his most devoted readers to double over in laughter, his work is persistently humorous. Perhaps the most salient aspect of this humor can be defined in negative terms: a relatively high number of sentences in the poetry seem to "ask" *not* to be taken seriously as the direct expression of information that matters. For the seasoned reader of Ashbery, invisible (sometimes visible) quotation marks form around any statement that is the slightest bit portentous. Noticing that a poem in the recent ***Shadow Train*** (1981)[1] begins with the exhortation, "Trust me," one chuckles and realizes that this poet's language can, most of the time, only be trusted to be *un*trustworthy. And even when an Ashbery poem ends with a solemn, lyrical tone, all of the playfulness invariably preceding it tends to make the reader suspect that the coda, too, should be interpreted ironically.

Many of Ashbery's readers have pointed to his refusal to make "serious" statements as a central feature of the poetry, but none have fully explored the essentially comic attitude that stems from that choice or the full range of humorous effects that largely derive from it. According to David Shapiro, author of the first book-length treatment of the poet,

> Ashbery's poetry is humorously and melancholically self-reflexive and sees itself as a provisional, halting critique of naäive and degraded referential poetries. . . . Ashbery deflates our expectation of sense, of presence, by giving us again and again the playful zone of *deferred sense.*[2]

Throughout his book, Shapiro tends to emphasize the melancholic and confrontational aspects of Ashbery's "decentering" activity rather than its abundantly humorous side: "The imagination in Ashbery speaks of a constantly agitated *agon.* . . ."[3] Granting that some Ashbery poems like **"Europe"** and sizable chunks of poems like **"The Skaters"** do evoke the agitation that Shapiro finds, I would consider the mock-agonistic more prevalent than the agonistic.

David Lehman, I believe, comes closer to Ashbery's dominant tone in a characterization of his irony:

> At home with an essential homelessness among ideologies and programs, adrift and yet secure in the houseboat of his days, he has resisted the temptation to fill

up vacancies with reassuring convictions. . . . What Ashbery calls "a tongue-and-cheek attitude" permits him to find a certain congeniality in situations of maximum uncertainty. . . . [4]

If Ashbery welcomes uncertainty with open arms, and he does, it is also with a powerful sense of fun.

In "Fresh Air: Humor in Contemporary American Poetry," John Vernon perceives two "camps" of poetic humorists and places Ashbery firmly in one of them: "The humor of these poets" (who include Kenneth Koch, James Tate, and others in the New York school, of which Ashbery is a charter member, and several Beat poets) "hovers between surrealism and a kind of epistemological skepticism, a refusal to mean or to respect meaning."[5] Vernon believes that this "camp" has adopted premises very similar to the omnitextual deconstructive philosophy of Jacques Derrida:

> If we unpeel all the layers of language around us, tracing words back to their sources in other words, and still other words, what we find behind it all is not a "world" or "reality" or a presence of any kind, but simply an absence. . . . If there's a gap between words and things, then why not release words to play on their own, joke around, display themselves, invent, shuffle, entertain?[6]

I would certainly agree that deconstruction provides fruitful approaches to Ashbery's texts, but the notion of "freeplay" discussed above is a limited version of both the philosophical practice and of the creation of humor in the poetry. A fuller description would account for ways in which the tendency of "words to play on their own" and "joke around" *comes up against* the awareness of "a 'world' or . . . presence" that *really exists* outside the realm of language. The possibility of relative descriptive accuracies within provisionally established contexts allows for the "jocoserious" *dislodging* of anticipated congruities and continuities. Take, for example, these blatantly "referential" opening sentences of the recent **"Qualm"**:

> Warren G. Harding invented the word "normalcy,"
> And the lesser known "bloviate," meaning, one
>   imagines,
> To spout, to spew aimless verbiage. He never
>   wanted to be president.
> The "Ohio Gang" made him. He died in the Palace
>
> Hotel in San Francisco, coming back from Alaska,
> As his wife was reading to him, about him,
> From *The Saturday Evening Post*.
>
> (***Shadow Train***)

Several of these details can be found in history texts; the only two elements revealing poetic invention on Ashbery's part are the assumed definition of "bloviate"—with the striking alliteration and assonance—and the use of a quatrain break to separate "Palace" and "Hotel," thus deflating Harding's "stature." Though the first two lines are "about" words, we cannot efface their connection to "Poor Warren" Harding, ranked by many historians as the

worst and most inept president the United States ever had.

Humor lies in Ashbery's careful selection and juxtaposition of details. We hear nothing of Harding's accomplishments in the White House (perhaps because there were none), and the only significant event of "Poor Warren's" abbreviated term, the Teapot Dome Scandal, goes unmentioned. Instead, Ashbery chooses a bizarre way of remembering a political leader—as one who coined two quaint words that passed out of currency soon after his death, like the poems of a minor poet. But one of the words makes possible the evocation of a historical irony: if Harding promised a "return to normalcy" after the turmoil of the First World War, it can be said that the phrase ultimately turned on him and exposed his comic insufficiency as someone *too normal* (mediocre) to tackle the presidency's severe challenge. To make matters even more incongruous—and that is Ashbery's specialty—whereas most politicians must utilize all of their resources and determination to be elected president, Harding's bumbling passivity, exploited by the unsavory "Ohio Gang," brought him to a pinnacle "he never wanted."

Even the circumstances of "Poor Warren's" death serve as a source of humor for Ashbery. The parallelism, "to him, about him," underscores the somewhat narcissistic pose of a president who spent his last moments paying attention to his own publicity (spoon-fed by his wife, of course) rather than thinking about affairs of state. There is also the possibility that Harding was so appalled to learn from the *Saturday Evening Post* about his abysmal performance as chief executive that it killed him. In the poem's third quatrain, the absurdity of Harding's small place in history is further accentuated when Ashbery gives the late president a modern mythological status: ". . . a new gold star / Flashes like confetti across the intoxicating early part / Of summer . . ." (***Shadow Train***).

A superficial reading of **"Qualm"** might conclude that Ashbery is merely taking aim at an easy target to elicit a few chuckles, but the title of the poem seems to indicate otherwise. Perhaps the misgiving is that alien forces shaping one's experience, coupled with the reifying language of gossip-mongering journalism (or pop-historical thumbnail sketches), can inflate a simple person with common weaknesses and predilections into a ludicrous spectacle. If the speaker is indeed articulating a **"Qualm,"** he relies on humor rather than anger to communicate a desire for change in the perspectives fostered by and in his media-drenched society.

Excessive generalization is one of the prime targets of Ashbery's comic thrust. His illustrious precursor, Wallace Stevens, obliquely aimed his potent comic darts at rigid attitudes of philosophical, spiritual, and aesthetic orthodoxy. Fond of poking fun at the inhuman immobility of ceremonial statues, which he seemed to link with a metaphysics of eternal stasis, Stevens used description and ironic commentary (". . . a permanence, so rigid / That it made the General [Du Puy] a bit absurd, / Changed his true flesh to an inhuman bronze. / There never had been, never could be, such / A man.")[7]) and wild surrealistic imagery (". . . the marble statues / Are like newspapers blown by the wind.")[8]) to put forth his humorous perspectives. In **"Credences of Summer,"** understatement was used to mock the dull, obsessive pursuit of "plain reality" in ultra-rural "Oley": "One of the limits of reality / Presents itself in Oley when the hay, / Baked through long days, is piled in mows. It is / A land too ripe for enigmas, too serene."[9] And in **"The Man on the Dump,"** Stevens reserved the most hyperbolic of caricatures for trite, sugary hyper-romanticism:

> The green smacks in the eye, the dew in the green
> Smacks like fresh water in a can, like the sea
> On a cocoanut—how many men have copied dew
> For buttons, how many women have covered
>   themselves
> With dew, dew dresses, stones and chains of dew,
>   heads
> Of the floweriest flowers dewed with the dewiest
>   dew.[10]

In such poems as **"Daffy Duck in Hollywood,"** Ashbery has employed most of these techniques for similar purposes, but a few new strategies can be found in his bag of tricks. Unlike Stevens, Ashbery dares to begin some of his poems with the most banal general statements imaginable—and he pretends, for a little while, to mean them. Here is a diluted modern version of Emersonian/Whitmanian confidence:

> I am still completely happy.
> My resolve to win further I have
> Thrown out, and am charged by the thrill
> Of the sun coming up. Birds and trees, houses,
> These are but the stations for the new sign of
>   being
> In me that is to close late, long
> After the sun has set and darkness come
> To the surrounding fields and hills.
>
> (*The Double Dream of Spring*)

Soon, this rhetoric of exaltation has been "sullied" by the sudden appearances of several other kinds of discourse, including colloquial throwaways, advertising hype, and military terminology, and the concept of "complete" visionary happiness grows vaguer by the minute. Indeed, at the end of the poem, with its acknowledgement of "the incredible violence and yielding / Turmoil that is to be our route," (*The Double Dream of Spring*) the initial statement has proven comically insufficient. A similar process of "decomposition" occurs in the later **"Collective Dawns,"** which features an equally outrageous beginning:

> You can have whatever you want.
> Own it, I mean. In the sense
> Of twisting it to you, through long, spiralling
>   afternoons.
> It has a sense beyond that meaning that was
>   dropped there
> And left to rot.
>
> (*Houseboat Days*)

The seductive immediacy of the opening line is necessarily qualified in the next breath: "having" turns into the narrower and slightly less satisfying "owning," which in turn undergoes further qualification in the less wholesome word, "twisting." Not really stable ownership at all, this "twisting" signifies the act of coercion, a psychological rather than a legal transaction, and the power-play takes valuable time to be resolved: "long, spiralling afternoons."

By the middle of the poem's second strophe, however, the will to power has failed the imagined "consumer." Some unidentifiable mayhem is confiscating even the possessions that have always been taken for granted: "They say the town is coming apart. / And people go around with a fragment of a smile / Missing from their faces" (*Houseboat Days.*) The rest of **"Collective Dawns"**—which does not "collect" anything but keeps losing or discarding whatever it has "picked up"—skips haphazardly among moments of mild hopefulness, jerky collapses, and "a weird ether of forgotten dismemberments" (*Houseboat Days*). Not only can "you" not "have whatever you want," but the possibility of having *anything* for keeps is severely questioned.

Whereas Stevens generally began his poems portentously, no matter how whimsical the tone later became, Ashbery in **"Crazy Weather"** makes an absurdly hackneyed conversational phrase the point of departure for a powerful lyric:

> It's this crazy weather we've been having:
> Falling forward one minute, lying down the next
> Among the loose grasses and soft, white, nameless
>   flowers.
> People have been making a garment out of it,
> Stitching the white of lilacs together with lightning
> At some anonymous crossroads. The sky calls
> To the deaf earth. The proverbial disarray
> Of morning corrects itself as you stand up.
> You are wearing a text.
>
> (*Houseboat Days*)

The poet breathes zany new life into a lump of banality by ignoring its figural status and by taking it as a literal (surreal) truth. Since the weather often serves as a scapegoat for people's inner dissatisfactions and as a topic of discussion for those who have nothing to say to each other, the extended personification proves comically apt: the weather can be viewed as a loud drunk or madman whose erratic behavior is a source of annoyance.

Of course, the weather *is* an external force beyond human control. But Ashbery, as close to the realm of cognitive psychology as he is to an awareness of "textuality," demonstrates how people try to foster the illusion that they have mastered such forces by "translating" them into human terms. The "soft, white, nameless flowers" are safely classified as "lilacs," and the meteorological insanity is brought under control when the weather is transformed by an act of will into a material that functions solely to protect and adorn human beings. The "anonymous crossroads" where this transformation may occur, we find, turns out to be the primal scene of the poem itself, the great chiasmus where "endless' "tropical" substitutions occur. This comic, Derridean moment of naming (and un-naming) is enhanced when we realize that the word "text" derives from the Latin verb "texere," which means "to weave." In the woven fabric of this text, genuine differences between the "lightning" and "lilacs" as referents are obscured by their similarities as signs—by the link of alliteration and the not-so "anonymous crossroads" of metaphor and metonymy. Since the "origin" of interpretation has been uncovered as an irreducible dynamism, the seriousness of generalization, much less cliché, as a mode for the achievement of static interpretive truth is boisterously exploded.

Many of Ashbery's readers have pointed to his refusal to make "serious" statements as a central feature of the poetry, but none have fully explored the essentially comic attitude that stems from that choice of the full range of humorous effects that largely derive from it.

—Thomas A. Fink

Although explosions do occur in Stevens' poems ("It was / In the genius of summer that they blew up / The statue of Jove among the boomy clouds."[11]), the modulation from assertion to "decreation" (deconstruction?) is rarely as swift or as stunning as in quite a number of Ashbery poems. In the recent **"Hard Times,"** for instance, after two quatrains full of conventional "wisdom" like "the power of this climate is only to conserve itself," Ashbery seems to be going along with the pessimistic view of life expressed by his speaker—without questioning the latter's simplistic rhetoric—until, in the middle of the third quatrain, the stream of prosey, general, avuncular admonitions is abruptly halted: "Get it? And / He flashed a mouthful of aluminum teeth in the darkness / To tell however it gets down, that it does, at last" (**Shadow Train**). At once sinister and laughably grotesque, the image of this automatic smile instantly unmasks the self-styled adviser as someone with little of substance to say who loves to hear himself say it. The illumination of aluminum reflects no universal truth or specific fact; it turns back upon its source as a physical indication that the vapid rhetoric of **"Hard Times"** is comically ineffective in helping anyone during decidedly "hard times."

It is one thing to say that a poet humorously punctures massive generalities; it is quite another to argue that the same poet maintains a comic outlook even when describing potential sources of major anxiety and even tragedy. In Ashbery's long poem, **"The Skaters,"** the themes of individual loneliness, the irreparable loss of an aesthetic or theological guiding principle, evidence of pervasive human selfishness, the dread of death, and a persistently menacing world situation comprise a sizable portion of the thirty pages; nevertheless, I submit that the poem *refuses*

the high seriousness of tragedy and the lugubriousness of black humor time and again.

One of Ashbery's ways in **"The Skaters"** of blunting negative emotional forces and of allowing a comic *dis*equilibrium to hold them in check is the technique of cutting quickly from one trope, image, or discursive passage to another. The poet speaks of "the rhythm of the series of repeated jumps, from abstract into positive and back to a slightly less diluted abstract. / Mild effects are the result" (**Rivers and Mountains**). Whenever the speaker seems about to sustain a consideration of a serious topic, such as poverty ("How to excuse it to oneself? The wetness and coldness? Dirt and grime? / Uncomfortable, unsuitable lodgings, with a depressing view?"), he brings in another topic out of left field: "But to return to our tomato can— those spared by the goats / Can be made into a practical telephone, the two halves being connected by a length of wire. / You can talk to your friend in the next room, or around corners" (**Rivers and Mountains**). Comic ingenuity is surely no cure for poverty, but it can serve as a diversion from its bitterness. Of course, diversion itself, and not social meliorism, can be considered the actual subject of this poetic transition: the movement of the text is like the movement of a mind through its perceptions and reflections.

Aside from "the rhythm of the series of repeated jumps," Ashbery uses incongruities produced by an irreducibly double perspective (as opposed to a relentless single focus) to make sure that a predominantly comic textual atmosphere prevails over the possibilities of anguish or staid seriousness. This doubleness does not foster a "New Critical" balance or "reconciliation of opposites"; the humor "spotlights" the incompleteness of any one viewpoint, attitude, or synthesis. In part III of **"The Skaters,"** a "professional exile's" alienation from world politics is expressed with memorable incongruity:

> The headlines offer you
> News that is so new you can't realize it yet. A
>   revolution in Argentina! Think of it! Bullets
>   flying through the air, men on the move;
> Great passions inciting to massive expenditures of
>   energy, changing the lives of many individuals.
> Yet it is all offered as "today's news," as if we
>   somehow had a right to it, as though it were a
>   part of our lives
> That we'd be silly to refuse. Here, have another—
>   crime or revolution? Take your pick.
>
> (**Rivers and Mountains**)

Simultaneously, the speaker can imagine the enormity of conflict in a relatively small and underdeveloped nation (and the complex ramifications of this event on "the lives of many individuals"), and he can acutely appreciate how commercial packaging has trivialized the event and thus drained it of significance in his eyes. As appalling as it may seem to realize that one is deriving quotidian "entertainment" from "massive expenditures" of human suffering, the absurdity of the situation can make one laugh and thus *accept* its *current* inevitability, since some news is preferable to none and since media packaging will not be changed overnight.

Some readers believe that Ashbery is a programmatic ironist who uses poetry to feel superior to everyone and everything. The poet presents this viewpoint in **"The Skaters"** in order to refute it:

> You who automatically sneer at everything that
>   comes along, except your own work, of course,
> Now feel the curious force of the invasion; its
>   soldiers, all and some,
> A part of you the minute they appear. It is as
>   though workmen in blue overalls
> Were constantly bringing on new props and taking
>   others away: that is how you feel the drama
>   going past you, powerless to act in it.
>
>   (*Rivers and Mountains*)

Ashbery demonstrates in this passage that, no matter how ironic one may choose to be, uncontrollable forces can often chop the ego down to size. The comic freshness of the simile about the stage crew stems from its utterly pedestrian quality: rather than finding cosmic superpowers cowing the poor little ironist with their awesome strength, we picture ordinary young men ignoring him quite matter-of-factly as they perform a dull, routine, and seemingly endless task. "Powerless to act" in a grand drama—such as one concerning world affairs—this witness is not even potent enough to have the tiniest influence behind the scenes.

In Ashbery's writing, the sudden evaporation of individual mastery is often represented as an absurd, sometimes grotesque stripping away of physical substance or as the reification of a formerly living element. An example of each kind of figuration can be found in the space of a few lines in the zany **"Variations, Calypso and Fugue on a Theme of Ella Wheeler Wilcox."** The passage describes what it is like to lose the security of "some tested ideals, some old standbys" and to have "nothing to put in their place. . . ."

> For later in the vast gloom of cities, only there you
>   learn
> How the ideas were good only because they had to
>   die,
> Leaving you alone and skinless, a drawing by
>   Vesalius.
> This is what was meant, and toward which
>   everything directs:
> That the tree should shrivel in 120-degree heat, the
>   acorns
> Lie around on the worn earth like eyeballs, and the
>   lead soldiers shrug and slink off.
>
>   (*The Double Dream of Spring*)

The quaint reference to Vesalius, rarified by our temporal distance from the anatomical "artist," converts what would otherwise be a horrifying image into a wildly funny evocation of the simultaneous embarrassment and joyous sense of ridiculousness experienced by someone "caught with his pants down." Ashbery, of course, tropes on the tired trope of "naked uncertainty"; skinlessness in his work often turns out to be more of an adventure than an agony. The poet, formidable surrealist that he frequently is, seizes upon the similarity in shape of "acorns" and "eyeballs" in order to convey the seemingly physical clumsiness and uselessness of a mind stripped of insight or "vision." The humor of that clumsiness, as well as the wit inherent in the choice of simile, outweighs any sense of loss in the lines: it would be extremely difficult to justify citing this passage as an example of black humor.

As I noted earlier, the collision between decentered textual "play" and gestures toward extra-textual actuality sets off a great deal of the comedy in Ashbery's poems. To identify an easily discernible manifestation of this process, there is a cross fire involving the formal (and situational) impediments to communication and the implicit opportunities for communication through language. **"Wet Casements"** provides a *tangible* example of such a conflict. In the poem Ashbery's speaker apostrophizes a person whose name was first mentioned

>   at some crowded cocktail
> Party long ago, and someone (not the person
>   addressed)
> Overheard it and carried that name around in his
>   wallet
> For years as the wallet crumbled and bills slid in
> And out of it. I want that information very much
>   today,
>
> Can't have it, and this makes me angry.
>
>   (*Houseboat Days*)

These lines reenact a miniature comedy of mediation: to establish contact with the person addressed in the poem, the speaker must at the very least find out his or her name; to discover that name, he must have access to a piece of paper on which it has been written; to obtain the information on the paper, he must track down the person who has it; finally, the name must be legible (after all the years), the man must still have the piece of paper, and he must be willing to turn over the information to the speaker. Once in close proximity to the name he now desires so urgently, the speaker finds it ludicrous and infuriating that so many stages—probably impossible to negotiate—lie between himself and his telos. Equally absurd is the fact (or conjecture) that the prized piece of paper (valuable only because of the purest chance) has lain, totally useless to anyone including its owner, in a deteriorating wallet for such a long time.

To curse and say, if only communication had been direct (then all would have worked out perfectly) is to forget that some form of mediation is *always* built into an exchange between two or more people. The speaker consciously utilizes this fact of experience in announcing his determination to express his negative emotions in the form of a work of art: "I shall use my anger to build a bridge like that / Of Avignon, on which people may dance for the feeling / Of dancing on a bridge" (*Houseboat Days*). The recipients of this communication make *their own* use of it, as the creator expects and wants, and, in turn, they create another work of art, a palimpsest, that the speaker can use for *his* own purpose of self-identification and validation: "I shall at last see my complete face / Reflected not in the water but in the worn stone floor of my bridge." One finds humor in the simultaneous terseness and hyperbole of this assertion and in the conscious swerving away from the fate of Narcissus.

At times, Ashbery employs the actual form of his poems to comment on difficulties of communication. The long *"Fantasia on 'The Nut-Brown Maid,'"* like the old British ballad noted in its title, is written in the form of a dialogue between "He" and "She," and yet the two characters hardly engage in ordinary conversation. The spatial proximity of passages labeled with two separate pronouns cannot mandate a dialogue in writing any more than two people (not signifiers) can be forced to exchange thoughts just because they have been seated together. Sometimes it is difficult to tell the two voices apart; both display rapid, often unaccountable, shifts in tone and subject matter, and both intersperse bizarre imagery with commonplaces. Each wanders chiefly in a labyrinth of semiprivate language. Immersed in tall tropes and cloudy conceptualizing, "He" and "She" find no time to "listen" attentively to each others' fears and longings.

The double-columned **"Litany"** takes the meta-communication of **"Fantasia"** a significant step further. In the latter poem, one might imagine the two speakers being able to listen to one another, but in the former, they are usually speaking at the same time! In fact, the author's note prefacing **"Litany"** makes it clear that conversation between the two speakers is out of the question: "The two columns of 'Litany' are meant to be read as simultaneous but independent monologues" (*As We Know*). The poem's form, then, calls for speculation about the communication between author and reader.

Needless to say, readers of poetry are accustomed to concentrating on one voice at a time, even if they encounter many different voices in the course of a long poem like *The Waste Land* or **"The Skaters."** But one might ask why poetry cannot be more faithful to a reality that is not so unified; whenever someone speaks, countless others are also speaking elsewhere. Why should poetry give the illusion that only one of those voices has something important to say at a given time? Perhaps Ashbery's movement in **"Litany"** from a single column of verse to twin columns signals an acknowledgment that all limits on poetic utterance and the production of meaning in general are arbitrary and can be obliterated.

One does not have to be another Samuel Johnson, however, to find epistemological problems with Ashbery's prefatory instructions. For the single reader who encounters **"Litany"** in print—let us forget about the inconceivable idea of making sense of the poem while two people are reading it aloud—simultaneous understanding of the columns is virtually impossible. He may choose to read a few lines from one column and then a few from the other or to read one whole column before turning to the other,

but moving down both at once does not work for someone whose mind cannot function as a split screen or stereo system. (Whose does?) No matter how one decides to go through the poem—and all such decisions are equally arbitrary—his necessary adherence to the temporality of reading will always force him to pretend that what the author has designated as spatial contiguity is really temporal sequence. Therefore, one cannot read the poem without doing violence to the "layout" of Ashbery's stated intention.

Of course, the poet himself has played a joke on the reader by placing him at one remove from a completeness of "meaning" from the moment he begins the poem. Possibilities of poetic utterance comically (and drastically) outpace the reader's perceptual capabilities, just as a totality of events that could occur in one room in a few seconds would prove too much for one individual to assimilate: ". . . a multitude of glittering, interesting / Things and people attack one / Like a blizzard at every street-crossing / Yet remain unseen, unknown, and undeveloped . . ." (*As We Know*). And, recalling that Ashbery had entitled a previous long poem **"Fragment,"** we can discern another facet of the joke: that **"Litany,"** however ungraspable, is but a subatomic particle compared to the babel-like totality of all the voices sounding in the world at the same time.

Appropriately, a humorous anecdote about the absurdity of failed communication concludes the poem's right-hand column:

> But you are leaving:
> Some months ago I got an offer
> From Columbia Tape Club, Terre
> Haute, Ind., where I could buy one
> Tape and get another free. I accept-
> Ed the deal, paid for one tape and
> Chose a free one. But since I've been
> Repeatedly billed for my free tape.
> I've written them several times but
> Can't straighten it out—would you
> Try?
>
> (*As We Know*)

The kind of tape mentioned here is the means by which a spoken communication can be recorded for posterity. Having sought a bargain in communication, the speaker has implicitly been denied it (consciously or unintentionally) by those who promised it, and he has been unable to "straighten out" the nuisance through another form of contact, a letter. When impefect modes of communication (and motives for it) are involved, something can easily go awry.

But the final note sounded by this voice is not one of annoyance; he asks "you" to help him break through the communication barrier. It is as though the poet confesses that he cannot quite manage the complexities of his experience and wants the reader to sort out the poem's tangled "messages" so that the *writer himself* will benefit from what he has written. Once again, though, Ashbery's refusal to be serious, his essentially comic spirit, comes to the fore: the "you" he mentions is not "leaving"; he has never been there in the first place! Ashbery is playfully spot-lighting the *illusion* of direct communication between reader and writer. Lines of a poem may "pretend" to be one half of a conversation, but this "voice" is only some writing on a page. This is not to say that one cannot pose or solve problems through written correspondence, but how seriously is a reader likely to take a request in a published poem after all?

The comic dimension of Ashbery's poetry cannot usefully be placed in any convenient literary category. As in existentialist or absurdist literature and in black humor in general, Ashbery's personae are not in harmony with nature and society and lack a sense of internal coherence, but the sustained bleakness and near-despair that go along with these realizations in the former categories are largely absent from Ashbery's "rhythm of the series of repeated jumps" in which "mild effects are" frequently "the result." The exhaustion resulting from much of Beckett's writing is not evident even in such laboriously reflective Ashbery texts as **"Clepsydra"** and **"Fragment,"** which are full of sprightly new beginnings after impasses. Elements of comedy of morals, manners, and ideas, and social and surreal comedy can be found in Ashbery's work, but no single category predominates, and the poet does not roll them into a spuriously unified whole, since there are antagonisms between these approaches. Even to speak of a comedy of deconstruction does not quite work, because at times Ashbery's humor has more to do with our direct awareness of extra-textual (phenomenal) collapses than metaphysical ones.

If we were to try to paste the above-mentioned labels on other comic modern writers like James Joyce, Jorge Luis Borges, W. H. Auden, and A. R. Ammons, we would probably face equally massive difficulties. And if we then attempted to place these figures, along with the subject of this essay, in a "community" of anomalous comic authors, we would find their points of contact with one another insufficient for substantial generalizations. Due to the complexity of their narrative forms and unconventional uses of "real" and surreal materials, it is extremely difficult to pinpoint philosophical attitudes in the humor of Joyce and Borges, though many have tried. Auden's comic detachment from human folly, as Justin Replogle has suggested,[12] is somehow permitted in the later work by the poet's belief in Christian redemption, a notion only to be parodied in Ashbery. As for Ammons, his Emersonian leanings tend to give the description of nature a much less ironic "status" than Ashbery does. Furthermore, merely including Ashbery among the "New York School" humorists obscures the areas that clearly differentiate him from his friends, Frank O'Hara and Kenneth Koch, both of whom have permitted various forms of sentimentality much stronger credibility in their work than does Ashbery in his.

In order to avoid a rhetorical dead end, we might "conclude" that, in a reading of Ashbery's poetry, "comedy" is the vague word used to characterize the mischievous, protean force that slips away from our *serious* pursuit of formulations for it.

Notes

1 Page references to my citations from Ashbery's work are included in my text. The following books are cited: *Rivers and Mountains* (New York: Holt, Rinehart and Winston, 1966); *The Double Dream of Spring* (New York: Dutton, 1970); *Houseboat Days* (New York: Viking, 1977); *As We Know* (New York: Viking, 1979); *Shadow Train* (New York: Viking, 1981).

2 David Shapiro, *John Ashbery: An Introduction to the Poetry* (New York: Columbia Univ. Press, 1979), p. 1.

3 *Ibid.,* p. 13.

4 "The Shield of a Greeting: the Function of Irony in John Ashbery's Poetry," in David Lehman, ed., *Beyond Amazement: New Essays on John Ashbery* (Ithaca, N.Y.: Cornell Univ. Press, 1980), p. 126.

5 Sarah Blacher Cohen, ed., *Comic Relief: Humor in Contemporary American Literature* (Urbana: Univ. of Illinois Press, 1978), p. 305.

6 *Ibid.*

7 *The Collected Poems of Wallace Stevens* (New York: Knopf, 1977), p. 391.

8 *Ibid.,* p. 473.

9 *Ibid.,* p. 374.

10 *Ibid.,* p. 202.

11 *Ibid.,* p. 482.

12 Justin Replogle, *Auden's Poetry* (Seattle: Univ. of Washington Press, 1969), p. 216.

John Ashbery with Paul Munn (interview date 1990)

SOURCE: An interview in *New Orleans Review,* Vol. XVII, No. 2, Summer, 1990, pp. 59-63.

[*In the following interview, Ashbery discusses influences on his work, his creative process, and his poetic philosophy.*]

[Munn]: *Besides writing poetry, what are your current projects?*

[Ashbery]: I was fortunate enough to get a MacArthur fellowship, which has relieved me of the necessity of earning a living for five years at least. But during this time it seems that I have agreed to write a number of articles, essays, art reviews, and so on, all of which I procrastinate about, and I can't seem to do anything with the time I am procrastinating about these other things. Basically I have written more or less the same amount of poetry I normally would have if I had been working at a job. I'm trying to get out from under these other commitments, and when I do that I would like to try to write some different kinds of things. I wrote some plays years ago in the fifties which I never really did anything with, although I still like them. And I would like to go back and do something in that form. And also I would like to write some fiction, which I haven't really done, except for a novel I collaborated on with the poet James Schuyler, called *A Nest of Ninnies,* which was published—which I don't really consider to be a novel. It was really a kind of game we played to amuse ourselves, never expecting when we began it at a very young age, both of us, that anyone would ever publish it. I'd like to try to write some fiction with the idea of publishing it rather than from the standpoint of its never seeing the light of day—which was the understanding I wrote the other one out of.

I've never enjoyed writing art criticism. For a long time it was the only way I seemed to be able to make a living, especially when I was living in France for ten years. There I wrote for the *International Herald Tribune* for five years. And although this wasn't enough to live on—they only gave $15 an article when I began working for them; it was up to $30 by the time I left five years later, so I actually got a 100% raise somewhere along the line—nevertheless, this enabled me to write other things about art and I was able to subsist that way. But I have always been a somewhat reluctant art critic. And now I would like to think that I'm not going to write any more art criticism. To celebrate this I have completed a book of my art writing. As long as I was in the business of writing it, I didn't want to publish it, because I was afraid some reviewer would come along and attack it and I would lose my job. But I no longer have this to worry about.

I'm interested in your selection process for the **Selected Poems***? How did you decide what to include and exclude? Did others take part in determining what finally went into your* **Selected Poems***?*

No, I selected them myself. I've had friends and other people—who knew my work—not be happy with the selection because of things I've left out. No one has yet complained about anything I have included, but I suppose there are complaints on that side too. But there were some poems that I realized were fairly well known, so far as any are, which I never really liked and therefore didn't include. There were others which I did like but which seemed somewhat repetitive of other poems which I like slightly better. I didn't intend this to be a sort of codex or ultimate choice, since my other books are in print, and I had no intention of disavowing any of the ones that are not included in the book.

If you were to put together a collected works, are there any poems that you would exclude? I'm thinking of the later W. H. Auden, who rethought his career. Would you rethink yours or throw out some poems or re-edit?

I think this is about as much of a collected poems as I'll ever do, and so, in a sense, I've already done or not done whatever that is. And I don't think I've been too harsh on my early work, one reason being that I felt that Auden did a kind of disastrous number on himself, leaving out many of his most cherished poems. This seems to be a congenital affliction of writers who reach a certain age. Henry James also kind of massacred or re-did some of his early works which were better in the original version. So I'm leery of doing this. I don't think, I hope, at any rate, that I wasn't too harsh on early works, which I can see flaws in but which nevertheless seem to have a kind of redeeming freshness, which maybe later works, which are in some ways better, wouldn't have. It's kind of a narrow line you have to follow in doing something like that, I guess.

So you don't feel a strong self-censoring or self-editing impulse, then, as you look back at the earlier work?

Well, much of it had already happened before the books were published. It takes a long time for a book of poetry to come out. Sometimes the poems in it are five years old or more when a book finally appears, so you've had ample time for self criticism or winnowing out. I certainly have written a lot more than I have actually published.

Critics have seen sources or analogues for your poetry in a considerable range of poets, and even composers and painters: Rimbaud, Whitman, Wallace Stevens, the current Language poets, John Cage, and Jackson Pollock are just a few. You have expressed an early admiration for Auden and Elizabeth Bishop. How important do you feel it is for readers such as us to be familiar with these earlier poets in order to get at your work?

I would hope not at all. Because even though I've been influenced by many different poets and artists and things not even related to the arts, I would not like to feel that a knowledge of any source material is necessary or even desirable before reading my work; I think that's true of any writer that one admires. It's interesting afterwards if you wish to go back and see where these things originated, but I hope at any rate that it's not a condition of reading my work.

Do you have any tips if there were someone in the audience who was just beginning to read your work? Is there any advice you might give them to facilitate their way into your work?

Well, much has always been made about how difficult my poetry is. I never thought of this until it was first pointed out to me. It has been many times since. This has become a kind of self-fulfilling prophecy, I think. This reputation of being difficult I think discourages people from looking at my work. I found in a number of cases that people who somehow have never heard of me and who don't even read poetry and happened on it have read it with enjoyment and not found it puzzling or enigmatic. I'm thinking particularly of a handyman who occasionally worked for me who heard indirectly that I was a writer and went to the library and found some of my books. Then he began collecting them, even insisting on first editions, even though I don't think he ever [had] read anything before, not *any* book. I could see that he was really very fervently involved in these poems. That doesn't happen, everyday, of course, but I think it can happen, and perhaps one suggestion would be to pretend that you haven't heard that it's very difficult, to read it and see what happens. And also not to worry if you don't understand it. It doesn't make that much difference. There are other things in life. And not to look for a structure or a framework underneath it. But as they say, go with the flow, which I hope is there.

From your example, you almost suggest that those of us who have sought a structure and applied the traditional ways of looking at poetry might actually be handicapped a little bit, and this other person you were talking about had an advantage by coming to it without preconceptions about how he should read.

That could be. He was perhaps an extreme example, but other people more literate than he have occasionally come up to me and said, "People are always saying your work is so difficult, but I think it means something to me." I've never quite understood about understanding anyway or about the meaning of poetry. Eliot, I believe, said that you don't have to understand poetry to enjoy it, and I think that's true. And I think the converse might be true as well. In fact, it's necessary not to understand it in order to enjoy it. I don't get much pleasure out of poems that offer no resilience or crunch, where you can tell almost from scanning the poem exactly what the message is, something like "The Star Spangled Banner," even though that has a few obscurities in it. In fact, I find that much so-called clear poetry is full of murkinesses that I seem to be the only one to pick up on.

Maybe this next question will lead into the murkiness in what's often thought to be more clear poems. Some of your poems might be characterized and have been characterized as anti-voice poems. By that I mean that your poems resist being thought of as speech originating from a presumed personality, attitude, or clear situation. I can think of a few poems of yours where you seem to have a poetic speaker who is a relatively consistent "I" and is also grounded in a time and place. **"The Instruction Manual"** *is one.* **"Self-Portrait in a Convex Mirror"** *may be another.* **"Evening in the Country"** *and* **"Ode to Bill"** *also seem to have that sense of the present speaking voice, relatively coherent. In any of these poems, were you aware—and this is a psychological question which may not help us with these poems—of the Wordsworthian, Yeatsian, and maybe Frank O'Hara background—the personality poet? Were you consciously playing off that in these sorts of poems?*

I don't think I was even in those examples that you just cited. I've never really had much of an idea of who I am, and I feel that Rimbaud put it very well when he said, "Je est un autre": "I is an other," meaning using "I" in the third person as someone who's not speaking that statement. I am constantly using different voices without being aware of it, of different people who seem to be talking in these poems without bothering to indicate to the reader where one stops and another one starts up again because

I'm interested in a kind of polyphonic quality that attracts me in music. I seem to be somewhat notorious for what I have come to think of as the floating pronoun. I coined this from my own practice. I didn't mean it to be that way. But it often seems to be enough to know that "you" is someone that the speaker is addressing, that "he" or "she" is someone who is neither of these two people, that "we" could be a number of people, including the speaker of the poem, the person he may be talking to, and all possible readers as well. For me this is actually enough. And it seems to be an attempt, possibly a misguided one, at a kind of more realistic approach toward what one learns, what one sees, hears, and what happens, what one's mind does during the course of a day, something like that. I'm interested in the movement of the mind, how it goes from one place to the other. The places themselves don't matter that much; it's the movement that does.

I have one more question before we turn to reading and talking about **"At North Farm,"** *You have written in a considerable variety of forms, some of which seem to be your own nonce forms or free verse, others of which are traditional or derived from traditional forms—quatrains, couplets, prose poems, and sestinas, for example. You have spoken yourself of "the tyranny of the line" ["The Experience of Experience: A Conversation with John Ashbery," with A. Poulin, Jr.,* Michigan Quarterly Review *20 (1981): 254]. One way of looking at your work might be to see it as a continual struggle with or response to form. Please excuse the baldness of this question: Why write a sestina?*

Well, that's a very complicated form which I first discovered in Auden and in Elizabeth Bishop, although many poets, particularly twentieth-century ones, have used the form. And that's a kind of a special case, really. I often use this as an assignment for students because the complexity of the form involves making so many conscious decisions that one's unconscious is kind of left free to go ahead and proceed with the poem, which is as it should be. Eliot said something like meaning in poetry is like the piece of meat that the burglar throws to the watchdog so that he can get at the treasure or whatever he's looking for. Frequently, it has a kind of therapeutic effect on students. When they get all done and realize that they have fitted all the pieces into place and stand back, they suddenly realize that they have written a poem while they thought that they were just solving a puzzle. There are not too many forms that I find useful for that kind of exercise. The canzone, which is actually a more constrained version of the sestina, has sometimes produced interesting work in class and the villanelle, which I have assigned. I have never actually been able to write a successful one myself, but I've had students who have done so. But when you get into the sonnet and things like that, these are forms that are really too loose to have this liberating effect that I'm looking for, especially in teaching. I don't use these forms such as the sestina very much for myself anymore. I probably did when I was younger, when I was finding it more difficult to write and used them as a kind of exercise to get going.

[At this point, by agreement, he read the first poem in his *A Wave,* "At North Farm."]

At North Farm

Somewhere someone is traveling furiously toward
    you,
At incredible speed, traveling day and night,
Through blizzards and desert heat, across torrents,
    through narrow passes.
But will he know where to find you,
Recognize you when he sees you,
Give you the thing he has for you?

Hardly anything grows here,
Yet the granaries are bursting with meal,
The sacks of meal piled to the rafters.
The streams run with sweetness, fattening fish;
Birds darken the sky. Is it enough
That the dish of milk is set out at night,
That we think of him sometimes,
Sometimes and always, with mixed feelings?

I'll tell you a little bit about how I happened to write the poem, although I would caution you against thinking that this is the key to the poem, because it doesn't have any key, like all poetry. Frequently, I find that questions in a situation such as this are actually someone asking for the recipe, and the recipe is always in my head. I can't give it to anybody, just like one's grandmother. The title, **"At North Farm,"** although it could [have] come from anywhere, actually was suggested by the Finnish epic folk poem the *Kalevala,* which you may know from some of Sibelius's tone poems. They were based on a fascinating body of folklore, copied down in the nineteenth century but actually much older. North Farm in the epic is a place near hell but not in it, and it's always referred to with the epithet "gloomy and prosperous North Farm." And as I recall there are always a lot of beautiful serving girls there, whom the hero, Lemminkainen, is very attracted to; he is always dropping in at North Farm to see what's cooking. So the "gloomy and prosperous," I think, gives you a little note to the stasis in the second part of the poem. Although nothing grows there— it's not fertile—nevertheless it's full of the evidence of fertility, such as these sacks of meal, fish in the streams, and so on.

The first part of the poem, I think, seems to me to come from some cinematic memory, maybe *Lawrence of Arabia,* somebody galloping across a desert stream. And "will he know where": this person is heading in your direction, but there's some doubt as to whether you are actually going to meet up and whether you will receive the thing that he has for you. It might also have been a kind of memory of that legend that's mentioned in the beginning of "Appointment in Samarra," by John O'Hara, where the man says he has to go to Samarra to avoid death, and death comes and says, "I have an appointment with him there." At any rate it's something ominous, I think, and it reflects a relationship that I had at the time that I wrote it with a person whom I felt to be sort of fascinating but somewhat alarming at the same time. There are a lot of people like that one encounters in the course of one's life—not too many perhaps. I think the idea is that somebody, maybe

one of these maids-in-waiting, is waiting back there at the farm where nothing ever happens, where it's fertile but somehow sterile, waiting for this kind of electrifying arrival of a messenger of something, we don't know quite of what. The dish of milk is traditional in fairy tales, something you set out at night to pacify the elves so they won't spoil your crops. It's an image I also use in another poem called **"Hop O'My Thumb."** A lot of my imagery comes from fairy tales and things I read when I was young, which impressed me more than much of what I've read since. The line in the other poem is "Nocturnal friendliness of the plate of milk left for the fairies / Who otherwise might be less well disposed."

I wrote this poem with great ease. And I enjoyed writing it a lot. I enjoyed the feeling. I was somehow able to use clichés, like "at incredible speed," "birds darken the sky," "travelling day and night," that sort of thing, that kind of very colloquial, not quite clichéd speech which I found at that moment very appealing. I frequently find colloquial, overheard speech to have a kind of beauty that I'd like to steal and put in my poetry. This was one case where I felt that I had been able to do that. At the end, this ambiguous person seems to be the thing that everything hinges on— "That we think of him sometimes"—which is immediately contradicted by "Sometimes and always, with mixed feelings," again a further feeling of contradiction. So it's left up in the air whether the person is going to arrive and what will happen when he does; and that's very often the case.

It sounds as though I'm a victim of too much reading when I'm hearing Yeats and Keats all through the second movement. I'm thinking particularly of Keats' "high-piled books, in charactery, / [which] Hold like rich garners the full ripened grain," and the closing stanza of **"To Autumn,"** *which has that sublime stasis, that end of the season fruition. And maybe even Yeats' "The young / In one another's arms, birds in the trees / —Those dying generations—at their song, / The salmon-falls, the mackerel-crowded seas"—that sense of richness and the sensuous life, which is there, but that's certainly my head.*

That might well be. We all have read these poems. They are all part of our subconscious, if not our conscious. I'm frequently finding that I'm rewriting something that I read thirty years ago and had completely forgotten. Perhaps indeed the Yeats line was in the back of my mind. I was also thinking of the Welsh epic poem the *Mabinogion,* where there's a scene [in which] I think a lot of soldiers are disguised as sacks of meal as in *Ali Baba and the Forty Thieves,* and the unfortunate warrior comes and accosts this man surrounded by sacks of meal. He is about to put him to the sword and the man says, "There is in this sack another type of meal," and then at that point, as I recall it, the armed men all jump out of the flour sacks. But even though this is material that I used, I don't know that it proves anything. It doesn't make the poem any better or worse. That's why I don't have footnotes or explanations as to where all these things came from. I don't think it matters.

Steven Meyer (review date 1995)

SOURCE: "Ashbery: Poet for All Seasons," in *Raritan,* Vol. XV, No. 2, Fall, 1995, pp. 144-61.

[*In the following review, Meyer provides a laudatory assessment of* Hotel Lautréamont *and* And the Stars Were Shining.]

For upwards of two decades now, since the acclaim that greeted his 1975 collection *Self-Portrait in a Convex Mirror*, John Ashbery has been the United States' preeminent poet, with books selling in the tens of thousands, both at home and abroad. In a recent issue of the British journal *PN Review,* two dozen poets and critics set out to "appraise the mark this American writer" has made and continues to make in Britain—a mark, we are told, that differs appreciably from his influence in the United States. Among the sources of Ashbery's widespread popularity is a feature of his work that he does not share with other contemporary writers and which might therefore account for some of his individual appeal. This is a quite exceptional openness to the influence of earlier writers, especially the first two generations of this century's English-speaking poets. It is this continuity with the poets largely responsible for making modern poetry consequential for readers today that makes Ashbery so recognizably a poet of consequence himself.

Along with his receptivity to the work of other poets, Ashbery exhibits an equal willingness to draw on the unexpected turns of demotic speech, with which most readers are no doubt more familiar than they are with the tropes of poetry. In poem after poem he demonstrates that everyday usage contains as much grist for poetry as poetry itself does. In adapting the language he finds around him, whether the language of poets or of personal and social life, Ashbery applies a technique that one finds described exactly, if somewhat outrageously, by Isidore Ducasse, the nineteenth-century French writer who called himself the Comte de Lautréamont. "Plagiarism is necessary," Ducasse wrote: "it is implied in the idea of progress. It clasps an author's sentence tight, uses his expressions, eliminates a false idea, replaces it with the right idea." Few writers have been as assiduous, or as unembarrassed, in their pursuit of the *bon mot* as Ashbery, who would have had to look no further than Auden and Stevens and Eliot to find exemplary plagiarists.

Indeed, the title of Ashbery's 1992 collection, *Hotel Lautréamont*—in deliberate contrast with Rimbaud's "Splendide-Hotel," "erected," as Rimbaud has it, in the splendid isolation "of ice and of polar night"— presents a trope of a man as a hotel where other people stay for a short while and then move on. This permeability of borders, and boarders, is central to Ashbery and his sense of "himself." In a crucial statement, dating from 1976, he observed that "what moves me is the irregular form—the flawed words and stubborn sounds, as Stevens said, that affect us whenever we try to say something that is important to us." It is this sense of a necessary incompleteness in poetry that he insists on, for such "irregular form" is what

enables the poetry to survive the circumstances of its own composition—and so make room both for the reader and for the later poet, who is always first a reader.

Perhaps one imagined that Eliot's *Four Quartets* was a paragon of completeness; so Ashbery in *Hotel Lautréamont* offers us an additional "Quartet." Similarly, to complement "Ash Wednesday" we are presented with **"Just Wednesday."** (Ashbery, as he often does, plays on his name here, modestly removing it from Eliot's great poem. Now, just how modest is this?) Donne's "A Valediction: Forbidding Mourning" is transformed into **"A Mourning Forbidding Valediction,"** in which the nine quatrains of the original poem, odd and even lines rhyming, are replaced by seven eight-line stanzas, each with the rhyme scheme *abcd cbad*. This magnificent poem alone is worth the purchase of the volume. And what of Stevens, whom Ashbery has called his favorite poet? The 1942 "Notes Toward a Supreme Fiction," surely as great a poem as has been written in this century, consists of three parts: "It Must Be Abstract," "It Must Change," "It Must Give Pleasure." Ashbery, refusing to be silenced by these peremptory judgments, contributes his own obiter dictum: **"It Must Be Sophisticated,"** "O what book shall I read now?" he wonders near the end of this truly wonderful poem: "for they are all of them new, and used, / when I write my name on the flyleaf."

Although he never lets one forget that one is reading poetry, not overhearing conversation, Ashbery certainly doesn't want his readers to feel that the concerns which engage him are exclusively literary and merely a matter of reading and responding to books "new, and used." In the same way, he wants his poems to speak to and for as broad a spectrum of his contemporaries as possible. Such ambitions have a precise genealogy. English-language poetry of the last two hundred years—ever since Wordsworth's insistence on using "the real language of men" rather than "the arbitrary and capricious habits of expression . . . frequently substituted for it by Poets"—turns on an ongoing tension between aristocratic and democratic conceptions of the reading public. Is the poetry written for the privileged few or the unexceptional many? Pound and Yeats are perhaps the most powerful modern proponents of a poetic aristocracy, which may account for Ashbery's relative lack of interest in them.

Wordsworth, in calling the volume he coauthored with Coleridge *Lyrical Ballads,* was responding to the late eighteenth-century revival of interest in English and Scottish ballads, a tradition of poetry that predated the Renaissance establishment of a "heightened" English and which seemed to speak for society as a whole in a way that poetry since the Renaissance had not. "Research has shown," the title poem of *Hotel Lautréamont* begins, in one of Ashbery's preferred manners, that of the academic spinner of clichés, "that ballads were produced by all of society / working as a team. They didn't just happen. There was no guesswork. / The people, then, knew what they wanted and how to get it. / We see the results in works as diverse as 'Windsor Forest' and 'The Wife of Usher's Well.'" The latter poem is a traditional Scottish ballad, whereas the former, an early production of Alexander Pope's, is composed in his trademark rhymed couplets. As such, it hardly qualifies as a ballad; yet, like "The Wife of Usher's Well," it invites precious little guesswork, and the forest world it portrays is the sort of "golden" world, "harmoniously confused: / Where Order in Variety we see, / And where, tho' all things differ, all agree," that can only be "produced by all of society / working as a team."

"Hotel Lautréamont" is not itself written in traditional ballad stanzas—it is rather a pantoum, an elaborate verse form of Malay origin that was introduced into French early in the nineteenth century and later adapted to English— but it testifies to the increasing importance the ballad has acquired in Ashbery's poetry. The long poem, "Fantasia on 'The Nut-Brown Maid,'" for instance, which appeared in the 1977 collection *Houseboat Days,* is modeled on the ballad alluded to in the title; and in the 1987 *April Galleons*, the poem "Forgotten Song" begins with variants of lines from several ballads and includes a passage from a third as well. In *Hotel Lautréamont*, besides the title poem, Ashbery has included a magical and quite-impossible-to-forget song. "The Youth's Magic Horn." Like so much of Ashbery's work of the last decade—after an almost-fatal spinal infection he experienced in 1982—this poem is a "dump" or lament at approaching death. It is divided into two sections of six quatrains each, with the much shorter second and fourth lines of each quatrain repeated throughout each section as a refrain. "First in dreams," the second section begins, "I questioned the casing of the gears the enigma presented / *You're a pain in the ass my beloved* / The twa corbies belched and were gone, song veiled sky that day / *I have to stop in one mile.*" The "twa corbies" are two ravens that, in the Scottish ballad of that name, are overheard discussing the meal they are about to make of "a new-slain knight."

It is not possible in so brief an excerpt to reproduce the beauty that emerges out of this medley of grating language and excruciating pain, since it depends on the song's cumulative effect, but the juxtaposition of dream and ballad in these lines does suggest the significance of Ashbery's concern with ballad form. The same juxtaposition is to be found in W.H. Auden's introduction to Ashbery's first book, *Some Trees*, which Auden selected as the 1956 winner of the Yale Series of Younger Poets. Auden suggests that any poet "working with the subjective life"— particularly poets who, like Ashbery, are "concerned with the discovery that in childhood largely, in dreams and daydreams entirely, the imaginative life of the human individual stubbornly continues to live by the old magical notions"—will be "tempted to manufacture calculated oddities, as if the subjectively sacred were necessarily and on all occasions odd." Here Auden is warning Ashbery against another "youth" with a "magic horn" whose influence may readily be discerned in such poems in *Some Trees* as the aptly-named "Popular Songs." This poet is the younger Auden.

Whenever Ashbery, who wrote an undergraduate honors thesis on Auden, finds himself addressing the importance the older poet had for him, he always makes a point of insisting that it was the early Auden who played the decisive role, the so-called "English" Auden of the 1930s— author, among many other works, of such ballads as "O what is that sound" and "As I walked out one evening." It is not ballads like these, however, that Auden is warning Ashbery against. Rather it is the poet of the 1932 miscellany, *The Orators,* who is to be watched out for; and in an interview with the *Paris Review* in the early 1980s, Ashbery made it quite clear that the message had been received. After noting that Auden "was of two minds about my own work," he added: "You'll remember, though, that he once said in later life that one of his early works, 'The Orators,' must have been written by a madman." It was not the flamboyant discontinuities of the work, the "calculated oddities," that demonstrated the writer's madness, but the fact that in this remarkable anthology of verse and prose forms the twenty-four-year-old Auden had tried to combine the dreamlike rhetoric of "an inner mythological life" with the public formats of the ode and the ballad, or, as he titled two sections of the work, the "journal of an airman" with an "address for a prize-day."

"The problem for the modern poet, as for everyone else today," Auden suggested in 1938, shortly before he left Europe for America, "is how to find or form a genuine community." As Ashbery puts it in "Hotel Lautréamont": "It remains for us to come to terms with *our* commonality." The traditional ballad represents for Ashbery, as it did for Auden, the poetry of "a community united in sympathy." The central task for the modern poet, then, is to try to create works that function the way ballads do, only for a community in which the shared experience is the feeling, as Ashbery described it in 1972, of everything "slipping away from me as I'm trying to talk about it." "A sense of permanent unraveling," he has also called it. One consequence of the resulting "simultaneity of conflicting states of being" is that for the poet, attentive above all to the play of language about him, the composition of modern life takes the form of an indefinitely extended "mix" of discourses: high, low, middle, whatever.

In the summer of 1955, shortly after being notified of his selection by Auden for the Yale Series, Ashbery left New York, where he had been living since his graduation from Harvard in 1949, to spend a year in France on a Fulbright. Between 1955 and late 1965 he lived continuously in France except for the 1957-58 school year which he spent back in New York as a graduate student in French literature at N.Y.U. If, as Ashbery has suggested, French writing played a relatively small role in his "experimenting with language" during these years, this was because the major role was performed by another American who half a century earlier had made Paris her home: Gertrude Stein. Thus he observes of novelist and former *Paris Match* columnist Pierre Martory—whose first collection of poetry, *The Landscape Is Behind The Door,* translated and introduced by Ashbery, was published last year—that "his take on [things French] has something distinctly and irreverently American about it." When they met, Martory, with whom Ashbery lived during much of the decade, "was reading Emily Dickinson, Eliot and Gertrude Stein."

In a 1957 review of Stein's posthumously published *Stanzas in Meditation,* Ashbery described the poetry he would come to write. Only he did so by describing Stein's work:

> Like people, Miss Stein's lines are comforting or annoying or brilliant or tedious. Like people, they sometimes make no sense and sometimes make perfect sense or they stop short in the middle of a sentence and wander away, leaving us alone for awhile in the physical world, that collection of thoughts, flowers, weather, and proper names. And, just as with people, there is no real escape from them. . . . Sometimes the story has the logic of a dream . . . while at other times it becomes startlingly clear for a moment, as though a change in the wind had suddenly enabled us to hear a conversation that was taking place some distance away. . . . In its profound originality, its original profundity, this poem that is always threatening to become a novel reminds us of the late novels of James . . . which seem to strain with a superhuman force toward "the condition of music."

There is no better, no more concise, description of Ashbery's subsequent poetry—despite the tremendous stylistic differences that one encounters in the thirty years of writing between his second book, *The Tennis Court Oath*, and *Hotel Lautréamont*. Ashbery includes here all the figures that he will use again and again in describing his own work: the everyday discontinuities of meaning and sentence structure, the dream-logic, the snatches of conversation, the music. These are all extrapoetic experiences that seem particularly suited to describing what he called in 1972 "the movement of experiencing" or "the experience of experience," and it was precisely this general sense of experience that he suggested fifteen years earlier was Stein's primary concern in *Stanzas in Meditation.* "It is usually not events which interest Miss Stein, rather it is their 'way of happening,' and the story of *Stanzas in Meditation* is a general, all-purpose model which each reader can adapt to fit his own set of particulars." Stein's work offered Ashbery a way of accommodating Auden's warning about confusing private dream and public ballad. Ashbery's poetry would henceforth be "about the privacy of everyone," the way experience feels to anyone.

The poems collected in *The Tennis Court Oath*, which like *Hotel Lautréamont* is dedicated to Martory, represent Ashbery's first attempts to think Stein through on his own terms, that is, in his own terms. Indeed, it is the nature of his terminology that most clearly distinguishes Ashbery from Stein. Whereas Stein, at least in *Stanzas in Meditation,* confined herself to "colorless connecting words such as 'where,' 'which,' 'these,' 'of,' 'not,' 'have,' 'about,' and so on" ("though now and then Miss Stein throws in an orange, a lilac, or an Albert to remind us that it really is the world, our world, that she is talking about"), Ashbery includes everything—every word and sequence of words—he can find. If Stein entertains the same range of events in her work, nonetheless she insists on using her own language: making over the received words, and in the process making the particular events as hard to discern as possible. What defines Ashbery's language as his own, by contrast, is its openness to the language of others. This is his signature. The poems are "his" because the lines are everybody's.

"Back from his breakfast, thirty-five years ago, / he stumbles, finds in the sun a nod that's new." So begins the exquisite **"And Socializing"**—and it is back to this era of "future memories," with its potent combination of party-going and poetry-writing, that Ashbery returns again and again in *Hotel Lautréamont*. The American original for this blending of the social and the poetic is, of course, the author of "Song of Myself," and on several occasions in the 1992 collection Ashbery takes the work of Whitman as his starting-point. He even stages an encounter, in **"A Driftwood Altar,"** with the writer who so memorably identified himself as "a trail of drift and debris": "Of all those who came near him at this stage, only / a few can describe him with any certainty: a drifter / was the consensus, polite with old people, indifferent to children, extremely interested in young adults, / but so far, why remember him? And few did, / that much is certain. I caught up with him / on a back porch in Culver City, exchanged the requisite nod, / shirt biting the neck . . ." Whitman, it will be recalled, concluded his epoch-defining "Song" by leaving everything up in the air: "Failing to fetch me at first keep encouraged, / Missing me one place search another, / I stop somewhere waiting for you."

Ashbery's references to past poetry are frequent, but they are rarely obscure. Unlike Eliot or Pound, he is not interested in impressing the reader with a vast range of esoteric knowledge. On the contrary, it is his range of common usage, the way he joins idioms that too often appear mutually exclusive, which is so impressive. He prefers to use language he can expect the reader to be relatively familiar with, so that the transformations worked on it will be recognizable. Hence the high proportion of titles and first lines in his literary allusions. The two most familiar titles in Whitman's oeuvre, for instance—*Leaves of Grass,* the name of the collected poems, and "When Lilacs Last in the Dooryard Bloom'd," the elegy for Lincoln—are all that a reader needs in order to grasp what Ashbery is after when, in **"Notes From the Air,"** reference is made to "some stranger's casual words" that concern "the square of barren grass that adjoins your doorstep." Similarly, in the superb **"Wild Boys of the Road,"** one passes directly from "the tin / posy in the doorjamb," wonderfully characterized as being "as unconcerned as if this were a hundred and fifty years ago"—as if Whitman's "poesy" had yet to be written—to the poem's final sentence which, seventy-five words long, begins "The leaves are too little at the top" and ends on the sobering note of "stone plinths with fringe of grass." The enumerative and almost infinitely expandable sentence quite literally frames the "stone plinths"—the gravestones of those Ashbery is elegizing, including himself—with perhaps the most resonant phrase in American literature: "leaves . . . of grass."

In speaking of the long prose poems gathered in the 1972 *Three Poems*, Ashbery has observed that "I would be able to write just a couple of pages at a time. I would be left with an overwhelming anxiety, not knowing whether I was ever going to be able to finish this thing or what on earth I was going to put in it." If Ashbery's poetry avoids, in Richard Howard's words, "the invoked anxiety of a closed form," there still remains the need to come up with an ending for the "open" work. Moreover, as Ashbery suggests, how to end is only half the problem; the other half is the perplexing business of just "how to continue"—which, as it happens, is the title of the final poem in *Hotel Lautréamont*.

"Oh there once was a woman / and she kept a shop / selling trinkets to tourists / not far from a dock / who came to see what life could be / far back on the island." So unfolds the first of the five stanzas of this song, with its parties and friends and lovers, "a marvel of poetry / and irony." The simplicity of the language, the generalized model it presents, the explicit concern with unity as well as with the contradictions of "our commonality," all these mark the poem as a contemporary ballad. As such, it is a fitting companion piece to a work like Elizabeth Bishop's "The Burglar of Babylon." Written in traditional ballad stanzas, Bishop's poem takes as its subject "the death of a Brazilian bandit in which emotionally charged ellipses build up to a tragic grandeur"—as Ashbery has put it—beginning and ending with the lines, "On the fair green hills of Rio / There grows a fearful stain: / The poor who come to Rio / And can't go home again." In the modern world the country has become part of the city, and with it has come a pressing need for something resembling the traditional ballad.

Ashbery, like Bishop, seeks to reintroduce us in his "general, all-purpose" poem to this new world in which we are all living and dying—poets and party-goers as well as the poor in the "fair green hills"—and hence to reintroduce us to one another. That is all. There is no particular message. But the poetry does have something to tell us, all the same. By its own example, it demonstrates "how to continue" much as **"The Instruction Manual,"** in *Some Trees*, had done. ("As is my way, I begin to dream, resting my elbows on the desk and leaning out of the window a little, / Of dim Guadalajara! City of rose-colored flowers! / City I wanted most to see, and most did not see, in Mexico!") This is a poetry that not only instructs us to continue but shows how we may do so, even when it seems that "we are in the departure / mode": how to continue, that is, as inhabitants of what Ashbery, in a phrase entered twice in this *Hotel*'s register, calls "our example, earth."

In his most recent collection, published last winter, Ashbery seems to have removed his attention from the earth to the stars—beginning with the title, *And the Stars Were Shining*. Does this mean that he has gone transcendental? I have to confess that when I first read these poems I thought that the poet, after more than forty years of gentle rigor, was finally showing signs of fatigue. The poems really did seem mechanical, as they have so often been accused of being: automatic, insubstantial, forced. I was especially confused by the twenty-four-page title poem, which consists of thirteen sections of varying lengths. These are sufficiently various that I wondered what difference it would make if they were treated as separate poems and given individual titles instead of being numbered—

hence instead of being parts of the poem, **"And the Stars Were Shining,"** merely parts of the book *And the Stars Were Shining*.

I mention this initial response because I suspect that it is the sort of experience which readers who distrust—and more, *dislike*—Ashbery's writing typically have. Needless to say, the first impression was mistaken. The writing is exactly the kind that one should, by now, have come to expect from this poet: whatever's not expected. The problem is that having learned to expect the unexpected doesn't necessarily make it any easier to accept. In the latest poems, it is the halfhearted, almost blasé, gestures that Ashbery seems intent on making which prove so deceptive, the recycled imagery of a "middle" state between life and death (stars, sea, island, dream, night). Instead of *Hotel Lautréamont*'s fierce meditations on death—mixing acceptance and disbelief, indelicacy and despair—these poems seem merely to offer token resistance. No "purgatory of words," such as one finds in the 1991 book-length poem *Flow Chart*, just a couple of shining stars resting on their laurels, drinking beers and, as one is informed late in the new collection, "shooting the breeze with night and her swift promontories."

Yet "token resistance" is Ashbery's own phrase, the title of the opening poem. In his relaxed way, he's pursuing what animates the ordinary, not its elevation—in effect, bringing the stars down to earth. In a recent interview he thus observed, concerning the collection's title (which directly translates *E lucevan le stella,* the aria that Cavaradossi, the painter and lover of Tosca in Puccini's opera *Tosca,* sings before his execution), that "one day" he had "thought of the title in Italian and thought of it being translated into English and it was kind of funny in English . . . a sort of unnecessary bit of information. The fact that they were shining." In Ashbery's new poetry, as in all successful poetry, the poet concentrates on what the mind hungry for information, especially information about which it can be certain, supposes to be unnecessary bits of info. The "present, with its noodle parlors / and token resistance" is still life; and to deny, or resist, this embarrassing fact is to place oneself above life, which is what Ashbery—stars and all—won't do, if he has any say in the matter.

"So must one descend from the checkered heights / that are our friends," Ashbery's poem of "token resistance" concludes: "needlessly / rehearsing what we will say / as a common light bathes us, / / a common fiction reverberates as we pass / to the celebration. Originally / we weren't going to leave home. But made bold / somehow by the rain we put our best foot forward. / / Now it's years after that. It / isn't possible to be young anymore. / Yet the tree treats me like a brute friend; / my own shoes have scarred the walk I've taken." It's not just Ashbery's shoes that have scarred this particular walk, however. "There was a time," Wordsworth's immortal Ode begins, "when meadow, grove, and stream, / The earth, and every common sight / To me did seem / Apparelled in celestial light . . . The Youth, who daily farther from the East / Must travel, still is Nature's Priest, / And by the vision splendid / Is on his way attended; / At length the Man perceives it die away, / And fade into the light of common day." Against Wordsworth's opposition of "common" and "celestial" Ashbery offers his token (that is to say, exemplary) resistance—collapsing the distinction in a "common light" that still leaves room for Wordsworth's "common fiction" of uncommon splendor.

Originally we weren't going to leave home. But made bold somehow by the rain we put our best foot forward. Now it's years after that. It isn't possible to be young anymore. This is Wordsworth's and Ashbery's common predicament. Where they part company is in their responses, as witnessed in the divergent perceptions of a "single" tree. First, Wordsworth: "But there's a Tree, of many one, / A single Field which I have looked upon, / Both of them speak of something that is gone." Then Ashbery, two hundred years later: "Yet the tree treats me like a brute friend." With his brutal honesty, Ashbery obliges one to attend to the present moment instead of the Wordsworthian life at a remove. "Our life is but a sleep and a forgetting," Wordsworth sometimes imagines. And Ashbery? "It was as if all of it had never happened, / my shoelaces were untied, and—am I forgetting anything?" Bringing to a close both *And the Stars Were Shining* and **"And the Stars Were Shining,"** these lines testify to Ashbery's extraordinarily surefooted appropriation of Wordsworth in the volume, for it is as if Wordsworth were speaking, yet the words come out Ashbery's.

Ashbery grew up on a farm outside Rochester—spending many weekends in town, where his grandfather was chairman of the University of Rochester physics department—and he has said that "the one thing I wanted to do was get the hell out of where I was and go to a city, preferably New York, and that's what I ended up doing." In a nostalgic frame of mind he muses not on "the growing Boy," as Wordsworth did or like the more conventionally Romantic Martory, but on his years as a "young adult." The poet's state of mind isn't exactly nostalgic, however, because it doesn't face in just one direction. The young adult he remembers is the young adult whom, as a child, he imagined he would become. This complex, Janus-faced temporality is probably the most distinctive feature of Ashbery's poetry, much more so than the often-commented-upon play with personal pronouns. At different points in his career the play of time (in the sense that one speaks of the play of light) has itself taken distinctive forms, as it does again in *And the Stars Were Shining*.

Ashbery's relation with Martory plays an exemplary role here. Martory has said that when they lived together he showed Ashbery his poems "without putting any pressure on him, and he didn't seem to pay any attention. . . . He did do that later, much later . . . [and] seems to have discovered suddenly that I am a poet." This new attention to Martory's poetry is one aspect of the renewed attention that, in the writing of the last decade, Ashbery has directed toward the period of his youth. This extended period may be characterized as a time of schooling, and further divided into three parts: first, the years that Ashbery's grandfather, as he has put it, "took over my edu-

cation"; second, his formal training at Deerfield Academy, Harvard, and Columbia; third, the self-reeducation that occurred during the years in Paris.

It is in his schooling, in fact, that Ashbery's differences with Wordsworth can most clearly be observed. For whether one takes the Ode as one's touchstone, with Nature understood as "that immortal sea / Which brought us hither," or earlier poems in which Wordsworth describes "the growth of mental power" as a consequence of his schooling in a difficult and glorious Nature, he always insists that it is to Nature that one owes one's imaginative capabilities and hence capacity for heightened ("poetic") consciousness. Wordsworth's Nature—embodied if not fully realized in a countryside that exists beyond the reach of an unsympathetic and unsympathetically portrayed city—is precisely where Ashbery feels least at home. Concerning his own country home, a Victorian mansion he has been restoring for the past fifteen years to resemble his grandfather's house in Rochester, he has said: "I kind of like the fact that I have a house in upstate New York and I have the advantage of no longer being a child and also of being able to get to New York City whenever I want and very easily."

In this way Ashbery is able, even outside his poetry, to resolve the conflict he experienced so strongly as a child between country and city, a divide that Wordsworth wished, if anything, to widen. As I suggested earlier, the decisive collapse of this distinction, with country moving in on the city and city moving out into the countryside, serves as a defining characteristic of modern life and modern poetry. The sun now rises, as Ashbery observed two decades ago, in a suburbia that stretches beyond the horizon, "the morning holocaust become one vast furnace." Still, the true site of exile for Ashbery—and in this he stands opposed to all forms of primitivism, Romantic or Modernist—is the cityless country. What sets his work off from most poetry written today is that in it country and city are accompanied by temporal cousins that are inseparable not only from the two intersecting spatial grids but also from each other. When city and country meet, two distinct forms of temporality collide, linear and cyclical: time that's organized minute by minute—day to day, week to week, month to month—or by season ("Next thing you know it's winter"). Filofax vs. *Farmer's Almanac*. The unyielding movement of *then and now* and the turning back on itself of *then is now*.

Ashbery's poetry serves as an extreme yet nonetheless composed form of reverie, something along the lines of Keats's "Was it a vision, or a waking dream? . . . Do I wake or sleep?" One consequence is that the seasons and cycles of the pastoral city receive the attention due them. The soul "isn't engaged in trade," Ashbery attests in the superb **"Not Planning a Trip Back"**: "it's woven of sleep and the weather / Of sleep." Yet neither is it absolutely disengaged. Day-to-day rhythms are conjoined with the very differently patterned day-to-night-to-day rhythms. As he proposes in **"Just For Starters,"** effectively setting the stage for Keats: "I don't know what got me to write this poem / or any other (I mean why does one write?), /

unless you spoke to me in my dream / and I replied to your waking / and the affair of sleeping and waking began."

The "inhabited landscapes" of Martory's poetry are alternately foreign and local, rural and urban, actual place and painted (or filmed) representation. It's much more difficult to specify the exact nature of Ashbery's settings; still, one can assert that, like Baudelaire's "Landscape," a ravishing translation of which is included in Ashbery's 1984 collection, *A Wave*, every landscape in *And the Stars Were Shining* is cityscape. What distinguishes Ashbery's poetry from both Martory's and Baudelaire's is not the subject matter but the quantity and range of his unsettling juxtapositions, the "motion" with which the riddling **"Like a Sentence"** concludes, "etched there, shaking to be free."

A sort of informal formality has always characterized Ashbery's poetry—the way, for instance, his longer poems incorporate seemingly arbitrary formal schemes, whether the length of the line, the number of lines per stanza, or even, as in a work like the 313-line **"Clepsydra,"** the sheer absence of stanzas or strophes. The form remains recognizably arbitrary, artificial, yet it becomes integral to the particular work. It's this *in*formalism that Ashbery stretches almost to the breaking point in **"And the Stars Were Shining."** In formal terms nothing holds this baker's dozen of sections together, which range from twelve lines to a hundred and thirty, divided into strophes of varying lengths, with even a rhymed quatrain—a variant on the common measure of hymns—thrown in for good measure: "where not too much ever happens, / / *except growing up, hook by hook, / year after tethered year. / And in the basement, that book, / just another thing to fear.*"

"I've never really done this before," Ashbery acknowledges at the beginning of section 8. "See, I couldn't do it . . . See, I can try again." "There is still another thing I have to do," section 11 opens: *"I've never been able to do this"* (Ashbery's italics). Just what *this* is—"this icon. That walks and jabbers / fortuitously or not"—becomes clearer in the next-to-last section, which concludes: "the hothouse beckons. / I've told you before how afraid this makes me, / but I think we can handle it together, / and this is as good a place as any / to unseal my last surprise: you, as you go, / diffident, indifferent, but with the sky for an awning / for as many days as it pleases it to cover you. / That's what I meant by 'get a handle,' and as I say it, / both surface and subtext subside quintessentially / and the deadletter office dissolves in the blue acquiescence of spring."

The "you" in these lines may refer to the reader or to some unidentified third party, but surely it's addressed "quintessentially" to the words on the page, "my last surprise," dead letters dissolving in "blue acquiescence." This poem, and the entire volume, is composed under the sign of Death, "a life of afterwords," its presiding spirit the still scandalously underappreciated American poet Laura Riding, whose writing Ashbery has worked diligently to publicize. Riding, who died at the age of ninety in 1991, was the author of such important poems as "The Judgement," "The Life of

the Dead," and "Death as Death." In the early 1940s she stopped writing poetry when she concluded that it was impossible to remove the poet, who never means exactly what the words seem to say, from the poetry. Two of Ashbery's poems in the present volume, **"World's End"** and **"Footfalls,"** complement poems of Riding's with identical or nearly identical titles ("World's End," "Footfalling"). Behind the four-stanza pantoum **"Seasonal"** in *Hotel Lautréamont*, in which Ashbery contemplates "what a lying writer knows," can be discerned the harsh truths of Riding's withering prose poem, "Poet: A Lying Word."

Now, in **"And the Stars Were Shining,"** Ashbery keeps pace with Winter. "It was the solstice," the poem opens, "and it was jumping on you like a friendly dog." The sun, and with it the passage of time, does not stand still, despite the fact that that is what "solstice" literally means. During the first eleven sections of the poem the season remains constant; this is a poem of winter, of *undoing,* but not, like the more insistently analytic poetry of the late fifties, with the objective of "taking poetry apart." In contrast to Eliot in *The Waste Land* ("I had not thought death had undone so many"), Ashbery stands firmly on the side of life and the life of poetry. "It was their / funeral, and they should have had a say in its undoing."

When, at the end of the poem's penultimate section, Spring is observed to "acquiesce"—presumably to anything one wants, hope springing eternal—and then in the last section, thirteenth month of a long winter, the interlocutor is told that "Summer won't end in your lap" (meaning both *Summer won't come to an end with you* and *you won't be settling down with Summer*), these are *prospective* seasons. The speaker stands outside their orbit even if his writing may not: "So—if you want to come with me . . ." He remains in his poetry and yet can envision, *pace* Riding, the poetry surviving his death. Here, "at the end," Ashbery composes himself in the face of his own death, and not, as in so many of his previous poems, in confronting the deaths of others. On this occasion time is neither cyclical (it remains winter, never quite making it to spring) nor linear (it remains winter, after all). It's time to end, unless the poet has forgotten something, in which case it's time to move on.

Jody Norton (essay date 1995)

SOURCE: "'Whispers out of Time': The Syntax of Being in the Poetry of John Ashbery," in *Twentieth Century Literature,* Vol. XLI, No. 3, Fall, 1995, pp. 281-305.

[*In the following essay, Norton analyzes Ashbery's verse in relationship to the major modes of linguistic theory and philosophy, in particular contemporary gay theory.*]

The meaning of a word is its use in the language.
—Ludwig Wittgenstein, *Philosophical Investigations*

The poem is you.

—John Ashbery, *Shadow Train*

In describing John Ashbery's poetry, Paul Breslin speaks of a contemporary attenuation of the sense of an occasion for poetry, "since all occasions are really only the one occasion of consciousness meditating on its own frustrations." He continues,

> As Ashbery writes in **"The Painter,"** "Finally all indications of a subject / Began to fade, leaving the canvas / Perfectly white" (*Some*). With very few exceptions, Ashbery's poems are meditations on an epistemological blankness, portraits of the whale's forehead.

But if Breslin is right about the blankness of the episteme, he is describing no more than the point (after the deconstruction of epistemology) where Ashbery's poetry—and all other postmodern literature—really begins.

If Hegel is, as Jacques Derrida claims, "the last philosopher of the book and the first thinker of writing," John Ashbery is the last poet of the subject and the first poet of the free predicate—the link between *The Waste Land,* read as a *post*modern poem (that is, as a polyphony of voices, rather than as a shoring of the fragments of the Great Tradition), and the Language poets—Charles Bernstein, Lyn Hejinian, Ron Silliman, Leslie Scalapino—who shift the formal focus of poetry definitively away from the personal subject and onto language itself as culture's open book.[1] Ashbery's principal concern—a concern that mirrors its poststructuralist theoretical moment—is to explore the shifting configurations of subjectivity, which take place not only in, but as, language. Poetic thinking, for Ashbery, is reflection: the subject, as thinking being, reflects on his own subjectivity, and in doing so reflects that subjectivity—which is no more fixed or consistent than thought itself.[2]

Ashbery's language is characterized both by self-reflexivity and by an irreducible temporicity. Because of the formal, theoretical, and thematic centrality of language in his poetry, Ashbery's work cannot be understood outside the context of contemporary philosophy of language, and especially the work of Heidegger, Derrida, and Wittgenstein. For Ashbery, as for these other philosopher/poets, questioning subjectivity, questioning language, is something that we, as subjects of language, do.

Questioning subjectivity, in Ashbery's poetry, ultimately both avoids and becomes the more particular questioning of gay being. Although the problematic of gay desire appears and disappears in Ashbery's poetry, like the opalescent colors of a pearl—as though the poet were both willing and unwilling that it should be visible—it is a crucial, if subtle, illuminant among the polyphonic voices of his text.

Ashbery's subject has been explained by critics in various ways, as the timeless horizon of subjectivity ("the limit of the world—not a part of it" [Wittgenstein *Tractatus,* qtd. in Koethe]), as "primarily a function, not an entity—a function that is manifest in our assertions of desire or our investments in things" (Altieri *Self*), or as "the play of

analogies organized by . . . artistic energies" (Altieri "John Ashbery"). The common element in each of these accounts is the lack of a self-sameness of subject and self-representation that would enable a full self-knowledge. The subject (or self, or agent, depending on the account) cannot directly know "himself," as subject, but only as object or, speaking more precisely in grammatical terms, as complement.[3]

Over and over in Ashbery's poetry, self-knowledge as constituted by a series of reflective glimpses, cinematic in their framed brevity, but lacking any governing directorial intention, gives rise to a sense of subjectivity as structural process, or syntax.[4] The thinking of the subject as syntactical process slides readily into the thinking of process as life. Self and life become conflated as transformation, bound only by "a weathered child's alphabet" (*Rivers*) and "our miserable, dank span of days" (*Three*).[5] **"Drunken Americans,"** from *Shadow Train*, exemplifies Ashbery's speculative—and cautionary—poetics:

> I saw the reflection in the mirror
> And it doesn't count, or not enough
> To make a difference, fabricating itself
> Out of the old, average light of a college town,
>
> And afterwards, when the bus trip
> Had depleted my pocket of its few pennies
> He was seen arguing behind steamed glass,
> With an invisible proprietor. What if you can't own
>
> This one either? For it seems that all
> Moments are like this: thin, unsatisfactory
> As gruel, worn away more each time you return to
>   them.
> Until one day you rip the canvas from its frame
>
> And take it home with you. You think the god-given
> Assertiveness in you has triumphed
> Over the stingy scenario: these objects are real as
>   meat,
> As tears. We are all soiled with this desire, at the
>   last moment, the last.

That "I saw the reflection," and not "myself," in the mirror, indicates tacitly that seeing "doesn't count" as self-cognition, or at least, "not enough / To make a difference"—to define the speaker categorically. This reflection, structuring a difference that doesn't count as one, is a fabrication, suggestive yet illusory—a kind of redaction of the mirror stage, but from the joyless perspective of the adult.[6]

"Afterwards . . . He ["I"? "The reflection"?] was seen arguing." Considering the title of the poem, one forms an image of a bar, but the location—given "afterwards," "steamed glass," and the invisibility of the proprietor— suggests the hazy reflection of memory, daydream, or dream. "What if you can't own / This one either?" the speaker asks, once again expressing doubt as to the possibility of possessing a reliable vision of himself—one which would continue to "count."

"All / Moments are like this": originally reflective, never of transparent value, their provisional, "unsatisfactory" capacity to serve as emblems of exchange for a remorselessly transient real is further worn away, like the inscriptions on coins, each time they are manipulated in the present (the moment of currency). The frustration of this insidious wearing leads to a violent imaging of a violent wish to "rip the canvas from its frame," and to "take it home with you"—to make one of these moments fully your own. "You think" that through a kind of Nietzchean sleight-of-hand, "you" will triumph. Yet this wish can be fulfilled only as fantasy (or figure). And the multiple ironies inherent in a making real of the moment, fantasized as a theft of the imaginary (the fabric-ated) are clear.

The statement that "these objects [moments] are real as meat, / As tears" takes the form of a direct and apparently unironic assertion by the speaker. Yet to the extent that it is read without irony, its irony is only redoubled: for meat (flesh and blood) and tears (painful feelings) are every bit as conditional, as ephemeral, as "Moments" and reflections—or if they are not, that "not" is "not enough / To make a difference." The closing line of the poem asserts that we are all of us, "at the last moment," "soiled with this desire" to assert control—to make ourselves immortal (though the lastness of this moment—and hence, the possibility of any final or essentializing event—is undercut by the repetition of "the last").

Ashbery's use of four personal pronouns ("I," "He," "You," "We") and "it", and his continuous shifting of tenses, help him to represent, respectively, the syntagmatic indeterminacy of subjectivity and the considerably greater complexity of that indeterminacy when its diachronic, or historic, dimension is taken into account. The problematic of the subject is encoded in the multiple usages of "it," some form of which appears in each stanza: "it doesn't count," "its few pennies," "it seems," "its frame," and "take it home." For Ashbery, the subject is the indefinite antecedent behind the (im)personal pronoun *it*.[7]

Heidegger's argument that language is co-originary with Being in relation to *Dasein* (the specifically human way of "being there" in the world) seems at first to present a useful theoretical paradigm for Ashbery's linguistic hypostatizations of the self; and to some extent it does do so. Heidegger's refusal to elide language's structural (not merely mechanical) role in philosophical thinking, and his insistence that, far from manipulating language from a position of ontological priority and superiority, man is in fact produced by and from language, are crucial models of Ashbery's poetic practice. However, while Ashbery refuses to invest in either philosophical or psycho-spiritual absolutes, Heidegger annunciates an undeclared theology of the word.

Being, in Heidegger's text, disseminates itself in a series of concept/essents, that are not, at one level, essential (that is, not synonymous with Being) but that ultimately expand into synonymous essences. Language, for example, is a way of naming/thinking "what is in essence" (*Poetry*); and in "The Origin of the Work of Art" we find

that "Language itself is poetry in the essential sense." All art, in fact, "is poetry," and poetry, it turns out, "is the saying of the unconcealedness of what is." Here, the standard, dictionary sense of the words poetry, art, and language exists in a kind of duck/rabbit ambiguity with the idolatrous imagos of the same words. The status of such terms is typically resolved by Heidegger through a kind of reductive tautology: language is only (essentially) language insofar as it is Language, poetry is (essentially) Poetry, etc. And all of these, finally, are the Same. Language, Heidegger will say, when it is Language, "at one great moment says one unique thing, for one time only" (*What*).

Ashbery effectively follows Saussure and Derrida, and opposes Heidegger, in understanding language as a matter of differences which are ultimately inessential. Ashbery's postmodernity—his sense that identity is constructed out of words that cannot be capitalized—is exactly what sets him apart from Heidegger, for whom it is a point of faith—or if one would rather, a matter of unconscious desire/denial—that Being is transcendental.[8]

> Everything in language is substitute
> —Jacques Derrida, *Of Grammatology*

Taking up Saussure's principle that "in language there are only differences" (Saussure), Derrida notes the importance of spacing as the condition of difference both within language and within the subject: "Spacing is the impossibility for an identity to be closed on itself, on the inside of its proper interiority, or on its coincidence with itself. The irreducibility of spacing is the irreducibility of the other" (*Positions*). Representation both divides the subject from "himself," in that no representation, as such, can be self-perceived, and divides the "himself," in that the subject cannot be conceived independently of the Other. Yet only under these conditions can subjectivity come to be, as self-conception. The subject is "an effect inscribed in a system of *différance*"—which for poetry is the system of language. The subject, finally, "is a 'function' of language" (*Margins*).

To think of oneself, then, is to think not of "oneself" but of a figure or sign of oneself. Derrida writes, "From the moment that there is meaning there are nothing but signs. We *think only in signs*" (*Grammatology*). Henry Staten points out,

> "The thing itself is a sign" does not mean "there isn't really any 'thing itself'"; nor does it mean "the thing is really all in your mind"; nor "there are really only words—we can't get outside of words." It means approximately this: "Let us consider the experience of what we call 'things themselves' as structured more like the experience of signs than like the experience of an idealized 'full presence.'" (*Wittgenstein*)

But in the case of the subject, the "thing itself"—the human being—exists *in his subjectivity* only as he is named: that is, the sign signifies a reality it creates by making that "reality" apprehensible to consciousness. And because consciousness—"our moment of attention" (Ashbery *Self-Portrait*)—is ephemeral, subjectivity constantly gives way.

If the subject is shaped by language, language is shaped by syntax. Syntax can be described as both the formation of motion and the motion of formation. Still, the moment of motionlessness, of the formation *in* motion, must, in a certain sense, be the moment of syntax. This moment of difference (difference in a "hard" sense, as distinction, rather than *différance,* which has the "soft" sense of the spacing that *creates* value) is the moment of meaning. But meaning, if it is to be more than arbitrary nomination, must involve the attribution of qualities, and/or the specification of relations. This is where the asyntactical syntax of the linking verb *to be* finds its place. The syntactical form X is Y is unique. It allows the proposition of a timeless (slipped) equivalence between two signifieds and it is the uniform tacit or explicit syntax of metaphor.

Ashbery frequently makes use of this nominative mode to produce what Derrida calls "savage metaphors." According to Derrida, if I say

> "I see giants," that false designation will be a literal expression of my fear. For in fact I see giants and there is a sure truth there, that of a sensible cogito. . . .

> Nevertheless, what we interpret as literal expression in the perception and designation of giants, remains a metaphor that is preceded by nothing either in experience or in language. (*Grammatology*)

For Ashbery any metaphor for the subject will be a savage metaphor—that is, a literal expression of a seeming or appearance. Since one can only realize oneself in terms of such appearances, each of the manifold tentative figurations in Ashbery's poetry, in its limited way, articulates a virtual subject.

Some of these savage metaphors are impressionistic—for example, Derrida's (Rousseau's) giants—and often, also like the latter, they express fear. The following is from **"The New Spirit"**:

> you will have to take apart the notion of you so as to reconstruct it from an intimate knowledge of its inner workings. How harmless and even helpful the painted wooden components of the Juggernaut look scattered around the yard, patiently waiting to be reassembled!

>   (*Three*)

Here the indication is that a self which is "together" is dangerous, destructive in its very wholeness.

The speaker continues,

> with everything sorted and labeled you can keep an eye on it a lot better than if it were again free to assume protean shapes and senses, the genie once more let out of the bottle, and who can say where all these vacant premises should end?

Like *Juggernaut* ("lord of the world"), the word *genie* conjures up images of power and the potential for destruction, even if the "shapes and senses" the genie may assume are ontologically "vacant premises."

Between Ashbery's nominative, or metaphoric, mode and his predicative, or metonymic, mode (in which the relations of equivalence established by the verb *to be* are disrupted by convoluted, faulty, or disjunctive syntax, or the use of non-linking verbs, or by the combination of divergent claims in a single predication) there exists a figurative middle mode, strictly speaking neither metaphoric nor metonymic, which employs what I will call the meta-simile, or is/as structure. In this hybrid figure the "is" of metaphor and the "as" of simile are combined to produce a statement which paradoxically asserts the reality of figuration: X exists, but only (nonobjectively) in its aspect as, or in its figuration as, Y.[9]

Ashbery writes, in **"Litany,"** *"All life / Is as a tale told to one in a dream / In tones never totally audible / Or understandable."* Where Macbeth's tale, told by an idiot, signifies nothing, Ashbery's subject asserts that life *is,* but exists *as* (in the form of) a fiction within a fiction—that is, as a structure of meaning (*"the novel / We had been overhearing"*) given to one within a structural illusion (dream—hence the *auto*biographical nature of the tale).

Ultimately, for Ashbery, syntax is mimetic at once of the subject and of the impossibility of a stable predication of the subject—even as syntax. One of the conditions of possibility of syntactical structure is the expenditure of time—sentences "take" time to speak or write—more (usually) than words, which take more than their phonemes (if they consist of more than one), and so forth. At the same time, on the semantic level, syntax constitutes a retaining structure. Meaning depends on our holding the earlier words of a sentence in mind while we read the later ones; and reading a sentence, a paragraph, a chapter, etc., often involves both mental review of what has gone before and, to a lesser extent, anticipation of what will follow. Meaning is not, therefore, produced along a rigidly unidirectional spatio-temporal axis, nor can it, as Husserl and Derrida have shown, exist significantly for us as pure presence. Meaning necessarily involves an indefinite structural and temporal extension/duration, or retention/protention, whether one is speaking of morphemes or of complete works of literary art. One never exactly names, then, one temporizes.

Yet in a way uncannily similar to Heidegger's description of *Dasein* as never quite *Dasein,* but as the moment of the *becoming* of *Dasein,* the subject for Ashbery often seems somehow to "be" as spatio-temporal-material-energic-figural passage itself—one needs only to note his affection for images of waves ("set free on an ocean of language that comes to be / Part of us, as though we would ever get away" [*Wave*] and flames ("a flame yourself / Without meaning, yet . . . / . . . living / In that flame's idealized shape and duration" [*Double*]). Thinking and writing poetry *can,* in a partial, meta-similic way, mime the subject in process. The subject, while he can never be fully objectified in language, can be enacted as his very transitivity.

To follow Ashbery's interrogatory reflections for any length of time is to be made inescapably aware of his speakers' relentless desire to arrive, amidst the "*blizzard / Of speculation,*" at some understanding of their subjectivity, momentary though it may be. In the closing lines of **"The New Spirit,"** Ashbery refers to

> the major question that revolves around you, your being here. And this is again affirmed in the stars: just their presence, mild and unquestioning, is proof that you have got to begin in the way of choosing some one of the forms of answering that question, since if they were not there the question would not exist to be answered.
>
> (***Three***)

Despite the self-satirical effect of this less-than-earnest play with "questions" which are not questions at all, the point beneath the amusement is a serious one. "Being here" is an unavoidable question, urged simply and powerfully by experience, and one feels pressured "to begin . . . choosing some one of the forms of answering" (cf. "Why are there essents rather than nothing?" the opening sentence of Heidegger's *Introduction to Metaphysics*).

Ashbery writes, in **"Litany"**:

> Who cares, anyway, about
> What it is or what it was like?
> You must be made to care. Yes,
> I am mad, I think, and I do care.
> I can't help it. I am mad,
> And don't care.

In an internal dialogue reminiscent of Wittgenstein's curious conversations with himself in the *Investigations*, Ashbery's speaker drives himself to the most uncharacteristic admission that "I do care. / I can't help it."[10] For Ashbery, the question of being cannot ultimately be separated from the impulse of caring. This feeling-like-an-I, and caring, is a fundamental motivation of his poetry.

For Ashbery's caring is a caring of the speaker not just about, but for, himself—the kind of care that alone makes possible the caring for another. This one-who-cares can know himself as the subject of love only through accession, not to a language of desire, but to desire as language. In this connection it is striking that Ashbery, who is gay, should so curiously efface from his poems the question of a specifically gay desire / gay language, a question equally strikingly absent from the criticism of his work, with the exception of John Shoptaw's recent book.[11]

Ashbery's poetry is not entirely without allusion to gay sexuality. In his prose poem **"Description of a Masque,"** Little Boy Blue is described as "apparently performing an act of fellatio" on Little Jack Horner (*Wave*). Typically, however, Ashbery's language and images are neither sexual nor erotic in any obvious way.

There are several possible ways of accounting for Ashbery's disconnection from the contemporary problematic of homosexuality—a sexuality that has been called, among other things, the origin of "a species" (Foucault *History*) and a crucial formation in "that remorseless mockery of Philistine common sense and bourgeois realism which is modern art" (Steiner, qtd. in Dollimore). One is that Ashbery chooses to avoid allowing his poems to run the risk of being collapsed from broadly applicable meditations on the instability of postmodern subjectivity into personalist ruminations on the plight of a "disposable" minority. Ashbery has remarked, for example, that "I do not think of myself as a gay poet." Another is that the thinking of subjectivity as language tends to discourage a preoccupation with being in its psychosomatic materiality.

On the other hand, it is possible to suggest that the problematic of gay being *is* in fact represented in the very tenuousness of the subject position in Ashbery's poetry. David Bergman discusses the frequent relative egolessness of the gay writer, in Eriksonian terms:

> Since for Erikson "ego identity is the awareness . . . of selfsameness and continuity," and since the homosexual's sense of himself does not "coincide with the sameness and continuity of one's *meaning for significant others*". . . the result is a "negative identity."

> This negative identity is *not* merely an inversion of selfhood—being the opposite of what others expect one to be—but rather an absence of identity—no one can point the gay child toward a model of who he is.

Bergman is actually describing not a lack of models so much as a discrepancy between the gay individual's "sense of himself" and the constructions according to which he is read by others. The effect is a dissonance, which is likely to manifest itself in the individual both as the feeling that one is "not right," and as the feeling that one is not *one*—i.e., a recognizable person, who counts—at all.

In an oft-quoted passage from the *Craft* interview Ashbery says,

> I guess I don't have a very strong sense of my own identity and I find it very easy to move from one person in the sense of a pronoun to another and this again helps to produce a kind of polyphony in my poetry.

An amorphous, or polymorphous, sense of identity is conductive to the production of multiple voices, but not to the imagination of a definite speaker.[12]

It can be argued, simultaneously, that Ashbery's "skepticism about the representative adequacy of language," to borrow Eve Kosofsky Sedgwick's phrase (qtd. in Chadwick), amounts to a tacit critique of the inherent homophobia of stable representation in general—that discourse constructed as a system of binary oppositions leaves no room for a way of sexual being that *comes between* "male" and "female," the gendered polarities of heterosexual desire.

Jonathan Dollimore notes that

> sexuality in its normative forms constitutes a 'truth' connecting inextricably with other truths and norms not explicitly sexual. This is a major reason why sexual deviance is found threatening: in deviating from normative truth and the 'nature' which underpins it, such deviance shifts and confuses the norms of truth and being throughout culture.[13]

> Who am I after all, you say despairingly
> once again
> —John Ashbery, *Three Poems*

Of all of Ashbery's poems, **"Self-Portrait in a Convex Mirror"** is the least self-protective, the least ironic, and the most forthright in its utterance of its speaker's desire to know. Yet even in this poem, at once a portrait of the Ashberyan subject, of the beautiful Renaissance male whose own self-portrait teases out the speaker's, and of an emphatic attraction so strong it "Makes hot tears spurt," gay desire sounds only as a discreet harmonic. **"Self-Portrait"** is, first of all, a poem of speculation in Ashbery's customary two blended senses of (1) thinking the nature of the subject, and (2) thinking/writing as reflective of, and ultimately as constituting, the subject.

To ascertain that Ashbery sees himself as a twentieth-century double, or reflection, of the sixteenth-century Italian painter one need only glance at the title of the book (which doubles the title of the poem) and the cover photograph of the author, wearing "the same / Wraith of a smile" he attributes to Parmigianino (*Self-Portrait*). Vasari's "'he set himself / With great art to copy all that he saw in the glass'," written in description of Parmigianino and quoted early in the poem by Ashbery, is thus to be taken as descriptive of Ashbery's speaker, and moreover as a reflection of the high seriousness, both moral and artistic, with which the poet himself approaches his project.

Although the problematic of gay desire appears and disappears in Ashbery's poetry, like the opalescent colors of a pearl—as though the poet were both willing and unwilling that it should be visible—it is a crucial, if subtle, illuminant among the polyphonic voices of his text.

—*Jody Norton*

What Parmigianino "'saw in the glass'," according to Ashbery's speaker, was "Chiefly his reflection, of which the portrait / Is the reflection once removed." Thus, within the first twenty lines of this 552-line poem we find Ashbery making a clear statement of the first of his two controlling ideas on the subject: that an attempt to produce a formulation of subjectivity is necessarily reflective—that

is, distanced from both the materiality and the experience of the individual. This distance, in its irreducible separation of the individual from "himself" as subject, is death, structurally. The image is "embalmed" by "the strict / Otherness."

The "soul" establishes itself in the liveliness of the image, yet—and here is Ashbery's second major idea of the subject—"the soul is not a soul," but merely a representation, present only during "our moment of attention." The subject, in short, possesses no essentiality or principle. "The surface is what's there," in the mirror, "And nothing can exist except what's there." Furthermore, "there are no words for the surface, that is, / No words to say what it really is."

"Self-Portrait" is in part an elegy for the soul—for a time when the soul existed by virtue of its own Wittgensteinian self-certainty, its own assumption of itself (a time when one would not have dreamed of confusing a portrait or image with the soul, or conversely, of attempting misguidedly, perhaps even blasphemously, to prove the existence of the soul through a painted image of the body).[14] Yet the soul, and the problem of how to demonstrate (or perhaps to conjure), through an instantaneous reflection, the existence of an essence which is radically distanced by the very *structure* of reflection are primarily Parmigianino's problems. For Parmigianino, the impossible project of picturing the soul issues ironically in the successful representation of the Renaissance self.

For Ashbery, on the other hand, the problem is to realize the subject in the indirect, abstract medium of language. If something unspecified is missing, as indeed it must be, from Parmigianino's portrait of his soul—its missing reflected in the portrait's moving expression of "tenderness, amusement and regret"—something specific is missing in **"Self-Portrait"**: the instantaneity of the visual image, and the identificatory gestalt it makes possible. **"Self-Portrait in a Convex Mirror"** can, in fact, be read as an elegy for the mirror stage—for a time when one lived in the simple assumption of one's own existence. For though the Lacanian infant is not without an awareness of difference from his mirror image, his anxiety concerning the lack of synonymy between himself and his image never coalesces into a fundamental doubt as to his own existence. With the evaluation of the oedipal split, and the accession to language, however, the unity of the psyche is irrevocably shattered, and difference is finalized: "This otherness, this / 'Not-being-us' is all there is to look at / In the mirror."

Within the represented world of the poem, there is a subtle but powerful homoerotic component in the speaker's attraction to the figure of Parmigianino, for the beauty of whom the speaker borrows Vasari's description, "'rather angel than man'." The poem continues,

> Perhaps an angel looks like everything
> We have forgotten, I mean forgotten
> Things that don't seem familiar when
> We meet them again, lost beyond telling,
> Which were ours once. . . .

you could be fooled for a moment
Before you realize the reflection
Isn't yours.

Here the beauty of the painter—coded chastely as angel-ic—kindles a scopophilic engagement with his image, both as reflection of the subject and as that subject's erotic double. At the same time, Parmigianino's beauty recalls the fluid indifferentiation of the mirror stage, for which sexual union, according to Lacan, is only a metaphor. The speaker's gaze repeats the lost vision in which we first recognize our own beauty in the beauty of an other.[15]

Inherent in Ashbery's complex, muted representation of gay desire as a dynamic relationship between subject, other, and self-as-other, in the context of his more general refusal to allow his speakers the safety and propriety of stable form, is the enactment of a radical—and generalizable—insight: that gayness, as a shared condition of being marked by various configurations of desire for members of the "same" sex, emblematizes—in a certain sense *is*—the recognition that human identity, in its sexual composition as in other respects, does not conform to any general set of culturally inscribed parameters.

Early in **"Self-Portrait"** Ashbery's speaker, reflecting on, and identifying with, the maddening distantiation, the *lack* of identity, that the act of self-identification involves—a distantiation that Rimbaud, on the brink of another modernism, finely articulated as *Je est un autre*—speaks of Parmigianino's as

the face
On which the effort of this condition reads
Like a pinpoint of a smile . . .
A perverse light whose
Imperative of subtlety dooms in advance its
Conceit to light up: unimportant but meant.

This "perverse light," in which alone Ashbery's poetry yields its "unimportant" gay reading, is a metaphor both for gayness as a way of being sexual that plays with the erotics of sameness as well as difference, and for Ashbery's formal procedure as a kind of gay poetics.

"Self-Portrait" is intensely a poem of time, in both its synergies and its aporias. The speaker's effort to determine his subjectivity can be consciously structured only out of past passages of that subjectivity: "The tale goes on," Ashbery writes, "In the form of memories deposited in irregular / Clumps of crystals." "My guide in these matters is your self / Firm, oblique, accepting everything" (71), says Ashbery's speaker, referring to Parmigianino but effectively recalling another Ashberyan image of subjectivity, **The Picture of Little J. A.,"** with its "hard stare, accepting / Everything" (*Some*). Yet what is most apparent to Ashbery's speaker is not, finally, his continuity with these images (despite the fact that "you could be fooled for a moment / Before you realize the reflection / Isn't yours"), but "The distance between us."

If each of these versions of subjectivity is transient, "Like a wave breaking on a rock, giving up / Its shape in a gesture which expresses that shape," "their importance / If not their meaning is plain." They serve "to nourish / A dream which includes them all"—the dream of an enduring, proper, fully real identity. And if such a dream can never actually be fulfilled, nevertheless it can provide us with a sustaining dimensionality. As Ashbery's speaker puts it,

Why be unhappy with this arrangement, since
Dreams prolong us as they are absorbed?
Something like living occurs, a movement
Out of the dream into its codification.

It is clear all the same why one *should* be unhappy, in Ashbery's speaker's view: without a valid identity it is only "Something like living" that occurs, not real life.

If hypothetical structurations of the subject are ontologically hollow, however, if their "locking into place" is even "'death itself'," nevertheless "the 'all'" of "the 'it was all a dream' / Syndrome . . . tells tersely / Enough how it wasn't." First of all, the real of being is "Like a dozing whale on the sea bottom / In relation to the tiny, self-important ship / On the surface" (the identificatory fiction of the subject). Second, even the chameleon subject, considered as the historical sequence of structurations of the individual, "Was real, though troubled," a "waking dream." The continuity of this existence is textual and temporal, however, rather than metaphysical. "Each part of the whole," each successive deposit "falls off," over time, and is aware of its past formation only "in cold pockets / Of remembrance." "'Death itself,'" finally, the provisional stability of the self-portrait in image or word, is life *As We Know* it.

The boy who cried "wolf" used to live there.—
John Ashbery, **"Litany"**

Ashbery's sense of the subject as a becoming-structure-going-past that can never stabilize itself as a durable presence, that involves a certain originary separation of the individual from himself as the condition of its presencing, and whose hypostatizations often appear most clearly legible when they have taken on the strangeness of the past, lends Ashbery's work a touch of pathos which is not always fended off with a joke. For example, the image of the subject—"This profile at the window"—Ashbery writes, is "The picture of hope a dying man might turn away from, / Realizing that hope is something else, something concrete / You can't have" (*Houseboat*).

This impression of the oppressive lostness of the self inevitably creates a host of echoes in Victorian and Modernist poetry. "For what wears out the life of mortal men?" Arnold asks in "The Scholar-Gipsy," and replies, "'Tis that from change to change their being rolls." The Scholar-Gipsy, having made the romantic choice of vision over ambition, and hence possessed of "perennial youth," is much to be admired and envied, despite Arnold's speaker's derogation of him as a "truant boy." His life is one of "unclouded joy," while we, who live "a hundred different lives," "pine, / And wish the long unhappy dream would end."

If, in Wallace Stevens's "Tea at the Palaz of Hoon," there is a certain braveness and possibility to "I was the world in which I walked" (Stevens) such a world holds, for "men, and earth and sky . . . / . . . sharp, / Free knowledges, secreted until then, / Breaches of that which held them fast" (Stevens). The disruption of "that which held them fast" (cf. Heidegger's fourfold of man and divinities, earth and sky) is such a central fact of experience for Stevens's imagination that his entire *oeuvre* may be read as a consideration of "the odd morphology of regret" (Stevens). For if "what I saw / Or heard or felt came not but from myself" there can be no absolute or objective source of validation of truth or value. Without a participatory relation with such a source we know neither who we are nor where we belong. We live, then, paradoxically, in a self-created place "That is not our own and, much more, not ourselves." "Life is a bitter aspic," he concludes, in "Esthetique du Mal," "We are not / At the centre of a diamond."

Yet if Ashbery's speaker can feel a certain "sadness as I look out over all this and realize that I can never have any of it, even though I have it all as I in fact do" (*Three*), he is protected from nostalgia, in a way that Arnold and Stevens are not, by the very passage of literary and historical time. For Arnold romantic vision is credible but no longer obtainable. For Stevens the spiritual *was* credible, but is no longer—and Stevens suffers precisely because of the reality of that incredibility. Ashbery, however, due in part to his coming at the post-Freudian, post-phenomenological theoretical moment that he does, has no sense that the romantic, the spiritual, the transcendental ever *has* existed as an existential possibility. For Ashbery the "unclouded joy" of the Scholar-Gipsy is "balmy felicity. The world of Schubert's lieder" (***Rivers***), where "balmy" invokes its colloquial British sense, "daft."

Ashbery's radically constructionist view of subjectivity links him in important ways to the second generation of postmodernists—the Language poets.[16] In his poststructuralist understanding of language as the indeterminate field on which we elaborate our psycho-social reality, and in his postmodern, post-Bakhtinian sense of culture as a cacophony of dissonant social languages, conflicting ideologies, and wildly mutating modes of representation, Ashbery should be understood as both a precursor and contemporary of the Language poets in what Marjorie Perloff calls "the poetics of indeterminancy."[17]

Yet there are significant differences between Ashbery and the Language poets as well, particularly on the issues of the relation of the poetic subject to language, the reader/text relation, and the temporicity of the poem. Lyn Hejinian writes:

> As Francis Ponge puts it, "Man is a curious body whose center of gravity is not in himself." Instead it seems to be located in language, by virtue of which we negotiate our mentalities and the world.

This sounds deceptively close to Ashbery's sense of the subject/language relation. However, whereas Ashbery remains interested in strategies of self-determination within language (his last link with the Romantic tradition), Hejinian and the other Language poets tend to view any rhetoric of the self as colonialist in its drive to dominate meaning through voice.[18] They prefer what Bruce Andrews calls "a non-imperial or language-centered writing" ("Text").

Charles Bernstein asks us to compare two possible views of what poetry is: "In the one, an instance (a recording perhaps) of reality/fantasy/experience/event is presented to us through the writing. In the other, the writing itself is seen as an instance of reality/fantasy/experience/event" ("Stray"). The shared perspective of the Language poets is that, in James Sherry's words, "spoken or written language is not a box for meaning—it is the content(s)."

Ashbery's urge to locate subjectivity, however transiently, runs counter not only to the Language poets' interest in language as "object-in-itself" (Grenier, qtd. in Nicholls), but also (in their view, at least) to their emphasis on poetry as a reader-responsive mode. Bernstein notes that much twentieth-century writing (and this would certainly include Ashbery's) has been centrally concerned with "the mapping of consciousness, an investigation implicitly involved with the nature of 'mind' and 'self'" ("Writing"). He goes on to argue that "this conception of reading/writing shares with more impersonal forms a projection of the text as sealed-off from the reader." The Language poem, on the other hand, "is open to the world and particularly to the reader" (Hejinian). It "calls upon the reader to be actively involved in the process of constituting its meaning, the reader becoming neither a neutral observer to a described exteriority or to an enacted interiority" (Bernstein "Writing").[19]

Whether or not one agrees that poetry which seeks to explore consciousness is necessarily "sealed-off from the reader" (it is axiomatic for Ashbery, for example, that "there is . . . no seeing without interpretation" [Bernstein "Writing"]), it is evident that to the extent that language itself, as a cultural phenomenon, becomes the impersonal speech of poetry, voice tends to disappear.[20]

Bruce Andrews speaks of the Language poets' desire to create "A semantic atmosphere or milieu, rather than the possessive individualism of reference" ("Text"; qtd. in Nicholls). Yet although this "semantic . . . milieu" will no doubt be historically and culturally determined, history and finally time itself tend to disappear when language becomes voiceless. Without a syntax of being, memory, reflexivity, and consequently subjectivity are not possible; and with subjectivity goes the possibility of political and intellectual agency. The final irony for an anti-colonial, liberatory poetic is to find itself generating a literature incapable of addressing the problem of the subject in his/her historical/theoretical location. Because of this destructed relation to history, the less successful Language poetry comes to seem oddly formalist and atemporal in ways uncomfortably suggestive of the more mechanistic strains of second-generation Modernist poetry.

Time remains timely for Ashbery, even as it resolves itself into a kind of mortified timelessness for Heidegger and, in a different way, for the Language poets. "It"—life, the subject, whatever "it" is—can "come about / . . . / only in the gap of today filling itself / . . . / in the idea of what time it is / when that time is already past" (**Self-Portrait**). Versions of the subject occur as provisional conceptualizations or figurations which must remain incomplete precisely to the degree to which they are completions—that is, more or less static representations within the structure of language.

As for the present, "This nondescript, never-to-be defined daytime," "You can't live there" (**Self-Portrait**). Living, the process of existing in the passage of time, casts "no shadow, / No reflection in the mirror." It would even only be possible "As a refugee from all this"—that is, if one could escape the sequence of semantic graspings that conscious codifications of the subject represent. For in formulating an objectification of the subject, a "This is how things are," as Wittgenstein writes of the general form of propositions, "One thinks that one is tracing the outline of the thing's nature over and over again, and one is merely tracing round the frame through which we look at it."

Yet living, for Ashbery, is also an Orphic dying-to-know, in which one cannot help killing the thing one loves/is. Ashbery writes in **April Galleons**, "It hurts, this wanting to give a dimension / To life, when life is precisely that dimension." As for Heidegger *Dasein* is (in its theoretical efficiency) a giving of dimension which can never be as itself, so to be human for Ashbery is, ultimately, and complicatedly, to "see yourself growing up around the other, posited life, afraid for its inertness and afraid for yourself, intimidated and defensive" (**Three**). The subject is both a massive "ball / of contradictions" and a "hollow, empty sphere."

Both Heidegger and Ashbery arrive at *Dasein*/subjectivity as the moment of division, but whereas for Heidegger this moment is, despite his disclaimers, ontological, for Ashbery "the carnivorous / Way of these lines is to devour their own nature, leaving / Nothing but a bitter impression of absence" (**Rivers**). For both, the subject is "whispers out of time" (**Self-Portrait**)—the hesitant articulation which is the saying of being. But while for Heidegger saying is an appropriating, or "setting-itself-into-work of truth" (*Poetry*) which "gathers mortals into the appropriateness of their nature" (*On the Way*), for Ashbery the saying of the subject produces "an endless confusion of fair and variegated forms . . . self-important and self-convoluted shapes" which add "disconcertingly up to zero" (**Three**).

If for Heidegger "Language is the house of being," for Ashbery it is a house of mirrors, "pure / Affirmation that doesn't affirm anything" (**Self-Portrait**). Narcissus's tragedy lay in his failure to complete the circuit of self-representation—to recognize himself *as* himself. The success of John Ashbery's tragicomic enterprise is grounded on his recognition that self-representation is *only* a circuit—that subjectivity is less like the Cartesian *cogito* than like a

wooden nickel: not something to be counted on, but to be played with (sometimes duplicitously).

At the same time, as I have argued, Ashbery's poetry comprises an affirmation of instability as the very condition of a liberatory conception of gay being. **"Self-Portrait,"** in all its elegaic grandeur, in all its regret for the passing of a soul which it can never actually imagine to have existed, can be read as a precursive vision of the sex-positive queer of the nineties. One of the central analytical insights of contemporary queer theory is that sexual ambiguity and gender dissonance are nothing less than emblematic of the fundamental polysexuality of all human beings. Judith Butler writes:

> Identifications are multiple and contestatory, and it may be that we desire most strongly those individuals who reflect in a dense or saturated way the possibilities of multiple and simultaneous substitutions, where a substitution engages a fantasy of recovering a primary object of a love lost—and produced—through prohibition. Insofar as a number of such fantasies can come to constitute and saturate a site of desire, it follows that we are not in the position of *either* identifying with a given sex *or* desiring someone else of that sex; indeed, we are not, more generally, in a position of finding identification and desire to be mutually exclusive phenomena.

In the liminality and transience of Ashbery's poetic identities, as in the anti-categorical work of contemporary queer theorists, you discover "Not the truth, perhaps, but—yourself" (**Three**).

Notes

[1] I use the word "subject" (alternatively "speaker") to specify the biologically/socially constructed agency whose voice enunciates some or all of the language of a poem.

"Consciousness" specifies mind, thought as indeterminately comprised of individual subjectivity and a collective linguistic and cultural context.

Pieces of language that seem not to originate from a particular subjectivity can be attributed to a generalized cultural consciousness reproduced in the poem by the author.

[2] Because I assume that Ashbery's subjects are male—and sometimes specifically gay male—(except where they are represented by the ungendered "it"), and for the sake of economy, I have generally used masculine pronouns. I recognize the political implications of this normalization, and the limitations it places on the range of possible readings of the poems.

[3] In the more challenging versions of this subject/complement relation, the agentic element itself is non-simple. Andrew Ross notes, for example, the contemporary epistemological shift "in which linguistic subjectivity is accepted as given and necessary." After Lacan's revisioning of Freud's theories of the formation of the ego, after Foucault's critique of the subject, after Derrida's critique of subjectivity, agency itself, in Ashbery's poetry as in poststructuralist theory generally, comes to be understood as de-

pendent on symbolic structuration within a social field in which language functions both as the architectonic foundation of culture and its principal production. Hence, no purely individual intentionality can be posited. As Stephen Fredman writes, "Ashbery operates from the central American premise that the self is a shared entity, that through language, consciousness is both individual and collective" (114).

Many of the most acute and interesting critics of contemporary poetry have written on Ashbery. The accounts I have found most useful, overall, are Charles Altieri *Self* (132-64), Stephen Fredman (99-133), John Koethe, Marjorie Perloff (248-87), Richard Stamelman, and Alan Williamson (116-48).

[4] In this Ashbery follows the implications of Nietzsche's critique of Descartes:

> "There is thinking: therefore there is something that thinks": this is the upshot of all Descartes' argumentation. But that means positing as "true *a priori*" our belief in the concept of substance—that when there is thought there has to be something "that thinks" is simply a formulation of our grammatical custom that adds a doer to every deed. In short, this is not merely the substantiation of a fact but a logical-metaphysical postulate. (268)

[5] The shaping and reshaping of meaning as a characteristic of Ashbery's poetic language has been noted by numerous critics. See Altieri *Self* 149, Kalstone 171, and Perloff 262.

[6] See Jacques Lacan's essay, "The mirror stage as formative of the function of the I as revealed in psychoanalytic experience," in *Ecrits* 1-7.

[7] David Kalstone writes that "The blurring of personal pronouns, their often indeterminate reference" is, for Ashbery, a way of "trying to be true not only to the mind's confusions but also to its resistance of stiffening formulations" (183). David Bergman remarks that Ashbery's "weak selfhood," which he suggests may be linked to Ashbery's homosexuality, "leads to his characteristic ambiguity of pronoun reference" (46). See my discussion of the thematic of gay sexuality below.

[8] Gerald Bruns complains that Derrida's work on Heidegger in *Margins of Philosophy* has led to a reductive view of the latter as "a failed deconstructionist who wants to go back behind the discourse of inferential reasoning to recover a primordial 'alliance of speech and Being in the unique word, in the finally proper name'" (4). Bruns calls this view "a caricature of Heidegger's thinking" (198). Yet Bruns later makes quite a different statement:

> As philosophers can claim to have found nothing in Heidegger, so both theologians and deconstructionists can claim to have uncovered onto-theological motives in him. I myself would not be surprised by the existence of these motives; quite possibly they are among Heidegger's dirty secrets. (210)

Jurgen Habermas notes,

> When one lets oneself be as affected by the circumstances of contemporary history as Heidegger does, and nonetheless progresses, as if with the force of

gravity, into the dimension of essential concepts, the truth claim of inverted foundationalism becomes rigidified into a prophetic gesture. (162)

[9] Henry Staten writes:

> Metaphysics in its most pervasive form is the tendency to think that "All *X* is really *Y*." . . . The Wittgensteinian alternative, if we were to put it as a formula, would be something like: "In certain contexts, it is more accurate (or sometimes simply, more useful) to treat *X* in terms of *Y*." ("Wittgenstein" 282)

Wittgenstein points out that "'Seeing as . . .' is not part of perception. And for that reason it is like seeing and again not like" (*Philosophical* 197e).

[10] Cf. "Teach us to care and not to care / Teach us to sit still." T. S. Eliot, "Ash-Wednesday" (Eliot 84).

Voice in Ashbery's poetry has been variously explicated. See Bloom, McClatchy, Fredman, and Ross. Thomas Gardner, through a series of quotations which are difficult to paraphrase, speaks of Ashbery as having "absorbed and internalized" "the world's 'many uttering tongues'" (145). I would agree with this if we can understand Whitman's "many uttering tongues" as practically synonymous with Bakhtin's concept of voice as a personal idiom which can combine multiple ideological languages. It seems to me that Bakhtin is the clearest theoretical guide to conceptualizing voice in Ashbery. Although Bakhtin is notorious for denying linguistic range to the lyric poem, his concepts of language, ideology, dialogism, polyphony, heteroglossia, double-voiced discourse, and centripetal/centrifugal forces within language are all of great potential use in thinking about the multivalent construction of Ashbery's poems.

[11] One looks in vain in the major pieces on Ashbery by Perloff, Altieri, Perkins, Ross, Kalstone, Williamson, Howard, von Hallberg, and Fredman for any mention of the presence or absence of gay desire in Ashbery's work.

David Shapiro describes "Self-Portrait in a Convex Mirror" as "a love poem to the image seen within, image of artist-virtuoso and young artist" (7). Shapiro, however, seems to understand the poem's gay eroticism as less important than—indeed, almost a metaphor for—its narcissistic structure: "the poem is one of endless narcissistic possibility and impossibility" (7). In this reading, the poem becomes less homoerotic than autoerotic.

John Shoptaw argues that Ashbery's work is "misrepresentative," and that his mode of misrepresentation is "homotextual." Ashbery's poems are characterized by "distortions, evasions, omissions, obscurities and discontinuities" (4) whose "homotextuality" derives, on the one hand, from Ashbery's leaving "himself and his homosexuality out of his poetry" (4) (thus, presumably, creating the possibility of homosexual subtexts) and, on the other, from the socio-political conditioning of the McCarthy era. However, since Shoptaw sees homotextuality as a formal procedure whose applicability is not necessarily limited to sexual thematics, it is unclear in what way this technique of "cryptography" comprises a specifically homosexual rhetoric, the more so as Shoptaw insists that Ashbery's poetry "provides no secret passage to a coterie of gay readers who 'catch' its specially encoded hidden meaning" (4).

[12] I do not address the question of the relation of the author of the poem to its subject or speaker—a relation which, in quasi-autobiographical poetry, is always vexed. Any autobiographical writing, no matter how candid, is inevitably fictional; and on the other hand, no fiction is ever without the formal presence of its author. In this essay I assume only (1) that there is a difference between the historical individual Ashbery and his poetic speakers, and (2) that these speakers undoubtedly express aspects of the psychic economy of their creator.

[13] Michael Warner describes heterosexuality as "the modern discursive organization of sex that treats gender difference as difference in general" (202). On gay theory and sex/gender difference see Boone and Cadden, and Fuss.

[14] Wittgenstein writes, "Even if the most trustworthy of men assures me that he *knows* things are thus and so, this by itself cannot satisfy me that he does know. Only that he believes he knows" (*On Certainty* 20e). He adds, "The difficulty is to realize the groundlessness of our believing" (24e).

[15] In his reading of the speaker's attraction to the figure of Parmigianino, Shoptaw notes both the "enchantment of self with self" (*Self-Portrait* 72) and the search for "the self in another and . . . the other in oneself" (Shoptaw 181-82). But Shoptaw does not attempt to analyze the incompatibility of Freud's theoretically unsatisfactory description of homosexuality in "On Narcissism" (Freud actually theorizes homosexuality more convincingly elsewhere) with the attraction to an other as such that narcissim, strictly speaking, precludes. Lacan's conception of the mirror stage offers an explanation of the self-other relation that accounts for its reflexive character as a dynamic exchange, rather than a static contradiction. Shoptaw refers to the mirror stage at one point, but does not distinguish it from narcissism (see 184).

Freud discusses the genesis and character of homosexuality in *Three Essays* and "Psychogenesis," as well as in "Psycho-Analytic." Kaja Silverman analyzes Freud's theories of male homosexuality at length.

[16] For the purposes of this brief discussion, I will take as representative of the category Language poets those authors whose work appears in Ron Silliman's collection or Douglas Messerli's anthology.

[17] Recent critical works in which connections between Ashbery's writing and that of the Language poets are asserted or implied include Fredman; Andrews "Misrepresentation"; Silliman, Watten, et al.; Waldrop; Nicholls; and Reinfeld.

[18] The exception in Ashbery's *oeuvre*, perhaps, is the radically nonsequential poetry of *The Tennis Court Oath*, which is referred to with approval in Language poetics. See Andrews "Misrepresentation."

[19] Analyzing Charles Bernstein's "The Simply," Jerome McGann writes, "The ultimate subject of a text like this is the reader" (36).

[20] Peter Nicholls warns that "to reject the 'voice' is not only to deny the imperial claims of the lyric self, but also to court an extreme of tonelessness which effaces social discourse in 'style'" (125). The ironically depoliticizing (because dehumanizing) effect of the Language poets' radical renunciation of personality in language, and the emotional and aesthetic aridity that are apt to plague resolutely voiceless forms of writing, are the chief risks the Language project takes.

Works Cited

Altieri, Charles. "John Ashbery and the Challenge of Postmodernism in the Visual Arts." *Critical Inquiry* 14 (1988): 805-30.

———. *Self and Sensibility in Contemporary American Poetry.* New York: Cambridge UP, 1984.

Andrews, Bruce. "Misrepresentation (A Text for *The Tennis Court Oath* of John Ashbery)." In Silliman 520-29.

———. "Text and Context." In Andrews and Bernstein 31-38.

——— and Charles Bernstein. *The L=A=N=G=U=A=G=E Book.* Carbondale: Southern Illinois UP, 1984.

Arnold, Matthew. *Matthew Arnold: Poetry and Prose.* Ed. John Bryson. Cambridge: Harvard UP, 1967.

Ashbery, John. *April Galleons.* New York: Viking, 1987.

———. *As We Know.* New York: Viking, 1979.

———. *The Double Dream of Spring.* 1970. New York: Ecco, 1976.

———. *Houseboat Days.* New York: Viking, 1977.

———. *Rivers and Mountains.* 1966. New York: Ecco, 1977.

———. *Self-Portrait in a Convex Mirror.* New York: Viking, 1975.

———. *Shadow Train.* New York: Viking, 1981.

———. *Some Trees.* 1956. New York: Ecco, 1978.

———. *The Tennis Court Oath.* Middletown, Conn.: Wesleyan UP, 1962.

———. *Three Poems.* New York: Viking, 1972.

———. *A Wave.* New York: Viking, 1984.

Bergman, David. *Gaiety Transfigured: Gay Self-Representation in American Literature.* Madison: U of Wisconsin P, 1991.

Bernstein, Charles. *The Sophist.* Los Angeles: Sun & Moon, 1987.

———. "Stray Straws and Straw Men." In Andrews and Bernstein 39-45.

———. "Writing and Method." In Silliman 583-98.

Bloom, Harold. *Figures of Capable Imagination.* New York: Continuum-Seabury, 1976.

Boone, Joseph A., and Michael Cadden, eds. *Engendering Men: The Question of Male Feminist Criticism.* New York: Routledge, 1990.

Breslin, Paul. *The Psycho-Political Muse: American Poetry since the Fifties.* Chicago: U of Chicago, P, 1987.

Bruns, Gerald. *Heidegger's Estrangements: Language, Truth, and Poetry in the Later Writings.* New Haven: Yale UP, 1989.

Butler, Judith. *Bodies That Matter: On the Discursive Limits of "Sex."* New York: Routledge, 1993.

Chadwick, Joseph. "Toward Gay Reading: Robert Gluck's 'Reader.'" In Easthope and Thompson 40-52.

Derrida, Jacques. *Margins of Philosophy.* Trans. Alan Bass. Chicago: U of Chicago P, 1982.

———. *Of Grammatology.* Trans. Gayatri Chakravorty Spivak. Baltimore: Johns Hopkins UP, 1976.

———. *Positions.* Trans. Alan Bass. Chicago: U of Chicago P, 1981.

Dollimore, Jonathan. *Sexual Dissidence: Augustine to Wilde, Freud to Foucault.* New York: Oxford UP, 1991.

Easthope, Antony, and John O. Thompson, eds. *Contemporary Poetry Meets Modern Theory.* Toronto: U of Toronto P, 1991.

Eliot, T. S. *Selected Poems.* New York: Harcourt, 1967.

Foucault, Michel. *The History of Sexuality: Volume I: An Introduction.* Trans. Robert Hurley. New York: Random, 1980.

Fredman, Stephen. *Poet's Prose: The Crisis in American Verse.* New York: Cambridge UP, 1983.

Freud, Sigmund. *The Ego and the Id.* Trans. Joan Riviere. Ed. James Strachey. New York: Norton, 1960.

———. *Leonardo da Vinci and a Memory of His Childhood.* Trans. Alan Tyson. Ed. James Strachey. New York: Norton, 1964.

———. "Psycho-Analytic Notes on an Autobiographical Account of a Case of Paranoia." *The Standard Edition of the Complete Psychological Works of Sigmund Freud.* Ed. James Strachey. Vol. 12. London: Hogarth, 1958. 1-82.

———. "The Psychogenesis of a Case of Homosexuality in a Woman." *Sexuality and the Psychology of Love.* Ed. Philip Rieff. New York: Macmillan-Collier, 1993. 123-49.

———. *Three Essays on the Theory of Sexuality.* Trans. and Ed. James Strachey. New York: Basic, 1962.

Fuss, Diana, ed. *inside/out: Lesbian Theories, Gay Theories.* New York: Routledge, 1991.

Gardner, Thomas. *Discovering Ourselves in Whitman: The Contemporary American Long Poem.* Urbana: U of Illinois P, 1989.

Grenier, Robert. "Tender Buttons." In Andrews and Bernstein 204-07.

Habermas, Jurgen. *The Philosophical Discourse of Modernity.* Trans. Frederick Lawrence. Cambridge: MIT Press, 1987.

Heidegger, Martin. *An Introduction to Metaphysics.* Trans. Ralph Manheim. New Haven: Yale UP, 1959.

———. *On the Way to Language.* Trans. Peter D. Hertz. 1971. New York: Harper, 1982.

———. *Poetry, Language, Thought.* Trans. Albert Hofstadter. 1971. New York: Harper, 1975.

———. *What Is Called Thinking?* Trans. J. Glenn Gray. New York: Harper, 1968.

Hejinian, Lyn. "The Rejection of Closure." *Writing/Talks.* Ed. Bob Perelman. Carbondale: Southern Illinois UP, 1985. 270-91.

Howard, Richard. *Alone with America.* New York: Atheneum, 1971.

Kalstone, David. *Five Temperaments.* New York: Oxford UP, 1977.

Koethe, John. "The Metaphysical Subject of John Ashbery's Poetry." In Lehman *Beyond Amazement* 87-100.

Lacan, Jacques. *Ecrits: A Selection.* Trans. Alan Sheridan. New York: Norton, 1977.

Lehman, David, ed. *Beyond Amazement: New Essays on John Ashbery.* Ithaca, N.Y.: Cornell UP, 1980.

———. *Ecstatic Occasions, Expedient Forms.* New York: Macmillan. 1987.

McClatchy, J. D. *White Paper: On Contemporary American Poetry.* New York: Columbia UP, 1989.

McGann, Jerome. "Charles Bernstein's 'The Simply.'" In Easthope and Thompson 34-39.

Messerli, Douglas, ed. *"Language" Poetries.* New York: New Directions, 1987.

Nicholls, Peter. "Difference Spreading: From Gertrude Stein to L=A=N=G=U=A=G=E Poetry." In Easthope and Thompson 116-27.

Nietzsche, Friedrich. *The Will to Power.* Ed. Walter Kaufman. Trans. Walter Kaufman and R. J. Hollingdale. New York: Random, 1968.

Packard, William, ed. *The Craft of Poetry: Interviews from* The New York Quarterly. New York: Doubleday, 1974.

Perkins, David. *A History of Modern Poetry: Modernism and After.* Cambridge: Harvard UP, 1987.

Perloff, Marjorie. *The Poetics of Indeterminacy: Rimbaud to Cage.* Princeton: Princeton UP, 1981.

Reinfeld, Linda. *Language Poetry: Writing as Rescue.* Baton Rouge: Louisiana State UP, 1992.

Ross, Andrew. *The Failure of Modernism: Symptoms of American Poetry*. New York: Columbia UP, 1986.

Saussure, Ferdinand de. *Course in General Linguistics*. Ed. Charles Bally, Albert Sechehaye, and Albert Riedlinger. Trans. Wade Baskin. 1959. New York: McGraw, 1966.

Sedgwick, Eve Kosofsky. "A Poem Is Being Written." *Representations* 17 (1987): 110-43.

Shapiro, David. *John Ashbery: An Introduction to the Poetry*. New York: Columbia UP, 1979.

Sherry, James. "Postscript." In Andrews and Bernstein 46-47.

Shoptaw, John. *On the Outside Looking Out: John Ashbery's Poetry*. Cambridge: Harvard UP, 1994.

Silliman, Ron, ed. *In the American Tree*. Orono, Me: National Poetry Foundation, 1986.

———, Barrett Watten, et al. "for CHANGE." In Silliman 484-90.

Silverman, Kaja. *Male Subjectivity at the Margins*. New York: Routledge, 1992.

Stamelman, Richard. "Critical Reflections: Poetry and Art Criticism in Ashbery's 'Self-Portrait in a Convex Mirror.'" *New Literary History* 15 (1984): 607-30.

Staten, Henry. *Wittgenstein and Derrida*. Lincoln: U of Nebraska P, 1984.

———. "Wittgenstein and the Intricate Evasions of 'Is.'" *New Literary History* 19 (1988): 281-300.

Steiner, George. *On Difficulty and Other Essays*. New York: Oxford UP, 1978.

Stevens, Wallace. *The Palm at the End of the Mind*. Ed. Holly Stevens. New York: Random, 1972.

Von Hallberg, Robert. *American Poetry and Culture, 1945-1980*. Cambridge: Harvard UP, 1985.

Waldrop, Rosemarie. "Shorter American Memory of the American Character According to Santayana." In Lehman *Ecstatic* 196-97.

Warner, Michael. "Homo-Narcissism; or, Heterosexuality." In Boone and Cadden 190-206.

Williamson, Alan. *Introspection and Contemporary Poetry*. Cambridge: Harvard UP, 1984.

Wittgenstein, Ludwig. *On Certainty*. Ed. G. E. M. Anscombe and G. H. von Wright. Trans. Denis Paul and G. E. M. Anscombe. 1969. New York: Harper, 1972.

———. *Philosophical Investigations*. Trans. G. E. M. Anscombe. 3rd ed. New York: Macmillan, 1968.

———. *Tractatus Logico-Philosophicus*. Trans. D. F. Pears and B. F. McGuiness. London: Routledge, 1961.

FURTHER READING

Criticism

Altieri, Charles. "John Ashbery and the Challenge of Postmodernism in the Visual Arts." *Critical Inquiry* XIV, No. 4 (Summer 1988): 805-30.

> Contends that critics should view Ashbery as an innovative modern artist rather than as a poet working solely within literary tradition.

Applewhite, James. "Painting, Poetry, Abstraction and Ashbery." *The Southern Review* XXIV, No. 2 (Spring 1988): 272-90.

> Places Ashbery's *A Wave* among the work of twentieth-century painters and poets.

Bloom, Harold, ed. *Modern Critical Views: John Ashbery*. New York: Chelsea House, 1985, 264 p.

> Critical essays on Ashbery's work written by such critics as Bloom, Helen Vendler, Richard Howard, Douglas Crase, Charles Berger, and David Kalstone.

———. "John Ashbery: The Charity of the Hard Moments." *Salmagundi*, Nos. 22-23 (Spring-Summer 1973): 103-31.

> Overviews Ashbery's work at mid-career.

Keeling, John. "The Moment Unravels: Reading John Ashbery's 'Litany'." *Twentieth Century Literature* XXXVIII, No. 2 (Summer 1992): 125-51.

> Analyzes the role of recognition/misrecognition in Ashbery's poem.

Leckie, Ross. "Art, Mimesis, and John Ashbery's 'Self-Portrait in a Convex Mirror'." *Essays in Literature* XIX, No. 1 (Spring 1992): 114-31.

> Examines the use of mimesis in "Self-Portrait," comparing it to Wallace Stevens's "An Ordinary Evening in New Haven."

Lehman, David, ed. *Beyond Amazement: New Essays on John Ashbery*. Ithaca, N.Y.: Cornell University Press, 1980, 294 p.

> Contains selected essays that address common questions and misunderstandings regarding Ashbery's works.

Mohanty, S. P. and Monroe, Jonathan. "John Ashbery and the Articulation of the Social." *Diacritics* (Summer 1987): 37-63.

> Focuses on the "individualist idealism" of Ashbery's poetry and describes this idealism in relation to his long poem *A Wave*.

Monroe, Jonathan. "Idiom and Cliché in T. S. Eliot and John Ashbery." *Contemporary Literature* XXXI, No. 1 (Spring 1990): 17-36.

Links Eliot to Ashbery through the utilization of literary and popular culture into their verse.

Ross, Andrew. "The Alcatraz Effect: Belief and Postmodernity." *Substance* XIII, No. 1 (1984): 71-84.

Illustrates postmodern belief in art by explicating Ashbery's "Self-Portrait in a Convex Mirror."

Schultz, Susan, ed. *The Tribe of John: Ashbery and Contemporary Poetry.* Tuscaloosa: University of Alabama Press, 1995, 280 p.

Comprehensive survey of critical reaction to Ashbery's verse.

Stamelman, Richard. "Critical Reflections: Poetry and Art Criticism in Ashbery's 'Self-Portrait in a Convex Mirror'." *New Literary History* XV, No. 3 (Spring 1984): 607-30.

Interprets Ashbery's poem as a demystification of Parmigianino's painting of the same title as well as a commentary on art itself.

Additional coverage of Ashbery's life and career is contained in the following sources published by The Gale Group: *Contemporary Literary Criticism,* **Vols. 2, 3, 4, 6, 9, 13, 15, 25, 41, 77;** *DISCovering Authors: Poets Module;* *Contemporary Authors,* **Vol. 5-8R;** *Contemporary Authors New Revision Series,* **Vols. 9, 37, 66;** *Dictionary of Literary Biography,* **Vols. 5, 165, and** *Major Twentieth-Century Writers.*

Thom Gunn
1929-

(Full name Thomson William Gunn) English poet, critic, editor, and essayist.

INTRODUCTION

An English poet who has lived in the United States since 1955, Gunn has combined in his writing characteristics of both formal, traditionally structured poetry and relaxed, modern free verse. Although Gunn continues to be better known in England than in the United States, he undoubtedly belongs to the Anglo-American tradition which includes such notable poets as T. S. Eliot, Ezra Pound, and W. H. Auden.

Biographical Information

Gunn was born in 1929 in Gravesend, Kent, England. He began writing sketches and fiction at an early age. As a student and poet at Cambridge in the early 1950s, Gunn shared many concerns with such writers as Donald Davie, Philip Larkin, and others who have been collectively referred to as The Movement. In 1954 Gunn moved to California and enrolled at Stanford University, where he studied under the poet and critic Yvor Winters. In the early 1960s Gunn taught at the University of California at Berkeley and became involved with the radical counterculture in San Francisco. His experiences with LSD and his new insights provided the material for many of the poems in *Moly* and *Jack Straw's Castle.* He continues to live in California.

Major Works

Gunn's early work displays a predilection for tightly rhymed and metered verse and a rejection of the neoromanticism favored in England in the 1940s. The poems in his first collection, *Fighting Terms,* were written at Cambridge and reveal his attempt at stylistic sophistication and hard realism. Although such dominant concerns as the quest for personal identity and meaning in human existence have remained constant, his topics, imagery, and style have changed. The poems comprising *My Sad Captains* exhibit this shift and the book is considered a major transitional point in Gunn's career. *Passages of Joy,* his 1982 collection, contain what many critics consider his most revealing poems up to the 1992 publication of *The Man with Night Sweats.* Written between 1982 and 1988, the poems in the collection range widely in style and incor-

porate both free and traditional verse grouped into four sections. The volume was awarded the Lenore Marshall/ *Nation* Poetry Prize in 1992.

Critical Reception

Many critics fault Gunn's early verse as affected and cerebral. As his style developed, some commentators expressed regret over his move away from formal literary traditions, though his poems are frequently praised for their heightened clarity, directness and precision of control. It has been noted that his verse has become progressively more personal and revealing; in the critically praised collection, *The Man with Night Sweats,* reviewers laud its unsentimental examination of the personal and social effects of AIDS, the deaths of friends and lovers, and neglected members of modern American society. He is considered an insightful and deft chronicler of contemporary culture, and his later verse is often praised for its energy and topicality as well as its exploration of such diverse themes as existentialism, identity, sexuality, the debilitating effects of AIDS on the homosexual community, and the relationship between humans and nature.

PRINCIPAL WORKS

Poetry

Fighting Terms 1954
The Sense of Movement 1957
My Sad Captains, and Other Poems 1961
Selected Poems [with Ted Hughes] 1962
Positives [with Ander Gunn] (photography and verse) 1966
Touch 1967
Poems, 1950-1966 1969
Moly 1971
Jack Straw's Castle 1976
Selected Poems 1950-1975 1979
The Passages of Joy 1982
The Man with Night Sweats 1992
Collected Poems 1994

Other Major Works

Occasions of Poetry: Essays in Criticism and Autobiography (essays) 1982

Shelf Life: Essays, Memoirs, and an Interview 1993

CRITICISM

G. S. Fraser (essay date 1961)

SOURCE: "The Poetry of Thom Gunn," in *The Critical Quarterly,* Vol. 3, Winter, 1961, pp. 359-67.

[*In the following essay, Fraser contrasts Gunn's poetry to that of Philip Larkin.*]

Thom Gunn is often classed as a Movement poet but though he first became known about the same time as the other poets of that group, around 1953, he belongs to a younger generation. He is seven years younger than Kingsley Amis and Philip Larkin, four years younger than John Wain, three years younger than Elizabeth Jennings. Born at Gravesend in 1929, the son of a successful Fleet Street journalist, Herbert Gunn, Thom Gunn was educated at University College School in London and at Trinity College, Cambridge. At Cambridge he had the sort of career which often precedes literary distinction, editing an anthology of undergraduate verse, being president of the University English Club, and taking a first in both parts of the English tripos. The Fantasy Press published his first pamphlet of verse when he was still an undergraduate, in 1953,

and his first volume, *Fighting Terms,* in 1954, shortly after he had taken his degree.

His second volume, *The Sense of Movement,* came out in 1957, published by Faber's, and won him a Somerset Maugham Award. Between 1954 and 1957, he had been teaching and studying at Stanford University in California, being much influenced by Professor Yvor Winters. He used his Somerset Maugham award to spend some time in Rome. His most recent volume, *My Sad Captains,* came out this year. He now teaches English at Berkeley in San Francisco. He visits England reasonably frequently, but nobody could call his poems insularly English. Italian painting, Californian scenes and characters, Greek mythology, French literature and philosophy frequently give him the pegs to hang his poems on. In his work there is nothing of the insularity or the distrust of cultural or philosophic themes that, in different ways, marks Amis and Larkin. He resembles these two only in his admirable care for lucidity of poetic thought and language. He is not weakly jocular as these two sometimes are, nor on the other hand has he the humour which is one of their strengths. He is often a witty poet, in the sense of being concise and epigrammatic, but he is never heartily familiar in tone. He keeps at a certain cool distance from the reader. His poetry also is less a poetry either of acceptance of society, as Larkin's is, or of sharp social criticism, like that of D. J. Enright, than a poetry of firm assertion of the romantic will.

With Larkin, he seems to me the best poet of the group that became known around 1953, and a contrast with Larkin may help to bring out some of his central qualities. What Larkin seems to me to be repeatedly saying in many of his best poems is that a sensible man settles for second-bests. One of Larkin's best poems, for instance, is about being tempted to give up a safe, dull job for the sake of wild adventure and firmly, and the reader is meant to feel rightly, resisting the temptation; several other good poems, on the other hand, are about being tempted by love or by the spectacle of happy domesticity into some permanent kind of emotional relationship, but retreating, since Larkin as a poet needs a kind of freedom which is not wild, but which does depend on a firm cutting down of the number of one's personal relationships and emotional commitments. Larkin, one might say, is the poet of emotional economy. The title poem of his volume *The Less Deceived* (a poem about a girl being kidnapped and raped in the mid-Victorian age) is both about how we should not waste our sympathy where it cannot help and also about how the young man in the story may have felt an even sharper grief than the girl's when he had done his wild, fierce, wicked thing and burst into "fulfilment's desolate attic".

Larkin's tender poem about old horses at grass seems fundamentally to be about the idea that such real freedom as most of us can hope to enjoy in life will be the freedom of pensioned retirement, with no continuing social function, with enough to eat, and with some pleasant memories. His poem about looking at a girl friend's snapshot album is fundamentally about how cherished images are in some ways better than difficult continuing relationships;

and the poem about the flavourless town where he grew up is, on the other hand, about how we should not fake up pleasant memory images where there are none. The total effect is that of a certain bleakness. When I think of Larkin I always think of Henry James's great short story, "The Beast in the Jungle": about a man who is so overshadowed by the sense of some nameless horror or terror that may jump on him if he takes risks with life, that he never takes any risks. When the beast does jump, it jumps, not as actual terror, but as the sudden awareness that a long life crippled by fear and caution has been wasted. The hero has never dared the high dive, never swum at the deep end. And it is too late now. There is a splendid relevant sentence of Elizabeth Bowen's: "One is empowered to live fully: occasion does not offer". Larkin's poetry is about not affronting the unoffered occasion. Gunn's is about snatching at occasion, whatever the risks, and whether it offers or not.

Outer order and personal stability, for Larkin, depend on our swallowing our gall. Gunn refuses to do this. I am proud to remember that, in 1953, when he was still an undergraduate, I included three early poems of his in an anthology called *Springtime.* The three poems I chose happened to illustrate, luckily, certain themes and attitudes that were to be recurrent. The first, about the world of the Elizabethan poet, began

> It was a violent time. Wheels, racks and fires
> In every poet's mouth, and not mere rant". . .

Gunn insisted in this poem that the heroic attitude, which he sees as behind all notable poetry, should be stimulated, not quenched, by a threatening age. It is the poet's business to make tragic sense of it all:

> In street, in tavern, happening would cry
> "I am myself, but part of something greater,
> Find poets what that is, do not pass by
> For feel my fingers in your *pia mater:*
> I am a cruelly insistent friend;
> You cannot smile at me and make an end."

The second poem I chose was called **"Helen's Rape"** and what it expressed might be called a nostalgia, though tinged a little with irony, for the kind of primitive violence that sees itself as moved by a divine force. This poem began:

> Hers was the last authentic rape:
> From forced content of common breeder
> Bringing the violent dreamed escape". . .

The "forced content" (meaning constrained contentment but carrying an overtone of enforced *containment*) is that which Helen enjoyed as an ordinary *hausfrau,* a "common breeder" or junior matron, with Menelaus. The "violent dreamed escape" is Helen's rape, or abduction, by Paris, but she had dreamt of a more genuinely divine abduction, or rape, like that of her mother Leda or of Europa. The real age of the gods is already past, and though Paris was inspired by Aphrodite, or moved by a divine madness, he had to soothe common-sense critics, and to pretend that he abducted Helen for political reasons, in retaliation for a similar abduction by the Greeks of a Trojan princess, his aunt. At the end of the poem, Gunn brings in the idea that only a simulacrum of Helen was taken to Troy and that the real Helen was wafted to Egypt. And yet even a distant Helen would know the harrowing griefs which even her image had brought on Troy.

So, at least, I interpret the very difficult last stanza:

> Helen herself could not through flesh
> Abandon flesh; she felt surround
> Her absent body, never fresh
> The mortal context, and the mesh
> Of the continual battle's sound.

The reference might just be, however, not to the legend of Helen in Egypt but simply to the idea that because Paris was only a hero, not a god, his carnal love could not transform her carnality into the divine. I think Gunn possibly ought to have put a comma after "fresh". If the reference is to Egypt, the meaning will be: "Though bodily transported to Egypt Helen could not remain aware of the havoc which Paris's love of her body had wrought: even absent in Egypt she felt herself surrounded and sullied ('never fresh') by the lust and violence of the Trojan war". Or it may be that a comma should not be added after "fresh" but omitted after "body" and that what she felt surrounding her Egyptian body was the "mortal context", the circumstances of death, which are never fresh, not so much in the sense that they are not refreshed or refreshing, but in the sense that they have been there from the beginning, they never started.

The puzzles of such a stanza suggest that though Gunn is learnedly lucid he is never likely to be a popular writer. The reader of this short poem is expected to have a very detailed knowledge of Greek mythology, as the reader of the one about Elizabethan poetry needs a detailed knowledge of Elizabethan literature and history. They were the only two poems in *Springtime* to which I felt I had to add notes.

The third poem I chose, **"Carnal Knowledge"**, stated a third recurring theme, the idea that sexual love can rarely, whether or not this is a good thing, break down, or merge, the essential separateness of two people. The stanzas had an excessively clever Empsonian refrain,

> You know I know you know I know you know,

alternating as,

> I know you know I know you know I know,

but in the last stanza this was truncated:

> Abandon me to stammering, and go;
> If you have tears, prepare to cry elsewhere—
> I know of no emotion we can share.
> Your intellectual protests are a bore
> And even now I pose, so now go, for
> I know you know.

This was a more awkward, a more undergraduate poem than the others, and I feel that even today Gunn is never quite at his best when he writes of personal relationships. But implicit in the poem, though not brought cleanly through, was a theme which he was soon to use more powerfully, not a half regret at the great difficulty of breaking down separateness, but a horror at the idea that such a breaking down, such a merging, should ever be possible at all.

I included in another anthology, *Poetry Now,* a poem which expressed perhaps less humanly but certainly more powerfully than **"Carnal Knowledge"** this horror of merging. Two men have been sharing a bed (or the two men may be different aspects of the poet's one personality) and one of them gets up in the small hours, looks out at the moon, and declaims:

> 'Inside the moon I see a hell of love.
> There love is all, and no one is alone.
> The song of passion deafens, as no choice
> Of individual word can hold its own
> Against the rule of that anonymous noise.
> And wait, I see more clearly; craters, canals,
>
> Are smothered by two giant forms of mist
> So that no features of the land remain.
> Two humming clouds of moisture intertwist
> Agreed so well, they cannot change to rain
> And serve to clean the common ground beneath.
>
> Singing there fell, locked in each other's arms,
> Cursed with content, pair by successive pair,
> Committed centuries to lie in calms
> They stayed to rot into that used-up air
> No wind can shift, it is so thick, so thick!'
>
> The ringing voice stopped, but as if one must
> Finish in moral, stumbled on and said:
> 'In that still fog all energy is lost.'
> The moonlight slunk on, darkness touched his head.
> He fell back, then he turned upon the pillow.

It will be noted that in this passage, as in the earlier passage about Helen, the word "content" which generally carries a strong pro-feeling in English poetry ("sweet content"), carries a strong anti-feeling; similarly the word "calms" instead of suggesting "calm after storm" recalls the rotting, glistering sea on which the ship lay becalmed in "The Ancient Mariner". Literary reminiscence and counterpoint is one of Gunn's main instruments. The giant lovers transformed into clouds might remind us of Ixion attempting to embrace Juno, but the line,

> Singing there fell, locked in each other's arms,

gains extra force if one recalls Paolo and Francesca. The line that gives the moral, "In that still fog all energy is lost" recalls an urgent line of Spender's: "Drink here of energy, and only energy". The attack, however, as in Spender's case, is not so much on the stuff of which romantic love is made as on its self-centredness and stupe-

fying effect. The clouds could dissolve into rain and "clean the solid earth beneath", or the self-centredness of love, perhaps, could be translated into a socially useful emotion or at least a psychologically useful one; the "solid earth beneath" may be the permanent personality and the twisted cloud figures projections of an attempted romantic escape from that. When the speaker turns on his pillow at the end, he may perhaps be turning not towards the sleep of exhaustion but to make love; in which case, perhaps, he has not found his own eloquence practically persuasive. But the love, as between two men, would be, by definition, sterile. This seems to me one of the most powerful of Gunn's earlier poems, with an almost Dantesque quality of visionary horror.

I know, however, few people who share this admiration. And I know of many admirers of another early poem from ***Fighting Terms,*** which strikes me as comical, but unconsciously so (Gunn, as I have said, has plenty of wit of the severer kind, but almost no humour). We have seen that separateness, self-sufficiency, energy even as something that inspires to restless movement with no clear purpose, are positive values for Gunn; so, sometimes, and it seems to me less attractively, are domination and ruthlessness. The early poem which strikes me as unconsciously self-parodic is called **"A Village Edmund"**. Edmund is Edmund in *King Lear* and we are to think also of Gray's "village Hampden" in the *Elegy.* Edmund is admittedly the most humanly sympathetic of all Shakespeare's villains, but Gunn's "rough and lecherous" village counterpart of him seems to me, as it were, a Tony Hancock part:

> One girl he fancied as much as she fancied him.
> 'For a moment,' she thought, 'our bodies can bestride
> A heaven whose memories must support my life.'
> He took her to the deserted countryside,
> And she lay down and obeyed his every whim.
>
> When it was over he pulled his trousers on.
> 'Demon lovers must go,' he coldly said.
> And walked away from the rocks to the lighted
>   town.
> 'Why should heaven,' she asked, 'be for the dead?'
> And she stared at the pale intolerable moon.

What spoils this as serious poetry is not, however, so much the callowness of the attitude as the weakness of the writing; the melodramatic novelettish language of the girl; the stiltedness of phrases like "obeyed his every whim": the conscious manly toughness of the line about pulling his trousers on, and the at once coy and trite narcissism (for I take it the poet is emotionally identifying himself with Edmund) of "he *coldly* said". The pale intolerable moon of the last line, for that matter, is very much out of some old romantic property-box. Gunn's failures of tone and feeling do not come from an excessive chumminess or prosiness (as, say, Amis's or Larkin's failures of that sort might come) but from an occasional self-admiring melodrama or sentimentality. They are more like the failures of Stephen Spender (who seems to me a better poet at his best than he is generally made out to be, and who seems to me also temperamentally in some ways not unlike Gunn, who has gone out of his way in one poem to attack him); in many ways, in fact, Gunn is more like a nineteen-thirties' than a nineteen-fifties' poet. His are poems without a Muse, or the Muse rather is a male Muse, village Edmunds, warriors in byrnies, black-jacketed James Dean characters roaring through small American towns on motor-cycles. But a fine intellectual discipline can make something universal out of this, as it might seem in itself, somewhat dubious material.

Let me take as an example of what seems to me a very notable success on Gunn's part, the first poem in his 1957 volume, *The Sense of Movement.* This is called **"On the Move"** and these young men on motor-cycles are vividly the topic but savingly in the end not the theme of the poem. The theme, rather, is Sartrean existential humanism. I want to examine in turn the last three lines of each of the five eight line stanzas. In these last three lines, in each stanza, Gunn presses from particulars towards a persuasive generality, which becomes progressively more firmly defined; he presses towards the stating of a moral. In the first stanza, the poet vividly observes birds on the edge of a dusty American road, birds which "follow some hidden purpose", while the poet himself is vainly "seeking their instinct, or their poise, or both". He sums it up:

> One moves with an uncertain violence
> Under the dust thrown by a baffled sense
> Or the dull thunder of approximate words.

"Baffled sense" is not there, or only partly, what it might be in Keats, sensuous apprehension baffled by trying to reach beyond itself, but baffled intellectual apprehension; the baffled sense of what it is all about.

In the second stanza, the boys on motor-cycles, anticipated already in the first stanza in the dust and the scariness of the birds, roar by. And we are told of them in the last three lines:

> In gleaming jackets trophied with the dust,
> They strap in doubt—by hiding it, robust—
> And almost hear a meaning in their noise.

The baffling dust here becomes a trophy, a prize, of pointless speed; and the noise of the motor-cycles (in communication theory *noise* is contrasted with *sound,* and means any interference with the transmission of the message) becomes paradoxically for them a kind of communication. Very often in Gunn apparently simple and ordinary words like "meaning" and "noise" can, in their juxtaposition, carry in this way a lucid paradox.

In the third stanza, Gunn points out that the motor-cyclists are not riding towards any known goal but as fast as possible away from a known and frustrating background. It is they who scare the birds across the fields but it is inevitable that even a right natural order should yield to even a subrational human will. And there is this to be said for the motor-cyclists, that they are emblems of a larger human condition:

> Men manufacture both machine and soul,
> And use what they imperfectly control
> To dare a future from the taken routes.

The idea behind these admirably compact lines is Sartre's that man creates himself, creates his "soul", by arbitrary but important choices. His choices cannot be made in complete foreknowledge of their consequences ("use what they imperfectly control"). But what is even more worrying is that the *general* consequences of all possible choices might be thought to be boringly worked out already. This abstract philosophical idea is beautifully translated into properly poetic language. The "taken" routes are at once the routes daringly taken, or undertaken, by the young motor-cyclists to create a future and they are also the routes, the roads there on the map, which would not be there at all if they had not been "taken" dully by generations of men already. Again, very plain, apparently obvious words produce a paradox.

The fourth stanza justifies the choice of the motor-cyclists as at least a partial solution of the human problem. Man is not necessarily at odds with the world because he is not purely an animal. Nor is he damned because, half but only half an animal, he has to rely not on "direct instinct" but on movements--say, movements of history or politics--which carry him on part of the way, even though in the end movement "divides and breaks":

> One joins the movement in a valueless world,
> Choosing it, till, both hurler and the hurled,
> One moves as well, always toward, toward.

What one moves "toward" is not to be abstractly defined, but one is moving away from that which one has found valueless (but there is also the Sartrean idea that value is imposed by choice, not there in the world to compel choice). One may be moving towards value.

In the fifth and last stanza, the cyclists vanished, the "self-defined, astride the created will". (Again notice how a philosophical concept is beautifully translated into a poetical conceit, the "manufactured" soul finding its emblem, or symbol, in the "manufactured" motor-cycle.) The cyclists are right, for Gunn, to burst through and away from towns which are no homes either for the naturalness of birds or the stillness of saints who, like birds, "complete their purposes". The justification of these "rebels without a cause" is that our civilized world, the world, say, which Larkin sadly accepts, has in its frustrating complication no home for either naturalness or holiness. And when one is, however restlessly and violently, "on the move",

> At worst one is in motion; and at best,
> Reaching no absolute, in which to rest,
> One is always nearer by not keeping still.

Gunn is not in any ordinary sense of the word a religious poet, but he is (both in the ordinary and to some degree in the literary sense of the word) a metaphysical poet. The kinds of metaphysics that interest him are very different from those that interest Eliot, say, yet there are obvious broad affinities between the pattern of argument in this poem and some of the patterns of argument in *Four Quartets*.

I have thought it better in this article to examine what one might call the broad human interest of Gunn's poetry, taking three or four sample poems as pegs to drape my exposition round, rather than to review, or re-review his volumes in detail, or to go in detail into the verbal texture of his work. Swiftness, directness, lucidity, beautifully exact dramatic or logical construction in a poem, mark his work much more than richness of imagery or any sort of lyrical cry; the kind of technical-appreciative words one would use about his verse are supple, muscular, "on the move". But his deep authenticity comes from range of curiosity, an undefeatedness of spirit, and a swift readiness to make choices, without any hesitant bother about how the choices will be socially taken. If Larkin is a fine poet born, in a sense, middle-aged, Gunn is a poet who should have a peculiarly direct appeal not for angry, but for fierce, young men.

M. L. Rosenthal (essay date 1967)

SOURCE: "Contemporary British Poetry," in *The New Poets: American and British Poetry Since World War II*, Oxford University Press, 1967, pp. 251-56.

[*In the following excerpt, Rosenthal surveys the themes of Gunn's early verse.*]

[Thom Gunn is an American-involved British poet] who has for a number of years taught at the University of California in Berkeley. In his first book, *The Sense of Movement* (1957), Gunn showed a fascinated interest in the world of the tough, leather-jacketed young motorcyclists and their slightly sinister, apparently pointless activity:

> On motorcycles, up the road, they come:
> Small, black, as flies hanging in heat, the Boys,
> Until the distance throws them forth, their hum
> Bulges to thunder held by calf and thigh.
>
> In goggles, donned impersonality,
> In gleaming jackets trophied with the dust,
> They strap in doubt—by hiding it, robust—
> And almost hear a meaning in their noise.
>
> Exact conclusion of their hardiness
> Has no shape yet, but from known whereabouts
> They ride, direction where the tires press.". . .

Where [the British poet Charles Tomlinson] is concerned with the precise ambience and impact of a given scene or personality, and with its proper idiom (rhythmically as well as in phrasing), and relates these concerns to his passion for the integrity of cultural heritage and of natural materials, Gunn turns his similar talents in other directions. He is attracted to the life of action, as a theme and

as a way of meeting the world. And beyond that, as in the poem '**On the Move**' just quoted, whose epigraph is *'Man, you gotta Go,'* he is something of a 'metaphysical' poet. '**On the Move**' begins by observing that there is 'hidden purpose' in the sudden movements of birds—'the blue jay scuffling in the bushes,' a 'gust of birds' that 'spurts across the field,' 'the wheeling swallows.' We can discover their meaning, but to gain 'their instinct, or their poise, or both' in human affairs is to move 'with an uncertain violence,' under 'dust thrown by a baffled sense,' amid 'the dull thunder of approximate words.' Then come the motorcyclists of the quoted passage, as if to embody the abstract thought behind these images. After the close-up of 'The Boys,' Gunn devotes the second half of his poem to contemplation of the human significance of their kind of concentrated action:

> It is a part solution, after all.
> One is not necessarily discord
> On earth; or damned because, half animal,
> One lacks direct instinct, because one wakes
> Afloat on movement that divides and breaks.
> One joins the movement in a valueless world,
> Choosing it, till, both hurler and the hurled,
> One moves as well, always toward, toward.". . .

'**On the Move**' is the opening poem of *The Sense of Movement*. It is followed by an allegorical poem, '**The Nature of an Action**,' which turns the issue of 'movement' inward much as Herbert does with the issue of free will in '**The Collar**.' The speaker describes his passage from the habits of passivity and introspection under the domination of the overwhelming power of tradition to a more active state, 'directed by the compass of my heart.' Painfully he moves through a short, narrow corridor, from the room of the past to the room of the future. The passage takes twenty years, full of doubt about his existence or the existence of anything else, until he finds the proper 'handle in the mind'—his will—to open the second door. The furnishings inside are the same as in the first; the only difference lies in the changed character of his presence among the room's

> . . . heavy-footed chairs,
> A glass bell loaded with wax grapes and pears,
>
> A polished table, holding down the look
> Of bracket, mantelpiece, and marbled book.". . .

A youthful preciosity and intellectual self-consciousness marks the greater number of Gunn's poems in this early book. The two opening poems break into the clear, however, as do a few others. '**Human Condition**' is another metaphysical contemplation, this time on the imprisoned state of that 'pinpoint of consciousness,' the individual self. '**The Unsettled Motorcyclist's Vision of His Death**' is a vivid 'vision' indeed, of the risk of 'being what I please.' It is an assertion, as well, that even the very concretely imagined death of the symbolic motorcyclists (sinking into marshland out of a stubborn refusal to yield to circumstances) is merely a confrontation of volitionless nature by man's invincible will. '**Lines for a Book**' is written in Audenesque, half-ironic praise of the 'toughs' of history as opposed to the men of mere sensibility ('I praise the overdogs from Alexander / To those who would not play with Stephen Spender'). **'Market at Turk,'** a sympathetic close-up of a hoodlumish San Franciscan, celebrates the young ruffian's poised readiness—purposeless yet oriented toward some undefined and dangerous violence. **'In Praise of Cities'** is a 'love song' on the changeableness, the surprises, the tantalizing promise and hardness of the great cities in the image of an infinitely varied woman. Amid the echoes of Yeats, Auden, Crane, and other masters, these poems show signs of a power of concentration and of an ability brutally to suppress self-indulgence and sentimentality, in the interest of testing forbidden sympathies and of pursuing realities outside the over-protected and over-civilized private self.

To a certain degree the promise was fulfilled in Gunn's second book, *My Sad Captains* (1961), but really in only two poems, **'In Santa Maria del Popolo'** and the title poem. The former is Gunn's most successful poem, in combined subtely, power, and intricate yet subdued patterning. The poem contemplates a painting by Caravaggio 'on one wall of this recess.' It is a painting of Saul fallen from his horse and 'becoming Paul,' and one must wait until evening when the sun becomes 'conveniently oblique' to see it fully. At first, while waiting,

> I see how shadow in the painting brims
> With a real shadow, drowning all shapes out
> But a dim horse's haunch and various limbs,
> Until the very subject is in doubt.

Then the whole scene emerges—'the act, beneath the horse,' of transformation, with an 'indifferent groom' present and Saul sprawling, 'foreshortened from the head, with hidden face,' among a 'cacophony of dusty forms' and making a mysterious 'wide gesture of the lifting arms' during his convulsive fit. Content with the external details, the possibly symbolic gesture, the sense of 'candor and secrecy inside the skin' that he was able to convey, the painter leaves the scene a mystery. Gunn remembers other paintings of Caravaggio's—the hard city types in them—and the artist's murder ('for money, by one such picked off the streets'). Turning, 'hardly enlightened,' from the chapel to the church's dim interior, he sees the people praying:

> Mostly old women: each head closeted
> In tiny fists holds comfort as it can.
> Their poor arms are too tired for more than this
> —For the large gesture of solitary man,
> Resisting, by embracing, nothingness.

So Gunn in this poem closes in on a multiple and sympathetic view of the human condition. He discovers his driving motif in the movement from the darkness within the painting to the darkness of meanings revealed by the painting itself when it comes into full view, and then to the vulnerability of the worshipers in their dark setting and in the poor comfort of their prayers and their phys-

ical attitudes; and so the final pair of lines, abstract as they are, becomes the largest statement of what the human gesture in the face of 'nothingness' creates or means. The poem **'My Sad Captains'** reaches through to a comparable insight, but in quite different terms. The 'sad captains' are a few friends and a few historical figures who have come to be spiritual models to the poet:

> . . . They were men
> who, I thought, lived only to
> renew the wasteful force they
> spent with each hot convulsion.". . .

But now

> they withdraw to an orbit
> and turn with disinterested
> hard energy, like the stars.

Gunn's preoccupation with existential emptiness on the one hand, and with the assertion of meaning through sheer will or willful action on the other, brings him in **'My Sad Captains'** to the same essential confrontation as does **'In Santa Maria del Popolo,'** but without the merciful buffer of anything like the Caravaggio painting. The 'message,' in the spirit perhaps of Williams's 'El Hombre,' is a desolate courage that stakes everything on pure energy. As in the earlier volume, the poems that stand out—in particular, these two—are so sharply differentiated from the rest that the latter for the most part seem mere exercises by comparison. At any rate, the lesser pieces are on 'set' themes—the difficulty of reaching past lust to love, the 'compact innocence, child-like and clear,' that made the Nazi stormtrooper the peculiarly unshakable monster he was, the fate of a middle-aged rake, and so on. Derivative notes, especially from Auden but also at times from Edwin Muir and others, constantly interfere with Gunn's own voice in poems like **'The Byrnies'** and **'Modes of Pleasure'** that are otherwise imaginative and psychologically stirring.

Merle E. Brown (essay date 1973)

SOURCE: "A Critical Performance of Thom Gunn's `Misanthropos'," in *The Iowa Review,* Vol. 4, No. 1, Winter, 1973, pp. 73-87.

[*In the following essay, Brown asserts that the repetitive and interconnected structure of* "Misanthropos" *reflects Gunn's poetic philosophy.*]

If one attends to his own experience of reading poems rather than to that of hearing a poet read poems in a crowded hall, he will, I believe, agree that the performance to which a poem summons him is not so much a public recitation as it is a form of criticism analogous to the performing arts. If the poet is a performing self, as Richard Poirier claims, if no work of art comes alive except in the presence of an audience, as R. G. Collingwood argues, if the reader of poems must accept these claims, nonetheless he will modify them because of his recognition that the poet is always his own first audience.[1]

The echoing quality of all poetic language depends on the presence of this primary audience, on the felt presence of the poet as his own first listener, and this essential echo is drowned out and rendered inaudible by the assumption that the life of poetry depends on its metropolitan audiences which are reached through our great publishing firms and on those crowds who are gathered together by the business of organizing poetry reading circuits. Unless misled by the prospect of a cash reward, no poet would think he was reciting his poems in order that they might be heard. For he could not even compose a poem unless it were heard in the very act of composition. The experience of reading poems to oneself and especially reading them silently must reveal that the listening presence of the poet has to be attended to just as much as his speaking presence. One cannot, in fact, even hear the words of poetry unless he also attends to the echoing into silence which is, at a conceptual level, the poet's act of shaping the poem. A poet works with his words in order to articulate that innermost feeling which determines the quality of his self, his world, and his experience. His words work poetically only in so far as they are the echo of that upsurge of feeling. A reader of those words can respond to them as echoingly resonant only to the extent that he also attends to the echo of that echo, to the over-arching action which is the poet's own attending to his words as echoing the deepest impulsion of his experience.

Words working poetically are neither transitive nor intransitive. They do not, like words used practically or intellectually, have the reason for their being in the conventional patterns and structures and frameworks to which they refer, even though they may include such transitive references. Nor are they self-subsistent, only internally referential, elements of an autonomous artifact, a fiction, a sort of entertaining make-believe. They are rather, in their essential nature, the echo of being as an upsurge of feeling and are in turn echoed by the becoming which is the poet's act of shaping that feeling into an articulated vision.

Quite apart, then, from being read and attended to critically by another person, a poem is itself an active community constituted by the poet as speaker and the poet as listener, by the poet expressing his deepest sense of himself and his world and the poet listening to and criticizing that expression. The poem circles in widening waves, out from its elemental feeling, as the poet speaks listening and, having listened, speaks further until he has exhausted his capacity for composition.

For at least the past twenty-five years, as part of the macadamization of literary studies, critics have been busy crushing out the communal life of the poem by reducing its being and its becoming, its feeling and its thinking, to what I should call its non-being, its status as a self-subsistent object. Once objectified in this way, the poem may then be said to have, in René Wellek's terms, a single structure of determination, the grasp of which leads us to its proper meaning.[2] Once reduced to an artifact, the poem calls for an interpretation in the manner of E. D. Hirsch, Jr., a delimitation of its intrinsic and extrinsic genres, accomplished by reference to the linguistic ambience of the poem, now treated as an object among objects. With the poem rendered lifeless and the process of interpretation itself doing nothing to revive it, critics have been led unavoidably, in order to retain some sense of themselves as alive, into widening circles of entrapment. Hirsch himself will locate Wordsworth's Intimations Ode within the vast framework of Schelling's philosophy. Raymond Williams, like many another neo-historicist, will view each objectified literary work in the light of a massive social and political movement, his version of which he calls The Long Revolution. Northrop Frye, radical structuralist that he is, will back away from the painting fixed on the wall until it blurs with more and more of its neighbors, "all reduced to one form and one size," to a single structure, a repetition, only, with variations, capped by his favorite myth. With the poem's echoing in widening waves blocked out, the critic must undertake his own spiralling out, with the consequence that the warmth and light of the poem diminishes to the point where it averages out with all other poems in grains of dust. There are, of course, secondary values accruing from such critical strategies. But all rest upon a deep-seated error, the conception of the poem as a corpus, the direct touch of which is death. The pain of that touch, or a horror at its numbness, when it should have been so vital, is what set them off on their long slow trips, on which they passed no humans, until each arrived, a final man upon a final hill, in a state of ataraxia, of apatheia, unperturbed by the touch of the dead poem or by any recollection of the joyful pain of touching the living poem.

If we do leave the green slopes of our isolation and vacate the empty centers of our structuralistic, historicistic, phenomenological webs, and approach a genuine poem with some sense of its vital activeness, we will find in its smallness an illumined largeness realizing, as few other experiences can, the full being of human community. The experience must surely be a painful one, partly because of our own bad habits, but also because of the painful element in all genuine community. We may even have to learn to memorize poetry again, so that we can truly join our breath with the poet's, giving the poem time to germinate in the dust of our own natures until we feel its deep surge and over-arching action. The closer we get to a poem, the more fully we experience the world as it is in the articulation of the poet, the more painful our sense of his otherness from ourselves is almost sure to become. At some point in our attention not just to what the poet says, but also to the way in which he attends to what he says, we will be forced to recognize that neither his mouth nor his ears are ours and, even while at one with the poem, we will move out of it into our own sense of experience in the effort to hear and feel its resonances as distinct from and at times at odds with those of the poem. At this stage, in this *concordia discors,* at one with the poem and distinct from it, opening up to ourselves our own natures as part of our experience of opening up the innermost nature of the poet and his world, with the poem qualifying and judging us as we qualify and judge it, in this vital interplay we will experience the living pulse of human community as it is and as it might be, but ah, as it is, as it is. And then, at last, we will be ready to perform the poem critically.

It is not possible to work out the critical performance of a poem by means of direct encounter, by what children call a "stare-down," and thus it is that I have moved with indirection toward Thom Gunn's **"Misanthropos,"** in spite of the lines with which Gunn concludes the poem:

> You must
> If you can, pause; and, paused,
>
> Turn out toward others, meeting their look at full,
> Until you have completely stared
> On all there is to see. Immeasurable,
> The dust yet to be shared.

Each of the seventeen poems of which **"Misanthropos"** is composed echoes the others, and all of them interinanimate each other. But if one would sense the surge of feeling that gives life and unity to the whole, he must attend to the interlinking action of Gunn's mind. Just as the final man of the poem, who has become its first man, can affirm that you must "Turn out toward others, meeting their look at full, / Until you have completely stared / On all there is to see," only if you have the capacity to pause, so we can stare into these final lines of the poem with understanding only if we can pause to hear the deepest echoes of the whole as they roll up and break into this final affirmation.

The skeletal pattern of **"Misanthropos"** is not hard to discern nor is discerning it important, when compared to the question, "do these bones live?" But noting it has mnemonic value and is a first step in coming as close to the poem as possible. The pattern is derived ultimately from Vico's eternal course and recourse of nations. The decadence of any nation or civilization is a state of disintegration. In the final stage of Rome, the citizens retreat to the hills, each one a final man upon his final hill. The accepted hierarchy of value collapses, each man carries off his own fragmentary version of it to his own hill, no one sees anyone else, and it is only the wind that utters ambiguous orders from the plain. Chaucer's pilgrims may stand as representative of another such recourse of decadence. But such decadence is virtually indistinguishable from the innocence with which a new recourse of nations begins. Thus, as Toynbee has shown, the Holy Roman Empire springs out of the isolated monasteries and mountain citadels and Germanic tribes which represent the final stage of the fall of the Roman Empire. And Chaucer's pilgrims are full of innocent exuberance and self-confidence. Now Gunn, in **"Misanthropos,"** is working with just this moment of transition in the eternal course and recourse of nations, the moment of decadence as it turns into the moment of innocence.

But Gunn responds to this pattern in an extremely personal way. He feels, and I think he is right to feel so, that all his poetry written prior to the volume *Touch* (The University of Chicago Press, 1967), in which **"Misanthropos"**

is the central poem, was fundamentally decadent. His first volume, *Fighting Terms* (1954), was written while he was still an undergraduate, and Charles Tomlinson found it to be clever and precious, an adolescent forcing of talent, much as F. R. Leavis had found Auden's early verse to be.[3] His first poem of that volume, **"Carnal Knowledge,"** begins with the clause, "Even in bed I pose," and includes the line, "You know I know you know I know you know," which should sum up adequately the cleverness and preciosity of the early Gunn.[4] In the third poem of **"Misanthropos,"** Gunn as listener recognizes the similarity between the early Gunn and the final man in these lines:

> But the curled darling who survives the war
> Has merely lost the admirers of those curls
> That always lavished most warmth on his neck;
> Though no one sees him, though it is the wind
> Utters ambiguous orders from the plain,
> Though nodding foxgloves are his only girls,
> His poverty is a sort of uniform.

Even in isolation he adopts a role and poses. He remains the same as the one who "Curled my hair, / Wore gloves in my cap." By wearing dark glasses, he was able to stand, "an armed angel among men." He fussed affectedly over the question of whether he was spy or spied on, "master, / or the world's abject servant." I do not intend, by noting these echoes in **"Misanthropos"** from earlier poems, to suggest that the poem is basically a conversation with those poems. Contrary to the position of Thomas Whitaker, I am convinced that no genuine poem is such a conversation.[5] A poem is essentially a dialectical dialogue between the poet speaking and the poet listening, the poet expressing and the poet criticizing; any conversational echoes with other poems which it may include are strictly subordinate to that primary dialogue. Thus the man referred to in **"Misanthropos"** as "the curled darling who survives the war," though he resembles a Gunn who could say "Even in bed I pose," is transformed by a feeling of loathing and disgust which is absent from the earlier poem. If it were insisted that the poem is a conversation with another poem outside it, then one would be forced to say that in the poem itself the conversation is fraudulently partisan, and whatever genuine conversation one claimed to exist would be the concoction of the critic rather than the creation of the poet.

When Gunn came to America in 1954 he avoided that deepening of affectation to which Auden succumbed, by going to Stanford and coming under the severe tutelage of Yvor Winters. Once there Gunn peeled off that delicate fastidiousness which would cause Philip Larken to be terrified of riding a motorcycle for fear he might tear his pants. Gunn heard the call, "Man, you gotta Go," and joined the Boys, "In goggles, donned impersonality." It is clear that, in *The Sense of Movement* (1957), Gunn does not "strap in doubt," as the Boys do, but the last lines of **"On the Move,"**

> At worst, one is in motion; and at best,
> Reaching no absolute, in which to rest,
> One is always nearer by not keeping still.

indicate that, for all his doubt, for all his knowledge that the Boys are "Small, black, as flies hanging in heat," he can come up with no alternative to riding in the "direction where the tires press," and thus accepts their way even though with a despairing cynicism. The passage echoing **"On the Move"** in the fifth poem of **"Misanthropos"** is dominated by a quite different feeling:

> thickets
> crowd in on the brown earth gap
> in green which is the path made
> by his repeated tread, which,
>
> enacting the wish to move,
> is defined by avoidance
> of loose ground, of rock and ditch,
> of thorn-brimmed hollows, and of
> poisoned beds. The ground hardens.
>
> Bare within limits. The trick
> is to stay free within them.
> The path branches, branches still,
> returning to itself, like
> a discovering system,
> or process made visible.

Here Gunn places the despairing cynicism of his decadence with a fine, discriminating disgust. The Boys were really just going around in circles. And their act was craven. Like our master structuralists, concocting patterns as remote as possible from the thickets of genuine poetry, they treaded out their discovering systems, returning upon themselves, merely to avoid the fearful things moving at the edges of their minds. Nor is there, in **"Misanthropos,"** any of that sentimental indulgence with which **"Lines from a Book"** closes:

> I think of all the toughs through history
> And thank heaven they lived, continually.

Gunn has achieved that moral discrimination of which Leavis despaired in Auden and which Tomlinson feared Gunn would not attain.

He has even surpassed the hard heroizing of the title poem of his next volume, *My Sad Captains* (1961):

> They were men
> who, I thought, lived only to
> renew the wasteful force they
> spent with each hot convulsion.
> They remind me, distant now.
>
> True, they are not at rest yet,
> but now that they are indeed
> apart, winnowed from failures,
> they withdraw to an orbit
> and turn with disinterested
> hard energy, like the stars.

As early as the fourth poem of **"Misanthropos,"** Gunn recognizes that such heroes are modelled on the move-

ment of the moon ("And steady in the orbit it must go.") and the Milky Way ("A luminous field that swings across the sky,") and that they represent an "envy for the inanimate." In the fourteenth poem, the first man's desire to be "Inhuman as a star, as cold, as white, / Freed from all dust" is placed as a form of cowardice, an unwillingness to accept the dust of life itself. Yvor Winters complained that the Gunn of *A Sense of Movement* and *My Sad Captains* usually had a "dead ear."[6] If his own sense of experience had not been so close to that of Gunn's, Winters might have realized, as Gunn does in **"Misanthropos,"** that the deadness went much deeper than the ear.

It was not, however, the Viconian pattern or Gunn's personalization of that pattern which sprung him free of his deadness, but rather, I think, his discovery that his decadence was "wholly representative." Gunn makes that recognition throughout **"Misanthropos."** His withdrawal first into affectation and then into isolated hardness ran parallel to a mass reaction to the Second World War. When the relief of the end of the war had exhausted itself, men turned away from each other in disgust. The humanized air which held the nation together in its united war effort suddenly became dry and empty. Even hitch-hikers were abandoned to themselves. "Each colourless hard grain" was "now distinct, / In no way to its neighbour linked." College students writing essays about what sort of man they would like to have survive a nuclear holocaust were in truth working out the desire to be "The final man upon a final hill." It was not their fear of the future but their disgust for the past which made them open this "disused channel / to the onset of hatred." Nor was the hysterical construction of fall-out shelters, an act usually accompanied by an image of oneself gunning down his improvident neighbors who implored him for a breath of unpoisoned air, really a sign of providence so much as it was an expression of misanthropy, a dream in which one was at last free of the smudge of other men. Some such realization resounds throughout **"Misanthropos"**: we had all withdrawn into an isolated state of ataraxia where we could live imperturbably, untouched by pain, "evil's external mark," unaware that if pain is the mark of evil, it is also the mark of goodness, the mark of "A man who burnt from sympathy alone."

That Gunn could find a way out of such a state, in which he had "grown / As stony as a lizard poised on stone," is not so remarkable as it might at first appear, especially to Americans. For, unlike us, he had behind him an experience in England following upon the First World War much like what happened to us only after the Second. Think, for example, of Yeats' ataraxic "An Irish Airman Foresees His Death" or of his desire to be taken up in the stone mosaics of Byzantium. Think too of Ezra Pound's major English poem, "Hugh Selwyn Mauberley," a poem written out of a state of paralysis from which there seemed to be no exit, whether into a Pre-Raphaelite dreamworld or into an impossibly depraved society run by the Mr. Nixons. Or consider whether the most influential English poem of the century, Eliot's *Four Quartets,* is not in truth written out of a deep state of ataraxia, being the sustained and repeatedly realized withdrawal from earthly, engaged experience, even a withdrawal from the crumbling language of the poem itself. Once Eliot had abandoned personal, sexual love in the poem "La figlia che piange," mustn't he be viewed as the exemplary final man upon the final hill, for whom every personal face is but a mask beyond which one moves into "the still point of the turning world"?

Even more important to the change that takes place for Gunn in **"Misanthropos"** is the criticism of F. R. Leavis and of the journal *Scrutiny,* which was a focus of literary intelligence in England from 1932 to 1952. Nothing in American criticism is comparable to Leavis' battle against the disintegration of his society and the impersonalization of both its social experience and its art. Leavis fought these heavy driftings not from the outside, rebelliously and violently, but from within, burning with good will and sympathy. He has never, for example, reneged on his claim that Eliot is one of the greatest of English poets. Compare his cautious and tentative and delicate criticism of Eliot with the blasts of Yvor Winters or with Quentin Anderson's recent claim, bordering as it does on hysteria: "The notion of the impersonality of art became the refuge of the infantile demand to rule the whole world."[7] Anderson's immediate targets are Emerson, Thoreau, Whitman, and Henry James, and the hundreds of thousands who gathered at Woodstock. But he is being exacerbated by the hidden foe of foes, T. S. Eliot. At least when set beside Leavis, Anderson seems to have no capacity to pause, and, having paused, to turn out toward others. In spite of himself, he appears as one more imperial self raging against imperial selves. Whereas for over thirty years Leavis did what Matthew Arnold tried to do but could not: by the free play of his mind, with his ideas of great poetry as both personal and impersonal and his conception of an English tradition as embodying such excellence, he made possible the recent resurgence of English poetry, among the finest representatives of which, in addition to Gunn, are Donald Davie, Jon Silkin, and Charles Tomlinson. Not, of course, that Gunn has found the way out of his stony isolation simply by following Leavis' precepts. He is an original poet, and, for all the resemblances between his recent poetry and the ideals Leavis advocates and certain poems by Davie, Silkin, and Tomlinson, the beating impulsion and the curve of action of **"Misanthropos"** are distinctly Gunn's own.

Even so, if Gunn had not had in his background Leavis' opposition to the impersonality and self-abnegation of Eliot, it seems likely that he would have fallen under the spell of that peculiarly imperialistic form of misanthropy to be found in so much of the very finest of contemporary American poetry. He could easily have turned into the path of Robert Bly, as James Wright did, temporarily, and tried to abandon his keen intellect and self-awareness. Bly would have us abandon ourselves utterly in order to move to the deepest point of our brain, where it dissolves into oneness with the God in Nature. He would have us move back to that still point at the heart of the wilderness and live and write poetry out of that impersonal center. Or Gunn might have followed Gary Snyder beyond the high point of his mountain retreats into an oriental form of ataraxia. At the very least he would have fallen in with

Allen Ginsberg's feeling that "All separate identities are bankrupt." Without Leavis' constant warnings he would have missed the odd likeness between the violence at the center of the vision of those poets who reject our society and the destructive acts committed in the name of that society. He would have missed the similarity between the perspective those poets take on the society they reject and the perspective of that society on the basis of which its leaders make it move.

The very form of "Misanthropos," the way its parts echo each other, grows out of Gunn's sense that the poet's individuality, in the act of composing the poem, is communal.

—Merle Brown

With all his misanthropy and with all the sympathy he shows for this American form of misanthropy, Gunn is able to resist this deepest revulsion for men with a disgust more intense than the sympathy he feels for it. Gunn articulates this complex mixture of sympathy and disgust in the twelfth poem, **"Elegy on the Dust,"** which is the high point of **"Misanthropos,"** the point at which the last man turns into the first man. The poem is a stunning articulation of the vision of men in society as a bowl of dust, "vexed with constant loss and gain," "a vaguely heaving sea," a graveyard which is a sea of dust. At the beginning of **"Misanthropos,"** the final man was being a contemporary Englishman in his refusal to build a watch tower. But here he has moved to America and looks outward from his retreat, taking into his view the hill, the wooded slope, and the vast expanse of dust beyond it. He has made the transfer which Lawrence's Lou Witt makes at the end of "St. Mawr."[8]

"Elegy on the Dust" ends with this visionary judgment on man in a modern mass nation state:

> Each colourless hard grain is now distinct,
>   In no way to its neighbour linked,
> Yet from wind's unpremeditated labours
>   It drifts in concord with its neighbours,
> Perfect community in its behaviour.
>   It yields to what it sought, a saviour:
> Scattered and gathered, irregularly blown,
>   Now sheltered by a ridge or stone,
> Now lifted on strong upper winds, and hurled
>   In endless hurry round the world.

The poem might seem to be merely a vision of man's ultimate form of decadence, that last stage in a Platonic cycle of degeneration at which a mobocracy turns into tyranny. Men are seen in the poem at their very lowest, averaged out in indistinguishable "grains of dust / Too light to act, too small to harm, too fine / To simper or betray or whine." In such a mobocracy, where even those who sought distinction hard are levelled with the rabble, in absolute uniformity, men are ready for a savior, a tyrant, who will windily hurl them "In endless hurry round the world." But instead of sharing this vision of Marcuse of the complete bankruptcy of our civilization, Gunn attends to its articulation with his keen, critical ear and turns the poem into a condemnation of that vision for which he has so much sympathy. The ultimate form of decadence turns out to be not what is seen, but the vision itself. As Raymond Williams has argued so persuasively, men exist as a mass only in the eye of the beholder. It is the beholding of men as a bowl of dust, as a mobocracy turning into a tyranny, not the men beheld in such a way, which is decadent.

One senses the special judgmental turn which Gunn is giving the vision in the way he works certain allusions into the poem. For example, in this part of the second stanza:

> Beneath it, glare and silence cow the brain
> Where, troughed between the hill and plain,
> The expanse of dust waits: acres calm and deep,
> Swathes folded on themselves in sleep
> Or waves that, as if frozen in mid-roll
> Hang in ridged rows.

Gunn is clearly echoing Wordsworth, and especially in the "acres calm and deep" the line "Ne'er saw I, never felt, a calm so deep!" from the sonnet "Composed upon Westminster Bridge." But he is doing more than simply alluding to the line; he is also judging Wordsworth's vision of London as organically beautiful only when all its citizens are asleep as an expression of imperialistic misanthropy. With Wordsworth so deeply studied and felt, Gunn could not fail to recognize the way in which the viewer personally determines the nature of the view. That the line "And vexed with constant loss and gain" in the next stanza echoes Wordsworth's sonnet "The world is too much with us" simply confirms how Gunn has learned from but then gone beyond the poet whom Galway Kinnell is now echoing somewhat uncritically. Of course, Marvell is present too, especially in the allusions to his most misanthropic and misogynous poem, "The Garden," as the lines "Interdependent in that shade" and "Are all reduced to one form and one size" echo the lines "Annihilating all that's made / To a green thought in a green shade." But the dominant allusion of the second of Gunn's lines just quoted is to Pound's "Hugh Selwyn Mauberley."

> here

> The graveyard is the sea, material things
> — From stone to claw, scale, pelt and wings—
> Are all reduced to one form and one size

echo these lines from Pound's "Envoi":

> I would bid them [the woman's graces] live
> As roses might, in magic amber laid,

> Red overwrought with orange and all made
> One substance and one colour
> Braving time.

Gunn senses that Pound's advocacy of the eternal beauty of art over the transiency of ordinary experience, summed up as it is as "Siftings on siftings in oblivion," is just a step short of going off to Italy and becoming an advocate of the Duce. It is Gunn's disgust for this disgust for men in society that turns the **"Elegy on the Dust"** away from being just one more imperial vision and into an extremely personal expression of Gunn's revulsion for such imperialism. It is the vision of men as a smudge of dust, this way of seeing men, which must be buried, the reducing of men to such a state, not men thus reduced, which must be abandoned. Gunn knows too much about Pound, he knows what Leavis recognized in him and what Donald Davie, following Leavis' lead, demonstrated in his book *Ezra Pound: Poet as Sculptor,* to be willing to follow after Ginsberg, Snyder, and Bly.

My reading of the **"Elegy"** as an expression of disgust for the vision of men as a bowl of dust instead of as a direct expression of that vision is reinforced by echoes in the **"Elegy"** from the poem just before it, the Epitaph for Anton Schmidt, and by the echoes of the **"Elegy"** itself in the poem which follows it, **"The First Man."** There is no irony in Gunn's admiration for Anton Schmidt, whose greatness depends on his not having mistaken "the men he saw, / As others did, for gods or vermin." The vision of the **"Elegy"** clearly mistakes the men viewed for vermin and the viewer for a god. Furthermore, the first man of the 13th poem is presented as Gunn's vision of the man who has had the vision of the **"Elegy,"** "An unreflecting organ of perception." That man can perceive men as a disgusting smudge because he does not reflect on what such a vision implies about himself. What it implies for Gunn is that, just as the men viewed in the **"Elegy"** disappear into the dust of a society blown "In endless hurry round the world" by a windy tyrant, so the visionary of the **"Elegy,"** that imperial self, that "transcendental eyeball," is finally to be seen "darkening in the heavy shade / Of trunks that thicken in the ivy's grip." And this image of the first man, of this American innocent, this barbarian who may be what must follow after the decadence of Europe, this appalls Gunn as much as it did the poet here being echoed, Wallace Stevens. The 11th poem of Stevens' "The Man With The Blue Guitar" is the rejection of its vision of men dissolving into a thicket of time, where they are caught as flies, "Wingless and withered, but living alive." At this point Gunn must make his final choice: to accept the disappearance of man as an individual into the dust of society or the heavy shade of nature or to reaffirm the value of that man as distinctive. His choice, as is obvious from the 14th poem, is the second: he must stare upon men as a smudge until they come so close to him that the outlines of the smudge break away from it and the men turn into individuals.

Only as a result of doing this does he realize in direct experience that as he gazes upon a man, he is himself gazed upon, as he touches another, he is himself touched, and that his own self and his whole world are enlarged and enlivened by this interaction. Gunn does not simply assert this but works it out experientially by means of echoes. The first man's affirming in the 17th poem that you must pause, if you can, echoes and is even learned from the scratched man's pausing in the 16th poem. The first man's revulsion from the stale stench, the hang-dog eyes and the pursed mouth of the scratched man in the 16th poem echoes the scratched man's response to the first man when he first sees him in the 15th poem:

> The creature sees him, jumps back, staggers, calls,
> Then, losing balance on the pebbles, falls.

The effect of Gunn's restraint in this passage—we aren't quite sure what the lines imply and may even feel them to be empty—is that our sense of the repulsiveness of the first man and Gunn's sense of his own repulsiveness coincide with the first man's momentary revulsion from the scratched man even as he grips his arm. Although Gunn's movement out of isolation at the end of **"Misanthropos"** includes such moments of felt insight, it is harsh and painful. There is no moment of explosive joy as there is at the end of Stevens' "Esthétique du Mal," when Stevens realizes that human life is made up of

> So many selves, so many sensuous worlds,
> As if the air, the mid-day air, was swarming
> With the metaphysical changes that occur,
> Merely in living as and where we live.

Gunn's use of the word "stared" to express the way in which we must connect with others suggests harshness. And his last words, "Immeasurable / The dust yet to be shared" come out with a grudging sigh. But Gunn has made his recognition and affirmation. And the poems which follow **"Misanthropos"** in *Touch,* especially the last one, **"Back to Life,"** and many poems in his most recent volume, *Moly,* show that he mean it.

The innermost sense of experience which forces Gunn to pull himself out of his isolation still remains to be explained. What forces him to affirm the value of human community is, I believe, his sense that his own nature as an individual is communal, even when he is most isolated. Observing the first man, in the 13th poem, "darkening in the heavy shade / Of trunks that thicken in the ivy's grip," he sees that his very existence as an individual, composed of himself as self-aware observer and himself as a rudimentary man, is about to be annihilated. It is his commitment to himself as a community, as both spy and spied on, which forces him finally to turn out toward others. The final choice is between dissolving into nature and rejoining men. Gunn chooses the second because of his growing awareness that the very essence of himself as an individual is communal and that he will not survive in any form at all if he becomes one with nature.

As early as the second poem of **"Misanthropos,"** Gunn reveals the doubleness of his individuality as poet and the last man quite emphatically. In contrast to the first poem of the sequence, in which Gunn as poet talks out his sense of himself as the last man, presented in the third person, in the second poem Gunn speaks as the last man in the first person to his echo, which of course is Gunn as poet. This conversation concludes thus:

> Is there no feeling, then, that I can trust,
> In spite of what we have discussed?
>   Disgust.

The form of the whole of **"Misanthropos"** is implicit in these lines. The experience of the last man is based upon disgust, upon misanthropy. But the nature of this disgust is articulated in marvellously varied discussions carried on between the last man and his echo or, to reverse the coin, between Gunn as poet and himself as last man. Gunn's shifting from poem to poem between the last man as objectively third person and as subjectively first person can be explained in no other way. It is in passing through "what we have discussed" that Gunn is enabled to move from disgust to trust and thus begin the last poem with:

> Others approach. Well, this one may show trust
> Around whose arm his fingers fit.

The trust of this last poem never breaks free from a need that it be discussed or even, for that matter, from an element of disgust. Thus, the poet, in expressing the last-man-become-first-man's willingness to trust the scratched man, also implies his grave doubts as to whether the man is worthy of such trust. Even the internal community of the second poem, moreover, is itself full of disgust. To get the tone of the poem right one needs to add to each echoing word the phrase "you poor fool." Thus, even though the basic movement of **"Misanthropos"** is from isolated disgust through discussion to communal trust, there is an internal community involved in the initial disgust just as there is an element of disgust in the trust of the final external community.

Once the reader recognizes the explicitly communal nature of the isolated individual as presented in the second poem, he can then see this community as implicitly present even in the first poem, which begins:

> He avoids the momentous rhythm
> of the sea, one hill suffices him
> who has the entire world to choose from.
>
> He melts through the brown and green silence
> inspecting his traps, is lost in dense
> thicket, or appears among great stones.

Although one probably begins the poem merely spying on the last man, who "lives like / the birds, self-contained they hop and peck," further readings are sure to convince him that the poem contains, along with the man we spy on, its own spy, the echoing, controlling presence of the poet. Unlike the last man, the last man's echo, the poet Thom Gunn, proves himself capable of the momentous rhythm of the sea. The first clause of the poem, with its anapestic rhythm and with the first line running on into the second is a sea-like rhythm. But having set this rhythm in motion, the poet then drops it abruptly, with the second clause, "one hill suffices him," working iambically and in a syntax at odds with that of the first clause, so that there is no build-up by way of clauses rhythmically and syntactically parallel. Similarly, in the second stanza the first line is a return to the momentous rhythm of sea-like anapests, but here the expected run-on effect of the first stanza is frustrated; one must pause after "silence" and begin again with "inspecting his traps." The poet as spy does, in other words, have a watch tower. He is not self-contained as the spied-upon man is; he looks beyond that self-containment to glimpse the rhythm the last man avoids, introducing it only to break it down, so that we sense not just the isolation of the man, but also that from which he is isolated.

The communal nature of **"Misanthropos"** is shared, it seems to me, by all genuine poems, and is why John Crowe Ransom was wrong when he said: one cannot write a love poem while he is in love and that is why Elizabeth Barrett Browning's sonnets are loving but unpoetic. The truth is rather that one must be both in love and out of love to write a love poem. To write a poem on himself as a man who widens his salitude till it is absolute. Gunn had to be both in that solitude and in community. In other words, the very writing of the poem forces him into internal communal relations which work against his desire for absolute solitude. **"Misanthropos"** is distinctive because it is a genuine poem based upon the realization of the communal doubleness inherent in all poetic sincerity. The very form of the poem, the way its parts echo each other, grows out of Gunn's sense that the poet's individuality, in the act of composing the poem, is communal. And it is this sense of the communal nature of the poet as individual, even when pushed to an extreme isolation by disgust, which leads Gunn to reject the American desire for dissolving into nature and to turn out toward other human beings.

Gunn's **"Misanthropos"** has a cinematic counterpart in Antonioni's *Zabriskie Point.* Like Gunn, Antonioni explored with fascination our desire to be "on the move" and to throw ourselves into simple, bodily love affairs, and he found them to be expressive of the deeper desire to end up in "this universal knacker's yard," at point zero, all levelled in dissolute couplation on the desert. Though Antonioni draws back from this lure to dissolution, the vision he moves back to is very much like the imperially decadent vision of Gunn's **"Elegy on the Dust."** This explains, I think, why *Zabriskie Point* disgusted its American audiences but was extremely popular in Europe. Gunn, in contrast, rejects not just the "vaguely heaving sea" of dust which is America seen from a final hill, but also the vision itself, as a deeper form of decadence than that which it contains and repudiates. Even so, Gunn's final position is not so very stirring. **"Misanthropos"** is pitched at a thin high extreme of self-consciousness. It is clear that the man who wrote this poem is the same man who wrote **"The Corridor,"** in which the "I" spies through a keyhole at two people making love and then realizes that he the spy is himself being spied upon by a figure in a mirror at the end of the hall. But though the poem is resolutely self-conscious, it does move with the force of necessity

beyond itself and into communion with others, whose otherness is more painful and also more vital than the otherness contained within the poet's individuality. The community achieved is minimal, but it is also essential.

One cannot leave the poem without a glancing reminder of what it implies about the critical maneuvers that have been so popular during the past twenty-five years. Once the poem is taken into the blood stream, wouldn't a critic be too ashamed to wear dark glasses and, "Between the dart of colours" to wear a darkening and perceive "an exact structure, / a chart of the world"? Too many things are moving "at the edges of the mind" to leave him content to be treading out a path "like / a discovering system, / or process made visible." Nor, once he has watched with Gunn's disgust the paradisal

> cells swimming in concert
> like nebulae, calm, without effort,
>
> great clear globes, pink and white.

is he likely to be satisfied with utopian and visionary criticism or, like Harold Bloom, to condemn Yeats' "Sailing to Byzantium" on the grounds that it fails to achieve oneness with the visionary company.[9] He would recognize that Yeats' poem comes alive just because the visionary company, the "great clear globes," and the ladies of Byzantium are violated by "the intruder with blurred outline" who touches and holds "in an act of / enfolding, possessing, merging love." The intruder may cause pain like a devil, but, without such a spark of fire, even sympathy cannot burn.

Criticism that moves to touch and hold a poem will be not only interpretive, but also appreciative. Interpretation alone is more like memorizing notes than performing them. A musician does not try simply to get the notes right. He must play in such a way as to articulate the living value of the notes, to realize, far beyond the score itself, the vital act of sound in movement which is the composer's creation. It is true, of course, that a critical performance lacks the immediacy of a musical performance. For the critic and his audience must always return to the text of the poem itself and work out the values in it which the critic can at best only hint at and point toward. Even so, I agree with Roger Sessions that, in their purpose and value, literary criticism and musical performance are fundamentally the same.[10] What the critic may learn from the musician is that he can expose and evoke a poem with any fullness only if he is willing to evoke and expose himself at the very same time. The critic who fashions for himself a frock from the skins of mole and rabbit, who writes in hiding, with sovereign impersonality, who tries to interpret and appreciate a poem in such a way that the poem is not permitted in turn to interpret and judge him, will touch neither the poem nor himself. He must listen long and carefully not just to the poem but also to himself until he too speaks with a voice of his own, if he would ever hope to converse with the intimate dialogue that every genuine poem is. He can learn from the musician that he himself must venture creatively if he would hope to touch the creativity of the poems of his concern. I am not suggesting that schools of criticism should model themselves on the great conservatories. But to the extent that those conservatories are committed not to technical perfection, but to a form of performance in which one realizes himself in the very act of evoking the living composition in all its otherness, it does seem to me that they provide a vital and meaningful model worthy of our emulation.[11]

Notes

[1] See chap. 14 of Collingwood's *The Principles of Art* (Oxford, 1938) and Poirier's *The Performing Self* (Oxford, 1971).

[2] Wellek, "Kenneth Burke and Literary Criticism," *The Sewanee Review* (Spring, 1971), 187-188.

[3] Tomlinson, "Poetry Today," *The Modern Age,* vol. 7 of *The Pelican Guide to English Literature* (Penguin, 1963), p. 473.

[4] In the three editions of *Fighting Terms* (1954, 1959, 1962) "Carnal Knowledge" has been much revised.

[5] Whitaker, "Voices in the Open: Wordsworth, Eliot, & Stevens," *The Iowa Review* (Summer, 1971), 96-112.

[6] Winters, *Forms of Discovery* (Swallow, 1967), p. 345.

[7] Quentin Anderson, *The Imperial Self* (Knopf, 1971), p. 203.

[8] See Poirier's superb analysis of "St. Mawr" in *A World Elsewhere* (Oxford, 1966). pp. 40-49.

[9] Harold Bloom, *Yeats* (Oxford, 1970), pp. 344-349.

[10] See chap. 3 of Roger Sessions, *Questions About Music* (Harvard, 1970).

[11] The antagonism of Hindemith against performers, expressed in chap. 7 of his *Autobiography.*

Clive Wilmer   (essay date 1980)

SOURCE: "Definition and Flow: Thom Gunn in the 1970s," in *British Poetry Since 1970: A Critical Survey,* edited by Peter Jones and Michael Schmidt, Persea Books, 1980, pp. 64-74.

[*In the following essay, Wilmer discusses the influences on Gunn's work, in particular such poets as Yvor Winters, William Carlos Williams, and Ezra Pound.*]

Thom Gunn's *My Sad Captains,* first published in 1961, has two sections quite distinct in character, the first consisting of poems in traditional metres, the second of apparently lighter pieces in syllabic verse. Gunn has since renounced syllabics in favour of free verse, but his publications still require the reader to accept that metrical poems are different in kind from poems in 'open' forms.

D.H. Lawrence, in the Preface to the American edition of his *New Poems* (an essay whose influence Gunn has acknowledged), arguing the case for such a distinction, wrote of free verse as pre-eminently the medium of present-tense meditation, of perception in the process of taking form. By contrast—so he argued—the great stanzaic poems deal with ends and beginnings, past and future:

> It is in the realm of all that is perfect. It is of the nature of all that is complete and consummate. This completeness, this consummateness, the finality and the perfection are conveyed in exquisite form: the perfect symmetry, the rhythm which returns upon itself like a dance where the hands link and loosen and link for the supreme moment of the end.". . . But there is another kind of poetry: the poetry of that which is at hand: the immediate present. In the immediate present there is no perfection, no consummation, nothing finished. The strands are all flying, quivering, intermingling into the web, the waters are shaking the moon. There is no round consummate moon on the face of running water, nor on the face of the unfinished tide.

Though Gunn's poetry is hardly dance-like, it certainly used to be remarkable for rhythms returning upon themselves, for the finality of its meditations; yet at the same time what did it celebrate but flux, risk, the unpredictable future, the unfinished artefact? Although much of its interest lay in the tension between form and content, one is hardly surprised to learn that Gunn has come increasingly to admire a poetry which possesses the very qualities that move him in life. All that the poetry of Whitman and Lawrence, Williams and Snyder must have lacked to so skilled and deliberate an artificer was a sense of the necessary and inevitable artificiality of poetry, the supreme fiction.

When Gunn finally discarded the somewhat arbitrary discipline of syllabic verse in the mid-sixties, it was mainly to William Carlos Williams that he turned for a model of free-verse prosody: the right choice, surely, for few modern poets have combined Williams's level of craftsmanship with such apparent informality. Now, ten years later, in *Jack Straw's Castle* (1976), the relationship between Gunn's two modes is becoming clearer. In the metrical poems the rhythms are looser, the language more conversational, the structures based more on sequences of perception than on patterns of logical thought. The free verse gains in authenticity from Gunn's sense of how a poem is made and how its making must relate to what already exists in the world. A sense of the limits of both flux and artifice is built into the poetry. Lawrence was original in his insistence that the two kinds of prosody fulfil different functions and must therefore continue to co-exist. Metre will still be called upon to embody the products of concentrated thought, to give the semblance of immutable form to (relatively) immutable verities. For this it depends on an element of predictability in its movement. Free verse, however—if it is wholly distinct from metre, as Lawrence's is and Williams's—depends on the opposite, on our inability to predict the rhythmic outcome. Gunn, like Williams, plays on this, tantalizing the reader with weak line-endings and long sinuous sentences broken into short lines. This procedure emphasises the overall rhythm (as against the line-as-unit) and suggests the hesitancy of the human voice as it shapes its utterances. The poem seems to discover its meanings as it proceeds, as if it were a sequence of thought enacted before us, affected by the moment: we seem to acquire a new awareness of thought (and poem) as *process*. This method—exemplified by a poem as early as **'Touch'**, published in 1967—enables Gunn not only to describe the world, but at the same time to dramatize the ways in which we come to know it, in terms which point ultimately to his own beliefs about its nature.

But there is nothing especially new about such discoveries. On the contrary, they are based on ideas associated with the adolescence of the modern movement. Their importance for us lies in the fact that Gunn, as a poet once associated with quite different attitudes to the function of poetry, has rediscovered them for himself. When he wrote *My Sad Captains,* Gunn was virtually a disciple of that implacable anti-Modernist, Yvor Winters, whose continuing influence on him has been considerable. Yet Gunn today can write of Ezra Pound as 'probably the greatest poet we have had in this century'; and any poet who turns to Williams as a model must ultimately come to terms with a Poundian view of literature.

Winters, a classicist and neo-humanist in the Jonsonian mould, held that a good poem was a rational structure composed of connected propositions, to which form was the objective equivalent. As such, he rejected the irrationalist assumptions of Modernist poetics as firmly as the Right-wing politics associated with its founders. For politically Winters was the most redoubtable of liberals. He held that political and literary irrationalism make men the victims of their history and experience. Poetry was only of value if its end was understanding; the poem was not a kind of secondary organism that partakes of life, but a skilfully contrived artefact set apart from the flux it seeks to evaluate. But Winters's view of understanding itself often seems excessively restricted; he always considers it in terms of completed perceptions and achieved ideas. For Gunn, ideas and understanding are more closely entwined in the process of language. He has written of Gary Snyder that 'like most serious poets he is mainly concerned at finding himself on a barely known planet in an almost unknown universe, where he must attempt to create and discover meanings. Discovery of a meaning is always also the creation of it, and creation is an act of discovery.' Then, of one specific poem, 'it is. . . . a series of pictorial perceptions made by a man embedded in time, who advances into the sensory world opened by his waking'. This conception of poetry and the terms Gunn uses are largely dependent on Winters's example. What he adds is a greater respect for the force of sensuous and instinctual awareness.

Gunn would now probably agree with Donald Davie who, in a recent study of Pound, takes issue with Winters's view of the *Cantos* but finds his objections to them illuminating. Winters, he writes,

> conceiving of an idea as that which could be stated in the form of a proposition, recorded his experience of

reading the *Cantos* by saying, 'we have no way of knowing whether we have had any ideas or not'." . . . if we take account of what he understood 'idea' to be, Winters' remark is one of the few valuably exact formulations that we have of what reading the *Cantos* amounts to, and feels like.

For Pound an idea was not a proposition but 'The *forma, the immortal concetto'* which Allen Upward had described in these words: 'The idea is not the appearance of a thing already there, but rather the imagination of a thing not yet there. It is not the look of a thing, it is a looking forward to a thing'.

Gunn rejects Wintersian 'propositions' in favour of something rather like Pound's *forma* in a poem called **'The Outdoor Concert'**. The title is a play on words: the 'concert' is both a musical performance and an experience of unity. The poem describes a 'secret' at the heart of a shared experience, a kind of synthesis. The act of discovery is not a lonely quest but the participation of one man in a group.

> The secret
> is still the secret
>
> is not a proposition:
> it's in finding
> what connects the man
> with the music, with
> the listeners, with the fog
> in the top of the eucalyptus,
> with dust discovered on the lip.

A proposition will not embrace the multiplicity of experience—nor indeed will any formulation—but to perceive *connections* is also a form of understanding. The poem constructs a *web*—an organic image which, since the poem is in free verse, may remind us of Lawrence. In more mechanical terms we might call it a diagram. *Jack Straw's Castle* does in fact contain a poem called **'Diagrams'**, which is written in strict heroic couplets and, with fourteen lines, recalls that most elaborately artificial of forms, the sonnet. We can now perceive how Gunn's preoccupation with reason and volitional form has developed. He is now concerned with 'models' of thought—as Poundian an interest as it is Wintersian, for what are Pound's ideograms but models, the matrices on which ideas are formed?

The ideogram in Pound's theory, though related to rhythm, is primarily a matter of content, of images and ideas. It was of no interest to Winters. And I doubt that Winters's scrupulous distinctions between metre ('the arithmetical norm, the purely theoretic structure of the line') and rhythm ('controlled departure from that norm') would have appealed to Pound. But both conceptions are of relevance to Gunn (and to many more of us). His own conception of metre remains as mathematical as Winters's; metre is, he has written, 'an unbodied abstraction', then goes on, like Winters, to emphasize that the life of a poem depends on it. For Gunn and Winters, all structures, whether of language or society, are frameworks which sustain a life, though—of their very nature—quite separate from it.

When we read Pound, however, we experience an attempt to push the artefact as close to the given world as it will go. The rhythms of speech are attuned to those of nature. The very structure of the *Cantos* is fragmentary, as if they had been worn down by the wind and water whose acts of erosion they so insistently and delectably evoke. Yet no reader could ever pretend that the hand and mind of the artificer seemed absent from the enterprise, whatever its aspirations or shortcomings. Moreover, though the overall structure of the work may appear loose, the individual details are remarkable for their hardness and definition. It must have been tensions of this sort that first made Pound's poetry available to Gunn.

Of the book that preceded *Jack Straw's Castle* Gunn has written—in language that might have been used to register his admiration for Pound—that 'It could be seen as a debate between the passion for definition and the passion for flow.'. . . Yet that book, *Moly* (1971), seemed to mark a retreat from the open forms he had developed in *Touch* (1967). The passion for definition is most in evidence in the elegant formality of the rhymed stanzas; that for flow in the varieties of energy they contemplate. But 'the *sense* of movement', of energy, has changed. Gone are the uniformed heroes for whom the will 'cannot submit /To nature, though brought out of it.' In their place are the surfers of '**From the Wave**'. Though, like the tearaways of '**On the Move**,' they become what they are through movement, they do so by adapting themselves to nature. Their skill and balance enable them to act in concord with the waves—and these are qualities which require a harmony between knowledge and instinct, consciousness and action.

The debate to which Gunn referred is continued in the group of metrical poems that make up the first section of *Jack Straw's Castle.* The free verse poems in the other two sections approach similar problems from a different angle; there definition is arrived at, not imposed. '**The Plunge**' tries in its language to enact the process of acquiring knowledge by total immersion. A diver plunges into a pool and stays under till he can take no more, till he reaches the limits of the self. This discovery of limits is a discovery of definition, of essential form. 'How much more can the body / take?' he asks, driving himself to the point where process must stop and formulation begin. For '**Thomas Bewick**', immersion in the detail of the natural world is like a return to the womb. The umbilical cord that binds him to the rest of the material universe not yet cut, he is conscious but not yet individual.

> Drinking from
> clear stream and resting
> on the rock he loses himself
> in detail,
>
>   he reverts
> to an earlier self, not yet
> separate from what it sees,

> a selfless self as difficult
> to recover and hold as to
> capture the exact way
> a burly bluetit grips
> its branch (leaning forward)
> over this rock
>   and in
> The History of British Birds.

Immersion in process reaches its limit in a new kind of permanence—the book for which Bewick's name is remembered, capitalized and visually set apart from the rest of the poem. The rhythm enacts the flow of experience into record.

If such poems are necessarily composed in open form, how do they differ from those written in traditional prosody? What Gunn has discovered through free verse has inevitably affected his standard metre, sometimes to its detriment. His attempts at the conversational can be banal: 'More meteors than I've ever set eyes on' for example. Or rhythmically confusing: the line, 'It doesn't matter tomorrow. Sleep well. Heaven knows', is only theoretically a pentameter; it is impossible to *hear* five feet, iambic or otherwise. But just at the edge of clumsiness, there are some felicitous variations, as in a mimetic view of a watersnake: 'I see a little snake alert in its skin /Striped head and neck from water, unmoving, reared'. The precariousness of such failures and successes is part of the whole debate between flux and definition, the intrusion of 'natural' rhythms into the fixities of traditional prosody.

The debate is initiated by the first three poems in *Jack Straw's Castle.* One of these, '**Diagrams**', explores the illusion of permanence and the containment of flux. A skyscraper is being built. In its unfinished state it resembles a mesa, as if it were not an artefact at all but a permanent feature of the landscape. To the European reader, both mesa and skyscraper evoke the American landscape; this is important, for Gunn, though English by birth, is now deeply concerned with the United States as a political and geographical entity. Significantly, the men at work on the steel mesa are aboriginal Americans:

> On girders round them, Indians pad like cats,
> With wrenches in their pockets and hard hats.

Their agility expresses their closeness to the environment, mesa or skyscraper. The human embodiment of American 'nature', they are engaged in creating the human contribution to that landscape. They are the presiding deities of *Jack Straw's Castle,* moving like animals among provisional human artefacts, yet equally at home in the given world. Gunn shows them poised between permanence and flux, rather as a Renaissance poet might show man poised between earth and air:

> They wear their yellow boots like moccasins,
> Balanced where air ends and where steel begins,
> Sky men.'. . .

Their boots—products of industrial society, used for work among that society's structures—are worn like the shoes they would wear on a real mesa. The building they are erecting, though intended as a fixed and stable thing, appears as it grows to absorb and transform the energies that surround it. It becomes a 'giant' that 'grunts and sways', rising into the air: 'And giving to the air is sign of strength.' As in **'From the Wave'**, to bend to the power of the elements is to derive strength from them. But the ordinary meaning of 'give' is also present: the building appears to seep energy into the air. The contrast with the solitary heroes to whom Gunn bade farewell in **'My Sad Captains'** could not be greater:

> They were men
> who, I thought, lived only to
> renew the wasteful force they
> spent with each hot convulsion.

The consumption of their energy was magnificent but, ultimately, waste. For Gunn today, the transformation of energy is 'sign of strength', the adaptation of self to environment.

Though Gunn's poetry is hardly dance-like, it certainly used to be remarkable for rhythms returning upon themselves, for the finality of its meditations; yet at the same time what did it celebrate but flux, risk, the unpredictable future, the unfinished artefact?

—Clive Wilmer

The diagrams of the title are cranes and exposed girders, but I take it that Gunn is also thinking of other structures that bear upon the poem's meaning—notably, the grid of its own metre. And most of these recent metrical poems are concerned with moments in which fluidity takes on permanent form. Such permanence is illusory but necessary. American permanence, in a political sense, is embodied in its constitution, which itself has its origin in revolutionary change. Gunn is not a political poet in the sense of being 'committed'—he is primarily concerned with identities and relations we think of as pre-political, with 'finding himself on a barely known planet in an almost unknown universe'. But as Camus (one of his most honoured heroes) discovered, freedom and choice do not exist in abstract purity; once a man is oppressed, he discovers his political nature whether he will or no. It was under Camus's influence, in *My Sad Captains*, that Gunn first tried to show how the individual's choices may operate in society. Like Camus, he was thinking of an extreme kind of society, though, unlike him, he had not lived in one. The political positions adopted are therefore limited in application, though quite clear: specifically anti-fascist, broadly anti-totalitarian. The rational individualism of **'Claus von Stauffenberg, 1944'** might be called liberal. It is strange to recall that Gunn's early poems were often accused of fascism—especially in the light of his recent testimony that as an undergraduate (when he wrote *Fighting Terms*) he was a pacifist and a Fabian socialist. The violence of those poems is examined outside a social context and not proposed as a good. The dissolution of self in the group and the adoption of various 'uniforms' are choices made voluntarily by individuals. The heroic stance is precisely that: a stance, a posture by which a man defines his identity: it is frozen action, the fluid given the appearance of permanence. If Gunn seemed obsessed with Nazism—its history, postures and regalia—this has something to do with growing up in time of war and reaching manhood when the struggle was over. *Not* having fought in that war is the context a recent poem like **'The Corporal'** requires. So, in *My Sad Captains* and *Touch,* Gunn criticizes his earlier stances in such a way as to acquit himself of this accusation. Since *Touch,* his politics have become decidedly American. It is possible to read the Arcadian world of *Moly* as a new version of the American dream—the New World as the second Eden. But such an Arcadia must become mere escapism in the years of the Vietnam war and Nixon's presidency, if actual political issues are not faced. *Jack Straw's Castle* is the only book of Gunn's which shows the need to deal with contemporary history. 'Nixon's era', with its corruption and rigidity, is regarded as a betrayal of the system of institutionalized change on which the United States was founded. **'Iron Landscapes'**, the one poem to deal directly with these issues, is brilliantly written, but flawed and problematic.

It is a meditation on an antiquated iron pier and a girdered ferry-building beside the Hudson River. Gunn's newly-acquired modernism is in evidence, not least in the rhythmic flexibility.

> A girdered ferry-building opposite,
> Displaying the name LACKAWANNA, seems to ride
>
> The turbulent brown-grey waters that intervene:
> Cool seething incompletion that I love.

In these lines, the iambic pentameter is the norm from which the rhythm departs. The first and fourth lines are regular. The other two depart from that pattern, much as the non-verbal facts they attempt to encompass elude verbal formulation. In the first of these, the capitalized name (does this too have Indian associations?) fits so awkwardly into the line that the hard physical intractability of the other artefact comes alive to us. (Gunn's admiration for similar rhythmic and verbal angularities in Thomas Hardy comes to mind: 'They present things with immediate authority.') Variation in the third line achieves a different effect: we feel the elusive fluidity of the perception by contrast with the formulaic precision of the regular line that follows. Regularity, of course, is appropriate to commentary, to formulations necessarily of the mind.

It is not just a matter of rhythm. Free verse enacts a different kind of thought and thinking. If we look at some of Gunn's best early poems—at **'Innocence'** or **'The Annihilation of Nothing'**—we are struck not only by the exactness of the metre (in contrast with the awkwardness of **'Iron Landscapes'**) but, more, by the perfection of the argument. *Too* perfect, you might think, too coherent to allow for the fluidities, the innate contradictions of the subject. Life is almost imprisoned by the subject, not enlarged. But in this poem we are able to follow the poet's train of thought as the different elements that compose the argument are brought together. It is not, as in the free verse, a poetry of process. The different elements have been prefabricated, as it were, into blocks. Our attention is drawn less to thought-as-process than to the way experience is shaped into form and formula, to become idea, concept, belief, opinion.

The poem begins with the 'bare black Z' of the pier and the poet beneath it, looking across the river to the ferry-building. The zigzags of the iron structures 'come and go' in the water, become fluid in the water's reflection of them. Separate perceptions are brought together, not by volition but by contingency. This provokes the central paradox, the conflict between Gunn's passions for definition and for flow. Then a third perception comes into play. Glimpsed downstream, the Statue of Liberty provokes reflections on the present state of the nation. Gunn has just declared his 'passion for definition', having earlier declared his love for its opposite, 'Cool seething incompletion'.

> But I'm at peace with the iron landscape too,
> Hard because buildings must be hard to last
> —Block, cylinder, cube, built with their angles true,
> A dream of righteous permanence, from the past.
>
> In Nixon's era, decades after the ferry,
> The copper embodiment of the pieties
> Seems hard, but hard like a revolutionary
> With indignation, constant as she is.
>
> From here you can glimpse her downstream, her far
>   charm,
> Liberty, tiny woman in the mist
> —You cannot see the torch—raising her arm
> Lorn, bold, as if saluting with her fist.

Thus from stability and flux, iron and water, the poem moves on to an historical plane: the rigidity of reactionary government is now set against the principle of change on which the Constitution is founded. First, the identification of buildings with institutions is made; the dream from the past is, among other things, the dream of the original revolutionaries whose Utopia is embodied in another metal artefact, the statue. The difficulty is that they created their liberal revolution in the image of the old order: they tried to institutionalize change. Today's revolutionaries aspire to base new societies on change, but their weakness (implicit here or not?) is their failure to recognize the human need for fixities. The poem ends with an image of the old revolution (the statue) transformed into the new (the clenched-fist salute), and 'Liberty' is neither permanent nor fluctuating but *constant,* a principle existing in time with changing manifestations, itself unchanging.

Inevitably writing of this sort raises questions. After all, these are matters we argue vehemently about, yet the poem—though it appears to take sides—is an unresolved embodiment of the issues. This is a case where we *need* Wintersian propositions but are left with a web of gestures, even of prejudices. For example, the poem depends on the assumption (which I happen to share) that the Nixon era was a bad time; but this is something we need to be persuaded of. A similar doubt infects the poem's technique. Is Gunn being relaxed and flexible, or merely clumsy? Does the rhyme 'ferry'/'revolutionary' work? Yet the rhythmical counterpoint in the last stanza is as beautiful and assured as anything in Gunn's work. His gaucheries sometimes seem Hardyesque authentications of his honesty; here he is most fluent where difficulties need to be raised, where the thought should meet with most resistance from the verse. It is a convincing conclusion to a line of thought but, finally, no more than a gesture—and it is a good many years now since Gunn first questioned the validity of 'the large gesture of solitary man'. In his earlier work, stance, pose and gesture were important as moments of stasis through which people established their identities, breaking temporarily free from 'movement'. Moreover, these stances, though they involved commitment to action, did not involve action in terms of the stance. The fetishistic dandy with the swastika-draped bed in **'The Beaters'** is in no sense a Nazi. But in **'Iron Landscapes',** the emotion compels us to identify with a pose which is intended to issue in specific actions with public implications and, however much one may sympathize with such a response to the Nixon era, one must ask what essential difference there is between the clenched fist and a Nazi salute. True, one is a gesture of resistance, the other of oppression. But both are salutes; both call for public violence; both deny the validity of rational discussion. Of course, it is not Gunn's purpose to declare a commitment or to invoke the detail of political argument. It is a fine poem, and not the least of its virtues is that it is able to provoke such questions and to show historical patterns growing from the matrices of feeling the landscape represents. It shows American society as necessarily based on the dialectic of permanence and change, the very dialectic which determines the creative tensions of Gunn's poetry.

We have reached a stalemate: one though, as it seems to me, that is at the root of modern poetry. **'Iron Landscapes'** attempts a reconciliation between the fluidity of the modern (free verse and all that goes with it) and the monumental qualities of the classical (the metred stanza). Whatever one makes of the metric, it should be clear that the internal structure is Modernist, almost Poundian; for it is concerned not with ideas but with the raw material of thought. It is significant that the internal structure resolves itself in a gesture: which is precisely the weakness of much of Pound's poetry. But what Gunn brings to this new Modernism is respect for the classical as a living concern. Whatever we make of the clenched fist, there is no mistaking the fundamentally liberal position of **'Iron Landscapes'**, a position reinforced by, for example, his version of colonization in the sequence called **'The Geysers'**. The Indian workers of **'Diagrams'** belong to a race displaced and humbled by colonialism, yet—as **'The Geysers'** shows—*all* human habitations are colonies. The perpetual challenge faced by the liberal is how to make such colonies humane, how to establish a fruitful harmony between man the artificer and man the creature. Gunn is a highly civilized artist—hence his continuing loyalty to the old forms. Despite his enthusiasm for the new, he does not welcome—as some writers whose names have been misleadingly linked with his appear to do—the collapse of our civilization. Rather he sees change and the capacity for change as *the* essential qualities of a living civilization, and so celebrates its continuity.

Jay Parini   (essay date 1982)

SOURCE: "Rule and Energy: The Poetry of Thom Gunn," in *The Massachusetts Review,* Vol. 23, Spring, 1982, pp. 134-51.

[*In the following essay, Parini maintains that Gunn is able to balance his energetic approach to language and theme with traditional forms to create "a tense climate of balanced opposition."*]

In an early poem addressed to his mentor, Yvor Winters, Thom Gunn writes:

You keep both Rule and Energy in view,
Much power in each, most in the balanced two:
Ferocity existing in the fence
Built by an exercised intelligence.

These potentially counterdestructive principles exist everywhere in his work, not sapping the poems of their strength but creating a tense climate of balanced opposition. Any poet worth thinking twice about possesses *at least* an energetic mind; but it is the harnessing of this energy which makes for excellence. In Gunn's work an apparently unlimited energy of vision finds, variously, the natural boundaries which make expression—and clarity—possible.

The exact balance of Rule and Energy occurs rarely enough in even the greatest poets. For the most part, a superabundance of either principle damages the final product, so that one is left wishing that, say, Ginsberg had Rule equal to his Energy or, conversely, that Wilbur had less control over more content. This is not meant to disparage either poet, both of whom have on many occasions achieved the precarious balance of great art. My purpose here is to suggest how Gunn, over roughly a quarter century, has effected a balance of Rule and Energy all his own, creating in the process a body of poems able to withstand the closest scrutiny.

Gunn has lived in the U.S., mostly in San Francisco, since his graduation from Cambridge in 1953. But his early poems, especially, reflect his British heritage and the interest in "formalist" poetry characteristic of poets identified with the so-called Movement. "What poets like Larkin, Davie, Elizabeth Jennings, and I had in common at that time was that we were deliberately eschewing Mod-

ernism, and turning back, though not very thoroughly, to traditional resources in structure and method," says Gunn. This return to traditional resources was common to the period of the early fifties in general, not only in England, as the work of Ransom, Roethke, Wilbur and Lowell shows.

The traditionalist bent of Gunn's first book, *Fighting Terms* (1954), tugs in opposition to his rebellious themes. The poet most often invokes a soldier persona, an existential warrior in the act of self-definition. **"The Wound"** is among the best poems here, the first in the book; its speaker is variously Achilles or "the self who dreamt he was Achilles" (Gunn's description):

The huge wound in my head began to heal
About the beginning of the seventh week.
Its valleys darkened, its villages became still:
For joy I did not move and dared not speak;
Not doctors would cure it, but time, its patient skill.

The slightly "sprung" pentameter, the emblem of the wound that runs through the poem, and the hallucinatory progress of the narrator/persona together produce the wonderful tautness found in Gunn's earliest verse. Achilles's "real" wound is the death of his friend, his lover, Patroclus:

I called for armour, rose, and did not reel.
But, when I thought, rage at his noble pain
Flew to my head, and turning I could feel
My wound break open wide. Over again
I had to let those storm-lit valleys heal.

The poem represents a young man's effort, via the form of dramatic monologue, to distance himself from his subject; this stage is crucial in any poet's development. The beginning writer rarely has sufficient space between himself and his material. The use of a persona helps, for it allows the poet to search for a sympathetic alter-ego, to study himself indirectly, safely. The poem acts as a grid through which the light of self-expression passes; with luck, something of the poet's true nature remains.

The warrior-lover figure in these poems is self-consciously aggressive at times, but Gunn succeeds by sheer force of will in a poem like **"Carnal Knowledge,"** his most striking early poem:

Even in bed I pose: desire may grow
More circumstantial and less circumspect
Each night, but an acute girl would suspect
My thoughts might not be, like my body, bare.
I wonder if you know, or, knowing, care?
You know I know you know I know you know.

The speaker knows himself to be a poseur, and self-contempt gathers through the poem, leading ultimately to feelings of inadequacy: "I know of no emotions we can share." He asks her, then, to abandon him to his ineffectual stammering. Gunn affects a simplicity of diction reminiscent of the Elizabethan "plain style," but it is also the casual diction of an adolescent, full of a young lover's painful self-consciousness and disposition to emotional complexity. **"Carnal Knowledge,"** owing to its sheer verbal dexterity, stays in the mind where many of the poems in *Fighting Terms* fade.

Among the accomplished poems from this early phase of Gunn's career is **"Tamer and Hawk,"** which treats of the Rule/Energy conflict in tightly rhymed trimeter stanzas (though the last line in each has two instead of three feet):

> I thought I was so tough,
> But gentled at your hands
> Cannot be quick enough
> To fly for you and show
> That when I go I go
> At your commands.

The poem is a swift, bold stroke; its central conceit is a subtly worked-out metaphor—the hawk is possessed by but in turn possesses the tamer: "You but half-civilize, / Taming me in this way." The theme of possession and control, of the positive and negative aspects of any intense relationship (whether between man and woman or poet and his language), has rarely found more distinct expression. **"Tamer and Hawk"** is equal to anything in Gunn's later volumes, and it points the way to the direction of his next book.

The Sense of Movement (1957) fulfills the promise of Gunn's first book, displaying a new range of assimilated (or half-assimilated) voices and refining, somewhat, the central metaphor of his work—the conflict of intellect and emotion. Having left Cambridge, Gunn passed nearly a year in Rome and went to California, where he has remained. More importantly for his work, he began reading Yeats, whom he later refers to as "the second most disastrous influence after Milton." Yeats is disastrous because unassimilable; the Yeatsian cadences can only be parodied, not imitated; Yeatsian mannerisms possess a fatal attraction for young poets because they are too easily mimickable. But this overstates the case (as does Gunn).

The Yeatsian manner lent a new richness to Gunn's verse. His most widely anthologized poem, **"On the Move,"** derives explicitly from the master:

> The blue jay scuffling in the bushes follows
> Some hidden purpose, and the gust of birds
> That spurts across the field, the wheeling swallows
> Have nested in the trees and undergrowth.
> Seeking their instinct, or their poise, or both,
> One moves with an uncertain violence
> Under the dust thrown by a baffled sense
> Or the dull thunder of approximate words.

The attribution of "some hidden purpose" to the animal world, the seeking of "signs," the epithet "wheeling," the intense feelings controlled by a blank verse that is heavily enjambed: these traits recall Yeats, specifically, though the influence is not overbearing. On the contrary, Gunn

adds something of his own to a great modern tradition (as do Roethke and Larkin in *their* own ways).

"On the Move" opens for examination throughout the volume one of Gunn's central ideas: that *action* is crucial to existential self-definition and that individual freedom depends, necessarily, upon the freedom of others. Poets are rarely philosophers; they "lift" ideas which seem compatible, which affect their sensibility and set their own language in motion. Gunn's arguments come, explicitly, from Sartre's lecture *L'Existentialisme est un humanisme*:

> When a man commits himself to anything, fully realizing that he is not only choosing what he will be, but is thereby at the same time a legislator deciding for the whole of mankind—in such a moment a man cannot escape from the sense of complete and profound responsibility. There are many, indeed, who show no such anxiety. But one affirms that they are merely disguising their anguish or are in flight from it.

So Gunn's heroes race up the highway "as flies hanging in heat." Their uniforms—leather jackets and goggles--lend an impersonality which is terrifying to spectators. "They strap in doubt—by hiding it, robust— / And almost hear a meaning in their noise." Yet Gunn admires them: "Men manufacture both machine and soul," he asserts. This supreme existential notion, that *soul* as well as machine has its ontological basis in the creative will, lifts **"On the Move"** out of the realm of commonplace observation or glorification of the motorcyclists. "It is a part solution, after all," the poet says. The Boys are, at least, self-defined; they have *chosen* their form of life. Gunn concludes the poem:

> At worst, one is in motion, and at best,
> Reaching no absolute, in which to rest,
> One is always nearer by not keeping still.

A Zen master would no doubt object; nevertheless, Gunn isolates an important "belief" of our times: that motion is itself a positive quality, a denial of death, an assertion of will over inert matter.

Much of *The Sense of Movement* was written while Gunn studied at Stanford under Yvor Winters, and these poems reflect his teacher's aesthetic to some extent. To Winters, says Gunn, poetry "was an instrument for exploring the truth of things, as far as human beings can explore it, and it can do so with greater verbal exactitude than prose can manage." Yet Gunn's notion of poetry goes well beyond the narrow strictures of Winters, admitting a wider range of feeling. Indeed, his belief that reality inheres in the particulars of experience almost works against Winters's dedication to abstract reason. Gunn's poetry is not intellectual, finally; rather, it explores concrete reality in a sensuous manner. The worst poems in this book, in fact, could be called "arguments." They make assertions about the human condition (as in **"Vox Humana"**) such as the following: "Much is unknowable." The best work here embodies the texture of Gunn's own life, as in **"At the Back of the North Wind"**:

All summer's warmth was stored there in the hay;
Below, the troughs of water froze: the boy
Climbed nightly up the rungs behind the stalls
And planted deep between the clothes he heard
The kind wind bluster, but the last he knew
Was sharp and filled his head, the smell of hay.

His sense-receptors come alive here, pricked by experience, registered in tough, clear language. These traits carry over into his next, and better, book.

My Sad Captains (1961) can, without strain, be called a "watershed" in Gunn's career. Its two parts neatly separate the early style (formal poetry about the creative will and self-determination) and the later, freer style (largely concerned with the interplay of man and nature and the necessity of love). Gunn never abandons metrical verse, but the echoes of Yeats and others disappear. *Captains* is possibly Gunn's strongest book to date.

Part I bears an epigraph from Shakespeare's *Troilus* relevant to my overall theme: "The will is infinite and the execution confined, the desire is boundless and the act a slave to limit." Again, Gunn's preoccupation with Rule and Energy surfaces. The book opens with one of his finest poems, **"In Santa Maria del Popolo,"** a meditation on Caravaggio's famous "Conversion of St. Paul." In the painting Paul makes a crucial existential choice, and this appealed to the younger Gunn; Paul sprawls before his horse, arms uplifted:

I see him sprawl,
Foreshortened from the head, with hidden face,
Where he has fallen, Saul becoming Paul.
O wily painter, limiting the scene
From a cacophony of dusty forms
To the one convulsion, what is it you mean
In that wide gesture of the lifting arms?

Gunn's conception of an existential moment widens with this poem; where previously his self-defining heroes asserted themselves willfully, even recklessly (as in **"The Beaters,"** a poem about sadists), here the poet focuses on the act of contrition as an heroic gesture. Saul *limits* himself in becoming Paul, much in the way Caravaggio limits his scene to "the one convulsion" or the way Gunn himself concentrates on one image. These acts of limitation, in effect, gather the energies which might otherwise disperse.

The Gunn who celebrated soldiers and motorcyclists is not quite finished, however; most of the remaining poems in Part I resurrect earlier personae. **"Innocence"** treats of a young soldier's schooling in indifference, "A compact innocence, child-like and clear, / No doubt could penetrate, no act could harm." The irony here can, indeed, be called an advance from the early celebration of the soldier-hero. **"Black Jackets"** represents a critique of the heroic mode of *The Sense of Movement*; the red-haired boy who drove a van on weekdays is metamorphosed on Sundays—becoming *not* an individual hero but a parody of the rebel he affects, no longer possessing even the sim-

ple virtue of movement which implies a physical if not metaphysical inclination toward the future:

He stretched out like a cat, and rolled
The bitterish taste of beer upon his tongue,
And listened to a joke being told:
The present was the things he stayed among.

Part I is the culmination of Gunn's early style, participating in the same mode it criticizes.

The last stanza of **"Waking in a Newly-Built House"** could serve as an epigraph to Gunn's mature style:

Calmly, perception rests on the things,
and is aware of them only in
their precise definition, their fine
lack of even potential meanings.

From here on, Gunn will aim more to describe than to prescribe experience. The poems in Part II, written in syllabics, move beyond the rigid expectations of formal verse; syllabics force on the poem a nerve-wrackingly regular irregularity: the reader *feels* the arbitrary restraint of a given number of syllables per line. When syllabics work, the effect is stunning, unsettling: the lines seem cut off like fingers, raw, unbandaged.

"Flying Above California" takes up the theme of perception, extending it:

Sometimes
on fogless days by the Pacific,
there is a cold hard light without break

that reveals merely what is—no more
and no less. That limiting candour,

that accuracy of the beaches,
is part of the ultimate richness.

"That limiting candour" is a new restraint, a new Rule to harness Gunn's Energy of vision. The poet longs to see *beyond* what is there; he wants description to give way to revelation. But seeing things "exactly as they are" (in Wallace Stevens's phrase) places a necessary formal restraint upon the poet; he must learn to keep his eye on the object. *"La poète,"* says André Gide, *"est celui qui regarde."* The hard light of sustained attention will yield, for Gunn, a batch of his finest lyrics.

"Considering the Snail" seems to me the best poem in this book. The poet's vision here filters through a wide-angle lens: "The snail pushes through a green / night." A deep image unifies the poem, this magnified view of a creature moving "in a wood of desire, / pale antlers barely stirring / as he hunts." Gunn's old interest in *will* emerges for reconsideration. There is no will here, perhaps: "I cannot tell," he admits, "what power is at work, drenched there / with purpose." Gunn examines the life-force at its most elemental level, and this snail's low fury is not finally of a different substance from that of the gang-boys

Gunn catches the sense of impending transformation in the opening poems, such as **"Rites of Passage,"** where he says that "Something is taking place." Now "Horns bud bright in my hair. / My feet are turning hoof." The transformation even into a pig is complete in **"Moly,"** the title poem. Having failed to discover that miraculous and saving flower, the narrator has become, literally, a pig, transmogrified by Circe: "I push my big grey wet snout through green, / Dreaming the flower I have never seen."

"For Signs" follows, a remarkable poem written with that luminous clarity which always attends Gunn at his best:

> In front of me, the palings of a fence
> Throw shadows hard as board across the weeds;
> The cracked enamel of a chicken bowl
> Gleams like another moon; each clump of reeds
> Is split with darkness and yet bristles whole.
> The field survives, but with a difference.

The poet's eye is passive here, the eye of an Impressionist painter, wide, open to fluctuations of atmosphere and light. But the imagination, as Coleridge observed, takes what is given and transforms it, dissolves and recombines that object; "the real is shattered and combined," says Gunn. Outward vision gives way, rapidly, to inward: "I recognize the pale long inward stare." The process of continuous creation cannot be checked, but it has its own laws, seen here as analogous to zodiacal fluctuations, this "Cycle that I in part am governed by." The poem ends cleanly and with force:

> I lean upon the fence and watch the sky,
> How light fills blinded socket and chafed mark.
> It soars, hard, full, and edged, it coldly burns.

"From the Wave" is a central poem in **Moly,** though a modest one. Its theme is controlled innocence, balance; though ostensibly a poem about surfing, its theme again is Rule and Energy, this time with a new metaphor. One could easily substitute poets for surfers in the following passage:

> Their pale feet curl, they poise their weight
>   With a learn'd skill.
> It is the wave they imitate
>   Keeps them so still.

A line from Theodore Roethke comes to mind: "This shaking keeps me steady." Herein lies the paradox of art, that true art is eternal but created out of the temporal; the finer the balance of antinomies, the finer the poem. "Balance is triumph in this place, / Triumph possession," Gunn concludes. Capturing the innocence of the surfers, men wedded temporarily to nature, "Half wave, half men," the poet himself rides easily on the waves of his emotion, tracking the waves steadily with artful poise. He affects a model of linguistic control.

The antinomies of motion and stillness give way, in **"Tom-Dobbin,"** to the parallel opposition of mind and instinct;

Gunn creates a centaur-like figure: half man, half horse. Only in the moment of orgasm does fusion take place:

> In coming Tom and Dobbin join to one—
> Only a moment, just as it is done:
> A shock of whiteness, shooting like a star,
> In which all colours of the spectrum are.

Gunn explores this paradoxical union in a five-part sequence, in effect a meditation on the possibility of union between lovers, "Selves floating in the one flesh we are of."

Many of the later poems in **Moly** re-create the mood of the late sixties: drugs, hard rock music, ecstatic experiences—all are evoked, beautifully. Gunn has written movingly of this period in his prose as well:

> And now that the great sweep of the acid years is over,
> I cannot unlearn the things that I learned during them,
> I cannot deny the vision of what the world might be like.
> Everything that we glimpsed—the trust, the brotherhood,
> the repossession of innocence, the nakedness of spirit—is
> still a possibility and will continue to be so.

Moly culminates in **"Sunlight,"** a poem of lyric grace and verbal control. "What captures light belongs to what it captures" sums up Gunn's meaning; he captures sunlight, his metaphor for that luminous concentration of experience in language which is called poetry; the poem demonstrates Gunn's miraculous poise, his balance of conflicting powers. The sun's "concentrated fires / Are slowly dying," but this matters only a little. "The system of which the sun and we are part / Is both imperfect and deteriorating." And yet, the sun "outlasts us at the heart." He ends by hymning the sunflower, the "yellow centre of the flower" which inherits the light, transforms color and shape, "Still re-creating in defining them." Of the flower, he asks:

> Enable us, altering like you, to enter
> Your passionless love, impartial but intense,
> And kindle in acceptance round your centre,
> Petals of light lost in your innocence.

In a sense, **Jack Straw's Castle** (1976) is an extension of **Moly.** The poems spring from the same source, that quasi-mystical sense of "continuous creation." These latest poems examine, especially in the eleven-part title sequence, the consequence of heightened self-consciousness and the necessity of human community and communication. Gunn ranges widely here, from his English past to his Californian present, but a strange new continuity obtains, as if the poet's life had ceased from previous linearity. Past and present now inform each other—exist simultaneously in the Bergsonian *durée* of the poem.

"The Geysers," a four-part sequence, is the heart of **Jack Straw's Castle,** and its language is richly descriptive, physical, imagistic:

> This is our bedroom, where we learn the air,
> Our sleeping bags laid out in the valley's crotch.

I lie an arm-length from the stream and watch
Arcs fading between stars.

The poet loosens, gradually, his grip on self-consciousness, and the poetry itself loosens; meters break down as barriers break; the poet enters that liminal border between himself and others in the bathhouse:

> torn from the self
> > in which I breathed and trod
> I am
> > I am raw meat
> > > I am a god

An attitude of benevolence and communal love emerges as a solution to self-confinement.

Yet its obverse, self-entrapment, obsesses the poet in the title poem, **"Jack Straw's Castle."** Whereas self-containment was, in his earlier books, seen as a positive move in the direction of existential self-definition, now only anxiety attends this limitation:

> isn't there anyone
> anyone here besides me
>
> sometimes I find myself wondering
> if the castle is castle at all
> a place apart, or merely
> the castle that every snail
> must carry around till his death

Within the metaphorical castle, hero Jack examines each room in turn, especially the cellars. One cannot be sure whether these are *real* rooms or the rooms of each dream; "dream sponsors" occur, such as Charles Manson and the Medusa, adding to the nightmarish quality of the poem. In fact, the poem may be thought of as a descent into the infernal regions of the unconscious mind. Jack drops into levels of subliminal mentality, digging away roots, delving into the foundations of selfhood, entering into a pure world of necessity where "They, the needs, seek ritual and ceremony / To appease themselves." The hero gets trapped here, temporarily, where there is "nothing outside the bone / nothing accessible." He says,

> I sit
> trapped in bone
> I am back again
> where I never left, I sit
> in my first instant and where
> I never left
> petrified at my centre.

Led by the demonic killer, Manson, who appears a second time, Jack assumes that something other than himself exists, even as the mere existence of evil implies a moral context. A strange staircase appears, the symbolic exit to another realm; but there is another temporary setback when this staircase ends at a sheer drop-off, with "bone-chips which must / at one time have been castle" heaped below it.

It is finally the urge to contact a reality beyond the castle's boundaries which brings the sequence to its tensely beautiful and haunting conclusion. Jack wakens to realize that someone is in bed with him; he is no longer alone: "So humid, we lie sheetless—bare and close, / Facing apart, but leaning ass to ass." This merest contact, ass to ass, is a hinge between Jack and something other, a bridge, a way out. Is it a dream or not? He shrugs: "The beauty's in what is, not what may seem." And in any case, "With dreams like this, Jack's ready for the world." So the poem ends, not conclusively, but with some optimism.

In essence, the sequence re-creates in miniature the entire journey Gunn has undertaken from *Fighting Terms* to the present, from self-consciousness to an outward turning; he recognizes the possibilities for love, for attachment to the beautiful and terrible flux of "continuous creation" in which all that matters is what Dorothy Parker, referring to Hemingway, called "grace under pressure," what I call a delicate balance of Energy and Rule.

The final section of *Jack Straw's Castle* exhibits some of Gunn's finest work to date, including **"Autobiography,"** which recollects the poet's adolescence in Hampstead:

> The sniff of the real, that's
> what I'd want to get
> > how it felt
> to sit on Parliament
> Hill on a May evening
> studying for exams skinny
> seventeen dissatisfied
> > yet sniffing such
> a potent air, smell of
> grass in heat from
> the day's sun

"The Cherry Tree" moves from literal memoir to mythic time; Gunn takes the tree for his metaphor of self-transformation, the organic metaphor of inclusion; for as the tree grows, it appropriates its surroundings, it participates in the flux:

> it starts as a need
> and it takes over, a need
> to push
> > push outward
> from the centre, to
> bring what is not
> from what is, pushing
> till at the tips of the push
> something comes about

From metrical to free verse, Gunn shows himself capable of mastering his experience, of translating *chronos* into *mythos,* of creating a language at once energetic and supremely under control.

Already Gunn is a poet of considerable status in contemporary British poetry. He has added to the language a handful of lyrics which may well survive the terrible winnowing process of time. And surely his struggle for existential self-affirmation, his reaching beyond self-confinement into the realm of community and love are central to our time if we do not wish to become barbarians. His effort to rule by intelligence the natural energies which lead, too often, to self-mutilation and, worse, the destruction of others, is exemplary. Thom Gunn is, in short, an essential poet, one for whom we should be grateful.

Michael Hulse (essay date 1983)

SOURCE: "The Repossession of Innocence," in *Quadrant,* Vol. XXVII, No. 4, April, 1983, pp. 65-9.

[*In the following essay, Hulse explores the role of innocence in Gunn's verse.*]

That generation of poets that emerged in Britain during the 'fifties, from start to finish of that long decade—how easy it has been for us to pretend we saw them clearly, and how little excuse they have given us for the pretence! There is Larkin, stiffening as he reaches sixty, but still interesting in the little he publishes. There is Enright, refining his ironic line with unfailing if inadequate urbanity. There is Elizabeth Jennings, bland, featureless, still writing poems. And Donald Davie, surviving his changes with an air of wear and tear that is elderly and authoritative. And Silkin with his mythic vision, and Ted Hughes with *his*: Hughes, most pleasing of them all to the Academy, famously fabricating his unrelenting myths at almost the same pace as Peter Redgrove.

Hughes alone can keep entire university industries alive. And then there is the man whose name was at one time inseparably linked to that of Hughes: Thomson William Gunn, of Gravesend and Hampstead and Cambridge, in 1956 labelled "a tough thinker writing for intellectual toughs like himself", today looking quite the opposite of tough *or* intellectual, and looking if anything rather adrift in his San Franscisco life.

> At worst, one is in motion; and at best,
> Reaching no absolute, in which to rest,
> One is always nearer by not keeping still.

Certainly Gunn has not kept still; but the perception of movement that gave subtlety to **'On the Move'**, in *The Sense of Movement* (1957), no longer informs his recent work, in which "boys and girls / whoosh by on skate boards", and it is far from clear what it might be that Gunn is nearer *to*.

The qualities that distinguished Thom Gunn's poetry at its best have been widely glossed and described, not least by the poet himself, who said of *Moly* in 1971 that the collection might be seen as "a debate between the passion for definition and the passion for flow." This polarity was used by Gunn's advocate, Clive Wilmer, for the title of a widely-read essay, in which Wilmer, commenting on the poem **'Iron Landscapes'** (in *Jack Straw's Castle,* 1976), added that "the dialectic of permanence and change" is

"the very dialectic which determines the creative tensions of Gunn's poetry." Thom Gunn himself has done much to confirm this view of his work, particularly in the following sentences from his essay 'My Life up to Now', where the fundamental polarity is shown to be intimately related to a wider vision:

> But my life insists on continuities—between America and England, between free verse and metre, between vision and everyday consciousness. So, in the 'sixties, at the height of my belief in the possibilities of change, I knew that we all continue to carry the same baggage: in my world, Christian does not shed his burden, only his attitude to it alters. And now that the great sweep of the acid years is over, I cannot unlearn the things that I learned during them, I cannot deny the vision of what the world might be like. Everything that we glimpsed—the trust, the brotherhood, the repossession of innocence, the nakedness of spirit—is still a possibility and will continue to be so.

There have been various critics who agree with Alan Bold that Gunn "can, in fact, be staggeringly naive", and Donald Davie, writing recently in the *London Review of Books,* expressed concern at finding Gunn "still starry-eyed about the acid dropping sixties"; but I think we are helped further toward an understanding of what makes Gunn's poetry work when it is successful and fail when it is bad if we consider how much in his basic "dialectic" is an attempt at "the repossession of innocence".

Innocence is the touchstone even in the earliest of Gunn. In *Fighting Terms* (1954) the nostalgia for "an undeniable good" in **'A Kind of Ethics',** for "right meanings" in **'For a Birthday',** reads like an annotation of the second poem in the book, **'Here Come the Saints'**:

> Here come the saints: so near, so innocent,
> They gravely cross the field of moonlit snow;
> We villagers gape humbly at the show.
> No act or gesture can suggest intent.
> They only wait until the first cock crow
> Batters our ears, and with abrupt and violent
> Motions into the terrible dark wood they go.

That is the whole poem. It is slight and was rightly dropped from the *Selected Poems 1950—1975,* but it is worth noticing because, behind the Audenesque ending, behind the emblematic design of darkness and snow and cock crow, behind the rather arthritic theatricals ("gravely cross", "gape humbly", the abruptness and violence of those motions), there is a clear sense that the *impulse* of the poem was one of concern. The otherness of innocence is enacted here as it is in **'Looking Glass'**, where the poet writes: "I still hold Eden in my garden wall." Less persuasively, no doubt: but the root concern is recognisably the same.

And it is recognisably the same in that first book's first and major poem, **'The Wound'**, which Gunn has referred to as "my first real poem". The poem has been widely reprinted, so here I quote only the last of its five stanzas:

> I called for armour, rose, and did not reel.
> But, when I thought, rage at his noble pain

Flew to my head, and turning I could feel
My wound break open wide. Over again
I had to let those storm-lit valleys heal.

With its Trojan War background and its foregrounding of
the figure of Achilles, and especially in its strong reminiscence throughout of Shakespear'e Patroclus—"Those
wounds heal ill that men do give themselves"—this poem
enigmatically invites (and rebuffs) speculation as to what
is *meant* by the wound. I think exploration must be guided by Patroclus, in so far as considering the wounds that
men do to themselves in connection with what that final
stanza appears to posit as a form of mental anguish brings
us very quickly to the nature of knowledge. The fourth
stanza of the poem gives us this: "I was myself: subject
to no man's breath." This is clear enough, militarily, as
far as it goes; it also suggests very strongly the *absence*
of the reported knowledge conveyed by cackling Ther-
sites a line or so later. Such absence is repose, is peace:
"my belt hung up, sword in the sheath." The sword, in
such conditions, knows no purpose; and we remember
briefly that loaded word "intent" in **'Here Come the
Saints'.** The wound that heals worst is knowledge, with
all the hurtful intent that knowledge brings with it. The
absence of knowledge is a pure purposeless peace.

This does not explain away the highly unsatisfactory riddle of **'The Wound',** but I think it at least suggests that
the core of the poem is the question of innocence and
knowledge, Eden and exile. I say this without any wish to
reduce the extremely pleasing suggestiveness which Gunn's
ambiguity produces. But, if we see this, Gunn's development through his next volumes at once becomes more
meaningful. *The Sense of Movement* is no longer leather
fetishism and Sartrian talk of the will, *My Sad Captains*
(1961) is no longer syllabic fascinations alone. If we go
along with Gunn's statement, in his essay on Hardy, that
all good writing is the product of obsession (and of course
we should be aware of the limitations of this view), then
we can see his own obsession as being with the nature of
innocence and everything in those two volumes as a discourse, from one angle or another, on innocence. The
famous motorcycle poems—**'On the Move'** and **'The
Unsettled Motorcyclist's Vision of His Death'**—imply
a context for "the created will" as well as an envy for the
"ignorance" of plants. Gunn has assured us that he is glad
to have grown up without a religion; nonetheless, the myth
of the Fall is present in his early poetry as an implicit
texture, from the pun of **'Carnal Knowledge'** through to
the paradox of 'Innocence', in which the will, fully directed by a sense of purpose, becomes insensitive even to evil,
and innocence, which "No doubt could penetrate, no act
could harm", becomes the very opposite of innocence,
looking upon a Nazi crime with subhuman unconcern.

The years from *My Sad Captains* to *Touch* (1967) mark
Gunn's most important widening of scope, not only in the
addition of syllabic and free verse forms to the metrical
precision of the 'fifties, but also in the colouring of the
idea of innocence in shades of compassion and trust.
Compassion of a kind was already in **'Considering the
Snail'** in 1961:

                    I would never have
        imagined the slow passion
        to that deliberate progress.

And trust becomes the thematic centre of poems like
'**Touch**' or '**The Discovery of the Pacific**' (in *Moly*) just
as the abuse of it links **'Confessions of the Life Artist'**
(in *Touch*) with **'The Idea of Trust'** (in *Jack Straw's
Castle*).

One particularly revealing poem from this period of San
Francisco openness, of confidence, LSD and aimlessness,
is '**Three**', published in 1971 in *Moly*:

        All three are bare.
    The father towels himself by two gray boulders,
        Long body, then long hair,
    Matted like rainy bracken, to his shoulders.

        The pull and risk
    Of the Pacific's touch is yet with him:
        He kicked and felt it brisk,
    Its cold live sinews tugging at each limb.

        It haunts him still:
    Drying his loins, he grins to notice how,
        Struck helpless with the chill,
    His cock hangs tiny and withdrawn there now.

        Near, eyes half closed,
    The mother lies back on the hot round stones,
        Her weight to theirs opposed
    And pressing them as if they were earth's bones.

        Hard bone, firm skin,
    She holds her breasts and belly up, now dry,
        Striped white where clothes have been,
    To the heat that sponsors all heat, from the sky.

        Only their son
    Is brown all over. Rapt in endless play,
        In which all games make one,
    His three-year nakedness is everyday.

        Swims as dogs swim.
    Rushes his father, wriggles from his hold.
        His body, which is him,
    Sturdy and volatile, runs off the cold.

        Runs up to me:
    Hi there hi there, he shrills, yet will not stop,
        For though continually
    Accepting everything his play turns up

        He still leaves it
    And comes back to that pebble-warmed recess
        In which the parents sit,
    At watch, who had to learn their nakedness.

The key, as so often with Gunn, who has been reluctant
to abandon his early love of the concluding apophtheg-
matic note, is in the ending. In the word "learn" we are

again being invited to consider the nature of knowledge, to consider the wound that takes so long to heal. The wound is knowledge; knowledge is the loss of innocence; and the impulse of the poem is its wish to repossess that lost innocence. The boy scampers to and fro in instinctual acceptance, while his parents, though naked too, are differentiated by their poses of grinning, of watching, and by the stripes on their bodies. There is indeed a sadness in their nakedness, since a lost innocence can never be relearnt: the mere world tells us so, for how can innocence be repossessed through knowing? If the poem has a certain clumsiness, it still succeeds in its central image of parents and child as emblems of paradise lost. The ideas, Gunn has said, came first; he was, he says, "preoccupied by certain related concepts", which he defines as "trust, openness, acceptance, innocence". The chance meeting on the beach gave him the embodiment. "In what sense might you say that innocence can be repossessed," he had wondered; and the chance meeting suggested Edenic nakedness as an apt emblem of repossession, or at least the attempt to repossess.

Jack Straw's Castle showed Gunn in the mid 'seventies not much further than this: nakedness in 'The Geysers' is still a key emblem, and in fact it is possible to see this volume as the turning point at which the quest for innocence becomes little more than a naive acceptance of unthinking. The obsession that gave power to 'The Wound' and 'On the Move' and 'Considering the Snail' and 'The Discovery of the Pacific', even to 'Three', has been transformed into a disturbing passivity in the face of experience. 'The Outdoor Concert' makes much of "the secret", 'Autobiography' speaks of "The sniff of the real" as if such a phrase were unproblematic, and in this absence of the pressure of thought upon his own perceptions Gunn betrays a lack of fidelity to his own most productive obsession. In *The Passages of Joy,* the poet's first collection for six years, this trend is regrettably confirmed.

1982 has seen the publication of a new book of poetry by Thom Gunn and a collection of prose pieces, both critical and autobiographical, written over a period of nearly two decades and now published as *The Occasions of Poetry.*

The Thom Gunn who emerges from these two books is not a major figure, either as poet or as critic, and the reader who meets Gunn for the first time in this work may well be puzzled to discover that a reputation of some weight is behind this writer's words.

That Gunn the critic is lacking in authority is the lesser surprise, I expect, since no one has ever supposed him to be remarkable for insight. *The Occasions of Poetry* collects short reviews of Gary Synder, Rod Taylor, Dick Davis and James Merrill, reprints essays on William Carlos Williams and Robert Duncan, and anthology introductions to Fulke Greville and Ben Jonson, and a lecture on Hardy's use of ballad forms". . . and then passes on to forty pages of autobiographical fragments. There is little point in demonstrating the lack of scholarly discipline in Gunn's essays: his manner is too naive, and smacks rather too much of impatience, for his achievement ever to be any-

thing but literary journalism, at times perhaps of a sophisticated kind. Possibly we are surprised if we remember that Gunn joined the English department at Berkeley, California, in 1959, and left in 1966, a year after being given tenure: what, we wonder, had he published in those years, that a university of high standing should wish him to teach on its staff full-time? *The Occasions of Poetry,* however, knows nothing of the academic career-maker: only unambitious journalistic work is reprinted.

This said, certain stray remarks remain in the mind after one puts down this book. I am not thinking only of silly assertions, such as "Robert Hunter's words for the Grateful Dead or Robbie Robertson's for the Band are good ballads and good poems by any standard." The excessive trust that we all agree on what is "good", and that the phrase "by any standard" is uncontroversial, need no comment. But there are other statements which, because they are superficially less contentious, need careful consideration all the more. One such is Gunn's view, in the piece on Hardy, that ballad poetry and the reflective lyric share a tonality, defined as "economy and impersonality", and proceed from a common root. This view can be supported, but only with carefully chosen examples, for the majority of poems that can be described as reflective lyric—such as Gray's 'Elegy'—are as different as anything can be from ballads such as 'Edward' or 'Sir Patrick Spens'. Gunn suppresses the inconvenient evidence. Or again: in his introduction to Jonson's poetry, Gunn writes:

> . . . all poetry is occasional: whether the occasion is an external event like a birthday or a declaration of war, whether it is an occasion of the imagination, or whether it is in some sort of combination of the two". . . The occasion in all cases—literal or imaginary—is the starting point, only, of a poem, but it should be a starting point to which the poet must in some sense stay true.

This looks attractive at first glance: but in fact it very soon proves to be an insight of considerable limitation, one devoid of the liberating effect of critical wisdom. What, after all, do we gain by generalising the term "occasional" in this way? The term traditionally has a fairly precise meaning, so that it can be used as a tool in analysis; in Gunn's usage that exactness is lost and the tool becomes useless. The attraction of the idea is only brief, for its implications are counterproductive.

Clive Wilmer suggests in his introduction to *The Occasions of Poetry* that Gunn has written "criticism of lasting interest" (which I do not think is the case) and that Gunn, by virtue of his practice as a poet, is a particularly good reader of other poets' work. This second observation works better in reverse, for it seems to me that it is *from* the responses to other poetry *toward* his own poetry that we see the most interesting patterns emerging. In the 1965 Williams essay, for example, Gunn praises "a habitual sympathy" and sees Williams' "stylistic qualities" as governed by "a tenderness and generosity of feeling which make them fully humane". This was when Gunn was writing *Positives* (1966) and *Touch* (1967), collections in which a naively generous sympathy begins to move to the forefront of Gunn's poetry. Again: in 'My Life up to Now' Gunn writes of metre and free verse:

> Rhythmic form and subject-matter are locked in a permanent embrace: that should be an axiom nowadays. So, in metrical verse, it is the nature of the control being exercised that becomes part of the life being spoken about. It is poetry making great use of the conscious intelligence, but its danger is bombast—the controlling music drowning out everything else. Free verse invites a different style of experience, improvisation. *Its* danger lies in being too relaxed, too lacking in controlling energy.

This reminds us of Gunn's concern, writing of Snyder, that looseness may lead to dullness, that "the accidental world itself might take over the poem". This concern reflects the troubles in which Gunn as technician has found himself, to an ever greater degree, since the mid-sixties.

What then of Gunn the poet in 1982? *The Passages of Joy* is a bad, boring book, the least endearing Gunn has written. It is bad because the pursuit of innocence has been filtered through that "habitual sympathy" to become a big sentimental gesture which announces that it wishes to love and understand the world, but which loses power by its very inclusiveness. It is bad because this sentimentality is confused with a scale of humane values, and therefore produces poems that are at one of two extremes: either they merely record series of impressions, or they attempt heavy-handed didactic lessons. As to the first, Peter Porter recently wrote in *The Observer:* "He does not strike me as having the right ear to make a success of poems which are essentially vignettes of casual urban life." And as to the second, I think Gunn's didacticism could best be described as a kind of Frisco Vernon Scannell: **'Sweet Things'** and **'As Expected'** are good examples of what I mean.

And this badness becomes boring because that tension of definition and flow, the dialectic of permanence and change, has been complacently removed. The implication of this is upsetting: it suggests that Gunn has settled into a self-satisfaction that poet of **'On the Move'** could never have countenanced. And in practice it means that the long loose poems are less under control than ever: the accidental world takes over, and that dullness results that is the concomitant of any uninspired improvisation.

Lest this seem unfair, here is the second half of a poem called **'New York'**:

> I return to a sixth floor
> where I am staying: the sun
> ordering the untidy kitchen,
> even the terraced black circles
> in the worn enamel are bright,
> the faucet dripping,
> the parakeets chirping quietly
> domestic about their cage,
> my dear host in the bed and
> his Newfoundland on it, together

> stretching, half-woken, as
> I close the door.

>   I calm down,
> undress, and slip
> in between them and think
> of household gods.

I promise that this poem is among the better half of the collection. What is bad here is present not only in the wholly disproportionate title nor even in the pretence of the final line, where we merely want to ask what Gunn was *really* thinking. The badness is the absence of any pressure whatsoever on the part of a shaping spirit. That absence can be defended, certainly, if we say it remains true to the random, unstructured character of actual experience: but a defence of this kind has always seemed to me extremely weak, since it admits that nothing has been *done,* nothing *made* by the poet, beyond the elements of notation. To suppose that this elementary notation will then interest a reader, who presumably encounters similar experience and, if called upon to do so, can verbalise that experience in precisely the same manner—this, I think, is arrogant. It is an arrogance that is dismally self-satisfied: and the line that ends with "and", a line so utterly unconcerned about the demands a reader may feel impelled to make, only reinforces this impression.

I should not care to be misunderstood on this. I am not complaining about free verse, like a stuffy Edwardian; I am regretting that complacent, undisciplined misuse of it, a misuse which Gunn himself acknowledges to be the commonest flaw in open forms. My own opinion is that Gunn has an ear that belongs *between* the extremes: metre tempts him toward glibness of an Empsonian Fifties kind, and free forms bring out his self-indulgent worst. But the syllabics that gave many poems in *My Sad Captains, Touch* and *Moly* their air of moving uncramped within generous confines (and yet confined): these, I think, favoured Gunn's strengths most systematically. Innocence cannot be repossessed, of course, but the gesture of making the attempt to repossess it is an important and central one in Gunn, and its wistful halftruthfulness is distorted by clear-cut forms as well as by looseness.

I began by saying that it is difficult to see those poets who emerged in the 'fifties at all clearly, and Gunn perhaps poses some of the trickiest problems. Still, one thing is clear: Gunn has moved, and his movement has been all in one direction, so that in 1982, when—as Donald Davie has said—Gunn seems to have forgotten all he had ever learnt from the Elizabethans and Metaphysicals, I feel he has followed too far his principle of the 'sixties: "better, always, to accept too much than too little." Such acceptance, true, can be a kind of innocence. But it is an innocence that puts an end to poetry.

Paul Giles   (essay date 1987)

SOURCE: "Landscapes of Repetition: The Self-Parodic Nature of Thom Gunn's Later Poetry," in *Critical Quarterly,* Vol. 29, No. 2, Summer 1987, pp. 85-99.

[In the following essay, Giles examines the function of self-parody in Gunn's more recent poetry.]

One of the side-effects of the recent appointment of Ted Hughes as British Poet Laureate was to emphasise how far his compatriot Thom Gunn has diverged from the native English tradition. Although Hughes and Gunn were yoked together by the 1962 Faber *Selected Poems* and have become a pairing institutionalised by school syllabuses in England, Gunn now says he has 'almost nothing in common' with Hughes;[1] and indeed, if eyebrows were raised when Hughes delivered his pagan drench for the christening of Prince Harry, those brows might well have changed colour entirely had Gunn been called upon to consider the royal ceremony in terms of the dishevelled American urban landscapes which have characterised his latest work. Such cultural estrangement is, in many ways, not surprising bearing in mind Gunn has lived continuously in the United States (mostly in California) since graduating from Cambridge in 1953; nor is it surprising that the poetry Gunn has produced in the 1980s has been more in keeping with an American rather than an English literary idiom. Nevertheless, Gunn's American persona has been by no means universally welcomed in England: reviewing his 1982 collection *The Passages of Joy* in the *Times Literary Supplement,* for instance, Ian Hamilton accused Gunn of 'awkwardness' and 'narcissim' and said that most of these poems seemed to lack a 'genuine' quality.[2] But on closer inspection we find it is just this creative exploitation of narcissism which is currently engaging Gunn's poetic energies: he has spurned the 'genuine' landscapes of Ted Hughes for the elaborate artifices, the self-portraits in convex mirrors, more typical of John Ashbery. The purpose of this essay will be to focus upon Gunn's more recent poetry, some of it as yet uncollected, and, by identifying how this playfully narcissistic or self-parodic strain operates, to demonstrate how Gunn is now writing within a sophisticated postmodernist framework.

I

Parody depends upon a willing admission of dualism, an acknowledgement of the comic discrepancy between a primary ideal and a secondary reflection; and this kind of comedy was on the whole not evident in Gunn's first two books, *Fighting Terms* (1954) and *The Sense of Movement* (1957), which are probably still his most famous collections. Here dualism was an interloper, an obstruction to the poet's dream of re-attaining a state both passionate and Innocent, prelapsarian and pre-Saussurian:

I have reached a time when words no longer help. . .
Description and analysis degrade,
Limit, delay, slipped land from what has been. . .
All my agnostic irony I renounce
So I may climb to regions where I rest
In springs of speech, the dark before of truth

('For a birthday')

Necessarily expelled from this 'dark before of truth', however, Gunn found himself in the pincer grip of every kind of dualism: between reason and instinct, between the object signified and the verbal signifier, between self and the mirrored or posed self. The heroes of this early poetry—Elvis Presley, Lofty in the Palais de Danse, the motorcyclist riding into the walls of rain—are (supposedly) 'toughs' who refuse to truckle to the intrusions of effeminate human sensibility: the unsettled motorcyclist suppresses rumination in favour of violent, existential action. Nevertheless, the *mise en abime* of '**Carnal knowledge**'—'You know I know you know I know you know'— is typical of that uneasy fragmentation which pervades *Fighting Terms* and *The Sense of Movement*: indeed, the energy of this poetry derives largely from its internal tension, the way it feeds upon its own contradictions and is forever chasing its own tail, forever trying to accomplish the impossible task of renouncing its own agnostic irony by transcending its own linguistic system. But in Gunn's next collection, *My Sad Captains* (1961), a change of emphasis is apparent: '**Considering the Snail**' is a witting self-parody of the poet's earlier self-projection, the motorcyclist defining himself by belligerently joining 'the movement in a valueless world'. In contemplating the snail, Gunn is in fact reflecting upon himself:

He
moves in a wood of desire,
pale antlers barely stirring
as he hunts. I cannot tell
what power is at work, drenched there
with purpose, knowing nothing.
What is a snail's fury?

This comic bathos represents the snail as an objectified alternative self. Whereas in '**Carnal Knowledge**' the dislocating irony is tortuously wrapped inside a poem attempting to surmount that irony, in '**Considering the Snail**' Gunn willingly embraces a conception of parody along with the dualisms inherent within parodic form. Dualism implies doubling and division, and so the desire of *Fighting Terms* to erase contradictions and re-attain some form of primal unity has now been superseded by Gunn's recognition of the obdurate nature of fragmentation, ambiguity and open-endedness within the terrestrial world.

Throughout his later collections, Gunn has continued to meditate upon his own yearning for the security of absolute meaning: '**Baby song**', in the 1976 collection *Jack Straw's Castle,* caustically celebrates 'the private ease of Mother's womb' ('Why don't they simply put me back / Where it is warm and wet and black?'); but the significant fact here is the poem's title, 'Baby song'—for by signalling how infantile this desire is, the poet once again trains an ironic light upon his own performance. *Jack Straw's Castle* contains another self-parodic poem, '**Behind the Mirror**', which might have been seized upon eagerly by the late Jacques Lacan:

I and the reflected self seemed identical twins,
alike yet separate, two flowers from the same
  plant. . .
Narcissus glares into the pool: someone glares
  back. . .

He escapes, he does not escape, he is the same,
  he is other.
If he drowned himself he would be one with
  himself". . . one flower,
one waxy star, giving perfume, unreflecting.

The 'mirror stage', for Lacan, occurs when a child, recognising his own image in the mirror, emerges from the 'imaginary' order of plenitude and wholeness into the 'symbolic' order necessarily imbued with otherness and absence. Thus in **'Behind the Mirror'** Gunn/Narcissus recounts a nostalgic wish to become 'one with himself', to obliterate difference; but again the poem operates parodically, to distance the pull of regression, because Gunn knows that in the end Narcissus can never be 'unreflecting'. There is a pun here on *unreflecting*: Narcissus wants to avoid seeing his own image 'reflected' in the pool; but he also hopes to be 'unreflecting' in a mental sense, endowed with the same preference for instinct over reflection that characterised Gunn's heroes in his poems of the 1950s. So 'unreflecting' is just what this poem's final word is not: on the contrary, the word punningly reflects upon itself, splits itself into two; and this neatly encapsulates the sense of irony in this poem, whereby the longing to retreat into an unreflecting situation **'Behind the Mirror'** is itself subjected to parodic linguistic reflection.

There are many other examples of this self-parodic tendency in Gunn's recent work. He himself has commented upon how in **'Sweet Things'** (from the 1982 collection *The Passages of Joy*) the mongoloid street urchin sitting outside a laundromat comes to mirror the poet's own desire for sweetness:[3]

> 'Gimme a quarter!?' I
> don't give it, never have, not to him,
> I wonder why not, and as I
> walk on alone I realize
> it's because his seven-year-old mind
> never recognizes me, me
> for myself, he only says hi
> for what he can get, quarters to
> buy sweet things, one after another. . . .

This mentally-defective child disturbs Gunn because he is a dark reflection of the author of *Fighting Terms*: someone never content to allow objects an autonomous existence, but always determined to manipulate them forcibly so as to extract (in the mongoloid's case) sweet things, or (in Gunn's case) the moral equivalent of sweet things: that is, aphorisms and meanings designed to protect his own troubled ego.

II

We find in **'Sweet things'**, then, Gunn parodying his own manic need to hammer out meanings from the world around him. In a 1986 interview with Graham Fawcett, Gunn voiced his awareness of the inevitable shadow between worldly event and literary meaning by declaring he had never quite found in poetry 'the correct incantation of a past feeling'. The saccharine signifier can never do justice to the rough-hewed signified: 'it gets a little too smooth', said Gunn, 'even when I'm talking about difficulties'.[4] So it is one of the functions of the self-parody in Gunn's work to constitute a radical challenge to traditional notions of poetic meaning. This was an idea first broached in his aptly-named **'Waking in a newly-built house'**, the poem which began the second part of *My Sad Captains*:

> Calmly, perception rests on the things,
> and is aware of them only in
> their precise definition, their fine
> lack of even potential meanings.

Such lack of even potential meanings is characteristic of the shift in emphasis within Gunn's poetry which *My Sad Captains* heralded. The first part of the collection consists of poems in classical and regular forms revolving upon Gunn's established axis of romantic freedom compromised by the circumscriptions of language and civilisation, and prefaced by an epigraph from *Troilus and Cressida* ('The will is infinite and the execution confined, the desire is boundless and the act a slave to limit'); the second part, however, took as its epigraph two sentences from Fitzgerald's *Last Tycoon*: 'I looked back as we crossed the crest of the foothills—with the air so clear you could see the leaves on Sunset Mountains two miles away. It's starting to you sometimes—just air, unobstructed, uncomplicated air.' Gunn's choice of Fitzgerald's description of what is unobstructed and uncomplicated suggests his new-found concern with how 'the things themselves are adequate', to quote again from **'Waking in a newly-built house.'** The influences at work here imply that American poetic heritage which Gunn has increasingly affiliated himself with: the journey away from ideas towards the specificity of concrete objects is reminiscent of Pound and William Carlos Williams, while the looser, more amorphous forms in which these poems of the 1960s are cast brings to mind the 'free verse' of Charles Olson and Robert Duncan. But Gunn's free verse differs from that of Olson and Duncan in so far as it invariably contains a latent dialectic whereby the new, freer idiom is implicitly arguing with the old standards of formal restraint. The 1967 *Touch* collection offers many examples of this: throughout the book there is a play around the idea of edge and edgelessness:

> As I support her, so, with
> my magnificent control,
> I suddenly ask: 'What if
> she has the edge over me?'

Thus **'Confessions of the life artist.'** Gunn's artificer wonders whether the natural life enjoyed by his model might not be superior to the 'magnificent control' asserted by his own artistry. The artist creates hard edges; but the model 'has the edge' in a metaphorical sense. In *Touch,* there is a conceptual progression away from fabricated edges towards a raw edgelessness: **'Berlin in ruins'** starts by asserting the city 'has an edge, or many edges', but it then goes on to discuss how the fanatical order associated with Berlin's Nazi era has now crumbled away. And this redundant social order becomes associated here with the 'stiff laurel' of Gunn's earlier verse forms, which tended forcibly to be contorted into a classical order, so that this passage into free verse is equated with the poet's psychological abandonment of the paraphernalia of violence. Gunn now prefers to 'touch' natural objects, as in **'Snowfall'**:

> . . . what the ice-packed heel must press
> Not quite resistant, not quite palpable,
> I find an edgelessness.

The final poem in **Touch** is appropriately entitled **'Back to life.'** But here we encounter a paradox: for the idea of returning **'Back to life'** through the medium of art is as much of a contradiction in terms as Gunn's proposed flight **'Behind the mirror.'** **'Back to life'** suggests a yearning after the kind of innocence sought for in **Fighting Terms,** a time when words no longer help and the duplicities of language can be cast aside. The difference is that in **Fighting Terms** this paradox disturbed Gunn and he attempted to cancel it, whereas in **Touch** he accepts the inexorable paradox and begins indeed to welcome it and to explore its poetic possibilities. In **Touch,** this manifests itself through a series of oxymorons, as Gunn openly flaunts the paradoxical nature of his art: he declares his intention to create a poetry of 'live marble' (in **'The girl of live marble'**); and in **'The kiss at Bayreuth'** we find another example of the kind of self-contradictory play mentioned earlier, where the resisting edges of art come up against the unresisting, swaying edgelessness of life:

> Colours drain, shapes blur, resisting,
> details swim together, the mass
> of the external wobbles, sways,
> disintegrating.". . .

We can say, then, that Gunn's poetry in **Touch** is engaged in a deliberate process of self-contradiction or self-parody in order to draw the reader's attention to the equivocal status allotted by the author to the whole idea of aesthetic artifice. We can say furthermore that the implicit dialectic in **Touch** between Gunn's earlier and later work—the way **'Berlin in ruins'** re-examines the imagery of **The Sense of Movement,** for example—is another instance of Gunn exploiting a parodic dualism to focus upon how poetic meanings become disintegrated and deconstructed: by reflecting upon his own earlier work, Gunn reveals its provisional and illusory condition. The critic Paul Fussell once wrote that the mistake of William Carlos Williams and other writers of 'free verse' was a naive inability to apprehend how their literary constructions are as much of a linguistic convention as the classical pentameters of Pope and Dryden; but Gunn rejects such naivety because he manipulates his free verse (and his sense of paradox) not in the hope of approaching some imaginary Innocence but rather parodically to destabilise and undermine meanings which have been conventionally pre-established.[5] **'Words'**, in Gunn's 1971 collection **Moly,** ends with a clean oxymoron signalling how the text distances itself from the claustrophobic confines of logical linguistic meaning:

> I was still separate on the shadow's ground
> But, charged with growth, was being altered,
> Composing uncomposed.

We are close here to the radical ambiguity and open-endedness advocated by Roland Barthes in **The Pleasure of the Text**: for Barthes, the conception of paradox operates to circumvent a punitive rationality and finality, that obsession with closure he associated with inquisitors of order such as Sade, Fourier and Loyola. By contrast, said Barthes, 'in the text of pleasure, the opposing forces are no longer repressed but in a state of becoming: nothing is really antagonistic, everything is plural'.[6] Gunn's 1982 collection **The Passages of Joy** includes a poem entitled **'Interruption'** where the author inspects his own reflection in the glass as he meditates upon his latest creative enterprise:

> . . . what makes me think
> The group of poems I have entered is
> Interconnected by a closer link
> Than any snapshot album's?

Gunn's parodic rupturing of his own text is commensurate with the abrasive open-endedness of **The Passages of Joy,** which presents the reader with snapshots of American life—the amusement arcade, the San Francisco streets—and carefully refuses to annotate, finalise or affix moral significance. Another poem in this collection, **'Song of a camera'**, makes explicit Gunn's rejection of the confections of poetic meaning:

> I cut the sentence
> out of a life
> out of the story
> with my little knife. . .
>
> so that another
> seeing the bits
> and seeing how
> none of them fits
>
> wants to add
> adverbs to verbs
> A bit on its own
> simply disturbs

Note the lack of punctuation here: we find no logical sequence, merely free-floating fragments. And 'A bit on its own / simply disturbs' could be the keynote of **The Passages of Joy** itself, with its random urban landscapes and disturbing sense of contingency.

III

This fragmentation or parody of textual meaning works in tandem with the way in which Gunn's poems parodically interrogate the idea of authorial identity. One example of Gunn's skill in ironising his own obsessions can be found in the title poem of the **Jack Straw's Castle** collection. Here we find the narrator brooding upon his imprisonment within the 'castle' of the ego:

why can't I leave my castle
he says, isn't there anyone
anyone here besides me

sometimes I find myself wondering
if the castle is castle at all
a place apart, or merely
the castle that every snail
must carry around till his death

The solipsism here recalls much of Gunn's earlier work, which despaired of matching internal fantasy with external fact; but in this poem Gunn deploys two tricks of language to undercut his castellated self. Firstly, the oxymoron of the title, **'Jack Straw's castle'**, reminds us that Jack Straw—the vagrant peasant leader of the Middle Ages—was the last person likely to possess a castle of his own, and so this oxymoron serves to burlesque the poet's implicit claims to isolation and autonomy. And secondly there is a pun on **'Jack Straw's castle'** which contradicts the author's mental imprisonment, for (though the poem does not openly admit this) Jack Straw's Castle is the name of a roundabout and well-known public house on the edge of Hampstead Heath in London, where Gunn was brought up and where many of his autobiographical pieces are set. The actuality of the location has the effect of demonstrating how the poetic voice must necessarily be left incomplete: the punning revelation of the objective fact of Jack Straw's Castle provides a guarantee of the insufficiency of the author's solipsism within the framework of his poem; and so it exemplifies Gunn's adroitness in mirroring or ironising his own narcissism.

Gunn's reflexive energies have not been directed only against his own poetry. **'Taylor Street'** (from *Touch*) deliberately mimics William Carlos Williams, for instance; while **'Considering the snail'** imitates or mirrors the style of Marianne Moore, so that the idea of parody contained within that latter poem is matched by the parodic nature of its form. In his book *The Survival of Poetry*, Martin Dodsworth took exception to this 'derivativeness' on Gunn's part, seeing it as the kind of 'susceptibility or even submissiveness before other people, and indeed before the world of things' that was intimately connected with the poet's more general themes of domination and submission;[7] and this charge of lacking a humanist centre of self has been levelled against Gunn by other critics, Colin Falck for instance:

> The real growing-points for Gunn's poetry. . . "must almost certainly be the points where the human faith and sympathy he longs for are already faintly present". . . he might at the same time be able to get himself clear of today's fashionably neo-primitive dissolution of the moral and social being into his constituent compulsions and energies and become a late and much-needed recruit to the battered ranks of humanism.[8]

Reviewing **Jack Straw's Castle** in the *Times Literary Supplement*, John Bayley raised similar questions about the dislocated aspects of Gunn's poetic identity by remarking: 'Gunn's poetry has often seemed to me to be not quite "real," to be, as it were, counterfeiting poetry with a highly accomplished and covertly malignant skill.'[9] For Gunn, however, such a dichotomy between 'real' and 'counterfeiting' is invalid; 'what we must remember', he wrote in his essay on Ben Jonson, 'is that artifice is not necessarily the antithesis of sincerity'—the truest poetry can be the most feigning.[10] Thus the elaborately contrived, parodic element in Gunn's work should not be dismissed as merely a decadent linguistic game, because this lapse in the poet's status as originator of his textual world— the death of the author, in Barthes' celebrated phrase— is typical of much postmodernist writing in recent years. **'Taylor Street'** and **'Considering the snail'** are indeed 'counterfeiting poetry', as Bayley would say; but this note of counterfeiting is not the result of some defect in Gunn's character (as Dodsworth suggested) but is rather designed to call into question our old notions of human identity. It is an interesting variation on the critic Harold Bloom's doctrine of the 'strong poet': whereas for Bloom the Romantic poet seeks to make space for his own identity to flourish by the process of concealing his poetic ancestors, for Gunn in **'Taylor Street'** and **'Considering the snail'** (and other poems) the open admission of ancestors and hence the constant adjacency of parody undermines any possibility of the (illusory) withdrawal of poetry into a hermetically—sealed, self-sufficient world.[11] Gunn's paradoxes and self-reflexive strategies prevent any possible retreat **'Behind the mirror'**: his poetry exposes itself to the variations of *reflection* in every sense.

IV

In his 1979 autobiographical essay 'My life up to now', Gunn wrote how in his work 'it has not been of primary interest to develop a unique poetic personality', and he acknowledged that 'This lack in me has troubled some readers'. Gunn attributed this sense of impersonality to his neoclassical inclinations, his willingness to be as 'derivative' as Ben Jonson and to 'borrow' from all kinds of different sources: 'I rejoice in Eliot's lovely remark that art is the escape from personality.'[12] An escape from humanist personality Gunn's work certainly is, but more than this, it embodies the kind of escape from the unified conception of a subjective self which is typical of postmodernist thinking. The dismantling of the ego in the critical writings of Barthes, Lacan and Foucault has become familiar to English-speaking audiences; less so, perhaps, is the work of Gilles Deleuze, whose 1972 book *Anti-Oedipus: Capitalism and Schizophrenia* rejected the 'imperialism' of Freudian analysis, with its emphasis upon neurosis and lack, substituting instead the idea of the psyche as a schizo-system in which things do not connect: Deleuze, like Foucault, was intent upon abolishing the autonomy of the subject and replacing it with a more impersonal (and, according to Deleuze, liberating) notion of the flow of desire: 'every "object" presupposes the continuity of a flow; every flow, the fragmentation of the object'.[13] In literary terms, these dislocations and discontinuities have manifested themselves in that interrogation of poetic meaning and identity we find most famously in postmodernist writers such as John Ashbery. As Charles Altieri has noted,

Ashbery 'turns self-reflexiveness into a metaphysical poetry', deploying a self-parodic dualism to undermine 'rhetorics that claim naturalness':[14]

> By refusing the vain poses of definite thoughts, the poem produces a self-consciousness capable of moving from perception to reflection, from immediacy to self-criticism to the opportunities for linguistic play that the multiple folds of consciousness allow. . . For Ashbery the mind stands toward its own knowing in the condition of infinite regressiveness that Derrida shows is the dilemma inherent in trying to know about the language we use in describing our knowledge.[15]

Gunn's poetry of the last twenty years is in a similar idiom, because it is grounded upon reflexive doubling and the transition between points of difference. Reflexive doubling is not an all-encompassing explanation of Gunn's work, and it can of course be seen in various conceptual contexts. For instance, in the second section of '**Misanthropos**', the long poem at the centre of *Touch,* dualism was apprehended pessimistically: the narrator, a 'courier after identity', found himself frustrated by the jarring homonyms at the end of each stanza which fragmented his poetic quest into a series of hollow, echoing puns, linguistic emblems of division:

> I passed no human on my trip, a slow one.
> Is it your luck, down there, to know one?
> > No one.

In *Moly,* by contrast, the transitions between points of difference contribute to a lucid transcendentalism which becomes a secularisation of Ralph Waldo Emerson's belief in the Oversoul:

> Water, glass, metal, match light in their raptures,
> Flashing their many answers to the one.
> > ('Sunlight')

Moly describes a universe where objects which are apparently isolated and fragmented become redeemed by 'the unifying spirit of nature:'. . . each clump of reeds / Is split with darkness and yet bristles whole ('**For signs**'). The re-working here of Emerson's Neoplatonism displays Gunn's most obvious debt to a specifically American poetic tradition. 'We live', said Emerson, 'in succession, in division, in parts, in particles. Meantime within man is the soul of the whole.'[16] This transposition of terrestrial objects into an Idealist harmony is also apparent in two of Gunn's most recent poems: in '**Outside the diner**', first published in 1984, the shabby and apparently casual figure of a tramp drinking muscatel is endowed ultimately with a luminous splendour:

> A poor weed,
> unwanted scraggle tufted
> with unlovely yellow,
> persists between paving stones
> marginal to the grid
> bearded face turned toward light.[17]

And in the 1985 '**Philemon and Baucis**', with its epigraph from William Carlos Wiliams, 'love without shad-

ows', the shadowy nature of division and separation has once more been transcended. Dualism is admitted, but overcome:

> Two trunks like bodies, bodies like twined trunks
> Supported by their wooden hug. Leaves shine
> In tender habit at the extremities.
> Truly each other's, they have embraced so long
> Their barks have met and wedded in one flow
> Blanketing both.[18]

If '**Misanthropos**' represents Gunn's reflexive echo-chamber at its most hollow, '**Philemon and Baucis**' portrays it at its most fulfilling, as each body chimes with the other. Many of Gunn's most recent poems, however, do not attempt to subsume these differences within some higher power but instead take a postmodernist delight in flaunting the difference, the shadow, which is always threatening to compromise the poet's conclusive meaning. A poem published in 1985 actually called 'The differences' broods retrospectively on a love-affair as the focus for a meditation upon ideas of unity and separation ('I have not crossed your mind for three weeks now').[19] And Gunn's 1982 collection was not entitled *The Passages of Joy* for nothing: the phrase itself comes from Samuel Johnson's poem 'The vanity of human wishes'—'Time hovers o'er impatient to destroy / And shuts up all the Passages of Joy'—but in Gunn, one of its significations is the joyful delight the poet takes in the idea of passage, metamorphosis, transition. For Johnson, the flow of time tended destructively to annihilate joy; but for Gunn, the flow of time positively contributes to it. The poem '**Crosswords**' in this collection epitomises this celebration of fluidity and open-endedness: starting from an image of crossword puzzles, the poem moves on to consider the 'cross words', the mutual disagreements and antagonism, expressed between two lovers. But this antagonism then comes to be welcomed, as it eventually provides the spark for their relationship:

> How glad I am to be back at your school
> Where it's through contradictions that I learn.
> Obsessive and detached, ardent and cool,
> You make me think of rock thrown free to turn
> At the globe's side, both with and not with us,
> Keeping yourself in a companionable
> Chilled orbit by the simultaneous
> Repulsion and attracton to it all.

The author's declaration that 'contradictions' furnish the basis of his education is supported by the oxymoronic construction of this stanza: *Obsessive, detached; ardent, cool; Repulsion, attraction.* These oxymorons provide another connotation for the title '**Crosswords**': words that cross, that contradict each other's sense. In this way, oxymoron contributes to Gunn's programme of self-parody, for oxymoron mocks any attempt at final meaning: poetic closure is abandoned in favour of the radical multiplicity of self-reflexive poetry. In his 1976 poem '**Iron landscapes (and the Statue of Liberty)**' Gunn specifically associated this open-endedness with the half-formed constructions of the American landscape—'Cool seething incompletion that I love'—and Christopher Ricks has similarly written of how this sense of what is evanescent and passing is a particular quality of American English:

> The point is not that British English is insensitive to time (no language can ever be); rather that, because it gives a less important role than does American English to the ephemeral or transitory or obsolescent, there are certain effects occluded from it. . . [American English has] this particular poignancy, of a language acknowledging that much of it is not long for this world.[20]

One good example of Gunn's introduction of the ephemeral and transitory occurs in his 1984 poem **'To a friend in time of trouble',** as yet uncollected. The end of the poem focusses upon the mind of the troubled friend being released from tension:

> It finds that it has lost itself upon
> The smooth red body of a young madrone,
> From which it turns toward other varying shades
> On the brown hillside where light grows and fades,
> And feels the healing start, and still returns,
> Riding its own repose, and learns, and learns.[21]

If *still* in that penultimate line is a noun, the friend has been calmed by returning to a state of still, serenity, lack of motion. But if *still* is an adverb, we find the healing returns continuously: the pun operates to disallow any hope of final quietude but sanctions instead the healing as a process of constant repetition: a movement which is supported by the doubling-up of the final phrase 'and learns' in the last line of the poem, and also by the pattern of the rhyme-scheme where each line is designed to chime with the next.

'To a friend in time of trouble' in fact demonstrates how Gunn's self-parodic idiom can function with a clear ethical intent. By inserting the disturbed friend into a landscape of repetition, a poetic hall of mirrors, the narrator implicitly liberates him from self-obsession by reminding him how these troubles are not a burden unique to himself. The passage away from solipsism towards a recognition of the multifarious nature of the world becomes equated with Gunn's progression into multiple meanings: it is the same kind of moral awareness as Altieri located in Ashbery's convex mirrors, 'a lucidity that keeps one from narcissistic illusions and / cheap emotional indulgences'.[22] We recall how in the recent interview with Graham Fawcett Gunn remarked once more that 'the correct incantation of a past feeling' is something he has never quite re-discovered in any poem; but whereas the Gunn of *Fighting Terms* felt himself under threat from this ineradicable difference, the Gunn of the 1980s thrives on such difference, sporting with the gap between signifier and signified, between artistic form and the random, formless areas of human experience. We can see from his critical essays that Gunn has always been attracted to dualistic writers: he praised Hardy's poetry for its 'reflective mode' and 'emotional reaction to ideas', while Ben Jonson was applauded for 'the extremes between which he moves so easily', blending 'wild anarchic vigour' with classical restraint;[23] and Scott Fitzgerald also received Gunn's approbation for bringing 'romanticism' and 'intelligence' into conjunction:

> [Fitzgerald] and I have something like the same strategies in common. He's a big old romantic, and you can tell from his first books just how awful and slushy that romanticism could be, but then he suddenly became more artistic and aware. Like Stendhal, as he gets older he gets more intelligent, but his intelligence doesn't destroy the romantic figures; it abets them". . . Fitzgerald's terrific in describing these wonderful girls and they come to life in a way that you can't deny them, but he's retaining his irony and criticism. The irony, as with Stendhal, doesn't undercut the romanticism, it actually reinforces it, and I think this is what I've been doing throughout.[24]

To blend romanticism with irony is to reconcile self-parody with ethical intent, perhaps even to locate self-parody as being at the very heart of ethical intent. Moral purpose becomes intimately connected with an idiom of reflection, because the creative interrogation of egocentric identity and meaning liberates Gunn's poetry from the atmosphere of claustrophobic narcissism which hovered around his early work. It is interesting to note that the 1976 essay by Colin Falck (cited earlier) which accused Gunn of lacking an ethical sense was described by the poet himself as 'a wonderful piece". . . very sympathetic and helpful';[25] and yet there is little sign of Gunn turning away from that 'dissolution of the moral and social human being' which Falck lamented. Gunn has indeed assimilated Falck's caution against poetic hedonism, but instead of regressing into older forms of humanism or English moral seriousness he has advanced into a postmodern, Americanised sensibility where 'passion and compassion' (Altieri's phrase) are able to emerge as parody self-reflexively turns the language of romanticism back against itself in a recognition of the arbitrary and contingent condition of human life, the arena of difference, incompletion and loss.[26] As Gunn said of Fitzgerald, this sense of irony paradoxically sets the author free to indulge to the full his extravagant romanticism, because he knows this romanticism will always be controlled by a sardonic intelligence: again, whereas in Gunn's early poetry the head and the heart tended to pull in opposite directions, now they complement each other perfectly. The image which recurs in Gunn's poetry to express this idea of conceptual equilibrium is physical balance: the narrator of **'From the wave'** in *Moly* proclaims 'Balance is triumph in this place' as he watches surfers in the Pacific; while the 1984 poem **'Skateboard'** celebrates the way a punk youth on a skateboard weaves his way through the urban jungle, preserving once more his essential balance:

> Darts, doubles, twists.
> You notice how nimbly
> the body itself has learned
> to assess the relation between
> the board, pedestrians,
> and immediate sidewalk.[27]

The image is again an implicit comment upon Gunn's own poetic practice: for by a similar process of doubling and twisting, Gunn's recent work has engaged in a creative exploitation of narcissism so as to fuse irony with romanticism, self-parody with ethical resolution.

Notes

1 See *Viewpoints: Poets in Conversation with John Haffenden* (London: Faber, 1981), p. 54. This interview was first published in *Quarto*, No. 8 (July 1980), pp. 9-11.

2 Ian Hamilton, 'The call of the cool', *Times Literary Supplement*, 23 July 1982, p. 782.

3 Graham Fawcett, *Thom Gunn's Castle*, BBC Radio 3, 4 March 1986.

4 *Ibid.*

5 See Paul Fussell, 'Some critical implications of metrical analysis' (1965), rpt. in *William Carlos Williams: a Critical Anthology*, ed. Charles Tomlinson (Harmondsworth: Penguin, 1972), pp. 315-17.

6 Roland Barthes, *The Pleasure of the Text* (1975), trans. Richard Miller (London: Cape, 1976), p. 31.

7 Martin Dodsworth, 'Thom Gunn: poetry as action and submission', in *The Survival of Poetry: a Contemporary Survey*, ed. Martin Dodsworth (London: Faber, 1970), p. 196.

8 Colin Falck, 'Uncertain violence', *New Review*, 3, No. 32 (Nov. 1976), pp. 40-1.

9 John Bayley, 'Castles and communes', *Times Literary Supplement*, 24 Sept. 1976, p. 1194.

10 Thom Gunn, 'Ben Jonson' (1974), rpt. in *The Occasions of Poetry* (London: Faber, 1982), p. 111.

11 See Harold Bloom, *The Anxiety of Influence: a Theory of Poetry* (New York: Oxford University Press, 1973).

12 Thom Gunn, 'My life up to now' (1979), rpt. in *Occasions of Poetry*, p. 186.

13 Gilles Deleuze and Felix Guattari, *Anti-Oedipus: Capitalism and Schizophrenia* (1972), trans. Robert Hurley, Mark Seem, Helen R. Lane (London: Athlone Press, 1984), p. 6.

14 Charles Altieri, *Self and Sensibility in Contemporary American Poetry* (Cambridge: Cambridge University Press, 1984), p. 163; p. 132.

15 *Ibid.*, p. 136; p. 140.

16 Ralph Waldo Emerson, *Complete Works* (Boston: Houghton Mifflin, 1903), II, 269.

17 Thom Gunn, 'Outside the diner', *Critical Quarterly*, 26, Nos. 1 and 2 (1984), p. 17.

18 Thom Gunn, 'Philemon and Baucis', *PN Review*, 12, No. 1 (1985), p. 36.

19 Thom Gunn, 'The differences', *PN Review*, 12, No. 1 (1985), pp. 35-6.

20 Christopher Ricks, 'American English', in *The Force of Poetry* (Oxford: Oxford University Press, 1984), pp. 427-8; p. 432.

21 Thom Gunn, 'To a friend in time of trouble', *PN Review*, 11, No. 2 (1984), p. 14.

22 Altieri, p. 209.

23 Thom Gunn, 'Hardy and the ballads' (1972), rpt. in *Occasions of Poetry*, p. 101; p. 78; 'Ben Jonson', p. 106; p. 110.

24 *Viewpoints*, p. 55.

25 *Viewpoints*, p. 49.

26 Altieri, p. 134.

27 Thom Gunn, 'Skateboard', *Critical Quarterly*, 26, Nos. 1 and 2 (1984), p. 18.

Martin Dodsworth   (essay date 1989)

SOURCE: "Gunn's Rhymes," in *PN Review*, Vol. 16, No. 2, 1989, pp. 33-4.

[*In the following essay, Dodsworth examines Gunn's use of rhyme, contending that it "is intimately related to his whole style and outlook, and is worth looking at for that reason."*]

Thom Gunn's development as a poet has been slow, and is clearly defined; he began with rhyme, then added a form of half-rhymed syllabic verse in his third book, **My Sad Captains,** and finally went on to develop his own, characteristic free verse. Although the syllabic form has disappeared from his work, he remains faithful to rhyme; his last full-length book, **The Passages of Joy,** is largely in free verse, but its second section is exclusively rhymed, and rhyme crops up elsewhere in its pages. The way Gunn uses rhyme is intimately related to his whole style and outlook, and is worth looking at for that reason.

Gunn likes to rhyme monosyllables with monosyllables. The preference is already manifest in **Fighting Terms**; checking through the first thirteen poems of that book (in its first edition, to be precise), I found that out of a total of 132 rhymes, 88 used monosyllables exclusively—*said / bed / dead*, for example. This is not generally regarded as a very exciting kind of rhyme. Of course, English is not a language with a plenitude of rhymes, and this fact may excuse a poet who relies heavily on monosyllables, even if it does suggest a mechanical exercise undertaken in order to maintain the rhyme-scheme: *bat / brat / cat / drat / fat / flat*, and so on. But can it excuse the poet's using rhyme at all when there are unrhymed forms available?

In using monosyllables so freely for his rhyming, Gunn seems to have been chiming with the poetic spirit of the time; another Cambridge poet, like Gunn associated with the Movement and like Gunn published by the Fantasy Press at Oxford, Donald Davie, in *his* first book of poems also uses them liberally. The first thirteen poems of his *Brides of Reason* rhyme exclusively on monosyllables 77 times out of the total 140. Even so Davie does not make so high a score as Gunn's. Practice elsewhere among *New Lines* poets seems to be more variable (they do not, of course, all use rhyme any way), though there is no doubt that a clipped and clearly audible rhyme was a part of the recall-to-order aesthetic of many, if not most, of them. Although Gunn did not meet Yvor Winters until after **Fighting Terms** was published in 1954, it seems not impossible that Gunn and Davie were already reflecting Winters's practice in this habit of monosyllabic rhyme—see, for example, the four poems which follow one another in Winters's *Collected*: 'On Rereading a Passage from John Muir', 'The Manzanita', 'Sir Gawaine and the Green Knight' and 'An October Nocturne'. Winters's criticism was certainly acceptable in Cambridge when Davie and Gunn were about, and Davie started to explore American literature quite early on—he ended up writing the introduction to the 1978 English edition of Winters's poems. In that introduction he associates Winters above all with "considered utterance", and the meaning of Gunn's rhymes in the early poems, like those of Davie, has something to do with a considered decisiveness admired for its own sake, as well as with the more general feeling in the Movement "against romanticism". Gunn uses monosyllabic rhymes not because he cannot find ones that are more complex but because monosyllables suit the *ethos* of his verse.

His rhymes tell us that that *ethos* has not changed. In **The Passages of Joy** the proportion of monosyllabic rhymes is much the same as it was in **Fighting Terms**; 92 of its 158 rhymes are of this kind. By contrast, Davie's use of rhyme is now far different from what it was. He has, of course, been a consistent experimenter with verse-form; the point is that even when he does use rhyme nowadays, he uses it in unpredictable and extremely various ways. In 'The Battered Wife' section of his *Collected Poems 1971-1983,* for example, it is impossible to determine what is exactly intended as rhyme and what is not, because his play with poetic sound has, in the years since *Brides of Reason,* become so much more complex. To take one example, 'Fare Thee Well' is a poem of five eight-line stanzas in which the following words find themselves at the line-end in the course of the poem: *tempest-whipped, shipped, tripped, wrapped, gripped, outstripped, slipped, accept, equipped.* Obviously something is going on here with an affinity to the kind of word-play associated with rhyme, but equally obviously the affinity is not an identity, not just because half-rhyme is involved (elsewhere I have counted that as rhyme when there seemed to be an expectation that one should do so) but also because the positioning of these words in the poem is unpredictable and assymetrical, and to that extent at odds with the structure of the poem. "Accept", it seems to me, is offered as something that may or may not be a rhyme. Such a practice is far removed from that of *Brides of Reason*; it is indicative of a change in the poet's mode of feeling towards and within his medium. No such change is visible in Gunn.

This fidelity to past practice in Gunn is a sign of strength and weakness. It is akin to that other fidelity he shows, a fidelity to 'his' subject-matter: adolescence, existential isolation, the exercise of will, the creation of identity. He has saturated this subject-matter with Gunnian feeling, and the result is poetry of great power. At the same time, his *oeuvre* suffers from a lack of spaciousness. Movement, like development, is difficult. The ease with which Gunn's three styles can be identified suggests the effort involved for him in developing technically; Gunn is unlike Davie in that he likes to know where he is in a poem, likes to know whether he is offering a rhyme or not. The ambiguous status of "accept" in the Davie poem is inconceivable in Gunn; but it is integral to the imaginative spaciousness that Gunn's poetry is able to intimate (for example, in **'Touch'**) but hardly to achieve.

Rhyming on monosyllables is associated in Gunn with the Movement rejection of Romantic sloppiness and a more particular, perhaps Cambridge, cult of decisiveness, closely related to his interest in the will. It also stands for a keeping faith with the self that was responsible for his earliest poems. There is even more to it than this, however. The preference for monosyllabic rhyme seems also to connect with attention to the thing in itself in the modern manner. A free-verse poem in **The Passages of Joy**, **'Expression'**, is interesting in this regard. It describes the satisfaction taken by the poet in regarding an early Italian altar-piece after reading the "very poetic poetry" (which is also posturing and self-concerned) of his juniors:

> Solidly there, mother and child
> stare outward, two pairs of matching eyes
> void of expression.

Alongside this, one might put the affirmation of Gunn's essay on Williams: "it is a humane action to attempt the rendering of a thing, person, or experience in the exact terms of its existence"—that is, I take it, without attempting the expressiveness of those younger poets who have nauseated Gunn in his own poem. Monosyllabic rhymes are a principle of order and decision; they are the audible equivalent of a defining line. But they imply the minimum "expressiveness" possible by being just about as unexciting as a rhyme can be. They point to what the line contains.

As usual, you pays your money and you takes your choice. Gunn's poetry may not show much in the way of development, but its attentiveness to things "in the exact terms" of their existence scarcely wavers:

> Separate in the same weather
> The parcelled buds crack pink and red,
> And rise from different plants together
> To shed their bud-sheaths on the bed. . .

In this respect there is a likeness in Gunn to the Wordsworth of *Lyrical Ballads.* In 'The Thorn' monosyllabic rhyme is used extensively for the rendering of things as they are, without the poet's obtrusively investing them with his own personality:

> There is a Thorn—it looks so old,
> In truth, you'd find it hard to say
> How it could ever have been young,
> It looks so old and grey.
> Not higher than a two years' child,
> It stands erect, this aged Thorn;
> No leaves it has, no prickly points;
> It is a mass of knotted joints,
> A wretched thing forlorn.
> It stands erect, and like a stone
> With lichens it is overgrown.

It is this likeness, which, as in Wordsworth, exposes the poet to charges of naivety and lapse of taste (see, for example, in *The Passages of Joy,* the remarkable poem 'The Miracle'). It remains, also, an abiding strength in Gunn's poetry.

Neil Powell   (essay date 1989)

SOURCE: "Loud Music, Bars, and Boisterous Men," in *PN Review,* Vol. 16, No. 2, 1989, pp. 39-41.

[*In the following essay, Powell determines the role of sexuality in Gunn's poetry.*]

Though he will probably cringe at the thought, Thom Gunn is the most distinguished living English gay poet, and after Auden the most significant English gay poet of the century. That's the sort of statement to make any poet cringe, which is why I want to get rid of it at the outset. It could all too easily seem to imply that writers can be sorted by sexuality into separate compartments, or that homosexual writers address a limited constituency of homosexual readers, neither of which must be the case. Gunn's sexuality matters to his readers partly because it has been, increasingly, a major theme in his work, and partly because his writing career spans and reflects a period of profoundly unsettling changes in the complex relationship between gay men and the rest of society.

Gunn is a poet who frequently revisits his past styles and refreshes himself with disparate influences, yet his work does roughly seem to divide into three phases or movements which I'll call containment, liberation, and openness. The first phase comprises the poems in *Fighting Terms* (1954), *The Sense of Movement* (1957), and part of *My Sad Captains* (1961). The superficial similarities between most of these poems are immediately apparent, and they concern characteristics which his early readers would readily have identified as Gunnish (thus, ironically, labelling and placing him in a way that the content of the poems is at pains to discourage): regular, iambic verseforms; metaphysical abstraction overlaid with echoes of Yeats and Sartre; recklessly inspired combinations of historical and contemporary allusiveness.

Yet beneath these superficial characteristics run two obsessive, related themes: debates of the divided self, and the making of a personal iconography. *Fighting Terms* presents a procession of double consciousnesses or divided selves: Achilles and Lofty, ancient and modern soldiers wounded by memories which divide their actions from their thoughts; the brash exterior ("Even in bed I pose") and the hurt mind ("I saw that lack of love contaminates") in 'Carnal Knowledge'; the role-reversing tamer and hawk; the man in the snowy street looking up at his window and calling his own name in 'The Secret Sharer'; derelict present and edenic past in 'Looking Glass'; heroic action and introspective cunning in 'The Beach Head'; innocence instructed by experience in 'Incident on a Journey'; "submissive" Shelley and "masterful" Byron in 'Lerici'. And in two poems of this period, the homosexual dimension of this concept becomes explicit. One is 'Without a Counterpart', where the speaker wakes, frightened and apparently alone, to imagine a vast bleak landscape whose features—"Two reed-lined ponds", "a long volcano", "prickly turf"—gradually resolve into the eyes, mouth and stubble of a lover's face. In fact the poem *does* have a counterpart in 'Light Sleeping', which Gunn wrote in 1953 but excluded from *Fighting Terms* (it appears in *The Missed Beat* [1976]): two men are in bed; one wakes to a nightmare vision; but this time the other is awake and observes everything. Suddenly sitting bolt upright, he meditates on the moon and redefines the terms of Sidney's famous sonnet in *Astrophil and Stella*. He sees "a hell of love" as the cause of the moon's "sad steps", while Sidney's anguished question, "Do they above love to be loved, and yet / Those lovers scorn whom that love doth possess?" is answered by Gunn's vision of lovers "locked in each other's arms, / Cursed with content, pair by possessive pair": for Gunn, conventional love is by definition hellish because possessive, and the moon can only provide confirmation, not consolation.

'Light Sleeping' is in retrospect an important and revealing poem: Gunn was probably right to leave it out of *Fighting Terms* precisely because it appears to decode, and thus damagingly to limit, other poems in the book. The divided self is not, after all, an exclusively homosexual theme, but it is one of special significance for gay men, for whom the concepts of 'What I am' and 'What I want' are apt to blur and interchange. In his 'containment' phase, Gunn kept his sexuality fairly veiled to give the poems maximum universality—an entirely honourable stance, though probably not one which the gay poet in the late twentieth century can sustain for ever. The divided self poems offer one way of being truthful and evasive at the same time; the icon poems provide another.

Those in the know (to borrow Gunn's own phrase from his essay on Robert Duncan) would have had no difficulty in seeing what Gunn was up to in his second book, *The Sense of Movement,* but a sizeable number of readers must have assumed that, for example, the bikers in 'On the Move' were solely objects of identification rather than objects of desire, whereas much of the poem's energy derives from the fact that they are both. Similarly, in 'Elvis Presley', the rather implausible, wearily detached opening stance ("this one, in his gangling finery / And crawling sideburns") is soon complicated by hints of more subjective interest ("Our idiosyncrasy and our likeness", "posture for combat"). *The Sense of Movement* owes much of its effectiveness to the way in which Gunn's literary and philosophical ideas at this time were running exactly in parallel with his sexual metaphors: there are Yeats's masks, Sartre's 'will', and the profound influence of Yvor Winters, with whom Gunn was working and who, though hostile to much homosexual writing, provided ideas of rigour, discipline and impersonality which suited Gunn very well. The word 'will' recurs in the book, carrying Sartrian or Wintersian overtones but also (as in the erotic, and syllabic, **'Market at Turk',** where the hustler's "bootstraps and Marine belt" are "reminders of the will") a more obviously sexual, Shakespearian resonance. Yet not all the icons are contemporary or fetishistic: from Achilles in *Fighting Terms,* through Julian, Jesus, St Martin, Alexander, Socrates and Brutus in *The Sense of Movement,* to St Paul and the "sad captains" themselves, there are also the "few with historical names". Often these figures serve to depersonalise and objectify Gunn's own ideas, but in the remarkable **'In Santa Maria del Popolo'**, which opens *My Sad Captains,* something more intimate and complex happens: it is about the conversion of St. Paul as perceived by Caravaggio as perceived by Gunn, and the 'I' who turns (punningly) "hardly enlightened" from the painting in the chapel to the congregation in the church is a vulnerable, implicated figure. The poem's final icon is not the divided self of Saul/Paul nor the immensely attractive existential-homosexual figure of Caravaggio but "the large gesture of solitary man, / Resisting, by embracing, nothingness".

My Sad Captains is a rewardingly transitional book. In a poem such as the second **'Modes of Pleasure'** ("Why pretend / Love must accompany erection?"), sexual frankness is still straining after the epigrammatic, and the result is a winsome bravado, charming but not quite convincing. But in **'A Map of the City'**, Gunn stands back to take possession of San Francisco, fertile cruising-ground for "my love of chance", and to be possessed by it:

> By the recurrent lights I see
> Endless potentiality,
> The crowded, broken, and unfinished!
> I would not have the risk diminished.

The sense of liberation, of simple fresh air, which invigorates particularly some of the syllabic poems in *My Sad Captains* is overwhelming: and it perhaps needs to be said at this point, though not in a limiting sense, that a gay poet is still a gay poet when he's not writing about sex. The sexual liberation which Gunn found in California permeates poems like **'Lights among Redwood'** and the most sensuous poem in the book, **'Flying above California'**, celebrating light, plants, mere names ("Such richness can make you drunk").

Gunn's next book, *Positives,* was the result of a year's return to England and a collaboration with his photographer brother, Ander. The finest creative result of this period is in fact a much later poem (**'Talbot Road'**), and the poem-captions in *Positives* are designedly and necessarily low-key: one, opposite a photograph of a boy in a cafe, restates with engaging directness a sub-text from **'Elvis Presley'**. The boy is "a rough young animal" who knows that "Youth is power" and who "makes, now, / a fine gesture, inviting / experience to try him". The poem, and indeed *Positives* as a whole, anticipates two subsequent developments in Gunn's work: the gradual substitution of ordinary, often unnamed people for the earlier icons, and the movement towards a hesitant, exploratory free verse.

That is the mode Gunn adopts for **'Touch'**, the title-poem of his 1967 collection and one which has a double-edged significance. The striking point about it ought to be its novelty—a first-person love poem, addressed to a lover in bed, and not involving a narrator, a historical figure, or a dream (even so, the lover is addressed as a sexless "you", is already asleep, and the cat got there first). Still more striking, however, is the fact that Gunn had managed to produce four previous books without including such a poem: it was still, even in the late sixties, a difficult kind of poem for a writer of his stature to publish, and anyway Gunn's talent didn't easily adapt to intimate informality. The most unequivocally successful single poem in *Touch,* **'Pierce Street'**, is formal, descriptive and meditative in the light-and-shade manner of **'In Santa Maria del Popolo'**; while his next book, *Moly* (1971), joyously liberated by sunlight and LSD, is the most formally iambic of all his later collections.

One can see why. For Gunn, liberation demands constraint almost as much as constraint demands liberation. In *Moly,* sexual freedom is transmuted—through drugs, flowers, music, places, people—into hectic, benign celebration: it takes all Gunn's iambic discipline to hold it in place, but he succeeds marvellously. In poems (among his very best) such as **'The Fair in the Woods'**, **'Flooded Meadows'**, **'Grasses'**, **'The Messenger'** and **'Sunlight'**, the sexuality is implicit because genuinely liberated, carried on a wave of articulate optimism.

Given the political and social changes of the seventies and eighties, it couldn't last: the transition from *Moly* to *Jack Straw's Castle* (1976) is, precisely, the transition from dream to nightmare. Yet the fragmented, nightmare title-sequence (whose origins Gunn describes in the autobiographical essay, 'My Life up to Now') ends in a deliberate, iambic gesture of affirmation and also of defiance:

> The beauty's in what is, not what may seem.
> I turn. And even if he were a dream
> —Thick sweating flesh against which I lie curled—
> With dreams like this, Jack's ready for the world.

"Ten years ago," Gunn told W.I. Scobie in 1977, "it wouldn't have occurred to me to end the title poem in *Jack Straw's Castle* as I do." Partly because he couldn't, but also because he needn't have done so: it is the gestures of repression, like the Christopher Street raid and the closure of the Sonoma County Geysers (or in England the *Gay News* blasphemy trial and the more recent Section 28 of the Local Government Act) which urge the gay poet towards the dangerous but necessary stridencies of sexual propaganda. Gunn is aware of both danger and necessity, but these are easy matters to misjudge. In *Jack Straw's Castle,* for instance, Gunn tamed some stridencies in the poems, depriving '**Fever**' of both general tanginess and specific detail (like "joints and amyl"), and losing altogether one section of '**The Geysers**' with its rather charming digression on the variousness of male nipples and its beatific final vision of America as "One great brave luminous green-gold meeting place". On the other hand, he included in his most recent full-length book, *The Passages of Joy* (1982), one sexual poem, '**The Miracle**', in which the failure of tone is as complete as it was in much earlier pieces like '**Lofty in the Palais de Danse**' (*Fighting Terms*) and '**The Beaters**' (*The Sense of Movement*): all three are weakened by an apparent inability to perceive, or to distance through irony, the potential absurdity of their subjects.

The successes among Gunn's recent sexually open poems are of two distinct kinds, though unified by the most consistent thread in his literary career—as always, his best writing occurs when physicality and the world of ideas, impulse and intellect, most closely reinforce each other. One kind of poem is the free verse anecdote which, lacking the more obvious shapings of metre and rhyme, especially needs the shaping discipline of the intellect. Thus, in '**The Idea of Trust**', the anecdote about "pretty" Jim who stole from the people he lived with is given unexpected sharpness by the meditation on trust and freedom (expressed in suitably ruminative, hesitant verse) which it provokes. That effect, it has to be said, is rather less in evidence in *The Passages of Joy,* where the anecdotes are more often left to speak for themselves, though the observation in poems such as '**Bally *Power Play**'* and '**Slow Waker**' is affectionate and acute.

The main strength of *The Passages of Joy* is in the other kind of poem—extended, reflective, retrospective. '**Talbot Road**', relaxed and almost prosy but in its accumulation of evocative detail absolutely compelling, recalls the magical mid-sixties year Gunn spent in London. '**Transients and Residents**' remembers an assortment of friends until interrupted by a piece of elegant self-analysis which moves in from the garden and the study to a self-portrait of the author himself:

> Starting outside,
> You save yourself some time while working in:
> Thus by the seen the unseen is implied.
> *I like loud music, bars, and boisterous men.*

At last, you might think, the real Thom Gunn, until a couple of lines later he points out that these are things "That help me if not lose then leave behind, / What else, the self." He emerges from the self-portrait as an attractive, plausible ventriloquist, nothing how in letters he mimics the style of his correspondents and concluding, "I manage my mere voice on postcards best".

He emerges, too, as a continuously youthful poet, in a way which has sometimes disconcerted his readers. And here, I think, it is for once proper to insist on the distinctness of the homosexual view of life: it is, after all, a simple fact that most heterosexuals, as parents and then as grandparents, have their social roles and responsibilities quite clearly defined by age in a way that gay men don't. Socialising homosexuals, on the other hand, tend to inhabit a world of bars and boys and pop music which cuts across the changes of attitude which otherwise come with age: it would be self-deluding to view this as the secret of eternal youth, but at best it allows a risk-taking receptiveness, and Gunn has always liked to be (as he says in '**New York**') "high / on risk". During the Reagan/ Thatcher years, the complex politics of gay life have become still more fraught with paradox: for instance, shadowed by AIDS, *populist* sentiment appears to have grown more homophobic while *popular* culture (as in the Communards, Erasure, Pet Shop Boys and so on) has grown more conspicuously gay-influenced. Gunn's need to provide an increasingly direct chronicle of gay life springs in part from this sort of tension.

"But my life insists on continuities," he has said, and he is right. He has always been blessed with that intelligent desire to shock which springs from essential gentleness, and on re-reading *The Sense of Movement* seems now a far more outrageous book than *The Passages of Joy,* largely because its explosive contents are wrapped in such disarmingly well-mannered verse forms. I suspect he wanted to be a bad boy from the moment he returned to London from war-time evacuation and began "eyeing the well-fed and good-looking G.I.s who were on every street"; and with Gunn, as is so often the case, the bad boy is of course the brightest in the class.

Robert Pinsky (essay date 1989)

SOURCE: "Thom Gunn," in *PN Review,* Vol. 16, No. 2, 1989, pp. 42-3.

[*In the following essay, Pinsky explores the theme of home in Gunn's verse.*]

I am writing without any books at hand by Thom Gunn or anyone else, a few days before a complicated move— from the East Coast back to California, then back to Massachusetts—feeling distinctly not at home. Since Gunn, whom I admire immensely, has a special relation to the idea of being at home, I will take that as the theme for these paragraphs.

There is a poise in Gunn's poetry, a confidence without much swagger, that is like the bearing of a creature at home in its surroundings. Yet in the way that Elizabeth Bishop cast herself as a traveler in the world—nearly anonymous, focused on sensation, a temporary presence— Gunn sometimes conveys the reserve and intimacy of a visitor, a mingled privacy and attention, focused on the space between souls, a provisional presence. Gunn's poems achieve a quality of being at home while on the move, but without the plodding caution of the turtle. The calm wildness of a cat, possibly, or of some imagined Zen master. (One might write "of a cat or a Zen master" if the tutelary Gunn spirit of honesty and accuracy were not hovering nearby, asking with a polite, not quite derisive smile what do I know about Zen masters.)

And to qualify "cat" a little, I think I mean the quality that made jazz musicians coin the term as alluding to a guy or bloke, with an emphasis on feral dignity, self-possession, readiness and possibly reckless skills. Also a keen sensitivity to atmosphere, the ability to make oneself at home.

Gunn's existential motorcycle toughs roaring through stanzas of jagged symmetry and keen meticulous sentences; the elegant iambic cable of his **'Tamer and Hawk'**, stretched over the Yeatsian short lines with a lilt I memorized from his first book, when I was in college; the free-verse equivalent governing the savage, telling enjambments of **'My Sad Captains'** ("all / the past lapping them like a / cloak of chaos"); his poem about the dog, from inside her mind; poems from the inside of Old English; of LSD; his great essay on Hardy and the English ballad, his essays on Marianne Moore and Rod Taylor, on Yvor Winters and Basil Bunting, his celebrations of Robert Duncan and of J.V. Cunningham; the great elegies and meditations on San Francisco's AIDS epidemic, some of them in the grave, passionate diamond-perfect measures of Ben Jonson, some in street music—a range and size of work equaled by very few living poets.

The truly mysterious poise that runs through it could be described as the power to be at home with the alien or unlikely: with various metrical extremes and modes; with the manners of various kinds of people, like Odysseus; with many countries and cities and cultures; at home with a kind, unsentimental holding back of judgment; but also at home exercising his judgment, mentioning serenely that he thinks some much praised book is very badly written, or that (say) some lyrics by the Talking Heads are very good. *Moly* is a book about being at home even in transformation, in distortion.

Absurd to think of Thom Gunn as an expatriate: San Francisco is his home city as few people find homes. He lives in his house and garden in a way that combines the English gift for coziness with California's elegant openness to air. The atmosphere of his house, familial but with a sense of privacies and amiable distinctions within the familial, reminds me of the happy mixture of being alone while with others on the bus that he chooses to ride across the Bay, between work in Berkeley and home in San Francisco. The subdued community of the bus—where Gunn often works on poems—is different from the busy island of a car in a way somehow like the pace and closeness of Gunn's imagination: the non-driver who wrote "One is always nearer by not keeping still".

I think he rides the generational trolley car of fame with a kind of amused impersonality, too. (Cary Grant's image: he talks somewhere about actors getting on the trolley and, with a certain amount of savage fighting not to fall off, riding it.) Thom Gunn is a kind of model for how to take the ups and downs of that ride. Happy to live without courting the coteries, alliances and constituencies that sometimes buoy reputations synthetically, he also seems incapable of the kind of self promotion that allows some artists to explain their importance to others. He once fell into friendly conversation for half an hour with a woman in a bar, telling one another their occupations and so forth; when she left, her parting wish to him was "I hope you get published some day". Thom I think mistakes the point of this story: he seems to think it illustrates how very much most people assume that poetry is not published. But what is striking about it is that he didn't drop any phrases along the lines of "my publisher" and so forth.

How to explain this absence of self-promotion in one who has so very little to be unpretentious about? Maybe Thom Gunn's sense of the ridiculous is too strong for boasting. It is hard to imagine a pompous message written on the back of the post cards he ferrets out somewhere: fifties workers in white smocks preparing a health tonic called something like VitaGreen; a wig company's advertisement, the same woman three times modeling the same stiffly styled wig in colors called 'Autumn Haze', 'Sun Drip', 'Mink'.

But to say 'sense of proportion' would imply smallness. Only an extremely ambitious writer could have made as many unforgettable poems as Thom Gunn, reaching in new directions with each book. That is why the idea of being at home, which is to say at home with himself, seems germane to me. The word 'expatriate' evokes tremendously wrong images of self-conscious exile or making a point or of being in, while not of, the dwelling place. Thom Gunn seems to live inside the rhythms and meanings and structures of our English language with a fresh, venturesome eagerness, and a mastery that make being merely an American poet or an English one seem beside the point. As Thom Gunn has written of Hardy's work in relation to Hardy's character, "It is a happy embodiment".

Clive Wilmer with Thom Gunn (interview date 1995)

SOURCE: "The Art of Poetry," in *The Paris Review,* Vol. 37, No. 135, Summer, 1995, pp. 142-89.

[*In the following excerpted interview, Gunn discusses his writing process, the main influences on his poetry, and the major themes and stylistic concerns of his work.*]

CLIVE WILMER: *I wonder if we could begin with a brief description of how you live? I get the feeling, for instance, that you're quite fond of routine.*

THOM GUNN: Well, if you haven't got a routine in your life by the age of sixty-two, you're never going to get it. I spend half the year teaching and half the year on my own. I like the idea of scheduling my own life for half the year, but by the end of that time I'm really ready to teach again and have somebody else's timetable imposed on me, because I'm chaotic enough that I just couldn't be master of myself for the entire year. It would leave me too loose and unregulated. As I say, I'm eager to teach again in January and then, during the term, very often I'll think of ideas for writing on but I usually don't have time to work them out. By the time I can work them out at the end of the term, I've either lost them or else I've got them much more complex and intense, so that's good too. I like the way my life has worked out very well. I live with some other men in a house in San Francisco. Somebody once said: "Oh, you've got a gay commune." I said: "No, it's a queer household!"—which I think was a satisfactory answer. Right now there's only three of us there. There *were* five: one of them left and one of them died of AIDS. But we really fit in well together. We really do work as a family: we cook in turn—stuff like that—we do a lot of things together.

Do you have a writing routine?

When anybody says, "Do you have a routine?," I always say piously it's very important to have one, but in fact I don't. I write poetry when I can and when I can't, I write reviews, which I figure at least is keeping my hand in, doing some kind of writing. Finally, however difficult it is, it does make me happy in some weird way to do the writing. It's hard labor but it does satisfy something in me very deeply. Sometimes when I haven't written in some time, I really decide I'm going to work toward getting the requisite fever, and this would involve, oh, reading a few favorite poets intensively: Hardy, for example, John Donne, Herbert, Basil Bunting—any one of a number of my favorites. I try to get their tunes going in my head so I get a tune of my own. Then I write lots of notes on possible subjects for poetry. Sometimes that works, sometimes it doesn't. It's been my experience that sometimes about ten poems will all come in about two months; other times it will be that one poem will take ages and ages to write.

Do you tend to work very hard on poems—revising and so on?

It depends on the poem. Some poems come out almost right on the first draft—you really have to make very few small alterations. Others you have to pull to pieces and put together again. Those are two extremes: it might be anything between them. For instance, I have a poem called **"Nasturtium."** I worked at it for ages and then decided it was just terrible. I only kept about one line, but then I rewrote the poem from a slightly different idea—I don't remember the difference between the two, but it was a completely different poem from the first draft, and I think it only has about one or two lines in common with it. Only the last two lines, I think.

When you start writing a poem, do you ever have a form in your head before you write, or do you always discover the form in writing?

Again, sometimes I do, sometimes I don't. For example, a poem called **"Street Song."** Part of the idea of that poem

was to write a modern version of an Elizabethan or Jacobean street song. So of course I knew it was going to rhyme, that it might have some kind of refrain, it was going to be a particular kind of poem. Other poems I don't really know what they're going to be like, and I will jot down my notes for them kind of higgledy-piggledy all over the page, so that when I look at what I've got maybe the form will be suggested by what I have there. That's *mostly* what happens with me. I don't start by writing a couplet or something, knowing the whole thing's going to be in couplets—though even *that* has happened.

I know that you quite consciously and deliberately draw on other writers and writings in your poems. Could you describe that process a little? Do you quite ruthlessly plagiarize or pilfer?

Yes, yes, yes. Well, T.S. Eliot gave us a pleasing example, didn't he, quoting from people without acknowledgement? I remember a line in *Ash Wednesday* which was an adaptation of "Desiring this man's art and that man's scope." When I was twenty, I thought that was the most terrific line I'd read in Eliot! I didn't know that it was a line from Shakespeare's sonnets. I don't resent that in Eliot and I hope people don't resent it in me. I don't make such extensive use of unacknowledged quotation as Eliot does, but every now and again I'll make a little reference. This is the kind of thing that poets have always done. On the first page of *The Prelude,* Wordsworth slightly rewrites a line from the end of *Paradise Lost*: "The earth is all before me" instead of "The world was all before them." He was aware that many an educated reader would recognize that as being both a theft and an adaptation. He was also aware, I'm sure, that a great many of his readers wouldn't know it was and would just think it was original. That's part of the process of reading: you read a poem for what you can get out of it.

Actually, though, what you do much more often is model your poems on other poems.

Well, I grew up when the New Criticism was at its height, and I took some of the things the New Critics said very literally. When I read (let's say) George Herbert, I really do think of him as being a kind of contemporary of mine. I don't think of him as being separated from me by an impossible four hundred years of history. I feel that in an essential way this is a man with a very different mind-cast from mine, but I don't feel myself badly separated from him. I feel that we're like totally different people with different interests writing in the same room. And I feel that way of all the poets I like.

Donald Davie says of you in Under Briggflatts *that you don't use literary reference, as Eliot does, "to judge the tawdry present." He finds that refreshing.*

I don't regret the present. I don't feel it's cheap and tawdry compared with the past. I think the past was cheap and tawdry too. One of the things I noticed very early on—and I probably got it from an essay by Eliot—was that the beginning of Pope's "Verses to the Memory of an Unfortunate Lady" is virtually taken from the beginning of the "Elegie on the Lady Jane Pawlet" by Ben Jonson. Now I don't think most of Pope's readers would have realized that. I don't think Jonson was that much read in Pope's time. I may be wrong. . . So I figured that was a very interesting thing to be able to do. But no, I don't do it in the way Eliot and Pound do—to show up the present. I do it much more in the way I've described Wordsworth or Pope as doing it.

Are there any particular influences that have been consistently—or intermittently—important for you?

The first poet who influenced me in a big way—in poems that never got into print—was W.H. Auden. I'm speaking about when I was about nineteen or twenty. He's someone I'm profoundly grateful to for giving me by his example the feeling that I could write about my experience. Anne Ridler, I think, said this many years ago: that his example enabled her to write. That's what his example did for me: it made things seem easy, and the poetry I wrote then— I doubt if any of it exists any longer—was riddled with Audenesque mannerisms. But he was tremendously helpful to me. He's not been an influence I've gone back to, however. The biggest two influences after him were, in my first year as an undergraduate, John Donne and Shakespeare. I read Donne en masse and understood him for the first time. I had tried reading him in my teens and I guess I just wasn't mature enough to know what to do with it. Suddenly I could see, and it was tremendously exciting. Then, that summer vacation, I read all of Shakespeare. I read everything by Shakespeare and doing that adds a cubit to your stature. He's so inventive with language. It's the idea of concepts and experience going into language, and going into *exciting* language—of *creating* the language for your poem as you're writing it. Of course, both of those influences have returned. Who has not been influenced by Shakespeare? Even somebody who doesn't like the influence, somebody like Pound, is influenced ultimately. Then, of course, Yeats was an influence". . .

Let me put a more specific question. Could you name anybody who has extended your sensibility—opened you up to things in experience that you were not sufficiently aware of?

Anybody I enjoy reading has always done this. A literary influence is never just a literary influence. It's also an influence in the way you see everything—in the way you feel your life. I'm not sure that this affected my poetry, but I read Proust when I was about twenty, just before I went to Cambridge. (We went to university rather late in those days. We had to do national service first, you should remember.) Of course, when you read all of Proust, you live in a Proustian world for a moment. You know, that bus conductor may be homosexual! So may your grandfather—or anybody maybe! I remember when I went to Chartres for the first time, I was all set to have a Proustian disappointment and I didn't! Instead I had absolute delight; it was even better than I expected it to be. But every writer does this to you to some extent. Auden, Donne, Shakespeare, Yeats—I was about to say Yvor Winters: all of these modified the way in which I see the

whole of my experience. I don't think there's any one person more than others. And I don't lose them: I never lost Donne, I never lost Yeats really. William Carlos Williams came later on.

I don't regret the present. I don't feel it's cheap and tawdry compared with the past. I think the past was cheap and tawdry too.

—*Thom Gunn*

Can we take Williams as an example? You got interested in his work in—what?—the late fifties. Shortly afterwards your poetry began changing a lot and started including things from the world which it hadn't included before.

It's very interesting you should say "things from the world." Up to about halfway through *My Sad Captains*— that is, my first two-and-a-half books—I was trying to write heroic poetry. There are interesting reasons for this. When I was at Cambridge, as I've said, I was very much influenced by Shakespeare, and of course much of Shakespeare deals with the heroic of a certain kind. This was emphasized by the fact that I was at Cambridge with a particular generation of talented actors and directors. Some of them went on to become famous—people like Peter Wood, Peter Hall and John Barton, who directed remarkable productions of *Coriolanus,* of *The Alchemist,* of *Love's Labour's Lost,* of *Edward II*: all sorts of Elizabethan and Jacobean plays. My great friend Tony White was an actor in many of those. I was in some sense trying to write, with Sartre's help, a modern equivalent to heroic poetry. The influence of Williams altered everything. I'd been reading him a bit, but I couldn't incorporate that influence until I started to write in syllabics, and that was about 1959 perhaps—the poems from the second half of *My Sad Captains.* There I found a way, with William's help, of incorporating the more casual aspects of life, the non-heroic things in life, that are of course a part of daily experience and infinitely valuable. I suppose I could have learned that from Hardy too but I wasn't very influenced by him at that time. I'd read and liked some Hardy, but you can't always incorporate your learning from a poet at the time when you first start admiring that poet. Then I got into rather a mess with my next book, *Touch,* and some of that book seems to me distinctly inferior in that I really wasn't quite sure how to connect the poetry of everyday life and the heroic poetry (which is greatly to oversimplify the two kinds). But I wanted to make some kind of connection. I maybe started to do so when I wrote a longish poem called **"Misanthropos,"** which is included in that book.. . .

In those early books you establish almost a kind of map of terms and conceptions which stay with you all through,

though they get more ghostly and more complex later on.
They're things like the will and energy, and the figure of
the soldier, and the concept of self, and posing, and this
whole idea of risk as something which helps to define the
self. Is that something that you're conscious of as you
work—that you have this structure, almost, that you build
on?

Well, I don't think conceptually about my poetry very
much. I try not to think as a critic, I try not to think of
key words: otherwise I would start being overly self-
conscious about using them. But some of them I just
can't avoid noticing, and of course they're also life-im-
ages. Now the idea of the soldier: my childhood was full
of soldiers. I tried to write about this in a poem called
"The Corporal." I was ten at the beginning of World
War Two and sixteen when it ended, so my visual landscape was full of soldiers. Of course, I became a soldier
for two years of national service and so that was another
kind of soldier. It was a strange kind of role I had to
measure myself against. And the idea of the will: there's
a poem in **The Man with Night Sweats** called **"The**
Differences" and in the last two lines I say that I

> *think back on that night in January,*
> *When casually distinct we shared the most*
> *And lay upon a bed of clarity*
> *In luminous half-sleep where the will was lost.*

So that is not *willed* love at all. This was a very conscious reference back to my over-use of the word *will* in
my early books. I'm saying in a sense that I'm no longer
the same person as I was then, and I'm pleased that I'm
not the same person. So there is a certain consciousness
of themes but, at the same time, there's a certain blessed
unconsciousness. There was a review, for which I was
profoundly grateful, in the *Times Literary Supplement* by
Hugh Haughton: he was reviewing my recent book, **The**
Man with Night Sweats, and he traced the imagery of
embracing and touching and holding hands—and even embracing oneself at one point. That was extraordinary: it
was all there. That was not planned, it was due to the
consistency of my own mind. We all have that kind of
consistency of course. It's a question of opening yourself
up to what you really want to say, to what for you is the
truth, and you come out with consistent images in that
way. I've not been aware of that, I've really not been
aware of that, and of course the embrace is in half the
poems in the book. I was glad I didn't find that out till the
book was finished! So one does not operate in complete
rational awareness of what one's doing all the time, and I
don't want to. I seem to write awfully rational poetry, but
I want there to be a considerable amount of strength given
from what is not conscious into the consciousness there—
that kind of energy. (I won't talk about the unconscious.)
I've noticed recently I've been particularly attracted by
various things in visual art or in poetry that I explain to
myself as being a mixture of the extremely sophisticated
and the primitive. I was just pointing out this morning
some lines from Spenser's "Epithalamion." They're the
ones about who is it "which at my window peeps." It is
the moon, who "walks about high heaven all the night."

It's a wonderfully sophisticated and ornate kind of poetry,
and suddenly this tremendously physical, almost anthro-
pomorphic image of the moon walking around the sky. It's
so magnificent! I find them wonderfully beautiful lines! I
think that kind of thing happens in some way in all the art
I like. I'd like that to happen in my poetry. I think that
sometimes when my poetry comes off—anybody's poetry
when it comes off—it's making use of two strengths at
once: a very conscious arranging strength, keeping things
in schematic form, but also the stuff you can call primitive
or unconscious.

So you have the controlling mind or intellect, but it's a
control that's prepared to allow things to slip in". . .

Yes, *allowing,* very good word, yes. It's a control that will
still allow things to slip under. Welcomes them in fact.

Going back to the soldier for a minute, one rather
striking thing about that figure is the way it estab-
lishes an atmosphere for those early books. At the
time there was a lot of talk, much of it rather vacuous,
about violence in those poems. I remember Ted Hugh-
es saying somewhere that he thought this emphasis
on violence superficial and what was much more im-
portant in your work was tenderness. Don't the two
things go together?

Of course, of course. I can quote from **"The Missing,"** a
passage in which I'm speaking about a sense of "the gay
community" (a phrase I always thought was bullshit, until
the thing was vanishing). In **"The Missing"** I speak about
the "Image of an unlimited embrace," and I mean partly
friends, partly sexual partners, partly even the vaguest of
acquaintances, with the sense of being in some way part
of a community.

> *I did not just feel ease, though comfortable:*
> *Aggressive as in some ideal of sport,*
> *With ceaseless movement thrilling through the*
>   *whole,*
> *Their push kept me as firm as their support.*

Take that image of sport. (Somebody pointed out that I
constantly use the word *play* in **The Man with Night**
Sweats, which is—again—something I wasn't completely
aware of.) If you use the idea of sport, you think of the
violence of the push, yes, but there's an ambiguity: an
embrace can be a wrestler's embrace or it can be the
embrace of love. There's tremendous doubleness in that
image, which I have used elsewhere in fact: the idea of the
embrace which can be violent or tender. But if you look
at it at any one moment, if it's frozen, it could be either,
and maybe the two figures swaying in that embrace are
not even quite sure which it is. Like Aufidius and Coriolanus: they embrace, they're enemies. They embrace in
admiration at one point. It's ambiguous because the two
things are connected. It could turn, at any moment, from
the one to the other, I suppose.". . .

You once said to me that free verse and metrical verse are
different in kind. Did you mean by that that, from your

point of view as a writer, to write in free verse is almost as different from writing in meter as it is again from writing in prose?

Yes, as a form, given the essential difference that prose is enormously expansive and that most good poetry tends to be condensed. That makes for the major difference. But otherwise, yes, I think there is as much difference. You know, I've been reading for the first time a bit of Glyn Maxwell, whom I like very much. I originally got his book because I read a terrific poem of his called "Dream but a Door." That poem and a great many of the other poems I've read so far seem to be in what I would call proper meter, as opposed to sloppy meter.

In 1961 you published a book, **My Sad Captains,** *in which this difference in kind was acknowledged by the structure of the book and, except for your last collection, you've followed that pattern ever since. However, in* **My Sad Captains** *the non-metrical section is in syllabics, not free verse. How did you start writing in syllabics?*

I admired a lot of American poetry in free verse but I couldn't write free verse. The free verse I tried to write was chopped-up prose, and I could see that was no good. Then I thought of ways in which I could learn how to write in something that was not metrical, that did not have the tune of meter going through it. Once you've got the tune in your head it's very difficult to get it out. Then, somehow or other I heard about syllabics and discussed them a bit with Winters, and I found a terrific example in some poems by Donald Hall about Charlotte Corday. Donald Hall, as opposed to (let's say) Robert Bridges or Marianne Moore, was not using a long syllabic line. His was a short line and the great virtue of this, for me, was that it was not in what we understand as a meter, which involves combinations of stressed and unstressed syllables. It was virtually in free verse or prose, arranged in lines, but each line simply depended on a mechanical count. I found the short line adaptable and interesting. After a while, when I was writing in (for example) the seven-syllable line, which was my favorite, I found that I could recognize or could think up a line of that length without counting the number of syllables. I'd check on it—yes, there were seven—but it had a kind of tune of its own. This was interesting. Anyway, I was halfway to writing in free verse and then I did, later on, in my next book, go into free verse itself. I don't think I have written any syllabics since the poems in **"Misanthropos"** in *Touch.*

Was there anything you could do in syllabics that you can't do in free verse?

I'm not sure. I must say I'm quite pleased with the poem called **"My Sad Captains."** I think I hit on something there but it's not something I've been able to repeat. There's something going on there with the sounds that I'm amazed I was able to achieve. I don't think I've ever done that in free verse. I don't think I could do it in syllabics again. I certainly couldn't do it in meter: it's not a metrical effect.

It's sometimes struck me that, in syllabic verse, you get closer to prose than you do in free verse.

I don't know. It seems to me that a good deal of D.H. Lawrence's free verse is very close to prose. I like it for that. Some is more incantatory, some is more biblical, but some of it is not. It depends which poet you're speaking about: there are so many different *kinds* of free verse. There's a different kind for every poet using it in fact.

As if each writer had to invent his or her own?

Yes, though of course Pound invented several kinds. Williams invented one kind in his youth and another kind— I don't think so good—in his old age. Stevens invented one amazingly subtle kind. Winters invented a kind all of his own.

Do you think yours is a different kind again?

I try to make it so. I hope it is.

But is there a principle that you follow?

No, it just depends on my ear.

We're about to touch on the point where form and content relate to one another. When you look at **My Sad Captains,** *it's not just a formal difference between the first and second halves of the book, but a difference in the kind of content.*

It seems to me that the freer forms—and that includes syllabic—are hospitable to improvisation or the feel of improvisation. Lawrence puts this wonderfully in his famous essay "Poetry of the Present." He speaks of free verse as poetry of the present: that is, it grabs in the details and these are probably very casual details of the present, of whatever is floating through the air, whatever is on the table at the time, whatever is underfoot, however trivial— trivial but meaningful. Whereas metrical verse, he says— I think rightly—metrical verse has the greater finish, because in a sense it deals with events or experience or thinking that are more finished. "Finished" in both senses: in a punning sense, it's also more over and done with. He calls it "poetry of the past." (He also calls it "poetry of the future" but I've never understood what he means by that.) But there is the idea of the completed thought; there is what we nowadays call the idea of closure. So the freer forms invite improvisation and are hospitable to the fragmentary details of one's life, as opposed to the important completed thoughts and experiences of one's life. The freer forms are less dramatic, I think, and more casual.

Taking **My Sad Captains** *as a whole, it's a much more humanistic book than the previous two.*

I was less of a fascist. I had been a Shakespearean, Sartrean fascist! I was growing up a little, I wasn't quite so juvenile. I was very much influenced by Sartre, as everybody realized and as I was not sorry for everybody to realize. I was in quest of the heroic in the modern world—

whether I succeeded or not—and that was a slightly fascistic quest because the heroic is so often a martial kind of virtue. Well, by the time I got to *My Sad Captains* I was growing up a bit. . . I suppose I acknowledge other kinds of life in the first poem in the book, **"In Santa Maria del Popolo,"** in that I'm speaking about the old women as well as the heroic gesture that's "Resisting, by embracing, nothingness."

I become very conscious in that book that religion is an option not open to you.

I'm not very spiritual!

Yes, but I'm asking you about a quality of language, I think. There are certain poems in the first part of **My Sad Captains** *which are metaphysical in content. They seem to invite inquiry into purpose and meaning in experience, yet the possibility of purpose and meaning seems closed off for you. You know: "Purposeless matter hovers in the dark" and so on.*

Oh I agree. Of course, this was somewhat different when I came to write *Moly,* when I took LSD. LSD certainly extends your awareness into other areas. It's chemical: it may be simply that you're not seeing round corners but you just think you are. You tend to think that these other areas are spiritual—and they may be. There's at least one poem, **"The Messenger,"** in which I speak about angels: "Is this man turning angel as he stares / At one red flower. . .?" I was playing with the idea. I don't think I was being irresponsible. It is still a question, and it's not a question that I answer in the poem. The poem where I most overtly take up religious terms—spiritual terms would be better— is a poem called **"At the Centre,"** which I now think is rather a pompous poem. This came out of my biggest acid trip. I took a colossal amount and stood with my friend Don Doody on a roof from which you could see the sign of a brewery, which had on the top of it a magnificent image in neon lights, even during the day, of a huge glass. The outline was permanently there, but it would fill up and drain with yellow lights, as if it were a filling-up glass of beer that would suddenly vanish and then fill up again from the bottom. This of course became a fantastic image for. . . Existence Itself! I think it comes into the poem with all the talk of flowing and stuff. And there I was indeed having, in that experience, a rather defiant conversation with a God whom I did not believe existed! There was one very funny thing happened during that day. I've only been able to admit it in recent years. (This was about 1968.) At one point, in this grandiloquent way that I had, I said to God: "What does it all mean?" Suddenly—this was a genuine hallucination—what seemed like a plastic bubble of shit crossed the sky. I did not admit this to my companion but I do remember saying: "No, oh no, not that. I do not want to believe that life is shit!" And I rejected that hallucination. But of course, the hallucination came from *me* in the first place. I'm not saying that the experiences in *Moly* were not genuine and I wouldn't disown anything in *Moly.* In fact, I still think of it as my best book, though few others have thought so. I think these experiences elicited my best poetry from me.

The last poem in **Moly,** *"Sunlight," is in form a kind of religious poem—in a way that* **"At the Centre"** *isn't. I mean, it's a sort of hymn.*

And the sun is like a god. At the same time, I do say in the poem that it has flaws and it's all going to burn out one day. So I'm qualifying it there.

So it's finite.

It's finite, yes, but to take a line of Stevens's from "Sunday Morning": "Not as a god, but as a god might be."

The other thing in **Moly,** *of course, is metamorphosis, and that reminds one of paganism.*

Yes, well the whole theme of the book is metamorphosis. Almost every poem I think. That was LSD, of course. It did make you into a different person. The myths of metamorphosis had much more literal meaning for me: the idea that somebody could grow horns, that somebody could turn into a laurel tree, or that somebody could be centaur (in the **"Tom-Dobbin"** poems—Tom is me of course), or turn into an angel. In the hallucinations—or more likely, distortions—that you saw under the influence of LSD, things did change their shape. You know, you could see bumps on somebody's forehead perhaps—I never did— but that's the kind of thing you could see that might resemble horns. You saw other possibilities.

Was there also a literary source? Were you thinking of Ovid?

Of course, yes. But I don't know if I'd read Ovid yet. Where I first got the myths was from Nathaniel Hawthorne's two retellings of them in *Tanglewood Tales* and *A Wonder-Book for Boys and Girls.* Often when people think I'm deriving from Ovid, I'm actually deriving from those books, which I read in my childhood. But he got them from Ovid.

We've skated over your previous book, **Touch.** *A lot of that was written during a year's visit to London, wasn't it?*

It wasn't actually. I'll tell you what I wrote on that year's visit. I wrote a good deal of **"Misanthropos,"** but it was about half written before I came. It was certainly all sketched out, so I was in a sense filling in blanks. I also wrote **"Confessions of the Life Artist"** and all of *Positives*—but those are just captions, those were easy.

They're quite important though, aren't they? Weren't they your first poems in free verse?

I think they probably were, yes. I remember thinking to myself rather pompously at the time that I was trying to adapt William Carlos Williams for the English—as if Charles Tomlinson had not been doing that for some years before me! I had very great difficulty in the years when I was writing the poems that went into *Touch.* There was a lot of time that went by when I just wasn't able to write. . .

I either couldn't write anything or I was writing poetry that got printed but didn't ultimately seem good enough to put in the book. I still wouldn't want to reprint them. They seem melodramatic or phony or something.

The book strikes me as transitional. Would you say it was because around that time—possibly through coming to London—you were becoming more decisively American than British? You lay yourself open to American influences. . .

I suppose that's right. How interesting! Yes. You know, people don't always think of themselves that clearly, so I need someone like you to tell me this kind of thing and I can assent to it. I'm not being ironic when I say this. It's just that we all know how difficult it is to stand back from ourselves and to perceive the pattern in our own lives, which may be perfectly obvious to other people. I do indeed think that's true. Yes.

Was it difficult to accept that you could write that sort of "open" poetry?

No, though change is always difficult. It's so true what you're saying. While I was in England I wrote an essay about William Carlos Williams, which later got into my prose book *The Occasions of Poetry.* So I did a lot of reading of Williams for that. And I discovered Snyder while I was here in England. I read *Riprap,* which I found in Foyle's bookshop in London. It had been out for four or five years but I hadn't yet read it. Creeley I didn't like at that time. I had to read more of him and eventually came to like him a very great deal. But he didn't make sense for me somehow, until I'd read him more thoroughly.

And Robert Duncan?

Oh yes, and Duncan was all mixed up with my acquaintance with him of course. The three writers who have influenced me *personally*—in a combination of their work and their character in other words through friendship—have been Yvor Winters, Christopher Isherwood and Robert Duncan. With two of those, Winters and Duncan, I was really just a listener. I call myself a friend but I wasn't a friend in that there wasn't much reciprocation between us. I don't think Winters or Duncan knew me very well. Partly, with Duncan, because he talked so much! He talked all the time—fascinatingly—and didn't give you much time to answer. Or when you did have a chance to answer, it was about ten minutes too late. Duncan was aware of this and was always making jokes against himself because of it. He had one very funny story about Olson. He said: "When I first met Olson, we found there was an immediate problem, because he liked to talk all the time and I liked to talk all the time, but we solved it at once by talking simultaneously!" But I don't think Duncan knew me very well. I was perfectly happy: I *learned* from him. Having lunch with him or spending an afternoon with him was such an extraordinary experience. I would go away with my head teeming with ideas and images and I'd write them down in my notebook and feel like writing poetry. I usually didn't and I didn't write Duncan-type

poetry in fact, but he was a tremendously fertilizing influence. He was that kind of influence on everybody.

Winters and Duncan, though, seems an extraordinary contrast.

I have sometimes said to myself: "I am the only person in the world ever to have dedicated poems to both Winters and Duncan." They hated each other. They didn't meet but they hated each other. When they referred to each other it was with contempt, though I must say Duncan was a little more respectful at times of Winters for his sheer consistency. Of course, as I said before, Winters was what we would nowadays call homophobic.

That seems not to have bothered you, though?

Well, most people were homophobic; whole departments of English were! You couldn't be honest then. Sometimes young people say to me: "Why were you in the closet in those days?" I was in the closet because I would not only have lost my job, I'd have been kicked out of America and consequently would not have been able to live with my lover. That was a very practical reason for my behavior, dishonest though it may have been. I suppose there was even a danger of going to prison at certain times, because the act of having sex with another man was illegal in many states. So there was no question of my being frank with Winters, though I think latterly he must have realized. He certainly didn't at the period of our greatest contact. I didn't see that much of him once I had left Stanford.

Well, I don't think conceptually about my poetry very much. I try not to think as a critic, I try not to think of key words: otherwise I would start being overly self-conscious about using them.

—*Thom Gunn*

Can we return to the contrast with Duncan?

Yes. Winters tried to be a complete rationalist, though he was in fact a tremendous romantic. Nobody would be that much of a rationalist unless they were really romantic. Duncan was a joyful irrationalist, even liking to write nonsyntactical sentences which could be looked at from each end! It could be very irritating: looked at from each end they'd have different meanings. Suddenly the syntax can change. . .

How do you think it is that you absorb such contrasts into your personality without losing the coherence of your writing?

I've never had any trouble with that. When I was reading what they nowadays call the canon of English literature to get a degree here at Cambridge, I had no difficulty in reading Pope with appreciation and Keats with appreciation, though they stood for completely different things. I, in a sense, read them as living writers. They were living in that they were speaking directly to me. I'm aware of all that's wrong with reading unhistorically. Nevertheless, one does read unhistorically. Primarily it's Pope or Keats speaking to me, Thom Gunn. I was aware that they would not have wanted to have anything to do with each other, but I never had difficulty in reconciling people who were in themselves irreconcilable. I'm a very unprincipled person. People like to talk so much about poetics now and theory. I don't have theory. I expect my practice could be brought down to theory but I'm not interested in doing that. Maybe if I ever get famous enough, somebody will do it for me!

Can you summarize what you learned from Duncan? There's a poem dedicated to him in your next book, **Jack Straw's Castle.**

It's not the best example though. I think the poem where I used Duncan most was **"The Menace."** I put on different voices, I am somewhat dislocated. . . His greatest poem he speaks of as a mosaic, "A Poem Beginning with a Line by Pindar." Actually it's something like Pound's way of writing—by juxtaposition of fragments. **"The Menace"** is written in this way: there is free verse, there is even kind of nursery-rhyme regular verse, there is prose and there is a freedom of form that I learned from him. It's deeper than just form, of course. Put it this way: the main difference between Winters and Duncan was that Winters was deliberately a poet of closure and Duncan deliberately a poet of process. Duncan spoke of writing as a process in which, if you were a good boy, things would come to you during the writing. The most interesting parts. Of course, they're both right to some extent, but they were making different emphases. I think in my practice I have become more interested in this idea of writing as a process and being open to things happening to you while you're writing—I mean things coming out of your imagination.

In the second half of your career, you seem to have become preoccupied with those ideas of openness and closure. Somewhere, talking about **Moly,** *you refer to "definition" and "flow," which are analogous to openness and closure.*

They are analogous. I play with these notions particularly in a poem called **"Duncan,"** which is about his death. The last lines of the poem recapitulate the Venerable Bede's famous story about the sparrow flying through the feasting hall. I see the hall as some barns are nowadays, with open gables at each end: that is, both open and closed. It depends whether you're inside or outside. They're inside a building, and Bede's analogy is that this is a man's life. But if you see it under the aspects of eternity—of the whole sky as being what you're in—then you're never inside. I'm playing with the notion of insideness and outsideness.

The subject of that poem, **"Duncan,"** *is a writer who takes the view from the outside, but the poem itself is in a strict traditional stanza form. Is that also important, that not only are you preoccupied with openness and closure but that you marry the two in different ways?*

I've always been trying to, yes. Donald Davie once said that he wanted to combine the influences in himself of Pound and Winters. I remember rather sarcastically remarking in print that this was like trying to abide by the principles of Hitler and Gandhi at the same time. But Donald was right! One can do this kind of thing; if one believes in the validity of the different poetries, then one can in some way marry or digest whatever is in them. Yes, I feel very much at ease in metrical and rhyming forms. I feel a certain freedom in them. I don't feel that they are constricting. I feel I can play tricks with them that open them up.

There are two moments in your relatively recent writing when you seem to fall back on closure and on meter. One is in **Moly** *and the other is in* **The Man with Night Sweats,** *the elegiac poems about AIDS victims. . .*

I know why I did that in **Moly.** I've spoken about it so often that I'll simply summarize it by saying that I was trying to deal with what seemed like the experience of the infinite, deliberately using a finite form in dealing with it because I was afraid that it would not be dealt with at all in a form that also partook of the non-finite. I don't know why I've been attracted to it recently. It's not just with the AIDS poems. It's in the poems I was writing for about four years before I started on any of those. The first of the AIDS poems was **"Lament"** and that's in couplets. It just came to hand, it just seemed to me a useful form, but it was also that because I'd been writing in rhyme and meter so much, so concentratedly, for the previous four years.

Do you think that writing **"Lament"** *in couplets established that as the kind of form you would use for the rest of them?*

That's probably right.

Let's go back to **Jack Straw's Castle.** *A lot of that book, particularly the title poem, seems to me to represent the bad face of the* **Moly** *experience.*

That was deliberate. Much of **Moly** was about dreams; this was about nightmares. Maybe I should explain who Jack Straw is. There's one of many songs that I like from the Grateful Dead called "Jack Straw" and I used to wonder what an American could make of the phrase "Jack Straw." There's an English pub called Jack Straw's Castle and an English reader might know that Straw was one of the leaders of the Peasants' Revolt. But Americans couldn't be expected to know that. So I looked "Jack Straw" up in the dictionary and found that it means a worthless person—legally "a man of straw," a person of no account. Also I was reading Dante at the time, so lots of references to the *Inferno* come in. There are heaps of literary references in that poem, but it's absolutely unnecessary for anybody to know. It was just fun doing them. The kittens changing into the Furies came from *Through the*

Looking Glass, when the kittens change into the Red Queen and the White Queen and so on. There's a bit from *Kidnapped* when David Balfour's walking up some stairs and suddenly there's a great gap. But yes, you're right, the drug dreams of *Moly* have all gone sour in *Jack Straw. . .*

I suppose I was trying to say that **Jack Straw's Castle** *feels less optimistic than* **Moly.** *Also, Robert Wells was telling me that he'd noticed in a lot of your poems a preoccupation with sequences of rooms, with houses and cellars and so on, which have a somewhat claustrophobic effect.*

You'd have to ask a shrink about that. It's a common enough metaphor for a person's body or a person's mind. It's like a house and there are rooms, there are half-hidden rooms in it, there are attics where nobody ever goes. . . I expect Freud speaks about it somewhere. You might almost say it was a cultural metaphor rather than an individual one. I do dream a lot about houses and about rooms, but I've always assumed everybody did.

Two other things happen in **Jack Straw's Castle** *that hadn't obviously happened in your work before. One is that there's a series of poems which are clearly autobiographical, in which you're looking back mainly on your childhood and adolescence. The other is that it's the book in which you come out as a homosexual. I wondered if there was any connection between that and the secret rooms: you know, the opening-up.*

Probably, probably. In the following book I use it as a metaphor in a poem called **"Talbot Road,"** where I speak about the canals which are there all over London, but you never know they're there unless you happen to be on the top of a bus: they're hidden behind walls and fences mostly. Yes, it's not unconnected. Of course, I came out sexually because, when everybody came out sexually, it became safe enough legally for the first time. In 1974 I was in New York, and there was the gay parade there. I didn't particularly want to go on it, but I was staying with somebody who was going on it and who would really have felt considerable contempt for me if I hadn't gone. I went on it so that he would think well of me. I was delighted by it! I was walking along in it and I kind of floated forward and backward a bit, so I was sometimes walking with my friend and sometimes not, and there was this wonderful little man who looked like a bank clerk. He was wearing a suit and he said he was from Hartford, Connecticut, and I thought: "Yes, that's terrific. That's what it's all about, isn't it?" I was delighted by it. Or as they nowadays say, "empowered!"

But how did it then come into the poetry?

I admitted it in, whereas formerly I had covered it over or disguised it or excluded it. I was now *able* to include it. For one thing, if I'd brought it in when I first started to publish, I don't think periodicals or possibly even book publishers would have found my work publishable. Things were that different in 1954. It was good reasoning; it was not just cowardice. I mean, it was cowardice as well, but

there was good reason not to write openly. Only a few very unusual people like Robert Duncan and Angus Wilson did write openly, and even with Angus Wilson I think it was only implicit—nobody could have been that interested in gay behavior without being gay himself. So that's how it happened. The end of **"Jack Straw's Castle"** where I'm in bed with a man—it would not have ended that way twenty years before. I'd have found some other way of dealing with it. Mind you, I never lied. I never wrote about a woman as a disguise for a man, the way Tennessee Williams in a sense did in his plays.

So the women in **Fighting Terms**. . .

The women in *Fighting Terms* were real women, yes. But I was guilty of using the Audenesque *you* to cover both sexes, which is what I think Alan Sinfield means when he speaks about "universality," which we were always taught at school was something we should be finding in our reading. Sinfield says that, when you use *you,* Auden could say it was the universal *you,* which could be applied to anybody, but in fact we are going to think it's a woman—and probably a white woman too! It's something I have a great distaste for, the word *universality.* My attitude to it is slightly different from Alan's—or rather, I come to a dislike of it through a different approach. Of course, this is something I was taught at school—this is something my students were taught at school. I started to have trouble with it when I would say to a student who was reading (let's say) *Othello,* "What value is this play to us? Why should you be interested in Othello?" And they would say—a little too glibly, I thought— "Oh, it's universal!" Well, one thing the situation of Othello is not is universal! In his position as the black commander of a white army, or in his marriage, or in his very dubious connection with Iago. That's unique. I suppose one might say that there are sentiments voiced in the play that could be universalized. I mean, if we were in that position— though I have certainly never felt jealousy of that sort myself—we could feel "What oft was thought, but ne'er so well expressed." But it seems to me that, in a larger sense, the idea of universality depends on a notion of similarity. That is, people like Hamlet particularly, men like Hamlet, young men like Hamlet, because they identify with Hamlet, because they are similar to Hamlet. But in my own experience, what I get from reading is both similarity and dissimilarity, likeness and difference. I think I probably read more for difference than I do for likeness. Appealing to universality seems to obscure this (for me) rather important mixture. I reached this conclusion quite independently and now I find that it's a very fashionable notion indeed! I find that all the critics nowadays are against universalizing.

There's a review of The Passages of Joy *by Donald Davie, where he somewhat recants on an earlier statement he had made in which he had praised you for renouncing what he calls "the glibly deprecating ironies" of much modern British poetry and going back to "that phase of English in which the language could register without embarrassment the frankly heroic." He's talking about the influence of Shakespeare and Marlowe on your work.*

But in this particular review he suggests that something has happened to your poetry which involves your sacrificing that rhetorical force. It's quite clear, though he doesn't directly say so, that what he means is that by admitting to homosexuality in your poems you have somehow given up a poetic advantage.

Yes. I'm terrifically grateful for that essay and for everything Donald has written about me. I think it has been consistently insightful. Nevertheless, his particular point there is that coming into the open about homosexuality—not *being* homosexual, but *speaking* about it openly—has been a diminishing force in my poetry. I don't see that at all and I don't quite understand how it operates in his mind, as if the subject matter were so *modern* that there can be no influence from any poet earlier than (I think he says) Whitman. Well, there *is* Marlowe! There are others whom one knows were homosexual. There are also most of Shakespeare's sonnets. We don't know what Shakespeare's primary sexual preferences were, but he does rather more than take up the subject. So it's not without precedents. I don't agree with his main assumption there. Nevertheless, he's got a right to his evaluation of that particular book. It's true that there's probably more free verse in that book and, if we're dealing with traditions, the tradition of free verse doesn't go back very far. So, when I'm writing free verse, I'm writing in a comparatively modern tradition. He connects the two in a way that I think is wrong, but he does it very intelligently. I don't think he'll any longer be able to make that connection in light of *The Man with Night Sweats.* Let me say that I also respect Donald so much that something that was in my mind the whole time I was writing this new book was: how can I show him that he's wrong?!

I wonder if I can play devil's advocate at this point? Take an early poem of yours, **"The Allegory of the Wolf Boy"** *from* **The Sense of Movement.** *It seems to me very clear now—though it wasn't when I first read it—that that poem is about being a homosexual.*

Indeed it is.

The poem is, to use Davie's word, "resonant." It's almost as if the not-owning-up is precisely what makes it so resonant, I suppose this is related to what we've just been saying about the universal: that from the particular experience of being homosexual, it seems to establish resonances which all of us can feel as human beings.

There's no real answer to this. I think you probably overvalue that poem a bit, but I'll admit your general point: that sometimes strategies of evasion—that does sound very 1990s, doesn't it?—may contribute to what makes a poem successful. In fact, whatever you have going, including the obstacles, contribute to the making of a poem, even the obstacle of having to write with some baby yelling in the next room or something like that. That kind of very obvious difficulty is something you may have to overcome and it may end with some benefit to the poem. I'd go further and say that one of the things that makes for good writing is getting to a certain point and getting

stuck in the elucidation of an idea or whatever you're writing about—the description of a thing, some imagery, or even choosing a word—and you have to stop and think maybe for weeks. *That* very likely may be a strength in the poem. But it doesn't mean that you have to *invite* obstacles. If you did that, you could invite them so successfully that you'd never write a poem. There are always plenty of obstacles in writing, and I don't think that being honest about one's sexuality is something to be avoided because the need for evasion is a useful obstacle.

There's a splendid phrase on the blurb of one of your books that comes from a review by Frank Kermode. He calls you "a chaste and powerful modern poet." You said earlier on that your poems were moral evaluations of a life some people would find immoral. There's something paradoxical here. What is it in your language that invites such a word as chaste?

I can't really comment on that because I don't know what the principles are that make me choose one word rather than another. I choose a word that seems to me more appropriate, more meaningful. But we all do that, don't we? And we end up with different styles. I do know that, extremely unfashionably, I admire the qualities of somebody like Isherwood—of what I would call a "transparent" style. Now the word *transparent,* as you know, is much frowned on by most critics nowadays. They don't like that at all. I *love* it! I think that's what it's all about. I certainly think that's what I *want* it to be about. Obviously I want more than clarity. I'm raising questions all the way with each of these words, with each questionable abstraction! But you see what I mean? I'm aiming to get through—most of the time—on a first reading if possible. I do not want to be an obscure poet. I do not want even to be as obscure a poet as Lowell, though I may often be so. That's in no sense a derogatory comment on Lowell; he's just a little more difficult at times than I am.

What do you mean exactly by transparency?

Transparent to my meaning. Of course, there is an implied contradiction with what I was saying before about poetry as process. There's the whole question raised of how much meaning you have before you sit down to write and how it gets altered in the process of writing. But you do start with some knowledge of what you're going to say after all. It may well not be what you end up saying, but it often is related to what you say. Yes, transparent. . . as though you're looking through a glass at an object. That's what the word implies. So the words are the glass to my mind. My mind is the fish in the tank behind the glass.

Isn't it also that you want a style that allows something to come into the poem which has nothing to do with you? You want the world in the poem. You don't want just Thom Gunn in it.

Oh, indeed, yes. I see what you're saying: it's not just the fish but it's all behind the fish as well.

One of the things that happens in **The Passages of Joy**

is that there are lots of other people in the book—there, as far as I can see, for their own sake.

I liked the idea of a populated book. I've always liked the idea of a book of poems as a kind of. . . if not a world, a country in a world. One of my impulses in writing is the desire to possess my experience and to possess *all* my experiences—my funny and trivial experiences too. I like to bring in people on the street. I was thinking that, if the romantics had "effusions" and certain of the modernists had "observations"—*Prufrock and Other Observations,* Marianne Moore's book *Observations*—what I'm trying to do is *record.* I'm recording the past, I'm also recording the present and I'm recording the world around me and the things that go through my mind. One of the things I want to record is the street, because the streets that I move through are part of my life that I enjoy and want to *possess.* I don't any longer think of a poem as "loot," but I do think of it as in some sense possessing something.

The streets are very much San Francisco streets, aren't they—particularly in the last few books?

Increasingly, yes. This started with *Touch,* though. There are bits of San Francisco in *Touch:* you know, **"Pierce Street," "Taylor Street," "The Produce District."** And probably more with each book. It thrilled me to write a litany of names in **"Night Taxi,"** the last poem in *The Passages of Joy.* There are two lines where I take four extreme points in the city:

> *China Basin to Twin Peaks,*
> *Harrison Street to the Ocean.*

I loved doing that. It's pure litany, it's not meaningful. But it gave me a feeling of possession or achievement— to have found a place for those names.

This is terribly surprising for an expatriate really, but it makes you almost a regional poet, like Thomas Hardy in "Wessex Heights." It's almost as if you'd invented roots for yourself.

I *have* invented roots. There must be some kind of seaweed that's rooted in one place and then floats to another place and puts down the same roots!

The other great theme in **The Passages of Joy** *is friendship.*

That was quite self-conscious too. It must be the greatest value in my life. This is not a literary influence, though I admire Ben Jonson very much and he likes to write about friendship. I write about love, I write about friendship. Unlike Proust, I think that love and friendship are part of the same spectrum. Proust says that they are absolutely incompatible. I find that they are absolutely intertwined.

Has AIDS had a fundamental effect on your poetry?

Anything as big as that must have had some fundamental effect, but I can't measure it and I'm not sure what it

would be. I've had to attend at the deathbeds of quite a few friends. On the other hand, what I'm especially focusing on is not the *kind* of death they had. What most of these poems have in common as a subject is the way people face death. It's not the only thing I'm writing about in them but it seems to be one of the main things.

Take **"The Man with Night Sweats"** *itself. You have the image of the flesh as a shield in that, and it reminds me of things you said when you were young and were writing about soldiers. It's as if the invasion of this virus has called into question a lot of assumptions that your poetry had been built on up till then.*

I suspect the word *shield* is something of a dead metaphor as I use it there, but it certainly calls into question the whole concept of taking risks. The same is true of the following poem, **"In Time of Plague."** I'm not much of a risk-taker myself but I've always found the taking of risks rather admirable in a wonderful and showy kind of way. And that's exactly one of the things one can't do any longer in one's sexual behavior because taking risks can have mortal consequences now. The worst consequence before would have been a completely curable disease—since the invention of penicillin after all. It was a fruitful kind of risk. I'm also implying what we know about even children taking risks. Children take risks in their games, which ultimately strengthen their bodies. So there's a kind of pattern in our knowledge that active behavior is sometimes a bit physically risky. You know, when you go swimming, you could get drowned. But that is ultimately a strengthening thing and suddenly it isn't any longer. This is something that those two poems have in common: they had to go together in the book, though I don't think I wrote them together.

"In Time of Plague" *takes it a bit further. . .*

That poem is absolutely true. I changed the names.

In that poem the love of risk is also a love of death, isn't it?

Yes, and I say "I know it, and do not know it," and "They know it, and do not know it." We know several things at once, and we also don't know each of them. We also sometimes act as if we didn't know.

Another theme, which seems to have grown through your work, and which flourishes in a special way in **The Man with Night Sweats,** *is the theme of dereliction. There are a lot of tramps in the book. . .*

I've always been interested in the life of the street. I suppose it's always seemed to me like a kind of recklessness, a freedom after the confinement of the home or the family. This goes way, way back to my teens even. There was a poem which started with the words "Down and out," that being (I thought romantically) a kind of freedom. In my second book there is a poem called **"In Praise of Cities"** where I play with this idea in a rather Baudelairean kind of way. There is the promiscuity of the streets, which can hold promise of a sexual promiscuity as well, which is exciting. I love streets. I could stand on the street and look at people all day, in the same way that Wordsworth could walk around the lakes and look at those things all day. As soon as Reagan pushed the nutcases out on to the street in California, turning them back to the "community," which means turning them out on to the streets in fact, the composition of the people on the streets began to change a good deal. So I wrote about that. There's a funny case in my recent book where I wrote about a character I call "Old Meg"—after Keats, who was writing after Scott—and I found that, at about the same time, my friend August Kleinzahler, who lives a few blocks away from me, had written about (we concluded) the same person. He called her Mrs. B, which says something about the difference between him and me I suppose: I make a rather literary antecedent and he makes up a name.

Do you suffer badly from writer's block?

Well, everybody does, I suppose. Or there are very few writers who don't. Even Duncan, who I thought wrote continuously and easily: there were two years when he didn't write anything. There are certain times when you are absolutely sterile, that is, when words seem to mean nothing. The words are there, the things in the world are there, you are interested in things in the same way and theoretically you can think up subjects for poems, but you simply can't write. You can sit down at your notebook with a good idea for a poem and nothing will come. It's as though there is a kind of light missing from the world. It's a wordless world, and it's somehow an empty and rather sterile world. I don't know what causes this, but it's very painful.

Do you think that the periods of fecundity are in any way related to these dry periods?

It might be that you have to go through dry periods so as in a sense to store things up. Maybe it's like a pregnancy. Sometimes I think it is and sometimes I don't. It'd be very nice to get up every day and write a new poem. I'm sure every poet would like to do that, but it's not possible. It may be that you've had some imaginative experience that's going to become a poem and it just has to become more a part of you. It has to stew, it has to cook until it's ready, and maybe there's nothing else to write about in-between. You've just got to cook away until it's ready to be taken out of the oven.

T.S. Eliot, when he was interviewed for The Paris Review, *was asked whether he thought his poetry belonged to the tradition of American rather than British literature. I wonder if I can put the same question to you in reverse?*

I call myself an Anglo-American poet. If it's a question of the poets I admire, there's a tremendous number of both British and American poets whom I admire greatly. I think I'm a weird product of both. I'm not like the other products, but then we're none of us like each other. Most American poets at least *know* all the British poets and there's some kind of a relation there. Probably that's a little less true of British poets, though they're pretty well-read in the American modernists and probably Whitman

and Dickinson as well. So I'm not sure that it's any longer a particularly meaningful question.

What do you feel about the situation of poetry in the English language at the moment?

There's always a lot to be unhappy with at any time. We look back on the best of the romantics or the Elizabethans or any period. We don't remember there was an incredible amount of junk being written too. The Elizabethans seem so good, and there are so many good ones. There were also very many bad ones. At times it seems to me that all the giants have died, but maybe it always seems like that. People like Eliot and Pound and Stevens and Williams and even Yeats were around for part of my life—I suppose I was already reading a bit of poetry at the age of ten, which was when Yeats died. Then the following generation died early. Crane died very early and Winters didn't exactly live into old age. People like Lowell and Berryman destroyed themselves in various ways. But there are a great many youngish poets or poets of my own generation whom I enjoy reading very much and find exciting and like to explore. If I mention a few names, these are no surprise to anybody because I've written about them. In America I very much admire Jim Powell and August Kleinzahler. In Britain I'd like to mention the present interviewer! And I like Robert Wells's poetry a great deal and Tony Harrison's and there are younger people: I mentioned Glyn Maxwell, whom I'm reading right now and who strikes me as very energetic and wonderfully crazy in a really good kind of way. And then there are surprises, of course, like W.S. Graham. I discounted him for so many years. I thought he was just an imitator of Dylan Thomas—and he probably was at first. But meanwhile he was creeping up from behind and, when we all rediscovered him something like twelve years ago, that was quite a revelation. Of course, Basil Bunting only died the other day, and he was a giant. So this isn't altogether a bad time to be living. I've no idea what the time looks like: how it measures up against other times, or even what it's shaped like—who the big ones are and who the small ones. I'd just rather follow my personal interests and enthusiasms.

FURTHER READING

Criticism

Bartlett, Lee. "Thom Gunn." In *Talking Poetry: Conversations in the Workshop with Contemporary Poets.* Albuquerque: University of New Mexico Press, 1987, pp. 88-101.

Gunn discusses the contemporary state of poetry, his interest in traditional poetic forms, and the influences on his work.

Bradley, Jerry. "Thom Gunn." In *The Movement: British Poets of the 1950s.* New York: Twayne Publishers, 1993, pp. 117-28.

Offers a thematic and stylistic overview of Gunn's verse.

Gewanter, David. "An Interview with Thom Gunn." *Agni,* No. 36 (1992): 289-99, 300-09.

> Gunn discusses stylistic concerns, expatriation, and his role within the gay community.

Giles, Paul. "From Myth into History: The Later Poetry of Thom Gunn and Ted Hughes." In *Contemporary British Poetry: Essays in Theory and Criticism,* edited by James Acheson and Romana Huk. Albany: State University of New York Press, 1996, pp. 143-73.

> Compares the later verse of Ted Hughes and Thom Gunn.

Martin, Robert K. "Fetishizing America: David Hockney and Thom Gunn." In *The Continuing Presence of Walt Whitman: The Life after the Life,* edited by Robert K. Martin. Iowa City: University of Iowa Press, 1992, pp. 114-26.

> Contends that both artists "make use of a constructed vision of America as part of an implicit critique of their European and British heritage and as a model for a socially sexuality."

Sinfield, Alan. "Thom Gunn in San Francisco: An Interview." *Critical Survey* 2, No. 2 (1990): 223-30.

> Gunn discusses his sexuality and its consequences on his work.

Additional coverage of Gunn's life and career is contained in the following sources published by Gale Group: *Contemporary Authors* Vols. 17-20; *Contemporary Authors New Revision Series* Vols. 9, 33; *Contemporary Dictionary of British Literary Biography* 1960-Present; *Contemporary Literary Criticism* Vols. 3, 6, 18, 32, 81; *Dictionary of Literary Biography* Vol. 27; *DISCovering Authors: Poets Module; International Contemporary Authors New Revisions* Vol. 33; and *Major Twentieth Century Writers* Vol 1.

Galway Kinnell
1927-

American poet, novelist, translator and essayist

INTRODUCTION

A writer of lyric free verse, Galway Kinnell is among the post-war generation of American poets including Robert Bly, James Wright, James Dickey and W.S. Merwin. Like them, he incorporated more experimental language in his poetic verse. While Yeats was most notably an early influence, Whitman, Frost, and Rilke also inspired him; Whitman's *Song of Myself,* seen in *The Avenue Bearing the Initial of Christ into the New World* and Rilke's *Duino Elegies* in the ten-part *The Book of Nightmares* are two such examples. Preoccupied with death and man's relationships with nature, Kinnell writes toward resolving questions of immortality by creating a "panentheistic" theology in his verse. Kinnell won both the Pulitzer Prize and the American Book Award for *Selected Poems* in 1982. As Charles Bell said of his former student, "Of all the poets born in the twenties and thirties, Galway Kinnell is the only one who has taken up the passionate symbolic search of the great American tradition."

Biographical Information

Born in Providence, Rhode Island, in 1927, Kinnell grew up near Pawtucket, and his Christian upbringing figures into much of his early work. He served in the U.S. Navy from 1945-46, and in 1948 he graduated *summa cum laude* from Princeton University, where Charles Bell served as an important mentor, as did W.S. Merwin. "He wrote poems; I wrote verse," he said of Merwin. Kinnell earned an M.A. from the University of Rochester in 1949, supervising the University of Chicago's downtown liberal arts program from 1951-54 and thereafter serving as Fulbright Professor at the Universities of Grenoble, Iran, Nice, and Sydney, Australia. Before settling into academic life, he worked registering black voters in the South in 1962. His first publication, *What a Kingdom It Was,* appeared in 1960. He went on to hold numerous poet-in-residency positions, awards and grants, among them the National Institute of Arts and Letters Award, 1962; two Guggenheim Fellowships, 1962, 1974; a Rockefeller Foundation grant, 1968; a National Endowment for the Arts Grant, 1969-70; a MacArthur Fellowship; in addition to his Pulitzer Prize and American Book Award for *Selected Poems,* in 1983. Kinnell married Ines Delgado de Torres and has two children, Maud Natasha and Fergus. He lives in Vermont and is among the eminent leaders of the Creative Writing Program at New York University.

Major Works

Included in his first published work, *What a Kingdom It Was* (1960), is one of Kinnell's best known poems, the long, Whitmanesque "The Avenue Bearing the Initial of Christ into the New World." Reflecting the plight of fellow urban residents, primarily Jewish, of Avenue C in New York City, the panacea for them as well as for all humanity becomes a need for reconciliation and a recognition of the universality of suffering. Transcendence accomplished through the intercession of everyday objects emerges as another solution, a theme that characterizes Kinnell's work. Likewise, religious symbolism common to his poetry and a unique vision surface in this volume. *While Flower Herding on Mount Monadnock* (1964) did not represent new developments in Kinnell's writing; however, *Body Rags* (1968) extends his concern for loss and privation to an even darker realm, that of death. In two of Kinnell's most often anthologized poems, "The Porcupine" and "The Bear," the speaker identifies with two suffering, dying animals. If violence, death and nothingness are the essence of life and art, then as Kinnell writes in "The Bear," the only answer is intensity of experience.

The book-length poem *The Book of Nightmares* (1971) mollifies the poet's dark vision of death and rebirth by fire. Beginning with the birth of his daughter and ending with the birth of his son, Kinnell ties the ten sections of the book to the cycles of a human existence forced to reforge connections that have been broken by a society without community. As a carefully crafted sequence, it contains the poet's anxiety for the fragile lives brought into a world of "nightmares" and death, and captures his compassion for them. As a result, joy and sorrow, and life and death, become intertwined.

After nine years, *Mortal Acts, Mortal Words* (1980) was published, representing a shift in Kinnell's concerns. The angels and abysses of *The Book of Nightmares* give way to images from his private life, and with a lighter tone and looser style, he conversely is able to achieve greater emotional impact and thematic resonance in this collection. Throughout Kinnell hits the high and low notes of "the music of grace," a central motif, which sings out his belief in immersion in experiences of mortality. It is music to "touch and feel, things and creatures," "to heal," rather than the poetry of dreams and memories that vanish.

Selected Poems (1982) gathers work from Kinnell's five major collections to 1980, including poems from as early as 1946. It acts as both an introduction to as well as a "full dossier" of his writing. Winning the Pulitzer Prize prompted critics to reappraise his career, most noting three phases in his growth: the first two volumes forecasting the "major phase" of *Body Rags* and *The Book of Nightmares;* with *Mortal Acts, Mortal Words* beginning the last, "less ferocious" stage. *The Past* (1985) and *Imperfect Thirst* (1990) fall into the last stage. Appearing in *The Past,* "The Fundamental Project of Technology," treats the bombing of Hiroshima and Nagasaki, again touching on a theme vital to Kinnell: modern man's attempts to dominate nature and "purge" human nature of its "animal characteristics," in particular of death. *The Past* also takes up again the metaphor of music as an analogy for poetry itself, with animals serving as the true angels that mediate God for man. "The Seekonk Woods" is Kinnell's exploration of his own past. *Imperfect Thirst,* like previous collections, is concerned with the domestic, his life in smalltown Sheffield, Vermont, and simply "saying in its own music what matters most."

Critical Reception

That Kinnell has made a lasting mark on American poetry there is no doubt. With *What a Kingdom It Was* came a change in American poetry. Ralph Mills wrote: "[I]t departed from the witty, pseudomythic verse, . . . of the 1950s to arrive at the more authentic, liberated work of the 1960s." "The Avenue Bearing the Initial of Christ into the New World" and *The Book of Nightmares* are generally considered his strongest works, with those following *Selected Poems* being termed "weaker," "uneven," or, as a *Village Voice* review described *The Past,* even guilty of too much "bad philosophizing" or "simple cutesiness." However, some critics defend his work since *The Book of Nightmares,* like Jay Parini who "finds a luxurious whole-

ness, a sense of grace" in the poetry that has turned less formal, increasingly personal. Thus the Kinnell of *Mortal Acts, Mortal Words* expresses an even "purer wish to live" and, as Peter Stitt notes, "an expressed love for the created world." Robert Hass, in response to *Selected Poems,* concludes, "Kinnell is widely read by the young who read poetry. If this were a different culture he would simply be widely read. . . . The common reader—the one who reads at night or on the beach for pleasure and instruction and diversion—who wants to sample the poetry being written in [his] part of the 20th century could do very well beginning with Galway Kinnell's *Selected Poems.*" Susan B. Weston sees his poetry as "utterly healthy,. . . . precisely because it confronts horrors—drunks dying of cirrhosis; war and destruction; the communal nightmare of a failing culture; the individual nightmare of the failure of love— along with all that is lovely and loving. . . . Kinnell's gift is a cursed awareness of time—not just of individual mortality but of geological time," the "facets of the single gem, the human condition. . . ."

PRINCIPAL WORKS

Poetry

What a Kingdom It Was 1960
Flower Herding on Mount Monadnock 1964
Poems of Light 1968
Body Rags 1968
Far Behind Me on the Trail 1969
The Hen Flower 1970
First Poems 1946-1954 1970
The Book of Nightmares 1971
The Shoes of Wandering 1971
The Avenue Bearing the Initial of Christ into the New World: Poems 1946-1964 1974
Three Poems 1976
Brother of My Heart 1977
Fergus Falling 1979
There Are Things I Tell to No One 1979
Two Poems 1979
Mortal Acts, Mortal Words 1980
The Last Hiding Places of Snow 1980
Angling, A Day, and Other Poems 1980
Selected Poems 1982
Woodsmen 1982
The Fundamental Project of Technology 1983
The Seekonk Woods 1985
The Past 1985
When One Has Lived a Long Time Alone 1990
Three Books: Body Rags: Mortal Acts, Mortal Words: The Past 1993
Imperfect Thirst 1994

Other Major Works

Black Light (novel) 1966
Walking Down the Stairs: Selections from Interviews 1978

The Poems of Francois Villon [translator] 1977; reprinted, 1982

The Essential Whitman [editor] 1987

On the Motion and Immobility of Douve: Poems by Yves Bonnefoy [translator] 1968; reprinted, 1992

CRITICISM

Louise Bogan (review date 1961)

SOURCE: A review of *What a Kingdom It Was,* in the *New Yorker,* Vol. 37, No. 7, April 1, 1961, pp. 29-31.

[*In the following excerpt, Kinnell's first book of verse is commended for its direct, colloquial language unfettered by contemporary influences.*]

Galway Kinnell's . . . first book of poems, *What a Kingdom It Was* is remarkably unburdened by this or that current influence. Kinnell is direct and occasionally harsh, and he keeps his syntax straight and his tone colloquial. His chief concern, we soon discover, is the enigmatic significance, more than the open appearance, of Nature and man. **"Freedom, New Hampshire,"** an elegy for his brother—a full realization of country boyhood, in ordinary terms, with a boy's confrontation of cruelty and unreasonable happiness left intact—is also an affirmation of immortality. Kinnell's longest and most pretentiously titled poem, **"The Avenue Bearing the Initial of Christ Into the New World,"** deals with a most difficult subject—life in a city slum. Here pitfalls abound—sentimentality, insincerity, the possibility of mixed and unresolved feelings of pity and guilt. Kinnell bypasses all these. City streets are for a time his home; he feels the vitality of their people; he responds with extreme sensitiveness to multiple sights, sounds, smells; without any furtive condescension, he places Avenue C in the human context. Sympathy, identification, insight sustain this long poem in every detail, and Kinnell chooses his details with startling exactness.

Sherman Hawkins (essay date 1963)

SOURCE: "Galway Kinnell: Moments of Transcendence," in *The Princeton Library Chronicle,* Vol. 25, No. 1, 1963, pp. 56-70.

[*In the following essay, a brief biography of Kinnell followed by an appraisal of his early work is presented.*]

Galway Kinnell was born in 1927 in Providence, Rhode Island, and raised in Pawtucket. He came to Princeton in the summer of 1944 and after only one semester joined the Navy. Six months later he returned to Princeton in the V-12 program and graduated at midyears in 1948. He then took an M.A. at the University of Rochester. His life since then has followed an alternating pattern common among American poets of his generation: teaching and travel, academic appointments and foreign fellowships. For two years he taught at Alfred University, and for three more he was Director of the Liberal Arts Programs at University College in the University of Chicago. Then in 1955 a Fulbright Fellowship took him to Paris to translate the poetry of Villon, and he stayed for another year as a lecturer at the University of Grenoble. In 1957 he came back to America and to New York University, first as a research associate and then as a teacher in the adult education program. In 1960 he was appointed Fulbright Professor at the University of Teheran, and the journey there and back took him around the world. The same year, Houghton Mifflin brought out his first volume of verse, **What a Kingdom It Was.**[1] In 1961 he was again in France, working on his translation of Villon, which will be published by The New American Library (Mentor Books). Since the spring of 1962, he has been living in New York and Vermont, giving poetry readings at various colleges and working on his second volume of poems, **Flower Herding on Mount Monadnock,** which will appear next year. This summer he worked for CORE, registering Negro voters in Louisiana. He has received a fellowship from the Guggenheim Foundation for his poetry and also an award from the National Institute of Arts and Letters.

In a review of the poetry of Charles Bell, Kinnell wrote: "It is good to see bold and rational verse appearing after years of experiment on the verbal level. . . . It is as though what we used to call the 'avant-garde' has scoured the Victorian decay and narrowing, making it possible for poets now to re-attach themselves, with purity of language and greatly broadened subject matter, to the continuing tradition of Western poetry." Such "re-attachment," he declared, is "not a reversion but a fruitful and needed going forward." This statement suggests Kinnell's own practice and intention. The tradition to which his best poetry "re-attaches" is that of transcendental and religious meditation—what Kinnell might call "sacred poetry." But if his work may be considered "rational" in its attachment to tradition, it is "bold" in its continuing development towards a more radical insight and a freer style. Today, indeed, Kinnell considers himself "a kind of unknown avantgarde."[2] His poetry is thus a "going forward": to understand its progress we need to consider the changes in his poetic models and theories as well as in the poetry itself.

The most important influences in his verse are those of Frost, Yeats, and Whitman. All three poets share a surface simplicity and a preference for the idiomatic and colloquial, the grace and toughness of actual speech—what Kinnell calls purity of language. But each is also felt as an individual presence: Frost in Kinnell's recourse to nature as norm and enigma, the special locus of revelation; Yeats in the structural deployment of image and symbol; Whitman in an intense social consciousness and a "oneness with all things." New England landscapes, recurrent imagery of birds, the free flowing line and the deliberately unpoetic catalogue—these stylistic trademarks are as reminiscent as the manner of individual poems: that of Frost in **"First Song,"** of Yeats in **"Descent,"** of Whitman in **"The Avenue Bearing the Initial of Christ into the New**

World." Frost is an early and Whitman a more recent model, but the influence of Yeats has been continuous.

It was at Princeton that Kinnell read Yeats for the first time, with overwhelming effect. "I tried to make them all sound like Yeats. No one else could have told I was imitating Yeats, but if they didn't sound like Yeats to me, I didn't think they were poems. It took a long time to get over that." But in Kinnell's earliest published lyrics, the influence of Frost is even more evident in the natural settings, the deftly rhyming stanzas, the personal and retrospective mode. It was Whitman who changed his notion of what a poem is, showing that the lines laid down by Frost are not the only ones "or that it is perhaps wrong to have lines at all." Frost has compared free verse to tennis without a net; Kinnell admits that meter and rhyme are the best way to play the game, "but what if it is not a game but a war?" For Kinnell, every poem is now part of the poet's life, and his rhymes and rhythms have become increasingly free as he seeks to achieve a more authentic utterance, "to throw the responsibility for the poem wholly on speech itself." Today he considers Whitman the significant influence in his writing. "They speak of Gertrude Stein and Ezra Pound as having purified the language, but Whitman's language—smack in the nineteenth century—seems to me more alive than Pound's. I can't read nineteenth-century English poetry now: every word has been dipped in nostalgia. But in Whitman ordinary and average things are seen in a sacred light. He was the really democratic poet, who standing among the streets, finds the sacred exists there."

This shift from Frost to Whitman marks a shift in attitude to poetry itself. Kinnell explained his earlier theories in the preface to a selection of his work in *The Beloit Poetry Journal*. His main thesis was stated in the title: "Only meaning is truly interesting. . . ." Kinnell argued that in much modern poetry, the emphasis on brilliant verbal effects of individual lines and images detracts from the meaning of the poem and the sense of the whole. Such poetry is an imitation of language rather than of nature. Style should be transparent like a window, so that the effect derives from the action or idea described, not from the language of description. He praised Charles Bell for verse stripped of the obvious devices of poetry, nearly as bare as prose. His own **"Spring Oak,"** a straightforward description, was deliberately written in "a style that is almost the absence of style."

A change is evident in Kinnell's review of Larry Eigner. He admires Eigner's poetry "for its closeness to things, its sense of their mystery and realness. . . ." At his best he writes in a state of grace with respect to the real, an openness and trust between himself and the world, by which the two blur and real objects keep dissolving towards a deeper, stranger reality. His best lines are less invented descriptions than the acts themselves of this contact." It is a rare gift: "Many poets, of course, write of common, despised objects, but Eigner comes close to making these things the personages of a sacred poetry." This is the kind of poetry Kinnell is trying to write today. Narrative and description (in the usual sense) have almost disappeared.

The words no longer form a transparent window; they seem to be "pressed very close to the thing, as if to a mould": each line is an act of contact. Things cease to be objects and take on a life of their own, become personages; there is "explicit consideration of the mystery of being."

No doubt Kinnell still believes that only meaning is truly interesting, but there has been a shift in the meaning of "meaning." In his preface he wrote that the meaning of a poem "though it may be dimly predicted, emerges only in the creative act. The organizing principle comes into full being simultaneously with its embodying detail. In the successful process there is a unifying light, a single vision of meaning, what might be called its tragic illumination." Such moments of enlightenment occur in "the mysteries of life as well as of poetry": Kinnell set out to recreate them "directly, simply, even reverently." Now if a poem reenacts a moment of enlightenment in the poet's life, then it is a recreation; it is mimetic. But if the meaning is only dimly perceived beforehand and the "unifying light" evolves in the creative act, then the poem itself becomes the moment of enlightenment: it is visionary. Of course these concepts of meaning are not mutually exclusive. In the attempt to recreate a moment of enlightenment, its meaning may change and grow, so that the finished poem becomes the fulfillment of the moment of experience. Many of Kinnell's poems seem to result from this double process of recreation and creation. It will not do to divide his poetry into two chronological periods or generic types, the mimetic and the visionary. Nevertheless, the distinction of vision and mimesis is useful: the tension between these impulses and their constantly shifting relationship seem to affect the form and style of individual poems, the line of Kinnell's development, even his deepest intuitions of meaning.

This interplay is obvious in the poems themselves. **"The Avenue Bearing the Initial of Christ"** is crowded with objects accurately sensed: the propane-gassed bus making its way through the streets with "big, airy sighs," a red kite wriggling like a tadpole, a pushcart market with its icicle-shaped carrots and "alligator-skinned / Cucumbers, that float pickled / In the wooden tubs of green skim milk." This kind of vivid sensory precision has become a minimum requirement in recent poetry. But in Kinnell's poems, these real objects are transfigured by intimations of deeper, stranger, reality: the tadpole kite, as it "crosses / The sun, lays bare its own crossed skeleton." Kinnell's poetry is grounded in reality, but it works constantly towards such moments of illumination, often in climaxes marked by rhetorical device and heightened diction. Mimesis becomes vision as we read.

In many poems this transfiguration takes the form of an ascent from the real to the ideal. The pattern is consciously Platonic. Kinnell's more ambitious poems, with their deliberate repetition of imagery, their frequent division into contrasting sections, their progression towards a synthesizing moment of vision, recall the strategy of certain poems by Yeats. But they are also modelled on the Platonic dialogue, which—considered as a work of art—Kinnell believes to be one of the great poetic forms. "It proceeds as a poem proceeds, using dialectic, images, characters. By the end the whole thing has been raised to a new level: every statement is transformed, has a meaning beyond itself, like the phrases at the end of a great poem." Platonism thus provides a typical structure and a tacit metaphysic for a poetry which is always moving from the reality into the mystery of things.

If the poem ends in the heavens, however, it must begin with things of earth. A poetry like that of Bell which seeks "redemptive beauty in experience" implies an ugliness that needs to be redeemed. The conjunction of the poetic and the unpoetic is a commonplace of modern verse, and this juxtaposition is already a poetic habit in Kinnell's **"First Song,"** with its contrasts of dung and music, its cornstalks metamorphosed into violins, its paradoxical affirmation of the "sadness of joy." In these early poems, Kinnell felt a need to make claims for the beauty of life, and the dung and cornstalks are necessary to save these claims from sentimentality. With the growing recognition that "life is uglier and more beautiful, both, than at that time I understood," the antitheses grow more extreme. The intuition of the sacred involves its opposite; the visionary imagination hungers for that which challenges its transfiguring power—objects not merely common but despised. Thus in **"Easter"**—itself an early poem—death confers an unresurrecting grace upon a nurse who has been almost ritually defiled: "Raped, robbed, weighted, drowned." **"Where the Track Vanishes"** enacts the myth of ascent from earth to heaven, but the goatherd who toils up the mountainside is Pierre le Boiteux, yellow-toothed, hamstrung, hideous in every way. Yet with this increasing stress on the unclean and deformed goes an increasing range of metamorphosis. Pierre becomes Boötes, the heavenly Herdsman; the fields into which he wades are constellations; the track to the churchyard leads out among the stars:

> Where the track vanishes the first land begins.
> It goes out everywhere obliterating the horizons.
> We must have been walking through it all our lives.

So by the tragic principle, negation evokes the vision which affirms. Perhaps this is one reason—artistic rather than biographical—why the recurring subject of these poems is death, for death is the final obstacle, the last enemy to be overcome by the imagination. It is a measure of Kinnell's achievement—and his honesty—that his elegiac poems end with the transcendence and reconciliation proper to the form while actually affirming the personal finality of death.

Kinnell's double commitment to the naturalistic and the visionary shapes and informs his first volume of collected verse. It is divided into four sections, corresponding in sequence to the kinds of poem which have interested him at different times. Each section is arranged chronologically, with the first poems of section II antedating the earliest of section I, and the last of section II postdating the first of section III. But the shape of the book is not quite that of Kinnell's poetic evolution. Many of his early lyrics—including **"Spring Oak,"** his exemplar of the transparent style, and **"Indian Bread,"** a poem he contributed to a collection honoring Robert Frost—do not appear in *What a Kingdom It Was.* This early verse tends to the mimetic: descriptive or narrative in form, firmly controlled in structure, realistic and clear in style. A number of poems, like those which form the first section of *What a Kingdom,* deal with an imagined boyhood and young manhood in the Middle West.[3] The six poems are arranged symmetrically: an introduction, two contrasted pairs of poems, and a conclusion. The unifying action is initiation. **"First Song"** tells how at dusk in Illinois—a halfway point in space and time—a boy's first song of happiness "woke / His heart to darkness and into the sadness of joy." In the central poems this ambivalent awareness becomes a growing recognition of the divine and the daemonic in nature and in man. **"Westport,"** a conclusion which is also a beginning, sets the static oppositions of **"First Song"** in motion, heading from east to west, from dark afternoon to a bright evening, and out of evening into night. But this is more than a metaphor of growing up, for here the action of initiation, with all its threat and promise, is extended to the youth of a society, the expansion of the American frontier. This shift from the individual to the community is repeated in the volume as a whole.

The second section, despite an occasional fine poem or significant pairing (**"Easter,"** or **"Alewives Pool"** and **"Leaping Falls"**), is the most heterogeneous and least impressive in the book. It is a collection of short lyrics, very different in subject, tone, and quality. The third section is more unified, consisting of six longer poems divided into parts, predominantly elegiac in mood and mode. The next to last, **"Freedom, New Hampshire,"** is a formal elegy for the poet's brother: personal, nostalgic, touching in its restraint of feeling and its refusal of any supernatural solution. In complement and contrast, the final poem in this section, **"The Supper After the Last,"** treats death impersonally, as a problem in metaphysics. The poem enacts the transition from the mimetic to the visionary: it is centrally concerned with margins and horizons, and here real objects actually do blur and resolve towards deeper, stranger realities. A whitewashed house in sunlight, a jug of water and a chair, the blind cat and "red-backed passionate dog" are rendered with the precision of an Andrew Wyeth, only to be transmuted into a vista out of Dali:

> The witnesses back off; the scene begins to float in
>   water;
> Far out in that mirage the Saviour sits whispering to
>   the world,
> Becoming a mirage. The dog turns into a smear on
>   the sand.
> The cat grows taller and taller as it flees into space.

When Kinnell had to select a poem for an anthology called *Poet's Choice,* he chose **"Supper After the Last."** It makes a fresh start: "I mean towards a poem without scaffolding or occasion, that progresses through images to a point where it can make a statement on a major subject." Such a poem must evolve its moment of insight in the act of its making: it is purely creative. Here, then, the shift from mimesis to vision is complete. If the book ended here, we could perhaps trace the Platonic structure which

Kinnell observes in Bell's volume of poems, progressing from physical details to symbolic meanings, from concrete to abstract. But there remains a fourth section, which consists of a single poem, **"The Avenue Bearing the Initial of Christ into the New World."** And this poem too makes a fresh start. Kinnell acknowledges a debt to *The Waste Land* and to Baudelaire, but the most striking influence is that of Whitman. Here at last the real and ideal are not juxtaposed in contrast or set in transcendent sequence: they blend and mingle; they become one.

The import of this change is clear only on the level of meaning. But poetic meaning is elusive, and our statements about it must be tentative. Kinnell seems to be a religious poet without religion. That is, his intuitions of the sacred do not seem based on any credal affirmation or institutional faith. He was brought up a Congregationalist, but today he finds churches irrelevant. His notions of transcendence, he asserts, derive from Plato and the Transcendentalists, especially Thoreau. Christianity, like Yeats's *Vision,* serves as a source of imaginatively potent words and images, grounded in a total and consistent myth. It has two advantages over Yeats's system: Christianity is a public mythology; and in current literary usage, exploitation need not imply belief. But the matter is not all that simple. Kinnell's deep instinct for the suffering and rejected does not derive from Plato or Thoreau. The figure of Jesus haunts these poems. A short story called "The Permanence of Love" dramatizes this ambivalence in the encounter of the unbelieving protagonist and a nun—significantly a *petite soeur de Jésus.*

The same attraction and withdrawal are expressed in **"First Communion"** and **"To Christ Our Lord,"** poems juxtaposed in the first section of *What a Kingdom It Was.* In **"First Communion"** a boy is repelled by the inadequacy of institutional religion and its rituals, the conjuration of Jesus into grape juice and "inferior bread." He tells Christ

> I would speak of injustice. . . .
> I would not go again into that place.

The world of nature, burning in late summer and late afternoon, offers a truer "parable" of death and continuity. **"To Christ Our Lord"** also contrasts dogma with natural parable. The "Christmas grace" is merely "long-winded," but in slaying and devouring a living creature, the boy experiences what he missed in his first communion. Love stirs within him even as he kills, but "There had been nothing to do but surrender, / To kill and eat; he ate as he had killed, with wonder."

> At night on snowshoes on the drifting field
> He wondered again, for whom had love stirred?
> The stars glittered on the snow and nothing
>   answered.
> Then the Swan spread her wings, cross of the cold
>   north,
> The pattern and mirror of the acts of earth.

Here Christianity and Platonism, "cross" and "pattern," seem to merge: the killing and eating is a sacrament, a finite repetition of the ideal, eternal act of sacrifice. Kinnell's title is the subtitle of **"The Windhover,"** and his wild turkey, like Hopkins' falcon, is emblematic of "Christ Our Lord." But Hopkins' bird is most dangerous and beautiful in stooping, the descent into flesh. The boy in Kinnell's poem looks to the heavenly pattern, the disincarnate Swan. It is more than the difference between the heavenly Logos and the incarnate Christ: it is the difference between Christian incarnation and Platonic transcendence—the point at which Augustine found Platonism, the most Christian of pagan philosophies, to be unchristian.

In much of Kinnell's poetry, then, the intuition of the sacred sets matter against spirit, concrete against abstract. But working against this instinctive dualism is an equally instinctive kinship with all suffering, an impulse which finds expression in his short story as the wish to serve. Countering the upward spiral of transcendence, of the "flesh made word," his poetry also moves outward, horizontally, in sympathy with the commonest forms of life. This is the expanding consciousness of Whitman, who found the sacred not among the stars but in the streets. So in **"The Avenue Bearing the Initial of Christ,"** the kingdom is realized among the perishing humanity of Avenue C. It is a vision of desolating ugliness. Kinnell has ceased to make claims for the beauty of life: "It seems to me now that to become one with a person, or thing, or event and to set it down in its fullness is itself sufficient, or transcends the need for making claims." So in this poem the poet has disappeared; the observer has become one with his subject; there is only the Avenue and the fullness and movement of its life. The tragic illumination of the poem does not come in any cumulative revelation but in "moments of transcendence" drifting in "oceans of loathing and fear," traffic lights blinking through darkness and rain. The representation of reality is uncompromising: walking up Avenue C today, one finds many of the signs Kinnell quotes—Blozstein's Cutrate Bakery, Little Rose Restaurant, Kugler's Chicken Store, Natural Bloom Cigars. But the holy is incarnate in the real. The fourteen divisions of the poem are the fourteen stations of the cross, down the fourteen intersections of Avenue C to the Power Station and East River at the end. So the word is made flesh: at the point where Christ meets Mary his mother, there appears a senile crone dispensing newspapers. Veronica's handkerchief is a stained grocery wrapper; the deposition is accomplished by a garbage truck. This is not symbolism but immanence: fish are simultaneously the traditional figure for Christ and actual gaping carp, crucified upon a wooden counter. An old rabbi is Jacob with his sons; even the vegetables in market carts are omens and images of our condition. The action of the poem is ordeal: as the devotee follows the stations of the cross, sharing in imagination the passion of Christ, so the observer—poet or reader—follows Avenue C. A day passes; the Avenue stretches "From the blind gut Pitt to the East River of Fishes"; and these motions in time and space become the archetype of all human movement. It is the life of man from darkness into dark, from the blind gut to the deep river. It is Israel in exile—the Jews, Negroes, Puerto Ricans who have become God's chosen people because they are despised and rejected of men—bearing, like the Avenue itself, the initial of the suffering man. "From the four-teenth station," writes Kinnell, "one looks back down the whole street and sees it transfigured, but also entirely real." In this transfiguration of reality, death and suffering are not transcended or denied. But against them is set the untiring laughter of the blood, the song of the Jews as they went out of their ghettos to destruction:

> In the nighttime
> Of the blood they are laughing and saying,
> Our little lane, what a kingdom it was!

Notes

[1] Two significant misprints occur in this edition. In the next to last line of "The Supper after the Last" on p. 64, "Steps" should be "Step" (an imperative). In "The Avenue Bearing the Initial of Christ into the New World," the order of fourth and fifth lines from the top of p. 83 has been reversed.

[2] Quotations not from Mr. Kinnell's poems or essay are from conversation or correspondence with the author.

[3] For all their realism, these poems should not be read as autobiographical. James R. Hurt has shown that the best known of them, "First Song," is based on a passage in *Wayfaring Stranger* by Burl Ives. See *The Explicator*, XX, No. 3 (November 1961), 23, and the references given there to previous discussions of the poem.

Michael Benedikt (review date 1968)

SOURCE: A review of *Body Rags*, in *Poetry*, Vol. CXIII, No. 3, pp. 188-91.

[*In the following excerpt, Benedikt notes a radical shift in Kinnell's work that moves from a preoccupation with urban life toward that which was to become a hallmark of the poet's verse, a celebration of nature.*]

. . . In his third book, **Body Rags,** Galway Kinnell has effected one of the most radical transformations of both matter and manner we have. His first two collections, with their perturbed pictures of the junk-ridden modern city, and their relatively straightforward presentations of the land-scape, seemed to recommend withdrawal from the urban syndrome in favor of nature. Now, we feel the breadth of his interpretation of the natural ideal. **"Night in the Forest"** is about an overnight camping trip, but one would hardly locate conservationism at the core of its concern:

> A woman
> sleeps next to me on the earth. A strand
> of hair flows
> from her cocoon sleeping bag, touching
> the ground hesitantly, as if thinking
> to take root.

The intensity of this yearning is almost supernatural. Still stranger are the particular natural aspects to which atten-

tion is directed. Kinnell writes about features ordinary nature poets, who are apt to moralize, deplore. "I can rejoice," he writes, "that everything changes, that / we go from life into life / and enter ourselves / quaking / like the tadpole, his time come, tumbling toward the slime." The romantic image of landscape is absent, and regions of rocks, roots, and seethings prevail. They represent, I think, arenas of intense natural struggle, areas where change is most conspicuous.

The leap from the crags of landscape to those of the body is a short, not to mention traditional, one. Kinnell's analogies are surprising, involving common qualities of alteration. Even outward nature takes on an inwardness. **"The Porcupine,** a poem which might otherwise pass as a strong example of objective description, in its climactic moment relates quite directly to this:

> A farmer shot a porcupine three times
> as it dozed on a tree limb. On
> the way down it tore open its belly
> on a broken branch, hooked its gut,
> and went on falling. On the ground
> it sprang to its feet, and
> paying out gut heaved
> and spartled through a hundred feet of goldenrod
> before
> the abrupt emptiness.

When in **"Testament of the Thief,"** all that the poet bequeaths is summarized as "this map of my innards", it is a serious matter. When, in **"One Who Used To Beat His Way,"** the narrator becomes ill and "gets a backed-up / mouthful of vomit-cut liquor, [mumbling] 'Thanks God,'" it is no joke. There is a thankfulness for, a sense of the worth of, essences.

As the long quotation above may suggest, the poetry itself moves according to some internal—not to mention intestinal—principle. One feels that the body, like the landscape and its animals, is partly a metaphor for the nature of poetry. The porcupine poem is followed by one about the poet's fight with a bear; after he kills it, he *enters* it. The poem closes (and the book ends) with the hunter imagining himself spending his life wondering "what, anyway, / was that sticky infusion, that rank flavor of blood, that poetry, by which I lived." The sole outright *ars poetica* in **Body Rags** insists on the identity of raw nature and true poetry. **"The Poem"** begins:

> On this hill, crossed
> by the last birds, a sprinkling
> of soil covers up the rocks
>
>   . . . . .
>
> The poem too
> is a palimpsest, streaked
> with erasures, smelling
> of departure and burnt stone.

The "burnt", "rank", bitter flavor seems to me to come not out of any established sense of the "ironical", as cultivated in the most pervasive poetics of the early part of our century (those of Eliot and his immediate followers), but as the result of an attempt to reduce—or elevate—art to essence. One of the most remarkable passages in **"The Poem"** expresses this ambition. It closes commenting on one of the most celebrated of all lines in verse, Villon's "où sont les neiges d'antan" (Kinnell has translated Villon, and there are references to that flesh-haunted medieval throughout this book, straight through to its title). The American poet answers the French poet's "where" with his own "here":

> Here is a fern-leaf binding *utter* to the image of
>   *illume,*
> here is a lightning-split fir the lines down its good
>   side
>   becoming unwhitmanesque and free,
> here is *unfulfilled* reflected as *mellifica* along the
>   feather of a crow,
> here is a hound chasing his bitch in trochaic
>   dimeter brachycatalectic,
>
>   . . . . .
>
> here is an armful of last-year's snows.

That a strong, lofty art can become a kind of rock, a reality to rest upon, is a remarkable, thoroughly modern assertion; this kind of elevation of the role of the intellect is of course exactly the opposite of the poetic view of, say, the generation of Eliot. These poems have what I would call (borrowing a phrase from certain contemporary, post-minimalist sculptors) an "object quality". Much of *Body Rags* not only asserts possibility, but is memorable enough to demonstrate it. . . .

Galway Kinnell with *The Ohio Review* (interview date 1972)

SOURCE: An interview with Galway Kinnell, in *The Ohio Review*, Vol. XIV, No. 1, Fall 1972, pp. 25-38.

[*In the following interview conducted after the publication of* The Book of Nightmares, *Kinnell discusses this long poem, as well as the influence of Yeats and Rilke on his work in general.*]

[OHIO REVIEW]: *Public poetry readings enjoy an unusual popularity nowadays, and you seem to present your poetry very successfully at your own readings, judging from audience response. Also you seem to be giving a good many readings of late. I wonder, do you think that for your poetry, as you conceive it, the printed page is essential?*

[KINNELL]: Yes, it is essential. *We* forget. But the printed page remembers. Gutenberg deprived us of verbal memory, but it's all right, perhaps even better, to have little memory but to have many books, since they can remember so much more than we can, provided that what we read passes into that part of us which would have remem-

bered it—if we still were able to remember. Also, the printed page is quite useful, for once one has abandoned counted meter and rhyme, it's the only way by which the individual lines, the rhythmic units, can keep their integrity.

That seems particularly true, I think, with longer poems like your **Book of Nightmares**—*written in units over a period of time. How long did it take you to do* **The Book of Nightmares**?

Four years.

And you see it as one poem that you worked on for four years?

Yes. I conceived of it as a single poem at the start.

Why is it so symmetrical—ten poems, seven parts each?

Well, I had already been writing poems in seven parts . . .

Yes, **"The Porcupine,"** *for example.*

And these, too, started coming out in seven parts. Some, of course, could as easily have been eight or six parts, so I just brought them all into seven parts. That there are ten sections I suppose is in tribute to *The Duino Elegies.*

Is seven a magical number to you?

It is, although I don't know why. In general, with magical things, one finds it hard to account for them or to believe in them theoretically; but in fact they are often impressive. Such as astrology. When I meet a Leo, for example, I can often recognize him at once. I find that strange because the theoretical basis of astrology doesn't impress me.

How important do you see narrative as being for your work, for your poetry?

I used to depend more on narrative than I do now. I would like a poem to be able to be free of narrative. *The Duino Elegies,* for example, the supreme modern poem, is supreme partly because it doesn't have a shred of narrative in it.

You see narrative then as a crutch? Something you've depended upon and want to transcend? Narrative seems so much the sense of the journey, the sense of forward motion in your poems, especially **Body Rags.**

Yes, my poems have depended a lot on narrative. Certain ones, like **"The Avenue Bearing the Initial of Christ into the New World,"** don't use narrative. Other poems, like **"The Bear,"** are sheer stories. If a poem could be free of narrative altogether, it would at least open the possibility that some truth could be said directly rather than by parable. It would be nice if there were poems that could teach the way Rilke does, the way much of the best of Whitman does.

Do you think there would be any consequent loss of that sense of personal emotional involvement that inheres in the kind of narrative you do—by the excision of the narrative, by movement beyond or away from the narrative?

One's self has to be completely in the poem. Whether the narrative is what holds it there or not, I don't know. I don't think so. But it's harder to write a poem which is not narrative, and we in this country are so attached to narrative, aren't we? The story is so much the basis of our conversations and much of our poetry. Of course, when I speak of a poem without narrative, I don't mean one which is without a progression. We were thinking of some kind of outward narrative rather than psychic progression.

Kind of an ontological order as opposed to a chronological order? Is that what you're talking about? How do you order a long poem if it's not in a sequence of things, steps, 1-2-3-4-5-6-7?

I would think it would be a progression of consciousness rather than of events.

I find that kind of progression-consciousness in "**The Porcupine.**"

Yes. That's one example.

When I asked the question about narrative I was thinking a little bit of a poem like "**Freedom, New Hampshire,**" *in which there are these narrative segments. Maybe the progression is another kind of progression, not a narrative progression, but narrative is the fundamental element out of which the units are constructed: each little narrative is itself the metaphor. To that extent, I was thinking that it was crucial to that kind of poem. So we may have been talking through each other for a minute—you might have been thinking I was considering some more truly external narrative.*

Well, no, I think I understood what you meant. The last section of that poem, however, is a narrative, and that's the section—at least the very end—which I would say begins to try to teach.

I'd like to go back to the original question about chronological order as opposed to psychological, ontological order. "**The Porcupine,**" *for example, as opposed to* "**The Bear**" *in* **Body Rags**. *Could you give us some names or some description of the kind of order, for example, that you see in* **The Book of Nightmares***? Is it a kind of organic order—one which, as you write the poem, orders itself? Is that what you mean?*

Well, you see, I think what I meant was, that with a narrative whatever happens is a consequence of an actual set of activities that's going on, and when the narrative is removed, then the consciousness is left on its own—it has no . . . nothing is telling it which way to go—it has to probe without maps, so to speak.

You mentioned briefly Rilke's influence. How about Yeats? Your two children are named after Yeats, in effect, after the life surrounding Yeats. How does he come into your poetry?

Well, Yeats had a great influence on me when I was in my early twenties, and I think that the kind of poem I wrote then—and probably still do—that is, of sections containing little narratives—probably came from Yeats as much as anybody, from something like "Among School Children," for example.

What is it that you find in Rilke, besides his ability to structure the long poem as he does it, that's so apparently influential and dynamic in your own life and work?

Well, Rilke writes nothing except that which is a matter of life and death for him. There is nothing trivial in his work; there's no idle commentary or dawdling on. He writes at the limit of his powers at all times, and then there are those moments when he starts writing beyond the limits of his powers, when his words grope off into space, trying to say the inexpressible, like the late quartets of Beethoven or passages in *King Lear*.

Can we return to the past, and get very personal? I have a sense when I read **The Book of Nightmares** *that somehow or other that poem shares its genesis with that of your children: the fact of their birth and developing life is a very crucial, essential part of it. Is that right?*

Yes.

Was that a part, really, of your conceiving of the thing—when you first began to think of the poem—as something that you were conscious of their life having brought you to?

Yes. I think when the poem began I knew that the first section would be about human birth, which in that case was the birth of my daughter. I didn't know until the form of the poem began to come clear that the last section would include the description of the birth of my son. So in the course of writing the poem Maud grew up to the age of two, and Fergus got born. That provided the framework of the poem. Everything that happens in between came during those years of their infancy.

Well, I was thinking that in addition to the kind of structural frame which that obviously provides there is also a kind of added urgency to the sense of transiency of human life, which, even in your poetry—where there has always been such a strong sense of that—became more intense.

That's true . . .

In other words, by having Maud and Maud's life there, you became either more sensitized to this or burdened by it?

Those little lumps of clinging flesh that babies are, and your great and inexplicable closeness to them, make you feel intensely the fragility of a person.

The Book of Nightmares *is dedicated to your children, and it seems to me a book for children. You just spoke of Rilke's Duino Elegies as teaching poems—I see that intention also in* **The Book of Nightmares**. *There's that* instructional quality: "I'm going to introduce you to this tragic sense, this understanding of duende, that your life is going to become."

Yes, but I also wanted that book, while it introduced all those things, to be a way of coping.

Absolutely. That's what I meant by instruction: "if you know this, if you learn this . . ." The Maud poem, the first poem, ends with, "And then / you shall open / this book, even if it is the book of nightmares." Still, you leave it as an affirmative poem.

Yes, I do. Though many feel it's a negative book.

There are many who think Lear, *which you mentioned a moment ago, is a very negative work, yet one of the things I've sensed from* Lear *is that the reason that it is so tragic is that what is affirmed is recognized as being so important, to the speaker and to the reader.*

Well, the curious thing about tragedy, Greek as well as Shakespearian, is that while practically everything that's said is destructive, yet the total effect is exalting. What it is that exalts is not really in the words—it's a spirit that moves the whole thing.

You revised a lot of the poems in **The Book of Night-mares.** *You rearranged passages, replaced and so forth, and revised in the sense of adding lines, dropping lines. Did you feel as they were published individually that they were not individual parts making the whole? Was that the reasoning behind it? Or did you just want to change each poem? Simply put, my question is, why did you revise?*

Well, I revise all the time, all my poems, quite a lot, and this poem more than others, I think, because there was not only the problem of making each passage live, but also there was this shifting around of parts and experimenting with the order of the parts, transposing back and forth.

You have as an epigraph to **The Book of Nightmares** *a quotation from Rilke:*

> But this, though: death,
> the whole of death,—even before life's begun,
> to hold it all so gently, and be good:
> this is beyond description!

How do you see the relationship of this epigraph to your book?

From one point of view, ***The Book of Nightmares*** is nothing but an effort to face death and live with death. Children have all that effort in their future. They have penetrating glimpses of death: through fatigue, sleep, their cuts and bruises, and the dangers their parents keep warning of, and also through their curiosity regarding birth and growth. But for the moment they live with death as the less self-conscious animals do, and that deep trust in the life rhythms, infantile as it is, yet provides the model for the trust they will struggle so hard to possess later on.

When I read your poems—the ones I like best—I sense that you manage to charge them with a total emotional intensity, and that then that emotional tension or freight is discharged or a resolution is made—an emotional, not intellectual, resolution. I feel that has something very much to do with the success of those poems. You get the charge, and then the emotional resolution of the charge. It has something to do with their being dramatic. Maybe something to do with the dramatization of a kind of narrative event. And also with the size of the poem. It has to be a longish poem to do that, perhaps. Do you have any theory about that, or any perspective of it in retrospect, in looking at your poems from the past?

Well, I don't know. I recognize what you say, and I think it's one reason I write long poems—that it is possible for them to begin and then wander around, search around for some way out, and to come to a climax and resolution. Small poems have always been difficult for me to write, difficult and frustrating also because I want that poem to be an organic thing, to have an inner drama, an inner rising line.

A growth to it?

Yes. And also to include the groping and wandering. A short poem exists outside of time—time doesn't play a role. Long poems are made out of time.

I find **"The Hen Flower"** *to be the most individual poem in* **The Book of Nightmares**—*I'm not sure why. One reason, perhaps, is that it's self-addressed: you're the only character in it in that sense, except for the hen, and yet, it seems to be the resolution of all those concerns in the whole* **Book of Nightmares**. *I guess my question is why is it in the second position?*

Well, the arrangement of ***The Book of Nightmares*** wasn't made entirely rationally, and so it isn't entirely explicable rationally. The reason is that **"The Hen Flower"** was the first poem I finished of the sequence, and thus it makes no reference backward. It's placed second because it addresses myself before I begin the journey of the poem, instructing myself to let go, to say all. In the third section, **"The Shoes,"** the actual journey begins.

A poem which you changed considerably, I think, especially the first part.

I changed that an awful lot.

"The Hen Flower" *is an interesting poem, I think, in that it is so obviously not about poetry, and yet, at the same time, is about poetry. Am I right? It seems to me that it's almost a statement of poetic credo for* **The Book of Nightmares.**

Yes. And again it's not.

Who do you think you are most like in your handling of free-verse, if anyone? You are without question a person very much in the old free-verse tradition.

Well, I've learned whatever I could from Whitman, as far as free-verse goes. I don't know of anyone elso who has moved me in terms of his rhythm. Whitman and the King James Bible.

That's a funny term, "free-verse," and, in a recent essay, you talk a lot about poetry being wasted breath, how we need the mimetic quality of the human voice in a one-to-one relationship with the raggedness of experience. Is that what you get from Whitman? that sense that this is a very human voice and has the openness of line and that all things are possible in this poem?

Yes. Whitman seeks the "perfect rectitude and insouciance of the movements of animals". . . and his lines have that—there's no way to systematize them. Their music includes very awkward sound—some of his most beautiful lines are rhythmically most awkward—and that makes them stronger. It means that what's being said, and the language in which it's being said, override any traditional music. It's the rhythm of what's being said.

The rhythm of what's being said?

Infants talk without words, using rhythms alone, and mothers who've had lots of children (or wet nurses) know how to talk back—they have their conversation. It's very Whitmanesque, and they understand each other perfectly. It means these rhythms are not ornaments of speech, but essential elements of the communication.

In an interview published in New York Quarterly you spoke of Ginsberg's Howl *as being important to you.*

Yes. When you asked me about who had influenced my line, my prosody—I said Whitman, but also Whitman through Ginsberg.

Yet, although you sweep the page, it's not an onslaught like Whitman or Howl. *Your line is kinetic, has much more a sense of break—angular, or bony, or something . . . But it moves to extremes rapidly—the long line and suddenly you break to one word.*

That's true—there are a lot of short lines. I was thinking of that music, that rhythm, that capacity of a line to be thrilling musically, and at the same time be awkward—just forced that way by what it had to say.

At the end of **Nightmares** *you say something in the Fergus poem, "if this is a poem . . ."*

"This poem, if we shall call it that."

Yes, "if we shall call it that." That seems to be calling into question what the poem is. Is that true? Are you doubting the whole sense of what a poem can do? Thinking of poetry as wasted breath?

No, I don't think I meant it that way. I suppose I meant something the same as Whitman meant when he said, "who touches this touches a man."

It's not self-deprecating or anything?

No.

In his essay on you in Alone With America, *Richard Howard says something about how your poetry resists these facile reductions to the organic metaphors of growth. And he says that you always, right in the early moments, articulated your concerns and your theme—all of which seems to me a very sensitive and sound observation. But even say that is true, I still wonder what you think about your growth toward this: some poetic idea or ideal you have for your poetry? For example, you spoke earlier about this pure poem: do you think you have matured or grown or changed radically as a poet or anything of that sort?*

I don't have an ideal which I try to fulfill. I doubt if anybody does. I remember when James Wright decided he was finished with the kind of poems he'd been writing in his early days. He said, "I'm through with that kind of poetry," and someone asked him, "Well, what kind of poetry are you going to write?" and he said, "I haven't the faintest idea." I think that whatever I do will be different from **The Book of Nightmares.** I've never had that feeling quite so strongly as I do with this book: that the book has been closed in some way on something, and that it would be impossible to open it again and extend it by a few more sections. As for the growth, or change, in my poetry from the beginning, it hasn't been radical. There've been no abrupt departures. It has changed a lot, but there aren't any visible seams, nor any holes. It just went along and changed itself without my ever wanting or asking it to. The second section of **The Book of Nightmares,** for example, resembles closely **"The Bear"** and **"The Porcupine."** And in **Body Rags,** there are poems exactly like ones in the previous book.

You say the concerns in your poetry remained essentially the same to a degree?

Yes. I'd hate to try to say what those concerns are, but I think they're the same.

To descend from the clouds for a moment, did you and Merwin write poems when you were at Princeton and show them to each other?

Merwin wrote poems, I wrote verse while we were at Princeton. We showed each other our work, and I'd say, "Those are real poems, Bill," and he'd say, "Those aren't, Galway." Merwin was prodigious. When he was nineteen, he was writing poems of enormous skill. It would depress me to compare his poems with my own clumsy writings. I was a much slower person. My poems were rather more forthright than his in what they were trying to say and much less capable of saying it. But it helped for Merwin to tell me those weren't poems. I learned from him. Charles Bell was also at Princeton at that time. Merwin and I and he got to know each other fairly well, and he encouraged us both and helped us.

Have you turned your hand seriously to fiction since Black Light?

No, I haven't, and I doubt if I will.

I suppose one could say, had you turned your hand seriously to fiction before Black Light*?*

Yes, I'd written several—I'd started several—novels, and finished one. The novel had always interested me. I think that what happened was that I gradually came to understand that poetry could say everything, or almost everything, I had wanted to say through a novel—that *I* had wanted to say. True novels can't be said in poems, but *Black Light* isn't a true novel—it's straining to be a poem at all its joints. I would rather write a poem than a novel—a large poem—and try to open, or increase, the weight that a poem can carry.

I want to ask a question about the speaking voice in your poems, especially in **The Book of Nightmares.** *Any time I read a James Wright poem I have a sense that there's no persona there at all, but Wright speaking directly— and I think this is true of a poet like Bly as well. But I still have the sense, even in* **The Book of Nightmares,** *that there is a hero in those poems, a character being created, as in a long story, and that he's going through certain experiences, and being confronted by certain tests, and that he will win or lose by the end of the story. Assuming he does lose, which he will in your poems, his life is being celebrated nevertheless.*

Yes, I think it's true. Just as a character is created in "Song of Myself." It's one of the added weights a poem can bear.

Well, I know you've been asked often about your use at times of the odd word, the out-of-the-way-word, and I'm going to try to ask an intelligent question about it. In one section of **The Book of Nightmares,** **"The Dead Shall Be Raised Incorruptible,"** *is the most striking occurrence of that in all of your poetry. Very near the beginning of that poem there is just a succession of, to the rest of us, essentially unknown words. That is obviously something you were doing for a reason. Do you mind talking about it?*

That particular list of strange words?

Yes, although you could go around to encompass the whole thing if you want to.

Well, the English language is a great language—it has so many more words than any other language, so few of which we even know, let alone use. I love it when I run across an archaic word that seems to me terribly expressive, I entertain the possibility of its resurrection. It's wrong to write only in those ordinary words that every language has, when there's so much richness still available. The list in that poem is a list of various words—some obsolete, some just rare—for refuse of one kind or another. I wanted to give a linguistic history of what was to follow in the poem. Of the blood-letting and waste, what the poem was about.

Who's your favorite non-English poet? Or is there one?

Not English you mean? Contemporary . . . well, I think Neruda, who's everybody's favorite.

Did you come to Neruda fairly early?

No, I didn't.

Like most everybody else, fairly late.

Fairly late, yes. You see, I don't read Spanish. I guess it was when I first met my wife, who is Spanish—about ten years ago. She used to read and explain to me Spanish poetry. We went through a lot of Neruda at that time.

Do you think contemporary poetry, in general, is moving toward, is getting into itself, more mystery? or more willingness, more openness to it?

Yes. That's the main search now (well, over the past fifteen years)—turning away from mere rational commentary, trying to find a way into mysterious life. Everyone who writes poetry in this country is a product of an unmysterious, technological society. So if one is to write from deep sources in himself, if he is to bring into his poetry his spiritual life, his poetry has to be an inner revolution, a means of changing himself inwardly. Already it's difficult for a young person, even more because on the one hand there are many ways into the spiritual realm being offered him, all of them tainted by the society, and at the same time poetry itself has suddenly become a "career," a way of getting ahead in the world. It's hard to seek a new spiritual life and, at the same time and by the same means, old-fashioned social status. As time goes on, probably the disparity between what modern man is, and what poetry has always asked a man to be, will get worse. If technological society doesn't in fact break down and collapse—as it well may—if it does survive and refine itself even farther, it may one day become impossible for poetry, in what will then be the old sense of the word, any longer to exist. Our connection with ritual and sacred traditions, the things which in humans are elaborations of instincts in animals, may be completely broken. Concrete poetry is the first sign of the other possibility, that to exist at all poetry will simply give up its old ambitions and adapt itself to what is, that it will simply become the expression of a reality from which all trace of the sacred has been removed. The visual arts have already gone a long way in this direction.

You were speaking earlier of the sense of the mystery and so forth in contemporary poetry, and a moving into that kind of dark, underground, Jungian, really surreal, territory. I don't see any of that surrealism, fantasia, going on in any of the things you've done so far. You don't use the simile, for example, much at all.

Yes, very little in my writing. I don't think the mystery of human life is apprehended only by surrealist poems. Even the French and Spanish poets gave up surrealism; what was useful for them was to be liberated by it, to pass through it. In this country, we have another, equally rich, tradition, of trying to evoke physical things, of giving them actual presence in a poem. Our language has more physical verbs and more physical adjectives than most others, and is more capable of bringing into reality—bringing into presence—those creatures and things that the world is made up of—through words bringing them to reality. If the things and creatures that live on earth don't possess mystery, then there isn't any. To touch this mystery requires, I think, love of the things and creatures that surround us, becoming one with them, so that they enter into us as Rilke says. They are transformed within us and our own inner life finds expression through them. The use of the term "inner life" means, of course, that one is not whole, one has an inner life and an outer life, and they don't come together. If a poem remains at the level of surrealism, possibly it means that no integration takes place, that the inner world and the outer world do not come together.

What is it about the simile that you mistrust or distrust, that makes you eschew it?

Well, I don't think things are often really like other things.

Too conscious?

They don't resemble other things. At some level all things resemble each other, but before one reaches that point it's necessary to respect the integrity of the separate creature. As Whitman says, speaking of appearances of things, "We use you, and do not cast you aside—we plant you permanently within us . . ." He means appearances, presences, not essences at all. Of course, in what I've said, I'm not criticizing surrealism. In talking about similes, I've been talking about the use of them descriptively.

What is the "advantage," aesthetic or otherwise, of the long poem over the short lyric?

In a very short poem time slows down, as it does in a music box that needs winding. If it's a very good poem it can come to rest on one moment, on the last note of the music box, and open that moment, seem to exist outside of time. The whole thing is rather delicate and magical. We Americans are deeply embedded in time and we aren't as good at that as, for instance, the ancient Chinese. But in the long poem it's possible to turn this limitation to good use. A person, or at least a personage, can begin to appear in the long poem, as in "Song of Myself," and also one can develop a series of events, of inner events, which can actually culminate, come to a fullness and climax, as in *Duino Elegies*. This culmination, though it's made of time, can also, in its way, transcend time.
I started writing long poems early . . . but I think everybody feels, eventually, that he's got to write a long poem. There's something so magnetic about the enterprise.

Don't you think that comes, in part, from the sense that to keep doing that thing that he has done so many times will not hold enough challenges, or surprises for the poet?

Yes. I do think a person has to go through a lot of changes, as Yeats did, for example. It's stultifying to keep writing from the same point of view the whole of one's life. That's

the reason most poets write their best things in their twenties and thirties. They keep on writing, but find that what they write after that is what they wrote before. Isn't that true?

There's a contemporary of Yeats who also went through those kinds of changes, perhaps not as famously as Yeats . . . D.H. Lawrence. He's a poet much influenced by Rilke. And with the animals and so forth of **Body Rags**, *I wondered how familiar you are with Lawrence's* Birds, Beasts, and Flowers?

I've already mentioned Rilke and Whitman, but I would mention Lawrence third among the germinal poets for modern times. I love his poetry. I love his love poems, and I love his animal poems. I don't like his didactic and social poems very much, the mental poems.

What sort of thing in Lawrence is it that you find most attractive?

In the love poems, it's that he does what Rilke talks about. Rilke talks about how lovers carry each other into the darkness, or into cosmic light. Lawrence's love poems—unlike Cummings', for example, which have two people loving each other—move into cosmic adoration, much like what happens in the fifth section of "Song of Myself," where there's some kind of paradigm of love experience in which love of a person dissolves into love of everything. Lawrence's is a dark and more mysterious experience. And in the animal poems, I like it that the animals remain animals throughout. They're not like Ted Hughes' animals, which become symbols too quickly. They have an incredible symbolic resonance all the way through without ever losing their animal reality.

I can't think of a poet before Lawrence who was able to do that.

Christopher Smart almost did that with his cat.

It's funny what a new life Christopher Smart has had in the last ten or fifteen years. All sorts of people have rediscovered and re-read him after a long obscurity.

Richard Howard is making an anthology of modern poetry in which each poet is to cite an older poem that's been important to him, which he will present along with the man's own poem. He said four or five people wanted to use Smart's cat poem. I don't know who finally got to use it.

What would be your poem?

Well, I wanted to use Rilke's *Ninth Elegy*, but the translations are too unsatisfactory, so I used sections of "Song of Myself."

You say that Ted Hughes' animals "become symbols too quickly." Do you see your bear or porcupine, for example, functioning as symbols—or are they simply part of a larger symbolic structure or "journey"?

For me those animals had no specific symbolic correspondences as I wrote the poems about them. I thought of them as animals. But of course I wasn't trying simply to draw zoologically accurate portraits of them. They were animals in whom I felt I could seek my own identity, discover my own bearness and porcupinehood. Depending on how well I succeeded, the reader would be able to do the same for himself, and the animals could have a symbolic resonance after all. But any specific correspondences would be those the reader would create and are not fixed by the poems.

I keep circling back to things—what is that talismanic sort of thing on the cover of **The Book of Nightmares**? *Who did those drawings?*

Well, they're all from books, generally fifteenth century.

Woodcuts?

Yes.

I assume they're your idea?

Yes. Some of them are from alchemical texts, some of them are from books on practical matters, like how to find water . . .

Yes, the dowsing rod.

The woodcut on the cover I saw reproduced in some book, and I knew I wanted it for the cover. I hadn't yet figured out who those two little angels were who were drawing words from the mouth of the man about to be devoured. I wrote the Library of Congress and asked them if there was a copy in the United States of the original book where that cut appeared. I was in Iowa City at the time, teaching. They wrote back and said there was only *one* copy in the United States, and that it was at the University of Iowa's medical library, in Iowa City. I went down the street and photographed it.

Incredible that you were there.

Yes.

Conrad Hilberry (essay date 1975)

SOURCE: "The Structure of Galway Kinnell's *The Book of Nightmares*," in *Field,* No. 12, Spring, 1975, pp. 28-46.

[*In the following essay, mythology as well as Kinnell's own comments on the poem's structure aid Hilberry in analyzing* The Book of Nightmares.]

Writing about Galway Kinnell's long poem, I feel as I imagine I might feel if I were lecturing about *Paradise Lost* with John Milton in the back of the hall. Why doesn't everybody just turn around and ask *him?* In fact, Kinnell has said some helpful things about the structure of *The Book of Nightmares* (e.g. in the *Ohio Review* interview, Fall 1972)—and may say more. But I suppose, like other

poets, he will leave a great deal unsaid. This, of course, is not coyness or obstinacy. When another person comments on a poem, we see that commentary as illuminating or not illuminating, right on certain points and wrong on others, etc. But no one sees it as the last word, equivalent to the poem itself. We always assume there is more to be said as the complexities of the poem take different configurations for other readers. But when a poet speaks about his own work, the statements sound with an uncomfortable finality. Who can dispute the man himself? And whenever a reading is taken as final, the poem is diminished.

I believe the best place to begin with a work as large as *The Book of Nightmares* is its structure. When the architecture of the book begins to come clear, when we have a confident sense of the movement of individual parts and the development of the whole poem as the parts build on each other, then there will be time to look more closely at recurring details or motifs, at variations of tone, at the texture of allusions, or at literary parallels. Certainly there will be things to be said about mythological elements. A glance at Joseph Campbell's *Hero with a Thousand Faces* draws to the surface countless pieces of myth in the poem: the road of trials through rocks and mountains, the helpful crone, the death of self, the descent into the underworld, the hero united with his missing female half, etc. But to begin with, what are the parts and how do they fit together?

I propose to look first at the structure of Poem I, **"Under the Maud Moon,"** in the belief that the structure of that poem is analogous, in a backwards way, to the structure of the whole book. I will go on, then, to the overall movement of the book and then back to look at several other individual poems in the context of the whole.

The first section of **"Maud Moon"** is a desolate one. It establishes the scene—Kinnell following a mountain path, lighting a fire, remembering a woman. (The speaker calls himself Kinnell.) Almost every detail reiterates a sense of brokenness, separation. He imagines tramps before him "unhouseling themselves on cursed bread." The tramps are doing the reverse of what the Eucharist intends; they are breaking themselves off from the sacred. So, too, with other details in this section. The woman is absent and Kinnell's hands hold only the empty space. The limbs, longing for the universe, snap, their embrace torn. The oath that made the universe one, holding together earth and water, flesh and spirit, is broken—resworn and broken over and over. Maud is not mentioned in this first section, nor is the song. The wholeness or oneness of the world is noticed only in its absence.

In the second section, the scene is the same—Kinnell is alone by the small fire in the rain. But he moves both back and forward in time, thinking back, by way of his singing, to the songs he used to croak for his daughter in her nightmares and forward to the bear out ahead of him, the one he will see later, nodding from side to side, eating flowers, his fur glistening in the rain. All three of the elements here, his daughter Maud, the bear, and the song, tend to bring some unity to the desolate brokenness of the first section. The child is closer than she will ever be again to the underlife, the "underglimmer of the beginning"; the bear moves with his own motion, perfectly at home among the blossom-smells on the rained earth; and the song, a love-note, "like the coyote's bark, curving off, into a howl," may bring us as close as we can come, with our torn speech, to a unison with the natural world.

The restorative elements are present again, and less hesitantly, in section 3. It moves back, in present tense now, to Maud waking in her crib. Throughout the section she is associated with plants, flowers: her hair sprouts out, her gums bud for her first spring, her green swaddlings tear and the blue flower opens. She is torn from the primal oneness, to be sure, but she is still natural, linked with flowers as the bear was in section 2. At the end of this section, she reaches into her father's mouth, to take hold of his song, to learn from him a second-best way toward wholeness.

Section 4, the center one of the seven sections, is crucial to the movement of "**Maud Moon.**" (This tends to be true of each of the poems; to understand its structure, notice the movement into and away from its fourth section.) Here Kinnell takes us back to wholeness, the child in the womb, flipping and overleaping, "somersaulting alone in the oneness under the hill." Here, for a while, the place is her own; she presses a knee or elbow along a slippery wall, "sculpting the world with each thrash." And the song she hears is not words spoken from mouth to ear but the stream of omphalos blood humming all about her. Effortlessly, she is the song. Without losing the gaiety, the comedy, of the child somersaulting "under the old, lonely bellybutton," Kinnell can slip in a phrase like "in remembrance," which must bring to mind Christian communion; inconspicuously he links the womb-leaping with the sacramental bread. Here flesh and spirit are put together—as they were not for the unhoused tramps in section 1.

A passage from Kinnell's essay "Poetry, Personality, and Death" (*Field*, Spring 1971, pp. 68-9) makes plain how much emphasis he intends to place on "the oneness under the hill":

> What do we want more than that oneness which bestows—which *is*—life? We want only to be more alive, not less. And the standard of what it is to be alive is very high. It was set in our infancy. Not yet divided into mind and body, our mind still a function of our senses, we laughed, we felt joyous connection with the things around us. In adult life don't we often feel half-dead, as if we were just brains walking around in corpses? The only sense we still respect is eyesight, probably because it is so closely attached to the brain. Go into any American house at random, you will find something—a plastic flower, false tiles, some imitation panelling—*something* which can be appreciated as material only if apprehended by eyesight alone. Don't we go sight-seeing in cars, thinking we can experience a landscape by looking at it through glass? A baby takes pleasure in seeing a thing, yes, but seeing is a first act. For fulfillment the baby must reach out, grasp it, put it in his mouth, suck it, savor it, taste it, manipulate it, smell it, physically be one with it. From

here comes our notion of heaven itself. Every experience of happiness in later life is a stirring of that ineradicable memory of once belonging wholly to the life of the planet.

Another sentence, from "The Poetics of the Physical World," (*Iowa Review,* Summer 1971, p. 121) explicitly follows our sense of oneness with the world back to the womb itself: "Isn't the very concept of paradise also only a metaphor? Our idea of that place of bliss must be a dream extrapolated from our rapturous moments on earth, moments perhaps of our infancy, perhaps beyond that, of our foetal existence."

The first three sections of Poem I have moved in toward the foetal somersaulting of section 4, the sense of "belonging wholly to the life of the planet." The last three sections move out again into the torn world. Chronologically, Maud's residence in the womb is the earliest event in "**Maud Moon**"; the first four sections moved progressively back in time to that original paradise. The next three sections move forward again to her birth, to her crying in the crib, and finally to a glimpse of her later life.

Section 5 is the birth. "Being itself" gives her into the shuddering grip of departure; separation is built into the nature of things. She skids out, in section 6, still clotted with celestial cheesiness, still glowing with the astral violet of the underlife. But they cut her umbilical tie to the darkness and her limbs shake as the memories rush out of them. She screams her first song and her arms clutch at the emptiness—as Kinnell's hands, in section 1, kept holding the empty space where the woman's face had been.

Section 7 becomes more distant, more reflective. Maud is now remembered in the past tense, as she was in section 2, after the more immediate present-tense birthing in the middle sections. Here Kinnell, still by the mountain fire presumably, thinks back to Maud in her crib and his own singing to her. The song itself is the main subject of this last section. It is no angel song but a blacker rasping; nonetheless it has cosmic allegiances. He learned the song under the Maud moon, when Sagittarius sucked the biestings, the first milk, of the cosmos. And he learned it from marshes where he could hear the "long rustle of being and perishing," where earth oozed up, "touching the world with the underglimmer of the beginning." The song carries intimations of a larger life beneath and above this one.

As the tramps in section 1 unhoused themselves on cursed bread, so here in the last section Kinnell foresees a time when Maud will be orphaned, emptied of wind-singing, with pieces of cursed bread on her tongue. The poem has moved from the brokenness and desolation of the first section into the miraculous "oneness under the hill" and back to separation and cold and curse again at the end. But in the last section there is the song, the poem, the ***Book of Nightmares,*** doing what it can to make connections. As Maud, crying in her crib, knew sadness "flowing from the other world," so she will remember the specter of her father, with ghostly forefathers behind him, singing to her in the nighttime. This section states, indirectly, the hope of the book: to be there, a raspy spectral voice reminding us that wholeness is at least conceivable, as Maud and the rest of us see the oath broken between flesh and spirit, between our lives and the life of the planet.

I have emphasized the symmetry of the first poem. The whole *Book of Nightmares,* though extremely various in its moods and inclusive in its details, is built on a similarly symmetrical pattern—in fact, the mirror image of the structure we have seen in **"Maud Moon."** That poem moves from fragmentation to wholeness and back to fragmentation; the whole book moves from Maud's birth with its affecting glimpse of the oneness we must have experienced in the womb or in infancy, to the relentless meditation on death in Poem V and the hellish picture of human depravity in Poem VI, and then back to the birth of Kinnell's son Sancho Fergus and the qualified celebration in the last poem. This symmetry is reinforced by details recurring in Poems I and X: the path, stream, and fire on the mountain, the bear, the two births, the constellation the Archer, references to communion, etc. More than that, some images or details that occur at the beginning or end of the book occur also in the desperate center parts but with connotations reversed. For example, as we have seen, the pregnant belly appears in an exuberant passage in the first poem. In the eighth poem, the swollen belly has similar connotations. But in Poems V and VI the belly is big with death. In VI, 5, the belly of a dead soldier "opens like a poison nightflower" reminding us, by contrast, of Maud's flowering in I, 3. Poem V, 5, develops more fully the deadly-birth image. Here the drunk dies, his flesh turns violet, and "the whine of omphalos blood starts up again, the puffed bellybutton explodes, the carnal nightmare soars back to the beginning."

A couple of other details similarly link the dead center of the book with the beginning or end. In II, 5, the Northern Lights flashed and disappeared until Kinnell thought he could "read the cosmos spelling itself, the huge broken letters shuddering across the black sky and vanishing." The comparable detail in V, 4, has none of this sense of ambiguity and wonder, no sense that the cosmos might magically flicker its meaning above the horizon. Here the message is manmade, definite, and final: "I saw the ferris wheel writing its huge, desolate zeroes in neon on the evening skies." One other instance: in VI, 2, the air force gunner, Burnsie, says,

> remember that pilot
> who'd bailed out over the North,
> how I shredded him down to catgut on his strings?
> one of his slant eyes, a piece
> of his smile, sail past me
> every night right after the sleeping pill . . .

That catgut comes back in X, 5 as the strings out of which the violinist draws his music.

Even these two small details, the writing on the night sky and the catgut, give some sense of the structural movement of the book. It begins aware of death and torn lives,

to be sure, but nonetheless buoyed up in the first two or three poems by glimmers of cosmic writing, remnants of celestial cheesiness, or intimations of the underlife. By V and VI, the book moves under "the absolute spell of departure," the neon zeroes of death. Men detest the sweat of their own bodies and shred other men to catgut because they love the sound of the guns and the feel of them in their hands. In the last poems love is again possible— under the pear tree which grows out of the boneyard, the aceldama bought with Judas's silver. Deeply acquainted with death, the wood and catgut will open again to love's singing.

The introduction of the mountain scene in I and the return to it in X leads Dennis McCarthy to argue (in conversation) that this place may be taken as the literal location of the poem, with all the rest being the hiker's mental journeying. This much is evident: as the book opens, Kinnell, the speaker, is making a fire on a path by a stream in the rain, remembering a woman whose face he has held in his hands, thinking of the bear he has not yet encountered out ahead of him, and, as he sings into the fire, thinking of his daughter. By the final poem he has climbed further up the mountain. The fire is now behind him, still flaring in the rain, and the stream is now skinny waterfalls that wander out of heaven and strike the cliffside. The bear that was out ahead is now present, his fur glistening in the rain, like Sancho Fergus' hair. Standing in the old shoes flowed over by rainbows of hen oil, Kinnell calls out toward the cliff and listens for an echo, hears the clatter of elk hooves, and looks down on the river below. This scene does contain many details that develop into prominent motifs as the book grows: the path, the stream, the bear, the stones, the woman who is his torn half and whom he has just left in Waterloo, Iowa, the fire, the daughter and son, even the old shoes and the hen—or at least the grease from the hen. It seems to me plausible to think of this as the literal setting of the poem, made intense partly by his having just let necessity draw him away from the woman in Waterloo. **"The Hen Flower," "The Shoes of Wandering,"** and the rest then become meditations triggered by elements in that literal scene. They are the imaginative or spiritual journey the speaker takes as he is climbing a few hundred yards or a mile or two up the mountain from the site of the fire to the clearing where the bear nods and turns.

One hesitates to push this reading too hard, for a couple of reasons. For one thing, even though the stream, the shoes, the hen, the children, the divided lovers, etc. recur throughout the book, there are few references between I and X to the mountain scene itself. (In fact, four: V, 4; VII, 4; VIII, 7; and IX, 1.) Can we travel through all the rich and emotional material in between and still hold in mind the mountain location? If Kinnell had intended us to do that, would he not have brought us back to that scene more often? Second, the description of Maud's birth in the first poem and Fergus' birth in the last gives a strong sense of time elapsed. (Probably our knowing that Kinnell wrote the book over a four-year period contributes, illegitimately, to that feeling.) But those reasons do not seem to me conclusive. There the hiker is, further up the mountain in the tenth poem, and if a reader finds it helpful to see the book as an internal journey, a series of meditations bracketed by the literal fire and bear on the mountain, I believe he is justified in doing so.

Now a few observations about Poems II, IV, VII, and X and their place in the progress of the book. Again, I am dealing with the general contours of these poems, their structure, saying little about the lovely modulations of tone and texture that draw the reader along, surprising him and engaging his feelings page after page.

If **"Maud Moon"** recalls the glimmers of the celestial, the intimations of immortality that we knew from before birth and still could touch in earliest childhood, **"The Hen Flower"** considers death and the mysteries, if any, that lie beyond it. It is as though Kinnell, in order to write Maud a true book for the days when she finds herself orphaned, must discover as much as can be known about death. He begins that exploration here in the second poem.

In the first and last sections of II Kinnell is sprawled face down on the mattress of hen feathers, aware of how little there is between himself and the long shaft of darkness shaped as himself, and wishing he could let go, throw himself on the mercy of darkness like the hen who woozes off when its throat is stroked, throws its head back on the chopping block, and longs to die. The "letting go" that Kinnell wishes to instruct himself in is probably, in part, a literal willingness to die when the time calls for it. It may be, as well, the death of the self that he speaks of in "Poetry, Personality, and Death" (pp. 72-74) as when in the deepest lovemaking "the separate egos vanish; the wand of cosmic sexuality rules." A paragraph from that essay may clarify this death-longing:

> The death of the self I seek, in poetry and out of poetry, is not a drying up or withering. It is a death, yes, but a death out of which one might hope to be reborn more giving, more alive, more open, more related to the natural life. I have never felt the appeal of that death of self certain kinds of Buddhism describe—that death which purges us of desire, which removes us from our loves. For myself, I would like a death that would give me more loves, not fewer. And greater desire, not less. Isn't it possible that to desire a thing, to truly desire it, is a form of having it? I suppose nothing is stronger than fate—if fate is that amount of vital energy allotted each of us—but if anything were stronger, it would not be acquiescence, the coming to want only what one already has, it would be desire, desire which rises from the roots of one's life and transfigures it.

"The Hen Flower" has its symmetries, as does **"Maud Moon,"** but the internal organization is different. Here, in sections 2 through 6, two views of death alternate, one prevailing for a section or a paragraph and then the other having its say. The first sees death as simple extinction, the cheeks of the axed hen caving in, the gizzard convulsing, the next egg skidding forth, ridding her of the life to come. This is the tone of the message in 5 in which the mockingbird sings the cry of the title, the tree holds the bones of the sniper, and the chameleon is not changed, not raised incorruptible, but remains the color of blood. It is

the tone of the paragraph in 6 in which the rooster groans out for Kinnell, as for the stonily doctrinaire Peter *it is the empty morning.* But playing off against this view of death as literal and final are those wonderful, halfcomic hen-resurrection passages—the one in which the beheaded hen waits for the blaze in the genes that according to gospel shall carry it back into pink skies, where geese cross at twilight honking in tongues. And the one in which the Northern Lights, seen through the spealbone of a ram, appear to spell mysteries against the black sky. And the one in which Kinnell flings high the carcass of the hen and watches the dead wings creak open as she soars across the arms of the Bear.

Section 4, at the center of **"The Hen Flower,"** takes us into the opened cadaver of the hen, back to the mystery of hen-death past the diminishing eggs toward the icy pulp of what is. There zero freezes itself around the finger. If there is any ambiguity here, it lies in our knowledge that zero is not only the end of the diminishing series of positive numbers but also the beginning of the series of negative numbers. But this may be too hopeful a reading for that cold cipher. Oneness was at the center of I; the center of II is zero.

In II Kinnell has instructed himself to let go, to throw himself on the mercy of darkness, "to say all," as he says in the *Ohio Review* interview (Fall 1972, p.30). In III, the dangerous journey begins. After a kind of vigil at the Xvarna Hotel (a Zoroastrian word, Kinnell says, meaning "hidden light"), he sets out, lost to his old self and aware of his inadequacy on this strange road where even the most elementary questions are a puzzle.

The fourth poem, **"Dear Stranger Extant in Memory by the Blue Juniata,"** is one of the most complex and difficult. The first three sections describe three different places where one might look for help or insight or guidance on the uncertain journey—and all three fail to provide it. No longer hoping for some mythic gatekeeper, or deskman, to swing open the steel doors and announce a new day, Kinnell still listens for the church's tinny sacring-bell, rung during the Eucharist at the elevation of the bread and wine. He hopes for some instruction from this old ceremony. But the *chime* is just *chyme,* a mass of semi-digested food. Instead of the bread and wine of our loves being transformed into the sacred body and blood, they are chewed and swallowed. The physical remains physical, subject to maggots. In section 2, Virginia is in touch with something supernatural, some force that can lead her hand to draw circles and figure eights and mandalas—all symbols of wholeness, infinity, or perfection. But she sees this magic not as benevolent but as terrifying and demonic. In 3, the natural landscape of rural America, the primal garden, has also lost its efficacy. The root-hunters are pulling up ginseng, violating the virginal woods so that they may sell artificial aphrodisiacs. (The first chapter of Malcolm Cowley's *Exile's Return,* titled "Blue Juniata," evokes just this sense of irrecoverable innocence, a lost world: "Somewhere the turn of a dirt road or the unexpected crest of a hill reveals your own childhood, the fields where you once played barefoot, the kindly trees, the landscape by which all others are measured and condemned.")

Section 4 provides a recipe for the only potion that we can hope may remake us. It is an unsavory concoction of salvaged bits of magic and religion, the fragments of belief or intution "that mortality could not grind down into the meal of blood and laughter." It is here, drawn through terrors by this imperfect magic, that we may find one more love, a face to be held in the hands, or one more poem whose title must be **"Tenderness toward Existence"** What stands against nothingness, the vacuum, here in section 4 is far more modest than the oneness asserted at the center of I. But it is something, a love or a poem to tie one to existence.

The world is not transformed by the potion. In the last three sections the Juniata (which flows through the Appalachians in south central Pennsylvania) is no longer blue or virginal, the sanctus bell dies against the sheetglass city, there is no second coming of resurrected hen, people do not share their darkness to make one light. As the primal garden of 3 becomes the dark shore of 5, so the letter of 2 is balanced by the even more desperate letter of 6. For Virginia, the super-natural holds nothing but terror. And the final section is Kinnell's acceptance of distances and wounds.

With the fifth poem, **"In the Hotel of Lost Light,"** the traveler becomes an intimate of death. In the sixth, **"The Dead Shall be Raised Incorruptible,"** he goes far beyond that, touching the very bottom of human depravity, especially American depravity. The deaths are no longer individual or personal; they have become institutional. (Both poems have the quality of legal documents—V a sort of death certificate, signed and dated in V, 7, and VI a last will and testament.) The title of VI is heavily ironic. In this poem, there is no sign that flesh will be changed, raised incorruptible. Corruption reigns. Only the prayer in the last section, "do not remove this last poison cup from our lips," may be intended without irony. Perhaps we must drink horror to the bottom of the cup if we are to have any hope of recovering from it.

Poem VII, **"Little Sleep's-Head Sprouting Hair in the Moonlight,"** opens with this sentence: "You scream, waking from a nightmare." Here the book wakes from the nightmare of VI. Maud, whom we have not seen since **"Maud Moon"** (except perhaps in IV, 5, if that is Maud crying in her bed by the Juniata) reappears, Kinnell's arms heal themselves holding her, and the tone changes to a relaxed, affectionate one. Death is still very much part of the poem, as it will be to the end, but now the emphasis shifts to the effect that the awareness of death has on our loves.

The center of VII seems to me to fall in section 5, rather than 4, and in general VII is less symmetrical than its predecessors. Perhaps the somewhat looser organization contributes to the change of pace and tone.

The subject of VII is permanence—or, rather, the inevitability of change. In the opening scene, Maud clings to her father as though he would never die, and in the second section Kinnell wishes he might hold Maud forever out of the world

of decay. But both of them sense the pre-trembling of a house that falls. In the restaurant, Maud shouted once, stopped all the devouring in midair—but only for a moment.

In section 4, Kinnell imagines the time, in 2009, when Maud will be the age he is now and will walk, as he is, in the rain, among the black stones that repeat one word *ci-gît* ("here lies . . .". In another glimpse of Maud's future, in 5, Kinnell sees her with a lover in a café at one end of the Pont Mirabeau, again re-enacting Kinnell's experience, thinking that the bridge arcs from love into enduring love. For Maud, as she lives these events for herself, Kinnell has one piece of advice—that she should reach more deeply into the sorrows to come, touch the bones under the face, hear under the laughter the wind across the black stones, not to lessen the intensity of the moment but to increase it. She should know that *here is the world:* this mouth, this laughter, these temple bones. The cadence of vanishing is the only measure she can dance to.

As section 4 and 5 moved forward in time, section 6 moves back to connect, in a lovely metaphor, Maud's mortality with that of Kinnell's father:

> I can see in your eyes
> the hand that waved once
> in my father's eyes, a tiny kite
> wobbling far up in the twilight of his last look:
> and the angel
> of all mortal things lets go the string.

Then he puts her back into her crib and promises that when he comes back (from climbing that stony mountain?) they will walk out together with the knowledge that *the wages of dying is love.* This idea, love's dependence on death, is critical in understanding the rest of the book. The force of it comes through clearly in this paragraph from "The Poetics of the Physical World" (p. 125):

> It is through something radiant in our lives that we have been able to dream of paradise, that we have been able to invent the realm of eternity. But there is another kind of glory in our lives which derives precisely from our inability to enter that paradise or to experience eternity. That we last only for a time, that everyone and everything around us lasts only for a time, that we know this, radiates a thrilling, tragic light on all our loves, all our relationships, even on those moments when the world, through its poetry, becomes almost capable of spurning time and death.

This meditation on mutability prepares us for **"The Call across the Valley of Not-Knowing,"** the book's strongest and most eloquent statement of the coming-together that is possible in love. Poem VIII is organized much as I is, moving from incomplete or partly broken love (the split half-persons Aristophanes speaks of in Plato's *Symposium*) toward a remembered moment of wholeness in section 4, and back to separation across the valley of not-knowing. But here the wholeness is not recalled from the womb but experienced in adult life—the coming together for a moment of body and thought, of man and unviolated nature, of love and the knowledge of death, of lover and lover.

"The Path among the Stones" (IX), for me the least energetic of the poems, recapitulates the movement of the whole book down into the dismal mineshaft where a man squats by his hell-flames and then, tentatively, back up.

The magnificent tenth poem, **"Lastness,"** has a structure of its own, but more important than this internal shape, perhaps, is its function in drawing together, into an ambiguous resolution, the themes and images that have twisted and grown through the whole book. The organization of X may be summarized very briefly: the first section reestablishes the mountain scene. The second and third sections present the positive and negative halves of the dichotomy that has played all through the book: wholeness is possible, yet everything breaks, falls apart, dies. The fourth section brings together those two opposites in the figure 10. The rest of the poem shows what follows from that conjunction of one and nothing, what kind of music, or poetry, may be sung out of it and what kind of life it implies.

Consider the cluster of images in each section. Even the first section, made of three direct sentences, holds the double vision that pervades the book. At this height, the stream is a series of skinny waterfalls, footpaths wandering out of heaven and shattering on the cliffside—reminiscent of the oath (I,1) sworn in the clouds and broken on earth, sworn and broken over and over. There is—and is not—a communion between the cosmos and our torn selves. Similarly, this section brings back all the water and fire that have gone before. The desolation of wet ashes, cursed bread in the rain, is eased by a twig fire, kindled out of a particular human love but, now that the self does not clutch for its own so greedily, part of a less personal vitality that keeps flaring up in a dying world.

Section 2, a touchstone if there ever was one, catches up in the bear and Sancho Fergus all the poem's images of what it is to belong wholly to the life of the planet. Here is the primal garden (IV), the blossoming of brain and body under the knowledge of tree (VIII) encompassed in the glistening of this new birth. The man watching the bear from the fringe of the trees is still a death-creature, still capable of the perversions and violations catalogued in poem VI, but at this moment he can become bear watching bear. That innocence echoes in the pride and freshness of Sancho Fergus' birth. Though Fergus' smile acknowledges disasters to follow, the force of this section is wonder at the glistening oneness of bear fur, boy fur, and the grasslands and fern of the newborn planet.

As Kinnell walks toward the cliff, in section 3, calling out to the stone, the stone calls back—and then does not, turns to stone, sending nothing back. He stands between the answer and nothing, as he stood in **"The Hen Flower"** between the resurrected hen soaring across the arms of the Bear and the cold cadaver of hen, the icy pulp of what is. This is where the shoes have stood all along; this is where the journey into the future must

be made—between the answer and nothing. At the end of the section, the negative half of the truth bears in more heavily. He learns again what he has been learning throughout the book, that *To Live* has a poor cousin, who pronounces the family name *To Leave.* In a clatter of elk hooves, the empyrean has emptied itself of whatever eternal truths it may have held. The truth now is that the earth is all there is and the earth does not last. The journey stops here. Living brings you to death, there is no other road.

The central section of the tenth poem pulls together all the ones and zeroes that have gone before: the oneness under the hill, the oneness of two loving halves put together, the oneness, perhaps, of man and bear and boy and planet in X, 2; and the freezing zero of hen corpse, the desolate neon zeroes of the ferris wheel, the zeroes the skipped wafer-stone leaves on the water. There can be no resolution. One and zero walk off the pages together, one creature side by side with the emptiness. The two need each other. Our brightness, gathered up out of time, takes some of its radiance from the fact that it will end, leaving nothing behind. And the death that resides in old cars, rivermist, and constellations is a beginning, too, as in the woodcut on the cover of *Book of Nightmares* new words are drawn out of the mouth of the man about to be devoured by the raven.

Out of love and the awareness of death, one and zero, comes the only music worthy of us. The ladies and gentlemen in the chandeliered room may look as though they would never die, but the violinist who puts the irreversible sorrow of his face into the palm of the wood knows better. As the rasping song of **"Maud Moon"** is at once a love-note and a howl, so the violinist's music knows the waves of holy desire of VIII and the flesh of the pilot, in VI, shredded to catgut. It is made out of the sexual wail of back-alleys and the sliced intestine of cat.

The book is not just song, or poem, but a life as well (as Kinnell says in response to a question about X, 6 in the *Ohio Review* interview). We are left with an image of how one may live: the sky-diver, floating free, opening his arms into the attitude of flight, as he obeys the necessity and falls. He has come back to the instructions of **"The Hen Flower,"** to let go, to throw himself on the mercy of darkness. The ambiguity persists to the end. The worms on his back are still spinning forth the silk of his loves and already gnawing away at them. And for a son whose father's body will be laid out, both reactions are fitting: Don't cry! Or else, cry.

In reply to Robert Frost's dictum that writing free verse is like playing tennis with the net down, Kinnell writes, "It is an apt analogy, except that the poem is less like a game than like a journey. . . ." ("Poetics of the Physical World," p. 114) Kinnell's poems have frequently been journeys literally, as well as figuratively. Even in his first book, *What a Kingdom It Was,* **"Westport," "Where the Track Vanishes,"** and **"The Descent"** are all traveling poems. So is **"The Bear."** So are many others. But *The Book of Nightmares* is the big journey, the one that encompasses the whole passage of our lives. The scope of its motion makes one think of *Paradise Lost* or the *Odyssey.* It is the hiker's journey up the mountain (on the Olympic Peninsula, Kinnell says), but inside that journey the poem travels back to the beginning, to the unborn child complete in its dark world or even further back to man before he had evolved away from the bear, when he was wholly at one with the planet. It moves through separation and knowledge of death into the collective depravity and wanton destruction of the Vietnam war. But it leads out of that slough, too, by way of Maud and Fergus, and love for a woman, and a hoarse song.

The traveler reaches no destination. In an interview in the *Iowa Review* (Spring 1970, p. 129) Kinnell says,

> One of the blessings of being my age is that you need not talk about the *purpose* of your life. When one is young, one perhaps longs for a goal or purpose. But life itself is insulted by having to be justified by a goal; life *is,* and that is all there is to it. And to open oneself to the rhythm of being born and dying, while it is awful, since it means facing your terror of death, it is also glorious, for then you are one with the creation, the cosmos.

When one and zero walk off the end of the poem's pages together, they are not headed toward a conclusion. The lone creature can only keep on journeying, side by side with the emptiness. But now, at the poem's end, the journey reverberates with cosmic terror and grandeur.

Al Poulin, Jr., and Stan Samuel Rubin (interview date 1976)

SOURCE: An interview with Galway Kinnell, in *The American Poetry Review,* Vol. 5, No. 4, January 1976, pp. 6-7.

[*In the following interview, Kinnell discusses* The Book of Nightmares *as well as the earlier* What A Kingdom It Was.]

[INTERVIEWER]: **"First Song"** *is the first poem in your first book,* **What a Kingdom It Was.** *It elicits an obvious first question. What kinds of impulses originally necessitated your writing poetry and under what kinds of circumstances did you start writing?*

[KINNELL]: I remember wanting to write poetry long long before I had even attempted to write a poem. I suppose from the age of twelve on I knew that was all I wanted to do. It was a kind of funny situation, because I didn't have any idea if I could do it at all. It wasn't until I was around eighteen that I began to write what you might call "seriously". As for the original impulses, I'm not sure. I do know that I lived a kind of double life: my relations with everyone I knew, my brother, sisters, parents, friends, and so on—and a secret life with the poems that I would read late at night. It seemed to me that in those poems I had a deep communication, found my own most private feelings shared—much more than in the relationships I had in the world. In poetry it might

be possible to say the things and express the things I didn't find it possible to in regular life.

Do you recall what poems you were reading?

A lot of Edgar Allen Poe. Also Emily Dickinson. Shelley. Wordsworth. Kipling. Housman. A jumble of poets. I preferred them romantic, and sentimental if possible.

Did you read Whitman early?

Yes, but I didn't understand Whitman when I read him early. It was only when I was in my mid-twenties that I discovered him. Then he meant very much to me, and he still does. It could be Whitman isn't a poet for young people. He's rapturous all right, but maybe not corny enough, to compete with someone like Kahlil Gibran. Also he's extremely physical, and perhaps young people don't like that, they want so hard to see beyond physical things.

Besides reading, what other kinds of events or experiences influenced your work? In his review of **What a Kingdom It Was,** *James Dickey stated: "Perhaps to a degree more than is true of other poets, Kinnell's development will depend on the actual events of his life." How accurate was Dickey's prediction?*

I do not know whether it's the case with other people's poetry, but my own does stay pretty close to the experiences of my life, and probably it has come to do so even more in my last two books. My children, for example, appear quite a lot in *The Book of Nightmares.* I think in the book Dickey was reviewing certain of the poems were completely invented. So there was perhaps a certain prescience in his remark.

But reading your poems one doesn't have the sense, as one does with the more personal poets—Lowell, Plath or Sexton—that this is an actual, real person speaking. There is always the sense of a kind of persona in the poem. I mean, one doesn't feel one's getting to know Galway Kinnell the private person.

That may be true, it's not something I could judge. Insofar as I use my own life in my poems I think of it as like other's lives. I change things, sometimes to make the experience sharper, to bring out something, but often to universalize an experience, to take away details that keep it merely autobiographical.

I'm not sure I agree that one doesn't feel one is getting to know you through your poetry. But there's something interesting there: you said that as a youth you felt that you were leading a kind of double life, and the notion of persona seems very important to you. How do you relate your ego in your own life to the beyond-ego you wish to achieve in your poetry, to the notion of an exploratory ego you discuss in your essay, "Poetry, Personality, and Death"?

I would think that if a poem succeeds in transcending the ego, it would then become accessible to others. It's when one sets forth one's own experiences exactly as they were, simply because that's how they were, that readers may find themselves no longer participants but forced a bit into the role of spectators.

You've said that the poem comes in part out of the poet's desire to be changed, out of his struggle with his own nature. Is the death of the ego a recognizable point in a poem; is it a place you go through when you're writing a poem?

I think that in some great poems, like Whitman's "Song of Myself," a reader goes from one individual, Whitman, to some deep self that's within us all. There is in Whitman a kind of continual sinking down into the "death of the self," if we can use the phrase, and it is one of the things that make the poem so glorious. As we read such poems, we learn about opening ourselves, we practice it. When we come to the line, "I was the man, I suffered, I was there," we already understand what it is to disappear into someone else. The final action of the poem, where Whitman dissolves into the air and into the ground is, I suppose, one of the ultimate moments of self-transcendence in a poem.

It seems to me that when the poet is writing he or she is engaging in some kind of public gesture. When you're dealing with this enormously private emotion and being that absolutely private self, doesn't it cause a number of problems and necessitate a great energy to move from that very personal emotion and transform it into a public gesture? Those seem almost irreconcilable.

I don't suppose I would think of the word "transform" right away. I'd use the term "going deeper" instead—going deeper until you reach a level where your own personality isn't there any more, where you're just a person. If you could go even deeper, you'd not be a person, you'd be an animal; and if you went deeper still, you'd be a blade of grass, eventually a stone. If a stone could speak, your poem would be its words.

That makes me think of the topic of death which runs throughout your poetry. It seems to have some special meaning for you.

It has a special meaning for me, probably for everyone. It has two sides to it. One, the extinction we fear, and the other, the stage in the lifecycle in which we need to have almost as much trust as we do in the moment of birth. There's a conflict within us. I think I deal so much with death in my poetry in order to try to deal with the conflict.

It also seems to me as if you almost feel at times that the moment of death is the moment of heightened clinging to life. I know you've written about Emily Dickinson's "I Heard a Fly Buzz when I Died."

Yes that's what Emily Dickinson was doing when she wrote the poem: imagining that she was dying, imagining the heightened intensity she would feel when she left everything she loved. In my case, the last section of *The Book of Nightmares* was written in something like that state.

This is something, then, that we should be able to do continuously?

Hegel says, "The life of the spirit is not frightened at death and does not keep itself pure of it. It lives with death and maintains itself in it." Yves Bonnefoy uses this as the epigraph to his wonderful book *On the Motion and Immobility of Douve.*

I find myself disagreeing with both of you. My reading of **The Book of Nightmares** *suggests an equal strain of transcendence of some kind. There's a profound traditional religious attitude toward death; if not life after death, then at least some form of transcendence, both in the newer poems as well as in the earlier ones. There is the motion from the river to the sea in your Easter poem, for example, and similar kinds of transcendence in other poems. There are always those transformations.*

Yes. I think that halfway through my first book of poems I ceased to look for that kind of transcendence. A lot of the poems in the last half of the book are struggles to be rid of the desire for heaven.

In another interview you said that 'the dream of every poem is to be a myth', and I wonder if any orthodox mythology is viable today, and if not, what then are the materials of a more contemporary myth.

I doubt if old myths, born in other circumstances, in other times, in other cultures, can be very alive for us. When I said, "The dream of every poem is to be a myth", I don't know if I meant myth in exactly the old sense. Perhaps "prayer" is more like it. The poem wants to be a kind of paradigm of what a person might wish to say in addressing the cosmos—I suppose the old myths were a bit like that. This, or something like this, is what John Logan must mean when he speaks of the "sacramental character" of poetry.

In regard to that, your poem, **"The Dead Shall Be Raised Incorruptible,"** *has perhaps more of what might be termed "political" content, social content, than almost any of your other poems. What motivated that poem?*

One writes out of obsessions. The political agony of this country, has obsessed, haunted the consciousness, and the conscience, at least since the Vietnam war began, and for many people in this country well before that. I wrote that poem out of the same drive that led almost every poet in this country to turn to political subjects. Many of the poems we wrote weren't particularly good poems, or even interesting politically. Some were. But the main thing is they had to be written. I think my own poem probably fails, but it did force me to try to understand what had become of our respect for life. That we could kill on such a large scale without any sensible reason at all. I'm not sure the poem even makes it clear, but as I wrote it I did learn there's a connection between our feeling, propagated by advertising, that the human body is repulsive until treated with deodorants, vaginal sprays, armpit-shaving, and the rest, and our indifference about killing Asians, whose bodies presumably remain in the state of nature. A kind of hygienic equivalent of the Crusaders' lack of compunction about killing heathens.

I asked you that because it is a kind of exception in **The Book of Nightmares**, *and yet it clearly relates to the nightmare you're speaking of. It's not the way you normally write or the kind of theme you normally handle.*

That's probably true, although in the previous book there is a long poem called **"The Last River"** which is also political, and a good deal longer. You see, what I wanted to do in *The Book of Nightmares,* in regard to politics, as well as in regard to other elements that come into the poem, was to bring from the central core of the poem a sort of light on to—well, I could say any subject whatever, that any one of those ten sections could have been about anything at all, that would be its pretext, and this light, this core, would be strong enough to gather even the most unrelated into the poem.

What, exactly, would you say is that central core?

I was afraid you might ask me that!

Why do you think so many poets have been working on long poems and sequences recently?

The desire for a poem in which you can say everything, in which there is nothing that won't fit.

That's very close to what Ginsberg is trying to do and, of course, it recalls Whitman, doesn't it—to include the entire universe?

I suppose that Pound has been more responsible than anyone for the way the long poem has developed. For myself, while I want a poem that can include everything, I don't want to abandon what I think of as its organic form—where the poem isn't made by accretion, by adding lines and stanzas, sections and books, and so on, indefinitely, as *Paterson* and the *Cantos* were made. I want a long poem to be an organism—to be born, to grow, to come to a certain flowering and climax.

While reading **The Book of Nightmares,** *which I did read as one poem—I couldn't put it down because the voice was continuous and gripping—I felt that something's happened to your relationship with time. I don't know how, perhaps your children may have something to do with that.*
What do you feel has happened?

A sense that a particular kind of affirmation of natural life that one gets reading your earlier poems is somewhat modulated here. Even in the opening poem, **"Under the Maud Moon,"** *there is a real consciousness of time-future, I think, in a way that I don't precisely sense in your earlier work. For example, the last image in the book: "see if you can find/the one flea which is laughing." Somehow that's a little more tentative than, say, the poem* **"The Fly,"** *I wonder if that means anything to you?*

Perhaps. For myself, *The Book of Nightmares,* for all that tentative and fearful quality you correctly see in it, is more affirmative than anything else I've written. I can't say more than that. Anyway I'm the last person to be able to judge.

In your essay, "The Poetics of the Physical World," *you spoke of the dichotomy between "the poetics of heaven" and "the poetics of the physical world," but in* **The Book of Nightmares** *you seem to have managed a reconciliation between them.*

I came to feel very free in writing that poem. I felt I could say anything. I could set down the very worst, anything, no matter what, I could evoke in the poem the most revolting presences, and I could do this in total faith that something was sustaining the whole poem that would not allow it to be a record of self-disgust, or hatred of nature, or fear of death, or loneliness, or defeat, but rather ultimately a restorative and healing and, if I can use the word, a happy poem.

There's been a great change in the structure of your poems from **What a Kingdom It Was** *to* **The Book of Nightmares** *and I'm rather fascinated by some of them. In "The Poetics of the Physical World," you say that for the modern poet rhyme and meter, having lost their sacred and natural basis, amount to little more than mechanical aids for writing. First of all, I'm intrigued by why they've lost their sacred and natural basis for the modern poet or for you.*

Oh, I'm just guessing. I guess that the Elizabethans must have heard something going on in existence that seemed akin to rhyme—the rhyme in their poems was a way of acknowledging it and sharing in it. We don't hear anything like that. We see that we're a race living for a while on a little planet that one day will die, in a space and time that we don't know anything about, that we probably won't ever know anything about, since our brains apparently are the wrong kind for knowing such things. It's a lot of things, beautiful, baffling, thrilling, frightening. I don't think it rhymes. Oh, this is just guessing . . .

Isn't that dangerously close to the belief that truth actually is beauty, or that whatever is true and looks like a poem necessarily is one?

How does it suggest that?
In the most basic terms, what, then, differentiates art from life?

I suppose it's that art contains a special fervor, a special light—it comes from a different level of being from "prose", from "talk", whether it's written out in the shape of a poem or not, whether it's even written down, or just spoken once by one person and forgotten . . .

You quote from C.M. Bowra's Primitive Songs *in several places. What do those kinds of poems mean to you?*

I quoted those poems hoping they would serve as contrasts to nineteenth century English poetry, which by its conventions often gives us a standard "poetic" way to feel about things. The poems from *Primitive Songs,* partly perhaps because they're in plain translations, seem to be psychologically more true.

Is this a good place for poets generally to go, then?

I think so. I think conventional English poetry is the worst place for a young poet. There are absolutely glorious poems in that tradition, of course, and anyone who wants to be a poet will know them. But to steep oneself at an early age in this tradition isn't a good idea. Precisely because the tradition is so attractive, those "poetic", distorting qualities take a fierce hold and one day you discover you have an awful lot to unlearn. It would be better to read poets a little outside the tradition—poets who are too individual and eccentric to have this effect—poets like Smart, Blake, Dickinson, Tuckerman, Clare, Melville. And poetry that's in another language doesn't have this effect either, at least if you can read it in the original, or if it's in translations that respect the literal meaning and don't try to reproduce the form. (Translation is O.K. in the case of the very greatest poems. What gets strained out is the mortal beauty, the message from heaven comes through. I'm not sure that's true—maybe it's the other way around.)

Perhaps a poem like "In Memoriam"—one of those big sloppy poems which I don't think you or very many readers have much affection for—is in a sense a kind of parallel to **The Book of Nightmares** *in terms of Tennyson's attempt to work out his unanswerable questions. Only I think he does it with less honesty and less success.*

I don't know. It's not a poem that moves me very much, but it's one I respect a great deal for the enterprise it represents. It's rare to find poets who want to confront, in all their complexity, all the facets of their most painful emotions. I don't think the poem succeeds—in part, maybe in large part, because of the terribly limiting, pretty, form it's written in.

Would you care to discuss what you're currently working on beyond **The Book of Nightmares**?

That's what I've asked myself. I thought of this poem as one in which I could say *everything,* everything that I knew or felt. Now that it's finished, now that some time has passed since it's been finished, I don't quite know what I shall write. Just now I'm writing some prose.

Are you experiencing fear?

No. Not yet. I feel tired. I have to wait until I feel an energy that wants to come out in words.

Might you be relieved in some way if you didn't feel the same sort of need that motivated **The Book of Nightmares**?

I don't think so. I really didn't want to let that poem go. I felt that I could spend the rest of my life writing it and developing it and perfecting it. So I clung to it and had to force myself to get rid of it, though I knew I would feel this unsettling emptiness for a long time afterwards. I would like to feel as totally consumed again.

Does that mean you don't feel that the writing of prose makes the same sort of demands on you?

No. It's the working out and setting down of opinions.

In the course of our conversation you've agreed that traditional mythology and symbology are no longer viable; you suggested that the formal and inner conventions of poetry must be discarded; and in "The Poetics of the Physical World" you state that formal beauty is an impediment to the discovery of glory. I wonder, what is there left?

Besides all those things I so foolishly threw out? I don't know. Maybe it's as well not to know. It may be that the fewer conventions, the fewer guides, we have, the more chance there is to come to some new place. I imagine it's better not to write merely conventional poems, that will come out competent, pleasing, more or less ornamental. I imagine it's better not to do that, but to do something bolder even at the risk of writing horrible poems, if it seems to you that in that way lies a possibility of finding that great thing you may be after of finding glory.

Charles Bell (essay date 1980)

SOURCE: "Kinnell, Galway," in *Contemporary Poets,* 3rd Ed., New York: St. Martin's Press, 1980, pp. 835-37.

[*In the following excerpt, Bell relates his intimate knowledge of his former student's career, up to and including* The Book of Nightmares.]

In the winter of 1946-47, when I was teaching at Princeton University, a dark-shocked student, looking more like a prize fighter than a literary man, showed me a poem, maybe his first. I remember it as a Wordsworthian sonnet, not what the avant-garde of Princeton, Blackmur or Berryman, would have taken to—old diction, no modern flair. But the last couplet had a romantic fierceness that amazed me. The man who had done that could go beyond any poetic limits to be assigned. I was reckless enough to tell him so.

I was to lecture at Black Mountain that summer. He took a bit of his G.I. money and came along. Apart from some works of mine which seemed to move him, it was to Yeats that he gave himself with the totality that has always characterized him. By the fall he had written the first form of a four-page poem, **"A Morning Wake among the Dead"** (later called **"Among the Tombs"**), which foreshadowed in volcanic latency all his later long poems. The death-haunted, tragic Kinnell had already spoken, though it would take years for the fact to be recognized.

In form, Kinnell was still using a romantic and Miltonic pentameter almost totally remade under impacts from Donne and the moderns—meter purposely broken up, rhymes concealed—a demonic wrestling with traditional measures. His matter was the reaffirmation of the Promethean and pioneer daring of America, to which I also, after the neo-Augustinian resignations of the war, was committed. He wrote a whole volume of Western poems which did not find a publisher, though some of them, revised, appear in the first sections of *What a Kingdom It Was.*

About 1956 Kinnell was able to get abroad. It was not too late for his "Prairie" style to be infused with French modernism, though without losing its passionate immediacy. The most remarkable fruit of this is **"The Supper after the Last,"** in *What a Kingdom,* a symbolist vision and statement, at one time Promethean-romantic and mysteriously avant-garde.

Kinnell's break with traditional form has continued, leading to his espousal of free verse as the only possible medium for an American poet. It is significantly to Whitman that he has returned, with some inspiration from William Carlos Williams. But anyone who will take the twisted rhymes of the earlier Kinnell and set them beside the free verse of recent works—that staggering diptych of animal poems, **"The Porcupine"** and **"The Bear"** in *Body Rags*—will sense how far everything that has occurred, both in content and form, was within the province of the original Apocalyptic vision of **"A Morning Wake among the Dead."**

What distinguishes that vision from anything else on the contemporary scene is its continuation of the titanism of the last century—whatever flamed from Goethe's *Faust* through Melville, Nietzsche, Rimbaud, to Rilke, Yeats, Jeffers. There is a sense in which Galway Kinnell has remained faithful to this heritage, though for a long time it handicapped him among those of a more oblique and verbal trend, poets who grew up as it were after Pound. Thus a review of *Body Rags* (in the *New York Review of Books*) spent most of its time complaining that Kinnell didn't write like Berryman—as if he hadn't had his chance at that and decided early against it.

Within Kinnell's passionate and personal vein, two drifts have revealed themselves, that of the longer poem prefigured in **"A Morning Wake," "The Avenue Bearing the Initial of Christ,"** and **"The Last River,"** and that of clarified small lyrics aimed at an ultimate transparency. The lyrical tendency reaches its earliest perfection in **"First Song"** ("Then it was dusk in Illinois") as in the other tender pieces (**"Island of Night," "A Walk in the Country"**) published in Rolfe Humphries' *New Poems* though not included by Kinnell in any of his volumes. So too with **"Spring Oak,"** a poem that illustrates Kinnell's critical pronouncement in his Beloit "Self-Study": "Only meaning is truly interesting." Even in *Body Rags* there are such distillates, **"The Falls"** and **"How Many Nights."** Reading them, as the "Self-Study" had also said, is "like opening a window on the thing the poem is talking about":

How many nights
have I lain in terror,
O Creator Spirit,
Maker of night and day,

only to walk out

the next morning over the frozen world
hearing under the creaking of snow
faint, peaceful breaths . . .
    . . . snake,
bear, earthworm, ant . . .

and above me
a wild crow crying *"yaw yaw yaw"*
from a branch nothing cried from ever in my life.

Against such poems, the underworld involvement of **"The Last River"** goes another road, groping through caves and antres of "the flinty, night-smelling depths," "waiting by the grief-tree of the last river."

Kinnell's second book, *Flower Herding on Mount Monadnock,* as the title suggests (strange the Indian name for that solitary mountain on a peneplane should hold the Greek root of the One), is largely in the lyrical mode. Even the Wagnerian love-death has wonderfully refined itself in **"Poems of Night":** "A cheekbone. / A curved piece of brow, / A pale eyelid / Float in the dark, / And now I make out / An eye, dark, / wormed with the far-off, unaccountable lights." While the title poem and **"Spindrift"**—"Sit down / By the clanking shore/Of this bitter, beloved sea"—stand at the pinnacle of the poignantly pure and deeply transparent.

At the moment I have before me various sketches of *The Book of Nightmares.* For oceanic participation, the section on childbirth (**"Maud Moon"**) goes beyond anything Kinnell has done before:

It is all over, little one,
the flipping
and overleaping,
the watery
somersaulting alone in the oneness
under the hill, under
the old, lonely bellybutton pushing forth again
in remembrance, all over,
the drifting there furled like a flower, pressing
a knee down the slippery
walls, sculpting the whole world, hearing
a few cries from without not even as promises, the
    stream
of omphalos blood humming all over you.

What distinguishes this from the work of any other poet (though parallels can be found: Roethke, Rilke, even Whitman) is the intuitive immediacy of its entrance into pre-birth and subhuman organic nature.

Of all the poets born in the twenties and thirties, Galway Kinnell is the only one who has taken up the passionate symbolic search of the great American tradition.

Hank Lazer (review date 1980)

SOURCE: A review of *Mortal Acts, Mortal Words,* in *Ironwood,* Vol. 16, Fall, 1980, pp. 92-100.

[*In the following review, Lazer praises* as having "lighter" and "looser" poems than the much-acclaimed, unified work that preceded it, The Book of Nightmares.]

In "The Age of Criticism," Randall Jarrell writes that "most people understand that a poet is a good poet because he does well some of the time." That certainly is the case with Galway Kinnell's writing and with Kinnell's latest book. I'm sure that some readers will find it inferior to **The Book of Nightmares,** possibly because **Mortal Acts, Mortal Words** is lighter, less unified, and looser. But these two books are different. **Mortal Acts, Mortal Words** is a collection of poems, in fact, of several different kinds of poems. **The Book of Nightmares** is a book of poems, a single sequence of poems intended to be read as a unified whole.

At their finest, Kinnell's new poems, as with many of his earlier poems, are testaments of faith. The second section of **"There Are Things I Tell to No One,"** one of the best poems in **Mortal Acts, Mortal Words** is the heart of Kinnell's faith:

> I say "God"; I believe,
> rather, in a music of grace
> that we hear, sometimes, playing to us
> from the other side of happiness.
> When we hear it, when it flows
> through our bodies, it lets us live
> these days lighted by their vanity
> worshipping—as the other animals do,
> who live and die in the spirit
> of the end—that backward-spreading
> brightness. And it speaks in notes struck
> or carressed or blown or plucked
> off our own bodies: *remember*
> *existence already remembers*
> *the flush upon it you will have been,*
> *you who have reached out ahead*
> *and taken up some of the black dust*
> *we become, souvenir*
> *which glitters already in the bones of your hand.*

It is fair to say that, like the previous passage, much of Kinnell's best poetry is Rilkean. It is *not* fair to say, therefore, that Kinnell is derivative. It just so happens that Rilke helped to stake out some rather elemental, crucial territory in the life/death interface. And Kinnell enters that territory too, but by his own vision or, as might be said, by his own lights.

There are, throughout this book, happy, glorious, celebratory lines. The poet takes a great and rich joy in this world: "no matter what fire we invent to destroy us, /ours will have been the brightest world ever existing." And there is still the death-hiss, still the world of dread and dissolution. But the advance that **Mortal Acts, Mortal Words** marks is in Kinnell's greater certainty of those impermanent but perfect moments of celebration. In this book the poet can say with conviction that "I have always felt / annointed by her love," and he can declare that "I am in the holy land."

But, again, to return to **"There Are Things I Tell to No One,"** it is the earned sureness of this poetry that I admire: "In this spirit /and from this spirit, I have learned to speak / of these things, which once I brooded on in silence." Like Walt Whitman, Kinnell's great service is to show us that life, our life, is holy:

> Yes, I want to live forever.
> I am like everyone. But when I hear
> that breath coming through the walls,
> grace-notes blown
> out of the wormed-out bones,
> music that their memory of blood
> plucks from the straitened arteries,
> that the hard cock and soaked cunt
> caressed from each other
> in the holy days of their vanity,
> that the two hearts drummed
> out of their ribs together,
> the hearts that know everything (and even
> the little knowledge they can leave
> stays, to be the light of this house),
>
> then it is not so difficult
> to go out, to turn and face
> the spaces which gather into one sound, I know
>   now, the singing
> of mortal lives, waves of spent existence
> which flow toward, and toward, and on which we
>   flow
> and grow drowsy and become fearless again.

I am proud to be corny and say that Kinnell, with such poetry, can deepen our appreciation of that great, brief gift: life. And he can also help us in that Rilkean task: to read the word "death" without negation.

The key fact for Kinnell is the uniqueness of each creature, life, moment, love. That is, as he writes in **"52 Oswald Street,"** Kinnell draws his strength "from unrepeatable life." He writes with a great eye for the specific, particular beauty of this world:

> the pelvic bones of a woman
> lying on her back, which rise
> smoothed by ten thousand years
> on either side of the crater
> we floated in, in the first life,
> that last time we knew
> more of happiness than of time.

For Kinnell, moments of epiphany and transcendence occur only by our becoming deeply familiar with the world. We transcend, that is, move to the realm of floating, first life, and that last time, only by being joined to the physical world.

That specific, intense union with the physical world must be accomplished by more than mere sight or vision. In his essay, "Poetry, Personality, and Death," which originally appeared in *Field* and is now available in *A Field Guide to Contemporary Poetry and Poetics,* Kinnell explains:

Don't we go sightseeing in cars, thinking we can experience a landscape by looking at it through glass! A baby takes pleasure in seeing a thing, yes, but seeing is a first act. For fulfillment the baby must reach out, grasp it, put it in his mouth, suck it, taste it, manipulate it, smell it, physically be one with it. From here comes our notion of heaven itself. Every experience of happiness in later life is a stirring of that ineradicable memory of once belonging wholly to the life of the planet.

Yes, for Kinnell in his poetry too, seeing is but a first act, and no poem better illustrates that fact in his new book than **"Saint Francis and the Sow,"** which, with its single, long, gorgeous sentence, requires quotation in its entirety:

> The bud
> stands for all things,
> even for those things that don't flower,
> for everything flowers, from within, of self-blessing;
> though sometimes it is necessary
> to reteach a thing its loveliness,
> to put a hand on its brow
> of the flower
> and retell it in words and in touch
> it is lovely
> until it flowers again from within, of self-blessing;
> as Saint Francis
> put his hand on the creased forehead
> of the sow, and told her in words and in touch
> blessings of earth on the sow, and the sow
> began remembering all down her thick length,
> from the earthen snout all the way
> through the fodder and slops to the spiritual curl of
>   the tail,
> from the hard spininess spiked out from the spine
> down through the great broken heart
> to the blue milken dreaminess spurting and
>   shuddering
> from the fourteen teats into the fourteen mouths
>   sucking and blowing beneath them:
> the long, perfect loveliness of sow.

"Saint Francis and the Sow" is a remarkable poem, fit to join company with Kinnell's finest animal poems of bear and porcupine. At the heart of Kinnell's work is the understanding that "sometimes it is necessary / to reteach a thing its loveliness." It is by way of hand and word, touch, snout, tail, spine, heart, and teat that the poet's, and our own, sacramental relationship to the world is achieved.

Aside from the perfect adjectives—creased forehead, thick length, earthen snout, spiritual curl, great broken heart, and blue milken dreaminess—there are several other features that intrigue me about this poem. The first is the long sentence and the adventurous, correct line breaks—both features of this entire volume. In other poems of the single long sentence, as in **"The Rainbow,"** Kinnell is able to give us a compressed, united experience. If a moment can be said to have duration, Kinnell gives us a long moment. And in the musical elaboration of a single sentence, Kinnell allows the moment to labor, dance, and play toward its fit and powerful conclusion. When Kinnell's long sentences click, as in **"Saint Francis and the**

Sow," "After Making Love We Hear Footsteps," "The Last Hiding Places of Snow," and "Flying Home," the long sentences convey the beauty of Kinnell's reading voice and the poems sound like rich, even-tempered blessings. An additional feature of the poem, and a feature worth noting in general about Kinnell's work, is the way, especially in the last line, Kinnell resists the impulse to create metaphors or similes out of the physical world.

I think that this resistance to metaphor and simile is one feature that sets Kinnell's work apart from some of the contemporaries—Robert Bly, especially—with whom Kinnell's work is often linked. In an interview with Wayne Dodd and Stanley Plumly, to be found in *Walking Down the Stairs,* a collection of interviews with Kinnell recently released from the University of Michigan Press's fine Poets on Poetry Series, Kinnell is asked what it is that he mistrusts about simile. His answer:

> I don't think things are often really like other things. At some level all things *are* each other, but before that point they are separate entities. Also, although they are common, as you say, in surrealist poetry, similes perhaps have the effect of keeping the irrational world under rational supervision. Perhaps the words "like" and "as if" draw a line through reality and say in effect, "Here we are no longer speaking of the real world— here we indulge our imaginations."

Kinnell, as in **"Saint Francis and the Sow,"** insists on the perfection and uniqueness of the world that is. Thus, a difference between Kinnell and Bly, analogous to a difference between Whitman and Thoreau. Bly, like Thoreau, through metaphor and simile, or through what we now more loosely refer to as the image, creates symbols for the inner, spiritual world of man. Bly and Thoreau side more closely with Emerson's maxims in "Nature":

> Particular natural facts are symbols of particular spiritual facts. Nature is the symbol of spirit. . . . The use of natural history is to give us aid in supernatural history; the use of the outer creation, to give us language for the beings and changes of the inward creation.

Kinnell's sense of correspondence and symbolism in nature is closer to the side of Whitman when, at the end of section 13 of "Song of Myself," he cautions,

> And do not call the tortoise unworthy because she
>   is not something else,
> And the mocking bird in the swamp never studied
>   the gamut, yet trills pretty well to me,
> And the look of the bay mare shames silliness out
>   of me.

If anything, Kinnell is more rigorous than Whitman in respecting the integrity and otherness of the creature world.

Thus, at the end of **"The Gray Heron,"** where Kinnell even allows himself to throw in a "like," our dominant impression is of the difference between the lizard world and the human world. The poet, where he expected to find the heron he had seen, instead finds

. . a three-foot-long lizard
in ill-fitting skin
and with linear mouth
expressive of the even temper
of the mineral kingdom.
It stopped and tilted its head,
which was much like
a fieldstone with an eye
in it, which was watching me
to see if I would go
or change into something else.

In the finest short poems in *Mortal Acts, Mortal Words,*
"**Daybreak,**" which I quote in its entirety, Kinnell does
allow himself a very precise comparison:

On the tidal mud, just before sunset,
dozens of starfishes
were creeping. It was
as though the mud were a sky
and enormous, imperfect stars
moved across it as slowly
as the actual stars cross heaven.
All at once they stopped
and as if they had simply
increased their receptivity
to gravity they sank down
into the mud; they faded down
into it and lay still; and by the time
pink of sunset broke across them
they were as invisible
as the true stars at daybreak.

But the more important analogy, between terrestrial and
celestial heavens, is resisted. That correspondence (or
contrast) remains outside the poem. Again, it is Kinnell's
judicious adjectives—enormous, imperfect, actual, and
true—that do so much in this poem, and that finally link
together the opposite worlds of mud and sky, sunset and
daybreak, imperfect starfish and true stars, our world and
the other world. And the linking takes place so quickly,
"all at once." It is just what Robert Frost says of the true
poem in "A Figure a Poem Makes": "Like a piece of ice
on a hot stove the poem must ride on its own melting."
But what dominates Kinnell's poem, and Kinnell's poems
throughout his career, is precision of description. The realm
of correspondence is usually only implied.

Part of this wonderful particularity throughout Kinnell's
career comes from his insistence on bringing to life old,
nearly dead words. In *Mortal Acts, Mortal Words* Kinnell
gives us the gritty substance of certain special verbs:
wastreled, dismouthed, moil, and curvetting, among the
most arresting in the text. Like his brother, Whitman, who
in a key line in "Song of Myself" uses "athwart" ("You
settled your head athwart my hips and gently turned over
upon me") and later in the poem says, "My foothold is
tenoned and mortised in granite," Kinnell too has a special fondness for the tangible but unusual verb.

The main weakness with *Mortal Acts, Mortal Words* is that
there are a fairly large number of poems that feel like filler.

Many of these weaker poems—poems with humor, or extensive word-play, or poems rooted in domestic life—add range
to Kinnell's work, but they simply do not stand up to re-
reading. Though they add a necessary contrast or counterpoint to the overall collection, finally, poems such as "**Angling, A Day,**" "**In the Bamboo Hut,**" "**Lava,**" "**Crying,**"
"**Les Invalides,**" "**On the Tennis Court at Night,**" and
"**Looking at Your Face,**" for this reader, don't make it.

In terms of the occasional failings in *Mortal Acts, Mortal
Words* a pertinent poem to take a look at is "**The Still
Time.**" It is a poem weakened and blurred by its many
plurals and vague, general terms: those summer nights, the
steps of my life, everything that drove me crazy, and all
the old voices. There are still beautiful moments in the
poem, as when at the end of the next to the last stanza
Kinnell writes,

as though a prayer had ended
and the changed
air between the palms goes free
to become the glitter
on common things that inexplicably shine.

In this passage it is "*a* prayer," but even that release of air
gets a bit blurred by the plural "things." Kinnell concludes
the poem by saying,

And all the old voices
which once made broken-off, chocked, parrot-
    incoherences,
speak again,
this time on the palatum cordis, all of them
saying there is time, still time,
for those who can groan
to sing,
for those who can sing to heal themselves.

It is the whole choir of old voices that weakens the specific,
odd beauty of "broken-off, choked, parrot-incoherences." *A*
voice singing to heal itself, *one* parrot-incoherence carefully listened to, would be much more effective.

I belabor this point because such a weakness in the lesser
poems casts into some doubt the strength of Kinnell's
writing. That strength is his bold and beautiful endings. In
the weaker poems the big endings feel more like rhetorical habit than the earned or urgent necessity of the poem
itself. More often, though, in *Mortal Acts, Mortal Words,*
the poem seems to rise naturally and easily to its strong
ending. In already strong poems, such as "**Saint Francis
and the Sow,**" "**There Are Things I Tell to No One,**"
"**The Sadness of Brothers,**" or "**The Rainbow,**" the
ending simply takes the poem one notch higher.

At the end of "**Fisherman,**" a poem consisting of words
to a friend whose wife has died, obviously an inherently
risky topic in terms of the subjects's potential for sentimentality, Kinnell's last stanza is:

I don't know how you loved
or what marriage was and wasn't between you—
not even close friends understand anything of that—

but I know ordinary life was hard
and worry joined your brains' faces in pure, baffled
    lines
and therefore some deepest part of you has gone
with her, imprinted into her—imprinted now
into that world which only she doesn't fear any
    longer,
which you too will have ceased fearing—
and waits there to recognize you into it
after you've lived, lived past the sorrow,
if that happens, after all the time in the world.

This ending attains an eloquence as it labors upstream, battling all its qualifications, its obstacle course of buts, therefores, and whiches. But what rescues and exalts the ending is the qualification present in the last line: "if that happens." It is such a qualification that makes this ending feel at once moving and comforting, lofty and judicious.

So, too, in the marvelous poem **"The Apple Tree."** Kinnell speaks earlier in the poem about the moment

When the fallen apple rolls
into the grass, the apple worm
stops, then goes
all the way through and looks out
at the creation unopposed, the world
made entirely of lovers.

And Kinnell ends the poem by saying,

The one who holds still and looks out,
alone
of all of us, that one may die mostly of happiness.

Again, I suggest that it is the double sense of "may" and the qualification implied by "mostly" that deepens this ending.

There is a more important point to be made about these endings than their employment of careful qualifications. Kinnell's strong endings are tied to a more comprehensive vision: his own special vision of death. As in **"The Apple Tree,"** where the apples "fail into brightness" and where Kinnell explains that "we die / of the return-streaming of everything we have lived," Kinnell's own endings to poems are part of a backward-spreading brightness. As Kinnell points out in **"There Are Things I Tell to No One,"** endings are a way of tying us to beginnings:

Just as the supreme cry
of joy, the cry of orgasm, also has a ghastliness to it,
as though it touched forward
into the chaos where we break apart, so the death-
    groan
sounding into us from another direction carries us
    back
to our first world.

By the very nature of endings we learn how inextricably and closely linked are those seeming opposites, life and death, which by our fear we mistakenly wish to keep apart.

As in **"The Choir"** where "eyes, nostrils, mouth strain together in quintal harmony / to sing Joy and Death well," Kinnell's own endings present an analogy for Kinnell's vision of our own ending. The glorious, humane, fine-sounding conclusions to Kinnell's poems are, finally, to be linked to the "return-streaming" and to "that backward-spreading / brightness" that Kinnell has spent a career pointing out to us.

Mortal Acts, Mortal Words presents us with a passionately moral poetry, but it is not priggish nor self-righteous. In this book we get the sense of a man saying directly, eloquently, and emotionally the things he knows. He tells us the few repeated facts and conjectures that he believes matter. Toward the end of **"Flying Home,"** the last poem in the book, we land in an "imponderable world." And I believe that Kinnell's humility, the admission of a word such as "imponderable," is not the last bit phony. In the finest poems of ***Mortal Acts, Mortal Words,*** as in **"Daybreak,"** we witness the perfect correctness of the slow starfish who moves through the mud and is suddenly receptive to gravity.

Charles Molesworth (revew date 1983)

SOURCE: A review of *Selected Poems,* in *Commonweal,* Vol. 110, No. 5, p. 157.

[*In the following excerpt, Molesworth hails* Selected Poems, *a thirty-five-year retrospective of Kinnell's career, as a "paradigm of one of the major shifts in postwar poetry."*]

. . . In Galway Kinnell's ***Selected Poems*** thirty-five years of poetry definitely originates in a single, identifiable sensibility. From the largely ironic and structured ***First Poems,*** on through the ecstatic longing for transcendence in ***Body Rags*** (1968) and ***The Book of Nightmares*** (1971), Kinnell's career develops as a paradigm of one of the major shifts in postwar poetry. This shift affected the work of many poets directly, such as Robert Bly and James Wright, but it also indirectly altered the major idiom of American poetry, moving as it did toward a language of empathy and celebration. Drawing on various sources such as Rilke, Whitman, Lawrence, and Frost, Kinnell's poetry gained prominence because of its Romantic scale and yearning. Throughout all of his volumes, this poet has known a central paradox:

It is written in our hearts, the empti-
    ness is all.
This is how we have learned, the em-
    brace is all.

Emptiness answered by embrace: these are for Kinnell an emotion and a bodily gesture, a physical condition and a spiritual response. The balance of this formulation doesn't guarantee the truth of its scope, its desire to know and say "all," but it embodies that desire. Large scope has to reside in balance, the balance of any lyrical utterance. Those poems from the middle of the journey—**"The Porcupine,"** **"The Bear,"** and **"The Last River"**—brought to perfection one strain of the American sublime, that imperious, empathetic invasion of nature with its need to infinitize the ego and yet to gather all details, all sensory awareness. Even when Kinnell's asceticism veers towards masochism, and his religious temper mingles with secular celebration, we have work that must be attended to if we are to measure our poetry at its fullest. As in Wordsworth's "Immortality Ode," we are given "fallings from us, vanishings" as the source of our knowledge. Kinnell's best poems plunge us into a darkness that is more than sufficient, and their light is made bearable only by their music. . . .

Madeleine Beckman (essay date 1983)

SOURCE: "Galway Kinnell Searches for Innocence," in *Saturday Review,* September/October 1983, pp. 14-16.

[*In the following essay, Beckman gives an overview of Kinnell's career in light of his having received the Pulitzer Prize for* Selected Poems.]

When Galway Kinnell showed his early poem **"First Song"** to the poet William Carlos Williams in the late 1950s, Williams told the younger poet that he had no business writing poems about "cornstalk violins" because he had never played one, nor should he write about fields in Illinois, where he had never lived. Williams suggested that Kinnell, who was living on New York's Lower East Side, take a pad and pencil and jot down notes about the neighborhood where he lived and walked, and write poems about what he knew best.

Following Williams' advice, Kinnell absorbed his neighborhood, specifically Avenue C between 14th Street and Houston Street. What emerged was a long, Whitmanesque, fourteen-part poem, **"The Avenue Bearing the Initial of Christ Into the New World."** For Kinnell the poem was a breakthrough. Now, more than twenty years later, Kinnell has published eight volumes of poetry, one novel, four translations, and has been anthologized with the world's greatest poets.

Among the awards Kinnell has received are a grant from the American Academy and Institute of Arts and Letters in 1962, a Guggenheim Fellowship in 1963, the Brandeis Creative Arts Award in 1969, the Shelly Memorial Award in 1973, the Award of Merit Medal for Poetry in 1975, the Herald Morton Landon Award for translation of poetry in 1979, the American Book Award (co-winner with Charles Wright) in April 1983, and most recently the 1983 Pulitzer Prize for his book *Selected Poems.*

In his acceptance speech for the Award of Merit, Kinnell said: "We know from the briefest glance at the past that poets who are honored in their time are often forgotten soon thereafter, that poets ignored while they live often come to great honor later on. I needed to remind myself of this principle frequently during that period of my life—a

long time, it seemed—when hardly anyone noticed my poetry. Now that I stand on this stage today I would just as soon forget it. But it's too late! I've learned it too well."

Kinnell is not quite sure why he won the Pulitzer. "I don't even know who the judges were," he says. "I meant to ask why they gave it to me, but I forgot." Kinnell does not think that his work will change because of the prize; he does, however, believe that his life will be made a little easier: he will give fewer readings for more pay.

Although the Pulitzer has created publicity for the poet, the prize has had little effect on his attitude toward himself. "I've seen many prizes come and go and I haven't paid too much attention to them," he says. He is pleased with having won the prize, but has not taken it as seriously as many people think he should. "The thing that did affect me about the poetry prize was the great outpouring of letters, telegrams, and telephone calls from all over the country. People I've known at some stage in my life, but also many people I don't know at all . . . what one correspondent called 'all your unmet friends.' So that wave of affection that did come through all those messages did affect me."

Kinnell was born in 1927 in Providence, Rhode Island, and grew up in the small milltown of Pawtucket, Rhode Island. At 15 he moved from Pawtucket to attend Wilbraham Academy. In 1948 he graduated summa cum laude from Princeton University with a bachelor's degree. A year later he earned a master's from Rochester University.

Today Kinnell divides his time between New York City, where he is director of NYU's creative writing program, and Sheffield, Vermont, where he and his wife Inez and their children Maud, 16, and Fergus, 14, have a home. (The children's names were taken from W.B. Yeats, who Kinnell says has had the most influence on his work, along with Rainer Marie Rilke.)

Kinnell at 56 is a burly man who has deep-set eyes that seem protected by his bushy eyebrows. He carries a bit of the New England countryside with him, even in Manhattan. His muscular physique gives him the appearance of a manual laborer, but his white shirt and khaki trousers confirm his academic attachment.

Kinnell likes living in New York City. "In New York I never feel separated from the anxiousness of the present moment," he says. "It's one reason why I want to live here. I don't know how permanently, but that's where I want to live for the moment. One of the reasons is that one is completely in touch with what is most difficult in human life, which is loneliness and poverty combined. Failed struggle—the sense of the whole class of crushed people, crushed individuals—is impossible not to meet every day. Living in New York keeps me in a state of anxious connection."

If Kinnell is striving to be a part of the world, to feel and interact, to be involved in relationships and to affirm his connectedness with the animal kingdom, he has achieved this goal in his poetry and in his social contributions as a teacher and political activist. In *Babel to Byzantium* the poet and novelist James Dickey wrote, "Galway Kinnell cares about everything." Not only does Kinnell have a passion *for* and devotion *to* poetry, he extends these same feelings to his friends and students, to political issues, and to the natural world around him.

In 1963 Kinnell worked as a laborer for CORE (Congress for Racial Equality) in Hammond, Louisiana; in the late Sixties he was active in poetry readings protesting the Vietnam War; in 1982 he organized a protest against nuclear arms called "Poetry Against the End of the World"; and in 1982 he was among the poets reading in "An Evening to Support Humanitarian Relief for the Children of Lebanon." "I think that Galway feels a poet is not just a private human being," says poet and colleague Jane Cooper, "but that a poet has public responsibilities."

When Kinnell writes a poem, he does not mean to make it political, but the relationships he observes *are* political. In the poem **"Vapor Trail Reflected in the Frog Pond,"** the narrator, a Vietnamese villager, hears "America singing," the song being the crackling of rifles mixed with a bomber plane's drone:

> The old watch: their
> thick eyes
> puff and foreclose by the moon. The young,
> heads
> trailed by the beginnings of necks,
> shiver,
> in the guarantee they shall be bodies.
>
> In the frog pond
> the vapor trail of a SAC bomber creeps,
>
> I hear its drone, drifting, high up
> in immaculate ozone.

The poem deals with "the sacred character of human life," Kinnell says. He believes that a sacred force exists that exemplifies itself in everything, and that this force sometimes shows itself in destruction. "When one animal eats another, that definitely has to do with the interchange of life, the dependency of one living creature on another," he says. "I think the problem with us today is that we have gone crazy. Human destruction is of a different order from every other form of destruction ever known on earth, because it's an act of madness. . . . The original and continuing function of poetry has been to counteract technological madness and to reconcile the human being once again with existence."

Listening to him talk about nuclear war, society, and his poetry, one must remember that despite his awards and position, Kinnell finds it difficult to identify with all the "hoopla" about himself. The floor of his cubbyhole office is strewn with publications: *Science 82, American Poetry Review.* A rolled-up mattress lies in the corner on the floor next to a coat-tree. On the windowsill sits an empty plastic soda bottle with a bouquet of dead flowers, gath-

ering dust. Next to the window hang a small watercolor landscape, with the $8.75 price tag still on the frame, and a black-and-white photograph of Kinnell playing with Maud and Fergus as young children. A Junior Delux portable typewriter; circa 1935, looking too small for his hands, sits on his desk practically hidden beneath piles of papers and letters. "This office is the state of my mind," says Kinnell, standing amid the mess.

His office is not the only indication of his battle with disorganization; his writing habits are haphazard as well. Kinnell writes at random intervals because his life is random. "If I had a patron to support me I'd have regular writing habits." Usually he writes his poems with a pen on scraps of paper. "If they're written on napkins and I find some shredded pulp in my pocket, I know that that one is not going to materialize into a poem," he says impishly. Kinnell writes when he can—on trains, at bus depots—carrying with him his portable typewriter.

It is hard-to believe that the poem **"The Bear"** was written either on a train or in a bus depot. This work has been analyzed and criticized more than any other of Kinnell's poems. The ninetyfour-line poem, divided into seven parts, is modeled after an Eskimo method of catching bears. In the poem the narrator pleads with the natural world for absolution of man's transgression—that of killing the bear for warmth and food. In the second stanza, the process of killing the bear begins:

> I take a wolf's rib and whittle
> it sharp at both ends
> and coil it up
> and freeze it in blubber and place it out
> on the fair way of the bears.

The last stanza brings the metaphor of the bear closer to Kinnell's own life:

> . . . the rest of my days I spend
> wandering: wondering
> what, anyway,
> was that sticky infusion, that rank flavor of
> blood, that poetry, by which I lived?

Kinnell says the poem is a metaphor for his writing process. Hearing him recite **"The Bear,"** one feels as if in the presence of a shaman who moves without his own control into a deeper place not quite earthbound. Watching Kinnell recite this poem, the listener can be distracted by the intensity of the performance. In an interview in 1975, Kinnell said that once when he announced the title at a reading, a rustle went through the auditorium and he felt as if he could have paused, nodded, and gone on to the next poem without anyone's noticing, because they all knew the poem.

Kinnell memorizes poetry, both his and others', because he believes that a poem does not really enter the reader until he memorizes it. At a recent memorial reading of the work of James Wright, Kinnell was the only guest poet to recite from memory. At another reading he recited his fourteen-part **"The Avenue Bearing the Initial of Christ"** without missing a beat or stumbling on a word. He thinks that he is probably the only poet ever to fall asleep during his own reading. In an interview he said, "I just folded my arms on the lectern and fell asleep. I suppose the audience thought I had fallen into a poetic swoon!"

Kinnell does not take critics seriously. One poem that they have frequently misinterpreted is **"Under the Maud Moon"** from the *Book of Nightmares.* In a 1976 interview with Kinnell, the interviewer interpreted the poem as either Kinnell's admission of defeat or his commitment to tragedy. Kinnell explained that the opposite was true: what he had meant to convey was his hope that when his daughter came upon hard hours in her life she could turn to the poem for help. The poem combines a man's feelings about birth and a father's adoration of his new daughter. Kinnell achieves a universal feeling by writing about his personal experience.

In the poem's fourth part, Kinnell talks about the daughter who is about to be born:

> It is all over,
> little one, the flipping
> and overleaping, the watery
> somersaulting alone in the oneness
> under the hill, under
> the old, lonely bellybutton. . . .

In Part VII he recalls how he used to go to her room at night to comfort her:

> I used to come to you
> and sit by you
> and sing to you. You did not know,
> and yet you will remember,
> in the silent zones
> of the brain, a specter, descendant. . . .

The last stanza of the poem is Kinnell's obvious wish that his daughter will continue to be comforted by her father even after he is gone:

> . . . may there come back to you
> a voice,
> spectral, calling you
> *sister!*
> from everything that dies.
> And then
> you shall open
> this book, even if it is the book of nightmares.

Whatever Kinnell writes about, whether it is bomber planes or lovemaking, his voice and the sensuousness of his poems are uncompromising. A recent poem, **"Blackberry Eating,"** is simple, direct, and less metaphorical than most of his poems:

> I love to go out in late September
> among fat, overripe, icy blackberries
> to eat blackberries for breakfast,
> the stalks very prickly, a penalty
> they earn for knowing the black art
> of blackberry-making; and as I stand among

> them
> lifting the stalks to my mouth, the ripest berries
> fall almost unbidden to my tongue,
> as words sometimes do, certain peculiar words
> like *strengths* or *squinched*
> many-lettered, one-syllabled lumps,
> which I squeeze, squinch open, and
>   splurge well
> in the silent, startled, icy, black language
> of blackberry-eating in late September. . . .

The voice in **"Blackberry Eating"** is playful and sensuous, combining the child and the man. It strives for an innocence that Kinnell realizes he cannot attain, because "being truly innocent is knowing everything."

For Kinnell, innocence has nothing to do with age. He says he does not feel his 56 years, though he will not deny that thoughts of "moving deathward" are with him. "There's a certain sense that when one is young you'll have time to accomplish everything in your life that you want to accomplish," he says. "But then when you get older, you have feelings you'll cease to be before 'your pen has gleaned your teeming brain.' It's true that Keats said that line when in his twenties; that was because of a premonition of a shortness of his life. But I think anybody in their late fifties is bound to feel the way I do. There are bound to be things I will not be able to get done. I guess that's better than running out of things to do."

Andrew Hudgins (essay date 1985)

SOURCE: "'One and Zero Walk Off Together': Dualism in Galway Kinnell's *The Book of Nightmares,*" in *American Poetry,* Vol. 3, No. 1, Fall 1985, pp. 56-71.

[*In the following essay, HUdgins notes that a dualistic stance toward death—both the rational perception of our own extinction as well as our mystical union with the universe after death—is traced through* The Book of Nightmares.]

In *The Book of Nightmares* Galway Kinnell explores from a contemporary perspective one of the great themes of romantic poetry: What is the proper human response to death? For Kinnell the answer to that question is complicated by his being possessed of a deep spiritual longing while living in an existential world. And death, that ultimate existential fact, is the stumbling block to spiritual aspirations because it implies utter nullity. But even with life ending in the apparent finality of death, people often intuit a harmony beyond death, a unity in the universe. Kinnell, in an interview, has stated the dichotomy succinctly: "death has two aspects—the extinction, which we fear, and the flowing away into the universe, which we desire—there is a conflict within us that I want to deal with."[1] Or to state the proposition in explicitly Freudian terms, people are torn between a drive toward life and a drive toward death. Behind this dualism, however, lies a deeper one; the rational mind looks at the world and sees that life, to all evidence, ends with death, while the irrational mind intuits a mystical oneness in death.

Throughout *The Book of Nightmares* Kinnell struggles with the separation of the conscious and unconscious aspects of the mind, trying to develop a coherent view of life and death, and his examination of his own ambivalences leads him to unravel a string of connected dualities—conscious and unconscious, rational and irrational, mind and body, and ultimately life and death. Like Carl Jung, Kinnell feels that in the modern world the logical mind has grown too powerful at the expense of the unconscious. He therefore exalts the wisdom of the body which taps into the unconscious, but finds the mind often blocks his access to it. All though the volume the poet honestly confronts both sides of the dichotomy, and never slides off into glib lyricism or the intellectual fuzziness of fashionable mysticism.

The book begins with Kinnell, after the birth of his daughter Maud, going out into the woods, where "by this wet site / of old fires," he starts a fire for his daughter:

> for her,
> whose face
> I held in my hands
> a few hours, whom I gave back
> only to keep holding the space where she was,
>
> I light
> a small fire in the rain.[2]

While the fire built on the ashes of an earlier fire hints at immortality through one's offspring, the speaker's main concern is about having brought a life, represented by the fire, into a world hostile to it. In spite of the rain, as an act of affirmation, he is able to start the fire. As the wood burns, the deathwatch beetles inside it "begin running out of time" (p. 3). Relishing the wordplay of *deathwatch,* Kinnell introduces a theme he will return to frequently: In the hour of our birth is the hour of our death. But why? The answer, which he will expand on later, is implicit in his description of what happens when the rain falls on the fire. The fire changes the rain as people's attitude to their suffering can change it into a means of attaining wisdom:

> The raindrops trying
> to put the fire out
> fall into it and are
> changed: the oath broken,
> the oath sworn between earth and water, flesh and
>   spirit,
>   broken,
> to be sworn again,
> over and over, in the clouds, and to be broken
>   again,
> over and over, on earth.
>
>   (p. 4)

In transcending earthly suffering and rising into the clouds, flesh and spirit join, but on earth, which is imperfect and subject to mortality, the joining breaks down, resulting in the uneasy division of the human psyche between mind

and body. At death, however, one returns to the universe, unity is restored, and the oath is sworn anew.

The harmony to be found in death can also be seen, though it fades rapidly, in newborn children. The poet's thoughts return to his daughter, who was born just hours ago. Before birth she was whole, "somersaulting alone in the oneness" of the womb (p. 5). Kinnell's description of the child as she is separated from oneness by birth is powerful and moving:

> she skids out on her face into light,
> this peck
> of stunned flesh
> clotted with celestial cheesiness, glowing
> with the astral violet
> of the underlife. And as they cut
>
> her tie to the darkness
> she dies
> a moment, turns blue as a coal,
> the limbs shaking
> as the memories rush out of them.
>
>   (p. 6)

The memories of the collective unconscious are lost or made subservient to the rational mind, and the child dies for a moment, suspended between the life of the unconscious mind and the life of the conscious mind. Once she is born, she is inevitably thrust into the emptiness that follows the loss of the oneness she enjoyed in the womb. While the doctors hold her up by the feet, she draws her first breath, "the slow, / beating, featherless arms / already clutching at the emptiness" (p. 7). Forced out of the harmony and fullness of the womb, she instinctively embraces the emptiness of the existential world.

Later, the poet hears Maud crying in her crib and attributes her crying to "a sadness / stranger than ours, all of it/ flowing from the other world" (p. 7). Behind this description and the description of Maud at birth—"clotted with celestial cheesiness, glowing/ with the astral violet / of the underlife"—I hear the voice of Wordsworth, another poet who felt intimations of immortality when recollecting early childhood and who described children as born "trailing clouds of glory" that diminish as the conscious mind grows.[3] The longer Maud lives, the more she loses of the dark knowledge of the unconscious from which she came and to which she may, perhaps, return. To provide for Maud when she needs that knowledge and finds herself cut off from it by the blindness of her own rational mind, Kinnell sings to her so, when the time comes,

> you will remember,
> in the silent zones
> of the brain, a specter, descendant
> of the ghostly forefathers, singing
> to you in the nighttime—
>
>   (p. 7)

The song she will hear is not the bright song of the unconscious mind but the dark song of the unconscious, which speaks through dream and nightmare, telling us the often frightening truths that we have forgotten. The songs that come back to Maud will be

> not the songs
> of light said to wave
> through the bright hair of angels,
> but a blacker
> rasping flowering on that tongue.
>
> (p. 7)

Kinnell is really giving himself the advice he addresses to his infant daughter: Trust the voice of the unconscious as it sings to you in the night.

In **"The Hen Flower,"** the second of ten sections of *The Book of Nightmares,* the poet meditates on death and the human inability to embrace death's inevitability. In the dead hen—the hen flower—that he holds in his hand, the poet sees a parallel to the human situation. When asked in an interview why he is so fond of bird imagery, Kinnell responded that "like everyone" he experiences "the contest between wanting to transcend and wanting to belong."[4] The hen's situation is more complicated, even, than that, and oddly comic too because, though winged and built for flight, it cannot fly. Similarly, humans, though they long to transcend their own earthbound nature, are held to earth by the weight of their bodies.

At the same time that he wants to transcend, the poet longs to live the purely animal life of the hen and not worry about death until it is immediately at hand.[5] "If only / we could let go," he exclaims, and "throw ourselves / on the mercy of darkness, like the hen" (p. 11). But letting go is easy for the hen; it has no rational mind to keep it from being a good animal. In another image, though, the poet merges the two aspects of the psyche when he uses the rational mind to see the world through the body of an animal. Looking through the thin, lucent part of a ram's spealbone—the shoulderblade, a bone sometimes used by primitives as a means of divination—he has a vision of nature and natural processes unchanged by death:

> I thought suddenly
> I could read the cosmos spelling itself, . . .
> and in a moment,
> in the twinkling of an eye, it came to me
> the mockingbird would sing all her nights the cry of
>   the rifle,
> the tree would hold the bones of the sniper who
>   chose not to
>   climb down,
> the rose would bloom no one would see it,
> the chameleon longing to be changed would remain
>   the
>   color of blood.
>
> (p. 13)

He has his moment of existential insight, but he cannot let go, cannot accept what he sees. In despair at his vision, the poet takes the body of a chicken killed by weasels and flings it into the air in a grotesque simulation of flying, as if to assure himself that death will provide the gift of flight that the chicken—and he—was denied in life. The effect, of course, is just the opposite. Again he tells himself to "let go" and accept death, even though he is afraid of it; after all, everyone and everything is afraid of dying, of nonexistence: "even these feathers freed from their wings forever /are afraid" (p. 15).

Deciding to put his fear behind him, the poet, in **"The Shoes of Wandering,"** begins his existential quest. Where is he going? He knows only that he must first lose his way. What is he looking for? He knows only that he will not find it. His quest is not his alone but the quest everyone makes in trying to come to terms with life. In what seems to be a reference to the archetypal nature of his search, the poet goes to a Salvation Army store and, after sampling "these shoes strangers have died from" (p. 19), he buys shoes for his journey:

> I discover
> the eldershoes of my feet,
> that take my feet
> as their first feet, clinging
> down to the least knuckle and corn.
>
> (p. 19)

As he wears the used shoes, walking "on the stepping-stones/ of someone else's wandering" (p. 19), he trusts the instinctive wisdom of the body. When he becomes frightened that he may have lost the way, he remembers the Crone who said *"the first step . . . / shall be/ to lose the way"* (p. 19). To find what he is seeking, he will have to forsake the established paths of the rational mind and pick his way across the "swampland" (p. 21) of the unconscious.

> On the journey, every step is
>
>   a shock,
> a shattering underfoot of mirrors sick of the itch
> of our face-bones under their skins,
> as memory reaches out
> and lays bloody hands on the future, the haunted
> shoes rising and falling
> through the dust, wings of dust
> lifting around them, as they flap
> down the brainwaves of the temporal road.
>
> (p. 21)

As he walks down the road, the "wings of dust" around his feet hint at the possibility of a limited transcendence rising from the fear of death. The poet expounds on the connection between wings and feet when he goes on to ask:

> Is it the foot,
> which rubs the cobblestones
> and snakestones all its days, this lowliest
> of tongues, whose lick-tracks tell
> our history of errors to the dust behind,
> which is the last trace in us
> of wings?
>
> (pp. 21-22)

The urge to transcend has been, in many ways, deflected into an earthbound restlessness. But the quest is both internal and external; it is not solipsistic. If it were, the poet would have a much easier time deluding himself about his ability to transcend himself. The poet's sense of the outside world is too sharp for any such self-deception. Also, he is clearly aware of the dangers of solipsism and is prepared to avoid them. Though he "longs for the mantle / of the great wanderers" (p. 22) of myth and legend who always, whatever mistakes they made, found the way, he knows the Crone—the outside voice—is right when she tells him, *"you will feel all your bones / break / over the holy waters you will never drink"* (p. 23).

The problem of delusion is examined in more detail in section IV, **"Dear Stranger Extant in Memory by the Blue Juniata."** In this section, Kinnell reacts to the claims of mystics with irony and some mockery, but it is irony that is sympathetic and even partially self-directed because he would like to believe in these shortcuts to the infinite. Kinnell quotes, in the poem, from letters he has received from Virginia, a mystic. Explaining who Virginia is, Kinnell says in an interview:

> Virginia is an actual person I've had a long correspondence with. She is a mystic, a seer. She is one of those born without the protective filtering device that allows the rest of us to see this humanized, familiar world as if it were all there is. She sees past the world and lives in the cosmos.[6]

This statement may at first sound like approval of Virginia, but, though Kinnell does no doubt admire her, it is worth pointing out that their first and only meeting was unsuccessful. Through letters, Virginia and Kinnell had to "reestablish an intimacy, though we now knew it was in part illusory, being purely platonic."[7] The same criticism applies to Virginia's mysticism, which leads her to reject the world she actually lives in. While Kinnell is compelled by courtesy to be polite in his statements about the actual Virginia, the stance of the poem, as I read it, is that Virginia, with her single-minded commitment to the cosmos is as wrong as those who can only see the world "as if it were all there is."

Two letters from Virginia are quoted in the fourth section of *The Book of Nightmares.* In the first of them she describes a session of automatic writing and her reaction to it. As her hand grows numb, she finds herself drawing, without conscious control, circles, figure eights, and mandalas. She drops the pencil, tries to relax, and then:

> I felt my mouth open. My tongue moved, my breath wasn't my own. The whisper which forced itself through my teeth said, *Virginia, your eyes shine back to me from my own world.* O God, I thought. My breath came short, my heart opened. O God, I thought, now I have a demon lover.

> Yours, faithless to this life,

> Virginia

(p. 28)

The sentence about the demon lover is wonderfully comic. That is not to imply, however, that Kinnell does not sympathize very deeply with Virginia's desire to be one with the universe; indeed, he shares it. But he realizes that that desire comes at the expense of the body. Virginia herself admits as much in her second letter when she says,

> God is my enemy. He gave me lust and joy and cut off my hands. My brain is smothered with his blood. I asked why should I love this body I fear. He said, *It is so lordly, it can never be shaped again—dear, shining casket. . . .* Forgive my blindness.

> Yours, in the darkness,

> Virginia

(pp. 30-31)

Virginia seems to be apologizing for her earlier excesses in response to Kinnell's yearning but cautious question: "Can it ever be true— / all bodies, one body, one light / made of everyone's darkness together?" (p. 30).

As if to reemphasize that his journey is inward, section V, **"In the Hotel of Lost Light,"** opens with the speaker still in the bed he was sleeping in when, in section III, he began his journey. Having taken the Crone's advice and lost the way that is illuminated by the light of the intellect, he resides now in the "Hotel of Lost Light." While lying in bed in his room, he sees and identifies himself with a fly

> whining his wings,
> concentrated wholly on
> *time, time,* losing his way worse
> down the downward-winding stairs, his wings
> whining for life as he shrivels
> in the gaze
> from the spider's clasped forebrains, the abstracted
>   stare
> in which even the nightmare spatters out its horrors
> and dies.

(p. 35)

The poet lost on his inward quest is represented by the fly lost on its downward spiral, and what makes the fly shrink is the "abstracted stare" that comes from the spider's brain. The proposed analogy is that the conscious mind is to the unconscious mind as a spider is to a fly: the latter is the prey of the former.

But Kinnell also realizes that the conscious mind is indispensable to our understanding of our situation and that the light it provides must be brought to bear, sympathetically, on the nurturing darkness of the unconscious. The rub is that light shone on darkness destroys the darkness. The poet's task—the human task—is to reconcile the irreconcilable.

"The Dead Shall Be Raised Incorruptible," section VI, is a grim consideration of what happens when the healthy impulses of the unconscious are repressed by adherence to a conscious creed. The result is "Christian man," who revels in violence and death. The Biblical quotation that

Kinnell takes for the title of this section pinpoints the false reasoning that has led to the Christian susceptibility to violence. Saying that "the dead shall be raised incorruptible" implies that people in their human, embodied form are corrupt—that mortality and moral failing are intrinsically linked. Kinnell maintains, in other words, that Christianity is based on contempt for the body. This section also seeks to establish a Freudian connection between anality and "Christian man," who is afflicted by, as Kinnell speaks for him, "my iron will, my fear of love, my itch for money, and my madness" (p. 44). The madness derives from Christian man's development being arrested in the anal phase, something that is made clear in the beginning of the section, where the speaker sees a corpse smoking in a field and reacts with a list of words that make explicit the connections between death, dirt, food, and money:

> carrion,
> caput mortuum,
> orts,
> pelf,
> fenks,
> sordes,
> gurry dumped from hospital trashcans.
>
> (p. 41)

At the center of this emphasis on decay and its scenes of warfare is a savage attack on the mentality that has produced these abominations. Using a form derived from Villon's *Testament,* which he has translated into English, Kinnell speaks as Christian man in "the Twentieth Century of my trespass on earth" (p. 42). He recounts the people whom he has killed, including "a whole continent of red men for living in unnatural community / and at the same time having relations with the land" (p. 42). Later in his testament, in one of the sharpest stabs of the volume, he leaves "my flesh to the advertising man, / the antiprostitute, who loathes human flesh for money" (p. 43).

There is something, though, some living essence, that resists death. An unidentified voice, apparently that of a wounded GI, says:

> *my neck broken I ran*
> *hold my head up with both hands I ran*
> *thinking the flames*
> *the flames may burn the oboe*
> *but listen buddy boy they can't touch the notes!*
>
> (p. 44)

The same point is made, even more dramatically, by an image that frames this section of the book; the section begins and ends with the image of a burning corpse, perhaps a victim of napalm: *"Lieutenant! / This corpse will not stop burning!"* (pp. 41 and 45).

After the nightmare of section VI, the poet turns to his daughter, and his love for her, as Robert Langbaum points out,[8] restores him: "my broken arms heal themselves around you" (p. 49). Section VII primarily consists of the poet's meditations on his daughter and his advice to her. Remembering when he heard her tell a flower not to die, he

says he would, if he could, keep her from dying. But, by calling her with odd and compelling tenderness *"O corpse-to-be"* (p. 50), he acknowledges that she—like everyone—will die:

> perhaps this is the reason you cry,
> this the nightmare you wake screaming from:
> being forever
> in the pre-trembling of a house that falls.
>
> (p. 50)

Already she seems to grasp and be disturbed by the existential realization that life has no intrinsic meaning.

As Maud grows, the poet sees her entering the Freudian anal phase, in which the mind strives to dominate, even exclude, nature; he sees that she might become estranged from nature and the body, might even become as dangerously divorced from nature as to be like "Christian man." He remembers a time when, in a restaurant, Maud climbed into his lap and cried at the food, *"caca! caca! caca!"* (p. 50). The child reacts so enthusiastically to the restraints of the anal phase that Kinnell fears she might, like Christian man, get stuck there, confusing nourishment and excrement. The connection is made much clearer when Kinnell describes the reaction of the other diners to his daughter's cry: "each spoonful / stopped, a moment, in midair, in its withering / steam" (p. 50). The image evokes the opening lines of the previous section, lines that are followed by the list of archaic or unusual words that have associations with anality: "A piece of flesh gives off / smoke in the field" (p. 41).

Kinnell can foresee a time when these natural maturing processes will cut Maud off from nature. He imagines her standing in a field,

> the raindrops
> hitting you on the fontanel
> over and over, and you standing there
> unable to let them in.
>
> (p. 51)

When and if this alienation occurs, he advises her to let her knowledge of death and "the sorrows / to come" cause her to embrace the present. In short, his advice is *carpe diem:*

> learn to reach deeper
> into the sorrows
> to come—to touch
> the almost imaginary bones
> under the face, to hear under the laughter
> the wind crying across the black stones. Kiss
> the mouth
> which tells you, *here,*
> *here is the world.* This mouth. This laughter. These
>   temple
>   bones.
>
> The still undanced cadence of vanishing.
>
> (p. 52)

The insight implicit in this passage is stated explicitly as the section ends. Out of the pain and suffering caused by death there arises one compensation: *"the wages / of dying is love"* (p. 53).

From this crucial insight, the poet progresses to **"The Call Across the Valley of Not-Knowing,"** a title that brings to mind Kierkegaard's "leap to faith." Though Kinnell does not leap across his valley, he calls across it and receives in reply intimations that harmony is possible in the world beyond. Occassionally he experiences something that lets him sense the possibility of wholeness, as he did once while in love with a woman whom he thinks of as the other half that completes his divided nature. The allusion, of course, is to Plato's speculation that the two sexes were once united beings whose union made them powerful enough to challenge the gods. Kinnell found, briefly, the half that made him whole but had to leave her because of "cowardice / loyalties, all which goes by the name of 'necessity'" (p. 58)—reasons in which mind dominates instinct.

Expanding on the idea that "the wages of dying is love," he sees that it is death and suffering that gives us the power to reach, temporarily, beyond ourselves and feel flashes of oneness, even though we are not with the exact other half we are looking for and have to settle for our "misfit":

> it must be the wound, the wound itself,
> which lets us know and love,
> which forces us to reach out to our misfit
> and by a kind
> of poetry of the soul, accomplish,
> for a moment, the wholeness the drunk Greek
> extrapolated from his high
> or flagellated out of an empty heart,
>
> that purest,
> most tragic concumbence, strangers
> clasped into one, a moment, of their moment on
>   earth.
>
>   (p. 58)

The union of two people in love and in sex is the closest people come to experiencing the integration of mind and body, but it is also tragic—it will not last, it hints at a unity that everywhere else eludes those seeking it. But in one such moment of love Kinnell has a vision of total integration. He thinks of a time when he and his wife were young and "not yet / dipped into the acids / of the craving for anything" (p. 58). They lay under a pear tree, "on the grass of the knowledge / of graves" (p. 59), where they felt perfect harmony of mind and body, felt the perfect interpenetration of the two opposing aspects of the self:

> And the brain kept blossoming
> all through the body, until the bones themselves
>   could think,
> and the genitals sent out wave after wave of holy
>   desire
> until even the dead brain cells
> surged and fell in god-like, androgynous fantasies—

> and I understand
> the unicorn's phallus could have risen, after all,
> directly out of thought itself.
>
>   (p. 59)

As if to emphasize that this vision is a vision and not the normal state of affairs, the poet recounts the story of a Southern sheriff in a civil-rights march, curses and spits. What he remembers most about the sheriff, though, is "the care, the almost loving, / animal gentleness of his hand on my hand" (p. 59) as he was finger-printed. The sheriff's racist beliefs have overwhelmed and perverted his natural kindness, or, to put it another way, his mind has been tainted by pernicious ideas that have squelched the natural goodness that still resides in his body. He has let his mind become so alienated from his body that, in effect, he no longer has a body:

> Better than the rest of us, he knows
> the harshness of that cubicle
> in hell where they put you
> with all your desires undiminished, and with no
>   body to
>   appease them.
>   (pp. 59-60)

Cut off from the body, he is cut off from that which brings people together, that which affirms life even in the face of death. If we listen, even standing in a field "where the flesh / swaddles its skeleton a last time / before the bones go their way without us," we still might hear

>   even then,
> the bear call
> from his hillside—a call, like ours, needing
> to be answered—and the dam-bear
> call back across the darkness
> of the valley of not-knowing
> the only word tongues shape without intercession,
>
> *yes . . . yes . . . ?*
>
>   (p. 61)

The only word the body forms without the intercession of the brain is one of affirmation and the instinctive but tentative response of one human being to another.

If section VIII considers the relationship of humans to the beyond, **"The Path Among the Stones"** explores the relationship of people to the present, inanimate world, and the poet ponders the curious fact that he himself has been inanimate and will be again. At one point he speaks of arrowheads; they are

>   stones
> which shuddered and leapt forth
> to give themselves into the broken hearts
> of the living,
> who gave themselves back, broken, to the stones.
>
>   (p. 65)

Later, in an image that provides the descent into the underworld of this inner epic, the poet imagines entering the earth—a reversal of the arrowhead entering the human body. Going down into the earth, he encounters an old man who is foolishly using hi intellect—the light at his forehead—in an attempt to avoid death. Inevitably he fails:

> An old man, a stone
> lamp at his forehead, squats
> by his hell-flames, stirs into
> his pot
> chopped head
> of crow, strings of white light,
> opened tail of peacock, dressed
> body of canary, robin breast
> dragged through the mud of battlefield, wrung-out
> blossom of caput mortuum flower—salts
> it all down with sand
> stolen from the upper bells of hourglasses . . .
>
> (p. 67)

The amused irony of "salts it all down" reveals the poet's response to the old man's efforts. The attempt, by logic, to conjure from their dead bodies the birds' ability to fly, and therefore to transcend the world, is doomed to failure; as is the attempt to extract immortality from the unexpended sand in the top section of the hourglass. All these efforts, the poet says, result in "nothing. / Always nothing" (p. 67). Immediately, however, he sees that something is gained by the striving, even, perhaps especially, if failure is unavoidable. Climbing up from the underground, he realizes the struggle has taken him to the essence of life: "I find myself alive / in the whorled/ archway of the fingerprint of all things" (p. 68).

At this insight, "the hunger / to be new lifts off" (p. 68) his soul; at long last he seems to have reconciled himself to mortality. He sees in the sacrifice of his life, a sacrifice every human has to make, the chance for a greater realization of self than would otherwise be possible:

> Somewhere
> in the legends of blood sacrifice
> the fatted calf
> takes the bonfire into his arms, and *he*
> burns *it*.
>
> (p. 68)

To understand this enigmatic passage, I find an observation by Jungian scholar Marie Louise von Franz helpful. Speaking of sacrifice, von Franz says, "It is *the* possibility for the ego to experience the superior presence and reality of the self."[9] By suffering, the ego realizes that it is not paramount but is part of a larger whole; and by sacrifice it acknowledges that fact. Therefore, it is through suffering and sacrifice that people move toward the integration of the psyche. This pragmatic insight is what the book has been working toward throughout the first nine sections.

With **"Lastness,"** the tenth and final section, the book comes full circle; but it more closely resembles a Mobius strip than it does a circle. While the setting the poet has returned to is more or less the same—the fire he started in the first section is "somewhere behind me" (p. 71)—and while time

has passed, what seems to be the same bear is performing what seem to be the same actions he performed then. This odd wrinkle in time points up the inner nature of the poet's journey. He returns to the same place and events and finds that though they have remained the same, he has changed. He has a more profound and empathetic feeling for the world around him. His mind reaches out and he becomes the bear he is watching. The scene also suggests the ease that the poet has acquired with the natural side of himself:

> He sniffs the sweat
> in the breeze, he understands
> a creature, a death-creature
> watches from the fringe of the trees,
> finally he understands
> I am no longer there, he himself
> from the fringe of trees watches
> a black bear
> get up, eat a few flowers, trudge away, . . .
>
> (pp. 71-72)

By imagination, he breaks down the subject—object dichotomy and abridges his alienation from the world outside himself. The circular movement of the volume takes the speaker back to where he began, but in his internal odyssey he has come out in a different place. The process of suffering has allowed him the opportunity to acquire knowledge, perhaps wisdom, and to achieve glimpses of himself as a whole person.

But that sense of unity is momentary and far from absolute. About this last section, the poet asserts:

> This is the tenth poem
> and it is the last. It is right
> at the last, that one
> and zero
> walk off together,
> walk off the end of these pages together
> one creature
> walking away side by side with the emptiness.
>
> (p. 73)

This stunning and witty image powerfully brings together the ideas of individuation and death, personal oneness and existential emptiness. To some extent, then, the dichotomy that has defined his struggle through the first nine sections of the book is resolved. He has achieved some integration of his own psyche, but then there rises a new dichotomy: The whole man lives in an empty world. The human condition is to be suspended between the two extremes, but in the end the poet has a stronger sense of his oneness than he has ever had before.

How, then, does this knowledge reflect itself in an attitude toward life? How does a sense of oneness exist "side by side with the emptiness"? The answer is embodied in the image of a skydiver who is both one and divided as he plummets through the air toward the ground, as we—all of us—plummet through life toward death. His life is a

> concert of one
> divided among himself,

this earthward gesture
of the sky-diver, the worms
on his back still spinning forth
and already gnawing away
the silks of his loves, who could have saved him,
this free floating of one
opening his arms into the attitude
of flight, as he obeys necessity and falls . . .

(p. 75)

He is compelled to assume the "attitude / of flight" though he knows the transcendence he longs for is impossible. The best he can hope for is that the worms, which represent his fear of death, don't eat away the parachute of "his loves, who could have saved him."

The imagery here becomes a bit ungainly as the poet tries to jam too much information into it, to qualify the image. But the poet's risking awkwardness to be as exact as possible points up a very great strength of the book: its honesty. Kinnell never slides into a facile vision of mystique unity. And what tenuous unity he does attain is matched by the emptiness without. But the zero added to the one raises it to a higher power, forming a new and much higher number than they do separately.

Notes

[1] Galway Kinnell, *Walking Down the Stairs: Selections from Interviews* (Ann Arbor: University of Michigan Press, 1978), 23.

[2] Galway Kinnell, *The Book of Nightmares* (Boston: Houghton Mifflin, 1971), 3. Page citations of all subsequent quotations from this book will be given parenthetically in the text of the article.

[3] Other instances of Wordsworth's influence on Kinnell are mentioned in Robert Langbaum, "Galway Kinnell's *The Book of Nightmares,*" *American Poetry Review* 8 (March-April 1979), 30.

[4] Galway Kinnell, "An Interview with Galway Kinnell," conducted by Thomas Gardner, *Contemporary Literature* 20 (1979), 427.

[5] Langbaum, 30.

[6] *Walking Down the Stairs,* 108.

[7] *Walking Down the Stairs,* 109.

[8] Langbaum, 31.

[9] Marie Louise von Franz, *C. G. Jung: His Myth in Our Time,* trans. William H. Kennedy (New York: Putnam, 1975), 229.

David Kleinbard (essay date 1986)

SOURCE: "Galway Kinnell's Poetry of Transformation," in *The Centennial Review,* Vol. XXX, No. 1, pp. 41-56.

[*In the following essay, Kleinbard examines* **The Book of Nightmares**, *specifically, as an example of Kinnell's poetry of a joyful acceptance of mortality as well as death's redemptive power.*]

At the time of its publication in 1971 Galway Kinnell's *The Book of Nightmares* was praised as an evocation of a national trauma, the Vietnam war and its effects on this country. Now, after more than a decade, it seems more remarkable as an expression of private experience in visionary images. Cumulatively these images develop an epic scope and a timeless range of reference reminiscent of Kinnell's models, "Song of Myself" and *Duino Elegies.* Kinnell has said that *The Book of Nightmares* is an account of a journey whose starting point is dread and that "the book is nothing but an effort to face death and live with it."[1] This does not mean stoic acceptance, but a rediscovery of the child's capacity for living with time, decay, and death "almost as animals do." Recurrently these ten poems suggest that one can "surrender to existence" only by letting go of the dread of extinction.

For Kinnell, as for Whitman and Rilke, dying is a return to the "oneness" with the world which we lose at birth. As he says in an interview, it may be seen as "the flowing away into the universe which we desire. . . ." (*Walking,* p. 23). Kinnell's most compelling poem on this theme is **"The Last Hiding Places of Snow,"** an elegy for his mother published in *Mortal Acts, Mortal Words.* Drawing upon the traditional associations between the foetal "underlife" and death as a return within maternal earth or nature[2], this poem recognizes not only the power but the danger of the longing to be with the mother again, particularly when the mother's desire for reunion, her desire to engulf her child, nurtures that longing in him:

My mother did not want me to be born;
afterwards, all her life, she needed me to return.
When this more-than-love flowed toward me, it
   brought darkness;
she wanted me as burial earth wants—to heap itself
   gently upon but
      also to annihilate—
and I knew, whenever I felt longings to go back,
that is what wanting to die is. That is why dread
   lives in me,
dread which comes when what gives life beckons
   toward death,[3]

This mother's "more-than-love" is all the more fearful because she is dead. Dying is the only way to be reunited with her. In the darkness of the woods Kinnell hears his mother's sorrows and her love sighing and moaning:

from the darkness of spruce boughs,
from glimmer-at-night of the white birches,
from the last hiding places of snow,
a breeze,
that's all, driving across certain obstructions:
every stump speaks,
the spruce needles play out of the air
the sorrows cried into it somewhere else.[4]

In the resonant simplicity with which it lets one hear and feel the living presence of the dead in nature **"The Last Hiding Places of Snow"** has powers of evocation which bring to mind T. S. Eliot's concept of the "auditory imagination," "the feeling for syllable and rhyme, penetrating far below the conscious levels of thought and feeling, invigorating every word; sinking back to the most primitive and forgotten, returning to the origin and bringing something back," combining "the most ancient and the most civilized mentality."[5]

As the elegy suggests, Kinnell's conception of death and of the longing for the various forms of darkness which his poems define is at least partly a response to the "mother-love" which "every stump / speaks" and "the spruce needles play out of the air." This "more-than-love" exerts such a strong pull towards death because it has such power to protect and redeem.

The memory of his mother's love crying out of the darkness in the woods makes the poet feel "annointed" and "lighted" as if by sunlight in the deserted house of the world from which she is gone, so that he can wander through any "foulnesses" and "contagions" "and find my way back and learn again to be happy."[6]

The dead mother's sorrows cried out of "the last hiding places of snow" recall the strange sadness of the poet's infant daughter in **"Under the Maud Moon,"** the first poem in *The Book of Nightmares.* When she cries, Maud's sadness flows "from the other world," "the darkness" of the foetal life "in the oneness under the hill, under / the old, lonely belly button" (pp. 7 and 5). Here, too, Kinnell draws on traditional associations between the foetus' existence and death, mother and earth.

Thinking of this incomprehensible sadness from "the other world," the poet remembers that he used to sing to his daughter the song that he learned listening to the "long rustle of being and perishing" on riverbanks where the marshy land sent up "the underglimmer / of the beginning" (pp. 7-8). The "underglimmer / of the beginning" recalls "the astral violet / of the underlife" which Maud brings with her at birth. This may be the glimmer of the moon and the stars in the "cold streaks" which the "earth oozes up" (p. 8). But "underglimmer" also brings to mind the glow of marsh gas as these are the marshes along the "riverbanks." The marsh fire rises from the decay of dead things, but it is also "the underglimmer/of the beginning" of life under the soil where the decay nurtures new sprouts and newly hatched creatures. For Kinnell it is a sign of the unity of "being and perishing."

Maud's birth, too, has helped to teach him that the processes of dying, change, growth, ripening, aging, death, and decay are vital and inextricable elements of life, of living. The song which has begun to glimmer in Kinnell's mind at the time of her birth, his "only song," is a response to this discovery. Rilke, whose influence is pervasive in *The Book of Nightmares,* formulates the same wisdom in terms which offer a clear and precise statement of Kinnell's implicit argument:

And so you see, it was the same with death. Experienced, and yet in its reality not to be experienced . . . never rightly admitted by us . . . death, which is probably so near us that we cannot at all determine the distance between it and the life-center within us without its becoming something external, daily held further from us. . . . Now this might still have made a kind of sense had we been able to keep God and death at a distance, as mere ideas in the realm of mind; but Nature knew nothing of this removal we had somehow accomplished—if a tree blossoms, death blossoms in it as well as life, and the field is full of death, which from its reclining face sends out a rich expression of life. . . . love too takes no heed of our divisions. . . . Lovers do not live out of the detached here-and-now; as though no division had ever been undertaken, they enter into the enormous possessions of their heart, of them one may say that God becomes real to them and that death does not harm them: *for being full of life, they are full of death* (the italics are the poet's).[7]

Implicitly, like Rilke's *Duino Elegies* and his *Sonnets to Orpheus,* the ten poems of *The Book of Nightmares* are saying that a culture which ignores the closeness of death to "the life-center within us" shuts out a large part of the richness of existence. The "ladies and gentlemen who would never die" in the tenth poem, "Lastness," recall the people in Rilke's tenth Duino Elegy who throng the market of empty diversions and drink a bitter beer called "Deathless," which is sweetened by ever new distractions.

At the end of **"Under the Maud Moon"** Kinnell imagines his daughter in the future, "orphaned," tasting the "cursed bread" which is the knowledge of death. He expresses the hope that out of the bitterness and emptiness of this experience a voice will come back to her, "spectral, calling you / *sister!* / from everything that dies" (p. 8).

Here the awakening to death is reminiscent of "Out of the Cradle Endlessly Rocking," where Whitman recalls his response as a boy to the song of a mocking bird grieving for its dead mate. The bird's grief in bringing the boy the awareness of death makes him hear "a thousand singers, a thousand songs, clearer, louder and more sorrowful than yours," and hear them with such imaginative empathy that "A thousand warbling echoes have started to life within me, never to die."

At the end of his poem Whitman recalls that it was the consciousness of death which first enabled him to see the bird as his "dusky demon and brother" and to "fuse" his song "With the thousand responsive songs at random, / My own songs awakened from that hour."

The dominant theme of *The Book of Nightmares* might well be defined by the last words of the seventh poem, which is also devoted to Maud: *"the wages of dying is love"* (the italics are the poet's).

Earlier I mentioned Kinnell's statement that *The Book of Nightmares* is an account of a journey whose starting point is the dread of death. The journey, which gets underway in the third poem, **"The Shoes of Wandering,"** takes the protagonist (really the poet, himself) through a series of encounters with death. Like Dante at the beginning of *The Divine Comedy,* he has lost his way. But unlike the voyager in *The Divine Comedy,* he affirms his confusion as the "first step" towards finding a new way of living (p. 19).

The poet makes his journey in a pair of secondhand shoes bought at a Salvation Army store, and these become a metaphor for his desire to leave behind the life he's led. He tells us that the stranger who first wore these shoes "died from" them (p. 19). This leaves one wondering. Did they cause his death? Did *they* wear *him* out? In casting off the shoes, the poem suggests, the stranger shed a part of himself or an earlier existence.

In the last part of **"The Shoes of Wandering"** a crone gazing into the crystal ball of Kinnell's skull tells him that he lives "under the Sign / of the Bear" (pp. 22-3). His fantasy of wearing shoes that a stranger has "died from" recalls his earlier poem, **"The Bear,"** in which he imagines that by crawling into the dead animal he may find out what it's like to be a bear and absorb some of its nature. The shoes of wandering will take him into another life. This is primitive magic. It's also a metaphor for casting yourself upon the mercy of the darkness, for letting instinct take you on "this path / inventing itself" (p. 22). The poet longs to join the great wanderers, like Whitman, Lawrence, and Rilke, whose "lamp," he believes, was "pure hunger and pure thirst," ". . . whichever way they lurched was the way" (p. 22).

In the fifth poem, **"The Hotel of Lost Light,"** the quester, who has wandered in the shoes of the stranger, lies in the bed where an unknown drunk has died in a freeway motel room. He watches a fly dying in the web of a spider that becomes, as Kinnell describes it, a fearful embodiment of death and destructiveness.

Lying in his bed, the quester seeks to identify himself with the drunk who cast off all the confinements of middle-class life along with its comforts and saving graces before casting off in death even the confinement of the self-conscious ego.

He assures those of us who recoil from this descent into **"The Hotel of Lost Light"** that "*To Live*/has a poor cousin, / . . . who pronounces the family name / *To Leave . . .*" and changes her body rags each visit, as the poet dies to an earlier existence when he sets off on the freeway of his imaginative life, finding his way to a new birth of poetry (p. 37).

In his journeying Kinnell's protagonist calls to mind Rilke's surrogate in *The Notebooks of Malte Laurids Brigge.* Malte commits himself to a life of desperate poverty after coming to Paris, associating with homeless, uprooted grotesques, husks, the sick, and the dying in the belief that only by going through an experience as fearful and radical as death or madness, no less complete in its destruction of customary logic and meaning and of all the familiar links between words and the things they name, can one come to the new and different ways of perceiving and thinking

about oneself and the world which are the primary source of genius.

The last three poems in **The Book of Nightmares** follow Kinnell's acknowledged model, the *Duino Elegies,* more closely than poems I through VII (see *Walking,* pp. 35 & 41). The eighth, **"The Call across the Valley of Not-Knowing,"** takes up Rilke's concept of "the open," the focal theme of the eighth Duino Elegy. The ninth, **"The Path among the Stones,"** is concerned with the idea of transformation, the main subject of Rilke's ninth elegy. The tenth, **"Lastness,"** recalls the tenth Duino Elegy's exploration of a fantastical realm of death and lamentation.

For Rilke, the experience of "the open" obliterates boundaries and barriers which commonsense puts between the living and the dead.

In the eighth Duino Elegy Rilke defines this kind of consciousness paradoxically, likening it to the life within the womb. A small insect, such as the gnat, he says, lives as if it never left the womb (*"die immer bleibt im Schoosse,"* "which always remains in the womb," line 53). For it the infinitely spacious and timeless world is like a "maternal body" within which, completely secure, "it does nothing but leap for joy."[8]

The eighth elegy contrasts human and animal consciousness. Rilke observes that we take children and turn them away from the timeless existence which animals enjoy, free from the prospect of death. We face them into a world constricted by mental constructs and distinctions, such as time; oppositions between self and other, subjective and objective, human and natural; moral and social prescriptions; ideas of property and possession.

Haunted by death, we "are always taking leave" (line 75). At home nowhere, we live like tenants subject to eviction at any time. Unlike the small insects in their womb of security, we are "spectators" or "onlookers" always and everywhere, without relief.

Free from our deadening self-consciousness, our super-egoburdened lives, the more primitive animals live without any sense of being watched over in *"das Reine, Unuberwachte,"* "the pure, unwatched-over," which Rilke also calls *"Nirgend ohne Nicht,"* "nowhere without not," an existence which is completely free in the absence of spatial limitation, time, and any form of negation (11, 17-18). Being nowhere in particular, one has the feeling of being everywhere, of encompassing and flowing all through the cosmos, as in this description of a mystical experience:

> . . . the cry of a bird . . . did not, so to speak, break upon the barriers of his body, but gathered inner and outer together into one uninterrupted space. . . . That time he had shut his eyes, so as not to be confused in so generous an experience by the contour of his body, and the infinite passed into him so intimately from every side, that he could believe he felt the light reposing of the already appearing stars within his breast.[9]

Though the eighth poem in *The Book of Nightmares* is a variation on Rilke's focal theme in the eighth Duino Elegy, it has none of the weightiness of metaphysical implication which interested Heidegger in Rilke's letters and poems about "the open."[10] In its focus on a close personal relationship Kinnell's approach to this theme is characteristically different from Rilke's.

"The Call across the Valley of Not-Knowing" contrasts Kinnell's marriage with an ideal, largely imagined relationship with a woman he met once in Waterloo, Iowa. The comparison and contrast between the reality of marriage and the ideal of the imagined relationship develop around the Greek myth that our primordial ancestors were hermaphrodites, that these were torn in half, and the longings of men and women for each other arise out of the desire to be reunited with one's lost other half and the craving for psychic wholeness which the primordial hermaphrodites must have enjoyed.

Kinnell's marriage, like so many others, has brought together "two mismatched halfnesses." At the beginning of the poem the poet is lying beside his wife, whose pregnancy both connects and separates them. She "sleeps on / happy, / far away in some other, / newly opened room of the world" (p. 57).

Though he feels excluded from this "newly opened room" and thinks of his wife and himself as "mismatched halfnesses," in her blissful pregnancy she becomes for him a luminous and sensuous image of wholeness and plentitude::

> Her hair glowing in the firelight,
> her breasts full,
> her belly swollen,
> the sunset of firelight
> wavering all down on one side, my wife sleeps on. . . .
>
> (p. 57).

In part 6 of the poem Kinnell imagines a meeting between himself and the "woman of Waterloo." They meet "in our own country," a phrase which suggests metaphorically that they are at home with each other and consequently also feel at home in the world. They look "into each other's blindness" (p. 60). This inversion, typical of Kinnell, calls to mind D. H. Lawrence's conception of the blind, mindless instinctiveness of passionate lovemaking and Kinnell's remark during an interview that Lawrence's "best love poems move into mystery . . . into acts of cosmic adoration" (*Walking,* p. 54).

If this had been a real meeting, the poet imagines, he might have "moved / from then on like the born blind,/their faces gone into heaven already" (p. 60). In this ultimate vision of psychic wholeness the poem conceives of a life lived entirely by the sure wisdom of instinct in unreflective, unselfconscious bliss like that of the pregnant mother's waking sleep or the foetus in the darkness of his underlife or the gnats leaping for joy in the womb of Rilke's cosmos.

In a deceptively simple passage, which recalls **"The Hen Flower,"** the second poem in *The Book of Nightmares,*

the faces of the poet and the woman of Waterloo incline toward each other "as hens / incline their faces / when the heat flows from the warmed egg back into the whole being" (p. 60). This comparison with the hen and the egg giving back the maternal warmth implicitly links the poet and the woman of Waterloo with the pregnant mother and her foetus in part 1 of the poem, and in particular it links them with the sense of wholeness and fullness which she enjoys.

But **"The Call across the Valley of Not-Knowing"** does not set up a simple contrast between the marriage and imagined perfection. Paradoxically, the mismatch of marriage so intensifies the pain of the open wound, which is the consciousness of being fragmentary, incomplete and insufficient, that it "forces us to reach out to our misfit / and by a kind of poetry of the soul, accomplish / for a moment the wholeness" defined by the myth of the hermaphrodite (p. 58).

In part 4 of the poem Kinnell recaptures one such moment in which he and his wife experience an ecstatic intimacy with nature and each other:

> we two
> lay out together
> under the tree, on earth, beside our empty clothes,
> our bodies opened to the sky,
> and the blossoms glittering in the sky
> floated down
> and the bees glittered in the blossoms
> and the bodies of our hearts
> open
>
> (p. 59).

"the bodies of our hearts" suggests that the division between sublimated feeling and egocentric desire was healed and that these were fused in this ecstatic experience. The next verse paragraph in part 4 has the brain "blossoming all through the body . . ." (p. 59). This conceit describes the cure of that basic evil, the split between body and mind. With characteristic wit Kinnell imagines that as a result of the brain's blossoming all through the body, "the bones themselves could think."

The healing of the rift between reflective thought and instinctive body and the curing of the sense of alienation from all other human beings and from nature frees sexual desire from the infection of sin, guilt, and shame: "and the genitals sent out wave after wave of holy desire" (p. 59). The line reveals how close Kinnell comes in this poem to the spirit in which Blake radically revised the mythology, the values, and the visionary expectations of traditional religion.

The new sense of self which the experience generates reverses the puritanical myth of the fall of the sexes into hostility through their sexuality. It takes the form of "androgynous fantasies" which are "god-like." With this result the remembered ecstatic communion of the husband and wife brings to a culmination the poem's development of the myth of hermaphroditic wholeness. Kinnell's celebration of their "god-like, androgynous fantasies" calls to mind the traditional conception of poetic genius as hermaphroditic. The most memorable American expression of this idea is the daring image of the poet's narcissism in "Song of Myself":

> I mind how once we lay such a transparent summer
>   morning.
> How you settled your head athwart my hips and
>   gently turn'd over
>   upon me,
> And parted my shirt from my bosom bone, and
>   plunged your tongue
>   to my bare-stript heart.
> And reach'd till you felt my beard, and reach'd till
>   you held my
> feet.
> Swiftly arose and spread around me the peace and
>   knowledge that
> pass all the argument of the earth,
> And I know that the hand of God is the promise of
>   my own,
> And I know that the spirit of God is the brother of
>   my own . . .

(The "you" in this passage is "my soul").

Such openness and tenderness toward oneself, other persons, and all things in nature as **"The Call across the Valley of Not-Knowing"** defines are essential to the poet's gift for transformation. The ninth poem in *The Book of Nightmares,* **"The Path among the Stones,"** manifests this gift with consummate mastery.

Thinking about Whitman, Kinnell conceives of the poet as a kind of shaman who can transform himself into anything, not only another person or an animal, but even a stone (*Walking,* p. 23). Mastering the language to describe what it is to be stone would be among the most difficult tasks of the poet seeking to encompass all existing things. Accomplishing this task would involve such complete absorption and transmutation of the qualities of stone into one's physical and mental being that, in the words of Rilke, the stone will have "turned to blood within us, to glance and gesture, nameless and no longer to be distinguished from ourselves."[11] If the poet accomplishes this transformation, the language of his poems "truly accords to the stones their own existence" (*Walking,* p. 63). "If a stone could speak your poem would be its words" (*Walking,* p. 23). This is the primary aim of **"The Path among the Stones."**

In part 3, the poet discovers "great, granite nuclei, / glimmering . . . with ancient inklings of madness and war" (p. 67). Kinnell may be thinking of megaliths such as those at Stone-henge. The giant rocks seem images of irrationality and violence within nature and within himself, irrationality radiating through all human culture and history.

"Ancient inklings of madness and war" also brings to mind "Ancestral voices prophesying war" which Kubla Kahn hears through the tumult of the sacred river in Coleridge's poem about the fearful shaping and destroying power of poetic genius.

These "inklings of madness" and violence prepare for the poet's descent, in part 4, into a place filled with "everything I ever craved and lost," where "hell-flames" burn up out of a brew full of dismembered parts of bodies, reminiscent of the broth made by the witches in Shakespeare's tragedy of insane destructiveness, *Macbeth* (p. 67).

The broth is stirred by an old man with a stone lamp on his brow, who seems to be associated with time as he salts his concoction with sand "stolen from the upper bells of hour glasses." It is time that dismembers and devours all things.

Having descended into this hell of craving and loss, dismemberment and devouring time, having, perhaps, attained to something like the kind of understanding that Dante found in hell, the poet emerges in part 5, surprisingly "alive" and finds himself "in the whorled / archway of the fingerprint of all things, / skeleton groaning, / blood strings wailing the wail of all things" (p. 68).

This is to say that through his journey represented in the eight preceding poems and its microcosm in the four preceding parts of this poem, he has become so closely identified with "everything that dies," that their voices have all become part of his own wailing, part of the "concert of one / divided among himself," as he calls his "music" in the next poem, **"Lastness"** (p. 75).

"The whorled / archway of the fingerprint of all things" means literally that stone, in its fossils, contains the prints of all forms of life. But the line also alludes to and echoes a passage in the preceding poem, **"The Call across the Valley of Not-Knowing,"** as so many lines in **"The Path among the Stones"** allude to earlier passages in the book, gathering major themes and motifs and metaphors of the first eight poems into a coherent culmination.

"the whorled archway of the fingerprint of all things" echoes "whorls / and tented archways" of fingerprints, which is one of the images of openness in **"The Call across the Valley of Not-Knowing"** (p. 59). They open into "the tabooed realm, that underlife/where the canaries of the blood are singing."

Kinnell is remembering being fingerprinted by a southern sheriff, a jailer who seems a projection of himself. He imagines that this jailer knows better than anyone else the hell experienced in a cell "with all your desires undiminished, and with no body to appease them" (p. 60).

But the jailer's sense of the life in the men whose fingerprints he presses into the police-blotter becomes a way out of that hell. The poet's fantasy is that the memory of all those hands the jailer took in his hands with "almost loving, / animal gentleness" to fingerprint them will make him feel the creation touching him all over his body. In this way he will enter, through "the whorled archways of /all those / fingerprints" the "underlife," (his own and theirs), the "darkness" of ordinarily buried consciousness where the "moan of wind / and the gasp of lungs" and the wailings and sighs of all beings "call to each other" in communion (p. 60).

Now that he has stood in that archway and has learned the sounds and other resonances of "all things" in his very bones and "bloodstrings," in the last two parts of **"The Path among, the Stones"** the poet achieves the task of transformation, which gives to all things a new life and at the same time, as he says, "accords to" them "their own existence" in his poem (p. 68).

The image of this transformation is the "eerie blue light" of "the hunger/to be new," which lifts off his soul and "blooms / on all the ridges of the world" (p. 68). In achieving this metamorphosis the passionate imagination consumes the "bonfire" of destructiveness, of "madness and war," in its own fire of creative energy (pp. 68, 67).

Having arrived at this version of the saving power of poetic genius, Kinnell concludes the poem with images which are metaphors for the healing love of all things for one another and metaphors for the resurrection of the dead to life.

In part 3 of **"The Path among the Stones"** the stones send up "ghost-bloom / into the starlight . . . / . . . seeking to be one / with the unearthly fires," the stars (p. 66). But their reflected light falls back, an image of the poet's sadness at his inability to sing in the register of the glorious and sublime and of his need to express the existence of ordinary things, "the glitter of the bruised ground" (p. 66).

In part 7 of the poem the stones attain their yearning, but not because they ascend. Instead, the stars "kneel down in the star-form of the Aquarian age: / a splash / . . . on the grass of this earth even the stars love, splashes of the sacred waters . . ." (p. 68). Literally the rain or dew of early morning reflects the light of "the last scattered stars," including the constellation Aquarius, the water-bearer, sign of our eleventh-hour epoch.

Speaking about the ninth Duino Elegy in one of his interviews, Kinnell observed, "Rilke says, in effect, 'Don't try to tell the angels about the glory of your feelings, or how splendid your soul is; they know all about that. Tell them . . . something that you know better than they, tell them about the things of this world'" (*Walking,* p. 35). The stars, "unearthly fires," in **"The Path among the Stones,"** are images of the glory and splendor of the visionary imagination. Their kneeling on the grass expresses the love of the visionary imagination for the ordinary things of this world. The dew or rains which transfigure these things with the reflected fire of the stars are "sacred," healing waters.

As Seamus Heaney says of another poem, these lines "cunningly" make their "cast" and raise "Blake in the pool of the ear."[12] They echo lines from "The Tiger": "When the stars threw down their spears, / And water'd heaven with their tears." This echo reflects the close affinity between the concluding stanzas of this poem and Blake's writings.

For, the concluding stanzas of the **"The Path among the Stones"** express a visionary conception of the world's redemption which is shaped by feelings and ideas that derive from the Bible and Christian eschatology as well as the religious and visionary literature that has grown out of them.

Despite this heritage (Kinnell's earliest poems are explicit expressions of his Christian background), like Blake's visions of the world's redemption, this one creates a universe without a deity. Implicitly the poet's imagination has taken the place of the Divine Savior who resurrects the dead.

In the last stanza of **"The Path among the Stones,"** the stones, which have been the protean central metaphor developing the argument and journey of the poem through an extraordinarily fertile and coherent variety and range of images and meanings, are grave markers. Here, however, they are not symbolic of death, but have been transformed with delicacy and limpid simplicity into moving images of the miraculous new life which poetic genius can bring to a dead world in a nightmarish time:

> So below: in the graveyard
> the lamps start lighting up, one for each of us,
> in all the windows
> of stone
>
> (p. 68).

Notes

[1] Galway Kinnell, *Walking Down the Stairs* (Ann Arbor: Michigan University Press, 1978), pp. 46-7, Hereafter this book will be designated *Walking* and the page(s) will be indicated in parentheses in the text.

[2] Galway Kinnell, *The Book of Nightmares* (Boston: Houghton Mifflin, 1971), p. 6. Hereafter page numbers will be indicated in parentheses in the text.

[3] Galway Kinnell, *Mortal Acts, Mortal Words* (Boston: Houghton Mifflin, 1980), pp. 42-3.

[4] *Ibid.,* pp. 41-2.

[5] T. S. Eliot. *The Use of Poetry and the Use of Critisicm* (Cambridge: Harvard University Press, 1933).

[6] *Mortal Acts, Mortal Words,* p. 42.

[7] *Letters of Rainer Maria Rilke, 1910-1926,* trans. Jane Bannard Green and M. D. Herter Norton (New York: Norton, 1947, 1948), pp. 148-9.

[8] I have consulted Leishman-Spender, MacIntyre, and Garney-Wilson translations of the *Duino Elegies* before translating them for this essay.

[9] Rainer Maria Rilke. *Duino Elegies,* trans. J. B. Leishman and Stephen Spender (New York: Norton. 1939). p. 126.

[10] See Martin Heidegger, *Poetry, Language, Thought,* trans. and introd. Albert Hofstadter (New York: Harper & Row, 1971), chapter 3, "What Are Poets For?"

[11] Rainer Maria Rilke, *The Notebooks of Malte Laurids Brigge,* trans. M. D. Herter Norton (New York: Norton, 1949), p. 27.

[12] Seamus Heaney, *Preoccupations: Selected Prose 1968-1978* (New York: Farrar, Straus and Giroux, 1980), p. 157.

Harold Beaver (review date 1986)

SOURCE: "Refuge in the Library, on the Farm and in Memories," in *The New York Times Book Review,* March 2, 1986, pp. 14-15.

[*In the following excerpt, Beaver praises* The Past *for its moments of "absorbed attention," Kinnell's ability to affix the present into the past and vice versa.*]

[In his work,] Galway Kinnell enriches each anecdote. Always there is a narrative frame and skeletal story—a place, a time, a character:

> *When the little sow piglet squirmed free,*
> *Gus and I ran her all the way down to the swamp*
> *and lunged and floundered and fell full-length*
> *on our bellies stretching for her—and got her!—*
> *and lay there, all three shining with swamp slime—*
> *she yelping, I laughing, Gus—it was then I knew*
> *he would die soon—gasping and gasping.*

In *The Past,* Mr. Kinnell nails down the present into the past and transfixes the past into the present:

> *Here I heard the terrible chaste snorting of hogs*
> *trying to re-enter the underearth.*
> *Here I came into the curve too fast, on ice, and*
> *being new to these winters, touched the brake*
> *and sailed into the pasture.*
> *Here I stopped the car and snoozed while two small*
> *children crawled all over me.*
> *Here I reread* Moby Dick *(skimming big chunks,*
> *even though to me it is the greatest of all novels)*
> *in a single day, while Fergus fished.*

The touch is always personal, sometimes opening like a letter—"We loaf in our gray boat in the sunshine. / The Canadian Pacific freight following the shoreline blows a racket of iron over Lake Memphramagog"—sometimes like an anecdote told at the fireside:

> *In those first years I came down*
> *often to the frog pond—formerly,*
> *before the earthen dam gave way,*
> *the farm pond—to bathe, standing*
> *on a rock and throwing pond water over me,*
> *and doing it quickly because of the leeches.*

For the theme in *The Past* is always reminiscence, commemoration, resuscitation. It ends with elegies for his friends and fellow poets Richard Hugo and James Wright. He looks back to childhood, his first love, his growing children and the breakup of a marriage. Mood and setting

interpenetrate with a masterly economy, as in **"The Old Life"**:

> *The waves collapsed into themselves*
> *with heavy rumbles in the darkness*
> *and the soprano shingle whistled*
> *gravely its way back into the sea.*
> *When the moon came from behind clouds*
> *its white full-moon's light*
> *lightly oiled the little beach stones*
> *back into silence. We stood*
> *among shatterings, glitterings,*
> *the brilliance. For some reason*
> *to love does not seem ever*
> *to hurt any less. Now it happens*
> *another lifetime is up for us,*
> *another life is upon us.*
> *What's left is what is left*
> *of the whole absolutely love-time.*

Always there is this landscape with figures. Always the landscape embodies emotion without a hint of pastoral extravagance or natural fallacy. For his special gift is an absorbed attention. The impulse is a retreat into the past, away from the technological future, the nuclear flash. "I think," he writes, "I want to go back now and live again in the present time, back there / where someone milks a cow and jets of intensest nourishment go squawking into a pail." "Now" is where past and present interpenetrate. One poem, **"First Day of the Future,"** ends, less jubilant than Thoreau:

> *But I guess I'm here. So I must take care. For here*
> *one has to keep facing the right way, or one sees*
> *one dies, and one dies.*
> *I'm not sure I'm going to like it living here in the*
> *future.*
> *I don't think I can keep on doing it indefinitely.*

Phoebe Pettingell (review date 1988)

SOURCE: A review of *The Past,* in "On Poetry: Songs of Science," *The New Leader,* Vol. LXVIII, No. 16, pp. 19-20.

[*In the following excerpt reviewing* The Past, *Pettingell highlights Kinnell's "biological perception of the world".*]

History was the controlling trope for 19th-century writers: Novelists, essayists, poets, and playwrights all affirmed their hopes for mankind's progress, or their fears about the decline and fall of civilization, by pointing to the record. The discoveries of Darwin and Einstein seem, at first glance, to have shifted our metaphor to science. Even Biblical fundamentalists who reject evolutionary theory will often subscribe to "Social Darwinian" demonstrations of survival of the fittest in the marketplace. Though physics may be too technical for a mass audience, "relativity" has revolutionized moral attitudes. But literature still frequently shrinks from science. Old-fashioned narratives continue to treat time as if it operated like a piece of thread unwinding from a spool, and man as if he were a unique phenomenon of nature. In *The Past* Galway Kinnell reports a dinner table discussion on this problem with Richard Hugo shortly before his death:

> We agreed that eighteenth-and nineteenth-century poets almost had to personify, it was like mouth-to-mouth resuscitation, the only way they could imagine to keep the world from turning into dead matter.

> And that as post-Darwinians it was up to us to anthropomorphize the world less and animalize, vegetablize, and mineralize ourselves more.
> We doubted that pre-Darwinian language would let us.

Although Kinnell has not invented an evolutionary mode of speech, his poems certainly exemplify a way of thinking that has embraced a biological perception of the world. Much of *The Past* was inspired by personal changes in his life: divorce, children growing up, the death of friends. Yet his consideration of these losses forms around his conviction that man is part of the animal kingdom, and must be stripped "back down / to hair, flesh, blood, bone, the base metals," to be seen for what he is.

Kinnell is a descendant of Rilke, the poet who first suggested that the material world may be superior to the heavenly one. In **"The Olive Wood Fire,"** Kinnell borrows his mentor's sense that God no longer watches over the world by describing how he used to rock his son, Fergus, before the fireplace when the boy had awakened from nightmares. The flames remind the father of the horrors of the Vietnam war as seen on television:

> One such time, fallen half-asleep myself,
> I thought I heard a scream
> —a flier crying out in horror
> as he dropped fire on he didn't know what or
>   whom,
> or else a child thus set aflame—
> and sat up alert. The olive wood fire
> had burned low. In my arms lay Fergus,
> fast asleep, left cheek glowing, God.

This vision of a childlike deity who sleeps through human horrors manages to combine Christian iconography with 20th-century agnosticism.

Speaking both of history and of his own youth, Kinnell recalls that "back then, dryads lived in these oaks; / these rocks were altars, which often asked / blood offerings." This personification of nature remains dear to many contemporary poets, who see themselves as shamans. Kinnell has abjured it, however. In **"The Seekonk Woods,"** his image for a kind of afterlife becomes the stink of a muskrat-skin cap that cannot lose the scent of its dead animal. A lucky person can, like James Wright, feel kinship with "salamanders, spiders and mosquitoes," and so imaginatively pick up "back evolutionary stages"—rather like dropped stitches in knitting, evidently. In **"The Waking,"** lovers during the act imagine that they are demi-gods lost in an arcadian landscape, but must come to "and remember they are bones and at once laugh/naturally again."

The irony of Darwin's title, *The Descent of Man,* was not lost on the language-conscious Victorians, who felt that in this new perspective they had suffered a fall from the hope of Divine ordinance, especially an eternal life of which the earthly one was merely a shadow. *The Past* is an attempt to reconcile oneself to the fact that one cannot re-enter times that are gone. "I have always intended to live forever, / but even more, to live now. The moment/ I have done one or the other, I here swear, / I will come back from the living and enter/death everlasting: consciousness defeated." In Kinnell's post-Darwinian world, truth means facing the knowledge that our lifecycle consists of no more or less than growth, propagation and decay, and that we fulfill our function by living it:

> The rails may never meet, O Fellow Euclideans,
> for you, for me. So what if we groan?
> That's our noise. Laughter is our stuttering
> in a language we can't speak yet. Behind,
> the world made of wishes grows dark. Ahead,
> if not tomorrow then never, shines only what is. . . .

Granville Taylor (essay date 1988)

SOURCE: "From Irony to Lyricism: Galway Kinnell's True Voice," in *Critical Essays on Galway Kinnell,* New York: G.K. Hall & Co., 1996, pp. 218-25.

[*In the following essay, Taylor traces Kinnell's "poetic evolution," from a Christian theology to a sacramentalism that elevates "numinous moments,".*]

To read the poetry of Galway Kinnell is to witness a poetic evolution. The Kinnell canon includes nine volumes of poetry and offers a paradigm for the present-day romantic struggling to free himself from his Christian inheritance yet to affirm that the world contains order, meaning, and the sacred. Kinnell's poetry begins with an attempt to reconcile Christian theology, particularly the resurrection, with human mortality and suffering. As this effort proves futile, he surrenders explicitly Christian references in favor of a natural theology that views the world as sacramental and emphasizes immanence over transcendence. Natural theology does not define the Absolute as a Being. Instead of Christian theism, Kinnell's notion of God is of Being itself which is embedded in creation. There is no transcendent realm over against creation. We might call Kinnell's sense of the holy a nontheistic sacramentalism, or echo Nathan Scott in calling it "panentheism."[1] Charles Altieri offers perhaps the clearest description:

> For the postmoderns, meaning and significance tend to depend on the immanent qualities manifested in the particular. As Olson put it, meaning is "that which exists through itself," or in Roethke's terms, "intensely seen, image becomes symbol"—a symbol is not a way of raising particulars to higher orders of significance . . . but

a particular charged with numinous force. This does not mean there are no universals, only that the universals that matter are not conceptual structures but energies recurring in numinous moments.[2]

In short, Kinnell's poetry develops from Christian to natural theology, from irony to lyricism, and from pessimism to affirmation and joy. The initial poems depict the gulf between the contingencies of existence and the assertions of Christian theism. As he drops theistic references, his vision becomes sacramental and brings the holy into his poems.

Although raised a Congregationalist, Kinnell is most authentic as a romantic, not a Christian poet. The romantic is, more than anything else, alone. The old gods or myths are no more. One is left to discover meaning on personal terms. The romantic existence is, therefore, unmediated. No longer does one have the Incarnation or God-man as mediator; no longer are there rituals which recreate sacred time. One faces, as George Steiner says, a "world gone flat."[3] Yet an unmediated world is also a world of possibilities, for it can be made profane or sacred. John S. Dunne points out:

> The modern man . . . finds his hell and purgatory on earth in the form of despair, and he seeks accordingly to find his heaven upon earth too, perhaps in some ideal change of circumstances or inwardly in some kind of inner assurance.[4]

The task, therefore, is to create one's own mythos and entails a fundamental redefining of the connectedness of human-world-divine to discover what, if any, sacred realm remains. Whereas the orthodox Christian's relation to the world is a derivative of the relation to the Christ, the romantic seeks to discover a relation to the world that allows or even causes the sacred to be revealed.

In his first two volumes, *First Poems* and *What a Kingdom It Was,* Kinnell essentially fights the wrong battle. He argues against his religious upbringing instead of accepting romanticism. It is as if Kinnell has to kill his parental ghosts before he can speak in his own voice. The protagonists of these poems cling to a mediated existence and, in so doing, confront the inadequacy of the Christian mythos for the complexities of contemporary existence. They continue to look for transcendence in a flat world and to look in vain. The result is a poetry which is ironic, pessimistic, and unromantic. Not surprisingly, an orthodox critic like Donald Davie claims that in these poems Kinnell "should not having turned his back on Christian dispensation, continue to trade surreptitiously in scraps torn arbitrarily from the body of doctrine he has renounced."[5]

The central problem is death. For Kinnell, theology is at best an evasion of human mortality and at worst a delusion:

> Theology and philosophy, with their large words, their abstract formulations, their airtight systems, which until recently they imagined forever, deal with paradigms of eternity. The subject of the poem dies.[6]

Kinnell's point is that to begin with a myth is to begin from the wrong direction. Conceptualization dilutes one's sense of reality; it distorts one's vision. Because existence does not fit a system, the early poems are filled with irony. Kinnell depicts the dilemma in these terms: "The poetics of heaven agree to the denigration of pain and death; in the poetics of the physical world these are the very elements."[7] The poetics of heaven offer explanations; the poetics of the physical world offer one a sense of existence, Elsewhere, Kinnell says, "What do we want more than that oneness, which bestows—which is—life? We want only to be more alive, not less."[8] For him, to be alive is to relinquish one's preconceptions of existence and to accept the inevitable duality of existence: joy/pain and life/death. These first poems, therefore, demonstrate the inadequacy of the poetics of heaven.

"Easter" is representative. The focus of the poem is death—specifically the death of a "virgin nurse." "Raped, robbed, weighed, drowned," her body drifts below the river's surface. Although the poem's protagonist wishes a resurrection for her—"In the floating days may you discover grace"—the poem offers little hope of its occurrence. In this world, rather:

> Death is everywhere, in the extensive
> Sermon, the outcry of the inaudible
> Prayer, the nickels, the dimes the poor give,
> And outside, at last, in the gusts of April.[9]

Death, therefore, is unalterable and pandemic. Humankind can wait and pray for resurrection, but there is little chance that anyone will emerge from the tomb. The only hint of any afterlife is the sea, the body's final destination. It signifies a return to universal nature. The thrust of the poem, however, is to demonstrate the distance between theology and existence. Death exists in the very sermon that denies its reality. The body does not rise but will forever drift. If grace is to occur, it will not negate death's finality. Grace is possible in Kinnell's world, but to occur it must be translated from Christian to natural theology. The later volumes contain such occurrences because by then the translation is complete.

The style of the poem is also quite different from those that follow. Its formality is uncharacteristic. Kinnell feels that "rhyme and meter, having lost their sacred and natural basis, amount to little more than mechanical aids for writing."[10] These devices made sense if one believed in a "natural harmony" or sought "to call back in poetry, the grace disappearing from everything else."[11] The contemporary poet is not interested in either endeavor. Living an unmediated existence, he cannot go by any models but seeks to create a new voice—a voice that "does not subjugate speech, but conforms to its irregular curves, to the terrain itself."[12] That Kinnell here adopts rhyme indicates both the inauthenticity of this voice and an attempt, modelled on the concept of Easter, to fit a dynamic reality into a static form.

An equally clear example of Kinnell's ironic use of Christian subjects is **"The Supper After the Last."** Christ returns in the poem, but his message is, surprisingly, that death is final:

      . . . Your
Lech for transcendence?
I came to prove you are
Intricate and simple things
As you are, created
In the image of nothing

                                    (p. 101)

Here the poet points to future poems. To understand the essence of Christ's message—that one is to become a vehicle for and a receiver of grace—is paradoxically to let go of theology. Humans are miraculous as they exist. Instead of hoping for redemption beyond this world, one is to look for it within this world. In short, grace will be immanent and not transcendent.

To deny death, therefore, is to block grace from occurring. The poem opens with an example of the futility of such a gesture:

      . . . Near shore
A bather wades through his shadow in the water.
He tramples and kicks it; it recomposes

                                    (p. 100)

At the poem's end, the Christ returns to affirm the permanence of the shadow or death:

    I cut to your measure the creeping piece of darkness
    That haunts you in the dirt. Step into the light—
    I make you over. I breed the shape of your grave in
      the dirt

                                    (p. 102)

The Christ has not come promising resurrection but death and, as a result, the tone of the poem is dark and ironic. Kinnell presents the attempt of translating the language of faith into the actuality of existence as doomed to failure. As the Christ of the poem admits, the distance is too great: "You are the flesh; I am the resurrection" (p. 102). Whatever the nature of the Christ, whatever the claims of theology, humankind's dilemma remains a certain extinction with no promise of an afterlife. As long as one hopes for a heaven above time, one misses the fullness of the present. Eternity is to be found existentially. Kinnell writes elsewhere:

    In the desolation of the universe, the brief, tender acts,
    the beauty that passes, which belong to life in the
    world, are the only heaven.[13]

His religious vision, then, is an inversion of orthodoxy. Instead of "The Word was made flesh," his poem **"The Descent"** claims, "In the cry / *Eloi! Eloi!* flesh was made word" (p. 92). Creation is not an expression of an already existent deity. Rather, in its depth creation gives expression to the sacred. The Christ was not the Word in the beginning, but becomes the word by fully being flesh. In his essay, Kinnell explains, "Zeus on Olympus is a theological being; the swan who desires a woman enters the province of poetry. In *Eloi, Eloi, laura sabacthani,* so does Jesus."[14] The universe is dynamic and demands the "poetics of the physical world" for expression of its sa-

cred dimension. To put this differently, grace can be found if one lives a full existence in the present moment. Like rhyme and meter, theology leads to a false existence and a false poetry. In those moments in the gospels when Jesus was living authentically, he gave expression to wondrous poetry. Christ crucified can be a mediator but not Christ resurrected.

The poetry of the early Kinnell is, therefore, unsatisfactory because he has yet to find his true voice. He points to a sacramental view of the world and suggests that an attentiveness to the very things and beings of life brings one into a participation of mystery. Existence is to be an ongoing revelation of a natural grace, but his revelation only occurs if one accepts death. These early poems hint at this vision but fail to give it adequate expression because of their concern with showing the inadequacy of a Christian concept of resurrection and immortality. Irony, after all, is rarely a vehicle for grace. This Kinnell is actually closer to Robinson Jeffers than to Thoreau, Williams, or Roethke. It is only after he discards all Christian references and relinquishes his attempt at reconciliation that he joins his true literary ancestors.

The poems in *Mortal Acts, Mortal Words* are radically different from the earlier work. Instead of ironic, they are lyrical. Instead of the futile attempt to make the Word flesh, these begin with the flesh and sometimes discover the words of grace. In these poems, however, grace is not expressed in words but in music. The logic of this metaphor is obvious. Music is nonverbal and is, therefore, based on nonrepresentational logic. Since music does not separate subject and object, the poet can more easily express an existent unity of fundamental connectedness to the universe. Lastly, music exists in time. It begins and ends. One can become part of it while it lives, but there is no delusion that it points to an existence above time.

Kinnell is not, of course, the creator of this metaphor. Since Ptolomaic cosmology music has been associated with divine order. Henry David Thoreau, however, is Kinnell's most immediate precursor. *Walden* describes Emerson's self-reliant person as one who steps "to the music which he hears, however, measured or far away."[15] In his essay "The Service," Thoreau indicates the true source of harmony: "To the sensitive soul the universe has her own fixed measure and rhythm, which is its measure also and constitutes the regularity and health of its pulse."[16] To discover the sacred is to align oneself with the rudimentary rhythms that pervade the world. These can only be found by attending to the particulars of nature. For Thoreau, grace enables one to align the inner sense of order with an outer, but for Thoreau there is a greater sense of an external order than with Kinnell. The cost of giving up theism is that meaning increasingly becomes solely existential and private. Thoreau equates the personal harmony with the Universal. The modern or postmodern poet wonders if perhaps music does not come from the heavens but only from the self. Thoreau offers a metaphor for grace, but Kinnell extends the metaphor by making grace more private.

"There Are Things I Tell to No One" offers the most explicit expression of this image:

I say "God"; I believe,
rather, in a music of grace
that we hear, sometimes, playing to us,
from the other side of happiness.
When we hear it, when it flows
through our bodies, it lets us live
these days lighted by their vanity
worshipping—as the other animals do,
who live and die in the spirit
of the end—that backward-spreading
brightness. And it speaks in notes struck
or caressed or blown or plucked
off our own bodies.[17]

The "music of grace" is Kinnell's "flesh made word." It comes from the body and flows through the body. As the agent of grace, the music affirms the essential connectedness of creation in time. It sounds not from the other side of life but from the other side of happiness. It enables us to worship the life force in "the spirit of the end."

Later in the poem, the music again sounds and reunites the persona with life's rhythms:

Yes. I want to live forever.
I am like everyone. But when I hear
that breath coming through the walls,
grace-notes blown
out of the wormed-out bones,

. . . . .

then it is not so difficult
to go out, to turn and face
the spaces which gather into one sound. . . . [18]

The essential music of existence brings grace. Its rhythm connects the human with that which is essential and, in so doing, shows the sacramental nature of reality. The depth of life is founded on the fact of death; the "grace-notes" are "blown / out of the wormed-out bones." As Kinnell says elsewhere:

Everyone who truly sings is beautiful
Even sad music
requires absolute happiness:
eyes, nostrils, mouth strain together in quintal
    harmony
to say Joy and Death well.[19]

The music, or poetry, comes from harmonizing death with life.

The stylistic differences between earlier and later poems are obvious as the content. Instead of a tight formal stanza and rhyme, the poems are in free verse and employ a speech rhythm. Most of all the perspective of the persona is subjective. He is looking through existence to discover meaning instead of down on existence from a detached position.

Perhaps Kinnell's most affirmative poem is **"The Still Time."** The poem opens with a frank expression of faith:

I know there is still time—
time for the hands
to open, for the bones of them
to be filled
by those failed harvests of want,
the bread imagined of the days of not having.[20]

"Still" has its double meaning: "yet" and "not moving." Each sense expresses Kinnell's faith in the powers of creation for renewal. The bread of life is immanental, in time. The hope is not for life after death but a deepening of life before; that is, for *chronos* to change to *kairos*.

The poem ends with a passage that echoes Hopkins' celebration for the sheer mystery and wonder of existence:

as though a prayer had ended
and the changed
air between the palms goes free
to become the glitter
on common things that inexplicably shine.

And all the old voices,
which once made broken off, choked, parrot-
    incoherences,
speak again,
this time on the palatum cordis, all of them
saying there is time, still time,
for those who groan
to sing,
for those who can sing to heal themselves.[21]

This is a world of participation: human with natural and the living with the dead. The common things shine inexplicably. Again the flesh becomes word. The final result is to sing or to join in the natural rhythm. The world, therefore, is sacramental; it is the vehicle for grace. Grace in this context satisfies "our deepest desire, which is to be one with all creation."[22] Kinnell typically insists upon the mixture of joy and pain. It is "those who groan" who sing. Moreover, in an unmediated world, one must heal oneself—albeit with creation's help. **"The Still Time"** shows the possibilities for a religious view that remains faithful to human mortality yet affirms the possibility of ecstasy in time.

There are, then, two Galway Kinnells. As long as he seeks to emulate Milton and to "justify the ways of God to man," the poet can only write in a voice that is ironic, pessimistic, and, finally, false. All that he affirms is the fact of death. When he alters his direction and focuses on the flesh itself, the poet's voice is lyrical, affirmative and true. The world becomes sacrament; creation becomes a choir that sings of "Joy and Death."

Kinnell's career demonstrates the difficulty of remaining true to the givens of modern existence while using the Christian myth as a paradigm. Perhaps in a world of Vietnam, Cambodia, and Ethiopia all one can see is Christ crucified. For Kinnell this leads to irony. For others it might lead to apologetics. A few certainly can still see such occurrences and witness the resurrection. Galway Kinnell's poetic development is not paradigmatic for all contemporary poets, nor does it demonstrate that poetry can no longer be orthodox. Rather, Galway Kinnell's poetry shows that the sacred dimension can be found in contexts which are not explicitly Christian and even explicitly non-Christian. His poems call for an expansion of interpretations of grace and sacrament. Dietrich Bonhoeffer once stated that the modern task is discovering how to speak "in a secular fashion of God."[23] In his later poems Galway Kinnell has made such a discovery.

Notes

[1] Nathan Scott, *The Wild Prayer of Longing: Poetry and the Sacred* (New Haven: Yale University Press, 1971), p. 58.

[2] Charles Altieri, *Enlarging the Temple: New Directions in American Poetry during the 1960's* (Lewisburg: Bucknell University Press, 1979), p. 42.

[3] George Steiner, *In Bluebeard's Castle* (New Haven: Yale University Press, 1971), p. 55.

[4] John S. Dunne, *A Search for God in Time and Memory* (Notre Dame: University of Notre Dame Press, 1977), p. 216.

[5] Donald Davie, "Slogging for the Absolute," in *On the Poetry of Galway Kinnell: The Wages of Dying,* ed. Howard Nelson (Ann Arbor: University of Michigan Press, 1987), p. 151.

[6] Galway Kinnell, "The Poetics of the Physical World," *The Iowa Review,* 2 (1971), p. 125.

[7] Kinnell, p. 119.

[8] Galway Kinnell, "Poetry, Personality, and Death," in *Claims for Poetry,* ed. Donal Hall (Ann Arbor: University of Michigan Press, 1982), p. 230.

[9] Galway Kinnell, *The Avenue Bearing the Initial of Christ into the New World* (Boston) Houghton Mifflin, 1974), p. 58. All further references to this work appear in the text.

[10] Kinnell, "Poetics," p. 113.

[11] Kinnell, "Poetics," p. 113.

[12] Kinnell, "Poetics," p. 120.

[13] Kinnell, "Poetics," p. 122.

[14] Kinnell, "Poetics," p. 125.

[15] Henry David Thoreau, *Walden and Other Writings* (New York: The Modern Library 1981), p. 290.

[16] Henry David Thoreau, "The Service," in *Reform Papers,* ed. Wendell Glick (Princeton: Princeton University Press, 1973), p. 11.

Richard J. Calhoun (essay date 1992)

SOURCE: "The Poetic Milieu of Galway Kinnell: From Modernism to Postmodernism and Neoromanticism," in *Galway Kinnell,* New York: Twayne Publishers, 1992, pp. 8-16.

[*In the following essay, Calhoun places Kinnell is placed among his predecessors and contemporaries as well as his poetic influences.*]

Born in 1927, Galway Kinnell was one of a generation of American poets who were trying to establish themselves as published poets at a time when the modernist practice in poetry and the formalist New Criticism theory, in vogue during their college years, had come under attack. It is important to see his poetry in the context of the transition that was taking place when he began writing from modernism to postmodernism. Four decisive events that signified change in the 1950s were the appearance of Charles Olson's antiformalist *Projective Verse* manifesto in 1950; the publication of Philip Larkin's personal poetry in *Poems* in England in 1954; the sensationalism of Allen Ginsberg's Beat protest poem *Howl* in 1956; and the impact of Robert Lowell's apparently confessional *Life Studies* in 1959. By the late 1950s and the early 1960s Allen Ginsberg and Gary Snyder were gurus for the Beat Movement; Robert Bly, James Wright, and Louis Simpson were exemplars for the Deep Image Movement; Charles Olson, Robert Creeley, and Robert Duncan were supporters of a movement away from formalism to freer, open forms in poetry. These poets were clearly becoming the new generation of poets in the late 1950s and early 1960s. Robert Lowell, Randall Jarrell, and John Berryman, a decade older, were designated as "Middle-Generation" poets who were now busily restructuring their previous modernist ironic mode and impersonal poetic personae. For the lack of a more precise name, *postmodernism* was the term soon fashioned by critics to depict new directions in poetry. It was a time when the pendulum had perceptibly swung away from the professed antiromanticism of Eliot and formalist practice of the New Criticism to a new fashion of neoromantic exploration and self-discovery in theme and in technique.

The modernist theories targeted by this critical restyling were the formalist theory of T. S. Eliot, identifying poetry as autotelic and impersonal, with poets ideally finding "objective correlatives" for their personal feelings; and the formalist New Criticism of the 1940s which instructed readers how to read and poets how to write poems in the ambiguous and ironic modernist style. The late 1950s and early 1960s are the most convincing dates for a watershed moment for the beginning of the decline of modernism and formalism. There was a reaction to the overemphasis on poetry as a craft and the poem as linguistic artifact. It was a time for rejoinders in critical theory and in poetic practice to a prevailing view that modern poetry belonged in the traditions of seventeenth-century metaphysical poetry with its irony and wit, and of nineteenth-century symbolism with its emphasis on private symbols and its taste for myth.

Behind modernistic critical theories had been a cultural attitude towards history which found, in Eliot's language, a "chaos and anarchy" in modern times, contrasting sharply with the accepted and meaningful rituals characteristic of a more traditional past. Juxtaposition of past and present in Joyce's *Ulysses* or in Eliot's *The Waste Land* was designated by Eliot as the "Mythical Method." Monroe K. Spears, in a valuable interpretation, has found the outstanding characteristic of modernism to be various forms of discontinuity—between the present and the accepted values of the past, between the poet hiding behind the mask of his persona and his poem as artifact, and within the poem, a chaos of form to reflect an age in chaos.[1]

The main targets of postmodernist practice were the modernist doctrines that the persona in the poem has to be divorced from the poet and that a poem is an art object that distances itself from life. Reacting to the modernist assumption that the poet creates a persona, the postmodernists of the 1960s took the view that the speaker should be perceived as the poet. The reader is no longer to presuppose that the *I* is an invented character. In their extremely personal confessional poetry, Robert Lowell, Anne Sexton, and Sylvia Plath wrote about personal afflictions which would ordinarily have been reserved for private communication to an analyst.

Commenting on the dominant mood of the last 25 years of postmodernism, David Perkins determines that the "salient characteristics of contemporary American poetry are, in general, that it is or seems spontaneous, personal, naturalistic, open in form and antagonistic to the idea of form, intellectually skeptical yet morally concerned and sometimes even righteous, and imbued with feelings of vulnerability, yet with the humor of resignation, acknowledging helplessness."[2] Clearly, any aesthetic distance from personal revelation provided by irony is gone. Recognizing this change, Perkins identifies the two conspicuous traits of postmodernist poetry in this manner: the poem appears to be personal and it gives also the semblance of spontaneous speech. With some recent poets there has been a further reaction against the view of poetry as artifact through an attempt to recapture the mythologizing mind of primitive peoples. In the 1960s the attitudes of many poets became simultaneously personal and political with the outbreak of social protest from concern over nuclear arms, segregation, Vietnam.

Postmodernism and Open Forms

If the poet has been returned to poetry, what then are the major structural forms of the postmodernist poetry of the last 30 years? David Perkins identifies the forms of recent poetry as a mixture of the old and the new, with a preference for the freer forms: "traditional and free verse in narrative, dramatic monologue, long meditation, list, catalogue, and lyric, including sonnet, song, chant, litany, spell, and mantra." (Perkins, 345). Galway Kinnell's own work began as relatively formal and structurally intricate poems, but he soon moved to a simpler diction, to a looser line, and to an overall freer structure. He has tried to write lyrics sustaining a music that stays true to the inner shape of the poem but never venturing too far from a sense of the speaking voice. Among literary historians there has always been some uncertainty as to whether postmodern-

ism has attempted to nullify modernism completely or to carry it on to a more radical stage. In the fifties and sixties poets like Charles Olson, Robert Creeley, and Robert Duncan may have thought that they were only carrying the poetic revolution begun about 1910 forward to another stage of development. The early poetic work of Ezra Pound and William Carlos Williams provided the specific models for what they were attempting. Even though a postmodernist, Kinnell probably had little feel of participating in a recognizable postmodernist rebellion. By the time he began publishing, the irony, wit, and impersonality characteristic of modernist practice and justified by new critical theory had simply passed out of fashion. Kinnell's poetry evidences this passing. One of the passages that David Perkins uses in his definitive history of modern poetry to illustrate the transformation that had taken place in American poetry is fittingly taken from **"Little Sleep's-Head Sprouting Hair,"** in Kinnell's ***Book of Nightmares*** (1971).

> learn to reach deeper
> into the sorrows
> to come—to touch
> the almost imaginary bones
> under the face, to hear under the laughter
> the wind crying across the black stones. Kiss
> the mouth
> which tells you, *here,*
> *here is the word.* This mouth. This laughter. These
> temple bones.
>
> (*BN,* 52)

Kinnell as Neoromantic

Perkins's point is well made that verse like this by Kinnell could not have been written earlier, in the 1940s and early 1950s. It is not entirely the poet; it is also the age that makes the poetry. Galway Kinnell is a postmodernist poet of importance and almost as distinctive a stylist as James Dickey. Kinnell's style was always a bit too personal and too romantic for the modernist taste of the fifties, more a new poetry of the sixties rather than the old poetry of the fifties and the forties. If it means anything to call him a neoromantic, it at least underscores his fascination with death. If Kinnell were a religious poet more inclined to traditional mythology, it would be easy to describe his concern mythically as a fascination with the journey to death, a kind of symbolic descent into hell, with a possible resurrection; but his stress is even closer to a more basic and more primitive one on death as a return to a preconscious or prehuman state. Kinnell's version of the myth is primitive and pre-Christian, simply emphasizing the individual's participation in a natural and universal process. It also owes something to a romantic "one life" belief that our deepest desire is "to be one with all creation" and for transgressions requiring a propitiatory act. Kinnell shares with James Dickey a fascination with imagining the conscious mind reuniting with its unconscious underpinnings, with the human vision regaining a way of seeing characteristic of the nonhuman. There is, however, a difference in scale. If Dickey would like to become the sea gull he empathizes with both in his poetry and in his prose, Galway Kinnell would become one with the more corporeal bear he imagines in his poetry.

Galway Kinnell's usual method of discerning our sameness with everyone and with everything is by delving more deeply into himself, not just into any better self, but even into his worst self, discovering in the process that what he had thought was personal is in fact universal. He is interested in inciting primitive archetypes, "the archaic and primitive ritual dramas," in order to minister to the fissures in the psyche of modern man. Kinnell is best treated as a postmodernist neoromantic, but he still has a modernist concern with at least hinting at the creation of myth in his poetry and echoing Eliot's alarm over a dissociation of sensibility, the old Cartesian split between thought and feeling, from which both modern poet and modern man suffer.

In his attitude towards death Kinnell actually turns out to be as much realist as romantic. He faces death, as Emily Dickinson did, and as Robert Frost did not, with only the hope of the continuity of life left to mediate the thought of death, acknowledging there is nothing that can resurrect the dead. For in Kinnell's poetry the traditional theme of the continuity of life cannot adequately compensate for an individual death, such as his brother's death remembered in several poems, most poignantly in the elegy **"Freedom, New Hampshire"**:

> But an incarnation is in particular flesh
> And the dust that is swirled into a shape
> And crumbles and is swirled again had but one
>   shape
> That was this man. When he is dead the grass
> Heals what he suffered, but he remains dead
> And the few who loved him know this until they
>   die.
>
> (***WKIW***, 61)

The only compensation for Kinnell is that dying may be an entrance into the mystery, a return to the unconscious and the preconscious; but this possibility can never quite compensate for loss of identity, for the death of the conscious self. Kinnell comprehends death as well as other matters in his poetry often in terms of what poststructuralist criticism identifies as "binary oppositions," with pain and fear as strongly felt as any compensating faith can be. I find little specific evidence that he consciously utilizes the depth psychology myths of Carl Gustav Jung, much read in the 1950s; but he does believe that we must face something like the Jungian shadow, involving the unconscious and the forces of primitive darkness, before any regeneration or return to psychic health. The most positive gain possible for humankind in his poetry is the wonder and awe that come from a grasping of the wholeness and oneness of life. He writes in his essay "Poetry, Personality, and Death": "The death of the self I seek, in poetry and out of poetry, is not a drying up or withering. It is a death, yes, but a death out of which one might hope to be reborn more giving, more alive, more open, more related to the natural life" (*PPD*, 222). Kinnell clearly rejects the mysticism of Eastern Buddhism with its aspiration to be purged of fleshly desire. He is concerned with physicality, and he envisions a death that would impart "greater desire, not less".

As a poet Galway Kinnell is in the tradition of the poetry of empathy of Whitman, and more recently, that of the actual exchange of identity of James Dickey. He writes in admiration of Whitman:

> It's one of the things that makes "Song of Myself" glorious. As we read this poem, we have to open ourselves if we are to get anything at all out of it. When we come to the lines "I was the man, I suffered, I was there," we already understand what it is to disappear into someone else. The final action of the poem, where Whitman dissolves into the air and into the ground, is for me one of the great moments of self-transcendence in poetry. (*WDS*, 22-23)

Kinnell calls his version of Whitmanesque empathy a feeling of "kinship," and, influenced by the French existentialism of the fifties, even identifies it as "a terrible kinship." It is terrible because it requires a loss of identity and the death of the self. With such preoccupations Kinnell might seem to be fixedly a morbid and death-obsessed poet, one whose preoccupations are with "the relation of the self to violence, transience, and death." But to him death actually has a dual meaning. It is "the flowing away into the universe, which we desire" (*PPD*, 209), as well as the extinction, which we fear. Whitman, as a nineteenth-century romantic, sees death as the greatest moment; Kinnell, as a twentieth-century neoromantic, accepts it more realistically as an "insoluble moment."

James Dickey cherishes the Biblical word *beheld* and uses it to indicate a new, more intense way of seeing things. Kinnell does not use this exact word, but he definitely wants to catch some of the same sense of seeing more intensely one's relationship to nature and to things in this world in the manner that Dickey denoted with his use of the word *beheld*.

Kinnell is aware that his view of death differs from that of many twentieth-century poets. Charles Molesworth suggests that the line most critical of Frost in Kinnell's fine poem **"For Robert Frost"** is that the older poet was "not fully convinced that he was dying."[3] He writes, "a man, what shall I say, / Vain, not full convinced he was dying . . ." (*FH*, 25). The perspective of Kinnell's persona, unlike Frost's, must constantly include an awareness that he is dying, for the process of living is also dying; "burning" is his favorite metaphor. There is a key statement in his essay "The Poetics of the Physical World": "The poetics of heaven agrees to the denigration of pain and death; in the poetics of the physical world these are the very elements" (*PPW*, 119). Kinnell's poetry embraces a physical world that requires an awareness of the relentless ongoing of time and accepts the "denigration of pain and death."

Kinnell also records in "The Poetics of the Physical World": "Of course, the desire to be some other thing is itself suicidal, involving as it must a willingness to cease to be a man, to be extinct" (*PPW,* 123). But this is only one half of Kinnell's message; he does not have a simple wish for extinction so much as he has a complex urge for a union with what is also loved. His desire is for more, not less life.

Benjamin De Mott once relegated James Dickey to what he called "the 'more life' school" of poetry.[4] The same simplistic classification could be fashioned, with more justification, for Kinnell. Charles Molesworth equates what Kinnell was trying to do with what Theodore Roethke had sought to accomplish in his poetry, even quoting Roethke in "Open Letter," published posthumously in *On the Poet and his Craft.* Molesworth relates of Kinnell: "He must scorn being "mysterious" or loosely oracular, but be willing to face up to a genuine mystery. His language must be compelling and immediate; he must create an actuality" (Molesworth, 102).

Molesworth also warns of a danger in Kinnell's poetry: he risks being either sentimental or "loosely oracular" when he rejects irony. He is successful only when he achieves "the immersion of empathy" (*Molesworth,* 104). Kinnell is aware of the risk of being "loosely oracular"; and, if he is truly a neoromantic, he nevertheless has a very unromantic belief that the ego hinders true poetry if a poet cannot go beyond mere solipsism. The poet supplies a need all of us have. We need to come to terms with ourselves and with our natural environment. At its best there is a terrible honesty in most postmodernist poetry. This honesty is a characteristic of Galway Kinnell's best poetry. To be convincing Kinnell often goes in his poetry from words to expressive gestures and on to symbolic acts.

Although it is easy to recognize Galway Kinnell as an important post-modernist poet, it is extremely difficult to categorize his style. He certainly cannot be simply pigeonholed—any more than James Dickey can—as a Black Mountain poet, a New York poet, a Beat poet, or a San Francisco poet. Perkins includes him with poets he describes as "against civilization," with an atoning interest in myth and archetypal symbol, with such poets as Robert Bly, W. S. Merwin, Gary Snyder, and Louise Glück. These poets share with the surrealists an impulse to escape from the limitations of a personal voice and of naturalistic immediacy, to speak from a "deeper, more universal level of feeling and experience" (Perkins, 559-60); and they often focus their poems on dreams. Kinnell and these poetic colleagues are neoromantics who oppose civilization by promoting a return to nature and to primitive conditions without any compensating romantic delusions that this state is necessarily better than the civilized state. Nature is perceived as the wilderness, specifically, as the trails of the West by Gary Snyder, or the farm country of Minnesota by Robert Bly; or the wilderness is depicted as the scene in interactions between people and animals in Kinnell's poetry. To all these poets, certainly including Galway Kinnell, nature is the unconscious as opposed to the conscious mind.

The Anxiety of Influences

Granted Galway Kinnell's poetry initiates in a poetic milieu that marked a change in literary styles from modernism to postmodernism, there remains the question of what older established and peer poets he read in the fifties were specific influences on his poetry. At Princeton his early enthusiasm was for the great modernist Yeats, which fellow student poet W. S. Merwin shared. Yeats was the textbook example then of a great modern poet. Later came an enthusiasm for Walt Whitman and Emily Dickinson, whose reputations were being established in the fifties as nineteenth-century poets who were, nevertheless, modern in significant though different ways. This decade welcomed, at long last, a good edition of Dickinson's poetry and sympathetic studies of Whitman as the first great American modernist. In the 1950s both were being reread from a twentieth-century perspective, and in new and better editions of their poetry. For Kinnell, after these influences, with his knowledge of the language, there was the attraction of the French symbolists and postsymbolists poets that he read extensively while he was on a Fulbright in France. In philosophy the existentialism of Jean-Paul Sartre and Albert Camus, a strong influence in America in the fifties, was undoubtedly reinforced by his sojourn in France. Kinnell's early published poems clearly reflect the "God is dead" existentialism of the time since God is acutely absent from his poetic cosmos. There is much *weltschmerz* about this in Kinnell's poems, which probably comes from his somewhat later reading of Rilke, who is certainly a major influence and whom Kinnell regards as the greatest poet of the twentieth century, even above Yeats.

The movement in Kinnell's own poetry towards freer and looser poems undoubtedly results in part from the influence by a radical movement of which he became an observer—the open forms philosophy of Charles Olson and the Black Mountain poets, whose quarters he inhabited the summer before his graduation at Princeton. He soon abandoned stanzas and meters for free verse, his early penchant for romantic diction for a more contemporary speech.

Existentially, as a seriously thinking poet in the fifties, Galway Kinnell wanted to show that he too had ultimate concern (so much admired at the time) about poetry and about life. The influence remained after the passing of the decade. He has achieved this goal of gravity almost to his detriment. About these matters Kinnell has been his own spokesman often in his poetry but also in his prose.

Richard J. Calhoun (essay date 1992)

SOURCE: "*The Past* and Other Works," in *Galway Kinnell,* New York: Twayne Publishers, 1992, pp. 111-16.

[*Calhoun's explication of the poems in* When One Has Lived a Long Time Alone *follows in this excerpt.*]

In Galway Kinnell's tenth major book of poetry, **When One Has Lived a Long Time Alone,** which appeared in late 1990 from a new publisher, Alfred A. Knopf, he confronts his own solitariness from other people, including family, and ultimately that terminal loneliness, his own mortality. A key line in the volume might well be "everything sings and dies," but it could also be "everything dies and sings," the decisive perception from **"Flower of Five Blossoms"** (*WOHLLTA,* 52). Dying is a characteristic humankind share with other creatures, but singing is a resource that the poet finds in people. In these poems Kinnell writes of loss, separation, death, aloneness after the break-up of the family he has celebrated in the antecedent poems. His trademark, the long poem, appears; but he also shows his ability to complete and master the short poem.

When One Has Lived a Long Time Alone contains 22 poems, divided into four parts, the first three with seven poems each, and the fourth part consisting entirely of the long title poem, **"When One Has Lived a Long Time Alone."** Three of the shorter poems strike me as especially fine, **"Judas-Kiss," "The Cat,"** and **"The Perch."** I would also praise the shortest poem in the volume, doubtless Kinnell's shortest ever good poem (a scant seven lines), **"Divinity."** Love is, once again, the only assurance against loneliness. In this poem Kinnell designates the ultimate escape from aloneness as that intimacy consummated with "the woman" at the moment he "touches through to the exact center" and "his loving friend becomes his divinity" (*WOHLLTA,* 46). In **"The Vow,"** his second shortest poem, consisting of eight brief lines, the lover leaves but their vow, "though broken," remains as a trace of eternal love "to give dignity to the suffering / and to intensify it" (*WOHLLTA,* 43).

Kinnell's tone is appropriately somber and reflective, for poems that disclose that love ends in suffering; but in **"Oatmeal,"** where Kinnell imagines sharing a bowl of porridge with John Keats, a rare, but welcome, show of humor occurs: "I am aware it is not good to eat oatmeal alone. / Its consistency is such that it is better for your mental health if / somebody eats it with you" (*WOHLLTA,* 37). The oatmeal-eating Keats confesses that two of his best lines from "To Autumn," which he recites, came to him "while eating oatmeal alone." The knowledge that both poets share, romantic and postmodern, is that poems, the natural tendency to sing, can result from being alone.

The title poem, **"When One Has Lived a Long Time Alone,"** specifies the loneliness of living by oneself as so potent that to retain the presence of another he hesitates to swat the fly or to strike the mosquito, and even lifts the toad "from the pit too deep to hop out of," and helps the swift stunned from crashing into the glass to "fly free" (*WOHLLTA,* 59). For companionship he may even grab the snake behind the head, hold him, and observe him. Or he may listen at morning to "mourning doves / sound their *kyrie eleison*" (*WOHLLTA,* 64). He, "as the conscious one," being human becomes the consciousness for the live creatures of nature around him, the red-headed woodpecker, "clanging out his music / from a metal drainpipe," or the grouse drumming his sound from deep in the woods (*WOHLLTA,* 65). He even relishes the "unlikeables" of nature—the pig, the porcupine—and with a touch of misanthropic loneliness he confesses that "one finds one likes / any other species better than one's own" (*WOHLL-TA,*

66). "Sour, misanthropic," he momentarily accepts the loneliness of forgetting one's own kind. But this mood passes, and the conclusive lesson from these denizens of nature is that one mates with one's own kind and his prayer becomes a wish to revert to one's own kind, "to live again among men and women" and to come back "to that place where one's ties with the human / broke" where lovers speak and stand "in a halo of being made one" (*WOHLL-TA,* 69).

There are poems of the loneliness of memory, the memories of his father and of his wife. The seven-part **"Memories of My Father"** counters his feeling of aloneness by contending that "Those we love from the first / can't be put aside or forgotten, / after they die they still must be cried / out of existence" (*WOHLLTA,* 11). He will return to the house and to memories of his father, and he expects to stop to hear someone singing whether it is his father or "someone I don't know." Kinnell still believes in the continuation of the act of singing, of the poignant human importance of giving form to one's feelings.

Another memory poem needed to sing his father out of existence, **"Kilauea,"** bears the name of the Hawaiian volcano and opens with an image of a stone found with two holes in it, which recalls a skull. He is reminded of his father's brow and of his "sprinting to get to death / before his cares could catch up / and kill him" (*WOHLL-TA,* 6). A small rainbow forms around him, its two ends almost touching his feet. He wonders if he could consequently be the pot of gold at the end of the rainbow. The poem ends with two memories of his father: the first of him in the cellar shoveling in "a new utopia of coal," delivering clanking noises to the radiator pipes; the second stropping his razor and shaving in the bathroom, hooting out "last night's portion of disgust" in song (*WOHLLTA,* 7).

"The Auction" begins with the aloneness of the poet whose sleeping wife "lies in another dream," covered by a quilt "like a hill / of neat farms" (*WOHLLTA,* 12), and moves on to his own dreams about the chest "the color of blood / spilled long ago" sold at auction with the instruction that *"All the old love letters go with it, all go!"* Though the words live on, the lovers lie asleep "in the scythed, white-fenced precinct / on the Heights," with "their alphabets / now two scatterings of bones" (*WOHLLTA,* 14). **"The Massage"** contrasts the intimacy of the physical contact of the body and the two busy hands of the massager—"How could anyone / willingly leave a world where they touch you / all over your body?" (*WOHLLTA,* 16)—and the distractions of external world sounds, including the urgent sound of an ambulance or police siren that leads to thoughts of cadavers on a slab and their last massage in preparation for the funeral. **"The Man on the Hotel Room Bed"** is a grim picture of night loneliness: "He feels around—/ no pillow next to his, no depression / in the pillow, no head in the depression" (*WOHLLTA,* 20). The only consolation for his solitariness is that alone he cannot be abandoned. This is "a man lying alone to avoid being abandoned, / who wants to die to escape the meeting with death" (*WOHLLTA,* 21).

"Agape" contrasts a man's desire to touch a woman and a patient willingness to wait until he can be instructed by a priestess "on love rightly understood" (*WOHLLTA*, 31). He realizes that, as time passes, like all things, she will age and yet he is fearful of what the test of touch may reveal: "I don't want / to know that on the other / side of the pillow nobody / stirs" (*WOHLLTA*, 32).

There are poems on other women, actual and perhaps mythological. **"Who, on Earth"** is both a discovery of a skate, lying on the sand of a beach, sucking holes, and a vivid waking dream, with the vision of a woman, mermaid-like, "up to her waist in a pool, / singing" (*WOHLLTA*, 33). The skate, dying, presses down into the sand, "trying to fall into heaven / inside earth" but is overwhelmed by the force of the waves that inevitably drag off its carcass, "leaving bubbles which pop" (*WOHLLTA*, 34). An analogy is made with the boy harangued by his mother and "icy-shouldered" by his father who "can only fall in loneliness / with . . . but . . . who, / on earth?" (*WOHLLTA*, 35).

"The Cat," which appeared as Kinnell's contribution to the "Fortieth Anniversary Issue" of the *Beloit Poetry Journal,* is indirectly a personal story about his interest in, as his host announces, "someone . . . a woman in your life. . . ."[2] But his concern is fixed on the treatment of the cat: "It is an awful thing you are doing. . . . When you lock her up / she becomes dangerous" (*WOHLLTA*, 26). It is both a cat and yet, in consequence, a mythological creature so that neither he nor his host can let it know its effect on them. Both he and his host are seized as if by "an electric force." His hands "flopping at his sides," while his host pretends, "I am washing the dishes":

> I realize that he is trying to make the cat to believe
> he is not in a seizure but washing the dishes.
> If either of us lets on about the seizure
> I know for certain the cat will kill us both.
>   (*WOHLLTA,* 26)

In one of two *New Yorker* poems, **"The Perch,"**[3] there is once more the memory of a woman friend and of a favorite perspective, "a fork in a branch / of an ancient, enormous maple," for looking out "over miles of valleys and low hills" (*WOHLLTA*, 41). Later, accompanied on skis by the woman, he concentrates on the trunk of the tree "contoured by the terrible struggles of that time when it had its hard time," aware "that some such time now comes upon me." He hears a rifle fired several times and regards this sound as

>   percussions
> of the custom of male mastery
> over the earth—the most graceful,
> most alert, most gentle of the animals
> being chosen to die.
>   (*WOHLLTA,* 42).

The poem concludes with the grace of a glance, as the woman "looked up—the way, from low / to high, the god blesses. . . ."

Kinnell sustains in the context of these poems his former preoccupation with time. In the second *New Yorker* poem, **"Judas-Kiss,"**[4] he knows that it "goes away eventually," once in a while "skips a day," even "a whole year can get lost." But time "basically sits there" (*WOHLLTA*, 18). The only way to rush the process of departing is through death. For this finality there will be a human recognition, a sign of shared humanity, even if what is bestowed is by the nature of death's solitariness, a false Judas kiss.

>   Then somebody,
> an ex-spouse, the woman downstairs,
> or maybe the UPS man, will happen by,
> discover the collapsed creature,
> and, never mind if it sleeps through
> its last clutches, bend down,
> and with the softest
> part of the face, which hides
> the hardest, Judas-kiss it,
> with a click, like a conductor's
> ticket punch, this one here, God
> of our Fathers, this one is the one.
>
>   (*WOHLLTA*, 18-19)

"Farewell" is a poem based on Haydn's "Farewell Symphony," during the performance of which musicians in ones or twos gradually fold up their music and depart. It is a superb musical metaphor for poems concerned with aloneness and thoughts of mortality.

> The orchestra disappears—
> by ones, the way we wash up on the unmusical
>   shore,
> and by twos, the way we enter the ark where the
>   world goes on
>   beginning.
>   (*WOHLLTA*, 53)

As the last two violinists remain "who have figured out what / they have figured out by sounding it upon the other," he sees the face of his old departed friend Paul Zweig, "—who went away, his powers intact, into Eternity's Woods alone" (*WOHLLTA,* 54).

Kinnell can be personal and yet suggestively archetypal, and, surprisingly, he can achieve a felt communication of something significant even in the short lyric, a matter that used to cause him some difficulty. The most significant development in his recent poetry is a matter of intensity. Galway Kinnell no longer believes that everything in his poetry must burn with the fierce flames of intensity. More ordinary human life as a subject has the consequence of getting the feel of a warmer humanity into the poems. Death remains a key subject, but here it is the deaths of contemporaries, of friends, of fellow poets, and contemplation of his own approaching death. But the subject is no longer quite as solemn. To follow up on "December Day in Honolulu" the wail of a cat can be interpreted as communicating the continuity of the cat's "wail" or the poet's song as revealing that "one singer falls but the next steps into the empty place and sings" (*TP*, 35). There is a calmer acceptance, not necessarily of anything momentous but of anything, everything. . . .

Thomas M. Disch (review date 1995)

SOURCE: "Poetry Roundup: *Imperfect Thirst*" in *The Castle of Indolence,* New York: Picado, 1995, pp. 208-21.

[*In the following excerpt, Disch calls* Imperfect Thirst *Kinnell's "comfy" poetry.*]

Readers with only a casual, or dutiful, interest in poetry seek out poets they can be comfortable with. Shades of the schoolhouse begin to close round such readers when poems require too much deciphering. So, according to their temperaments, they will gravitate to poets of amiability or moral earnestness, whose work they will reward with a knowing chuckle or an approving nod.

Among contemporary poets few can rival Galway Kinnell for sheer amiability. The press kit accompanying his twelfth collection, *Imperfect Thirst,* declares, "One of the foremost performers on the poetry circuit, Kinnell inevitably draws enormous crowds with his readings." He is a Pulitzer winner, a MacArthur fellow, and the poet laureate of Vermont, where Hugh Schultz, who owns the Wheelock Village Store, has saluted the poet as "a hometown body" and "a heckuva nice guy, real easy going, low-key." If ever a poet had to be found to endorse a new brand of bran flakes, here is the man.

In the world according to Kinnell death is, unproblematically, an aspect of life in Vermont.

> In the other animals the desire to die comes when
> existing wears out existence.
> In us this desire can come too early, and we kill
> ourselves, or it may never come, and we have to
> be dragged away.
> Not many are able to die well, not even Jesus going
> back to his father.
> And yet dying gets done—and Eddie Jewell coming
> up the road with his tractor in the back of a truck
> and seeing an owl lifting its wings as it alights
> on the ridgepole of that red house, Galway, will
> know that now it is you being accepted back into
> the family of mortals.

"The Biting Insects"

One might ask of such a death where its sting is, but surely a poet is entitled to imagine his own death in whatever terms he likes. There is nothing wrong with being comfy. Comfy feels good, and it is Kinnell's mission as a poet to share his good feelings with his readers, as when at the close of another poem, "The Music of Poetry," Kinnell finds himself.

> . . . here in St. Paul, Minnesota, where I lean
> at a podium trying to draw my talk to a close,

> or a time zone away on Bleecker Street in New
> York,
> where only minutes ago my beloved may have
> put down her book and drawn up her eiderdown
> around herself and turned out the light—
> now, causing me to garble a few words
> and tangle my syntax, I imagine I can hear
> her say my name into the slow waves
> of the night and, faintly, being alone, sing. . . .

Karen Maceira (essay date 1995)

SOURCE: "Galway Kinnell: A Voice to Lead Us," in *The Hollins Critic,* Vol. XXXII, No. 4, October, 1995, pp. 1-15.

[*In the following essay, Kinnell's career is surveyed in light of the publication of* Imperfect Thirst.]

In this last decade of an apocalyptic century, many of us begin to search for the voices who can lead us away from despair for humanity and toward hope for the next era. The publication of Galway Kinnell's latest book, *Imperfect Thirst,* provides an opportunity to review the career of a poet who may turn out to be one of those voices. Few writers have embraced the contemporary existential view of life with as much grace and affirmation as Kinnell. In his poetry, he has made the shift successfully from the theistic framework of our forebears to the secular one our culture has claimed as its own, a shift, for Kinnell, that does not leave behind the sacred but weaves it into the very air we breathe. He is a poet who has taken the material of the self, delivered into our laps mid-century like an uncertain fetus, and taught it that it can survive, even flourish, on the earthly elements of human love and the knowledge of death. This affirmation stands as his major achievement. But Kinnell's contribution to American poetry touches formal aspects as well as content. An already acknowledged master of free verse, he displays in this latest book an even greater ability to put into practice his own definition of poetry, "Saying in its own music what matters most."

Kinnell's has been a quiet career. Allied with none of the various schools of poetry which often monopolize the attention of critics, his work has only in the last several years begun to receive the serious critical consideration it deserves, despite the Pulitzer awarded his *Selected Poems* in 1983. Born in 1927, he came to maturity at the beginning of the postmodern movement away from the tigher forms and distanced, ironic voices which predominated in American poetry in the earlier decades of this century. Kinnell began by writing traditional verse, though even his early poems displayed characteristically aggressive rhythms. In one essay of Howard Nelson's collection, *On the Poetry of Galway Kinnell: The Wages of Dying,* Charles Bell, an early teacher at Princeton and a lifelong mentor and friend, speaks of the poet's first efforts: "In form, Kinnell was . . . using a romantic and Miltonic pentameter almost totally remade under impacts from Donne and the moderns—meter purposely broken up, rhymes concealed— a demonic wrestling with traditional measures" (26).

But even as early as his first book, *What a Kingdom It Was,* Kinnell began to alternate the use of free verse with iambic pentameter in some of the long, multipart poems which were the hallmark of the first half of his career, and when he did, he employed the same kind of discordant musicality in free verse as he did in pentameter. **"Freedom, New Hampshire,"** an elegy for Kinnell's older brother, Derry, who was killed in an automobile accident at age 32, evinces some characteristics of this musicality. Kinnell uses onomatopoeia, repetition and clustered stresses to make sound echo and enhance the sense of what he is saying. In part three of the poem, he describes some childhood pastimes shared with Derry, here involving the making of music on combs, ultimately referring, as his poems usually do, to darkness and mortality:

> Though dusk would come upon us
> Where we sat, and though we had
> Skirled out our hearts in the music,
> Yet the dandruffed
> Harps we skirled it on
> Had done not much better than
> Flies, which buzzed, when quick
> We trapped them in our hands,
> Which went silent when we
> Crushed them, which we bore
> Downhill to the meadowlark's
> Nest full of throats
> Which Derry charmed and combed
> With an Arabian air, while I
> Chucked crushed flies into
>
> Innards I could not see. . . .

Another long poem in the same book, **"The Avenue Bearing the Initial of Christ into the New World,"** brought him recognition. Composed of fourteen sections ranging from eight to sixty-one lines each, the poem is an ironic commentary on the reality of an immigrant neighborhood in New York City, a reality unredeemed by either Christ or the American democratic ideal. The tone of the poem is modernist; Kinnell's narrator is a distanced, omniscient voice, reminiscent of Eliot's in *The Waste Land,* who describes the dense, squalid life of the "Jews, Negroes, (and) Puerto Ricans" of Avenue C. The narrator not only sees the exterior reality, but also the interior one:

> The figures withdraw into chambers overhead—
> In the city of the mind, chambers built
> Of care and necessity, where hands lifted to the
>   blinds,
> They glimpse in mirrors backed with the blackness
>   of the world
> Awkward, cherished rooms containing the familiar
>   selves.

This interior reality is isolated and bereft of grace. In a reinterpretation of the Old Testament Abraham and Isaac story, Kinnell says,

> A child lay in the flames
> It was not the plan. Abraham

> Stood in terror at the duplicity.
> Isaac whom he loved lay in the flames.
> The Lord turned away washing
> His hands without soap and water
> Like a common housefly.

Here, Kinnell associates the figure of the fly with betrayal of the spirit. In later poems, written after he has made the existential shift to acceptance of an unmitigated death, he uses the fly as a symbol of the last of earthly vitality. In his essay **"The Poetics of the Physical World,"** Kinnell discusses the fly in Emily Dickinson's poem "I heard a Fly buzz—when I died." He says, "The poetics of heaven agrees to the denigration of pain and death; in the poetics of the physical world these are the very elements." He adds, "The most ordinary thing, the most despised, may be the one chosen to bear the strange brightening, this last moment of increased life."

In "Skunk Hour," the poem which closes *Life Studies,* the landmark book published just a year before Kinnell's first book, a normally "despised" animal is also used by poet Robert Lowell as a figure of affirmation, though the mother skunk and her "column of kittens" in that poem represent an "ambiguous" affirmation, Lowell's own word to describe it. Important differences exist between the two poets; Kinnell, for one thing, hasn't explored the self in terms of mental illness in the way that Lowell was compelled to do. And while Lowell returned to the undergirding of traditional form in the unrhymed sonnets which comprise most of his books after *Life Studies,* Kinnell for the most part has continued to move further away from traditional form. Both poets, however, represent the postmodern trend towards a dependence on the self for redemption, a salvation likely to come from identification with the least of earth's creatures.

Kinnell concludes this section of **"Avenue C"** with the only passage in the entire poem in which the narrator, still an unidentified, disembodied voice, speaks directly:

> Maybe it is as the poet said,
> And the soul turns to thee
> O vast and well-veiled Death
> And the body gratefully nestles close to thee—
>
> I think of Isaac reading Whitman in Chicago,
> The week before he died, coming across
> Such a passage and muttering, Oi!
> What shit! And smiling, but not for you—I mean,
>
> For *thee,* Sane and Sacred Death!

Whitman would turn out to be the major influence in Kinnell's work. But while he invokes Whitman here and mimics Whitman's use of inclusive catalogue in the poem, Kinnell is not yet prepared to fully embrace Whitman's affirmative vision and still operates within the ironic mode. Granville Taylor is right when he says that for Kinnell

> Existence is to be an ongoing revelation of a natural
> grace, but his revelation only occurs if one accepts

death. These early poems hint at this vision but fail to give it adequate expression because of their concern with showing the inadequacy of a Christian concept of resurrection and immortality. Irony, after all, is rarely a vehicle for grace (*Christianity and Literature.* Summer, 1988).

Kinnell moves closer to a vision of "natural grace" in the poems of his second book, *Flower Herding on Mount Monadnock,* and especially in his third book, *Body Rags,* published in 1968. The title of this latter book recalls Yeats ("the foul rag and bone shop of the heart"; "A tattered coat upon a stick") with whom Kinnell shares an Irish heritage, and who provided him an important early model. Kinnell attributes his interest in long, sectioned poems to Yeats. But Kinnell departs from Yeats in a fundamental way. In "Sailing to Byzantium," Yeats yearns for the sublimation of the mortal, the transient, into the permanence of art:

> Once out of nature I shall never take
> My bodily form from any natural thing,
> But such a form as Grecian goldsmiths make
> Of hammered gold and gold enameling.

Kinnell, on the other hand, asserts:

> . . . for a man
> as he goes up in flames, his one work
> is
> to open himself, to be
> the flames

No permanence exists, no possibility of anything except the warmth and illumination of what is. But instead of the limitations of human life leading to meaninglessness, the major limitation, death, leads Kinnell to an assertion of the value of a fragile existence, providing a basis for his neo-romanticism. (Both Richard Calhoun, in *Galway Kinnell,* and Lee Zimmerman, in *Intricate and Simple Things,* discuss Kinnell as a neo-romantic.) Kinnell's neo-romanticism is characterized by many of the traditional tenets of that movement—belief in the importance of the imagination and of the natural world, rejection of prescribed parameters for subject matter and form—with the crucial addition necessary in our era, the ability to come to affirmation despite no hope of an afterlife. Contemporary neo-romanticism does not contrast with realism; instead, the new romantic vision embraces and incorporates a realistic perception. Indeed, affirmation gains validity from the ability to gaze unwaveringly at the worst, and most of the poems in *Body Rags* take on this function.

Two of the poems, **"Vapor Trail Reflected in the Frog Pond"** and **"The Last River,"** deal with political issues. In the first one, Kinnell conveys his condemnation of the Vietnam War and its political era, invoking again the voice of Whitman in an ironic manner:

> And I hear,
> coming over the hills, America singing,
> her varied carols I hear:

crack of deputies' rifles practicing their aim on stray
    does at night,
sput of cattleprod,
TV groaning at the smells of the human body,
curses of the soldier as he poisons, burns, grinds,
    and stabs
rice of the world,
with open mouth, crying strong, hysterical curses.

This 34 line, three part poem of varied line lengths reveals a general tendency of the poems in *Body Rags.* Though sectioned poems still predominate (17 of 23), many poems are shorter on average, and there is one poem, **"The Burn,"** comprised of a single long stanza, a form Kinnell turns to increasingly in later work, and almost exclusively in *Imperfect Thirst.* Kinnell's movement toward simpler form goes back to Whitman's influence. In his introduction to *The Essential Whitman,* a book published in 1987, he says,

> Under Whitman's spell I stopped writing in rhyme and meter and in rectangular stanzas and turned to longlined, loosely cadenced verse; and at once I felt immensely liberated. Once again, as when I first began writing, it seemed it might be possible to say everything in poetry. Whitman has been my principal master ever since.

For Kinnell, internal form, the argument of the poem, is just as important as external form, perhaps even more important. He says, in his self-edited collection of interviews, *Walking Down the Stairs (WDS)* published in 1978, "poetry is a matter of vision and understanding, even awkwardly expressed, if need be . . ." (78).

One of the most interesting poems in *Body Rags,* **"The Last River,"** explores Kinnell's experience as a civil rights worker in Louisiana in 1963. The poem takes place in a jail cell, where Kinnell spent a week as a result of his voter registration activities, and it depicts a Dantean journey. Kinnell chooses Thoreau as his guide, but where Dante's poem ends in Paradise with the immortality of the spirit, Thoreau can leave Kinnell only a legacy of death: "For Galway alone / I send you my mortality." Kinnell chooses Thoreau so that he can point out Thoreau's transgression in "Seeking . . . love/without human blood in it, / that leaps above / men and women, flesh and erections." Thoreau held to the eastern belief in the wisdom of ridding the self of desire. He says in *Walden,* "We are conscious of an animal in us, which awakens in proportion as our higher nature slumbers. It is reptile and sensual, and perhaps cannot be wholly expelled; like the worms, which even in life and health, occupy our bodies." Thoreau was not impressed with Whitman, as one can imagine, knowing Whitman's blatantly sexual poems. Kinnell has Thoreau repent and realize that "he [Thoreau] loved most [his] purity." For Kinnell, Whitman's embrace of human sensuality provides one basis for affirmation.

Sensuality, because it pertains to the body, provides a connection with the animal world, and it is here that Kinnell finds another basis for affirmation, a possibility for transcendence. Kinnell says, "If the things and creatures that live on earth don't possess mystery, then there isn't any. To touch this mystery requires, I think, love of the things and creatures that surround us: the capacity to go out to them so that they enter us" (*WDS* 52). ***Body Rags*** concludes with two animal poems which have been among the most popular of Kinnell's, **"The Bear"** and **"The Porcupine."** In both, the poet ultimately *becomes* the animal, especially in terms of a fearless acceptance of the physical. In **"The Bear"** the speaker eats bear feces soaked in blood. In **"The Porcupine"** Kinnell describes what a porcupine (read *human being*) loves:

> Adorer of ax
> handles aflow with grain, of arms
> of Morris chairs, of hand
> crafted objects
> steeped in the juice of fingertips,
> of surfaces wetted down
> with fist grease and elbow oil,
> of clothespins that have
> grabbed our body rags by underarm and crotch . . .
> Unimpressed-bored—
> by the whirl of the stars, by *these*
> he's astonished, ultra-
> Rilkean angel!

By the end of the poem, the speaker has become the porcupine:

> the fatty sheath of the man
> melting off
> the self-stabbing coil
> of bristles reversing, blossoming outward—

In these two animal poems, Kinnell has left behind his ironic voice. He is making his way toward "natural grace." But the journey involves a descent into the darkness of mortality which he accomplishes in his next book, ***The Book of Nightmares,*** a descent which yields the greatest possibility of transcendence in the births of his children.

Kinnell began writing ***The Book of Nightmares*** with Rilke in mind. He explains, speaking of the *Duino Elegies:*

> In the Ninth Elegy, Rilke says, in effect, 'Don't try to tell the angels about the glory of your feelings, or how splendid your soul is, they know all about that. Tell them something they'd be more interested in, something that you know better than they, tell them about the things of the world.' So it came to me to write a poem called 'The Things.' Like the *Elegies* it would be a poem without plot, yet with a close relationship among the parts, and a development from beginning to end" (*Walking Down the Stairs* 35).

What began as a single ten-part sequence, after Rilke's poem which is in ten parts, eventually became the book length poem which many consider Kinnell's best work. Kinnell retains Rilke's ten-part organization, further dividing each part into seven sections. As a whole, the poem represents a meditation on spiritual isolation and corporeal decay, as well as on the one thing which ultimately rescues human existence from meaninglessness and despair—love, in this case, a parent's love for his children. But the rescue does not wipe away terror and loneliness. The "I" of the poem dwells alternately within the uncompromising reality of the natural world and the sordid confines of seedy hotel rooms, which, for Kinnell, represent the hell of human isolation. And the affirmation which rises is "a love-note/twisting under my tongue,/ like the coyote's bark,/curving off, into a/howl." The affirmation provided by twentieth-century neo-romanticism still frames a tragic view of life, In "Poetry, Personality and Death," Kinnell quotes Simone Weil: "Love is not consolation, it is light."

The most beautiful passage of ***The Book of Nightmares*** is also certainly among the loveliest and most compelling passages in contemporary American poetry—Part VII, **"Little Sleep's-Head Sprouting Hair in the Moonlight,"** which describes the father coming to answer his small daughter's cries in the night:

> 1
>
> You scream, waking from a nightmare.
>
> When I sleepwalk
> into your room, and pick you up,
> and hold you up in the moonlight, you cling to me
> hard,
> as if clinging could save us. I think
> you think
> I will never die, I think I exude
> to you the permanence of smoke or stars,
> even as
> my broken arms heal themselves around you.

The innocent faith of the child and the knowledge through experience of the adult become one, yielding the powerful bond of love between them.

> 2
>
> I have heard you tell
> the sun, *don't go down,* I have stood by
> as you told the flower, *don't grow old,*
> *don't die.* Little Maud,
> I would blow the flame out of your silver cup,
> I would suck the rot from your fingernail,
> I would brush your sprouting hair of the dying
>   light,
> I would scrape the rust off your ivory bones,
> I would help death escape through the little ribs of
>   your body,
> I would alchemize the ashes of your cradle back
>   into wood,
> I would let nothing of you go, ever. . . .

Here Kinnell's passionate, sincere voice sounds a note as far from irony as possible. He satisfies his definition of poetry, rising to the ability to "get past the censors in one's mind and say what really matters without shame or exhibitionism" (*WDS* 105).

Part VII concludes:

7

Back you go, into your crib.

The last blackbird lights up his gold wings:
  farewell.
Your eyes close inside your head,
in sleep. Already
in your dreams the hours begin to sing.

Little sleep's-head sprouting hair in the moonlight,
when I come back
we will go out together,
we will walk out together among
the ten thousand things,
each scratched too late with such knowledge, *the*
  wages of dying is love.

The nature of salvation here differs radically from the traditional Christian one. For Kinnell, it is a salvation into mortality, not immortality. The epigraph that he uses from Rilke at the beginning of the book explains:

But this, though: death,
the whole of death,—even before life's begun,
to hold it all so gently, and be good:
this is beyond description!

Acceptance of death allows the freedom to live in a spirit of grace and simplicity. And a special power inheres in the birth of one's child—the self and yet not-self—for although salvation must be self-referenced, it must also lead outwardly, away from solipsistic obsession. Kinnell says in Part IV,

So little of what one is threads itself through the
  eye
of empty space.

Never mind.
The self is the least of it.

In *The Book of Nightmares,* Kinnell said he would sing "not the songs / of light said to wave/through the bright hair of angels, / but a blacker/rasping flowering on that tongue." In the interim between that book and *Mortal Acts, Mortal Words,* Kinnell seems to have given himself permission to sing the "songs of light," as well. The distinguishing characteristic of this 1980 book is its intense lyrical quality,

exemplified in poems such as **"Saint Francis and the Sow,"** **"After Making Love We Hear Footsteps," "Wait"** and **"There Are Things I Tell to No One."** The poems are overall much shorter and simpler in design.

In the first poem mentioned above, Kinnell turns to a full, neo-romantic acceptance of what is. He states, "everything flowers from within, of self-blessing." Everything (including everyone) must by necessity endorse his own life which is, like the sow's, homely, broken and earthy because it is mortal, vulnerable:

as Saint Francis
put his hand on the creased forehead
of the sow, and told her in words and in touch
blessings of earth on the sow, and the sow
began remembering all down her thick length,
from the earthen snout all the way
through the fodder and slops to the spiritual curl of
  the tail,
from the hard spininess spiked out from the spine
down through the great broken heart
to the sheer blue milken dreaminess spurting and
  shuddering
from the fourteen teats into the fourteen mouths
  sucking and blowing
        beneath them:
the long, perfect loveliness of sow.

Kinnell's short lyric poems have sometimes been held in less esteem than his long poems. But their simplicity is often deceptive. In **"Saint Francis and the Sow,"** while Kinnell seems to be speaking of something less significant, he is actually making clear the connection of the earthly with the spiritual, that they are one and the same, thus setting out a rationale for his uncompromising acceptance of the physical. He does this partly through the use of sound. The sounds in "from the earthen snout all the way / down through the fodder and slops . . ." typify the hard, Anglo-Saxon edges Kinnell like to put on his often stark descriptions of the physical. But "the spiritual curl of the tail" follows immediately with its lilting, "L" sounds. Who else would think to call the curl of a pig's tail "spiritual"? And yet, as soon as we read it, we know we have always believed it to be so.

Mortal Acts, Mortal Words contains several elegies— for Etheridge Knight, for friend Allen Planz, another for his brother Derry, and for his mother. Her poem, called simply **"Goodbye,"** ends with lines which sum up Kinnell's philosophy: "It is written in our hearts, the emptiness is all. / That is how we have learned, the embrace is all."

Reading *The Past,* I enjoyed the gentle, and for Kinnell rather rare, humor of the first poem, **"The Road Between Here and There"** (Maud and Fergus, both names associated with Yeats, are Kinnell's children):

Here I reread Moby Dick, skimming big chunks, in

a single day, while Maud and Fergus fished.
Here I abandoned the car because of a clonk in the
motor and hitchhiked (which in those days in
Vermont meant walking the whole way with a
limp) all the way to a garage where I passed the

afternoon with ex-loggers who had stopped by to
oil the joints of their artificial limbs and talk.
Here the barn burned down to the snow. "Friction,"
one of the ex-loggers said. "Friction?" "Yup, the
mortgage, rubbing against the insurance policy."

But the poem that struck me hard, **"Man Splitting Wood in the Daybreak,"** did so because it possesses a fearless emotion all too rare in contemporary American poetry. Instead of the pseudo-sophistication and cynicism concerning the ability of language to communicate that many writers now cling to like a new god (as if something *could* hold back death, after all), I found genuineness of feeling:

We could turn to our fathers,
but they protect us only through the unperplexed
looking-back of the numerals cut into headstones.
Or to our mothers, whose love, so devastated,
can't, even in spring, break through the hard earth.
Our spouses weaken at the same rate we do.
We have to hold up our children to lean on them.
Everyone who could help goes or hasn't arrived.
What about the man splitting wood in the daybreak,
who looked strong? That was years ago. That man
was me.

The Past came out in 1988, when Kinnell was 61, an age at which one naturally assumes the past contains more of one's life than the future, an age given to contemplation of that past, and there is a meditative quality to these poems. In the last poem, a three-and-a-half page, single-stanza meditation called **"The Seekonk Woods,"** Kinnell returns to the subject of "what is," which opened *Body Rags* twenty years earlier. Vision has matured and developed after the passage of a generation in time, but the consistency of the message and the same distinctive diction and rhythms come through. The poem opens:

When first I walked here I hobbled
along ties set too close together
for a boy to step naturally on each.
When I grew older, I thought, my stride
would reach every other and thereafter
I would walk in time with the way
towards the meeting place of rails . . .

And it closes

The rails may never meet, O fellow Euclidians,
for you, for me. Never mind if we groan.
That is our noise. Laughter is our stuttering
in a language we can't speak yet. Behind,
the world made of wishes goes dark. Ahead,

if not now then never, shines only what is.

The present moment, the embrace, is what counts.

After breaking with traditional meter and the long, sectioned poem in *The Past,* Kinnell returns to both in his 1991 book, *When One Has Lived a Long Time Alone.* The title poem consists of eleven parts, each of which contains thirteen iambic pentameter lines. The poem can be viewed as a recounting of the part of Kinnell's Dantean journey which readies him to enter Paradise, the realm of love. Perhaps, then, we can see it as his Purgatorio. This poem comes after poems like the already mentioned **"Wait,"** which is an argument against suicide, and **"The Man Splitting Wood in the Daybreak,"** which communicates the loneliness and isolation after divorce. As he says in part ten, he learns, after long solitude and the company only of animals, that all creatures "live to mate with their kind." In part eleven he says, after the estranged one returns to "live again among men and women," that "they (the man and woman) stand in a halo of being made one: kingdom come," signaling entrance to Paradise. In this book and in poems since, Kinnell has explored the paradise of sexual love.

Some critics, attributing a lessening of intensity to Kinnell's poems after *The Book of Nightmares,* have concluded that his career has since gone into decline. While I see that book as a seminal work both for Kinnell and for contemporary American poetry, I see his work since not as a diminution of poetic powers, but as a satisfying and fitting extension of knowledge and ability gained, both in content and form. *Imperfect Thirst* bears this out, containing poems which display a mature talent at its height, poems which are deadly serious yet full of the tenderness born out of an emotional courage which comes, if one is fortunate, with age. Kinnell's defication to the clarity of the internal argument of the free verse poem has never produced better work. His wide-ranging lines of thought are as certain as spider's silk, lending an enriching complexity and delicacy to his message.

The book begins with **"The Pen,"** a poem which quickly brought to mind a personal story. After a reading a couple of years ago, I approached Kinnell to have him sign a book of his poems. I held out the book along with my Bic pen. To my surprise, he looked rather alarmed and swiftly drew out a small leather pouch containing an obviously fine fountain pen. I felt immediately embarrassed at my transgression, though he, always gracious, obviously *did not* intend to cause me discomfort. **"The Pen"**, therefore, had special significance for me, and I smiled as I read it.

The poem illustrates the ease with which Kinnell assumes what is true and important for him is so for everyone, an ability to include personal details as though they were universal references: "the pen dreams of paper, and a feeling of pressure comes into it, and, like a boy dreaming of Grace Hamilton, who sits in front of him in the fifth grade, it could spout." It also confirms that Kinnell can now speak of even the darker elements of his own life without taking himself too seriously, a charge some critics have made in the past: "I called it 'my work' when I would spend weeks on the road, often in the beds of others./This Ideal pen, with vulcanite body, can't resist dredging up the waywardness of my youth./Fortunately pens run out of ink." But mostly this poem, like so many others in the book, demonstrates how Kinnell can take a far-reaching, meditative approach and bring all the components together satisfyingly and without fanfare.

In one group of poems, the Sheffield Ghazals, Kinnell again illustrates a new mastery in terms of leaving behind the self-consciousness which some critics have pointed to in earlier work. He addresses himself, using his own name near the end of each poem. Kinnell did this in **"The Last River"** and *The Book of Nightmares,* to name two previous examples, and there it seemed awkward and overly self-important, but here, perhaps because the Ghazal form *requires* self-address, the technique fits, enhancing the touching effect of each poem:

> Not many are able to die well, not even Jesus going
> back to his father
> And yet dying gets done—and Eddie Jewell coming
> up the road with
> his tractor on a flatbed truck and seeing an owl
> lifting its
> wings
> as it alights on the ridgepole of this red house,
> Galway, will
> know that now it is you being accepted back
> into the family
> of mortals.

This poem also shows, again, Kinnell's ability in this book to address his mortality, but not be ruled by it.

Kinnell, and the reader, have a lot of fun in some poems even while mindful of serious issues. **"The Deconstruction of Emily Dickinson"** vents his frustration with language cynics. **"Holy Shit"** quotes many other thinkers on the subject before Kinnell delivers his own message:

> Of course, as cummings'
> Olaf, 'whose warmest heart recoiled at war,'
> declared, 'there is some s. I will not eat.'
> Like the s. of having to print it as *s.*
> Or of imagining we are a people who don't die,
> who come out of the sky like gods and drop
> not shit but bombs on people who shit.

"Holy Shit" may be a surprise in terms of its range of humor, but not in that it addresses the physicality of human existence or makes the political statement in the last three lines quoted above. But the subject Kinnell addresses in **"Lackawanna,"** parental sexual abuse, is a surprise, simply because it is a new subject for him. Kinnell concentrates on the effects throughout a life, even throughout generations, of the memory of such an act:

> It may be that the past has the absolute force
> of the law that visits parent upon child
> unto the third or fourth generation, and the
> implacability
> of vectors, which fix the way a thing
> goes reeling according to where it was touched.
> What is called spirit may be the exhaust-light
> of toil of the kind a person goes through
> years later to take an unretractable step
> out of that room. . . .

It is a great pleasure to see this master poet grow beyond the parameters of his own accomplishments and weaknesses of the past. Kinnell has never been easy to categorize; he remains a dynamic and surprising poet. But one thing does remain constant: Kinnell's bonedeep confidence in the human—after Darwin and Nietzsche, after Marx, after the great wars, the racial atrocities and assassinations of this century, after the marginalization of the human in practically every arena—reverberates throughout his work.

The closer we get to the millennium, the harder we look for those voices who can lead us away from cynicism. It may be that those who can lead us now are the quiet ones who've had sense enough to stay close to the earth, close to the music of love and desire, close to a language the body remembers. After reading *Imperfect Thirst,* and re-reading his other books, I am more convinced than ever that Galway Kinnell is one of those voices.

FURTHER READING

Bibliography

Calhoun, Richard J. *Galway Kinnell.* New York: Twayne Publishers, 1992. 144 pp.
    A ten-page "Selected Bibliography" is included.

Hawkins, Sherman. "A Checklist of the Writings of Galway Kinnell." *The Princeton University Library Chronicle* 25, No.1 (1963): 65-70.
    An extensive list of pieces by and about the poet up to the publication of *Flower Herding on Mount Monadnock.*

Biography

Calhoun, Richard J. *Galway Kinnell.* New York: Twayne Publishers, 1992. 144 pp.
    A chronology precedes Chapter One, "A Poet's Life and Backgrounds."

Criticism

Comito, Terry. "Slogging Toward the Absolute." *Modern*

Poetry Studies VI, No. 2 (Autumn 1975): 189-192.

A favorable review of *The Avenue Bearing the Initial of Christ into the New World.*

Derricotte, Toi. *"Imperfect Thirst." Prairie Schooner* LXXI, No. 2 (Summer 1997): 188-91.

Some verse in the volume is noted as Kinnell's self-questioning.

Flint, R.W. "At Home in the Seventies." *Parnassus* VIII, No. 2 (January 1980): 51-62.

Reviews both *Mortal Acts, Mortal Words* and *Walking Down Stairs: Selections from Interviews.*

Goldensohn, Lorrie. "Approaching Home Ground: Galway Kinnell's *Mortal Acts, Mortal Words,"* in *The Massachusetts Review: A Quarterly of Literature, the Arts and Public Affairs* Vol. 25, No. 2 (Summer 1984): 303-21.

Explores language that is grounded in "the ordinary object as the right carrier for meaning."

Hoffman, Daniel. "Poetry: Dissidents from Schools." *Harvard Guide to Contemporary American Writing.* Cambridge, MA: Harvard UP, 1979, pp. 566-70.

Kinnell is included in a chapter on poets who broke with the formalist tradition of the fifties.

Howard, Richard. "Changes." *Partisan Review* XXXVIII, No. 4 (Winter 1971-72): 484-90.

The Book of Nightmares is reviewed.

Kinnell, Galway. "The Poetics of the Physical World." *The Iowa Review* II, No. 2 (Summer 1971): 113-26.

Kinnell discusses poetry as the language of "heaven" that confronts death.

—. "Poetry, Personality, and Death." *Field* No. 4 (Spring 1971): 56-75.

Kinnell's exploration of the "self" assumed by the contemporary poet.

Logan, John. "The Bear in the Poet in the Bear." *The Nation* CCVII, No. 8 (September 16, 1968): 244-5.

A thorough review of *Body Rags.*

Pettingell, Phoebe. "Sane and Sacred Death." *The New Leader* LXV, No. 17 (September 27, 1982): 16-17.

Kinnell's *Selected Poems* is praised as a retrospective of poems celebrating mortality.

Rich, Adrienne. "Poetry, Personality, and Wholeness: A Response to Galway Kinnell." *Field* No. 7 (Fall 1972): 10-18.

The feminist critic's response to Kinnell's essay, "Poetry, Personality, and Death."

Stitt, Peter. "Stages of Reality: The Mind/Body Problem of Contemporary Poetry." *The Georgia Review* XXXVII, No. 1 (Spring 1983): 201-210.

Includes a section contrasting Kinnell's and Mark Strand's verse.

Tuten, Nancy L., ed. *Critical Essays on Galway Kinnell.* New York: G.K. Hall & Co., 1996.

Includes 27 reviews of Kinnell's work as well as ten essays.

—. "'For Robert Frost':" Form and Content in the Poetry of Galway Kinnell." *His "Incalculable" Influence on Others: Essays on Robert Frost in Our Time.* Victoria, B.C.: University of Victoria, 1994, 97-104.

Examines Kinnell's response to the problem of form as set down by Frost.

Van Duyn, Mona. "Vision, Celebration, and Testimony." *Poetry* CV, No. 4 (January 1965): 264-69.

A review of *Flower Herding on Mount Monadnock.*

Weston, Susan B. "To Take Hold of the Song: The Poetics of Galway Kinnell." *The Literary Review* XXXI, No. 1 (Fall 1987): 73-85.

A study of Kinnell's poetics of transcendence in *The Book of Nightmares.*

Zimmerman, Lee. *Intricate and Simple Things.* Urbana, IL: U of IL P, 1987, 247 pp.

Six chapters each on Kinnell's volumes through *The Past,* through which author "charts shifting relationships between isolation and belonging," the Romantic project of the self in the world, vis-a-vis three opposing pairs of poets: Wordsworth and Keats; Whitman and Dickinson; Eliot and William Carlos Williams.

Interviews

Hilgers, Thomas and Michael Molloy. "An Interview with Galway Kinnell." *Modern Poetry Studies* XXI, Nos. 1-2 (Autumn 1982): 107-12.

Kinnell talks about inspiration, animals in his poetry, poets of his generation, among other topics.

Landsfeld, Karla, Jackson, John, and Cheryl Sharp. "Galway Kinnell." *American Poetry Observed: Poets on Their Work.* Ed. Joe David Bellamy. Chicago: University of Illinois Press, 1984, pp. 134-42.

The writing process as well as Kinnell's private life are discussed.

McKenzie, James J. "To the Roots: An Interview with Galway Kinnell," *Salmagundi* XXII, No. 23 (Spring/Summer 1973): 207-221.

Kinnell discusses his early attempts at writing as well as various American poets.

Additional coverage of Kinnell's life and career is contained in the following sources published by Gale Group: *Contemporary Literary Criticism,* Vols. 1, 2, 3, 5, 13, 29; *Contemporory Authors* 9-12R; *Contemporary Authors New Revision Series,* Vols. 10, 34, 66; *Dictionary of Literary Biography,* Vol. 5; *Dictionary of Literary Biography Yearbook,* Vol. 87; and *Major Twentieth Century Authors.*

Alexander Pope
1688-1744

English poet, critic, translator, and essayist.

INTRODUCTION

Deemed the perfecter of the English heroic couplet, Pope is considered the foremost writer of the Augustan Age and one of the most forceful poetic satirists of all time. His verse is viewed as the ultimate embodiment of eighteenth-century neoclassical ideals. These ideals, such as order, beauty, sophisticated wit, and refined moral sentiment, are exemplified throughout his verse, but particularly in such works as *An Essay on Criticism* (1711) and the mock-heroic poem *The Rape of the Lock* (1712). Like these works, virtually all of Pope's writings are concerned with the moral, social, and intellectual state of humanity, which he considered of utmost relevance to his craft. Pope's most controversial work and most often considered his masterpiece, *The Dunciad* (1728), severely satirizes London writers who Pope believed had unjustly maligned him or who he considered contributors to the dissolution of Augustan ideals in England. Although satire, inspired by that of Roman poet Horace, represents much of his literary corpus and claim to critical praise, Pope is also highly revered for his monumental translations of Homer's *Iliad* and *Odyssey* and for his critical discussions of poetry and aesthetics.

Biographical Information

Pope was born in London and was the only child of a moderately wealthy linen merchant, Alexander, and his second wife Edith. Under the Anglican rule of William of Orange and Mary Stuart, who ousted the Catholic monarch James II in the year of Pope's birth, Pope's family, like all Roman Catholics living in England at the time, faced numerous restrictions. They were, for example, forbidden by law to practice their religion openly, to hold public office, or to attend public schools and universities. Also enacted at this time was a law prohibiting Catholics from residing within ten miles of London, and so the Popes relocated to nearby Windsor Forest, beside the Thames. Under these circumstances, Pope received his education irregularly through private tutors and Catholic priests but was largely self-taught. By the age of twelve, he was already well versed in Greek, Roman, and English literature and diligently emulated the works of his favorite poets. At this time, though, Pope contracted a tubercular condition from infected milk, which caused permanent curvature of the spine and severely stunted growth; as a result, he attained a maximum height of only four feet, six inches, and throughout adulthood was so physically disabled that he required daily care. Yet, this did not deter Pope from the literary life he sought. By his teens, after voluminous reading of the classics, he had come to regard the heroic couplets of John Dryden as the highest, most sustained form of English poetry yet produced, and so he decided to pattern his verse after this Restoration master. During periodic visits to London at this time, Pope met three of Dryden's contemporaries: the poet William Walsh, and dramatists William Wycherley and William Congreve. Through the influence of these writers, Pope's manuscript of his early bucolic poems, the *Pastorals,* captured the attention of publisher Jacob Tonson, then Britain's leading publisher, and in 1709 the *Pastorals* appeared in Tonson's *Poetical Miscellanies.* Pope later became friends with Whig writers Joseph Addison and Richard Steele, publishers of the *Spectator,* and contributed poems and articles to their journal during the next few years. Pope's growing understanding of the commercial aspects of publishing and his established position as the prominent poet of the age led him to obtain enough money to render him the first independently wealthy, full-time writer in English history. Pope's huge financial and literary successes enraged less-fortunate London writers and critics. Due to his success, as well as his Catholic religion and unpopular Tory politics, Pope attracted abusive critical and personal attack with nearly every new literary venture he began. He closely oversaw the publication of virtually everything he wrote, often editing and reissuing his works in updated and collected volumes. During his later years, Pope began revising his poems in preparation of a complete, edited edition of his works. He died in 1744 of acute asthma and dropsy before completing this task.

Major Works

Pope's first published poetic work, the *Pastorals,* a series of four poems named after the seasons, is consciously affined with the verse of Virgil, Edmund Spenser, John Milton, and Dryden. This sequence was inspired by Pope's youth in Windsor Forest and idealizes shepherd life. *An Essay on Criticism* is at once a treatise of literary theory and working manual of versification. It is divided into three parts: part one creates a vision of the golden era of art and criticism, part two presents a vision of decay and disorder in literary criticism, and part three puts forth a means of reformation and restoration in literary endeavors, emphasizing in particular the basic precepts of clarity, impartiality, and public responsibility. Composed at the age of twenty-three, this work rendered literary London awestruck, for it displayed not only a precocious mastery of the couplet form but originated a wealth of impeccably expressed eighteenth-century sentiments, including "To err is human, to forgive divine" and "A little learning is a dangerous thing," which have since become firmly embedded in English and American culture. *The Rape of the Lock* was first published in two cantos in 1712 and expanded to five cantos in 1714. This work is ostensibly based on a real-life incident that occurred in 1711, when a young man publicly cut a lock of hair from the head of a young, beautiful female relation. *The Rape of the Lock* was written on the request of a friend to heal the estrangement between the two families. Influenced by the fusion of high humor and moralization characteristic of the *Spectator,* the charming, slightly irreverent depiction of English high society in *The Rape of the Lock* quickly endeared the poem to readers throughout the country. "Eloisa to Abelard" (1717) is poem based on a well-known tragic love story between Pierre Abélard, a French philosopher and theologian, and Héloïse, a pupil twenty-one years his junior who became his lover, the mother of his child, and later his secret wife. When her family learned about the relationship, they had Abélard castrated; he became a monk and Héloïse became a nun. Pope's poem is written in the form of a letter from Héloïse to Abélard years after their separation and addresses the conflict between love of God and love of man. Until the publication of *The Dunciad,* Pope had refrained from wholesale refutation of critical and personal attacks, but pent-up anger at being caricatured as an ape, a madman, and a literary scoundrel, as well as growing impatience with what he saw as a widespread profanation of the writer's responsibility to society, led him to the tradition of satire which was to become his focus for the remainder of his career. In the

first edition of *The Dunciad,* Pope designated as his chief victim Lewis Theobald, a writer who had heavily criticized Pope for his emendations and modernizations of Shakespeare. The following year, Pope published *The Dunciad, Variorum,* which included mock-pedantic footnotes intensifying his attack on the reputations and abilities of a host of London critics and writers. In 1743, Pope expanded *The Dunciad* to four books and broadened its satirical scope to encompass the whole of English society, which he believed by then to be near moral collapse: "Lo! thy dread Empire, CHAOS is restored; / Light dies before thy uncreating word; / Thy hand, great Anarch! lets the curtain fall; / And Universal Darkness buries all." *An Essay on Man* (1734) is a philosophical poem that addresses the nature of humankind, God's design for the world, and the role of humankind within this system. Pope incorporated numerous philosophical and theological theories into this work, particularly those of two influential thinkers, Lord Shaftesbury, who believed that man was by nature social and benevolent, and Thomas Hobbes, who believed man was selfish and impelled by passion and self-preservation. *An Essay on Man* is generally optimistic in tone, with Pope declaring at the conclusion of the poem: "And all our knowledge is, OURSELVES TO KNOW."

Critical Reception

Since Pope's death, the merit of his literary achievements has been hotly debated. During the second half of the eighteenth century, such critics as Joseph Warton, William Warburton, and Samuel Johnson all accorded Pope high status as a gifted versifier, critic, and translator. Yet, none deemed his major poems poetry in its highest form. Such appraisals foreshadowed the prominent nineteenth-century critical viewpoint, that of Pope as a crafty wordsmith who was oblivious to the "highest" poetic subjects—the documentation of personal experience and the natural world, subjects with which Romantic poets concerned themselves. Recapitulating this stance near the end of the century, Matthew Arnold asserted that the works of Pope and his literary predecessor, Dryden, represented classics of English prose rather than poetry. However, the emergence of new critical methodologies in the twentieth century, along with the publication of a complete edition of Pope's works and a resurgence in Augustan literature, has helped vindicate Pope as a classic English poet and widely broadened the public's understanding and appreciation of his works. Despite having been written during Pope's adolescent and early adult years, such poems as the *pastorals,* "Verses to the Memory of an Unfortunate Lady," *Windsor-Forest,* and "Eloisa to Abelard," have been highly acclaimed since their first appearance as exemplary poems of beauty, human passion, and suffering. The charge that Pope abandoned these concerns to his detriment in later years has been refuted by modern scholars who emphasize the workings of not only a keen intellect but of a feeling, fully sensitive individual as well. Although these works have been labeled trite or historically unimportant in comparison to Pope's major works, they remain outstanding initial demonstrations of the poet's control of meter and language. Undoubtedly Pope's most publicly cherished work is *The Rape of the Lock.* Celebrated as a masterstroke of English originality in his lifetime and scrutinized as an ethereal curiosity in the nineteenth century, it has, in the present century, attracted profuse, diverse interpretation, from character analyses to examinations of Pope's political motivations and extensive literary allusions to *The Iliad, The Aeneid,* and *Paradise Lost.* Perhaps the approach that has most illuminated this work in relation to Pope's others is that which focuses on his concurrent acceptance of and satiration of high English society. At present, Pope's literary reputation is exceedingly high. He ranks as the unquestioned master of the heroic couplet, and this, combined with his keen satiric and moral sensibility, affords Pope an exalted position as one of the most proficient and powerful versifiers of all time.

PRINCIPAL WORKS

Poetry

Pastorals 1709; published in *Poetical Miscellanies: The Sixth Part*
An Essay on Criticism 1711
"The Messiah" 1712; published in the journal *The Spectator*
* *The Rape of the Lock* 1712; published in *Miscellaneous Poems and Translations*
Windsor-Forest. To the Right Honourable George Lord Lansdown 1713
The Rape of the Lock. An Heroic-Comical Poem. In Five Cantos 1714
The Temple of Fame: A Vision 1715
"Eloisa to Abelard" 1717; published in *The Works of Mr. Alexander Pope*
** "Verses to the Memory of an Unfortunate Lady" 1717; published in *The Works of Mr. Alexander Pope*
The Dunciad. An Heroic Poem. In Three Books 1728
The Dunciad, Variorum. With the Prolegomena of Scriblerus. 1729; revised and enlarged
An Epistle to the Right Honourable Richard Earl of Burlington 1731
Epistles to Several Persons 1731-35
Satires and Epistles of Horace, Imitated 1733-37
An Essay on Man, Being the First Book of Ethic Epistles. To Henry St. John L. Bolingbroke 1734
An Epistle From Mr. Pope, to Dr. Arbuthnot 1735
An Epistle to a Lady: Of the Characters of Women 1735
Epilogue to the Satires, In Two Dialogues 1738
The New Dunciad: As It Was Found in the Year 1741 1742
The Dunciad, In Four Books 1743
The Twickenham Edition of the Poems of Alexander Pope. 11 vols. 1939-69

Other Major Works

The Iliad of Homer. 6 vols. [translator] (poetry) 1715-20
The Works of Mr. Alexander Pope (poetry and criticism) 1717

The Odyssey of Homer. 5 vols. [translator; with William Broome and Elijah Fenton] (poetry) 1725-26
The Works of Shakespear. 6 vols. [adaptor] (poetry) 1725
"Peri Bathous; or, The Art of Sinking in Poetry" (criticism) 1727; published in *Miscellanies: The Last Volume*
Mr. Pope's Literary Correspondence for Thirty Years; from 1704 to 1734 (letters) 1735
The Works of Mr. Alexander Pope, Volume 2 1735
Letters of Mr. Alexander Pope, and Several of His Friends (letters) 1737
The Works of Alexander Pope. 9 vols. (poetry and criticism) 1751
The Prose Works of Alexander Pope: The Earlier Works, 1711-1720 1936
The Correspondence of Alexander Pope (letters) 1956
The Prose Works of Alexander Pope: The Major Works, 1725-1744 1986

---

*This version of *The Rape of the Lock* was published in two cantos.
**This work is also referred to as "Elegy to the Memory of an Unfortunate Lady."

CRITICISM

John Dennis (essay date 1711)

SOURCE: "Reflections Critical and Satyrical, Upon a Late Rhapsody, Call'd, An Essay Upon Criticism," in *The Critical Works of John Dennis: 1692-1711,* Vol. 1, edited by Edward Niles Hooker, The John Hopkins Press, 1939, pp. 396-422.

[*Dennis was a minor eighteenth-century writer who is generally esteemed for his literary criticism. However, his several unusually abusive attacks on the character and writings of Pope have largely diminished his posthumous status in the field. In the following excerpt, taken from Dennis's first pamphlet attack on Pope,* Reflections Critical and Satyrical, Upon a Late Rhapsody, Call'd, An Essay Upon Criticism *(1711), he lambasts Pope for what he considers the immoral, imprecise, and insipid thought presented in* An Essay on Criticism.]

'Tis now almost seven Years, since I happen'd to say one Morning to a certain Person distinguish'd by Merit and Quality, that wherever the *Italian Opera* had come, it had driven out Poetry from that Nation, and not only Poetry, but the very Tast of Poetry, and of all the politer Arts; and that if the same Protection and Encouragement were continued to the *Opera,* by which it was then supported, the same Calamity would befal *Great Britain* which had happen'd to the Neighbouring Nations. As 'tis hard to find a Man more quick or more penetrating, than the Person to whom I spoke this; he immediately enter'd into that Sentiment, and soon after withdrew that Encouragement which he had given to the *Italians.* All that I foretold, and more than all hath happen'd. For such Things, such monstrous Things have been lately writ, and such monstrous Judgments pass'd, that what has been formerly said has been sufficiently confirm'd, that 'tis impossible an Author can be so very foolish, but he will find more stupid Admirers.

A most notorious Instance of this Depravity of Genius and Tast, is the Essay upon which the following Reflections are writ [*An Essay on Criticism*], and the Approbation which it has met with. I will not deny but that there are two or three Passages in it with which I am not displeas'd; but what are two or three Passages as to the whole? . . . The approving two or Three Passages amongst a multitude of bad ones, is by no means advantageous to an Author. That little that is good in him does but set off its contrary, and make it appear more extravagant. The Thoughts, Expressions, and Numbers of this Essay are for the most part but very indifferent, and indifferent and execrable in Poetry are all one. But what is worse than all the rest, we find throughout the whole a deplorable want of that very Quality, which ought principally to appear in it, which is Judgment; and I have no Notion that where there is so great a want of Judgment, there can be any Genius.

However, I had not publish'd the following Letter, but had suffer'd his Readers to have hugg'd themselves in the Approbation of a Pamphlet so very undeserving, if I had not found things in it that have provok'd my Scorn, tho' not my Indignation. For I not only found my self attack'd without any manner of Provocation on my side, and attack'd in my Person, instead of my Writings, by one who is wholly a Stranger to me, and at a time when all the World knew that I was persecuted by Fortune; I not only saw that this was attempted in a clandestine manner with the utmost Falshood and Calumny, but found that all this was done by a little affected Hypocrite, who had nothing in his mouth at the same time but *Truth, Candor, Friendship, good Nature, Humanity,* and *Magnanimity.*

'Tis for this Reason that I have publish'd the following Letter, in which if I have not treated the Author of the *Essay* with my usual Candor, he may thank himself and this good-natur'd Town. For having observ'd with no little Astonishment, that Persons have been censur'd for ill Nature, who have attempted to display the Errors of Authors undeservedly successful; tho' they have done this with all imaginable Candor, and with the best and noblest Designs, which are the doing Justice, the Discovery of Truth, and the Improvement of Arts; while Writers of Lampoons and infamous Libels, whose Anonymous Authors have lain lurking in the dark, sometimes in Clubs, and sometimes solitary, like so many common Rogues and Footpads, to ruin the Fortunes, and murder the Reputations of others; have been caress'd and hugg'd by their thoughtless Applauders, and treated as if they had been the most vertuous and the best natur'd Men in the World; having observ'd all this with no little astonishment, I at last found out the reason of it, which is, because the Attempts of Libellers and Lampooners hurt only those whom they attack, and delight the rest of the Readers; whereas they who expose by a just Criticism the Absurdities of foolish fortunate Authors, attack all those who commend and admire those Authors, and disturb perhaps by open-

ing their Eyes, no fewer than a thousand Fops in the good Opinion which they have conceiv'd of themselves. 'Tis for this Reason that I have endeavour'd to comply with this wise and good natur'd general Disposition of Minds, and to make amends for the Ill-nature of my Criticism, by the Allurements of my *Satyr.* . . .

I am inclin'd to believe that [the *Essay*] was writ by some young, or some raw Author, for the following Reasons.

First, He discovers in every Page a Sufficiency that is far beyond his little Ability; and hath rashly undertaken a Task which is infinitely above his Force; a Task that is only fit for the Author, with the just Encomium of whose Essay my Lord *Roscommon* begins his own.

> Happy that Author whose correct Essay
> Repairs so well our old *Horatian* way.

There is nothing more wrong, more low, or more incorrect than this Rhapsody upon Criticism. The Author all along taxes others with Faults of which he is more guilty himself. He tells us in the very two first Lines, that

> 'Tis hard to say if greater want of Skill.
> Appear in writing, or in judging ill.

Now whereas others have been at some Pains and Thought to shew each of these wants of Skill separately and distinctly, his comprehensive Soul hath most ingeniously contriv'd to shew them both in a supreme Degree together.

Secondly, While this little Author struts and affects the Dictatorian Air, he plainly shews that at the same time he is under the Rod; and that while he pretends to give Laws to others, he is himself a pedantick Slave to Authority and Opinion, of which I shall give some Instances.

In the beginning of his Essay he lays down this Maxim:

> Let such teach others who themselves excel,
> And censure others who have written well.

Where he would insinuate, that they alone are fit to be Criticks who have shewn themselves great Poets. And he brings in *Pliny* to confirm by his Authority the Truth of a Precept, which is denied by matter of Fact, and by the Experience of above Two thousand Years. . . .

Another Instance which I shall give of his being a Slave to Authority and Opinion, is the servile Deference which he pays to the Ancients. . . .

> Still Green with Bays each ancient Altar stands
> Above the reach of sacrilegious Hands,
> Secure from Flames, from Envy's fiercer Rage,
> Destructive War, and all devouring Age.
> See from each Clime the Learn'd their Incense
>   bring,
> Hear in all Tongues triumphant Pœans ring!
> In Praise so just let ev'ry Voice be join'd,
> And fill the general Chorus of Mankind. . . .

[A] third infallible mark of a young Author, is, that he hath done in this Essay what School-boys do by their Exercises, he hath borrow'd both from Living and Dead, and particularly from the Authors of the two famous Essays upon Poetry and Translated Verse; but so borrow'd, that he seems to have the very Reverse of *Midas*'s noble Faculty. For as the coursest and the dullest Metals, were upon the touch of that *Lydian* Monarch immediately chang'd into fine Gold; so the finest Gold upon this Author's handling it, in a moment loses both its lustre and its weight and is immediately turn'd to Lead.

A fourth thing that shews him a young man, is the not knowing his own mind, and his frequent Contradictions of himself. His Title seems to promise an Essay upon Criticism in general, which afterwards dwindles to an Essay upon Criticism in Poetry. And after all, he is all along giving Rules, such as they are, for Writing rather than Judging. In the beginning of the 8th Page the Rules are nothing but Nature.

> These Rules of old discover'd, not devis'd,
> Are Nature still, but Nature methodiz'd.

But no sooner is he come to the 10th Page, but the Rules and Nature are two different things.

> When first great *Maro,* in his boundless mind,
> A Work t' outlast immortal *Rome* design'd,
> Perhaps he seem'd above the Critick's Law,
> And but from Nature's Fountains scorn'd to
>   draw.

But in the last Line of this very Paragraph they are the same things again.

> Learn hence for ancient Rules a just Esteem,
> To copy Nature is to copy them.

But to this he will answer, That he is guilty of no Contradiction, that he is only shewing that *Virgil* was guilty of Error and Ignorance; who first absurdly began to write his *œneis,* and afterwards sate down to learn the Rules of Writing; which when he began to write that Poem, he took to be things distinct from Nature; but that after he had wrote part of it, he fell to the reading of *Homer,* and that undeceiv'd him. That while he is talking of *Virgil*'s Error and Ignorance, he is making a Parade of his own incomparable Wisdom and Knowledge; and not contradicting himself, but *Virgil,* or rather making him appear inconsistent with and contradicting himself: for that tho' *Virgil* took the Rules and Nature to be distinct from each other, for his own part he is wiser, and knows better things. Now is not this a very modest and a very judicious Gentleman?

A fifth Sign of his being a young Author is his being almost perpetually in the wrong. And here in relation to the foregoing passage, I might desire to ask him one or two civil Questions. First, who acquainted him with that noble Particularity of *Virgil*'s Life, that he designed to write his *œneis* without Art? Had he it from ancient or modern Authors, or does he owe it to a noble Effort of his own sagacious Soul? If *Virgil* had so little Knowledge of the Rules of his own Art, and so very little true Judgment within him, as to be capable of such an Extravagance, an Extravagance which, says this Essayer, nothing but the reading of *Homer* was able to correct, how comes he so far to have surpass'd his Master in the admirable Contrivance of his Poem? But secondly, what does he mean by *Maro*'s designing a Work to outlast immortal *Rome?* Does he pretend to put that Figure, call'd a Bull, upon *Virgil?* Or would he ambitiously have it pass for his own? 'Tis no wonder that one who is capable of imputing so great an Extravagance to *Virgil,* should be capable of writing himself without any manner of meaning.

Whenever we find a Simile, the first Line of it is like a Warning-piece, to give us notice that something extraordinary false or foolish is to follow. We have one in the 6th Page, where the former and the latter part have not the least relation, and bear not the least proportion to one another.

> As on the Land while here the Ocean gains,
> In other Parts it leaves wide sandy Plains:
> Thus in the Soul while Memory prevails,
> The solid Power of Understanding fails;
> Where Beams of warm Imagination play,
> The Memory's soft Figures melt away.

Here the Soul in the third Verse is made to answer to Land in the first, and Memory to Ocean, which in the fourth Verse is chang'd for Understanding; tho' in this Simile the Author shews neither Memory nor Understanding; for there are as many Absurdities in it as there are Lines. At this rate a man may make a thousand Similes in an hour! Any thing may become like to any thing. . . . But what a thoughtless Creature is this Essayer, to deny in these very Rhimes, by which he pretends to shew both Poetry and Criticism, the co-existence of those Qualities, without which 'tis impossible to be both Poet and Critick? Besides, how wrong is this; and how many Persons have I known who have had all these Qualities at the same time in a very great degree? What follows is more wrong and more absurd:

> One Science only will one Genius fit,
> So vast is Art, so narrow Human Wit.

Is not this a rare Pretender to Poetry and Criticism, who talks at this rate, when all the World knows that 'tis impossible for a Man with only one Science to be either Poet or Critick? Which is so much the more unlucky, because the very Fathers of Poetry and Criticism *Homer* and *Aristotle,* whom he mentions so often in this Essay, are believed to have had all the Sciences. 'Tis now between Two and three thousand Years since *Aristotle* wrote his Morals, his Politicks, his Rhetorick, and his Poetick; and three of these are the very best in their kinds to this very day, and have infinitely the Advantage of all those several thousand Treatises that have been writ since. . . .

But what most shews him a very young Author, is, that . . . he has the Insolence of a Hero, and is a downright

Bully of *Parnassus,* who is ev'ry moment thund'ring out Fool, Sot, Fop, Coxcomb, Blockhead, and thinks to hide his want of Sense by his pretended Contempt of others, as a Hector does his want of Courage by his perpetual blustring and roaring; and is sagaciously of Opinion, that he arrogates so much Sense to himself as he imputes Folly to other People. . . .

I find . . . that in the compass of one Page, which is the thirty first, he has Libell'd two Monarchs and two Nations. The two Monarchs are King *Charles* and King *William:* The two Nations are the *Dutch* and our own. The *Dutch* we are told are a parcel of Sharpers, and we are downright Bubbles and Fools. King *Charles* the Second was too much a Libertine, and too much an Encourager of Wit for him; King *William* the Third was too much a *Socinian.* But tho' he has without Mercy condemn'd the Reigns of the foremention'd Monarchs, he is graciously pleas'd to pass over in silence that which comes between them. In the beginning of the 12th Page, we find what that is which so happily reconcil'd him to it, and that was the Dispensing Pow'r, which was set on foot in order to introduce and to establish Popery, and to make it the National Religion. Now I humbly conceive that he who Libels our Confederates, must be by Politicks a *Jacobite;* and he who Libels all the Protestant Kings that we have had in this Island these threescore Years, and who justifies the Dispensing Pow'r so long after we are free'd from it, a Pow'r which as was hinted above was set on foot on purpose to introduce Popery: He who justifies this when he lyes under the Tye of no Necessity, nor ev'n Conveniency to approve of it, must, I humbly conceive, derive his Religion from St. *Omer*'s, as he seems to have done his Humanity and his Criticism; and is, I suppose, politickly setting up for Poet-Laureat against the coming over of the Pretender, which by his Insolence he seems to believe approaching, as People of his Capacity are generally very sanguine. . . .

This little Author may extol the Ancients as much and as long as he pleases, but he has reason to thank the good Gods that he was born a Modern. For had he been born of *Græcian* Parents, and his Father by consequence had by Law had the absolute Disposal of him, his Life had been no longer than that of one of his Poems, the Life of half a day. Instead of setting his Picture to show, I have taken a keener Revenge, and expos'd his Intellectuals, as duly considering that let the Person of a Gentleman of his parts be never so contemptible, his inward Man is ten times more ridiculous; it being impossible that his outward Form, tho' it should be that of downright Monkey, should differ so much from human Shape, as his immaterial unthinking part does from human Understanding. How agreeable it is to be in a Libel with so much good Company as I have been, with two great Monarchs, two mighty Nations, and especially the People of Quality of *Great Britain,* and this Libel compos'd by a little Gentleman, who has writ a Panegyrick upon himself! Which Panegyrick if it was not writ with Judgment, yet was it publish'd with Discretion, for it was publish'd in Mr. *W*———'s Name; so that by this wise Proceeding he had the Benefit of the Encomium, and Mr. *W*———had the Scandal of the

Poetry; which it brought upon him to such a degree, that 'tis ten to one if ever he recovers the Reputation of a good Versifyer. And thus for the present I take my leave of you and of this little Critick and his Book; a Book throughout which Folly and Ignorance, those Brethren so lame and so impotent, do ridiculously at one and the same time look very big and very dull, and strut, and hobble cheek by jowl with their Arms on Kimbo, being led and supported, and Bully-back'd by that blind Hector Impudence.

William Hazlitt (essay date 1818)

SOURCE: "On Dryden and Pope," in *Lectures on the English Poets and the English Comic Writers,* edited by William Carew Hazlitt, George Bell and Sons, 1894, pp. 91-113.

[An English essayist, Hazlitt was one of the most important critics of the Romantic age. In the following excerpt from an essay originally published in 1818, he discusses Pope's verse as an incomparably refined body of work which must, nevertheless, be placed outside the English tradition of "natural" verse established by Geoffrey Chaucer, William Shakespeare, and John Milton.]

Dryden and Pope are the great masters of the artificial style of poetry in our language, as . . . Chaucer, Spenser, Shakespeare, and Milton, were of the natural; and though this artificial style is generally and very justly acknowledged to be inferior to the other, yet those who stand at the head of that class ought, perhaps, to rank higher than those who occupy an inferior place in a superior class. They have a clear and independent claim upon our gratitude, as having produced a kind and degree of excellence which existed equally nowhere else. . . .

The question, whether Pope was a poet, has hardly yet been settled, and is hardly worth settling; for if he was not a great poet, he must have been a great prose-writer; that is, he was a great writer of some sort. He was a man of exquisite faculties, and of the most refined taste; and as he chose verse (the most obvious distinction of poetry) as the vehicle to express his ideas, he has generally passed for a poet, and a good one. If indeed by a great poet we mean one who gives the utmost grandeur to our conceptions of nature, or the utmost force to the passions of the heart, Pope was not in this sense a great poet; for the bent, the characteristic power of his mind, lay the clean contrary way: namely, in representing things as they appear to the indifferent observer, stripped of prejudice and passion, as in his [*Essay on Criticism*] or in representing them in the most contemptible and insignificant point of view, as in his Satires; or in clothing the little with mock-dignity, as in his poems of Fancy; or in adorning the trivial incidents and familiar relations of life with the utmost elegance of expression and all the flattering illusions of friendship or self-love, as in his *Epistles.* He was not, then, distinguished as a poet of lofty enthusiasm, of strong imagination, with a passionate sense of the beauties of nature, or a deep insight into the workings of the heart; but he was a wit and a critic, a man of sense, of observation, and the world, with a keen relish for the elegances of art, or of nature when embellished by art, a quick tact for propriety of thought and manners as established by the forms and customs of society, a refined sympathy with the sentiments and habitudes of human life, as he felt them within the little circle of his family and friends. He was, in a word, the poet, not of nature, but of art; and the distinction between the two, as well as I can make it out, is this. The poet of nature is one who, from the elements of beauty, of power, and of passion in his own breast, sympathises with whatever is beautiful, and grand, and impassioned in nature, in its simple majesty, in its immediate appeal to the senses, to the thoughts and hearts of all men; so that the poet of nature, by the truth, and depth, and harmony of his mind, may be said to hold communion with the very soul of nature; to be identified with, and to foreknow, and to record the feelings of all men at all times and places, as they are liable to the same impressions, and to exert the same power over the minds of his readers that nature does. He sees things in their eternal beauty, for he sees them as they are; he feels them in their universal interest, for he feels them as they affect the first principles of his and our common nature. Such was Homer, such was Shakespeare, whose works will last as long as nature, because they are a copy of the indestructible forms and everlasting impulses of nature, welling out from the bosom as from a perennial spring, or stamped upon the senses by the hand of their Maker. The power of the imagination in them is the representative power of all nature. It has its centre in the human soul, and makes the circuit of the universe.

Pope was not assuredly a poet of this class, or in the first rank of it. He saw nature only dressed by art; he judged of beauty by fashion; he sought for truth in the opinions of the world; he judged of the feelings of others by his own. . . .

In his smooth and polished verse we meet with no prodigies of nature, but with miracles of wit; the thunders of his pen are whispered flatteries: its forked lightnings, pointed sarcasms; for "the gnarled oak" he gives us "the soft myrtle:" for rocks, and seas, and mountains, artificial grass-plats, gravel-walks, and tinkling rills: for earthquakes and tempests, the breaking of a flower-pot or the fall of a china-jar: for the tug and war of the elements or the deadly strife of the passions we have

> Calm contemplation and poetic ease.

Yet within this retired and narrow circle how much, and that how exquisite, was contained! What discrimination, what wit, what delicacy, what fancy, what lurking spleen, what elegance of thought, what pampered refinement of sentiment! It is like looking at the world through a microscope, where everything assumes a new character and a new consequence, where things are seen in their minutest circumstances and slightest shades of difference; where the little becomes gigantic, the deformed beautiful, and the beautiful deformed. The wrong end of the magnifier is, to be sure, held to everything; but still the exhibition is highly curious, and we know not whether to be most

pleased or surprised. Such, at least, is the best account I am able to give of this extraordinary man, without doing injustice to him or others. It is time to refer to particular instances in his works. *The Rape of the Lock* is the best or most ingenious of these. It is the most exquisite specimen of *filigree* work ever invented. . . . It is made of gauze and silver spangles. The most glittering appearance is given to everything, to paste, pomatum, billets-doux, and patches. Airs, languid airs, breathe around; the atmosphere is perfumed with affectation. A toilette is described with the solemnity of an altar raised to the Goddess of Vanity, and the history of a silver bodkin is given with all the pomp of heraldry. No pains are spared, no profusion of ornament, no splendour of poetic diction, to set off the meanest things. The balance between the concealed irony and the assumed gravity is as nicely trimmed as the balance of power in Europe. The little is made great, and the great little. You hardly know whether to laugh or weep. It is the triumph of insignificance, the apotheosis of foppery and folly. It is the perfection of the mock-heroic! . . .

The Rape of the Lock is a double-refined essence of wit and fancy, as the *Essay on Criticism* is of wit and sense. The quantity of thought and observation in this work, for so young a man as Pope was when he wrote it, is wonderful: unless we adopt the supposition, that most men of genius spend the rest of their lives in teaching others what they themselves have learned under twenty. The conciseness and felicity of the expression are equally remarkable. Thus in reasoning on the variety of men's opinion, he says;

> 'Tis with our judgments, as our watches; none
> Go just alike, yet each believes his own.

Nothing can be more original and happy than the general remarks and illustrations in the *Essay:* the critical rules laid down are too much those of a school, and of a confined one. . . .

If he had no great faults, he is full of little errors. His grammatical construction is often lame and imperfect. In [*Eloisa to Abelard*], he says:

> There died the best of passions, Love and Fame.

This is not a legitimate ellipsis. Fame is not a passion, though love is: but his ear was evidently confused by the meeting of the sounds "love and fame," as if they of themselves immediately implied "love, and love of fame." Pope's rhymes are constantly defective, being rhymes to the eye instead of the ear, and this to a greater degree not only than in later, but than in preceding writers. The praise of his versification must be confined to its uniform smoothness and harmony. In the translation of the *Iliad,* which has been considered as his masterpiece in style and execution, he continually changes the tenses in the same sentence for the purposes of the rhyme, which shows either a want of technical resources, or great inattention to punctilious exactness. But to have done with this.

The epistle of *Eloisa to Abelard* is the only exception I can think of to the general spirit of the foregoing remarks;

and I should be disingenuous not to acknowledge that it is an exception. The foundation is in the letters themselves of Abelard and Eloisa, which are quite as impressive, but still in a different way. It is fine as a poem: it is finer as a piece of high-wrought eloquence. No woman could be supposed to write a better love-letter in verse. Besides the richness of the historical materials, the high *gusto* of the original sentiments which Pope had to work upon, there were perhaps circumstances in his own situation which made him enter into the subject with even more than a poet's feeling. The tears shed are drops gushing from the heart: the words are burning sighs breathed from the soul of love. Perhaps the poem to which it bears the greatest similarity in our language, is Dryden's "Tancred and Sigismunda," taken from Boccaccio. Pope's Eloisa will bear this comparison; and after such a test, with Boccaccio for the original author, and Dryden for the translator, it need shrink from no other. There is something exceedingly tender and beautiful in the sound of the concluding lines:

> If ever chance two wandering lovers brings
> To Paraclete's white walls and silver springs, &c.

The ***Essay on Man*** is not Pope's best work. It is a theory which Bolingbroke is supposed to have given him, and which he expanded into verse. But "he spins the thread of his verbosity finer than the staple of his argument." All that he says, "the very words, and to the self-same tune," would prove just as well that whatever is, is *wrong,* as that whatever is, is *right.* The ***Dunciad*** has splendid passages, but in general it is dull, heavy, and mechanical. . . .

His Satires are not, in general, so good as his Epistles. His enmity is effeminate and petulant from a sense of weakness, as his friendship was tender from a sense of gratitude. I do not like, for instance, his character of Chartres, or his characters of women. His delicacy often borders upon sickliness; his fastidiousness makes others fastidious. But his compliments are divine; they are equal in value to a house or an estate. . . .

Pope's letters and prose writings neither take away from nor add to his poetical reputation. There is, occasionally, a littleness of manner and an unnecessary degree of caution. He appears anxious to say a good thing in every word, as well as every sentence. They, however, give a very favourable idea of his moral character in all respects; and his letters to Atterbury, in his disgrace and exile, do equal honour to both. If I had to choose, there are one or two persons—and but one or two—that I should like to have been better than Pope!

Dryden was a better prose-writer, and a bolder and more varied versifier than Pope. He was a more vigorous thinker, a more correct and logical declaimer, and had more of what may be called strength of mind than Pope; but he had not the same refinement and delicacy of feeling. Dryden's eloquence and spirit were possessed in a higher degree by others, and in nearly the same degree by Pope himself; but that by which Pope was distinguished was an essence which he alone possessed, and of incomparable value on that sole account.

Lord Byron (letter date 1821)

SOURCE: A letter to [John Murray] on February 7, 1821, in *The Works of Lord Byron: Letters and Journals,* Vol. V, edited by Rowland E. Prothero, Charles Scribner's Sons, 1901, pp. 536-60.

[*An English poet and dramatist, Byron is considered one of the most important versifiers of the nineteenth century. In the following excerpt from a letter which refutes the points made in W. L. Bowles's lukewarm introduction to an 1806 edition of Pope's works, Byron acclaims Pope as one of the most prominent and talented figures in English literary history.*]

The depreciation of Pope is partly founded upon a false idea of the dignity of his order of poetry, to which he has partly contributed by the ingenious boast,

> That not in fancy's maze he wandered long,
> But *stooped* to Truth, and moralised his song.

He should have written 'rose to truth.' In my mind, the highest of all poetry is ethical poetry, as the highest of all earthly objects must be moral truth. Religion does not make a part of my subject; it is something beyond human powers, and has failed in all human hands except Milton's and Dante's, and even Dante's powers are involved in his delineation of human passions, though in supernatural circumstances. What made Socrates the greatest of men? His moral truth—his ethics. What proved Jesus Christ the Son of God hardly less than his miracles? His moral precepts. And if ethics have made a philosopher the first of men, and have not been disdained as an adjunct to his Gospel by the Deity himself, are we to be told that ethical poetry, or didactic poetry, or by whatever name you term it, whose object is to make men better and wiser, is not the *very first order* of poetry; and are we to be told this too by one of the priesthood? It requires more mind, more wisdom, more power, than all the 'forests' that ever were 'walked for their description,' and all the epics that ever were founded upon fields of battle. The Georgics are indisputably, and, I believe, *undisputedly,* even a finer poem than the Aeneid. Virgil knew this; he did not order *them* to be burnt.

> The proper study of mankind is man.

It is the fashion of the day to lay great stress upon what they call 'imagination' and 'invention,' the two commonest of qualities: an Irish peasant with a little whisky in his head will imagine and invent more than would furnish forth a modern poem. If Lucretius had not been spoiled by the Epicurean system, we should have had a far superior poem to any now in Existence. As mere poetry, it is the first of Latin poems. What then has ruined it? His ethics. Pope has not this defect; his moral is as pure as his poetry is glorious.

In speaking of artificial objects, I have omitted to touch upon one which I will now mention. Cannon may be presumed to be as highly poetical as art can make her objects.

Mr. B. will, perhaps, tell me that this is because they resemble that grand natural article of Sound in heaven, and Similie *(sic)* upon earth—thunder. I shall be told triumphantly, that Milton made sad work with his artillery, when he armed his devils therewithal. He did so; and this artificial object must have had much of the Sublime to attract his attention for such a conflict. He *has* made an absurd use of it; but the absurdity consists not in using *cannon* against the angels of God, but any *material* weapon. The thunder of the clouds would have been as ridiculous and vain in the hands of the devils, as the 'villainous saltpetre:' the angels were as impervious to the one as to the other. The thunder-bolts become sublime in the hands of the Almighty, not as such, but because *he* deigns to use them as a means of repelling the rebel spirits; but no one can attribute their defeat to this grand piece of natural electricity: the Almighty willed, and they fell; his word would have been enough; and Milton is as absurd, (and, in fact, *blasphemous.*) in putting material lightnings into the hands of the Godhead, as in giving him hands at all.

The artillery of the demons was but the first step of his mistake, the thunder the next, and it is a step lower. It would have been fit for Jove, but not for Jehovah. The subject altogether was essentially unpoetical; he has made more of it than another could, but it is beyond him and all men.

In a portion of his reply, Mr. B. asserts that Pope 'envied Phillips,' because he quizzed his pastorals in the *Guardian,* in that most admirable model of irony, his paper on the subject. If there was any thing enviable about Phillips, it could hardly be his pastorals. They were despicable, and Pope expressed his contempt. If Mr. Fitzgerald published a volume of sonnets, or a *Spirit of Discovery,* or a *Missionary,* and Mr. B. wrote in any periodical journal an ironical paper upon them, would this be 'envy?' The authors of the *Rejected Addresses* have ridiculed the sixteen or twenty 'first living poets' of the day, but do they 'envy' them? 'Envy' writhes, it don't laugh. The authors of the *R. A.* may despise some, but they can hardly 'envy' any of the persons whom they have parodied; and Pope could have no more envied Phillips than he did Welsted, or Theobald, or Smedley, or any other given hero of the **Dunciad.** He could not have envied him, even had he himself *not* been the greatest poet of his age. Did Mr. Inge *'envy'* Mr. Phillips when he asked him, 'How came your Pyrrhus to drive oxen and say, "I am *goaded* on by love?"' 'This question silenced poor Phillips; but it no more proceeded from 'envy' than did Pope's ridicule. Did he envy Swift? Did he envy Bolingbroke? Did he envy Gay the unparalleled success of his *Beggar's Opera?* We may be answered that these were his friends—true: but does *friendship* prevent *envy?* Study the first woman you meet with, or the first scribbler, let Mr. B. himself (whom I acquit fully of such an odious quality) study some of his own poetical intimates: the most envious man I ever heard of is a poet, and a high one; besides, it is an *universal* passion. Goldsmith envied not only the puppets for their dancing, and broke his shins in the attempt at rivalry, but was seriously angry because two pretty women received more attention

than he did. *This is envy;* but where does Pope show a sign of the passion? In that case Dryden envied the hero of his MacFlecknoe. Mr. Bowles compares, when and where he can, Pope with Cowper—(the same Cowper whom in his edition of Pope he laughs at for his attachment to an old woman, Mrs. Unwin; search and you will find it; I remember the passage, though not the page); in particular he requotes Cowper's Dutch delineation of a wood, drawn up, like a seedsman's catalogue, with an affected imitation of Milton's style, as burlesque as the *Splendid Shilling.* These two writers, for Cowper is no poet, come into comparison in one great work, the translation of Homer. . . .

> **Pope is the moral poet of all civilisation; and as such, let us hope that he will one day be the national poet of mankind. He is the only poet that never shocks; the only poet whose *faultlessness* has been made his reproach**
>
> —***Lord Byron***

I will submit to Mr. Bowles's own judgement a passage from another poem of Cowper's, to be compared with the same writer's Sylvan Sampler. In the lines "to Mary,"—

> They *needles,* once a shining store,
> For my sake restless heretofore,
> Now rust disused, and shine no more;
>   My Mary!

contain a simple, household, *"indoor,"* artificial, and ordinary image; I refer Mr. B. to the stanza, and ask if these three lines about *"needles"* are not worth all the boasted twaddling about trees, so triumphantly requoted? and yet, in *fact,* what do they convey? A homely collection of images and ideas, associated with the darning of stockings, and the hemming of shirts, and the mending of breeches; but will any one deny that they are eminently poetical and pathetic as addressed by Cowper to his nurse? The trash of trees reminds me of a saying of Sheridan's. Soon after the "Rejected Address" scene in 1812, I met Sheridan. In the course of dinner, he said, "L. B., did you know that, amongst the writers of addresses, was Whitbread himself?" I answered by an enquiry of what sort of an address he had made. "Of that," replied Sheridan, "I remember little, except that there was a *phoenix* in it."—"A phoenix!! Well, how did he describe it?"—*Like a poulterer,"* answered Sheridan: "It was green, and yellow, and red, and blue: he did not let us off for a single feather." And just such as this poulterer's account of a phoenix is Cowper's—a stick-picker's detail of a wood, with all its petty minutiæ of this, that, and the other.

One more poetical instance of the power of art, and even its *superiority* over nature, in poetry; and I have done:— the bust of *Antinous!* Is there any thing in nature like this marble, excepting the Venus? Can there be more *poetry* gathered into existence than in that wonderful creation of perfect beauty? But the poetry of this bust is in no respect derived from nature, nor from any association of moral exaltedness; for what is there in common with moral nature, and the male minion of Adrian? The very execution is *not natural,* but *super*natural, or rather *super-artificial,* for nature has never done so much.

Away, then, with this cant about nature, and "invariable principles of poetry!" A great artist will make a block of stone as sublime as a mountain, and a good poet can imbue a pack of cards with more poetry than inhabits the forests of America. It is the business and the proof of a poet to give the lie to the proverb, and sometimes to *"make a silken purse out of a sow's ear,"* and to conclude with another homely proverb, "a good workman will not find fault with his tools." [With all the] faults of Pope's translation, and all the scholarship, and pains, and time, and trouble, and blank verse of the other, who can ever read Cowper? and who will ever lay down Pope, unless for the original? Pope's was 'not Homer, it was Spondanus;' but Cowper's is not Homer either, it is not even Cowper. As a child I first read Pope's Homer with a rapture which no subsequent work could ever afford, and children are not the worst judges of their own language. As a boy I read Homer in the original, as we have all done, some of us by force, and a few by favour; under which description I come is nothing to the purpose, it is enough that I read him. As a man I have tried to read Cowper's version, and I found it impossible. Has any human reader ever succeeded? . . .

I look upon this as the declining age of English poetry; no regard for others, no selfish feeling, can prevent me from seeing this, and expressing the truth. There can be no worse sign for the taste of the times than the depreciation of Pope. It would be better to receive for proof Mr. Cobbett's rough but strong attack upon Shakespeare and Milton, than to allow this smooth and 'candid' undermining of the reputation of the most *perfect* of our poets, and the purest of our moralists. Of his power in the *passions,* in description, in the mock heroic, I leave others to descant. I take him on his strong ground as an *ethical* poet: in the former, none excel; in the mock heroic and the ethical, none equal him; and, in my mind, the latter is the highest of all poetry, because it does that in *verse,* which the greatest of men have wished to accomplish in prose. If the essence of poetry must be a *lie,* throw it to the dogs, or banish it from your republic, as Plato would have done. He who can reconcile poetry with truth and wisdom, is the only true *'poet'* in its real sense, 'the *maker,*' 'the *creator,*'—why must this mean the 'liar,' the 'feigner,' the 'tale-teller?' A man make and create better things than these.

I shall not presume to say that Pope is as high a poet as Shakespeare and Milton, though his enemy, Warton, places him immediately under them. I would no more say this than I would assert in the mosque (once Saint Sophia's), that Socrates was a greater man than Mahomet. But if I say that he is very near them, it is no more than has been asserted of Burns, who is supposed

To rival all but Shakespeare's name below.

I say nothing against this opinion. But of what *'order,'* according to the poetical aristocracy, are Burns's poems? There are his *opus magnum,* 'Tam O'Shanter,' a *tale;* the Cotter's Saturday Night, a descriptive sketch; some others in the same style: the rest are songs. So much for the *rank* of his *productions;* the *rank* of *Burns* is the very first of his art. Of Pope I have expressed my opinion elsewhere, as also of the effect which the present attempts at poetry have had upon our literature. If any great national or natural convulsion could or should overwhelm your country in such sort as to sweep Great Britain from the kingdoms of the earth, and leave only that, after all, the most living of human things, a *dead language,* to be studied and read, and imitated by the wise of future and far generations, upon foreign shores; if your literature should become the learning of mankind, divested of party cabals, temporary fashions, and national pride and prejudice;—an Englishman, anxious that the posterity of strangers should know that there had been such a thing as a British Epic and Tragedy, might wish for the preservation of Shakespeare and Milton; but the surviving World would snatch Pope from the wreck, and let the rest sink with the people. He is the moral poet of all civilisation; and as such, let us hope that he will one day be the national poet of mankind. He is the only poet that never shocks; the only poet whose *faultlessness* has been made his reproach. Cast your eye over his productions; consider their extent, and contemplate their variety:—pastoral, passion, mock heroic, translation, satire, ethics,—all excellent, and often perfect. If his great charm be his *melody,* how comes it that foreigners adore him even in their diluted translations? But I have made this letter too long. Give my compliments to Mr. Bowles.

James Russell Lowell (essay date 1871)

SOURCE: "Pope," in *Literary Essays,* Vol. IV, Houghton Mifflin and Company, 1897, pp. 1-57.

[*Lowell was a celebrated American poet and essayist, and an editor of two leading journals,* The Atlantic Monthly *and the* North American Review. *In the following excerpt from an essay originally published in 1871, Lowell favorably evaluates Pope's verse.*]

I confess that I come to the treatment of Pope with diffidence. I was brought up in the old superstition that he was the greatest poet that ever lived; and when I came to find that I had instincts of my own, and my mind was brought in contact with the apostles of a more esoteric doctrine of poetry, I felt that ardent desire for smashing the idols I had been brought up to worship, without any regard to their artistic beauty, which characterizes youthful zeal. What was it to me that Pope was called a master of style? I felt, as Addison says in his Freeholder when answering an argument in favor of the Pretender because he could speak English and George I. could not, "that I did not wish to be tyrannized over in the best English that ever was spoken." The young demand thoughts that find an echo in their real and not their acquired nature, and care very little about the dress they are put in. It is later that we learn to like the conventional, as we do olives. There was a time when I could not read Pope, but disliked him on principle, as old Roger Ascham seems to have felt about Italy when he says, "I was once in Italy myself, but I thank God my abode there was only nine days."

But Pope fills a very important place in the history of English poetry, and must be studied by every one who would come to a clear knowledge of it. I have since read over every line that Pope ever wrote, and every letter written by or to him, and that more than once. If I have not come to the conclusion that he is the greatest of poets, I believe that I am at least in a condition to allow him every merit that is fairly his. . . . Pope as a literary man represents precision and grace of expression; but as a poet he represents something more,—nothing less, namely, than one of those eternal controversies of taste which will last as long as the imagination and understanding divide men between them. It is not a matter to be settled by any amount of argument or demonstration. There are born Popists or Wordsworthians, Lockists or Kantists, and there is nothing more to be said of the matter.

Wordsworth was not in a condition to do Pope justice. A man brought up in sublime mountain solitudes, and whose nature was a solitude more vast than they, walking an earth which quivered with the throe of the French Revolution, the child of an era of profound mental and moral movement, it could not be expected that he should be in sympathy with the poet of artificial life. Moreover, he was the apostle of imagination, and came at a time when the school which Pope founded had degenerated into a mob of mannerists who wrote with ease, and who with their congenial critics united at once to decry poetry which brought in the dangerous innovation of having a soul in it.

But however it may be with poets, it is very certain that a reader is happiest whose mind is broad enough to enjoy the natural school for its nature, and the artificial for its artificiality, provided they be only good of their kind. At any rate, we must allow that the man who can produce one perfect work is either a great genius or a very lucky one; and so far as we who read are concerned, it is of secondary importance which. And Pope has done this in the **Rape of the Lock.** For wit, fancy, invention, and keeping, it has never been surpassed. I do not say there is in it poetry of the highest order, or that Pope is a poet whom any one would choose as the companion of his best hours. There is no inspiration in it, no trumpet-call, but for pure entertainment it is unmatched. . . .

Elsewhere he has shown more force, more wit, more reach of thought, but nowhere such a truly artistic combination of elegance and fancy. His genius has here found its true direction, and the very same artificiality, which in his pastorals was unpleasing, heightens the effect, and adds to the general keeping. As truly as Shakespeare is the poet of man, as God made him, dealing with great passions and innate motives, so truly is Pope the poet of society, the delineator of manners, the exposer of those motives which

may be called *acquired,* whose spring is in institutions and habits of purely worldly origin. . . .

The theory of the poem is excellent. The heroic is out of the question in fine society. It is perfectly true that almost every door we pass in the street closes upon its private tragedy, but the moment a *great* passion enters a man he passes at once out of the artificial into the human. So long as he continues artificial, the sublime is a conscious absurdity to him. The mock-heroic then is the only way in which the petty actions and sufferings of the fine world can be epically treated, and the contrast continually suggested with subjects of larger scope and more dignified treatment, makes no small part of the pleasure and sharpens the point of the wit. The invocation is admirable:—

> Say, what strange motive, Goddess, could compel,
> A well-bred lord to assault a gentle belle?
> O say what stranger cause, yet unexplored,
> Could make a gentle belle reject a lord?

The keynote of the poem is here struck, and we are able to put ourselves in tune with it. It is not a parody of the heroic style, but only a setting it in satirical juxtaposition with cares and events and modes of thought with which it is in comical antipathy, and while *it* is not degraded, *they* are shown in their triviality. . . . The mythology of the Sylphs is full of the most fanciful wit; indeed, wit infused with fancy is Pope's peculiar merit. . . . Throughout this poem the satiric wit of Pope peeps out in the pleasantest little smiling ways, as where, in describing the toilet-table, he says:—

> Here files of pins extend their shining rows,
> Puffs, powders, patches, Bibles, *billet-doux.* . . .

But more than the wit and fancy, I think, the perfect keeping of the poem deserves admiration. Except a touch of grossness, here and there, there is the most pleasing harmony in all the conceptions and images. . . .

In short, the whole poem more truly deserves the name of a creation than anything Pope ever wrote. The action is confined to a world of his own, the supernatural agency is wholly of his own contrivance, and nothing is allowed to overstep the limitations of the subject. It ranks by itself as one of the purest works of human fancy; whether that fancy be strictly poetical or not is another matter. If we compare it with the "Midsummer-night's Dream," an uncomfortable doubt is suggested. The perfection of form in the **Rape of the Lock** is to me conclusive evidence that in it the natural genius of Pope found fuller and freer expression than in any other of his poems. The others are aggregates of brilliant passages rather than harmonious wholes.

It is a droll illustration of the inconsistencies of human nature, a more profound satire than Pope himself ever wrote, that his fame should chiefly rest upon the **Essay on Man.** It has been praised and admired by men of the most opposite beliefs, and men of no belief at all. Bishops and free-thinkers have met here on a common ground of sympathetic approval. And, indeed, there is no particular faith in it. It is a droll medley of inconsistent opinions. It proves only two things beyond a question,—that Pope was not a great thinker; and that wherever he found a thought, no matter what, he could express it so tersely, so clearly, and with such smoothness of versification as to give it an everlasting currency. Hobbes's unwieldy Leviathan, left stranded there on the shore of the last age, and nauseous with the stench of its selfishness,—from this Pope distilled a fragrant oil with which to fill the brilliant lamps of his philosophy,—lamps like those in the tombs of alchemists, that go out the moment the healthy air is let in upon them. The only positive doctrines in the poem are the selfishness of Hobbes set to music, and the Pantheism of Spinoza brought down from mysticism to commonplace. Nothing can be more absurd than many of the dogmas taught in this *Essay on Man.* For example, Pope affirms explicitly that instinct is something better than reason:—

> See him from Nature rising slow to art,
> To copy instinct then was reason's part;
> Thus, then, to man the voice of nature spake;—
> Go, from the creatures thy instructions take;
> Learn from the beasts what food the thickets
>   yield;
> Learn from the birds the physic of the field;
> The arts of building from the bee receive;
> Learn of the mole to plough, the worm to weave;
> Learn of the little nautilus to sail,
> Spread the thin oar, or catch the driving gale.

I say nothing of the quiet way in which the general term "nature" is substituted for God, but how unutterably void of reasonableness is the theory that Nature would have left her highest product, man, destitute of that instinct with which she had endowed her other creatures! As if reason were not the most sublimated form of instinct. The accuracy on which Pope prided himself, and for which he is commended, was not accuracy of thought so much as of expression. . . .

However great his merit in expression, I think it impossible that a true poet could have written such a satire as the *Dunciad,* which is even nastier than it is witty. It is filthy even in a filthy age, and Swift himself could not have gone beyond some parts of it. One's mind needs to be sprinkled with some disinfecting fluid after reading it. I do not remember that any other poet ever made poverty a crime. And it is wholly without discrimination. De Foe is set in the pillory forever; and George Wither, the author of that charming poem, "Fair Virtue," classed among the dunces. And was it not in this age that loose Dick Steele paid his wife the finest compliment ever paid to woman, when he said "that to love her was a liberal education"?

Even in the *Rape of the Lock,* the fancy is that of a wit rather than a poet. . . .

Joseph Warton, in summing up at the end of his essay on the genius and writings of Pope, says that the largest part of his works "is of the *didactic, moral,* and *satiric;* and, consequently, not of the most *poetic* species of *poetry;* whence it is manifest that *good sense* and *judgment* were

his characteristical excellences rather than *fancy* and *invention.*" It is plain that in any strict definition there can be only one kind of poetry, and that what Warton really meant to say was that Pope was not a poet at all. . . .

It will hardly be questioned that the man who writes what is still piquant and rememberable, a century and a quarter after his death, was a man of genius. But there are two modes of uttering such things as cleave to the memory of mankind. They may be said or sung. I do not think that Pope's verse anywhere sings, but it should seem that the abiding presence of fancy in his best work forbids his exclusion from the rank of poet. The atmosphere in which he habitually dwelt was an essentially prosaic one, the language habitual to him was that of conversation and society, so that he lacked the help of that fresher dialect which seems like inspiration in the elder poets. His range of associations was of that narrow kind which is always vulgar, whether it be found in the village or the court. Certainly he has not the force and majesty of Dryden in his better moods, but he has a grace, a finesse, an art of being pungent, a sensitiveness to impressions, that would incline us to rank him with Voltaire (whom in many ways he so much resembles), as an author with whom the gift of writing was primary, and that of verse secondary. No other poet that I remember ever wrote prose which is so purely prose as his; and yet, in any impartial criticism, the *Rape of the Lock* sets him even as a poet far above many men more largely endowed with poetic feeling and insight than he.

A great deal must be allowed to Pope for the age in which he lived, and not a little, I think, for the influence of Swift. In his own province he still stands unapproachably alone. If to be the greatest satirist of individual men, rather than of human nature, if to be the highest expression which the life of the court and the ball-room has ever found in verse, if to have added more phrases to our language than any other but Shakespeare, if to have charmed four generations make a man a great poet,—then he is one. He was the chief founder of an artificial style of writing, which in his hands was living and powerful, because he used it to express artificial modes of thinking and an artificial state of society. Measured by any high standard of imagination, he will be found wanting; tried by any test of wit, he is unrivalled.

Leslie Stephen (essay date 1873)

SOURCE: "Pope as a Moralist," in *The Cornhill Magazine,* Vol. XXVIII, No. 167, November, 1873, pp. 583-604.

[*Many scholars consider Stephen the most important literary critic of the Victorian Age after Matthew Arnold. In the following excerpt, Stephen judges the moralistic quality of Pope's verse.*]

The extraordinary vitality of Pope's writings is a remarkable phenomenon in its way. Few reputations have been exposed to such perils at the hands of open enemies or of imprudent friends. In his lifetime "the wasp of Twickenham" could sting through a sevenfold covering of pride or stupidity. Lady Mary and Lord Hervey writhed and retaliated with little more success than the poor denizens of Grub Street. But it is more remarkable that Pope seems to be stinging well into the second century after his death. His writings resemble those fireworks which, after they have fallen to the ground and been apparently quenched, suddenly break out again into sputtering explosions. The waters of a literary revolution have passed over him without putting him out. Though much of his poetry has ceased to interest us, so many of his brilliant couplets still survive that probably no dead writer, with the solitary exception of Shakspeare, is more frequently quoted at the present day. It is in vain that he is abused, ridiculed, and even declared to be no poet at all. The school of Wordsworth regarded him as the embodiment of the corrupting influence in English poetry; more recently M. Taine has attacked him, chiefly, as it would seem, for daring to run counter to M. Taine's theories; and, hardest fate of all, the learned editor [A. W. Ward] who is now bringing out a conclusive edition of his writings has had his nerves so hardened by familiarity with poor Pope's many iniquities, that his notes are one prolonged attack on his author's morality, orthodoxy, and even poetical power. We seem to be listening to a Boswell animated by the soul of a Dennis. And yet Pope survives, as indeed the bitterness of his assailants testifies. When controversialists spend volumes in confuting an adversary who has been for centuries in his grave, their unconscious testimony to his vitality is generally of more significance than their demonstration that he ought to be insignificant. Drowning a dead rat is too dismal an occupation to be long pursued; and whilst we watch the stream descending, we may generally assume that the rat has still some life in him.

Pope, moreover, has received testimonies of a less equivocal kind. Byron called him, with characteristic vehemence, the "great moral poet of all times, of all climes, of all feelings, and of all stages of existence"; though it is not less characteristic that Byron was at the same time helping to dethrone the idol before which he prostrated himself. Ste.-Beuve, again, has thrown the shield of his unrivalled critical authority over Pope when attacked by M. Taine; and a critic, who may sometimes be overstrained in his language, but who never speaks as a critic without showing the keenest insight, has more recently spoken of Pope in terms which recall Byron's enthusiasm. "Pope," says Mr. Ruskin, in one of his Oxford lectures, "is the most perfect representative we have, since Chaucer, of the true English mind"; and he adds that his hearers will find, as they study Pope, that he has expressed for them, "in the strictest language and within the briefest limits, every law of art, of criticism, of economy, of policy, and finally of a benevolence, humble, rational, and resigned, contented with its allotted share of life, and trusting the problem of its salvation to Him in whose hand lies that of the universe." These remarks are added by way of illustrating the relation of art to morals, and enforcing the great principle that a noble style can only proceed from a sincere heart. "You can only learn to speak as these men spoke by learning what these men were." When we ask impartially what Pope was, we may possibly be inclined to doubt the com-

plete soundness of the eulogy upon his teaching. Meanwhile, however, Byron and Mr. Ruskin agree in holding up Pope as an instance, almost as the typical instance, of that kind of poetry which is directly intended to enforce a lofty morality. To posses such a charm for two great writers, who, however different in all other respects, strikingly agree in this, that their opinions are singularly independent of conventional judgments, is some proof that Pope possessed great merits as a poetical interpreter of morals. Without venturing into the wider ocean of poetical criticism, I will endeavour in this article to inquire what was the specific element in Pope's poetry which explains, if it does not justify, this enthusiastic praise.

I shall venture to assume, indeed, that Pope was a genuine poet. Nor do I understand how any one who has really studied his writings can deny to him that title, unless by help of a singularly narrow definition of its meaning. It is sufficient to name the ***Rape of the Lock,*** which is allowed, even by his bitterest critics, to be a masterpiece of delicate fancy. . . . But a delicate fancy is a delicate fancy still, even when employed about the paraphernalia of modern life; a truth which Byron maintained, though not in an unimpeachable form, in his controversy with Bowles. We sometimes talk as if our ancestors were nothing but hoops and wigs; and forget that human passions exist even under the most complex structures of starch and buckram. And consequently we are very apt to make a false estimate of the precise nature of that change which fairly entitles us to call Pope's age prosaic. In showering down our epithets of artificial, sceptical, and utilitarian, we not seldom forget what kind of figure we are ourselves likely to make in the eyes of our own descendants.

Whatever be the position rightly to be assigned to Pope in the British Walhalla, his own theory has been unmistakably expressed. He boasts

> That not in fancy's maze he wandered long,
> But stooped to truth and moralised his song.

His theory is compressed into one of the innumerable aphorisms which have to some degree lost their original sharpness of definition, because they have passed, as current coinage, through so many hands.

> The proper study of mankind is man.

The saying is in form about identical with Goethe's remark that man is properly the only object which interests man. The two poets, indeed, understood the doctrine in a very different way. Pope's interpretation was narrow and mechanical. He would place such limitations upon the sphere of human interest as to exclude, perhaps, the greatest part of what we generally mean by poetry. How much, for example, would have to be suppressed if we sympathised with Pope's condemnation of the works in which

> Pure description holds the place of sense.

A large proportion of such poets as Thomson and Cowper would disappear, Wordsworth's pages would show fearful gaps, and Keats would be in risk of summary suppression. We may doubt whether much would be left of Spenser, from whom both Keats and Pope, like so many other of our poets, drew inspiration in their youth. Fairyland would be deserted, and the poet condemned to working upon ordinary commonplaces in broad daylight: The principle which Pope proclaimed is susceptible of the inverse application. Poetry, it really proves, may rightly concern itself with inanimate nature, with pure description, or with the presentation of lovely symbols not definitely identified with any cut and dried saws of moral wisdom; because there is no part of the visible universe to which we have not some relation, and the most ethereal dreams that ever visited a youthful poet "on summer eve by haunted stream" are in some sense reflections of the passions and interests that surround our daily life. Pope, however, as the man more fitted than any other fully to interpret the mind of his own age, inevitably gives a different construction to a very sound maxim. He rightly assumes that man is his proper study; but then by man he means not the genus, but a narrow species of the human being. "Man" means Bolingbroke, and Walpole, and Swift, and Curll, and Theobald; it does not mean man as the product of a long series of generations and part of the great universe of inextricably involved forces. He cannot understand the man of distant ages; Homer is to him not the spontaneous voice of a ruder age, but a clever artist, whose gods and heroes are consciously-constructed parts of an artificial "machinery." Nature has, for him, ceased to be inhabited by sylphs and fairies, except to amuse the fancies of fine ladies and gentlemen, and has not yet received a new interest from the fairy tales of science. The old ideal of chivalry merely suggests the sneers of Cervantes, or even the buffoonery of Butler's wit, and has not undergone restoration at the hands of modern romanticists. Politics are not associated in his mind with any great social upheaval, but with a series of petty squabbles for places and pensions, in which bribery is the great moving force. What he means by religion often seems to be less the recognition of a divine element in the world than a series of bare metaphysical demonstrations too frigid to produce enthusiasm or to stimulate the imagination. And, therefore, he inevitably interests himself chiefly in what is certainly a perennial source of interest—the passions and thoughts of the men and women immediately related to himself; and it may be remarked, in passing, that if this narrows the range of Pope's poetry, the error is not so vital as a modern delusion of the opposite kind. Because poetry should not be brought into too close a contact with the prose of daily life, we sometimes seem to think that it must have no relation to daily life at all, and consequently convert it into a mere luxurious dreaming, where the beautiful very speedily degenerates into the pretty or the picturesque. Because poetry need not be always a pointblank fire of moral platitudes, we occasionally declare that there is no connection at all between poetry and morality, and that all art is good which is for the moment agreeable. Such theories must end in reducing all poetry and art to be at best more or less elegant trifling for the amusement of the indolent: and to those who uphold them, Pope's example may be of some use. If he went too far in the direction of identifying poetry with preaching, he was not wrong in assuming that

poetry should involve preaching, though by an indirect method. Morality and art are not independent, though not identical; for both, as Mr. Ruskin shows in the passage just quoted, are only admirable when the expression of healthful and noble natures.

Taking Pope's view of his poetical office, there remain considerable difficulties in estimating the value of the lesson which he taught with so much energy. The difficulties result both from that element which was common to his contemporaries and from that which was supplied by Pope's own idiosyncrasies. The commonplaces in which Pope takes such infinite delight have become very stale for us. Assuming their perfect sincerity, we cannot understand how anybody should have thought of enforcing them with such amazing emphasis. We constantly feel a shock like that which surprises the reader of Young's *Night Thoughts* when he finds it asserted, in all the pomp of blank verse, that

> Procrastination is the thief of time.

The maxim has rightly been consigned to copybooks. And a great deal of Pope's moralising is of the same order. We do not want denunciations of misers. Nobody at the present day keeps gold in an old stocking. When we read the observation,

> 'Tis strange the miser should his cares employ
> To gain the riches he can ne'er enjoy,

we can only reply in the familiar French, *connu!* We knew that when we were in petticoats. . . .

We cannot give him credit for being really moved by such platitudes. We have the same feeling as when a modern preacher employs twenty minutes in proving that it is wrong to worship idols of wood and stone. But, unfortunately, there is a reason more peculiar to Pope which damps our sympathy still more decidedly. It cannot be fairly denied that all recent inquiries have gone to strengthen those suspicions of his honesty which were common even amongst his contemporaries. Mr. Elwin has been disgusted by the revelations of his hero's baseness, till his indignation has become a painful burden to himself and his readers. Speaking bluntly, indeed, we admit that lying is a vice, and that Pope was in a small way one of the most consummate liars that ever lived. He speaks, himself, of "equivocating pretty genteelly" in regard to one of his peccadilloes. But Pope's equivocation is, to the equivocation of ordinary men, what a tropical fern is to the stunted representatives of the same species in England. It grows until the fowls of the air can rest on its branches. His disposition, in short, amounts to a monomania. That a man with intensely irritable nerves, and so fragile in constitution that his life might, without exaggeration, be called a "long disease," should defend himself by the natural weapons of the weak, equivocation and subterfuge, when exposed to the brutal horseplay common in that day, is indeed not surprising. But Pope's delight in artifice was something phenomenal. He could hardly "drink tea without a stratagem," or, as Lady Bolingbroke put it, was a politician about cabbages and turnips; and certainly he did not despise the arts known to politicians on a larger stage. . . .

The insincerity which degraded Pope's life detracts from our pleasure in his poetry. Take, for example, the *Epistle to Dr. Arbuthnot,* which is amongst his most perfect works. Some of the boasts in it, as we shall presently remark, are apparently quite justified by the facts. But what are we to say to such a passage as this?—

> I was not born for courts or great affairs;
> I pay my debts, believe, and say my prayers;
> Can sleep without a poem in my head,
> Nor know if Dennis be alive or dead.

Admitting his independence, and not inquiring too closely into his prayers, can we forget that the gentleman who could sleep without a poem in his head called up a servant four times in one night of "the dreadful winter of Forty" to supply him with paper, lest he should lose a thought? Or what is the value of a professed indifference to Dennis from the man distinguished beyond all other writers for the bitterness of his resentment against all small critics; who disfigured his best poems by his petty vengeance for old attacks; and who could not refrain from sneering at poor Dennis, even in the Prologue which he condescended to write for the benefit of his dying antagonist?

Thus we are always pursued, in reading Pope, by disagreeable misgivings. We don't know what comes from the heart, and what from the lips; when the real man is speaking, and when we are only listening to old commonplaces skilfully vamped. There is always, if we please, a bad interpretation to be placed upon his finest sentiments. His indignation against the vicious is confused with his hatred of personal enemies; he protests most loudly that he is honest when he is "equivocating most genteelly;" his independence may be called selfishness or avarice; his toleration simple indifference; and even his affection for his friends a decorous picture which will never lead him to the slightest sacrifice of his own vanity or comfort. A critic of the highest order is provided with an Ithuriel spear, which discriminates the sham sentiments from the true. As a banker's clerk can tell a bad coin by its ring on the counter, without need of a testing apparatus, the true critic can instinctively estimate the amount of bullion in Pope's epigrammatic tinsel. But criticism of this kind, as Pope truly says, is as rare as poetical genius. Humbler writers must be content to take their weights and measures, or, in other words, to test their first impressions, by such external evidence as is available. They must proceed cautiously in these delicate matters, and instead of leaping to the truth by a rapid intuition, patiently inquire what light is thrown upon Pope's sincerity by the recorded events of his life, and a careful cross-examination of the various witnesses to his character. They must, indeed, keep in mind Mr. Ruskin' excellent canon,—that good fruit, even in moralizing, can only be borne by a good tree. Where Pope has succeeded in casting into enduring form some valuable moral sentiment, we may therefore give him credit for having at least felt it sincerely. If he did not always act

upon it, the weakness is not peculiar to Pope. Time, indeed, has partly done the work for us. In Pope, more than in almost any other writer, the grain has sifted itself from the chaff. The jewels have remained after the flimsy embroidery in which they were fixed has fallen into decay. Such a result was natural from his mode of composition. He caught at some inspiration of the moment; he cast it roughly into form; brooded over it; retouched it again and again; and when he had brought it to the very highest polish of which his art was capable, placed it in a pigeonhole to be fitted, when the opportunity offered, into an appropriate corner of his mosaic-work. . . .

Pope was more than a mere literary artist, though he was an artist of unparalleled excellence in his own department. He was a man in whom there was the seed of many good thoughts, though choked in their development by the growth of innumerable weeds. And I will venture, in conclusion, to adduce one more proof of the justice of a lenient verdict. . . . Pope, we have seen, is recognised even by judges of the land only through the medium of Byron; and therefore the *Universal Prayer* may possibly be unfamiliar to some readers. If so, it will do them no harm to read over again a few of its verses. Perhaps, after that experience, they will admit that the little cripple of Twickenham, distorted as were his instincts after he had been stretched on the rack of this rough world, and grievous as were his offences against the laws of decency and morality, had yet in him a noble strain of eloquence significant of deep religious sentiment.

Matthew Arnold (essay date 1880)

SOURCE: An introduction to *The English Poets: Chaucer to Donne,* Vol. I, edited by Thomas Humphry Ward, 1880. Reprint by Macmillan Company, 1920, pp. xvii-xlvii.

[*Although Arnold was a poet and a commentator on the social and moral life in England, he was essentially an apologist for literary criticism. In the following summary, recognized as the quintessential nineteenth-century view of Pope, he discusses the poet and his literary predecessor, John Dryden, as writers of classic English prose, not poetry.*]

Are Dryden and Pope poetical classics? Is the historic estimate, which represents them as such, and which has been so long established that it cannot easily give way, the real estimate? Wordsworth and Coleridge, as is well known, denied it, but the authority of Wordsworth and Coleridge does not weigh much with the young generation, and there are many signs to show that the eighteenth century and its judgments are coming into favour again. Are the favourite poets of the eighteenth century classics?

It is impossible within my present limits to discuss the question fully. And what man of letters would not shrink from seeming to dispose dictatorially of the claims of two men who are, at any rate, such masters in letters as Dryden and Pope; two men of such admirable talent, both of them, and one of them, Dryden, a man, on all sides, of such energetic and genial power? And yet, if we are to gain the full benefit from poetry, we must have the real estimate of it. I cast about for some mode of arriving, in the present case, at such an estimate without offence. And perhaps the best way is to begin, as it is easy to begin, with cordial praise.

When we find Chapman, the Elizabethan translator of Homer, expressing himself in his preface thus: 'Though truth in her very nakedness sits in so deep a pit, that from Gades to Aurora and Ganges few eyes can sound her, I hope yet those few here will so discover and confirm, that, the date being out of her darkness in this morning of our poet, he shall now gird his temples with the sun,'—we pronounce that such a prose is intolerable. When we find Milton writing: 'And long it was not after, when I was confirmed in this opinion, that he, who would not be frustrate of his hope to write well hereafter in laudable things, ought himself to be a true poem,'—we pronounce that such a prose has its own grandeur, but that it is obsolete and inconvenient. But when we find Dryden telling us: 'What Virgil wrote in the vigour of his age, in plenty and at ease, I have undertaken to translate in my declining years; struggling with wants, oppressed with sickness, curbed in my genius, liable to be misconstrued in all I write,'—then we exclaim that here at last we have the true English prose, a prose such as we would all gladly use if we only knew how. Yet Dryden was Milton's contemporary.

But after the Restoration the time had come when our nation felt the imperious need of a fit prose. So, too, the time had likewise come when our nation felt the imperious need of freeing itself from the absorbing preoccupation which religion in the Puritan age had exercised. It was impossible that this freedom should be brought about without some negative excess, without some neglect and impairment of the religious life of the soul; and the spiritual history of the eighteenth century shows us that the freedom was not achieved without them. Still, the freedom was achieved; the preoccupation, an undoubtedly baneful and retarding one if it had continued, was got rid of. And as with religion amongst us at that period, so it was also with letters. A fit prose was a necessity; but it was impossible that a fit prose should establish itself amongst us without some touch of frost to the imaginative life of the soul. The needful qualities for a fit prose are regularity, uniformity, precision, balance. The men of letters, whose destiny it may be to bring their nation to the attainment of a fit prose, must of necessity, whether they work in prose or in verse, give a predominating, an almost exclusive attention to the qualities of regularity, uniformity, precision, balance. But an almost exclusive attention to these qualities involves some repression and silencing of poetry.

We are to regard Dryden as the puissant and glorious founder, Pope as the splendid high-priest, of our age of prose and reason, of our excellent and indispensable eighteenth century. For the purposes of their mission and destiny their poetry, like their prose, is admirable. Do you ask me whether Dryden's verse, take it almost where you will, is not good?

> A milk-white Hind, immortal and unchanged,
> Fed on the lawns and in the forest ranged.

I answer: Admirable for the purposes of the inaugurator of an age of prose and reason. Do you ask me whether Pope's verse, take it almost where you will, is not good?

> To Hounslow Heath I point, and Banstead
>   Down;
> Thence comes your mutton, and these chicks my
>   own.

I answer: Admirable for the purposes of the high-priest of an age of prose and reason. But do you ask me whether such verse proceeds from men with an adequate poetic criticism of life, from men whose criticism of life has a high seriousness, or even, without that high seriousness, has poetic largeness, freedom, insight, benignity? Do you ask me whether the application of ideas to life in the verse of these men, often a powerful application, no doubt, is a powerful *poetic* application? Do you ask me whether the poetry of these men has either the matter or the inseparable manner of such an adequate poetic criticism; whether it has the accent of

> Absent thee from felicity awhile . . .

or of

> And what is else not to be overcome . . .

or of

> O martyr souded in virginitee!

I answer: It has not and cannot have them; it is the poetry of the builders of an age of prose and reason. Though they may write in verse, though they may in a certain sense be masters of the art of versification, Dryden and Pope are not classics of our poetry, they are classics of our prose.

George Saintsbury (essay date 1916)

SOURCE: "Alexander Pope and His Kingdom," in *The Peace of the Augustans: A Survey of Eighteenth Century Literature as a Place of Rest and Refreshment,* G. Bell and Sons, Ltd., 1916, pp. 43-104.

[Saintsbury has been called the most influential literary historian and critic of the late nineteenth and early twentieth centuries. His studies of French literature have established him as a leading authority on such writers as Guy de Maupassant and Honoré de Balzac. In the following excerpt, Saintsbury praises the superior phrasing and wit in Pope's verse, despite the many faults he perceives in the poet's work.]

There is a tendency which, being human, is like most human things not unpardonable, but like many human things rather irritating—to try to make out that everything is something else. In illustration of this a rather well-known Frenchman once wrote a book, not without merit, on *Le Romantisme des classiques;* and, to append small things to great in the old manner, a distinguished American once endeavoured, good-humouredly enough, to prove "Rymerism" in the present humble writer, who had declared his adhesion to Macaulay's dictum that Rymer was the worst critic who ever lived. To rise again to the great, it is notorious that the character of Pope—not so much his personal character, for that is now pretty well beyond dispute, as the character of his poetry—has always been a favourite subject for wrangling and paradox and self-contradictions. In his own day his superiors, such as Swift, and his equals, whether jealous or not, such as Addison, had no doubt about his greatness, while the very "Grub Street" vermin, whom he foolishly provoked and persecuted, evidently regarded him with almost as much envy and secret admiration as hatred. The long and fitful battle on the "Is Pope a poet?" question was at nearly all its revivals a battle of feints, paradoxes, and topsy-turvifications; not a few of his assailants or "discounters," such as Warton, make observations and reservations which would rather astonish those who take them, unread, as wholly on the Romantic side; more than one of his defenders, such as Byron, adopt lines of defence which admit of dangerous flank attack; and as has been already indicated, his latest partisans have continued the process by ringing changes on the ambiguities of words like "nature," "wit," and the like. In such a case it is perhaps best to state frankly the views of the present writer. It seems to him:

I. That to deny poetry to Pope is absurd.

II. That any one who denies him something like a chief if not the chief place in his own division of poets, unquestionable as such, will have his work cut out to make the denial good.

III. That Joseph Warton was perfectly right in his main position—that Pope was not *transcendently* a poet: though Warton frequently blundered and faltered in maintaining this.

Those who *simpliciter* deny poetry to Pope must needs deny, as a major, the definition or description of poetry elsewhere given; and it is a fallacy to reply that this position ought to be generally established first. For, as Dante says, startlingly to some but with incontestable truth, "the business of science is not to prove but to explain its subject"; or, in other words, the axioms and postulates with which we start it are not its problems or theorems. Now that Pope displayed at least two of the qualifications to be laid down as necessary for the poet—vivid expression of his actual subjects and artistic use of such metre as he actually employed—is simply undeniable. To urge that there are large ranges of subject which he perhaps could not, and certainly did not treat; and that there was only a limited region of metre in which he was

at home, would at best be legitimate in reference to the third position—his claim to poetical transcendency. It is practically "out of order" and irrelevant as regards the first and second. Moreover, his extraordinary felicity of expression, and his wonderful command of such metre as was congenial to him, appear to have been, according to the hackneyed phrase of poets, not merely congenial but congenital. Since he was not "the least liar" (as all poets are, according to the other tag) but the most lying of all poets and persons, we cannot accept absolutely the dates which he gives us of his precocities. But we certainly have no remains of what the elder Mr. Pope may have censured as "bad rhymes," and there is no doubt that some which must have been early are astonishingly good. It was as if Pope had been served heir by Providence to Dryden; and had entered upon his inheritance and begun to improve it in certain directions almost before Dryden died.

To part, and what some may think (to use an everlastingly treacherous word) the "greatest" part, of the inheritance he did not indeed succeed. He could not forge and wield the Olympian thunderbolt of Dryden's couplet; even had he been able to do so he could not have charged it with the massive strength of Dryden's sense. But he might possibly claim the Apollonian darts, though it is to be feared that they could deserve the epithet of "mild" only in the hypereuphemistic sense of the Greek itself; for they were never very kindly, and were frequently poisoned. His processes of refinement of form are extremely simple, though idle partisanship, or the mere desire to be different, has sometimes denied this. In practice he never quite abandoned the license of Alexandrine and triplet, but he reduced it more and more; he emphasised, to the point of making a sort of continuous crease down the page, the importance of the central pause; he redoubled the antithesis between verbs, adjectives, substantives in the two halves of the same line; he increased the separation of the couplets; he toned off the final rhymes to as light a character as possible; and indulged very seldom in "wrenched accent" (trochees for iambs) or in trisyllabic feet. These are the simple, almost the sole rules for the construction of the "fiddle." That the "rosin"—the application of which allows the thing in all but a few cases to escape the monotony whereunto in other hands it usually fell—is more of a secret is true; but it also is not quite undiscoverable or unanalysable.

This secret is, indeed, a sort of *secret de Polichinelle*—a position which hardly anybody has denied, though it cannot be said that everybody has exactly apprehended it. It lies in the fact that Pope, with a consummate command of one form of poetical, that is to say metrical, expression, had an even more consummate command of the manners of diction and phrase which are suited to that form; and a third faculty—less real but almost more specious than either of the others—of presenting thought—or the appearance of thought—which was once more exactly suitable to the words, and the verse, and the actual material subject. In this last point his extreme superficiality has long been more or less admitted, except by an Old Guard of partisans whose small stronghold of prejudice is perhaps impregnable, but can be simply left alone, as it has "no military importance." He practically never thinks for himself or sees for himself, while, except in some touches of personal affection and many more of personal resentment and spite, he scarcely ever feels for himself. It is always what somebody else has thought, the *communis sensus* of some particular nation, ancient or modern, or it may be both, that Pope expresses so well, with such admirable "wit" in the various meanings which he himself attaches to the word. It has been recognised a hundred times that the famous couplet, the component parts of which have just been woven into prose, exactly describes him on the best side of his stuff. There is of course a side not so good. Lady Mary was perfectly right as to fact when she told how her original admiration of the *Essay on Criticism* ceased when she found it was all stolen from the ancients; except that, if she had herself known a little more, she might have perceived that most of it was stolen or borrowed at second-hand. Warburton knew perfectly well what he was doing when he plastered and varnished and buttressed with comment and exposition Pope's well meant, admirably expressed, but sometimes almost non-sensical and still more often platitudinous attempts to build a mansion of Bolingbroke's half-baked bricks and his own untempered mortar in the *Essay on Man.* The amiable endeavours to discover in *The Dunciad* a generous defence of good literature against those who disgraced it become distressingly inapposite, when one remembers that there is practically in the whole book, whether as originally constructed or as recast later, nothing, till you come to the fine but utterly disconnected close, except personal and sometimes far from honest caricatures of individual writers obnoxious to the poet, some of them quite harmless, most quite insignificant, and hardly any, except Curll, in any way a "disgrace to literature." There *is* something first-hand in that strange **"Elegy on an Unfortunate Lady,"** which is the one mystery still remaining after generations of unremitting and generally damaging investigations. But elsewhere, with the possible exception of *The Rape of the Lock,* in the comic, to serve as pendant to the *Elegy* in the tragic vein, the whole of Pope's work may be called translation, and not merely the *Statius,* the *Homer,* and the other confessed instances. It is always, and not merely when he has a book before him, that he seems to be working from some brief, carefully and extensively drawn up for him by a clever "devil," chipping into final form a statue blocked out by an intelligent, but himself not very original "ghost." Carlyle, harshly but not perhaps unjustly, declared that there was not one great thought in all the hundred volumes of Voltaire. It would be scarcely rash to say that there is not an original thought, sentiment, image, or example of any of the other categories of poetic substance to be found in the half a hundred thousand verses of Pope. But even here the triumphant *sense* of the century saved him from mere silliness always, and nearly (not quite) always from mere *galimatias;* while his quintessential possession of its own peculiar form of wit infused something into the very matter of the thought or subject which, till you examine it rather carefully, may look like originality.

But if not wholly, yet still to some extent to be separated from this "stuff and substance" of wit, as well as (with the same proviso) from the, in its own way, unrivalled supremacy of versification above admitted, there remains—and for our purpose remains as of supreme importance—that wonderful faculty of mere expression, of command over diction and phrase, which has been all but universally allowed him. His limits, even in this way, may not be very wide; he never delves beneath the surface for hidden wealth of suggestion or soars into the ether for unexpected flights of it. But, in his own way and under his own conditions, it is almost impossible for him to make a mistake, or if he has made one at first (the "Atticus" is a specimen) not to correct it. The thought may be trifling, obvious, at times rather base; the sentiment may be plainly insincere; the very wit, when you roll it over a little on your mind's tongue, may be slightly vapid; the very verse, if you go on too long with it, may impress you with a sense of monotonous mannerism. There are often bad rhymes (not including those affected by change of pronunciation) to disgust one sort of taste; there is only too frequently bad blood to disgust another. But, with the rarest exception, the phrasing is triumphant, and those who can once perceive and submit themselves to its supremacy never rebel. . . .

[Though] it may be a sad fact to the moralist, it is a certain one for the student of life and literature that, even with the power of enjoying both, you may tire of far "greater" poets than Pope before you tire of him, and that you may revisit him more frequently and with far more confidence than you can revisit them.

Even yet enough may not have been said on him. Hackneyed as **"The Messiah"** is, and obvious as it is at once that without Isaiah and Virgil Pope's page would be simply a blank, it is a not easily tiring or tired-of diversion to see with what gusto he sets about the work of refashioning his borrowed matter, clothing it with his own version of his greater and lesser originals' thoughts, and displaying throughout a perfect triumph of *technique.* Johnson was not merely, as he often was, prejudiced but definitely unjust (which he was seldom) and ungrateful (which he was more rarely still) in belittling the poem. For even while putting it above the *Pollio,* he ascribed *all* the merit of the improvement to the borrowings from a poet so incomparably greater than either Virgil or Pope himself as Isaiah. Pope's manner is only like that of the Roman with a very considerable difference, but it is poles asunder from that of the Hebrew. His own style of diction might easily be expected to seem hard and cold beside the delicate and almost effeminate art of Virgil, tawdry and frigid beside the splendour, the magnificence, the actually divine sublimity of Isaiah. But experience and practice tell us that though difference may sometimes imply inferiority, it never necessarily implies badness; and then we perceive what a triumph in its own line and way **"The Messiah"** is—in the skilful motion of its climax, the just selection and keeping, the completeness and adequacy of the whole thing. If, once more, you confine yourself to the feeble and puerile, "I don't like this: I want something else," the piece may rank low with you; if you ask the one question of criticism, "Has the man done what he wanted to do, and done it well?" you cannot refuse the answer, *"Optime!"* On the other hand there are some who—despite Wordsworth's vouchsafing an, it is true, not very cordial exception from condemnation—do not find much refreshment in *Windsor Forest;* and the **"St. Cecilia"** piece affords others or the same an interesting critical *lemma* in the question, "Why does Pope, who had succeeded not ill in competition with men so different from himself as Virgil and Isaiah, fail so grossly in one with a prophet and master of his own?" But there is no need of more detailed criticism. A delightful writer and true poet of our own day, himself the modern laureate of the eighteenth century, has, adopting the lesser Alexander's own phrase, declared that—

> [He] throw[s] for wit, and poetry, and Pope.

For Pope, as an exponent of wit *in* poetry, we all may throw caps and money, votes and voices. Nor is that wit of the noisy or flashy order which sooner or later tires. The salt of *mere* wit is resalted with common sense; and that again with a certain purely intellectual quality difficult positively to define, for, as granted above, it is lacking in depth, in height, in originality, in several other good things, but easy to perceive and not evanescent. And so, though he enjoyed little rest or refreshment himself, he has provided much for others.

Edith Sitwell (essay date 1930)

SOURCE: *Alexander Pope,* Cosmopolitan Book Corporation, 1930, 368 p.

[*Sitwell was a twentieth-century English poet who, extremely cognizant of the value of sound and rhythmic structure in poetry, experimented widely in these areas in her verse. In the following excerpt from her biography of Pope, she examines several passages from Pope's works to demonstrate various aspects of the poet's technical skill.*]

Sir Leslie Stephen, in his life of Pope, complains of the monotony of Pope's technique—as though the heroic couplet, with its infinite and subtle variation (especially in the hands of Pope)—were all of one depth, of one height, of one texture. . . .

The stupidly despised *Essay on Criticism* leads us to understand with what care and infinite subtlety Pope studied and worked at his texture:

> But when loud surges lash the sounding shore,
> The hoarse, rough verse should like the torrent
>   roar:
> When Ajax strives some rock's vast weight to
>   throw,
> The line too labours, and the words move slow:
> Not so, when swift Camilla scours the plain,
> Flies o'er th' unbending corn, and skims along the
>   main.

The dipping and bending of that line is miraculous. No swallow ever flew more lightly.

The **"Ode on Saint Cecilia's Day"** shows how stiff and unaccustomed Pope felt himself to be when he was not working in couplets. The poem contains beautiful lines, with occasional appalling lapses; it contains this splendor:

> Thy stone, O Sisyphus, stands still
>   Ixion rests upon his wheel,
>   And the pale spectres dance!
> The Furies sink upon their iron beds,
> And snakes uncurl'd hang list'ning round their
>   heads.

The first two lines are magnificent; the subsequent lines less so, but still fine, the poem contains also this lovely verse:

> By the hero's armed shades,
> Glitt'ring thro' the gloomy glades,
> By the youths that died for love,
> Wand'ring in the myrtle grove,
> Restore, restore Eurydice to life:
> Oh take the husband, or return the wife!

But the last line comes as a shock; it is difficult to see how so great a poet could reconcile himself to such bathos. The admiration for respectability which was such a moving power in his life, must have been at work here. . . .

As an example of Pope's so-called monotony, let us take the difference between **The Rape of the Lock,** with its infinite variations, and **The Dunciad,** with its enormous variations of height and depth, speed, and heavy consciously dulled sloth. **The Rape of the Lock,** this miraculous poem, which has been most foolishly described as a work in silver filigree, is light, variable and enchanting as a little summer wind blowing down the golden spangles of the dew from the great faunal trees—the whole poem might have been woven by the air-thin golden fingers of Pope's sylphs. This thin and glittering texture, how did it ever come into being? The lines differ in no wise from the wings of the sylphs, as they float above the barge:

> Some to the sun their insect-wings unfold,
> Waft on the breeze, or sink in clouds of gold;
> Transparent forms, too fine for mortal sight,
> Their fluid bodies half dissolved in light.
> Loose to the wind their airy garments flew,
> Thin glitt'ring textures of the filmy dew,
> Dipped in the richest tincture of the skies,
> Where light disports in ever-mingling dyes;
> While ev'ry beam new transient colours flings,
> Colours that change whene'er they wave their
>   wings.

Those lines are the only fitting description of the poem itself; it is impossible to describe it in other terms. And yet Pope has been held to be deficient in beauty! . . .

It has been the fashion to regard only the tempests of fury, and not the strange murky and Tartarean beauty of *The Dunciad,* although it is one of the greatest poems in our language. Yet it is just as beautiful in its own way, and just as strange, as "The Ancient Mariner." It has been held not to be, only because it is a satire, and people whose liking for poetry is a purely sentimental one, are unable to believe that beauty is not dependent upon subject alone.

How enormous are the opening lines, with the thick, muffled, dull thud of the alliterating "M's":

> The mighty mother, and her son, who brings
> The Smithfield muses to the ears of kings.

The sound is thick, gross, and blind as stupidity itself. Then take the lines:

> Fate in their dotage this fair idiot gave,
> Gross as her sire, and as her mother grave,
> Laborious, heavy, busy, bold, and blind,
> She rul'd, in native anarchy, the mind.

The "G" sounds in the first and last words of the second line, give a designedly unwieldy lumbering gait to the line, a gait indicative of the subject; the next line, with its appalling deafening blows, caused by the alliterative "B's," placed so close together, has an overwhelming effect of power.

If we compare those varying lines with those I have quoted from *The Rape of the Lock,* I do not see how it is possible, for any but the most insensitive, to uphold that Pope is monotonous. . . .

We might as well complain that the world is monotonous because it is round, and because it circles round the sun, as complain of the monotony of Alexander Pope.

One example of his "monotony" is his use of the cæsura. Now the cæsura has, for the purposes of convenience, been held to be of uniform length and depth. But this is not so. And Pope places the cæsura, the pause (of varying depths), not only to vary the *music* of his verse, but so as to heighten the meaning. As when, in the *Epistle to Dr. Arbuthnot,* he says:

> The dog-star rages! nay, 'tis past a doubt,
> All Bedlam, or Parnassus, is let out:
> Fire in each eye, and papers in each hand,
> They rave, recite, and madden round the land.

In this, the slightness of the pauses in the second line give the effect of a disheveled procession streaming past one. In the fourth line, the fact that the first and second verbs are alliterative, and rather long-sounding, with their hard "R's," and that the third verb begins with a thick thumping "M," gives the degree of irritation which was felt by the poet.

But to return to the cæsura. If we examine these lines from *The Dunciad:*

> One cell there is, conceal'd from vulgar eye,
> The cave of poverty and poetry.

> Keen, hollow winds howl thro' the bleak recess,
> Emblem of music caus'd by emptiness,

we shall find that the slightness of the cæsura, in the third line I have quoted—a cœsura so shallow as to be hardly perceptible—gives it a strange chilliness, which is added to by the little cold wind of the two words beginning with "H" in the third line, the last of these two words, because it is a one-syllabled word and has a long vowel-sound, being louder than the two-syllabled short-voweled "hollow."

Compare the slightness of the cæsura here with the violence of the pause, the violence of the antithesis in the last line of these couplets from the *First Epistle of the First Book of Horace:*

> To either India see the merchant fly,
> Scared at the spectre of pale poverty!
> See him, with pangs of body, pangs of soul,
> Burn through the tropic, freeze beneath the pole!

How perfectly he fits his substance to his meaning. Take, for instance, these lines, which convey, in spite of the perfect structure of the heroic couplet, a sense of the formlessness of primeval matter (the lines are from *The Dunciad*):

> Till genial Jacob, or a warm third day,
> Call forth each mass, a poem or a play:
> How hints, like spawn, scarce quick in embryo lie,
> How new-born nonsense first is taught to cry,
> Maggots half-form'd in rhyme exactly meet,
> And learn to crawl upon poetic feet.

These lines, and the eight lines which follow, have a perfectly deliberate, and most unpleasant, softness—the softness of corruption. . . .

In Pope's minor poems, there is not much to examine. Yet *Eloisa to Abelard* although it is not one of Pope's most successful poems, has been, I think, rather underrated, for it is in many ways a moving poem. Unfortunately, the skilled use of the antithesis, of which Pope and Dryden were our greatest masters, was not suitable to this subject:

> I mourn the lover, not lament the fault

this gives the emotion an epigrammatic effect which lessens and falsifies the emotion.

Yet how real and how moving is this:

> Ah hopeless, lasting flames! like those that burn
> To light the dead, and warm th' unfruitful urn.

The poem is very quiet and restrained, the restraint is moving; but I am not quite sure that it was *meant* to be as quiet as it is—that the quietness is not a result of Pope's ill-health—(his physical debility could never be guessed from *The Dunciad* or *The Rape of the Lock*!)

I am not qualified to judge of the translations from Homer as *translations.* May I not, therefore, be allowed to regard them, not as translations, but as evidences of Pope's great poetic genius? The translation of the Odyssey is bathed in the azure airs of beauty that come to us from an undying sea. The lines and the heroes walk with the pomp and majesty of waves.

In the Odyssey we do not find the astonishing variations in texture that we find in **The Dunciad,** nor the incredibly subtle variations of **The Rape of the Lock.** The poem is more uniform, but had it been otherwise, the technique would have been unsuited to the matter.

W. H. Auden (essay date 1937)

SOURCE: "Pope," in *From Anne to Victoria: Essays by Various Hands,* edited by Bonamy Dobrée, Cassell and Company, Limited, 1937, pp. 89-107.

[*Auden was an English poet and critic who belonged to the generation of British writers strongly influenced by the ideas of Karl Marx and Sigmund Freud; he considered social and psychological commentary important functions of literary criticism. In the following excerpt, Auden offers a general appraisal of Pope's verse.*]

As a poet, [Pope] was limited to a single verse form, the end-stopped couplet; his rare attempts at other forms were failures. To limitation of form was added limitation of interest. He had no interest in nature as we understand the term, no interest in love, no interest in abstract ideas, and none in Tom, Dick and Harry. . . .

Pope was interested in three things, himself and what other people thought of him, his art, and the manners and characters of society. Not even Flaubert or Mallarmé was more devoted to his craft. "What his nature was unfitted to do, circumstance excused him from doing"; and he was never compelled to write to order, or to hurry over his work. He missed nothing. If he thought of something in the midst of the night, he rang for the servant to bring paper; if something struck him during a conversation, he would immediately write it down for future use. He constantly altered and rewrote, and always for the better. The introduction of sylphs and gnomes into the **Rape of the Lock,** and the conclusion of the **Dunciad** were not first thoughts. . . .

The beauties and variety of his verse have been so brilliantly displayed by others, notably Miss Sitwell, that I shall confine myself to considering two popular ideas about Pope. That his language is either falsely poetic, or "a classic of our prose" and that his poetry is cold and unemotional. The question of poetic diction was the gravamen of the Romantic's charge. The answer is that Pope and his contemporaries were interested in different fields of experience, in a different "nature." If their descriptions of cows and cottages and birds are vague, it is because their focus of interest is sharp elsewhere, and equal definition over the whole picture would spoil its proportion and obscure its design. They are conventional, not because the poets

thought that "the waterpudge, the pilewort, the petty chap, and the pooty" were unpoetic in their naked nature and must be suitably dressed, but because they are intended to be conventional, a backcloth to the more important human stage figures. When Pope writes in his preface to the *Odyssey,* "There is a real beauty in an easy, pure, perspicuous description even of a low action," he is saying something which he both believes and practises. . . .

Those who complain of Pope's use of periphrasis, of his refusal to call a spade a spade, cannot have read him carefully. When he chooses he is as direct as you please.

> So morning insects that in muck begun
> Shine, buzz, and flyblow in the setting sun.

And when he does use a periphrasis, in his best work at least, it is because an effect is to be gained by doing so.

> While China's earth receives the smoking tide.

To say that Pope was afraid to write, as Wordsworth might have written,

> While boiling water on the tea was poured

is nonsense. To the microscopic image of tea-making is added the macroscopic image of a flood, a favourite device of Pope's, and the opposite kind of synthesis to Dante's, "A single moment maketh a deeper lethargy for use than twenty and five centuries have wrought on the emprise that erst threw Neptune in amaze at Argo's shadow."

There are places in Pope, as in all poets, where his imagination is forced, where one feels a division between the object and the word, but at his best there are few poets who can rival his fusion of vision and language.

> Chicane in furs, and casuistry in lawn

> Bare the mean heart that lurks beneath a star.

> How hints, like spawn, scarce quick in embryo lie,
> How new-born nonsense first is taught to cry,
> Maggots half-formed in rhyme exactly meet,
> And learn to crawl upon poetic feet.
> Here one poor word an hundred clenches makes,
> And ductile Dulness new maeanders takes;
> There motley images her fancy strike,
> Figures ill paired, and Similes unlike. . . .

Like Dante, Pope had a passionate and quite undonnish interest in classical literature. The transformation of the heroic epic into **The Rape of the Lock** and the **Dunciad,** is not cheap parody; it is the vision of a man who can see in Homer, in eighteenth century society, in Grub Street, similarities of motive, character, and conduct whereby an understanding of all is deepened. Rams and young bullocks are changed to folios and Birthday odes, and

> Could all our care elude the gloomy grave
> Which claims no less the fearful than the brave

For lust of fame I should not vainly dare
In fighting fields, nor urge thy soul to war

becomes

O if to dance all night and dress all day,
Charmed the small pox, or chased old age away;
Who would not scorn what housewife cares pro-
    duce,
Or who would learn an earthly thing of use?

Literature and life are once more happily married. We laugh and we love. Unlike Dryden, Pope is not a dramatic poet. He is at his best only when he is writing directly out of his own experience. I cannot feel that his Homer is anything but a set task, honourably executed: the diction gives it away. But show him the drawing-rooms where he longed to be received as a real gentleman, let him hear a disparaging remark about himself, and his poetry is beyond praise. The *Essay on Man* is smug and jaunty to a degree, until we come to Happiness and Fame

All that we feel of it begins and ends
In the small circle of our foes and friends.
To all beside as much an empty shade
An England living, as a Caesar dead.

Pope knew what it was to be flattered and libelled, to be ambitious, to be snubbed, to have enemies, to be short, and ugly, and ill, and unhappy, and out of his knowledge he made his poetry, succeeded, as Rilke puts it, in

transmuting himself into the words.
Doggedly, as the carver of a cathedral
Transfers himself to the stone's constancy.

John Butt (essay date 1945)

SOURCE: "The Inspiration of Pope's Poetry," in *Essays on the Eighteenth Century,* Oxford University Press, 1945, pp. 65-79.

[*In the essay below, Butt examines the inspiration behind Pope's poetry, including "the inspirations drawn from fancy, morality, and books."*]

The twentieth-century reader is beginning to discover that there is enjoyment to be obtained from the poetry of Pope, but he is still in danger of misunderstanding what Pope was trying to express and the methods he used. The radical misunderstanding is that though the meaning of Pope's poetry seems so easy to grasp, it requires as active and intelligent co-operation from the reader as the work of more recognizably difficult poets. Many poems—many great poems—require in the first place little more than the reader's sympathy, his receptivity, his power of experiencing normal human emotions. We need only to have been glad at the sight of a field of daffodils to appreciate 'I wandered lonely as a cloud' and to receive from it all, or almost all, that Wordsworth has to communicate. And we

need no particular training or sophistication to be excited by Keats's 'Ode to Autumn' or by *Hamlet.* Study will enrich our appreciation, but it is possible to enjoy reading much Elizabethan and much nineteenth-century poetry with no other equipment than keenness of sensibility, because our power of seeing and feeling is the most obvious part of that common ground of experience which we share with Shakespeare, Keats, and Wordsworth, and from which their poetry sprang.

But the common reader, fresh from the excitement of romantic poetry, is troubled as soon as he begins to read Pope. He finds some things to please him: the pathos of such a line as

To help me thro' this long Disease, my Life,
                    [*Epistle to Arbuthnot*]

or the rapture of

Belinda smil'd, and all the World was gay,
                    [*Rape of the Lock*]

or the accuracy (to call it no more) of

The spider's touch, how exquisitely fine!
Feels at each thread, and lives along the line.
                    [*Essay on Man*]

Equally apparent is Pope's 'fine and delicate imagination', as his friend the Earl of Orrery described it. Nothing more than a sympathetic and receptive mind is required to appreciate such a couplet as this, describing the activities of eastern magicians:

These stop'd the Moon, and call'd th' unbody'd
    Shades
To Midnight Banquets in the glimmering Glades,
                    [*Temple of Fame*]

and perhaps nothing more than an alert mind to notice Pope's fondness for words such as *glimmering* in that couplet, which with its suggestion of something imperfectly seen is charged with romantic associations and possibilities. The alert reader will remember 'the glimmering light' in such an unpromising context as the *Essay on Criticism;* or the sylphs in *The Rape of the Lock,* 'trembling for the Birth of Fate'. The recurrence of 'trembling' is especially remarkable: the Priestess trembles before she begins the sacred rites of pride; the shrines tremble as Eloisa takes the veil [*Eloisa to Abelard*]; and later in that poem, when Eloisa kneels before the altar in religious ecstasy, one thought of Abelard puts all the pomp to flight:

Priests, Tapers, Temples, swim before my sight:
In seas of flame my plunging soul is drown'd,
While Altars blaze, and Angels tremble round.

In each of these instances the word is used to signify the uncontrollable reaction to some more than human activity, an essentially romantic effect most readily pleasing to the unsophisticated reader. But the unsophisticated reader will find comparatively little of this in Pope, and his pleasure in it will be modified by what will appear peculiar in Pope's imaginative and descriptive writing; peculiar, that is, when compared with the imaginative and descriptive writing of Shakespeare, Wordsworth, and Keats.

With two exceptions, the passages quoted above are taken from poems written before 1717, the year in which Pope collected and published his early work. In these poems his imagination had been specially active: devising fanciful situations in the *Pastorals* and *The Rape of the Lock;* creating a new race of beings called sylphs; placing the sculptured figures of the **'Elegy to the Memory of an Unfortunate Lady'** and *Eloisa to Abelard* in a variety of exquisitely passionate poses; describing idealized scenes in the *Messiah, Windsor Forest,* and *The Temple of Fame,* as lavish with his gold paint as Sir John Vanbrugh decorating Blenheim Palace, dropping it on the breast of a pheasant, on the scales of a carp, on the roofs of Mexican palaces [*Windsor Forest*], on the façade of Fame's temple [*Temple of Fame*], on chariots [*Rape of the Lock*], and on the girdles of goddesses [*Windsor Forest*], and even having enough to spare for a lake of liquid gold in *The Rape of the Lock;* then setting these off with crystal domes and countless silver ornaments, and breathing upon them Arabian gales [*Temple of Fame*] and the aromatic souls of flowers, [*Windsor Forest*] till the scenes were as gorgeously rococo as any Man of Taste could require.

After 1717 Pope preferred to subdue his powers of imagination. Looking back upon this early poetry in later years, he regarded it with indulgent condescension as a youthful excess. He liked to think that he had not wandered long in Fancy's maze (the distinction between Fancy and Imagination was not yet recognized), but had soon stooped like a falcon upon Truth and moralized his song. The association of description and fancy implied, and the dissociation of description and truth, are worth remarking. Pope's method in description never was to keep his eye on the object and to describe that object so accurately either by realistic or impressionistic means that the description corresponded with what other men might see. He preferred to describe something laid up in his imagination, something more splendid than could be seen by anyone else. What he describes are such scenes as I have already indicated, scenes bedizened with gold and silver—something quite unnatural, as unnatural as the decoration of Lycid's hearse; for neither Milton nor Pope wished to limit themselves to the comparatively mean resources of nature. Truth of description, like all other aspects of truth, Pope reserved to strengthen his moral purpose. The fineness of the spider's touch is part of his argument that 'throughout the whole visible world, an universal order and gradation in the sensual and mental faculties is observed, which causes a subordination of creature to creature, and of all creatures to Man'. The dab-chick, which

> waddles thro' the copse
> On feet and wings, and flies, and wades, and hops,
> [*Dunciad*]

was described so precisely to make the appearance of one of the dunces more ridiculous. To appreciate Pope's imaginative description, therefore, we must be prepared to forget for the moment our breeding in naturalistic poetry. So much co-operation is essential to avoid misunderstanding.

But though Pope allowed himself more licence in description than later poets have done, he allowed himself less licence in expounding a rule of life and the truth as he understood it. Pope was no revolutionary. He had no Utopian system to offer. He had no wish to reconstruct society. Instead, he fell in with the spirit of the times, which was to conserve and consolidate what had been won by the revolutionary struggles of the previous century. His ethical position resembles Addison's not a little. The writings of both men were intended to produce a higher level of culture and a greater social decency in the new middle class, which was just then growing up. Their methods were different—Addison preferred persuasion and raillery, Pope preferred satire: but their motives were the same. The influence of the *Tatler* and the *Spectator* on Pope's way of thinking was considerable. It was perhaps from these periodicals that he acquired his views on literature as a corrective to morals; and, as Professor Sherburn has observed, *The Rape of the Lock* would have been almost impossible before raillery on the fair sex had been made popular by Steele and Addison.

But we cannot merely say that the intention and inspiration of Pope's original poetry after he had escaped from Fancy's maze were ethical, for to say no more than that might suggest that Pope was imagining some ideal society and expounding some ideal rule of life. His intention and inspiration were not so revolutionary. Indeed, all his moral poetry was directed to improving the existing social state. His inspiration was therefore both ethical and topical. We shall not fully appreciate the magnificent praise of humility and political probity in the *Epilogue to the Satires* until we know something of the so-called 'patriotic' movement of the late thirties, a movement started by a few honest but gullible members of the parliamentary opposition, inspired by Bolingbroke, who hoped to end the jobbery and corruption of Walpole's government. Similarly, the numerous passages in praise of retirement and the simple life should be read in the light of Pope's compulsory retirement as a Roman Catholic and a Tory sympathizer. Our full understanding and enjoyment of the *Essay on Man* will depend to some extent upon our knowledge of the tenets of Bolingbroke and other deistic philosophers; and the epistle to Burlington, *On the Use of Riches,* cannot be fully appreciated without at least some recognition of contemporary taste in architecture and gardening. This applies even more to the casual references throughout these later poems. When at the end of the *Epilogue to the Satires* Pope thinks of himself as the last to draw a pen for freedom, because 'Truth stands trembling on the edge of Law', he is alluding to the press censorship which the government was threatening in 1738. The reason why the Law's thunder is hurled on Gin in the same poem will not be appreciated by one who has not seen Hogarth's celebrated picture 'Gin Lane' or who has not read of the disastrous effects on the physique of the population of the sale of cheap gin and the riots which followed the attempt to curtail its distribution. Or why should Pope compare Addison's fear of rivals to the Turk's, who could bear no brother near the throne? [*Epistle to Arbuthnot*] The answer is that Pope was retorting upon Addison the very same rebuke with which Addison had started his review of the *Essay on Criticism* in the *Spectator,* and was adapting for that purpose three lines of Denham's poem on John Fletcher's works quoted by Addison on that occasion:

> Nor needs thy juster Title the foul guilt
> Of Eastern Kings, who to secure their reign,
> Must have their Brothers, Sons, and Kindred slain.

Without that particular knowledge, some of the point and effectiveness is lost.

A commentary when reading Pope's later works is therefore essential, 'a necessary evil' as Dr. Johnson said of commentaries on Shakespeare, something to be cast aside and ignored when the reader starts a later reading of the poem. Pope was quite well aware of the topical difficulty of his poems, as he showed by setting an example in annotation. Few of his later works were issued without explanatory notes, and as further editions appeared when the immediate occasion of many lines had been forgotten, the notes were increased in number. It is inevitable that the common reader should neglect what is merely topical in the literature of former ages, when there is so much being written by his contemporaries which more nearly concerns him. He must therefore be assured of the compensations for his trouble in tackling the antiquarian problems of Pope's later poetry before he pays it much attention.

To say merely that Pope's ethical and topical poetry transcends its occasions is asking too much of a reader's faith. Yet this is the result of Pope's treatment of his materials. A tempting example of this transcendence is the striking applicability (though it must be allowed to be mere coincidence) of Pope's political poetry to the political state of England just before the present war. Walpole had an unassailable parliamentary majority behind him; he had the moneyed interests on his side and the poets and the wits against him; and he was trying to avoid war by methods which the Opposition did not approve of. It is therefore not surprising that we can read to-day with a certain relish such irony as this addressed to the head of the government:

> Oh! could I mount on the Mæonian wing,
> Your Arms, your Actions, your Repose to sing!
> What seas you travers'd! and what fields you
>   fought!
> Your Country's Peace, how oft, how dearly bought!
> How barb'rous rage subsided at your word,
> And Nations wonder'd while they dropp'd the
>   sword!
> How, when you nodded, o'er the land and deep,
> Peace stole her wing, and wrapt the world in sleep;
> Till Earth's extremes your mediation own,
> And Asia's Tyrants tremble at your Throne.
>
> ['*Epistle to Augustus*']

But the historical parallel here is a mere coincidence: Pope's ethical and topical poetry is often more profoundly and more permanently true. In contemporary extravagances and follies, Pope always sees the abuse of a general principle. In Timon's tasteless display of wealth or in Sir Balaam's mercenary spirit he sees a neglect of the rule of simple living: in the variety of Wharton's escapades [*Moral Essay*], an immoderate desire of admiration. And the converse is equally true: in Lyttelton he sees the type of the incorruptible politician, or in Ralph Allen's secret philanthropy [*Epilogue to the Satires*] a model of what every charitable man should be. These particular examples are, like a nightingale or a Grecian urn to Keats, the exciting perceptions which moved Pope to the expression of something which has universal significance. Their purpose in his poetry is to give illustrative force to the expression of universal truths.

It is worth remarking that a comparison of earlier and later versions of a poem will show that Pope's method in revision was often to omit unnecessary particulars and to generalize. Thus the 'Irish Poetess' of an early version of the *Epistle to Dr. Arbuthnot,* a reference either to Mrs. Barber or to Mrs. Sykins, later becomes the 'maudlin Poetess', and by omitting the only direct reference to his quarrel with Addison he converted his character-sketch of Addison into 'Atticus', the type of all insincere yet influential men of letters.

Often Pope's method of generalizing seems to have been to conflate two characters. Thus Bufo, the mean and tasteless patron in the *Epistle to Dr. Arbuthnot,* seems to be a conflation of Halifax and Bubb Dodington; Pitholeon, the sponging poet, a conflation of Welsted and Cooke; Atossa, the termagant in the *Characters of Women,* a conflation of the Duchess of Buckingham and the Duchess of Marlborough. No doubt it was economical and guarded to lampoon two people in one character, because if either protested Pope could declare the character was intended for the other. Such a reflection may have appealed to him, but of course Pope knew that he was more certain of describing a universal type by taking characteristics from a number of people than by confining himself to one. This should be a warning against an attempt to define each of Pope's characters as invariably the character of one of his contemporaries.

The problem whether to use his contemporaries' characters as his examples or to invent imaginary characters continually exercised Pope's mind. He discussed it again and again both in his poems and in his letters, but his attitude is briefly summarized in a passage from a letter to his friend Caryll: 'I shall make living examples, which enforce best'—enforce, of course, the universal truth whether the character be vicious or virtuous. Pope would seem to have agreed with Milton that Virtue needs no fanciful decoration to set off her beauty. His verse, whenever he reflects on virtuous behaviour, is quite unadorned. The swell of emotion is enough to carry such passages, as when he cries, in the *Epilogue to the Satires:*

> Yes, I am proud; I must be proud to see
> Men not afraid of God, afraid of me:

Safe from the Bar, the Pulpit, and the Throne,
Yet touch'd and sham'd by *Ridicule* alone.

But it must not be supposed that his delight in sensuous description, so evident in the early poems, was extinguished when he ceased to make Fancy the intention of his poetry. He always took a trembling delight in the observation of beauty, and though the beauty of a virtuous action now chiefly detained him, he still had his use for sensuous experiences and fancies:

To happy Convents, bosom'd deep in vines,
Where slumber Abbots, purple as their wines:
To Isles of fragrance, lilly-silver'd vales,
Diffusing languor in the panting gales:
To lands of singing, or of dancing slaves,
Love-whisp'ring woods, and lute-resounding waves.

But for the second line, one might well suppose that these lines are to be found in *Windsor Forest* or the *Pastorals.* In fact, they are part of Pope's satirical argument in the fourth book of the *Dunciad,* and are a description (like the Bower of Bliss in the second book of the *Faerie Queene*) made to show how the young can be debauched by sensuality. It is a triumph of Pope's virtuosity that he reserves most of this later sensuousness for his satirical verses, as though he were trying to rid them of any taint of irritation, or demonstrating with what gracious ideas his mind was filled when he conceived these lampoons. This is especially true of the *Dunciad,* where Pope's enemies and the traditional enemies of good taste and sense are flayed in his most grave and imaginative poetry. Here we find Shadwell in the limbo of forgotten poetasters 'nod[ding] the Poppy on his brows', and Lord Hervey, now renamed Narcissus,

prais'd with all a Parson's pow'r,
Look'd a white lilly sunk beneath a show'r,

and Pope's arch-pedant reclining in sensuously Spenserian repose:

As many quit the streams that murm'ring fall
To lull the sons of Marg'ret and Clare-hall,
Where Bentley late tempestuous wont to sport
In troubled waters, but now sleeps in Port.

In these lines the imaginative beauty is as evident as the mischievous pun, and surely gave Pope as much delight. One is bound to ask what was the nature of Pope's animosity against Theobald as he wrote the *Dunciad.* Was he really considering Theobald at all when he described him in that beautiful couplet?

Him close she curtain'd round with vapours blue,
And soft besprinkled with Cimmerian dew.

Or was he any longer consumed with anger when he described the altar of books which Theobald erected as a sacrifice to the Goddess, and concluded his description with an allusion to the duodecimo edition of Theobald's translation of Sophocles?

Quarto's, Octavo's, shape the less'ning pyre,
And last, a little Ajax tips the spire.
[*The Dunciad Variorum* (1729)]

It is difficult to reconcile the poet who cared for such thrilling precision with the vicious little satirist of popular imagination. If there is petulance there, it is petulance recollected in tranquillity.

In these and in many a more extensive passage in the *Dunciad,* Pope is working at two levels. At one he is avenging the wrongs done to good sense and culture by contemporary dunces, and attempting with partial success to make his own particular revenge of universal significance; at another level he is satisfying his imagination with poetry which is beautiful in itself, apart from any satiric significance.

There is another sense in which Pope's verses may be said to have differences of level, differences most easily illustrated from the *Imitations of Horace.* In the first 'Imitation', for example, he is making a particularly clever rendering of the first satire of Horace's second book and at the same time defending himself from certain specific charges, and in the **'Epistle to Augustus'** he is turning Horace's praise of Augustus into ridicule of George II and at the same time making some astute judgements on poets of his own and previous generations. As a critic of Pope has expressed it, 'The *Imitations of Horace* show the poet bound hand and foot and yet dancing as if free' [G. Tillotson, in *Essays in Criticism and Research*]'. But such a dance could only be performed by one who had had constant practice in earlier measures:

True ease in writing flows from art, not chance,
As those move easiest who have learn'd to dance.
[*Essay on Criticism*]

All his life Pope had been active in verse translation. He was an accomplished translator long before he started on the *Iliad.* Translation, in fact, had been his early training. He told Spence that as a boy he read eagerly through a great number of English, French, Italian, Latin, and Greek poets, not with any system, but dipping in here and there, and whenever he met with a passage or story that pleased him more than ordinary, he endeavoured to imitate it, or translate it into English: 'this', he said, 'gave rise to my Imitations published so long after'. It was by these translations and imitations that he shaped his own original work. 'My first taking to imitating', he told Spence, 'was not out of vanity, but humility: I saw how defective my own things were; and endeavoured to mend my manner, by copying good strokes from others'. This, according to his own account, must have been evident in his first extensive poem, an epic of 4,000 lines on Alcander, Prince of Rhodes, which he kept by him until 1722, when he burnt it on Bishop Atterbury's advice. 'I endeavoured in this poem', he said, 'to collect all the beauties of the great epic writers into one piece: there was Milton's style in one part, and Cowley's in another; here the style of Spenser imitated, and there of Statius; here Homer and Virgil, and there Ovid and Claudian'. The revealing account of his method in this early poem is to some extent true of his method in every poem he wrote. To call it plagiarism is too crude. It is better to connect it with Pope's imaginative, ethical, and topical inspiration, and call it Pope's literary inspiration, the appreciation of which presents one more difficulty to the common reader.

Literary inspiration is not essentially different from inspiration derived from life. The reading of a book can be an emotional experience as much as the sight of a field of daffodils, as Keats found when he looked into Chapman's Homer. Literary experience, therefore, is part of a store of emotional experiences upon which the poet can draw for his work. There is this difference, however, that whereas most emotional experiences will be recollected in some form unconnected with words, a literary experience will return with some memory of the words which the writer has used. There is also the frequent possibility of literary experiences mixing with other experiences, of our recollecting at some emotional crisis the literary expression which had once before been given to it. Thus it seems possible that when Gray, in whom literary inspiration was as powerful as it was in Pope, stopped to contemplate some elm, the description of that tree in *Comus* recurred to his mind,

> Or 'gainst the rugged bark of some broad Elm,

and the tree and Milton's description were thereafter so indissociably connected, that when in turn he came to mention the tree in the *Elegy,* 'Beneath those rugged Elms' became the inevitable choice of words.

Like Gray's, Pope's ideas and emotions were closely associated with the expression which former writers had used in similar circumstances. Regret at the too quick passing of years seems to have recalled to Pope Milton's sonnet on his twenty-third birthday as being, perhaps, the best expression which that emotion had received, so that even when Pope had Horace's words before him in the 'Imitation' of the second Epistle of Horace's second book, it was to Milton that he turned when he wrote

> This subtle Thief of Life, this paltry Time,
> What will it leave me, if it snatch my Rhime?

And when in the **'Messiah'** he needed to versify Isaiah's description of the earth bringing forth its earliest fruits as offerings to the new-born child, he passed over Isaiah and Virgil, whom he was ostensibly imitating, to choose a passage from the ninth book of *Paradise Lost:*

> The humid flow'rs, that breath'd
> Their morning incense,

which in his digesting memory he transmuted to

> See Nature hastes her earliest wreaths to bring,
> With all the incense of the breathing spring.

Canto 4 of *The Rape of the Lock* ends with Belinda's despairing cry at her misfortune. She wishes she had never visited Hampton Court and had rather lived in some distant northern land, where she could have kept her charms from mortal sight; and as Pope searched for an image to describe beauty in concealment, it was Waller's lines he associated with this idea. In 'Go, Lovely Rose', Waller had written

> Tell her that's young
> And shuns to have her graces spied,
>   That hadst thou sprung
> In deserts, where no men abide,
> Thou wouldst have uncommended died.

And Pope adapted them to his purpose as follows:

> There kept my Charms conceal'd from mortal Eye,
> Like Roses that in Desarts bloom and die.

Here as well two different levels may be observed in the poetry. The more apparent level is the beauty of expression, the less apparent is the pleasure which our memories have in associating Pope's words with a former poet's. A quotation from *Guardian* No. 12, a paper which has been attributed to Pope, may serve to reinforce this:

> But over and above a just Painting of Nature, a learned Reader will find a new Beauty superadded in a happy Imitation of some famous Ancient, as it revives in his Mind the Pleasure he took in his first reading such an Author. Such Copyings as these give that kind of double Delight which we perceive when we look upon the Children of a beautiful Couple; where the Eye is not more charm'd with the Symmetry of the Parts, than the Mind by observing the Resemblance transmitted from Parents to their Offspring, and the mingled Features of the Father and the Mother.

It has been assumed in commenting on the three passages quoted above that Pope's imitation was intentional. It may not have been, for a poet may not know whom he is imitating. But when Pope did know, his frequent (if not invariable) practice was to quote his source in a footnote, thus indicating once more the way in which editors must annotate his work.

Pope's indication of his sources serves many purposes. It is an acknowledgement of indebtedness. More important, it demonstrates Pope's inheritance of traditional ideas passed on from one reputable writer to another; this is especially true of the *Essay on Criticism* with its footnote references to Cicero, Horace, Persius, and Quintilian, and of the *Dunciad* with its reminders of grave epic parallels to Pope's ridiculous incidents. But most important, the acknowledgement of indebtedness invites comparison between the earlier and later expression of the idea. The Augustan age was an age of consolidation, an age when men stopped to chew and digest the experiences of former ages. Pope was best serving the men of his generation by giving the expression of those experiences 'an agreeable turn', a turn so agreeable, in fact, that we may often remember Pope though we forget his originals.

It should not be supposed that the three inspirations of Pope's work, the inspirations drawn from fancy, morality, and books, exist separately in his poetry and are never associated. On the contrary, the variety of levels in his poetry shows that he could satisfy more than one poetical impulse within the limits of the same verse. Occasionally, indeed, his inspiration is a blend of all three. When Pope revised *The Rape of the Lock* for the first collected edition of his works in 1717, he added a passage of twenty-six lines to the fifth canto, which will serve for illustration. The revision of his works had been a respite from the translation of Homer, in which he had proceeded at that time as far as the twelfth book of the *Iliad*. This book describes an attack upon the Greek entrenchments by the Trojan forces, the success of which was largely owed to the valour of Sarpedon. Sarpedon had encouraged his friend Glaucus in a speech which Pope had translated and published separately some years before; but it was doubtless the occasion of fitting the speech into its place in the translation of the twelfth book at that time, which suggested that an imitation of it might suitably be put into the mouth of the grave Clarissa before the battle begins in canto v of *The Rape of the Lock.* Here are the two passages, Homer translated first:

> Why boast we, *Glaucus!* our extended Reign,
> Where *Xanthus'* Streams enrich the *Lycian* Plain;
> Our num'rous Herds that range the fruitful Field,
> And Hills where Vines their purple Harvest yield,
> Our foaming Bowls with purer Nectar crown'd,
> Our Feasts enhanc'd with Music's sprightly Sound?
> Why on those Shores are we with Joy survey'd,
> Admir'd as Heroes, and as Gods obey'd?
> Unless great Acts superior Merit prove,
> And vindicate the bount'ous pow'rs above.
> 'Tis ours, the Dignity they give, to grace;
> The first in Valour, as the first in Place:
> That when with wond'ring Eyes our martial Bands
> Behold our Deeds transcending our Commands,
> Such, they may cry, deserve the sov'reign State,
> Whom those that envy, dare not imitate!
> Could all our Care elude the gloomy Grave,
> Which claims no less the fearful than the brave,
> For Lust of Fame I should not vainly dare
> In fighting Fields, nor urge thy Soul to War.
> But since, alas! ignoble Age must come,
> Disease, and Death's inexorable Doom;
> The Life which others pay, let us bestow,
> And give to Fame what we to Nature owe;
> Brave tho' we fall, and honour'd if we live,
> Or let us Glory gain, or Glory give!

Homer burlesqued follows:

> Say, why are Beauties prais'd and honour'd most,
> The wise Man's Passion, and the vain Man's Toast?
> Why deck'd with all that Land and Sea afford,
> Why Angels call'd, and Angel-like ador'd?
> Why round our Coaches crowd the white-glov'd
>   Beaus,
> Why bows the Side-box from its inmost Rows?
> How vain are all these Glories, all our Pains,
> Unless good Sense preserve what Beauty gains:
> That Men may say, when we the Front-box grace,

> Behold the first in Virtue, as in Face!
> Oh! if to dance all Night, and dress all Day,
> Charm'd the Small-pox, or chas'd old Age away;
> Who would not scorn what Huswife's Cares
>   produce,
> Or who would learn one earthly Thing of Use?
> To patch, nay ogle, might become a Saint,
> Nor could it sure be such a Sin to paint.
> But since, alas! frail Beauty must decay,
> Curl'd or uncurl'd, since Locks will turn to grey,
> Since painted, or not painted, all shall fade,
> And she who scorns a Man, must die a Maid;
> What then remains, but well our Pow'r to use,
> And keep good Humour still whate'er we lose?
> And trust me, Dear! good Humour can prevail,
> When Airs, and Flights, and Screams, and Scolding
>   fail.
> Beauties in vain their pretty Eyes may roll;
> Charms strike the Sight, but Merit wins the Soul.
>   [*The Rape of the Lock,*]

The grave Clarissa's speech is both an imaginative episode in *The Rape of the Lock* and a parody of Homer. But it is an unusual parody, for while the memory of Homer's lines produces a ludicrous effect as it is read, the good sense of it, so elegantly expressed, opens 'more clearly the Moral of the Poem', as Pope explained in a note. Pope is stooping unerringly to Truth, although he is still wandering in Fancy's maze. It is the many-layered richness of such a passage as that which demands our profoundest admiration for his poetry.

Notes

[2] *Moral Essay,* iv. 99 ff.
[3] Ibid. iii. 339 ff.

[4] Ibid. i. 178 ff.

[5] *Imit. Hor.* Ep. I, i. 29.

[6] *Epilogue to the Satires,* i. 135 f.

F. R. Leavis (essay date 1947)

SOURCE: "Pope," in *Revaluation: Tradition and Development in English Poetry,* George W. Stewart Publishers, Inc., 1947, pp. 68-100.

[*Leavis was an influential contemporary English critic. In the following excerpt, he suggest paths toward a more judicious, comprehensive assessment of Pope's accomplishment than was generally accorded it during the nineteenth century.*]

Pope has had bad luck. Dryden, fortunate in the timeliness of Mr. Mark Van Doren's book, was enlisted in the argument against the nineteenth century. It was an opportunity; the cause was admirable and *Homage to John Dryden* admirably served it (though Mr. Eliot, who—or so it seems to me—has always tended to do Dryden something more than justice, was incidentally, perhaps accidentally, unfair to Pope). The homage announcing, on the other hand, Pope's rehabilitation was left to Bloomsbury, and Pope, though he has more to offer the modern reader than Dryden and might have been enlisted in the argument with certainly not less effect, was taken over, an obvious property, by the post-war cult of the *dix-huitième*—an opportunity for Lytton Strachey and Miss Sitwell.

Such attention as he has received from critics qualified to appreciate him—an aside from Mr. Middleton Murry, a note by Mr. Edgell Rickword, a paragraph or two of Empsonian analysis—has been casual. It is true that what is offered by these three critics (and there is not a great deal more to record) would, if considered, be enough to establish an intelligent orientation to Pope. And Pope's achievement being so varied, I can hardly pretend to attempt more than this. Keeping in view the purpose of the book and the necessary limits of space, I can aim at little more than to suggest coercively the re-orientation from which a revaluation follows; if more, to indicate something of Pope's range and variety.

'Re-orientation,' here, envisages in particular the classification 'satirist.' It may be no longer necessary to discuss whether satire can be poetry, and we may have entirely disposed of Matthew Arnold; nevertheless, when Pope is classed under 'Satire' it is still with a limiting effect, as if he did only one kind of thing, and that involving definite bounds and a restricted interest. So there is point in considering to begin with a poem of an excellence that is obviously not satiric.

The rare fineness of the **"Elegy to the Memory of an Unfortunate Lady"** has not had the recognition it deserves. It is praised commonly (when praised) for a `pathetic' power distinguishing it from the body of Pope's work, but this does not appear to recommend it even to Miss Sitwell. In fact, though to condemn the manner as declamatory is no longer the thing, there is something about it that is found unengagingly outmoded. I remember to have heard, incredulously, a theory, purporting to come from a critic of high repute, that is worth mentioning because it calls attention to certain essential characteristics of the poem. The theory was that Pope opened in all solemnity, but finding it impossible to continue in so high-flown a strain without smiling at himself (he had, after all, a sense of humour), slipped in a qualifying element of burlesque and achieved a subtle total effect analogous to that of *Prufrock.* The evidence? Well, for example, this:

> As into air the purer spirits flow,
> And sep'rate from their kindred dregs below;
> So flew the soul to its congenial place,
> Nor left one virtue to redeem her Race.

The percipient reader, one gathered, smiled here, and, if it were pointed out that 'dregs' turned 'the purer spirits' into a ludicrous metaphor, the less percipient would smile also.

Nevertheless, the reader who sees the relevance here of remarking that Pope was born in the seventeenth century will not be inclined to smile any more than at

> But ah! my soul with too much stay
> Is drunk, and staggers in the way

in Vaughan's *The Retreat.* If it had never even occurred to one that the image could strike any reader as funny, it is not because of the lulling effect of Pope's orotund resonances, but because, by the time one comes to the lines in question, one has been so potently reminded of Pope's Metaphysical descent. The preceding lines are actually those quoted by Mr. Middleton Murry as illustrating the Metaphysical element in Pope:

> Most souls, 'tis true, but peep out once an age,
> Dull sullen pris'ners in the body's cage:
> Dim lights of life, that burn a length of years
> Useless, unseen, as lamps in sepulchres;
> Like Eastern Kings a lazy state they keep,
> And close confin'd to their own palace, sleep.

Mr. Murry's observation is just. Pope is as much the last poet of the seventeenth century as the first of the eighteenth. His relationship to the Metaphysical tradition is aptly suggested by his **Satires of Dr. Donne Versified:** bent as he was (with Dryden behind him) on being the first 'correct' poet, Metaphysical 'wit'—the essential spirit of it—was at the same time congenial to him, more so than to Dryden; and what is suggested in the undertaking to 'versify' Donne he achieved in his best work. In it subtle complexity is reconciled with 'correctness,' his wit is Metaphysical as well as Augustan, and he can be at once polite and profound.

In the passage first quoted one is not merely solemnly impressed by the striking images; their unexpectedness and variety—the 'heterogeneous ideas' that are 'yoked together'—involve (on an adequate reading) a play of mind and a flexibility of attitude that make such effects as that of 'dregs' acceptable when they come: there is an element of surprise, but not the shock that means rejection (complete or ironically qualified) of the inappropriate. Seriousness for Pope, for the Metaphysicals, for Shakespeare, was not the sustained, simple solemnity it tended to be identified with in the nineteenth century; it might include among its varied and disparate tones the ludicrous, and demand, as essential to the total effect, an accompanying play of the critical intelligence. So in these lines of Pope: the associations of 'peep' are not dignified, and one's feelings towards the 'souls' vary, with the changing imagery, from pitying contempt for the timorous peepers, through a shared sense (still qualified with critical contempt, for one is not oneself dull and sullen) of the prisoners' hopeless plight, and a solemn contemplation in the sepulchral couplet of life wasted among shrivelled husks, to that contempt mixed with humour and a sense of opulence that is appropriate to the Kings lazing in their palaces.

The Kings are at least dignified, and they make the transition to the complete dignity of the Lady, who enters again in the next couplet:

From these perhaps (ere nature bade her die)
Fate snatch'd her early to the pitying sky.
As into air the purer spirits flow, *etc.*

But her dignity is not a precarious one, to be sedulously guarded from all possibly risible associations. The 'mean' element in the texture of the previous passage can be safely carried on in 'dregs.' The very violence of this, directed as it is upon her contemptible family ('her Race'), draws the attention away from the value it gives, retrospectively, to 'spirits,' though enough of this value is felt to salt a little, as it were, the sympathetically tender nobility that is opposed to 'dregs.'

Indeed, the successful reconciliation of so formally exalted a manner with such daring shifts and blends is conditioned by this presence of a qualifying, seasoning element. This presence is wit. We have a clear sense of its being generated (to take the process at its most observable) in the play of thought and image glanced at above, from 'Most souls' to 'sleep.' The changes of tone and attitude imposed on the reader (consider, for instance, that involved in passing from 'souls' to 'peep' in the first line) result in an alertness; a certain velleity of critical reserve in responding; a readiness for surprise that amounts in the end to an implicit recognition, at any point, in accepting what is given, of other and complementary possibilities. It becomes plain, in the light of such an account, why we should find ourselves describing as 'mature' the sensibility exhibited by verse in which wit is an element, and also why, in such verse, a completely serious poetic effect should be able to contain suggestions of the ludicrous such as for Gray, Shelley or Matthew Arnold would have meant disaster. . . .

The commentary called for by the exalted decorum of the *Elegy* is . . . implicitly provided by Pope himself:

'Tis Use alone that sanctifies Expense,
And Splendour borrows all her rays from Sense.

Pope was at one with a society to which these were obvious but important truths. So supported, he could sustain a formal dignity such as, pretended to, would make a modern ridiculous. 'Use' represents robust moral certitudes sufficiently endorsed by the way of the world, and 'Sense' was a light clear and unquestionable as the sun. . . .

After various tones of declamation, we pass through . . . to the deeply moving final paragraph, in which the strong personal emotion, so firmly subdued throughout to the 'artificial' form and manner, insists more and more on its immediately personal intensity.

It is time now to turn to the satirist. What in the foregoing page or two may have appeared excessively elementary will be recognized, perhaps, in its bearing on the satire, to serve at least some purpose. For, granting Pope to be pre-eminently a satirist and to enjoy as such what favour he does enjoy, one cannot easily find good reasons for believing that an intelligent appreciation of satiric poetry is much commoner to-day than it was among the contempo-

raries of Matthew Arnold. Elementary things still need saying. Such terms as 'venom,' 'envy,' 'malice' and 'spite' are, among modern connoisseurs, the staple of appreciation (it is, at any rate, difficult to find anything on Pope in other terms): . . . we are in the happy position of being able, quite imperturbably, to enjoy the fun. . . . We sit at our ease, reading those *Satires* and *Epistles,* in which the verses, when they were written, resembled nothing so much as spoonfuls of boiling oil, ladled out by a fiendish monkey at an upstairs window upon such of the passers-by whom the wretch had a grudge against—and we are delighted. The Victorians disapproved; Bloomsbury approves: that is the revolution of taste.

It is, in some ways, a pity that we know so much about Pope's life. If nothing had been known but the works, would 'envy,' 'venom,' 'malice,' 'spite' and the rest have played so large a part in the commentary? There is, indeed, evidence in the satires of strong personal feelings, but even—or, rather, especially—where these appear strongest, what (if we are literate) we should find most striking is an intensity of art. To say, with Leslie Stephen and Lytton Strachey, that in the character of Sporus Pope 'seems to be actually screaming with malignant fury' is to betray an essential inability to read Pope.

But one has to conclude from published criticism that the nature of Pope's art is very little understood. Just as I reach this point there comes to hand the following, by an American critic: 'A familiar charge often brought against Shelley is lack of discipline, but in such charges one must always know what the poet is trying to control. If, as in the case of Pope, it is the mere perfection of a regulated line of verse, the problem becomes one of craftsmanship.' A 'mere perfection of a regulated line of verse' is not anything as clearly and precisely indicated as the critic, perhaps, supposes; but that he supposes Pope's technique ('craftsmanship' being plainly depreciatory) to be something superficial, some mere skill of arranging a verbal surface, is confirmed by what he goes on to say: Pope's 'recitation of the dogmas of his day is hollow,' and 'in his day as in ours it is a relatively simple matter to accept a ritual of devotion as a substitute for an understanding of basic moral values.'

An 'understanding of basic moral values' is not a claim one need be concerned to make for a poet, but that Pope's relation to the 'basic moral values' of the civilization he belonged to was no mere matter of formal salute and outward deference has been sufficiently shown above, in the discussion of the close of *Epistle IV.* When Pope contemplates the bases and essential conditions of Augustan culture his imagination fires to a creative glow that produces what is poetry even by Romantic standards. His contemplation is religious in its seriousness. The note is that of these lines, which come in *Epistle III* not long after a vigorous satiric passage and immediately before another:

Ask we what makes one keep and one bestow?
That Pow'r who bids the Ocean ebb and flow,
Bids seed-time, harvest, equal course maintain,

Thro' reconcil'd extremes of drought and rain,
Builds life on Death, on Change Duration founds,
And gives th' eternal wheels to know their rounds.

The order of Augustan civilization evokes characteristically in Pope, its poet, when he is moved by the vision of it, a profound sense of it as dependent on and harmonious with an ultimate and inclusive order. The sense of order expressed in his art when he is at his best (and he is at his best more than most poets) is nothing merely conventional or superficial, explicable in terms of social elegance and a pattern of verse. His technique, concerned as it is with arranging words and 'regulating' movements, is the instrument of a fine organization, and it brings to bear pressures and potencies that can turn intense personal feelings into something else. 'His "poetic criticism of life,"' says Lytton Strachey, gibbeting solemn fatuity, 'was simply and solely the heroic couplet.' Pope would have found it hard to determine what precisely this means, but he certainly would not have found the fatuity Arnold's, and if the Augustan idiom in which he expressed much the same commonplaces as Arnold's differed from the Victorian, it was not in being less solemn.

> Ask you what Provocation I have had?
> The strong Antipathy of Good to Bad

—we may not accept this as suggesting adequately the moral basis of Pope's satire, but it is significant that Pope could offer such an account: his strength as a satirist was that he lived in an age when such an account could be offered.

The passages of solemnly exalted imagination like those adduced above come without incongruity in the midst of the satire—the significance of this needs no further insisting on. What does need insisting on is that with this capacity for poised and subtle variety goes a remarkable command of varied satiric tones. The politeness of the Atticus portrait is very different from that of the *Rape of the Lock* (a work that, in my opinion, has enjoyed more than justice); the intense destructive vivacity of the Sporus portrait is different from that of the attack on Timon; the following (which is very far from an exception) is enough to dispose of the judgment that 'Pope was witty but not humorous'—the theme is Paper Credit:

> Had Colepepper's whole wealth been hops and
>   hogs,
> Could he himself have sent it to the dogs?
> His Grace will game: to White's a Bull be led,
> With spurning heels and with a butting head.
> To White's be carry'd, as to ancient games,
> Fair Coursers, Vases, and alluring Dames.
> Shall then Uxurio, if the stakes he sweep,
> Bear home six Whores, and make his Lady weep?

The story of Sir Balaam at the end of *Epistle III* is, again, quite different—but one cannot by enumerating, even if

there were room, do justice to Pope's variety. Indeed, to call attention to the satiric variety as such is to risk a misleading stress. . . .

A representative selection of passages would fill a great many pages. A selection of all Pope that one would wish to have by one for habitual re-reading would fill a great many more. Is it necessary to disclaim the suggestion that he is fairly represented in short extracts? No one, I imagine, willingly reads through the *Essay on Man* (Pope piquing himself on philosophical or theological profundity and acumen is intolerable, and he cannot, as Dryden can, argue interestingly in verse); but to do justice to him one must read through not merely the *Epistles,* but, also as a unit, the fourth book of the *Dunciad,* which I am inclined to think the most striking manifestation of his genius. It is certainly satire, and I know of nothing that demonstrates more irresistibly that satire can be great poetry.

An adequate estimate of Pope would go on to describe the extraordinary key-position he holds, the senses in which he stands between the seventeenth and the eighteenth centuries. Communications from the Metaphysicals do not pass beyond him; he communicates forward, not only with Johnson, but also (consider, for instance, *Eloïsa to Abelard*) with Thomson and Gray. It was not for nothing that he was so interested in Milton.

Maynard Mack (essay date 1949)

SOURCE: "Wit and Poetry and Pope," in *Alexander Pope,* edited and with an introduction by Harold Bloom, Chelsea House Publishers, 1986, pp. 9-12.

[*Mack is a critic well known for his work on Pope. In the following excerpt from an essay originally published in his* Pope and His Contemporaries *(1949), Mack discusses the mockheroic metaphor in Pope's works, particularly in* The Rape of the Lock *and* The Dunciad.]

The great pervasive metaphor of Augustan literature, including Pope's poetry, is the metaphor of tone: the mockheroic. It is very closely allied, of course, to the classical or Roman myth . . . and is, like that, a reservoir of strength. By its means, without the use of overt imagery at all, opposite and discordant qualities may be locked together in 'a balance or reconcilement of sameness with difference, of the general with the concrete, the idea with the image, the individual with the representative, the sense of novelty and freshness with old and familiar objects'—the mock-heroic seems made on purpose to fit this definition of Coleridge's of the power of imagination. For a literature of decorums like the Augustan, it was a metaphor with every sort of value. It could be used in the large, as in *Joseph Andrews, Tom Jones, The Beggar's Opera, The Rape of the Lock, The Dunciad,* or in the small—the passage, the line. It could be set in motion by a passing allusion, not necessarily to the classics:

Calm Temperance, whose blessings those partake,
Who hunger, and who thirst, for scribling sake;

by a word:

Glad chains, warm furs, broad banners, and broad
faces;

even by a cadence:

And the fresh vomit run for ever green.

Moreover, it was a way of getting the local, the ephemeral, the pressure of life as it was lived, into poetry, and yet distancing it in amber:

That live-long wig, which Gorgon's self might own,
Eternal buckle takes in Parian stone.

It was also a way of qualifying an attitude, of genuinely 'heroicizing' a Man of Ross, a parson Adams, a Schoolmistress, yet undercutting them with a more inclusive attitude:

Rise, *honest* Muse! and sing the Man of Ross

Above all—and this, I think, was its supreme advantage for Pope—it was a metaphor that could be made to look two ways. If the heroic genre and the heroic episodes lurking behind **The Rape of the Lock** diminish many of the values of this society, they also partially throw their weight behind some others. Clarissa's speech is an excellent case in point. Her words represent a sad shrinkage from the epic views of Glaucus which reverberate behind them, views involving real heroism and (to adapt Mr. Eliot's phrase) the awful daring of a real surrender. Still, the effect of the contrast is not wholly minimizing. Clarissa's vision of life, worldly as it is when seen against the heroic standard, surpasses the others in the poem and points, even if obliquely, to the tragic conflict between the human lot and the human will that is common to life at every level.

This flexibility of the mock-heroic metaphor is seen in its greatest perfection in the **Dunciad.** There are, indeed, three thicknesses of metaphor in this poem: an overall metaphor, in which the poem as a whole serves as vehicle for a tenor which is the decline of literary and human values generally; a network of local metaphor, in which this poem is especially prolific; and in between, the specifically mock-heroic metaphor which springs from holding the tone and often the circumstances of heroic poetry against the triviality of the dunces and their activities. But what is striking about this metaphor in the **Dunciad,** and indicative of its flexibility, is that it is applied quite differently from the way it is applied in the **Rape of the Lock.** There, the epic mode as vehicle either depresses the values of the actors, as with Belinda, or somewhat supports them, as with Clarissa. Here, on the contrary, one of the two lines of development (the comic) grows from allowing the actors to depress and degrade the heroic mode, its dignity and beauty. Again and again Pope builds up in the poem effects of striking epic richness, only to let them be broken down,

disfigured, stained—as the word 'vomit' stains the lovely movement and suggestion of the epic line quoted above. Thus the diving and other games in Book II disfigure the idea of noble emulation and suggest the befoulment of heroic values through the befoulment of the words and activities in which these values are recorded. Thus the fop's Grand Tour in IV mutilates a classical and Renaissance ideal (cf. also Virgil's Aeneas, to whose destined wanderings toward Rome the fop's are likened) of wisdom ripened by commerce with men and cities. Indeed, the lines of the whole passage are balanced between the ideal and the fop's perversions of it:

A dauntless infant! never scar'd with God.
Europe he saw, and Europe saw him too.
Judicious drank, and greatly daring dined;

or between related ideals and what has happened to them:

To happy Convents, bosomed deep in Vines,
Where slumber Abbots, purple as their Wines.

or between epic resonances, the epic names, and the sorry facts:

To where the Seine, obsequious as she runs,
Pours at great Bourbon's feet her silken sons.

This is one line of development in the **Dunciad.** The other is its converse: the epic vehicle is gradually made throughout the poem to enlarge and give a status of serious menace to all this ludicrous activity. Here the epic circumstance of a presiding goddess proved invaluable. Partly ludicrous herself, she could also become the locus of inexhaustible negation behind the movements of her trivial puppets; her force could be associated humorously, but also seriously, with the powerful names of Chaos, Night, Anti-Christ, and with perversions of favourite order symbols like the sun, monarchy, and gravitation. Here, too, the epic backgrounds as supplied by Milton could be drawn in. Mr. C. S. Lewis has remarked of *Paradise Lost* that 'only those will fully understand it who see that it might have been a comic poem'. The **Dunciad** is one realization of that might-have-been. Over and above the flow of Miltonic echoes and allusions, or the structural resemblances like Cibber's (or Theobald's) Pisgah-vision based on Adam's, or the clustered names of dunces like those of Milton's devils, thick as the leaves that strew bad books in Grubstreet—the **Dunciad** is a version of Milton's theme in being the story of an uncreating Logos. As the poem progresses, our sense of this increases through the calling in of more and more powerful associations by the epic vehicle. The activities of the dunces and of Dulness are more and more equated with religious anti-values, culminating in the passage on the Eucharist. . . . The metaphor of the coronation of the king-dunce moves always closer to and then flows into the metaphor of the Day of the Lord, the descent of the anti-Messiah, the uncreating Word. Meantime, symbols which have formerly been ludicrous—insects, for instance, or sleep—are given by this expansion in the epic vehicle a more sombre cast. The dunces thicken and become less individual, more anonymous, expressive of blind inertia—bees in swarm, or locusts blackening the land. Sleep becomes tied up with its baser physical manifestations, with drunkenness, with deception, with ignorance, with neglect of obligation, and finally with death. This is the sleep which *is* death, we realize, a *Narrendämmerung,* the twilight of the moral will. And yet, because of the ambivalence of the mock-heroic metaphor, Pope can keep to the end the tension between all these creatures as comic and ridiculous, and their destructive potentiality in being so. Certainly two of the finest puns in any poetry are those with which he continues to exploit this tension at the very end of the poem, when Dulness finally *yawns* and Nature *nods.*

Thomas R. Edwards (essay date 1963)

SOURCE: "The Mighty Maze: *An Essay on Man,"* in *Alexander Pope,* edited and with an introduction by Harold Bloom, Chelsea House Publishers, 1986, pp. 37-50.

[*Edwards was an American educator who has written extensively on poetry and politics. In the following essay, originally published in his* This Dark Estate: A Reading of Pope *(1963), he discusses problems in reasoning in* An Essay on Man, *concluding that "no one could deny that the poem would be better if its argument were more consistently reasoned . . . [but its] poetic failure is the curious measure of its human success."*]

Pope is shown confronting a difficult poetic problem in ***An Essay on Man*** (1729-1734). As an "official" argument for philosophical optimism the poem cannot avoid simplification and direct statement; yet there are signs in the verse that Pope was uncomfortable with didactic strategies. He was not a very gifted thinker, if by that word we mean someone capable of clear and sound consecutive reasoning; by accepting the didactic role, he incurred an obligation to be rational that he could not fulfill. Yet the ***Essay,*** even though it is unsound at its avowed center, cannot be dismissed simply as a failure. The poem is partly redeemed by just those aspects of temperament and sensibility that made Pope's didacticism unsuccessful. By this I mean that the didactic impulse (whether it originated in Pope or in Bolingbroke makes no difference) is thwarted in the poem partly by the views of experience and expression that I have called Augustan. Though the ***Essay*** lacks thoroughgoing doctrinal coherence, still in some important ways it succeeds as a poem, even at the expense of its philosophy. What we have, I think, is a case of sensibility opposing and finally killing doctrine, as Pope's grasp of real experience stubbornly resists the use of such experience as a vehicle for rational abstraction. But sensibility kills doctrine only that it may assert positive values of its own, values firmly rooted in direct apprehension of the beautiful complexity of actual things.

The Voice of God

In the opening address to Bolingbroke we seem, as has often been remarked, to overhear one of the participants in a conversation between well-bred Augustans. The contempt for the vulgarity of worldly aspirations in "leave all meaner things / To low ambition and the pride of Kings"; the discreet parenthetical admission that life is short and futile, followed by urbanely stoic determination to make the most of it; the action, an observant ramble through the woods and gardens of the world; the Chesterfieldian resolution to restrain mirth but to be "candid" about human folly whenever decorum permits—every detail works to define the speaker and his unheard companion as eighteenth-century gentlemen of leisure and cultivation. The extended metaphor of the world as a "Wild" or a "Garden" works nicely—in its rich variety the world exists to be explored by sophisticated men of sound judgment, who "expatiate" over it intellectually just as they range over their estates hunting beasts and birds. "Nature's walks" will mean more as the poem progress; Pope has his eye on actual nature at the same time that his inner eye contemplates a larger, more abstract nature. But what is most significant here is simply the decorum of tone with which the subject is introduced.

This tone of urbane detachment is conversational, but without any of the colloquial raciness of rhythm and idiom so common in the satires. "Awake, my St. John" is a rather lofty kind of informality, and in fact the conversational element in the passage soon is counterpointed by another sort of speech: "Say first, of God above, or Man below / What can we reason, but from what we know?" These lines may be addressed to Bolingbroke, posing a rhetorical question as prelude to discussing a topic on which they generally agree, but it is hard not to feel that Bolingbroke has lost most of his dramatic individuality and become something like the epic muse. The dramatic situation changes and Bolingbroke disappears for a time as Pope pays his ironic respects to the astronautical fancies of John Wilkins and the Royal Society and to the Lucretian image of the speculative philosopher as supernatural voyager. It is obviously impossible for ordinary human reason to achieve such clear perception of the universe, and the consequent irony in "thy pervading soul" indicates a shift of situation. The "thee" being addressed is no longer Bolingbroke but "Presumptuous Man." Conversation becomes oratory, a change predicted by the elevation of tone in the opening line; and it is at the oratorical level that the poem will mainly conduct its argument.

This shift of tone is of course not complete. The conversational beginning persists in the inner ear throughout the poem, providing an implicit context for the oratory. We are both Pope's equals, sharing Bolingbroke's gratification at having our own ideas expressed so handsomely for us, and also his pupils, resisting in our ignorant pride the messages of reason that are being delivered. The didactic poet runs the danger of not being able to justify his knowledgeable tone. He must sound just a little like God, which is all right when the subject is crop rotation or beekeeping, something in which his *expertise* (or lack of it) can be assessed; but if he ventures upon high speculation, where authority is a more uncertain matter, his voice may grow uncomfortably pontifical. Pope often does talk like God in the *Essay.* His subject commits him to saying that human consciousness cannot comprehend orders of being higher than its own, and yet he must himself at times speak as if the whole hierarchy were visible to him: "All Nature is but Art, unknown to thee; / All Chance, Direction, which thou canst not see." The frame of conversation eases some of this pontificality. Our double identity in the poem—as the speaker's peers and as his congregation—allows us to feel the full weight of the sermon even as we participate in its delivery. Although we take the preacher seriously, we usually can remember that he is not a fanatic but a gentleman like us.

Still, our suspicions are not wholly allayed by the interplay of tones. When the voice becomes markedly aloof and judicative we tend to distrust it, and it does so too frequently to allow complete reconciliation. Pope's decision to cast the *Essay* in the form of direct and "sincere" moralizing involved a considerable problem of rhetoric. Disinterested sincerity in Swift, for example, is almost always a sign of irony, as Martin Price notes:

> The mask of impartiality, if it were not qualified by humor, was as much a questionable type as were those of partisan zeal. Constant claims of "modest proposals" to "universal benefit" were keys to pretentious and specious disinterestedness. "I burnt all my Lord———'s letters," Swift wrote to Betty Germain, "upon receiving one where he had used these words to me, 'all I pretend to is a great deal of sincerity,' which indeed, was the chief virtue he wanted."

Pope's later satires brilliantly demonstrate moral involvement; we are persuaded that he has chosen the right cause and that his vehemence marks a powerful and admirable indignation. The mask of cool disengagement, as worn by an Addison or a Chesterfield, seems unpleasantly lifeless when set next to Swift's or Pope's vigorous expressions of commitment. By choosing the disengaged man for his *persona* in the *Essay* Pope took on a difficult task, and the poem succeeds as much in the breaking of this dramatic fiction as in the observing of it.

Human Limits and Natural Harmony

The theme of the *Essay on Man* is the familiar one of reconciling the apparent chaos of natural experience with man's intimations of ultimate order. The traditional concept of the "correspondences," the analogies that connect the human world with the natural below and the divine above, operates in the poem as a distinctly uncertain possiblity. "Presumptuous Man" has questions to put to nature, but nature, while it seems in its variety to embody some principle of significant order, cannot tell him precisely what that order is. Both nature and man are ignorant, that is, but only man is cursed by the yearning to know. His "knowledge," as the passage on "the poor Indian" reveals, is essentially derived from mythmaking; the Indian simply projects, in all innocence, a "heaven" that is an idealized version of his known world. The results are not "true," but they serve the purposes of consolation, and the Indian, for all his pastoral naïveté, is happier than

civilized man. It is the same predicament that so vexes Swift—one scarcely wants to be a fool, yet one suspects that ignorance and delusion are the only sources of serenity in a world which will not bear too much scrutiny.

Pope will not settle, however, for this view in its purest, most desperate form. Analogy *can* give a general sense of man's place in the scheme; man cannot look directly upward to the ultimate source of order, but he can look downward and make metaphors for his own lot from the relationships he perceives in the lower orders of the Scale of Being. But metaphor was not knowledge to the post-Hobbesian mind, and a steady skeptical undercurrent qualifies Pope's dogmatism. To assume, as Whitehead did, that Pope "was untroubled by the great perplexity which haunts the modern world," that he was "confident that the enlightened methods of modern science provided a plan adequate as a map of the 'mighty maze,'" is to ignore the complexity of Pope's view, as the lines on Newton show. Newton could answer all questions except the most important ones, those that concern the "movement of his Mind," "his own beginning, or his end." The irony places science in the right human perspective—Newton's unfolding of natural law must be contemplated in relation to his inability even to "describe," much less "explain," his own position in a universe of time and change.

This criticism of "reason" becomes explicit in the rest of Epistle II. It is a mistake to view the poem through the Victorian lens of "an age of prose and reason." As Professor Lovejoy observes, the most influential authors of the eighteenth century

> made a great point of reducing man's claims to "reason" to a minimum, and of belittling the importance of the faculty in human existence; and the vice of "pride" which they so delighted to castigate was exemplified for them in any high estimate of the capacity of the human species for intellectual achievement, or in any of the more ambitious enterprises of science and philosophy, or in any moral idea which would make pure reason (as distinguished from natural "passions") the supreme power in human life.

One of the strongest forces drawing Pope away from a simple confidence in reason is his understanding that like any human faculty, it operates within the confines of "the lurking principle of death." The phrase appears only as a simile within a passage whose main subject is the power of a "ruling passion" to undermine mental health; but the idea of life being a gradual dying reminds us of that area of the whole scheme which reason cannot investigate. Reason has its value, but Pope takes the Platonic view of it as "guard," not "guide," in a world whose springs of action are passionate.

In short, all that man can know about the processes of time and change are their fragmentary effects on nature and himself. His sense of his own identity, which he yearns to define in relation to these processes, must remain disconnected and dim. There is thus a tragic paradox in Pope's use of the Scale of Being, which has lost its former metaphoric potency as a true ladder by which man might transcend his earthly condition. The concept suggests that man is a part of a cosmic perfection, but he can never experience that perfection while he remains man. The problem for the moralist lay in man's discontent with his lot. If it is a condition of his middle status, how can he be censured for feeling discontent? And yet, the whole tenor of the poem insists, it is disastrous to him to feel it! Analogy is not a solution; to know something by analogy is painfully unlike knowing it by experience, and it is for experience of perfection that man yearns. But Pope's job in the ***Essay*** is to forbid despair; he evades this impasse, not very consistently, by occasionally giving ground before the theological pressure that bears on his position: "Hope humbly then; with trembling pinions soar; / Wait the great teacher Death, and God adore!" While one may "adore" perfection in this world, only in some world to come can one *know* it—if then.

Such difficulties in defining the ultimate reality lead Pope's sermon to its essentially negative center. Whatever man should be in this world, he should at least not be proud. He is neither the center nor the master of nature. The dangers of pride are clear in I, where the ironies rebuke the arrogant anthropocentrism of supposing that the creatiorr exists to serve man and mirror his feelings; it is equally clear in this fine "anti-pastoral" passage:

> Is it for thee the lark ascends and sings?
> Joy tunes his voice, joy elevates his wings:
> Is it for thee the linnet pours his throat?
> Loves of his own and raptures swell the note . . .
> The hog, that plows not nor obeys thy call,
> Lives on the labours of this lord of all.

The couplets play off the imagined nature invented by human pride against the real nature which exists as much for its own purposes as for man's. The natural world is full of life and feeling, but it is independent of "this lord of all." But there are consolations in man's position:

>   he only knows,
> And helps, another creature's wants and woes.
> Say, will the falcon, stooping from above,
> Smit with her varying plumage, spare the dove?
> Admires the jay the insect's gilded wings?
> Or hears the hawk when Philomela sings?

Nature is not responsive to man, but man is responsive to nature in a way that no merely natural creature can be. Through his unique gifts of compassion and esthetic appreciation he can penetrate into nature and so in a sense participate in it. He achieves a moral dignity that no other creature can have, but by submitting to, not dominating over, the rest of creation. He is in fact a part of nature, though not in the way he would like to be. He is "Fix'd like a plant on his peculiar spot, / To draw nutrition, propagate, and rot." While his place in the Scale involves painful complexities of feeling from which the lower orders are free, he can nonetheless relate his own life and death to the rhythms of nature. The simile denies man's cherished illusions of freedom, even as it offers compen-

sation in vegetable simplicity. Although reason distinguishes man from the other creatures, the "fruits" of virtue grow from "savage stocks"—the "wild Nature" working at man's roots is ultimately the same nature that gives productive life (and death) to the nonhuman creation.

The analogies of nature thus point down and not up. Man will find his place in the scheme not by yearning for higher status but by accepting his relationship with the lower creatures. Still, to know that man and nature are parts of a single order is not to resolve man's yearning for a direct, intimate bond with the things of this world. In Epistle III Pope postulates such a bond, in the pastoral innocence of Eden or the Golden Age from which man fell. Despite Hobbes, "the state of Nature was the reign of God." Human history has represented a decline from this primal perfection, as man created the social arts, commerce, secular government, and ultimately tyranny and superstition through the exercise of reason. These inventions stemmed from natural promptings to imitate the lower creatures, and thus were not originally wrong; the turning point, the beginning of man's alienation from nature, came when superstition replaced "charity" with "zeal" and secular power no longer had to reflect a spiritual order that was fundamentally benevolent. Faced with such chaos, man was "Forc'd into virtue thus by Self-defence"; through the inspired examples of the poet and the lawgiver the "shadow," if not the "image," of true divinity was rediscovered, and secular organization again became a metaphor for the great hierarchy of nature. The pyramids of "Beast, Man, or Angel" and of "Servant, Lord, or King" regained their congruence, with each order topped by the single point which is God.

Epistle III does not of course afford a very satisfying account of moral history. Nor is it poetically the strongest section of the ***Essay***. Some of Pope's metaphors ring false; how true is it to say, for instance, that the "Ant's republic" provided a model for human society, or even (reading not historically but "mythically," as we probably should) that it affords a very enlightening analogy? Pope has his difficulties in leading the poem in a positive direction, for all the assurance of his tone. Yet in the great passage on social harmony he comes as close as he can to solving the problem of the whole poem, through an Augustan appeal to the traditional concept of the *concordia discors*. Harmony is simply a special condition of discordance, and as Maynard Mack observes, the metaphor's power in the ***Essay*** stems from a doubleness associated with the figure from earliest classical times: "the image brought together in one perspective man's present suffering and his faith, the partial and the whole views; [and suggested] that in some higher dialectic than men could grasp the thesis and antithesis of experienced evil would be resolved." One may wish that the image were more solidly developed out of the argument of Epistle III, but its power is undeniable. The stability of even the best human society resides in a rather precarious balance of stresses, but that even a limited harmony is conceivable in the secular world consoles us if we take that harmony as an echo, however faint, of the grand but unhearable cosmic composition. The original intimacy of man and nature vanished when man lost his innocence, but in a social order that is properly attuned to the order of nature, a measure of intimacy can be restored.

The Power of Time

This is as close as the ***Essay*** comes to expressing anything like "optimism" in our ordinary sense of the word. It is not very close, we see, when we ponder Pope's implicit comparison of the poem with *Paradise Lost*. The Fall of Man was marked by his subjugation to Sin and Death, which is to say to *time* and its fundamental enmity to human value. It is the fact of time, Professor Lovejoy argues, that ultimately invalidates the concept of the Scale of Being:

> A world of time and change . . . is a world which can neither be deduced from nor reconciled with the postulate that existence is the expression and consequence of a system of "eternal" and "necessary" truths inherent in the very logic of being. Since such a system could manifest itself only in a static and constant world, and since empirical reality is not static and constant, the "image" (as Plato called it) does not correspond with the supposed "model" and cannot be explained by it. *Any* change whereby nature at one time contains other things or more things than it contains at another time is fatal to the principle of sufficient reason.

Milton reconciles a temporal world to cosmic immutability by appealing to the orthodox concept of Redemption: because of the sacrifice of Christ, man can look forward to an eventual translation out of time into a realm of being which is perfectly changeless. The ***Essay on Man*** seems at times to yield to theological pressure, but Pope must generally exclude specific Christian doctrine. Whether or not he believed in the redemption of souls, in the ***Essay*** his subject is not eternity, which cannot be known, but this world and how to endure it. And the possibilities of earthly experience seem far from cheerful.

Epistle IV is especially rich in allusions to death, which strikes capriciously, without regard for "justice." Even though by Pope's time the idea of an impersonal, mechanistic universe must have seemed considerably less terrible than it had to Shakespeare or Donne, the concept still could not have been a very comfortable one to entertain. Pope in fact does not entertain it fully; his rhetoric is addressed to the enormous task of making natural impersonality a source of comfort. Falkland, Turenne, and Sidney did not die *because* they were virtuous; nature cannot recognize either virtue or vice. But because the universe does not observe moral law, as men know it, does not mean that it obeys *no* law: "Think we, like some weak Prince, th' Eternal Cause / Prone for his fav'rites to reverse his laws?" The answer is "no"—the analogy of earthly order to supernal points out the weakness of the former only to assert the consoling perfection of the latter.

But this appeal to the "externalist pathos," the emotional power of the idea of immutability upon man's sense of his own involvement in time, cannot fully subdue the sobering fact of human mortality:

> What's Fame? a fancy'd life in others breath,
> A thing beyond us, ev'n before our death.
> Just what you hear, you have, and what's unknown
> The same (my Lord) if Tully's or your own.
> All that we feel of it begins and ends
> In the small circle of our foes or friends.

In this paraphrase of ***The Temple of Fame*** Pope again sees personal fame as sorry compensation for the necessity of dying. The lines, to be sure, state a positive view of personal relations, which Pope always cherished: "The only pleasure which any one either of high or low rank must depend upon receiving," he wrote to Ralph Allen, "is in the Candour or Partiality of Friends and that Smaller Circle we are conversant in." But this is tacit recognition that the pleasures of friendship are fleeting; they are valuable, they are in fact all that one has, but like everything else they will soon pass. Nor is wisdom any more reliable. When Pope returns to gentlemanly conversation with Bolingbroke, it is only to place rueful emphasis on the futility of "Parts superior." Wisdom leads finally to frustration and loneliness:

> Truths would you teach, or save a sinking land?
> All fear, none aid you, and few understand.
> Painful preheminence! yourself to view
> Above life's weakness, and its comforts too.

As wise man, Bolingbroke stands as symbol of man's dissatisfaction with his mixed nature and his ambiguous role in creation. The cost of intelligence is fearfully high: "'Tis but to know how little can be known."

Hierarchy and Experience

The description of Bolingbroke has implications for the reader as well. Pope's rhetorical aim has been to put us in Bolingbroke's position, to improve our understanding so as to reveal how limited understanding must be. It is flattering to be admitted to such company, but the reader's new point of view is a difficult one—the "optimism" of the poem involves a serious recognition of its own limitations and of the oppositions that are all too likely to overcome it. But Pope's "official" theme will not permit so complex a view to prevail, and this inhibition leads to a crucial poetic difficulty. In Section vi of Epistle IV he undertakes to demolish "the false scale of Happiness" that prevents most men from understanding their roles in the true scale of Being. "External goods" cannot prevent "human Infelicity"—"the perfection of Virtue and Happiness consists in a conformity to the ORDER OF PROVIDENCE here, and a resignation to it here and hereafter." The trouble is that the false scale, since one knows it through immediate experience, lends itself more readily to poetic particularization than does the hypothetical, unexperienced "true" hierarchy.

The ***Essay*** both faces up to the difficult facts of human experience and attempts to make them bearable by assigning them functions in a hierarchical order. An appeal to hierarchy draws its rhetorical power from the useful changes of name that are made possible, and we not that Pope's arguments usually hinge on such redefinition:

Respecting Man, whatever wrong we call,
May, must be right, as relative to all.

Cease then, nor ORDER Imperfection name.

All Nature is but Art, unknown to thee.

Modes of Self-love the Passions we may call.

Know then this truth (enough for Man to know)
"Virtue alone is Happiness below."

Man, that is to say, tends to call things by their "wrong" names, and in so doing he confirms his own unhappiness, since he cannot make his vocabulary jibe with any consoling conceptual scheme of order. God, however, calls things by their "right" names. If man can translate his words for experiences into a vocabulary that fits an imaginative hierarchy extending beyond the limits of his knowledge, most of his anxiety about the human condition will turn out to have been the result of terminological muddles.

Like any example of sophisticated rhetoric, then, the *Essay* draws much of its persuasive force from a view of language that is fundamentally magical. The translation of our names for experiences into a new vocabulary is a therapeutic act, for to change the name is to change the "fact"—or at least to make it bearable—by providing a new context of ideas and feelings in which to contemplate it. Pope again is God, for he knows the right names. At the same time, however, this transformation of terms adds to our sense that the poem is "enclosed" by the speaking voice of an individual human being with whom we have a particular social relationship. The semantic shifts appeal to common sense: we share with Pope a firm identity within a community of intelligence and taste, and so he can confidently invite us to agree with him about names, since a defining characteristic of a community is the mutual acceptance of "proper" vocabularies. For example, we share his amusement at the Neo-Platonists who call "quitting sense" "imitating God" Like "Eastern priests," they are somehow exotic, not a part of the community, and his manner of addressing us defines us as persons who share his belief that "sense" plays a vital part in any activity, religion not excepted. Once we have agreed about the right name for one kind of experience, we are inclined to accept the speaker's judgment about names in cases which are further from communal assumptions. Although the tone of such transformations is usually didactic, it is softened by our sense that we have come to occupy much the same ground from which Pope speaks.

But Pope's appeal to an explicit hierarchy of values involves him in poetic difficulties. In the *Essay* he expresses the complexity of human experience in a world that is at best indifferent to man; but he also attempts to resolve complexity into simplicity by relating experience to a predefined system of absolute values. In passages like Pride's speech in Epistle I there is no poetic problem, since the "right" attitude is developed out of an initial "wrong" view which is nevertheless fairly (even beautifully) expressed. Both complexity and simplicity are there, in

the verse, and the adjustment between them is dramatized as argument. But as the poem draws to its close, Pope must increasingly derogate the false scale in order to emphasize the finality of the true one, as in the passage on the need for human love to "rise from Individual to the Whole":

Self-love but serves the virtuous mind to wake,
As the small pebble stirs the peaceful lake;
The centre mov'd, a circle strait succeeds,
Another still, and still another spreads,
Friend, parent, neighbor, first it will embrace,
His country next, and next all human race. . . .

Pope has no better luck than any other eighteenth-century moralist in bridging the gap between self-love and social. The metaphor seems arbitrary—Addison would have called the play on "wake" and "stir" an example of false wit, dependent upon "resemblance of words" rather than of ideas, and there is nothing else to persuade us that self-love and pebbles are analogous—and it seems positively muddled unless we exclude the entire metaphorical vehicle from the "it" which embraces friends, parents, and the like. This passage is the climax of Pope's final affirmation of the true scale, and it simply does not work when we measure it against the Johnsonian description of the fate of the worldly, the great "glory, jest, and riddle" section that begins Epistle II, or any of the other passages in which Pope treats human experience with full respect for its complexity. When he rises from the individual to the whole something unfortunate happens to his verse.

The trouble seems due not only to Pope's weakness in rational argument but also to the nature of his subject. Whitehead said that both the Greek and medieval Christian views of nature were essentially "dramatic," which is to say they supposed a nature that worked toward purposes which could in some way be understood by human beings and that included human experience in its operation. The nature Pope has to work with is a very different one. He can deal dramatically with experiential reality in all its complexity, but in the *Essay* he must also transcend experience to knowledge of permanence and order; and since his "climate of opinion" presupposes a cosmos which is not dramatic but mechanistic, and thus largely foreign to human experience, his invocations of supernatural order are seldom fully convincing. When he can find in the natural world some evidence of the Scale—when he deals with the "esthetic" order his senses perceive—the *Essay* achieves its great poetic triumphs by fusing rhetoric and imaginative particularity. At such moments metaphor functions meaningfully, for the grand tenor is elucidated by solidly realized vehicles. But when natural experience is left behind in the attempt to prove that one knows what one insists is beyond knowledge, an attempt that must rely on rhetoric alone, the *Essay* loses much of its power. Mechanism is not only unattractive as an idea, it is also nearly impossible to dramatize in experiential terms. It is immediate experience that sustains Pope's Augustan mediations, and when doctrinal considerations exert their thinning or confusing tendencies on the experiential vehicle, he shows his weakness in the kind of poetic reasoning that a Dryden or a Wordsworth might bring off. His tendency to resort to conventional pietism illustrates this weakness. He tries to soften the concept of mechanism by hinting that the Christian God is at the controls, but this scrambles his argument; for example, at the end of the poem, when he declares that virtue is not only the sole source of earthly happiness but also a way to ascend to God, we uneasily feel that he has come close to contradicting his earlier assertion that the quality of human life, *as man knows it,* has no relevance to the ultimate reality. But the main problem is a literary and not just a logical one. It is not that Pope tries to make us know what he himself has called unknowable, but that the quality of the knowledge we receive is flawed by his inability to manage an abstract poetic idiom. When he treats the "true Scale" his language is less rich, less interesting, and above all less intelligible than when he expresses the perplexing imperfections of actual experience. His sensibility was attuned to the concrete, the immediate, and the *Essay* is not fully alive at the moments when its oratory loses touch with natural particulars.

The poem finally seems most interesting when read not as philosophy but as an expression of a conflict between views of reality as excitingly terrible and as ultimately orderly and peaceful. In such a reading one sees Pope as a man whose strong sense of the value of order makes experienced disorder a dreadful thing to consider, and who yearns for an imaginative myth of cosmic immutability to sustain and console him. The myth does not work perfectly, to be sure; when the poetic speaker invokes a hierarchy that he has not fully grasped imaginatively, the poem falters, regaining its stride only when he returns to the world he can experience directly. But another kind of drama emerges from this conflict of experience and speculation, a drama in which a human being tries out ways of coming to terms with his situation and finds that though none are entirely adequate some work better than others. A man who was wholly convinced by his own vision of order would not need to test it so often against actuality; Pope's poetic concern for real things and real feelings (another way of saying his humanity) refuses to surrender to his speculations, and the result is poetry. The poetry is intermittent, to be sure. When Mr. Mack calls the *Essay on Man* the greatest speculative poem in English between *Paradise Lost* and *The Prelude,* we think as much of the decline such poetry suffered in the eighteenth century as of Pope's achievement. No one could deny that the poem would be better if its argument were more consistently reasoned, if the didactic impulse were more cogently realized. But such "intentional" success would have taken the *Essay* even further from the Augustan mode's complex adjustment of ideal and actual, and the poem's poetic failure is the curious meausre of its human success.

Thomas R. Edwards (essay date 1971)

SOURCE: "Visible Poetry: Pope and Modern Criticism," in *Twentieth-Century Literature in Retrospect,* edited by Reuben A. Brower, Harvard University Press, 1971, pp. 299-321.

[*Below, Edwards provides an overview of twentieth century critical reaction to Pope's works.*]

It was only ninety years ago that Arnold pronounced Dryden and Pope "classics of our prose." In 1880 Shaw was twenty-four, Yeats fifteen, Joyce two years unborn and Lawrence five; as Arnold suspected, a new literary age was dawning, one that would find his view of the Augustan poets no more congenial than many of his other views. But modern criticism was shaped by the need to answer Arnold, and our idea of Pope owes more than we like to admit to the Arnoldian terms it rejects.

The terms themselves are of course almost embarrassingly vulnerable: "Are Dryden and Pope poetical classics? Is the historic estimate, which represents them as such and which has been so long established that it cannot easily give way, the real estimate? Wordsworth and Coleridge, as is well known, denied it; but the authority of Wordsworth and Coleridge does not weigh much with the younger generation, and there are many signs to show that the eighteenth century and its judgments are coming into favor again. Are the favorite poets of the eighteenth century classics?"

Few others abide our question as meekly as Dryden and Pope, that is; but in fact these questions are rather feeble. The favorite poets of the eighteenth century were not Dryden and Pope at all, but Homer, Shakespeare, and Milton, Arnold's and everyone's favorites; and it is a slippery logic that would make the high estimate of the Augustans both a "long established" piety and an irritating fad of an impertinent new age. Yet if both "the historic estimate" and "the younger generation" have the suspicious rustle of the straw-man, still, our answers to Arnold on this matter have led to confusions of our own, not least the assumption that he spoke for an "official" Victorian culture unanimously insensitive or hostile to the Augustans. He himself assumed no such thing—his tone is defensive, if belligerently so.

Victorian taste resists casual definition—there was so *much* of it—but Arnold's age was of several minds about Pope. Arnold himself was restating a standard eighteenth-century view: that of, for example, Joseph Warton's insistence that "ethical poetry" like Pope's, however excellent of its kind, was of a lower order than the poetry of Shakespeare, Spenser, and Milton [*Essay on the Genius and Writings of Pope* (1756, 1782)]. (Johnson's defense of Pope tacitly conceded the point.) What Warton was saying in the 1750's Wordsworth was still saying in the 1830's: "if the beautiful, the pathetic, and the sublime be what a poet should chiefly aim at, how absurd it is to place these men [Dryden and Pope] amongst the first poets of their country! Admirable are they in treading their way, but that way lies almost at the foot of Parnassus" [*Letters of the Wordsworth Family,*]. (In the same remark, however, he admitted that "to this day I believe I could repeat, with a little previous rummaging of my memory, several thousand lines of Pope.") This historic estimate was memorably summed up, a decade before Arnold's remarks, by a Victorian belles-lettrist improbably named John Dennis, in whom Pope's Appius indeed lived on in softer forms of passion: "He has written none of the verses which children love, nor any lines which grown-up people care to croon over in moments of weakness or sorrow. [No Touchstones, in fact?] In his works the wit o'ertops the poetry, the intellect gets the better of the heart, and thus he wins admiration from his readers rather than affection" ["Alexander Pope," in *Frazier's Magazine* (May 1870)].

But of course there was another line on Pope kept alive in appreciative remarks by Byron, De Quincey and others, the line taken by Thackeray in *The English Humourists* (1853):

> In considering Pope's admirable career, I am forced into similitudes drawn from other courage and greatness, and into comparing him with those who achieved triumphs in actual war. I think of the works of the young Pope as I do the actions of young Bonaparte or young Nelson. In their common life you will find frailties and meannesses, as great as the vices of the meanest men. But in the presence of the great occasion, the great soul flashes out, and conquers transcendent. In thinking of the splendour of Pope's young victories, of his merit, unequalled as his renown, I hail and salute the achieving genius, and do homage to the pen of a hero.

This sees Pope less as poet than as Representative Man, but Thackeray's "admirable career" at least has more generous intentions than Wordsworth's "admirable are they in treading their way," Dennis' "admiration . . . rather than affection," Arnold's own "admirable for the purposes of the high priest of an age of prose and reason." And an even higher heroic tone was being taken by Swinburne in the same year "The Study of Poetry" appeared:

> And what a spirit it was! how fiery bright and dauntless! . . . It rouses the blood, it kindles the heart, to remember what an indomitable force of heroic spirit, and sleepless always as fire, was inclosed in the pitiful body of the misshapen weakling whose whole life was spent in fighting the good fight of sense against folly, of light against darkness, of human speech against brute silence, of truth and reason and manhood against all the banded bestialities of all dunces and all dastards, all blackguardly blockheads and all blockheaded blackguards, who then as now were misbegotten by malignity on dulness. ["A Century of English Poetry," *Fortnightly Review* (October 1880),]

One sees what Arnold had to contend with. Yet it was convenient for the twentieth-century estimate of Pope, in its beginnings in Bloomsbury, to take Arnold's estimate as representing the nineteenth century in toto. Lytton Strachey and Virginia Woolf admired the feeling rationality of Pope and his contemporaries—what Strachey, who aspired to it himself, appreciatively called "civilization illuminated by animosity"—largely because it so neatly rebuked the muddle of high principles, pomposity, and aggressive coarseness of taste in the Victorian ancestors they were so anxious to live down. In the charming prank she called a biography of Pope, Edith Sitwell put the new mood with characteristic verve:

A large section of the public has not yet recovered from the cold, damp mossiness that has blighted the public taste for the last fifty or even sixty years; and to these people, Pope is not one of the greatest of our poets, one of the most loveable of men, but a man who was deformed in spirit as in body . . . This general blighting and withering of the poetic taste is the result of the public mind having been overshadowed by such Aberdeen-granite tombs and monuments as Matthew Arnold—is the result, also, of the substitution of scholar for poet, of school-inspector for artist. [*Alexander Pope* (1930)]

One loves Pope in order to punish those one does not love, and the famous deformities make the preference all the more cruel— "What can such a nice girl see in him?" poor Arnold is imagined jealously asking. Bloomsbury does to public taste, in Arnold's name, what Arnold in his day did to public taste in Pope's name.

Now if compelled to choose, which of us would not prefer Arnold's "culture" to Lytton Strachey's "civilization," even if it meant losing Pope? High seriousness is at least serious, if rather high. But the idea of such a choice is a nice historical irony—Arnold wins the argument, in effect, by establishing the terms in which even Pope's better champions, outside Bloomsbury, show that he loses it. For Eliot and Pound, though their main stakes were elsewhere, Pope could be invoked to show a "hard" sensibility that measured the softness of a received and debased tradition. (If Pope, of all people, was good, then Milton, Shelley, and Tennyson were really out of luck.) For Empson, whose *Seven Types* in 1930 gave him more attention than anyone except Shakespeare and put him to some of the best "close reading" he's received, Pope was excellent proof of the complexity of motive good poetry reveals. For Leavis, Pope carried the healthy seventeenth-century "line of wit" farther than Eliot's scheme allowed, while embodying a positive integrity of culture and imagination that later ages would try to vulgarize or destroy. For American "New Critics" like Brooks and Tate, Pope demonstrated the "anti-Platonic" energy of wit and paradox. For Geoffrey Tillotson Pope showed the validity of "period" conventions of style we had forgot how to understand; for Maynard Mack he showed the rhetorical operations of the neoclassical genres, especially satire; for Reuben Brower he showed how poetry is made of other poetry, particularly the classical poets Pope's age felt in their brains as we feel Joyce and Eliot in ours; for a current generation of scholar-critics he shows how poetry contains the stuff of intellectual history, the philosophical, religious, political, and economic assumptions of an age. For Marshall McLuhan (to end a tiring list with a bang) the ***Dunciad*** gives a true account of how Gutenbergian typography detaches words from their meanings and ushers "the polite world back into primitivism, the Africa within, and above all, the unconscious."

This summary is of course cavalier and superficial; the study of Pope has been one of the finest achievements of our age of critical redefinition. Yet that achievement is significantly colored, and inhibited, by Arnold's terms. We deny that Pope was, in Arnold's sense, the high priest of an age of prose and reason by substituting for "prose and reason" qualities more to our taste—and to Arnold's, some of them. We find "imagination" in the wit of his imagery, organizational control rather than pedantry in his allusions, moral and metaphysical seriousness in his "social" attitudes and ironies; in general he serves as a useful corrective to a too narrow idea of poetry. Quite so, these findings are right—yet in effect we may only have redefined "prose and reason" as *something better* for Pope to be the high priest of, some other state of mind and culture he positively and masterfully can represent.

Our age understands more than Arnold about the nature of Pope's materials, the expressiveness of his poetic "prose" and the issues at play beneath the surface of his "reason"; but I doubt that we have sufficiently asked whether his *relation* to those materials is priestlike. Does our approval of Pope mean as much as it seems to? Do we read him for pleasure as we do other great poets? Do students find him as exciting as we tell them they should? Do teachers fight and scheme to teach him as they do to teach Shakespeare, Blake, Yeats, Chaucer, Milton, Wordsworth? In short, does Pope occupy minds today as something more than a little treasury of marvelous passages, and of brilliant exegetical moments in the masters of modern criticism? We can "analyze" his verse beautifully, appreciate his relation to his culture ancient and modern, see how the genres contributed to his art; but have we really grasped the pleasures, and the difficulties, of his poems as whole literary experiences?

I want to suggest that Pope's perspective on his own "civilization," what Arnold meant by prose and reason, was in its own way no less questioning and skeptical than Arnold's perspective on his, or ours on our own. And Pope's perspective is implicit in his way of organizing his materials, in the demands his "extensive" kind of poetry makes on the mind as one reads. My example will be Epistle II of the *Essay on Man,* a poem which, more than Pope's others, presents itself as reasoned, sequential discourse and seems to deny itself the digressive excitements of satire. Here Pope is as close as he ever gets to talking like a high priest, an official spokesman who knows the answers and aims to tell the truth for his reader's own good. Though sequential interpretation can be tedious, it may be useful to look through the Epistle part by part, to see what its way of progressing suggests about Pope's relation to his own poetic art.

Epistle II begins memorably with the great "glory, jest, and riddle" passage, which from its location both summarizes the attack in Epistle I on "Presumptuous Man" for failing to apprehend the implicit order in creation and establishes the ground for what follows, the account of passion's role in human experience:

> Know then thyself, presume not God to scan;
> The proper study of Mankind is Man.
> Plac'd on this isthmus of a middle state,
> A being darkly wise, and rudely great:
> With too much knowledge for the Sceptic side,
> With too much weakness for the Stoic's pride,
> He hangs between; in doubt to act, or rest,

> In doubt to deem himself a God, or Beast;
> In doubt his Mind or Body to prefer,
> Born but to die, and reas'ning but to err;
> Alike in ignorance, his reason such,
> Whether he thinks too little, or too much:
> Chaos of Thought and Passion, all confus'd;
> Still by himself abus'd, or disabus'd;
> Created half to rise, and half to fall;
> Great lord of all things, yet a prey to all;
> Sole judge of Truth, in endless Error hurl'd:
> The glory, jest, and riddle of the world!

Maynard Mack's notes for these eighteen lines in the "Twickenham" edition run to more than a hundred lines of small type, with dozens of references to Pascal, Montaigne, Hooker, Milton, Robert Gould, Bezaleel Morrice, and other thoughtful worthies. Pope was well aware of the ethical traditions behind him, and Mack admirably explains the relation of Epistle II to the philosophical design of the whole poem. Yet that design seems more coherent in Mack's exegesis than it does in reading the poem; in this passage one feels a complexity of attitude that derives from the "background" but that also expresses a particular, dramatically "located" state of mind which the ideas themselves don't wholly account for.

That confident, magisterial first couplet seems to settle things—now that we know our proper study, all should be well. Yet what follows is unsettling. We are the pitifully confused thing we should study; and how can it hope to study itself? The antithetical, oxymoron-ridden verse patterns emphasize man's isthmian place in the creation, the terrible paradoxes of his nature—our nature. But once "Man" becomes "he," a third person both poet and reader can stand aside from, the paradoxes seem not to be personally menacing problems but the substance of a familiar and intelligible human situation. The contradictions in man's nature, that is, become material for speculative conversation—this is the voice of someone who "talks that way" and with whom we can thus be fairly comfortable, though (like Rosenkrantz and Guildenstern listening to "what a piece of work is a man") we risk something by assuming we know how to take such a message from such a voice.

But the rather abrupt rise of sarcasm in the following attack on speculative intellect—"Go, wondrous creature! mount where Science guides"—disturbs the reader's new-found composure. We can accept the general proposition that man is an absurd mixture of jarring natures, we've heard *that* before, but it hurts when intellectual heroes like Newton and Boyle (to say nothing of Plato!)—men we admire and are proud to claim as fellow creatures—are put to ridicule. And indeed the indulgence in an exhilarating Juvenalian, or Swiftian, animus ("Go, teach Eternal Wisdom how to rule—/ Then drop into thyself, and be a fool!") does yield to a kind of control:

> Superior beings, when of late they saw
> A mortal Man unfold all Nature's law,
> Admir'd such wisdom in an earthly shape,
> And shew'd a NEWTON as we shew an Ape.

This puts Newton in his place, but it's not simply a ludicrous place. It makes some sense to value apes for their surprising and charming resemblances to us, and there's some comfort in hearing that "superior beings" aren't wholly unlike us in their pleasures. If Newton thinks the universe centers upon him, then the lines are a terrible affront; but if he understands (as Pope wants us to do) that the creation is a design of overlapping hierarchies in which apes, men, and superior beings have a mutual relation that shames none of them, he will find the remark as complimentary as it is satirical and limiting.

> **Modern criticism has excellently told the main truth about pope, that he is a poet, that the great moments are fully imagined, complex, rich in evoked faling, mature in moral intelligence.**
>
> —*Thomas R. Edwards*

The point is that this opening section is made up of movements and countermovements of feeling, false starts, interruptions, and collisions. The poetic mind that examines man's isthmian nature also demonstrates it in its own noticeable shifts of emphasis and outlook. Elsewhere in this volume Paul J. Alpers speaks of the "seamless" effect of Milton's blank verse, one's sense that new material grows out of what has gone before without evident transitions or connections, like a tapestry endlessly unrolling before the eye. Pope's couplet verse, here and elsewhere, works quite differently—passages are being arranged as we watch, visibly put together for maximum effect like pieces of furniture in a large room, or like ideas in the Lockeian mind. (Even the self-containment of Pope's couplets suggests that "parts" are being arranged, that the verse moves not through "organic" growth but through a conscious and even ostentatious "art.") This is not, of course, mere "interior decoration," but the process of a poetry that confesses and makes a virtue of the uncertain, provisional nature of its own effects. The making of a rational doctrine—what Pope's prose "Arguments" for the four Epistles try to convey—is as much upset as advanced by a moment like the Newton-ape passage, which is less a contribution to the "thought" of the poem than a cue to a properly complex response to it, a response that in a way is also a resistance to the thought.

I am suggesting that Pope's is an art that makes visible its own difficulties in achieving structural coherence and doctrinal clarity. Epistle II shows him trying to accommodate doctrine to moral imagination, by finding and releasing elements in the traditional psychology of reason-and-passion that could support his own interest in irrational energy without sanctioning utter mindlessness. From Newton he moves rather abruptly to "Self-love" and "Reason" as the defining terms of isthmian self-awareness. It is not an exciting stretch of poetry, but in his analogies for self-love—the spring of motion in the mind's clockwork without which human life would be only a vegetable cycle, a kind of mental eyesight that takes short but intense views—one can at least see him searching for the best that can be said for unregulated passion, and the verse finally does wake up a bit:

> In lazy Apathy let Stoics boast
> Their Virtue fix'd; 'tis fix'd as in a frost,
> Contracted all, retiring to the breast;
> But strength of mind is Exercise, not Rest:
> The rising tempest puts in act the soul,
> Parts it may ravage, but preserves the whole.
> On life's vast ocean diversely we sail,
> Reason the card, but Passion is the gale;
> Nor God alone in the still calm we find,
> He mounts the storm, and walks upon the wind.

As usual when the issue crystalizes into an object, a human embodiment of error like the lazy Stoic, Pope gets down to poetic business, here that of finding and sustaining a tone feelingly vigorous enough to support the claims being made for the value of passionate activity.

The culminating analogy for the relation of Reason and Passion comes here, and it stresses the difficult complexity of their interaction:

> Passions, like Elements, tho' born to fight,
> Yet, mix'd and soften'd, in his [God's] work unite:
> These 'tis enough to temper and employ;
> But what composes Man, can Man destroy?
> Suffice that Reason keep to Nature's road,
> Subject, compound them, follow her and God.
> Love, Hope, and Joy, fair pleasure's smiling train,
> Hate, Fear, and Grief, the family of pain;
> These mix'd with art, and to due bounds confin'd,
> Make and maintain the balance of the mind:
> The light and shades, whose well accorded strife
> Gives all the strength and colour of our life.

Reason, God's "work," operates on the passions like a painter mixing and modifying his colors, creating balance out of elements that would glaringly clash if no such composing art held them in accord. The analogy was commonplace in ethical theory, and one sees why. Where the writer or musician in effect makes something of nothing—the words or sounds he "creates" are not the paper and ink he uses—the painter organizes what already exists. The finished painting is only the paint he began with, though wonderfully modified by what he has done with it. The passage says quite directly that such an ethical "art" is possible and desirable. Our life *can* be beautiful if we let reason exercise its composing powers. The conventionality of the terms—"fair pleasure's smiling train," "the family of pain"—does seem tacitly to confess that such an art ends in virtual cliché, like allegorical painting: the balanced mind isn't very novel or glamorous. But "the strength and colour of our life" ends the passage with a hopeful touch of vividness and affirmation.

But the Epistle is less than half finished, and this resolved mood is shadowed by the pages yet unturned, the lines we know remain to be read. Incompleteness was hinted at by "confin'd" and "strife," the rhyme words that may not be entirely appeased by their echo in "mind" and "life." (The rhymes indeed make us remember, not forget, the tension implicit in "balance.") And the next passage, though it begins with assured delight in a work compatible with the art of reason ("Pleasures are ever in our hands and eyes"), soon runs into a challenging qualification: "All spread their charms, but charm not all alike." Minds are not regular and uniform; receptivity to the objects of rational pleasure differs from man to man, and in each man one "master Passion" lurks, "like Aaron's serpent," to crowd out the other passions that should be part of the balanced whole. "The ruling passion is the manifestation of God's power," says the "Twickenham" note on Aaron's serpent, but as "Man" we consider the allusion as much from the viewpoint of Pharaoh and his magicians—it's an unnatural mystery that shakes our belief in the dignity of our own powers—as from Moses' and God's viewpoint. And this return to uncertainty is confirmed by lines 133-144, where the "lurking principle of death" in the youngest and healthiest constitution is the figure for the ruling passion, "the Mind's disease" which, fed by imagination, concentrates in one spot the "vital humour" that should nourish the whole psychic economy. The "dang'rous art" of imagination subverts the art of reason and we are back on the dark isthmus, in the chaos of thought and passion we supposed the analogy with art had transformed into "the balance of the mind."

This seems to be the crux of the ethical problem. Reason, which should control and guide natural impulse into integration of the self, seems in practice only a grim judge condemning our folly without helping us overcome it: "What can she more than tell us we are fools?" Epistle II manfully seeks a positive answer, but Pope's art in effect shows that it really has no answer—that the reason of the ethical poet, the authority by which he condemns bad men and praises good ones, is always provisional and ad hoc, an unprovable instinct that acts powerfully in negative modes but is virtually helpless to accomplish its purpose of satiric correction. To tell the rational truth about Sporus, Cibber, Atticus, Atossa, or Timon is to punish them so severely as to fix them in their defiant antipathy to truth and nature; and all the Men of Ross in the world won't lead them back to virtue's paths once Pope's reason has pronounced sentence upon them. In practice we either rationalize our vices into self-justification or conceive a horror of self from which there's no exit into positive, active virtue.

In short, the isthmian mood returns in the middle of Epistle II in a form that strikes closer to home than the large ethical commonplaces we admired but were so well able to bear in the opening lines. The verse of the middle sections is quieter, more abstract and discursive, than the high rhetoric earlier; but if anything this makes the mood harder to resist, less "placeable" as poetic or philosophical mannerism. Even so, Pope works hard at mitigating this dark idea of reason's practical impotence. "Nature" is invoked as authorizing a view of reason as "no guide, but still a guard"; all men are at least consistent in their individual passionate fixations, though the consistency may be trivial or pathetic and ultimately self-defeating:

> Thro' life 'tis follow'd, ev'n at life's expence;
> The merchant's toil, the sage's indolence,
> The monk's humility, the hero's pride,
> All, all alike, find Reason on their side.

Reason is simply that which transmits natural energy into usable social forms; like delicate fruits grafted on "savage stocks . . . the surest Virtues thus from Passions shoot, / Wild Nature's vigor working at the root" as anger is transformed to "zeal and fortitude," avarice to "prudence," pride and shame to "Virtue" (chastity), and so on. Reason is less a faculty than a disposition of mind, a channel through which passion flows and, in its passage, is purified into "civilized" behavior—virtue comes, as it were, not from repression but from sublimation.

Pope tries hopefully to see the passivity of reason both as transformational medium and as the instrument that measures the resulting differentiation between "negative" impulse and "positive" virtue: "This light and darkness in our chaos join'd / What shall divide? The God within the mind." Yet this couplet sums up a passage on the virtuous potential of villainy that seems very precarious (Nero and Cataline are so established in their evil roles by history as to make the thought that they *could* have been good seem empty theorizing—"Nero reigns a Titus, if he will," but he won't, he didn't) and from the metaphor of sorting out emerges a new and less hopeful appeal to the mixing of effects in painting:

> Extremes in Nature equal ends produce,
> In Man they join to some mysterious use;
> Tho' each by turns the other's bounds invade,
> As, in some well-wrought picture, light and shade,
> And oft so mix, the diff'rence is too nice
> Where ends the Virtue, and begins the Vice.

These lines are a kind of miniature of the larger movement of the poem. The positive claim for the "mysterious use" of extremes is made; but what follows dwells not upon the use, the achievement of "balance," as above, but the mystery, in four lines of concession that pull against the hopeful commonplace. Here painting signifies not integration of opposites but the impossibility of telling light from shade, virtue from vice, in a well-made picture of human character. As usual, Pope's dialectic moves away from synthesis when it seems to have been achieved— it unresolves what had seemed settled. Though we (addressed as "Fools!") are immediately warned that we know very well the difference between vice and virtue, this stubborn common sense appeals not to reason but, as the "Twickenham" note says, to an "intuitive" apprehension that vice and virtue exist and are different. We get so used to our own vices as to think them less dreadful than our neighbors, but this is only because custom and self-interest film over the ugliness we naturally recognize at first sight.

This section of the epistle seems a jumble of claims, concessions, and qualifications that is almost impossible to follow as "argument." But we miss the point, I think, if we simply judge Pope a bad philosopher and the poem therefore faulty. Rather, in Pope's very visible difficulty in reconciling the ethical doctrines philosophers offer us, something significant is expressed. A poet's mind lets us see what it is doing—making poetry out of lumps of philosophy that resist becoming poetry. The mind that can't quite resolve these ideas into coherent unity is a recognizably human one, by no means immune to the weakness and error it finds in the mind of "Man." Whatever we make of the argument, we can follow the ethical poet's refusal to ignore or sentimentalize human folly as it struggles against his determination to salvage from the chaos some basis (almost any will do) for continuation of life within that chaos. The qualification and redirection of points, the shifts of tone and mood, express not mere confusion but a visible and meaningful dissatisfaction with what one can say, what one has said, about the nature of moral consciousness. Pope shares some of Eliot's understanding of the hopelessness, and the absolute necessity, of philosophical poetry, where each attempt at truth is

> a new beginning, a raid on the inarticulate
> With shabby equipment always deteriorating
> In the general mess of imprecision of feeling,
> Undisciplined squads of emotion.
>
> T. S. Eliot, "East Coker"

Pope's view of "emotion" is less austere than this, but despite its assertive moments the general tone of the *Essay on Man* is anything but confident and cheerful. Not the substance of a doctrine, but the activity of trying to formulate it satisfactorily—and only partly succeeding, and knowing that the success is only partial—is what Pope most powerfully expresses.

The making of poetry out of resistances to one's own doctrinal impulses is especially clear and impressive in the last section (VI) of Epistle II. In a long passage Pope first seems to arrive at the goal, a mood (if not a coherent argument) that sums up and turns to positive account the hesitations and contradictions that have accumulated. All men are virtuous *and* vicious in idiosyncratic ways, but "Heaven's great view is One, and that the Whole"—God counteracts our weakness by assigning to each man the "happy frailty" that suits his station. The "glory, jest, and riddle" formula is converted into terms that seem to answer and resolve it—"[Heaven] builds on wants, and on defects on mind, / The joy, the peace, the glory of Mankind"—and Pope goes on to praise Society as the gift of heaven that puts passion and weakness into a reciprocal play that serves all needs:

> Wants, frailties, passions, closer still ally
> The common int'rest, or endear the tie:
> To these we owe true friendship, love sincere,
> Each home-felt joy that life inherits here:
> Yet from the same we learn, in its decline,
> Those joys, those loves, those int'rests to resign:

Taught half by Reason, half by mere decay,
To welcome death, and calmly pass away.

There is still a half-turn ("Yet from the same . . .) from positive to qualifying negative, but the dying fall delicately makes death seem a necessary and acceptable completion of "life." The Epistle could end here.

But of course it doesn't, and the thirty-four concluding lines are astonishing in this context—as well as being, independent of context, one of Pope's finest pieces of poetry. "Half by Reason, half *by mere decay*" recalls something the analysis of reason and passion has largely obscured, the biological imperative, so to speak, that shadowed the opening lines but had little part in the ethical speculations that followed. Life reconciles you to the self you are—such has been the Epistle's hopeful burden—but the result looks different from another perspective:

> The learn'd is happy nature to explore,
> The fool is happy that he knows no more;
> The rich is happy in the plenty giv'n,
> The poor contents him with the care of Heav'n.
> See the blind beggar dance, the cripple sing,
> The sot a hero, lunatic a king;
> The starving chemist in his golden views
> Supremely blest, the poet in his muse.

Happiness may indeed compensate for our deficiencies, but a world of dancing blindmen, singing cripples, drunks and madmen convinced of their own heroic grandeur, obsessed alchemists and "inspired" poets, is no happy prospect to the rational reader. This is the world of Swift's "Digression on Madness," the world of the misers in *To Bathurst* who starve themselves to fatten their bank accounts, the world of the poor compulsive scribbler in *Arbuthnot* who "lock'd from Ink and Paper, scrawls / With desp'rate Charcoal round his darken'd walls," the world of nonsense that oozes from the inner sanctuary of Dulness herself:

> Hence the Fool's paradise, the Statesman's scheme,
> The air-built Castle, and the golden Dream,
> The Maid's romantic wish, the Chymist's flame,
> And Poet's vision of eternal fame.
>
> (*Dunciad,*)

Such happiness heartbreakingly feeds on delusion and suffering, and the visionary intensity of Pope's "See" mixes rapt fascination with an almost unbearable pitying wisdom—*this* is what heaven offers to make our isthmian lot endurable!

At this moment it is hard to value the doctrinal point, that passionate self-deception is God's way of allowing man to live at all. Once you know what Pope knows in these lines, their consoling power mostly disappears. He does try to regain the "philosophical" perspective:

> See some strange comfort ev'ry state attend,
> And Pride bestow'd on all, a common friend;
> See some fit Passion ev'ry age supply,
> Hope travels thro', nor quits us when we die.

But the terms and implications clash with the doctrine. That persistent "Hope" is what sustains the Dunces, the obsessed women of *To a Lady,* the lost souls at the end of *To Cobham* whose hopeful deaths merely re-enact the compulsive follies that ruined their lives. "Some *strange* comfort" is not said by someone who takes much comfort in it himself, and while "a common friend" tries to mean a mutual, impartial one, it comes close to meaning an indiscriminate one, notoriously available to all like a common alehouse or a common whore. (A friend who's everyone's friend seems no friend at all; and of course the antecedent for all this is *Pride.*) And what follows offers strange comfort indeed:

> Behold the child, by Nature's kindly law,
> Pleas'd with a rattle, tickled with a straw:
> Some livelier play-thing gives his youth delight,
> A little louder, but as empty quite:
> Scarfs, garters, gold, amuse his riper stage;
> And beads and pray'r-books are the toys of age:
> Pleas'd with this bauble still, as that before;
> 'Till tir'd he sleeps, and Life's poor play is o'er!

Jaques' "strange eventful history" of the ages of man is seen here with more compassion but equal melancholy; for Pope "Life's poor play" defines man less as actor than child, indulged by "kindly" nature and unable to grow up to put away childish things. Again, the voice that speaks knows better, yet can't really insist on its superior wisdom—we have not been reconciled to the isthmian state but made to feel its inadequacy and folly even more poignantly.

And this discontent, what the poem vows to talk us out of, is not appeased but further exacerbated by the final reappearance of the analogy with painting, which now stresses the illusory quality of the attitudes that sustain us:

> Mean-while Opinion gilds with varying rays
> Those painted clouds that beautify our days;
> Each want of happiness by Hope supply'd,
> And each vacuity of sense by Pride:
> These build as fast as knowledge can destroy;
> In Folly's cup still laughs the bubble, joy;
> One prospect lost, another still we gain;
> And not a vanity is giv'n in vain;
> Ev'n mean Self-love becomes, by force divine,
> The scale to measure others wants by thine.
> See! and confess, one comfort still must rise,
> 'Tis this, Tho' Man's a fool, yet GOD IS WISE.

The doctrine is adequately preserved—man's folly proves God's wisdom in giving comforts even to foolish creatures. But the final couplet is imaginatively less "final" for coming after such a vision of human futility. To see and confess one's folly requires that one be wise enough to recognize it as folly and desire something better—yet according to the poem that desire is itself foolish. The difficult argument leads back to its beginning, the dark isthmus from which both mainlands are always poignantly visible but unattainable. Still, if the proper study is circular and frustrating, the proper student, the reader, has learned

something. He now can see what is left unsaid by pronouncements about The Human Condition; he knows that "philosophy" as doctrinal product matters less than the activity of trying to produce it, the continual redefining and shifting of emphasis required to think seriously about the case.

When one asks what post-Arnoldian criticism of Pope has not sufficiently taken account of, so simple a matter as the poems' length comes to mind. The Horatian imitations, for example, are all longer than their originals, on average more than fifty percent longer; and if some of the excess is due to the relative prolixity of an uninflected language, still, English isn't that much wordier than Latin, and the concision of Pope's couplet English is proverbial. It is rather startling to realize that the **Dunciad** is longer than "Prufrock," *The Waste Land, Ash-Wednesday* and *Four Quartets* combined, and even the shorter major poems run to several hundred lines. And the scale is not supported by the devices one expects in long poems. No full-length story is told, at least not in any direct and efficient way; the perspectives of history or allegory are incompletely developed when they figure at all; there is, apart from **Eloisa to Abelard,** no intensive representation of a particular consciousness "personally" involved in its own experience. (The voice in **Arbuthnot** and the other "personal" satires is at least as much "the satirist" as he is "Pope.") It is usually hard to grasp the connection between a passage in Pope while reading it and a significant whole order of progression in the poem. There seems something provisional, potentially alterable, about the arrangement of parts; and of course Pope often did write "parts," passages that would later be fitted into poems, and many of his best works were rewritten, rearranged, added to or cut down, as second thoughts suggested new possibilities.

The lengthiness of the poems makes him a nuisance to anthologists, who must either print inferior shorter poems, truncate several of the masterpieces, or print one or two major poems in entirety and so exclude other aspects of a richly various body of work. And the anthologists' problem is in a way our critical problem too, since even learned readers mostly possess the poetic tradition as a kind of big personal anthology of favorites into which short poems fit better than long ones unless the latter are broken up into storable and retrievable "beauties." Pope belongs in that anthology, and prominently, but the great moments fit better than the poems. Or, if one abandons the anthology and gets down to work on Pope himself, it is easier and tidier to transform long and relatively "unstructured" works into a synthetic order made of selected passages, which when released from the whole context are more available for one's purposes—image tracing, genre definition, allusion hunting, intellectual historiography, whatever it is we "do." These things are worth doing, they help us to understand Pope as Arnold or even Johnson couldn't; but our sense of parts may interfere with an understanding of whole poems.

My account of Epistle II of the **Essay on Man** may roughly suggest a way of thinking about what Pope's long poems are like. By this account, the poem is a collection of moments assembled to cast light on or even interfere with each other. Some of the moments are memorable in themselves, others tend to fade when the eye leaves the page. And their order may seem tentative and logically loose—we remember what we remember not as a progressive, unfolding design but as a complex overlaying of conflicting attitudes and feelings that are not perfectly governed by the poem as formal object or generic instance. *The Rape of the Lock* is a well-made poem, perhaps Pope's most brilliant "design"; yet one remembers better the moments of excessive intensity—the sad and curiously useless wisdom of Clarissa's speech, for example, as it picks up earlier, glancing suggestions of the futility and pathos of merely "social" existence—than the splendid moments that grasp and place social details in the teasingly ironic main picture. The *Essay on Criticism* rehearses the standard neoclassical literary dicta, but only (as Empson shows) through jokes about Wit confessing that the kind of writer Pope is, while superior to the mere witlings who mostly make up the world of poetry and criticism, is yet from the perspective of truly great writers, the Ancients, rather small potatoes; what the Rules don't teach is finally more important than what they do. The *Essay on Man* and the *Moral Essays* represent a struggle between an ethical theory and a particular awareness of vice and folly that the theory can't quite take care of; the *Epistle to Arbuthnot* and the *Epilogue to the Satires* dramatize the virtual impossibility of reforming uncivilized behavior with the resources of civilized irony; the *Dunciad* is so confusing in plot and action because it is so insistent and thorough in detail, because the "myth" of Dulness can't wholly accommodate the passion of Pope's response to actual dunces or his fascination with the processes of degeneration that his "civilization" compels him to abhor.

Pope's poetry, that is, has less (though less is not nothing) to do with the neoclassical qualities of formal order, reasoned argument, logical coherence of parts, urbanity of manner, than we have tended to suppose. His verse is more than a way of presenting the data and skills of "Augustan" literary culture. I am convinced that the poems are not harmonious, resolved wholes, and that they are none the worse as poems therefore. They don't make sense taken as narrative or discursive orders like *Paradise Lost* or *The Prelude;* they do make "dramatic" sense only if one conceives of wit and poetry and Pope in terms that do more than turn the tables on Arnold. The past changes as we change, obviously, and the twentieth century might want to think Pope more like Eliot and Pound and the Stevens of the longer poems than like Milton or Wordsworth. If we think of his as a "visible" art—one that depends on recognizing and participating in logical and emotional discontinuity, juxtaposition of contradictory tones and moods, imperfect adjustment of feeling to convention—we might understand and enjoy him better.

So large and vague a suggestion of course solves nothing; I mean only to suggest that our view of Pope may be too comfortable, that his poems pose more difficulty than they seem to. One doesn't want to have to put on an imaginary periwig to read him, coming to him only by forgetting who and where we really are. On the other hand, too much "relevance" is worse than none at all—Pope is not *simply* a "modern" poet, and we must see and respect his differences from us because they are what he has to teach us. His poetry is not just a collection of fine passages, yet it really won't do to claim for it the "thematic" or "structural" or "imagistic" integrity we have invented to describe Shakespeare or the novelists or the lyric poets. He is more than the drawing-room wit his enemies think him, yet views of him as Swinburnian hero or McLuhanesque pivotal mind run into his own skeptical amusement about such pretensions even in himself. If he was in some sense a Christian poet, his religious moments usually sound like rhetorical devices; and his beliefs, such as they may have been, don't strongly bear on the subjects and moods his poetry takes as its imaginative province.

It may be better to accept these contradictions than to try to resolve them, seeing him as an artist imperfectly convinced that his own art worked, or that any human art could achieve its highest intentions. In the poems assertion and denial, positive hope and worldly skepticism, visibly confront and criticize each other. Progressive design turns back on itself questioningly, so that "endings" are usually inconclusive or despairing, as in *To Bathurst,* the *Epilogue,* or the *Dunciad.* Or, when the positive note is struck, as at the end of *The Rape of the Lock,* the *Essay on Man, To Burlington,* or *Arbuthnot,* one at least recognizes that it has been hard earned, that something has had to be left out to make the final major chord feasible. This is not to claim for him some tragic sense of life, only a wonderful power of perceiving the limits of secularized imagination and of letting *us* see that he sees them.

Modern criticism has excellently told the main truth about Pope, that he is a poet, that the great moments are fully imagined, complex, rich in evoked feeling, mature in moral intelligence. But the criticism is most useful and interesting when it asks how the poems render a mind at work— Empson and Brower are especially helpful here—and as yet it hasn't taken this direction often and fully enough. We know a great deal about Pope's "civilization," the cultural materials, ideas of personal style, and assumptions about literary manner and intention out of which he made poems. But it is not the mere possession of ideas and techniques, but possessing them in particular, potentially unstable ways that defines his civilization, which remains open to its discontents, the difficult possibilities its official tenets and assumptions tend to exclude. If he believed in prose and reason, it was because they were impossible; if he was a high priest, his sermons show his awareness that the church might fall on him at any moment. In a way, as Arnold saw, he was the wrong man to have taken on the task of realizing in English the shape and substance of what his age took to be the "classical" state of mind; in another way, that very wrongness is what makes his poems so compelling and potentially so congenial to the twentieth century, if—as of course I have failed to do, too—it can ever get Arnold out of its head.

G. Douglas Atkins (essay date 1983)

SOURCE: "'Gracing These Ribalds': The Play of Difference in Pope's *Epistle to Dr. Arbuthnot*", in *Reading Deconstruction/Deconstructive Reading,* University Press of Kentucky, 1983, pp. 118-35.

[*In the essay below, Atkins offers a deconstructionist reading of* Epistle to Dr. Arbuthnot, *focusing on the relation of the self to the other.*]

An Epistle to Dr. Arbuthnot is normally read as Pope's defense of himself and justification of his satire, as—in other words—his *apologia pro satura sua.* In the prose "Advertisement" that precedes the poem, Pope describes his aim, in fact, in legal terms as an indictment, establishing an adversarial situation and pitting himself and his word against certain others, their changes, and their "truth": "This Paper is a Sort of Bill of Complaint, begun many years since, and drawn up by snatches, as the several Occasions offer'd. I had no thoughts of publishing it, till it pleas'd some Persons of Rank and Fortune . . . to attack in a very extraordinary manner, not only my Writings (of which being publick the Publick judge) but my *Person, Morals,* and *Family,* whereof to those who know me not, a truer Information may be requisite." After making clear his own desire to tell the truth, Pope proceeds to describe himself as "divided between the Necessity to say something of Myself, and my own Laziness to undertake so awkward a Task." This confession of self-division is perhaps more suggestive, and important, than has hitherto been recognized. These two kinds of difference, that external form consisting of difference between (say) Pope and those he indicts, and the internal form representing self-division and rendering certain conventions problematical, will be my focus here. I shall attend, that is, to the story told by the play of difference in *Arbuthnot.* My effort, hardly exhaustive, will be exploratory and speculative.

I begin with Pope's defense, which consists in large part of a series of strategies designed to establish him as a "good man." He differentiates, for example, his background, motives, and character from those of "the Race that write," maintaining that, unlike the "Clerk, foredoom'd his Father's soul to cross, / Who pens a Stanza when he should *engross,*" he "left no Calling for this idle trade, / No Duty broke, no Father dis-obey'd. Depicting himself as a good man, Pope claims to rise above the level of "slashing *Bentley*" and "piddling *Tibalds,*" proceeding to adduce a list of illustrious friends to prove the difference; from them, he asserts, "the world will judge of Men and Books, / Not from the *Burnets, Oldmixons,* and *Cooks.*"

Pope focuses strategically on this matter of friendship as a means of establishing his virtue and his difference. Perhaps his most effective and economical rhetorical use of friendship appears in the choice of John Arbuthnot as "recipient" of his "epistle" and as interlocutor. As is well known, Pope draws on a tradition suggested in Ecclesiasticus 6:16 ("A faithful friend is the medicine of life") and developed by Plutarch, who, in a disquisition entitled "How to Know a Flatterer from a Friend," uses as a recurrent motif the comparison of a good friend to an able physician. Of course, Arbuthnot was by profession a physician (he had, in fact, been physician to Queen Anne), and if one accepts the view expressed by Sir William Temple, Pope is especially blessed in having a doctor as a friend: "In all Diseases of Body and Mind, 'tis happy to have an able Physician for a Friend, or a discreet friend for a Physician; which is so great a blessing that the Wise Man will have it to proceed only from God." That Arbuthnot was a satirist as well as a physician (he wrote the *History of John Bull,* coauthored with Pope and Gay *Three Hours after Marriage,* and was a member of the Scriblerus Club) allows Pope to suggest also the familiar notion that the satirist is, despite appearances to the contrary, a physician and a friend. Finally, because Arbuthnot was widely respected, Pope is able to draw on a tradition perhaps deriving from Aristotle's *Ethics* and to suggest that his friendship with such a man evidences his own virtue. When this good man speaks in the poem as interlocutor, therefore, his words carry considerable weight and authority. In his five short "speeches," Arbuthnot urges caution and restraint, warning against the naming of individuals, but he also assists in his friend's satire on Sporus.

The terms this particular friend enables Pope to exploit, "physician," "satirist," and "friend," serve indeed as focal structuring devices for the defense. The idea that links the first two here, "friend" is also the concept that differs from while connecting two other terms crucial to the poem's thematic development and Pope's strategies of defense. The terms appear together in lines 206-7: "A tim'rous foe, and a suspicious friend, / Dreading ev'n fools, by Flatterers besieg'd." Pope, of course, opposes "friend" to "foe," and the other term, "flatterers," is both distinguished from and linked to "foes"; indeed, the construction of line 104, which brings together the conclusion of Arbuthnot's warning concerning names and Pope's response thereto, illustrates the similarity and difference of the terms: "'But Foes like these!'—One Flatt'rer's worse than all." Pope's claims may, then, be described as follows: Because the satirist is a physician of sorts, he is ultimately a friend, even of those he lashes, intending to cure them of their follies and vices: "This dreaded Sat'rist *Dennis* will confess / Foe to his Pride, but Friend to his Distress." A satirist obviously differs from a flatterer, who, Pope insists, is ultimately a foe (Bufo well illustrates the point).

Though I have no doubt oversimplified in summarizing, the above represents, I think, Pope's basic line of argument in *An Epistle to Dr. Arbuthnot.* Indeed, Pope's defense exhibits many of the qualities Margaret W. Ferguson [in *The Literary Freud: Mechanisms of Defense and the Poetic Will*] claims as characteristic of the tradition of defenses of poetry; being classifiable as neither disinterested art nor disinterested critical commentary, becoming in fact "active rather than passive advocates for what we might call the claims of the ego," these defenses, according to Ferguson, act as "protection against external threats to the ego's task of defending itself against internal threats." It is impossible to do justice here to Ferguson's subtle and complex argument, and I have no intention of trying to apply her arguments to **Arbuthnot** in any consistent way, though a certain parallel will emerge between my argument below and her claim that the usual poetic defense "involves a complex double movement of attack and courtship." But of course, Pope's "Bill of Complaint" is more than merely defensive. To use J. Paul Hunter's helpful terms, in this poem satiric apology turns into satiric instance—one of several turns we shall consider. From the very beginning, indeed, Pope is concerned to draw straight, distinct, and unmistakable lines between himself and those others.

The poem opens, of course, with Pope seeking shelter from the would-be poets who besiege him wherever he goes. In escaping into his own home, Pope signals the desire for physical distance that is itself a sign of his desire for literary and moral differentiation. Outside, he maintains, with the poetasters lunacy rages, from which he would sequester and protect himself. The immediate danger Pope fears is contamination or infection; thus he laments, "What *Drop* or *Nostrum* can this Plague remove?". This seemingly innocent metaphor, like all other figures, carries great weight, for the medical plague has become, as here, a metaphor for a social plague. Indeed, it functions as a "generic label for a variety of ills that . . . threaten or seem to threaten the very existence of social life." [René Girard, *"To Double Business Bound,"* 1978.] In texts as divergent as *Oedipus Rex, Troilus and Cressida,* and Camus's 1948 novel, the plague acts as part of a thematic cluster that involves epidemic contamination and eventually the dissolving of differences. If Pope cannot cure the plague or be inoculated against it, he can at least reduce the possibility of infection by quaranteening himself and perhaps thus maintaining the difference that the plague threatens to collapse.

Pope preserves his difference not only by escaping from the "plague" but also by establishing his difference from others who, he argues, lack sufficient difference. The desire to differentiate himself takes several forms. Some of these we have already glimpsed, including the differences in background, motive, and character he draws between himself and "the Race that write." Naming is another basic means of differentiation, perhaps the simplest, and Pope indulges in naming the specific targets of his satire, despite Arbuthnot's warnings. Pope's most elaborate and effective means of differentiation, which happens to be his main offensive strategy, the famous linked portraits of Atticus, Bufo, and Sporus, is designed to advance the defensive strategy of establishing Pope as an alternative—indeed, as a true friend and a good man.

Before turning to these portraits, it is necessary to examine carefully Pope's desire for difference and the implications of his wish for clear and absolute distinctions. Such desire appears to be masculine, Pope wanting from the outset to establish what he later calls his "manly ways." To be a good man and a true friend is, according to Pope's strategy, to be distinct, to possess a clear identity—in short, to be different. Difference is the male quality, the presence of the penis. Pope's fear of the loss of difference may be seen, then, as fear of the loss of his maleness, or

castration. It is the fear that he will become, in fact, what Sporus was turned into: an in-different male, a male who was castrated and then treated as a woman, "one vile Antithesis. / Amphibious Thing!" In Pope's case, however, it is not so much castration as intercourse with him, feminized, that threatens: "What Walls can guard me, or what Shades can hide? / They pierce my Thickets, thro' my Grot they glide." The judgment rendered by Pope, after being "Seiz'd and ty'd down to judge," certainly carries sexual overtones: "'Keep your Piece nine years,'" an imagined suitor's reaction to which extending the implication ("'The Piece you think is incorrect: why take it, / I'm all submission, what you'd have it, make it'"). Feminized, Pope withdraws from these suitors and their assaults, declaring in the poem's opening lines, "Shut, shut the door, good *John!* fatigu'd I said, / Tye up the knocker, say I'm sick, I'm dead," "knocker" perhaps being the penis.

The enigmatic ferminization, or attempted feminization, of Pope cannot be understood, I contend, apart from the metaphorical treatment of writing in **Arbuthnot.** Pope of course claims that, whereas for the "Witlings" writing is a compulsion and a drive akin to madness, for him it is both a burden and a moral obligation. He also treats writing in sexual terms, as when he notes that "ev'ry Coxcomb knows me by my *Style*" and when he counsels to "'Keep your Piece nine years,'" "Piece" being both the written text and the sexual instrument and *"Style"* suggesting the *stylus* or penis. The references to Gildon's "venal quill," to Bufo "puff'd by ev'ry quill," and to "each gray goose quill" that a patron may bless, as well as to "slashing *Bentley,* indicate the relation of pen to penis— writing, according to Freud, entailing "making a liquid flow out of a tube onto a piece of white paper" and so assuming "the significance of copulation." The mob of would-be poets courting favor and Pope are thus said "To spread about the Itch of Verse and Praise." Pope makes clear that the writer with his pen(is) seeks pen-etration and satisfaction. As a result of Pope's own (masculine) writing, moreover, "Poor *Cornus* sees his frantic Wife elope, / And curses Wit, and Poetry, and *Pope.*"

Further, Pope depicts his own reception as a writer in terms that define writing as a masculine act and the response to a writer as feminine. Pope indeed describes his own writing in sexual terms ("The Muse but serv'd to ease some Friend, not Wife,") the suggestion of homosexuality being (anachronistically) supported by the statement that his friends "left me GAY." If writing and writers are masculine, and the response sought feminine, we can appreciate why Pope as would-be patron, courted for favor, is being treated as female. He becomes the sexual object pursued by the "Witlings."

Recalling the Freudian implications of eyes and sight, we can appreciate too the nature of Pope's withdrawal from the poet-suitors as he summarizes that withdrawal: "I sought no homage from the Race that write; / I kept, like *Asian* Monarchs, from their sight." Withdrawing, Pope refuses to mingle with the poetasters. He thus rejects the role of woman they seek to impose upon him: he will not be turned into their lover, their host, their patron.

Pope attempts, then, to preserve his difference (phallus) in the face of the dunces' aim to make him a patron-woman who can satisfy their desires as writer-males. He preserves his difference not only by withdrawing but also by establishing clear and distinct difference from others. Pope's most effective strategies of differentiation, and his most strenuous attacks, occur in the portraits of Atticus, Bufo, and Sporus, in which the language of sexuality and the sexuality of language are unmistakable.

The first portrait is of Atticus, whom Pope lashes for his failure to achieve distinct identity:

> . . . were there One whose fires
> True Genius kindles, and fair Fame inspires,
> Blest with each Talent and each Art to please,
> And born to write, converse, and live with ease:
> Shou'd such a man, too fond to rule alone,
> Bear, like the *Turk,* no brother near the throne,
> View him with scornful, yet with jealous eyes,
> And hate for Arts that caus'd himself to rise;
> Damn with faint praise, assent with civil leer,
> And without sneering, teach the rest to sneer;
> Willing to wound, and yet afraid to strike,
> Just hint a fault, and hesitate dislike;
> Alike reserv'd to blame, or to commend,
> A tim'rous foe, and a suspicious friend,
> Dreading ev'n fools, by Flatterers besieg'd,
> And so obliging that he ne'er oblig'd;
> Like *Cato,* give his little Senate laws,
> And sit attentive to his own applause;
> While Wits and Templers ev'ry sentence raise,
> And wonder with a foolish face of praise.
> Who but must laugh, if such a man there be?
> Who would not weep, if *Atticus* were he!

Different from the manliness Pope praises, Atticus appears weak, indistinct, unwilling to take a definite stand. He accedes to flattery, and if he attacks, it is barely. Unable to be really different, Atticus is not sufficiently masculine. Lacking in confidence, he fears competition for "the throne" and indeed hates the very "Arts" by which he has "risen" to that place.

With the second portrait the situation is more complicated. From more than one perspective Bufo is the central portrait—and arguably the most important difference Pope establishes in *Arbuthnot.* Bufo's importance derives in part from his similarity to Pope, particularly as the poet appears early on in the poem, courted by the flattering dunces. Pope's aim, of course, is to claim essential difference in this situation of similarity, thereby differentiating himself as true friend from the false friend (and foe) that Bufo the patron is. The theme of the portrait thus concerns the relationship of flatterer and flattered or, to use analogous terms, host and parasite. Clearly, the plagues of poetasters surrounding Bufo, like "the Race that write" courting Pope, are parasites. But just as clearly the patron-flattered-host Bufo functions also as a flatterer-parasite on what initially appear to be parasite-poetasters: for if as host Bufo feeds the "undistinguish'd race" of "Wits," he is fed in turn by the very parasites he feeds, feeding

on the parasites, changing places with them in a "see-saw between *that* and *this,*" and so finally becoming identifiable as neither simply parasite nor host, flatterer nor flattered, but as both.

> Proud, as *Apollo* on his forked hill,
> Sate full-blown *Bufo,* puff'd by ev'ry quill;
> Fed with soft Dedication all day long,
> *Horace* and he went hand in hand in song.
> His Library, (where Busts of Poets dead
> And a true *Pindar* stood without a head)
> Receiv'd of Wits an undistinguish'd race,
> Who first his Judgment ask'd, and then a Place:
> Much they extoll'd his Pictures, much his Seat,
> And flatter'd ev'ry day, and some days eat:
> Till grown more frugal in his riper days,
> He pay'd some Bards with Port, and some with Praise,
> To some a dry Rehearsal was assign'd,
> And others (harder still) he pay'd in kind.
> *Dryden* alone (what wonder?) came not nigh,
> *Dryden* alone escap'd this judging eye:
> But still the Great have kindness in reserve,
> He help'd to bury whom he help'd to starve.

The sexual language we have noted elsewhere in *Arbuthnot* appears here, too. For the portrait treats the relationship of male-female, as well as that of patron-poet and parasite-host. As the opening lines of the portrait indicate, what Pope feared does happen to a patron: "full blown" and "puff'd by ev'ry quill," Bufo becomes female in hosting the would-be poets. Yet he gets his revenge on the emasculating writers by becoming the castrated-castrating woman, for in his library (or womb) lie "dead" poets, including Pindar, who "stood without a head." Are these writers merely "spent"? Or is it that, feminized, Bufo feminizes, turning the masculine writer into a female if he is allowed to have his way? Perhaps it is both. With the male-female relationship, in any case, as with those others it treats, the Bufo portrait dramatizes the turning of one thing into another, destabilizing, indeed, differences usually arrested as distinct oppositions.

If Atticus is neither quite one thing nor fully another, neither adequately friend nor identifiably foe, Sporus is, more dramatically than Bufo, *both* one thing *and* another. According to one of the shrewdest commentators on the poem, Sporus is, therefore, "the very reverse of the divine reconciliation of opposites" [Thomas E. Maresca, *Pope's Horatian Poems,* 1966]. Assumed to represent John Lord Hervey, well known for effeminacy of both manner and appearance, Sporus is an "Antithesis" and an "Amphibious Thing," both male and female, oscillating "between *that* and *this*":

> Yet let me flap this Bug with gilded wings,
> This painted Child of Dirt that stinks and stings;
> Whose Buzz the Witty and the Fair annoys,
> Yet Wit ne'er tastes, and Beauty ne'er enjoys,
> So well-bred Spaniels civilly delight
> In mumbling of the Game they dare not bite.
> Eternal Smiles his Emptiness betray,

As shallow streams run dimpling all the way.
Whether in florid Impotence he speaks,
And, as the Prompter breathes, the Puppet squeaks;
Or at the Ear of *Eve,* familiar Toad,
Half Froth, half Venom, spits himself abroad,
In Puns, or Politicks, or Tales, or Lyes,
Or Spite, or Smut, or Rymes, or Blasphemies.
His Wit all see-saw between *that* and *this,*
Now high, now low, now Master up, now Miss,
And he himself one vile Antithesis.
Amphibious Thing! that acting either Part,
The trifling Head, or the corrupted Heart!
Fop at the Toilet, Flatt'rer at the Board,
Now trips a Lady, and now struts a Lord.
Eve's Tempter thus the Rabbins have exprest,
A Cherub's face, a Reptile all the rest;
Beauty that shocks you, Parts that none will trust,
Wit that can creep, and Pride that licks the dust.

According to Aubrey Williams [in *Poetry and Prose of Alexander Pope,* 1969], the name "Sporus" derives from the youth that the emperor Nero caused to be castrated and then, treating him as a woman, eventually married. Certainly, Pope's portrait presents Sporus as having lost his difference. He seems, in fact, to have succumbed, somewhat like Bufo, to pressures Pope has resisted, and that failure in Sporus no doubt accounts in part for the vigor of Pope's attack. Sporus both attacks and flatters, and so his efforts evidently cancel each other out. He is self-divided, opposing forces colliding within him. According to Pope, he is, then, impotent and empty.

Taking the portraits together, we notice a certain progression: whereas Atticus is not male enough, Bufo appears feminized, and Sporus is divided, being both male and female. The straight lines Pope has sought blur in Atticus, curve in Bufo, and become indeterminate, undecidable in Sporus. To them Pope aims to be an effective alternative, with his "manly ways." He has, of course, acted in an apparently "manly" way in setting up these differences in hopes of preserving his difference. Having established that difference, in part by showing his difference from those lacking difference, Pope now exhibits some interesting differences from himself, at least from himself as he has appeared in the poem.

Though they are by no means radical breaks, important differences appear immediately following the Sporus portrait. To begin with, there is the change to third-person narration, indicative of the indirectness that replaces the directness we have noted. The accompanying change in tone is also marked, Pope now appearing patient and long-suffering, receiving rather than giving blows and apparently no longer so intent on the kind of differentiation evident earlier. For "Virtue's better end," he claims, he withstood

The distant Threats of Vengeance on his head,
The Blow unfelt, the Tear he never shed;
The Tale reviv'd, the Lye so oft o'erthrown;
Th' imputed Trash, and Dulness not his own;
The Morals blacken'd when the Writings scape;

The libel'd Person, and the pictur'd Shape;
Abuse on all he lov'd, or lov'd him, spread,
A Friend in Exile, or a Father, dead.

Two verse paragraphs later Pope extends the argument, maintaining that he has actually befriended his attackers:

Full ten years slander'd, did he once reply?
Three thousand Suns went down on *Welsted*'s Lye:
To please a *Mistress,* One aspers'd his life;
He lash'd him not, but let her be his *Wife:*
Let *Budgel* charge low *Grubstreet* on his quill,
And write whate'er he pleas'd, except his *Will;*
Let the *Two Curls* of Town and Court, abuse
His Father, Mother, Body, Soul, and Muse.

The shift in these paragraphs in tone and from first- to third-person are but two of several significant internal differences that the remainder of the poem develops. To continue, the verse paragraph from which I have just quoted closes with Pope's praise of his father and mother for their tolerance and forbearance—qualities the son has not displayed, at least through the Sporus passage. Whereas the poet passed judgment, assigned blame, and launched often-scathing attacks, his "Father held it for a rule / It was a Sin to call our Neighbour Fool, / That harmless Mother thought no Wife a Whore." Obviously, such passages are designed to show the injustice of the attacks on Pope's family, but I think more is going on. For one thing, the following portrait of Pope's deceased father develops the differences between father and son, offering, indeed, a clear criticism of the poet as he appeared earlier in the poem. Presented as a kind of hero, the elder Pope is given the name the poet had sought for himself: "The good Man." Hero and *vir bonus,* the father is yet a *naif:* unlike his son, he was never involved in civil or religious controversy and never offered such a "Bill of Complaint" as is ***An Epistle to Dr. Arbuthnot.*** In phrases that inevitably recall his earlier depiction of "this long Disease, my Life," Pope even contrasts his father's lifelong healthfulness with his own illness and physical deformities:

Born to no Pride, inheriting no Strife,
Nor marrying Discord in a Noble Wife,
Stranger to Civil and Religious Rage,
The good Man walk'd innoxious thro' his Age.
No Courts he saw, no Suits would ever try,
Nor dar'd an Oath, nor hazarded a Lye:
Un-learn'd, he knew no Schoolman's subtle Art,
No Language, but the Language of the Heart.
By Nature honest, by Experience wise,
Healthy by Temp'rance and by Exercise:
His Life, tho' long, to sickness past unknown,
His Death was instant, and without a groan.

Pope proceeds to pray that he be allowed to live and die like his father; if so, "Who sprung from Kings shall know less joy than I." His father thus represents for Pope simplicity, naturalness, and innocence of discord, strife, and rage—in short, the pastoralism that the poet supposedly forsook as "not in Fancy's Maze he wander'd long, / But stoop'd to Truth, and moraliz'd his song." Whether Pope now wishes to return to "Fancy's Maze," there appears a nostalgic longing for simplicity and escape that connects with the desire evidenced in the poem's opening to get away from the "plague" of poetasters. Though he sought to appear "the good man," Pope now appears different from "the good man." What does this say about his effort to establish and preserve his difference?

We approach an answer to that question by noting that Pope seems desirous of leaving behind the burden of writing, a masculine activity that is in the poem, as we have seen, aggressive, differentiating, and indeed divisive. In deemphasizing writing, Pope seems to put penis, as well as pen, away, for very little sexual language appears in later sections of *Arbuthnot.* Withdrawing from writing-sex, Pope, "sick of Fops, and Poetry, and Prate, / To *Bufo* left the whole *Castalian* State." Having done so, he turns to his surviving but aged mother. Despite his earlier resistance to the attempted feminization of him, as well as his determined insistence on his "manly ways," Pope now depicts himself as nurse and mother to her. In effect, he changes places with his mother:

> Me, let the tender Office long engage
> To rock the Cradle of reposing Age,
> With lenient Arts extend a Mother's breath,
> Make Languor smile, and smooth the Bed of Death,
> Explore the Thought, explain the asking Eye,
> And keep a while one Parent from the Sky!

At poem's end, then, Pope evidently rejects the divisive life of writing for the immediacy, naturalness, and supposed peace of home and family. Pope thus withdraws, adopting his father as model and ideal and apparently hoping to repeat the innocence he represents. In so doing, Pope completes, it seems, the pattern established at the opening of the poem. But much more is happening, as we have begun to see. In several ways Pope comes to differ from "himself," appearing divided, just as his poem does. Pope implicitly admits that his desire of difference has produced precisely difference from at least one major ideal and goal. Moreover, shortly after adopting his father as ideal, Pope—in a quite different sense— adopts his mother, indeed mothering her; though his father is an ideal (even if nonassertive, nondifferentiating, and so only problematically masculine), Pope becomes a mother. If this is so, if difference thus plays with our desire, what difference does the desire of difference make in those oppositions around which *Arbuthnot* is constructed?

It begins to appear that binary oppositions are illusory. Consider, for instance, Pope's desire all along to project "manly ways" and to resist the feminization apparent in the poetasters' efforts to make him their patron. In spite of himself, Pope reveals throughout certain supposedly feminine traits. For as he defends his hard-hitting truth-telling, Pope resembles a coquette: he asks, coyly, "You think this cruel?" and "Whom have I hurt?" Further, when he admits, "If wrong, I smil'd; if right, I kiss'd the rod," the *double entendre* establishes his own position as female. Moreover, the act of withdrawing, apparent in the opening couplet and culminating in Pope's focus at

poem's end, seems a feminine act. Pope not only withdraws, of course, but, as we have seen, he also becomes nurse and mother. Thus differentiating, a masculine act, and withdrawing, a feminine one, result in the same loss of difference and the turn into the femininity Pope sought to avoid.

But "turn" can be misleading if it suggests a change from one stable and absolute identity into another. "Oscillation" may be better, for even when female qualities seem most apparent in Pope, they exist alongside and in oscillation with masculine ones. There are no absolute differences—and so no radical breaks in *Arbuthnot* before and after the Sporus portrait. Thus, even as he adopts his father as (nonassertive and nondifferentiating) model and ideal, Pope continues the (masculine) desire of clear, straight lines, for he posits his father as an absolute: innocent, simple, and natural. Pope thus substitutes one kind of absolute, one kind of distinctiveness, for another.

It seems that male and female qualities are actually coterminous in Pope as appears at poem's end when he is both drawn to his father and acts as mother. This is, of course, precisely what Pope objected to (and perhaps feared) in Sporus especially. It is to the Sporus portrait that I want now, in concluding, to return.

The internal split within the antithetical Sporus is obvious, but what that self-division signifies—and implies for Pope's own situation—may not be. Does it spell emptiness and impotence, as Pope declares? To begin with, consider that the name "Sporus" also suggests "spore," which comes from the New Latin *spora* (seed, spore), which derives from the Greek sense of both seed and the act of sowing, itself traceable to the word *speirein,* meaning "to sow." A spore is "a primitive usually unicellular resistant or reproductive body produced by plants and some invertebrates and capable of development into a new individual in some cases unlike the parent either directly or after fusion with another spore" *(Webster's New Collegiate Dictionary).* Whereas Sporus as a historical reference suggests the doubleness Pope emphasizes in the portrait, the etymology of the word denotes fertility and productiveness. This second, positive meaning is always in the word as a shimmering or trace that prevents the meaning from lying still or being unequivocal.

Though we may insist, with Pope, on Sporus' impotence, we can also insist on his at least potential fertility. That potential may, in fact, be seen as realized in Pope's satire. For within the poem the fertility is no longer merely potential but manifest and productive of satire. In a sense, Pope places Sporus, though not unproblematically, in the role of male to Pope's own female ability to produce.

The negative side of the coin that is Sporus, which represents Pope's declaration of Sporus' lack of difference as impotence, is simply but half the story. The other side shows how an internal split, an oscillation "between *that* and *this,"* can be positive and productive. The self-divi-

Hair, which I always mention with Reverence). The Human Persons are as Fictitious as the Airy ones; and the Character of *Belinda,* as it is now manag'd, resembles You in nothing but in Beauty. . . .

Addressed to Arabella, the letter is undoubtedly intended as an apologia to Pope's feminist readers. Following what Susan Schibanoff calls [in "Taking the Gold out of Egypt: The Art of Reading as a Woman," in *Gender and Reading*] the "well-established *topos* of manuscript literature," Pope hoped to "relieve the problems that the anti-feminist text [might cause] the female reader." But, rather than relieving problems, the letter actually makes the poem more offensive:

Authorial apologies to the female reader for anti-feminist texts are . . . something other than heart-felt laments. They are attempts both to intimidate her and . . . to immasculate her. They warn her that the written traditions of antifeminism have contemporary guardians and custodians who will not allow these texts to disappear.

Pope's duplicity is apparent from the first sentence. His claim that the poem is written for Arabella is false. The person to whom Pope actually addresses the poem is his friend John Caryll. Arabella's story, told to Pope by Caryll, may have "inspired" the poem, but it is Caryll and other males who are his "intended readers." Pope's anti-feminism appears full-blown in the second sentence: the poem is intended to "divert a few young ladies, who have good sense and good humor enough to laugh not only at their sex's little unguarded follies, but at their own." The choice of "divert" is perfect: Pope hopes to divert attention away from his act of misogynous judgment and focus it on what he calls the "folly" of female *nature.* Like the more or less formalist readers with whom reader-response criticism argues, Pope attempts to present activity and relationship as some reified, unchanging "nature." At this point the feminist reader must begin the "succession of decisions" that ultimately will determine her interpretation of the text. She must resist the text's seduction by referring to her own field of experience, becoming what might be called an "unintended reader"—the reader the text is designed to mislead.

Pope claims that his intention in revising *The Rape of the Lock* is to complete the poem by adding the *"Machinery."* Rather than simply explaining the change, Pope uses the revisions as an excuse to position and define his female readers in such a way that their only recourse is to imagine themselves as male readers—to "immasculate" themselves. He explains to his uneducated female readers the workings of *"Machinery,"* which he uses in imitation of the "ancient Poets," whose tendency to blow trivialities out of proportion is reminiscent of "modern Ladies." His audience for such a statement is not Arabella; rather it defines the readers as men who will appreciate the joke. When he explains the "hard Words" that women readers probably will not understand, this "male" laughter increases. The resisting reader knows, however, that Pope's humor illustrates the fact that women did not know the es-

oteric terminology of epic machinery because they were denied the opportunity to learn it. Only a small percentage of Pope's female readers could have had any training in the classics. Pope is not doing women readers a favor; he is openly ridiculing women for a lack created by the patriarchal society he represents and inviting *all* his readers to join in his misogyny. The laughter becomes louder as the "lessons" continue. Pope cannot identify his Rosicrucian source without a condescending reference to women's novel-reading, an activity that has made them so silly they might read non-fiction with a novelistic title and not know the difference.

Buried near the end of the letter is Pope's most revealing comment—a comment that ties him, and his poem, to [what Ellen Pollak calls] the eighteenth-century "cult of passive womanhood." His linking of Belinda to the Sylphs can be read as a warning to all women that they will only enjoy the protection of male society as long as they co-operate in the "inviolable preservation" of their chastity. The woman who strays loses the protection of the same society that led her astray in the first place.

Ironically, it is the strength of Pope's determination to preserve the status quo that most clearly reveals his weakness. He does not insult woman because she is inferior but because he fears the power her "otherness" symbolizes—those "secret Truths" known only to "Maids and Children." The site of her chastity is a dark place that men can only visit, leaving fragments of themselves and getting momentary pleasure in return. Woman's "chastity" represents a gap in her access to the mysterious powers of Nature. As long as she is kept chaste, the object of male desire, woman cannot know her own innate power as subject. If, as Sherry Ortner convincingly asserts [in "Is Female to Male as Nature Is to Culture?" in *Woman, Culture, and Society,* 1974], "Culture" is associated with the male and "Nature" with the female, the greatest fear of a phallocentric Culture, with only a tenuous hold on its power, must be that Nature will someday regain her supremacy. This is why Pope must stress such points as the artificiality of Belinda's "purer" blushes, created by rouge, not by Nature. It is crucial that woman be separated from Nature—kept in her place, threatened with ostracism, convinced of her ignorance, denied knowledge of her strength beyond cultural forms.

Once the phallocentric code of Pope's letter has been broken, reading the text of the poem itself produces a field of meaning quite different from the traditional interpretation. Rather than identifying with the "hero" who restores order to the (male) text and disapproving of Belinda, as the immasculated reader might have done, the de-immasculated reader's allegiance is reversed. She no longer reads against herself as "other" but with Belinda, the "other" against whom Pope writes.

To read "with" Belinda is difficult—everything in Pope's poem resists such reading—yet such a reading can reveal what Patrocinio Schweickart calls the "dual hermeneutic" of feminist reader-response: "a negative hermeneutic that discloses [male writers'] complicity with patriarchal ideology, and a positive hermeneutic that recuperates the utopian moment . . . from which they draw a significant portion of their emotional power." In Pope, the feminist negative hermeneutic is quite easily deployed because, in part, the mock-epic is a layered text that self-consciously uses its own negative moment satirically. In mock-epic, one layer, the "story" (or stories), is applied on top of a second, the "epic" implied by the form of the "discourse." In *The Rape of the Lock,* the primary story concerns an attack on the person of the vain Belinda, who worships at the altar of her toilet. Belinda goes on a day's outing—after spending hours in preparation. She expects a relaxing day of cards and gossip. In the midst of an innocent game of ombre, Belinda is attacked by an "admirer" who snips off one of her locks—one of two designed to show off her "smooth Iv'ry Neck." Pandemonium reigns. Belinda demands the return of the lock; she appeals to her foppish beau, Sir Plume, for assistance, but he, of the "unthinking Face," can only rap his snuffbox and mumble to himself. Ultimately, after much ado about nothing the lock rises magically into the heavens, to inscribe "mid'st the Stars" the name of Belinda. The uppity woman is put in her place; the status quo is restored.

At the level of the discourse, however, this rather unextraordinary plot is elevated to a higher plane. Belinda is not an ordinary woman but an earthly goddess, watched over by a "Guardian *Sylph,*" who is able to enlist the aid of all modes of divine "machinery." From the Vergilian invocation ("What dire Offence from am'rous Causes springs, / What mighty Contests rise from trivial Things, / I sing") to the Ovidian metamorphosis of the lock at the end of the poem, Pope superimposes the trivial story of Belinda onto the classical epic format. Belinda's toilet, for instance, has religious significance and magical powers. As Aeneas was "armed" with the power to conquer his enemies, so Belinda is armed with "Files of Pins" that "extend their shining Rows" and regiments of "Puffs, Powder, Patches, Bibles, [and] Billet-doux." As Aeneas was protected by his shield, Belinda is protected by her petticoats—a "sev'nfold Fence," "arm'd with Ribs of Whale." Canto III contains the epic digression of the Games, followed by the fatal attack on the lock that forces Belinda (as Achilles was forced by the death of Patroclus) to take arms and rally her troops against the sea of trouble stirred up by her attacker. Canto V is the final battle:

> Fans clap, Silks rustle, and tough
>   Whalebones crack;
> Heroes' and Heroines' shouts confus' dly
>   rise,
> And bass and treble Voices strike the Skies.
> No common Weapons in their Hands are
>   found;
> Like Gods they fight, nor dread a mortal
>   Wound.

Finally, the gods intervene and, in imitation of the story of Romulus who ascended to the heavens during a rainstorm, carry the sacred lock heavenward.

On this level, the story is trite; attaching it to a classical form of discourse makes it seem even more superficial. Society has proved to be vain, frivolous, wasteful, lazy, and shallow. Waging "war" over a lock of hair highlights the effeminate character of a social system peopled by emasculated men and uppity women, all of whom have forgotten their "natural" places. The popularity of *The Rape of the Lock* has lasted for nearly three centuries because of Pope's masterful use of the heroic couplet, because of the cleverness with which he layered the trivial, momentary story onto the universal, timeless epic, and because the poem is based on a phallogocentric "joke" that readers of both sexes have been taught to understand as "funny"—a reading perpetuated in the twentieth century by the New Critics. Cleanth Brooks, for example, suggests that Belinda's "histrionics" are merely a "passing show, the product of an overwrought virginal mind whose hypocrisies her male admirers . . . can afford to treat with humorous indulgence."

The negative satirical reading of Pope's poem, however, can be resisted by a self-conscious feminist reading that aims, through its negative hermeneutic, to uncover the more or less unconscious misogyny that governs *The Rape of the Lock.* The immasculated reader is easily seduced by Pope's phallogocentric satire. Taught to read as a man, she unwittingly elevates "male difference" to the level of "universality" and reduces "female difference" to "otherness" (Schweickart). Because her interpretation of the text is regulated by her need to belong to a male-dominated academic/intellectual community, she reads against herself—against her otherness. In reading *The Rape of the Lock* the immasculated reader identifies with the "hero" who restores order to the (male) text, rather than with Belinda, the other who refuses to be silent. Even the most "liberated" immasculated reader may be victimized by her own liberation. Belinda is, after all, hardly a sympathetic figure—she is the epitome of unliberated womanhood; her values run counter to any sort of "feminist" ideology. Perhaps, in some way, she deserves what she gets. By thus indicting Belinda's otherness, condoning her loss of power, the immasculated reader increases her own lack of power. She participates, figuratively, in her own castration.

The feminist reader must develop an even more powerful instrument than the "lost" phallus—a double-edged sword with which she can resist the text's intention and read it from both phallocentric and gynocentric perspectives. Just as the coded "apology" of Pope's letter to Arabella can be understood beyond the literal apology, so the poem itself can be reread from the perspective of its heroine. By running her sword between the layers of the male text, the feminist reader can locate the sub-text(s) that evade the immasculated reader.

A feminist re-reading of *The Rape of the Lock* exposes a sub-text layered in between the primary story and the epic form of the discourse, a sub-text that articulates female power in its very otherness. Belinda, whose locks give her a great deal of power, is raped (with scissors) by a "hero" who lacks power. By figuratively castrating Belinda—the "other" who (at least in western culture) should *lack* power—the "hero" regains control of his society. This is the root of the phallogocentric joke: Belinda, the woman who has appropriated masculine power, is put in her place; the threat to the eighteenth century's "myth of passive womanhood" has been eliminated. From the feminist reader's perspective, however, the joke is not on Belinda but on the "man's man" who thinks he can destroy her power by merely cutting off an imaginary penis. Or, rather, there is no "joke" at all, but rather the *marked* difference between human desire (including blushes) and the narrow and life-denying range of possible articulations of that desire presented in the poem. Pope moves epic contests to the arena of sexual relations as a joke, but within this joke there is, I will argue, an unrealized "utopian" possibility of humanizing, by sexualizing, human relations.

Such lost possibilities are suggested by the very insistence of Pope's negative hermeneutic. ***The Rape of the Lock*** seems to be centered around an insignificant battle in the war between the sexes. Both men and women characters are made to look foolish; no one is actually hurt physically. But that center does not hold: the "joke" is played out at the expense of Belinda, and all women who forget their "places"; the underlying message of the joke is deadly serious. Belinda has learned well the lessons taught her by a male-dominated society. She is vain, lazy, superficial, and artificial. She knows it is only her outward appearance in which men are interested, and she gains power by making herself as attractive an object as possible. Like the women Luce Irigaray describes in *This Sex Which is Not One,* Belinda has been conditioned to believe that "the penis [is] the only sexual organ of recognized value," and, thus, she has taken advantage of "every means available to appropriate that organ for herself." She knows that her power lies in an outward display of sexuality, figuratively represented by two locks which "graceful hung behind"; Pope's negative hermeneutic is grotesque in its insistence: rather than one sex organ, Belinda has grown two. Like the "universal," supposedly "ungendered" reader Pope's discourse implies, she not only has the sexual power of the female, but she has appropriated that of the male as well.

Such grotesquery calls for the "mock" violence of the poem, which reveals the powerful violence that is the price of the "universal" man lurking below the joke: the Baron, the hero who refeminizes Belinda and restores the fictive community to its "rightful" order, is applauded for his action because his victim "asks for it." Such violence is so usual that a critic like Brooks can say, "Pope knows that the rape has in it more of compliment than of insult." In this way, in mockery, we are taught that the Baron is not "predestined to be a rake at heart"; he is just momentarily overwhelmed by Belinda's female beauty, which Pope feared as a form of "sexual aggression," believing that female sexuality inspired desire in members of both sexes.

But rape is not a "compliment"; it is, as Margaret Higonnet asserts [in "Speaking Silences: Women's Suicide," in *The Female Body in Western Culture*], an attempt to destroy a woman by attacking the thing that gives her her identity as a woman:

Much like love or lost love, rape has been affiliated with the breakdown of a woman's identity. The focus on chastity, of course, involves that precisely which distinguishes woman as woman, and does so in terms of possession by a man, fetishistically. If woman is taken to be a commodity, rape means total devaluation: reified, then stolen, she has no essence left to justify her continuing existence.

The "hero" realizes that the only way he can possess the most prized possession of the powerful Belinda is through "Fraud or Force"—a solution Pope (and his masculine and immasculated readers) presumably condoned. The Baron takes out his scissors—an instrument that unites in its design the phallus (closed) and the vagina (opened). Imitating his version of the female power he so fears—the woman who can cut him off from Nature, just by closing her legs together—the Baron "spreads the glitt'ring *Forfex* wide, / T'inclose the Lock; now joins it, to divide." In a sort of reverse rape, the hero castrates the too-powerful female, returning her to a position of powerlessness. She will not even be allowed to retain the remaining lock, which now hangs limp and "the fatal Shears demands." What the negative hermeneutic reveals is a kind of Hobbesian reduction of all nature to warfare, all power to control.

Toward the end of the poem, the "nymph" Clarissa steps forward to deliver a sermon on the theme of *carpe diem,* reminding Belinda that

> To patch, nay ogle, might become a Saint,
> Nor could it sure be such a Sin to paint.
> But since, alas! frail Beauty must decay,
> Curl'd or uncurl'd, since Locks will turn to
>   grey;
> Since painted or not painted, all shall fade,
> And she who scorns a Man, must die a Maid;
> What then remains, but well our pow'r to
>   use,
> And keep good Humour still whate'er we
>   lose?

This would seem to be a good lesson—why should women worry about anything so silly as their hair? And from the male perspective—in this world of war of all against all—it is silly. Men grow more powerful with age; grey hair becomes a sign of maturity, experience and increased value. When a woman's hair changes to grey, however, she loses value in the eyes of those same men. She is old, used up, less valuable as a commodity. It is not the lesson of *carpe diem* but that of the age-old double standard that Clarissa's speech teaches and Pope's readers have accepted. Jove, the male god (of course), is sent to decide the fate of Belinda and her lock. He "[w]eighs the Men's Wits against the Lady's Hair; / The doubtful Beam long nods from side to side; / At length the Wits mount up, the Hairs subside." In defiance, the women still insist on the return of the lock, but Jove's "machinery" intercedes to remove it permanently from woman's grasp. The raped lock will hang forever in the heavens, a "universal," unattainable prize. Intended to remind women of Belinda's heavenly reprimand, the astro-lock becomes, for the resisting reader, a symbol of the lengths to which the guardians of a phallocentric culture will go to retain control of the "sex which is not one."

This reading of *The Rape of the Lock* as a story of reverse penis envy is "resistant" in that it turns the violence and almost palpable misogyny of the poem back on itself. Thus, it is hard to imagine how a positive and sympathetic feminist reading might recuperate a more generous vision of human life in Pope's narrative. Readers could, as Fetterley says, identify with the male power of Pope's world, but now more widely conceived in its "utopian power." That is, the feminist reader can find within Pope's mocking violence the possibility of imaging "nature" very different from the dominant discourse of Pope's age. Such a reading is negative in that it seeks to outline "the thing which was not" (to quote Swift's Houyhnhnms) in the way Pope saw the would—but in imaging a sexual rather than a bloody epic as the overriding metaphor for human life (as Blake did later in the century), it is possible in Schweickart's "utopian" sense. In other words, the very fact that Pope translates epic warfare into sexual warfare contains within it the possibility of reconceiving human life and "nature" in terms of "utopian" love rather than universal strife. Of course, Pope literally cannot conceive of such a reading, but a feminist rereading can apply a positive hermeneutic even to Pope.

> **Canonical texts like *The Rape of the Lock*
> must be re-read by women (and men) from
> a feminist perspective. Such a re-reading
> produces a considerably different story
> than the traditional one and reveals a new
> layer in an already multi-layered text.**
>
> **—Kate Beaird Meyers**

Such a reading suggests what Schweickart calls "domination-free discourse." In her essay "Engendering Critical Discourse," Schweickart re-evaluates, from a feminist perspective, the "ideal speech situation" outlined by Jürgen Habermas in "Wahrheitstheorien." According to Habermas, the ideal speech situation exists if "the opportunity to select and employ speech acts [is] equitably distributed among all the participants of the discourse," with "no internal or external structures that impose nonreciprocal obligations on the participants or allow some of them to dominate others"; and if there are no "constraints on communication . . . [e]verything—specific assertions, theoretical explanations, language-systems, and theories of knowledge—must be open to question." The result of discourse occurring under these circumstances is, Hebermas believes, as close to truth (or at least true consensus) as it is possible to come.

The difficulty Schweickart finds in this model is that it is based on the ideals of the Enlightenment, with the "universality" that is the foundation of Pope's irony:

It links rationality and truth with liberty, equality . . . *and* fraternity. It is, in short, an ideal that has been abstracted from the discourse of the brotherhood . . . [embodying] masculine interests and intuitions—a masculine sense of self and the intersubjectivity or man-to-man relationships.

Habermas, like Pope and most male reader-response theorists, supposes a commonality of knowledge, a supposition that does not take into account the question of sexual difference. In the critical discourse surrounding reader-response theory, gender must be recognized as [what Schweikart calls] a "locus both of difference and power" in the act of interpretation. Sexual difference must be acknowledged as legitimate grounds for literary interpretation; the power of validation must be distributed equally among all participants. The recognition of gender as a major factor in the reading process will help capture at least a glimmer of a different world—Schweickart's "utopian moment." It will also help generate the kind of "playful pluralism" Kolodny sees as crucial to recognizing the "various systems of meaning and their interaction" within a text. Such pluralism will not only aid in the de-immasculation of women readers but will help make up for anything that might be lacking in the male reader's reading experience as well.

Joanne Cutting-Gray and James E. Swearingen (essay date 1992)

SOURCE: "System, the Divided Mind, and the *Essay on Man*," in *Studies in English Literature, 1500-1900,* Vol. 32, No. 3, Summer, 1992, pp. 479-94.

[*In the essay below, Cutting-Gray and Swearingen reinterpret* An Essay on Man, *stating that the poem anticipates modern ideas about human nature.*]

Nothing more clearly marks the character of the eighteenth century than the extreme differences with which persons of serious and judicious mind responded to Pope's *Essay on Man.* The famous contrasting responses from thinkers inclined neither to idolatry or to caviling demonstrate both the enthusiasm and controversy which the poem stirred and point to a duality that lay at the heart of the age itself. Notwithstanding the inevitable controversies over the philosophic content of the poem and in spite of their doctrinal differences, a multitude of disparate groups responded to the poem as though it expressed their own conception of an orthodox view of the creation. English Pietists, Deists, traditional Protestants, French Catholics, as well as German theologians and philosophers apparently found something in the poem that they could share.

Even to this day, the poem draws an unusually wide spectrum of responses and evokes a question raised in its own time. Is the *Essay* an event of tradition in the sense that it hands over a body of thought—a picture of the world—in an act of preservation, or does it also give up and unwittingly betray what it seeks authoritatively to preserve? When Pope recommends the poem as a more concise argument for commonplace truths than a "dry and tedious" philosophical treatise, in point of doctrine, he makes an uneasy compromise with the past by incorporating the less than orthodox views of Lord Bolingbroke, Spinoza, Leibniz, and biblical interpreter Anthony Collins. Furthermore, the chronological gap between Pope's day and ours makes the unrecognized betrayal of what he most wishes to advocate an important part of the present life of the poem. Only in part, then, can its popularity be attributed to its being [as Maynard Mack has stated] the "poetic definition to the problem of man's nature and God's justice outside the sphere of religious allegory, heroic drama, and scriptural story, where they had for the most part been confined before.

To say, as Pope himself did, that the **Essay** steers between the extremes of the new rage for mathematical certainty and the older traditions of faith, as though it offered a cautious eclecticism, understates the achievement of the poem in bringing out something historically decisive but concealed in that figure of opposition. In calling upon Heidegger's analysis of the "Age of the World Picture" [in "The Age of the World Picture," in *The Question Concerning Technology and Other Essays,* 1977], we will argue that exactly at the points where the poem is vulnerable to criticism, something subtle, something decisive for the future of thought occurs that is visible only to the retrospection of later readers.

The argument will be that even though the poem appeared to be a catalogue of the familiar, in fact it described something quite new. According to Heidegger, "to be new is peculiar to the world that has become picture," a world enframed by Man, the subjective center who projects it. Pope gave voice to this rift in the early modern mind. To historical retrospection this shift from a world open to one who apprehends to a world pictured by the one who represents is not simply a change in the way one views the world: "The world picture does not change from an earlier medieval one into a modern one, but rather the fact that the world becomes picture at all is what distinguishes the essence of the modern age." In charting the primary challenge to the way both world and man are changed in essence by a new criterion of knowledge, Heidegger enables us to clarify the double allegiance of a poem that gives voice to an unstable duality not only in Pope's age but in our time as well. Furthermore, such a duality provides the impetus to system and to our modern systematizing mentality.

What the early modern era found unusually appealing was less Pope's use of old ideas than the frame around them— not the form of the **Essay** but its peculiarly modern way of enframing the familiar which shifts from the immediacy of the given world to the mediation of a theoretical map of nature. Through a process that presupposes an orderly universe, the poem "essays" or tests the value and purity of its ideas, an eighteenth-century meaning of the word "essay" that lifts "mere" poetry into the realm of serious thought and grants it an authority denied it by the new spirit of enlightenment. Pope says that "The gen'ral ORDER

. . . Is kept in Nature, and is kept in Man," rendering change according to "laws" and subjecting [What Heidegger calls] chaos to rule. Both Nature and Man are "kept" in place as "objects of a representing that explains."

The well-known contradictions in this *tour de force* of systemic thinking show that, at times, it is conspicuously weak in simple intellectual orderliness. Not only does the poem describe human nature outside the lexicon and genres of traditional theological discussion; the famous opening metaphor from landscape architecture puts the commonplace truths in an entirely new narrative setting and supplies an important clue to how the poem puts "Man" in the context of nature externalized. Pope invites St. John to join him in wandering over the "scene of Man,"

> A mighty maze! but not without a plan;
> A Wild, where weeds and flow'rs promiscuous shoot,
> Or Garden, tempting with forbidden fruit.

When Pope tells us ahead of time that he connects his poem with *Paradise Lost,* the "mighty maze" seems to parallel those puzzles that confounded Milton's pagan Greek thinkers, in "wand'ring mazes lost." However, the old religious and philosophical riddles, representing man's search into the mysteries of life, are safely enclosed within the completely managed figure of landscape architecture. For all its intricate turnings, the maze is arranged in an order, the garden crafted to appear as a labyrinth, and the entire "scene" planned, not by God, the celestial architect, but by Man, the landscape architect. Hence the use of these figures departs from their traditional role in accounting for Nature and the ways of God, thereby creating an initial rift in traditional thought. The description of the scene as a garden, echoes of Eden and the "forbidden fruit," suggests that the scene is problematic and the poem a new theodicy. Set within a landscape design, however, the old moral and theological question of evil— less a question of wickedness than an error in thought— appears rational and solvable. Such a setting forth within a represented design or frame, world become picture, would not have been possible for the Ancient Greeks, for the Middle Ages, or even for Milton. The world is now explicitly "placed in the realm of man's knowing and of his having disposal, and that it is in being only in this way" (Heidegger). The frame of the poem sets up nature to exhibit itself as a coherence of forces calculable in advance.

While the poem seems to situate the traditional mythic account of man within a historically real, rather than artificial or fictional context, it is "natural," that is, free from affectation or artifice, only in the sense that the planned English landscape with its managed surprises, concealed bounds, and crafted contrasts appears as a "Wild," spontaneous and unplanned. The figure of the hunt extends the range of the landscape metaphor and its "map" over a description of the speaker's action. The hunter expresses confidence in his complete knowledge of the quarry he stalks: man who "blindly creeps" and "sightless soars."

Together let us beat this ample field,
Try what the open, what the covert yield;
The latent tracts, the giddy heights explore
Of all who blindly creep, or sightless soar;
Eye Nature's walks, shoot Folly as it flies,
And catch the Manners living as they rise.

Here is man pitted, not against a cosmic question or an unfathomable God, but against himself as "ample field" to beat, eye, try, explore, catch, shoot, vindicate, and naturalize. Man is presented dramatically as problematical and divided, both surveyor and hunter of his own species, quarry and site to be surveyed, and not as harmonious dweller within a seamlessly unfolding "scene." Heidegger observes, "In that man puts himself into the picture in this way, he puts himself into the scene, i.e., into the open sphere of that which is generally and publicly represented. Therewith man sets himself up as the setting in which whatever is must henceforth set itself forth, must present itself, i.e., be picture." In such a scene or picture, "the position of man is conceived as a world view."

As many have noted before, the problem here is not the universe within which man exists; but man himself. The Harvard Manuscript contains a marginal note in Pope's hand stressing the thematic and structural importance of these initial figures representing the mind of man: "The 6th, 7th, and 8th lines allude to the Subjects of This Book, the General Order and Design of Providence; the Constitution of the human mind." If the scene is the "constitution" of the mind, then by horticultural arrangement the mind is a human construction which appears unplanned only to the untrained or unstable eye. To those with singular vision, who "see worlds on worlds" and "Observe how system into system runs" the invisible design presupposes the naturally intelligible and visible. Every appearance of surprise, doubt, and half-knowledge confronting the mind in its frailty actually follows the design as when, in the **Epistle to Burlington,** the architecture of the landscape,

Calls in the country, catches opening glades,
Joins willing woods, and varies shades from shades,
Now Breaks, or now directs th'intending Lines,
Paints as you plant, and, as you work, designs.

Man is the self-constructed scene, and what wants justifying is no longer God, but the interior of man-divided into both subject and object of a world projected by him. The world can only become picture when man becomes *subjectum* at its center: "The more extensively and the more effectually the world stands at man's disposal as conquered, and the more objectively the object appears, all the more subjectively, i.e., the more importunately, does the *subiectum* rise, up [Heidegger]." The universe and the species now externalized as Nature are actually grounded in this doubled *subjectum* or "Mind." Thus Pope's new narrative setting completely alters the traditional genre upon which it is based and reverses the narrative of human experience from a God's eye view to that of the plan and context of man. We will ponder what it means to project a blueprint of the world and then move—not into the world—but into the plan.

Two parallel developments help explain this "new" phenomenon: first, the revolutions in biblical hermeneutics and, second, the new science, each seizing upon the methodizing impulse to project the world as a system or picture. Both disciplines, scientific and religious, embraced this theoretical framework that provided a way to analyze and thus "picture" religious revelation with certainty—a duplicity they embraced no matter how they differed in their actual interpretation of the biblical narrative. In order to discover how such a contradictory understanding of the world could be readily accepted, we need briefly to recall the radical shift in biblical hermeneutics.

In *The Eclipse of Biblical Narrative: A Study in 18th and 19th Century Hermeneutics,* Hans W. Frei describes the reversal that took place at the end of the seventeenth century between biblical narrative and the new secular narrative of history. Earlier, worldly experience had been interpreted by reference to a veridical biblical story that moved forward in a continuous historical sequence of Old and New Testaments, from creation to apocalypse. According to the conventional understanding, life moved within the biblical story. When the Bible no longer provided access *to* the world but resided *within* the world, it had to correspond to secular experience. The real events of history assume their own authority and incorporate their own autonomous temporal framework, though still conceived as being under God's providence. Hence, the historiographical investigation of so-called myth compensated for the loss of faith. In this light we can understand why an age of historiography would make the claim for a literal, historical Jesus in the work of such thinkers as Spinoza, Cocecius, and Bengel. Rending the veil between biblical and historical worlds results in the secular spirit's coming to occupy the sacred Ark of the Covenant. Since the eighteenth century generally held that the Bible could be understood by following empirical principles of interpretation common to all texts, meaning became detachable from the biblical story, and referred no longer to the spiritual world. In the gap of unreliability caused by this disintegration of biblical authority, it became possible for a work like **An Essay on Man,** which does not pretend to the status of theological dogma, to occupy the space once reserved for Christian tradition as the locus of truth and measure of practice.

Not only did biblical narrative suffer a loss of authority in the wake of the Copernican revolution, but accounts of ordinary sensory experience also came under suspicion and, even among empiricists, needed vindication. In empiricism, the meaning of common-sense experience tends to dissolve into the elementary thinking of sense data as when Locke derives all mental functions from "ideas" of sensation. Because empiricism lacks confidence in the truth of experience, even systematic observation is insufficient to confirm elementary sensation. Observation depends on faith in method. The effort to reduce experience to the presumed literalism of the senses, to dissolve in scepticism the commonplace narratives of communal experience, displaces faith in traditional narratives to a new faith in systems of explanation. The goal is no longer to order human experience; it is to discover what lies behind the commonplace. Under the compulsion of projecting a system of explanation, perception and the common sense based on it prove weak and coarse. In two contradictory but related moves hermeneutics sacrificed the revelatory power of a narrative of faith for the sake of an empirical method of interpretation, while the new science weakened its observation of the sensory and particular for the sake of faith in a method of intellectual certainty. Thus, the confident tone of Pope's speaker-hunter, as when he promises to "Laugh where we must, be candid where we can," begins to waver, and he must "wrangle" with the question, whether "God has plac'd him [Man] wrong?" Repetition of "must" suggests that the beast of suspicion may be lurking in the "coverts" of man. In other words, the coherent and commanded hinges upon the hypothetical and uncertain:

> Of Systems possible, if 'tis confest
> That Wisdom infinite must form the best,
> Where all must full, or not coherent be,
>
>   . . . . .
>
> Then, in the scale of reas'ning life, 'tis plain
> There must be, somewhere, such a rank as Man.

Only *if* it is "confest," i.e. agreed upon and assumed ahead of time, that "Wisdom infinite must form the best" system, can there be, and even must there be, "somewhere, such a rank as Man." Trying to shake off a sense of dread, Pope argues that man cannot comprehend the intelligible universe in its complexity: "Tis but a part we see, and not a whole." Yet the remainder of the poem explains these things more or less fully, even though, as Maynard Mack claims, "Pope's subject is not the visible universe but the intelligible manifested in the invisible." The rest of the poem attempts to make verisimilar what it dividedly assumes and pleads *must*, or at least, ought to be so.

What most seriously betrays the tradition is not simply the new narrative setting for old truths, nor the substitution of secular narrative for biblical revelation, not even the weakened observation of the sensory based on empirical faith, but rather the system which projects these divisions in thought. Instead of a representative picture of the world or even an empirical description, the poem offers a world picture. Nature is no longer rendered in its particularity. Even where Pope writes most movingly, we are not simply immersed in the immediacy of the created order. Dr. Johnson clearly defines [in *A Dictionary of The English Language,* 1755] the modern phenomenon of system and systemic thinking that Pope adds and presupposes: "1. Any complexure or combination of many things acting together. 2. A scheme which reduces many things to regular dependence or co-operation. 3. A scheme which unites many things in order." The *Essay* offers a system, "strong connections, nice dependencies, / Gradations just," which stands between us and a concrete world. Only in our own day are we gaining sufficient distance from the anthropocentric mind to see that this eloquent announcement of the world as the scene of man requires one to distinguish between the systematic and the orderly. Here is a new and important idea of *mimesis* as a representational scheme presumed to be nature itself. This, surely, is nature methodized.

This frame of reference makes the plan of the poem striking. The human becomes the primary sub-ject: the being and truth of all that is, appears grounded on man as the relational center of the world. The chain of being should "vindicate the ways of God to Man" by outlining what belongs to and what properly happens in the sphere of nature. Instead, it becomes a picture of nature fixed by a projection, as when the landscape blueprint displaces nature itself. When "Nature deviates"—"Th' exceptions few; some change since all began"—it constitutes a problem and calls for "vindication" of the whole scheme. The picture, no mere copy, encloses the world in a frame and sets it before an observer who "reveal[s] the real, in the mode of ordering, as standing-reserve" (Heidegger). The observer sees the world only as his own projection, an entirely new belief based upon a duplicity of system.

When the poem insists on human subordination and dependency in the grand scheme, it mocks the pride that makes itself "the God of God" and judge of the universe: "Know then thyself, presume not God to scan; / The proper study of Mankind is Man." And yet the satire derives its power from a dual allegiance, for the thoroughly anthropocentric representation designates the human as the privileged center of reference who explains and evaluates everything. In responding to the double allegiances that we have traced in hermeneutics and science, the satirist in a sense belongs to both parties. However central man's position on the presumed chain, he is diminished by his elevation—"Created half to rise, and half to fall; / Great lord of all things, yet a prey to all." Paradoxically, the one who falls prey is also the one who projects the map in which he resides. For all the discussion of reason, the passions, and happiness, the represented being is of necessity an entity alongside others on the objective scale.

It would be a serious misunderstanding to regard this rift in thought as a weakness in the poem or the poet. Rather, when in Epistle 1 he refutes the notion that man is the center, Pope eloquently articulates this conflict:

> Ask for what end the heav'nly bodies shine,
> Earth for whose use? Pride answers, "Tis for mine:
> "For me kind Nature wakes her genial pow'r,
> "Suckles each herb, and spreads out ev'ry flower."

He pours scorn on the head of Pride as it concludes the speech in unrestrained self-absorption:

> "For me, the mine a thousand treasures brings;
> "For me, health gushes from a thousand springs;
> "Seas roll to waft me, suns to light me rise;
> "My foot-stool earth, my canopy the skies."

By contrast with this voice of pride, "To reason right," he says, "is to submit." The poem at once denies that the ether of human understanding extends to the boundaries of the cosmos, and it devotes most of its lines to filling out the picture of that cosmos.

In a subtle departure from a long tradition that interprets nature hierarchically, Pope projects his theoretical model upon nature and divides systemic thought from the tradition. For the Greeks the term "theory" referred to clear-sightedness in ordinary intercourse with things; but in the intellectual economy of the modern age, theory has become an abstract framework under the dominion of "man."

Again the poet mocks what he cannot but share:

> Go, wond'rous creature! mount where Science
>   guides,
> Go, measure earth, weigh air, and state the tides;
>
> . . . . .
>
> Go, teach Eternal Wisdom how to rule—
> Then drop into thyself, and be a fool!

As a useful point of contrast, we may remember that Aristotle attended to the actual behavior of natural phenomena without deciding in advance on what terms he would observe them. He let things address him without commanding them. But Newton's famous phrase, *hypothesis non fingo,* says that a hypothetical basis of procedure is not arbitrary. The new science requires a procedure based on a prior framework of representation so that intellectual calculation frames even the constancy of change. In spite of his opposition to the new science, Pope will deal with the "unruly" passions in Epistle 2 by assimilating them to their place in an overall representation of reality, bringing them under a rule. The importance of Pope's announcement of the age of anthropology, surely a new science, cannot be over-emphasized. The more the world becomes picture the more does observation of the world change into a doctrine of man, an anthropology.

Well might the *Essay* strike a sympathetic chord in an era that instinctively decides in advance on what terms and under what conditions phenomena are to be observed. The more we regard the world as an object at our disposal, as an object of desire, the more observation turns into anthropological dogma: "Anthropology is that interpretation of man that already knows fundamentally what man *is* and hence can never ask who he *may be*" (Heidegger). Where world is picture, every detail of the picture points back to the being who projects it, as the book of nature had once pointed to its Author. Instead of our being an idea in the mind of God, as Bishop Berkeley says, God becomes a creature of our picture. The new god who must be vindicated and upon whom everything else is grounded, is man. Where everything reveals itself causally to Man, "God can, for representational thinking, lose all that is exalted and holy, the mysteriousness of his distance" (Heidegger). The divine becomes the familiar, personalized deity of those who define the concealed and ineffable in terms of full knowledge.

Once we have realized how the systematizing impulse makes man the creator, something else stands out that makes *An Essay on Man* a new event in its age and an important one in ours. The poem subtly proclaims a new faith and attempts to mediate the rift that puts revelation and even the revelatory capacity of the senses in doubt.

In grafting together two conflicting allegiances—the age-old Christian vision and the theory of scientific experiment—it begins to ponder whether the human subject is indeed the sole possibility for truth as the new doctrine of knowledge proclaims. Hence, the being who confidently yields from "covert" and "giddy heights" the "Manners living as they rise" undergoes a surprising change that can no longer be concealed by the projected plan. Plagued by doubt—"Chaos of Thought and Passion, all confus'd"—man becomes the oxymoronic being of the famous opening thirty lines of Epistle 2, "darkly wise, and rudely great," with "too much knowledge" and "too much weakness."

> He hangs between; in doubt to act, or rest,
> In doubt to deem himself a God, or Beast;
> In doubt his Mind or Body to prefer,
> Born but to die, and reas'ning but to err.

Here uneasily side by side are the systematizing mentality and the old sense of wonder. The challenge is to see the difference between projecting blueprints of the "mighty maze" of a changing world and celebrating the ineffability of things, with a willingness to live in ignorance, to surrender to the risks inherent in the flux of the world.

Just as Descartes and the biblical interpreters who followed his method needed both certainty and mystery to reconcile unlimited knowledge with an inscrutable God, so the poem maintains an ancient sense of ineffability as a brake against the pride of the new rationality: "See! and confess, one comfort still must rise, / 'Tis this, Tho' Man's a fool, yet GOD IS WISE." With man as both theological center, proud system maker, and empirical doubter, the plan of providence must be rationally discernible yet partially inscrutable, and therefore irreducible to a full explanation that would fuel human pride and crush religious faith: "Trace Science then, with Modesty thy guide; / First strip off all her equipage of Pride." The striking paradox is that the more the poem "confesses," i.e. acknowledges faith or belief, the more it encounters doubt and expresses anxiety. Presupposing the world as picture deploys the very tension it is designed to circumvent. The system-maker not only needs mystery in order to preserve the wonder that total explanation would expunge; he needs mystery as the impetus for his systematizing. Hence, the uncertainty of faith destabilizes the poem, and in effect, the whole system.

If what we have described in Epistles 1 and 2 is true, we must ask how systemic thinking relates to the remaining epistles. Do they return from the abstraction of the projected plan to the phenomenological world? Or do they continue the illusion of direct access to experience when in fact the poem substitues a map for phenomena? In other words we need to ask about the practical consequences of what we have described as systemic thinking and its contradictory impulses upon the configuration of the human (Epistle 2), on political life (Epistle 3), and on human happiness (Epistle 4). Under the rule of system, and the figure of the landscape maze in Epistle 1, practical life remains theoretical, an imposition of conceptual categories on experience. As Pope draws closer to the concrete in Epistles 2-4 however, he reveals how particular conceptual categories intrude between him and the world he seeks to describe.

When, for example, Epistle 2 documents the "Well accorded strife" of the passions, it portends the collapse of system: "Two Principles in human nature reign; / Self-love, to urge, and Reason, to restrain." These lines describe Reason and Passion as though they were simply inner facts. In other words, when Pope treats theoretically derived categories as though they were phenomenological (spirit, faculties, wit, nature, habit, virtue), any attempt to maintain the exclusivity of the elements collapses before what is inextricable in "our chaos." The positing of reason and passion as "original" features of experience prevents asking about the constitution of these inner events in a way that would alleviate the tension in the poem. Thus, the "ruling" entity, passion, exercises rule over its opposite reason yet is essentially "unruly."

The poem adheres to reason while departing from it. Only when passion already belongs to rational comportment can it be conceptualized in opposition to reason. Thus Pope both excludes and includes passion in the field of rational activity. Fixed meanings gradually dissolve into a relativism of perspective as when he questions the categories of vice and virtue: "But where th' Extreme of Vice, was ne'er agreed: / Ask where's the North? at York, 'tis on the Tweed."

The well-known inconsistencies of Epistle 3 serve an unexpected end. We may either describe Pope's thought as inconsistent or recognize that the system casts a shadow, hints at something inevitably concealed in its revealing as when he posits in advance what he subsequently purports to be unable to know. He can assert that self-fulfillment serves the good of Society, that God "bade Self-love and Social be the same." At the same time he suggests that "jarring int'rests of themselves create / Th' according music of a well-mix'd State" (Locke's mixed constitution). The conceptual formulation misses the contingencies of "jarring int'rests." Whenever he resituates a mode of experience in the system, contingency gets displaced, excluded. But when he turns to face phenomena themselves, we get a glimpse of what representation cannot catch, something that remains inevitably concealed.

The poem that articulates the passion for a new rationality, reducing mystery to a maze and the maze to a map, finally over-reaches that conceptual project by bringing out something unexpected and hidden in systemic thinking itself. The transformation of an unverifiable Christian faith into an equally unverifiable faith in system produces a profound distrust of experience, the very legacy of suspicion inherent in the new model of biblical interpretation. But where system reaches its limit, poetic thinking itself extends beyond system and acknowledges the need for faith and hope as "Nature plants in Man alone / Hope of known bliss, and Faith in bliss unknown."

In the very act of advocacy, *An Essay on Man* overturns an ancient experience of man and nature making the poem the voice of its age and giving unforgettable form to its divided mind. The eloquence of these memorable couplets sets the *Essay* alongside Descartes's *Meditations* and Rousseau's *Confessions* as spiritual exercises for a secular age. Where Descartes had transformed the believer into a sceptic, where Rousseau later requires sincerity in a priesthood of secular believers, Pope offers a testament of a new faith in system that casts a fleeting shadow of doubt, in Heidegger's phrase, a "saving power" of questionableness, over systemic thinking.

Shef Rogers (essay date 1995)

SOURCE: "Pope, Publishing, and Popular Interpretations of the *Dunciad Variorum,* in *Philological Quarterly,* Vol. 74, No. 3, Summer, 1995, pp. 279-95.

[*In the essay below, Rogers provides a publishing history of the various editions of* The Dunciad, *stating that they show Pope was "a brilliant poet and acute businessman, sensitive to the follies of the world and highly current with contemporary printing and bookselling practice."*]

Alexander Pope has often been portrayed, both during his lifetime and in this century, as a plotting, spiteful little man who used his pen to exact vengeance upon friend and foe alike, often for petty transgressions. Nowhere, according to such critics, is Pope's true nature more evident than in the multiple versions of his *Dunciad Variorum.* Samuel Johnson asserted that the poem was an elaborate means of revenge, in which Pope "endeavoured to sink into contempt all the writers by whom he had been attacked" [*Lives of the English Poets*]. I would like to offer an argument challenging these traditional views of Pope and of his motivations for endlessly revising his greatest poem. Much of my argument hinges on bibliographical details or publishing negotiations that have only recently become available, as well as on a comparison with the composition practice of Pope's close friend and memorialist, Joseph Spence.

The charges against Pope stem from his first satire on the dunces, "Peri Bathous," published in the third volume of the Pope-Swift *Miscellanies* on 8 March 1728, about ten weeks before the *Dunciad.* Like most satiric works of the day, this parody of Longinus' treatise on the sublime usually referred to its victims only by initials (though Pope often provided identifications for his direct quotations). Responses and speculations regarding the intended victims followed, and were frequently inaccurate. Where I would argue that Pope simply used deliberately vague references to avoid charges of libel, Pope's critics have argued that his use of initials and asterisks was part of a larger plan to elicit attacks on himself in order to justify his creation of the *Dunciad.* Edna Leake Steeves [in *The Art of Sinking in Poetry,* 1952] is representative in her accusation against Pope:

> [in *The Art of Sinking in Poetry,* 1952] We may surmise that Pope had it in mind . . . to use "Peri Bathous"

as a sprat to catch a whale, or, more properly, as ground bait to bring the fish to his net. Certainly Pope anticipated the responses which the initials . . . would incite, and quite possibly he planned beforehand the strategy for the War of the Dunces.

Would that this were so—Pope would indeed be a genius of the highest order, particularly since of the four pamphlet attacks on Pope published between "Peri Bathous" and the *Dunciad,* not one mentioned Pope's satire m "Peri Bathous." Lewis Theobald did manage to launch a quick retort at the end of March in Mist's *Weekly Journal,* but a single shot can hardly be characterized as a war (nor was it for this minor provocation alone that Theobald found himself crowned King of the Dunces). Yet scholars persist in inventing such a confrontation, even when it leads to illogical conclusions. Describing the *Weekly Journal* attack, Theobald's biographer, R. F. Jones, claims that "Pope was evidently satisfied with the rather poor results of the provocative treatise on the **"Bathos,"** for on May 18, 1728, appeared *The Dunciad.*" The causal link presented here is nonsensical: why, if a poet wished to provoke responses, would a single retort contained within a larger work be deemed satisfactory? Surely Pope was capable of penning a truly provocative satire had he so desired, or of stalling the publication of the *Dunciad* until later responses had been published and could be cited as justification.

Nonetheless, from an initial assumption of a planned series, scholars go on to assert that Pope knew before he published the *Dunciad* that he would compose the *Dunciad Variorum.* Their arguments rest on two "facts," one of which is an error, the other, as I see it, an overly strong interpretation. The first "fact" is invoked by R. K. Root and his followers, who claim on the basis of the introductory letter to the 1729 *Dunciad Variorum* that:

> The *Dunciad* of 1728 was deliberately intended to be an "imperfect" copy; and to further this design there is a glaring misprint in the very first word of the first line, which reads:

> BOOK and the man, I sing . . .

According to Root, this is a setup, since we know from a letter of January 1728 that the line was supposed to read "Books." Root claims that the singular first word enables Pope to fulfil his Publisher's concluding statement: "If it provoke the Author to give us a more perfect edition, I have my end." However, in 1982 David Vander Meulen finally sorted out the order of printing of the 1728 *Dunciad*s, showing that the duodecimo version, which contains the correct reading, "Books," was printed first, before the octavo version which must have lost the "s" in reformatting the pages. Pope may have overlooked the error in the octavo format, given that he had apparently considered a singular reading in his earlier drafts in order to emphasise his satiric focus on a single book, Theobald's *Shakespeare Restored.* By 1728, however, Pope had chosen to use the plural form, probably in order to restore parallelism with Virgil's original and to acknowledge that his victims were more diverse and prolific than could be

captured by a singular noun. Whatever the thinking behind the change, it is clear from the bibliographical evidence that the first edition read "Books" and was therefore not in need of perfecting in subsequent editions.

The *Dunciad Variorum,* in all its versions, endures as a testimony to the uniquely ambivalent combination of social, legal, literary, and personal variables that shaped, and reshaped, Pope's verse.

—Shef Rogers

The second fact upon which Pope scholars rely comes from Swift's letter to Pope of 1 June 1728, in which Swift writes, "The doctor told me your secret about the Dunciad, which does not please me, because it defers my vanity in the most tender point, and perhaps may wholly disappoint it." Since the doctor, Patrick Delany, had left England in mid-May, he must have been entrusted with the secret before the 18th, when the *Dunciad* was published. Thus, Pope's detractors argue, the poet intended, before he ever published the *Dunciad,* to revise the poem, presumably in order to incorporate new dunces who had revealed themselves in the meantime, just as was supposed to have happened between the publication of "Peri Bathous" and the appearance of the *Dunciad.* However, this view rests upon the single ambiguous sentence cited above: Sherburn glosses the word secret to mean "that a larger (*variorum*) edition was in preparation, and that the inscription of the poem to Swift was deferred to it." I would argue less broadly that the secret simply refers to the omission of the dedicatory lines referring to Swift. Pope recognized that publication of such a dedication would be taken as a sign of his authorship, and preferred for the moment to maintain anonymity. Swift feared complete disappointment, because he was uncertain the lines would ever see print. Not until more than a month after publication, on the 28th of June, did Pope request that Swift contribute annotations, after seeing the first responses to the *Dunciad* and after being asked for keys to the text by Swift, by a well-informed patron, the Earl of Oxford, and by the King himself. As friends and foes alike misinterpreted his poem, Pope must have realized that he would have to find a way to clarify his satire.

However, clarification entailed legal risks, risks Pope sought to eliminate. By the time the *Dunciad Variorum* appeared in 1729, Pope had consulted with lawyers to ensure not only that he was safe from prosecution, but also that his printers and booksellers would not be subject to imprisonment. In order to secure protection for them, Pope concocted a scheme involving false warrants of authorship, resulting in a delay in legal registration with the Stationer's Company. This care led to problems in 1743, when Pope wished to republish material from the *Dunciad Var-*

iorum as part of his ***Dunciad in Four Books,*** because of uncertainty regarding the beginning of the 14-year copyright term for the 1729 material. Having originally published the ***Dunciad Variorum*** on 10 April 1729. Pope expected copyright to revert to him in mid-April 1743. Pope's bookseller, Gilliver, however, only officially received copyright of the ***Dunciad Variorum*** on the 16th of October, 1729 and as a result his term of copyright lasted until late in 1743. It is no accident that the ***Dunciad in Four Books*** appeared two weeks after the expiration of Gilliver's copyright (which had subsequently been sold to Lintot). I would argue that Pope was justifiably frustrated by the difficulties involved in reclaiming his copyright, since it had been his careful arrangements in 1729 that had originally determined the late date of copyright transfer. Having looked after their interests in the first instance, Pope no doubt felt he deserved similar cooperation from his booksellers.

As well as legal complications, the desire for clarification led to bibliographical experimentation. Pope had to cloak his need for clarification under some more clever excuse than a mere concession that he had simply misjudged his audience. So, as James McLaverty [in "The Mode of Existence of Literary Works of Art: The Case of the *Dunciad Variorum," Studies in Bibliography* 37 (1982)] has brilliantly proved, he consulted contemporary models and settled upon the variorum format used in the *Oeuvres* of Boileau. The variorum format also naturally suggested ridicule of recent scholarly editions in that format, and allowed Pope to indulge his long-standing desire to "correct the taste of the town in wit and criticism" by being satirist and critic simultaneously.

Finally, the variorum format naturally suited Pope's own composition habits, in which he collected and jotted down the inane comments or verses of others, as well as his own verses, on any handy scraps of paper. Swift vividly captures this practice in his short poem, "Dr. Sw--to Mr. P--e, While he was writing the *Dunciad:*

> Now Backs of Letters, though design'd
>   For those who will more need 'em,
> Are fill'd with Hints, and interlin'd
>   Himself can hardly read 'em.
>
> Each Atom by some other struck,
>   All Turns and Motions tries,
> Till in a Lump together stuck.
>   Behold a *Poem* rise!

Swift may perhaps exaggerate, but such a method of composition is evident in surviving Pope manuscripts and the poet confesses in letters to reusing his own lines as examples of dullness. I attribute this constant revisiting of his own scraps and ideas to Pope's broglio method. The Italian word broglio is defined by James McLaverty as probably meaning "that things are moved about, rearranged." The term introduces notes collated by Jonathan Richardson, Jr. in 1728 and 1736 editions of the ***Dunciad Variorum,*** where it appears in the title-page explanation that "This Book corrected from the First Broglio MS. as the Ed. 1736 is from the Second." Unfortunately, the Pope

manuscripts from which Richardson copied his notes do not survive, but I propose to offer a parallel example that I believe represents what Pope sent to Richardson and helps to explain why Pope was so grateful for Richardson's assistance. If the Spence parallel is apt, Richardson had to transcribe the contents of a sheaf of loose and various sheets, perhaps even in various hands, into a single volume, placing material appropriately and imposing order on a jumble of notes drafted hastily in little or no sequence.

My example comes from a long manuscript poem by Pope's close friend and admirer, Joseph Spence. Spence's work is entitled *The Charliad* and, like Pope's poem, relies on extensive mock-scholarly annotation to convey its satiric force. The title itself purports to derive from a pseudo-scholarly combination of Italian and French, *ciarlare babiller,* "which signifies to talk w[ithou]t ye drudgery of Thinking." Although it is not possible to determine an absolute date for Spence's initial efforts on *The Charliad,* datable references all follow the publication of the ***Dunciad Variorum.*** Unlike Pope, Spence never published his poem, but his manuscripts survive to display his method of composing a variorum-format satire. I believe that Spence's work provides a suggestive analogy to Pope's own composition practice, a practice which involved collecting scraps and jotting down absurd literary remarks whenever encountered, then compiling all these notes into a single volume; in a word, the broglio method.

Spence's poem survives in two manuscripts. University of Chicago MS 70 includes the earlier of the two versions and reads like a typical fair copy of a poem. It forms part of a longer octavo volume which contains some of Spence's other efforts at poetry and a sheaf of blank pages at the end awaiting the entry of further items. The other manuscript, British Library Additional MS 25,897, is a very different collection, devoted solely to material related to *The Charliad.* A slim, large quarto, the bound MS consists of a sheaf of originally loose papers of different size, color, and quality. The book opens with an expanded version of the poem, in a relatively clean copy, but this is followed by a medley of undigested potential epigraphs, poetry, and notes, some rejected from the poem, some never incorporated at all, and some perhaps still to be included. This material is recorded on various sorts of paper, in various colors of ink, capturing Spence's efforts at particular moments. Notations and ideas that have been worked into the main text are crossed through and, as in the Broglio MSS, a reader can watch a couplet or theme evolving down the page through successive drafts. One leaf of the MS (f. 51) consists of a title-page from an Italian work, perhaps torn out for scrap paper during one of Spence's three periods as chaperone for the Grand Tour. Several sheets are in another hand and were at one time clearly folded in a letter, just as notes requested by Pope from Swift and other members of the Scriblerian circle, as well as from Thomas Sheridan, and later from Warburton, would have been posted. The authors of Spence's postal contributions are identified only by Roman pseudonyms, but they were clearly well informed of the content of Spence's poem and the general aim of his satire. Spence, less known and less hated than Pope, must have been able to circulate his manuscript without fear of interception, whereas Pope, though equally desirous of support, could only solicit contributions from his friends once printed texts were available to them after 1728, and even then could not identify his contributors for fear of involving them in endless attacks by the dunces. Only in the 1751 edition of the *Dunciad* are we allowed to distinguish the contributions of Warburton and Pope, though even then many of the 1751 notes are attributed to joint authorship or credited to "Scribl."

Because of Pope's reticence to identify his collaborators (or their reticence to be identified), the *Dunciad* appears primarily as the work of Martinus Scriblerus, but this fiction of authorship must constantly be regarded as a corporate creation. Any theory of composition that romantically imagines Pope as the spiteful poet alone in his grotto cannot account for the virtually ceaseless revision of the *Dunciad.* (David Vander Meulen has undertaken the Herculean task of a full bibliography of all the versions of the poem, revealing that the poem exists in at least thirty-three separate editions and about sixty impressions and issues by the time Warburton edits the first posthumous collections of Pope's *Works* in 1751). On the other hand, a theory of composition envisioning a broglio collection can explain both why lines within the *Dunciad* refer to events as early as 1719-20 and why ideas included in Richardson's transcriptions of the broglios turn up in other poems, such as the *Epistle to Burlington.*

With such an understanding of Pope's composition practice in mind, we can see why it was necessary for the poet to announce in his preface to the original *Dunciad* that "there may arise some obscurity in Chronology from the *Names* in the Poem, by the inevitable removal of some Authors, and insertion of others, in their Niches." Curll, immediately after the publication of the 1728 poem, presented this practice as another sign of Pope's malicious nature: *"The* DUNCIAD, *it seems, is to mimic a* Weather-Glass, *and vary every impression as the Author's Malice* increases *to One, or* abates *to Another."* However, I would stress once again that these changes are not products of Pope's boundless spite, but rather the result of a particular method of composition that collected evidence of folly in all its forms as Pope constantly sought to keep his poem up to date. One could even push this argument to its logical extension and claim that Pope possessed such freedom to substitute names precisely because he held little personal resentment against some of his victims. So long as a victim was readily identifiable as an appropriate embodiment of a particular vice, that person's name was suitable, whether or not Pope had ever been wronged by the individual. No doubt revision was more interesting, though, when the new victim was both a personal enemy and the epitome of a particular fault, particularly if that person's name was the topic of current scandal.

Not content merely to update his internal references to accord with contemporary events, Pope also attempted to coordinate his publication dates with public events of significance for his poem. One of the most important revela-

tions of Vander Meulen's work on the *Dunciad* has been to show that Pope, having ascertained through a lawsuit against Lintot that copyright of the 1729 *Dunciad Variorum* reverted to him on the 16th of October, waited a further two weeks, until the 29th of October, to release the 1743 *Dunciad in Four Books,* in order to align his poem with an historical event already anticipated in his new version—George II's sixtieth birthday—and with a date that had been an important element in the poem ever since 1728—Lord Mayor's Day. Pope may have consoled himself over the bookseller's reluctance to yield copyright with the knowledge that he could at least unite poetry with history, if only for a day, as he once more made an aesthetic and satiric virtue of an externally-imposed necessity.

In addition, he could console himself with his wealth. Despite complaints by Samuel Richardson and others about purchasing multiple editions of Pope's poem, any member of the literary world who wished to stay current really had to check the latest edition for changes. However, I should also emphasize Pope's consideration for his readers—he carefully ensured that each new work or revision came out in formats to match editions of his earlier works, even editions published by his previous booksellers, so that his readers could complete their sets at minimum expense. As Gilliver advertised in the octavo *Works II* on 24 April 1735:

> And whereas Bernard Lintot having the property of the former Volume of Poems, would never be induced to publish them compleat, but only a part of them, to which he tack'd and imposed on the Buyer a whole additional Volume of other Men's Poems. This present Volume will with all convenient Speed be published in Twelves at 5s. that the Buyer may have it at whatever price he prefers, and be enabled to compleat any Sett he already has, even that imperfect one printed by Lintot.

More discerning readers, who had already purchased *The Essay on Man* or the *Satires of Horace* in the larger quarto format, "could return them and receive the quarto *Works II* for 15s," as opposed to the full price of one guinea. For an author whose *Works* alone came to possess a copyright value which exceeded the combined copyrights of Milton and Shakespeare, such consideration for his readers seems relatively generous.

Cynics would no doubt dismiss this generosity as yet another example of Pope cloaking self-interest in the undeserved guise of public good. They would consider his marketing techniques simply good business, and argue that his sales were enhanced by the ability to complete sets at reduced prices. I would agree that Pope's practices were certainly beneficial to himself and usually beneficial to his booksellers, but I would wish to place Pope's motivations within a larger context. As a poet writing in a period of unprecedented uncertainty about the legal rights and professional status of authors, Pope devoted enormous energy to manipulating the networks of production, distribution, and consumption of his texts. Terry Belanger, in a broad survey of the shifting practices of eighteenth-century publishing, has described Pope as a watershed figure, one of the first to adapt the new possibilities to his advantage.

But Belanger emphasized that Pope was also unusual in his success; generally the new structures worked to the advantage of booksellers rather than authors. Alvin Kernan has concisely captured [in *Samuel Johnson and The Impact of Print,* 1987] the paradox that Pope, as author of the **Dunciad,** both feared and exploited:

> the existence and identity that print gave to the writer with one hand it took away with the other, for if widely circulated printed books made authors real to themselves and others, and made the *idea* of the author a social fact, then the very number of books published guaranteed, with rare exceptions like Johnson, that the individual writer would exist only momentarily.

Although Scriblerus' claim that his poem resulted from the unfortunate coincidence of living at a time when "Paper . . . became so cheap, and printers so numerous, that a deluge of authors cover'd the land" exaggerated current reality, it did capture the Augustans' nervous awareness that publishing was increasing rapidly and was providing public forums for all sorts of voices. Even worse, in Pope's eyes, the expansion of the market actually encouraged lesser writers to take up quill and paper in order to fill the pages of periodicals, newspapers, and a wide range of book-length publications. A sufficient literary market existed to make possible payment for writing, but the possibility of being a professional writer conflicted with the tradition ideal of writing as a gentlemanly pursuit undertaken in leisure. "Throughout the period, writers labeled each other 'mercenary scribblers' as the most damning epithet possible, perpetuating the low status of the writing profession even as they realized that the age of patronage was passing . . . [Claudia Newell Thomas, "Alexander Pope and 'The Publick in General,'" 1985] Yet the textual density of Pope's **Dunciad Variorum** depends upon the abundance of his rivals' printed comments: the 1729 text includes 19 pages of "Testimonies of Authors" as well as copious quotations in the notes, all culled from other printed publications. Pope gathered these items primarily as a means of justifying his response or accusations, but they also helped to swell his own volume and increase its price.

Nor was Pope above such financial calculations and careful accounting of each page in his creative ventures. He understood the value of original work and fulfilled his contracts to the letter of the law, often digging up older works to fill out the required number of sheets for a volume. That was why he submitted "Peri Bathous" to the *Miscellany* volume in the first place, and also why he probably altered his footnotes to the **Variorum** to endnotes in the 1735 **Works.** Warburton seems to have adopted this trick from Pope's model, for he writes to his printer, Knapton, that, having eliminated some notes in order to reduce the printing and sales costs for the small octavo 1753 edition, they consider

> That what notes are left be not printed, as in all the other Edns., under each page: but all together at the end of each poem, to which they belong; and the notes of the Dunciad at the end of each Book, as in Mr. Pope's q[uart]o edns. both of his Poems & Homer. My reasons are these, first it will be a variety from the other Edns. but principally I think the small chara[c]ter of the notes in the specimen you have, deforms & hurts the beauty of the Edn. it appears to be much more elegant to have nothing but verses in the page or nothing but prose, besides if the notes be thrown together as I propose they will be in the same letter with the text, which will make the Edn. more beautifull, & what is of still more consequence will swell it out a little more, which it will want to be.

Pope should have derived great satisfaction from turning his enemies' accusations of mercenary ends into yet more material to swell his **Dunciad** and enrich himself.

But Pope's printing strategies were not limited to simple (and comparatively inexpensive) adjustments of layout. He was quite willing to tie up (literally) substantial quantities of set type, as he did with the type for his letters to Wycherley from 1728 to 1735, and to store unused sheets from various editions to incorporate wherever possible at a later date. This willingness created innumerable bibliographic difficulties, some of which were evident even during Pope's own lifetime, others of which have only been analyzed by recent scholars. Johnson, once more, was partially responsible for diverting attention from the economic aspects of Pope's constant revision, by stressing the poet's desire to excel: "[Pope] was never content with mediocrity when excellence could be attained. . . . [T]o make verses was his first labour, and to mend them was his last." But in between, Pope clearly devoted much time and effort to the complexities of imposition and potential uses for unsold sheets.

Nonetheless, Pope did strive for excellence, and not all of his publishing ploys were directed at immediate profit. His choice of the Boileau format, appreciation of Elzevier typefaces, and abandonment of catchwords in the **Dunciad Variorum** all attested to Pope's desire to associate his text with those of the classics. In addition, Maynard Mack has argued that Pope's addition of annotation to his poems in **Works II** (1735) was an assertion of status. Pope himself was more explicit about his ambitions in his request to Warburton to become his editor, starting with the 1743 four-book **Dunciad:** "I have a particular reason to make you Interest your self in Me & My Writings. It will cause both them & me to make the better figure to Posterity." While Warburton's 1751 edition of Pope's **Works** created as many difficulties as it solved, Warburton was faithful to his author's typographical preferences and continued Pope's practice of issuing his works in varying formats for different audiences. The fifth volume of Warburton's edition, the one containing the **Dunciad,** appeared in a large octavo format with five new illustrations, but was also published in an unillustrated small octavo from which text was pared by not identifying the authors of notes, and by parting with at least thirty of Warburton's own annotations. The strict economies of publisher limitations impinged on even the greatest of poets and most assertive of editors, because both Warburton and

Pope understood the financial value of the poet's every word and recognized the need to please diverse audiences. Only by making it possible for all readers to adorn their bookshelves with complete sets of his works could Pope assure himself a physical as well as spiritual presence among the shelves of the literary canon. In a world where the increasingly shrill demands of new works appealed for space, a substantial presence on the shelf was in itself a symbol of esteem. Thus, although Pope clearly wished to avoid the derogatory accusation of being a mercenary, he also wished to ensure that he achieved the best possible income from his original compositions, and was quite happy to exploit the proliferation of publishing even as he decried it. I would urge that we not only acknowledge but also appreciate Pope's cleverness in adopting the technology and legal rights available to him, rather than scorn him for his financial savvy. Though his contemporaries often berated him for his economic success, their objections hardly prove that Pope was either malicious or wrong, since had he been less crafty in his negotiations we would probably fault him for failing to recognize his own worth or participate in the new literary markets to his advantage.

So far, then, I have sketched a picture of Pope as an author initially trying to extricate himself from the problem of how to ensure that his satire is understood without incurring charges of libel, an author fully aware of his legal rights, ever conscious of the potential for profit, considerate of his consumers, and generally supportive of his booksellers, both current and former. Such an image hardly accords with the malicious toad portrayed by Pope's own enemies, or with the more recent view of Pope as a farsighted provocateur, launching a verbal war against his enemies in order to create ever more cruel and clever satires about them. Instead, I would argue for an image of Pope as a brilliant poet and acute businessman, sensitive to the follies of the world and highly current with contemporary printing and bookselling practice. Using Jerome McGann's terminology, I would maintain that Pope's ceaseless revisions reveal concern with both the linguistic and bibliographic codes, but I would attribute his concern with bibliographic code as much to a desire for money and reputation as to a desire for meaning. I would also argue that the case of Pope's ***Dunciad*** provides a rich challenge to editors concerned with the relations between versions and intentions, that it reveals just how much criticism can be misled by literary commentary and instructed by bibliographical detail, and that it undermines traditional views of the Augustan age as stable. What looks in any single version like a massively inert and definitive monument to Dulness proves from a diachronic perspective to be an endlessly mutating conglomeration of disparate, carefully preserved instances of folly and misguided pride. I have no doubt that Pope sought stability, and that one function of the variorum apparatus was to fix meaning and parody the new scholarship, but having recognized that the very instability he feared could yield a solid financial return and enable him to sustain his attack on folly with greater accuracy, Pope made the best of necessity.

In concluding, I should point out that I doubt this is the sort of defense Pope would desire, since a fuller understanding of his compositional methods and financial and legal entanglements undermines his stance as morally superior to his Grub-Street rivals, who were themselves seeking to exploit the system just as Pope had. Viewed as an opportunistic insider taking advantage of and even altering the legal system and printing practices to suit his own ends, rather than as a resentful outsider resorting to the only avenue of protest available to him, Pope becomes an engaged Augustan, part of the vibrant mercantilism and social fragmentation which his masterpiece claims to resent and resist. While Pope was undoubtedly an outsider in many respects and while he would almost certainly prefer us to accept his self-presentation in ***Epistle to Arbuthnot,*** he has left enough traces of his behind-the-scenes activities to allow us to sketch an alternative backdrop against which to view his drama of Dulness. Thus the ***Dunciad Variorum,*** in all its versions, endures as a testimony to the uniquely ambivalent combination of social, legal, literary, and personal variables that shaped, and reshaped, Pope's verse.

FURTHER READING

Bibliographies

Guerinot, J. V. *Pamphlet Attacks on Alexander Pope 1711-1744.* New York: New York University Press, 1969, 360 p.
    Descriptive bibliography of nearly one hundred sixty critical attacks on Pope and his works that appeared during his lifetime.

Lopez, Cecelia L. *Alexander Pope: An Annotated Bibliography, 1945-1967.* Gainesville: University of Florida Press, 1970, 154 p.
    Lists studies about Pope and his works.

Tobin, James Edward. *Alexander Pope: A List of Critical Studies Published from 1895 to 1944.* New York: Cosmopolitan Science and Art Service Co., 1945, 30 p.
    Secondary bibliography.

Biographies

Mack, Maynard. *Alexander Pope: A Life.* New Haven: Yale University Press, 1985, 975 p.
    Comprehensive biography.

Quenell, Peter. *Alexander Pope: The Education of Genius, 1688-1728.* New York: Stein and Day, 1968, 278 p.
    Biography of Pope's life through the publication of the first edition of *The Dunciad.*

Sherburn, George. *The Early Career of Alexander Pope.* Oxford: Clarendon Press, 1934, 326 p.
    Account of Pope's life through 1727.

Criticism

Aden, John M. *Pope's Once and Future Kings.* Knoxville: University of Tennessee Press, 1978, 218 p.

Examines political and satirical themes in Pope's verse published prior to 1728.

Barnard, John, ed. *Pope: The Critical Heritage.* London and Boston: Routledge and Kegan Paul, 1973, 544 p.
  Excerpted and annotated critical essays on Pope's writings, dating from 1705 to 1782.

Bateson, F. W., and N. A. Joukousky, eds. *Alexander Pope: A Critical Anthology.* Middlesex, England: Penguin Books, 1971, 512 p.
  Excerpts of representative criticism by and about Pope from 1706 to 1968.

Boyce, Benjamin. *The Character Sketches in Pope's Poems.* Durham, N.C.: Duke University Press, 1962, 141 p.
  Comparative and evaluative examination of character sketches in Pope's poems.

Brooks, Cleanth. "The Case of Miss Arabella Fermor." In *The Well Wrought Urn: Studies in the Structure of Poetry,* pp. 74-95. New York: Reynal and Hitchcock, 1947.
  Detailed explication of *The Rape of the Lock* that centers on the character Belinda.

Brower, Reuben Arthur. *Alexander Pope: The Poetry of Allusion.* Oxford: Clarendon Press, 1978, 368 p.
  Examines Pope's attention to form and his recurrent use of literary allusions in his works.

Clark, Donald B. *Alexander Pope.* New York: Twayne Publishers, 1967, 180 p.
  Presents "a coherent, unified interpretation" of Pope's major poems.

Dixon, Peter, ed. *Alexander Pope.* London: G. Bell and Sons, 1972, 342 p.
  Collection of critical essays.

Durant, David S. "Man and Nature in Alexander Pope's *Pastorals.*" *Studies in English Literature, 1500-1900* XI, No. 3 (Summer 1971): 469-85.
  Argues that Pope wrote the *Pastorals* to explain his future abandonment of the genre.

The Eighteenth Century: Theory and Interpretation 29, No. 2 (Spring 1988).
  Special issue on Pope edited by David B. Morris. Includes essays by such critics as Morris, Susan Staves, and Carey McIntosh.

Engell, James. "Wealth and Words: Pope's *Epistle to Bathurst.*" *Modern Philology* 85, No. 4 (May 1988): 433-46.
  Examines "two key social systems of signification and value, money and language," in *Epistle to Bathurst.*

Erskine-Hill, Howard. *Pope: "The Dunciad."* London: Edward Arnold, 1972, 72 p.
  Historical approach to understanding *The Dunciad.* Erskine-Hill finds it "a poem so subtle, rich, and at times so surprising, that the critic determined to see his subject in order may find himself engaged almost entirely in

unfolding and exploring."

——*The Social Milieu of Alexander Pope: Lives, Example, and the Poetic Response.* London and New Haven: Yale University Press, 1975, 344 p.
  Study of Pope's poetry in relation to the Augustan society that fostered it.

Ferraro, Julian. "The Satirist, the Text and 'The World Beside': Pope's *First Satire of the Second Book of Horace Imitated.*" *Translation and Literature* 2 (1993): 37-63.
  Provides a close reading of the manuscript materials for Pope's *First Satire of the Second Book of Horace Imitated* in order to show "a new and revealing account of [Pope's] response to his model."

Francus, Marilyn. "An Augustan's Metaphysical Poem: Pope's *Eloisa to Abelard.*" *Studies in Philology* LXXXVII, No. 4 (Fall 1990): 476-91.
  Argues that *Eloisa to Abelard* is a hybrid of Augustan and metaphysical models.

Franssen, Paul. "Pope's Janus-Faced Imagery." *Dutch Quarterly Review* 20, No. 1 (1990): 19-36.
  Examines metaphysical imagery in Pope's works.

Guerinot, J. V., ed. *Pope: A Collection of Critical Essays.* Englewood Cliffs, N.J.: Prentice-Hall, 1972, 184 p.
  Collection of critical essays that includes such works as "Rhetoric and Poems" by William K. Wimsatt, Jr., "The Cistern and the Fountain: Art and Reality in Pope" by Irvan Ehrenpreis, and "The Satiric Adversary" by John M. Aden.

Hammand, Brean S. *Pope.* Sussex, England: The Harvester Press, 1986, 218 p.
  Study of Pope in which Hammand notes that "the project of [this] book is to extend the direction of recent Pope studies by considering what is often a missing term in historical and scholarly treatments—Pope's ideology."

Ingrassia, Catherine. "Women Writing/Writing Women: Pope, Dulness, and 'Feminization' in the *Dunciad.*" *Eighteenth Century Life* 14, No. 3 (November 1990): 40-58.
  Offers a feminist reading of *The Dunciad,* concluding that the poem reveals "a symbolically emasculated man's personal and professional anxiety about the increasing power of creative and mercenary male and female writers."

Jackson, Wallace, and R. Paul Yoder, eds. *Critical Essays on Alexander Pope.* New York: G. K. Hall, 1993, 200 p.
  Collects essays on Pope published after 1980. The essays are general in nature and attempt to place Pope in a broader perspective.

Mack, Maynard. "Pope's Copy of Chaucer." *Evidence in Literary Scholarship: Essays in Memory of James Marshall Osborn,* edited by René Wellek and Alvaro Ribeiro, pp. 105-21. Oxford: Clarendon Press, 1979.
  Discusses the influence of Geoffrey Chaucer on Pope and his works.

Mallett, Phillip. "If Pope Be Not a Satirist." *Forum for*

Modern Language Studies XXX, No. 4 (October 1994): 316-28.

> Maintains that the moral authority in Pope's verse is implicit in his poetic technique.

Morris, David B. "Virgilian Attitudes in Pope's *Windsor-Forest*." *Texas Studies in Literature and Language* XV, No. 2 (Summer 1973): 231-50.

> Discusses the influence of Virgil on Pope's early verse, particularly *Windsor-Forest*.

Nash, Richard. "Translation, Editing, and Poetic Invention in Pope's *Dunciad*." *Studies in Philology* LXXXIX, No. 4 (Fall 1992): 470-84.

> Argues that a more "literal conception" of Pope's later versions of *The Dunciad* "can shed light on Pope's satire of Lewis Theobald."

Nicholson, Colin, ed. *Alexander Pope: Essays for the Tercentenary*. Aberdeen: Aberdeen University Press, 1988, 264 p.

> Collection of essays by such critics as H. T. Dickinson, Peter France, and Alastair Fowler.

Payne, Deborah C. "Pope and the War against Coquettes; or, Feminism and *The Rape of the Lock* Reconsidered—Yet Again." *The Eighteenth Century: Theory and Interpretation* 32, No. 1 (Spring 1991): 3-24.

> Feminist reading of *The Rape of the Lock* in which Payne focuses on gender fragmentation.

Piper, William Bowman. "The Conversational Poetry of Pope." *Studies in English Literature, 1500-1900* X, No. 3 (Summer 1970): 505-24.

> Examines Pope's conversational poems, written between 1730 and 1738, concluding, "taken as a group, [these conversational poems] give dramatic illustrations of the possibilities and the limitations of public discourse."

Pollak, Ellen M. "Pope and Sexual Difference: Woman as Part and Counterpart in the 'Epistle to a Lady.'" *Studies in English Literature, 1500-1900* 24, No. 3 (Summer 1984): 461-81.

> Discusses Pope's depiction of women in *Epistle to a Lady*.

Quinsey, K. M. "'Am'rous Charity': *Eros* and *Agape* in *Eloisa to Abelard*." *Renascence* XXXIX, No. 3 (Spring 1987): 407-21.

> Maintains that *Eloisa to Abelard* plays out the conflict between love of man and love of God.

Rogers, Pat. *An Introduction to Pope*. London: Methuen and Co., 1975, 180 p.

> Overview of Pope and his works.

——"Rhythm and Recoil in Pope's *Pastorals*." *Eighteenth-Century Studies* 14, No. 1 (Fall 1980): 1-17.

> Outlines and explains repetitive effects used in the *Pastorals*.

——"Wit, Love, and Sin: Pope's *Court Ballad* Reconsidered." *Eighteenth Century Encounters: Studies in Literature and*

Society in the Age of Walpole, pp. 56-74. Sussex, England: The Harvester Press, 1985.

> Reconsiders the *Court Ballads,* concluding that "the poem is shot through with contemporary references" and is "more daring and more verbally inventive than previous accounts have allowed."

——— *Essays on Pope*. Cambridge: Cambridge University Press, 1993, 263 p.

> Collects essays written on Pope over a twenty-five year period.

Root, Robert Kilburn. *The Poetical Career of Alexander Pope*. Princeton: Princeton University Press, 1938, 248 p.

> Examination of Pope's most notable poetic works.

Rousseau G. S., and Pat Rogers, eds. *The Enduring Legacy: Alexander Pope Tercentenary Essays*. Cambridge: Cambridge University Press, 1988, 286 p.

> Essay collection that includes works by such critics as David B. Morris, Pat Rogers, and Howard Erskine-Hill.

Rudd, Niall. "Variation and Inversion in Pope's *Epistle to Dr. Arbuthnot*." *Essays in Criticism* XXXIV, No. 3 (July 1984): 216-28.

> Examines classical influences in *Epistle to Dr. Arbuthnot,* including the works of Horace and Lucilius.

Smith, Molly, "The Mythical Implications in Pope's 'Epistle to a Lady.'" *Studies in English Literature, 1500-1900* 27, No. 3 (Summer 1987): 427-36.

> Discusses Pope's portrayal of Martha Blount in *Epistle to a Lady*.

Solomon, Harry M. "Reading Philosophical Poetry: A Hermeneutics of Metaphor for Pope's *Essay on Man*." *The Philosopher as Writer: The Eighteenth Century,* edited by Robert Ginsberg, pp. 122-39. Cranbury, N.J.: Associated University Presses, 1987.

> Analysis of Pope's use of metaphor in *An Essay on Man*.

Spacks, Patricia Meyer. "Fictions of Passion: The Case of Pope." *Studies in Eighteenth-Century Culture,* 20 (1990): 43-53.

> Discusses Pope's exploration of "ruling passion" in *An Essay on Man* and *Epistles to Several Persons*.

Stephanson, Raymond. "The Love Song of Young Alexander Pope: Allusion and Sexual Displacement in the *Pastorals*." *English Studies in Canada* XVII, No. 1 (March 1991): 21-35.

> Examines psychological subtexts in the *Pastorals*.

Szilagyi, Stephen. "Pope's 'shaggy Tap'stry': A Discourse on History." *Studies in Eighteenth-Century Culture* 20 (1990): 183-95.

> Analyzes the relationship between literature and history in *The Dunciad*.

Terry, Richard. "'Tis a sort of . . . Tickling': Pope's *Rape* and the Mock-heroics of Gallantry." *Eighteenth Century Life*

18, No. 2 (May 1994): 59-74.

   States that *The Rape of the Lock*'s "representation of female life articulates a pervasive male discourse of gallantry or 'fair-sexing,' a discourse that contains mock-heroic properties."

Thompson, James. "Pope's *Unfortunate Lady* and Elegiac Form." *Rhetorics of Order/Ordering Rhetorics in English Neoclassical Literature,* edited by J. Douglas Canfield and J. Paul Hunter, pp. 120-33. Newark: University of Delaware Press, 1989.

   Argues that differences between Pope's "Unfortunate Lady" and previous and subsequent funeral elegies can be ascribed, at least in part, "to changing concepts of the elegy as an ordering rhetoric."

Tillotson, Geoffrey. "Pope and the Common Reader." *The Sewanee Review* LXVI, No. 1 (January-March 1958): 44-78.

   Examines how Pope's wish to reach the common reader affected "the choice of his medium and the art with which he used it."

Weber, Harold. "'One Who Held It in Disdain': The Tragic Satirist in Pope's Final Words." *Criticism* XXII, No. 1 (Winter 1980): 25-39.

   Concludes that Pope's tone in "Epilogue to the Satires," is substantially different than in the rest of the *Imitations of Horace.*

. . . . "The Comic and the Tragic Satirist in Pope's *Imitations of Horace.*" *Papers on Language and Literature* 16, No. 1 (Winter 1980): 65-80.

Examines Pope's unconventional treatment of comic and tragic themes in his *Imitations of Horace.*

Wheeler, David. "'So Easy to Be Lost': Poet and Self in Pope's *The Temple of Fame.*" *Papers on Language and Literature* 29, No. 1 (Winter 1993): 3-27.

   Argues that *The Temple of Fame* is the only poem from Pope's early career that is "psychologically self-revelatory."

White, Douglas H., and Thomas P. Tierney. "*An Essay on Man* and the Tradition of Satires on Mankind." *Modern Philology* 85, No. 1 (August 1987): 27-41.

   Discusses satirical elements in *An Essay on Man,* concluding that the work "does what it does through the agency of wit rather than dialectic."

Williams, Aubrey L. *Pope's Dunciad: A Study of Its Meaning.* London: Methuen and Co., 1955, 162 p.

   Historical and interpretive study of the development of *The Dunciad* through its four major editions.

. . . . "A Hell for 'Ears Polite': Pope's *Epistle to Burlington.*" *ELH* 51, No. 3 (Fall 1984): 479-503.

   Examines unity of theme and vision in *Epistle to Burlington.*

Woodman, Thomas. "Pope: The Papist and the Poet." *Essays in Criticism* XLVI, No. 3 (1996): 219-33.

   Discusses how Pope's religious background influence his works.

Additional coverage of Pope's life and career is contained in the following sources published by Gale Group: *Concise Dictionary of British Literary Biography 1660-1789; Discovering Authors; DISCovering Authors: British Edition; DISCovering Authors: Canadian Edition; DISCovering Most-Studied Authors; DISCovering Poets; Dictionary of Literary Biography,* Vols. 95, 101, and *World Literature Criticism.*

Alfred (Victor) de Vigny
1797-1863

French poet, short story writer, dramatist, and novelist

INTRODUCTION

Vigny was a pioneer of the French Romantic movement whose work received considerable critical acclaim but little popular support. The author of influential plays and prose fiction, today his reputation rests primarily on his poetry. His major poetic works are distinguished by his innovative use of traditional forms, his intense concentration on poetic technique, and his determination to explore philosophical ideas in metaphor and verse. Although overshadowed by contemporaries such as Lamartine and Hugo, Vigny is still ranked among the great French poets of the nineteenth century.

Biographical Information

Vigny was born in the Loches in the Touraine region of France to aristocratic parents who, though once wealthy, had lost their fortune during the French Revolution. The family moved to Paris where Vigny was raised among other families nostalgic for the *ancien régime* of pre-Revolutionary France. In 1814, he followed family tradition and joined the Royal Guard, in which he served for thirteen years. Near the end of his military service, Vigny married Lydia Bunbury, the daughter of a rich and eccentric Englishman. Her father disapproved of Vigny and promptly disinherited her. Lydia became a chronic invalid shortly after their marriage, and Vigny became involved with several other women, including the great Romantic actress Marie Dorval. Disillusioned by politics, failed love affairs, and his lack of recognition as a writer, Vigny withdrew from Parisian society after 1840. In 1845, following several unsuccessful attempts, he was elected to the prestigious literary society, Académie française. Three years later, Vigny retreated to the family home at Charente, for which the French critic Charles Augustin Sainte-beuve coined the famous phrase "tour d'ivoire" or "ivory tower." There, he lived quietly until his death.

Major Works

Vigny began and ended his literary career with poetry. His first two published collections were *Poèmes* (1822) and *Éloa; ou, La soeur des anges, mystère* (1824). The ten works in these two volumes were among the twenty-one poems included in *Poèmes antiques et modernes* (1826). The dominant genre in this collection is the *poème,* which Vigny defined as "compositions in which a philosophical thought is staged under an epic or dramatic form." Though the structure is dramatic, each *poème* is tightly restricted in scope, showing only one episode and its effect on no

more than two characters. Vigny's *poèmes* are characterized by their stoical pessimism: Their principal themes include God's indifference to humanity, women's deceit, inexorable fate, and the poet's alienation from a mediocre world. Vigny divided the poems in this collection into three groups: "Livre mystique" (mystical poems), "Livre antique" (ancient poems), and "Livre moderne" (modern poems). The "Livre antique" is further divided into "Antiquité biblique" (biblical poems) and "Antiquité homérique" (Homeric poems). "Le cor," based on the medieval legend of Roland, is acclaimed for its evocation of atmosphere, particularly the description of the sound of the hero's horn in the woods. For many critics, "Moïse" is an outstanding example of Vigny's use of the *poème* to dramatize an idea through symbols. "Moïse" has been described as Vigny's pronouncement on the position of the Romantic poet in nineteenth-centuy society. Like the prophet, the poet is chosen for his artistic gift but must pay for his talent by becoming an outcast.

Most critics agree that Vigny's greatest literary achievement is the collection of poems that marked the end of his literary career: *Les destinées: Poèmes philosophiques* (1864). The eleven poems of *Les destinées* were composed between 1839 and 1863. The genre is an extension or transformation of the *poème,* in which Vigny opened up the originally tight dramatic structure to allow more thematic exposition. He refined and developed the ideas present in earlier works, including his ambivalent feelings toward women and nature and the role of the poet in an increasingly mechanized world. The philosophical problem that governs *Les destinées* is the ruptured relationship between humanity and its creator. While the early pieces are characterized by an attitude of stoical resignation, the later poems, particularly "L'esprit pur," Vigny's last work before his death, reflect his rejection of an earlier Christian interpretation of fate and his renewed confidence in the human spirit. Vigny combined his interest in philosophical thought with a passion for perfecting poetic form. His goal in *Les destinées* was to rework and condense themes and images until he achieved a "hard, brilliant diamond" in each of the poems. Commentators agree that his technical skill is responsible for the purity of the greatest poems in this collection: "La maison du berger," "La mort du loup," "Le Mont de Olivier," "La bouteille à la mer," and "L'esprit pur."

Critical Reception

Although Vigny was regarded as an innovator and a leader during the early years of the Romantic movement, his small poetic output cost him his initial prominence. His work was largely neglected until the early twentieth century, when scholars began a critical re-evaluation. Today, critics remain divided about the extent of Vigny's achievement in poetry. Albert Thibaudet calls the tercets of *Les destinées* "the most lastingly luminous poems, the fixed stars of French poetry." Others praise not only the texture of the verse but the dramatic pleasures of the poetry—including the highly visual descriptions of the setting and the stirring action in poems such as "la mort du loup." Some critics, however, consider Vigny's poems uneven in quality; his verse has been described as awkward, prosaic, and obscure. J.M. McGoldrick criticizes "Le Mont des Oliviers" as a "series of heterogeneous impressions" that contribute to "the organic disunity of the poem." Other critics, such as Stirling Haig and Frank Paul Bowman, read these conflicts and contradictions as ambiguities that support rather than disrupt the coherence of Vigny's poetry. Harry Kurz praises "the depth and originality of his imaginative spirit," and many readers have admired the struggle in Vigny's poetry between despair over the human condition and faith in the eventual triumph of the human spirit. Others criticize his didacticism and his tendency toward what W.N. Ince calls "over-simple, dogged symbolism." Many scholars, however, would agree with Ince, who writes of Vigny: "He is a great and original poet: it is often by the criteria implied by his best poems that his shortcomings can best be seen."

PRINCIPAL WORKS

Poetry

Poëmes 1822
Éloa; ou, La soeur des anges, mystère 1824

Poèmes antiques et modernes 1826
*Les destinées: Poèmes philosophiques (poetry) 1864

Other Major Works

Cinq-Mars; ou, Une conjuration sous Louis XIII (novel) 1826
[*Cinq-Mars; or, A Conspiracy under Louis XII,* 1847; also published as *The Spider and the Fly,* 1925]
Le more de Venise [translator, from the drama *Othello* by William Shakespeare] (drama) 1829
La maréchale d'Ancre (drama) 1831
Les consultations du Docteur Noir: Stello; oui, Les diables bleus, Première consultation (short stories) 1832
[*Stello: A Session with Doctor Noir,* 1963]
Quitte pour la peur (drama) 1833
Chatterton (drama) 1835
Servitude et grandeur militaires (short stories) 1835
[*The Military Necessity,* 1953; also published as *The Military Condition,* 1964]
Oeuvres complètes. 7 vols. (poetry, short stories, novel, and drama) 1837-39
Théâtre complet du comte Alfred de Vigny (drama) 1848
Alfred de Vigny: Journal d'un poète (journal) 1867
Oeuvres complètes. 8 vols. (poetry, short stories, novel, and drama) 1883-85
Correspondance de Alfred de Vigny, 1816-1863 (letters) 1905
**Shylock [translator, from the drama *The Merchant of Venice* by William Shakespeare] 1905
Daphné (*Deuxième consultation du Docteur Noir*) (unfinished novel) 1913

*Many of these poems were originally published in the journal *Revue des deux mondes between 1843 and 1854.*
**This work was written in 1830.

CRITICISM

James Doolittle (essay date 1957)

SOURCE: "The Function of 'La colère de Samson' in *Les destinées,*" in *The Modern Language Quarterly,* Vol. 8, No. 1, March, 1957, pp. 63-8.

[*In the following essay, Doolittle argues that* 'La colère de Samson' *belongs in the thematic progression of* Les destinées *as a representation of one stage of "the gradual emergence of spirit from the matrix of tradition and substance."*]

There is no doubt that Vigny intended to include **"La Colère de Samson"** in *Les Destinées.* Yet the colossal figure of Samson, knowingly and voluntarily bowing to the weaknesses of his own nature, and the voluptuous portrait of the empty-headed and utterly selfish Dalila seem out of place in a group of poems representing man's disdainful and morally triumphant struggle against the enormous, impersonal powers of Nature, Destiny, and God. Available documents show that from 1849 until his death in 1863 Vigny made this poem a part of each of his several plans for the group which became *Les Destinées.*[1] Our questioning of the poem must, therefore, be limited to asking in what way it furthers the over-all intention of the group.

It should be plain to any reader of Vigny that throughout his work his major preoccupation, as in the case of any true poet, is with the nature of humanity and humanity's place in the universe. It should be equally plain that he scorns the mass of mankind and confines his interest to a most noble and rare type, an *homme d'élite* whom it is difficult to describe otherwise than as a distillate of man's highest potentialities. I think it is fair to say of his writings in general that they seek to represent, or define, and then to evaluate, the nature and operations of this type. Certainly this is the most important objective of *Chatterton, Stello,* and *Daphné,* of many of the **Poèmes antiques et modernes,** and above all of the masterpieces *Servitude et grandeur militaires* and **Les Destinées.**

As one follows this endeavor through Vigny's work, one becomes aware of a wide variation in the roles attributed to what for convenience I shall call his hero. Proceeding chronologically, we find, for example, that the hero in the early poem **"Héléna"** is a militant and spectacular leader of a nation and a civilization, in **"Le Déluge"** a representative of humanity in defiance of an arbitrary and insensate divinity, in *Stello* and *Daphné* an aloof but exalted intellectual and spiritual prophet, in *La Canne de jonc* an obscure and devoted soldier, in **"La Flûte"** a poor man "aveuglé J'esprit"—and so on.

The hero's nature, on the other hand, remains essentially constant, changing only in the direction of increased detail and clarity of definition. This character is a composite, a duality, a double protagonist, set against an infinitely more powerful antagonist. Thus Cinq-Mars and de Thou are indispensable to one another in opposition to Richelieu, Héléna and Mora against the Truk, Julien and Libanius against human history. Stello and the Docteur-Noir oppose together a bourgeoisie-dominated society, as do Chatterton and the Quaker. Emmanuel's defiance of God, in **"Le Déluge,"** is given its meaning by Sara. It is obvious that Eloa, the angel whose rather surprising femininity is so carefully stressed by Vigny, would have no significance without Satan. And I need hardly remind the reader of the pairing of the Berger with the mysterious Eva.

While the dual hero is usually represented by two persons, most often a male-female couple, there are instances, such as **"Le Mont des Oliviers,"** in which the hero, while still dual, is not a couple, and others, like **"La Bouteille à la mer"** or **"La Mort du loup,"** where at least one partner is not even a person. But the duality device itself persists from one end of Vigny's work to the other.

This duality seldom constitutes a person, i.e., a creation of human character. Each hero, rather, is a pair of idealized qualities or notions, a pair of symbols, perhaps, of certain grand ideas or intellectual aspirations. Thus the **Héléna** of 1822 presents Héléna and her lover Mora, prophetess-apostle and military leader respectively:

> Deux âmes, s'élevant sur les plaines du monde,
> Toujours l'une pour l'autre existence féconde,
> Puissantes à sentir avec un feu pareil,
> Double et brûlant rayon né d'un même soleil,
> Vivant comme un seul être, intime et pur mélange. . . .

This inseparable couple goes into battle: "L'ange exterminateur vient, guidé par la foi." While neither member of the pair could be effective without the other, the poem's title, as well as its text, makes it plain that the leading principle is the feminine one, the incomprehensible one of faith and values spiritual, rather than the easily understood idea of force.

An analogous dichotomy is expressed in the concluding chapter of *Stello* (1832), where Vigny asks if Stello does not resemble "quelque chose comme le *sentiment,*" the Docteur-Noir "quelque chose comme le *raisonnement.* Ce que je crois," he goes on, "c'est que si mon cœur et ma tête avaient, entre eux, agité la même question, ils ne se seraient pas autrement parlé." We recall that it is the poet who provokes the reasoner to speak, not the other way around. The "question" in *Stello* is that of the composition, the proper function and attitude in society of the poet-prophet leader of mankind, the man of genius. We gather that he must be possessed of both head and heart and that his activity must spring from a certain, or rather uncertain, not clearly definable, proportion between these two not clearly defined faculties.

The head-heart duality is somewhat more fully described in a passage from the casket scene of *Shylock* (1828), the only passage in the translations from Shakespeare, by the way, which differs substantially from its original. Bassanio, finding nothing to guide his choice of caskets, says that man can rely only upon his heart to find out truth. The term *cœur* is here explicitly differentiated from mind, the faculty of reason, and from the senses, the faculty of force; it is distinguished also from soul, the faculty of religious faith. It designates instead a mysterious faculty of *conscience,* desire, instinct, giving rise to an otherwise unaccountable penchant, caprice, emotion; and the source of *cœur* finally is said to be "les Cieux." In other words, only through this faculty, incomprehensible in its origin and in its works, can eternity, perfection, ultimate truth, be revealed to man.[2]

Cœur, conscience, feeling, and the mysterious apprehension of the ideal are all brought together in the well-known passage on honor in *La Canne de jonc* (1835): "L'Honneur, c'est la conscience, mais la conscience exaltée.—C'est le respect de soi-même et de la beauté de sa vie porté jusqu'à la plus pure élévation et jusqu'à la passion la plus ardente." *Honneur* resides in man's bosom "comme un second cœur où siègerait un dieu. De là," the passage continues, "lui viennent des consolations intérieures d'autant plus belles, qu'il en ignore la source et la raison véritables; de là aussi des révélations soudaines du Vrai, du Beau, du Juste: de là une lumière qui va devant lui."

Conscience, passion, light, revelation of the True, the Beautiful, the Just, mystery, consolation, source of moral strength—these attributes of the *cœur* of Stello and Bassanio, of the *honneur* of the humble heroes of *Servitude,* are all ascribed to the patroness of *Les Destinées,* the feminine partner in the "**Maison du Berger**", to Eva. To them the characterization of Eva adds others: love, capricious authority, disillusionment with *le vulgaire,* the "divine faute" (which I take to mean the original sin of Eve: the pursuit of knowledge). The whole character is summed up in one line: "L'enthousiasme pur dans une voix suave." Such, for the *Poèmes philosophiques,* is the second essential element, the feminine component, the motivating principle, of the *homme d'élite,* the philosopher-poet for whom the jewel of Poetry illuminates "les pas lents et tardifs de l'humaine Raison," thus making of him the interpreter and prophet, the Berger, the Shepherd of mankind.

The single exception in *Les Destinées* to the usage of the dual hero is "**La Colère de Samson**."[3] Unlike the other examples I have mentioned, the Samson-Dalila pair does not seem to constitute a protagonist; on the contrary, the action of each partner is opposed to that of the other. And the poem differs in other ways from the rest of the *Poèmes philosophiques.* For instance, the characterization of Samson departs fundamentally from Vigny's customary handling of his man against destiny. And the radical difference in the presentation of Dalila from that of the other women in the group calls for justification; this is usually supplied (oversimply, I think) by making Dalila stand for the enslaving love which is one of the crosses laid upon man by Fate.

Of Eva's attributes, Dalila possesses only that of capricious authority. Her power is the power of sheer materiality. To the beauty of her body is added material treasure (bracelets, bands, golden rings). She is identified with a specific people or region (daughter of Hatsor), and with its religion: her breasts are "tout chargés d'amulettes anciennes"; in the temple festival she is placed beside the sacrificial heifer, crowned, and worshiped; she dies, with her gods and their altars, in the wreckage of the temple. She thus represents sensuality and venality adorned with trappings of an institutional religion.

Samson also bears a religious mark. He is a Nazarite, he believes in the ceremonial origin of his strength, he twice accuses Woman of ceremonial impurity, and his God is the Jehovah of the Pentateuch.

Like the Christ of "**Le Mont des Oliviers**", Samson is called shepherd, *pasteur.* By definition he is the leader of his people. His outstanding trait is his extraordinary physical strength, which presumably springs from the faithful observance of an arbitrary taboo. Yet, with his hair still uncut, "la force divine obéit à l'esclave": the physical strength does not have a moral counterpart. On the contrary, it is subservient, and willfully so, to Dalila.

Unlike the Samson of *Judges,* this one goes directly from his capture to the temple festival. His last feat of strength is accomplished despite his shaven head, nor does he make

any prayer. His strength, therefore, in fact depends not at all upon the observance of a taboo. His strength is and always was his own; in giving up his secret he has in reality given up nothing; he has merely acknowledged his total submission to the single, natural principle of physical force. For Samson and Dalila are almost identically composed: they are not a duality, but two aspects of a single essence.

If Samson's surrender is bitter to him, it is because he knows that he has wrought his own downfall by trying to follow an instinctive urge toward another principle. His wrath is expressed in an outcry against the fact that he is nothing but a physique, against the imposibility of satisfying his yearning for *conscience,* against the apparent refusal of nature and religion alike to permit him to be a man. He does not understand, however, that his failure lies in accepting prescribed formulas and depending upon traditional opinions and values instead of creating his own. He is indignant at being afflicted with the "besoin de caresse et d'amour," not comprehending that only through having this need and making it serve him is a man able fully to realize his manhood. Because Samson has sought, however unwittingly, for Eva, spirituality incarnate, and has found only Dalila, he concludes that there is no Eva ("ce que j'ai voulu n'existe pas!"), and he logically holds God responsible for his monstrous vision of the Sodom and Gomorrha to come. The manner of both his life and his death is determined by his following the way of superstitious acquiescence to the forces of nature and of ritualistic tradition, rather than the way of "respect de soi-même et de la beauté de sa vie," of free-minded confidence in the resources of his own individuality. And as his life has been a failure, so his death accomplishes only destruction. Destruction of three thousand enemies and of a foreign religion, no doubt; destruction also of himself and of Dalila, the embodiment of the false principle responsible for his failure. His achievement, if such it be, is solely a negative one.

Samson's wrath is misdirected. His complaint can be justified only by his complete lack of comprehension of the nature and splendor of man's spiritual part, or else by admitting that the proper role of humanity is passive submission to the traditional formulations of Fate, Nature, God, or whatever one chooses to call the nonhuman forces affecting man. The group *Les Destinées* is an outspoken rejection of this principle; it should follow, then, that, whatever Vigny's intention for the poem in 1838-1839, the year of its composition, in the context of *Les Destinées* Samson is to be pitied, perhaps, but he must also be rejected and condemned, not glorified.

While we cannot be certain that the posthumous publication of the group by Ratisbonne in 1864 is in complete accordance with Vigny's wishes as to selection and order of the poems, it seems to me that there is no need to cavil either at the inclusion of "**La Colère de Samson**" or at its position in the sequence. Samson is set between the obscure American pioneer of "**La Sauvage**" and the silently fighting wolf. As a man, he is clearly inferior to both. He represents, I believe, the antipodes of the *homme d'élite.*

He sums up in a single treatment those other figures in the collection who are idolized or feared by the mass for their material strength: the harpies of **"Les Destinées,"** the demagogues, the false prophets, of **"Les Oracles,"** the warring red men of **"La Sauvage",** the czar of **"Wanda,"** the hunters of **"La Mort du loup,"** and even the poet's knightly and forgotten ancestors in **"L'Esprit pur."** If the movement of the group can be correctly called a gradual emergence of spirit from its matrix of tradition and substance, then the poem representing the nullity of physical force and consecrated opinion may well find its place in close proximity with those others, like **"Les Destinées," "Les Oracles," "La Sauvage,"** and **"La Mort du loup,"** which emphasize these things.

For Vigny the proper work of man is accomplished not because of, or in imitation of, nature and its creator, but in spite of them, over the opposition of the crushing, nonhuman forces which they exert eternally against man. Man's true strength lies not in the physique or the incoherent instincts of a Samson, but in his *conscience,* in his conscious, enlightened awareness of possessing a spirit by which the importance of things physical can be set at naught and the things themselves made to serve spiritual ends. Given the obstacles that *conscience* must overcome, the strength of man's spirit must be very great. Only the *homme d'élite* is so endowed. Only he can serve as a medium for the work of the human spirit, the work not of God, but of man, the work which is not that of destiny, but rather that by which destiny is annulled, the work not of nature, but of art.

NOTES

[1] The various projects for the group are presented by Fernand Baldensperger in the Pléïade edition of Vigny's works.

[2] *Shylock, le marchand de Venise* (1828), Act II, Scene ii (Pléïade edition, I, 502):

[3] And the outstanding exception in the work as a whole appears to me *Moïse,* whose exclusion from *Les Destinées* has surprised more than one reader. The group's opening poem, however, announces the Christian dispensation, not the Mosaic, as one of its basic materials. The figure of the man of flesh almost wholly subjugated by the spirit, and thereby isolated from ordinary human intercourse, is supplied by the Christ of *Le Mont des Oliviers.* *Moïse,* moreover, is heroic, even Byronic, in conception and character, while the Christ is philosophical in the sense, at least, of the group's subtitle. Splendid poem that it is, the early *Moïse* lacks the maturity and especially the originality, the peculiarly Vignesque quality, which characterizes *Les Destinées* throughout.

Harry Kurz (essay date 1963)

SOURCE: "The Centenary of a Poet," in *The American Legion of Honor Magazine,* Vol. 34, No. 2, 1963, pp. 73-86.

[*In the following excerpt, Kurz provides an overview of Vigny's poetic achievements.*]

. . . The passing of a century has strikingly increased his stature and has led to an ever-growing appreciation of the depth and originality of his imaginative spirit. His name is Alfred de Vigny.

Most American college men and women who took French will remember the name as that of the author of a poem popular in anthologies, **"Le Cor"** (The Horn). It recalls the betrayal of Roland at Roncevaux. To Charlemagne's nephew has been given the duty of guarding the Pyrenean pass as the Emperor crosses from Spain into France. Ganelon, the traitor, has arranged for an overwhelming attack by the Saracen horde. Vigny's poem relates this combat to the death, the refusal of proud Roland to blow his horn to summon aid, his mighty defiance even as he breathes his last into the horn which brings the French warriors back. The poem is a sonorus little masterpiece, evoking the wild echoes of this immortal fray between Moors and Christians. . . .

. . . The year 1826 was marked by the publication of another sheaf of poems, now including the one that Vigny liked the best among his works. This is the famous **"Moïse"** (Moses) which uses the symbolic form developed by the poet to convey memorably a profound philosophic truth. The basic theme of this poem is that the man of genius is separated from the milling crowd by his unique gift, has to suffer the loneliness imposed upon him by the drive of his mission. Here Moses ascends Mt. Nebo to speak with the Lord as the Jews below in the valley tremble at the blaze of fire circling the prophet's head till he is shrouded by the summit clouds. The centenarian Moses implores the Lord to release him from his arduous leadership of the Chosen People, which has lasted from the plagues in Egypt and the sundering of the Red Sea to this moment, half a century later, when the Promised Land extends before his gaze, a land he may not enter. His power has made him lonely and deprived him of the joys of human companionship. This noble stirring monologue is answered by reverberating thunders as the cloud lifts and reveals the summit without Moses. Below the new chief, Joshua, now advances, pale and silent, for he is the Leader chosen by the Lord. The image of the aged Moses, wearied with his powerful mission, beseeching rest in mortal slumber, is etched with masterful strokes by the poet and conveys unforgettably the consecrated loneliness of the truly great spirit, Jesus at Gethsemane, Abe Lincoln in the White House, and eventually Vigny himself as he matures and traces before those of his time and ours the divine mission entrusted to the poet. . . .

It is clear that a philosophic poet who wants to be appreciated must devise some brilliant and illuminating objective frame of reference for his ideas. Otherwise, he runs the risk of becoming abstruse and unread. Vigny, as we have remarked in **"Moïse,"** develops bold, clarifying human symbols to convey the deep thoughts he wishes to express. Of all his poems we have selected only six, matured over the years of the writer's life and published at intervals. Actually he composed about a dozen philosophic poems, the result of reflection as much as inspiration. Vigny's mind was much faster than his pen. We have an invaluable record of his cogitation and composition in the shape of his Journal which has been published in full only recently in a masterful Pléïade edition of the works by the late Fernand Baldensperger of the Sorbonne. As we analyze briefly these poems, the reader will see how Vigny gradually moved from early pessimism toward faith in the Idea or Ultimate Truth.

First in order comes **"La Sauvage"** (1834) which has its scene in America and is inspired by Tocqueville's *Democracy*. It tells the story of an Indian squaw and her children escaping from a Huron massacre of her tribe. She finally emerges into a stockaded clearing of a settler and is welcomed by him and his family on Christmas Day. The man reads aloud the story of the Nativity in this bare room decorated only by a framed ten word letter written by Washington, and a set of Shakespeare. The Indian mother will make her home with the white family and replace the fruitless nomadic life of her tribe by that of the agricultural civilization fashioned by the colonists based on respect for Work and Woman, labor and love, with faith in God. The settler is here pictured as an imposing prophetic figure, the pioneer, strong, steady, devout, with the wisdom of simplicity, and the conviction that Law is truly the way to Liberty.

Vigny was deeply interested in our country [America] and his *Journal* has a number of his reflections about us. We add here a few of his conclusions entered over the years as he directed his solitary gaze our way. He even planned to write a poem entitled *Oneida* dealing with another Indian mother and her son. In the main his thoughts are generalities, like:

"The history of the world is nothing else but the struggle of power against public opinion. When power is in accord with the desire of the people it is strong; when it opposes it, power crumbles."

"The public conscience judges everything. There is power in a people assembled."

Vigny mentions an English minister who submitted to his King a message "listing the expenses incurred by the President of the United States as compared with those of the King of England. It is obvious that the King in one year spends as much as the President in forty-five years. One of the greatest misfortunes that can befall a man is popularity. Popularity is a sure sign of weakness in some respect."

"The government least objectionable is the one that is least visible, that one feels the least and which costs the least."

The next poem, **"La Mort du Loup"** (Death of the Wolf) was included in the same collection as **"La Sauvage."** This is one of his best known works. It is divided into three parts. The first relates the hunt. The wolf ringed by hounds seizes one in his teeth while the hunters shoot and stab, till in the end the dead dog is dropped and the wild animal dies without a cry. The poet then considers the scene and is impressed by this silent death. This leads to the third section of the poem filled with admiration for this lesson in heroic attitude and dignified recognition of fate, without complaint. The wolf is transformed into the

symbol of stoic strength amidst agonies, the acceptance of our destiny without repining. Vigny translates the message of the animal's final look:

> "To groan, weep, or beg, is all equally cowardly.
> Perform with valor the long heavy task.
> In the career to which Fate has summoned you
> And then, like me, suffer and expire without a
>   word."

In 1844, the poet published a momentous poem called **"Le Mont des Oliviers"** (The Mount of Olives). This is a long monologue expressing the thought of Jesus at Gethsemane. He knows he is about to be crucified and in his lonely distress, with his disciples asleep below him, he speaks to His Father of Evil and Doubt which His death now will leave unanswered. His mission on earth is not finished as He reviews prophetically the coming ages filled with strife and untruth. In vain Jesus begs a respite; the heavens remain closed and silent. "Thy will be done," says the son of man as He beholds Judas and the Roman torches. The pity of Jesus for mankind is overwhelming and intensifies the harsh silence of the Lord. This distrust of a cruel indifferent Divinity before the obvious distress of our world is a theme oft recurring in many of our poet's writings. Even when age has matured him into a deeper understanding of human destiny and a more abiding faith in the ultimate goal of our existence, Vigny still has rebellion stirring within him. Some twenty years after he had set down this supplication of Jesus, a year before his own death, Vigny added a famous stanza to the **"Mount of Olives"** which he entitled *Silence*. In it he affirms once more the break between the Lord and his creation and answers His silence with his own. This defiance is reminiscent of the wolf's stoic death. He even goes so far in this challenge that in his Journal, he indicates that at the Last Judgment, it will not be mankind but God Himself who will be called upon to reveal to assembled humanity the meaning of life's contradictions and to justify Himself.

For posterity Vigny's greatest testament and the most difficult to analyze is the poem he titles **"La Maison du Berger"** (Shepherd's Home). He worked on it for six years before its publication in 1844. It is the most poignant with concentrated wisdom and has an underlying unity despite its diversity of thought. It begins with an invitation to retreat to nature from our complex society and its problems. As an example he cites the railroad and its thunderous speed. As an antidote to our dangerous and bewildering mechanical progress, he next pays a lovely tribute to Poetry and its lustrous mission in our lives. From Poetry he naturally turns to a tender invocation to Eva, idealized woman, the eternal feminine who will transform solitude by her charm. Here the poet in majestic tones expresses in a surprising change of tone from the beginning of his poem, his distrust of unfeeling nature, and his wish never to be left alone with her. He ends with an exaltation of the meaning of shared love and its miracle in our brief lives. The whole poem is filled with reverberations of pity for man whose only guidance is by the diamond-like glitter of pure poetry and the intimate joy of woman's companionship. Above all, the poet appreciates the dignity of human suffering. . . .

We have still three of his major poems to analyze briefly. These were published after his death. The first to be treated is **"Des Destinées"** (The Fates). The grim Sisters have kept their grip upon enslaved humanity till Christ came to free us. They ascend to ask God whether Fatality of the pagan world is to be replaced by the new dawn of Freedom in the Christian faith. The Almighty sends them back, decreeing that man is to remain uncertain. He may think he is master of his fate but his lot is written, "in the Book of the Divine" says the Orient, "in the Book of Christ" says our western world. The poem, composed in 1849, reveals how Vigny's mind is preoccupied with the problem of freedom of will. At this stage he seems to deny the freedom to choose. That is partly why the poet refrained from immediately publishing *Les Destinées,* groping toward a clearer concept of man's independence which he reveals more completely in *La Bouteille à la Mer.*

He also kept quietly in his papers another poem, very personal and bitter, which his literary heir will also publish after Vigny's death. This is **"La Colère de Samson"** (Samson's Anger). The chivalrous noble son, of a puritanical mother who warned him againt closer contact with actresses than that afforded by opera glass, nevertheless lost his balance when he first encountered Marie Dorval. It was the elder Dumas who presented him to this lively dame a year younger than the poet. She was then married to husband number two and the mother of two daughters. What attracted Vigny at once was her impetuous nature and magnetic personality. Her theater-director husband was complaisant and soon the poet's affair with her became current gossip. She looked up to Vigny with ardent admiration as one heaven-sent to advance her career, which he did. During the five years following their encounter, he wrote three plays for her and succeeded in securing her acceptance as a member of the troupe of the Théâtre Français. It was for her that Vigny in 1835 wrote his impressive play on Chatterton, in which Dorval played the role of Kitty Bell, wife of the gruff London merchant in whose house the starving poet lodges. At the end he poisons himself and falls dead in his doorway. Wretched Kitty's heart breaks as she tumbles down the stairway with a wild shriek and falls dead into the arms of a sympathetic Quaker, also a visitor in the household. Marie Dorval was perfect for the role and her audiences were aghast at her marvelous growing agitation throughout the play ending in this horrendous death. Marie and Alfred were transported by his success, but their joy wanes before the insistent realities of their existence. Vigny was held at home by a mother who had had a stroke, and a wife who was becoming paralyzed by her mysterious malady. Marie Dorval was able to neglect her husband and her daughters, but never her career. She took to touring the southland, even playing one night stands, sending to her lover pressed flowers from the bouquets presented to her. Finally reports of her infidelities filtered through to Vigny and he refused, despite her denials, to have anything further to do with her.

But her treason rankled after he had written words of farewell to her in 1838. On a trip to England to claim his wife's share of the inheritance left by father Bunberry, Vigny sketches the theme of a faithless woman plotting against her lover and so Delilah became the symbolic figure. The final poem was written in England but discreetly withheld from publication till after his death. As for la Dorval, she dropped out of the Comédie Française which forbade barnstorming. Her charm and energy lessened. In 1845 she made a final appearance in a low type melodrama and faced decline and poverty. She died suddenly in 1848 without ever receiving a sign of forgiveness from her poetic lover.

This bitter unrelenting harshness is obvious in **"Samson's Anger"** in which Delilah is the temptress who thrice has betrayed Samson only to discover that she still does not know the secret of his strength. At length, he is tired of her malicious cunning and prefers to end this perfidy by meeting his fate. The battle of the sexes have never been more ruthlessly spoken and Vigny's invective is almot a condemnation of all women. But we have seen now that this pessimism wore away, as is revealed in the figure of Eva in **"Shepherd's Home."** And in his own home, by his loving care of two helpless women, his beloved mother and his devoted wife, he slowly recovers his balance after his rupture with Mme. Dorval. Lydia's condition worsened after her mother-in-law's death in 1837, but the poet could write: "She is enabling me perhaps to redeem all my mistakes if Heaven is judging me." He kept her with him in her ailing state for 25 years after his mother's death. Lydia had a sudden heart seizure and died just before Christmas, 1862. Her last words were: "My dear Alfred, I am not suffering." These words comforted him when he became soon thereafter chained to his bed with a cancer that was to bring him welcome release on September 16, 1863. His body has its resting place by the side of his mother in the Montmartre cemetery.

It is appropriate to end with Vigny's last poem, **"L'Esprit pur"** (Pure Spirit), dated March 10, 1863. It is a final letter to Eva. The poet speaks simply of his honorable ancestors, of his own distinguished place in the long family record, and ends with a message to the coming generations hoping for their occasional questing glance at his philosophic poems as they look forward to the new spirit animating a changing world. Vigny knows that France will treasure his name among the immortals. Between 1834 and 1863, he has written eleven priceless intense poetic messages, a total of about 1,500 lines, but he has the assurance within him of the splendid integrity of his work. He has groped his way out of doubts and queries, has noted courageously the weakness of old faiths, and achieved a personal code based on honor and compassion. By those noble principles, he declares that man can affirm his liberty and integrity and gain the final victory of Pure Spirit. Vigny draws aside the curtain shrouding the Future and proclaims: "Ton règne est arrivé, Pur Esprit, roi du monde!"

Eva Kushner (essay date 1965)

SOURCE: "Vigny's View of History," in *Bulletin of the New York Public Library,* Vol. 69, No. 9, November, 1965, pp. 609-17.

[In the following excerpt, Kushner surveys Vigny's poetic examination of historical progress and his search for "the collective destiny of mankind."]

Historical Consciousness is one of the battle cries of French Romanticism. On the level of literary expression, this is shown by the historical reconstructions abounding in "couleur locale" with which every French Romantic writer filled his poems, novels, and plays. In depth, it manifests itself by the Romantics' keen and pathetic awareness of the historicity of man and all things created. The realization of historicity may elicit regret and merge with lamentations on the theme of "carpe diem," as the poet feels unable to accept the passing of time and the inherent fleetingness of human beings; in the words of Musset, summing up the theme of Lamartine's all to famous "Le Lac":

> Ces ruines du temps qu'on trouve à chaque pas,
> Ces sillons infinis de lueurs éphémères,
> Qui peut se dire un homme et ne les connaît pas?

Again, the realization of historicity may occur in a more hopeful form, that of belief in a gradual improvement of the condition of man, whether this is called perfectibility, as in the work of Madame de Staël, or whether it is regarded as the advent of light after its long struggle with darkness, as in Hugo's *Légende des siècles*. But whether the historical nature of man is viewed pessimistically or optimistically, the Romantic writer is acutely aware of it at all times. In fact, his interest in reconstructing the past stems directly from his feeling that the past has value in that it embodies the unfolding of human progress.

What is true in literature also holds for the historiography of the Romantic period, of which Collingwood says: "The scope of historical thought was vastly widened, and historians began to think of the entire history of man as a single process of development from a beginning in savagery to an end in a perfectly rational and civilized society."[1]

Now Vigny is, among the French Romantics, the most acutely curious inquirerer concerning the nature and orientation of the historical process. True, Victor Hugo is more explicit about his interest in history than is Vigny. Yet the writings of Vigny betray a consistent, stubborn determination, year after year, to reach the truth about the collective destiny of mankind. His novels are historical; so is one major play, *La Maréchale d'Ancre,* and so are many of his poems, if we consider the ***Poèmes antiques et modernes*** as historical in the more formal sense of historical setting and reconstruction, and the ***Poèmes philosophiques*** as historical in the sense of their symbolical portrayal of man's situation on earth as it evolves in the course of time. Curiously enough, the primacy of this thought has not been consistently studied by Vigny scholars, with the exception of Estève[2] who devoted to it a chapter, and Flottes[3] and Bonnefoy[4] by allusions. Yet it appears essential to classify and attempt to weave into a consistent picture the scattered data, many of these drawn from the *Journal d'un Poète,* which might indicate aspects of Vigny's view of history. . . .

. . . . .

Whatever definition Vigny may reach when he reflects upon history, his emotional attitude towards it as a poet is one of desperate love. History is the battle-ground of man against his destiny and the battle seems forever lost. Pessimistic and optimistic in turn as to its outcome, Vigny clings to sobriety in his speculations. The knowledge of history, as expressed in the writing of history, is within man's reach provided it is recognized that it can only be based on "conjectures upon events." As to the orientation of history, as to the final cause why an event takes one turn rather than another, these answers are forever hidden from us. "You say: history will decide, which means that it will say: I decide and will take action at random. But who will decide concerning history itself?"[12] History elucidates, but does not essentially explain, the long chain of events of which it already consists; and it explains even less about the future.

As a poet, Vigny is challenged by this very uncertainty because of the pathos he sees in it. In fact, he sees the poet as the challenger of the unknowable. Whether the unknowable conceals fate, destiny, or the providential hand of God, or even mere chance, Vigny's attitude towards it is one of constructive defiance. First, we are to confront courageously the horror of the human condition:

> Je ne sais d'assurés, dans le chaos du sort,
> Que deux points seulement, la Souffrance et la
>   Mort.
> Tous les hommes y vont avec toutes les villes.
> Mais les cendres, je crois, ne sont jamais stériles.[13]

The way to redemption passes through suffering, for mankind as well as for the individual. Knowing this, he who faces the situation with open eyes will labour towards improvement. That is why, in the second place, the attitude of constructive defiance consists in making the earth a home in the true sense. Such is the philosophy of the poem entitled **"La Sauvage"** which takes place in America and in which a settler's family converts an Indian girl, not only to Christianity but also to civilisation, that is, to the organizing of the earth's resources for man's greater benefit. This is also the reason why Vigny is attracted by the positive social philosophies of his time, such as that of Saint-Simon. The social contract is necessary. The social order is necessary. They are lesser evils. They are man's historical answer to a situation in which the odds are stacked heavily against him. To sum up, the word history has a two-fold meaning in the work of Vigny. It denotes first of all the art of writing history which comprises, in addition to historiography proper, historically based literature: novels, drama, poetry, which Vigny values more highly than bare accounts of events. Secondly, it denotes that which is the object of written history, namely the unfolding of human activity in the course of time. Thus, accepting the distinction between history as "res gestae" and "historia rerum gestarum," he is fully aware of the fact that the resurrection of the latter is and can only be performed through the former, with the consequent projection of the historian's subjectivity. Furthermore, this knowledge removes any feeling of inferiority or even of húmble self-effacement on the part of the creator of historical fiction, drama, and poetry when he compares his vision to that of the historiographer proper. In fact, he may well feel that his very subjectivity is the key to a more inspired, a truer vision.

Here we have to follow Vigny upon his own grounds which are indeed those of literary imagination, so as to catch a glimpse of his own vision of history through his literary writings. Keeping in mind the distinction between history as a literary activity and history as a chain of events, or sum-total of the past, present, and future, let us first of all consider the former. In his *Réflexions sur la vérité dans l'art,* Vigny sets forth his ideas concerning the writing of history. This text makes it immediately apparent that what Vigny has in mind when he speaks of reflective history is freedom for the historian to re-arrange the picture of the past so as to make its general pattern clear. We must of course bear in mind that the "Réflexions" were written partly in defence of the liberties that Vigny himself had taken with history in his novel *Cinq-Mars.* Furthermore, he asserts that he used the fictional form only because a treatise on the same problems and specifically upon the part played by Richelieu in the annihilation of the nobility would not have found as many readers. The fictional form is indeed regarded as being purely a question of presentation, a help to attractiveness and popularity.

> I cannot help setting forth these thoughts upon the freedom of the writer's imagination to gather up in its nets all the main figures of a century, and in order to give more common ground to their actions, to sometimes make the reality of facts yield to the IDEA that each of them must represent in the eyes of posterity; in short, my thoughts upon the differences that I see between the truth of art and the veracity of fact.[14]

Men, says Vigny, have two needs which are fulfilled by history: their love of truth and their love of the fable. History was born the day that one man told his life to another. The memory of sheer facts has no meaning apart from the moral lessons it may hold for the present. But so-called facts or events come to us in disjointed form. It is for the writer to endow them with consistency. For they have none of their own.

> The acts of the human family on the stage of the world may form a whole; but the meaning of this vast tragedy which it performs there will only be visible to the eye of God, till the *dénouement* which will perhaps disclose it to the last of men. All the philosophies have in vain laboured to explain it, forever rolling up their Sisyphus rock which never reaches the summit and always falls back upon them. And each philosophy builds its frail edifice upon the ruins of another. . . . [15]

The writer's only ambition can be, therefore, to recreate according to his own conception of ideal truth minute fragments of the unseizable whole of human history.

Here it may appear that Vigny joins the throng of those whom he condemns for sacrificing facts to pre-conceived

ideas. This however is not so. He claims this artistic freedom for the historian only with a view to limited studies and not on the universal scale of the ultimate meaning of human history. Concerning the latter, Vigny remains sceptically silent.

On the other hand, he has many intuitions as a poet concerning the poet's own participation in the course of history. Of these many have a profoundly pessimistic flavour. The most frequent symbol for mankind's destiny is that of a prison into which men are cast, not knowing by whom or for what crime. (It is not until Kafka with the story of K. waiting before the gate of the Law that we again see in literature such a tragic sense of condemnation.) Furthermore the evidence for man's trial has been lost, so that in a sense all is at any rate lost. There are, however, two possible attitudes men may assume in their prison. Utter lethargy, or anxiety. Utter lethargy is the attitude of the masses. Anxious solicitude is that of the leaders who just as in Plato's cave wish to alleviate the ignorance and suffering of the masses.

To Vigny the distinction between these two kinds of humanity is very important. He indeed shares Carlyle's feeling that "universal history is fundamentally the history of the great men who have laboured here." For Vigny however a truly great man is almost necessarily a thinker. A few have been both thinkers and leaders of men in a more demagogic sense: Moses, and Julian the Apostate, whom Vigny hero-worships because he sees in him an embodiment of the philosopher-king. It is interesting, however, that at the end of *Daphné* Julian fails, admitting the doom of a civilisation of which he was the most perfect representative, and surrendering the torch of civilisation to Christ with the famous words: "Tu as vaincu, Galiléen!" By implication, however, and more explicitly in other writings, Vigny believes that the Christian civilisation will in turn be superseded; in fact, he believes that in his own time it has been superseded by the advent of a godless democracy.

Thus history sees the rise and fall of civilisations; the struggle of the masses to gain power against those in power; or again, history may be defined as the history of liberty, a liberty which is never reached but always remains an object of desire; but above all history is through all these struggling forces man's groping endeavour to gain control of the forces which control him. What forces? Vigny only defines them negatively in that fate, destiny, and Providence are according to him the same forces, named differently by those who believe in God and those who do not. Man can never hope to vanquish the forces which surround him and act upon his will; but he has another hope which is his sublime compensation for the handicap of historicity. He has the whole realm of spirit, including the realm of artistic creation, to assert himself against his fate; and works of art survive the decline of civilisations. The realm of spirit also includes the power of thought by which, and here Vigny agrees with Pascal, man can at least measure and define the forces which are against him, and thus, surpass them:

L'invisible est réel. Les âmes ont leur monde
Où sont accumulés d'impalpables trésors.
Le Seigneur contient tout dans ses deux bras
   immenses,
Son Verbe est le séjour de nos intelligences
Comme ici bas l'espace est celui de nos corps.[16]

This means that according to Vigny the essence of man's life is not fully encompassed in his temporal vicissitudes. These are, as physical space is to the body, the sojourn, the "locus" of his activity. But, with Kant, Vigny believes that the innermost reality is not bound up with this, while he believes with Plato that the highest in man has its ultimate home in the Logos. Thus the earth, and man's becoming on earth, can only be an initial, and sorrowful, phase of a becoming the total meaning of which is resolved, not collectively, but in the final secrecy of individual souls.

Those who see beyond and above the testing-ground of history, the great men, can at least lead others to a reasonable *modus vivendi* upon it. This is Vigny's justification for unceasing effort towards political improvements, here and now.

Thus he rejects the views of all those who attempt in some manner to justify the existence of evil in history, in the belief that it may somehow contribute to a universal good: de Maistre, Herder, Ballanche. As with nature and with God, so with history, Vigny voluntarily maintains at all times an attitude of lucid, constructive, stoical despair.

Notes

[1] R. G. Collingwood, *The Idea of History* (Oxford, The Clarendon Press 1946).

[2] Edmond Estève, *Alfred de Vigny. Sa pensée et son art* (Paris 1923).

[3] Pierre Flottes, *La pensée politique et sociale d'Alfred de Vigny* (Paris, Les Belles Letters 1927).

[4] Georges Bonnefoy, *La pensée religieuse et morale d'Alfred de Vigny* (Paris, Hachette 1944).

[12] *Journal inédit* of 1855, quoted by Flottes, p 314.

[13] "Paris," in *Oeuvres complètes* I 165.

[14] *"Réflexions sur la vérité dans l'art"* II 20.
[15] II 20-21.

[16] I 179.

Giovanni Gullace (essay date 1969)

SOURCE: "Alfred de Vigny's Conception of Esthetics," in *Symposium*, Vol., XXIII, No. 3-4, Fall-Winter, 1969, pp. 265-276.

[*In the following essay, Gullace examines the tension in Vigny's aesthetic between poetry as a means for philosophical inquiry and poetry as an expression of emotion.*]

The development of esthetic theory in France is to be credited more to the practitioners of the arts than to philosophers or critics. Poets and artists seem, in fact, to have expressed more penetrating views on the nature of artistic creation than did the builders of esthetic systems. Alfred de Vigny's is a case in point. Among the men of his generation he is perhaps the most deeply concerned with the essence and the function of art. While Lamartine, Hugo, and Musset wrote mostly by pure instinct, in Vigny poetic creation always was accompanied by a keen theoretical awareness.

Vigny, however, left no systematic treatise on art or poetry; he never attempted to develop his ideas into a logical and coherent whole. They must therefore be gleaned from his works, especially his *Journal d'un Poète*. His thought can thus be reconstructed, allowing us a better insight into the true nature of his romanticism.

The poet seems to have entertained two conflicting notions of poetry—poetry as the expression of philosophical ideas, and poetry as the expression of feeling. And, strangely enough, he speaks of poetry as the expression of philosophical ideas when he is writing his **Poèmes antiques et modernes,** where his philosophical intentions are least pronounced; while he defines poetry as the expression of feeling when he is composing his last "poème philophique," **"L'Esprit pur."** In fact, he wrote in 1824, in reference to the relationship between philosophy and the works of imagination, "L'imagination donne du corps aux idées et leur crée des types et des symboles vivants qui sont comme la forme palpable et la preuve d'une théorie abstraite."[1] And in the preface for the 1829 edition of his poems he indicates that in these works "une idée philosophique est mise en scène sous forme épique ou dramatique."[2] But in his *Mémoires inédits* we find, under the date of 1862, the following statement: "La poesie est faite: Pour exprimer du cœur les pleurs et les soupirs plus que les pensers du cerveau."[3]

However, despite this apparent contradiction, Vigny remains basically consistent in thinking that poetry is the imaginative embodiment of philosophical ideas. Poetic creation is for him the highest activity of the mind, combining reflection with feeling and imagination. Poetry, thus, is philosophical thought animated by lyrical images: "La poésie est à la fois une science et une passion."[4] This implies no antithesis; on the contrary, the traditional antithesis between thought and feeling, reason and imagination, poetry and philosophy, originating in Plato's *Republic,* is here solved by bringing all these elements into a unified whole.

Some aspects of Vigny's thought can be traced to Plato, to whom he is unquestionably indebted. The absolute supremacy the poet attributes to the world of ideas over the world of concrete reality, his worship of pure intelligence, uncontaminated by material preoccupations, his conception of beauty as related to truth and goodness, and in general his vague idealism, are definitely reminiscent of Platonic philosophy. However, Vigny's views on art are substantially far removed from Plato's position, despite occasional analogies which critics have often over-emphasized. A comparison between their theories would reveal more differences than similarities. Vigny assigns to the poet a sort of messianic role: "Le poète cherche aux étoiles quelle route nous montre le doigt du Seigneur."[5] This great mission as "apôtre de la vérité"[6] is reserved by Plato only for the philosopher, the man who rises above the world of passions and appearances to the contemplation of the intelligible world. In Plato's republic Vigny, the poet, would not have been better off than under the July Monarchy, for his conception of art surely falls within the Platonic condemnation. "La poésie," writes Vigny, "est beauté suprême des choses,"[7] meaning that poetry is the realization of supreme beauty in the world of concrete reality. Art is a downward movement of contamination, from the purity of the essence to the impurity of its embodiments. For Plato, on the other hand, beauty is above the sphere of art; it is an intelligible essence which can only be attained by rising from the transient beauty of things, thoughts, and actions, to the sphere of pure forms.[8] This upward process is one of purification in which the mind gradually divests itself of all material concerns in order to rise to the contemplation of beauty in itself. Art belongs to the lower stage of knowledge, to the world of sense experience and imagination, where the ideal form of beauty still escapes us.

The Platonic antinomy between the imaginative activity of the poet and the intellective activity of the philosopher sets Vigny's views on art in direct opposition to Plato's esthetics. Vigny finds no reason why intellect should be denied to poets and imagination to philosophers. And in *Stello* he takes issue with Plato for having placed intellect above imagination.[9]

Vigny's conception of art, therefore, is more indebted to the idealistic philosophy of his own times than to Plato. It is in this philosophy that the traditional antithesis is somehow brought to an end, and reason and feeling, intellect and imagination are harmonized as constituent elements of the intrinsic unity of the subject. With Kant's *Critique of Judgment,* feeling and imagination acquire for the first time a positive function in the life of the mind; and the Kantian idea of art as the sensible and imaginative embodiment of rational concepts becomes a basic assumption accepted and developed further by post-Kantian idealists. For Schelling art is the true organon of philosophy; it is the realization of the infinite in the finite, the expression of the universality of things: "Beauty exists when the particular (the real) is so adequate to its concept that the latter, as infinite, enters the finite and presents itself to our contemplation in concrete form."[10] Hegel conceives of art as the symbol of the universal idea; the idea is the content of art, the sensible and imaginative configuration of the idea is its form. Artistic imagination does not stop at the external appearance of reality, but seeks the internal truth and rationality of it, in order to bring it to light. In a work of art, the ideal must enlighten the real. The artist must meditate the universal truth of the idea in all its implica-

tions before he can realize it in its concrete form. Reflection and feeling are the main characteristics of the artist.[11]

Although Vigny had no profound knowledge of idealist esthetic thought, this notion of art was so widespread among romanticists that it could not escape his attention. His direct philosophical source is perhaps Victor Cousin's *Du Vrai, du Beau et du Bien* which, in many ways, echoes the very esthetic principles of idealism. "La fin de l'art," writes Cousin, "est l'expression de la beauté morale à l'aide de la beauté physique. Celle-ci n'est que le symbole de celle-là."[12] And further on: "Ce qui fait l'art, c'est avant tout la réalisation de l'idée, et non pas l'imitation de telle ou telle forme particulière" (p. 177). These statements summarize Vigny's own esthetic principles. Poetry is the symbol of the idea, the visible form of an invisible world: "Concevoir et méditer une pensée philosophique; trouver dans les actions humanies celle qui en est la plus évidente preuve . . . voilà où doit tendre cette poésie épique et dramatique."[13] And he states further, more explicitly: "L'idée est tout. Le nom propre n'est rien que l'exemple et la preuve de l'idée."[14] But the idea lives only in its incarnations. Beauty, therefore, is not a pure essence to be intellectually contemplated in its abstractness, as in Plato's philosophy, but the beauty of things as realized by art, in which beauty lives concretely. It is not above art, but it belongs to the world of art.

In the light of these general views, Vigny's esthetics becomes clearly evident in his remarks concerning the faculties involved in the creative process. While it is common knowledge that artistic production is the work of genius, the faculties characterizing genius have been variously interpreted. For the classicists the idea of genius suggests the supremacy of reason, the obedience to established rules, the mastery of traditional techniques. With Kant, genius becomes a combination of feeling, imagination, and intellect.[15] Some of the Romantic poets consider genius to be an imaginative power, violator of all established rules and creator of its own. Victor Cousin writes in *Du Vrai, du Beau et du Bien* that genius is nothing but "le goût en action," and he points out that "trois facultés entrent dans cette faculté complexe qui se nomme goût: l'imagination, le sentiment, la raison" (p. 173). For Vigny the faculties constitutive of genius are the same as those indicated by Cousin. He writes in his *Journal d'un Poète* that genius is made up of four elements (strangely enough he mentions only three): "1. La conception du sujet et la création des personnages; 2. la composition; 3. le style (rien du 4ᵉ)" (p. 1389). All this involves reflection, imagination, and mastery of the technical means to realize the work of art. The work of genius is not the result of an entirely spontaneous and unconscious inspiration, of that divine madness described by Plato in his *Ion,* but a conscious process of construction. Such construction requires both inspiration and rational organization. Imagination, which enriches and expands the idea by fully unfolding its obvious and hidden meanings, is not governed by its own whim; it is guided by judgment:

> La logique est la source la plus sûre et la plus pure
> d'où puisse jaillir et couler l'imagination. Elle maintient

la marche et le langage des personnages inventés et donne à l'œuvre une solidité qui fait sentir à chaque pas la démonstration d'une pensée . . . L'imagination, née de la logique du jugement, fait les plus durables œuvres. Lorsque l'imagination part du fond même du laboratoire intime, où mûrissent, où se concentrent, où se retournent les délibérations de la raison, elle choisit le pur froment et le féconde. De là sortent les œuvres immortelles. (p. 1359)

A work of art based on unrestrained imagination and feeling, while being more spontaneous, would be formless; a work of art based on ideas and reason, while containing more logical truth, would be a lifeless philosophical discourse, completely unappealing to human sensibility. In either case the work would be a mutilated one, for its completeness lies in the synthesis of all vital energies, both instinctive and rational. "La poésie," remarked Vigny, "doit être la synthèse de tout" (p. 1223). But the poet, in order to reach the synthesis, must be able to master his subject-matter with his judgment; he must be able to harmonize all the conflicting elements:

La perpétuelle lutte du Poète est celle qu'il livre à son idée. Si l'idée triomphe du Poète et le passionne trop, il est sa dupe et tombe dans la mise en action de cette idée et s'y perd. Si le Poète est plus fort que l'idée, il la pétrit, la forme et la met en œuvre. Elle devient ce qu'il a voulu, un monument. (p. 1071)

Poetic creation is thus a sort of mediated process, voluntary and not unconscious. Imagination is not an irrational, effusive power opposed to judgment and reason, but a creative energy rationally guided toward a definite end. It cannot be eliminated from the life of the mind in favor of reason, and it cannot, on the other hand, govern by itself our mental activities. The traditional mistrust of imagination and the exaggerated Romantic reliance on it find in Vigny a conciliatory solution. Artistic creation is the interplay of all of our mental forces.

What best describes such a creation is the image of the circle. "Je pars toujours," writes the poet, "du fond de l'idée. Author de ce centre, je fais tourner une fable qui est la preuve de la pensée et doit s'y rattacher par tous ses rayons comme la circonférence d'une roue."[16] In this sense artistic creation is the process by which, from the fixity of the idea, the artist arrives at the variety of its expressive forms, from unity to multiplicity; in short, from the center to the circumference. It is the center that generates the circumference. In every work of art, Vigny maintains, there are two points of view, one philosophical, the other poetic:

Le point de vue philosophique doit soutenir l'œuvre d'un pôle à l'autre, précisément comme l'axe d'un globe, mais le globe dans sa forme arrondie et complète, avec ses couleurs variées et brillantes, est une image de l'axe de l'art, de l'art qui doit être en vue, en tournant autour de la pensée philosophique et l'emportant dans son atmosphère.[17]

The work of art is brought about by a pressure from the center to the surface of the globe. The artistic impulse comes from the idea which, once conceived or received by the mind, immediately sets the creative faculties in motion. As Vigny writes in *Journal d'um Poète:*

Lorsqu'une idée neuve, juste, poétique, est tombée de je ne sais où dans mon âme, rien ne peut l'en arracher; elle y germe comme le grain dans une terre labourée sans cesse par l'imagination. En vain je parle, j'agis, j'écris, je pense même sur d'autres choses: je la sens pousser en moi, l'épi mûrit et s'élève, et bientôt il faut que je moissonne ce froment et j'en forme, autant que je puis, un pain salutaire. (p. 1180)

Thought is the source of feeling: "La pensée éternelle est un feu dévorant"[18] The human heart is a dark chamber, the *Journal d'un Poète* tells us: "La mémoire et la pensée l'illuminent et y font paraître les sentiments. Sans la tête, ils s'éteignent" (p. 1127). Feeling, in its turn, is the source of imagination. The stronger the feeling accompanying thought, the more powerful the imagination which develops it into the work of art. Without feeling and imagination, thought would remain in its fixity, in the cold domain of philosophy; without thought, feeling and imagination would be almost empty. "Le cœur," Vigny points out, "n'est que l'écho du chant qui résonne en haut, sous les voûtes divines de la tête" (p. 1199). Those who are not moved by an idea are unfortunately bereft of artistic imagination.

Thought, feeling, imagination constitute the chain through which the work of art is realized. But it must be stressed that these elements are not externally related; their relationship is internal; they are within each other. Thought is the center and feeling and imagination are its concentric expansion. No idea is ever received by the mind of the artist passively, without a feeling of some sort; and feeling contains within itself the impulse to fancy, to invent the objects of its desire or to remove, in its fancying, the causes of its suffering.

This conception of poetic creation as a process of expansion from the center to the sphere gives such a process a regulated movement, a sort of direction or orientation. The images are linked to the idea and they revolve around it in ever wider circles with no danger of arbitrary dispersion in all directions. These views on the creative process led Vigny to the following lapidary definition: "La poésie, c'est l'enthousiasme cristallisé" (p. 1078)—a definition which suggests a state of exaltation of the idea in its outward movement to acquire a concrete and indestructible form in the work of art. Through poetry, which is the purest form of art, the idea emerges from the obscure regions of the mind and reveals itself in all its luminosity. "La poésie," writes Vigny, "est une volupté, mais une volupté couvrant la pensée et la rendant lumineuse par l'éclat de son cristal conservateur qui lui permettra de vivre et d'éclairer sans fin" (pp. 1139-40). Poetry, thus, performs a philosophical function—the preservation of thought:

Poésie, il se rit de tes graves symboles,
O toi des vrais penseurs impérissable amour!
Comment se garderaient les profondes pensées,

Sans rassembler leurs feux dans ton diamant pur
Qui conserve si bien leurs splendeurs condensées?

("**La Maison du Berger,**" vv. 195-199)

Pierre Moreau has remarked that symbolism follows two opposite movements: one from the idea to the images expressing it, the other from the images to the idea suggested by them. And he has pointed out that Vigny "a suivi ces deux démarches"—the first in his last works, the second in his earlier works.[19] Georges Poulet in his *Les Métamorphoses du Cercle*[20] emphasizes in Vigny the two opposite movements as two modes of the reciprocal relationship between the center and the circumference. But Poulet's description of this two-way relationship is not altogether convincing, especially when applied to Vigny's artistic creation. Poulet seems to use two conflicting theories in his analysis of the poet's mental processes—the idealistic and the sensationalistic. Idealism is characterized by the movement from the center to the periphery, from the ego to the external world, the latter being an expansion of the former; sensationalism, on the contrary, moves from the periphery to the center, from the external world to the ego which develops through its relation with the outer reality. Idealism is a centrifugal movement, while sensationalism is a centripetal one. Vigny's creative process definitely follows the idealistic principle; it is a unidirectional movement from the center to the circumference. Referring to his "manière de composer," Vigny in fact reiterates in *Journal d'un Poète* what he had said on various other occasions: "L'idée une fois reçue m'émeut jusqu'au cœur, et je la prends en adoration . . . puis je travaille pour elle, je lui choisis une époque pour sa demeure, pour son vêtement une nation" (p. 1355). The idea may come unexpectedly from an unknown source; it may come from an historical impression, a remembrance, an observation, a sensation. But the creative process begins when the idea enters the sphere of consciousness. The genetic principle of the circle is the center, for every circle implies the center. The great poets, according to Vigny, constructed their works by a process similar to that of Michelangelo:

> Ils posaient d'abord leur idée-mère, leur pensée souveraine, et la scellaient comme un roi pose la première pierre d'un temple; de ses larges fondations s'élevaient les charpentes fortes et élégantes avec leurs courbures célestes, leurs larges entrées et leurs passages dérobés, leurs vastes ailes et leurs flèches légères, et tout était ensuite recouvert d'une robe d'or ou de plomb, de marbre ou de pierre, sculptée et égayée d'arabesques, de figurines, de chapiteux, ou simple, grave, sombre, pesante et sans parure. Qu'importe! La forme extérieure n'est rien qu'un vêtement convenable qui se ploie, se courbe ou s'élève au gré de l'idée fondamentale; et toute la construction de l'édifice avec l'habileté de ses lignes ne fait que servir de parure à cette idée, consacrer sa durée et demeurer son plus parfait symbole.[21]

What seems, in *Les Métamorphoses du Cercle,* particularly objectionable in Poulet's interpretation of the relation between the center and the circumference is the statement that in Vigny "les termes relatés restent distincts l'un de l'autre et soient destinés à ne pas se confondre" (p. 236). This alleged distinction would perhaps imply that the two terms exist independently. If this is the case, their relation will be purely external and accidental, as between things. But the circle of mental life does not consist in the association of two independent elements by an extrinsic relationship. It is an intrinsic unity in which the center and the circumference are so closely interrelated that one would be meaningless without the other. Neither could exist without the other. The center is the entire circle in its abstract form; the circumference is the entire circle in its reality. The center is an abstract point realizing itself in the circumference, which is immanent in it. The creative process is not the result of an external activity, but the outcome of an inner virtuality. It is a growth from within and not from without.

Feeling and thought are not two independent entities entertaining an external relation, but they are one living reality. Feeling (and I mean here not a blind emotion, outside the sphere of consciousness, but an emotion conscious of its object) is the feeling of thought; they are therefore one within the other. Poetry is a synthesis. Philosophy when separated from the poetic language is a lifeless intellectual exercise. The truth of philosophy becomes alive in the work of poetry.

Vigny's esthetic views place him in a unique position in relation to romanticism. In many respects he seems to be much closer to symbolism than to romanticism. The importance he attaches to the musical quality of poetic creation offers an additional link between him and the symbolist poets. He describes poetry in *Journal d'un Poète* as the feeling and rhythm of thought, as "un élixir des idées" (p. 1192). He believes that: "Les vers sont enfants de la Lyre, / Il faut les chanter, non les lire." And he transcribes these lines by Le Brun le Pindarique with the following remarks:

> Tout est dans ce mot. Oui, il faut chanter . . . La Musique et la Poésie sont deux émotions semblables qui nous saississent le cœur par l'oreille. La peinture, émotion qui vient des yeux, est plus calme et plus durable par conséquent, l'autre est plus vive et plus courte. Le tort de l'imprimerie envers la Poésie a été de transporter son émotion de l'oreille aux yeux; elle l'a perdue.[22]

Poetry must be read aloud, for it completes itself in the act of reading, when meaning and harmony are fused in a whole. It could not be understood if separated from "l'harmonie dont elle est inséparable." Once in print, poetry loses much of its suggestive power, for, *Journal d'un Poète* informs us, "la poésie est issue de pensée et d'harmonie" (p. 1083). How could one feel the poetic emotion which must be transmitted "par l'organe de la voix humaine émue elle-même" (p. 1083)? In order to give the feeling of poetry it is necessary that the poet himself read his poems "comme les rapsodes de l'antiquité ou les trouvères du moyen âge" (p. 1083). Furthermore, Vigny conceives of poetry as made of short pieces (which reminds us of Poe's theory): "La poésie comme la musique fatigue par la durée;

comme l'émotion s'émousse par la durée"; therefore, "elle ne doit vivre que d'ellipse."[23]

These remarks foreshadow a conception of poetry which suggests rather than expresses, which leaves to the reader the pleasure of discovering, through the suggestion of music, what lies beyond the ellipses and the allusions of the poet: "Laisser à deviner," Vigny points out, "est le comble du génie."[24]

It appears sufficiently clear at this point that Vigny's conception of art is neither classic nor romantic in a narrow sense; it is the synthesis of both, for there is no art which is either intellectual reflection or spontaneous effusion of feeling. Art is rationality and sensibility in their intrinsic unity. By stressing the imaginative and emotional aspects of art, Vigny's romanticism did not set itself as the antithesis of classicism, but it added to classicism a new dimension. Vigny went beyond both classicism and romanticism, integrating the old with the new, classical reason with romantic sensibility. And it seems appropriate to say that 'il annonce le classicisme de Baudelaire, Mallarmé et Valéry."[35]

Such statements in *Journal d'un Poète* as "l'art est la vérité choisie" (p. 901), "chaque homme n'est que l'image d'une idée de l'esprit général" (p. 890), bring him very close to the classical tradition. Against the tendency of romanticism to identify art with life, Vigny asserts that "l'art n'est pas la vie même," but "le miroir de la vie, plus beau qu'elle-même" (p. 1274). Art does not copy life as it is, but aims at the realization of the ideal form of it: "Si le premier mérite de l'art n'était que la peinture de la vérité, le panorama serait supérieur à la *Descente de la croix*" (p. 901). His own example as a poet shows his resistance to the exaggerations of romanticism, such as the excessive effusion of the ego, and the unpolished directness of expression. "Gardons-nous bien," warns Vigny, "de porter trop loin ce caprice moderne qu'on pourrait nommer la *recherche de la personnalité*."[26] Sainte-Beuve justly remarked that the poet "ne donne jamais dans ses vers ses larmes à l'état de larmes; il les métamorphose."[27] He never displays his suffering directly, as would Lamartine or Musset. He transposes it into a fictional character or into a pagan or Christian myth. By this sort of "dédoublement" he can place himself outside his own inner world and contemplate it objectively; he can thus master and control it. *Journal d'un Poète* Vigny writes:

> Jamais mon esprit n'est plus libre que quand l'œuvre que je fais n'a nul rapport avec ma situation présente. Et j'ai toujours eu un tel effroi du présent et du réel dans ma vie que je n'ai jamais représenté par l'art une émotion douloureuse ou ravissante dans le temps même que je l'éprouvais, cherchant à fuir dans le ciel de la poésie cette terre dont les ronces m'ont à chaque pas déchiré les pieds trop délicats peut-être et trop faciles à faire saigner. (p. 903)

Life with its outbursts of passion, with its agonizing suffering, is thus transposed into art, into a serene image of life, better than life itself. Art is for Vigny a reflective act, not an immediate effusion of feeling. It is not only inspiration, but also technical effort to translate the ideal into a form of reality. He claims for himself as an artist two dominant qualities: "La conception et la composition" (p. 1063). And conception and composition are in Vigny always separated by a long period of inner labor which requires the concomitant energies of all the creative faculties. While conception may take place in a moment of enthusiasm, composition is always hard and laborious. Vigny never improvised, and he had little regard for poetic improvisation and facileness: "L'improvisation ne doit pas prétendre à la durée de la gloire. Elle ne peint pas, elle brosse, elle ne dessine pas, elle ébauche. La méditation seule bâtit pierre sur pierre et sur un plan médité" (p. 1223). When we compare the haughty negligence of Lamartine with the constant preoccupation of Vigny for artistic perfection, we can clearly see the real position of the latter in relation to romanticism: "Lamartine," Vigny says, "est un poète d'enivrement sans bornes, sans forme" (p. 894). But inebriation alone cannot create durable works; the poet needs the power of organization and a complete mastery of all of the technical means of expression. Vigny's unfaltering concern with the hard task of composition in order to achieve artistic perfection singles him out among the poets of his generation. He seems to have carried out almost perfectly Chénier's suggestion: "Sur des pensers nouveaux faisons des vers antiques."[28]

Between the estheticism of the "art for art's sake" theory and the utilitarian tendencies of romanticism, between a complete detachment from the concrete problems of life and a full commitment to the solution of these problems, Vigny's conception of art occupies a position which can reconcile and harmonize these opposite exigencies. The poet can neither divorce himself completely from practical life nor involve himself entirely in it. Poetry has a special and definite function—the preservation of the ideal which is the guiding light for mankind. "Toute œuvre d'art," he writes, "est un apologue"[29]. The apologue is nothing but the illustration of a truth for a high moral purpose. The poet must attend to the exercise of the mind, the noblest of all activities. He can best serve his high moral purpose, *Journal d'un Poète* teaches, by working within his own domain, and preventing the world of practical reality from interfering with his activity:

> La vocation du génie étant d'ouvrir sans cesse à l'esprit humain des voies nouvelles, par une chaîne d'idées dont les anneaux ne soient jamais interrompus et conduisent à une lumineuse conséquence sans soulever les passions et sans descendre au matériel des affaires, je pense que l'homme fort doit se concentrer tout entier dans la méditation solitaire et non se disperser dans les improvisations d'une tribune. Il doit viser au parfait, et l'improvisation est toujours imparfaite. (p. 905)

Vigny feels that "l'application des idées aux choses n'est qu'une perte de temps pour le créateur de pensées" (p. 975), for the creator can work more efficiently within his own sphere.

This attitude created the myth of a Vigny withdrawn to an ivory tower, to the regions of the "esprit pur" to avoid contamination with practical reality. But even when he writes that silence is for him "la poésie même" (p. 941), or when he speaks of "la pensée pure, l'exercice intérieur des idées et leur jeu entre elles" (p. 1337) as being the most satisfying activity, he is in no way estranging himself from the world of reality. Ideas are for him more important than facts. But he fully realizes that, without the facts, the ideas have no validity. Ideas cannot remain pure, with no relation to facts, for they would be silent and ineffectual. Vigny's "esprit pur" is in no way pure. It speaks through the work of art, through "l'écrit universel" which reveals and preserves the ideas. The exercise of the "esprit pur" is not a withdrawal to the ivory tower for the futile pleasure of a philosophical reflection for its own sake. From the tower, center of the poet's meditation, Vigny looks at the world not with indifference, but with a deep moral concern: the tower is a lighthouse. "La neutralité du penseur solitaire," he writes, "est une neutralité armée qui s'éveille au besoin."[30]

Notes

[1] *Journal d'un Poète, œuvres complètes* (cited hereafter as OC) (Paris: Gallimard [Bibliothèque de la Pléiade]), II, 1948, p. 880.

[2] *Poèmes antiques et modernes,* Ed. Edmond Estève (Paris: Hachette, 1914), p. 5.

[3] Paris: Gallimard, 1959, p. 363.

[4] *Journal d'un Poète, OC,* II, p. 1272.

[5] *Stello, OC,* II, p. 677.

[6] *Ibid.,* p. 803.

[7] *Journal d'un Poète, OC,* II, p. 1288.

[8] *Symposium. The Dialogues of Plato,* tr. by B. Jowett (New York: Random House, 17th ed., 1937), I, p. 335.

[9] *OC,* I, Chap. XXXVII, pp. 787-93.

[10] *Philosophier der Kunst, Sämtliche Werke,* V (Stuttgart, 1856), p. 382.

[11] *Philosophy of Fine Art,* tr. by Osmaston (London: Bell, 1920). See Introduction and Part I, *passim.*

[12] *Du Vrai, du Beau et du Bien* (Paris: Didier, 1883), p. 176.

[13] *Journal d'un Poète, OC,* II, p. 891.

[14] "La Vérité dans l'Art" (preface to *Cinq-Mars*), *OC,* II, p. 250.

[15] *Critique of Judgment,* tr. by G. H. Bernard (New York: Hafner, 1966), p. 160

[16] Letter to Edmon Biré, Sept. 4, 1847.

[17] *Journal d'un Poète, OC,* II, p. 1082.

[18] *Journal d'un Poète.* Notes et commentaires par Léon Séché (Paris: Mignot, n.d.), p. 228.

[19] *Les Destinées d'Alfred de Vigny* (Paris: Malfère, 1936), p. 149.

[20] Paris: Plon, 1961, chap. IX, pp. 231-42.

[21] "De la Propriété littéraire," *OC,* I, p. 916.

[22] *Journal d'um Poète,* ed. Léon Séché, p. 153.

[23] *Ibid.*

[24] *Mémoires inédits* (Paris: Gallimard, 1958), p. 383.

[25] Marc Eigeldinger, *Alfred de Vigny* (Paris: Seghers, 1965), p. 36.

[26] *OC,* I, p. 912.

[27] *Portraits contemporains* (Paris: Calmann-Lévy, n.d.), II, p. 63.

[28] *L'Invention,* v. 184.

[29] *Mémoires inédits,* p. 379.

[30] *Stello, OC,* I, p. 802.

W. N. Ince (essay date 1969)

SOURCE: "Some Simple Reflections on the Poetry of Alfred de Vigny," in *Symposium,* Vol., XXIII, No. 3-4, Fall-Winter, 1969, pp. 277-283.

[*In the following essay, Ince argues that Vigny is, most essentially, a didactic poet whose chief fault is a tendency toward "overt moralizing."*]

Vigny says his ambition is to write poetry in which "une pensée philosophique est mise en scène sous une forme Épique ou Dramatique."[1] He asserts: "Ce que je suis partout (je crois), c'est *moraliste* et *dramatique.*" He calls himself "une sorte de moraliste épique." More clearly still: "Concevoir et méditer une pensée philosophique; trouver dans les actions humaines celle qui en est la plus évidente *preuve;* la réduire à une action simple qui se puisse graver en la mémoire . . . —voilà où doit tendre cette poésie épique et dramatique à la fois."[2] The three important adjectives he uses to describe himself as a poet, *moraliste, épique,* and *dramatique,* will serve as useful headings for the considerations I have in mind.

First, *moraliste* and *épique.* I take the two adjectives together because they cannot really be dissociated when we are speaking of his poetry, which is, in Pierre Moreau's excellent phrase, "moraliste pour le fond, épique pour la forme."[3] The term *moraliste* describes Vigny much more accurately than *philosophe* or *penseur.* In his most characteristic, in his best and best-known poems, he seeks to convey some thought or message by means of a simple main symbol. Thus Moïse symbolizes or embodies the inevitable loneliness and suffering of the man of genius.

The wolf is the creature which lives and dies stoically independent and uncomplainingly proud, an example for man to follow. The bottle, or its contents, in **"La Bouteille à la Mer"** stands for poetry, or any work of genius, achieved at the cost of great suffering; it will eventually reach port, that is, be understood and appreciated by the brave genius's fellow-men and contribute to their enlightenment and well-being. Thus, because he has a main thought to communicate about the human condition, Vigny is a *moraliste*. More than this, by his own confession, his aim is strongly didactic: he conceives and ponders, he says, some "pensée philosophique"; he then quite consciously and deliberately looks for some event or action which will be a convincing proof of it; he next simplifies the thought inherent in the event or action to make it as striking and as memorable as possible. In fact, and almost inevitably, he is often led to choose some very well-known, easily understood, and vastly significant event, something with the obvious epic quality of the Flood or subjects like the crisis in the life of Moses, Samson, or the Man in the Iron Mask.

There are two simple essentials if, artistically speaking, Vigny's method is to stand a chance of real success. Firstly, the thought and the symbol need to fit perfectly. If they do not, the reader is made painfully aware that the poet has a thought to express, but that the symbol chosen is not an adequate illustration or embodiment of it; in fact, he is made aware that there are two things, symbol and thought. Secondly—this is, to some extent, my first point seen differently—the didactic element should not be too obvious. Poetry should appeal to the whole person—reason, imagination, sensibility—and I am quite aware of the unsatisfactory nature of these three classifications. It is true that overtly didactic poetry will usually contain figures and rhetoric and perhaps, to that extent, will influence the imagination and sensibility. But such poetry is going too far towards making a means of what should be an end in itself. In the best poetry, the poet is seeking to communicate something that has affected all of him: its expression is his principal concern. It is not just that too explicit moralizing or didacticism spoils the esthetic effect; that is too simplistic. In the last analysis, all art, certainly all literature, has and must have a moral and a didactic effect and stem from moral and didactic considerations. The paradox of literature, and even more of poetry alone, is that the less overt, the less explicit the moral or didactic element, the more effective the work.

We can look at this matter, in relation to Vigny's poetry, from another angle. There are different kinds of poetry. We do not perhaps object to poetry that is avowedly or frankly didactic (Boileau, Pope); we can accept it on its own terms. But the essential ideal in Vigny's simple symbolism entails an *implicit* didacticism, perceived by himself and perceivably by the reader.[4] In other words, we are less inclined to accept from him poems which present us with an uneasy alliance of his kind of symbolism and overt didacticism. Speaking generally, then, our two requirements are met in several poems, and this partly explains why they are good. In others, the two requirements are not met, and this helps to make them imperfect. I shall try to substantiate my views with what can be only a few instances.

In **"Moïse,"** Vigny's favorite poem, the didactic element or message fits perfectly with the symbol. There is no overt moralizing at all. The epic aspects of the crisis Moses has reached, all the grandeur and magnificence of his character and of the powers he has been granted are annexed to Vigny's personal attitude on the question of genius, so much so that we are not aware at all, while reading the poem, of "the poet's view" as such. There is perfect coincidence of symbol and thought. **"Le Déluge"** and **"La Prison,"** generally speaking, are two more examples of Vigny's method working well. He either keeps more or less to the facts of some well-known event, or else he reconstructs artistically and dramatically some well-known event, in such a way that his treatment and details do not clash with the event or myth as generally known or understood.

"Le Mont des Oliviers" is a different case. Until the silence passage was added after many years, it is true that there was no explicit intervention of the poet in the poem, as, say, in **"La Colère de Samson."** But it is surely impossible to close one's eyes to the fact that the details of Christ's prayers and attitude in Gethsemane have been totally changed: "He went away again the second time, and prayed, saying, O my Father, if this cup may not pass away from me, except I drink it, Thy will be done" (Matthew). Christ is referring to the cup of bitterness he will drink when he is betrayed and crucified. There is no animosity against God the Father. In Luke's version, "There appeared an angel unto him from heaven, strengthening him." Jesus has no doubts about the work he has done. This is clear in John's version: "These words spake Jesus, and lifted up his eyes to heaven, and said, Father, the hour is come: glorify Thy Son, that Thy Son also may glorify Thee: [. . .] I have glorified Thee on the earth: I have finished the work which Thou gavest me to do." There could not be a stronger contrast than the one between the Biblical Christ and Vigny's, reproachful and heartbroken that he has not been able to finish the task he (not God) had set himself: abolition of Doubt and Evil, establishment on earth of two smiling angels, "La Certitude heureuse et l'Espoir confiant." The important point for our present purpose is the reader's realization that symbol and thought do not fit; the message is seen as separate or separable from the symbol.

"La Mort du Loup" is a much-loved poem because it has many merits: a simple, clear, good story dramatically told; forceful appeal to our emotions; strong, energetic, lapidary, and gnomic[5] lines in the last section. But the symbol and the thought do not fuse. A wolf is not an adequate illustration of the "pensée philosophique" in the poem. A wolf, to the best of our knowledge, is far from thinking and feeling as we do. It does not face moral choices. It does not have a will and discernment sufficiently like those of human beings to carry the weight and significance of the message. The poem is top-heavy because of this fundamental flaw. So great are the poem's merits that, during our reading, it is only at a few points that the anthropomorphism becomes obtrusive (e.g., "la belle et sombre veuve"; a wolf which is seen as "studieuse et pensive"). Furthermore, despite the dense, originally energetic, and muscular poetry in the third section, the moralizing is too overt. The machinery of the poem creaks with the ponderous treatment of the subject; especially in the second section, where, after the splendid climax of the wolf's death, Vigny laboriously tells us that he is beginning to think.

"La Bouteille à la Mer" presents a different fault. There is perhaps not too much overt moralizing, but the symbol is surely too trivial and, above all, too poorly set up at the beginning. All the details about the bottle can be very fine in themselves. But they are not relevantly and significantly enough linked to the central message: the symbolism is not truly functional, it is mostly decorative.

Let us now turn to the third of those three adjectives I began with: *dramatique.* It is the most important of the three. It covers much in Vigny's poetic technique and, of course, is very closely bound up with the other two, particularly *épique:* the epic is inherently dramatic in such themes as the Flood and Christ on the Mount of Olives. Furthermore, Vigny's method is essentially dramatic in that a main idea is personified, embodied in the full sense of the word, in the symbol he uses and the story he tells. The supreme importance of the dramatic in Vigny's poetry is evident, if we bear in mind, as a minimum, the following points. Firstly, and most obviously, the amount of speech, monologue, or dialogue. Secondly, the structure of many of the poems and their fairly regular pattern: the scene is often set in an initial and usually brief descriptive passage, often dramatic in itself (cf. **"La Mort du Loup"** and the description in its first section, all of which forms a dramatic and minatory prelude to the fierce and poignant action to come), and then we witness the unfolding of a kind of plot, the events of the story (this is particularly true of **"Le Déluge,"** **"La Femme adultère,"** and **"La Mort du Loup"**). The manner in which the events unfold is also significantly dramatic; the most striking instances are perhaps **"La Femme adultère"** and **"Le Déluge."** Vigny's numbering of the sections in some of his poems emphasizes this aspect of scenes or tableaux. Finally, rhetoric, climax-building, and contrast (often for pathetic effect) have importance within the body of his poems (**"Moïse"** is one of the most obvious and best examples, though the declamation of Vigny's Christ and Samson also provide good illustration). These dramatic devices entail no shortcomings in Vigny's art; on the contrary, they are an integral part of his achievement and work excellently. Many of them, especially the rhetoric, declamation, and climax-building, are inherent not merely in his method, his manner of composition, but in his epoch. By style of thinking, feeling, and writing he has much in common with, say, Lamartine and Hugo.

When Vigny's method works, when his symbols are well chosen, and when the moral or didactic element is therefore able to be implicit, then a good, original poetry results, a poetry which has the style, note, range of preoccupations, and effects which stamp Vigny as Vigny. Vigny was soundly aware of the originality of his conception of the objective *poème,* symbolic in his manner, but his compositions show that he was not always able to achieve the ideal implicit in his vision, completely to free the precious diamond of his original poetry from the impurities and irrelevancies in the gangue.

Why, one is led to wonder, and how did Vigny come to reveal the shortcomings I have alleged? A full answer to this question would involve many considerations. He is perhaps too concerned to communicate ideas. It is worth recalling that he wrote detailed drafts in prose before actually composing his poems. We have seen that the communication of one central idea is inseparable from his method, and from the excellent aspects of his method, but it can be claimed that he starts too much from an idea to express. "Je pars toujours du fond de l'*Idée.* Autour de ce centre, je fais tourner une fable qui est la preuve de la pensée et doit s'y attacher par tous ses rayons comme la circonférence d'une roue."[6] Sometimes, the main idea in a poem does not seem to have gripped Vigny, does not seem to have fired his imagination enough to give that unity from which a certain poetic vision or creation, with its coherence, will come. There is not enough sure instinct in some parts of Vigny's poems: hence the impression, frequently remarked upon by critics from his time to now, of a sometimes labored, clumsy, even inept style. One example must suffice, from the first section of **"La Mort du Loup."** The wolves are observed playing silently:

> Et je vois au delà quatre formes légères
> Qui dansaient sous la lune au milieu des bruyères,
> Comme font chaque jour, à grand bruit, sous nos
>   yeux,
> Quand le maître revient, les lévriers joyeux.

Why this comparison between the hounds and the wolves? The hounds, as Vigny says, make a great deal of noise while "les enfants du Loup se jouaient en silence." So the comparison is for pathetic contrast, presumably. But the hounds are depicted as tamed animals, "animaux serviles dans le pacte des villes," to quote from the second section of the poem where Vigny sharply distinguishes between such animals and the proud, independent wolves. The comparison in the lines quoted is clumsy and inappropriate, even incoherent. His rhetoric and dramatic skill lead Vigny to aggravate his excessive concern with a central message. The symbolic force of **"La Mort du Loup"** and **"La Colère de Samson"** would perhaps have been greater still without the pompous generalizations at the end of these poems. "Seul le silence est grand, tout le reste est faiblesse" is a fine line of poetry, provided it is not thought about. A moment's reflection causes one to ask why then Vigny wrote his poem: we are plunged at once into the problem of the poem's anthropomorphism.

For any particular "pensée philosophique," Vigny says that he wants "la plus évidente preuve" and "une action simple." The "proof," we have seen, can be unconvincing: his love of ideas and his love of being a *moraliste* seem to render him incapable of appreciating subtly enough the relationship between the truth of art and other truths.[7] The "proof" can also seem *too* evident and *too* simple. He can try to put too much thought into a symbol that will not take such an amount (as in **"La Bouteille à la Mer"**). He can give the impression in his poetry (though rarely in his prose) of having a mediocre intelligence. A good poet does not have to be intellectual or very intelligent; but, after all, if we take Vigny on his own terms, it is ideas and thought that are so important. His over-simple, dogged symbolism, his overstatement of the moral, can unfortunately help to make him appear unaware of life's more obvious complexities and unappreciative of some of the truths, that, for perceptive and sensitive people, lie at the heart of things. Going further still we might claim that, along this line of enquiry, we reach the very heart of Vigny's uniqueness, of the original strength in him that is inseparable from the weakness. Ideas are the source of his power and also of a curiously pathetic, defensive precariousness: "Consolons-nous de tout par la pensée que nous jouissons de notre pensée même, et que cette jouissance, rien ne peut nous la ravir."[8] He and his poetry are in love with ideas, abstractions, as is evident from our reading of that poetry and from his prose writing about himself. "Quand on veut rester pur, il ne faut pas se mêler d'agir sur les hommes. L'application des idées aux choses n'est qu'une perte de temps pour les créateurs de pensées."[9] A wish to keep clear of political involvement and practical affairs can incur no criticism in the context of this paper. "Committed" poetry is not *ipso facto* better than any other. But Vigny's kind of purity can be bought at too high a price. He adored solitude, but such an adoration does not necessarily exclude a more intimate acquaintance with others and even with self than Vigny seems to have had. However embodied in his poems his abstractions may be, they can lack the warmth, cogency and greater complexity they would perhaps have had if the man had thought, felt, and lived more . . . deeply, less egocentrically, with subtler discrimination, more openheartedly, and more openmindedly. His poetry would have been even better if he had been more self-critical, if he had seen his own love of abstraction with greater detachment. He might then have developed a sense of humor and also been able to perceive some of the silly details that can mar parts of some poems (e.g., the butlers who go up, but never seem to come down, the staircases at the beginning of the third section of **"La Sauvage,"** or the sailors performing remarkable feats in the ninth stanza of **"La Bouteille à la Mer,"** high on their masts [clinging to them?], one hand holding a glass of wine for the toast, the other uncovering their heads in salutation). His notion of charity or love is understandably thought sublime, but, given the total impact of Vigny, it is too near to being charity at a distance, charity of the study, just the *idea* of charity.

But already we are leaving behind the poems themselves, though it is never easy and perhaps, beyond a certain stage, not desirable to try to separate the artistic from the moral. There is much in Vigny the poet to admire and to love, but he is too often the object of a fulsome, uncritical, and, from the strict viewpoint of poetry, unanalytically irrelevant praise. He is a great and original poet: it is often by the criteria implied by his best poems that his shortcomings can best be seen.

Notes

[1] "Préface," *Euvres complètes* (Paris: Gallimard, Bibliothèque de la Pléiade, 1950), p. 55.

[2] *Le Journal* (Paris: Gallimard, Pléiade, 1948), pp. 934, 1018, 891.

[3] *Les "Destinées" d' Alfred de Vigny* (Paris: Société française d'Éditions Littéraires et Techniques, Les Grands Evénements littéraires, 1936), p. 147.

[4] As Alison Fairlie writes in her *Baudelaire: Les Fleurs du Mal* (London: Edward Arnold, 1960), p. 20: "The finest images give a feeling not just of an ingenious intellectual parallel, but of a compelling and suggestive interaction of two things. This is perhaps why the technique of first describing of an object in detail or telling a story and then explaining the meaning rarely produces the best poetry. This frequent nineteenth-century device leaves us too conscious of the division between outer and inner worlds, and of the intrusion of an outside observer to explain and discuss."

[5] The adjective is from P.-G. Castex, *Vigny: L'Homme et l'œuvre* (Paris: Boivin, Connaissance des Lettres, 1952), p. 160.

[6] Letter to E. Biré, September 1847, quoted by Eigeldinger, *Alfred de Vigny* (Paris: Seghers, 1965), p. 64.

[7] See, for instance, Vigny's *Réflexions sur la Vérité dans l'Art, œuvres complètes,* 1948, pp. 19-25.

[8] *Le Journal,* p. 1009.

[9] *Le Journal,* p. 975.

Lloyd Bishop (essay date 1973)

SOURCE: "Jesus as Romantic Hero: *Le Mont des Oliviers,*" in *The French Review,* Vol. XLVI, No. 5, Spring, 1973, pp. 41-8.

[*In the following essay, Bishop defends the coherence of Vigny's portrait of Christ in* Le Mont des Oliviers, *arguing that Christ in the poem shares the religious doubts of Vigny and his contemporaries as well as their continuing need to believe.*]

Alfred de Vigny's famous poem on Christ in the Garden of Gethsemane has recently been attacked in an interesting article by J. M. McGoldrick for its "utter confusion," its "organic disunity."[1] The problem according to McGoldric lies in the characterization of Christ. The image the reader receives of the Savior, he says, is that of a series of heterogeneous impressions rather than a coherent personality, and "The message expounded does not always grow out of the plot that is supposed to illustrate it" (p. 510). McGoldric focuses his criticism on the poem's second section in which Christ pleads to his heavenly Father to dissolve mankind's metaphysical ignorance and doubt. Our purpose here is to demonstrate what most readers have implicitly felt: that the initial section of the poem does provide an adequate foundation for what follows and that the poem does offer a coherent, if unorthodox, image of Christ.

In the opening thirty-four lines Vigny is careful to stress Jesus' human side, his frail "mortal" nature. He is shown walking hurriedly and nervously while his disciples sleep. In the chill of the night he is "frissonnant comme eux."[2] He calls to his Father, but there is no answer. He is dumbfounded ("étonné") by this inexplicable silence. A "bloody sweat" breaks out on his face. He is "frightened." This emphasis on Jesus' human nature not only reflects the poet's traumatic reaction to Dr. Strauss's book on the life of Jesus, but it is essential for the thematic structure of the poem: it conditions the reader to accept and identify with Jesus as a purely human hero (one does not identify with a god).

At the end of the first section Jesus, remembering all he has suffered for thirty-three years and shocked ("étonné") by his Father's apparent indifference, "becomes man," that is, fully human. For the space of this brief, bitter moment Jesus is disowning his Father and renouncing his own divine nature. Pierre-Georges Castex mentions a fragment of a projected poem in which Vigny depicts Jesus proclaiming his purely human nature and ancestry: "Je ne suis pas le Fils de Dieu!"[3] Castex adds: "**Le Mont des Oliviers**" ne va pas aussi loin" (ibid.). But the poem does go that far. The suggestion of rebellion, of a conversion in reverse, is implicit in the force of the *passé simple:* "Jésus . . . devint homme" (i, 26-27) and "Eut sur le monde et l'homme une pensée humaine" (i, 32). The structural unity of the poem hinges on these lines. Jesus is going to identify with Man, he is going to see the problems of the human condition with human eyes. The importance of the epithet "humaine," coming at the rhyme, must not be overlooked; it introduces the second movement of the poem. The unorthodox monologue in section two is not a departure from but a development of what has preceded, it is what the poem is all about.

The central theme of section two is Jesus' complaint that he is being relieved of his mission before its completion:

> *Avant le dernier mot ne ferme pas mon livre.*

> (ii, 2)

> . . . . .

> *N'ayant que soulevé ce manteau de misère.*

> (ii, 50)

It is true that Jesus' attitude toward his mission is ambiguous, or rather, ambivalent:

> *Si j'ai coupé les temps en deux parts, l'une esclave*
> *Et l'autre libre;—au nom du Passé que je lave*
> *Par le Sang de mon corps qui souffre et va frémir*
> *Versons-en la moitié pour laver l'avenir!*

> (ii, 21-24)

In the first two lines Jesus claims to have already successfully divided time into two parts having absolved the Past and freed the future. Why then is the future (which is not dignified by a capital letter as is the Past) characterized in the final line as an unfinished task? If there is a real semantic distinction between "freeing" the future and "washing it clean," it must be this: thanks to the Crucifixion mankind will be redeemed from original sin, it will be given a fresh start, but will remain vulnerable. Christ anticipates the future, unabsolved sins still to come. Thus he seems to have doubts about the total efficacy of his Crucifixion. It's value seems to be solely retroactive. The Sacrifice seems premature. Despite the tactful tone, this amounts to nothing less than a lack of confidence in divine judgment: the Father has poorly timed the Crucifixion.

An even bolder passage follows:

> *Mal et Doute! En un mot je puis les mettre en*
>   *poudre,*
> *Vous les aviez prévus, laissez-moi vous absoudre*
> *De les avoir permis.—C'est l'accusation*
> *Qui pèse de partout sur la Création!—*

> (ii, 53-56)

Here Jesus sees his role not as Redeemer of mankind but as God's advocate. He suggests that God himself is on trial and is asked to give an accounting to mankind, an explanation of the many enigmas of his Creation. This reversal of God's role from judge to accused is expressed even more boldly in an outline of a projected poem that Vigny planned to call "Jugement dernier": "Ce sera ce jour-là que Dieu viendra se justifier devant toutes les âmes et tout ce qui est vie. Il paraîtra et parlera, il dira clairement pourquoi la création et pourquoi la souffrance et la mort de l'innocence, etc. En ce moment; ce sera le genre humain ressuscité qui sera le juge, et l'Eternel, le Créateur, sera jugé par les générations rendues à la vie." (PL, II, p. 1001). Here we see the full implications of "Jésus . . . devint homme" and "pensée humaine." In this tacit quarrel between God and Man Jesus is siding with the latter. If God will not speak in his own defense, let Jesus speak for Him, or let others, like Lazarus, who have seen the secrets of the other world.

The aggressiveness of the plea is startling in its boldness, but it is not inconsistent with the section that precedes nor the one that follows. Christ's yielding to his Father's will is presented in section three. The formal division itself suffices to indicate that the rebellious mood is over. The transition is further signalled by a change of epithet: "humaine," which closed the first section and introduced the second, now yields to "divin":

> *Ainsi le divin Fils parlait au divin Père*

> (iii, 1)

The resumption of the Father-Son relationship is underscored by the repetition of the epithet. However, Jesus' submission does not diminish his anguish, it "redoubles" it. Vigny nicely manages to effect the transition in accordance with the Biblical account without a drastic change in characterization. While submitting to his Father's will, Jesus does not relinquish his anguished quest for light:

> *Il se prosterne encore, il attend, il espère . . .*
> *Mais il renonce et dit: "Que votre volonté*
> *Soit faite et non la mienne, et pour l'Eternité!"*
> *Une terreur profonde, une angoisse infinie*
> *Redoublent sa torture et sa lente agonie.*
> *Il regarde longtemps, longtemps cherche sans voir.*
> *Comme un marbre de deuil tout le ciel était noir.*

> (iii, 2-8)

The basic problem, underlined by the final antithetical rhyme, remains unresolved. Looking at the poem in terms of its overall structure, one must allow that the poet has handled his transitions with care and subtlety.

The alleged disunity of the poem will disappear at once when one reads it as the description of a moment of crisis, a brief moment of dissent. The poem's essential structure is solid enough: an exposition in which Jesus suddenly empathizes with mankind's grievances, a central section in which he both articulates and symbolizes them, the resolution of the revolt (but not the anguish), and of course the defiant post-script on Silence uttered not by Christ but by the poet himself anxious to point up the moral.[4]

The exposition makes it clear that we are dealing with Jesus not as omniscient God-Man but as a purely human figure, in fact an archetypal Romantic Hero in revolt against the rules (in this case, silence) imposed upon him. In addition to the rebelliousness implicit at the end of section one and explicit in section two, Vigny's Jesus exhibits nearly all the other traits one associates with the Romantic Hero. He endures, for example, the solitude of the superior individual: "Jésus marchait seul" (i, 1). As in **"Moïse,"** the poet is careful to put symbolic distance between the hero and his followers. And Moses' lament:

> *Sitôt que votre souffle a rempli le berger*
> *Les hommes se sont dit: "il nous est étranger."*

> (PL, I, p. 9)

is paralleled by that of Jesus:

> *"Ne pouviez-vous prier et veiller avec moi?"*
> *Mais un sommeil de mort accable les apôtres.*
> *Pierre à la voix du maître est sourd comme les*
>   *autres.*

> (i, 18-20)

Jesus also possesses the brooding melancholy of the *beau ténébreux:* "Triste jusqu'à la mort, l'œil sombre et ténébreux" (i, 6). He is tracked down by Hernani's "destin insensé" thanks to the poem's first simile foeshadowing

the Crucifixion: "Vêtu de blanc ainsi qu'un mort de son linceul" (i, 2). An even bolder simile shows Jesus with bowed head "croisant les deux bras sur sa robe / Comme un voleur de nuit cachant ce qu'il dérobe; / Connaissant les rochers mieux qu'un sentier uni" (i, 7-9). Here we see the Romantic Hero as paria and outlaw. More often than not, the Romantic Hero is not just an outcast but an orphan, a bastard son, disowned or dispossessed. Typical examples are Hugo's Didier in *Marion Delorme:* "J'ai pour tout nom Didier. Je n'ai jamais connu / Mon père ni ma mère. On me déposa nu, / Tout enfant, sur le seuil d'une église. . . ." and Dumas' Antony: "Les autres hommes, du moins, lorsqu'un événement brise leurs espérances, ils ont un père, une mère! . . . des bras qui s'ouvrent pour qu'ils viennent y gémir. Moi! Moi! je n'ai pas même la pierre d'un tombeau où je puisse lire un nom et pleurer." (Happily absent from Vigny's moving figure of Christ is one of the less attractive traits of the Romantic Hero: self-pity.) The parallel here is poignant: Jesus' fitful cries to his Father fall on deaf ears: "Le vent seul répondit à sa voix" (i, 20).

In his *Journal* Vigny has expressed his admiration for those heroes who dare defy the gods: "Quand un contempteur des dieux paraît, comme Ajax, fils d'Oïlée, le monde l'adopte et l'aime; tel est Satan; tels sont Oreste et Don Juan. Tous ceux qui luttèrent contre le ciel injuste ont eu l'admiration et l'amour secret des hommes" (PL, II, 1001). The poet was furnished with more recent Romantic models in Byron's Manfred and Cain.[5] As Castex has indicated, this "caïnisme" or "prométhéisme" was an important Romantic theme on both sides of the Channel.

The weakest part of McGoldric's article is his criticism that Vigny "by a ruthless selection of material illustrative of a romantic obsession with the horrific" (p. 512) has "created a subject totally removed from both the letter and the spirit of the Gospels" (p. 510). Jesus' anticipation of his Crucifixion, for example, is criticized because certain details are not specifically found in the Gospel accounts ("Les verges qui viendront") or because they are mentioned "only" once (the cup of gall) or twice (the crown of thorns)! And surely McGoldric is over-straining to make a point when he speaks of Jesus' "morbid, pagan preoccupation with what Lazarus experienced in the nether world after dying" (p. 512).

McGoldric's main complaint seems to be the poem's lack of optimism and the fact that Jesus' monologue is not a theodicy but, rather, what Sartre has called, in *L'Idiot de la Famille,* "théologie négative." Vigny's Jesus incarnates a certain ambivalence or tension between two polar attitudes, theism and atheism, the dialectic of the central section yielding a synthesis that would best be termed anguished agnosticism. There is an acceptance of the existence of God as a working hypothesis, a vague "ground of being" but at the same time a harsh critique of that existence. Christ offers his complaint as constructive criticism, but the tone is one of tactful irony. There is an unspoken, but almost bitter question being formulated: "If You are really a loving Father, why do you behave like an absentee landlord?"

The poem's ambivalence reflects, on the one hand, the growing doubts of Vigny's mature years, and, on the other, his lingering need to believe. The death of his mother in 1837 provided the chief example of the cruelty of Creation, but at the same time stirred a need to believe in a final, transcendent Justice. Several entries made toward the end of 1837 in the *Journal d'un poète* reflect Vigny's effort to believe:

> *Mon Dieu! mon Dieu! avez-vous daigné connaître mon coeur et ma vie? mon Dieu! m'avez-vous éprouvé à dessein? Aviez-vous réservé la fin de ma pauvre mère commme spectacle pour me render à vous plus entièrement?*
>
> (PL, II, 1088)

> *Donnez-moi, ô mon Dieu! la certitude qu'elle m'entend et qu'elle sait ma douleur; qu'elle est dans le repos bien-heureux des anges et que, par vous, à sa prière, je puis être pardonné de mes fautes.*
>
> (PL, II, 1091)

Vigny's plea for certainty went unanswered, and his doubts were fueled by Strauss' *Vie de Jésus* anticipating Renan's more famous presentation of a de-deified Christ. Vigny had read the book by February of 1839, and the original manuscript of "Le Mont des Oliviers" is dated November 12 of the same year. The rendering of Jesus not only as purely human but as symbolic of mankind's religious doubts was inspired by Jean-Paul Richter's "Dream." Madame de Staël's translation of the key passage in which an anguished Christ speaks to the dreamer will give some idea of the stylistic as will as thematic similarity of the two pieces:

> *"J'ai parcouru les mondes, je me suis élevé au-dessus des soleils, et là aussi il n'est point de Dieu; je suis descendu jusqu'aux dernières limites de l'univers, j'ai regardé dans l'abîme . . . Relevant ensuite mes regards vers la voûte des cieux je n'y ai trouvé qu'un orbite vide, noir et sans fond."[6]*

Vigny's wavering religious stance was representative of a certain cross-current of belief-disbelief among many Christian intellectuals of the Romantic period that helps explain why "negative theology" surfaced so frequently during the nineteenth century. As Sartre says, in *L'Idiot de la famille:* "L'inspiration, originellement, relevait de Dieu; en France, après la déchristianisation de la bourgeoisie jacobine, la question se complique: Hugo, poète *vates,* preétend encore écrire sous la dictée d'en haut, mais beaucoup de romantiques—en particulier Musset—incertains, victimes d'un agnosticisme auquel ils ne se résignent pas, remplacent l',tre suprême, à la source de leurs poèmes, par la douleur de l'avoir perdu. . . ."[7] The conflicting demands of faith and reason, perhaps best exemplified in Kierkegaard's brave but intellectually anguished "leap" of faith, are already adumbrated in the religious anguish of many a Romantic Hero. Whether he leans toward theism or atheism, the Romantic Hero's *feelings* at least tend to be ambivalent. When he believes, he asks, like Vigny's Christ, who will help his unbelief. When he doubts, he asks, like Musset's Rolla, who will give him faith:

> *Jésus, ce que tu fis, qui jamais le fera?*
>
> *Nous, vieillards nés d'hier, qui nous rajeunira?*

And when Rolla laments:

> *Je ne crois pas, ô Christ, à ta parole sainte.*

the epithet is not sarcastic but nostalgic. Sarcasm, in fact, is reserved, just as earnestly as Blake's "Mock on, mock on, Voltaire, Rousseau," for the *philosophes* of the Enlightenment:

> *Dors-tu content, Voltaire, et ton hideux sourire*
>
> *Voltige-t-il encore sur tes os décharnés?*
>
> *Ton siècle était, dit-on, trop jeune pour te lire;*
>
> *Le nôtre doit te plaire, et tes hommes sont nés.*
>
> *Il est tombé sur nous, cet édifice immense*
>
> *Que de tes larges mains tu sapais nuit et jour.*

Voltaire's men had indeed been born, but the loss of faith left a vacuum, which, being abhorrent to nature, triggered a wistful nostalgic reaction and provided the Romantics with a new lyrical theme—metaphysical anguish—which has come to dominate the literature of the twentieth century with the successive failures of Science, Marxism, and Eastern Philosophy to fill the void or provide a rejuvenating faith. Latter-day Romantics—"hippies," "yippies," "Jesus-freaks," and what have you—continue the tradition not only by shocking the bourgeois but by ressurecting a purely human and anguished Jesus as "Superstar," an ambivalent term wavering between sarcastic and nostalgic irony, i.e., suggesting both adulation and deflation. Jesus' descent from God to Hero to Superstar (surely a stylistic notch below Hero) must be taken as one of the parameters of faith in the western world.

Sartre's characterization of Flaubert as an "agnostique-malgré-lui" (*L'Idiot,* p. 2077) would fit many a Romantic Hero before and since, and Flaubert's determination to "souffrir *en présence* du Dieu absent" (ibid., p. 2073; Sartre's italics) has an exact analogue in **"Le Mont des Oliviers"** the main poetic device of which is an ironic apostrophe to a God whose main attribute seems to be absenteeism. It is this ironic tension, as much as anything else, that holds the poem together.

Vigny's poetic right to make of his Christ a Romantic Hero, heir to the doubts of the Enlightenment and witness to the new critical exegesis of the Bible, should go without saying. But even judging the poem on its historicity, one need not see in it a violent departure from either the letter or the spirit of the Gospels. The poem deals not with an entire career but with one of the darkest moments in it.

The somberness, although not developed at length, is already present in the Gospel accounts.[8] And Mark's Gospel tells us that Christ will have an even more somber, bitter moment on the Cross when he cries out at the ninth hour: "Eli, Eli, lama sabacthane."

Notes

[1] J. M. McGoldric, "Vigny's Unorthodox Christ," *Modern Language Notes,* 85 (1970), 510-514.

[2] Alfred de Vigny, *Oeuvres complètes* (Paris: Gallimard, 1950), I, p. 153. Hereafter cited as PL for Pléiade edition.

[3] Pierre-Georges Castex, *"Les Destinées" d'Alfred de Vigny* (Paris: Société d'Édition d'Enseignement Supérieur, 1964), p. 113.

[4] The section on Silence is dated April 2, 1862, eighteen years after the first publication of "Le Mont des Oliviers" and one year before the poet's death.

[5] See Georges Bonnefoy, *La Pensée religieuse et morale d'Alfred de Vigny* (Paris: Hachette, 1944), p. 30.

[6] Quoted by Claude Pichois, *L'Image de Jean-Paul Richter dans les lettres françaises* (Paris: Corti, 1963), p. 257. Se also pp. 275-276 for specific stylistic similarities, which Pichois does not think considerable. What is significant, of course, is the characterization of Christ and the general atmosphere of despair.

[7] Jean-Paul Sartre, *L'Idiot de la famille* (Paris: Gallimard, 1971), II, 1960.

[8] "My soul is very sorrowful, even to death" (Mark 14:34 and Matthew 26:38). "And being in an agony he prayed more earnestly; and his sweat became like great drops of blood upon the ground." (Luke 22:44)

Henry F. Majewski (essay date 1976)

SOURCE: "Alfred de Vigny and the Poetic Experience: From Alienation to Renascence," in *Romantic Review,* Vol. LXVI, No. 1, 1976, pp. 268-89.

[*In the following essay, Majewski describes the transformation of Vigny's conception of the poet in society: from the portrait of the poet as a scapegoat and a victim in* Stello *to the poet as spiritual leader in "La Maison du Berger."*]

C. S. Lewis, Jung and others have analyzed the movement of the romantic consciousness in the experience of poetry as a desire to create through harmonious, symbolic language the image of a world which would be whole; that is coherent, ordered and beautiful. The essential rhythm of the poet's quest for wholeness can thus be seen in terms of the archetypal pattern of rebirth; the poems themselves manifest in their themes and structure a sense of evolution and spiritual discovery such as that of the *Ancient Mari-*ner or the *Prelude* of Wordsworth.[1] Legends, myths and poems usually containing the rebirth archetype exhibit a similar tripartite structure which is found in the initiatory rites and ceremonies of many peoples: a spiritual death, or refusal of the world defined as fatally imperfect and static, is followed by contact during a time of isolation and alienation with a source of spiritual meaning and beauty (such as new knowledge of the profound life of nature, love or God), which leads to a renewal of being or renascence on a higher plane of existence.

Images of mythical half-gods dying and resurrected, titans like Prometheus, often served the romantic poets to illustrate their themes of disenchantment with society, spiritual alienation, and finally, necessary revolt and change, even revolution. The theme of "la révolte sainte," for example, was actualized in Hugo's *Le Satyre* and *La Fin de Satan;* Michelet presented history as inevitable progress resulting from the dialectical struggle of man's liberty and genius against the fatalities of time. These works corroborate the thesis of critics[2] who see the romantic vision in terms of a rejection of the world as a mechanical, static, chain of being in favor of a world in the state of perpetual "becomingness," an organic process of evolution in which man, nature and God are parts of a meaningful whole.

Vigny's works, often dealing with much the same content as those of his romantic contemporaries, have suggested contradictory ideas, a prideful retreat to the ivory tower and even disappointment due to awkwardness in his poetic language. Sympathetic critics on the other hand have examined his poetic practices, the Icarian aspect of his concept of the poet, and have studied in depth his moral and religious ideas.[3] Germain's excellent *L'Imagination d'Alfred de Vigny* (Paris: Corti, 1962) provides us with an indispensable and thorough analysis of the ways in which Vigny imagines the world of objects and sensations, and offers a sensitive psychological portrait of his complex creative personality. Except for this latter study Vigny criticism remains fragmented, and we are left with the uneasy impression of a basic lack of unity or confusion in his work which is even attributed on occasion to the fact that Vigny was more "poète" than philosopher, although he claimed to be a philosophical poet.

It is precisely his concept of the poet and of poetry itself which seems to me to be at the heart of his work and of his experience as a writer. A closer reading of the texts concerned with the poet (specifically *Stello* and **"La Maison du Berger,"** as well as the *Journal d'un Poète*) will reveal, I believe, a recurrent structural pattern very similar to the dialectical or oppositional structure of many poems in Hugo, and inherent in Michelet's view of history, which gives unity and coherence to his writing. Expressed in these works is a strong confidence in the act of poetry, capable of leading to a "seconde vie," which makes of Vigny perhaps the major French exponent of the romantic poem as a process of spiritual discovery. Not only are poets and poetry the major subject of much of his work (an early example of highly self-conscious literature), but he chose to represent in his own world the needs of other unappreciated poets, and through an obstinate defense of poetry, the need for poetic idealism in an increasingly materialistic society. His misunderstood efforts in Parliament and through the *Académie Française* in favor of subsidizing young artists were part of a strong commitment to the social value of poetry.

There is very definitely a change in perspective between the publication of *Stello* (1830) and that of **"La Maison du Berger"** (1844), concerning the poet and the creative process. Even Germain fails to take this development into account when he considers to be conclusive Vigny's presentation of the artistic personality as dualistic and permanently divided into Docteur Noir and Stello, animus-intellect and anima-dreamer.

It is quite clear that in *Stello* Vigny presents the poet as the scapegoat of society. Like a Prometheus chained to the rock, he is devoured by the sense of his own uselessness and forced to renounce the "sacred fount" of life, to take refuge in the Ivory Tower in order to find spiritual nourishment through solitude. It becomes evident, however, that in **"La Maison du Berger"** we are presented with the liberation and regeneration of the poet, a Prometheus unbound, inspired by love and a new confidence in his own genius, prepared to create and participate in the life of man: "j'aime la majesté des souffrances humaines."

My essay will attempt to account for this transformation. From sacrificial victim of society's power to shepherd of men, from alienation and spiritual death to rebirth, the poet-Prometheus has been freed and his creative force renewed.

Not enough attention has been paid to the interesting variety of narrative techniques employed by Vigny in the writing of *Stello,* to the complexity of "point of view," and especially the dialectical structure underlying its composition. The work has the form of a dialogue or "consultation," actually an early example of a psychoanalytical session between doctor and patient, a form which Vigny repeated in *Daphné* (his unfortunately neglected version of the life of Julian the Apostate that parallels his own spiritual itinerary), and which he projected for other incompleted works. Within the outer dialogue between the Docteur Noir, realist, rationalist and cynic (also poet and repressed sentimentalist) and the poet-dreamer, Stello, there are three "récits" presenting the opposition between power and poetry in three different societies and in increasing complexity. The final "récit" actually presents four different kinds of "poet" from the viewpoint of the Docteur Noir who himself "sees" poetically. A series of binary oppositions or antitheses governs the dialogue and the "récits" contained within it, giving each part dramatic tension, suggesting the movement and struggle of ideas,[4] and finally producing the tragic consequences for poets and for poetry. The binary oppositions do not result in a new synthesis but rather the domination of thesis over antithesis, of power over poetry, and of the need for solitude and a refusal of life over participation and communion. Gilbert, Chatterton and André Chénier become tragic victims of the monarchical, parliamentarian and democratic grovernments respectively in the three "récits." Stello learns from the telling of the stories and his dialogue with the doctor that "la solitude est sainte," and that the poet must remain isolated and alienated if he is to survive.

What might be termed the romantic aspects of the narrative have been mentioned by critics, such as the Hugolian antithesis of the grotesque and the sublime in character and situation (e.g. the materialistic Lord Mayor and the spiritual Chatterton, the horrors of St. Lazare and the stoic resignation of the aristocrats during the terror). The use of local color and historical setting, a mixture of styles and even genres quite contrary to classical design have been singled out. It should be stressed that each récit has its characteristic tone or rather tones, since for example the Doctor changes his language and style as he describes in the first "récit" the frivolity of the court of Louis XV and then the pathetic suicide of Gilbert. He consciously adopts the tone and style of the period he is presenting and imitates the language of the actors of the scene, cryptic and witty when speaking of Louis XV, pedantic during the presentation of London's lord mayor, and gravely poetic concerning the Terror.

Point of view is complex and innovative. In the "récits" it is obviously the doctor-narrator who focuses on reality for his auditor and for the reader. The dialogue presents a double or rather triple point of view; the doctor's voice seems reliable about society, but nevertheless we are told by the narrator-persona of Vigny that the dreamer Stello is always superior to the reasoner. And yet Stello is presented as a "malade" almost driven mad by spleen. In fact the narrator-persona remains detached and through a use of ironic distance refuses a simple identification with either voice in the dialogue or part of the creative personality, head or heart. It is perhaps this irony which made the text so disconcerting to its early readers, but which gives it now a modern cast.[5] The author remains outside of his text since he cannot be identified entirely with either the coldly cynical doctor or the sometimes foolish dreamer. F. Germain's analysis of the dialogue as representing the divisions within the creative personality of Vigny is penetrating and convincing, and a reading of the *Journal* reveals the importance Vigny attached to the reflection of his own personality in his imaginary characters.[6] According to Germain the doctor (intellect-will-animus) finally purges the dreamer Stello (sentiment-anima) of the child's nightmare world within him through an exorcism by terror. His technique is to use the poison of bitter truth against the poison of despair, thus enabling him to understand his situation clearly, and hopefully to induce him to create his poetry without illusions.

It is not at all necessary to move from the text to its author in order to see the dialogue in terms of the dialectic between the sacred fount of life (Docteur Noir) and the Ivory Tower (Stello): the conflict between the search for the sources of creativity in the realities of the outside world as opposed to the discovery of meaning and beauty within the personality of the artist himself. The stated thesis of the book counsels only the latter course for art ("l'imagination ne vit que d'émotions spontanées"), and yet it is the Doctor who has lived the experiences of the dying poets, produced the "stories," and interpreted their significance. We are even told that he has his own malady, that of protecting young poets; and that he is given to poetic expression himself. He apostrophizes Death during Gilbert's agony and transforms his sensations of the scene of Chénier's execution into a series of poetic images of destiny and time: "la roue mythologique," "le cadran ensanglanté," "l'océan du peuple."

Vigny appreciates the paradoxical nature of truth almost as much as Diderot, and in fact the complex interaction of personalities found in Stello recalls *Le Neveu de Rameau*, another "novel" treating the problems of creativity. Just as there are at least two contrasting personalities within "moi," le Philosophe, and in the Neveu, "lui," Vigny suggests this second level of "dédoublement" in the Doctor and Stello. Voices of ego and alter-ego speak through both men. In the final "récit" he even develops a multiplicity of poetic personalities; Stello and the Doctor are "poètes" but so are the brothers Chénier, as well as Robes-pierre and Saint-Just in their fashion.

The theme of the divided self, the splitting off of the creative personality, has been attributed by existentialist criticism to the problem of the alienated artist in search of a public to which he can address himself. Sartre's analysis in *Qu'est-ce que la littérature?* is certainly corroborated by the situation of Stello. He is anguished primarily because he desires to write a political tract for a specific party and discovers his contribution is not desired, and that the nineteenth-century bourgeois public has only contempt for poets; in other words he suffers and requires the services of the psychiatrist-doctor precisely because he cannot engage his talent in a social commitment. His problem is therefore the opposite of that of Icarus; he has no public with which to communicate.

At least since Rousseau (*Rousseau, Juge de Jean-Jacques*) artists have expressed their inability to accept the conditions of society through a curious doubling of the personality. Since their desires for freedom and beauty are manifestly in contradiction with the dictates of reason, which readily grasps the necessary limitations and imperfections of society's conventions and laws, individual revolt takes the form of a divided self in an alienated personality.

Of course Vigny's example of the double personality (the Doctor and Stello) has other literary antecedents; Quixote and Panza, Faust and Mephistopheles as well as the Nephew (a "râté," rather than a "poète maudit") and the Philosopher. Vigny quite often suggests the satanic aspects of the doctor's cynicism, his despair, and omnipresence; Stello like Faust dreams of prophecy in poetry and power over men through knowledge.

In spite of these interesting points of reference the real significance of the dialogue can best be decoded from the complex system of relations and contrasts in the text. Vigny is preoccupied even more with the problem of creativity itself than with the situation of the artist in the world. He questions to what extent imagination (the center of creative activity) depends on direct contact with things and experience with others in order to begin to function. Or does it develop like an autonomous complex through the purity of spontaneous emotions in the spirit and memory of the individual artist? Inner life-outer life, (sentiment or reason), dreams and reality, solitude versus solidarity, idealism and objective observation, these are the sets of oppositions which best characterize Stello and the Doctor. At the most profound level the couple represents the struggle within the artist himself between his *idea,* the result of the work of the imagination, which here takes the form of the knowledge acquired by the Docteur Noir, and his own desires and dreams, in this case the contrary aspirations of Stello, the poet. In other words the dialogue takes place within the mind of the artist, as an integral part of the creative process:

> La perpétuelle lutte du Poète est celle qu'il livre à son idée. Si l'idée triomphe du Poète et le passionne trop, il est sa dupe et tombe dans la mise en action de cette idée et s'y perd. Si le Poète est plus fort que l'idée, il la pétrit, la forme et la met en œuvre. Elle devient ce qu'il a voulu, un monument.[7]

Stello's beliefs about the nature of poetry, which are not criticized by the doctor, constitute a clear statement of what we now call the romantic myth of poetry. In his "credo" he proclaims faith in the poet as the inspired guide of humanity, whose nature or God-given gift of poetic creation is a mysterious, sacred act of interpretation through imagination of the hidden meanings and secret unity of the world. He believes in his destiny, in the importance of love and enthusiasm as sources of creativity, and in the poet's mission to preserve necessary ideals in society. He sense in himself a strong creative power ("puissance secrète") and links poetry to prophecy. These familiar aspects of the romantic attitude toward poetry afford Stello the happiness of what Germain terms the "paradis intérieur," a satisfying awareness of the value of his vocation and his own worth. Surely more interesting, however, than this example of the romantic "Sacre de l'Ecrivain"[8] is Vigny's own myth-making.

One of his most important techniques in poetry and prose is the transformation of the facts of observation, feeling or an "idea" into a "fable" which contains and expresses meaning in all its complexity, richness and ambiguity. Myth for Vigny, (although he uses the term fable), is truth condensed, a form of language corresponding to the diamond, crystal, or treasure chest, material images he constantly uses to suggest the need for the writer to concentrate, purify and illuminate his thought through the discovery of the proper form or permanent container, that is mythic structure. Vigny's well-known formula "l'art, c'est la vérité choisie," can be best understood through his creative use of myth which for him both conceals and reveals the most profound aspirations, needs and unconscious desires hidden on the surface of man's experience. The myth of Samson, for example, becomes the expression not only of the superior man's eternal cry of distress, nor of the idea of disillusionment with woman's treachery, but suggests the secret knowledge that love itself is an illusion which man must learn to live without: "Donc, ce que j'ai voulu, Seigneur, n'existe pas!"[9]

In *Stello,* it seems to me, Vigny has forged a myth for his time, transforming the actual lives of his historical characters, and giving new forms to the theme of the "poète maudit" or "râté" already to be found in preromantic literature. The stories told by the Doctor in order to cure Stello of his ambition to act in society present three variations on the legend or myth of the scapegoat. In all current forms of governmental organization (monarchic, parliamentarian, democratic) the poet becomes a victim or martyr, and dies a real or symbolic and spiritual death. The scapegoat, however, has the stature of a half-god or titan; the mediocre Gilbert and the weak Chatterton are likened to Promethean beings (Chatterton's eyes are compared to "deux flammes comme Prométhée les dut puiser au soleil"[10]). The structure of each story is identical; the opposition between Power and Poetry, the materialistic gods of the present versus the spiritualistic rebels who look to the future, produces a tragic confrontation leading to sacrifice in the form of suicide or execution. Vigny has elevated the three stories, through metaphor and mythological allusion as well as the theme of the sacrifical victim, to the level of a myth containing a cruel and ambiguous truth about the poet and society. The poet-seer as Stello has presented him, with the approbation of the rational Docteur Noir, has been and will always be the victim of society because Power always negates Art; the artist is the natural enemy of authority since by definition his critical, prophetic and independent spirit is oriented to the future or the past whereas the representatives of authority concentrate on maintaining the order of the present. The spiritualistic poet is thus always useless and even dangerous in a materialistic society. The myth of the three stories conceals an even harsher truth; social order is seen as destructive of all manifestations of profound individuality: revery, genius, spirituality, the very sources of artistic creativity are destroyed through the conformity and tyranny of social power. Representative government fosters mediocrity while revolutionary democracy tyrannizes the artist; we have only to think of the situation of the writer in America, forced to popularize in order to succeed, or that of a Solzenitzhen hounded into exile, to grasp the relevancy of Vigny's legends.

In short the conclusions drawn by the two protagonists in the chapter "Tristesse et Pitié" develop the fundamentally anti-social or even anarchical significance of the text; all contemporary forms of social order are attacked as illogical, totalitarian, materialistic, and unjust. Vigny's narrators express the despair accompanying their loss of illusion when faced with the fatality of social order which systematically excludes and destroys the very sources of art. From this perspective the book anticipates the disillusionment of a Musset confronted with the collapse of traditional values in the *Confessions d'un enfant du siècle* (1834); but more philosophical in nature and modern in its anarchistic tendencies, it suggests the paradoxes of *Civilization and Its Discontents*. In fact in his *Journal* Vigny gives us an excellent résumé of that Freudian discourse:

> Dans l'individu est reconnu l'ennemi né de la Société
> s'il ne se contrefait ou ne se réforme avec effort. Donc
> la Société est *contraire* aux penchants naturels de

l'homme, mais l'espèce se détruit sans la société. Il faut donc pour la conserver renouveler sans cesse cet essai.

> Mais cet essai ne peut être que mauvais puisqu'il s'oppose toujours (dans un but de conservation) à notre nature qui *tend* sans cesse à la *destruction*.[11]

Vigny's thesis (because *Stello* is also a "roman à thèse") quite simply informs us that if the poet tries to offer his special knowledge to society, he will be condemned to a real or at least a spiritual martyrdom. This idea is the message contained in the fable of the sacrifice of the half-god of poetic genius which gives each story its structure and meaning: Prometheus is chained to the rock for having desired to give men the fire of knowledge and in so doing having rebelled against the authority of the gods.

The third story concerning Chénier is the most complex, and the most moving to the reader. Vigny succeeds in suggesting the tragic grandeur of the last days of the Terror without excessive pathos or grandiloquence. The Docteur Noir recollects the scene with a mixture of horror and fascination which is translated into some of the finest of Vigny's poetic prose. What interests us here, however, is Vigny's analysis of the poet in a revolutionary society. He presents André Chénier as a great artist who is conscious of the visionary aspect of his poetry, a somber, angry hero of revolt who has dared to write against the tyranny of the regime in the name of liberty, and now stoically awaits his execution. Vigny has apparently transformed his character completely, in accord with his flexible concept of the use of history in art,[12] to make of him a symbol of the ideal writer. In contrast to André Chénier is Robespierre, the anti-poet, representative of totalitarian power who has, however, the imaginative gift of prophecy (he foresees Napoleon's empire) and who wrote verses when he was young. He is sick with paranoia, and an assassin, but above all he illustrates the corruption of ideals in the hands of power. For not only does he oppose Chénier's brand of idealism, but he himself is an uncompromising idealist without human compassion or pity, with no sense of the need for moderation and indulgence. His idealism has rapidly become a tool for repression.

This danger to the essence of poetry (i.e. to the preservation of ideals and ideas through poetic symbol and fable) perverted through action in society is developed in more detail through the second group of antagonists. Saint-Just is a poet who has given himself to power; his maxims are presented as the naive, rousseauistic poetry of a sincere young moralist, who has attained power without having known life outside of books. His pitiless innocence, refusal of all compromise, and desire to live by absolute principles alone are transposed in the simple and tyranncal laws of his *Institutions* which Robespierre sees as inspired legislation. In other words he is a kind of Stello without the experience of the Docteur Noir. Solitude and purity without contact with humanity could thus produce a negative poetry of death, and we are back to the original problem of the proper balance between the inner and outer life, solitude and solidarity in the creative personality, posed by the couple Stello and the Doctor. Robespierre and Saint-Just are even more dangerous as perverted poets than as opponents of poetry. The final member of the quartet, Marie-Joseph Chénier, a man of talent, has compromised himself by consenting to lead an active, political life; it is easy to detect in this portrait of the weak and inefficacious brother of André the same kind of reproach addressed by Vigny to poets like Lamartine. Artistic talent in the service of politics leads only to a diminution of art and a compromise of principle.

Four poets and four different approaches to poetry, but only one genius who is sacrificed; the text "Un soir d'été" is one of the most beautiful Vigny ever wrote in which he dispenses with rhetoric in order to oblige the reader to share his horror before the absurd and tragic loss of human greatness:

> Après le trente-troisième cri, je vis l'habit gris tout debout. Cette fois je résolus d'honorer le courage de son génie en ayant le courage de voir toute sa mort: je me levai.

> La tête roula, et ce qu'il *avait là* s'enfuit avec le sang.[13]

The system of relationships in the poetic paradigm is complex and the points of view on poetry multiple. Stello's purity is reflected in that of Saint-Just, the Docteur Noir's experience in Robespierre's knowledge of men, the brothers Chénier point to the degradation of a compromise with society (Marie-Joseph), and the sacrifice of the true artist who tries to address his work and commit his idealism to the needs of society.

The fictional Docteur Noir himself eloquently opposes the position of a real writer, Joseph de Maistre, who attempted to justify massacre in the name of Christian expiation; he speaks for Life against all those who would excuse political murder and any sacrifice of humanity in the name of power and the authority of the state. His pessimistic analysis of the psychology of revolution (the reign of mediocre men who remain in power only through the elimination of all enemies) does not concern us here, except for the interesting and very modern parallel he draws between the mind of the revolutionary assassin and that of the "splénétique," or melancholy artist-dreamer. Both are sick with disgust and disillusionment in a corrupt society whose values they cannot accept. Both are dominated by the death wish and live in anger, fear and "spleen," which the revolutionary tries to sublimate by taking vengeance on others, while the poet contemplates suicide. The "émotion continue de l'assassinat" of a Robespierre is thus related to the "rêve maladif" of Stello in another cross-relationship on the complex paradigm of poets and their characteristics to be found in this novel.

F. Germain has analyzed with particular thoroughness the conclusions of *Stello* the "cure" effected by the Doctor and his ideas concerning poetry.[14] For my purposes it should be stressed that the Doctor proclaims his ordinance in a set of solemn maxims like an ancient oracle, in effect becoming a poet once again, speaking through a language of image and myth to present his code for the young artist. Through a series of examples from the past including that of Homer and Plato's poet excluded from the Republic, the Doctor elevates his concept to that of a universal myth—the poet is not only the eternal martyr but saint of society since his mission is to preserve the necessary ideals of the group, to guide its inner, spiritual life. Perpetual ostracism and solitude must be the accepted lot of the artist, who is, however, essential to every society for it is he who helps men fight the tide of the material, rational, and animal needs which constantly reduce and diminish the quality of human experience: his work is eminently and finally that of a civilizing force. Vigny's high conception of art is seen in this mystique of poetry which both Stello and the Doctor celebrate in the concluding chapters. All direct action or political activity by the poet is impossible. The application of his ideals to society's needs is left to others—the parliament, for example, should subsidize the impoverished artist. Thus Vigny in writing *Stello* has fulfilled his own function by indicating to society its need of the idealism of poetry, and the danger to poets from the hostility of power. Through the writing of *Stello* Vigny has actually realized the conception of art which has evolved through the dialogue of the doctor and the poet.

A very serious problem, nevertheless, remains; without active participation by the artist in the life of his time how does the idealistic work of art reach its public? The response is both "romantic" and modern. Considered superior to religion itself as a spiritual guide (because it remains pure and abstracted from quotidian life) the work of the poet produces communion among men which can move them to act. Poetry elevates the spirit of its readers through the emotions it touches of love and compassion ("pitié"); it is therefore addressed to man's emotional nature and in turn engenders emotion. Parallel to Sartre's concept of the work of art as part of a quest for freedom, appealing to the reader's need to overcome his own sense of contingency, Vigny's ideal work of art presents emotions which must cause "une profonde et même une douloureuse impression"[15] on its often unthinking and unfeeling readers. Art works are then symbols of emotion which act in turn on the emotions of the reader thus helping to create an increased awareness of reality or images of new realities. Vigny approximates the concepts of C. J. Jung, who thought that the authentic work of art helps to restore the psychic balance of a group, a society or even an epoch[16] because it furnishes the necessary images of conscious and unconscious levels of experience which the society has been repressing, but which it needs for wholeness. Vigny's society, becoming increasingly materialistic and industrialized, is losing its sense of individual spiritual values; Hugo and Nerval certainly responded to this situation through their efforts at religious syncretism, renewing images of God and the irrational world in works like *Aurélia* and *La Fin de Satan*. Vigny perhaps more than any other romantic sees the hope for the preservation of individual values in those of poetry. The work of art thus helps the group rediscover realities it has repressed or denied by presenting symbols which can transform its image of things and of itself.

Finally, and ironically, the very misfortune of the poet becomes a source of his happiness; through his work he has the hope of transcending time and conquering the fatality of death. The work preserves the essence of his personality, and although the poet is sacrificed in life, like the half-gods of the legends he lives again for the future. Anticipating the "Bénédiction" of Baudelaire, Vigny concludes *Stello* with this paradox, insisting that the poet is a guide for the future of mankind; he works for his posterity and that of society:

> Votre royaume n'est pas de ce monde sur lequel vos yeux sont ouverts, mais de celui qui sera quand vos yeux seront fermés.[17]

In the present, however, there remains the unalterable opposition, the tragic antithesis between the fatality of Power and the vulnerability of the poet.

In 1830 then, Vigny imagines the poet to be the tragic victim of an unjust order threatened by his idealism and to which he is sacrificed, just as in the ancient legends expiation and atonement necessitated the death of heroes in the name of a mysterious order of gods and nature. Most critics have, nevertheless, pointed to significant changes in idea and attitude from *Stello* to the ***Destinées*** (1864); Castex spoke of the development in Vigny's thought from a fundamentally tragic pessimism towards a humanistic optimism.[18] However, the sometimes contradictory themes of the poems have been disconcerting to many readers (praise of science, for example, in **"La Bouteille à la mer"**; its apparent condemnation in **"La Maison du berger"**). The problem stems again from too much concern with the intellectual content of the poetry instead of a careful examination of the structure of its themes and images. **"La Maison du berger"** (1842), which I propose to discuss in detail, was conceived by Vigny as the prologue to his collection, to be completed by a "réponse d'Eva." Much more than an introcution, and in addition to being his poetic masterpiece, it contains the major themes, preoccupations and ideas which are treated in various ways throughout the ***Destinées.*** It is significantly the one text in which the reader can observe the working of the imagination of the poet-narrator as he gives poetic form to the experience of discovery he has undergone, a work therefore to be compared with similar texts in English romantic poetry which reveal the mind of the poet structuring the world and thereby uncovering and discovering itself.

It is also a poem about poetry, but most importantly a poem which *is* the romantic experience of poetry: the form given to an experience of inner discovery, spiritual change or evolution; language which expresses the movement from the poet's situation of alienation to his integration in a new and higher order of being and knowing.

Like *Stello* most of the fables and myths of the ***Destinées*** contain stories which suggest a sacrifice, and are constructed according to antitheses or binary oppositions which permit no antithesis, only a tragic resolution forcing the acceptance of cruel but vital human truths. Already in the ***Poèmes bibliques et modernes*** youthful love was sacrificed in a corrupt world (**"Les Amants de Montmorency," "Le Déluge"**), innocence was abandoned in **"Eloa,"** and the need for human solidarity remained unsatisfied in **"Moise."**

The poems of *Les Destinées,* however, are much more uniformly dominated by sacrifice, and the presence of "mythes cruels" or "mythes consolants." In the series of "mythes cruels" there is **"La Colère de Samson"** whose myth contains the message that man must give up his ideal of human love; it is sacrificed to the bitter reality of his solitude and the perpetual war between the sexes. Man learns in **"Les Destinées"** the need to sacrifice his idea of personal freedon; Christianity with its emphasis on grace and predestination has brought only the illusion of liberty and represents no more than a modern version of ancient fatality. At the heart of the poet's disillusionment is the sacrifice of Christ (**"Le Mont des Oliviers"**) with the concomitant realization that man must depend on himself alone, that he is abandoned in an irrational world. When man confronts woman, and his own destiny as a being of will desiring freedom, or the supernatural; that is, when his ideals (love, free will, belief in a spiritual universe) are confronted with the fatalities of experience (Samson-Dalila, human will-the fates, Christ and God) the outcome is tragic and the human ideal is sacrificed.[19]

The need to abandon these ideals and illusions, the "cruel" truths contained in the myths are accompanied, however, with a positive affirmation. In each case the poet-narrator has made an intellectual and personal discovery: the stoic need to affirm his own strength, to purify his mind of illusion, to develop the inner resources of his personality, his own particular "genius." In other words the myths are contradictory and ambiguous; their truths are at once iconoclastic and destructive, and yet affirmative and even consoling. They imply the sacrifice of an important ideal but affirm the power of man's spirit:

> Arbitre libre et fier des actes de sa vie,
> Si notre cœur s'entr'ouvre au parfum des vertus,
> S'il s'embrase à l'amour, s'il s'élève au génie,
>
> Que l'ombre des Destins, Seigneur, n'oppose plus
> A nos belles ardeurs une immuable entrave,
> A nos efforts sans fin des coups inattendus![20]

Herein lies, it seems to me, the real explanation for Vigny's constant fascination with myth and his important role as a romantic mythologizer. He finds in myth, first of all, an extension of poetic language. Like symbol it is, for him, a crystallization of ideas, a permanent form in which to distill his own personal experience. Like symbol it permits him to suggest more than can be explained rationally, above all the ambiguous, paradoxical and contradictory truths which result from the poet's intuition, the world of his imagination and memory. Myths permit Vigny to pass from the limitations of the "moi" to Everyman; they become for him the revelations of the meaning of collective experience, symbolic interpretations of essential human situations which correspond to the deepest aspirations, desires and fears of men of his generation and of mankind. Being part of a long tradition they can be interpreted in diverse ways; therefore they demand the response of the reader at the level of his individual experience; like diamonds or crystals they give off light and meaning but contain mystery, are multilayered and difficult to penetrate. For Vigny, in the last analysis, myths are the creations of the imagination of poets and thinkers which contain, that is, conceal and reveal, metaphysical, spiritual or moral truths surpassing rational and scientific knowledge. Vigny's poetry certainly confirms R. Wellek's statement: "All the great romantic poets are mythopoeic, are symbolists whose practice must be understood in terms of their attempt to give a total mythic interpretation of the world to which the poet holds the key."[21]

The consoling myths of *Les Destinées* are characterized first by their modernity if not their originality: **"La Flûte," "La Bouteille à la mer," "L'Esprit pur"** and **"La Maison du berger"** contain stories about the present, and images taken from contemporary experience even though the underlying myths be ancient ones. In this instance they simply resemble poems of the "modern" section of Vigny's first collection. Far more important, however, is a new, different thematic structure. The work of the creative person, that of artist or scientist, the creations of the human spirit are now seen as the means to extend and actually overcome the rational, material and temporal limitations of existence. Instead of a tragic impasse resulting from the confrontation between man's aspirations and the fatalities of the world, a new synthesis results from this conflict, producing renewed confidence in man's creative power and his power to transform the world.

"La Flûte" evokes the power and permanence of the world of ideas through a Platonic contrast with the weakness of the flesh, thus encouraging and consoling the young "râté" who resembles Stello:

> Du corps et non de l'âme accusons l'indigence.
> Des organes mauvais servent l'intelligence
> Ils touchent, en tordant et tourmentant leur nœud,
> Ce qu'ils peuvent atteindre et non ce qu'elle veut.
> En traducteurs grossiers de quelque auteur céleste
> Ils parlent. Elle chante et désire le reste.
>
> . . . . .
>
> Votre souffle était juste et votre chant est faux.[22]

"L'Esprit pur" extols the products of human genius capable of endowing their creator with immortality and identifies creativity as the divine element in man:
> Ton règne est arrivé, PUR ESPRIT, roi du monde!
>
> . . . . Aujourd'hui, c'est L'ECRIT,
> L'ECRIT UNIVERSEL,, parfois impérissable,
> Que tu graves au marbre ou traces sur le sable,
> Colombe au bec d'airain! VISIBLE SAINT-
> ESPRIT![23]

"La Bouteille à la mer" presents an allegory of the acceptance and comprehension of a work of art by its readers in terms of the partial conquest of the destructive fa-

tality of the ocean through the knowledge of a sea captain's charts. The Captain dies in the storm ("Son sacrifice est fait"), but he is destined to have a second life in the immortality of his science:

> Il sourit en songeant que ce fragile verre
> Portera sa pensée et son nom jusqu'au port,
> Que d'une île inconnue il agrandit la terre,
> Qu'il marque un nouvel astre et le confie au sort,
> Que Dieu peut bien permettre à des eaux insensées
> De perdre des vaisseaux, mais non pas des pensées,
> Et qu'avec un flacon il a vaincu la mort.[24]

The element missing then, in *Stello* and in the pessimistic poems of *Les Destinées,* (those in the series of "mythes cruels"), is belief in the power of the created work itself and in the divine nature of creativity: for Vigny man has now become his own god and his works are proof of his divinity.

Indeed **"La Maison du berger"** presents the complete spiritual itinerary of the poet-narrator as he relates an experience of inner discovery; an experience with life and poetry from which he emerges renewed, regenerated, as if reborn. Liberated from his alienation, his period of spiritual death, he discovers himself ready to create, to attempt to write in the name of mankind, confident in his genius and the value and power of art. The rebirth of the poet, (for that is the central theme of the poem), aided by the love of Eva, ideal woman and muse, recalls the situation of Prometheus and Asia in Shelley's poem *Prometheus Unbound.* In fact **"La Maison"** is Vigny's version of the Prometheus legend as well as a retelling of the part of the story of Adam and Eve in which man is saved from the sin of narcissism through the regenerating force of woman's love.

The poem is constructed in dialectical form; in each of its three parts there is a series of antitheses, or contradictions whose conflict produces a new synthesis. The movement of themes and images corresponds to the flux of ideas in the poet's mind and here signifies change, growth and renewal.

Part I might best be called "évasion du spleen" and "invitation au voyage"; Part II, the discovery of an esthetic, and Part III, the poet's metaphysics. The poem begins the way *Stello* ends, with the poet expressing his isolation when faced with the fatalities of the modern world, and his despair with the tragic limitations of the human condition. Instead of Stello, the figure of a pure but an incommunicable light, the poet is a shepherd involved with life and the poem is addressed to a mysterious Eva, who seems to have replaced the Docteur Noir. Images of weight, suffering and slavery dominate the first stanzas, evoking Napoleon's exile and Prometheus bound to his rock; "âme enchaînée," "plaie immortelle," "rocs fatals," "aigle blessé," reinforce the effect of alienation and spiritual death which the poet feels in this "monde fatal, écrasant et glacé."[25]

Instead of the destructive nature of political power which dominated the text of *Stello,* the materialism and technology of modern civilization now menace the very sources of poetry. The city and science (with their product and sign the railroad) signify fatality here, and are placed in opposition to nature (a source of consolation and spiritual value), and revery (the impetus to poetic creation) which together evoke the possible happiness of escape with Eva. The interplay of themes and ideas, the conflict between the static fatality of the City and the sentimental appeal of Nature produce, however, in the central symbol of the work the idea of a new life in the moving house of the shepherd; neither limited to city or country, nor dominated by the excesses of modern technology the poet and his lover will travel through country and countryside into contact with the life of various peoples and collecting impressions for poetry. The shepherd dreams of becoming a guide for men.

The themes and images of the poetic structure are linked according to a logic suggesting the inner working of the poet's imagination. The theme of science which imposes ever new limits on man's freedom by eliminating chance and the unknown, and forcing conformity, "La science/ Trace autour de la terre un chemin triste et droit," (MB, 176) leads directly to a meditation on its antithesis, revery, that is the poetic world of imagination, beauty and mystery, the very center of his spiritual life. The danger of science and modern technology is precisely that it could destroy the sources of poetry: revery before the beauty of nature, imagination's contact with the mystery of experience. Part II thus develops as a long debate on the meaning and value of poetry whose very essence is threatened in modern society.

If the "thesis" in this section is now the possibility of political life and action, it is opposed by the "anti thesis" of pure poetry and thought, or the meditative life. The same set of binary oppositions which were found in *Stello* become this time the basis for a new synthesis about the role of the poet in society and the value of poetry. The true poet neither participates actively in political life nor does he isolate himself in holy solitude, he becomes, however warily, the guide or "shepherd" of humanity:

> Diamant sans rival, que tes feux illuminent
> Les pas lents et tardifs de l'humaine Raison!
> Il faut, pour voir de loin les peuples qui cheminent,
> Que le Berger t'enchâsse au toit de sa Maison.

> (**MB**, 178)

It is in Part II of the **"Maison"** that Vigny most profoundly develops his concept of the meaning and role of poetry, and resolves the seemingly insoluble paradoxes of *Stello*. The familiar images of the diamond, mirror, pearl and monument are used to convey Vigny's sense of the function of poetic forms; the symbols and myths must operate to concentrate and purify the "profondes pensées" of the artist. The poem thus becomes a durable condensation of the spirit or light of the individual poet, but also preserves the highest ideals of his civilization from the destruction of time:

> Ce fin miroir solide, étincelant et dur,
> Reste des nations mortes, durable pierre

> Qu'on trouve sous ses pieds lorsque dans la
>   poussière
> On cherche les cités sans en voir un seul mur.

> (**MB**, 178)

Poetry is considered to be superior to reason which functions by dividing and separating phenomena, since it is capable of grasping the highest synthetic truths through intuition and imagination; indeed, the poet through his revelations of the spiritual sense of life becomes the intuitive guide of human progress:

> Le jour n'est pas levé.—Nous en sommes encore
> Au premier rayon blanc qui précède l'aurore
> Et dessine la terre aux bords de l'horizon.

> (**MB**, 178)

The creative spirit of the poet represents for Vigny a kind of divinity in man, and through the exercise of this faculty in the poetic act he participates positively in the divine element of the universe:

> Mais notre esprit rapide en mouvements abonde:
> Ouvrons tout l'arsenal de ses puissants ressorts.
> L'Invisible est réel. Les âmes ont leur monde
> Où sont accumulés d'impalpables trésors.

> (**MB**, 179)

A religion of human genius has clearly replaced traditional Christianity for Vigny; he remains an idealist whose need for transcendence is now satisfied by the works of the "pure Spirit."[26]

There are consequently three ways in which poetry can transcend the fatalities of life: first, the work brings immortality to the poet himself; second, its form condenses and reveals the spiritual life of man, preserving his ideals against the danger of the collapse of temporary forms of civilization; and, finally, through its intuition of supreme truths it becomes the highest means to knowledge capable of guiding man to a better future.

If we return for a moment to the ordinance of the Docteur Noir at the end of *Stello*, the change in vision is striking. The Doctor had recommended to the young poet the necessary and sacred solitude of the ivory tower—the poet of **"La Maison"** is liberated and reborn through the love of Eva. Imagination, he said, thrives only on the spontaneous emotions of the artist—the poet now seeks to know and love "tout dans les choses créées" and during a long voyage with Eva will learn to admire "la majesté des souffrances humaines."

According to the Doctor his mission was to produce works, "utiles" in their very uselessness; his situation was to be "maudit" in the eyes of those in power, and to live without hope a destiny of pain and doubt. Instead, the poet of the **"Maison"** is confident that poetry may become the spiritual leader of science and reason, and he displays measured optimism concerning the future for himself and society.

The long period of stagnation, alienation and sterility experienced by the poet in **"La Maison"** (Part I) ends through contact with a new spiritual element, the very force of his own creative self, which produces new affirmation and strength (Part II). This force is, of course, poetry itself, and it is incarnated in the dream of Eva. The rebirth of the poet, his "poetic" health is thus achieved in Part III of "La Maison" through reunion with the woman, or anima, the redemptive figure, Eva, who now replaces Christ in the poet's world, saving him from death and helping him return to wholeness.

For Germain the ordinance of the Doctor implied the necessary division or separation of the two parts of the poet's personality. In order to survive, the animus— "volonté" must repress the feminine anima— "rêverie." The poet must in effect refuse life, or at least use his willpower to cure himself of the "rêve maladif" of communication and participation; in other words he must accept sterility in the name of purity, curtail the effects of revery (the very source of poetry) and concentrate solely on his craft.

The sacrifice of the feminine part of the poetic personality, the anima— "rêverie," which is the lesson of *Stello* in the last analysis, could only lead to a spiritual death. It is revived, however, in **"La Maison"** in the form of an overwhelming need for love as a necessary condition of creativity. Examined in the context of the conflict of ideas throughout the entire poem feminine symbols dominate the consciousness and creative imagination of the poet-narrator. Woman takes the form of nature, a goddess, a "voyageuse indolente," Diana, vestal virgin and priestess; she incarnates revery, the poet's muse, and most significantly poetry itself: "O toi des vrais penseurs impérissable amour!" (**MB**. 178). Spiritualized and yet profoundly human,[27] the mysterious Eva of Part III becomes the redemptive figure whose love makes it possible for the poet to find again his sense of wholeness; she not only symbolizes poetry, "L'enthousiasme pur dans une voix suave," (**MB**, 179), but also the fragility and impermanence of man and the possible grandeur of human suffering. Her delicate sensitivity, compassion and deep understanding of human values: "C'est à toi qu'il convient d'ouïr les grandes plaintes/Que l'humanité triste exhale sourdement" (**MB**, 180), are the necessary complement to the poet's intelligence and will; indeed these qualities are at the source of all creativity and their assimilation makes feasible the poet's reintegration in the world of men and nature:

> Eva, j'aimerai tout dans les choses créées,
> Je les contemplerai dans ton regard rêveur
> Qui partout répandra ses flammes colorées,
> Sur mon cœur déchiré viens poser ta main pure,
> Ne me laisse jamais seul avec la Nature,
> Car je la connais trop pour n'en pas avoir peur.

> (**MB**, 180)

The artist's empathetic penetration of or identification with the world of things and man, a quality considered by writers close to Vigny but as diverse as Diderot, Balzac and Baudelaire, to be essential to the creative process was

denied to Stello. It is now offered to the poet of **"La Maison"** as a function of the ability to love.

The dialectic of Part III is expressed in terms of an antithesis between the goddess of Nature, hostile, indifferent and eternal, and the fragile, impermanent, human woman. Nature moves ("roule") with the indifference to men of the railway trains of Part I; woman loves, suffers and knows the perishable but privileged beauty of the passing moment, of that which is always menaced by death, but alone has human value. The poet concludes from this contrast that what counts for man in his impermanence and contingency is to give meaning to a world which has none without him. The very fragility of woman makes him love men again and seek to illuminate the sense of human suffering against the beautiful but insensitive backdrop of nature:

> Viens du paisible seuil de la maison roulante
> Voir ceux qui sont passés et ceux qui passeront.
> Tous les tableaux humains qu'un Esprit pur
>   m'apporte
> S'animeront pour toi, quand devant notre porte
> Les grands pays muets longuement s'étendront.

> (**MB**, 181-182)

Eva thus figures the regenerative principle of love which brings the poet back to the sources of being, a love which is a means of access to knowledge and spiritual elevation and the necessary impetus to creativity. The last stanzas develop the image of the poet as a modern Prometheus[28] freed and reborn through the strength of love and confidence in the power of poetry. He enters a new life of knowing and becoming with the possibility of renewing his "genius" and reconciling himself with nature and men.

The poem itself is therefore an experience of rebirth in that the writing of it permits the poet to rediscover the ties which exist between the alienated self and the world of others and things; as the poet develops the language to express the world of coherence and beauty which his imagination discerns, a second life begins for him and a new reality born of his images, symbols and myths is created.

Vigny himself expressed this paradox of the archetypal rebirth pattern, which to me illuminates the sacrificial death of the poet in *Stello* and his subsequent renascence in *Les Destinées,* when he wrote the following lines. They are addressed to Antoni Deschamps, one of the many unfortunate young poets who were suffering from incomprehension and poverty, and who were beginning to consider Vigny, the successful playwright and poet, as the primary contemporary defender of poets and the cause of poetry:

> . . . J'ai souffert d'abord et gémi avec vous et j'ai admiré la beauté de vos sentiments, autant au moins que la beauté de vos vers; je l'admirais et je m'attristais avec vous, mais quand je me suis reculé de ce grand tableau de votre âme et quand je l'ai considéré avec des yeux plus sereins et moins troublés, je me suis senti heureux comme d'une seconde naissance qui vous aurait été donnée.

Croyez-moi, mon ami, vous voilà guéri. La Poésie qui vous avait perdu vous a sauvé. Vous conserverez toute la vie sur le front la trace du tonnerre, mais ce ne sera qu'une cicatrice, et votre âme est restée intacte sous ce front blessé.[29]

Notes

[1] Maud Bodkin in *Archetypal Patterns in Poetry* (Oxford, 1934) explains the special power of the rebirth archetype: ". . . we may say that all poetry, laying hold of the individual through the sensuous resources of language, communicates in some measure the experience of an emotional but supra-personal life; and that poetry in which we re-live, as such a supra-personal experience though in terms of our own emotional resources, the tidal ebb toward death followed by life renewal, affords us a means of increased awareness, and of fuller expression and control, of our own lives in their secret and momentous obedience to universal rhythms." (p. 89)

[2] In major statements about romantic theory Lovejoy, Peckham and Wellek have essentially accepted this concept. See A. Lovejoy, "Romanticism and Plenitude," *The Great Chain of Being* (New York: Harper and Brothers, 1963); M. Peckham, "Towards a Theory of Romanticism," *PMLA,* LXI (1951), 5-23; and R. Wellek, *Concepts of Criticism* (New Haven: Yale University Press, 1955).

[3] F. P. Bowman, "*The Poetic Practices of Vigny's* Poèmes Philosophiques," *MLR,* LX (1964), 359-368.

M. Schroder, *Icarus, The Image of the Artist in French Romanticism* (Cambridge: Harvard University Press, 1961).

G. Bonnefoy, *La Pensée religieuse et morale d'Alfred de Vigny* (Paris: Hachette, 1944).

A brief but impressive recent article from a phenomenological perspective by J. P. Richard on Vigny is found in his *Etudes sur le Romantisme* (Paris: Seuil, 1970).

[4] The interplay of ideas itself was for Vigny a major expression of creativity: "La Pensée seule, la Pensée pure, l'exercice intérieur des idées et leur jeu entre elles, est pour moi un véritable bonheur." Vigny, *Le Journal d'un Poète,* in *œuvres Complètes,* Ed. Pléiade, 2 Vols. (Paris, 1948), I, 1337. All future references to the work of Vigny are from the Pléiade edition.

[5] Vigny himself in an entry in the *Journal* of 1836 pointed out the role of irony in his largely misunderstood "Consultation": "Ce qui me surprendrait le plus, si quelque négligence des critiques pouvait surprendre, ce serait de voir que pas un d'eux ne s'est aperçu que l'originalité de *Stello* tient au mélange d'ironie et de sensibilité du Docteur Noir dans ses récits." (II, 1046-1047). In other references to *Stello* he notes the originality of its composition when compared to the taste for symmetrical patterns of unimaginative critics: "Je l'ai dit et pensé souvent, *Stello* a donné le vertige à la critique.—Personne n'a laissé voir qu'il eût senti ni le fond ni la forme même. Comment n'ont-ils pas vu qu'un livre de désespoir devait être désespéré dans sa forme même et dégoûté même de la symétrie des compositions ordinaires, qu'il devait laisser tomber ses récits et ses réflexions feuille à feuille comme un arbre qui se dépouille?" (II, 965). He also analyzes with remarkable precision the element of unresolved tension which constitutes the real originality of *Stello;* the opposition between sacred fount (Docteur Noir) and ivory tower (Stello), life and poetry, which defines the structural as well as the thematic levels

of the work: "Le Docteur Noir, c'est la vie. Ce que la vie a de réel, de triste, de désespérant, doit être représenté par lui et par ses paroles, et toujours le malade doit être supérieur à sa triste raison de tout ce qu'a la poésie de supérieur à la réalité douloureuse qui nous enserre; mais cette raison selon la vie doit toujours réduire le sentiment au silence et ce silence sera la meilleure critique de la vie." (II, 969).

[6] Speaking of his unhappy childhood in 1832 he explains the need he felt to repress his emotional nature: "—Une sensibilité extrême, refoulée dès l'enfance par les maîtres et à l'armée par les officiers supérieurs, demeura enfermée dans le coin le plus secret du cœur.—Le monde ne vit plus pour jamais que les idées, résultat du travail prompt et exact de l'intelligence.—Le Docteur Noir seul parut en moi, Stello se cacha." (II, 960). The "anima" side of his personality was thus contained under an iron mask and permanently controlled through extreme efforts of willpower: "J'étais né doué d'une sensibilité féminine. Jusqu'à quinze ans je pleurais, je versais des fleuves de larmes par amitié, par sympathie, pour une froideur de ma mère, un chagrin d'un ami, je me prenais à tout et partout j'étais repoussé. Je me refermais comme une sensitive." (II, 986).

He admits the continual presence of the two selves and their alternating influence on his actions and his writing, the animus— "moi philosophique" and the anima— "moi dramatique": Je dois donc dire que j'ai cru démêler en moi deux êtres bien distincts l'un de l'autre, le moi dramatique, qui vit avec activité et violence, éprouve avec douleur ou enivrement, agit avec énergie ou persévérance, et la *moi philosophique,* qui se sépare journellement de l'autre moi, le dédaigne, le juge, le critique, l'analyse, le regarde passer et rit ou pleure de ses faux pas comme ferait un ange gardien." (II, 1032).

In June of 1844 he defines and generalizes the significance of the two personalities: "Le Docteur Noir est le côté humain et réel de tout: Stello a voulu voir ce qui devrait être, ce qu'il est beau d'espérer et de croire, de souhaiter pour l'avenir: c'est le côté divin." (II, 1218).

[7] II, 1071.

[8] Title of P. Bénichou's recent study of the romantic concept of the writer. (Paris: Corti, 1973).

[9] I, 194.

[10] I, 656.

[11] II, 1196.

[12] See his defence of the historical novel, "Réflexions sur la vérité dans l'art" and his essay on *Chatterton,* "Dernière nuit de travail."

[13] I, 773.

[14] "Les Idées du Docteur Noir," Part VI of *L'Imagination d'Alfred de Vigny* (Paris: Corti, 1962), pp. 443-526.

[15] I, 583.

[16] C. J. Jung, "On the Relation of Analytical Psychology to Poetry" and "Psychology and Literature" found in *The Spirit in Man, Art, and Literature,* (New Jersey: Princeton University Press, 1966).

[17] I, 803.

[18] P. G. Castex, *Vigny, L'Homme et l'œuvre* (Paris: Boivin, 1952).

[19] The idea of sacrifice is at the core of Vigny's concept of morality;

he never ceased to admire the Christian concept of sacrifice, and the stoical renunciation of personal desires is a recurrent theme in the last pages of his *Journal.* In 1863 he writes of his devotion to his wife:

> Jamais mon esprit de sacrifice n'a trouvé de sentiment de reconnaissance proportionné, excepté dans la tendresse de Lydia pour moi. (II, 1381).

In one of the final entries he concludes that his life and work have been devoted to the celebration of the tragic sacrifice in modern society of the noble, the poet and the soldier. He reiterates the three great themes of his fiction and poetry, and provides a résumé of his understanding of the meaning of his life:

> Etant poète, J'ai montré l'ombrage qu'a du poète tout plaideur d'affaires publiques et le vulgaire des salons et du peuple.
>
> Officier, J'ai peint ce que j'ai vu: le gladiateur sacrifié aux fantaisies politiques du peuple ou du souverain.
>
> J'ai dit ce que je sais et ce que j'ai souffert. (II, 1390-91).

[20] "Les Destinées," *Poèmes Philosophiques* (I, 172).

[21] R. Wellek, "The Concept of Romanticism," *Concepts of Criticism,* (New Haven: Yale University Press, 1963), pp. 188-189.

[22] "La Flûte" (I, 202).

[23] "L'Esprit Pur" (I, 222).

[24] "La Bouteille à la mer" (I, 210).

[25] All references to "La Maison du berger" are to Volume I of the Pléiade edition of Vigny's works and will be designated hereafter in the text as MB.

[26] This concept of the human spirit as a dynamic, divine force is found delineated in the *Journal* as early as 1829:

> Soumettre le monde à la domination sans bornes des esprits supérieurs en qui réside la plus grande partie de l'intelligence divine doit être mon but—et celui de tous les hommes forts du temps. (II, 897)

[27] Eva is both goddess and child:

> Viens donc! le ciel pour moi n'est plus qu'une auróle
> Qui t'entoure d'azur, t'éclaire et te défend;
> La montagne est ton temple et le bois sa coupole.
> La terre est le tapis de tes beaux pieds d'enfant.
>
> (I, 180)

[28] The image of Prometheus is of course a recurrent one in romantic writing. Associated with Napoleon and with other figures of rebellion it was not considered too heroic to be applied to one's private experience as Vigny does occasionally in his *Journal.* In this entry he compares his stoic sense of duty and the sacrifice of himself during his army career to the suffering of Prometheus:

> —Je marchai une fois d'Amiens à Paris par la pluie avec mon Bataillon, crachant le sang sur toute la route et demandant du lait à toutes les chaumières, mais ne disant rien de ce que je souffrais. Je me laissais dévorer par le vautour intérieur. (II, 960)

[29] *Lettres à des poètes,* II, 996.

Stirling Haig (essay date 1978)

SOURCE: "The Double Register of "Les Destinées," in *Studi Francesi,* Vol. 64, 1978, pp. 104-6.

[*In the following essay, Haig analyzes the ambiguous imagery in* Les Destinées *of the relationship between humanity and the divine and concludes that the poem affirms Vigny's conviction "that hope is cruel folly."*]

The argument of the liminary poem of Vigny's most famous collection is well known. At the Savior's birth, the powers that Vigny syncretically terms *destinée* must temporarily relax their cruel hold over man; they appeal to the Lord (here called "Jéhovah", which for Vigny always means the terrible and vengeful God of the Old Testament), who reaffirms their subjugation of man. The Fates then return to their "proie éternelle" in the name of grace or Christian providence. The poem concludes with a question of metaphysical anguish: "Notre mot éternel est-il: C'ÉTAIT ÉCRIT?" an expression of the determinism that fundamentally governs the human lot in the world both ancient and modern, eastern and western[1].

With such a theme—man's duplicitous relationship with the Divinity—it is not surprising that the poem's imagery should be ambiguous, in the proper sense of working simultaneously in two opposing directions. In effect, in the course of the poem's forty-one tercets, there appear to be two antithetical semantic fields. Images of imprisonment yield (approximately at tercet 26) to images of liberation, and the latter would seem to be wholly inconsonant with the poem's assertion of an "epochal" change that turns out in reality to be merely illusory. For the Fates reassert their supremacy over humanity. No liberation takes place at all when the ancient world and its slavery are replaced by the Christian ethic.

The purpose of this note is briefly to examine the two sets of images, and to emphasize their underlying unity, for it is clear in the end that both belong to a single semantic field, and that their apparent opposition is intended to suggest divine perfidy[2].

The first field is that of limitation or circumscription. In the beginning of the poem, the moirai weigh heavily[3] upon man, who is presented as a beast of burden ("boeuf") who is literally subjugated ("le *joug* de plomb") by what Vigny will call the "poids de notre vie" in the opening line of **"La Maison du berger"**, the only poem in the collection in which escape is truly realized. The yoke causes man to trace a deep furrow in the course of his repetitive movements and restricts those movements to the narrow limits of a "cercle fatal", marked by deadlines ("Sans dépasser la pierre où sa ligne est bornée")[4]. Man, gathered with his fellows like a herd ("troupeau" is not explicitly pronounced until v. 64) is hobbled ("entraves") and his inflexible, eternal condition and burdensome existence are suggested by the mention of "airain" and "plomb". This drama is played out on a negative landscape— "Tous errant sans étoile en un désert sans fond"—suggesting unrelieved desolation and sterility. The unlighted setting, the relative paucity of descriptive vocabulary, seem to play a functional role here, as they point to the very *dénuement* of man. To this limited vocabulary we can add the relentlessness of the *terza rima* rhyme scheme[5]. *Terza rima* (rare in nineteenth-century France; Gautier and Leconte de Lisle make some use of it) is a self-perpetuating form that is unremitting in its *enchaînement;* it progresses, or rather moves forward, only within the strict limitations of predetermined repetition, and it is no doubt the notion of illusory change—for it cannot break with its own past—that makes it appropriate for this poem.

As the fate of the Fates hangs in an augural balance, the sempiternal, grinding movement of the sphere is suspended, and it is here that the second lexeme is introduced:

> Il se fit un silence, et la Terre affaissée
> S'arrêta comme fait la barque sans rameurs
> Sur les flots orageux, dans la nuit balancée.

This would appear to be a change in register, for the images of the sea and the swimmer suggest liberation and an end to passive, limited situations. All the traditional associations of the sea adventure, from the Homeric periplus to the demonic search of Rimbaud's *Bateau ivre*—which Vigny's poem anticipates to a largely unnoticed extent—come to mind. (This is indeed the code of liberation in the most optimistic poem of *Les Destinées, La Bouteille à la mer.*) "Ondes" and "eau" become the new *milieu,* replacing "désert", and the vocabulary of voyage and exploration dominates one whole line: "Cependant sur nos caps, sur nos rocs, sur nos cimes" (v. 106). Yet, these images of flow and extension are delimited or phrased in such a way—with pejorative modifiers—as to force them into the same negative mold as the prison network. The swimmer is "incertain", the waves are those of "[le] temps qui se mesure et passe", and the voyage is tipped precipitously toward the abyss: "Et, d'un coup, nous renverse au fond des noirs abîmes"[6]. So RESPONSABILITÉ will not replace FATALITÉ, man will not strike out on his own, and the non-reversal of the poem's semantic code (and hence of its message) is confirmed by the appearance of the image of the collar:

> Vous avez élargi le COLLIER qui nous lie,
> Mais qui donc tient la chaîne?—Ah! Dieu Juste, est-
> ce vous?
>
> (vv. 110-11)

COLLIER is an obvious and perhaps predictable variant of the *boeuf-joug-entraves* paradigm, and with its appearance there comes a fall back into the state of chains (here

that of domesticated animal) from which escape was always illusory.

Brooding and plangent, the double register of confinement of *Les Destinées* projects a failed escape. In the political context of 1849, the poem signals a multiplicity of failed aspirations. It is a reaffirmation of one of Vigny's oldest convictions, that hope is cruel folly. In 1832 Vigny had written "Il faut surtout anéantir l'espérance dans le coeur de l'homme" (II, 950). And in the same *Journal d'un poète,* for the same year, we find the transcription of the Docteur Noir's most pessimistie dictum on hope: "L'espérance est la plus grande de nos folies" (II, 945).

Notes

[1] Vigny attached great importance to the phrase C'ÉTAIT ÉCRIT, making it not only the conclusion but also the epigraph of this poem and of the collection as a whole. In *Le Malheur* which Vigny claims to have written in 1820, we find these verses:

> Vers les astres mon oeil se lève;
> Mais il y voit pendre le glaive
> De l'antique fatalité. (vv. 48-50)

Meditations are consigned to this theme in the *Journal d'un poète* as early as 1826: "D'où vient que, malgre le christianisme l'idée de la fatalite ne s'est pas perdue?" (Pléiade edition, II, 895) See also an entry for 1832 (II, 965) and one for 1860: "ce que l'antiquité nommait *Destin, Fatalite, Sort* et le Christianisme *Providence*" (II, 1353).

Yves Le Hir notes that the term "Jéhovah, est inconnu des premiers traducteurs et des auteurs profanes. Il ne doit pas remonter au-delà du XVIe siècle (*Styles,* Paris, Klincksieck, 1972, p. 146).

[2] As for perfidy, P.-G. Castex would seem to offer an opposing view in his commentary of *Les Destinées:* "Le second moment du poème définit l'esperance chrétienne" (Paris, Société d'Edition d'Enseignement Supérieur, 1964, p. 249).

[3] And alliteratively: the first tercet contains four words beginning with a "p". For the notion of weight in Vigny's works, see François Germain's compendious *thèse, L'Imagination d'Alfred de Vigny,* Paris, José Corti, 1961 [-1962], pp. 152-53, 161-86 (*L'Enfer*).

[4] "Borne" is repeated in v. 66, and "sillon" is reinforced by the image of v. 67: "Le *moule* de la vie était creusé par nous."

[5] James Doolittle terms its usage in this poem "deliberately plodding" (*Alfred de Vigny,* New York, Twayne, 1967, p. 98).

[6] Cf. Pascal: "tout notre fondement craque, et la terre s'ouvre jusqu'aux abîmes" (Brunschvicg 72); an earlier Pascalian note in this poem was the comparison of men to "ces condamnés à mort" (v. 65). For the prison theme in Vigny and its Pascalian resonances, see C. SAVAGE, *Cette prison nommée la vie: Vigny's Prison Metaphor,* "Studies in Romanticism", 9 (1970), pp. 99-113. Two figures of struggle neglected in my study are the *athlète* (vv. 24, 89, 101) and the Prometheus figure ("vautour", v. 16 and "proie éternelle, v. 94).

[*] I would like to acknowledge the gracious assistance of my colleagues

George Mauner, Francis and Lois boe Hyslop, Alain de Leiris, and James S. Patty, all of whom read this paper and offered valuable suggestions.

Laurence M. Porter (essay date 1978)

SOURCE: "Symbolic Gesture in Vigny's 'Poëme,'" in *The Renaissance of the Lyric in French Romanticism: Elegy,* "Poëme" *and Ode,* French Forum Publishers, Lexington, Kentucky, 1978, pp. 19-74.

[*In the following excerpt, Porter examines Vigny's "visual sensitivity" and traces his use of gesture and posture to illustrate character in his symbolic poetry.*]

. . . . .

III

At first, Vigny's poetic projects were determined mainly by the epic ambitions he shared with his contemporaries. In 1823, he planned to rival Hesiod by composing a "Théogonie chrétienne," "poëme immense qui achèverait l'œuvre du Dante et de Milton" by relating the history of humanity and the destinies of the world (10). The ***Poëmes antiques et modernes,*** fragmented into discontinuous episodes, are in a sense the debris of these unrealized epic projects. (Perhaps these projects should not be taken too literally, but rather considered as the poetic counterpart of fantasies of lost aristocratic dominance) (11). The few poems which might have stood alone as "philosophical" statements— **"Eloa," "Le Déluge,"** and **"Moïse"**—were submerged by the collection's time-bound title and by its diachronic division into prehistoric, pre-Christian, and post-Christian books. Vigny was dissatisfied with the outcome: he felt that he needed and lacked a suitable poetic vehicle for his ideas. "La Poésie n'a en France qu'une langue imparfaite, circonscrite et prude. La lyre française n'a que la corde de l'Elégie. Toutes les autres sont fausses ou absentes. Je les ai touchées toutes, on pourrait m'en croire" (12). The missing organizing principle, however— symbolic gesture in the context of kinetic metaphors— already was latent in Vigny's mind.

The autobiographical passages of the intimate, informal *Mémoires inédits* reveal how Vigny's mother, a devoted painter, developed his visual sensitivity and brought it to bear upon literature:

> Cette tête blonde [Vigny's] lui [to his mother] était confiée tout entière; elle la prit de mon père et s'en empara pour la remplir à son gré. Elle et lui ne la meublèrent que de beautés, si bien choisies, rangées, établies et scellées comme dans un arsenal et un musée qu'après tant d'années je les y retrouve encore en fermant les yeux et regardant à l'intérieur. Les premiers tableaux que virent mes yeux furent *la Sainte Famille,* de Raphaël, et une surtout où l'on voit un jeune ange aux cheveux bruns se pencher sur le berceau du Sauveur. . . . Cet ange m'était toujours présent et dès que je pris un crayon, je le voulus dessiner. . . . Avec

> les premières histoires de la Genèse, les chefs-d'œuvre m'étaient gravés dans la mémoire, le déluge ne m'apparut que dans la forme de la sombre inondation de Poussin, la pythonisse d'Endor m'amena l'ombre de Samuël conduite par celle de Salvator Rosa. . . . Si le soir, sous les lampes, mon père me lisait Homère, survenait Girodet aux yeux de flamme qui faisait passer sous la lumière les traits merveilleux de Flaxman. . . . Le matin, je voyais au Louvre *l'Apollon du Belvédère,* conquis par l'Empire, et le soir, il tirait devant moi les flèches de son carquois. [Goddesses, nymphs, and wrestlers] étaient mes compagnons d'enfance, j'avais autour de moi leurs statues et leurs moules, et les dessins qui les animaient et les alliaient aux beaux Troyens et aux Grecs. Cette grâce incomparable qui accompagne toutes leurs attitudes et ne les quitte ni dans la douleur ni dans la mort . . .

> (pp. 52-53; cf. 50 and 51)

This childhood training made Vigny keenly aware of people's postures and gestures. He had the habit of sketching people in later life (13) and throughout the *Mémoires inédits,* Vigny's painterly eye characterizes people and their ideas by means of recorded posture and gesture (14). The first time that Vigny describes real people in the *Journal d'un poète* he reports their gestures:

> Pendant la réponse de M. Daru [M. de Montmorency] ne cessait de rouler dans ses doigts le cahier de son discours, à la manière d'un bon écolier qui écoute attentivement la réprimande qu'on lui fait, n'osant détourner ses yeux de ceux du Directeur qui le traitait assez mal, et saluant de temps en temps d'un air d'intelligence docile. (*OC* II, 883: February 9, 1826)

This detailed notation is surprising because the *Journal d'un poète* is in general quite abstract, whereas gestures are concrete. To introduce the next story, a portrait of Walter Scott, Vigny observes: "Voir est tout pour moi. Un seul coup d'œil me révèle un pays et je crois deviner, sur le visage, une âme" (p. 883). Elsewhere, writing to Eugène Sue who had asked him whether the story of Captain Renaud in *Servitude et grandeur militaires* was true, Vigny describes the act of literary composition—as he did frequently—in terms of creating a statue: "Vous écrire tout ce qu'il y a d'alliage dans le métal de cette statue et qui a posé dans ma mémoire pour le bras ou la tête serait bien long" (15). So keen was Vigny's visual memory that he avoided encounters whose image he might not want to harbor in his mind. He writes that his mind was like a garden full of statues and that he,

> sentant mes recueillements, mes travaux, mon sommeil encombrés de ces images du passé et de ses statues d'êtres évanouis ou absents, rencontrant trop souvent debout sur les avenues de la pensée une scène importune de la vie, j'ai résolu de fuir dans le spectacle de la vie tout ce qui n'est pas digne de souvenir. . . .

> (*Mémoires inédits,* pp. 104-05)

In the post-aristocratic world, aristocracy could survive only in a concern for appearances, and Vigny fears being corrupted and debased by the contagion of the unworthy postures and gestures which he might witness.

His reliance on reporting gestures and postures so as to comment indirectly on a situation emerges most clearly from a comparison between Vigny's translation and Shakespeare's original text of *Othello*. He adds no fewer than thirty-seven notations of gesture and posture (16). Twenty-eight of these are confined to one key scene from each act (I, 3; II, 3; III, 9; IV, 10; V, 2 in Vigny's version), showing that Vigny does not apply the procedure of gestural notation mechanically, but rather reserves it for special effects at moments of great tension. Most of the added gestures are Othello's: the protagonist is thereby thrown into greater relief. Generally speaking, Vigny moves from dialogue to gesture during the climactic moments of his theater, showing that emotions have become so strong that they affect the body. This procedure, commonplace in theater, becomes striking in Vigny's prose works, for example during the confrontation between Richelieu and the king who wishes to be free of him in *Cinq-Mars* (*OC* II, 121-25), and during the confrontation between Napoleon and the Pope his prisoner in *Servitude et grandeur militaires* (*OC* II, 627-37).

Vigny was so aware of the expressive value of postures and gestures that he sometimes used them by preference to depict the moral status of those he described. Recalling the death of his own father, who for a long time had been crippled and bent by war wounds, Vigny wrote: "par une sorte de convulsion miraculeuse l'agonie le redressa et, au moment du dernier soupir, il devint plus grand et droit comme un soldat qui se rend à l'appel du jugement et va prendre son rang pour l'éternité" (*MI*, p. 47). A retrospective portrait of his father ends with the phrase: "et, dans chaque geste lent et naturel, le bon goût" (*MI*, p. 49). And when Vigny imagines encountering his ancestors in another world, he says: "Je dois vivre de manière à mériter qu'ils se lèvent quand j'entrerai" (*MI*, p. 38). In *Stello*, the Docteur Noir's geometrically regular gestures correspond to his hyper-rational habits of mind (*OC* I, 578), and regarding Kitty Bell, the narrator says: "l'ordre et le repos respiraient en elle, et tous ses gestes en étaient la preuve irrécusable" (*OC* I, 605).

Notations of gesture and pose come to provide vehicles even for Vigny's abstract thought in the political and philosophic spheres. He conceives that his proper role in the service of Louis-Philippe is to ask nothing of him, but "l'affermir et le mettre en état de se tenir debout, puis rentrer dans ma solitude et le regarder marcher . . ." (*MI*, p. 99). In *Stello* the narrator observes that "la Nation, humiliée, ployait le dos" (*OC* I, 723). In *De Mlle Sedaine et de la propriété littéraire*, Vigny sums up the anti-poets' arguments as recommending: "Courbez-vous sous tous les bâtons" (*OC* I, 883). And in *Cinq-Mars*, he notes a striking series of poses unconsciously adopted by De Thou as he responds to the thought of Descartes in the *Méditations métaphysiques* (*OC* II, 212).

IV

In 1825, concerning the memorable human types in epic and drama, Vigny had written: "L'imagination [y] donne du corps aux idées et leur crée des types et des symboles vivants qui sont comme la forme palpable et la preuve d'une théorie abstraite" (*JP*, p. 880). The genre of the "Poëme" proved too short to develop adequately a symbolic *character* such as Vigny describes here, but he soon came to realize that by replacing symbolic characters with symbolic *acts*, the "Poëme" could embody philosophical ideas as effectively as could longer genres. The work of preparing a second edition of the ***Poëmes antiques et modernes*** led Vigny to this decisive *prise de conscience*, and to a clear statement of his future aims on May 20, 1829 (the same year as his translation of *Othello*):

> Je viens de réunir mes poëmes qui ont la forme la plus sévère et forment un tout complet, ceux auxquels je crois de la vitalité par leur composition forte. Concevoir et méditer une pensée philosophique; trouver dans les actions humaines celle qui en est la plus évidente *preuve;* la réduire à une action simple qui se puisse graver en la mémoire et représenter en quelque sorte une statue et un monument grandiose à l'imagination des hommes, voilà où doit tendre cette poésie épique et dramatique à la fois.

> (*JP*, p. 891)

Here, "epic" means endowed with a universal significance concerning the history and destiny of man; "dramatique" refers to a poetic practice which condenses the manifold action of the epic into a single moement (17). Vigny's reference to a monumental statue of a single action shows him moving towards the notion of an exemplary human gesture or posture serving to embody philosophical ideas. The notion of "body language" was scarcely a novelty in Vigny's day. Quintilian's *Institutes of Oratory*, for example, had devoted many pages to it (Book 11, chapter 3, sections 65-183). Cicero, the seventeenth-century painter Le Brun, Lavater, and Sulzer (a German work translated as the *Théorie générale des beaux-arts*, s.v. "Geste") had discussed it. J.J. Engel's influential treatise, published shortly before Vigny was born, explained that the posture of the body at rest reveals perceptible traces of individual personality features, just as facial expressions do: "Le corps ne garde jamais la même position quand les idées changent d'objet" (18). (One recalls how insistently Diderot, who knew Engel's work, recommended the use of pantomine in the theater.) Basing himself on Engel, the Englishman Henry Siddons codified the relationships between gestures and intimate feelings, with the aid of a hundred engravings inspired by actual theatrical performances (*Practical Illustrations of Rhetorical Gesture and Action, Adapted to the English Drama* [London: Printed for Sherwood, Neely, and Jones, 1822]). But the intent of these precursors was the opposite of Vigny's. They were attempting to draw up a catalog in which one bodily attitude would be selected to illustrate each emotion. Actors could then represent these emotions in panoramic succession, to suit any dramatic situation. Vigny, on the other hand, began with the idea of a single, basic existential situation, for which the statuesque postures of his characters would provide moral commentary without the need of authorial intervention.

Vigny's desire to immortalize significant postures and gestures in a statue reflects a new trend, "the late eighteenth and nineteenth centuries' belief in sculpture, or statuary, as opposed to painting, as the art pre-eminently suited to idealistic subjects rendered in classical or classicizing style. Such a distinction between sculpture and painting had never been sharply or insistently drawn before." In this period the word *statue* by itself comes to suggest "grandeur or generality or definitiveness of form and expression" (19). In turn, this revival of the dominant art-form of antiquity reflects the style of the "Neoclassic stoic," the *exemplum virtutis* which the visual arts portrayed for bourgeois audiences, with moralizing fervor, from the mid-eighteenth century on (20). The English engraver John Flaxman, whose spare and linear style without spatial modeling was inspired by the Greek vases brought back to England by Sir William Hamilton, served as an intermediary between Greco-Roman sculpture and the public. He made a minimum vocabulary of statuesque poses widely familiar on the Continent, where he was popular (21); and Vigny, even on military maneuvers, carried a few of Flaxman's engravings with him, together with his Bible, as if they were "my household gods" (22). No doubt Vigny's powerful attachment to Flaxman's frozen visual vocabulary reflects "une velléité rétrograde, tendant à dissimuler ou à neutraliser la nouveauté angoissante des transformations techniques et économiques" (23) as well as the disruptive changes of the Revolution. The poetic statue expresses the desire to preserve the past intact.

For the most part, Vigny drew upon the same verbal and postural traditions as his precursors in verse narrative (Chénier, Delille, Millevoye, and Voltaire). The repertory of postures and gestures in this tradition is rather narrow. Eyes are fixed upon a distant or invisible object of yearning; a crowd drags a victim along; suppliants fall at the feet of an authority and embrance his knees; a prince's arm outstretched offers ceremonial welcome, protection, assistance, or pardon; the hero takes up his weapon (24). Many of the associated similes (the hero resists like a rock or an oak) go back to Homer and oral tradition. . . .

Vigny's decisive innovation in the "Poëme" was to achieve noteworthy concentration by focusing on his protagonists in a moment of crisis. Through the shorthand of posture and gesture, the manifold feats of the epic hero are represented by a single bodily reaction to the generalized oppressive authority which confronts them. Vigny's protagonists invariably assume one of four stances at a moment of crisis. (*a*) The key words *baisser, courber,* and *ployer* consistently express submission; (*b*) *porter, soutenir,* and *élever* express support (the hero holds a loved person or the symbol of an ideal aloft, out of the reach of on-rushing destructive forces); (*c*) *immobile, debout,* and *résister* express monolithic resistance; (*d*) *lancer* and *s'élancer* express an Icarian venture. By evoking a restricted number of postures, recurring in various contexts of crisis (and much less frequently elsewhere) throughout his poetic narratives, Vigny created a repertory of kinetic metaphors which constitute a hierarchy of heroism. The more erect the protagonist, in spite of the crushing weight of universal injustice, the more admirable he or she is.

Progressively in the later poems, Vigny freed his heroes from a specific historical or legendary setting. They thus

come to represent all men; their postures represent heroic deeds; and their choice of response to external forces, their bodily attitude, signifies a philosophical attitude consciously adopted in the face of a hostile or indifferent Nature, Fate, of God. Their postures determine their existential value. As Vigny explained, "la destinée [l'homme] enveloppe et l'emporte vers un but toujours voilé—le vulgaire est entraîné, les grands caractères sont ceux qui luttent" (*OC* II, 880). Even the most resolute may fall, but they will rise again. Vigny frequently associates his heroes with the myth of Sisyphus. Thus in his commentary on *Chatterton* ("Sur les représentations du drame joué le 12 février 1835 à la Comédie-Française," *OC* I, 848), he points out "la fierté de Chatterton dans sa lutte perpétuelle . . . son accablement chaque fois que le rocher qu'il roule retombe sur lui pour l'écraser."

Symbolic postures, moreover, are readily adaptable to didactic as well as to thematic purposes. They constitute a covert, universal rhetorical appeal, doctrinally neutral, to which an author's public can readily yield (compare the moral implications of words like "upright" and "supine"). Then they will later be better prepared to accept by contagion the remainder of the author's plea, for the values like service, solidarity, monarchy, or poetic creation, which he associates with his heroes (26).

V

As he gradually transformed his short epics to symbolic poetry, Vigny retained in his repertory the conventional epic postures of resistance and submission, because these, although static, can visually suggest a commentary on the moral stature of the protagonist. He also kept the standard epic verbs of venture ("lancer, s'élancer") because they can depict heroic resolve condensed into a single moment. But he added the upraised arm, sign of the hero's defiance of superior forces and inimical fate, to replace the verb lists and the series of successive heroic acts in his precursors' verse narrative. This upraised arm at times also acquired the abstract function of providing support for the ideal, becoming the visible, physical token of a moral commitment (27).

Byron's poetry offered Vigny a striking example of the use of this symbolic posture at the dramatic climax of verse narrative. The visible effects of Byron's influence on his poetry date from 1819— "La Femme adultère"— when the Pichot translation of Byron appeared. At that time, Vigny did not yet know English well enough to read it without the help of a French translation. But twelve of his first sixteen poems are in part Byronic (28). Once translated, the English poet had quickly become immensely popular throughout Europe; his *Tales* in particular taught Vigny "l'art de concrétiser, d'incarner, de vivifier . . . la pensée abstraite" (29).

Byron's poems of revolt frequently describe the protagonist's defiantly upraised and brandished arm. This posture literally gives the Byronic hero greater stature. In "The Island," the wounded mutineer Christian "Cast one glance back, and clench'd his hand, and shook / His last rage against the earth which he forsook." The raised arm is also described as a beacon to guide lesser men. In "The Siege of Corinth," the renegade Alp's bare right arm "gleams like a falling star" as he leads his heathen hosts on the assault:

> Unclothed to the shoulder it waves them on;
> Thus in the fight is he ever known:
>
> . . . . .
>
> Look through the thick of the fight, 'tis there!
> There is not a standard on that shore
> So well advanced the ranks before.

But the raised arm also singles the hero out for destruction:

> Now was the time, he waved his hand on high,
> And shook—Why sudden drops that plumed crest?
> The shaft is sped, the arrow's in his breast!
> That fatal gesture left the unguarded side,
> And Death hath stricken down the arm of pride
>
> (Lara 30)

Vigny suppressed the shaking and brandishing of this upthrust arm: the frenzied energy of its repeated violent movement would have destroyed the statuesque, monumental effect he sought from posture and gesture. But he preserved the gesture itself as a determined self-affirmation, voluntary and perilous, in the face of an inevitable defeat. He gave the affirmative gesture greater prominence by liberating it from the detailed descriptions of military valor in which Byron had embedded it. One cannot conclusively demonstrate direct textual borrowings; nor was Byron the only literary source for affirmative postures in Vigny's **"Poëmes."** But the *Tales* offered Vigny the most prestigious contemporary models of short verse narrative in which such postures become foci of meaning.

As Vigny's poetic career progressed, and as his sense of achievement as a poet began to compensate for his sense of failure as an aristocrat and soldier, he endowed his protagonists with increasingly affirmative gestures. At first the attitudes of submission predominate; eventually they are dissociated from the protagonists and embodied in surrogates; at the same time, the heroic affirmative gestures are associated with metaphors which give them increasing connotations of endurance . . . The *Poëmes antiques et modernes* and the first three *Destinées* in order of composition ("**La Mort du loup**," "**La Colère de Samson**," "**Le Mont des Oliviers**") describes a sinister world where men have no goal other than to endure. (The later *Destinées* become more optimistic.) Characteristically, they yield beneath external pressure ("baisser, courber, ployer, à genou"). For example, the assembled armies fall to the ground in submission to divine authority at the end of **"La Fille de Jephté"** and **"Le Trappiste"**; Moses' people drop to their knees before him in fear; the lovers of **"Le Déluge"** and the unfaithful husband of **"Dolorida"** kneel in supplication; the priest of **"La Prison"** urges the prisoner: "Souhaitez avec moi de tomber à genoux."

The most powerful heroes are tempted to react this way. The effort required to bear the burden of leadership is intense. Charlemagne's brow "porte en se ridant le fer de la couronne" (**"La Neige,"** *OC* I, 83). Moses and Samson both yearn to sink under the weight of their responsibilities, to rest their head upon a woman's breast. Samson explains:

> Mais enfin je suis las.—J'ai l'âme si pesante
> Que mon corps gigantesque et ma tête puissante
> Qui soutiennent le poids des colonnes d'airain
> Ne la peuvent porter avec tout son chagrin
>
> (*OC* I, 145)

And Moses says:

> J'ai marché devant tous, triste et seul dans ma
> gloire,
> Et j'ai dit dans mon cœur, "Que vouloir à présent?
> Pour dormir sur un sein mon front est trop pesant . . ."
>
> (*OC* I, 9)

Vigny exaggerates these men's loneliness (Moses married Jethro's daughter, and Vigny knew it) (31) as well as their prestige (Moses performs Joshua's miracles in Vigny's poem). But they do not veil their eyes or shrink back. Like the dying wolf, they contemplate their dominant adversary, man or God.

Aside from Moses and "Eloa's" Satan, however, the *Poëmes antiques et modernes* are peopled by lesser figures who keep silence and avert their gaze from their oppressor. Their stance reveals not only fear, but also an unwillingness to question, understand, or oppose authority. To look the oppressor in the face—to confront his injustice openly—would logically impel the victim to condemn him. This denial of a stable world order dependent on the oppressor would oblige the victim to forsake security, while making an heroic attempt to create his own order amid the moral chaos he would perceive around himself. Consequently, when Jephté learns that God demands the sacrifice of his only child, he raises his arm to hide his face. While he exclaims that his vengeful God kills the innocent, he does not question the divine edict. The Trappist makes the same gesture of hiding his face behind his robe when informed that the king for whom he is fighting has betrayed his supporters. He then accepts his role as sacrificial victim, rather than renounce the monarchical ideal which structures his moral universe. Satan himself, being momentarily overwhelmed by the radiance of Eloa's moral splendor, a reflection of the God who condemns him, veils his face with his wing. Soon he recovers, however, and reasserts his independence at the cost of having to fall back into the void. But he is an exception. Even when all is to end well, in the fairy-tale world of **"La Neige,"** Emma and Eginhard do not assert the dignity of their love and its rightful claims. Fearfully they kneel before Charlemagne, bowing their trembling heads and clasping their hands in supplication. The most powerful imagery of submission occurs in the poem **"Moïse."** While the prophet was climbing Mount Nebo to speak with God hidden in a cloud, the entire Hebrew nation

> Priait sans regarder le mont du Dieu jaloux;
> Car, s'il levait les yeux, les flancs noirs du nuage
> Roulaient et redoublaient les foudres de l'orage,
> Et le feu des éclairs, aveuglant les regards,
> Enchaînait tous les fronts courbés de toutes parts.

> (*OC* I, 10)

This brings to mind Jupiter's pyrotechnic farce in Sartre's play *Les Mouches.* Moses, unwillingly identified with divine authority, finds himself irremediably set apart from his trembling, submissive followers.

A head meekly bowed indicates some form of choice and consent, however strongly motivated by fear, on the part of the victim. Already in the *Poëmes antiques et modernes,* however, the innocent victim assumes not a passive role, but a self-sacrificial protection of an ideal. He then combines the functions of resistance and support which will devolve upon non-human transparent shields in the *Destinées.* He momentarily succeeds in holding an ideal aloft ("porter, soutenir, élever") above a menacing environment, but eventually is engulfed. Pathetically doomed to material failure, gloriously dedicated to the heroic enterprise which proves his value, his efforts effectively dramatize man's—and the poet's—existential situation. To represent the symbolic act of support, Vigny describes feats which, if taken literally, would demand intense physical effort of his heroes. In the only anecdote of the *genre troubadour* which he saw fit to assimilate to poetry, **"La Neige,"** Charlemagne's daughter tries to save her lover Eginhard from detection by carrying him across the new snow on her back. Until Emmanuel finally drowns in **"Le Déluge,"** "Longtemps sur l'eau croissante élevant ses deux mains, / Il soutenait Sara par les flots poursuivie" (*OC* I, 40). The warrior-monk of **"Le Trappiste"** exhorts his army faithfully to continue to serve their unfaithful king, saying:

> Quand même, nous brisant sous notre propre effort
> L'arche que nous portons nous donnerait la mort;
> Quand même par nous seuls la couronne sauvée
> Ecraserait un jour ceux qui l'ont relevée,
> Seriez-vous étonnés? et vos fidèles bras
> Seraient-ils moins ardents à servir les ingrats?

> (*OC* I, 95)

In the *Destinées,* both La Sauvage and Wanda's sister protectively carry their two children.

There are basically three main possible destinies for Vigny's heroes as they confront a hostile, oppressive world: humiliation, glorious defeat, or resistance. Each possibility raises problems of achieving a poetic treatment which simultaneously does justice to the superiority of the hero, yet preserves him from becoming inhuman. The historically realized possibility after 1789, the only one remaining for the aristocrat outside the salons, once the bourgeoisie has triumphed in the nineteenth century, is humil-

iation: the hero finds himself both physically and morally weaker than the new society, his adversary. Before writing the *Destinées,* Vigny had contemplated his own supposed martyrdom, that of the superior man insufficiently admired by the society he serves, in the three historically-situated figures of Aristocrat (*Cinq-Mars,* 1826), Poet (*Stello,* 1831-32), and Soldier (*Servitude et grandeur militaires,* 1835) (32). But after **"La Sauvage"** in 1843, settings of the poems are usually sufficiently vague that they no longer impose on the protagonists the non-poetic roles of warrior or statesman (33), although the captain-figure in **"La Bouteille à la mer"** (a prose version dates from 1846) reveals that Vigny still may envy and desire the prestige of the heroic adventurer and explorer—one recalls Vigny's undistinguished military career and his fretting during years of garrison stagnation (34). But the Captain's venture serves an intellectual purpose.

By 1848, moreover, Vigny's sense of worth as a creative artist began to free him from his earlier fixation on the prestige of his aristocratic heredity. In January of that year, he told the sculptor David d'Angers not to inscribe the title of Count upon his bust, since "si deux ou trois personnes dans la postérité savaient mon nom, ce serait celui du Poëte et non du Noble" (*JP,* p. 1264). Vigny definitely exorcises the aristocrat in his last poem, **"L'Esprit pur"** (35).

In the later *Poëmes antiques et modernes* and in the *Destinées,* Vigny lifts the onus of humiliation from his heroes as well as from himself by presenting his now unconsenting characters in manacles that are clearly no longer mind-forged. Severe oppression, now embodied in a tyrannical political order or in a perverse Providence, bears the responsibility for human bondage. Crushing weights render affirmative, upward gestures virtually impossible. Thus Providence intervenes in human affairs, inimically, as the huge fallen boulder in **"Le Cor"** (1825). Roland leaps atop it, and successfully resists the Moors, until the stone capriciously rolls over to squash him. There results an implicit parody of the emblem of the Wheel of Fortune, here allied as it were with the pagan armies against the hero. Divine malice will destroy the virtuous, the cosmic irony of the situation suggests, if their human enemies cannot do so unaided. Overhanging clouds menacingly support a vast rock above **"Paris"** (1831). A brutal onrush of mindless waves crushes ("écrase") the valliantly embattled "Frégate la Sérieuse," the ship of **"La Bouteille à la mer,"** and the whole earth in **"Le Déluge"** (36). "La Femme adultère," the captive in **"La Prison,"** the political prisoner in **"Wanda,"** the humbled Samson, and Eva's heart and soul in **"La Maison du Berger"** are wrapped in heavy chains.

In the *Destinées* Vigny, more than ever preoccupied by the subject of man's defeat at the hands of an inimical universe, accumulates leaden bonds and heavy darkness with compelling force. Immense animated statues grinding every mind and intention underfoot in the liminary poem, the *Destinées* "nous écrasaient de leur poids colossal" (*OC* I, 119). In **"La Mort du loup,"** hunting knives and spears transfix the dying animal to the ground, like a Stoic Christ on the cross. The *Destinées'* heroes would venture if they could. A thwarted spiritual élan intensifies the feeling of oppression. Weight is the demonic reverse of venture; "un élan nié," "un bond humilié" (37). So the poet-persona addresses his Eva in "**La Maison du Berger**":

Si ton cœur, gémissant du poids de notre vie,
Se traîne et se débat comme un aigle blessé,
Portant comme le mien, sur son aile asservie,
Tout un monde fatal, écrasant et glacé;

. . . . .

Pars courageusement, laisse toutes les villes:

. . . . .

Du haut de nos pensers vois les cités serviles
Comme les rocs fatals de l'esclavage humain.

(*OC* I, 123)

The massed stone and brick of urban concentrations becomes the material emblem of a great moral servitude. In the particularly somber atmosphere of "**Le Mont des Oliviers**" and "**Les Destinées**," human efforts can effect only a slight, momentary alleviation of it ("soulever") (38).

Thanks to the auto-analysis of *Stello* (1832), however, Vigny became able to dissociate his poet-persona from the figure of the humiliated victim (39). Cast forth into the outside world, the latter comes to be represented through surrogates like La Sauvage, Wanda's sister, Eva, the beggar of "**La Flûte**," and the young poet addressed in the added introductory stanza to "**La Bouteille à la mer.**" These last three figures are encouraged to take heart by the speaker, who has emancipated himself from their weaknesses.

More often, however, the heroes of the *Destinées* are able to undertake an active venture as their supreme gesture of self-affirmation. Compared to intrepid swimmers, they strike forth into chaos. Though they may drown, they impose a meaning on chaos: the human intention suggested by the direction they chose. The verbs "lancer" and "s'élancer" evoke this enterprise. The captive of "**La Prison**" (1821) already anticipates it, flinging his arm outward in a gesture of rebellion that preserves his dignity. Refusing the timorous priest's temptation to submit to an unjust order of things, he defiantly smashes his arm against the cell wall, symbol of this order, as he dies. Roland, "seul debout" in "**Le Cor**" (1825) also foreshadows the later imagery of venture. The Sisyphean metaphor associated with Roland reappears more explicitly in "**La Flûte**" (1843) of the *Destinées*. There the poet-persona urges his fellow men to strive:

J'aime, autant que le fort, le faible courageux
Qui lance un bras débile en des flots orageux

. . . . .

Ce Sisyphe éternel. . . .

(*OC* I, 151)

Again in the poem "**Les Destinées**," struggling mankind is a "nageur incertain."

Resistance and venture signify emotional self-control in the face of a hostile world. Vigny further enhances the stature of his self-possessed heroes by endowing them with intellectual superiority to that world. Unlike the Stoical wolf in the earliest *Destinée*, who dies "sans daigner savoir comment il a péri" (*OC* I, 148), the Captain of "**La Bouteille à la mer**" "voit les masses d'eau, les toise et les mesure, / Les méprise en sachant qu'il en est écrasé." The human intellect becomes a god. Four lines after the verses just cited, Vigny explains the general significance of his parable. When physical resistance to oppression is impossible, "le penseur s'isole et n'attend d'assistance / Que de la forte foi dont il est embrasé" (*OC* I, 157). Increasingly, the protagonists of the later-composed *Destinées* become intellectual heroes rather than "men of action." Even the vocabulary and attitudes of submission become intellectualized, in "**La Flûte**," so as to refer to a failure of creativity rather than to a material defeat. Speaking of his mental weakness, the beggar confesses that the radiance of an ambitious idea, barely glimpsed on the horizon, "écrase et fait ployer ma vue" (*OC* I, 151).

In four of the last seven *Destinées*— "**La Flûte**," "**La Maison du Berger**," "**La Bouteille à la mer**," and "**L'Esprit pur**"—the value of the creative act rather than of the material venture has become the principal subject. In yet another of these last poems, "**Les Oracles**," Vigny expresses his disgust at the self-serving scheming of revolutionaries, who are too impulsive and short-sighted to anticipate the consequences of their acts. He proclaims the wisdom of holding oneself aloof when one cannot participate in public life with honor. And he devotes a postscript half as long as the poem itself to celebrating the diamond, which here represents "the art of ideal things," "the most brilliant and enduring treasure" of all that survives the fall of our transient political empires (*OC* I, 137). With the aid of this diamond metaphor, Vigny's poetry flows into that broad romantic current of artistic self-consciousness which will become the dominant mode of Symbolist poetry.

Such self-contemplation has its risks. The more the "Poëme" protagonist withdraws from material adventures to become a timeless monument of philosophical significance, the more he loses concreteness, dramatic force, and psychological complexity. The immobility forced upon him by Vigny's enterprise of idealization protects his dignity but also traces limits around him, transforming his actions into static poses. Even the versification of successive *Destinées* changes in a way that seems calculated to suppress narrative spontaneity and consequently to inhibit the protagonists' freedom of action. Up to and including "**La Flûte**" (1843), the *Destinées* are written in alexandrine rhyming couplets, which can be accumulated at will and made to conform flexibly to any narrative progression of incidents. Vigny adopts his distinctive stanzas of seven alexandrines starting with "**La Maison du Berger**" (1844). These are used in all the remaining poems except "**Les Destinées**" (originally conceived in such stanzas) (40), where in its context the *terza rima* suggests an inexorable interconnection of events in a world ruled by fatality. After **"La Maison du Berger,"** all the stanzas are numbered. Since Vigny laboriously shaped his later verse out of preliminary prose sketches (41), the composition of his later poems suggests the carving of a diamond's facets, whose number and arrangement have been determined in advance. The effect of narrative spontaneity is sacrificed in favor of rigorous strophic form, corresponding to an inner, mental world controlled by the poet.

The heroes' freedom becomes further curtailed, both in the *Poëmes antiques et modernes* and the *Destinées,* when they adopt a posture of rocklike resistance ("immobile, debout, résister") to assert human stability in the face of overwhelming onslaughts from a surrounding sea of moral chaos. The rigidity of such a pose makes it inappropriate for a symbolic representation of human action. Ultimately, through his inflexibility, the hero becomes metaphorically identified with the very forces he resists. His strength makes him inhuman. As Samson puts it, ". . . la bonté de l'Homme est forte, et sa douceur / Ecrase, en l'absolvant, l'être faible et menteur" (*OC* I, 145). And at the end of his poem, Samson literally crushes Delilah to death. Likewise, the stance of heroic resistance in "La Bouteille à la mer" transforms the Captain into a simulacrum of the reefs which will smash his ship. Erect, calmly scornful of the threatening storm, he stands:

> . . . immobile et froid, comme le cap des Brumes
> Qui sert de sentinelle au détroit Magellan,
> Sombre comme ces rocs au front chargé d'écumes,
> Ces pics noirs dont chacun porte un deuil castillan.

(OC I, 158)

By itself, such a pose cannot represent an active, creative self-definition in the face of this world, nor does immobility allow mutual communication with other men. Vigny frequently avoids this impasse by separating resistance from the hero, and attributing it instead to an object or idea associated with him. "La Royauté résiste" ("endures"), says **"Le Trappiste."** Not he, but the Mont-Serrat on which he stands, becomes the dominant symbol of stoical resistance in that poem. It faces the onrushing clouds (in human terms, delusions, misfortunes, and the temptation of despair), "les brisant de son front, comme un nageur habile" (*OC* I, 90). It is the personified "Frégate la Sérieuse," rather than its captain, which holds steadfast as a rock against the onslaught of a large enemy fleet. And in **"La Bouteille à la mer,"** communication is effected by the message in the bottle, rather than by the rigid Captain (42).

Progressively throughout the *Destinées,* metaphors evoking objects or abstractions come intermittently to supplant the human postures of resistance and venture, to appropriate symbolically the functions of human posture. The bottle replaces a man as the intrepid swimmer, its thick glass enduring the blows of the icebergs and waves; a dove rather than a poet bears a message to other men; the diamond rather than the human mind sends forth the beacon

light of the pure intellect. But the capacity for movement and communication, although threatened, is not lost in this world of abstractions. Since Vigny still uses the same key words to describe the action of these non-human symbols as he had earlier used to describe the heroes' postures, the latter remain recognizable. Transferred to rock, bottle, dove and gem, freed from its impermanence and frailty, the human stance achieves poetic apotheosis as an immortal monument of self-affirmation. At the same time, the arrangement of the individual poems within the published *Destinées* makes their dominant symbols progress from intense oppressive weight (**"Les Destinées"**) to extreme lightness and mobility in the soaring dove (**"L'Esprit pur"**—see Castex, p. 303). And two master symbols, the dove's unbounded flight and the radiance streaming from the diamond, continue to represent the outflowing significance of the human venture.

In one sense, the previous paragraph and the following one do nothing more than briefly recapitulate a discussion of Vignian symbols which can be found in François Germain's splendid book, in a far richer and profounder form. But the reader should remember the context of genre history in which those two paragraphs have been placed. Vigny's *Poëmes antiques et modernes* discover symbolic posture as a shorthand for the manifold heroic actions of the epic. The later *Destinées* detach the two most heroic in Vigny's hierarchy of postures—resistance and venture— from the protagonist and embody them simultaneously in the diamond. (The diamond, of course, functions also as the ultimate avatar of the transparent shield for a treasure, which motif Germain has masterfully traced throughout Vigny's *Oeuvre.*) The continued association of the diamond with the poet-prophet, and with the same kinetic verbs used previously for the heroic gesture, preserve a tenuous connection between the diamond symbol and its distant origins in the short narrative poem.

To elaborate, the diamond's radiance preserves in a secular and inhuman form the glowing transfigured countenance of the prophets such as Moses in the *Poëmes antiques et modernes.* First, the liminal poem of the *Destinées* transfers the image of a shining face from the religious to the secular plane. It replaces divinely inspired Biblical figures with all men who have been liberated from servitude through an act of will, and transformed by an intellect which "transporte à des hauteurs sublimes / Notre front éclairé par un rayon du ciel" (*OC* I, 122). Then **"La Maison du Berger"** transposes the same attribute of luminosity from a human to an inanimate subject, to the diamond set in the roof of the shepherd's rolling hut. Although inanimate, this diamond is not immobilized: it travels through the world with the shepherd (43). It provides a beacon of visionary inspiration for other men (cf. the significant title "Stello" meaning "star"), who must follow as best they can the light of inspiration, slowly and with difficulty, by exercising their limited, communal faculty of reason:

> Diamant sans rival, que tes feux illuminent
> Les pas lents et tardifs de l'humaine Raison!
> Il faut, pour voir de loin les peuples qui cheminent,

Que le Berger t'enchâsse au toit de sa Maison.

(*OC* I, 128)

Similarly in **"Les Oracles"** (1862), the active transitive verb "lancer" applied to the diamond preserves the suggestion of an arm outthrust in militant and creative defiance. The gem's rays "Ne cessent de lancer les deux lueurs égales / Des pensers les plus beaux, de l'amour le plus pur" (*OC* I, 137). Thus the human gesture originally depicted by "lancer" acquires the non-human advantages of enduring protective stability and tireless outward venture in all directions simultaneously.

Notes

[10] *OC* II, 876 and 878: "Le Journal d'un Poète" [*JP*].

[11] See Pierre Flottes, *La Pensée politique et sociale d'Alfred de Vigny* (Paris: Les Belles Lettres, 1927).

[12] *JP*, p. 887 (1828). "Elegy" no doubt alludes to Lamartine, whom Vigny both detested and admired. Several of Vigny's poems imply a dialogue with Lamartine. See also *JP*, pp. 1041, 1072, and 1096.

[13] Vigny, *Servitude et grandeur militaires*, *OC* II, 601 and 604.

[14] *MI*, pp. 115, 119, 139, 213-15, 217, 243. Marc Citoleux has an excellent, learned chapter on the visual arts as sources of inspiration for Vigny's "Poëmes" (pp. 605-39). He points out that Vigny continually speaks of himself as if he were a sculptor or a painter (p. 608).

[15] Letter of August 26, 1843, cited by Henri Guillemin, *M. de Vigny, homme d'ordre et poète* (Paris: Gallimard, 1955), p. 177.

[16] Barry Vincent Daniels, a theatrical historian, interprets Vigny's added notations of gesture as "une tentative d'assimiler les techniques de la pantomime 'naturelle' chez les comédiens anglais." See his "Shakespeare à la Romantique: 'Le More de Venise' d'Alfred de Vigny," *RHT*, 27 (1975), 138.

[17] Vigny's former epic ambitions were not forgotten: they were transferred to prose. Two months after completing *Stello* in 1832, he wrote: "Je me suis toujours trouvé le génie *épique*. . . . Mais comme l'une des conditions de ces vastes conceptions est l'étendue, et que l'étendue en vers français est insupportable [because of the monotony of regular rhyme and rhythm?], il m'a fallu la tenter en prose: de là *Cinq-Mars*, *Stello* . . ." (*JP*, p. 958. Cf. p. 972).

[18] J.J. Engel, *Idées sur la geste et l'action théâtrale*, 2 vols. (Paris: Barrois, 1788-89), I, 113. Originally *Ideen zur Mimik*. This work has been called the most significant of the eighteenth-century treatises on gesture. See Herbert Josephs, *Diderot's Dialogue of Gesture and Language: "Le Neveu de Rameau"* (Columbus: Ohio State University Press, 1969).

[19] See Webster Smith, "Definitions of *Statua*," *The Art Bulletin*, 50 (1968), 266.

[20] See Robert Rosenblum, *Transformations in Late Eighteenth Century Art* (Princeton: Princeton University Press, 1967), p. 50.

[21] See Rosenblum, pp. 158 and 171; David Irwin, *English Neoclassical Art: Studies in Inspiration and Taste* (London: Faber and Faber, 1966), pp. 27-28, 63 and 65.

[22] Marc Citoleux, *Alfred de Vigny, persistances classiques et affinités étrangères* (Paris: Champion, 1924), p. 621, citing Vigny's *Correspondance*, p. 9 (letter from 1824).

[23] Jean Starobinski, "La Vision de la dormeuse," *Nouvelle Revue de Psychanalyse*, 5 (Spring 1972), 23.

[24] For detailed discussions of these precursors' influence on Vigny, see the references cited in note 2, and also Robert de Souza, "Un Préparateur de la poésie romantique (L'Abbé Delille, 1738-1813)," *MdF*, 285 (July 1938), 298-327.

[26] See Kenneth Burke, *Language as Symbolic Action* (Berkeley: University of California Press, 1966), p. 296. See also Susanne K. Langer, *Feeling and Form* (New York: Scribner's, 1953), pp. 174-75; Francis Hayes, "Gestures: A Working Bibliography," *Southern Folklore Quarterly*, 21 (December 1957), 218-317; and Burke, *The Philosophy of Literary Form: Studies in Symbolic Action* (Baton Rouge: Louisiana State University Press, 1967), pp. 4-50.

[27] For an abstract thematic interpretation of kinetic imagery in Vigny's poetry, mainly divorced from the notion of posture, see Jean-Pierre Richard, "Vertical et horizontal dans l'œuvre poétique de Vigny," *Critique*, 26 (February 1970), 99-114. "Dans son projet . . . la poésie vignyenne est donc une *élévation*" (p. 101). Richard's interpretation is sensitive but schematic, blurring distinctions between individual poems.

[28] Emile Lauvrière, *Alfred de Vigny, sa vie et son œuvre*, 2 vols. (Paris: B. Grasset, 1945), I, 103n.

[29] Estève, *Byron*, pp. 360 and 388.

[30] *The Poetical Works of Lord Byron* (London: Oxford University Press, 1960). "The Island," iv, 339-40, p. 365; "The Siege of Corinth," vv. 821-38, p. 328; "Lara," ii, 379-83, p. 316. See also "The Giaour," vv. 241-42, p. 254; "The Corsair," i, 570, p. 285, and ii, 285-86, p. 290; "Lara," ii, 466-71, p. 317.

[31] François Germain, *L'Imagination d'Alfred de Vigny* (Paris: Corti, 1962), p. 257.

[32] Concerning the martyred soldier, see the fine articles by Albert Smith, "Vigny's 'Le Cor': The Tragedy of Service," *SIR*, 7 (1968), 159-65, and by Stirling Haig, "Conscience and Antimilitarism in Vigny's *Servitude et grandeur militaires*," *PMLA*, 89 (January 1974), 50-56.

[33] Cf. Germain, p. 492.

[34] Cf. Germain, p. 317: "Si Vigny s'est rêvé soldat, c'est pour nier l'infériorité dont il souffrait; et c'est parce que cette infériorité . . . l'humiliait qu'il imagine des autorités humiliantes."

[35] Pierre-Georges Castex, *"Les Destinées" d'Alfred de Vigny* (Paris: SEDES, 1964), pp. 276 and 280-82.

[36] "Le Déluge" somewhat imitates Byron's verse drama *Heaven and Earth*.

[37] Richard, p. 104.

[38] Compare Eloa's plaintive question to Satan as she plummets with him into the abyss: "N'est-ce pas Eloa qui soulève ta chaîne?" (*OC* I, 31).

[39] Germain, pp. 459-63 *et passim.*

[40] Castex, pp. 292-94.

[41] Guillemin has studied and published such sketches by Vigny for "La Colère de Samson," "La Sauvage," "La Flûte," "Wanda," "La Bouteille à la mer," and "Les Destinées," as well as a plan for the arrangement of the entire collection. See his *M. de Vigny,* pp. 65-87.

[42] To be sure, the poet-persona of "L'Esprit pur" also assumes this pose: "Je reste. Et je soutiens encor dans les hauteurs, / Parmi les maîtres purs de nos savants musées, / L'IDEAL du poète et des graves penseurs" (*OC* I, 172). But it is appropriate here. For this protagonist becomes a permanent monument to Vigny's career, now ended. He need not be human. Figuratively combining rocklike stability and protective support, preserving a message, he epitomizes a poetic triumph, "Calme bloc ici-bas chu d'un désastre obscur."

[43] There is a good discussion of the shepherd-figure in Vigny's poetry in James Doolittle, *Alfred de Vigny* (New York: Twayne, 1967), pp. 77-78 and note 87, pp. 137-38.

Martha Noel Evans (essay date 1983)

SOURCE: "Mirror Images in 'La Maison du berger,'" in *The French Review,* Vol. LVI, No. 3, February, 1983, pp. 393-99.

[In the following essay, Evans cites recent psychoanalytic theories about the self and examines the mirror imagery in "La Maison du berger" as metaphors of human consciousness.]

That homely object the mirror has played over the centuries an extraordinarily rich metaphoric role. At various times a figure of human vanity, an image of the mimetic function of art, or a mythic emblem of self-consciousness, it has lately been elaborated and enriched as a metaphor of human consciousness by psychoanalysts like Jacques Lacan and Luce Irigaray. In his essay "Le Stade du miroir" [1] Lacan brilliantly condenses Hegel's description of self-consciousness and Freud's formulation of narcissism into a new mythic figure: the child before the mirror. In Lacan's view the process by which the child reaches self-consciousness always includes the splitting and projection of the self into an external image so that the self is first perceived as being *out there, in the mirror.* The formation of the Ego, one of the products of this defensive strategy, thus inextricably links visual processes with aggressive impulses.

In *Speculum de l'autre femme,* Luce Irigaray develops further the meaning of this myth by asserting that the child before the mirror must of necessity be a male. His other-

ness, i.e., his femaleness, is aggressively split off and projected into the inverted image of the mirror self. While Irigaray insists that the predominance of vision in the formation of identity is a peculiarly male characteristic, she does share two assumptions with Lacan: first, that the processes of vision are linked with aggressivity; and second, that the phenomenology of sight will yield a general logic and geometry defining the subject's relationship to space and finally to the outside world.

Lacan says in "Le Stade du miroir," "l'image spéculaire semble être le seuil du monde visible" (p. 95). As "the threshold of the visible world," the mirror takes on, then, a central hermeneutic role in the meaning of seeing. The ancient *vanitas* and *speculum mundi* have evolved into a *psyché,* a looking glass, in which we simultaneously look *out* and *into* ourselves. The mirror has become the image of the sighted psyche.

All of this seems a long way from Romantic poetry, but the psychoanalytic mirror will serve us well as we look at Alfred de Vigny's poem **"La Maison du berger"** (1844). The very lexicon of the poem, studded as it is with mirrors and sight imagery, seems to make an appeal to the reader to see the seeing in this poem. Vigny's belief in the Romantic notions of poetry as a concentrating mirror and in the poet as Seer is well known. I would like to go beyond these beliefs in order to examine, in the light of Lacan's and Irigaray's myths, what this poetry reflects and how the Seer sees.

"La Maison du berger" is in the form of a letter addressed by the poet to his mistress, Eva, pressing her to flee the city with him. But Vigny immediately introduces a new and curious modification of the traditional ethics of Romantic pastoralism. As the poet presents it, the corruption and moral decay attendant on urban life do not depend, as one might expect, on the superficiality and dishonesty of city dwellers, but rather on the inevitable and unavoidable visibility of the individual to the gaze of anonymous lookers:

> Si ton corps, frémissant des passions secrètes,
> S'indigne des regards, timide et palpitant;
> S'il cherche à sa beauté de profondes retraites
> Pour la mieux dérober au profane insultant,
> [. . .]
> Pars courageusement, laisse toutes les villes.
>
> (Vv. 15-18, 22)

In this passage, it seems to be the very visibility of his mistress that makes her morally vulnerable, as if she could be penetrated and possessed by these insulting looks. The poet paradoxically reveals the sadistic component of his own visual imagination and at the same time imagines the woman timidly palpitating under the powerful and oppressive gaze of the multitude. Vigny has supplanted the traditional ethics of pastoralism by another ethics inherent in what he conceives to be the power politics of vision. Eva's passion, for instance, is no more pure than the villainous desires of the city dwellers. What gives it its particular taint is its public visibility. The poet can therefore protect and purify his mistress by taking her away into hiding: "Viens y cacher l'amour et ta divine faute" (v. 47).

In this initial section of the poem, vision creates its own moral dynamics: it is a closed system, defined by extreme polarities and by either/or oppositions. To be seen is to be blinded and made powerless by the look of the other in a visual process of pre-emption and sexual debasement. The moral polarities set up here by Vigny promote *prostitution,* in its original etymological sense, to the position of major crime in urban social life: Eva is shamed by *standing forth* in the other's field of vision.

The logic and tone of the opening section lead us to expect that the proposed pastoral retreat will serve the purpose of establishing a form of interaction superior to the prostitution of city life. We expect Vigny to erect a third observation post from which he can watch both the seers and the seen. But although his physical retreat from society seems to propose this new triangular geometry to us, emotionally the poet remains within the dyadic struggle for visual mastery. His removal from society is not so much a liberation as a strategic retreat meant to enhance his position on the battlefield. Vigny does not spurn society's duel of looks but rather maneuvers in order to win it by reversing the direction of forces. He flees the self-alienation of visibility in order to achieve mastery as the Seer.

The poet's pastoral retreat is a feint, then, meant to enslave the multitudes who have enslaved him: "Du haut de nos pensers vois les cités serviles / Comme les rocs fatals de l'esclavage humain" (vv. 24-25). From his elevated position, the poet establishes his power by looking down on the multitudes, both physically and morally. He becomes "un roi de la Pensée,"[2] and his gift of poetic vision is defined in this moral scheme precisely by the dominance he achieves by being able to see without being seen.

The poet must thus be concealed, and the landscape he describes as his asylum is seen as a function of this need. By a process of emotional projection onto the visible world, Nature is turned into a reflection of the poet's desires. The place of hiding becomes itself a process of self-concealment: "La forêt a voilé ses colonnes profondes / La montagne se cache" (vv. 33-34).

The poet hides himself in the hiding of Nature. He takes refuge in the mobile shepherd's hut. But eventually he finds his surest asylum in an unexpected place, the gaze of his mistress:

Je verrai si tu veux, les pays de la neige,
Ceux où l'astre amoureux dévore et resplendit,
[. . .]
Que m'importe le jour? Que m'importe le monde?
Je dirai qu'ils sont beaux quand tes yeux l'auront
   dit.

(Vv. 57-58, 62-63)

The poetic process is here expressed entirely in terms of sight and vision. It is, in fact, a strangely *silent* process,

promoted only by Eva's will to see. In a wordless exchange, Eva provides the will to see while the poet furnishes the power of vision. By means of this symbiosis the poet becomes a passive instrument while maintaining his power of sight through the will of a blind other. The poet is thus safely shielded by Eva from the dangers of visibility. Her gaze becomes a mask for the poet to hide behind. And this mask has a double function: it protects the poet both from the hostile looks of others and from the responsibility of his own desire to be a Seer.

This desire, which appears here as a gift of love, reveals its root in the soil of aggressivity, affirming Lacan's assertion that altruism is always the product of a deeper wish to destroy: "le sentiment altruiste est sans promesse pour nous, qui perçons à jour l'aggressivité qui sous-tend l'action du philanthrope, de l'idéaliste . . . voire du réformateur" (p. 100).

The aggressivity underlying the will of this poetic idealist and pastoral reformer becomes extraordinarily clear in the following section of the poem. Having secured Eva as a mask, as the source of his sight, the poet unleashes a series of angry imprecations whose aggressive power produces images of hallucinatory brilliance. Vigny's poetry, which he calls elsewhere "le miroir magique de la vie" (*Journal,* II, 1192), seems rather here to turn into a carnival gallery of distorting mirrors, for everything the poet looks at becomes twisted into the grotesque shapes of corruption.

Seeing, here, is a process of laying bare, of penetrating and possessing, just as previously the gazes of the "profane insultant" violated Eva. Politicians, statesmen, even the Muse, appear to the poet as actors in the debasing drama of prostitution described earlier. As before, Vigny translates relationships of power inherent in social visibility into the language of promiscuous and sadistic sexuality. Even the virgin Muse is transformed by the poet's angry gaze into "une fille sans pudeur" singing like a street-walker "aux carrefours impurs de la cité" (vv. 155, 158). And what corrupted her, what made her bad, was precisely her solicitation, not of sex, but of the other's look: "Dès que son œil chercha le regard des satyrs / Sa parole trembla, son serment fut suspect" (vv. 150-51).

What the poet's second look at society reveals is that things are exactly the opposite of what they first seemed to be. As in the opening section of the poem, all reality is divided into a closed system of polar opposites; gradations are banished; hierarchies denied. All aspects of human life thus fall into mutually exclusive categories: love or hate, master or slave, virgin or prostitute. Looking at the world is like looking at a mirror where every image is reversed, turned around. Vigny literalizes this process of reversal and betrayal in an image of sexual inversion. As the final instance of the debauchery of the Muse, the poet pictures her in ancient Greece, perched happily in the midst of a pederastic festival: "Un vieillard t'enivrant de son baiser jaloux / [. . .] parmi les garçons t'assit sur ses genoux" (vv. 163, 165).

What is most interesting about this economy of projection, reversal, and inversion is that the poet participates blindly in his own process of vision. While presenting himself as the pastoral poet who is "above it all," he is actually the occasion for the very depravity he reviles. His own look prostitutes the object of his gaze. So while he thought to hide from the capricious and hostile power of the other's look, he has, in fact, hidden from his own aggression. Although the angry and debasing thrusts of his look are concealed from the poet's consciousness, they become paradoxically visible everywhere in the spectacle of the outside world. The poet's anger, which he does not acknowledge as his own, seems therefore to be coming at him *from the outside.*

This blind spot, the focus of the poet's denied aggression, becomes particularly visible in Vigny's dazzling diatribe against the railroad. The railroad appears first of all as the corrupt and sexually inverted counterpart of the shepherd's hut. While the rolling hut wanders free like the "mobile pensée" (v. 251) of the female mind, the phallic railroad reduces space into a network of constricting straight lines. This coldly predictable machine re-emerges, however, in the contradictory guise of a fiery bull that eats up men and boys. In the poet's double vision the steam engine is at once a scientific apparatus and a dangerous, perverse monster:

> Sur le taureau de fer qui fume, souffle et beugle,
> L'homme a monté trop tôt. Nul ne connaît encor
> Quels orages en lui porte ce rude aveugle.
> [. . .]
> Son vieux père et ses fils, il les jette en otage
> Dans le ventre brûlant du taureau de Carthage.

(Vv. 78-80, 82-83)

While the presentation of the railroad as a "chemin triste et droit" (v. 121) logically furthers the pastoral thematics of the poem, the ambivalence of Vigny's vision is overwhelmed by its own wildness. The mythical "dragon mugissant" (v. 90) devours its own impotent apparition as cold machinery, just as the monster's unseeing eye stares down the poet with the blindness of his own rage.

The poet's helplessness in the face of his own anger finally structures all knowledge in a paranoid mode. Vigny views the truth as a hostile force whose main property is to victimize him. This anguished sense of victimization, of undeserved betrayal, takes shape in the second apparition of Nature. The poet's aggression finally breaks out of its silent hiding place in Eva's gaze and speaks in the voice of a proud and punishing woman:

> "Je n'entends ni vos cris ni vos soupirs; à peine
> Je sens passer sur moi la comédie humaine
> Qui cherche en vain au ciel ses muets spectateurs,
> Je roule avec dédain sans voir et sans entendre."

(Vv. 285-88)

The split of the poet's consciousness is reified in this hallucinatory image of Nature where the actual relationship of self and other is at once proposed and denied. To the poet's bitter disappointment, Nature does not recognize him as her own; but, on the other hand, neither does the poet recognize her as his double. The poet's own blindness has made him invisible. The unseeing stare of his own image looks through him as if he were not there. The nightmare of reflexivity has been accomplished; the impalpable figure in the mirror has become the source of vision, while the Ego has dissolved into nothingness.

Significantly, this I/eye, this distanced self whom he does not recognize, is envisaged by the poet not as a "he" but as a "she," *la marâtre Nature,* an unnatural and perverse mother. What the poet has cut off from consciousness and rejected as a debasing component of his identity is therefore not only his aggression but also the female part of himself. The poet as "she" appears in two images in the poem: in the punishing but eloquent figure of Nature and in the passive, silent figure of Eva. In the last section of the poem, following the song of Nature, the themes of narcissism and split consciousness finally become explicit in the metaphor of the mirror.

Eva is described as a reflecting pool where God has forever fated narcissistic man to contemplate himself, "tourmenté de s'aimer, tourmenté de se voir" (v. 231). She thus becomes simultaneously a passive instrument of reflection and the place where the poet will inscribe his self-knowledge. Poetry, "ce fin miroir solide, étincelant et dur" (v. 200), and woman, "ce miroir d'une autre âme" (v. 234), merge in a bivalent symbol where love and vision blend in the single process of producing self-conscious poetic language. In his effort to forestall the dizzying process of self-contradiction and reversal, the poet here seeks unity as poetry looking at itself. Doubleness of vision seems at last evaded; subject and object, reflection and mirror, appear to fuse in the shining diamond of poetry's song.

But like someone trying in a quick turn to catch a glimpse of his own back, poetry's look at itself must of necessity be fleeting and oblique. In order to see as One, in order to see the One, the poet must try to immobilize this evanescent moment of first sight: "Aimez ce que jamais on ne verra deux fois" (v. 308). What one sees only once is "true" because it does not change: it is forever fixed in its initial appearance. The truth is made One, is made pure, only by its disappearance.

Once again, the poet's effort to escape the tormenting vision of his own Otherness is not achieved through synthesis and integration but rather by a repetition of the same denial that was the original source of his alienation. The poet can no more recuperate the denied part of himself by visualizing it *out there* in a female reflection than Narcissus could be requited by his own image in a pool. Eva's very function as reflection disables her as a healer of the poet's narcissistic wound; immobilized by her imagined passivity, she is powerless to desire. Her love therefore can find expression only in regret, in mourning:

appuyée aux branches incertaines
Pleurant comme Diane au bord de ses fontaines
Son amour taciturne et toujours menacé.

                                                    (Vv. 334-36)

At the end of **"La Maison du berger,"** the image of the mirror is itself split as it becomes the figure of an irreversibly divided consciousness. The aggression and dissolution inherent in self-enunciation splinter Vigny's mirror of poetry into two component parts. On the one hand, the quick-silver reflecting surface embodied in Eva, the moon-maiden, is the projection of the poet's passive femininity, of the silence and dissolution that threaten him, of the death that inhabits him. On the other hand, the poet isolates himself within the crystal covering of the mirror to become the pure, preserving Word, self-present and diamond-hard, never menaced by change or dissolution.

As a result of this final splitting, the poet remains an everlasting "pur esprit, roi du monde / [. . .] / visible Saint-Esprit,"[3] while his Other, woman, becomes the pool of banishment where the poet's frailty, his mortality, shimmers palely in the light reflected from the sun of his intellect. The female part of the mirror becomes the mercurial image of fleeting time while the male part represents the imperishable diamond of thought. He is the One, and she is the process of self-destruction that sustains his unity.

The two parts are contiguous without ever being joined, since fusion with his Other represents for Vigny a horrifying and repugnant union with his own death, with his own putrefaction. The preserving crystal and the quick-silver of mortality are separated by an infinitesimal space, the pressurized domain of fear and hostility whose purpose it is to keep death at a safe distance, *out there.*

But by exteriorizing his own death, Vigny has paradoxically and tragically cut himself off from his own vitality. In his attempt to localize his fear and anger in the outside world, he has, in fact, rendered himself defenseless against them. These feelings that threaten from within become hauntingly omnipresent without; they color all that the poet sees with a somber and heavily charged light. The triumphant figures of life and independence in **"La Maison du berger"** are persistently overshadowed by the specters of death and dependence. All expressions of love in this poem have, if I may use the term, a necrophilic halo. Nature, that sweet refuge, is also a tomb; the shepherd's hut, the symbol of Romantic revery, is called a "char nocturne" (v. 53); and the nuptial bed, erotic bower of pleasure, turns into a coffin-like "lit silencieux" (v. 56). The diamond of poetry itself becomes a dazzling and sadistic evil eye whose aggressive rays flutter fatally around the image of the mourning mistress, forever weeping, forever silent, forever dying.

Vigny experiences his relationship with the world as a duel with a persecuting Other. As the place where he can be most intensely alone and therefore most significantly in control of this duel, poetry becomes for Vigny a kind of therapeutic process of self-domination by dominating oth-

ers. But this poetry, which represents for Vigny the gift of sight, is also a focus of his own blindness. The mimetic function of poetry, this "miroir magique de la vie," is thus fragmented and undermined by its function as *psyché,* the narcissistic looking-glass. The mirror of life is dismantled in **"La Maison du berger"** in a personal mythology that will persist in Vigny's poetry. The reflecting quick-silver of the world, at once beautiful and menacing, is separated from the crystal protective surface, the diamond of poetry, which will sing its invulnerability in a language blanched by its own purity and impoverished by its very unity.

Notes

[1] *Ecrits* (Paris: Seuil, 1966), pp. 93-100.

[2] Vigny, *Le Journal d'un poète,* in *œuvres complètes,* Bibliothèque de la Pléiade (Paris: Gallimard, 1948), II, 1192.

[3] "L'Esprit pur" (1863), vv. 50, 56.

J. C. Ireson   (essay date 1984)

SOURCE: "Poetry," in *The French Romantics,* edited by D.G. Charlton, Cambridge University Press, 1984, pp. 113-162.

[*In the following excerpt, Ireson examines the relationship between French Romantic poetry and Vigny's experiments with poetic form.*]

Poetry appears to have enjoyed a favoured status in the Napoleonic and Restoration societies. The officer classes in the later years of the Empire seem to have viewed the writing of verse as a fashionable accomplishment; Joseph-Léopold Sigisbert Hugo, a general in Napoleon's army and latterly governor of a province in Spain, gave his son advice on prosody when Victor was serving his apprenticeship in the art. Vigny appears to have had little difficulty in combining, in the Parisian salons around 1820, the appeal of a fashionable officer with the prestige of a promising young poet. More importantly, the society of the returned *émigrés,* however reactionary in politics, had expectations of a revived artistic and literary culture, and although these expectations were circumscribed by monarchist and Catholic values, enforced contact with other European cultures had produced a general awareness of the limits of the former traditions and a desire to see the forms of art adapted to the new period.

In her work *De l'Allemagne* (1810), Mme de Staël had underlined the main factor inhibiting the progress of French poetry in a period of changing political and religious conditions: the failure of its form and language to evolve with the mental universe of the writer, and above all to give adequate expression to the lyrical genius of the race, so that for her the great lyricists of France are not to be found among the poets, but among the great prose writers such as Bossuet, Fénelon, Buffon and Rousseau. Yet, in the years following 1815, the poets most in vogue were, for lack of new models, the masters of verse of the eighteenth century: Delille and Parny, both recently dead, Voltaire, Fontanes, Lebrun, Lemercier, Viennet, Baour-Lormian and J. B. Rousseau. Little in the ideas and attitudes expressed in this poetry had direct relevance for the reading public of 1820. A restored monarchy, a restored aristocracy, automatically brought with them values which seemed new after the upheavals of the Revolution and the Empire; and legitimism and Catholic orthodoxy were the values to which the new writers subscribed. In poetry, three newcomers appeared whose impact determined the course of French poetry for several decades. These were Lamartine, Hugo and Vigny.

It is noteworthy that each initially chose poetry as his preferred form, and each appears to have considered throughout his life, despite achieving fame in other genres, that poetry was first among the literary arts, potentially the most powerful and the most universal. That potential remained, however, at the beginning of the 1820s, largely to be realised, or rediscovered. . . .

. . . Vigny's development as a poet is initially associated, as in the case of Lamartine and Hugo, with the renovation and advancement of an older form of poetry. His concern was principally with the *poème,* a form which, in the later eighteenth century, had been used to signify a short epic or heroic poem, and Vigny's intention was to adapt it to the ideas and style of his time. His experiments with the *poème* lasted between 1820 and 1829, during which period he also turned, more briefly, to another form, the *mystère,* probably from the examples given by Byron in *Cain* (1821) and *Heaven and Earth* (1822). Two other forms, the *élévation,* with which he experimented for a short time around 1830, and the *poème philosophique,* which preoccupied him from about 1839 to the year of his death (1863), were designed to permit the expression of ideas in a more complex way than was possible with the *poème* and the *mystère.*

It was probably his intention to form individual volumes from sequences of these individual types of poem. In the event, his first major volume of verse, *Poèmes antiques et modernes,* slowly built up in stages (*Poèmes,* 1822; *Poèmes antiques et modernes,* 1826; *Poèmes,* 1829; *Poèmes antiques et modernes,* 1837), combined *poèmes, mystères* and *élévations,* the unity of the book being obtained from the arrangement of the pieces in a historical order, twenty in all in the 1837 edition.

Of these twenty poems, thirteen bear the subtitle *poème.* One or two, such as '**Le Cor**', were originally written as experiments with the *ballade,* giving a lyrical tone and a medieval configuration and colouring, without too much concern for authenticity, to a heroic episode, in this case the stand of Roland and Oliver at Roncevaux. '**Madame de Soubise**', though published as a 'poème du xvie siecle', has all the marks of a *ballade* in the manner of Hugo: interesting stanza and metrical forms permitting both a heroic and lyrical interpretation of the subject (an event from the Saint Bartholomew massacre) and an attractive simulation of some mannerisms of the older language. The

difference occurs in the intention of the poet. Vigny goes beyond historical fancy towards the sense of events and the performance of the figures involved in them.

His *poème* is a historical genre. It is relatively short, rarely exceeding 200 lines in length, and presents a concentrated episode shown in its effect on one or two figures. The figures themselves represent varied human types, ranging from men of spiritual or political power (Moïse, Charlemagne) to representatives of the code of military service and honour (Roland and Oliver, the soldier-monk of the Trappist order, the Captain of the frigate *La Sérieuse*). The list extends further, to the victims of political persecution (the prisoner in the iron mask), to women capable of tragic action through passion (Dolorida), and to beings capable of surmounting physical frailty through acts of courage (Madame de Soubise; Emma, the young 'princesse de la Gaule' of '**La Neige**'). His use of known events to provide perspectives for human action is, of course, not new, and Vigny's starting point is, typically, a familiar episode from the Scriptures ('**Moïse**', '**La Fille de Jephté**', '**La Femme adultère**'), a historical or contemporary event ('**La Prison**', '**Le Trappiste**'), or even a *fait divers* of the period ('**Dolorida**'). His treatment of his subjects is original in the variety of the colour and tone of the episodes and in the evocation of personality in the human figures. Though some of the earlier pieces, such as '**La Neige**', subscribe to the fashion of a fairly cursory local colour, others, particularly those founded on biblical episodes, combine imaginative reconstruction with a remarkable degree of detail in allusions. The four major themes of '**Moïse**' are centred on four books of the Bible. Moïse's recall of the migration from Egypt to the promised land and the establishing of his leadership derives from twelve chapters of Exodus; his triumphs, miracles and final weariness of responsibility are presented by references to eight chapters from Numbers; his last acts and his death outside the promised land are based on seven chapters from Deuteronomy; the elegiac theme of complaint is a compound of allusions to eight chapters of the Book of Job. A similar technique, though less dominant in the poem, is found in '**La Femme adultère**'. The most important features of Vigny's *poème* are found, however, elsewhere than in the external techniques. Although the control of the structure of individual pieces is impressive, their best achievement is found in the use of a spectacle to suggest important ideas concerning the human condition. The interaction of the characters and the situation in which they are found is dramatic (at times, as in '**La Prison**', Vigny uses passages of dialogue). The characters react through gesture, which takes on a ritual and symbolic significance, and through action, which shows the disproportion between the individual human will and impulses on the one hand, and the ordering of events on the other, whether these events are determined by natural or providential forces. Each figure is shown at grips with a dilemma occurring either as the consequence of an action or the working of an unseen process. Occasionally, as in '**Le Bal**', where the glamour of the ballroom is contrasted with the tribulations that inevitably lie ahead, the dilemma is left vague and inescapable. In most cases, it is a trial that engages the responsibility and courage of an individual: hence the action of Moïse in seeking to confront Jehovah, the unavailing effort of the priest to make contact with the mind of the dying prisoner in the iron mask, the tragic jealousy of Dolorida, the fate of the 'femme adultère', saved but not redeemed by the intervention of Christ in the processes of the Judaic law, the Christian love of Mme de Soubise, stronger than the fanatical conflicts of her century. Over this whole sequence of *poèmes* broods a general question concerning human responsibility and fatality: to what extent can moral strength counter the play of unpredictable forces that threaten human life?[5] The sombre picture is relieved by one thing, the presence of sexual love, which is painted in the suave tones of amorous pleasure ('**Dolorida**', '**La Femme adultère**') and shown briefly in its more innocent and elevated forms as a force able to illuminate and sublimate life ('**La Neige**', '**Madame de Soubise**').

The *poème*, as conceived by Vigny, is valuable for its power of illustrating an idea in heroic and sentimental terms, and its symbolic capacity is considerable, since the actions and speeches of the characters are left, within the context of the events, to carry the import of the larger ideas with which he is concerned. But its objectivity is also a limitation, in that it makes the elaboration of an idea more difficult, when the poet is not free to comment directly upon it. This fact may explain to some extent his early interest in the *mystère,* not so much in the form of the medieval play, as met with, for example, in Gringoire's ill-fated *mystère* in *Notre-Dame de Paris,* but in a rather more modern guise. Reference has been made to the examples given by Byron, which are written in the form of plays. Vigny's two *mystères* are narrative pieces, combining several different techniques, of which dramatic effect is one of the most striking. '**Éloa**' and '**Le Déluge**' figure among seven *mystères* listed on the first page of his journal, under the date 1823. The heading, *Les Mystères, Poèmes,* shows some hesitation between the two forms, but seems to indicate a decision to keep within a strictly poetic frame. '**Le Déluge**' does not differ superficially from the form of '**Moïse**' or '**La Femme adultère**' ('**Éloa**' has its own form, being written in three cantos, with ornamental devices such as simile). The difference is found in the nature of the ideas, which are more specifically concerned with the divine ordering of the world and divine intervention in the course of human history. The figures are divine or semi-divine beings. As in Byron's *Mysteries,* a modern and personal interpretation is given to events drawn from the Judaeo-Christian tradition. Éloa, the female angel of pity, is largely a creation of Vigny himself, though the name occurs in a passage by Klopstock quoted by Chateaubriand in *Le Génie du christianisme.* The figure of Satan is probably influenced by Milton's depiction of the fallen angel, but distorted by Vigny by the prominence given to the sensual theme in the description of the ensnaring of Éloa. Both poems depict the conflict between human virtues and supernatural power. Éloa, created by God from a tear shed by Christ over the body of Lazarus, is enslaved by Satan and becomes part of fallen creation, unable to do more than strive to console a suffering world. In their meeting in the depths of Chaos, the divine innocence of Éloa stirs Satan almost to repentance:

> Ah! si dans ce moment la Vierge eût pu l'entendre,
> Si la célste main qu'elle eût osé lui tendre
> L'eût saisi repentant, docile à remonter . . .
> Qui sait? le mal peut-etre eût cessé d'exister.

The value of Christ's ministry in the world is ultimately in question here. The theme will appear again, in less symbolical terms, in Vigny's later poems. But at this stage his views seem dominated by a belief in a divine will, the principles and consistency of which remain concealed at all levels of creation.

'**Le Déluge**' is constructed on the account given in Genesis of the destruction of the world by the Flood as a divine punishment following the forbidden mingling of human beings and angels. The poem focuses on two beings—Emmanuel, half man, half angel, and Sara, of human stock—who put their human love before their lives, which could be saved by separation, and perish on Mount Ararat in the last moments of the Deluge. The Flood, frequently treated in painting and in literature, offered an opportunity for original treatment of descriptive effects, for a poignant lyricism intrinsic to the situation imagined by Vigny, and for a strong message universalising the theme. The descriptive effects of the poem are conceived in the form of a violent disruption of harmony: glimpses of the last moments of the 'perfect order' of the antediluvian landscape are followed by visual shots of the destruction of this order by the storm and the Flood, and of the behaviour of animals and men in the rising of the 'implacable sea', until the moment of ironic calm signalled by the rainbow. The lyricism is in the doomed innocence expressed in the dialogue of the lovers. The message of the poet is conveyed in a speech attributed to the angel, father of Emmanuel, who interprets the divine judgment:

> La pitié du mortel n'est point celle des Cieux.
> Dieu ne fait point de pacte avec la race humaine:
> Qui créa sans amour fera périr sans haine.

By 1829, Vigny's *Poèmes antiques et modernes* had almost taken their final shape, although the title was not yet firm. The philosophical ground-work of the collection was already laid; the historical intention was apparent, but not yet developed as completely as Vigny wished. The poems were arranged as individual fragments of a sequence designed to reflect stages of moral development from the beginnings of Judaism to the formation of modern Europe. Despite the presence of '**Le Bal**', '**Dolorida**' and '**La Frégate la Sérieuse**', Vigny was still looking for a form which would permit a more detailed presentation of the values of the modern world. An entry in his journal dated 20 May 1829 notes the difficulty of finding suitable forms of expression for modern subjects; he appears to have been thinking about the possibility of a new form from about 1827, calling it *élévation.* Two poems of this type were written: '**Les Amants de Montmorency**' (1830) and '**Paris**' (1831). Vigny defined the *élévation,* referring to these two pieces, in a letter to Camilla Maunoir in 1838: 'partir de la peinture d'une image toute terrestre pour s'élever à des vues d'une nature plus divine'. Both were published separately and brought into the *Poèmes antiques et modernes* of 1837 as the last two poems of the collection. **'Les Amants de Montmorency',** based on a newspaper account of the suicide pact of two lovers, is a lyrical projection of their state of mind during the last three days of their lives; it extends the theme of condemned or tragic love, to which he gives a special place in his vision of the complex forces that assail human life. **'Paris',** in which Vigny gives a detailed elaboration of his thoughts inspired by the modern capital city, starts with the 'image toute terrestre' of Paris viewed by night from a tower by the poet and a traveller. Abandoning the narrative formulation of the *poèmes,* he constructs this *élévation* on a dialogue between himself and the companion who is unfamiliar with the city. The dialogue arises from two images suggested to the traveller by the sight of its lamps and the smoke of its fires: a glowing wheel and a furnace. The poet develops the sense of these images. The wheel is the representation of the motive force transmitted by Paris to the nation, and of the radius of action of the capital. The idea of new things being forged is elaborated chiefly by reference to ideas. The work from which the shape of the future will emerge is the work of 'des Esprits', and the lamp is the symbol of their efforts. Vigny has in mind the action of four thinkers or schools of thought. Three of these, representing contemporary attitudes to religion (Lamennais), politics (Benjamin Constant) and doctrines of society (Saint-Simon), he sees as exponents of limited systems. Above them he places the effort of independent thinkers, presumably like himself, uncommitted and disinterested:

> Des hommes pleins d'amour, de doute et de pitié,
> Qui disaient: *Je ne sais,* des choses de la vie,
> Dont le pouvoir ou l'or ne fut jamais l'envie.

There is no more than a hint here of the values which he himself will seek to elaborate. Such elaboration will require long reflection, not only upon ideas themselves, but on the form and expression in which the ideas can take the most permanent shape.

For the present, Vigny's poetry remains a poetry of isolated ideas on moral and theological problems, and experiments with form appear to be his chief concern: 'Concevoir et méditer une pensée philosophique; trouver dans les actions humaines celle qui en est la plus évidente *preuve;* la réduire à une action simple qui se puisse graver en la mémoire et représenter en quelque sorte une statue et un monument grandiose à l'imagination des hommes, voilà où doit tendre cette poésie épique et dramatique à la fois' (*Journal d'un poète,* 20 May 1829). Nevertheless, the qualities of his poetry are already clearly established. Statuesque and grandiose according to his own formulation, his heroic verse is distinguished from near-contemporary examples such as Théveneau's *Charlemagne* (1816) and La Harpe's *Le Triomphe de la religion* (1814) by the vitality of the effects and the adjustment of technique to the formulation, without didacticism, of an individual idea. The features of that technique are to be found in the variation of tone and perspective (this is probably the dramatic intention referred to by Vigny), and the organisation of

images of physical action in such a way as to evoke both a moral crisis and a significant historical moment (**'Éloa',** for example, to all appearances purely symbolic in its action, also marks the destined role of the compassion brought by Christ to the world). . . .

Vigny . . . did not pursue the attempt at an epic formulation of his views on progress, though he never departed from his opinion, reaffirmed in 1839 in the *Journal d'un poète:* 'Il y a plus de force, de dignité et de grandeur dans les poètes *objectifs,* épiques et dramatiques . . . que dans les poètes *subjectifs* ou élégiaques.' But his principal intention was to use verse forms in order to express aspects of a fundamental question: how far had the Christian era freed itself from the superstitions of the ancient world, particularly from the notion of fatality? The indications are that by the end of the 1830s he had established his answer: Christ's mission in the world remained inconclusive; Christianity was a failed religion; and the modern world had to establish its own values that would lead it towards civilisation. From this period, his poetry concentrated mainly on this third point, and in elaborating his ideas, Vigny found it necessary to develop new techniques. These are the techniques of the *poème philosophique,* a term used by him to categorise his poems written from 1838 onwards.[24] Three of these were composed before 1840. They mark a turning point, a state between the *poème* and the *poème philosophique.* **'La Colère de Samson'** (1839), with its diatribe against treacherous love, remains within the sentimental range of the *poème,* which it pushes to the limit. **'Le Mont des oliviers'** (1839) would seem to belong to the *Poèmes antiques et modernes* by its trappings and by its sentimental formulation, but to another form of poem by the analytical scrutiny of the unsolved enigmas confronting the human mind. **'La Mort du loup'** (1838), still within the narrative range of the *poème* with its dramatic and strongly drawn effects, marks a new departure with its foreground use of the wild animals to inculcate an idea about modern societies.

The *Poème philosophique* is a freer form of the *poème* in that the author intervenes to develop his own views in greater detail within a context of imagery, but not necessarily controlled by a narrative. *Les Destinées* forms an extended, if fragmentary, meditation on the values of modern civilisation, the two pieces (**'Les Destinées'** itself and **'Le Mont des oliviers'**), 'set at the beginning of the Christian era', being presumably included for the purpose of illustrating the bleak religious situation of the modern world.

This situation is depicted sometimes by means of episodes, but also, and more effectively, by the projection of ideas through symbols, which are chosen to represent the quality of human effort: the bottle with information from the Captain's log sealed in it, returning through the ocean currents from the wreck of an expedition to map the coast of Tierra del Fuego; the diamond and the pearl, illustrating the qualities of poetry; the railway train, representing the progress of mechanical inventions. Fuller tableaux also are used. In **'La Sauvage'** and **'La Mort du loup',** the young Red Indian mother and the wolf are set in different ways against the values of European life. The symbolic object itself, as in **'La Flûte'**, can be the centre of a dialogue.

The underlying argument of *Les Destinées* concerns the extent to which human beings have the power to control their lives and the forces confronting them in the world. In individual poems, Vigny celebrates the modern capacity to dominate the environment, complete the exploration of the planet, open new areas for European settlement. He warns, in two apparently opposed sections of **'La Maison du berger'**, of the need to understand the relationship of man and nature. He is also the satirist of Louis-Philippe, the humanitarian opponent of the absolutist régime of the Tsar, and the pessimistic observer of the slow progress towards civilisation. He defends poetry, which he sees, in the 1840s, as declining in prestige, presenting it as the most powerful form in which language can be used to illuminate the minds of one's fellow citizens. **'La Maison du berger'** is a meditation on the poet, on the social and intellectual independence necessary to him, and on the function of poetry. And the function of poetry is the concluding theme of his last poem, **'L'Esprit pur'**. Poetry, the expression of an ideal of nobility in both senses of the term, is, as Vigny conceives it, the best symbol of a new era in which the work of the mind will take over from the disorderly conflicts of an age of wars, and in which the written word will remain the repository of the values of a civilisation.

By its themes and techniques, even more than by the late moment of its publication (1864), *Les Destinées* moves out of the Romantic period, although features of the sensibility of the 1820s still remain. Contemporary by its date of publication with the middle years of the Parnassian movement, it overlaps the work of the Parnassians by its quest for intellectual values in religious history and for a strong, disciplined form, which Vigny found in the seven-line stanza, used in five of the eleven poems, and which he made his own: a quatrain followed by a tercet, with a rhyming link provided between the two parts by the last line. The equation of the art of poetry with an ideal of beauty, referred to at a number of points in the *Journal d'un poète,* connects Vigny further with the poets of the succeeding school rather than with the Romantics of 1830, from whose concerted effort emerges the idea of a poetic language designed to increase the immediate communicative power of language, and not to strengthen its hieratic potential.

Notes

[5] A note in the *Journal d'un poète,* dated 1824, summarises Vigny's general position: 'Dieu a jeté—c'est ma croyance—la terre au milieu de l'air et l'homme au milieu de la destinée. La destinée l'enveloppe et l'emporte vers le but toujours voilé.—Le vulgaire est entraîné, les grands caractères sont ceux qui luttent'.

[24] In 1843, Vigny published four *poëmes* (Vigny's spelling) in *Revue des deux mondes:* 'La Sauvage', 'La Mort du loup', 'La Flûte', 'Le Mont des Oliviers'. The following year, 'La Maison du berger' was presented as the 'prologue' to the *poèmes philosophiques,* this term having appeared as the subtitle of the four already published. A sixth poem was published, also in *Revue des deux mondes,* in 1854: 'La Bouteille à la mer'. Vigny's final intention appears to have been to publish a volume under the title of *Les Destinées,* with *poèmes philosophiques* as a subtitle. This intention was carried out by Louis Ratisbonne in preparing the posthumous edition. This included five hitherto unpublished poems: 'Wanda' (written 1847), 'Les Destinées' (1849), 'Les Oracles' (1862), 'L'Esprit pur' (1863), and 'La Colère de Samson', which Vigny had left unpublished for twenty-four years.

Malcolm McGoldrick (essay date 1991)

SOURCE: "The Setting in Vigny's 'La Mort du Loup,'" in *Language Quarterly,* Vol. 29, No. 1-2, Winter-Spring, 1991, pp. 104-14.

[*In the following essay, McGoldrick shows how Vigny uses contrasting effects to construct the setting of "La Mort du Loup" so it contributes to the plot.*]

Vigny's poem **"La Mort du Loup"** recounts the tracking-down of a wolf, its mate, and two cubs, by a band of hunters with a pack of dogs. The wolf is pursued, easily cornered and caught off guard, and attacked by one of the dogs. It seizes the dog, and only releases it from the clutch of its jaws after the animal lies dead. Then, mortally wounded by knife and bullet wounds, it too lies down to die. In the poem's second and third sections, Vigny uses the wolf's death to spell out his message of stoic resignation and submission to fate exemplified by the wolf. The poem becomes a fable, and the wolf is extolled as an example for mankind. Because Vigny's critics have concentrated on the poem's moral lesson, they have paid relatively scant attention to the intrinsic merit of the setting in **"La Mort du Loup."** V.L. Saulnier and P.-G. Castex have included some descriptive notations about the setting in their critical commentaries.[1] However, they have not exhausted all the critical comment to be made about Vigny's setting, in which the atmosphere of suspense and murder is present as ". . . a dramatic and minatory prelude to the fierce and poignant action to come . . ." (Ince, 1969). In spite of the highly graphic depiction of the wolf's death, the landscape—together with an equally poignant skyscape—constitutes the real tableau of **"La Mort du Loup."**[2] My *terminus ad quem* is line 26 of the poem, with which the descriptive part of the poem's first section ends; the confrontation with the wolves sets the action in motion immediately afterwards.

There are no peripeteia in the details of the hunting of the wolves. The poem is a *coup de main,* whose outcome—the wolf's death—is announced in the poem's title. The atmosphere of tension is built up in and through the setting, rather than by action. This is done partly through images which suggest forceful impact rather than clarification and logical meaning. The imagery that the poet uses makes the tableau assume a nightmarish quality. The tightness and sobriety of individual descriptive details is due to Vigny's use of those aspects of tension alone which have immediate impact.

For example, from the very beginning of the poem we are introduced to a world of danger:

> Les nuages couraient sur la lune enflammée
> Comme sur l'incendie onvoit fuir la fumée,

The adjective "enflammée" in line 1, which qualifies "lune", introduces a larger-than-life quality into the description, and the parallel with fire an inauspicious element. Line 2 is almost in parenthesis to line 1, the symmetry of the comparisons being underscored by repetition of the preposition "sur" and the chiasmic structure of the couplet, with its verbs "couraient" and "fuir" placed immediately before and after the medial causura in lines 1 and 2 respectively. The forcefulness of the analogy between moon and fire is all the more powerful after the moon has been described as "enflammée". The scene portrayed comprises a dark setting on which a certain coloration is superimposed. In these lines Vigny creates the conditions for the wind which, we learn later, causes the weather vane to produce its shrill cry, itself a portentous symbol of the tragedy to come. No mention is made here of the wind, as this would be inconsistent with the tone of the passage, which at this point conveys the hushed stillness of the landscape. Silence is important for both hunters and wolves. The hunters depend on it to stalk their prey. Their progress is marked by respect for it: "Nous marchions, sans parler . . .", "Rien ne bruissait . . ." The wolves also depend on silence to avoid being descried by the hunters.

Just as Vigny uses both hushed stillness and shrill sounds in his tableau, so too he uses both elements of a chiaroscuro motif. Darkness is emphasized. It is required for and linked to the atmosphere of sinisterness. Dark and sinister clouds billow like smoke above a fire, producing a tone of danger. Dark woods extend to the horizon and are traditionally associated through fairy tales with sinister events.[3] The hunters depend for the success of their dark designs on both silence and cover of dark.

In contradistinction to darkness, moonlight is evoked. Its importance in setting the scene through the simile of a fire, which in turn introduces the clouds hurrying across the sky, cannot be overstated.[4] The moonlight, like the weather vane, assumes the value of an omen. It is the visual agency which allows the poet-hunter later to espy the wolf cubs dancing in the moonlight. Because of the moonlight the hunters have to hide their shotguns which reflect the light. The hunter depends on the light of a star to interpret the animal footprints in the sand.[5] Later, the wolf cubs are silhouetted, and the gleam in the eye of the wolf or she-wolf is the first glimpse that the hunter catches of his quarry.[6] The whole death scene also depends on the hunters having enough natural light to witness the events and the expression on the wolf's face: moonlight is required for the whole chiaroscuro effect.

Just as Vigny uses both darkness and light for effect, so too he uses spatial dimension and constriction. The very barrenness of the landscape is not allowed to escape participating in the poignancy of the atmosphere: although **"La Mort du Loup"** portrays a desolate landscape of "landes" which extend as far as the horizon, we read later

that ". . . les enfants du Loup se jouaient en silence, Sachant bien qu'à *deux pas, ne dormant qu'à demi,* / Se couche dans ses murs l'homme, leur ennemi" (italics in this quotation, and in following ones, are my own).

Shrill sounds and silence, the play of light and darkness, expanse and constriction, create for the reader an atmosphere of dramatic suspense. A variety of technical means also contributes to this effect. The subordinate clause in lines 6-7 intensifies the narration. Vigny frequently withholds the main clause of a sentence, holding the reader in suspense through a sometimes lengthy digression. In lines 9 and 10 bated breath is conveyed as a real impression through the break-up of the *hémistiches:* "Nous avons / écouté, // retenant / notre haleine / Et le pas / suspendu. //" The alliteration in "p" and the other surds (sounds that are uttered with the breath and not the voice) "b", and "s" in "suspendu", are reminiscent of a whisper. The logical order of sequence in the above lines would be: "le pas suspendu, nous avons écouté, retenant note haleine." In the adopted word-order, "listening" assumes priority, and "le pas suspendu" becomes almost a kind of ablative absolute. Bated breath and halted footsteps are in harmony with the hushed stillness of the setting in which they are found, with the atmosphere of which they are a part.

Suspense is once again created by the period and dash in line 10, which introduces six and a half lines of descriptive parenthesis before the action is resumed. Alliteration conveys the unnatural and awesome silence of "Ni le bois ni la plaine / Ne *p*oussaient un sou*p*ir dans les airs." Vigny's use of the plural "airs", and his general predilection for plurals and definite articles (his tableau consists of "les nuages", "la lune", "l'incendie", "la fumée", "les bois", "l'horizon") gives it an unreal quality of essence, of the ethereal rather than reality.[8] The vague effect created by the use of the definite article is of a universe of undefined shape and dimension.

In lines 10 to 16 in particular, Vigny creates both horizontal and vertical expanse:

> . . . Ni le bois ni la plaine
> Ne poussaient un soupir dans les airs; seulement
> La girouette en deuil criait au firmament.
> Car le vent, élevé bien au-dessus des terres,
> N'effleurait de ses pieds que les tours solitaires,
> Et les chênes d'en bas, contre les rocs penchés,
> Sur leurs coudes semblaient endormis et couchés.

Vigny places us in the midst of a wood-covered plain. The introduction of woods which stretch as far as the eye can see gives the tableau depth, yet defines its limit. Lines 12-16 depict the eeriness created by images in the physical setting which astound the reader's imagination. Solitary towers are to be found here. Once again Vigny uses the definate article and plural nouns even where this clashes with verisimilitude—the unlikelihood, for instance, of there being more than one of these towers in the midst of a desolate landscape—to impose upon the reader a deliberately unreal and nightmarish tableau. Mentioning the firmament creates both expanse and confinement.

After using the absence of wind to set the tone of stealth, Vigny here makes the wind an aural participant. This demonstrates the way in which he *creates* desolation and anguish. The verb "crier" on line 12 aptly renders the plaintive cry of the weather vane "en deuil", and creates a tone which is consonant with the setting. It adds to the value of "en deuil" by the common association both words have with bereavement. A word like "grincer" would be too technically precise and detract from the value of metaphor which both terms share: the cry of the weather vane connotes the wailing of mourners—imprecise yet suggestive.

Startling metaphors, the "pieds" referring to the undercurrents of wind which brush against the weather vane, and "coudes", the oaks nestling on their elbows, appearing "endormis et couchés", stand out in the description as glaringly incongruous. Symmetrical use of alliterationin the past participle "penchés" qualifying "chênes", and "couchés" which expands upon "coudes."

Many other stylistic and poetic properties assure the success of Vigny's attempt to create an imaginative *décor* that captivates the reader. Avoidance of a first-person narrative technique obviates a possible identification through sympathy between reader and narrator. The latter, being linked to his band of fellow hunters, mentions "nous" six times from the beginning of the narration onwards. Only from line 27 does he use the singular personal pronoun. He does, of course, elicit the reader's sympathy later, but not at this confrontational stage in the action. Nor is the specific function of the men in the setting revealed prematurely either. We are told only of ". . . les Loups voyageurs que nous *avions* traqués" The only person singled out for attention, before the perhaps inauspicious notation "*Trois* s'arrêtent" is "Le plus vieux des chasseurs", who probably conjures up an image of sagacity or shrewdness rather than one of aggression. Theirs is, admittedly, a foreboding presence, but for a long time it remains a purely minatory one. When the denouement comes about, it does so quite suddenly.

Vigny also makes effective use of assonance and explosive consonants (as well as of alliteration). He uses the conjunction "et" to give a conversational ring and the flavor of story-telling to his poem. He resorts to the historic present tense when the most crucial events in the progression of the hunt require the reader's full participation without any interval of time or tense coming between narrator and reader.

The setting in **"La Mort du Loup"** serves as more than a preparation for the tracking-down of the wolf and the unfolding of the plot. Much of the interest and enjoyment which the poem holds resides in its highly stylized setting in which all elements create tension, poignancy and a baleful atmosphere. Vigny achieves this by a masterful juxtaposition of contrasting effects: noise and silence, darkness and light, confinement and expanse, wilderness and the proximity of urban man (with their attendant values of nature and civilization), barrenness and luxuriant vegetation, prey and predator, realism and surrealism.

François Germain wrote of the poem: "**La Mort du Loup**" est moins un récit qu'une march funèbre.'"

Notes

[1] Alfred de Vigny, *Les Destinées,* edited by Verdun L. Saulnier (Geneva and Paris: Textes littéraires français, 1963); *Les Destinées,* commentées par Pierre-Georges Castex (Paris: Société d'édition d'enseignement supérieur, 1968).

[2] See J. O. Fischer (1977: 243): "Une des images les plus plastiques de Vigny, celle du loup mourant, ne présente pas un tableau réel, mais une scène théâtrale, l'image du loup stylisé en homme-héros pour préparer le parallèle final."

[3] François Germain, (1962: 67-8), makes the following comment about the poem: "La vérité idéale du poème est . . . celle de l'angoisse; et dés les premiers vers elle est irrécusable. Avant même de parler de chasse, Vigny crée un paysage inquiétant qui confine au cauchemar: lune de sang, nuages qui fuient, bois noirs, végétation qui reparaît dans tous les contes populaires quand on veut perdre un enfant ou égorger une jeune princesse, un parfait décor de meurtre."

[4] Norris J. Lacy (1976) comments on this simile (one of three that he treats): "It may reasonably be argued that the appearance of the moon and the clouds requires no visual clarification, but if Vigny's technique here does not clarify, it does intensify. Indeed, it not only conveys the vividness of the scene, but by moving from the serene and picturesque evocation of nature to the image of fire and smoke, it also establishes the mood and theme of the poem: violence superimposed on tranquillity."

[5] I am using the *varia lectio* which appears in the new Pléiade edition of the *Oeuvres complètes,* edited by François Germain and André Jarry (I, Paris: N.R.F., Gallimard, 1986, Bibliothèque de la Pléiade, p.74).

[6] J. Castex (1948: 271-274) states as a hunter: "Pas plus que ceux des lions et des panthères, les yeux du loup ne peuvent flamboyer, car ils ne sont pas phosphorescents par eux-mêmes." François Germain (1962: 66-7) underlines the inconsistencies of the poem as a logical exposition of a hunt.

[7] Clive Scott, in a perceptive study titled "The Designs of Prosody: Vigny's 'La Mort du Loup'" describes the 3+3+3+ trisyllabic measures in lines 9-11, in line 4, and elsewhere, as ". . . this spiritual space, the space of steadied self-collection, of undemonstrative aloofness, occupied by a sense of one's own worth and the self-justifying nature of that worth." This is in contradistinction to hemistichs of unequal measures (2+4, 4+2, 5+1, etc.) like line 12 (4+2+2+4, where the creaking weathercock is heard), which convey the sense of vicissitude. Each rhythmically different hemistich conveys a difference in focalization or point of view.

[8] Germain remarks (1962:491): "L'emploi systématique . . . de l'article défini invite à concevoir un univers où se donnent rendez-vous des essences; comme si Vigny remontait d'un objet particulier à l'Objet, et l'infinie diversité du monde se réduit à quelques archétypes."

Works Cited

Castex, J. 1948. Alfred de Vigny et la chasse au loup. *Revue des Sciences Humaines.*

Fischer, J. O. 1977. *"Epoque romantique" et réalisme: Problèmes méthodologiques.* Prague: Univerzita Karolova [Université Charles IV].

Germain, François. 1962. *L'Imagination d'Alfred de Vigny.* Paris: Corti.

Ince, W. N. 1969. Some reflections on the poetry of Alfred de Vigny. *Symposium.*

Lacy, Norris J. 1976. Simile in "La Mort du Loup." *University of South Florida Language Quarterly,* Nos. 1-2.

Scott, Clive. 1990. The designs of prosody: Vigny's "La Mort du Loup." In C. Prendergast, ed., *Nineteenth-century French Poetry. Introductions to Close Readings.* Cambridge U.P.

de Vigny, Alfred. 1986. *Oeuvres complètes.* Edited by François Germain and André Jarry. I, Paris: N.R.F., Gallimard, Bibliothèque de la Pléiade.

————. 1968. *Les Destinées, commentées par Pierre-Georges Castex.* Paris: Société d'édition d'enseignement supérieur.

————. 1963. *Les Destinées.* Edited by Verdun L. Saulnier. Geneva and Paris: Textes littéraires français.

Phillip A. Duncan (essay date 1992)

SOURCE: "Alfred de Vigny's 'La Colère de Samson' and Solar Myth," in *Nineteenth-Century French Studies,* Vol. 20, No. 3-4, Spring-Summer, 1992, pp. 478-81.

[*In the following essay, Duncan examines how Vigny combines elements of celestial mythology with psychological realism to add a "mythic dimension" to a story of romantic betrayal.*]

The Biblical account of the Nazarite, Samson, involves three levels of narrative. While it relates the amorous adventures of Samson and the treachery of Dalilah, its central reference is to the superhuman exploits of a hero whose life echoes the epic of Hercules in a neighboring culture. Additionally, Samson and Dalilah (as well as Hercules) behave as celestial deities anthropomorphized. Alfred de Vigny's **"La Colère de Samson"** virtually suppresses the elements of gigantism and the marvelous to focus on the human passion and pathos that mask a combat of male solar and female lunar principles.

Vigny's troubled liaison with the actress Marie Dorval provoked the poem. There seems no doubt that his passion was intense and that he expected uncompromising affection in return. In this he was cruelly disappointed by Marie's bisexual divagations. No doubt Vigny's own truculence contributed to her disenchantment with a severe and self-righteous companion. Marie's betrayals, her sexual and emotional inconstancy, are an issue in Vigny's transposition of his personal experience to the context of the Samson legend; but Dalilah's relationship with Samson in the poem depends more on political, religious and profit motives. Dalilah is the agent of her people, the

Philistines, who are committed to the subversion of a powerful enemy among the Hebrews. She strips Samson of the purity and strength emblematized by his unshorn hair, a mark of the zealot Nazarite. With the shearing of his hair and the implicit loss of masculinity as well as his God-given moral and physical powers, Samson is reduced to impotence and is led away to servitude and death. Dalilah betrays an implied professed love for Samson not so much for the sake of variety in pleasure, Marie's offense, but for personal gain and the benefit of the tribe.

Samson is Vigny as he sees himself—the anguished victim of feminine deceit. In Vigny's poem Samson is the ironic captive of his own love, or more accurately, passion, which is consistent with Jewish tradition that perceives him as allowing sensual pleasure to dominate his conduct. In the poem's central apostrophe Samson acknowledges that man is bred to carnal satisfaction:

> L'Homme a toujours besoin de caresse et d'amour;
>
> . . . . .
>
> Il rêvera partout à la chaleur du sein,
> Aux chansons de la nuit, aux baisers de l'aurore,
> A la lèvre de feu que sa lèvre dévore,
> Aux cheveux dénoués qui roule sur son front,
> Et les regrets du lit, en marchant, le suivront.[1]

Although he protests of woman that "c'est le plaisir qu'elle aime. . . ." (1. 66), it is he, himself, who sits bound by the arms of Dalilah, symbolically a prisoner of his own lust. However, beyond his need for woman's "caresses" is Vigny/Samson's need for woman's love. Samson's strength in this text apparently derives fundamentally not from divine anointment but from his presumption of Dalilah's love:

> Eternel! Dieu des forts! vous savez que mon âme
> N'avait pour aliment que l'amour d'une femme
> Puisant dans l'amour seul plus de sainte vigeur
> Que mes cheveux divins n'en donnaient à mon
>   coeur.
>
> (ll. 81-84)

His blinding at the hands of his captors is the symbolic actualization of his refusal to recognize the truth of her indifference, "Interdire à ses yeux de voir ou de pleurer." (1. 104) It is not the loss of his "cheveux divins" that emasculates him but his final realization that Dalilah's love is false and the fact that he has further expended his powers in repressing his anger and frustration:

> Toujours mettre sa force à garder sa colère
> Dans son coeur offensé, comme en un sanctuaire
> D'où le feu s'échappant irait tout dévoré,
> Interdire à ses yeux de voir ou de pleurer,
>
> (ll. 101-105)

What restores his strength in captivity is still another irony, his liberation from the need of Dalilah's love and from the need to contain his violent anger at his betrayal. Now "le feu s'échappant irait tout dévoré," (l. 103) and so the pillars of the temple of Dagon are thrust assunder in a cataclysmic demonstration of power restored. A solar fire bursts through the imprisoning bars of night.

While Vigny, in his poem, has personalized the human aspect of Samson and diminished his superhuman dimension, he has, simultaneously, enriched the latent allegory in this material of the rivalry between Night and Day. The poem opens with an exposition of place. In addition to suggesting a topography for the events, characteristics of the physical environment indicate the roles and something of the nature of the protagonists. The "shepherd" (Samson), heroic and solitary, (traits borrowed from the Biblical representation) is associated with lions. (l. 3) The lion's head has from ancient times been a solar icon. The halo of its mane imitates the "rays" of the sun and the tawny color is idealized as golden. Like the sun, the lion is represented as the solitary master of its realm. Hercules, the Greek Samson, with his twelve labors, is an acknowledged solar hero. In the first of his (adult) adventures he slew the lion of Nemea, skinned it and wore its head over his own so that his identity as the sun hero is clearly established in the myth. Samson, also the subject of twelve marvels, first slew a lion. His Hebrew name, "Shimshon," is derived from "Shemesh," the sun. To suggest the simultaneity of Samson, lion and the sun Vigny immediately adds in his introduction: "La nuit n'a pas calmé / La fournaise du jour dont l'air est enflammé." (ll. 3-4) Even though envelopped in darkness, an anticipation of Samson's blindness and captivity at the end of the poem, the sun's fierce heat and light and the hero's energy remain immanent. Following the masculine statement of the first four lines— solitude, gritty sand, lions, fiery sun, male courage—the conclusion of the stanza is a feminine modulation:

> Un vent léger s'élève à l'horizon et ride
> Les flots de la poussière ainsi qu'un lac limpide.
> Le lin blanc de la tente est bercé mollement;
> L'oeuf d'autruche, allumé, veille paisiblement,
> Des voyageurs voilés intérieure étoile,
> Et jette longuement deux ombres sur la toile.
>
> (ll. 5-10)

A soft wind ruffles the sand like waves on a pool and swells the sides of the tent to create the image of undulating water, a feminine essence. There is a further feminine presence in the liquid "l's" that lull these lines. Finally, to command this dark place there is an ostrich-egg lamp—a miniature moon to epitomize Artemis, lunar goddess or earth mother, who may adopt various guises. Her guise in "La Colère de Samson" is Dalilah, envoy of Dagon, god of vegetation and fertility, and in whose name resonates the Hebrew "laylah"—the night. In a diurnal allegory, Dalilah, sensual spirit of darkness, has seized and encompassed the regent of the day: "ses bras sont liés / aux genoux réunis du maître . . ." (ll. 12-13). The power of night has obscured the brilliant aura of solar majesty. His rays are extinguished (his head is shorn). The "rays" of his vision are destroyed in a bloody sunset and he is imprisoned in darkness where he awaits the res-

toration of his vigor at the return of day. Vigny has abridged the period of Samson's captivity in the poem (1) in the interests of concentrating dramatic impact, (2) because Dalilah's betrayal of Samson has purged him of his amorous servitude thus immediately restoring his moral and emotional wholeness, and (3) in order to compress the action into one nighttime to enhance the verisimilitude of one single solar cycle of decline and resurrection.

Samson's climactic destruction of the temple of Dagon and the symbolic daybreak is preceded elsewhere in the Biblical account (and alluded to in lines 94-95 of the poem) by another of his adventures which relates to his epic revenge and to his role as solar hero. Once when Samson was dallying with a prostitute in the town of Gaza, his enemies set an ambush for him. He was to be seized and killed at dawn. Somehow learning of the attack Samson forestalled it by uprooting the pillars holding the portals of the city, carrying off the entire gate assembly and installing it high on a hill near Mount Hebron. Dawn for the people of Gaza was signaled when the first rays of the sun entered the gates of the city. Samson had removed the break of day to a new location thus eliminating the trigger of the ambushers' assault. Closeted in this episode with an alter-Dalilah, he breaks out of his nocturnal confinement and brings first light where it falls naturally to high elevation by an act of great strength and violence and so reasserting his hegemony. Samson's explosive resolution of his contest with the Night—a shattering dawn which burst open the pillars of his somber prison—is an elaboration of the Gaza episode.

In the Book of Judges Samson is Shemesh humanized and martyred. Like Hercules, the Hebrew sun-hero comes to a human end and, like Hercules, is the victim of his all too human passions. Vigny knows his own weaknesses, but represents himself in his poem as a martyr of deception and betrayal. The latent allegory of the solar hero, as well as the Biblical reference, dignifies and redeems with a mythic dimension a confession of personal inadequacy.

Notes

[1] Alfred de Vigny, *œuvres complètes,* Ed. Paul Viallaneix (Paris: Aux Editions du Seuil [L'Intégrale], 1965) 98-99. ll. 39 and 44-48.

FURTHER READING

Biography

Doolittle, James. *Alfred de Vigny.* New York: Twayne Publishers, 1967. 154 p.
    Survey Vigny's works in the context of his era and the events of his life.

West, Anthony. "Alfred de Vigny." In his *Principles and Persuasions: The Literary Essays of Anthony West,* pp. 52-60. New York: Harcourt, Brace, and Co., 1957.

Offers a brief history of Vigny's life and career as well as a negative appraisal of his poetic accomplishments.

Criticism

Bowman, Frank Paul. "The Poetic Practices of Vigny's 'Poèmes philosophiques'." *The Modern Language Review* LX, No. 3 (July 1965): 359-68.

Argues that many of the qualities considered faults in Vigny's verse were actually part of the poet's effort to revise poetic form so it corresponded more closely with human experience.

Brandes, George. "De Vigny's Poetry and Hugo's 'Orientales'." In his *Main Currents in Nineteenth Century Literature: The Romantic School in France,* Vol. V, translated by Diana White and Mary Morison, pp. 81-9. William Heinemann, 1904.

Suggests that Vigny was distinguished by his "cult of pure intellect and his proud, stoic feeling of solitude."

Croce, Benedetto. "Alfred de Vigny." In his *European Literature in the Nineteenth Century,* translated by Douglas Ainslie, pp. 131-44. New York: Alfred A. Knopf, 1923.

Discuss Vigny's conception of the role of the poet, considers the pessimism of his poetry, and praises his poems for their intensity and profundity.

Denommé, Robert T. "Alfred de Vigny, Preacher in an Ivory Tower." In his *Nineteenth Century French Romantic Poets,* pp. 63-90. Southern Illinois University Press, 1969.

Offers a close reading of the sources, symbols, form, and theme of the most important poems in *Poèmes antiques et modernes* and *Les destinées.*

Dey, William Morton. "The Pessimism and Optimism of Alfred de Vigny." *Studies in Philology* XXXIII, No. 3 (July 1936): 405-16.

Relates images of hope and despair in Vigny's poetry with incidents in his life and concludes that his later poetry shows a growing optimism and increasing religious faith.

Doolittle, James. "Lines 65-66 of Vigny's *Moïse:* Another Suggestion." *Modern Language Notes* 80, No. 5 (December 1965): 624-8

Interprets a problematic couplet in Vigny's "Moïse" as referring to the "mystery of original sin."

Gerothwohl, Maurice A. "Alfred de Vigny on Genius and Women." *The Fortnightly Review* XCIII, No. DLIII (1 January 1913): 94-111.

Examines the depiction of genius and women in Vigny's "Moïse," "L'esprit pur," "Eloa," and "La colère de Samson."

Guérard, Albert. "Alfred de Vigny." In his *Fossils and Presences,* pp. 135-63. Palo Alto: Stanford University Press, 1957.

Criticizes Vigny for relying too heavily on technique, while admiring the technical facility evident in both his poetry and his prose.

Haig, Stirling. "Notes on Vigny's Composition." *The Modern Language Review* LX, No. 3 (July 1965): 369-73.

Offers a close analysis of Vigny's creative process in the writing of "La Colère de Samson" and "La Maison du Berger."

Hartman, Elwood. "Alfred de Vigny on Progress: An Optimistic Pessimist." *Proceedings: Pacific Northwest Conference on Foreign Language* Vol. XXI (April 1970): 27-33.

Suggests that Vigny, while often despairing in the face of humanity's daily struggle, continued to believe in historical progress and the eventual triumph of the spirit.

Lacy, Norris J. "Simile in 'La mort du loup'." *The USF Language Quarterly* XV, No. 1-2 (Fall-Winter 1976): 59-60.

Reads the ambiguous similes in "La mort du loup" as vehicles for Vigny's pessimistic vision of the human condition.

McGoldrick, J.M. "Vigny's Unorthodox Christ." *Modern Language Notes* 85, No. 4 (May 1970): 510-14.

Argues that the ambiguous depiction of Christ in "Le Mont de Oliviers" contributes to the "organic disunity of the poem."

McGoldrick, Malcolm. "Vigny's *Le Mont des Oliviers* and *Amos.*" *French Studies Bulletin* 32 (Autumn 1989): 5-8.

Examines Vigny's borrowing from the Old Testament in "Le Mont des Oliviers."

Mill, John Stuart. "Poems and Romances of Alfred de Vigny." In his *Essays on Poetry,* edited by F. Parvin Sharpless, pp. 75-137. Columbia, South Carolina: University of South Carolina Press, 1976.

Examines the social and historical conditions that influenced Vigny's poetry, particularly the effects of the Revolution of 1830.

Minogue, Valerie. "The Tableau in 'La Colère de Samson'." *The Modern Language Review* LX, No. 3 (July 1965): 374-78.

Studies the tension between visual and poetic elements in the pictorial descriptions in "La Colère de Samson."

Porter, Laurence M. "The Art of Verse Narrative in Vigny's 'La neige'." *Romance Notes* XI, No. 1 (Autumn 1969): 57-60.

Examines how Vigny "purged" his poetry of seventeenth-century poetic conventions and stylistic devices.

Porter, Laurence M. "Vigny's Influence on Mallarme's Early Poetry." *Romance Notes* XI, No. 3 (Spring 1970): 536-38.

Identifies in Mallarme some echoes of Vigny's verses.

Savage, Catharine. "Cette Prison Nommée La Vie': Vigny's Prison Metaphor." *Studies in Romanticism* Vol. IX, No. 2 (Spring 1970): 99-113

Traces the prison metaphor through Vigny's poetry and prose and connects this image to Vigny's family history as well as his personal experiences.

Smith, Albert B. "Vigny's 'Le cor': The Tragedy of Service." *Studies in Romanticism* Vol. VII, No. 3 (Spring 1968): 159-65.

Maintains that rather than being symbolic, "Le cor" is a narrative: a poetic review of physical and mental experience.

Thibaudet, Albert. "The Generation of 1820: Alfred de Vigny." In his *French Literature from 1795 to Our Era,* translated by Charles Lam Markmann, pp. 122-28. New York: Funk & Wagnalls, 1968.

Discusses Vigny's reputation, his use of myth, emotion, and philosophical ideas, as well as his depiction of love.

Brereton, Geoffrey. "Alfred de Vigny." In his *An Introduction to French Poets: Villion to the Present Day,* revised edition, pp. 112-21. London: Methuen & Co. Ltd., 1973.

Offers a mixed evaluation of Vigny's poetic accomplishment, criticizing his poems as "awkward, grotesque, unnatural as well as unspiritual."

Poetry Criticism
INDEXES

*Literary Criticism Series
Cumulative Author Index*

Cumulative Nationality Index

Cumulative Title Index

How to Use This Index

The main references

Calvino, Italo
   1923–1985 .... CLC 5, 8, 11, 22, 33, 39,
                                           73; SSC 3

list all author entries in the following Gale Literary Criticism series:

BLC = *Black Literature Criticism*
CLC = *Contemporary Literary Criticism*
CLR = *Children's Literature Review*
CMLC = *Classical and Medieval Literature Criticism*
DA = *DISCovering Authors*
DAB = *DISCovering Authors: British*
DAC = *DISCovering Authors: Canadian*
DAM = *DISCovering Authors: Modules*
      DRAM: *Dramatists Module*; *MST*: *Most-Studied Authors Module*;
      MULT: *Multicultural Authors Module*; *NOV*: *Novelists Module*;
      POET: *Poets Module*; *POP*: *Popular Fiction and Genre Authors Module*
DC = *Drama Criticism*
HLC = *Hispanic Literature Criticism*
LC = *Literature Criticism from 1400 to 1800*
NCLC = *Nineteenth-Century Literature Criticism*
PC = *Poetry Criticism*
SSC = *Short Story Criticism*
TCLC = *Twentieth-Century Literary Criticism*
WLC = *World Literature Criticism, 1500 to the Present*

The cross-references

See also CANR 23; CA 85-88;
   obituary CA116

list all author entries in the following Gale biographical and literary sources:

AAYA = *Authors & Artists for Young Adults*
AITN = *Authors in the News*
BEST = *Bestsellers*
BW = *Black Writers*
CA = *Contemporary Authors*
CAAS = *Contemporary Authors Autobiography Series*
CABS = *Contemporary Authors Bibliographical Series*
CANR = *Contemporary Authors New Revision Series*
CAP = *Contemporary Authors Permanent Series*
CDALB = *Concise Dictionary of American Literary Biography*
CDBLB = *Concise Dictionary of British Literary Biography*
DLB = *Dictionary of Literary Biography*
DLBD = *Dictionary of Literary Biography Documentary Series*
DLBY = *Dictionary of Literary Biography Yearbook*
HW = *Hispanic Writers*
JRDA = *Junior DISCovering Authors*
MAICYA = *Major Authors and Illustrators for Children and Young Adults*
MTCW = *Major 20th-Century Writers*
NNAL = *Native North American Literature*
SAAS = *Something about the Author Autobiography Series*
SATA = *Something about the Author*
YABC = *Yesterday's Authors of Books for Children*

Literary Criticism Series
Cumulative Author Index

Asturias, Miguel Angel 1899-1974 **CLC 3, 8, 13;
DAM MULT, NOV; HLC**
See also CA 25-28; 49-52; CANR 32; CAP 2;
DLB 113; HW; MTCW 1, 2
Atares, Carlos Saura
See Saura (Atares), Carlos
Atheling, William
See Pound, Ezra (Weston Loomis)
Atheling, William, Jr.
See Blish, James (Benjamin)
Atherton, Gertrude (Franklin Horn) 1857-1948
TCLC 2
See also CA 104; 155; DLB 9, 78, 186
Atherton, Lucius
See Masters, Edgar Lee
Atkins, Jack
See Harris, Mark
Atkinson, Kate .... **CLC 99**
See also CA 166
Attaway, William (Alexander) 1911-1986 **C L C
92; BLC 1; DAM MULT**
See also BW 2; CA 143; DLB 76
Atticus
See Fleming, Ian (Lancaster); Wilson, (Thomas)
Woodrow
Atwood, Margaret (Eleanor) 1939- **CLC 2, 3, 4,
8, 13, 15, 25, 44, 84; DA; DAB; DAC; DAM
MST, NOV, POET; PC 8; SSC 2; WLC**
See also AAYA 12; BEST 89:2; CA 49-52;
CANR 3, 24, 33, 59; DLB 53; INT CANR-24;
MTCW 1, 2; SATA 50
Aubigny, Pierre d'
See Mencken, H(enry) L(ouis)
Aubin, Penelope 1685-1731(?) .... **LC 9**
See also DLB 39
Auchincloss, Louis (Stanton) 1917- **CLC 4, 6, 9,
18, 45; DAM NOV; SSC 22**
See also CA 1-4R; CANR 6, 29, 55; DLB 2;
DLBY 80; INT CANR-29; MTCW 1
Auden, W(ystan) H(ugh) 1907-1973 **CLC 1, 2,
3, 4, 6, 9, 11, 14, 43; DA; DAB; DAC; DAM
DRAM, MST, POET; PC 1; WLC**
See also AAYA 18; CA 9-12R; 45-48; CANR 5,
61; CDBLB 1914-1945; DLB 10, 20; MTCW
1, 2
Audiberti, Jacques 1900-1965 **CLC 38; DAM
DRAM**
See also CA 25-28R
Audubon, John James 1785-1851 ... **NCLC 47**
Auel, Jean M(arie) 1936- **CLC 31, 107; DAM
POP**
See also AAYA 7; BEST 90:4; CA 103; CANR
21, 64; INT CANR-21; SATA 91
Auerbach, Erich 1892-1957 .... **TCLC 43**
See also CA 118; 155
Augier, Emile 1820-1889 .... **NCLC 31**
See also DLB 192
August, John
See De Voto, Bernard (Augustine)
Augustine 354-430 **CMLC 6; DA; DAB; DAC;
DAM MST; WLCS**
See also DLB 115
Aurelius
See Bourne, Randolph S(illiman)
Aurobindo, Sri
See Ghose, Aurabinda
Austen, Jane 1775-1817 **NCLC 1, 13, 19, 33, 51;
DA; DAB; DAC; DAM MST, NOV; WLC**
See also AAYA 19; CDBLB 1789-1832; DLB
116
Auster, Paul 1947- .... **CLC 47**
See also CA 69-72; CANR 23, 52, 75; MTCW 1

Austin, Frank
See Faust, Frederick (Schiller)
Austin, Mary (Hunter) 1868-1934 .. **TCLC 25**
See also CA 109; DLB 9, 78, 206
Autran Dourado, Waldomiro
See Dourado, (Waldomiro Freitas) Autran
Averroes 1126-1198 .... **CMLC 7**
See also DLB 115
Avicenna 980-1037 .... **CMLC 16**
See also DLB 115
Avison, Margaret 1918- .. **CLC 2, 4, 97; DAC;
DAM POET**
See also CA 17-20R; DLB 53; MTCW 1
Axton, David
See Koontz, Dean R(ay)
Ayckbourn, Alan 1939- . **CLC 5, 8, 18, 33, 74;
DAB; DAM DRAM**
See also CA 21-24R; CANR 31, 59; DLB 13;
MTCW 1, 2
Aydy, Catherine
See Tennant, Emma (Christina)
Ayme, Marcel (Andre) 1902-1967 ...... **CLC 11**
See also CA 89-92; CANR 67; CLR 25; DLB
72; SATA 91
Ayrton, Michael 1921-1975 .... **CLC 7**
See also CA 5-8R; 61-64; CANR 9, 21
Azorin .... **CLC 11**
See also Martinez Ruiz, Jose
Azuela, Mariano 1873-1952 .. **TCLC 3; DAM
MULT; HLC**
See also CA 104; 131; HW; MTCW 1, 2
Baastad, Babbis Friis
See Friis-Baastad, Babbis Ellinor
Bab
See Gilbert, W(illiam) S(chwenck)
Babbis, Eleanor
See Friis-Baastad, Babbis Ellinor
Babel, Isaac
See Babel, Isaak (Emmanuilovich)
Babel, Isaak (Emmanuilovich) 1894-1941(?)
TCLC 2, 13; SSC 16
See also CA 104; 155; MTCW 1
Babits, Mihaly 1883-1941 .... **TCLC 14**
See also CA 114
Babur 1483-1530 .... **LC 18**
Bacchelli, Riccardo 1891-1985 .... **CLC 19**
See also CA 29-32R; 117
Bach, Richard (David) 1936- .. **CLC 14; DAM
NOV, POP**
See also AITN 1; BEST 89:2; CA 9-12R; CANR
18; MTCW 1; SATA 13
Bachman, Richard
See King, Stephen (Edwin)
Bachmann, Ingeborg 1926-1973 .... **CLC 69**
See also CA 93-96; 45-48; CANR 69; DLB 85
Bacon, Francis 1561-1626 .... **LC 18, 32**
See also CDBLB Before 1660; DLB 151
Bacon, Roger 1214(?)-1292 .... **CMLC 14**
See also DLB 115
Bacovia, George .... **TCLC 24**
See also Vasiliu, Gheorghe
Badanes, Jerome 1937- .... **CLC 59**
Bagehot, Walter 1826-1877 .... **NCLC 10**
See also DLB 55
Bagnold, Enid 1889-1981 .... **CLC 25; DAM
DRAM**
See also CA 5-8R; 103; CANR 5, 40; DLB 13,
160, 191; MAICYA; SATA 1, 25
Bagritsky, Eduard 1895-1934 .... **TCLC 60**
Bagrjana, Elisaveta
See Belcheva, Elisaveta
Bagryana, Elisaveta .... **CLC 10**
See also Belcheva, Elisaveta

See also DLB 147
Bailey, Paul 1937- .... **CLC 45**
See also CA 21-24R; CANR 16, 62; DLB 14
Baillie, Joanna 1762-1851 .... **NCLC 71**
See also DLB 93
Bainbridge, Beryl (Margaret) 1933- **CLC 4, 5,
8, 10, 14, 18, 22, 62; DAM NOV**
See also CA 21-24R; CANR 24, 55, 75; DLB
14; MTCW 1, 2
Baker, Elliott 1922- .... **CLC 8**
See also CA 45-48; CANR 2, 63
Baker, Jean H. .... **TCLC 3, 10**
See also Russell, George William
Baker, Nicholson 1957- .. **CLC 61; DAM POP**
See also CA 135; CANR 63
Baker, Ray Stannard 1870-1946 ..... **TCLC 47**
See also CA 118
Baker, Russell (Wayne) 1925- .... **CLC 31**
See also BEST 89:4; CA 57-60; CANR 11, 41,
59; MTCW 1, 2
Bakhtin, M.
See Bakhtin, Mikhail Mikhailovich
Bakhtin, M. M.
See Bakhtin, Mikhail Mikhailovich
Bakhtin, Mikhail
See Bakhtin, Mikhail Mikhailovich
Bakhtin, Mikhail Mikhailovich 1895-1975 **CLC
83**
See also CA 128; 113
Bakshi, Ralph 1938(?)- .... **CLC 26**
See also CA 112; 138
Bakunin, Mikhail (Alexandrovich) 1814-1876
NCLC 25, 58
Baldwin, James (Arthur) 1924-1987 **CLC 1, 2,
3, 4, 5, 8, 13, 15, 17, 42, 50, 67, 90; BLC 1;
DA; DAB; DAC; DAM MST, MULT, NOV,
POP; DC 1; SSC 10, 33; WLC**
See also AAYA 4; BW 1; CA 1-4R; 124; CABS
1; CANR 3, 24; CDALB 1941-1968; DLB 2,
7, 33; DLBY 87; MTCW 1, 2; SATA 9;
SATA-Obit 54
Ballard, J(ames) G(raham) 1930- **CLC 3, 6, 14,
36; DAM NOV, POP; SSC 1**
See also AAYA 3; CA 5-8R; CANR 15, 39, 65;
DLB 14, 207; MTCW 1, 2; SATA 93
Balmont, Konstantin (Dmitriyevich) 1867-1943
TCLC 11
See also CA 109; 155
Baltausis, Vincas
See Mikszath, Kalman
Balzac, Honore de 1799-1850 **NCLC 5, 35, 53;
DA; DAB; DAC; DAM MST, NOV; SSC 5;
WLC**
See also DLB 119
Bambara, Toni Cade 1939-1995 . **CLC 19, 88;
BLC 1; DA; DAC; DAM MST, MULT;
WLCS**
See also AAYA 5; BW 2; CA 29-32R; 150;
CANR 24, 49; DLB 38; MTCW 1, 2
Bamdad, A.
See Shamlu, Ahmad
Banat, D. R.
See Bradbury, Ray (Douglas)
Bancroft, Laura
See Baum, L(yman) Frank
Banim, John 1798-1842 .... **NCLC 13**
See also DLB 116, 158, 159
Banim, Michael 1796-1874 .... **NCLC 13**
See also DLB 158, 159
Banjo, The
See Paterson, A(ndrew) B(arton)
Banks, Iain
See Banks, Iain M(enzies)

Banks, Iain M(enzies) 1954- .... **CLC 34**
See also CA 123; 128; CANR 61; DLB 194; INT
128

Banks, Lynne Reid .... **CLC 23**
See also Reid Banks, Lynne
See also AAYA 6

Banks, Russell 1940- .... **CLC 37, 72**
See also CA 65-68; CAAS 15; CANR 19, 52,
73; DLB 130

Banville, John 1945- .... **CLC 46, 118**
See also CA 117; 128; DLB 14; INT 128

Banville, Theodore (Faullain) de 1832-1891
NCLC 9

Baraka, Amiri 1934-**CLC 1, 2, 3, 5, 10, 14, 33,
115; BLC 1; DA; DAC; DAM MST, MULT,
POET, POP; DC 6; PC 4; WLCS**
See also Jones, LeRoi
See also BW 2; CA 21-24R; CABS 3; CANR 27,
38, 61; CDALB 1941-1968; DLB 5, 7, 16,
38; DLBD 8; MTCW 1, 2

Barbauld, Anna Laetitia 1743-1825 **NCLC 50**
See also DLB 107, 109, 142, 158

Barbellion, W. N. P. .... **TCLC 24**
See also Cummings, Bruce F(rederick)

Barbera, Jack (Vincent) 1945- .... **CLC 44**
See also CA 110; CANR 45

Barbey d'Aurevilly, Jules Amedee 1808-1889
NCLC 1; SSC 17
See also DLB 119

Barbour, John c. 1316-1395 .... **CMLC 33**
See also DLB 146

Barbusse, Henri 1873-1935 .... **TCLC 5**
See also CA 105; 154; DLB 65

Barclay, Bill
See Moorcock, Michael (John)

Barclay, William Ewert
See Moorcock, Michael (John)

Barea, Arturo 1897-1957 .... **TCLC 14**
See also CA 111

Barfoot, Joan 1946- .... **CLC 18**
See also CA 105

Baring, Maurice 1874-1945 .... **TCLC 8**
See also CA 105; 168; DLB 34

Baring-Gould, Sabine 1834-1924 .... **TCLC 88**
See also DLB 156, 190

Barker, Clive 1952- .... **CLC 52; DAM POP**
See also AAYA 10; BEST 90:3; CA 121; 129;
CANR 71; INT 129; MTCW 1, 2

Barker, George Granville 1913-1991 . **CLC 8,
48; DAM POET**
See also CA 9-12R; 135; CANR 7, 38; DLB 20;
MTCW 1

Barker, Harley Granville
See Granville-Barker, Harley
See also DLB 10

Barker, Howard 1946- .... **CLC 37**
See also CA 102; DLB 13

Barker, Jane 1652-1732 .... **LC 42**

Barker, Pat(ricia) 1943- .... **CLC 32, 94**
See also CA 117; 122; CANR 50; INT 122

Barlach, Ernst 1870-1938 .... **TCLC 84**
See also DLB 56, 118

Barlow, Joel 1754-1812 .... **NCLC 23**
See also DLB 37

Barnard, Mary (Ethel) 1909- .... **CLC 48**
See also CA 21-22; CAP 2

Barnes, Djuna 1892-1982 **CLC 3, 4, 8, 11, 29;
SSC 3**
See also CA 9-12R; 107; CANR 16, 55; DLB 4,
9, 45; MTCW 1, 2

Barnes, Julian (Patrick) 1946- **CLC 42; DAB**
See also CA 102; CANR 19, 54; DLB 194;
DLBY 93; MTCW 1

Barnes, Peter 1931- .... **CLC 5, 56**
See also CA 65-68; CAAS 12; CANR 33, 34,
64; DLB 13; MTCW 1

Barnes, William 1801-1886 .... **NCLC 75**
See also DLB 32

Baroja (y Nessi), Pio 1872-1956**TCLC 8; HLC**
See also CA 104

Baron, David
See Pinter, Harold

Baron Corvo
See Rolfe, Frederick (William Serafino Austin
Lewis Mary)

Barondess, Sue K(aufman) 1926-1977 **CLC 8**
See also Kaufman, Sue
See also CA 1-4R; 69-72; CANR 1

Baron de Teive
See Pessoa, Fernando (Antonio Nogueira)

Baroness V.
See Zangwill, Israel

Barres, (Auguste-) Maurice 1862-1923 **T C L C
47**
See also CA 164; DLB 123

Barreto, Afonso Henrique de Lima
See Lima Barreto, Afonso Henrique de

Barrett, (Roger) Syd 1946- .... **CLC 35**

Barrett, William (Christopher) 1913-1992
CLC 27
See also CA 13-16R; 139; CANR 11, 67; INT
CANR-11

Barrie, J(ames) M(atthew) 1860-1937**TCLC 2;
DAB; DAM DRAM**
See also CA 104; 136; CANR 77; CDBLB
1890-1914; CLR 16; DLB 10, 141, 156;
MAICYA; MTCW 1; SATA 100; YABC 1

Barrington, Michael
See Moorcock, Michael (John)

Barrol, Grady
See Bograd, Larry

Barry, Mike
See Malzberg, Barry N(athaniel)

Barry, Philip 1896-1949 .... **TCLC 11**
See also CA 109; DLB 7

Bart, Andre Schwarz
See Schwarz-Bart, Andre

Barth, John (Simmons) 1930-**CLC 1, 2, 3, 5, 7,
9, 10, 14, 27, 51, 89; DAM NOV; SSC 10**
See also AITN 1, 2; CA 1-4R; CABS 1; CANR
5, 23, 49, 64; DLB 2; MTCW 1

Barthelme, Donald 1931-1989**CLC 1, 2, 3, 5, 6,
8, 13, 23, 46, 59, 115; DAM NOV; SSC 2**
See also CA 21-24R; 129; CANR 20, 58; DLB
2; DLBY 80, 89; MTCW 1, 2; SATA 7;
SATA-Obit 62

Barthelme, Frederick 1943- .... **CLC 36, 117**
See also CA 114; 122; CANR 77; DLBY 85; INT
122

Barthes, Roland (Gerard) 1915-1980 **CLC 24,
83**
See also CA 130; 97-100; CANR 66; MTCW 1,
2

Barzun, Jacques (Martin) 1907- .... **CLC 51**
See also CA 61-64; CANR 22

Bashevis, Isaac
See Singer, Isaac Bashevis

Bashkirtseff, Marie 1859-1884 .... **NCLC 27**

Basho
See Matsuo Basho

Bass, Kingsley B., Jr.
See Bullins, Ed

Bass, Rick 1958- .... **CLC 79**
See also CA 126; CANR 53; DLB 212

Bassani, Giorgio 1916- .... **CLC 9**
See also CA 65-68; CANR 33; DLB 128, 177;
MTCW 1

Bastos, Augusto (Antonio) Roa
See Roa Bastos, Augusto (Antonio)

Bataille, Georges 1897-1962 .... **CLC 29**
See also CA 101; 89-92

Bates, H(erbert) E(rnest) 1905-1974 **CLC 46;
DAB; DAM POP; SSC 10**
See also CA 93-96; 45-48; CANR 34; DLB 162,
191; MTCW 1, 2

Bauchart
See Camus, Albert

Baudelaire, Charles 1821-1867**NCLC 6, 29, 55;
DA; DAB; DAC; DAM MST, POET; PC 1;
SSC 18; WLC**

Baudrillard, Jean 1929- .... **CLC 60**

Baum, L(yman) Frank 1856-1919 ..... **TCLC 7**
See also CA 108; 133; CLR 15; DLB 22; JRDA;
MAICYA; MTCW 1, 2; SATA 18, 100

Baum, Louis F.
See Baum, L(yman) Frank

Baumbach, Jonathan 1933- .... **CLC 6, 23**
See also CA 13-16R; CAAS 5; CANR 12, 66;
DLBY 80; INT CANR-12; MTCW 1

Bausch, Richard (Carl) 1945- .... **CLC 51**
See also CA 101; CAAS 14; CANR 43, 61; DLB
130

Baxter, Charles (Morley) 1947- . **CLC 45, 78;
DAM POP**
See also CA 57-60; CANR 40, 64; DLB 130;
MTCW 2

Baxter, George Owen
See Faust, Frederick (Schiller)

Baxter, James K(eir) 1926-1972 .... **CLC 14**
See also CA 77-80

Baxter, John
See Hunt, E(verette) Howard, (Jr.)

Bayer, Sylvia
See Glassco, John

Baynton, Barbara 1857-1929 .... **TCLC 57**

Beagle, Peter S(oyer) 1939- .... **CLC 7, 104**
See also CA 9-12R; CANR 4, 51, 73; DLBY 80;
INT CANR-4; MTCW 1; SATA 60

Bean, Normal
See Burroughs, Edgar Rice

Beard, Charles A(ustin) 1874-1948 **TCLC 15**
See also CA 115; DLB 17; SATA 18

Beardsley, Aubrey 1872-1898 .... **NCLC 6**

Beattie, Ann 1947-**CLC 8, 13, 18, 40, 63; DAM
NOV, POP; SSC 11**
See also BEST 90:2; CA 81-84; CANR 53, 73;
DLBY 82; MTCW 1, 2

Beattie, James 1735-1803 .... **NCLC 25**
See also DLB 109

Beauchamp, Kathleen Mansfield 1888-1923
See Mansfield, Katherine
See also CA 104; 134; DA; DAC; DAM MST;
MTCW 2

Beaumarchais, Pierre-Augustin Caron de
1732-1799 .... **DC 4**
See also DAM DRAM

Beaumont, Francis 1584(?)-1616**LC 33; DC 6**
See also CDBLB Before 1660; DLB 58, 121

**Beauvoir, Simone (Lucie Ernestine Marie
Bertrand) de** 1908-1986**CLC 1, 2, 4, 8, 14,
31, 44, 50, 71; DA; DAB; DAC; DAM MST,
NOV; WLC**
See also CA 9-12R; 118; CANR 28, 61; DLB
72; DLBY 86; MTCW 1, 2

Becker, Carl (Lotus) 1873-1945 ...... **TCLC 63**
See also CA 157; DLB 17

Berger, Melvin H. 1927- .... **CLC 12**
  See also CA 5-8R; CANR 4; CLR 32; SAAS 2;
  SATA 5, 88
Berger, Thomas (Louis) 1924-**CLC 3, 5, 8, 11,**
  18, 38; DAM NOV
  See also CA 1-4R; CANR 5, 28, 51; DLB 2;
  DLBY 80; INT CANR-28; MTCW 1, 2
Bergman, (Ernst) Ingmar 1918- ..**CLC 16, 72**
  See also CA 81-84; CANR 33, 70; MTCW 2
Bergson, Henri(-Louis) 1859-1941 . **TCLC 32**
  See also CA 164
Bergstein, Eleanor 1938- .... **CLC 4**
  See also CA 53-56; CANR 5
Berkoff, Steven 1937- .... **CLC 56**
  See also CA 104; CANR 72
Bermant, Chaim (Icyk) 1929- .... **CLC 40**
  See also CA 57-60; CANR 6, 31, 57
Bern, Victoria
  See Fisher, M(ary) F(rances) K(ennedy)
Bernanos, (Paul Louis) Georges 1888-1948
  TCLC 3
  See also CA 104; 130; DLB 72
Bernard, April 1956- .... **CLC 59**
  See also CA 131
Berne, Victoria
  See Fisher, M(ary) F(rances) K(ennedy)
Bernhard, Thomas 1931-1989 .. **CLC 3, 32, 61**
  See also CA 85-88; 127; CANR 32, 57; DLB 85,
  124; MTCW 1
Bernhardt, Sarah (Henriette Rosine) 1844-1923
  TCLC 75
  See also CA 157
Berriault, Gina 1926- ... **CLC 54, 109; SSC 30**
  See also CA 116; 129; CANR 66; DLB 130
Berrigan, Daniel 1921- .... **CLC 4**
  See also CA 33-36R; CAAS 1; CANR 11, 43,
  78; DLB 5
Berrigan, Edmund Joseph Michael, Jr.
  1934-1983
  See Berrigan, Ted
  See also CA 61-64; 110; CANR 14
Berrigan, Ted .... **CLC 37**
  See also Berrigan, Edmund Joseph Michael, Jr.
  See also DLB 5, 169
Berry, Charles Edward Anderson 1931-
  See Berry, Chuck
  See also CA 115
Berry, Chuck .... **CLC 17**
  See also Berry, Charles Edward Anderson
Berry, Jonas
  See Ashbery, John (Lawrence)
Berry, Wendell (Erdman) 1934-**CLC 4, 6, 8, 27,**
  46; DAM POET
  See also AITN 1; CA 73-76; CANR 50, 73; DLB
  5, 6; MTCW 1
Berryman, John 1914-1972**CLC 1, 2, 3, 4, 6, 8,**
  10, 13, 25, 62; DAM POET
  See also CA 13-16; 33-36R; CABS 2; CANR 35;
  CAP 1; CDALB 1941-1968; DLB 48; MTCW
  1, 2
Bertolucci, Bernardo 1940- .... **CLC 16**
  See also CA 106
Berton, Pierre (Francis Demarigny) 1920-
  CLC 104
  See also CA 1-4R; CANR 2, 56; DLB 68; SATA
  99
Bertrand, Aloysius 1807-1841 .... **NCLC 31**
Bertran de Born c. 1140-1215 .... **CMLC 5**
Besant, Annie (Wood) 1847-1933 ...... **TCLC 9**
  See also CA 105
Bessie, Alvah 1904-1985 .... **CLC 23**
  See also CA 5-8R; 116; CANR 2; DLB 26

Bethlen, T. D.
  See Silverberg, Robert
Beti, Mongo .... **CLC 27; BLC 1; DAM MULT**
  See also Biyidi, Alexandre
Betjeman, John 1906-1984**CLC 2, 6, 10, 34, 43;**
  DAB; DAM MST, POET
  See also CA 9-12R; 112; CANR 33, 56; CDBLB
  1945-1960; DLB 20; DLBY 84; MTCW 1, 2
Bettelheim, Bruno 1903-1990 .... **CLC 79**
  See also CA 81-84; 131; CANR 23, 61; MTCW
  1, 2
Betti, Ugo 1892-1953 .... **TCLC 5**
  See also CA 104; 155
Betts, Doris (Waugh) 1932- .... **CLC 3, 6, 28**
  See also CA 13-16R; CANR 9, 66, 77; DLBY
  82; INT CANR-9
Bevan, Alistair
  See Roberts, Keith (John Kingston)
Bey, Pilaff
  See Douglas, (George) Norman
Bialik, Chaim Nachman 1873-1934 **TCLC 25**
  See also CA 170
Bickerstaff, Isaac
  See Swift, Jonathan
Bidart, Frank 1939- .... **CLC 33**
  See also CA 140
Bienek, Horst 1930- .... **CLC 7, 11**
  See also CA 73-76; DLB 75
Bierce, Ambrose (Gwinett) 1842-1914(?)
  TCLC 1, 7, 44; DA; DAC; DAM MST; SSC
  9; WLC
  See also CA 104; 139; CANR 78; CDALB
  1865-1917; DLB 11, 12, 23, 71, 74, 186
Biggers, Earl Derr 1884-1933 .... **TCLC 65**
  See also CA 108; 153
Billings, Josh
  See Shaw, Henry Wheeler
<indexbody>Billington, (Lady) Rachel (Mary)**
  1942-   **CLC 43**
  See also AITN 2; CA 33-36R; CANR 44
Binyon, T(imothy) J(ohn) 1936- .... **CLC 34**
  See also CA 111; CANR 28
Bioy Casares, Adolfo 1914-1984 **CLC 4, 8, 13,**
  88; DAM MULT; HLC; SSC 17
  See also CA 29-32R; CANR 19, 43, 66; DLB
  113; HW; MTCW 1, 2
Bird, Cordwainer
  See Ellison, Harlan (Jay)
Bird, Robert Montgomery 1806-1854**NCLC 1**
  See also DLB 202
Birkerts, Sven 1951- .... **CLC 116**
  See also CA 128; 133; CAAS 29; INT 133
Birney, (Alfred) Earle 1904-1995 **CLC 1, 4, 6,**
  11; DAC; DAM MST, POET
  See also CA 1-4R; CANR 5, 20; DLB 88; MTCW
  1
Biruni, al 973-1048(?) .... **CMLC 28**
Bishop, Elizabeth 1911-1979**CLC 1, 4, 9, 13, 15,**
  32; DA; DAC; DAM MST, POET; PC 3
  See also CA 5-8R; 89-92; CABS 2; CANR 26,
  61; CDALB 1968-1988; DLB 5, 169; MTCW
  1, 2; SATA-Obit 24
Bishop, John 1935- .... **CLC 10**
  See also CA 105
Bissett, Bill 1939- .... **CLC 18; PC 14**
  See also CA 69-72; CAAS 19; CANR 15; DLB
  53; MTCW 1
Bitov, Andrei (Georgievich) 1937- ..... **CLC 57**
  See also CA 142
Biyidi, Alexandre 1932-
  See Beti, Mongo
  See also BW 1; CA 114; 124; MTCW 1, 2

Bjarme, Brynjolf
  See Ibsen, Henrik (Johan)
Bjoernson, Bjoernstjerne (Martinius)
  1832-1910 .... **TCLC 7, 37**
  See also CA 104
Black, Robert
  See Holdstock, Robert P.
Blackburn, Paul 1926-1971 .... **CLC 9, 43**
  See also CA 81-84; 33-36R; CANR 34; DLB 16;
  DLBY 81
Black Elk 1863-1950 **TCLC 33; DAM MULT**
  See also CA 144; MTCW 1; NNAL
Black Hobart
  See Sanders, (James) Ed(ward)
Blacklin, Malcolm
  See Chambers, Aidan
Blackmore, R(ichard) D(oddridge) 1825-1900
  TCLC 27
  See also CA 120; DLB 18
Blackmur, R(ichard) P(almer) 1904-1965**C L C**
  2, 24
  See also CA 11-12; 25-28R; CANR 71; CAP 1;
  DLB 63
Black Tarantula
  See Acker, Kathy
Blackwood, Algernon (Henry) 1869-1951
  TCLC 5
  See also CA 105; 150; DLB 153, 156, 178
Blackwood, Caroline 1931-1996**CLC 6, 9, 100**
  See also CA 85-88; 151; CANR 32, 61, 65; DLB
  14, 207; MTCW 1
Blade, Alexander
  See Hamilton, Edmond; Silverberg, Robert
Blaga, Lucian 1895-1961 .... **CLC 75**
  See also CA 157
Blair, Eric (Arthur) 1903-1950
  See Orwell, George
  See also CA 104; 132; DA; DAB; DAC; DAM
  MST, NOV; MTCW 1, 2; SATA 29
Blair, Hugh 1718-1800 .... **NCLC 75**
Blais, Marie-Claire 1939- **CLC 2, 4, 6, 13, 22;**
  DAC; DAM MST
  See also CA 21-24R; CAAS 4; CANR 38, 75;
  DLB 53; MTCW 1, 2
Blaise, Clark 1940- .... **CLC 29**
  See also AITN 2; CA 53-56; CAAS 3; CANR 5,
  66; DLB 53
Blake, Fairley
  See De Voto, Bernard (Augustine)
Blake, Nicholas
  See Day Lewis, C(ecil)
  See also DLB 77
Blake, William 1757-1827 .. **NCLC 13, 37, 57;**
  DA; DAB; DAC; DAM MST, POET; PC 12;
  WLC
  See also CDBLB 1789-1832; CLR 52; DLB 93,
  163; MAICYA; SATA 30
Blasco Ibanez, Vicente 1867-1928 .. **TCLC 12;**
  DAM NOV
  See also CA 110; 131; HW; MTCW 1
Blatty, William Peter 1928-**CLC 2; DAM POP**
  See also CA 5-8R; CANR 9
Bleeck, Oliver
  See Thomas, Ross (Elmore)
Blessing, Lee 1949-............................. **CLC 54**
Blish, James (Benjamin) 1921-1975 ..**CLC 14**
  See also CA 1-4R; 57-60; CANR 3; DLB 8;
  MTCW 1; SATA 66
Bliss, Reginald
  See Wells, H(erbert) G(eorge)
Blixen, Karen (Christentze Dinesen) 1885-1962
  See Dinesen, Isak

Brown, Dee (Alexander) 1908- ... **CLC 18, 47; DAM POP**
See also AAYA 30; CA 13-16R; CAAS 6; CANR 11, 45, 60; DLBY 80; MTCW 1, 2; SATA 5

Brown, George
See Wertmueller, Lina

Brown, George Douglas 1869-1902 **TCLC 28**
See also CA 162

Brown, George Mackay 1921-1996 **CLC 5, 48, 100**
See also CA 21-24R; 151; CAAS 6; CANR 12, 37, 67; DLB 14, 27, 139; MTCW 1; SATA 35

Brown, (William) Larry 1951- .... **CLC 73**
See also CA 130; 134; INT 133

Brown, Moses
See Barrett, William (Christopher)

Brown, Rita Mae 1944- **CLC 18, 43, 79; DAM NOV, POP**
See also CA 45-48; CANR 2, 11, 35, 62; INT CANR-11; MTCW 1, 2

Brown, Roderick (Langmere) Haig-
See Haig-Brown, Roderick (Langmere)

Brown, Rosellen 1939- .... **CLC 32**
See also CA 77-80; CAAS 10; CANR 14, 44

Brown, Sterling Allen 1901-1989 **CLC 1, 23, 59; BLC 1; DAM MULT, POET**
See also BW 1; CA 85-88; 127; CANR 26, 74; DLB 48, 51, 63; MTCW 1, 2

Brown, Will
See Ainsworth, William Harrison

Brown, William Wells 1813-1884 **NCLC 2; BLC 1; DAM MULT; DC 1**
See also DLB 3, 50

Browne, (Clyde) Jackson 1948(?)- ..... **CLC 21**
See also CA 120

Browning, Elizabeth Barrett 1806-1861 **NCLC 1, 16, 61, 66; DA; DAB; DAC; DAM MST, POET; PC 6; WLC**
See also CDBLB 1832-1890; DLB 32, 199

Browning, Robert 1812-1889 . **NCLC 19; DA; DAB; DAC; DAM MST, POET; PC 2; WLCS**
See also CDBLB 1832-1890; DLB 32, 163; YABC 1

Browning, Tod 1882-1962 .... **CLC 16**
See also CA 141; 117

Brownson, Orestes Augustus 1803-1876 **NCLC 50**
See also DLB 1, 59, 73

Bruccoli, Matthew J(oseph) 1931- ..... **CLC 34**
See also CA 9-12R; CANR 7; DLB 103

Bruce, Lenny .... **CLC 21**
See also Schneider, Leonard Alfred

Bruin, John
See Brutus, Dennis

Brulard, Henri
See Stendhal

Brulls, Christian
See Simenon, Georges (Jacques Christian)

Brunner, John (Kilian Houston) 1934-1995 **CLC 8, 10; DAM POP**
See also CA 1-4R; 149; CAAS 8; CANR 2, 37; MTCW 1, 2

Bruno, Giordano 1548-1600 .... **LC 27**

Brutus, Dennis 1924- . **CLC 43; BLC 1; DAM MULT, POET; PC 24**
See also BW 2; CA 49-52; CAAS 14; CANR 2, 27, 42; DLB 117

Bryan, C(ourtlandt) D(ixon) B(arnes) 1936- **CLC 29**
See also CA 73-76; CANR 13, 68; DLB 185; INT CANR-13

Bryan, Michael
See Moore, Brian

Bryant, William Cullen 1794-1878 **NCLC 6, 46; DA; DAB; DAC; DAM MST, POET; PC 20**
See also CDALB 1640-1865; DLB 3, 43, 59, 189

Bryusov, Valery Yakovlevich 1873-1924 **TCLC 10**
See also CA 107; 155

Buchan, John 1875-1940 **TCLC 41; DAB; DAM POP**
See also CA 108; 145; DLB 34, 70, 156; MTCW 1; YABC 2

Buchanan, George 1506-1582 .... **LC 4**
See also DLB 152

Buchheim, Lothar-Guenther 1918- ..... **CLC 6**
See also CA 85-88

Buchner, (Karl) Georg 1813-1837 .. **NCLC 26**

Buchwald, Art(hur) 1925- .... **CLC 33**
See also AITN 1; CA 5-8R; CANR 21, 67; MTCW 1, 2; SATA 10

Buck, Pearl S(ydenstricker) 1892-1973 **CLC 7, 11, 18; DA; DAB; DAC; DAM MST, NOV**
See also AITN 1; CA 1-4R; 41-44R; CANR 1, 34; DLB 9, 102; MTCW 1, 2; SATA 1, 25

Buckler, Ernest 1908-1984 ..... **CLC 13; DAC; DAM MST**
See also CA 11-12; 114; CAP 1; DLB 68; SATA 47

Buckley, Vincent (Thomas) 1925-1988 **CLC 57**
See also CA 101

Buckley, William F(rank), Jr. 1925- **CLC 7, 18, 37; DAM POP**
See also AITN 1; CA 1-4R; CANR 1, 24, 53; DLB 137; DLBY 80; INT CANR-24; MTCW 1, 2

Buechner, (Carl) Frederick 1926- **CLC 2, 4, 6, 9; DAM NOV**
See also CA 13-16R; CANR 11, 39, 64; DLBY 80; INT CANR-11; MTCW 1, 2

Buell, John (Edward) 1927- .... **CLC 10**
See also CA 1-4R; CANR 71; DLB 53

Buero Vallejo, Antonio 1916- .... **CLC 15, 46**
See also CA 106; CANR 24, 49, 75; HW; MTCW 1, 2

Bufalino, Gesualdo 1920(?)- .... **CLC 74**
See also DLB 196

Bugayev, Boris Nikolayevich 1880-1934 **TCLC 7; PC 11**
See also Bely, Andrey
See also CA 104; 165; MTCW 1

Bukowski, Charles 1920-1994 **CLC 2, 5, 9, 41, 82, 108; DAM NOV, POET; PC 18**
See also CA 17-20R; 144; CANR 40, 62; DLB 5, 130, 169; MTCW 1, 2

Bulgakov, Mikhail (Afanas'evich) 1891-1940 **TCLC 2, 16; DAM DRAM, NOV; SSC 18**
See also CA 105; 152

Bulgya, Alexander Alexandrovich 1901-1956 **TCLC 53**
See also Fadeyev, Alexander
See also CA 117

Bullins, Ed 1935- .. **CLC 1, 5, 7; BLC 1; DAM DRAM, MULT; DC 6**
See also BW 2; CA 49-52; CAAS 16; CANR 24, 46, 73; DLB 7, 38; MTCW 1, 2

Bulwer-Lytton, Edward (George Earle Lytton) 1803-1873 .... **NCLC 1, 45**
See also DLB 21

Bunin, Ivan Alexeyevich 1870-1953 . **TCLC 6; SSC 5**
See also CA 104

Bunting, Basil 1900-1985 **CLC 10, 39, 47; DAM POET**
See also CA 53-56; 115; CANR 7; DLB 20

Bunuel, Luis 1900-1983 .... **CLC 16, 80; DAM MULT; HLC**
See also CA 101; 110; CANR 32, 77; HW

Bunyan, John 1628-1688 ..... **LC 4; DA; DAB; DAC; DAM MST; WLC**
See also CDBLB 1660-1789; DLB 39

Burckhardt, Jacob (Christoph) 1818-1897 **NCLC 49**

Burford, Eleanor
See Hibbert, Eleanor Alice Burford

Burgess, Anthony CLC 1, 2, 4, 5, 8, 10, 13, 15, 22, 40, 62, 81, 94; DAB
See also Wilson, John (Anthony) Burgess
See also AAYA 25; AITN 1; CDBLB 1960 to Present; DLB 14, 194; DLBY 98; MTCW 1

Burke, Edmund 1729(?)-1797 . **LC 7, 36; DA; DAB; DAC; DAM MST; WLC**
See also DLB 104

Burke, Kenneth (Duva) 1897-1993 **CLC 2, 24**
See also CA 5-8R; 143; CANR 39, 74; DLB 45, 63; MTCW 1, 2

Burke, Leda
See Garnett, David

Burke, Ralph
See Silverberg, Robert

Burke, Thomas 1886-1945 .... **TCLC 63**
See also CA 113; 155; DLB 197

Burney, Fanny 1752-1840 .... **NCLC 12, 54**
See also DLB 39

Burns, Robert 1759-1796 .. **LC 3, 29, 40; DA; DAB; DAC; DAM MST, POET; PC 6; WLC**
See also CDBLB 1789-1832; DLB 109

Burns, Tex
See L'Amour, Louis (Dearborn)

Burnshaw, Stanley 1906- .... **CLC 3, 13, 44**
See also CA 9-12R; DLB 48; DLBY 97

Burr, Anne 1937- .... **CLC 6**
See also CA 25-28R

Burroughs, Edgar Rice 1875-1950 **TCLC 2, 32; DAM NOV**
See also AAYA 11; CA 104; 132; DLB 8; MTCW 1, 2; SATA 41

Burroughs, William S(eward) 1914-1997 **CLC 1, 2, 5, 15, 22, 42, 75, 109; DA; DAB; DAC; DAM MST, NOV, POP; WLC**
See also AITN 2; CA 9-12R; 160; CANR 20, 52; DLB 2, 8, 16, 152; DLBY 81, 97; MTCW 1, 2

Burton, Sir Richard F(rancis) 1821-1890 **NCLC 42**
See also DLB 55, 166, 184

Busch, Frederick 1941- .... **CLC 7, 10, 18, 47**
See also CA 33-36R; CAAS 1; CANR 45, 73; DLB 6

Bush, Ronald 1946- .... **CLC 34**
See also CA 136

Bustos, F(rancisco)
See Borges, Jorge Luis

Bustos Domecq, H(onorio)
See Bioy Casares, Adolfo; Borges, Jorge Luis

Butler, Octavia E(stelle) 1947- **CLC 38; BLCS; DAM MULT, POP**
See also AAYA 18; BW 2; CA 73-76; CANR 12, 24, 38, 73; DLB 33; MTCW 1, 2; SATA 84

Butler, Robert Olen (Jr.) 1945- **CLC 81; DAM POP**
See also CA 112; CANR 66; DLB 173; INT 112; MTCW 1

Butler, Samuel 1612-1680 .... **LC 16, 43**
　See also DLB 101, 126
Butler, Samuel 1835-1902 ... **TCLC 1, 33; DA; DAB; DAC; DAM MST, NOV; WLC**
　See also CA 143; CDBLB 1890-1914; DLB 18, 57, 174
Butler, Walter C.
　See Faust, Frederick (Schiller)
Butor, Michel (Marie Francois) 1926- **CLC 1, 3, 8, 11, 15**
　See also CA 9-12R; CANR 33, 66; DLB 83; MTCW 1, 2
Butts, Mary 1892(?)-1937 .... **TCLC 77**
　See also CA 148
Buzo, Alexander (John) 1944- .... **CLC 61**
　See also CA 97-100; CANR 17, 39, 69
Buzzati, Dino 1906-1972 .... **CLC 36**
　See also CA 160; 33-36R; DLB 177
Byars, Betsy (Cromer) 1928- .... **CLC 35**
　See also AAYA 19; CA 33-36R; CANR 18, 36, 57; CLR 1, 16; DLB 52; INT CANR-18; JRDA; MAICYA; MTCW 1; SAAS 1; SATA 4, 46, 80
Byatt, A(ntonia) S(usan Drabble) 1936- . **C L C 19, 65; DAM NOV, POP**
　See also CA 13-16R; CANR 13, 33, 50, 75; DLB 14, 194; MTCW 1, 2
Byrne, David 1952- .... **CLC 26**
　See also CA 127
Byrne, John Keyes 1926-
　See Leonard, Hugh
　See also CA 102; CANR 78; INT 102
Byron, George Gordon (Noel) 1788-1824 **NCLC 2, 12; DA; DAB; DAC; DAM MST, POET; PC 16; WLC**
　See also CDBLB 1789-1832; DLB 96, 110
Byron, Robert 1905-1941 .... **TCLC 67**
　See also CA 160; DLB 195
C. 3. 3.
　See Wilde, Oscar
Caballero, Fernan 1796-1877 .... **NCLC 10**
Cabell, Branch
　See Cabell, James Branch
Cabell, James Branch 1879-1958 ...... **TCLC 6**
　See also CA 105; 152; DLB 9, 78; MTCW 1
Cable, George Washington 1844-1925 **TCLC 4; SSC 4**
　See also CA 104; 155; DLB 12, 74; DLBD 13
Cabral de Melo Neto, Joao 1920- .... **CLC 76; DAM MULT**
　See also CA 151
Cabrera Infante, G(uillermo) 1929- **CLC 5, 25, 45; DAM MULT; HLC**
　See also CA 85-88; CANR 29, 65; DLB 113; HW; MTCW 1, 2
Cade, Toni
　See Bambara, Toni Cade
Cadmus and Harmonia
　See Buchan, John
Caedmon fl. 658-680 .... **CMLC 7**
　See also DLB 146
Caeiro, Alberto
　See Pessoa, Fernando (Antonio Nogueira)
Cage, John (Milton, Jr.) 1912-1992 ... **CLC 41**
　See also CA 13-16R; 169; CANR 9, 78; DLB 193; INT CANR-9
Cahan, Abraham 1860-1951 .... **TCLC 71**
　See also CA 108; 154; DLB 9, 25, 28
Cain, G.
　See Cabrera Infante, G(uillermo)
Cain, Guillermo
　See Cabrera Infante, G(uillermo)

Cain, James M(allahan) 1892-1977 **CLC 3, 11, 28**
　See also AITN 1; CA 17-20R; 73-76; CANR 8, 34, 61; MTCW 1
Caine, Mark
　See Raphael, Frederic (Michael)
Calasso, Roberto 1941- .... **CLC 81**
　See also CA 143
Calderon de la Barca, Pedro 1600-1681 **LC 23; DC 3**
Caldwell, Erskine (Preston) 1903-1987 **CLC 1, 8, 14, 50, 60; DAM NOV; SSC 19**
　See also AITN 1; CA 1-4R; 121; CAAS 1; CANR 2, 33; DLB 9, 86; MTCW 1, 2
Caldwell, (Janet Miriam) Taylor (Holland) 1900-1985 **CLC 2, 28, 39; DAM NOV, POP**
　See also CA 5-8R; 116; CANR 5; DLBD 17
Calhoun, John Caldwell 1782-1850 **NCLC 15**
　See also DLB 3
Calisher, Hortense 1911- **CLC 2, 4, 8, 38; DAM NOV; SSC 15**
　See also CA 1-4R; CANR 1, 22, 67; DLB 2; INT CANR-22; MTCW 1, 2
Callaghan, Morley Edward 1903-1990 **CLC 3, 14, 41, 65; DAC; DAM MST**
　See also CA 9-12R; 132; CANR 33, 73; DLB 68; MTCW 1, 2
Callimachus c. 305B.C.-c. 240B.C. . **CMLC 18**
　See also DLB 176
Calvin, John 1509-1564 .... **LC 37**
Calvino, Italo 1923-1985 **CLC 5, 8, 11, 22, 33, 39, 73; DAM NOV; SSC 3**
　See also CA 85-88; 116; CANR 23, 61; DLB 196; MTCW 1, 2
Cameron, Carey 1952- .... **CLC 59**
　See also CA 135
Cameron, Peter 1959- .... **CLC 44**
　See also CA 125; CANR 50
Campana, Dino 1885-1932 .... **TCLC 20**
　See also CA 117; DLB 114
Campanella, Tommaso 1568-1639 .... **LC 32**
Campbell, John W(ood, Jr.) 1910-1971 **CLC 32**
　See also CA 21-22; 29-32R; CANR 34; CAP 2; DLB 8; MTCW 1
Campbell, Joseph 1904-1987 .... **CLC 69**
　See also AAYA 3; BEST 89:2; CA 1-4R; 124; CANR 3, 28, 61; MTCW 1, 2
Campbell, Maria 1940- .... **CLC 85; DAC**
　See also CA 102; CANR 54; NNAL
Campbell, (John) Ramsey 1946- **CLC 42; SSC 19**
　See also CA 57-60; CANR 7; INT CANR-7
Campbell, (Ignatius) Roy (Dunnachie) 1901-1957 .... **TCLC 5**
　See also CA 104; 155; DLB 20; MTCW 2
Campbell, Thomas 1777-1844 .... **NCLC 19**
　See also DLB 93; 144
Campbell, Wilfred .... **TCLC 9**
　See also Campbell, William
Campbell, William 1858(?)-1918
　See Campbell, Wilfred
　See also CA 106; DLB 92
Campion, Jane .... **CLC 95**
　See also CA 138
Campos, Alvaro de
　See Pessoa, Fernando (Antonio Nogueira)
Camus, Albert 1913-1960 **CLC 1, 2, 4, 9, 11, 14, 32, 63, 69; DA; DAB; DAC; DAM DRAM, MST, NOV; DC 2; SSC 9; WLC**
　See also CA 89-92; DLB 72; MTCW 1, 2
Canby, Vincent 1924- .... **CLC 13**
　See also CA 81-84

Cancale
　See Desnos, Robert
Canetti, Elias 1905-1994 **CLC 3, 14, 25, 75, 86**
　See also CA 21-24R; 146; CANR 23, 61; DLB 85, 124; MTCW 1, 2
Canfield, Dorothea F.
　See Fisher, Dorothy (Frances) Canfield
Canfield, Dorothea Frances
　See Fisher, Dorothy (Frances) Canfield
Canfield, Dorothy
　See Fisher, Dorothy (Frances) Canfield
Canin, Ethan 1960- .... **CLC 55**
　See also CA 131; 135
Cannon, Curt
　See Hunter, Evan
Cao, Lan 1961- .... **CLC 109**
　See also CA 165
Cape, Judith
　See Page, P(atricia) K(athleen)
Capek, Karel 1890-1938 **TCLC 6, 37; DA; DAB; DAC; DAM DRAM, MST, NOV; DC 1; WLC**
　See also CA 104; 140; MTCW 1
Capote, Truman 1924-1984 **CLC 1, 3, 8, 13, 19, 34, 38, 58; DA; DAB; DAC; DAM MST, NOV, POP; SSC 2; WLC**
　See also CA 5-8R; 113; CANR 18, 62; CDALB 1941-1968; DLB 2, 185; DLBY 80, 84; MTCW 1, 2; SATA 91
Capra, Frank 1897-1991 .... **CLC 16**
　See also CA 61-64; 135
Caputo, Philip 1941- .... **CLC 32**
　See also CA 73-76; CANR 40
Caragiale, Ion Luca 1852-1912 .... **TCLC 76**
　See also CA 157
Card, Orson Scott 1951- **CLC 44, 47, 50; DAM POP**
　See also AAYA 11; CA 102; CANR 27, 47, 73; INT CANR-27; MTCW 1, 2; SATA 83
Cardenal, Ernesto 1925- **CLC 31; DAM MULT, POET; HLC; PC 22**
　See also CA 49-52; CANR 2, 32, 66; HW; MTCW 1, 2
Cardozo, Benjamin N(athan) 1870-1938 **TCLC 65**
　See also CA 117; 164
Carducci, Giosue (Alessandro Giuseppe) 1835-1907 .... **TCLC 32**
　See also CA 163
Carew, Thomas 1595(?)-1640 .... **LC 13**
　See also DLB 126
Carey, Ernestine Gilbreth 1908- .... **CLC 17**
　See also CA 5-8R; CANR 71; SATA 2
Carey, Peter 1943- .... **CLC 40, 55, 96**
　See also CA 123; 127; CANR 53, 76; INT 127; MTCW 1, 2; SATA 94
Carleton, William 1794-1869 .... **NCLC 3**
　See also DLB 159
Carlisle, Henry (Coffin) 1926- .... **CLC 33**
　See also CA 13-16R; CANR 15
Carlsen, Chris
　See Holdstock, Robert P.
Carlson, Ron(ald F.) 1947- .... **CLC 54**
　See also CA 105; CANR 27
Carlyle, Thomas 1795-1881 ...**NCLC 70; DA; DAB; DAC; DAM MST**
　See also CDBLB 1789-1832; DLB 55; 144
Carman, (William) Bliss 1861-1929 . **TCLC 7; DAC**
　See also CA 104; 152; DLB 92
Carnegie, Dale 1888-1955 .... **TCLC 53**
Carossa, Hans 1878-1956 .... **TCLC 48**
　See also CA 170; DLB 66

Chapman, George 1559(?)-1634 **LC 22; DAM DRAM**
See also DLB 62, 121

Chapman, Graham 1941-1989 .... **CLC 21**
See also Monty Python
See also CA 116; 129; CANR 35

Chapman, John Jay 1862-1933 .... **TCLC 7**
See also CA 104

Chapman, Lee
See Bradley, Marion Zimmer

Chapman, Walker
See Silverberg, Robert

Chappell, Fred (Davis) 1936- .... **CLC 40, 78**
See also CA 5-8R; CAAS 4; CANR 8, 33, 67; DLB 6, 105

Char, Rene(-Emile) 1907-1988 **CLC 9, 11, 14, 55; DAM POET**
See also CA 13-16R; 124; CANR 32; MTCW 1, 2

Charby, Jay
See Ellison, Harlan (Jay)

Chardin, Pierre Teilhard de
See Teilhard de Chardin, (Marie Joseph) Pierre

Charles I 1600-1649 .... **LC 13**

Charriere, Isabelle de 1740-1805 .... **NCLC 66**

Charyn, Jerome 1937- .... **CLC 5, 8, 18**
See also CA 5-8R; CAAS 1; CANR 7, 61; DLBY 83; MTCW 1

Chase, Mary (Coyle) 1907-1981 .... **DC 1**
See also CA 77-80; 105; SATA 17; SATA-Obit 29

Chase, Mary Ellen 1887-1973 .... **CLC 2**
See also CA 13-16; 41-44R; CAP 1; SATA 10

Chase, Nicholas
See Hyde, Anthony

Chateaubriand, Francois Rene de 1768-1848 **NCLC 3**
See also DLB 119

Chatterje, Sarat Chandra 1876-1936(?)
See Chatterji, Saratchandra
See also CA 109

Chatterji, Bankim Chandra 1838-1894 **N C L C 19**

Chatterji, Saratchandra .... **TCLC 13**
See also Chatterje, Sarat Chandra

Chatterton, Thomas 1752-1770 .. **LC 3; DAM POET**
See also DLB 109

Chatwin, (Charles) Bruce 1940-1989 **CLC 28, 57, 59; DAM POP**
See also AAYA 4; BEST 90:1; CA 85-88; 127; DLB 194, 204

Chaucer, Daniel
See Ford, Ford Madox

Chaucer, Geoffrey 1340(?)-1400 . **LC 17; DA; DAB; DAC; DAM MST, POET; PC 19; WLCS**
See also CDBLB Before 1660; DLB 146

Chaviaras, Strates 1935-
See Haviaras, Stratis
See also CA 105

Chayefsky, Paddy .... **CLC 23**
See also Chayefsky, Sidney
See also DLB 7, 44; DLBY 81

Chayefsky, Sidney 1923-1981
See Chayefsky, Paddy
See also CA 9-12R; 104; CANR 18; DAM DRAM

Chedid, Andree 1920- .... **CLC 47**
See also CA 145

Cheever, John 1912-1982 **CLC 3, 7, 8, 11, 15, 25, 64; DA; DAB; DAC; DAM MST, NOV, POP; SSC 1; WLC**
See also CA 5-8R; 106; CABS 1; CANR 5, 27, 76; CDALB 1941-1968; DLB 2, 102; DLBY 80, 82; INT CANR-5; MTCW 1, 2

Cheever, Susan 1943- .... **CLC 18, 48**
See also CA 103; CANR 27, 51; DLBY 82; INT CANR-27

Chekhonte, Antosha
See Chekhov, Anton (Pavlovich)

Chekhov, Anton (Pavlovich) 1860-1904 **T C L C 3, 10, 31, 55; DA; DAB; DAC; DAM DRAM, MST; DC 9; SSC 2, 28; WLC**
See also CA 104; 124; SATA 90

Chernyshevsky, Nikolay Gavrilovich 1828-1889 **NCLC 1**

Cherry, Carolyn Janice 1942-
See Cherryh, C. J.
See also CA 65-68; CANR 10

Cherryh, C. J. .... **CLC 35**
See also Cherry, Carolyn Janice
See also AAYA 24; DLBY 80; SATA 93

Chesnutt, Charles W(addell) 1858-1932 **T C L C 5, 39; BLC 1; DAM MULT; SSC 7**
See also BW 1; CA 106; 125; CANR 76; DLB 12, 50, 78; MTCW 1, 2

Chester, Alfred 1929(?)-1971 .... **CLC 49**
See also CA 33-36R; DLB 130

Chesterton, G(ilbert) K(eith) 1874-1936 **TCLC 1, 6, 64; DAM NOV, POET; SSC 1**
See also CA 104; 132; CANR 73; CDBLB 1914-1945; DLB 10, 19, 34, 70, 98, 149, 178; MTCW 1, 2; SATA 27

Chiang, Pin-chin 1904-1986
See Ding Ling
See also CA 118

Ch'ien Chung-shu 1910- .... **CLC 22**
See also CA 130; CANR 73; MTCW 1, 2

Child, L. Maria
See Child, Lydia Maria

Child, Lydia Maria 1802-1880 .... **NCLC 6, 73**
See also DLB 1, 74; SATA 67

Child, Mrs.
See Child, Lydia Maria

Child, Philip 1898-1978 .... **CLC 19, 68**
See also CA 13-14; CAP 1; SATA 47

Childers, (Robert) Erskine 1870-1922 **T C L C 65**
See also CA 113; 153; DLB 70

Childress, Alice 1920-1994 **CLC 12, 15, 86, 96; BLC 1; DAM DRAM, MULT, NOV; DC 4**
See also AAYA 8; BW 2; CA 45-48; 146; CANR 3, 27, 50, 74; CLR 14; DLB 7, 38; JRDA; MAICYA; MTCW 1, 2; SATA 7, 48, 81

Chin, Frank (Chew, Jr.) 1940- .... **DC 7**
See also CA 33-36R; CANR 71; DAM MULT; DLB 206

Chislett, (Margaret) Anne 1943- .... **CLC 34**
See also CA 151

Chitty, Thomas Willes 1926- .... **CLC 11**
See also Hinde, Thomas
See also CA 5-8R

Chivers, Thomas Holley 1809-1858 **NCLC 49**
See also DLB 3

Choi, Susan .... **CLC 119**

Chomette, Rene Lucien 1898-1981
See Clair, Rene
See also CA 103

Chopin, Kate . **TCLC 5, 14; DA; DAB; SSC 8; WLCS**
See also Chopin, Katherine
See also CDALB 1865-1917; DLB 12, 78

Chopin, Katherine 1851-1904
See Chopin, Kate
See also CA 104; 122; DAC; DAM MST, NOV

Chretien de Troyes c. 12th cent. - .... **CMLC 10**
See also DLB 208

Christie
See Ichikawa, Kon

Christie, Agatha (Mary Clarissa) 1890-1976 **CLC 1, 6, 8, 12, 39, 48, 110; DAB; DAC; DAM NOV**
See also AAYA 9; AITN 1, 2; CA 17-20R; 61-64; CANR 10, 37; CDBLB 1914-1945; DLB 13, 77; MTCW 1, 2; SATA 36

Christie, (Ann) Philippa
See Pearce, Philippa
See also CA 5-8R; CANR 4

Christine de Pizan 1365(?)-1431(?) .... **LC 9**
See also DLB 208

Chubb, Elmer
See Masters, Edgar Lee

Chulkov, Mikhail Dmitrievich 1743-1792 **LC 2**
See also DLB 150

Churchill, Caryl 1938- .... **CLC 31, 55; DC 5**
See also CA 102; CANR 22, 46; DLB 13; MTCW 1

Churchill, Charles 1731-1764 .... **LC 3**
See also DLB 109

Chute, Carolyn 1947- .... **CLC 39**
See also CA 123

Ciardi, John (Anthony) 1916-1986 **CLC 10, 40, 44; DAM POET**
See also CA 5-8R; 118; CAAS 2; CANR 5, 33; CLR 19; DLB 5; DLBY 86; INT CANR-5; MAICYA; MTCW 1, 2; SAAS 26; SATA 1, 65; SATA-Obit 46

Cicero, Marcus Tullius 106B.C.-43B.C. **C M L C 3**
See also DLB 211

Cimino, Michael 1943- .... **CLC 16**
See also CA 105

Cioran, E(mil) M. 1911-1995 .... **CLC 64**
See also CA 25-28R; 149

Cisneros, Sandra 1954- ... **CLC 69, 118; DAM MULT; HLC; SSC 32**
See also AAYA 9; CA 131; CANR 64; DLB 122, 152; HW; MTCW 2

Cixous, Helene 1937- .... **CLC 92**
See also CA 126; CANR 55; DLB 83; MTCW 1, 2

Clair, Rene .... **CLC 20**
See also Chomette, Rene Lucien

Clampitt, Amy 1920-1994 ...... **CLC 32; PC 19**
See also CA 110; 146; CANR 29; DLB 105

Clancy, Thomas L., Jr. 1947-
See Clancy, Tom
See also CA 125; 131; CANR 62; INT 131; MTCW 1, 2

Clancy, Tom ... **CLC 45, 112; DAM NOV, POP**
See also Clancy, Thomas L., Jr.
See also AAYA 9; BEST 89:1, 90:1; MTCW 2

Clare, John 1793-1864 . **NCLC 9; DAB; DAM POET; PC 23**
See also DLB 55, 96

Clarin
See Alas (y Urena), Leopoldo (Enrique Garcia)

Clark, Al C.
See Goines, Donald

Clark, (Robert) Brian 1932- .... **CLC 29**
See also CA 41-44R; CANR 67

Clark, Curt
See Westlake, Donald E(dwin)

Clark, Eleanor 1913-1996 .... **CLC 5, 19**
See also CA 9-12R; 151; CANR 41; DLB 6

Graham, Tom
See Lewis, (Harry) Sinclair
Graham, W(illiam) S(ydney) 1918-1986 . **C L C 29**
See also CA 73-76; 118; DLB 20
Graham, Winston (Mawdsley) 1910- . **CLC 23**
See also CA 49-52; CANR 2, 22, 45, 66; DLB 77
Grahame, Kenneth 1859-1932**TCLC 64; DAB**
See also CA 108; 136; CLR 5; DLB 34, 141, 178; MAICYA; MTCW 2; SATA 100; YABC 1
Granovsky, Timofei Nikolaevich 1813-1855 **NCLC 75**
See also DLB 198
Grant, Skeeter
See Spiegelman, Art
Granville-Barker, Harley 1877-1946 **TCLC 2; DAM DRAM**
See also Barker, Harley Granville
See also CA 104
Grass, Guenter (Wilhelm) 1927-**CLC 1, 2, 4, 6, 11, 15, 22, 32, 49, 88; DA; DAB; DAC; DAM MST, NOV; WLC**
See also CA 13-16R; CANR 20, 75; DLB 75, 124; MTCW 1, 2
Gratton, Thomas
See Hulme, T(homas) E(rnest)
Grau, Shirley Ann 1929- .... **CLC 4, 9; SSC 15**
See also CA 89-92; CANR 22, 69; DLB 2; INT CANR-22; MTCW 1
Gravel, Fern
See Hall, James Norman
Graver, Elizabeth 1964- .... **CLC 70**
See also CA 135; CANR 71
Graves, Richard Perceval 1945- .... **CLC 44**
See also CA 65-68; CANR 9, 26, 51
Graves, Robert (von Ranke) 1895-1985**CLC 1, 2, 6, 11, 39, 44, 45; DAB; DAC; DAM MST, POET; PC 6**
See also CA 5-8R; 117; CANR 5, 36; CDBLB 1914-1945; DLB 20, 100, 191; DLBD 18; DLBY 85; MTCW 1, 2; SATA 45
Graves, Valerie
See Bradley, Marion Zimmer
Gray, Alasdair (James) 1934- .... **CLC 41**
See also CA 126; CANR 47, 69; DLB 194; INT 126; MTCW 1, 2
Gray, Amlin 1946- .... **CLC 29**
See also CA 138
Gray, Francine du Plessix 1930-**CLC 22; DAM NOV**
See also BEST 90:3; CA 61-64; CAAS 2; CANR 11, 33, 75; INT CANR-11; MTCW 1, 2
Gray, John (Henry) 1866-1934 .... **TCLC 19**
See also CA 119; 162
Gray, Simon (James Holliday) 1936-**CLC 9, 14, 36**
See also AITN 1; CA 21-24R; CAAS 3; CANR 32, 69; DLB 13; MTCW 1
Gray, Spalding 1941-**CLC 49, 112; DAM POP; DC 7**
See also CA 128, CANR 74, MTCW 2
Gray, Thomas 1716-1771**LC 4, 40; DA; DAB; DAC; DAM MST; PC 2; WLC**
See also CDBLB 1660-1789; DLB 109
Grayson, David
See Baker, Ray Stannard
Grayson, Richard (A.) 1951- .... **CLC 38**
See also CA 85-88; CANR 14, 31, 57
Greeley, Andrew M(oran) 1928-**CLC 28; DAM POP**
See also CA 5-8R; CAAS 7; CANR 7, 43, 69; MTCW 1, 2

Green, Anna Katharine 1846-1935 . **TCLC 63**
See also CA 112; 159; DLB 202
Green, Brian
See Card, Orson Scott
Green, Hannah
See Greenberg, Joanne (Goldenberg)
Green, Hannah 1927(?)-1996 .... **CLC 3**
See also CA 73-76; CANR 59
Green, Henry 1905-1973 .... **CLC 2, 13, 97**
See also Yorke, Henry Vincent
See also DLB 15
Green, Julian (Hartridge) 1900-1998
See Green, Julien
See also CA 21-24R; 169; CANR 33; DLB 4, 72; MTCW 1
Green, Julien .... **CLC 3, 11, 77**
See also Green, Julian (Hartridge)
See also MTCW 2
Green, Paul (Eliot) 1894-1981 **CLC 25; DAM DRAM**
See also AITN 1; CA 5-8R; 103; CANR 3; DLB 7, 9; DLBY 81
Greenberg, Ivan 1908-1973
See Rahv, Philip
See also CA 85-88
Greenberg, Joanne (Goldenberg) 1932-**CLC 7, 30**
See also AAYA 12; CA 5-8R; CANR 14, 32, 69; SATA 25
Greenberg, Richard 1959(?)- .... **CLC 57**
See also CA 138
Greene, Bette 1934-........................... **CLC 30**
See also AAYA 7; CA 53-56; CANR 4; CLR 2; JRDA; MAICYA; SAAS 16; SATA 8, 102
Greene, Gael .... **CLC 8**
See also CA 13-16R; CANR 10
Greene, Graham (Henry) 1904-1991**CLC 1, 3, 6, 9, 14, 18, 27, 37, 70, 72; DA; DAB; DAC; DAM MST, NOV; SSC 29; WLC**
See also AITN 2; CA 13-16R; 133; CANR 35, 61; CDBLB 1945-1960; DLB 13, 15, 77, 100, 162, 201, 204; DLBY 91; MTCW 1, 2; SATA 20
Greene, Robert 1558-1592 .... **LC 41**
See also DLB 62, 167
Greer, Richard
See Silverberg, Robert
Gregor, Arthur 1923-........................... **CLC 9**
See also CA 25-28R; CAAS 10; CANR 11; SATA 36
Gregor, Lee
See Pohl, Frederik
Gregory, Isabella Augusta (Persse) 1852-1932 **TCLC 1**
See also CA 104; DLB 10
Gregory, J. Dennis
See Williams, John A(lfred)
Grendon, Stephen
See Derleth, August (William)
Grenville, Kate 1950- .... **CLC 61**
See also CA 118; CANR 53
Grenville, Pelham
See Wodehouse, P(elham) G(renville)
Greve, Felix Paul (Berthold Friedrich) 1879-1948
See Grove, Frederick Philip
See also CA 104; 141; DAC; DAM MST
Grey, Zane 1872-1939 ... **TCLC 6; DAM POP**
See also CA 104; 132; DLB 212; MTCW 1, 2
Grieg, (Johan) Nordahl (Brun) 1902-1943 **TCLC 10**
See also CA 107

Grieve, C(hristopher) M(urray) 1892-1978 **CLC 11, 19; DAM POET**
See also MacDiarmid, Hugh; Pteleon
See also CA 5-8R; 85-88; CANR 33; MTCW 1
Griffin, Gerald 1803-1840 .... **NCLC 7**
See also DLB 159
Griffin, John Howard 1920-1980 .... **CLC 68**
See also AITN 1; CA 1-4R; 101; CANR 2
Griffin, Peter 1942- ....**CLC 39**
See also CA 136
Griffith, D(avid Lewelyn) W(ark) 1875(?)-1948 **TCLC 68**
See also CA 119; 150
Griffith, Lawrence
See Griffith, D(avid Lewelyn) W(ark)
Griffiths, Trevor 1935- .... **CLC 13, 52**
See also CA 97-100; CANR 45; DLB 13
Griggs, Sutton Elbert 1872-1930(?) **TCLC 77**
See also CA 123; DLB 50
Grigson, Geoffrey (Edward Harvey) 1905-1985 **CLC 7, 39**
See also CA 25-28R; 118; CANR 20, 33; DLB 27; MTCW 1, 2
Grillparzer, Franz 1791-1872 .... **NCLC 1**
See also DLB 133
Grimble, Reverend Charles James
See Eliot, T(homas) S(tearns)
Grimke, Charlotte L(ottie) Forten 1837(?)-1914
See Forten, Charlotte L.
See also BW 1; CA 117; 124; DAM MULT, POET
Grimm, Jacob Ludwig Karl 1785-1863**N C L C 3**
See also DLB 90; MAICYA; SATA 22
Grimm, Wilhelm Karl 1786-1859 ..... **NCLC 3**
See also DLB 90; MAICYA; SATA 22
Grimmelshausen, Johann Jakob Christoffel von 1621-1676 ....**LC 6**
See also DLB 168
Grindel, Eugene 1895-1952
See Eluard, Paul
See also CA 104
Grisham, John 1955-...... **CLC 84; DAM POP**
See also AAYA 14; CA 138; CANR 47, 69; MTCW 2
Grossman, David 1954- .... **CLC 67**
See also CA 138
Grossman, Vasily (Semenovich) 1905-1964 **CLC 41**
See also CA 124; 130; MTCW 1
Grove, Frederick Philip .... **TCLC 4**
See also Greve, Felix Paul (Berthold Friedrich)
See also DLB 92
Grubb
See Crumb, R(obert)
Grumbach, Doris (Isaac) 1918-**CLC 13, 22, 64**
See also CA 5-8R; CAAS 2; CANR 9, 42, 70; INT CANR-9; MTCW 2
Grundtvig, Nicolai Frederik Severin 1783-1872 **NCLC 1**
Grunge
See Crumb, R(obert)
Grunwald, Lisa 1959-........................ **CLC 44**
See also CA 120
Guare, John 1938- ... **CLC 8, 14, 29, 67; DAM DRAM**
See also CA 73-76; CANR 21, 69; DLB 7; MTCW 1, 2
Gudjonsson, Halldor Kiljan 1902-1998
See Laxness, Halldor
See also CA 103; 164
Guenter, Erich
See Eich, Guenter

Guest, Barbara 1920- ....CLC 34
See also CA 25-28R; CANR 11, 44; DLB 5, 193
Guest, Judith (Ann) 1936- .. CLC 8, 30; DAM
NOV, POP
See also AAYA 7; CA 77-80; CANR 15, 75; INT
CANR-15; MTCW 1, 2
Guevara, Che ....CLC 87; HLC
See also Guevara (Serna), Ernesto
Guevara (Serna), Ernesto 1928-1967
See Guevara, Che
See also CA 127; 111; CANR 56; DAM MULT;
HW
Guicciardini, Francesco 1483-1540 ..... LC 49
Guild, Nicholas M. 1944- ....CLC 33
See also CA 93-96
Guillemin, Jacques
See Sartre, Jean-Paul
Guillen, Jorge 1893-1984 .... CLC 11; DAM
MULT, POET
See also CA 89-92; 112; DLB 108; HW
Guillen, Nicolas (Cristobal) 1902-1989CLC 48,
79; BLC 2; DAM MST, MULT, POET;
HLC; PC 23
See also BW 2; CA 116; 125; 129; HW
Guillevic, (Eugene) 1907- ....CLC 33
See also CA 93-96
Guillois
See Desnos, Robert
Guillois, Valentin
See Desnos, Robert
Guiney, Louise Imogen 1861-1920 .. TCLC 41
See also CA 160; DLB 54
Guiraldes, Ricardo (Guillermo) 1886-1927
TCLC 39
See also CA 131; HW; MTCW 1
Gumilev, Nikolai (Stepanovich) 1886-1921
TCLC 60
See also CA 165
Gunesekera, Romesh 1954- ....CLC 91
See also CA 159
Gunn, Bill ....CLC 5
See also Gunn, William Harrison
See also DLB 38
Gunn, Thom(son William) 1929-CLC 3, 6, 18,
32, 81; DAM POET; PC 26
See also CA 17-20R; CANR 9, 33; CDBLB 1960
to Present; DLB 27; INT CANR-33; MTCW
1
Gunn, William Harrison 1934(?)-1989
See Gunn, Bill
See also AITN 1; BW 1; CA 13-16R; 128; CANR
12, 25, 76
Gunnars, Kristjana 1948- ....CLC 69
See also CA 113; DLB 60
Gurdjieff, G(eorgei) I(vanovich) 1877(?)-1949
TCLC 71
See also CA 157
Gurganus, Allan 1947- ... CLC 70; DAM POP
See also BEST 90:1; CA 135
Gurney, A(lbert) R(amsdell), Jr. 1930-CLC 32,
50, 54; DAM DRAM
See also CA 77-80; CANR 32, 64
Gurney, Ivor (Bertie) 1890-1937 .... TCLC 33
See also CA 167
Gurney, Peter
See Gurney, A(lbert) R(amsdell), Jr.
Guro, Elena 1877-1913 ....TCLC 56
Gustafson, James M(oody) 1925- .....CLC 100
See also CA 25-28R; CANR 37
Gustafson, Ralph (Barker) 1909- ....CLC 36
See also CA 21-24R; CANR 8, 45; DLB 88
Gut, Gom
See Simenon, Georges (Jacques Christian)

Guterson, David 1956- ....CLC 91
See also CA 132; CANR 73; MTCW 2
Guthrie, A(lfred) B(ertram), Jr. 1901-1991
CLC 23
See also CA 57-60; 134; CANR 24; DLB 212;
SATA 62; SATA-Obit 67
Guthrie, Isobel
See Grieve, C(hristopher) M(urray)
Guthrie, Woodrow Wilson 1912-1967
See Guthrie, Woody
See also CA 113; 93-96
Guthrie, Woody ....CLC 35
See also Guthrie, Woodrow Wilson
Guy, Rosa (Cuthbert) 1928- ....CLC 26
See also AAYA 4; BW 2; CA 17-20R; CANR
14, 34; CLR 13; DLB 33; JRDA; MAICYA;
SATA 14, 62
Gwendolyn
See Bennett, (Enoch) Arnold
H. D. ....CLC 3, 8, 14, 31, 34, 73; PC 5
See also Doolittle, Hilda
H. de V.
See Buchan, John
Haavikko, Paavo Juhani 1931- .....CLC 18, 34
See also CA 106
Habbema, Koos
See Heijermans, Herman
Habermas, Juergen 1929- ....CLC 104
See also CA 109
Habermas, Jurgen
See Habermas, Juergen
Hacker, Marilyn 1942- .. CLC 5, 9, 23, 72, 91;
DAM POET
See also CA 77-80; CANR 68; DLB 120
Haeckel, Ernst Heinrich (Philipp August)
1834-1919 ....TCLC 83
See also CA 157
Haggard, H(enry) Rider 1856-1925 TCLC 11
See also CA 108; 148; DLB 70, 156, 174, 178;
MTCW 2; SATA 16
Hagiosy, L.
See Larbaud, Valery (Nicolas)
Hagiwara Sakutaro 1886-1942TCLC 60; PC 18
Haig, Fenil
See Ford, Ford Madox
Haig-Brown, Roderick (Langmere) 1908-1976
CLC 21
See also CA 5-8R; 69-72; CANR 4, 38; CLR 31;
DLB 88; MAICYA; SATA 12
Hailey, Arthur 1920-CLC 5; DAM NOV, POP
See also AITN 2; BEST 90:3; CA 1-4R; CANR
2, 36, 75; DLB 88; DLBY 82; MTCW 1, 2
Hailey, Elizabeth Forsythe 1938- ....CLC 40
See also CA 93-96; CAAS 1; CANR 15, 48; INT
CANR-15
Haines, John (Meade) 1924- ....CLC 58
See also CA 17-20R; CANR 13, 34; DLB 212
Hakluyt, Richard 1552-1616 ....LC 31
Haldeman, Joe (William) 1943- ....CLC 61
See also CA 53-56; CAAS 25; CANR 6, 70, 72;
DLB 8; INT CANR-6
Hale, Sarah Josepha (Buell) 1788-1879N C L C
75
See also DLB 1, 42, 73
Haley, Alex(ander Murray Palmer) 1921-1992
CLC 8, 12, 76; BLC 2; DA; DAB; DAC;
DAM MST, MULT, POP
See also AAYA 26; BW 2; CA 77-80; 136; CANR
61; DLB 38; MTCW 1, 2
Haliburton, Thomas Chandler 1796-1865
NCLC 15
See also DLB 11, 99

Hall, Donald (Andrew, Jr.) 1928-CLC 1, 13, 37,
59; DAM POET
See also CA 5-8R; CAAS 7; CANR 2, 44, 64;
DLB 5; MTCW 1; SATA 23, 97
Hall, Frederic Sauser
See Sauser-Hall, Frederic
Hall, James
See Kuttner, Henry
Hall, James Norman 1887-1951 ...... TCLC 23
See also CA 123; 173; SATA 21
Hall, Radclyffe
See Hall, (Marguerite) Radclyffe
See also MTCW 2
Hall, (Marguerite) Radclyffe 1886-1943TCLC
12
See also CA 110; 150; DLB 191
Hall, Rodney 1935- ....CLC 51
See also CA 109; CANR 69
Halleck, Fitz-Greene 1790-1867 ...... NCLC 47
See also DLB 3
Halliday, Michael
See Creasey, John
Halpern, Daniel 1945- ....CLC 14
See also CA 33-36R
Hamburger, Michael (Peter Leopold) 1924-
CLC 5, 14
See also CA 5-8R; CAAS 4; CANR 2, 47; DLB
27
Hamill, Pete 1935- ....CLC 10
See also CA 25-28R; CANR 18, 71
Hamilton, Alexander 1755(?)-1804 . NCLC 49
See also DLB 37
Hamilton, Clive
See Lewis, C(live) S(taples)
Hamilton, Edmond 1904-1977 ....CLC 1
See also CA 1-4R; CANR 3; DLB 8
Hamilton, Eugene (Jacob) Lee
See Lee-Hamilton, Eugene (Jacob)
Hamilton, Franklin
See Silverberg, Robert
Hamilton, Gail
See Corcoran, Barbara
Hamilton, Mollie
See Kaye, M(ary) M(argaret)
Hamilton, (Anthony Walter) Patrick 1904-1962
CLC 51
See also CA 113; DLB 191
Hamilton, Virginia 1936-CLC 26; DAM MULT
See also AAYA 2, 21; BW 2; CA 25-28R; CANR
20, 37, 73; CLR 1, 11, 40; DLB 33, 52; INT
CANR-20; JRDA; MAICYA; MTCW 1, 2;
SATA 4, 56, 79
Hammett, (Samuel) Dashiell 1894-1961CLC 3,
5, 10, 19, 47; SSC 17
See also AITN 1; CA 81-84; CANR 42; CDALB
1929-1941; DLBD 6; DLBY 96; MTCW 1, 2
Hammon, Jupiter 1711(?)-1800(?) .. NCLC 5;
BLC 2; DAM MULT, POET; PC 16
See also DLB 31, 50
Hammond, Keith
See Kuttner, Henry
Hamner, Earl (Henry), Jr. 1923- ....CLC 12
See also AITN 2; CA 73-76; DLB 6
Hampton, Christopher (James) 1946- . CLC 4
See also CA 25-28R; DLB 13; MTCW 1
Hamsun, Knut .... TCLC 2, 14, 49
See also Pedersen, Knut
Handke, Peter 1942-CLC 5, 8, 10, 15, 38; DAM
DRAM, NOV
See also CA 77-80; CANR 33, 75; DLB 85, 124;
MTCW 1, 2

Hanley, James 1901-1985 .... **CLC 3, 5, 8, 13**
See also CA 73-76; 117; CANR 36; DLB 191; MTCW 1
Hannah, Barry 1942- .... **CLC 23, 38, 90**
See also CA 108; 110; CANR 43, 68; DLB 6; INT 110; MTCW 1
Hannon, Ezra
See Hunter, Evan
Hansberry, Lorraine (Vivian) 1930-1965 **C L C 17, 62; BLC 2; DA; DAB; DAC; DAM DRAM, MST, MULT; DC 2**
See also AAYA 25; BW 1; CA 109; 25-28R; CABS 3; CANR 58; CDALB 1941-1968; DLB 7, 38; MTCW 1, 2
Hansen, Joseph 1923- .... **CLC 38**
See also CA 29-32R; CAAS 17; CANR 16, 44, 66; INT CANR-16
Hansen, Martin A(lfred) 1909-1955 **TCLC 32**
See also CA 167
Hanson, Kenneth O(stlin) 1922- .... **CLC 13**
See also CA 53-56; CANR 7
Hardwick, Elizabeth (Bruce) 1916- . **CLC 13; DAM NOV**
See also CA 5-8R; CANR 3, 32, 70; DLB 6; MTCW 1, 2
Hardy, Thomas 1840-1928 **TCLC 4, 10, 18, 32, 48, 53, 72; DA; DAB; DAC; DAM MST, NOV, POET; PC 8; SSC 2; WLC**
See also CA 104; 123; CDBLB 1890-1914; DLB 18, 19, 135; MTCW 1, 2
Hare, David 1947- .... **CLC 29, 58**
See also CA 97-100; CANR 39; DLB 13; MTCW 1
Harewood, John
See Van Druten, John (William)
Harford, Henry
See Hudson, W(illiam) H(enry)
Hargrave, Leonie
See Disch, Thomas M(ichael)
Harjo, Joy 1951- .... **CLC 83; DAM MULT**
See also CA 114; CANR 35, 67; DLB 120, 175; MTCW 2; NNAL
Harlan, Louis R(udolph) 1922- .... **CLC 34**
See also CA 21-24R; CANR 25, 55
Harling, Robert 1951(?)- .... **CLC 53**
See also CA 147
Harmon, William (Ruth) 1938- .... **CLC 38**
See also CA 33-36R; CANR 14, 32, 35; SATA 65
Harper, F. E. W.
See Harper, Frances Ellen Watkins
Harper, Frances E. W.
See Harper, Frances Ellen Watkins
Harper, Frances E. Watkins
See Harper, Frances Ellen Watkins
Harper, Frances Ellen
See Harper, Frances Ellen Watkins
Harper, Frances Ellen Watkins 1825-1911 **TCLC 14; BLC 2; DAM MULT, POET; PC 21**
See also BW 1; CA 111; 125; DLB 50
Harper, Michael S(teven) 1938- ..... **CLC 7, 22**
See also BW 1; CA 33-36R; CANR 24; DLB 41
Harper, Mrs. F. E. W.
See Harper, Frances Ellen Watkins
Harris, Christie (Lucy) Irwin 1907- .. **CLC 12**
See also CA 5-8R; CANR 6; CLR 47; DLB 88; JRDA; MAICYA; SAAS 10; SATA 6, 74
Harris, Frank 1856-1931 .... **TCLC 24**
See also CA 109; 150; DLB 156, 197
Harris, George Washington 1814-1869 **N C L C 23**
See also DLB 3, 11

Harris, Joel Chandler 1848-1908 **TCLC 2; SSC 19**
See also CA 104; 137; CLR 49; DLB 11, 23, 42, 78, 91; MAICYA; SATA 100; YABC 1
Harris, John (Wyndham Parkes Lucas) Beynon 1903-1969
See Wyndham, John
See also CA 102; 89-92
Harris, MacDonald .... **CLC 9**
See also Heiney, Donald (William)
Harris, Mark 1922- .... **CLC 19**
See also CA 5-8R; CAAS 3; CANR 2, 55; DLB 2; DLBY 80
Harris, (Theodore) Wilson 1921- .... **CLC 25**
See also BW 2; CA 65-68; CAAS 16; CANR 11, 27, 69; DLB 117; MTCW 1
Harrison, Elizabeth Cavanna 1909-
See Cavanna, Betty
See also CA 9-12R; CANR 6, 27
Harrison, Harry (Max) 1925- .... **CLC 42**
See also CA 1-4R; CANR 5, 21; DLB 8; SATA 4
Harrison, James (Thomas) 1937- **CLC 6, 14, 33, 66; SSC 19**
See also CA 13-16R; CANR 8, 51; DLBY 82; INT CANR-8
Harrison, Jim
See Harrison, James (Thomas)
Harrison, Kathryn 1961- .... **CLC 70**
See also CA 144; CANR 68
Harrison, Tony 1937- .... **CLC 43**
See also CA 65-68; CANR 44; DLB 40; MTCW 1
Harriss, Will(ard Irvin) 1922- .... **CLC 34**
See also CA 111
Harson, Sley
See Ellison, Harlan (Jay)
Hart, Ellis
See Ellison, Harlan (Jay)
Hart, Josephine 1942(?)- **CLC 70; DAM POP**
See also CA 138; CANR 70
Hart, Moss 1904-1961 **CLC 66; DAM DRAM**
See also CA 109; 89-92; DLB 7
Harte, (Francis) Bret(t) 1836(?)-1902 **TCLC 1, 25; DA; DAC; DAM MST; SSC 8; WLC**
See also CA 104; 140; CDALB 1865-1917; DLB 12, 64, 74, 79, 186; SATA 26
Hartley, L(eslie) P(oles) 1895-1972 **CLC 2, 22**
See also CA 45-48; 37-40R; CANR 33; DLB 15, 139; MTCW 1, 2
Hartman, Geoffrey H. 1929- .... **CLC 27**
See also CA 117; 125; DLB 67
Hartmann, Sadakichi 1867-1944 ..... **TCLC 73**
See also CA 157; DLB 54
Hartmann von Aue c. 1160-c. 1205 **CMLC 15**
See also DLB 138
Hartmann von Aue 1170-1210 .... **CMLC 15**
Haruf, Kent 1943- .... **CLC 34**
See also CA 149
Harwood, Ronald 1934- **CLC 32; DAM DRAM, MST**
See also CA 1-4R; CANR 4, 55; DLB 13
Hasegawa Tatsunosuke
See Futabatei, Shimei
Hasek, Jaroslav (Matej Frantisek) 1883-1923 **TCLC 4**
See also CA 104; 129; MTCW 1, 2
Hass, Robert 1941- ..... **CLC 18, 39, 99; PC 16**
See also CA 111; CANR 30, 50, 71; DLB 105, 206; SATA 94
Hastings, Hudson
See Kuttner, Henry

Hastings, Selina .... **CLC 44**
Hathorne, John 1641-1717 .... **LC 38**
Hatteras, Amelia
See Mencken, H(enry) L(ouis)
Hatteras, Owen .... **TCLC 18**
See also Mencken, H(enry) L(ouis); Nathan, George Jean
Hauptmann, Gerhart (Johann Robert) 1862-1946 .... **TCLC 4; DAM DRAM**
See also CA 104; 153; DLB 66, 118
Havel, Vaclav 1936- ..... **CLC 25, 58, 65; DAM DRAM; DC 6**
See also CA 104; CANR 36, 63; MTCW 1, 2
Haviaras, Stratis .... **CLC 33**
See also Chaviaras, Strates
Hawes, Stephen 1475(?)-1523(?) .... **LC 17**
See also DLB 132
Hawkes, John (Clendennin Burne, Jr.) 1925-1998 **CLC 1, 2, 3, 4, 7, 9, 14, 15, 27, 49**
See also CA 1-4R; 167; CANR 2, 47, 64; DLB 2, 7; DLBY 80, 98; MTCW 1, 2
Hawking, S. W.
See Hawking, Stephen W(illiam)
Hawking, Stephen W(illiam) 1942- **CLC 63, 105**
See also AAYA 13; BEST 89:1; CA 126; 129; CANR 48; MTCW 2
Hawkins, Anthony Hope
See Hope, Anthony
Hawthorne, Julian 1846-1934 .... **TCLC 25**
See also CA 165
Hawthorne, Nathaniel 1804-1864 . **NCLC 39; DA; DAB; DAC; DAM MST, NOV; SSC 3, 29; WLC**
See also AAYA 18; CDALB 1640-1865; DLB 1, 74; YABC 2
Haxton, Josephine Ayres 1921-
See Douglas, Ellen
See also CA 115; CANR 41
Hayaseca y Eizaguirre, Jorge
See Echegaray (y Eizaguirre), Jose (Maria Waldo)
Hayashi, Fumiko 1904-1951 .... **TCLC 27**
See also CA 161; DLB 180
Haycraft, Anna
See Ellis, Alice Thomas
See also CA 122; MTCW 2
Hayden, Robert E(arl) 1913-1980 **CLC 5, 9, 14, 37; BLC 2; DA; DAC; DAM MST, MULT, POET; PC 6**
See also BW 1; CA 69-72; 97-100; CABS 2; CANR 24, 75; CDALB 1941-1968; DLB 5, 76; MTCW 1, 2; SATA 19; SATA-Obit 26
Hayford, J(oseph) E(phraim) Casely
See Casely-Hayford, J(oseph) E(phraim)
Hayman, Ronald 1932- .... **CLC 44**
See also CA 25-28R; CANR 18, 50; DLB 155
Haywood, Eliza (Fowler) 1693(?)-1756 **LC 1, 44**
See also DLB 39
Hazlitt, William 1778-1830 .... **NCLC 29**
See also DLB 110, 158
Hazzard, Shirley 1931- .... **CLC 18**
See also CA 9-12R; CANR 4, 70; DLBY 82; MTCW 1
Head, Bessie 1937-1986 . **CLC 25, 67; BLC 2; DAM MULT**
See also BW 2; CA 29-32R; 119; CANR 25; DLB 117; MTCW 1, 2
Headon, (Nicky) Topper 1956(?)- ...... **CLC 30**
Heaney, Seamus (Justin) 1939- **CLC 5, 7, 14, 25, 37, 74, 91; DAB; DAM POET; PC 18; WLCS**
See also CA 85-88; CANR 25, 48, 75; CDBLB 1960 to Present; DLB 40; DLBY 95; MTCW 1, 2

Highwater, Jamake (Mamake) 1942(?)-**CLC 12**
See also AAYA 7; CA 65-68; CAAS 7; CANR
10, 34; CLR 17; DLB 52; DLBY 85; JRDA;
MAICYA; SATA 32, 69; SATA-Brief 30
Highway, Tomson 1951- **CLC 92; DAC; DAM
MULT**
See also CA 151; CANR 75; MTCW 2; NNAL
Higuchi, Ichiyo 1872-1896 .... **NCLC 49**
Hijuelos, Oscar 1951- **CLC 65; DAM MULT,
POP; HLC**
See also AAYA 25; BEST 90:1; CA 123; CANR
50, 75; DLB 145; HW; MTCW 2
Hikmet, Nazim 1902(?)-1963 .... **CLC 40**
See also CA 141; 93-96
Hildegard von Bingen 1098-1179 .. **CMLC 20**
See also DLB 148
Hildesheimer, Wolfgang 1916-1991 ... **CLC 49**
See also CA 101; 135; DLB 69, 124
Hill, Geoffrey (William) 1932-**CLC 5, 8, 18, 45;
DAM POET**
See also CA 81-84; CANR 21; CDBLB 1960 to
Present; DLB 40; MTCW 1
Hill, George Roy 1921- .... **CLC 26**
See also CA 110; 122
Hill, John
See Koontz, Dean R(ay)
Hill, Susan (Elizabeth) 1942-**CLC 4, 113; DAB;
DAM MST, NOV**
See also CA 33-36R; CANR 29, 69; DLB 14,
139; MTCW 1
Hillerman, Tony 1925- ... **CLC 62; DAM POP**
See also AAYA 6; BEST 89:1; CA 29-32R;
CANR 21, 42, 65; DLB 206; SATA 6
Hillesum, Etty 1914-1943 .... **TCLC 49**
See also CA 137
Hilliard, Noel (Harvey) 1929- .... **CLC 15**
See also CA 9-12R; CANR 7, 69
Hillis, Rick 1956- .... **CLC 66**
See also CA 134
Hilton, James 1900-1954 .... **TCLC 21**
See also CA 108; 169; DLB 34, 77; SATA 34
Himes, Chester (Bomar) 1909-1984**CLC 2, 4, 7,
18, 58, 108; BLC 2; DAM MULT**
See also BW 2; CA 25-28R; 114; CANR 22; DLB
2, 76, 143; MTCW 1, 2
Hinde, Thomas .... **CLC 6, 11**
See also Chitty, Thomas Willes
Hindin, Nathan
See Bloch, Robert (Albert)
Hine, (William) Daryl 1936- .... **CLC 15**
See also CA 1-4R; CAAS 15; CANR 1, 20; DLB
60
Hinkson, Katharine Tynan
See Tynan, Katharine
Hinton, S(usan) E(loise) 1950- .. **CLC 30, 111;
DA; DAB; DAC; DAM MST, NOV**
See also AAYA 2; CA 81-84; CANR 32, 62; CLR
3, 23; JRDA; MAICYA; MTCW 1, 2; SATA
19, 58
Hippius, Zinaida .... **TCLC 9**
See also Gippius, Zinaida (Nikolayevna)
Hiraoka, Kimitake 1925-1970
See Mishima, Yukio
See also CA 97-100; 29-32R; DAM DRAM;
MTCW 1, 2
Hirsch, E(ric) D(onald), Jr. 1928- ...... **CLC 79**
See also CA 25-28R; CANR 27, 51; DLB 67;
INT CANR-27; MTCW 1
Hirsch, Edward 1950- .... **CLC 31, 50**
See also CA 104; CANR 20, 42; DLB 120
Hitchcock, Alfred (Joseph) 1899-1980**CLC 16**
See also AAYA 22; CA 159; 97-100; SATA 27;
SATA-Obit 24

Hitler, Adolf 1889-1945 .... **TCLC 53**
See also CA 117; 147
Hoagland, Edward 1932- .... **CLC 28**
See also CA 1-4R; CANR 2, 31, 57; DLB 6;
SATA 51
Hoban, Russell (Conwell) 1925- ... **CLC 7, 25;
DAM NOV**
See also CA 5-8R; CANR 23, 37, 66; CLR 3;
DLB 52; MAICYA; MTCW 1, 2; SATA 1, 40,
78
Hobbes, Thomas 1588-1679 .... **LC 36**
See also DLB 151
Hobbs, Perry
See Blackmur, R(ichard) P(almer)
Hobson, Laura Z(ametkin) 1900-1986 **CLC 7,
25**
See also CA 17-20R; 118; CANR 55; DLB 28;
SATA 52
Hochhuth, Rolf 1931-.... **CLC 4, 11, 18; DAM
DRAM**
See also CA 5-8R; CANR 33, 75; DLB 124;
MTCW 1, 2
Hochman, Sandra 1936- .... **CLC 3, 8**
See also CA 5-8R; DLB 5
Hochwaelder, Fritz 1911-1986 **CLC 36; DAM
DRAM**
See also CA 29-32R; 120; CANR 42; MTCW 1
Hochwalder, Fritz
See Hochwaelder, Fritz
Hocking, Mary (Eunice) 1921- .... **CLC 13**
See also CA 101; CANR 18, 40
Hodgins, Jack 1938- .... **CLC 23**
See also CA 93-96; DLB 60
Hodgson, William Hope 1877(?)-1918**TCLC 13**
See also CA 111; 164; DLB 70, 153, 156, 178;
MTCW 2
Hoeg, Peter 1957- .... **CLC 95**
See also CA 151; CANR 75; MTCW 2
Hoffman, Alice 1952- .... **CLC 51; DAM NOV**
See also CA 77-80; CANR 34, 66; MTCW 1, 2
Hoffman, Daniel (Gerard) 1923-**CLC 6, 13, 23**
See also CA 1-4R; CANR 4; DLB 5
Hoffman, Stanley 1944- .... **CLC 5**
See also CA 77-80
Hoffman, William M(oses) 1939- .... **CLC 40**
See also CA 57-60; CANR 11, 71
Hoffmann, E(rnst) T(heodor) A(madeus)
1776-1822 .... **NCLC 2; SSC 13**
See also DLB 90; SATA 27
Hofmann, Gert 1931- .... **CLC 54**
See also CA 128
Hofmannsthal, Hugo von 1874-1929**TCLC 11;
DAM DRAM; DC 4**
See also CA 106; 153; DLB 81, 118
Hogan, Linda 1947- ... **CLC 73; DAM MULT**
See also CA 120; CANR 45, 73; DLB 175;
NNAL
Hogarth, Charles
See Creasey, John
Hogarth, Emmett
See Polonsky, Abraham (Lincoln)
Hogg, James 1770-1835 .... **NCLC 4**
See also DLB 93, 116, 159
Holbach, Paul Henri Thiry Baron 1723-1789
LC 14
Holberg, Ludvig 1684-1754 .... **LC 6**
Holden, Ursula 1921- .... **CLC 18**
See also CA 101; CAAS 8; CANR 22
Holderlin, (Johann Christian) Friedrich
1770-1843 .... **NCLC 16; PC 4**
Holdstock, Robert
See Holdstock, Robert P.

Holdstock, Robert P. 1948-................. **CLC 39**
See also CA 131
Holland, Isabelle 1920- .... **CLC 21**
See also AAYA 11; CA 21-24R; CANR 10, 25,
47; JRDA; MAICYA; SATA 8, 70;
SATA-Essay 103
Holland, Marcus
See Caldwell, (Janet Miriam) Taylor (Holland)
Hollander, John 1929-............. **CLC 2, 5, 8, 14**
See also CA 1-4R; CANR 1, 52; DLB 5; SATA
13
Hollander, Paul
See Silverberg, Robert
Holleran, Andrew 1943(?)- .... **CLC 38**
See also CA 144
Hollinghurst, Alan 1954- .... **CLC 55, 91**
See also CA 114; DLB 207
Hollis, Jim
See Summers, Hollis (Spurgeon, Jr.)
Holly, Buddy 1936-1959 .... **TCLC 65**
Holmes, Gordon
See Shiel, M(atthew) P(hipps)
Holmes, John
See Souster, (Holmes) Raymond
Holmes, John Clellon 1926-1988 .... **CLC 56**
See also CA 9-12R; 125; CANR 4; DLB 16
Holmes, Oliver Wendell, Jr. 1841-1935 **T C L C
77**
See also CA 114
Holmes, Oliver Wendell 1809-1894 **NCLC 14**
See also CDALB 1640-1865; DLB 1, 189; SATA
34
Holmes, Raymond
See Souster, (Holmes) Raymond
Holt, Victoria
See Hibbert, Eleanor Alice Burford
Holub, Miroslav 1923-1998 .... **CLC 4**
See also CA 21-24R; 169; CANR 10
Homer c. 8th cent. B.C.-**CMLC 1, 16; DA; DAB;
DAC; DAM MST, POET; PC 23; WLCS**
See also DLB 176
Hongo, Garrett Kaoru 1951- .... **PC 23**
See also CA 133; CAAS 22; DLB 120
Honig, Edwin 1919-........................... **CLC 33**
See also CA 5-8R; CAAS 8; CANR 4, 45; DLB
5
Hood, Hugh (John Blagdon) 1928-**CLC 15, 28**
See also CA 49-52; CAAS 17; CANR 1, 33; DLB
53
Hood, Thomas 1799-1845 .... **NCLC 16**
See also DLB 96
Hooker, (Peter) Jeremy 1941- .... **CLC 43**
See also CA 77-80; CANR 22; DLB 40
hooks, bell .... **CLC 94; BLCS**
See also Watkins, Gloria
See also MTCW 2
Hope, A(lec) D(erwent) 1907- .... **CLC 3, 51**
See also CA 21-24R; CANR 33, 74; MTCW 1, 2
Hope, Anthony 1863-1933 .... **TCLC 83**
See also CA 157; DLB 153, 156
Hope, Brian
See Creasey, John
Hope, Christopher (David Tully) 1944-**CLC 52**
See also CA 106; CANR 47; SATA 62
Hopkins, Gerard Manley 1844-1889**NCLC 17;
DA; DAB; DAC; DAM MST, POET; PC 15;
WLC**
See also CDBLB 1890-1914; DLB 35, 57
Hopkins, John (Richard) 1931-1998 .... **CLC 4**
See also CA 85-88; 169
Hopkins, Pauline Elizabeth 1859-1930 **T C L C
28; BLC 2; DAM MULT**
See also BW 2; CA 141; DLB 50

Knox, John c. 1505-1572 .... **LC 37**
See also DLB 132
Knye, Cassandra
See Disch, Thomas M(ichael)
Koch, C(hristopher) J(ohn) 1932- ..... **CLC 42**
See also CA 127
Koch, Christopher
See Koch, C(hristopher) J(ohn)
Koch, Kenneth 1925-CLC 5, 8, 44; DAM POET
See also CA 1-4R; CANR 6, 36, 57; DLB 5; INT
CANR-36; MTCW 2; SATA 65
Kochanowski, Jan 1530-1584 .... **LC 10**
Kock, Charles Paul de 1794-1871 ... **NCLC 16**
Koda Shigeyuki 1867-1947
See Rohan, Koda
See also CA 121
Koestler, Arthur 1905-1983CLC 1, 3, 6, 8, 15, 33
See also CA 1-4R; 109; CANR 1, 33; CDBLB
1945-1960; DLBY 83; MTCW 1, 2
Kogawa, Joy Nozomi 1935- .... **CLC 78; DAC;
DAM MST, MULT**
See also CA 101; CANR 19, 62; MTCW 2; SATA 99
Kohout, Pavel 1928-.......................... **CLC 13**
See also CA 45-48; CANR 3
Koizumi, Yakumo
See Hearn, (Patricio) Lafcadio (Tessima Carlos)
Kolmar, Gertrud 1894-1943 .... **TCLC 40**
See also CA 167
Komunyakaa, Yusef 1947- CLC 86, 94; BLCS
See also CA 147; DLB 120
Konrad, George
See Konrad, Gyoergy
Konrad, Gyoergy 1933- .... **CLC 4, 10, 73**
See also CA 85-88
Konwicki, Tadeusz 1926- .. CLC 8, 28, 54, 117
See also CA 101; CAAS 9; CANR 39, 59; MTCW 1
Koontz, Dean R(ay) 1945-CLC 78; DAM NOV, POP
See also AAYA 9; BEST 89:3, 90:2; CA 108;
CANR 19, 36, 52; MTCW 1; SATA 92
Kopernik, Mikolaj
See Copernicus, Nicolaus
Kopit, Arthur (Lee) 1937-CLC 1, 18, 33; DAM DRAM
See also AITN 1; CA 81-84; CABS 3; DLB 7; MTCW 1
Kops, Bernard 1926-.......................... **CLC 4**
See also CA 5-8R; DLB 13
Kornbluth, C(yril) M. 1923-1958 ..... **TCLC 8**
See also CA 105; 160; DLB 8
Korolenko, V. G.
See Korolenko, Vladimir Galaktionovich
Korolenko, Vladimir
See Korolenko, Vladimir Galaktionovich
Korolenko, Vladimir G.
See Korolenko, Vladimir Galaktionovich
Korolenko, Vladimir Galaktionovich 1853-1921
TCLC 22
See also CA 121
Korzybski, Alfred (Habdank Skarbek)
1879-1950................................. **TCLC 61**
See also CA 123; 160
Kosinski, Jerzy (Nikodem) 1933-1991CLC 1, 2, 3, 6, 10, 15, 53, 70; DAM NOV
See also CA 17-20R; 134; CANR 9, 46; DLB 2;
DLBY 82; MTCW 1, 2
Kostelanetz, Richard (Cory) 1940- .... **CLC 28**
See also CA 13-16R; CAAS 8; CANR 38, 77
Kostrowitzki, Wilhelm Apollinaris de 1880-1918
See Apollinaire, Guillaume

See also CA 104
Kotlowitz, Robert 1924- .... **CLC 4**
See also CA 33-36R; CANR 36
Kotzebue, August (Friedrich Ferdinand) von
1761-1819................................. **NCLC 25**
See also DLB 94
Kotzwinkle, William 1938- .... **CLC 5, 14, 35**
See also CA 45-48; CANR 3, 44; CLR 6; DLB
173; MAICYA; SATA 24, 70
Kowna, Stancy
See Szymborska, Wislawa
Kozol, Jonathan 1936-........................ **CLC 17**
See also CA 61-64; CANR 16, 45
Kozoll, Michael 1940(?)-..................... **CLC 35**
Kramer, Kathryn 19(?)-....................... **CLC 34**
Kramer, Larry 1935-CLC 42; DAM POP; DC 8
See also CA 124; 126; CANR 60
Krasicki, Ignacy 1735-1801 .... **NCLC 8**
Krasinski, Zygmunt 1812-1859 .... **NCLC 4**
Kraus, Karl 1874-1936 .... **TCLC 5**
See also CA 104; DLB 118
Kreve (Mickevicius), Vincas 1882-1954T C L C 27
See also CA 170
Kristeva, Julia 1941-........................... **CLC 77**
See also CA 154
Kristofferson, Kris 1936-.................... **CLC 26**
See also CA 104
Krizanc, John 1956-............................ **CLC 57**
Krleza, Miroslav 1893-1981 .... **CLC 8, 114**
See also CA 97-100; 105; CANR 50; DLB 147
Kroetsch, Robert 1927- CLC 5, 23, 57; DAC; DAM POET
See also CA 17-20R; CANR 8, 38; DLB 53; MTCW 1
Kroetz, Franz
See Kroetz, Franz Xaver
Kroetz, Franz Xaver 1946-................. **CLC 41**
See also CA 130
Kroker, Arthur (W.) 1945-.................. **CLC 77**
See also CA 161
Kropotkin, Peter (Aleksieevich) 1842-1921
TCLC 36
See also CA 119
Krotkov, Yuri 1917-............................ **CLC 19**
See also CA 102
Krumb
See Crumb, R(obert)
Krumgold, Joseph (Quincy) 1908-1980CLC 12
See also CA 9-12R; 101; CANR 7; MAICYA;
SATA 1, 48; SATA-Obit 23
Krumwitz
See Crumb, R(obert)
Krutch, Joseph Wood 1893-1970....... **CLC 24**
See also CA 1-4R; 25-28R; CANR 4; DLB 63, 206
Krutzch, Gus
See Eliot, T(homas) S(tearns)
Krylov, Ivan Andreevich 1768(?)-1844NCLC 1
See also DLB 150
Kubin, Alfred (Leopold Isidor) 1877-1959
TCLC 23
See also CA 112; 149; DLB 81
Kubrick, Stanley 1928- .... **CLC 16**
See also AAYA 30; CA 81-84; CANR 33; DLB 26
Kumin, Maxine (Winokur) 1925-CLC 5, 13, 28; DAM POET; PC 15
See also AITN 2; CA 1-4R; CAAS 8; CANR 1, 21, 69; DLB 5; MTCW 1, 2; SATA 12

Kundera, Milan 1929-CLC 4, 9, 19, 32, 68, 115;
DAM NOV; SSC 24
See also AAYA 2; CA 85-88; CANR 19, 52, 74;
MTCW 1, 2
Kunene, Mazisi (Raymond) 1930-
CLC 85
See also BW 1; CA 125; DLB 117
Kunitz, Stanley (Jasspon) 1905-CLC 6, 11, 14;
PC 19
See also CA 41-44R; CANR 26, 57; DLB 48;
INT CANR-26; MTCW 1, 2
Kunze, Reiner 1933-........................... **CLC 10**
See also CA 93-96; DLB 75
Kuprin, Aleksandr Ivanovich 1870-1938
TCLC 5
See also CA 104
Kureishi, Hanif 1954(?)- .... **CLC 64**
See also CA 139; DLB 194
Kurosawa, Akira 1910-1998CLC 16, 119; DAM MULT
See also AAYA 11; CA 101; 170; CANR 46
Kushner, Tony 1957(?)-CLC 81; DAM DRAM; DC 10
See also CA 144; CANR 74; MTCW 2
Kuttner, Henry 1915-1958 .... **TCLC 10**
See Vance, Jack
See also CA 107; 157; DLB 8
Kuzma, Greg 1944-............................. **CLC 7**
See also CA 33-36R; CANR 70
Kuzmin, Mikhail 1872(?)-1936 .... **TCLC 40**
See also CA 170
Kyd, Thomas 1558-1594LC 22; DAM DRAM; DC 3
See also DLB 62
Kyprianos, Iossif
See Samarakis, Antonis
La Bruyere, Jean de 1645-1696 .... **LC 17**
Lacan, Jacques (Marie Emile) 1901-1981C L C 75
See also CA 121; 104
Laclos, Pierre Ambroise Francois Choderlos de
1741-1803................................. **NCLC 4**
La Colere, Francois
See Aragon, Louis
Lacolere, Francois
See Aragon, Louis
La Deshabilleuse
See Simenon, Georges (Jacques Christian)
Lady Gregory
See Gregory, Isabella Augusta (Persse)
Lady of Quality, A
See Bagnold, Enid
**La Fayette, Marie (Madelaine Pioche de la
Vergne Comtes** 1634-1693 .... **LC 2**
Lafayette, Rene
See Hubbard, L(afayette) Ron(ald)
Laforgue, Jules 1860-1887NCLC 5, 53; PC 14; SSC 20
Lagerkvist, Paer (Fabian) 1891-1974 . CLC 7, 10, 13, 54; DAM DRAM, NOV
See also Lagerkvist, Par
See also CA 85-88; 49-52; MTCW 1, 2
Lagerkvist, Par .... **SSC 12**
See also Lagerkvist, Paer (Fabian)
See also MTCW 2
Lagerloef, Selma (Ottiliana Lovisa) 1858-1940
TCLC 4, 36
See also Lagerlof, Selma (Ottiliana Lovisa)
See also CA 108; MTCW 2; SATA 15
Lagerlof, Selma (Ottiliana Lovisa)
See Lagerloef, Selma (Ottiliana Lovisa)
See also CLR 7; SATA 15

See also BEST 89:4; CDBLB 1960 to Present;
DLB 87; MTCW 2

Le Clezio, J(ean) M(arie) G(ustave) 1940-**CLC 31**
See also CA 116; 128; DLB 83

Leconte de Lisle, Charles-Marie-Rene 1818-1894 .... **NCLC 29**

Le Coq, Monsieur
See Simenon, Georges (Jacques Christian)

Leduc, Violette 1907-1972 .... **CLC 22**
See also CA 13-14; 33-36R; CANR 69; CAP 1

Ledwidge, Francis 1887(?)-1917 ..... **TCLC 23**
See also CA 123; DLB 20

Lee, Andrea 1953- ..... **CLC 36; BLC 2; DAM MULT**
See also BW 1; CA 125

Lee, Andrew
See Auchincloss, Louis (Stanton)

Lee, Chang-rae 1965- .... **CLC 91**
See also CA 148

Lee, Don L. .... **CLC 2**
See also Madhubuti, Haki R.

Lee, George W(ashington) 1894-1976**CLC 52; BLC 2; DAM MULT**
See also BW 1; CA 125; DLB 51

Lee, (Nelle) Harper 1926-... **CLC 12, 60; DA; DAB; DAC; DAM MST, NOV; WLC**
See also AAYA 13; CA 13-16R; CANR 51;
CDALB 1941-1968; DLB 6; MTCW 1, 2;
SATA 11

Lee, Helen Elaine 1959(?)- .... **CLC 86**
See also CA 148

Lee, Julian
See Latham, Jean Lee

Lee, Larry
See Lee, Lawrence

Lee, Laurie 1914-1997 . **CLC 90; DAB; DAM POP**
See also CA 77-80; 158; CANR 33, 73; DLB 27;
MTCW 1

Lee, Lawrence 1941-1990 .... **CLC 34**
See also CA 131; CANR 43

Lee, Li-Young 1957- .... **PC 24**
See also CA 153; DLB 165

Lee, Manfred B(ennington) 1905-1971**CLC 11**
See also Queen, Ellery
See also CA 1-4R; 29-32R; CANR 2; DLB 137

Lee, Shelton Jackson 1957(?)-**CLC 105; BLCS; DAM MULT**
See also Lee, Spike
See also BW 2; CA 125; CANR 42

Lee, Spike
See Lee, Shelton Jackson
See also AAYA 4, 29

Lee, Stan 1922- .... **CLC 17**
See also AAYA 5; CA 108; 111; INT 111

Lee, Tanith 1947-................................. **CLC 46**
See also AAYA 15; CA 37-40R; CANR 53; SATA 8, 88

Lee, Vernon .... **TCLC 5; SSC 33**
<iSee also Paget, Violet
See also DLB 57, 153, 156, 174, 178

Lee, William
See Burroughs, William S(eward)

Lee, Willy
See Burroughs, William S(eward)

Lee-Hamilton, Eugene (Jacob) 1845-1907 **TCLC 22**
See also CA 117

Leet, Judith 1935- .... **CLC 11**

Le Fanu, Joseph Sheridan 1814-1873**NCLC 9, 58; DAM POP; SSC 14**
See also DLB 21, 70, 159, 178

Leffland, Ella 1931- .... **CLC 19**
See also CA 29-32R; CANR 35, 78; DLBY 84;
INT CANR-35; SATA 65

Leger, Alexis
See Leger, (Marie-Rene Auguste) Alexis
Saint-Leger

Leger, (Marie-Rene Auguste) Alexis Saint-Leger 1887-1975**CLC 4, 11, 46; DAM POET; PC 23**
See also CA 13-16R; 61-64; CANR 43; MTCW 1

Leger, Saintleger
See Leger, (Marie-Rene Auguste) Alexis
Saint-Leger

Le Guin, Ursula K(roeber) 1929-**CLC 8, 13, 22, 45, 71; DAB; DAC; DAM MST, POP; SSC 12**
See also AAYA 9, 27; AITN 1; CA 21-24R;
CANR 9, 32, 52, 74; CDALB 1968-1988;
CLR 3, 28; DLB 8, 52; INT CANR-32; JRDA;
MAICYA; MTCW 1, 2; SATA 4, 52, 99

Lehmann, Rosamond (Nina) 1901-1990**CLC 5**
See also CA 77-80; 131; CANR 8, 73; DLB 15;
MTCW 2

Leiber, Fritz (Reuter, Jr.) 1910-1992 . **CLC 25**
See also CA 45-48; 139; CANR 2, 40; DLB 8;
MTCW 1, 2; SATA 45; SATA-Obit 73

Leibniz, Gottfried Wilhelm von 1646-1716**LC 35**
See also DLB 168

Leimbach, Martha 1963-
See Leimbach, Marti
See also CA 130

Leimbach, Marti .... **CLC 65**
See also Leimbach, Martha

Leino, Eino .... **TCLC 24**
See also Loennbohm, Armas Eino Leopold

Leiris, Michel (Julien) 1901-1990 ...... **CLC 61**
See also CA 119; 128; 132

Leithauser, Brad 1953- .... **CLC 27**
See also CA 107; CANR 27; DLB 120

Lelchuk, Alan 1938- .... **CLC 5**
See also CA 45-48; CAAS 20; CANR 1, 70

Lem, Stanislaw 1921- .... **CLC 8, 15, 40**
See also CA 105; CAAS 1; CANR 32; MTCW 1

Lemann, Nancy 1956- .... **CLC 39**
See also CA 118; 136

Lemonnier, (Antoine Louis) Camille 1844-1913 **TCLC 22**
See also CA 121

Lenau, Nikolaus 1802-1850 .... **NCLC 16**

L'Engle, Madeleine (Camp Franklin) 1918-**CLC 12; DAM POP**
See also AAYA 28; AITN 2; CA 1-4R; CANR 3,
21, 39, 66; CLR 1, 14; DLB 52; JRDA;
MAICYA; MTCW 1, 2; SAAS 15; SATA 1,
27, 75

Lengyel, Jozsef 1896-1975 .... **CLC 7**
See also CA 85-88; 57-60; CANR 71

Lenin 1870-1924
See Lenin, V. I.
See also CA 121; 168

Lenin, V. I. .... **TCLC 67**
See also Lenin

Lennon, John (Ono) 1940-1980 ...**CLC 12, 35**
See also CA 102

Lennox, Charlotte Ramsay 1729(?)-1804 **NCLC 23**
See also DLB 39

Lentricchia, Frank (Jr.) 1940- .... **CLC 34**
See also CA 25-28R; CANR 19

Lenz, Siegfried 1926- .... **CLC 27; SSC 33**
See also CA 89-92; DLB 75

Leonard, Elmore (John, Jr.) 1925-**CLC 28, 34, 71; DAM POP**
See also AAYA 22; AITN 1; BEST 89:1, 90:4;
CA 81-84; CANR 12, 28, 53, 76; DLB 173;
INT CANR-28; MTCW 1, 2

Leonard, Hugh .... **CLC 19**
See also Byrne, John Keyes
See also DLB 13

Leonov, Leonid (Maximovich) 1899-1994**CLC 92; DAM NOV**
See also CA 129; CANR 74, 76; MTCW 1, 2

Leopardi, (Conte) Giacomo 1798-1837**NCLC 22**

Le Reveler
See Artaud, Antonin (Marie Joseph)

Lerman, Eleanor 1952- .... **CLC 9**
See also CA 85-88; CANR 69

Lerman, Rhoda 1936- .... **CLC 56**
See also CA 49-52; CANR 70

Lermontov, Mikhail Yuryevich 1814-1841 **NCLC 47; PC 18**
See also DLB 205

Leroux, Gaston 1868-1927 .... **TCLC 25**
See also CA 108; 136; CANR 69; SATA 65

Lesage, Alain-Rene 1668-1747 .... **LC 2, 28**

Leskov, Nikolai (Semyonovich) 1831-1895 **NCLC 25; SSC 34**

Lessing, Doris (May) 1919- **CLC 1, 2, 3, 6, 10, 15, 22, 40, 94; DA; DAB; DAC; DAM MST, NOV; SSC 6; WLCS**
See also CA 9-12R; CAAS 14; CANR 33, 54,
76; CDBLB 1960 to Present; DLB 15, 139;
DLBY 85; MTCW 1, 2

Lessing, Gotthold Ephraim 1729-1781 ... **LC 8**
See also DLB 97

Lester, Richard 1932- .... **CLC 20**

Lever, Charles (James) 1806-1872 . **NCLC 23**
See also DLB 21

Leverson, Ada 1865(?)-1936(?) .... **TCLC 18**
See also Elaine
See also CA 117; DLB 153

Levertov, Denise 1923-1997**CLC 1, 2, 3, 5, 8, 15, 28, 66; DAM POET; PC 11**
See also CA 1-4R; 163; CAAS 19; CANR 3, 29,
50; DLB 5, 165; INT CANR-29; MTCW 1, 2

Levi, Jonathan .... **CLC 76**

Levi, Peter (Chad Tigar) 1931- .... **CLC 41**
See also CA 5-8R; CANR 34; DLB 40

Levi, Primo 1919-1987 .. **CLC 37, 50; SSC 12**
See also CA 13-16R; 122; CANR 12, 33, 61, 70;
DLB 177; MTCW 1, 2

Levin, Ira 1929- .... **CLC 3, 6; DAM POP**
See also CA 21-24R; CANR 17, 44, 74; MTCW
1, 2; SATA 66

Levin, Meyer 1905-1981 .. **CLC 7; DAM POP**
See also AITN 1; CA 9-12R; 104; CANR 15;
DLB 9, 28; DLBY 81; SATA 21; SATA-Obit
27

Levine, Norman 1924- .... **CLC 54**
See also CA 73-76; CAAS 23; CANR 14, 70;
DLB 88

Levine, Philip 1928-**CLC 2, 4, 5, 9, 14, 33, 118; DAM POET; PC 22**
See also CA 9-12R; CANR 9, 37, 52; DLB 5

Levinson, Deirdre 1931- .... **CLC 49**
See also CA 73-76; CANR 70

Levi-Strauss, Claude 1908- .... **CLC 38**
See also CA 1-4R; CANR 6, 32, 57; MTCW 1, 2

Levitin, Sonia (Wolff) 1934- .... **CLC 17**
See also AAYA 13; CA 29-32R; CANR 14, 32;
CLR 53; JRDA; MAICYA; SAAS 2; SATA 4,
68

Lopez Portillo (y Pacheco), Jose 1920-**CLC 46**
See also CA 129; HW
Lopez y Fuentes, Gregorio 1897(?)-1966 **C L C 32**
See also CA 131; HW
Lorca, Federico Garcia
See Garcia Lorca, Federico
Lord, Bette Bao 1938- ....**CLC 23**
See also BEST 90:3; CA 107; CANR 41; INT 107; SATA 58
Lord Auch
See Bataille, Georges
Lord Byron
See Byron, George Gordon (Noel)
Lorde, Audre (Geraldine) 1934-1992 **CLC 18, 71; BLC 2; DAM MULT, POET; PC 12**
See also BW 1; CA 25-28R; 142; CANR 16, 26, 46; DLB 41; MTCW 1, 2
Lord Houghton
See Milnes, Richard Monckton
Lord Jeffrey
See Jeffrey, Francis
Lorenzini, Carlo 1826-1890
See Collodi, Carlo
See also MAICYA; SATA 29, 100
Lorenzo, Heberto Padilla
See Padilla (Lorenzo), Heberto
Loris
See Hofmannsthal, Hugo von
Loti, Pierre .... **TCLC 11**
See also Viaud, (Louis Marie) Julien
See also DLB 123
Louie, David Wong 1954- ....**CLC 70**
See also CA 139
Louis, Father M.
See Merton, Thomas
Lovecraft, H(oward) P(hillips) 1890-1937 **TCLC 4, 22; DAM POP; SSC 3**
See also AAYA 14; CA 104; 133; MTCW 1, 2
Lovelace, Earl 1935- ....**CLC 51**
See also BW 2; CA 77-80; CANR 41, 72; DLB 125; MTCW 1
Lovelace, Richard 1618-1657 ....**LC 24**
See also DLB 131
Lowell, Amy 1874-1925 ..... **TCLC 1, 8; DAM POET; PC 13**
See also CA 104; 151; DLB 54, 140; MTCW 2
Lowell, James Russell 1819-1891 ......**NCLC 2**
See also CDALB 1640-1865; DLB 1, 11, 64, 79, 189
Lowell, Robert (Traill Spence, Jr.) 1917-1977 **CLC 1, 2, 3, 4, 5, 8, 9, 11, 15, 37; DA; DAB; DAC; DAM MST, NOV; PC 3; WLC**
See also CA 9-12R; 73-76; CABS 2; CANR 26, 60; DLB 5, 169; MTCW 1, 2
Lowenthal, Michael (Francis) 1969- **CLC 119**
See also CA 150
Lowndes, Marie Adelaide (Belloc) 1868-1947 **TCLC 12**
See also CA 107; DLB 70
Lowry, (Clarence) Malcolm 1909-1957 **T C L C 6, 40; SSC 31**
See also CA 105; 131; CANR 62; CDBLB 1945-1960; DLB 15; MTCW 1, 2
Lowry, Mina Gertrude 1882-1966
See Loy, Mina
See also CA 113
Loxsmith, John
See Brunner, John (Kilian Houston)
Loy, Mina .... **CLC 28; DAM POET; PC 16**
See also Lowry, Mina Gertrude
See also DLB 4, 54

Loyson-Bridet
See Schwob, Marcel (Mayer Andre)
Lucan 39-65 .... **CMLC 33**
See also DLB 211
Lucas, Craig 1951- ....**CLC 64**
See also CA 137; CANR 71
Lucas, E(dward) V(errall) 1868-1938 **TCLC 73**
See also DLB 98, 149, 153; SATA 20
Lucas, George 1944- ....**CLC 16**
See also AAYA 1, 23; CA 77-80; CANR 30; SATA 56
Lucas, Hans
See Godard, Jean-Luc
Lucas, Victoria
See Plath, Sylvia
Lucian c. 120-c. 180 ....**CMLC 32**
See also DLB 176
Ludlam, Charles 1943-1987 ....**CLC 46, 50**
See also CA 85-88; 122; CANR 72
Ludlum, Robert 1927-**CLC 22, 43; DAM NOV, POP**
See also AAYA 10; BEST 89:1, 90:3; CA 33-36R; CANR 25, 41, 68; DLBY 82; MTCW 1, 2
Ludwig, Ken ....**CLC 60**
Ludwig, Otto 1813-1865 ....**NCLC 4**
See also DLB 129
Lugones, Leopoldo 1874-1938 ....**TCLC 15**
See also CA 116; 131; HW
Lu Hsun 1881-1936 ....**TCLC 3; SSC 20**
See also Shu-Jen, Chou
Lukacs, George ....**CLC 24**
See also Lukacs, Gyorgy (Szegeny von)
Lukacs, Gyorgy (Szegeny von) 1885-1971
See Lukacs, George
See also CA 101; 29-32R; CANR 62; MTCW 2
Luke, Peter (Ambrose Cyprian) 1919-1995 **CLC 38**
See also CA 81-84; 147; CANR 72; DLB 13
Lunar, Dennis
See Mungo, Raymond
Lurie, Alison 1926- ....**CLC 4, 5, 18, 39**
See also CA 1-4R; CANR 2, 17, 50; DLB 2; MTCW 1; SATA 46
Lustig, Arnost 1926- ....**CLC 56**
See also AAYA 3; CA 69-72; CANR 47; SATA 56
Luther, Martin 1483-1546 ....**LC 9, 37**
See also DLB 179
Luxemburg, Rosa 1870(?)-1919 ......**TCLC 63**
See also CA 118
Luzi, Mario 1914- ....**CLC 13**
See also CA 61-64; CANR 9, 70; DLB 128
Lyly, John 1554(?)-1606 **LC 41; DAM DRAM; DC 7**
See also DLB 62, 167
L'Ymagier
See Gourmont, Remy (-Marie-Charles) de
Lynch, B. Suarez
See Bioy Casares, Adolfo; Borges, Jorge Luis
Lynch, David (K.) 1946- ....**CLC 66**
See also CA 124; 129
Lynch, James
See Andreyev, Leonid (Nikolaevich)
Lynch Davis, B.
See Bioy Casares, Adolfo; Borges, Jorge Luis
Lyndsay, Sir David 1490-1555 ....**LC 20**
Lynn, Kenneth S(chuyler) 1923- ....**CLC 50**
See also CA 1-4R; CANR 3, 27, 65
Lynx
See West, Rebecca
Lyons, Marcus
See Blish, James (Benjamin)

Lyre, Pinchbeck
See Sassoon, Siegfried (Lorraine)
Lytle, Andrew (Nelson) 1902-1995 .....**CLC 22**
See also CA 9-12R; 150; CANR 70; DLB 6; DLBY 95
Lyttelton, George 1709-1773 ....**LC 10**
Maas, Peter 1929- ....**CLC 29**
See also CA 93-96; INT 93-96; MTCW 2
Macaulay, Rose 1881-1958 ....**TCLC 7, 44**
See also CA 104; DLB 36
Macaulay, Thomas Babington 1800-1859 **NCLC 42**
See also CDBLB 1832-1890; DLB 32, 55
MacBeth, George (Mann) 1932-1992 **CLC 2, 5, 9**
See also CA 25-28R; 136; CANR 61, 66; DLB 40; MTCW 1; SATA 4; SATA-Obit 70
MacCaig, Norman (Alexander) 1910-**CLC 36; DAB; DAM POET**
See also CA 9-12R; CANR 3, 34; DLB 27
MacCarthy, Sir(Charles Otto) Desmond 1877-1952 .... **TCLC 36**
See also CA 167
MacDiarmid, Hugh CLC 2, 4, 11, 19, 63; PC 9
See also Grieve, C(hristopher) M(urray)
See also CDBLB 1945-1960; DLB 20
MacDonald, Anson
See Heinlein, Robert A(nson)
Macdonald, Cynthia 1928- ....**CLC 13, 19**
See also CA 49-52; CANR 4, 44; DLB 105
MacDonald, George 1824-1905 ....**TCLC 9**
See also CA 106; 137; DLB 18, 163, 178; MAICYA; SATA 33, 100
Macdonald, John
See Millar, Kenneth
MacDonald, John D(ann) 1916-1986**CLC 3, 27, 44; DAM NOV, POP**
See also CA 1-4R; 121; CANR 1, 19, 60; DLB 8; DLBY 86; MTCW 1, 2
Macdonald, John Ross
See Millar, Kenneth
Macdonald, Ross ....**CLC 1, 2, 3, 14, 34, 41**
See also Millar, Kenneth
See also DLBD 6
MacDougal, John
See Blish, James (Benjamin)
MacEwen, Gwendolyn (Margaret) 1941-1987 **CLC 13, 55**
See also CA 9-12R; 124; CANR 7, 22; DLB 53; SATA 50; SATA-Obit 55
Macha, Karel Hynek 1810-1846 .....**NCLC 46**
Machado (y Ruiz), Antonio 1875-1939**TCLC 3**
See also CA 104; DLB 108
Machado de Assis, Joaquim Maria 1839-1908 **TCLC 10; BLC 2; SSC 24**
See also CA 107; 153
Machen, Arthur ....**TCLC 4; SSC 20**
See also Jones, Arthur Llewellyn
See also DLB 36, 156, 178
Machiavelli, Niccolo 1469-1527**LC 8, 36; DA; DAB; DAC; DAM MST; WLCS**
MacInnes, Colin 1914-1976 ....**CLC 4, 23**
See also CA 69-72; 65-68; CANR 21; DLB 14; MTCW 1, 2
MacInnes, Helen (Clark) 1907-1985 **CLC 27, 39; DAM POP**
See also CA 1-4R; 117; CANR 1, 28, 58; DLB 87; MTCW 1, 2; SATA 22; SATA-Obit 44
Mackay, Mary 1855-1924
See Corelli, Marie
See also CA 118

Manzoni, Alessandro 1785-1873 ..... **NCLC 29**
Map, Walter 1140-1209 .... **CMLC 32**
Mapu, Abraham (ben Jekutiel) 1808-1867
NCLC 18
Mara, Sally
See Queneau, Raymond
Marat, Jean Paul 1743-1793 .... **LC 10**
Marcel, Gabriel Honore 1889-1973 ... **CLC 15**
See also CA 102; 45-48; MTCW 1, 2
Marchbanks, Samuel
See Davies, (William) Robertson
Marchi, Giacomo
See Bassani, Giorgio
Margulies, Donald .... **CLC 76**
Marie de France c. 12th cent. -**CMLC 8; PC 22**
See also DLB 208
Marie de l'Incarnation 1599-1672 .... **LC 10**
Marier, Captain Victor
See Griffith, D(avid Lewelyn) W(ark)
Mariner, Scott
See Pohl, Frederik
Marinetti, Filippo Tommaso 1876-1944**T C L C
10**
See also CA 107; DLB 114
Marivaux, Pierre Carlet de Chamblain de
1688-1763 .... **LC 4; DC 7**
Markandaya, Kamala .... **CLC 8, 38**
See also Taylor, Kamala (Purnaiya)
Markfield, Wallace 1926- .... **CLC 8**
See also CA 69-72; CAAS 3; DLB 2, 28
Markham, Edwin 1852-1940 .... **TCLC 47**
See also CA 160; DLB 54, 186
Markham, Robert
See Amis, Kingsley (William)
Marks, J
See Highwater, Jamake (Mamake)
Marks-Highwater, J
See Highwater, Jamake (Mamake)
Markson, David M(errill) 1927- .... **CLC 67**
See also CA 49-52; CANR 1
Marley, Bob .... **CLC 17**
See also Marley, Robert Nesta
Marley, Robert Nesta 1945-1981
See Marley, Bob
See also CA 107; 103
Marlowe, Christopher 1564-1593 . **LC 22, 47;
DA; DAB; DAC; DAM DRAM, MST; DC
1; WLC**
See also CDBLB Before 1660; DLB 62
Marlowe, Stephen 1928-
See Queen, Ellery
See also CA 13-16R; CANR 6, 55
Marmontel, Jean-Francois 1723-1799 ...**LC 2**
Marquand, John P(hillips) 1893-1960 **CLC 2,
10**
See also CA 85-88; CANR 73; DLB 9, 102;
MTCW 2
Marques, Rene 1919-1979 ...... **CLC 96; DAM
MULT; HLC**
See also CA 97-100; 85-88; CANR 78; DLB 113;
HW
Marquez, Gabriel (Jose) Garcia
See Garcia Marquez, Gabriel (Jose)
Marquis, Don(ald Robert Perry) 1878-1937
TCLC 7
See also CA 104; 166; DLB 11, 25
Marric, J. J.
See Creasey, John
Marryat, Frederick 1792-1848 .... **NCLC 3**
See also DLB 21, 163
Marsden, James
See Creasey, John

Marsh, (Edith) Ngaio 1899-1982 . **CLC 7, 53;
DAM POP**
See also CA 9-12R; CANR 6, 58; DLB 77;
MTCW 1, 2
Marshall, Garry 1934- .... **CLC 17**
See also AAYA 3; CA 111; SATA 60
Marshall, Paule 1929- .... **CLC 27, 72; BLC 3;
DAM MULT; SSC 3**
See also BW 2; CA 77-80; CANR 25, 73; DLB
157; MTCW 1, 2
Marshallik
See Zangwill, Israel
Marsten, Richard
See Hunter, Evan
Marston, John 1576-1634**LC 33; DAM DRAM**
See also DLB 58, 172
Martha, Henry
See Harris, Mark
Marti, Jose 1853-1895**NCLC 63; DAM MULT;
HLC**
See also DLB 211
Martial c. 40-c. 104 .... **PC 10**
See also DLB 211
Martin, Ken
See Hubbard, L(afayette) Ron(ald)
Martin, Richard
See Creasey, John
Martin, Steve 1945- .... **CLC 30**
See also CA 97-100; CANR 30; MTCW 1
Martin, Valerie 1948- .... **CLC 89**
See also BEST 90:2; CA 85-88; CANR 49
Martin, Violet Florence 1862-1915 . **TCLC 51**
Martin, Webber
See Silverberg, Robert
Martindale, Patrick Victor
See White, Patrick (Victor Martindale)
Martin du Gard, Roger 1881-1958 . **TCLC 24**
See also CA 118; DLB 65
Martineau, Harriet 1802-1876 .... **NCLC 26**
See also DLB 21, 55, 159, 163, 166, 190; YABC
2
Martines, Julia
See O'Faolain, Julia
Martinez, Enrique Gonzalez
See Gonzalez Martinez, Enrique
Martinez, Jacinto Benavente y
See Benavente (y Martinez), Jacinto
Martinez Ruiz, Jose 1873-1967
See Azorin; Ruiz, Jose Martinez
See also CA 93-96; HW
Martinez Sierra, Gregorio 1881-1947**TCLC 6**
See also CA 115
Martinez Sierra, Maria (de la O'LeJarraga)
1874-1974 .... **TCLC 6**
See also CA 115
Martinsen, Martin
See Follett, Ken(neth Martin)
Martinson, Harry (Edmund) 1904-1978 **C L C
14**
See also CA 77-80; CANR 34
Marut, Ret
See Traven, B.
Marut, Robert
See Traven, B.
Marvell, Andrew 1621-1678 .... **LC 4, 43; DA;
DAB; DAC; DAM MST, POET; PC 10;
WLC**
See also CDBLB 1660-1789; DLB 131
Marx, Karl (Heinrich) 1818-1883 .. **NCLC 17**
See also DLB 129
Masaoka Shiki .... **TCLC 18**
See also Masaoka Tsunenori
Masaoka Tsunenori 1867-1902
See Masaoka Shiki

See also CA 117
Masefield, John (Edward) 1878-1967**CLC 11,
47; DAM POET**
See also CA 19-20; 25-28R; CANR 33; CAP 2;
CDBLB 1890-1914; DLB 10, 19, 153, 160;
MTCW 1, 2; SATA 19
Maso, Carole 19(?)- .... **CLC 44**
See also CA 170
Mason, Bobbie Ann 1940-**CLC 28, 43, 82; SSC
4**
See also AAYA 5; CA 53-56; CANR 11, 31, 58;
DLB 173; DLBY 87; INT CANR-31; MTCW
1, 2
Mason, Ernst
See Pohl, Frederik
Mason, Lee W.
See Malzberg, Barry N(athaniel)
Mason, Nick 1945- .... **CLC 35**
Mason, Tally
See Derleth, August (William)
Mass, William
See Gibson, William
Master Lao
See Lao Tzu
Masters, Edgar Lee 1868-1950 .. **TCLC 2, 25;
DA; DAC; DAM MST, POET; PC 1; WLCS**
See also CA 104; 133; CDALB 1865-1917; DLB
54; MTCW 1, 2
Masters, Hilary 1928- .... **CLC 48**
See also CA 25-28R; CANR 13, 47
Mastrosimone, William 19(?)- .... **CLC 36**
Mathe, Albert
See Camus, Albert
Mather, Cotton 1663-1728 .... **LC 38**
See also CDALB 1640-1865; DLB 24, 30, 140
Mather, Increase 1639-1723 .... **LC 38**
See also DLB 24
Matheson, Richard Burton 1926- ...... **CLC 37**
See also CA 97-100; DLB 8, 44; INT 97-100
Mathews, Harry 1930- .... **CLC 6, 52**
See also CA 21-24R; CAAS 6; CANR 18, 40
Mathews, John Joseph 1894-1979 ... **CLC 84;
DAM MULT**
See also CA 19-20; 142; CANR 45; CAP 2; DLB
175; NNAL
Mathias, Roland (Glyn) 1915- .... **CLC 45**
See also CA 97-100; CANR 19, 41; DLB 27
Matsuo Basho 1644-1694 .... **PC 3**
See also DAM POET
Mattheson, Rodney
See Creasey, John
Matthews, Greg 1949- .... **CLC 45**
See also CA 135
Matthews, William (Procter, III) 1942-1997
CLC 40
See also CA 29-32R; 162; CAAS 18; CANR 12,
57; DLB 5
Matthias, John (Edward) 1941- .... **CLC 9**
See also CA 33-36R; CANR 56
Matthiessen, Peter 1927-**CLC 5, 7, 11, 32, 64;
DAM NOV**
See also AAYA 6; BEST 90:4; CA 9-12R; CANR
21, 50, 73; DLB 6, 173; MTCW 1, 2; SATA
27
Maturin, Charles Robert 1780(?)-1824**N C L C
6**
See also DLB 178
Matute (Ausejo), Ana Maria 1925- .... **CLC 11**
See also CA 89-92; MTCW 1
Maugham, W. S.
See Maugham, W(illiam) Somerset
Maugham, W(illiam) Somerset 1874-1965**CLC
1, 11, 15, 67, 93; DA; DAB; DAC; DAM**

Medoff, Mark (Howard) 1940- .... **CLC 6, 23; DAM DRAM**
See also AITN 1; CA 53-56; CANR 5; DLB 7; INT CANR-5

Medvedev, P. N.
See Bakhtin, Mikhail Mikhailovich

Meged, Aharon
See Megged, Aharon

Meged, Aron
See Megged, Aharon

Megged, Aharon 1920- .... **CLC 9**
See also CA 49-52; CAAS 13; CANR 1

Mehta, Ved (Parkash) 1934- .... **CLC 37**
See also CA 1-4R; CANR 2, 23, 69; MTCW 1

Melanter
See Blackmore, R(ichard) D(oddridge)

Melies, Georges 1861-1938 .... **TCLC 81**

Melikow, Loris
See Hofmannsthal, Hugo von

Melmoth, Sebastian
See Wilde, Oscar

Meltzer, Milton 1915- .... **CLC 26**
See also AAYA 8; CA 13-16R; CANR 38; CLR 13; DLB 61; JRDA; MAICYA; SAAS 1; SATA 1, 50, 80

Melville, Herman 1819-1891 **NCLC 3, 12, 29, 45, 49; DA; DAB; DAC; DAM MST, NOV; SSC 1, 17; WLC**
See also AAYA 25; CDALB 1640-1865; DLB 3, 74; SATA 59

Menander c. 342B.C.-c. 292B.C. ..... **CMLC 9; DAM DRAM; DC 3**
See also DLB 176

Mencken, H(enry) L(ouis) 1880-1956 **TCLC 13**
See also CA 105; 125; CDALB 1917-1929; DLB 11, 29, 63, 137; MTCW 1, 2

Mendelsohn, Jane 1965(?)- .... **CLC 99**
See also CA 154

Mercer, David 1928-1980 **CLC 5; DAM DRAM**
See also CA 9-12R; 102; CANR 23; DLB 13; MTCW 1

Merchant, Paul
See Ellison, Harlan (Jay)

Meredith, George 1828-1909 ... **TCLC 17, 43; DAM POET**
See also CA 117; 153; CDBLB 1832-1890; DLB 18, 35, 57, 159

Meredith, William (Morris) 1919- **CLC 4, 13, 22, 55; DAM POET**
See also CA 9-12R; CAAS 14; CANR 6, 40; DLB 5

Merezhkovsky, Dmitry Sergeyevich 1865-1941 **TCLC 29**
See also CA 169

Merimee, Prosper 1803-1870 **NCLC 6, 65; SSC 7**
See also DLB 119, 192

Merkin, Daphne 1954- .... **CLC 44**
See also CA 123

Merlin, Arthur
See Blish, James (Benjamin)

Merrill, James (Ingram) 1926-1995 **CLC 2, 3, 6, 8, 13, 18, 34, 91; DAM POET**
See also CA 13-16R; 147; CANR 10, 49, 63; DLB 5, 165; DLBY 85; INT CANR-10; MTCW 1, 2

Merriman, Alex
See Silverberg, Robert

Merriman, Brian 1747-1805 .... **NCLC 70**

Merritt, E. B.
See Waddington, Miriam

Merton, Thomas 1915-1968 **CLC 1, 3, 11, 34, 83; PC 10**
See also CA 5-8R; 25-28R; CANR 22, 53; DLB 48; DLBY 81; MTCW 1, 2

Merwin, W(illiam) S(tanley) 1927- **CLC 1, 2, 3, 5, 8, 13, 18, 45, 88; DAM POET**
See also CA 13-16R; CANR 15, 51; DLB 5, 169; INT CANR-15; MTCW 1, 2

Metcalf, John 1938- .... **CLC 37**
See also CA 113; DLB 60

Metcalf, Suzanne
See Baum, L(yman) Frank

Mew, Charlotte (Mary) 1870-1928 ... **TCLC 8**
See also CA 105; DLB 19, 135

Mewshaw, Michael 1943- .... **CLC 9**
See also CA 53-56; CANR 7, 47; DLBY 80

Meyer, June
See Jordan, June

Meyer, Lynn
See Slavitt, David R(ytman)

Meyer-Meyrink, Gustav 1868-1932
See Meyrink, Gustav
See also CA 117

Meyers, Jeffrey 1939- .... **CLC 39**
See also CA 73-76; CANR 54; DLB 111

Meynell, Alice (Christina Gertrude Thompson) 1847-1922 .... **TCLC 6**
See also CA 104; DLB 19, 98

Meyrink, Gustav .... **TCLC 21**
See also Meyer-Meyrink, Gustav
See also DLB 81

Michaels, Leonard 1933- . **CLC 6, 25; SSC 16**
See also CA 61-64; CANR 21, 62; DLB 130; MTCW 1

Michaux, Henri 1899-1984 .... **CLC 8, 19**
See also CA 85-88; 114

Micheaux, Oscar 1884-1951 .... **TCLC 76**
See also DLB 50

Michelangelo 1475-1564 .... **LC 12**

Michelet, Jules 1798-1874 .... **NCLC 31**

Michels, Robert 1876-1936 .... **TCLC 88**

Michener, James A(lbert) 1907(?)-1997 **CLC 1, 5, 11, 29, 60, 109; DAM NOV, POP**
See also AAYA 27; AITN 1; BEST 90:1; CA 5-8R; 161; CANR 21, 45, 68; DLB 6; MTCW 1, 2

Mickiewicz, Adam 1798-1855 .... **NCLC 3**

Middleton, Christopher 1926- .... **CLC 13**
See also CA 13-16R; CANR 29, 54; DLB 40

Middleton, Richard (Barham) 1882-1911 **TCLC 56**
See also DLB 156

Middleton, Stanley 1919- .... **CLC 7, 38**
See also CA 25-28R; CAAS 23; CANR 21, 46; DLB 14

Middleton, Thomas 1580-1627 . **LC 33; DAM DRAM, MST; DC 5**
See also DLB 58

Migueis, Jose Rodrigues 1901- .... **CLC 10**

Mikszath, Kalman 1847-1910 .... **TCLC 31**
See also CA 170

Miles, Jack .... **CLC 100**

Miles, Josephine (Louise) 1911-1985 **CLC 1, 2, 14, 34, 39; DAM POET**
See also CA 1-4R; 116; CANR 2, 55; DLB 48

Militant
See Sandburg, Carl (August)

Mill, John Stuart 1806-1873 ..... **NCLC 11, 58**
See also CDBLB 1832-1890; DLB 55, 190

Millar, Kenneth 1915-1983 **CLC 14; DAM POP**
See also Macdonald, Ross
See also CA 9-12R; 110; CANR 16, 63; DLB 2; DLBD 6; DLBY 83; MTCW 1, 2

Millay, E. Vincent
See Millay, Edna St. Vincent

Millay, Edna St. Vincent 1892-1950 . **TCLC 4, 49; DA; DAB; DAC; DAM MST, POET; PC 6; WLCS**
See also CA 104; 130; CDALB 1917-1929; DLB 45; MTCW 1, 2

Miller, Arthur 1915- **CLC 1, 2, 6, 10, 15, 26, 47, 78; DA; DAB; DAC; DAM DRAM, MST; DC 1; WLC**
See also AAYA 15; AITN 1; CA 1-4R; CABS 3; CANR 2, 30, 54, 76; CDALB 1941-1968; DLB 7; MTCW 1, 2

Miller, Henry (Valentine) 1891-1980 **CLC 1, 2, 4, 9, 14, 43, 84; DA; DAB; DAC; DAM MST, NOV; WLC**
See also CA 9-12R; 97-100; CANR 33, 64; CDALB 1929-1941; DLB 4, 9; DLBY 80; MTCW 1, 2

Miller, Jason 1939(?)- .... **CLC 2**
See also AITN 1; CA 73-76; DLB 7

Miller, Sue 1943- .... **CLC 44; DAM POP**
See also BEST 90:3; CA 139; CANR 59; DLB 143

Miller, Walter M(ichael, Jr.) 1923- **CLC 4, 30**
See also CA 85-88; DLB 8

Millett, Kate 1934- .... **CLC 67**
See also AITN 1; CA 73-76; CANR 32, 53, 76; MTCW 1, 2

Millhauser, Steven (Lewis) 1943- **CLC 21, 54, 109**
See also CA 110; 111; CANR 63; DLB 2; INT 111; MTCW 2

Millin, Sarah Gertrude 1889-1968 .... **CLC 49**
See also CA 102; 93-96

Milne, A(lan) A(lexander) 1882-1956 **TCLC 6, 88; DAB; DAC; DAM MST**
See also CA 104; 133; CLR 1, 26; DLB 10, 77, 100, 160; MAICYA; MTCW 1, 2; SATA 100; YABC 1

Milner, Ron(ald) 1938- **CLC 56; BLC 3; DAM MULT**
See also AITN 1; BW 1; CA 73-76; CANR 24; DLB 38; MTCW 1

Milnes, Richard Monckton 1809-1885 **NCLC 61**
See also DLB 32, 184

Milosz, Czeslaw 1911- **CLC 5, 11, 22, 31, 56, 82; DAM MST, POET; PC 8; WLCS**
See also CA 81-84; CANR 23, 51; MTCW 1, 2

Milton, John 1608-1674 . **LC 9, 43; DA; DAB; DAC; DAM MST, POET; PC 19; WLC**
See also CDBLB 1660-1789; DLB 131, 151

Min, Anchee 1957- .... **CLC 86**
See also CA 146

Minehaha, Cornelius
See Wedekind, (Benjamin) Frank(lin)

Miner, Valerie 1947- .... **CLC 40**
See also CA 97-100; CANR 59

Minimo, Duca
See D'Annunzio, Gabriele

Minot, Susan 1956- .... **CLC 44**
See also CA 134

Minus, Ed 1938- .... **CLC 39**

Miranda, Javier
See Bioy Casares, Adolfo

Mirbeau, Octave 1848-1917 .... **TCLC 55**
See also DLB 123, 192

Miro (Ferrer), Gabriel (Francisco Victor) 1879-1930 .... **TCLC 5**
See also CA 104

p'Bitek, Okot 1931-1982**CLC 96; BLC 3; DAM MULT**
See also BW 2; CA 124; 107; DLB 125; MTCW 1, 2

Peacock, Molly 1947- .... **CLC 60**
See also CA 103; CAAS 21; CANR 52; DLB 120

Peacock, Thomas Love 1785-1866 .. **NCLC 22**
See also DLB 96, 116

Peake, Mervyn 1911-1968 .... **CLC 7, 54**
See also CA 5-8R; 25-28R; CANR 3; DLB 15, 160; MTCW 1; SATA 23

Pearce, Philippa .... **CLC 21**
See also Christie, (Ann) Philippa
See also CLR 9; DLB 161; MAICYA; SATA 1, 67

Pearl, Eric
See Elman, Richard (Martin)

Pearson, T(homas) R(eid) 1956- .... **CLC 39**
See also CA 120; 130; INT 130

Peck, Dale 1967- .... **CLC 81**
See also CA 146; CANR 72

Peck, John 1941- .... **CLC 3**
See also CA 49-52; CANR 3

Peck, Richard (Wayne) 1934- .... **CLC 21**
See also AAYA 1, 24; CA 85-88; CANR 19, 38; CLR 15; INT CANR-19; JRDA; MAICYA; SAAS 2; SATA 18, 55, 97

Peck, Robert Newton 1928-**CLC 17; DA; DAC; DAM MST**
See also AAYA 3; CA 81-84; CANR 31, 63; CLR 45; JRDA; MAICYA; SAAS 1; SATA 21, 62

Peckinpah, (David) Sam(uel) 1925-1984 **C L C 20**
See also CA 109; 114

Pedersen, Knut 1859-1952
See Hamsun, Knut
See also CA 104; 119; CANR 63; MTCW 1, 2

Peeslake, Gaffer
See Durrell, Lawrence (George)

Peguy, Charles Pierre 1873-1914 .... **TCLC 10**
See also CA 107

Peirce, Charles Sanders 1839-1914 **TCLC 81**

Pena, Ramon del Valle y
<indSee Valle-Inclan, Ramon (Maria) del

Pendennis, Arthur Esquir
See Thackeray, William Makepeace

Penn, William 1644-1718 .... **LC 25**
See also DLB 24

PEPECE
See Prado (Calvo), Pedro

Pepys, Samuel 1633-1703 .. **LC 11; DA; DAB; DAC; DAM MST; WLC**
See also CDBLB 1660-1789; DLB 101

Percy, Walker 1916-1990**CLC 2, 3, 6, 8, 14, 18, 47, 65; DAM NOV, POP**
See also CA 1-4R; 131; CANR 1, 23, 64; DLB 2; DLBY 80, 90; MTCW 1, 2

Percy, William Alexander 1885-1942**TCLC 84**
See also CA 163; MTCW 2

Perec, Georges 1936-1982 .... **CLC 56, 116**
See also CA 141; DLB 83

Pereda (y Sanchez de Porrua), Jose Maria de 1833-1906 .... **TCLC 16**
See also CA 117

Pereda y Porrua, Jose Maria de
See Pereda (y Sanchez de Porrua), Jose Maria de

Peregoy, George Weems
See Mencken, H(enry) L(ouis)

Perelman, S(idney) J(oseph) 1904-1979**CLC 3, 5, 9, 15, 23, 44, 49; DAM DRAM; SSC 32**
See also AITN 1, 2; CA 73-76; 89-92; CANR 18; DLB 11, 44; MTCW 1, 2

Peret, Benjamin 1899-1959 .... **TCLC 20**
See also CA 117

Peretz, Isaac Loeb 1851(?)-1915**TCLC 16; SSC 26**
See also CA 109

Peretz, Yitzkhok Leibush
See Peretz, Isaac Loeb

Perez Galdos, Benito 1843-1920 ..... **TCLC 27**
See also CA 125; 153; HW

Perrault, Charles 1628-1703 .... **LC 2**
See also MAICYA; SATA 25

Perry, Brighton
See Sherwood, Robert E(mmet)

Perse, St.-John
See Leger, (Marie-Rene Auguste) Alexis Saint-Leger

Perutz, Leo(pold) 1882-1957 .... **TCLC 60**
See also CA 147; DLB 81

Peseenz, Tulio F.
See Lopez y Fuentes, Gregorio

Pesetsky, Bette 1932- .... **CLC 28**
See also CA 133; DLB 130

Peshkov, Alexei Maximovich 1868-1936
See Gorky, Maxim
See also CA 105; 141; DA; DAC; DAM DRAM, MST, NOV; MTCW 2

Pessoa, Fernando (Antonio Nogueira) 1888-1935 **TCLC 27; DAM MULT; HLC; PC 20**
See also CA 125

Peterkin, Julia Mood 1880-1961 .... **CLC 31**
See also CA 102; DLB 9

Peters, Joan K(aren) 1945- .... **CLC 39**
See also CA 158

Peters, Robert L(ouis) 1924- .... **CLC 7**
See also CA 13-16R; CAAS 8; DLB 105

Petofi, Sandor 1823-1849 .... **NCLC 21**

Petrakis, Harry Mark 1923- .... **CLC 3**
See also CA 9-12R; CANR 4, 30

Petrarch 1304-1374 **CMLC 20; DAM POET; PC 8**

Petrov, Evgeny .... **TCLC 21**
See also Kataev, Evgeny Petrovich

Petry, Ann (Lane) 1908-1997 ..... **CLC 1, 7, 18**
See also BW 1; CA 5-8R; 157; CAAS 6; CANR 4, 46; CLR 12; DLB 76; JRDA; MAICYA; MTCW 1; SATA 5; SATA-Obit 94

Petursson, Halligrimur 1614-1674 .... **LC 8**

Peychinovich
See Vazov, Ivan (Minchov)

Phaedrus c. 18B.C.-c. 50 .... **CMLC 25**
See also DLB 211

Philips, Katherine 1632-1664 .... **LC 30**
See also DLB 131

Philipson, Morris H. 1926- .... **CLC 53**
See also CA 1-4R; CANR 4

Phillips, Caryl 1958- .. **CLC 96; BLCS; DAM MULT**
See also BW 2; CA 141; CANR 63; DLB 157; MTCW 2

Phillips, David Graham 1867-1911 . **TCLC 44**
See also CA 108; DLB 9, 12

Phillips, Jack
See Sandburg, Carl (August)

Phillips, Jayne Anne 1952-**CLC 15, 33; SSC 16**
See also CA 101; CANR 24, 50; DLBY 80; INT CANR-24; MTCW 1, 2

Phillips, Richard
See Dick, Philip K(indred)

Phillips, Robert (Schaeffer) 1938- ..... **CLC 28**
See also CA 17-20R; CAAS 13; CANR 8; DLB 105

Phillips, Ward
See Lovecraft, H(oward) P(hillips)

Piccolo, Lucio 1901-1969 .... **CLC 13**
See also CA 97-100; DLB 114

Pickthall, Marjorie L(owry) C(hristie) 1883-1922 .... **TCLC 21**
See also CA 107; DLB 92

Pico della Mirandola, Giovanni 1463-1494**L C 15**

Piercy, Marge 1936- .. **CLC 3, 6, 14, 18, 27, 62**
See also CA 21-24R; CAAS 1; CANR 13, 43, 66; DLB 120; MTCW 1, 2

Piers, Robert
See Anthony, Piers

Pieyre de Mandiargues, Andre 1909-1991
See Mandiargues, Andre Pieyre de
See also CA 103; 136; CANR 22

Pilnyak, Boris .... **TCLC 23**
See also Vogau, Boris Andreyevich

Pincherle, Alberto 1907-1990 .... **CLC 11, 18; DAM NOV**
See also Moravia, Alberto
See also CA 25-28R; 132; CANR 33, 63; MTCW 1

Pinckney, Darryl 1953- .... **CLC 76**
See also BW 2; CA 143

Pindar 518B.C.-446B.C. ...... **CMLC 12; PC 19**
See also DLB 176

Pineda, Cecile 1942- .... **CLC 39**
See also CA 118

Pinero, Arthur Wing 1855-1934 .... **TCLC 32; DAM DRAM**
See also CA 110; 153; DLB 10

Pinero, Miguel (Antonio Gomez) 1946-1988 **CLC 4, 55**
See also CA 61-64; 125; CANR 29; HW

Pinget, Robert 1919-1997 .... **CLC 7, 13, 37**
See also CA 85-88; 160; DLB 83

Pink Floyd
See Barrett, (Roger) Syd; Gilmour, David; Mason, Nick; Waters, Roger; Wright, Rick

Pinkney, Edward 1802-1828 .... **NCLC 31**

Pinkwater, Daniel Manus 1941- .... **CLC 35**
See also Pinkwater, Manus
See also AAYA 1; CA 29-32R; CANR 12, 38; CLR 4; JRDA; MAICYA; SAAS 3; SATA 46, 76

Pinkwater, Manus
See Pinkwater, Daniel Manus
See also SATA 8

Pinsky, Robert 1940-**CLC 9, 19, 38, 94; DAM POET**
See also CA 29-32R; CAAS 4; CANR 58; DLBY 82, 98; MTCW 2

Pinta, Harold
See Pinter, Harold

Pinter, Harold 1930-**CLC 1, 3, 6, 9, 11, 15, 27, 58, 73; DA; DAB; DAC; DAM DRAM, MST; WLC**
See also CA 5-8R; CANR 33, 65; CDBLB 1960 to Present; DLB 13; MTCW 1, 2

Piozzi, Hester Lynch (Thrale) 1741-1821 **NCLC 57**
See also DLB 104, 142

Pirandello, Luigi 1867-1936**TCLC 4, 29; DA; DAB; DAC; DAM DRAM, MST; DC 5; SSC 22; WLC**
See also CA 104; 153; MTCW 2

Pirsig, Robert M(aynard) 1928-**CLC 4, 6, 73; DAM POP**
See also CA 53-56; CANR 42, 74; MTCW 1, 2; SATA 39

Pisarev, Dmitry Ivanovich 1840-1868**NCLC 25**

Pix, Mary (Griffith) 1666-1709 .... **LC 8**
See also DLB 80

Shamlu, Ahmad 1925- ....**CLC 10**

Shammas, Anton 1951- ....**CLC 55**

Shange, Ntozake 1948-**CLC 8, 25, 38, 74; BLC 3; DAM DRAM, MULT; DC 3**
See also AAYA 9; BW 2; CA 85-88; CABS 3; CANR 27, 48, 74; DLB 38; MTCW 1, 2

Shanley, John Patrick 1950- ....**CLC 75**
See also CA 128; 133

Shapcott, Thomas W(illiam) 1935- ....**CLC 38**
See also CA 69-72; CANR 49

Shapiro, Jane ....**CLC 76**

Shapiro, Karl (Jay) 1913-**CLC 4, 8, 15, 53; PC 25**
See also CA 1-4R; CAAS 6; CANR 1, 36, 66; DLB 48; MTCW 1, 2

Sharp, William 1855-1905 ....**TCLC 39**
See also CA 160; DLB 156

Sharpe, Thomas Ridley 1928-
See Sharpe, Tom
See also CA 114; 122; INT 122

Sharpe, Tom ....**CLC 36**
See also Sharpe, Thomas Ridley
See also DLB 14

Shaw, Bernard ....**TCLC 45**
See also Shaw, George Bernard
See also BW 1; MTCW 2

Shaw, G. Bernard
See Shaw, George Bernard

Shaw, George Bernard 1856-1950 **TCLC 3, 9, 21; DA; DAB; DAC; DAM DRAM, MST; WLC**
See also Shaw, Bernard
See also CA 104; 128; CDBLB 1914-1945; DLB 10, 57, 190; MTCW 1, 2

Shaw, Henry Wheeler 1818-1885 ....**NCLC 15**
See also DLB 11

Shaw, Irwin 1913-1984 ..**CLC 7, 23, 34; DAM DRAM, POP**
See also AITN 1; CA 13-16R; 112; CANR 21; CDALB 1941-1968; DLB 6, 102; DLBY 84; MTCW 1, 21

Shaw, Robert 1927-1978 ....**CLC 5**
See also AITN 1; CA 1-4R; 81-84; CANR 4; DLB 13, 14

Shaw, T. E.
See Lawrence, T(homas) E(dward)

Shawn, Wallace 1943- ....**CLC 41**
See also CA 112

Shea, Lisa 1953- ....**CLC 86**
See also CA 147

Sheed, Wilfrid (John Joseph) 1930- **CLC 2, 4, 10, 53**
See also CA 65-68; CANR 30, 66; DLB 6; MTCW 1, 2

Sheldon, Alice Hastings Bradley 1915(?)-1987
See Tiptree, James, Jr.
See also CA 108; 122; CANR 34; INT 108; MTCW 1

Sheldon, John
See Bloch, Robert (Albert)

Shelley, Mary Wollstonecraft (Godwin) 1797-1851**NCLC 14, 59; DA; DAB; DAC; DAM MST, NOV; WLC**
See also AAYA 20; CDBLB 1789-1832; DLB 110, 116, 159, 178; SATA 29

Shelley, Percy Bysshe 1792-1822 ..**NCLC 18; DA; DAB; DAC; DAM MST, POET; PC 14; WLC**
See also CDBLB 1789-1832; DLB 96, 110, 158

Shepard, Jim 1956- ....**CLC 36**
See also CA 137; CANR 59; SATA 90

Shepard, Lucius 1947- ....**CLC 34**
See also CA 128; 141

Shepard, Sam 1943- **CLC 4, 6, 17, 34, 41, 44; DAM DRAM; DC 5**
See also AAYA 1; CA 69-72; CABS 3; CANR 22; DLB 7, 212; MTCW 1, 2

Shepherd, Michael
See Ludlum, Robert

Sherburne, Zoa (Morin) 1912- ....**CLC 30**
See also AAYA 13; CA 1-4R; CANR 3, 37; MAICYA; SAAS 18; SATA 3

Sheridan, Frances 1724-1766 ....**LC 7**
See also DLB 39, 84

Sheridan, Richard Brinsley 1751-1816 **N C L C 5; DA; DAB; DAC; DAM DRAM, MST; DC 1; WLC**
See also CDBLB 1660-1789; DLB 89

Sherman, Jonathan Marc ....**CLC 55**

Sherman, Martin 1941(?)- ....**CLC 19**
See also CA 116; 123

Sherwin, Judith Johnson
See Johnson, Judith (Emlyn)

Sherwood, Frances 1940- ....**CLC 81**
See also CA 146

Sherwood, Robert E(mmet) 1896-1955 **T C L C 3; DAM DRAM**
See also CA 104; 153; DLB 7, 26

Shestov, Lev 1866-1938 ....**TCLC 56**

Shevchenko, Taras 1814-1861 ....**NCLC 54**

Shiel, M(atthew) P(hipps) 1865-1947 **TCLC 8**
See also Holmes, Gordon
See also CA 106; 160; DLB 153; MTCW 2

Shields, Carol 1935- ....**CLC 91, 113; DAC**
See also CA 81-84; CANR 51, 74; MTCW 2

Shields, David 1956- ....**CLC 97**
See also CA 124; CANR 48

Shiga, Naoya 1883-1971 ......**CLC 33; SSC 23**
See also CA 101; 33-36R; DLB 180

Shikibu, Murasaki c. 978-c. 1014 .....**CMLC 1**

Shilts, Randy 1951-1994 ....**CLC 85**
See also AAYA 19; CA 115; 127; 144; CANR 45; INT 127; MTCW 2

Shimazaki, Haruki 1872-1943
See Shimazaki Toson
See also CA 105; 134

Shimazaki Toson 1872-1943 ....**TCLC 5**
See also Shimazaki, Haruki
See also DLB 180

Sholokhov, Mikhail (Aleksandrovich) 1905-1984 **CLC 7, 15**
See also CA 101; 112; MTCW 1, 2; SATA-Obit 36

Shone, Patric
See Hanley, James

Shreve, Susan Richards 1939- ....**CLC 23**
See also CA 49-52; CAAS 5; CANR 5, 38, 69; MAICYA; SATA 46, 95; SATA-Brief 41

Shue, Larry 1946-1985**CLC 52; DAM DRAM**
See also CA 145; 117

Shu-Jen, Chou 1881-1936
See Lu Hsun
See also CA 104

Shulman, Alix Kates 1932- ....**CLC 2, 10**
See also CA 29-32R; CANR 43; SATA 7

Shuster, Joe 1914- ....**CLC 21**

Shute, Nevil ....**CLC 30**
See also Norway, Nevil Shute
See also MTCW 2

Shuttle, Penelope (Diane) 1947- ....**CLC 7**
See also CA 93-96; CANR 39; DLB 14, 40

Sidney, Mary 1561-1621 ....**LC 19, 39**

Sidney, Sir Philip 1554-1586 . **LC 19, 39; DA; DAB; DAC; DAM MST, POET**
See also CDBLB Before 1660; DLB 167

Siegel, Jerome 1914-1996 ....**CLC 21**
See also CA 116; 169; 151

Siegel, Jerry
See Siegel, Jerome

Sienkiewicz, Henryk (Adam Alexander Pius) 1846-1916 ....**TCLC 3**
See also CA 104; 134

Sierra, Gregorio Martinez
See Martinez Sierra, Gregorio

Sierra, Maria (de la O'LeJarraga) Martinez
See Martinez Sierra, Maria (de la O'LeJarraga)

Sigal, Clancy 1926- ....**CLC 7**
See also CA 1-4R

Sigourney, Lydia Howard (Huntley) 1791-1865 **NCLC 21**
See also DLB 1, 42, 73

Siguenza y Gongora, Carlos de 1645-1700**LC 8**

Sigurjonsson, Johann 1880-1919 ....**TCLC 27**
See also CA 170

Sikelianos, Angelos 1884-1951 ....**TCLC 39**

Silkin, Jon 1930- ....**CLC 2, 6, 43**
See also CA 5-8R; CAAS 5; DLB 27

Silko, Leslie (Marmon) 1948-**CLC 23, 74, 114; DA; DAC; DAM MST, MULT, POP; WLCS**
See also AAYA 14; CA 115; 122; CANR 45, 65; DLB 143, 175; MTCW 2; NNAL

Sillanpaa, Frans Eemil 1888-1964 .....**CLC 19**
See also CA 129; 93-96; MTCW 1

Sillitoe, Alan 1928- ......**CLC 1, 3, 6, 10, 19, 57**
See also AITN 1; CA 9-12R; CAAS 2; CANR 8, 26, 55; CDBLB 1960 to Present; DLB 14, 139; MTCW 1, 2; SATA 61

Silone, Ignazio 1900-1978 ....**CLC 4**
See also CA 25-28; 81-84; CANR 34; CAP 2; MTCW 1

Silver, Joan Micklin 1935- ....**CLC 20**
See also CA 114; 121; INT 121

Silver, Nicholas
See Faust, Frederick (Schiller)

Silverberg, Robert 1935- . **CLC 7; DAM POP**
See also AAYA 24; CA 1-4R; CAAS 3; CANR 1, 20, 36; DLB 8; INT CANR-20; MAICYA; MTCW 1, 2; SATA 13, 91; SATA-Essay 104

Silverstein, Alvin 1933- ....**CLC 17**
See also CA 49-52; CANR 2; CLR 25; JRDA; MAICYA; SATA 8, 69

Silverstein, Virginia B(arbara Opshelor) 1937- **CLC 17**
See also CA 49-52; CANR 2; CLR 25; JRDA; MAICYA; SATA 8, 69

Sim, Georges
See Simenon, Georges (Jacques Christian)

Simak, Clifford D(onald) 1904-1988**CLC 1, 55**
See also CA 1-4R; 125; CANR 1, 35; DLB 8; MTCW 1; SATA-Obit 56

Simenon, Georges (Jacques Christian) 1903-1989**CLC 1, 2, 3, 8, 18, 47; DAM POP**
See also CA 85-88; 129; CANR 35; DLB 72; DLBY 89; MTCW 1, 2

Simic, Charles 1938-**CLC 6, 9, 22, 49, 68; DAM POET**
See also CA 29-32R; CAAS 4; CANR 12, 33, 52, 61; DLB 105; MTCW 2

Simmel, Georg 1858-1918 ....**TCLC 64**
See also CA 157

Simmons, Charles (Paul) 1924- ....**CLC 57**
See also CA 89-92; INT 89-92

Simmons, Dan 1948- ......**CLC 44; DAM POP**
See also AAYA 16; CA 138; CANR 53

Simmons, James (Stewart Alexander) 1933- **CLC 43**
See also CA 105; CAAS 21; DLB 40

Soedergran, Edith (Irene) 1892-1923 TCLC 31
Softly, Edgar
See Lovecraft, H(oward) P(hillips)
Softly, Edward
See Lovecraft, H(oward) P(hillips)
Sokolov, Raymond 1941- .... CLC 7
See also CA 85-88
Solo, Jay
See Ellison, Harlan (Jay)
Sologub, Fyodor .... TCLC 9
See also Teternikov, Fyodor Kuzmich
Solomons, Ikey Esquir
See Thackeray, William Makepeace
Solomos, Dionysios 1798-1857 .... NCLC 15
Solwoska, Mara
See French, Marilyn
Solzhenitsyn, Aleksandr I(sayevich) 1918-CLC
 1, 2, 4, 7, 9, 10, 18, 26, 34, 78; DA; DAB;
 DAC; DAM MST, NOV; SSC 32; WLC
See also AITN 1; CA 69-72; CANR 40, 65;
 MTCW 1, 2
Somers, Jane
See Lessing, Doris (May)
Somerville, Edith 1858-1949 .... TCLC 51
See also DLB 135
Somerville & Ross
See Martin, Violet Florence; Somerville, Edith
Sommer, Scott 1951- .... CLC 25
See also CA 106
Sondheim, Stephen (Joshua) 1930-CLC 30, 39;
 DAM DRAM
See also AAYA 11; CA 103; CANR 47, 68
Song, Cathy 1955- .... PC 21
See also CA 154; DLB 169
Sontag, Susan 1933-CLC 1, 2, 10, 13, 31, 105;
 DAM POP
See also CA 17-20R; CANR 25, 51, 74; DLB 2,
 67; MTCW 1, 2
Sophocles 496(?)B.C.-406(?)B.C.CMLC 2; DA;
 DAB; DAC; DAM DRAM, MST; DC 1;
 WLCS
See also DLB 176
Sordello 1189-1269 .... CMLC 15
Sorel, Georges 1847-1922 .... TCLC 91
See also CA 118
Sorel, Julia
See Drexler, Rosalyn
Sorrentino, Gilbert 1929- CLC 3, 7, 14, 22, 40
See also CA 77-80; CANR 14, 33; DLB 5, 173;
 DLBY 80; INT CANR-14
Soto, Gary 1952-.. CLC 32, 80; DAM MULT;
 HLC
See also AAYA 10; CA 119; 125; CANR 50, 74;
 CLR 38; DLB 82; HW; INT 125; JRDA;
 MTCW 2; SATA 80
Soupault, Philippe 1897-1990 .... CLC 68
See also CA 116; 147; 131
Souster, (Holmes) Raymond 1921- CLC 5, 14;
 DAC; DAM POET
See also CA 13-16R; CAAS 14; CANR 13, 29,
 53; DLB 88; SATA 63
Southern, Terry 1924(?)-1995 .... CLC 7
See also CA 1-4R; 150; CANR 1, 55; DLB 2
Southey, Robert 1774-1843 .... NCLC 8
See also DLB 93, 107, 142; SATA 54
Southworth, Emma Dorothy Eliza Nevitte
 1819-1899 .... NCLC 26
Souza, Ernest
See Scott, Evelyn

Soyinka, Wole 1934-CLC 3, 5, 14, 36, 44; BLC
 3; DA; DAB; DAC; DAM DRAM, MST,
 MULT; DC 2; WLC
See also BW 2; CA 13-16R; CANR 27, 39; DLB
 125; MTCW 1, 2
Spackman, W(illiam) M(ode) 1905-1990 C L C
 46
See also CA 81-84; 132
Spacks, Barry (Bernard) 1931- .... CLC 14
See also CA 154; CANR 33; DLB 105
Spanidou, Irini 1946- .... CLC 44
Spark, Muriel (Sarah) 1918-CLC 2, 3, 5, 8, 13,
 18, 40, 94; DAB; DAC; DAM MST, NOV;
 SSC 10
See also CA 5-8R; CANR 12, 36, 76; CDBLB
 1945-1960; DLB 15, 139; INT CANR-12;
 MTCW 1, 2
Spaulding, Douglas
See Bradbury, Ray (Douglas)
Spaulding, Leonard
See Bradbury, Ray (Douglas)
Spence, J. A. D.
See Eliot, T(homas) S(tearns)
Spencer, Elizabeth 1921- .... CLC 22
See also CA 13-16R; CANR 32, 65; DLB 6;
 MTCW 1; SATA 14
Spencer, Leonard G.
See Silverberg, Robert
Spencer, Scott 1945- .... CLC 30
See also CA 113; CANR 51; DLBY 86
Spender, Stephen (Harold) 1909-1995CLC 1, 2,
 5, 10, 41, 91; DAM POET
See also CA 9-12R; 149; CANR 31, 54; CDBLB
 1945-1960; DLB 20; MTCW 1, 2
Spengler, Oswald (Arnold Gottfried) 1880-1936
 TCLC 25
See also CA 118
Spenser, Edmund 1552(?)-1599 LC 5, 39; DA;
 DAB; DAC; DAM MST, POET; PC 8;
 WLC
See also CDBLB Before 1660; DLB 167
Spicer, Jack 1925-1965 . CLC 8, 18, 72; DAM
 POET
See also CA 85-88; DLB 5, 16, 193
Spiegelman, Art 1948- .... CLC 76
See also AAYA 10; CA 125; CANR 41, 55, 74;
 MTCW 2
Spielberg, Peter 1929- .... CLC 6
See also CA 5-8R; CANR 4, 48; DLBY 81
Spielberg, Steven 1947- .... CLC 20
See also AAYA 8, 24; CA 77-80; CANR 32;
 SATA 32
Spillane, Frank Morrison 1918-
See Spillane, Mickey
See also CA 25-28R; CANR 28, 63; MTCW 1,
 2; SATA 66
Spillane, Mickey .... CLC 3, 13
See also Spillane, Frank Morrison
See also MTCW 2
Spinoza, Benedictus de 1632-1677 .... LC 9
Spinrad, Norman (Richard) 1940- ..... CLC 46
See also CA 37-40R; CAAS 19; CANR 20; DLB
 8; INT CANR-20
Spitteler, Carl (Friedrich Georg) 1845-1924
 TCLC 12
See also CA 109; DLB 129
Spivack, Kathleen (Romola Drucker) 1938-
 CLC 6
See also CA 49-52
Spoto, Donald 1941- .... CLC 39
See also CA 65-68; CANR 11, 57
Springsteen, Bruce (F.) 1949- .... CLC 17
See also CA 111

Spurling, Hilary 1940- .... CLC 34
See also CA 104; CANR 25, 52
Spyker, John Howland
See Elman, Richard (Martin)
Squires, (James) Radcliffe 1917-1993 CLC 51
See also CA 1-4R; 140; CANR 6, 21
Srivastava, Dhanpat Rai 1880(?)-1936
See Premchand
See also CA 118
Stacy, Donald
See Pohl, Frederik
Stael, Germaine de 1766-1817
See Stael-Holstein, Anne Louise Germaine
 Necker Baronn
See also DLB 119
Stael-Holstein, Anne Louise Germaine Necker
 Baronn 1766-1817 .... NCLC 3
See also Stael, Germaine de
See also DLB 192
Stafford, Jean 1915-1979CLC 4, 7, 19, 68; SSC
 26
See also CA 1-4R; 85-88; CANR 3, 65; DLB 2,
 173; MTCW 1, 2; SATA-Obit 22
Stafford, William (Edgar) 1914-1993CLC 4, 7,
 29; DAM POET
See also CA 5-8R; 142; CAAS 3; CANR 5, 22;
 DLB 5, 206; INT CANR-22
Stagnelius, Eric Johan 1793-1823 ... NCLC 61
Staines, Trevor
See Brunner, John (Kilian Houston)
Stairs, Gordon
See Austin, Mary (Hunter)
Stalin, Joseph 1879-1953 .... TCLC 92
Stannard, Martin 1947- .... CLC 44
See also CA 142; DLB 155
Stanton, Elizabeth Cady 1815-1902 TCLC 73
See also CA 171; DLB 79
Stanton, Maura 1946- .... CLC 9
See also CA 89-92; CANR 15; DLB 120
Stanton, Schuyler
See Baum, L(yman) Frank
Stapledon, (William) Olaf 1886-1950TCLC 22
See also CA 111; 162; DLB 15
Starbuck, George (Edwin) 1931-1996CLC 53;
 DAM POET
See also CA 21-24R; 153; CANR 23
Stark, Richard
See Westlake, Donald E(dwin)
Staunton, Schuyler
See Baum, L(yman) Frank
Stead, Christina (Ellen) 1902-1983CLC 2, 5, 8,
 32, 80
See also CA 13-16R; 109; CANR 33, 40; MTCW
 1, 2
Stead, William Thomas 1849-1912 . TCLC 48
See also CA 167
Steele, Richard 1672-1729 .... LC 18
See also CDBLB 1660-1789; DLB 84, 101
Steele, Timothy (Reid) 1948- .... CLC 45
See also CA 93-96; CANR 16, 50; DLB 120
Steffens, (Joseph) Lincoln 1866-1936TCLC 20
See also CA 117
Stegner, Wallace (Earle) 1909-1993CLC 9, 49,
 81; DAM NOV; SSC 27
See also AITN 1; BEST 90:3; CA 1-4R; 141;
 CAAS 9; CANR 1, 21, 46; DLB 9, 206; DLBY
 93; MTCW 1, 2
Stein, Gertrude 1874-1946 TCLC 1, 6, 28, 48;
 DA; DAB; DAC; DAM MST, NOV, POET;
 PC 18; WLC
See also CA 104; 132; CDALB 1917-1929; DLB
 4, 54, 86; DLBD 15; MTCW 1, 2

Torsvan, Berwick Traven
See Traven, B.
Torsvan, Bruno Traven
See Traven, B.
Torsvan, Traven
See Traven, B.
Tournier, Michel (Edouard) 1924- **CLC 6, 23, 36, 95**
See also CA 49-52; CANR 3, 36, 74; DLB 83; MTCW 1, 2; SATA 23
Tournimparte, Alessandra
See Ginzburg, Natalia
Towers, Ivar
See Kornbluth, C(yril) M.
Towne, Robert (Burton) 1936(?)- .... **CLC 87**
See also CA 108; DLB 44
Townsend, Sue .... **CLC 61**
See also Townsend, Susan Elaine
See also AAYA 28; SATA 55, 93; SATA-Brief 48
Townsend, Susan Elaine 1946-
See Townsend, Sue
See also CA 119; 127; CANR 65; DAB; DAC; DAM MST
Townshend, Peter (Dennis Blandford) 1945-
CLC 17, 42
See also CA 107
Tozzi, Federigo 1883-1920 .... **TCLC 31**
See also CA 160
Traill, Catharine Parr 1802-1899 ... **NCLC 31**
See also DLB 99
Trakl, Georg 1887-1914 .... **TCLC 5; PC 20**
See also CA 104; 165; MTCW 2
Transtroemer, Tomas (Goesta) 1931- **CLC 52, 65; DAM POET**
See also CA 117; 129; CAAS 17
Transtromer, Tomas Gosta
See Transtroemer, Tomas (Goesta)
Traven, B. (?)-1969 .... **CLC 8, 11**
See also CA 19-20; 25-28R; CAP 2; DLB 9, 56; MTCW 1
Treitel, Jonathan 1959- .... **CLC 70**
Tremain, Rose 1943- .... **CLC 42**
See also CA 97-100; CANR 44; DLB 14
Tremblay, Michel 1942- . **CLC 29, 102; DAC; DAM MST**
See also CA 116; 128; DLB 60; MTCW 1, 2
Trevanian .... **CLC 29**
See also Whitaker, Rod(ney)
Trevor, Glen
See Hilton, James
Trevor, William 1928- **CLC 7, 9, 14, 25, 71, 116; SSC 21**
See also Cox, William Trevor
See also DLB 14, 139; MTCW 2
Trifonov, Yuri (Valentinovich) 1925-1981 **C L C 45**
See also CA 126; 103; MTCW 1
Trilling, Lionel 1905-1975 .... **CLC 9, 11, 24**
See also CA 9-12R; 61-64; CANR 10; DLB 28, 63; INT CANR-10; MTCW 1, 2
Trimball, W. H.
See Mencken, H(enry) L(ouis)
Tristan
See Gomez de la Serna, Ramon
Tristram
See Housman, A(lfred) E(dward)
Trogdon, William (Lewis) 1939-
See Heat-Moon, William Least
See also CA 115; 119; CANR 47; INT 119

Trollope, Anthony 1815-1882 **NCLC 6, 33; DA; DAB; DAC; DAM MST, NOV; SSC 28; WLC**
See also CDBLB 1832-1890; DLB 21, 57, 159; SATA 22
Trollope, Frances 1779-1863 .... **NCLC 30**
See also DLB 21, 166
Trotsky, Leon 1879-1940 .... **TCLC 22**
See also CA 118; 167
Trotter (Cockburn), Catharine 1679-1749 **LC 8**
See also DLB 84
Trout, Kilgore
See Farmer, Philip Jose
Trow, George W. S. 1943- .... **CLC 52**
See also CA 126
Troyat, Henri 1911- .... **CLC 23**
See also CA 45-48; CANR 2, 33, 67; MTCW 1
Trudeau, G(arretson) B(eekman) 1948-
See Trudeau, Garry B.
See also CA 81-84; CANR 31; SATA 35
Trudeau, Garry B. .... **CLC 12**
See also Trudeau, G(arretson) B(eekman)
See also AAYA 10; AITN 2
Truffaut, Francois 1932-1984 ....**CLC 20, 101**
See also CA 81-84; 113; CANR 34
Trumbo, Dalton 1905-1976 .... **CLC 19**
See also CA 21-24R; 69-72; CANR 10; DLB 26
Trumbull, John 1750-1831 .... **NCLC 30**
See also DLB 31
Trundlett, Helen B.
See Eliot, T(homas) S(tearns)
Tryon, Thomas 1926-1991 .. **CLC 3, 11; DAM POP**
See also AITN 1; CA 29-32R; 135; CANR 32, 77; MTCW 1
Tryon, Tom
See Tryon, Thomas
Ts'ao Hsueh-ch'in 1715(?)-1763 .... **LC 1**
Tsushima, Shuji 1909-1948
See Dazai Osamu
See also CA 107
Tsvetaeva (Efron), Marina (Ivanovna) 1892-1941 .... **TCLC 7, 35; PC 14**
See also CA 104; 128; CANR 73; MTCW 1, 2
Tuck, Lily 1938- .... **CLC 70**
See also CA 139
Tu Fu 712-770 .... **PC 9**
See also DAM MULT
Tunis, John R(oberts) 1889-1975 .... **CLC 12**
See also CA 61-64; CANR 62; DLB 22, 171; JRDA; MAICYA; SATA 37; SATA-Brief 30
Tuohy, Frank .... **CLC 37**
See also Tuohy, John Francis
See also DLB 14, 139
Tuohy, John Francis 1925-
See Tuohy, Frank
See also CA 5-8R; CANR 3, 47
Turco, Lewis (Putnam) 1934- .... **CLC 11, 63**
See also CA 13-16R; CAAS 22; CANR 24, 51; DLBY 84
Turgenev, Ivan 1818-1883 **NCLC 21; DA; DAB; DAC; DAM MST, NOV; DC 7; SSC 7; WLC**
Turgot, Anne-Robert-Jacques 1727-1781 .**L C 26**
Turner, Frederick 1943- .... **CLC 48**
See also CA 73-76; CAAS 10; CANR 12, 30, 56; DLB 40
Tutu, Desmond M(pilo) 1931- **CLC 80; BLC 3; DAM MULT**
See also BW 1; CA 125; CANR 67

Tutuola, Amos 1920-1997 **CLC 5, 14, 29; BLC 3; DAM MULT**
See also BW 2; CA 9-12R; 159; CANR 27, 66; DLB 125; MTCW 1, 2
Twain, Mark **TCLC 6, 12, 19, 36, 48, 59; SSC 34; WLC**
See also Clemens, Samuel Langhorne
See also AAYA 20; DLB 11, 12, 23, 64, 74
Tyler, Anne 1941- **CLC 7, 11, 18, 28, 44, 59, 103; DAM NOV, POP**
See also AAYA 18; BEST 89:1; CA 9-12R; CANR 11, 33, 53; DLB 6, 143; DLBY 82; MTCW 1, 2; SATA 7, 90
Tyler, Royall 1757-1826 .... **NCLC 3**
See also DLB 37
Tynan, Katharine 1861-1931 .... **TCLC 3**
See also CA 104; 167; DLB 153
Tyutchev, Fyodor 1803-1873 .... **NCLC 34**
Tzara, Tristan 1896-1963 **CLC 47; DAM POET**
See also CA 153; 89-92; MTCW 2
Uhry, Alfred 1936- **CLC 55; DAM DRAM, POP**
See also CA 127; 133; INT 133
Ulf, Haerved
See Strindberg, (Johan) August
Ulf, Harved
See Strindberg, (Johan) August
Ulibarri, Sabine R(eyes) 1919- **CLC 83; DAM MULT**
See also CA 131; DLB 82; HW
Unamuno (y Jugo), Miguel de 1864-1936
TCLC 2, 9; DAM MULT, NOV; HLC; SSC 11
See also CA 104; 131; DLB 108; HW; MTCW 1, 2
Undercliffe, Errol
See Campbell, (John) Ramsey
Underwood, Miles
See Glassco, John
Undset, Sigrid 1882-1949 **TCLC 3; DA; DAB; DAC; DAM MST, NOV; WLC**
See also CA 104; 129; MTCW 1, 2
Ungaretti, Giuseppe 1888-1970 **CLC 7, 11, 15**
See also CA 19-20; 25-28R; CAP 2; DLB 114
Unger, Douglas 1952- .... **CLC 34**
See also CA 130
Unsworth, Barry (Forster) 1930- .... **CLC 76**
See also CA 25-28R; CANR 30, 54; DLB 194
Updike, John (Hoyer) 1932- **CLC 1, 2, 3, 5, 7, 9, 13, 15, 23, 34, 43, 70; DA; DAB; DAC; DAM MST, NOV, POET, POP; SSC 13, 27; WLC**
See also CA 1-4R; CABS 1; CANR 4, 33, 51; CDALB 1968-1988; DLB 2, 5, 143; DLBD 3; DLBY 80, 82, 97; MTCW 1, 2
Upshaw, Margaret Mitchell
See Mitchell, Margaret (Munnerlyn)
Upton, Mark
See Sanders, Lawrence
Upward, Allen 1863-1926 .... **TCLC 85**
See also CA 117; DLB 36
Urdang, Constance (Henriette) 1922- **CLC 47**
See also CA 21-24R; CANR 9, 24
Uriel, Henry
See Faust, Frederick (Schiller)
Uris, Leon (Marcus) 1924- . **CLC 7, 32; DAM NOV, POP**
See also AITN 1, 2; BEST 89:2; CA 1-4R; CANR 1, 40, 65; MTCW 1, 2; SATA 49
Urmuz
See Codrescu, Andrei
Urquhart, Jane 1949- .... **CLC 90; DAC**
See also CA 113; CANR 32, 68

Vollmann, William T. 1959- .... **CLC 89; DAM NOV, POP**
See also CA 134; CANR 67; MTCW 2
Voloshinov, V. N.
See Bakhtin, Mikhail Mikhailovich
Voltaire 1694-1778 .. **LC 14; DA; DAB; DAC; DAM DRAM, MST; SSC 12; WLC**
von Aschendrof, BaronIgnatz
See Ford, Ford Madox
von Daeniken, Erich 1935- .... **CLC 30**
See also AITN 1; CA 37-40R; CANR 17, 44
von Daniken, Erich
See von Daeniken, Erich
von Heidenstam, (Carl Gustaf) Verner
See Heidenstam, (Carl Gustaf) Verner von
von Heyse, Paul (Johann Ludwig)
See Heyse, Paul (Johann Ludwig von)
von Hofmannsthal, Hugo
See Hofmannsthal, Hugo von
von Horvath, Odon
See Horvath, Oedoen von
von Horvath, Oedoen
See Horvath, Oedoen von
von Liliencron, (Friedrich Adolf Axel) Detlev
See Liliencron, (Friedrich Adolf Axel) Detlev von
Vonnegut, Kurt, Jr. 1922-**CLC 1, 2, 3, 4, 5, 8, 12, 22, 40, 60, 111; DA; DAB; DAC; DAM MST, NOV, POP; SSC 8; WLC**
See also AAYA 6; AITN 1; BEST 90:4; CA 1-4R; CANR 1, 25, 49, 75; CDALB 1968-1988; DLB 2, 8, 152; DLBD 3; DLBY 80; MTCW 1, 2
Von Rachen, Kurt
See Hubbard, L(afayette) Ron(ald)
von Rezzori (d'Arezzo), Gregor
See Rezzori (d'Arezzo), Gregor von
von Sternberg, Josef
See Sternberg, Josef von
Vorster, Gordon 1924- .... **CLC 34**
See also CA 133
Vosce, Trudie
See Ozick, Cynthia
Voznesensky, Andrei (Andreievich) 1933-**C L C 1, 15, 57; DAM POET**
See also CA 89-92; CANR 37; MTCW 1
Waddington, Miriam 1917- .... **CLC 28**
See also CA 21-24R; CANR 12, 30; DLB 68
Wagman, Fredrica 1937- .... **CLC 7**
See also CA 97-100; INT 97-100
Wagner, Linda W.
See Wagner-Martin, Linda (C.)
Wagner, Linda Welshimer
See Wagner-Martin, Linda (C.)
Wagner, Richard 1813-1883 .... **NCLC 9**
See also DLB 129
Wagner-Martin, Linda (C.) 1936- ...... **CLC 50**
See also CA 159
Wagoner, David (Russell) 1926- . **CLC 3, 5, 15**
See also CA 1-4R; CAAS 3; CANR 2, 71; DLB 5; SATA 14
Wah, Fred(erick James) 1939- .... **CLC 44**
See also CA 107; 141; DLB 60
Wahloo, Per 1926-1975 .... **CLC 7**
See also CA 61-64; CANR 73
Wahloo, Peter
See Wahloo, Per
Wain, John (Barrington) 1925-1994**CLC 2, 11, 15, 46**
See also CA 5-8R; 145; CAAS 4; CANR 23, 54; CDBLB 1960 to Present; DLB 15, 27, 139, 155; MTCW 1, 2
Wajda, Andrzej 1926- .... **CLC 16**
See also CA 102

Wakefield, Dan 1932- .... **CLC 7**
See also CA 21-24R; CAAS 7
Wakoski, Diane 1937-...**CLC 2, 4, 7, 9, 11, 40; DAM POET; PC 15**
See also CA 13-16R; CAAS 1; CANR 9, 60; DLB 5; INT CANR-9; MTCW 2
Wakoski-Sherbell, Diane
See Wakoski, Diane
Walcott, Derek (Alton) 1930- **CLC 2, 4, 9, 14, 25, 42, 67, 76; BLC 3; DAB; DAC; DAM MST, MULT, POET; DC 7**
See also BW 2; CA 89-92; CANR 26, 47, 75; DLB 117; DLBY 81; MTCW 1, 2
Waldman, Anne (Lesley) 1945- .... **CLC 7**
See also CA 37-40R; CAAS 17; CANR 34, 69; DLB 16
Waldo, E. Hunter
See Sturgeon, Theodore (Hamilton)
Waldo, Edward Hamilton
See Sturgeon, Theodore (Hamilton)
Walker, Alice (Malsenior) 1944-**CLC 5, 6, 9, 19, 27, 46, 58, 103; BLC 3; DA; DAB; DAC; DAM MST, MULT, NOV, POET, POP; SSC 5; WLCS**
See also AAYA 3; BEST 89:4; BW 2; CA 37-40R; CANR 9, 27, 49, 66; CDALB 1968-1988; DLB 6, 33, 143; INT CANR-27; MTCW 1, 2; SATA 31
Walker, David Harry 1911-1992 .... **CLC 14**
See also CA 1-4R; 137; CANR 1; SATA 8; SATA-Obit 71
Walker, Edward Joseph 1934-
See Walker, Ted
See also CA 21-24R; CANR 12, 28, 53
Walker, George F. 1947- ... **CLC 44, 61; DAB; DAC; DAM MST**
See also CA 103; CANR 21, 43, 59; DLB 60
Walker, Joseph A. 1935-**CLC 19; DAM DRAM, MST**
See also BW 1; CA 89-92; CANR 26; DLB 38
Walker, Margaret (Abigail) 1915-1998**CLC 1, 6; BLC; DAM MULT; PC 20**
See also BW 2; CA 73-76; 172; CANR 26, 54, 76; DLB 76, 152; MTCW 1, 2
Walker, Ted .... **CLC 13**
See also Walker, Edward Joseph
See also DLB 40
Wallace, David Foster 1962- ...... **CLC 50, 114**
See also CA 132; CANR 59; MTCW 2
Wallace, Dexter
See Masters, Edgar Lee
Wallace, (Richard Horatio) Edgar 1875-1932 **TCLC 57**
See also CA 115; DLB 70
Wallace, Irving 1916-1990 .. **CLC 7, 13; DAM NOV, POP**
See also AITN 1; CA 1-4R; 132; CAAS 1; CANR 1, 27; INT CANR-27; MTCW 1, 2
Wallant, Edward Lewis 1926-1962 **CLC 5, 10**
See also CA 1-4R; CANR 22; DLB 2, 28, 143; MTCW 1, 2
Wallas, Graham 1858-1932 .... **TCLC 91**
Walley, Byron
See Card, Orson Scott
Walpole, Horace 1717-1797 .... **LC 49**
See also DLB 39, 104
Walpole, Hugh (Seymour) 1884-1941 **TCLC 5**
See also CA 104; 165; DLB 34; MTCW 2
Walser, Martin 1927- .... **CLC 27**
See also CA 57-60; CANR 8, 46; DLB 75, 124
Walser, Robert 1878-1956 **TCLC 18; SSC 20**
See also CA 118; 165; DLB 66

Walsh, Jill Paton .... **CLC 35**
See also Paton Walsh, Gillian
See also AAYA 11; CLR 2; DLB 161; SAAS 3
Walter, Villiam Christian
See Andersen, Hans Christian
Wambaugh, Joseph (Aloysius, Jr.) 1937- **C L C 3, 18; DAM NOV, POP**
See also AITN 1; BEST 89:3; CA 33-36R; CANR 42, 65; DLB 6; DLBY 83; MTCW 1, 2
Wang Wei 699(?)-761(?) .... **PC 18**
Ward, Arthur Henry Sarsfield 1883-1959
See Rohmer, Sax
See also CA 108; 173
Ward, Douglas Turner 1930- .... **CLC 19**
See also BW 1; CA 81-84; CANR 27; DLB 7, 38
Ward, Mary Augusta
See Ward, Mrs. Humphry
Ward, Mrs. Humphry 1851-1920 ... **TCLC 55**
See also DLB 18
Ward, Peter
See Faust, Frederick (Schiller)
Warhol, Andy 1928(?)-1987 .... **CLC 20**
See also AAYA 12; BEST 89:4; CA 89-92; 121; CANR 34
Warner, Francis (Robert le Plastrier) 1937- **CLC 14**
See also CA 53-56; CANR 11
Warner, Marina 1946- .... **CLC 59**
See also CA 65-68; CANR 21, 55; DLB 194
Warner, Rex (Ernest) 1905-1986 .... **CLC 45**
See also CA 89-92; 119; DLB 15
Warner, Susan (Bogert) 1819-1885 . **NCLC 31**
See also DLB 3, 42
Warner, Sylvia (Constance) Ashton
See Ashton-Warner, Sylvia (Constance)
Warner, Sylvia Townsend 1893-1978 .. **CLC 7, 19; SSC 23**
See also CA 61-64; 77-80; CANR 16, 60; DLB 34, 139; MTCW 1, 2
Warren, Mercy Otis 1728-1814 ...... **NCLC 13**
See also DLB 31, 200
Warren, Robert Penn 1905-1989**CLC 1, 4, 6, 8, 10, 13, 18, 39, 53, 59; DA; DAB; DAC; DAM MST, NOV, POET; SSC 4; WLC**
See also AITN 1; CA 13-16R; 129; CANR 10, 47; CDALB 1968-1988; DLB 2, 48, 152; DLBY 80, 89; INT CANR-10; MTCW 1, 2; SATA 46; SATA-Obit 63
Warshofsky, Isaac
See Singer, Isaac Bashevis
Warton, Thomas 1728-1790 ...... **LC 15; DAM POET**
See also DLB 104, 109
Waruk, Kona
See Harris, (Theodore) Wilson
Warung, Price 1855-1911 .... **TCLC 45**
Warwick, Jarvis
See Garner, Hugh
Washington, Alex
See Harris, Mark
Washington, Booker T(aliaferro) 1856-1915 **TCLC 10; BLC 3; DAM MULT**
See also BW 1; CA 114; 125; SATA 28
Washington, George 1732-1799 .... **LC 25**
See also DLB 31
Wassermann, (Karl) Jakob 1873-1934**TCLC 6**
See also CA 104; 163; DLB 66
Wasserstein, Wendy 1950- .... **CLC 32, 59, 90; DAM DRAM; DC 4**
See also CA 121; 129; CABS 3; CANR 53, 75; INT 129; MTCW 2; SATA 94

White, E(lwyn) B(rooks) 1899-1985..**CLC 10, 34, 39; DAM POP**
See also AITN 2; CA 13-16R; 116; CANR 16, 37; CLR 1, 21; DLB 11, 22; MAICYA; MTCW 1, 2; SATA 2, 29, 100; SATA-Obit 44

White, Edmund (Valentine III) 1940- **CLC 27, 110; DAM POP**
See also AAYA 7; CA 45-48; CANR 3, 19, 36, 62; MTCW 1, 2

White, Patrick (Victor Martindale) 1912-1990 **CLC 3, 4, 5, 7, 9, 18, 65, 69**
See also CA 81-84; 132; CANR 43; MTCW 1

White, Phyllis Dorothy James 1920-
See James, P. D.
See also CA 21-24R; CANR 17, 43, 65; DAM POP; MTCW 1, 2

White, T(erence) H(anbury) 1906-1964**CLC 30**
See also AAYA 22; CA 73-76; CANR 37; DLB 160; JRDA; MAICYA; SATA 12

White, Terence de Vere 1912-1994 .... **CLC 49**
See also CA 49-52; 145; CANR 3

White, Walter
See White, Walter F(rancis)
See also BLC 3; DAM MULT

White, Walter F(rancis) 1893-1955 **TCLC 15**
See also White, Walter
See also BW 1; CA 115; 124; DLB 51

White, William Hale 1831-1913
See Rutherford, Mark
See also CA 121

Whitehead, E(dward) A(nthony) 1933- **CLC 5**
See also CA 65-68; CANR 58

Whitemore, Hugh (John) 1936- .... **CLC 37**
See also CA 132; CANR 77; INT 132

Whitman, Sarah Helen (Power) 1803-1878
NCLC 19
See also DLB 1

Whitman, Walt(er) 1819-1892**NCLC 4, 31; DA; DAB; DAC; DAM MST, POET; PC 3; WLC**
See also CDALB 1640-1865; DLB 3, 64; SATA 20

Whitney, Phyllis A(yame) 1903-**CLC 42; DAM POP**
See also AITN 2; BEST 90:3; CA 1-4R; CANR 3, 25, 38, 60; JRDA; MAICYA; MTCW 2; SATA 1, 30

Whittemore, (Edward) Reed (Jr.) 1919-**CLC 4**
See also CA 9-12R; CAAS 8; CANR 4; DLB 5

Whittier, John Greenleaf 1807-1892 **NCLC 8, 59**
See also DLB 1

Whittlebot, Hernia
See Coward, Noel (Peirce)

Wicker, Thomas Grey 1926-
See Wicker, Tom
See also CA 65-68; CANR 21, 46

Wicker, Tom .... **CLC 7**
See also Wicker, Thomas Grey

Wideman, John Edgar 1941-**CLC 5, 34, 36, 67; BLC 3; DAM MULT**
See also BW 2; CA 85-88; CANR 14, 42, 67; DLB 33, 143; MTCW 2

Wiebe, Rudy (Henry) 1934-.... **CLC 6, 11, 14; DAC; DAM MST**
See also CA 37-40R; CANR 42, 67; DLB 60

Wieland, Christoph Martin 1733-1813 **N C L C 17**
See also DLB 97

Wiene, Robert 1881-1938 .... **TCLC 56**

Wieners, John 1934- .... **CLC 7**
See also CA 13-16R; DLB 16

Wiesel, Elie(zer) 1928- . **CLC 3, 5, 11, 37; DA; DAB; DAC; DAM MST, NOV; WLCS**
See also AAYA 7; AITN 1; CA 5-8R; CAAS 4; CANR 8, 40, 65; DLB 83; DLBY 87; INT CANR-8; MTCW 1, 2; SATA 56

Wiggins, Marianne 1947- .... **CLC 57**
See also BEST 89:3; CA 130; CANR 60

Wight, James Alfred 1916-1995
See Herriot, James
See also CA 77-80; SATA 55; SATA-Brief 44

Wilbur, Richard (Purdy) 1921-**CLC 3, 6, 9, 14, 53, 110; DA; DAB; DAC; DAM MST, POET**
See also CA 1-4R; CABS 2; CANR 2, 29, 76; DLB 5, 169; INT CANR-29; MTCW 1, 2; SATA 9

Wild, Peter 1940- .... **CLC 14**
See also CA 37-40R; DLB 5

Wilde, Oscar 1854(?)-1900 **TCLC 1, 8, 23, 41; DA; DAB; DAC; DAM DRAM, MST, NOV; SSC 11; WLC**
See also CA 104; 119; CDBLB 1890-1914; DLB 10, 19, 34, 57, 141, 156, 190; SATA 24

Wilder, Billy .... **CLC 20**
See also Wilder, Samuel
See also DLB 26

Wilder, Samuel 1906-
See Wilder, Billy
See also CA 89-92

Wilder, Thornton (Niven) 1897-1975**CLC 1, 5, 6, 10, 15, 35, 82; DA; DAB; DAC; DAM DRAM, MST, NOV; DC 1; WLC**
See also AAYA 29; AITN 2; CA 13-16R; 61-64; CANR 40; DLB 4, 7, 9; DLBY 97; MTCW 1, 2

Wilding, Michael 1942- .... **CLC 73**
See also CA 104; CANR 24, 49

Wiley, Richard 1944-........................... **CLC 44**
See also CA 121; 129; CANR 71

Wilhelm, Kate .... **CLC 7**
See also Wilhelm, Katie Gertrude
See also AAYA 20; CAAS 5; DLB 8; INT CANR-17

Wilhelm, Katie Gertrude 1928-
See Wilhelm, Kate
See also CA 37-40R; CANR 17, 36, 60; MTCW 1

Wilkins, Mary
See Freeman, Mary Eleanor Wilkins

Willard, Nancy 1936- .... **CLC 7, 37**
See also CA 89-92; CANR 10, 39, 68; CLR 5; DLB 5, 52; MAICYA; MTCW 1; SATA 37, 71; SATA-Brief 30

William of Ockham 1285-1347 .... **CMLC 32**

Williams, Ben Ames 1889-1953 .... **TCLC 89**
See also DLB 102

Williams, C(harles) K(enneth) 1936- **CLC 33, 56; DAM POET**
See also CA 37-40R; CAAS 26; CANR 57; DLB 5

Williams, Charles
See Collier, James L(incoln)

Williams, Charles (Walter Stansby) 1886-1945
TCLC 1, 11
See also CA 104; 163; DLB 100, 153

Williams, (George) Emlyn 1905-1987**CLC 15; DAM DRAM**
See also CA 104; 123; CANR 36; DLB 10, 77; MTCW 1

Williams, Hank 1923-1953 .... **TCLC 81**

Williams, Hugo 1942-........................... **CLC 42**
See also CA 17-20R; CANR 45; DLB 40

Williams, J. Walker
See Wodehouse, P(elham) G(renville)

Williams, John A(lfred) 1925-**CLC 5, 13; BLC 3; DAM MULT**
See also BW 2; CA 53-56; CAAS 3; CANR 6, 26, 51; DLB 2, 33; INT CANR-6

Williams, Jonathan (Chamberlain) 1929-**C L C 13**
See also CA 9-12R; CAAS 12; CANR 8; DLB 5

Williams, Joy 1944- .... **CLC 31**
See also CA 41-44R; CANR 22, 48

Williams, Norman 1952- .... **CLC 39**
See also CA 118

Williams, Sherley Anne 1944-**CLC 89; BLC 3; DAM MULT, POET**
See also BW 2; CA 73-76; CANR 25; DLB 41; INT CANR-25; SATA 78

Williams, Shirley
See Williams, Sherley Anne

Williams, Tennessee 1911-1983**CLC 1, 2, 5, 7, 8, 11, 15, 19, 30, 39, 45, 71, 111; DA; DAB; DAC; DAM DRAM, MST; DC 4; WLC**
See also AITN 1, 2; CA 5-8R; 108; CABS 3; CANR 31; CDALB 1941-1968; DLB 7; DLBD 4; DLBY 83; MTCW 1, 2

Williams, Thomas (Alonzo) 1926-1990**CLC 14**
See also CA 1-4R; 132; CANR 2

Williams, William C.
See Williams, William Carlos

Williams, William Carlos 1883-1963**CLC 1, 2, 5, 9, 13, 22, 42, 67; DA; DAB; DAC; DAM MST, POET; PC 7; SSC 31**
See also CA 89-92; CANR 34; CDALB 1917-1929; DLB 4, 16, 54, 86; MTCW 1, 2

Williamson, David (Keith) 1942-........ **CLC 56**
See also CA 103; CANR 41

Williamson, Ellen Douglas 1905-1984
See Douglas, Ellen
See also CA 17-20R; 114; CANR 39

Williamson, Jack .... **CLC 29**
See also Williamson, John Stewart
See also CAAS 8; DLB 8

Williamson, John Stewart 1908-
See Williamson, Jack
See also CA 17-20R; CANR 23, 70

Willie, Frederick
See Lovecraft, H(oward) P(hillips)

Willingham, Calder (Baynard, Jr.) 1922-1995
CLC 5, 51
See also CA 5-8R; 147; CANR 3; DLB 2, 44; MTCW 1

Willis, Charles
See Clarke, Arthur C(harles)

Willis, Fingal O'Flahertie
See Wilde, Oscar

Willy
See Colette, (Sidonie-Gabrielle)

Willy, Colette
See Colette, (Sidonie-Gabrielle)

Wilson, A(ndrew) N(orman) 1950-..... **CLC 33**
See also CA 112; 122; DLB 14, 155, 194; MTCW 2

Wilson, Angus (Frank Johnstone) 1913-1991
CLC 2, 3, 5, 25, 34; SSC 21
See also CA 5-8R; 134; CANR 21; DLB 15, 139, 155; MTCW 1, 2

Wilson, August 1945-**CLC 39, 50, 63, 118; BLC 3; DA; DAB; DAC; DAM DRAM, MST, MULT; DC 2; WLCS**
See also AAYA 16; BW 2; CA 115; 122; CANR 42, 54, 76; MTCW 1, 2

Poetry Criticism
Cumulative Nationality Index

AMERICAN

Aiken, Conrad (Potter) **26**
Ammons, A(rchie) R(andolph) **16**
Ashbery, John (Lawrence) **26**
Auden, W(ystan) H(ugh) **1**
Baraka, Amiri **4**
Bishop, Elizabeth **3**
Bogan, Louise **12**
Bradstreet, Anne **10**
Brodsky, Joseph **9**
Brooks, Gwendolyn **7**
Bryant, William Cullen **20**
Bukowski, Charles **18**
Carruth, Hayden **10**
Clampitt, Amy **19**
Clifton, (Thelma) Lucille **17**
Crane, (Harold) Hart **3**
Cullen, Countee **20**
Cummings, E(dward) E(stlin) **5**
Dickinson, Emily (Elizabeth) **1**
Doolittle, Hilda **5**
Dove, Rita (Frances) **6**
Dunbar, Paul Laurence **5**
Duncan, Robert (Edward) **2**
Eliot, T(homas) S(tearns) **5**
Emerson, Ralph Waldo **18**
Ferlinghetti, Lawrence (Monsanto) **1**
Forche, Carolyn (Louise) **10**
Frost, Robert (Lee) **1**
Gallagher, Tess **9**
Ginsberg, Allen **4**
Giovanni, Nikki **19**
Gluck, Louise (Elisabeth) **16**
Hammon, Jupiter **16**
Harper, Frances Ellen Watkins **21**
Hass, Robert **16**
Hayden, Robert E(arl) **6**
H. D. **5**
Hongo, Garrett Kaoru **23**
Hughes, (James) Langston **1**
Jeffers, (John) Robinson **17**
Johnson, James Weldon **24**
Kinnell, Galway **26**
Knight, Etheridge **14**
Kumin, Maxine (Winokur) **15**
Kunitz, Stanley (Jasspon) **19**
Levertov, Denise **11**
Levine, Philip **22**
Lindsay, (Nicholas) Vachel **23**
Lorde, Audre (Geraldine) **12**
Lowell, Amy **13**
Lowell, Robert (Traill Spence Jr.) **3**
Loy, Mina **16**
Madhubuti, Haki R. **5**
Masters, Edgar Lee **1**
McKay, Claude **2**
Merton, Thomas **10**
Millay, Edna St. Vincent **6**
Momaday, N(avarre) Scott **25**
Moore, Marianne (Craig) **4**
Nash, (Frederic) Ogden **21**
Nemerov, Howard (Stanley) **24**
Olds, Sharon **22**
Olson, Charles (John) **19**

Ortiz, Simon J(oseph) **17**
Plath, Sylvia **1**
Poe, Edgar Allan **1**
Pound, Ezra (Weston Loomis) **4**
Rexroth, Kenneth **20**
Rich, Adrienne (Cecile) **5**
Robinson, Edwin Arlington **1**
Roethke, Theodore (Huebner) **15**
Rose, Wendy **13**
Rukeyser, Muriel **12**
Sanchez, Sonia **9**
Sandburg, Carl (August) **2**
Schwartz, Delmore (David) **8**
Sexton, Anne (Harvey) **2**
Shapiro, Karl (Jay) **25**
Snyder, Gary (Sherman) **21**
Song, Cathy **21**
Stein, Gertrude **18**
Stevens, Wallace **6**
Swenson, May **14**
Toomer, Jean **7**
Wakoski, Diane **15**
Walker, Margaret (Abigail) **20**
Wheatley (Peters), Phillis **3**
Whitman, Walt(er) **3**
Williams, William Carlos **7**
Wylie, Elinor (Morton Hoyt) **23**
Zukofsky, Louis **11**

ARGENTINIAN

Borges, Jorge Luis **22**

AUSTRALIAN

Wright, Judith (Arandell) **14**

AUSTRIAN

Trakl, Georg **20**

CANADIAN

Atwood, Margaret (Eleanor) **8**
Bissett, Bill **14**
Page, P(atricia) K(athleen) **12**

CHILEAN

Neruda, Pablo **4**

CHINESE

Li Ho **13**
Tu Fu **9**
Wang Wei **18**

CUBAN

Guillen, Nicolas (Cristobal) **23**

ENGLISH

Arnold, Matthew **5**
Auden, W(ystan) H(ugh) **1**
Behn, Aphra **13**
Belloc, (Joseph) Hilaire (Pierre Sebastien Rene Swanton) **24**
Blake, William **12**
Bradstreet, Anne **10**
Bronte, Emily (Jane) **8**
Brooke, Rupert (Chawner) **24**

Browning, Elizabeth Barrett **6**
Browning, Robert **2**
Byron, George Gordon (Noel) **16**
Carroll, Lewis **18**
Chaucer, Geoffrey **19**
Clare, John **23**
Coleridge, Samuel Taylor **11**
Day Lewis, C(ecil) **11**
Donne, John **1**
Dryden, John **25**
Eliot, George **20**
Eliot, T(homas) S(tearns) **5**
Graves, Robert (von Ranke) **6**
Gray, Thomas **2**
Gunn, Thom(son William) **26**
Hardy, Thomas **8**
Herbert, George **4**
Herrick, Robert **9**
Hopkins, Gerard Manley **15**
Housman, A(lfred) E(dward) **2**
Hughes, Ted **7**
Jonson, Ben(jamin) **17**
Keats, John **1**
Kipling, (Joseph) Rudyard **3**
Larkin, Philip (Arthur) **21**
Levertov, Denise **11**
Loy, Mina **16**
Marvell, Andrew **10**
Milton, John **19**
Montagu, Mary (Pierrepont) Wortley **16**
Owen, Wilfred (Edward Salter) **19**
Page, P(atricia) K(athleen) **12**
Pope, Alexander **26**
Rossetti, Christina (Georgina) **7**
Sassoon, Siegfried (Lorraine) **12**
Shelley, Percy Bysshe **14**
Sitwell, Dame Edith **3**
Smart, Christopher **13**
Smith, Stevie **12**
Spenser, Edmund **8**
Swift, Jonathan **9**
Swinburne, Algernon Charles **24**
Tennyson, Alfred **6**
Tomlinson, (Alfred) Charles **17**
Wordsworth, William **4**

FILIPINO

Villa, Jose Garcia **22**

FRENCH

Apollinaire, Guillaume **7**
Baudelaire, Charles **1**
Breton, Andre **15**
Gautier, Theophile **18**
Hugo, Victor (Marie) **17**
Laforgue, Jules **14**
Lamartine, Alphonse (Marie Louis Prat) de **16**
Leger, (Marie-Rene Auguste) Alexis Saint-Leger **23**
Mallarme, Stephane **4**
Marie de France **22**
Merton, Thomas **10**
Nerval, Gerard de **13**
Rimbaud, (Jean Nicolas) Arthur **3**

Nationality Index

PC Cumulative Title Index

Title Index

Title Index

Title Index

"How the Wallflower Came First" (Herrick) **9**:102

"How to Be Old" (Swenson) **14**:250, 288

"How to Die" (Sassoon) **12**:267, 285

"How to Enter a Big City" (Merton) **10**:337, 344

"How to Make a Good Chili Stew" (Ortiz) **17**:228, 233

"How Very Often at a Fashionable Ball" (Lermontov) **18**:297

"how we avoid prayr" (Bissett) **14**:32

"How We Danced" (Sexton) **2**:366

"How Yesterday Looked" (Sandburg) **2**:305

"Howard Lamson" (Masters) **1**:338

"Howarth Churchyard" (Arnold) **5**:33-4, 52

"Howl" (Ginsberg) **4**:44-9, 51, 57-61, 63-5, 67-70, 73-5, 79

Howl, and Other Poems (Ginsberg) **4**:73, 87

Howling at the Moon (Hagiwara Sakutaro)
    See *Tsuki ni hoeru*

"The Howling of Wolves" (Hughes) **7**:137, 142, 159

Hristos voskres (Bely) **11**:7, 24, 28, 31, 33

"Hsiang Consort" (Li Ho) **13**:51-2

"Hsin-i Village" (Wang Wei) **18**:362

"The Hudsonian Curlew" (Snyder) **21**:292, 297, 308

"Hue, carcan!" (Laforgue) **14**:93

Hugh Selwyn Mauberley (Pound) **4**:318-21, 330, 338-39, 341-42, 348

"Hughie At The Inn" (Wylie) **23**:311

"Hugo at Théophile Gautier's Grave" (Lowell) **3**:224

"Huhediblu" (Celan) **10**:124

"L'Huillier, si nous perdons ceste belle Princess" (Ronsard) **11**:250

"8e vision" (Lamartine) **16**:265

"The Human Abstract" (Blake) **12**:10, 34

"Human Affection" (Smith) **12**:310

"Human Applause" (Holderlin)
    See "Menschenbeitfall"

"Human Burning" (Aleixandre) **15**:19, 21

"Human Condition" (Gunn) **26**:185

"Human Cylinders" (Loy) **16**:322

"Human Grief" (Trakl)
    See "Menschliche Trauer"

Human Shows, Far Phantasies, Songs, and Trifles (Hardy) **8**:89

Human Wishes (Hass) **16**:215-17, 221-22

"A Humane Materialist . . ." (Smith) **12**:331

"L'humanitè" (Lamartine) **16**:266, 281, 293

"The Humanities Building" (Shapiro) **25**:322

"Humanity I Love You" (Cummings) **5**:90

"Humble Jar" (Song) **21**:344-48

"The Humble Petition of Frances Harris" (Swift) **9**:251, 296

"The humble Petition of poore Ben: To . . . King Charles" (Jonson)
    See "The humble Petition of poore Ben: To . . . King Charles"

"The Humble-Bee" (Emerson) **18**:79, 84-85, 93, 99

"Humiliation" (Blok) **21**:5, 15

"The Humming-Bird" (Dickinson) **1**:79

"The Humours" (Bradstreet)
    See "Of the Four Humours in Man's Constitution"

"Hunchback Girl: She Thinks of Heaven" (Brooks) **7**:53, 69, 80

"The Hunchback in the Park" (Thomas) **2**:394

"A Hundred Collars" (Frost) **1**:215

"Hunger" (Cullen) **20**:63, 76

"Hunger" (Rich) **5**:374

"Hunger in the South" (Neruda) **4**:282

"Hungerfield" (Jeffers) **17**:129, 136

Hungerfield and Other Poems (Jeffers) **17**:123, 136

"The Hunter" (Williams) **7**:360

"The Hunter of the Prairies" (Bryant) **20**:23

"The Hunter's Serenade" (Bryant) **20**:15

The Hunting of the Snark: An Agony in Eight Fits (Carroll) **18**:30-33, 40-49

"Hunting Watch" (Wang Wei) **18**:389

"Huntress" (H. D.) **5**:269

"The Huntress and Her Dogs" (MacDiarmid) **9**:191

Huntsman, What Quarry? (Millay) **6**:230-31, 233-34, 242

"Hurrah for Positive Science" (Whitman) **3**:384

"Hurrah for Thunder" (Okigbo) **7**:235, 247

"The Hurricane" (Bryant) **20**:15

"The Hurricane" (Finch)
    See "A Pindarick Poem upon the Hurricane"

"Hurry Up Please It's Time" (Sexton) **2**:367-68

"Hurt Hawks" (Jeffers) **17**:117, 129

"Hurt Hawks II" (Jeffers) **17**:110

"Hush'd Be the Camps To-day" (Whitman) **3**:418

"The Hyacinth Symphony" (Elytis) **21**:131

"L'hydre Univers tordant son corps écaillé d'astres" (Hugo) **17**:90

"L'hylas" (Ronsard) **11**:235

"Hyme" (Donne)
    See "Hymne to God my God, in my sicknesse"

Hymen (H. D.) **5**:266-70

"Hymme to God My God, in My Sicknesse" (Donne)
    See "Hymne to God my God, in my sicknesse"

"Hymn" (Ammons) **16**:27, 40, 57-8, 60, 63-5

"Hymn" (Dunbar) **5**:137

"Hymn" (Poe) **1**:446

"Hymn among the Ruins" (Paz)
    See "Himno entre ruinas"

"Hymn before Sunrise in the Vale of Chamouni" (Coleridge) **11**:48-9, 53, 55-8, 92

"Hymn from a Watermelon Pavilion" (Stevens) **6**:292

"Hymn IV" (Ammons) **16**:22

"Hymn of Apollo" (Shelley) **14**:167, 170

"Hymn of Death" (Lamartine)
    See "Hymne de la mort"

"Hymn of Not Much Praise for New York City" (Merton) **10**:344

"Hymn of Pan" (Shelley) **14**:167, 177

"Hymn of the Morning" (Lamartine)
    See "L'hymne du matin"

"A Hymn of the Sea" (Bryant) **20**:3, 13

"Hymn of the Waldenses" (Bryant) **20**:5

"Hymn to Adversity" (Gray)
    See "Ode to Adversity"

"Hymn to Aphrodite" (Sappho)
    See "Ode to Aphrodite"

"Hymn to Beauty" (Baudelaire)
    See "Hymne à la beauté"

"Hymn to Beauty" (Spenser)
    See "An Hymne in Honour of Beautie"

"Hymn to Death" (Bryant) **20**:4, 10, 13, 16, 18

"An Hymn to Diana" (Jonson) **17**:171,182, 207

"Hymn to Earth" (Wylie) **23**:304-306, 308, 311, 323

"An Hymn to God the Father" (Jonson) **17**:172

"An Hymn to Humanity" (Wheatley) **3**:338, 340-41, 348, 361, 363

"Hymn to Ignorance" (Gray) **2**:143, 155

"Hymn to Intellectual Beauty" (Shelley) **14**:166, 169, 177-8, 187, 217, 234, 237-8

"Hymn to Lanie Poo" (Baraka) **4**:15

"Hymn to Physical Pain" (Kipling) **3**:192

"Hymn to Proserpine" (Swinburne) **24**:316, 320, 338, 345-48

"An Hymn to the Evening" (Wheatley) **3**:361, 363

"An Hymn to the Morning" (Wheatley) **3**:361

"Hymn to the Seal" (Smith) **12**:295

"Hymn to the Supreme Being, on Recovery from a Dangerous Fit of Illness" (Smart) **13**:346

"Hymne" (Baudelaire) **1**:63

"Hymne à la beauté" (Baudelaire) **1**:71

"Hymne au Christ" (Lamartine) **16**:280, 293

"L'hymne au soleil" (Lamartine) **16**:277

"Hymne de Calaïs et de Zetes" (Ronsard) **11**:287

"Hymne de la mort" (Lamartine) **16**:283

"Hymne de la Mort" (Ronsard) **11**:226-27, 244, 269, 272-74

"L'hymne de la nuit" (Lamartine) **16**:262, 266, 292

"Hymne de l'ange de la terre apres la destruction de globe" (Lamartine) **16**:265, 281, 287

"Hymne de l'autonne" (Ronsard) **11**:230, 232-34, 267, 279

"L'Hymne de l'hiver" (Ronsard) **11**:266

"Hymne de Pollux et de Castor" (Ronsard) **11**:284, 287

"L'hymne du matin" (Lamartine) **16**:267, 279, 292

"Hymne du printemps" (Ronsard) **11**:242

"An Hymne in Honour of Beautie" (Spenser) **8**:331, 337

"An Hymne in Honour of Love" (Spenser) **8**:337

"Hymne of Beauty" (Spenser)
    See "An Hymne in Honour of Beautie"

"An Hymne of Heavenly Beautie" (Spenser) **8**:332, 336-37, 345

"An Hymne of Heavenly Love" (Spenser) **8**:329, 332, 336-37, 345

"Hymne of Love" (Spenser)
    See "An Hymne in Honour of Love"

"A Hymne to Christ, at the authors last going into Germany" (Donne) **1**:139

"Hymne to God my God, in my sicknesse" (Donne) **1**:140, 158

"A Hymne to God the Father" (Donne) **1**:138-39

"Hymnes" (Spenser) **8**:331

Hymnes (Ronsard) **11**:248

Hymnes (Spenser)
    See *Fowre Hymnes*

"Hymnes in Honor of Love and Beauty" (Spenser) **8**:331

Hymns (Ronsard)
    See *Hymnes*

Hymns and Spiritual Songs for the Fasts and Festivals of the Church of England (Smart) **13**:332, 340-42, 368

Hymns for Children (Smart)
    See *Hymns for the Amusement of Children*

Hymns for the Amusement of Children (Smart) **13**:340, 349, 361

Hymns for the Fasts and Festivals (Smart)

Title Index

Title Index

Title Index

Title Index

Title Index

Title Index

Title Index

ISBN 0-7876-3074-8

90000